Volume II

IDEAS, CONCEPTS, DOCTRINE:
Basic Thinking in the United States Air Force
1961-1984

by

Robert Frank Futrell

Air University Press
Maxwell Air Force Base, Alabama 36112-5532

December 1989

Library of Congress Cataloging-in-Publication Data

Futrell, Robert Frank.
   Ideas, concepts, doctrine; vol. I.

   Originally published: Maxwell Air Force Base, Ala.: Air University, 1971.
   Bibliography: p.
   Includes index.
   1. United States. Air Force—History. 2. United States—Military policy. 3. Military art and science—United States—20th century. 4. Aeronautics, Military—Study and teaching—United States I. Title.
   UG633.F84   1989   358.4'00973   89-165

ISBN 1-58566-029-9

First Printing December 1989
Second Printing September 1991
Third Printing September 2001
Fourth Printing September 2002
Fifth Printing September 2004

Disclaimer

This publication was produced in the Department of Defense school environment in the interest of academic freedom and the advancement of national defense-related concepts. The views expressed in this publication are those of the author and do not reflect the official policy or position of the Department of Defense or the United States government.

This publication has been reviewed by security and policy review authorities and is cleared for public release.

Air University Press
131 West Shumacher Avenue
Maxwell AFB AL 36112-6615
http://aupress.maxwell.af.mil

In Memory of

Maj General Haywood S. Hansell, Jr.
1903-1988

Architect of the American strategic air campaign against Germany and the father of the US Twentieth Air Force.

Contents

Chapter		Page
	DISCLAIMER	ii
	ABOUT THE AUTHOR	xi
	PREFACE	xiii
1	THE NEW FRONTIER: REDIRECTION OF DEFENSE STRATEGY	1
	Fiscal Policies and Military Forces	2
	Allegations of a Missile Gap	4
	Military Airlift and Strategic Mobility	10
	Effect of Election Debates on Military Policy	21
	The Kennedy Administration: Redefinitions of Defense Policy	22
	Kennedy-McNamara Quick-Fix Budget Amendments	26
	Limited Mobilization for the Berlin Crisis	35
	Emerging Strategy: Flexible Response and Multiple Options	39
	Five-Year Military Force Projection	43
	General LeMay Fears for Strategic Superiority	48
	Air Force Thinking on Limited War	56
	Emergence of the McNamara Strategy	58
	Notes	64
2	THE NEW FRONTIER: MATURITY OF FLEXIBLE RESPONSE	75
	Evaluations of the Cuban Missile Crisis	82
	Politico-Military Effects of the Cuban Crisis	86
	Strategic Debates of 1963	87
	Air Force Questions about the McNamara Strategy	91
	Rebuttal to Air Force Questions	98
	Vicissitudes of a Strategic Bomber Program	100
	Arms Control and Limited Nuclear Test Ban	102
	Maturity of the Strategy of "Controlled Flexible Response"	107
	McNamara and LeMay Dispute Strategic Requirements	108
	Continental Air and Missile Defenses	113

Chapter	Page
General-Purpose Forces Projections	117
Deputy Secretary Gilpatric Views the Future	123
Notes	125

3 THE AIR FORCE IN A CHANGING DEFENSE ENVIRONMENT ... 133

- Centralization of National Security Management ... 133
- Providing a NASA-Defense Interface ... 137
- Secretary McNamara and Defense Management ... 145
- Changing Air Force Views on Defense Unification ... 155
- Air Force Organizational Adjustments to Defense Reorganization ... 160
  - Air Force Reorganization of Doctrinal Pursuit ... 160
- Air Force Systems Command/Logistics Command Reorganization ... 163
- Continued Thinking about Air Doctrine ... 171
  - Challenges of Army Doctrinal Development ... 173
  - Beginnings of an Army Aviation Challenge ... 178
- Strike Command Tests of Army and Air Force Concepts ... 182
- Clarification of Responsibilities for Doctrine ... 189
- Defense Rationale on Science and Technology ... 193
- Secretary McNamara Revises Research and Development Priorities ... 196
- The McNamara Rationale on Research and Development ... 205
- Threats and Opportunities in Space ... 212
- Reflections on Military Space Requirements ... 226
- Future in Prospect: Project Forecast and Air Force Manual 1-1 ... 228
- Secretary Zuckert Describes Air Doctrine Guidelines ... 230
- August 1964: New Thoughts in Basic Air Doctrine ... 235
- Notes ... 236

4 INSURGENCY AND WAR IN SOUTHEAST ASIA ... 255

- Objectives and Strategy ... 255
  - Advisory Assistance to South Vietnam ... 257
  - Air Attacks against North Vietnam ... 259
  - Americans Join the In-Country Ground War ... 260
  - President Nixon and Vietnamization ... 263
  - Air Power and the 1972 Spring Invasion ... 266
  - Epitaph for the Republic of Vietnam ... 271

Chapter	Page
Organization and Operations	277
Command Organization Affecting Air Power	277
Counterair Battles Maintained Air Superiority	287
Aerial Interdiction and Close Air Support	298
Airmobility: US Air Force Transports and Army Helicopters	311
Evaluations of the Air War	316
Notes	323

5 STRATEGIC CHALLENGES TO AIR POWER, 1970-83 333

    Early Military Analysis of the Soviet Missile Threat 333
    Search for a United States Nuclear Strategy 337
    President Nixon Demands Selectivity and Flexibility in
        Targeting 342
    President Carter's Countervailing Strategy 352
        President Reagan Opts for Both Offense and Defense 364
    Articulation of the Strategic Triad Concept 384
    Struggle for a Long-Range Combat Aircraft 389
    Denigration and Re-creation of Strategic Defenses 427
    Notes 452

6 TWO DECADES OF TACTICAL AIR COMMAND
   DEVELOPMENT, 1964-84 467

    Early Emphasis on a European Nuclear Defense 467
    Ordering TACAIR Resources for Realistic Deterrence 476
    Response to the Soviet/Warsaw Pact Threat 490
    Fixed-Wing Air and Attack Helicopters in Controversy 516
    US Navy and Marine Corps Tactical Air 531
    The Tactical Air Command – Training and Doctrine
        Command 539
    Second Echelon Attack/AirLand Battle 546
        Electronics: Key to the Advancing Tactical Air Command
            Air Program 555
    Notes 567

Chapter		Page
7	**THE AIR FORCE IN THE DEFENSE DEPARTMENT**	583
	Continuing Complexities of Defense Organization	584
	The Blue Ribbon Defense Panel	587
	Personnel Cuts Affected Unified Commands and Organization	601
	Secretary Brown and the Steadman Report	606
	Reorganization Proposals Foster Service Interdependency	612
	Notes	617
8	**GLOBAL AIRMOBILITY FORCES**	623
	New Concepts and Requirements	623
	Strategic Airlift Support of Southeast Asia	629
	A New Maturity of Strategic Airlift: The C-5A Story	637
	The Israeli Airlift of 1973	641
	Airlift Consolidation and Specified Status for MAC	645
	The Modern Airlift Era	648
	Estimating Mobility Requirements Proves Difficult	648
	New Perspectives on Airlift Aircraft	652
	Organizing for Strategic Mobility	659
	Notes	669
9	**THE AIR FORCE IN SPACE**	677
	Discourse and Decisions on Manned Military Spacepower	677
	A New Air Force Policy of Space Applications	684
	Building a Space Command and Space Doctrine	689
	President Reagan's Strategic Defense Initiative	701
	Notes	704
10	**THE NEVER-ENDING QUEST FOR AIR FORCE DOCTRINE**	711
	Recognition of a Need for Dynamic Doctrine	711
	The Air Force Directorate of Doctrine, Concepts, and Objectives	717
	New Program Directions for Air Concepts and Doctrine	722
	Facing the Future: Cooperative Armed Forces Doctrine	740
	Notes	745
	INDEX	751

Illustrations

Table		Page
1	Strategic Defensive Forces	434
2	Military Airlift Command Passenger and Cargo Movement	634
3	Consignment of Military Air Cargo: Fiscal Years 1960–75	634
4	MAC International Civil Airlift Procurement: Fiscal Years 1960–75	635
5	United States Airlift/Sealift	643

About the Author

Dr Robert Frank Futrell

Robert Frank Futrell was a senior historian at the Albert F. Simpson Historical Research Center. He holds bachelor of arts and master of arts degrees from the University of Mississippi and a PhD from Vanderbilt University (1950). During World War II he served as historical officer of the AAF Tactical Center, Orlando, Florida, and assistant historical officer of Headquarters Far East Air Forces in the Philippines.

After World War II, Doctor Futrell joined the new Army Air Forces/United States Air Force Historical Office, which was moved from Washington, D.C., to the Air University, Maxwell AFB, Alabama, in 1949. At the Air University he was professor of military history and became emeritus professor at his retirement from the US Civil Service in 1974. He also retired as a lieutenant colonel from the Air Force Reserve.

Doctor Futrell is author of *The United States Air Force in the Korean War, 1950–1953*; *The United States Air Force in Southeast Asia, The Advisory Years to 1965*; and has authored and coauthored many other air history books and articles. Recently under contract with the Airpower Research Institute, he revised and updated one of his former works—*Ideas, Concepts, Doctrine: A History of Basic Thinking in the United States Air Force, 1907–1964*. Volume I updates and revises his previous book and covers the period through 1960; volume II picks up with 1961 and goes through 1984.

Preface

This history continues the story of United States Air Force ideas, concepts, and doctrine from the watershed of massive retaliation/flexible response that was occasioned in 1960. The first three chapters of this volume are in effect reprinted from the 1974 edition of *Ideas, Concepts, Doctrine*, and the following chapters have been added to bring this never-ending story up to 1984.

I joined the Air University Airpower Research Institute as a visiting professor of military history in September 1981 and completed research and writing for this study in January 1985. The original understanding regarding this work was that the research and writing would follow the same pattern as used in the older version, and this was conscientiously followed in this new second volume. Dr David MacIsaac, associate director for research, Airpower Research Institute, stimulated much of the thinking reflected in this extension of the story since 1964. The successive AUCADRE directors—Col Kenneth Alnwick, Col Donald Stevens, Brig Gen John Fryer, Jr., and Col Sidney Wise—maintained the strong climate of intellectual honesty necessary for the history.

Where many persons have provided information and assistance toward the writing of this history, the author assumes the responsibility for the errors of fact or of interpretation that may have escaped into print. A number of people at Air University Press worked hard to keep those errors under control. These include Dr Richard Bailey, my text editor for volume II; Agnes Wallner, my documentation editor, and her assistant, Anna Leavell; and the entire staff of the Production Division.

Like other Air Force historical studies, this history is subject to revision, and additional information or suggestions for corrections will be welcomed.

ROBERT F. FUTRELL
Visiting Research Fellow
Airpower Research Institute

CHAPTER 1

THE NEW FRONTIER: REDIRECTION OF DEFENSE STRATEGY

In the middle 1920s during the formative years of the Air Corps, Maj Gen Mason M. Patrick had been favorably impressed by Basil H. Liddell Hart's *Paris: Or the Future of War*. Based upon the experiences of World War I the British military commentator had spoken against the frontal assault doctrines of Napoleon and Clausewitz and in favor of direct action designed to break the ability and will to resist of a hostile nation. In 1960, at the height of the United States presidential campaign, Sen John F. Kennedy, the democratic candidate, found time to review a new book by Liddell Hart, entitled *Deterrent or Defense*. Kennedy endorsed Liddell Hart's grand theme, which was that "the West must be prepared to face down Communist aggression, short of nuclear war, by conventional forces." Kennedy observed that this same judgment was supported in other books by "responsible military leaders such as Generals [James M.] Gavin and [Maxwell D.] Taylor." In an expression of his own views on defense requirements, Kennedy stated that the United States (1) must guarantee that its deterrent was safe from sudden attack and capable of effective penetration of enemy defenses; (2) must bring rapidly into being the new generation of Polaris and Minuteman mobile missiles that "should diminish the need for hair-trigger decisions and should give the United States, and the world as a whole, a greater degree of stability"; (3) must "think through afresh" the military mission of the North Atlantic Treaty Organization and ensure that NATO had sufficient ground divisions "to provide a persuasive deterrent to the Russian temptation to seek a limited advance in Europe, on the assumption that the West's only protection is a nuclear attack the West would not use"; (4) must take steps to provide greater air and sea mobility for conventional Army and Marine forces not to fight limited wars but to remove the temptation for Moscow and Peking to attempt local aggression; and (5) must ensure that United Nations forces (such as had been used in the Middle East and the Congo) "must be ready for instant movement." Senator Kennedy also emphasized the importance of arms control negotiations. "The notion that the Free World can be protected simply by the threat of 'massive retaliation' is no longer tenable," Kennedy added.[1]

Senator Kennedy's review of the nation's defense requirements provided a convenient summary of the criticisms Democratic leaders were bringing against the military policies of President Dwight D. Eisenhower. These criticisms included dissatisfaction with the level of defense appropriations and with defense management, allegations that a concern for balanced budgets was causing a "missile gap," demands for increased conventional forces and for augmented airlift, and strong statements of a new need for civil defense. The Democratic dialogue on national defense would provide a background for the new national strategy of flexible response and multiple options that would be implemented when Kennedy assumed the presidency in January 1961.

Fiscal Policies and Military Forces

"It is a fact," stated Sen Lyndon B. Johnson on 11 March 1959 after hearing testimony on major defense matters as chairman of the Senate Preparedness Investigating Subcommittee, "that the strength of the Nation's security cannot be measured solely, or even primarily, in terms of money. . . . Throughout these hearings I have been unable to escape the conclusion that we are not doing enough, fast enough, or thoroughly enough."[2] Johnson indicated a grave fear that the Eisenhower defense budget ceilings might be jeopardizing security. Although defense spending under the Eisenhower administration had increased from $35.5 billion in fiscal year 1955 to $41.2 billion in fiscal year 1960, the Department of Defense (DOD) computed that in terms of constant value fiscal year 1953 defense dollars the net purchasing power of defense appropriations had decreased from $34.9 billion in fiscal year 1955 to $32.5 billion in fiscal year 1960.[3]

Following his retirement as Army chief of staff, Gen Maxwell D. Taylor criticized the defense budget ceilings, which he said were arbitrarily imposed by the Bureau of the Budget, and recommended budgeting by military task rather than by military service.[4] In another influential postretirement book, Lt Gen James M. Gavin charged that the United States would find itself in a "missile-lag period," which would be most critical in the years 1960–64. "Actually," Gavin remarked, "some of our most important missile programs have been slipping steadily because of the diminishing value of the dollar and the increased cost of labor and scientific help."[5] At the Rand Corporation a group of analysts headed by economist Charles J. Hitch proposed that the existing DOD financial management system did not "facilitate the relating of costs to weapon systems, task, and missions," did not "disclose the full time-phased costs of proposed programs," and did not "provide the data needed to assess properly the cost and effectiveness of alternative programs."[6]

Closely related to the defense budget ceilings were allegations that the National Security Council had failed to provide realistic strategic policies. General Taylor described the Basic National Security Policy papers issued annually as being "so broad in nature and so general in language as to provide limited guidance in practical application."[7] In an address made in September 1959, Paul H. Nitze charged that dissatisfaction with the National Security Council technique caused the Eisenhower administration to rely increasingly upon outside committees of private citizens to assist with policy review and formulation. These distinguished citizens groups included the Kelly, Sprague, Killian, Gaither, and Coolidge committees. Although charged to make important policy recommendations, these outside groups were necessarily powerless to perform an essential step in policy formulation: to help the fight to secure adoption of recommended policies within the government.[8] Despite the important role that Secretary of State John Foster Dulles played in national policy formulation, Sen Henry M. Jackson observed: "Judging by his appearances before Senate committees, Mr Dulles seemed not to be well informed on military scientific developments having an important bearing on foreign policy and tended to regard budgetary questions as being outside his proper concern."[9]

Speaking in support of the fiscal positions of the Eisenhower administration that had prevailed during his tenure as DOD comptroller, W. J. McNeil did not consider "the word 'ceiling' used in connection with the budget . . . a nasty word at all." Comptroller McNeil emphasized that governments had operated under budgetary ceilings in the past and doubtless would do so in the future. After studying the experience of the Truman administration, which had operated for a time during the Korean War without reference to fixed budgetary ceilings, McNeil recorded that the Eisenhower administration had determined that the defense plateau of the nation ought to cost "in the neighborhood of $35 to $40 billion a year."[10] Closely questioned about budgetary ceilings in February 1959, Secretary of Defense Neil H. McElroy was confident that the nation would be willing to pay whatever it needed for its security. But McElroy insisted that any country had "just so many resources," and he maintained that defense spending had to be computed in context with national requirements for schools, roads, aid to underdeveloped nations, and an advancing standard of living. McElroy said, "It is inherent in the obligation of an administration," to consider not only what its obligations are in national security but what its obligations are in the administration of the resources of the country for the various projects. He also explained:

> The thing that you try to do in defense is to determine what you need for your national security and to have enough cushion there so that you are not taking a substantial chance with the national security. If you are doing that, then that is all you should do and you should use the remaining resources for other constructive purposes.[11]

Since the Eisenhower administration believed that military force possessed flexibility, its key officials found it impossible to define "limited" or "general" war and impractical to design forces to participate in specialized forms of combat. Although Secretary Thomas S. Gates considered in March 1960 that increased amounts of money had been put into limited-war capabilities each year, he maintained: "Many people have tried to put our budget on a functional basis, and we have found it impossible to do so."[12] When pressed to state official definitions of limited and general war in 1959, DOD responded:

> With respect to the duration and scope of the action, and the selection of weapons to be used . . . there are an infinite variety of possible combinations. For this reason . . . there is no practical way in which we can precisely define limited and general war in

these specific terms, or even index all the possible situations which might fall into these two broad classifications.[13]

As a result of his experience as defense comptroller during the Truman and Eisenhower administrations, McNeil pointed out that any process of budgeting forces to perform specific defense tasks "would not be conducive to economy of force" and "tends to compartmentalize the forces. If we budget by certain weapons system type compartments," he urged, "it tends to freeze the use of forces thus supported.... I would far rather support the forces at the approximate level we thought would do the job and leave flexible the use of forces where, as, and if, necessary."[14]

Allegations of a Missile Gap

"The facts are," Sen Stuart Symington informed his colleagues on 27 January 1960, "that a very substantial missile gap does exist, and the administration is going to permit this gap to increase."[15] The gnawing apprehension that the Soviet Union enjoyed a substantial margin of superiority in missiles over the United States traced back to an interview with Nikita Khrushchev reported by James Reston in October 1957. "I think I will not be revealing any military secret," Khrushchev said, "if I tell you that we now have all the rockets we need: long-range rockets, intermediate-range rockets and close-range rockets." From this time onward, Khrushchev asserted that surface-to-air missiles had made bombers obsolete, good only for display in museums. He told press correspondents late in 1959:

> We do not want to scare anyone, but we can tell the truth—in saying that we have now stockpiled so many missiles and so many atomic and hydrogen devices that, if we were attacked, we could wipe all our probable enemies off the face of the earth.... In one year a plant that we visited produced 250 missiles with hydrogen warheads on the assembly line.[16]

Appearing before the Supreme Soviet in January 1960, Khrushchev asked for and received authority to reduce the manpower strength of the Soviet armed forces from 3,623,000 to 2,423,000 by the autumn of 1961.[17]

Based upon demonstrated technological achievements of the Soviets, US estimates made in 1958 credited the Soviet Union with the ability to possess a significant missile threat in the years 1960–63, when the United States would be missile limited. This estimate appeared additionally creditable because the Soviets had demonstrated an already developed long-range missile technology, although the delay in US missile programs was attributable to development rather than to production. One commonly accepted estimate in 1958 and 1959 was that the Soviets would possess a 3-to-1 superiority of intercontinental ballistic missiles over the United States in the early 1960s. Speaking in the Senate in 1958, Senator Kennedy announced:

> We are rapidly approaching that dangerous period which General Gavin and others have called the "gap" or the "missile-lag period"—a period, in the words of General Gavin, "in which our offensive and defensive missile capabilities will lag so far behind those of the Soviets as to place us in a position of great peril."[18]

As officially conceived for implementation in the winter of 1957–58, the Air Force ballistic missile program envisioned deployment of 4 Thor and 4 Jupiter intermediate-range ballistic missile (IRBM) squadrons to Europe between December 1958 and March 1960 and deployment of 9 Atlas and 4 Titan intercontinental ballistic missile (ICBM) squadrons at bases within the United States by January 1963. This force objective was not as large as the Air Force believed necessary. As supreme allied commander, Europe, Gen Lauris Norstad had requested the assignment of 10 IRBM squadrons to NATO, and the Air Force wanted to program 16 Atlas and 11 Titan squadrons instead of the force authorized. Early in 1958, however, Secretary McElroy was inclined to give emphasis to the deployment of the IRBMs. "I think that we become strongest," he said, "as of the time we have some IRBMs deployed in our allied countries in Europe and the Far East, ... where we have some Polaris submarines around the periphery of Europe, and where we have ICBMs which can be deployed in this country and have manned bombers."

The successful development of the solid-propellant SM-80 Minuteman would affect the ICBM program since this missile would be cheaper and easier to deploy in protected positions than the Atlas or Titan missiles.[19] In February 1958 McElroy announced that he strongly favored production of long-range missiles. He nevertheless stated three reasons for a cautious approach to missile production: he was reluctant to go into large-scale production until missile testing programs were more advanced; he expected great progress in the field of solid-propellant missiles and did not want to build up large inventories of early model missiles; and he wanted to avoid duplication in building inventories of different missiles. In short, McElroy wanted more time to test and to decide what missiles should be put into production.[20]

Even though he wanted more time to make decisions on the ICBMs, McElroy believed the DOD should take "a calculated risk and move faster than the testing results would in themselves justify" in preparing for operational deployments of Thors and Jupiters.[21] The negotiations for overseas bases, which were begun late in 1957 and actively prosecuted in the summer of 1958, dictated the extent of the IRBM programs. Great Britain agreed to accept four Thor squadrons (60 operational missiles), which would be manned by Royal Air Force personnel, with the United States retaining custody of the nuclear warheads. According to Gen Curtis E. LeMay the British were "never very enthusiastic about Thor as a weapon system," but this deployment was brought to completion early in 1960, when the 60th operational missile was airlifted to Great Britain.[22] France did not accept the Jupiter squadrons offered, but Italy accepted two squadrons (30 missiles) and Turkey agreed to take one squadron (15 missiles) of the Jupiter IRBMs.

Shortly after deployments to Italy were completed and while the establishment of missiles in Turkey was still in progress, a subcommittee of the congressional Joint Committee on Atomic Energy recommended on 11 February 1961 that the Italian Jupiters be replaced with mobile IRBMs and that the Turkish deployment should be halted. The subcommittee demonstrated that the thin-skinned, liquid-fueled Jupiters were particularly vulnerable to sabotage and would be easily destroyed by a Soviet first-strike missile attack. The committee recommended that a Polaris submarine operated by US personnel should be assigned to NATO in lieu of the 15 obsolete Jupiters slated for deployment to Turkey. At this time the United States did not have a Polaris submarine immediately available for such an assignment, and the Turkish government was unwilling to modify the existing agreement. Although Secretary of Defense Robert S. McNamara later would state that "the Turkish Jupiters should never have been placed in position," the United States proceeded with the agreed program, and the Jupiter missiles became operational in Turkey by about July 1962. As was the case in England, United States crews controlled the nuclear warheads for the missiles sited in Italy and Turkey.[23]

Despite a rising feeling of national concern about the predicted missile gap, President Eisenhower's fiscal year 1960 defense budget submitted to Congress in January 1959 called for 9 Atlas and 11 Titan squadrons to become operational by June 1963.

> The reason why the Defense Department does not plan to produce the same number of ICBMs that the Soviets are estimated to be capable of producing over the next few years is that, in the judgment of the president of the United States, the National Security Council, and the military experts of the Department, there is no particular logic in trying to match everything it is estimated our opponent might do.[24]

McElroy urged that there would be no gap in the nation's defense posture if all combinations of delivery systems were considered. He acknowledged that the United States had a capability to produce more of the first-generation missiles than it actually would produce, and he suggested that the Soviets, who would doubtless recognize the deficiencies of early type missiles, might not be willing to produce anything like the number which the national intelligence estimate credited them with an ability to produce.[25]

Before submitting the fiscal year 1960 budget to Congress, Secretary McElroy had cautiously sought and received a statement that the Joint Chiefs of Staff found no "serious gaps" in its "key elements." As far as missiles were concerned, the military leaders supported the administration's objectives when they appeared before congressional committees. When asked about the missile gap, General Taylor replied: "I would not be unduly concerned at this time because we have so many other compensatory weapons which can do the same job of putting bombs and missiles on target."[26] Adm Arleigh Burke agreed that the United States had sufficient strategic weapons. "I think," he said, "we do have too much retaliatory power, and I think that we should put more money into limited capability."[27] Gen

Thomas D. White called attention to the slow reaction time of the first-generation Atlas and Titan missiles and observed:

> I feel we should not increase the production of either of those missiles under the present circumstances when all factors including the manned bomber are considered plus the fact that the Minuteman, the second generation, the solid fuel missile is, shall we say, just around the corner.[28]

Speaking for the Strategic Air Command (SAC), Gen Thomas S. Power said: "I think you should produce the Atlas at the maximum logical, practical rate, because you are going to get it first. . . . I think we ought to get it as fast as we can, and get it on hardened sites." But Power was even more enthusiastic about the Minuteman, which would be built relatively cheap and could be deployed in large numbers either in hardened underground silos or on mobile railway trains.

> This is really the philosophy of deterrence in that we will have so many of these missiles. . . . Then it becomes mathematically impossible for an aggressor to destroy them all, and you will always survive with a percentage high enough to strongly deter him.[29]

Only Lt Gen Bernard A. Schriever, who admitted that he "would have to be considered as not necessarily biased but certainly perhaps narrow" in his viewpoint, strongly urged the need for more ballistic missiles and at an earlier date. Schriever contended that the Atlas and Titan missiles would be useful throughout the 1960s and would have "considerably greater growth potential than the Minuteman."[30]

Although they supported the Eisenhower ballistic missile program, General Power and the other Air Force leaders were apprehensive about the Soviet missile threat to the United States. On the basis of tangible evidence Power privately admitted that the United States knew the locations of the experimental and test missile sites in the Soviet Union, but he pointed out that the Soviets might not be deploying their operational missiles from the same type of relatively ponderous sites the United States was erecting.[31] To reduce the vulnerability of the Strategic Air Command, General Power sponsored the testing of an airborne alert posture during 1958. In this concept bomber crews flew courses and met aerial tankers at optimum points, which ensured that the bombers could attack an assigned target at any time they were in the air. Early in 1959 Power requested the Joint Chiefs of Staff to authorize SAC to begin a continuous airborne alert.[32] When he appeared before a subcommittee of the House Committee on Appropriations in February 1959 Power explained the airborne alert concept and added, "I feel strongly that we must get on with this airborne alert to carry us over this period."[33]

During the congressional hearings on the defense budget for fiscal year 1960, Democratic members found little satisfaction in the expectation that the United States would lag behind the Soviets in intercontinental missiles. In February 1959 the House Committees on Armed Services and on Appropriations asked for pertinent data on the possibility of matching the Soviets missile for missile. After the study, the Air Force recommended against a "crash program" in May but found it possible to plan for the orderly establishment of 17 Atlas squadrons, 12 Titan squadrons, and 3 Minuteman squadrons (150 missiles) by June 1963. In July Secretary McElroy announced that the Soviets possessed only 10 long-range weapons "at most," but Congress was in no mood to accept the administration's missile program. In August it accordingly voted an additional $85 million, looking toward eight additional Atlas squadrons and $87 million further to accelerate the Minuteman development program. Congress also added a section to the 1960 appropriation act authorizing the secretary of defense, upon the determination of the president, to provide for the cost of an airborne alert as an excepted expense.[34]

In preparation for his defense of the fiscal 1960 defense budget, Secretary McElroy had referred the individual service budgets to the Joint Chiefs of Staff, and they, as a corporate body, had advised McElroy that they "found no serious gaps in the key elements of the budget."[35] With such reassurance, McElroy informed the Senate on 17 June that he would probably spend any additional money appropriated for Minuteman but would impound any additional funds for Atlas.[36] Accepting the need to permit flexible decisions, the 1960 appropriation act authorized the secretary of defense to transfer funds to accelerate the missile programs he deemed advantageous. This action seemed doubly wise since Atlas tests conducted during the spring of 1959 were marked by a spectacular series of failures, leading General White to comment: "A faint heart in ... February to July 1959 could well have caused a program cancellation of Atlas." In the autumn of 1959 Atlas began "turning in a remarkable performance," and new and better informed decisions could be made on the ICBM programs. Prepared under the direction of Secretary of Defense Gates, the defense missile program for fiscal year 1961 called for 13 Atlas and 14 Titan squadrons and for funds to establish a production facility to manufacture 30 Minuteman missiles per month, this despite the fact that the Minuteman was still in research and development.[37]

In the last half of 1959 DOD also considered General Power's request that the Strategic Air Command should be augmented to undertake an air alert posture. Power specifically recommended that SAC should be given men, spare parts, and operating funds to permit a continuous air alert with one-fourth of its B-52 force. General White was unwilling to go along with Power's proposal that the continuous air alert be put into effect, but he recommended that SAC be provided an on-the-shelf capability to conduct the around-the-clock alert with one-quarter of its B-52s during national crisis. To make a long story short, the Joint Chiefs of Staff accepted air alert in principle, but they were not willing to accept the estimated $3-billion cost of Power's proposal. Shortly after he took office, Secretary Gates released $85 million to enable SAC to begin procurement of long, lead-time spare parts for an airborne alert, and he directed the Air Force to make plans for implementing an airborne alert program without increasing its manning level. As events subsequently worked out between Gates and the Air Force, the defense budget for fiscal year 1961 made provisions whereby the Strategic Air Command would have an emergency capability to maintain one-eighth of its B-52s on a continuous airborne alert. This action satisfied the Department of Defense and the Joint Chiefs of Staff, but it did not satisfy General Power. "I am compelled to reiterate," he wrote to White on 10 December 1959, "that the goal for a heavy force must be one-fourth. Any steps short of this, although certainly steps in the right direction, are based on a gamble too great to take—the security of the United States."[38]

As he defended the fiscal year 1961 defense budget on 13 January 1960, Secretary Gates emphasized that no "deterrent gap" was in prospect, but he conceded: "If we compare the estimated Soviet ICBM and sea-launched missile programs with plans for deployment of US ICBMs and Polaris missiles, we note that the Soviets may enjoy at times a moderate numerical superiority during the next three years."[39] Looking for new methods of evaluating the potential threat, Gates announced on 20 January that the National Intelligence Board (NIB) would begin to estimate projections of Soviet ICBM strength on the basis of "intent" rather than "capability." Based upon "intent" the revised national intelligence estimate accordingly reduced the number of long-range missiles the Soviets were expected to have by mid-1961 by 66 percent of the earlier accepted figure.[40]

The Eisenhower administration's assurances did not quiet public fear about the missile gap and what it could mean. In his book, *The Uncertain Trumpet*, published in January 1960, General Taylor argued: "My personal conclusion is that until about 1964 the United States is likely to be at a significant disadvantage against the Russians in terms of numbers and effectiveness of long-range missiles—*unless heroic measures are taken now*."[41] Speaking before the Economics Club of New York City on 19 January of the same year, General Power stated that with 300 intercontinental missiles the Soviet Union could virtually wipe out the 100 facilities from which the United States could launch aircraft or missiles. "With adequate and timely preparations for meeting added demands for support," Power added, "SAC can maintain an airborne alert long and effective enough to bridge what could otherwise become the most dangerous gap in our military posture since Pearl Harbor."[42] On the floor of the Senate on 27 January, Senator Symington urged that the unfavorable missile gap still existed even when new estimates based on Soviet intent rather than capability became the standard of prediction. "The truth is," he said, "that if we compare the ready-to-launch missiles attributed to the Soviets on the new intelligence basis with the official readiness program for US ICBMs, the ratio for a considerable length of time will be more than 3 to 1."[43]

Obviously seeking to allay public apprehension in late March 1960, DOD summarized its views in a 17-page letter sent to some 600 business leaders. "For more than a year now," the letter stated, "a few critics of the defense program have been successful to an incredible degree in confining discussion of our military strength to one single segment—the intercontinental ballistic missile."[44] From Gen Nathan F. Twining downward, Air Force officers who appeared before congressional committees supported the administration's viewpoint about the missile gap. "On the basis of all the information available, and in view of the mix and strategic locations of our retaliatory weapons systems," Twining said, "I just do not believe that any nation possesses the ability to destroy us, or attack us, without receiving unacceptable damage in return."[45] Even though General White first observed that he would like to see more ICBMs, more B-58s, and a number of other things if "we had more money," he submitted a written statement two days later to the House Subcommittee on Appropriations which declared:

> The Air Force has taken into account all the known aspects of the threat and the forces required to deter that threat, within the major parameters of time, numbers, and state of the art. The present mix of ICBMs . . . is in our judgment the best force obtainable within these limitations.[46]

Apparently seeking to head off a political issue, the Republican party platform adopted in the summer of 1960 pledged to accelerate missile programs, but the "missile gap" continued as a rich political issue. Both Senator Kennedy and Senator Johnson had been active critics of the Eisenhower defense program, and in the course of the presidential campaign Kennedy demanded "new defense goals" and attacked the Republican party for not doing enough in the "missile gap crisis."[47]

Military Airlift and Strategic Mobility

In his speeches two years prior to 1960 Senator Kennedy often expressed his conviction that the Soviets will take advantage of their growing strategic nuclear missile capability as a "shield from behind which they will slowly, but surely, advance — through Sputnik diplomacy, limited brushfire wars, indirect nonovert aggression, intimidation and subversion, internal revolution, increased prestige or influence, and the vicious blackmail of our allies." He maintained that the Soviets had "invalidated the original strategic concept of NATO by outflanking its key element — the deterrent power of the US Strategic Air Command." Kennedy criticized the Eisenhower administration for cutting the numbers and strength of Army and Navy ground forces and for failing to provide the airlift and sealift needed to give those forces swift mobility for deployment anywhere in the world.[48] As has been seen, General Taylor's proposal for a national military program of "flexible response" also emphasized the development of limited war forces deployed in theaters of operation, limited war reserves in the United States, and provision of sealift and airlift mobility for the limited war forces.[49]

On the philosophical level the Air Force did not deny that small wars might become more likely, but it was unable to accept the argument that since small wars might be more probable than a general war, the United States must devote more of its scarce resources and planning efforts to them. One Air Force speaker observed: "This is like an investment counselor advising the head of a family to buy automobile insurance before life insurance because he is more likely to dent his fenders than he is to die."[50] Speaking of the airlift problem on 27 January 1960, General White noted that it had been around a good many years and was solely attributable to the fact that no one had been able to establish a definite requirement for additional airlift within existing budgetary guidelines. "If there is to be more airlift," White added, "the only question is to establish a requirement for it, and provide the funds."[51]

Within the Department of Defense the problem of providing airmobility for the Army traced back to 1954–55, when the Army advanced the concept that limited war was the most likely threat to the United States. Within the Air Force the problem of military airlift involved the separate capabilities of tactical troop carrier aviation, whose previous mission was curtailed at the lower extremity by the Army's development of organic airlift, and of the Military Air Transport Service (MATS), whose capabilities were kept in check by civil air carriers' insistence that military air transportation unfairly and inefficiently competed with the Civil Reserve Air Fleet. Expenditures for transport aircraft also competed unfavorably for money and productive capability required to support combat aircraft.

During the Korean War the Air Force had accepted the Tactical Air Command's concept that intratheater troop carrier airlift forces should comprise heavy, medium, and assault troop carrier wings, the latter to be composed of a fixed-wing group and another rotary-wing group. Such a force would serve all theater airlift requirements from the front lines to the theater's rear area, and requisite units were programmed in the 137-wing Air Force objective. The Air Force procured C-124 aircraft for the heavy wings, C-119s for the medium wings, C-123s for the fixed-wing assault groups, and H-21 cargo helicopters for the rotary-wing assault groups. This program was changed even before it was completed. Late in 1954 the Army stated that it had no requirements for Air Force rotary-wing support within the combat zone.[52] Despite a successful employment of rotary-wing assault troop carrier squadrons in the "Sagebrush" maneuver in November and December 1955, the Air Force decided in January 1956 to concede superiority in rotary-wing air transport to the Army, this decision being based both upon the Army's manifest determination to possess its own combat-area air transport and a belief that helicopters were too short ranged and vulnerable to serve as assault aircraft. TAC dropped plans to activate additional rotary-wing assault troop carrier groups and inactivated the existing units of this type in July 1956.[53] As a part of the Department of Defense establishment of a single manager and industrial fund system for military airlift, TAC's C-124 wings and groups were transferred to MATS on 1 July 1957. These C-124s would continue to perform the same Army training maneuvers, DEW line support, and other nonscheduled tasks they had been performing previously.[54]

In May 1956 troop carrier capabilities met stated requirements for existing emergency war plans; nevertheless, Gen Otto P. Weyland considered the troop carrier end position in the 137-wing program marginal at best since the programming did not reflect growing demands for intratheater airlift.[55] Army officers stated that troop carrier deficiencies existed, but the Army did not make official requirements for added theater airlift units.[56] Early in 1957 Weyland also protested that the assignment of the C-124s to MATS would vastly complicate the TAC composite air strike force (CASF) deployments. As it happened, however, TAC began to profit from acquisition of new C-130A and C-130B Hercules troop carrier aircraft as replacements for C-119s. The versatile turboprop Hercules had good short-field characteristics, truck-bed loading heights, and an airdrop capability, and it appeared to be a suitable aircraft to replace the C-123 and the C-119. Interested in getting intercontinental transportation for its CASFs, TAC also placed a requirement for the development of a long-range version of the Hercules, designated the C-130E. The increased capabilities of the Hercules permitted reductions in regular troop carrier unit strength. With the retrenchment nearly completed in 1959 TAC possessed two wings of C-130s and two wings of C-123s. In the theaters, the United States Air Forces in Europe possessed one wing of C-130s and one wing of C-119s and was additionally supported by one squadron of MATS C-124s on rotational duty. The Pacific Air Forces had one wing of C-130s and was additionally supported by two MATS C-124 squadrons. To receive the troop carrier aircraft released from regular units, in November 1957 the Air Force programmed the strength of the Air Force Reserve at a force structure of 15 troop carrier wings. By 1959 the Air Force Reserve had 14 C-119 and 1 C-123 wings, all of which were available to TAC for airlift and for exercises and maneuvers with the Army.[57]

When the Military Air Transport Service was established in 1948, the Navy chose to maintain the organizational integrity of Marine Corps assault transport squadrons and Navy fleet logistic air wings. The two fleet logistic air wings (one being assigned to the Atlantic Fleet and one to the Pacific Fleet) provided special, immediate, and unpredictable airlift required by the fleet commanders.[58] By 1957 the Navy had 40 four-engine aircraft assigned to MATS and 112 transport planes (including 35 four-engine aircraft) assigned to fleet logistic air wings.[59] The Air Force followed the same pattern for the transportation of nuclear weapons. To provide expedited weapons delivery anywhere in the world, the Air Materiel Command activated three logistic support squadrons in the years 1952–54. These squadrons collectively possessed 36 C-124 aircraft in 1959. By 1959 the Strategic Air Command also employed 3 strategic support squadrons, each with 16 C-124 aircraft, to move nuclear weapons between its bases within the United States.[60]

Based upon the seminal thinking of Maj Gen William H. Tunner, who was then deputy commander of Air Materiel Command (AMC), and upon the work of Brig Gen John P. Doyle, Air Force director of transportation, the Air Force accepted a concept in 1953-54 that accelerated air delivery of high-value logistical support items (particularly aircraft engines) would result in large savings. These items ordinarily would have to be stocked in large quantities. The Air Force regulation on the use of air transportation, issued on 30 March 1954, described the objectives of the use of air transportation as being to develop a wartime capability for providing rapid and flexible deployment of men and materiel, to expedite the transaction of business, and to reduce the nonproductive time of men and materiel by a reduction in pipeline time.[61] Extending the policy throughout the government, the White House on 26 May 1954 directed all agencies to make wider use of air transportation.[62]

The Air Force's use of airlift for transporting engines and other high-value spares resulted in an estimated $1.5-billion savings in the purchase of spare equipment between 1955–58 and also permitted the closing of a number of overseas air depots.[63] It also posed a requirement for highly reliable special air transport services. Beginning in June 1954 the Air Materiel Command annually contracted with civil airlines for the services of some 54 C-46 logistics airlift (LOGAIR) aircraft, which were employed in scheduled flights between Air Force depots, air bases, and ports of aerial embarkation in the United States.[64] In July 1950, in addition to its organic air transport capabilities, the Navy instituted a contract air service – called QUICKTRANS – to facilitate logistical support within the United States. The Navy ordinarily accepted bids each year for these services without specifying the number of aircraft that the civil contractor would employ. In 1959, however, eight DC-4 (C-54) cargo aircraft were being used by the QUICKTRANS contractor.[65]

Although the Military Air Transport Service had been established in 1948 as the DOD air transport agency, the performance of this mission was necessarily affected by the proliferation of special-purpose transport organizations outside of its control. The mission of MATS required it to "provide under one authority, for the transportation by air of personnel (including the evacuation of sick and wounded), materiel, mail, strategic materials, and other cargoes for all agencies of the Department of Defense and as authorized for other Government agencies of the United States, subject to priorities and policies established by the Joint Chiefs of Staff."[66] War requirements for military airlift were dictated by the emergency war plans approved by the Joint Chiefs of Staff, and the routine usage of MATS airlift was allocated by the Joint Military Transport Committee. Except for the Navy transports assigned to it, MATS was funded and supported by the Air Force, and such new planes as it received came principally from appropriated Air Force funds.[67] Calling attention to the many duplicative air transport services that existed, the Hoover Commission on Governmental Organization recommended in 1955 that the secretary of defense merge all of the services within DOD (except for administrative aircraft, which ought to be "drastically reduced" in number) into MATS. It also recommended

> that the peacetime operations of the integrated MATS be restricted and realistically limited to persons and cargo carefully evaluated as to necessity for military air transportation and, only after commercial carriers have been utilized to the maximum practicable extent, should transportation on Service carriers be authorized.[68]

Issued on 7 December 1956 the DOD directive entitled "Single Manager for Airlift Service" designated the secretary of the Air Force as the single manager and directed him to work through MATS, which would be the single-manager operating agency. The directive sought to integrate into "a single military agency of the Department of Defense all transport type aircraft engaged in point-to-point service whose operations are susceptible of such scheduling, and such organizational and other transport aircraft as may be specifically designed by the

Secretary of Defense." As has been seen, the Air Force transferred TAC's C-124s to MATS, and the Navy similarly assigned 15 four-engine aircraft from its fleet logistic air wings to the single-management agency. When industrial funding was begun on 1 July 1958 MATS received a one-time appropriation of $75 million to use as a revolving fund that would be replenished as airlift was sold to service customers.[69] The reorganization of MATS on the single-manager industrial fund basis ended complaints that a considerable part of the military airlift traffic comprised items that did not require air movement, but the industrial fund also emphasized the airline characteristics of the military air service. Moreover, some 920 Air Force and Navy transport aircraft remained outside the control of MATS.[70]

The conversion of MATS to industrial funding did not affect the fact that its modernization aircraft would have to come from appropriated Air Force or Navy funds. When he was in command of MATS, Lt Gen Joseph Smith insisted that MATS required new jet transport aircraft. To handle outsized missile cargoes, MATS began to take delivery of 23 turboprop C-133 Globemaster III aircraft in August 1957. The C-97s replaced by the new C-133s were transferred to Air National Guard squadrons. When General Tunner took command of MATS on 1 July 1948, he also insisted on the need for modernized equipment but his planning brought him into quick competition with SAC. Tunner's studies indicated that the most feasible means of providing cargo-jet (C-jet) aircraft would be to purchase a quantity of "swingtail" C-135 planes. This was the same plane that the Strategic Air Command held in highest priority for procurement as the KC-135 tanker. Although SAC admitted that jet transports would speed the recovery and relaunching of poststrike and restrike forces, it was strongly opposed to a diversion of KC-135 resources, which would reduce the strength of its initial striking force. Speaking of the situation in July 1958, General LeMay said: "I would like to have some jet transports." But he immediately added: "If you gave us money now for jet airplanes, I would buy tankers, not airplanes for MATS. . . . I think we would increase our combat capability more in that manner than we would in augmenting the MATS fleet."[71] Gen Nathan F. Twining emphasized that the Joint Chiefs of Staff had an open mind in regard to airlift, but with only so much money available, he had to observe: "Somewhere the Joint Chiefs of Staff as a corporate body has to make up its mind [about] what you are going to buy."[72]

At the same time that it had a secondary priority to combat forces, the Military Air Transport Command was jealously regarded by many civil air carriers. From its establishment, MATS had figured its aircraft requirements during peacetime in terms of the capability it would require to perform a D-day mission. Under ideal circumstances the military air transport force maintained during peacetime would have equalled D-day requirements. Indeed, its aircrews would have been flown at wartime rates to be capable of surging to the wartime requirements without delay. The maintenance of such a fleet in peacetime, however, would have been very costly, and the most practicable means of augmenting military airlift involved use of planes from the Civil Reserve Air Fleet (CRAF). Even with such augmentation,

MATS would have to surge into all-out action on D-day and maintain a high tempo of operations for 30 days. This action posed a requirement for well-trained military crews, who needed to be flying at least 40 hours a month during peacetime to acquire proficiency.

MATS had learned from experience that it must exercise its system at a daily aircraft utilization rate of 6 hours if it was to meet wartime requirements. At the beginning of the Berlin airlift, for example, MATS had been operating its aircraft at about 4 hours a day, and it was able with priority effort to increase its rate to 5.5 hours a day at the end of 30 days. At the start of the Korean War, MATS was operating at a rate of 2-1/2 hours a day, and it was able to increase to only 4.3 hours during the first 30 days. In each instance, MATS was able to purchase civil airlift to augment its resources, but the civilian planes were unable to fly into either Berlin or Korea. During the Korean conflict the cost of the civil airlift amounted to $69,941,034 in fiscal year 1951, $68,951,344 in fiscal year 1952, and $70,843,376 in fiscal year 1953.[73] With the ending of the war in Korea government contracts for civil air transport rapidly decreased, but for two years shortages of civil airlift in an expanding economy allowed the civil carriers to maintain their prosperity. By 1956, however, civil airlines were receiving new equipment in large amounts, and the supply of civil airlift began to exceed demand. By flying MATS at a rate of slightly more than 4 hours a day in fiscal years 1956 and 1957, DOD was able to provide $43,269,349 and $49,746,935 in contracts, respectively, with the civil air carriers, but the civilian operators nevertheless needed more business. People, whom Assistant Secretary of the Air Force Dudley C. Sharp sadly said should have known better, began to describe MATS as "a billion dollar boondoggle," a "second family car," "plush," "excessively costly," "unnecessarily large," and, most frequently, "competitive with the carriers."[74]

In the spring of 1958 congressional committees investigated the MATS-CRAF problem. The House Committee on Government Operations recommended the modernization of the MATS fleet but it also recommended that MATS "should concentrate on outsized and special cargo traffic and technical missions, leaving to the civil air carriers the primary responsibility for the transportation of passengers and more conventional kinds of military cargo."[75] Concurrent hearings by the Senate Commerce Subcommittee arrived at similar conclusions. Speaking of MATS, Sen A. S. Monroney said: "Our quarrel is that they haven't got any special-duty equipment except the C-133 . . . while they are duplicating, and continuing to duplicate in new purchases, the passenger carrying capacity that is available in large amounts."[76] Seeking a solution to airlift problems, President Eisenhower asked the secretary of defense on 23 July 1958 to make a study of the military role performed by MATS in peace and war. During the year and a half that this study was under way in the Office of Assistant Secretary of Defense (Supply and Logistics) an extraordinary amount of attention was given to the future of MATS. According to General Twining the Joint Chiefs of Staff made 18 airlift studies during 1958, 3 of them major studies "about the size of the New York telephone book." "Airlift," Twining added, "has been studied and restudied more than any other single problem we have."[77]

Shortly after he assumed command over MATS, General Tunner stated a strong case for the assignment of jet aircraft to the military airlift command. These planes could be justified by their relatively low cost of operation, their ability to fly nonstop to Europe, and the personnel savings incident to their use. Tunner also announced criteria for an effective air transport force, namely the ability to be

> immediately available and responsive to tight military control . . . conditioned to operating as part of a military combat effort with attendant consideration of command and discipline . . . trained and ready to undertake flying in unusually hazardous conditions . . . prepare[d] . . . for use of very large volume capacity aircraft, and for the handling of large bulk and, frequently, very sensitive cargo loads . . . composed, in part, of aircraft which are readily convertible from cargo to passenger and to patient-evacuation use [and] able to shift operational effort over wide geographical ranges.[78]

Tunner recognized that MATS depended upon the Civil Reserve Air Fleet for augmentation, but he insisted that there was a hard-core military mission that must be performed by military crews flying modern aircraft. He maintained that these military planes must be flown at a peacetime rate of five hours a day to meet wartime surge requirements. This peacetime flying would generate air transportation, which in the interest of the national economy had to be used for the movement of defensive traffic.[79] The experience of MATS in the Lebanon and Taiwan crises in the autumn of 1958 bore out the need for military manning of a hard-core airlift. Tunner considered it inadvisable to send any transports into Lebanon and Taiwan that were not manned by military crews under military discipline. The case of Lebanon required no civil augmentation, but when cargo backed up at the San Francisco port during the Taiwan crisis, MATS sought civil assistance for a part-way shuttle to mid-Pacific bases. At this moment, however, civil airlines were in the midst of the tourist season and either demanded high prices for their services or refused to bid on government business. In November 1958 Trans World Airlines employees went on strike, and MATS had to take over all but four of TWA's contract flights.[80]

At the same time that MATS faced charges that it was in competition with civil air carriers, General Taylor expressed dissatisfaction with the availability of airlift for local war deployments. When they criticized airlift, Army officials did not focus on a shortage of airplanes. Gen Thomas D. White found it difficult to reconcile the different emphasis that Gen Maxwell D. Taylor placed on airlift inside and outside the Joint Chiefs of Staff.[81] In January 1958 Deputy Secretary of Defense Donald A. Quarles observed: "The air transport we now have provided does meet the Joint Chiefs of Staff requirements for air transport, but it does not meet the Army concept of what the air transport should be."[82] When asked to speak to these charges in February 1958, Taylor responded:

When I look at the four-engined aircraft — the so-called strategic aircraft available in all the services — in MATS, in the Navy, in the Air Force and in the Marines, and then look at the airlines I am impressed that we have large assets. The real question is: Do we have the means to assemble these assets fast enough, and when the time comes what will be the decision as to their allocation? Because there will be lots of customers for airlift. So with these question marks in my mind, I have difficulty in saying dogmatically, "Yes, there is enough or there is not enough."[83]

In a positive assessment of Army airlift requirements, Taylor asked the Joint Chiefs on 17 June 1958 to preallocate sufficient strategic airlift to deploy the spearhead elements of a two-division force — 5,840 personnel and 7,438 short tons of equipment.[84] By early 1959, however, the Army was contemplating a movement within 30 days of at least 2 of its 3 Strategic Army Corps divisions anywhere in the world by a combination of precommitted airlift and sealift.[85] As a result of the detailed studies made during 1958, General Twining testified that the Joint Chiefs of Staff agreed that airlift capabilities to meet general war requirements were "generally adequate" and that four of the five members agreed that airlift capabilities were also "adequate as a basis for planning to meet limited war situations." Twining added: "We are still working on this problem to meet General Taylor's views. But the problem here is that you can let your imagination run wild and have six or eight limited wars going on at one time."[86]

When they received General Taylor's specific airlift requirement in June 1958, the Joint Chiefs of Staff deferred final consideration of it, pending the submission of detailed transportation requirements from the unified and specified commanders during 1959.[87] Although action was thus suspended, the Air Force got agreement from DOD to include $50 million in its fiscal year 1960 budget for an "off-the-shelf" purchase of 10 turbojet transports (converted Boeing 707s or something similar) to begin the modernization of MATS.[88] Early in 1959 Senators Monroney and Symington advocated government assistance for the development of civil cargo aircraft, which they said was "essential, not only in terms of our specific defense needs, but also if we are to maintain our international leadership in commercial aviation."[89] On the other hand, Congress refused to appropriate the funds the Air Force requested for the procurement of an initial order of turbojet transports and added a provision to the defense appropriation that required $85 million of the funds voted to MATS to be made "available only for the procurement of commercial air transportation services."[90] Following another series of hearings in the spring of 1959, the House Committee on Government Operations repeated its earlier recommendation that MATS should concentrate on the handling of outsized and special cargo and technical missions and leave the transportation of passengers and the conventional military cargo to civil air carriers.[91]

The Joint Chiefs of Staff reopened their airlift studies early in 1959. They considered airlift requirements for a war that might begin under three assumed conditions: six months of mobilization followed by 60 days of general war; general war occurring without warning or prior mobilization (D-day and M-day coinciding); or the resumption of hostilities in Korea. On 15 October the Joint Chiefs of Staff reached an agreed position on airlift requirements on the basis of planning assumptions.[92]

The new Army chief of staff, Gen Lyman L. Lemnitzer, requested enough strategic air transportation (1) to lift at least two reinforced battle groups and their combat equipment to any trouble spot in the world within hours of the time the order to move was given; (2) to move by air within days enough troops and supplies to build a full division force with necessary logistical support in the combat area; and (3) to increase the size of the fighting force to two divisions within two to four weeks and to provide it with adequate supplies and supporting forces to conduct operations for an extended period of time. In regard to tactical airlift in both general and limited war situations, the Army required sufficient troop carrier airlift to lift and support the assault echelon of at least one airborne division.[93] The Joint Chiefs of Staff did not determine airlift requirements for limited wars other than the war in Korea. Once again, General White explained that "limited war variations were so infinite that you could not state a simple limited war requirement for airlift and . . . a hypothetical case was not one . . . upon which you can justify military requirements."[94]

Inasmuch as the Joint Chiefs of Staff did not state airlift requirements for limited war other than in Korea, Generals White and Lemnitzer agreed to tackle the problem at what Lemnitzer described as the "grassroot level."[95] On November 1959 the Air Force directed the commander of Tactical Air Command to serve as the sole contact with Department of Army commands for all Air Force airlift applied to joint airborne training. During a visit to Headquarters TAC and Headquarters Continental Army Command (CONARC) on 21 December, Generals White and Lemnitzer further agreed that TAC should be made the Air Force's single focal point not only for joint training but also for developing and testing of air plans for the deployment of CONARC forces in support of emergency or contingency war plans. White and Lemnitzer also agreed on the need for a joint planning group at the CONARC-TAC level, for a lower-level joint plans development group, and for a joint CONARC-TAC strike force headquarters that would be capable of rapidly deploying Army and Air Force units placed under it. Upon returning to Washington, they concluded an agreement under which the Army specified the forces and timing for a typical limited war deployment over a long line of communications to an area with limited logistical and command facilities, and the Air Force agreed to attempt to secure sufficient airlift to meet the Army requirements. As a matter of fact, the Air Force had the capability to move the specified number of people but not within the specified time parameters. The White-Lemnitzer agreement was set down and signed on 15 March 1960.[96]

Obviously exasperated with the long airlift controversy and wanting to get some matters "off my chest," General White spoke quite frankly on 27 January 1960:

> The airlift presently available meets the criteria established by the Joint Chiefs of Staff. . . . I would also submit that under the guidelines and total defense budget . . . the

> most important mission the Air Force has is the strategic retaliatory force. . . . I would also say that a proper air defense of this Nation is of a very high order of importance. . . . In addition to that, we have the tactical strike missions in support of the Army. . . . I sometimes think that the Air Force is impairing its own future by standing for the Nation in those very important roles. . . . They take an enormous part of our budget. Yet at the same time we are accused of not providing airlift. There are even suggestions that the airlift functions should go to some other service. . . . I say we want it and cannot get it within the budget guidelines and within the priorities. . . . If there is to be more airlift, the only question is to establish a requirement for it, and provide the funds.[97]

In the same month that General White got his opinions in the open, the long freeze on air transportation began to show signs of thawing.

In anticipation of changes in government airlift policy, on 4 January 1960 Secretary of the Air Force Dudley C. Sharp appointed a civilian committee headed by Gordon C. Reed to investigate the most advantageous method by which MATS could contract for commercial airlift, the number of hours of training exercises that MATS should fly to assure its readiness for emergency operations at 6 to 10 hours a day for 30 days, the dependability of the Air Force Reserve and Air National Guard for providing backup airlift to MATS, and the most advantageous equipment for the modernization of MATS. Working against a very short deadline, the Reed committee recommended that a greater proportion of MATS peacetime capability should be employed in training exercises. Even though the committee recognized that the one-year, competitive bids through which MATS negotiated for CRAF support provided airlift augmentation at the cheapest cost, it suggested that the CRAF operators could hardly modernize their aircraft under such circumstances. It therefore recommended that MATS procure transportation from certified and supplemental air carriers at civil tariff rates approved by the Civil Aeronautics Board. The committee also wanted to give certificated route carriers the right of first refusal to all defense traffic over their routes. The committee acknowledged that its recommendations would cost DOD a great deal more money, but it contended that they would make the CRAF operators better able to provide themselves with modern aircraft.[98] These recommendations were available early in February when a DOD study requested by Eisenhower in 1958 was released under the title of "The Role of Military Air Transport Service in Peace and War." Mindful that the feeling against MATS airline-type operations had become strong enough to block the modernization of military airlift capabilities, the Defense Department's report recommended that MATS withdraw from routine channel operations to the extent that the function could be performed effectively and at reasonable cost by commercial carriers without detriment to the hard-core military mission or unnecessary duplication of airlift services. The report recommended that MATS should "consist of a modern military air transport nucleus (hard-core) capable of meeting effectively those airlift requirements which by nature and timing must be moved by military aircraft."[99] Secretary Gates immediately accepted the report. "I have concluded," he informed the chairman of the Joint Chiefs of Staff, "that the level of airlift capability maintained within

MATS should, as an objective, be the minimum required to accommodate the Department of Defense hard-core airlift requirements, and that the peacetime operations of MATS should be geared primarily to hard-core mission support rather than regularly scheduled channel operations."[100]

As submitted to Congress early in January 1960, the DOD budget request for fiscal year 1961 included $120.4 million for modernized airlift, the amount comprising $70.4 million for the purchase of 25 C-130B medium range troop carrier aircraft and $50 million for the development of a new "uncompromised cargo aircraft" that would be able to perform either tactical or strategic airlift functions.[101] Obviously dissatisfied with these limited proposals during the annual military posture briefing presented to the House Armed Services Committee, Chairman Carl Vinson named Rep L. Mendel Rivers to head a special subcommittee to conduct "an inquiry into the adequacy, or inadequacy, of the national airlift, insofar as that national capability relates to the requirements of national defense."[102] When he appeared before the House Appropriations Subcommittee on 15 February, General Tunner posed requirements for aircraft modernization that far exceeded the administration's requests. Tunner submitted that 454 of the MATS aircraft were "obsolescent in speed, range and overall capability." He posed a requirement for three types of planes: an airplane for movement of outsized cargo which was already being met by the 50 C-133s on hand or on order, a modest number of fast-reaction planes for the support of nuclear strike forces, and, finally, "an austere workhorse airplane which will form the backbone of the military airlift forces." He proposed that the fast-reaction planes should be provided by off-the-shelf purchases of 94 swing-tail jet planes, of which 45 might well be cargo versions of the KC-135 tanker. He anticipated that MATS would need 188 "workhorse" aircraft, planes that would have to be developed as a result of a special operational requirement (SOR) and that would come into the MATS operating inventory in about five years.[103]

Looking back at the opening of the hearings of the Special House Subcommittee on National Military Airlift, Chairman Rivers would note on 8 March 1960 that "there was no sentiment whatsoever in the Defense Establishment for the support of interim modernization of MATS, and there was open hostility in some quarters outside of the Defense Establishment." For the first time, however, the military services jointly participated in a full discussion of the airlift problem.[104] While still taking testimony, the subcommittee decided to require MATS to expedite modernization, and on 30 March Rivers appeared before the House Appropriations Subcommittee and recommended a $50-million appropriation for the SOR development and an additional $335-million appropriation for the procurement of 50 C-135s and 50 C-130Bs with extended range (the latter subsequently designated as C-130Es).[105] At the conclusion of its hearings, the Rivers subcommittee found strategic airlift capabilities seriously inadequate in terms of requirements that would be encountered in the first 20 days of either general war without warning or limited war under any of the then-current planning assumptions. It recommended that the military transport and troop carrier forces be modernized, that MATS be limited to a hard-core mission, and that Air National Guard and Air Reserve units would continue to receive the planes released by the modernization programs. The committee also recommended that the CRAF be modernized (this to be facilitated by longer-term contracts based on negotiated terms that would be fair and reasonable to both parties) and that the responsiveness of CRAF crews to military requirements be increased either by legislation or by company-negotiated agreements against work stoppages.[106]

In its version of the fiscal year 1961 defense appropriation bill, the House of Representatives not only appropriated the originally requested $120.4 million but added $250 million for the procurement of 50 C-130s with extended range and an unspecified number of a cargo version of the C-135. This amount of money was more than DOD wanted, and in an appearance before the Senate Subcommittee on Appropriations Deputy Secretary of Defense Quarles asked that the additional amount be reduced to $150 million. The Senate reduced the additional $250 million to $190 million and provided that 50 C-130Es would be produced from this added sum. In its final bill, Congress specified that the $310.8 million voted for airlift modernization could not be diverted to other purposes, nor should any of the money be used for the procurement of aircraft to be used for scheduled passenger service. As matters worked out, the 50 C-130Es specified for mandatory purchase would cost about $170 million, and the additional funds voted by Congress thus would not permit the purchase of a meaningful number of C-135s.[107]

Although DOD proved unwilling to accept the total amount of airlift funds that Congress appeared willing to appropriate, General White nevertheless believed the airlift hearings by the Rivers subcommittee had been beneficial. Working closely together as the hearings progressed, Generals White and Lemnitzer agreed on what the Army wanted in the way of airlift and this, White said, "implies an Air Force obligation to do its reasonable best to get it." Even though the Joint Chiefs of Staff did not pass on the White-Lemnitzer agreement, White remarked that "in JCS deliberations in the future, at least the Army and the Air Force will be together on some subjects that we have not been together on in the past." White also welcomed the new attitude of Congress toward modernized airlift.[108]

Effect of Election Debates on Military Policy

In the evaluations of military posture during the heat of the presidential campaign of 1960, Senator Kennedy demanded "new defense goals" and attacked the Republican party for the "missile gap" and for "unrealistic limited war preparations." On the other hand, the Republican candidate, Vice President Richard M. Nixon, pledged to accelerate missile programs, to intensify development of an active civil defense, and to strengthen the military might of free-world nations.

Viewed on the record the election year debates of 1960 narrowed the military differences between the Republican and Democratic parties. Thus in August 1960 the Eisenhower administration released some $476 million previously appropriated for additional Polaris submarines, modernization of Army weapons, greater airlift capability, development of the B-70 as a weapon system, and increased capabilities for the SAC's airborne alert. In preparation of the national defense fiscal year 1962 budget, the Department of Defense required the services to accept the fiscal year 1961 budget as a starting point, but the services authorized them to present a "C" budget that exceeded the 1961 obligational authority by 5 percent and a "D" budget that included all other desirable priority items. On the basis of this guidance, the Eisenhower defense budget estimate for fiscal year 1962 totaled $44.9 billion, an increase of about 5 percent over the $43.2 billion appropriated for fiscal year 1961.[109] At the same time that the Eisenhower defense budget was being increased, Secretary of State Christian A. Herter, in an address in September 1960, stated new requirements for military forces that were significantly different from those that had been required under the massive retaliation strategy. Herter wanted the nation's foreign policy to prevent war, to reinforce historic trends that would reshape the world along constructive lines, and to move toward a world of law. This foreign policy required the United States to maintain an invulnerable strategic deterrent; to maintain "a secure and diversified capability for responding to, and suppressing, a wide variety of lesser threats to the peace"; to maintain collective security arrangements that would diminish the chance of conflict by miscalculation; and to seek "safeguarded arms reduction" that would "diminish the risk of war resulting from a continuing and spiralling arms race."[110]

Even though the Republican strategy appeared to be moving away from a transcendent emphasis on the strategic deterrent, President Eisenhower could not agree that his defense programs, kept under control by annual budget ceilings, had been inadequate for the security of the nation. In a final address to the American people on the eve of the inauguration of Kennedy, President Eisenhower warned:

> In the councils of government, we must guard against the acquisition of unwarranted influence, whether sought or unsought, by the military-industrial complex. . . . Only an alert and knowledgeable citizenry can compel the proper meshing of the huge industrial and military machinery of defense with our peaceful methods and goals, so that security and liberty may prosper together.[111]

The Kennedy Administration: Redefinitions of Defense Policy

Early in 1961, in the days before the new administration took office on 20 January, President-elect John F. Kennedy assembled the new men who would form his government for orientation briefings and informal talks about the affairs of state. In these talks, Robert S. McNamara, who was coming to Washington from the presidency of the Ford Motor Company to be secretary of defense, and Dean Rusk, who would become the new secretary of state, agreed that there were few great issues of military policy and posture that were not inextricably wedded to the field of foreign policy. As will be seen, their appreciation of this fact would lead to the establishment of closer and more intimate organizational relationships between the State and Defense Departments. In these early days, Kennedy also directed McNamara to recommend the size and type of military establishment required to protect national security without regard to arbitrary budget ceilings, and having done this, to take every possible action to provide the military establishment of the appropriate size and type at the lowest possible cost.[112] "I would say," McNamara recollected, "that a major instruction which I received from President Kennedy was to develop a defense program that would assure the security of our Nation without regard to arbitrary budget ceilings. I think this instruction by itself may have had much to do with the change in the program."[113]

In his State of the Union message delivered to Congress on 30 January 1961, President Kennedy stated that he had instructed Secretary McNamara to reappraise the entire United States defense strategy and that, pending this study, he had ordered quick action to increase military airlift capacity, step up the Polaris submarine program, and accelerate the missile programs.[114] In the reappraisal of the national defense strategy, one of the first concerns of the Kennedy administration was to inform itself in greater detail of the changes that were taking place in the structure and strategy of the Soviet armed forces.

Following his announcement in January 1960 that the size of the Red Army forces would be greatly reduced, Khrushchev had announced in May 1960 the establishment of a new rocket command as one of the five main directorates of the ministry of defense, on coequal level with ground, air, air defense, and naval forces. These Soviet actions appeared to be designed to adapt the Soviet forces to new military technology, including nuclear weapons and missiles.[115]

Assembled in Moscow in November 1960, a conference of world Communist parties addressed the problem of defining Communist strategy during an era of thermonuclear missiles, and Khrushchev reported the findings of the conference in a speech entitled "For New Victories of the World Communist Movement," delivered on 6 January 1961. After describing the horrors of thermonuclear war, Khrushchev concluded that Communist ideology no longer could regard a general thermonuclear war or even a limited war that would rapidly escalate into thermonuclear war as being a useful instrument of policy for the extension of world communism. Khrushchev nevertheless asserted that "liberation wars and popular uprisings" were "not only admissible but inevitable." To hasten the historical inevitability of the triumph of world communism, Khrushchev stated that the Soviets would support subversion, guerrilla, and insurgency wars, particularly in the emerging nations of the world.

Shortly after he took office, President Kennedy secured a detailed analysis of Khrushchev's speech, which he circulated among top governmental officials with instructions to "read, mark, learn, and inwardly digest." Referring to this speech, McNamara later commented that in it Khrushchev "stated as clearly as any one has ever stated, to my knowledge, the strategy of the Soviet Union."[116]

During his first fortnight in office, McNamara examined the relative missile capabilities of the United States and the Soviet Union. In August 1960 the official estimate of the number of ICBMs that the Soviets could be expected to have built by mid-1961 had been reduced again, so that the estimate was only 30 percent of what it had been at the beginning of the year.[117] McNamara soon determined, as he said, "that although there might have been a missile gap there certainly was no deterrent gap and that in any event there almost certainly would not be a missile gap at any time in the near future if this country pursued an appropriate missile procurement program."[118] On the evening of 6 February McNamara met with a group of news correspondents for an off-the-record background briefing, and in a clear violation of nonattribution, one of the correspondents subsequently quoted McNamara as having said there "appeared at this time no signs of a Soviet crash effort to build intercontinental missiles, though overall Russian military preparations were continuing at a rapid pace." McNamara subsequently retorted that this statement was an unwarranted publication that came "directly from our national intelligence estimates."[119]

At a press conference on 8 February, President Kennedy noted that DOD had not yet indicated whether there was an existing missile gap, but with the passing of time it became evident that the Soviets were procuring only a small fraction of the number of ICBMs that they had been believed capable of producing in 1959.[120] Exactly why the missile gap did not materialize remained a mystery. Looking back in 1964 General Schriever believed that the missile gap had existed in 1957 and 1958, even though the expected numbers of Soviet ICBMs did not materialize. "The threat, particularly in the ballistic missile area," he argued, *"was* real." Schriever believed that the Soviets had been ahead in the production of liquid-fueled missiles, but that they had been slow to make a breakthrough into solid-propellant technology.

> I personally believe that the solid-propellant breakthrough is the most important breakthrough since World War II. Relatively speaking it made it possible for us to mass-produce ballistic missiles. The Soviets were far down the line with a large liquid-fuel missile with which they are unable to match us in numbers. So it was this breakthrough that really has given us the upper hand in ballistic missiles.[121]

Facing the need for a revision in the Eisenhower defense budget, Secretary McNamara conceived that the defense budget had to "start with the political objective, the formulation of which is presented to us by the Secretary of State and upon which the President indicates his desires that we develop a military program that will support the political objective."[122] As announced by President Kennedy on 28 March 1961, the new basic US defense policies were as follows:

> 1. The primary purpose of our arms is peace, not war — to make certain that they will never have to be used — to deter all wars, general or limited, nuclear or conventional, large or small — to convince all potential aggressors that any attack would be futile — to provide backing for diplomatic settlement of disputes — to insure the adequacy of our bargaining power for an end to the arms race. . . .

2. Our arms will never be used to strike the first blow in any attack.... In the area of general war, this doctrine means that such capability must rest with that portion of our forces which would survive the initial attack. We are not creating forces for a first strike against any other nation....

3. Our arms must be adequate to meet our commitments and insure our security, without being bound by arbitrary budget ceilings.... We must, of course, take advantage of every opportunity to reduce military outlays as a result of scientific or managerial progress, new strategic concepts, a more efficient, manageable and thus more effective Defense Establishment, or international agreements for the control and limitation of arms. But we must not shrink from additional costs where they are necessary....

4. Our arms must be subject to ultimate civilian control and command at all times, in war as well as peace. ... This requires effective and protected organization, procedures, facilities, and communications in the event of attack ... as well as defensive measures designed to insure thoughtful and selective decision by the civilian authorities....

5. Our strategic arms and defenses must be adequate to deter any deliberate nuclear attack on the United States or our allies—by making clear to any potential aggressor that sufficient retaliatory forces will be able to survive a first strike and penetrate his defenses in order to inflict unacceptable losses upon him....

6. The strength and deployment of our forces in combination with those of our allies should be sufficiently powerful and mobile to prevent the steady erosion of the free world through limited wars; and it is this role that should constitute the primary mission of our overseas forces.... In most areas of the world, the main burden of local defense against overt attack, subversion and guerrilla warfare must rest on local populations and forces. But given the great likelihood and seriousness of this threat, we must be prepared to make a substantial contribution in the form of strong, highly mobile forces trained in this type of warfare, some of which must be deployed in forward areas, with a substantial airlift and sealift capacity and prestocked overseas bases.

7. Our defense posture must be both flexible and determined. Any potential aggressor contemplating attack on any part of the free world with any kind of weapons, conventional or nuclear, must know that our response will be suitable, selective, swift, and effective.... We must be able to make deliberate choices in weapons and strategy, shift the tempo of our production, and alter the direction of our forces to meet rapidly changing conditions or objectives at very short notice and under any circumstances.... To purchase productive capacity and to initiate development programs that may never need to be used ... adopts an insurance policy of buying alternative future options.

8. Our defense posture must be designed to reduce the danger of irrational or unpremeditated general war—the danger of an unnecessary escalation of a small war into a large one, or of miscalculation or misinterpretation of an incident or enemy intention. Our diplomatic efforts to reach agreements on the prevention of surprise attack, an end to the spread of nuclear weapons—indeed all our efforts to end the arms race—are aimed at this objective.[123]

These basic policies were used to direct the revision of the defense budget for fiscal year 1962, and they would continue to provide guidance to national defense posture, since the Kennedy administration would not issue the Basic National Security Policy papers that had annually guided the preparation of defense budgets during the Eisenhower era.

Kennedy-McNamara Quick-Fix Budget Amendments

Inside DOD the work of restructuring the national defense posture in terms of the characteristics of the forces desired by President Kennedy and (inferentially) by Secretary Rusk would be accomplished first by making "quick-fix" amendments to the 1962 fiscal year budget and then by preparing a longer-range five-year defense projection which would be offered to Congress with the fiscal year 1963 budget. To make the basic reappraisal of military strategy and capability directed by the president in his State of the Union address, McNamara appointed several special task groups, each under the direction of a senior government official and with representatives from the joint staff and the military services. The task group assigned to study strategic delivery system requirements was headed by Charles J. Hitch, assistant secretary of defense (comptroller). Paul H. Nitze, assistant secretary of defense for international security affairs, headed the task force that reviewed limited war requirements, and Dr Herbert F. York, who continued to be director of defense research and engineering, headed the task force that reviewed research and development projects.[124] Not content to depend on briefings and special studies for his information, McNamara also prepared 96 questions relating to defense projects—called "McNamara's Ninety-Six Trombones" by some—which he sent to the joint chiefs and the service departments for a response. His questions were subsequently expanded into some 150 research projects.[125] Accompanied by General Lemnitzer, who had become chairman of the Joint Chiefs of Staff on 30 September 1960, McNamara went to Omaha, Nebraska, late in February 1961 for briefings on SAC's strike planning and to discuss with General Power the means for increasing SAC's ground alert posture to 50 percent, thereby reducing its vulnerability.[126]

Both Hitch and Nitze were familiar with the counterforce strategy proposals, and, in addition to this, McNamara asked for a briefing on the subject of counterforce shortly after he took office. After hearing the briefing of SAC's strike plans, McNamara was said to have disliked what he called the "spasm war" that seemed inherent in an all-out salvo of nuclear weapons at the beginning of a general war.[127] After having become acquainted with counterforce and having studied the finite deterrent strategy favored by the Navy, McNamara noted that both strategic concepts stressed the requirement for highly survivable, second-strike forces and the importance of maintaining positive and secure command and control systems. As early as February, McNamara was inclined to accept some elements of counterforce among the building blocks in the new defense strategy because of the multiple options that it offered; but he did not believe the terms *finite deterrent* or *counterforce* were "used sufficiently consistently or precisely" to warrant their being applied to the revisions of the defense budget, which were submitted to Congress on 28 March 1961.[128]

Instead of emphasizing any particular strategy, the McNamara revisions to the Eisenhower budget followed the same categories of interest already made evident by the establishment of the task forces. The first categories of budget changes were focused on the development of strategic delivery systems for nuclear weapons that would survive an attack with sufficient power to destroy the enemy's warmaking capacity in a second strike. McNamara announced that it would be necessary to shift rapidly from the first-generation Atlas and Titan programs to second-generation solid-fuel Polaris and Minuteman missiles. The Eisenhower budget included funds for the construction of 5 Polaris submarines in fiscal year 1962 for a total of 19. Drawing upon fiscal year 1961 funds, President Kennedy had already authorized 5 additional Polaris submarines, and McNamara asked Congress to add 5 more to the 1962 funding, making a total of 29 Polaris submarines to be constructed. In view of the increase in Polaris submarines, McNamara stated that plans to mount Polaris missiles on the nuclear-powered cruiser *Long Beach* had been canceled. Where the Eisenhower budget had been funded for a 13-squadron Atlas program and a 14-squadron Titan program, McNamara advocated the deletion of 2 Titan squadrons in view of the funding of 12 Minuteman squadrons, each to possess 50 missiles that would be widely dispersed in well-hardened underground sites. The Eisenhower budget had programmed 3 squadrons of train-mounted mobile Minuteman missiles, but the cost of the mobile squadron was expected to be over 50 percent greater than that of a fixed-base squadron, and the revised budget deferred mobile Minuteman deployments. McNamara additionally recommended that the production capacity of Minuteman should be doubled, looking toward even greater procurement of these missiles for the future. The Polaris-Minuteman mix had been carefully thought out: the Polaris submarines appeared to be relatively invulnerable, but a Polaris deployment cost more than an equivalent Minuteman deployment, and there was an additional danger that some breakthrough in antisubmarine detection apparatus might reduce the invulnerability of the Polaris system. Both Polaris and Minuteman fitted into President Kennedy's defense criteria: "Polaris, and to a somewhat lesser degree Minuteman," McNamara pointed out, "are not dependent for their survival on a hair-trigger response to the first indications of a ballistic missile attack and, therefore, lend themselves to a more calculated and deliberate response." He suggested that these missiles would increase significantly the nation's deterrent power. "It is essential if the deterrent is to be a successful deterrent," he said, "that an enemy understand that we have developed a deterrent power which can survive a surprise attack with sufficient force to destroy an enemy and it is that element of credibility which makes it a deterrent."[129]

During World War II McNamara had served with Army Air Forces bomber units as a statistical control officer, and he remarked that it was difficult for him "to conceive of a time when we would not have them." Nevertheless, when judged according to the new defense criteria that strategic weapons had to be either survivable or capable of quick reaction, manned bombers did not compare favorable with the Minuteman or Polaris missiles. Speaking of manned bombers in April 1961, McNamara observed: "I think the evidence points to a declining emphasis on them, but I am not prepared personally at the present time to say for sure that they are on the way out."[130] With B-47s still in the inventory at the time the old B-36s were being phased out by new B-52s and the supersonic B-58s were becoming operational, the Air Force manned bomber strength reached its postwar peak of 1,800 aircraft in the 1957-59 time period. General White personally favored retention of the admittedly obsolescing B-47s as long as possible, since they could provide mass for a strategic air campaign, but he nevertheless agreed to phase out the B-47s at a rate of two wings of B-47s for each additional B-52 or B-58 wing added SAC's strength. Based upon the buildup to 14 B-52 wings and 2 B-58 wings, the number of Air Force strategic wings declined from 43 in mid-1959 to 37 in mid-1961, and the number of strategic bombers was reduced from 1,800 in 1957–59 to something over 1,500 in mid-1961.[131] In addition to normal bomb loads, later model B-52s were equipped to carry two AGM-77 Hound Dog missiles for use in stand-off attacks: the air-breathing Hound Dog had been successfully test launched from a B-52 in April 1959, and late in 1960 they were operationally available in one SAC wing. It was planned that the Hound Dog would be replaced by AGM-87A Skybolt air-launched missiles and that a B-52 would carry four of these 1,000-mile-range missiles. By employing Hound Dog and later Skybolt, the manned bombers would be able to penetrate through increasingly difficult Soviet surface-to-air missile defenses.[132]

Since the equipment of the planned number of SAC B-52 and B-58 wings would be completed with funds provided in prior year budgets, the Eisenhower defense budget for fiscal year 1962 did not contain funds for the procurement of additional strategic bombers. Based in part upon congressional insistence that the Air Force required the B-70 as a follow-on weapon system to the B-52 (Congress had voted an additional $265 million for the B-70 program in July 1960), the Eisenhower administration released funds for reinstatement of limited weapon system development of the B-70 in November 1960. In addition, the Eisenhower defense budget for fiscal year 1962 contained $358 million for the development of one stripped prototype XB-70 and two test-quality YB-70s, the latter to have weapon system capabilities. Given the $358 million for continuing development and adequate funding in subsequent years, the Air Force planned to have a B-70 combat wing in its inventory by August 1968.[133] In departmental considerations of the 1962 defense budget late in 1960, General White was willing to accept the cut-off in the B-58 program at two wings or 116 aircraft: although these planes had supersonic dash capabilities, they were very expensive, relatively short ranged, and unable to carry either Hound Dog or Skybolt missiles. At the same time, White argued against the decision to terminate B-52 production. Pending the demonstration of missile reliability and the availability of B-70s, White urged that B-52 production facilities should be kept in operation as a hedge and insurance against unforeseen events: he actually wanted to keep both of Boeing's B-52 lines open, but he was willing to settle for one line and for a modest feasible rate of continuing B-52 production — say about four planes per month.[134]

Already in difficulty during the Eisenhower administration, the Air Force manned strategic weapons program fared poorly in the defense reevaluations early in 1961.

> In reevaluating our general war position, our major concern was to reduce our dependence on deterrent forces which are highly vulnerable to ballistic missile attack or which rely for their survival on a hair-trigger response to the first indications of such an attack. Consequently, we sought to place greater emphasis on the second approach — the kind of forces which would ride out a massive nuclear attack and which could be applied with deliberation and always under control of the constituted authority.[135]

Since strategic bombers could not be deployed in a mode that gave them a good chance to survive an attack, they had to be launched into the air within a relatively short tactical warning time — about 15 minutes — or risk destruction on the ground. In an era in which the enemy would be able to launch an intercontinental ballistic missile attack with little warning, the number of bombers on an alert status and capable of immediate launching promised to be much more important than the total number of bombers available in the inventory. McNamara accordingly did not recommend the procurement of additional bombers in fiscal year 1962; he instead urged that the number of bombers maintained on constant alert be substantially increased. Only the B-52s were assumed to be suited to ground alert, and to provide the additional personnel that SAC would require to raise its ground alert posture from 33 percent to 50 percent, McNamara programmed a phaseout of B-47 wings faster than planned and the inactivation of the superseded Snark air-breathing, long-range missile wing in December 1961 rather than June 1963. The B-52s and B-58s would continue in the SAC inventory throughout the 1960s but no additional aircraft of these types would be procured.[136]

Based upon this same estimate of the situation relative to the vulnerability of bombers and the fact that ballistic missiles would be plentiful in 1968, McNamara conceived that the Air Force would not have a valid operational requirement for the B-70. Even though the B-70 would operate at Mach 3 at 70,000 feet altitude, it would not be able to employ Skybolt missiles. McNamara concluded that a B-52 equipped with Skybolt missiles would be "a more effective, efficient delivery system" in the late 1960s than the B-70. On the other hand, there were important advantages inherent in a mixed missile and bomber force, and — from a purely technical point of view — development of a B-70 would afford an opportunity to explore the many diverse problems involved in flying a large aircraft at great speed and at high altitudes. After weighing advantages and disadvantages, McNamara terminated the B-70 as a weapon system and limited the program to three XB-70 prototypes. He established a projected development ceiling of $1.3 billion, including $800 million from prior-year funds, for the XB-70 program, and reduced the funding requested for it during fiscal year 1962 from $358 to $220 million.

McNamara emphasized that President Kennedy had personally made the decision on the B-70 based upon recommendations that McNamara had made. McNamara also explained that his personal recommendations came out of exhaustive personal analyses and a two-day discussion of the problem with the secretaries and the Joint Chiefs of Staff.[137] The Eisenhower fiscal year 1962 budget had not included additional development funds for the Skybolt missile in the belief that the $150 million available in the 1961 appropriation could be stretched out, but McNamara believed the project should either be dropped or efficiently pursued and accordingly added $50 million for Skybolt development in the revised fiscal year 1962 budget.[138]

Although President Kennedy had committed himself to an improvement of limited-war capabilities, the DOD task force studying limited-war requirements ran into some initial difficulties. For one thing, the new Army chief of staff, Gen George H. Decker, called for a "man-for-man" ground force capability. "I think we should have the capability to fight man-to-man if the occasion demands it," he said, "and I am sure there will be times in the future when that will appear to be the best course of action."[139] In the revised 1962 defense budget submitted to Congress on 28 March 1961, Secretary McNamara allocated only small strength increases to the Army and Marine Corps. The Army would continue to be structured at 14 combat divisions, but it was allocated 5,000 additional spaces—3,000 of which were to be used to double the size of the Army special forces that were trained for guerrilla warfare.

To enhance the effectiveness, versatility, and readiness of limited war forces, however, McNamara emphasized a twin program aimed at increased mobility and the establishment of dual-conventional-atomic capabilities. Immediately after President Kennedy's State of the Union message in January, the Defense Department increased procurement of Lockheed C-130E transport aircraft from 50 to 99 planes, a part of the augmentation order comprising the deletion of 26 shorter-range C-130B troop carrier planes. The Defense Department also directed that 17 KC-135 jet tanker aircraft which were on the production lines should be turned into transport configurations and ordered 13 additional C-135s, making a total of 30 C-135s, which would become available at a rate of two per month beginning in June 1961. The revised defense budget also increased the Navy's appropriation for modernized sealift. Most of the changes in the limited-war program, however, enhanced nonatomic capabilities. McNamara explained:

> Even in limited war situations, we should not preclude the use of tactical nuclear weapons, for no one can foresee how such situations might develop. But the decision to employ tactical nuclear weapons in limited conflicts should not be forced upon us simply because we have no other means to cope with them.... What is being proposed at this time is not a reversal of our existing national policy but an increase in our nonnuclear capabilities to provide a greater degree of versatility to our limited war forces.[140]

The revised budget provided augmented funds for purchase of modern conventional weapons, including heavy orders of Bullpup missiles and nonnuclear bombs, and a substantial increase for research and development in conventional ordnance. Funds also were included for the improvement of the capabilities of F-105 tactical fighters to handle conventional ordnance and for the initial development of a new triservice tactical fighter. McNamara said:

> In general, what we are striving for is one fighter to fill the needs of all the services—a fighter which could operate from the larger number of existing smaller airfields all over the world and yet fly without refueling across the ocean, thus greatly increasing its value for limited war purposes.[141]

When he appeared before the House Subcommittee on Appropriations on 6 April 1961, McNamara was asked why "more bodies" had not been provided for the Army and Marines. Although he noted that limited-war studies had not been completed, he replied:

> Point No. 1, one of the most effective elements in any limited war are the guerrilla forces. We are proposing a more than double increase in guerrilla forces. I think that is a tremendous step forward. Point No. 2, a major factor affecting the effectiveness of a military force in limited war is mobility. We are proposing a very sizable increase in modern, long-range transport cargo aircraft.[142]

During a later hearing before the same committee, McNamara loosely defined "limited war" as "nonnuclear warfare."

> I think, by "limited" war we simply mean war that is carried on, for the most part, with nonnuclear weapons, and what we are proposing in the budget is a further emphasis on the procurement and potential use of such nonnuclear weapons in order to be better prepared to meet any situation.[143]

In their appearances before congressional committees in the spring of 1961, Eugene M. Zuckert, the new secretary of the Air Force, and General White, who was making valedictory appearances as Air Force chief of staff on 30 June, were gravely distrustful of the strategic implications of the forces envisioned by the revised defense budget.

> The Nation's military forces must be designed not just to wreak unacceptable destruction but to win.... Since America's defense objective is more than just survival, our forces must be designed and adequate to carry through the initial engagement with the will and means to put an end to the further use of force by an aggressor.... What you are going to do ... is to destroy his military potential.[144]

General White maintained "that a nation that is going to live has to make survival a part of its national policy. If it gets in a war it is going to try to win it." He admitted that winning a nuclear war would be difficult, but he urged that "we can't afford to have any other basic philosophy than that our military force is designed to win a war if it is forced upon us."[145] White conceived that a future nuclear war could be won only by concentrating forces against "those elements of enemy strength that can do the greatest damage to us, namely, his military forces."[146]

IDEAS, CONCEPTS, DOCTRINE

Among the members of the Senate Armed Services Committee, White encountered a friendly skepticism about the counterforce strategy—particularly its plan for a measured employment of force. "If you ever start using the atomic weapon," Chairman Richard Russell speculated, "I say there is no way to control it or to limit it, and I think you had better use the whole arsenal right after they hit us with the first atomic weapon."[147] White admitted that war always had been full of surprises and speculated that "in the next one . . . there will be more confusion, more surprises, and more uncertainty than ever existed in human history before," but he continued to endorse counterforce and provided the senators with the Air Force definition of the strategy. This written statement read:

> In the Air Force view, "counterforce" is a military concept for the design and employment of military forces to destroy, neutralize, or render impotent the military capabilities of an enemy force, under any circumstances by which hostilities may be initiated. It is not a "strike first" concept—it is a concept for the development of a capability to prevail under any conditions of attack. This concept has, as its central theme, the application of superior offensive and defensive military force against enemy strengths that directly threaten the continued freedom and security of the United States and her allies.
>
> Implementation of a counterforce strategy demands a well-integrated national military structure. This concept is both offensive and defensive—a point often misunderstood. It requires strategic offensive forces capable of surviving initial enemy attacks and of destroying enemy offensive strike forces and control and support structures. It requires defensive forces in depth to destroy enemy mass destruction weapons in flight and as far from the United States and its allies as possible. It also requires forward area forces which, in conjunction with our allies, can conduct initial holding action to deny enemy access and prevent the infiltration or overrun of friendly territory. The size and effectiveness of a military force necessary to defeat the enemy's military force are dependent upon the size and effectiveness of that enemy force. A civil defense effort to provide greater protection to our civilian population is an additional strength that complements this military concept.[148]

In a succinct summary of these same thoughts, White stated:

> Until such time as worldwide disarmament under a positive system of controls and inspection is achieved, the United States and its allies must be superior to . . . our enemies in decisive military power. They must possess the ability to destroy the military strength that would hurt us while, at the same time, minimizing damage to our own military forces, to this Nation and to our friends and allies as well.[149]

To General White the Soviet Union's growing aerospace weapons inventories and the many uncertainties that were likely to prevail in a period of uneasy peace and possible general war demanded that the United States maintain a proper mix of manned and unmanned weapons in its future aerospace forces. He realized the nation's defense posture would be greatly improved by the acquisition of intercontinental ballistic missiles; as a matter of fact, he disagreed with the decision to delete two squadrons of Titan missiles, since these missiles could carry large warheads that would be required against extremely hard targets. Without dismissing the value of mobility, White was willing to accept McNamara's decision to delay the mobile Minuteman to get as many missiles as soon as possible. He nevertheless insisted: "We will have to rely on manned weapons systems to perform vital war functions which require on-the-spot trained, human judgment." Manned bomber systems, for example, would be required to prosecute "hunter-killer" follow-up attacks against imprecisely located counterforce targets in the wake of an initial missile salvo. Beyond this, White maintained that there would be "two incontestable overriding mandates" for the continuation of manned systems. The first of these concerned the "simple but awesome decision to launch." Bomber aircraft could be launched at critical junctures, even on suspicion of impending attack. They could proceed to a prearranged line and loiter there and could either return or, if given an order, attack. "Consequently," White explained, "their operations do not pose the problem of finality of decision which must inevitably accompany the launching of ballistic missiles." White conceived that even a perfected missile would be "the most inflexible weapon you can have.... It has two modes — go; no go."

> The second mandate concerns the perpetual requirement for operational flexibility. In any future war there is the almost certain probability that events will not unfold exactly as planned. Thus, there will be a tremendous premium on systems which can look, and find, and report, and attack, and return, and attack again. We will always need systems which can search out and destroy mobile targets, as well as fixed or rapidly developing targets whose positions are uncertain or unknown until observed. We will also need a poststrike reconnaissance capability to assess the results of our attacks and to show the way to the most effective employment of succeeding strikes.[150]

White also feared the effect of missiles on the psychology of the nation and of the missile crews, the latter who would "have to sit there day after day ready to push the button . . . they will get a static, nondynamic frame of mind." He pointed out that there had been "invulnerable weapons systems in the past" — the Great Wall of China and the Maginot Line were examples — but they had not proven invulnerable, any more than missiles were apt to be.[151]

In response to questions directed at him by congressional committees, White presented a detailed commentary of the Air Force's view on McNamara's specific proposals on the bomber force. He favored the 50-percent ground alert for the B-52s, but he argued against the concomitant rapid phaseout of the B-47s.

> The B-47 is an obsolescing airplane, but in these critical times, particularly during the periods of known unreliability of missiles and this day of rather uncertain international situations, it would be my thesis as the Chief of Staff of the Air Force that we ought to maintain all of the strategic forces that we can in our inventory.[152]

He also repeated his recommendation that the B-52 production line ought to be kept open.[153]

In appearances before the House Armed Services Committee and the House Subcommittee on Appropriations in March and April 1961, General White drew upon his "responsibilities as Chief of Staff of the Air Force and as an aviator of more than 35 years' service in flying" to present the "philosophical side of the question" as to why the Air Force required a B-70 weapon system. Much of these presentations involved his unwillingness to see a situation develop in which the nation "would have to depend for its survival on missiles for nearly 100 percent of its offensive capability." Drawing upon history, White asserted:

> The word "bomber" . . . has historically been a nasty word, for various reasons. Every bombing system we have ever developed has had many obstacles put in its way. . . . I refer to the B-17, which was restricted for some years in its operating radius. I refer to the B-29, in World War II. The B-36 was controversial, but it is a fact that we had no wars while we had the B-36. And I would hate to think where we would be now if we didn't have the B-47s, the B-52s, and the B-58s.[154]

White emphasized the importance of mobility in the historic art of warfare. "We can't leave the only exploitation of the air to ballistic missiles," he said. "The ability to be over your target, over enemy territory, to have dynamics in our strategic systems is essential. The missile is too inflexible to be the whole part of it." Speaking particularly about the B-70, he suggested, "If we don't build this airplane, in a certain sense the science of aeronautics is dead, because this is a breakthrough of the heat barrier." The technology of the B-70 would have very great application to the development of a Mach-3 transport for civil employment. White also pointed out that the B-70 would serve as a "hunter-killer" that would be able to find targets and destroy them. In future international negotiations, atomic missiles might be outlawed: bombers, however, could not be outlawed unless civil aircraft were outlawed because any plane that could carry passengers could also carry a bomb. "I forecast, from a solemn point of responsibility upon me and a reading of history which I think need not be very deep, that the future is very likely to depend on something like the B-70," White concluded.[155]

During the House Armed Services Committee's extended hearings on military posture and procurement, Chairman Carl Vinson noted the growth of "a perceptible hesitancy in placing complete confidence and dependence in the ICBM for now or the near future." The committee believed that the bomber was a vehicle of known capability, whereas the only knowledge of the effectiveness of the ICBM came from extrapolation. "The committee," Vinson stated, "is unwilling to place the safety of this country in a purely academic attitude." In a discussion with Secretary McNamara, Vinson secured agreement that the DOD would initiate planning that would place the bomber in proper perspective with other weapons at least until 1970. McNamara further assured Vinson that there was no ironclad date for phasing out B-47 bombers. Despite these assurances Congress apparently felt that the Air Force ought to have some additional bombers. As finally enacted in August 1961 the Department of Defense Appropriations Act for fiscal year 1962 included an additional $180 million to increase the B-70 from prototype development to a weapon system program and an additional $514.5 million for the procurement of another wing of B-52 bombers.[156]

When he discussed the Air Force's requirement for bombers with a subcommittee of the House Committee on Appropriations in May 1961, General White indicated that DOD probably would not authorize additional bombers even if the money for them were appropriated. Secretary McNamara confirmed General White's prediction by stating that the Defense Department had enough bombers and would not need any more until 1967 or 1968.[157] Somewhat later McNamara pointed out that the three prototype B-70s would still be built under a low-cost program and that the first of the planes would have the same "fly date" as would the first plane under the high-cost program advocated by the Air Force.[158] Speaking in opposition to the B-70 as a weapon system, Dr Herbert F. York described the big question about the manned-bomber system as "not really a scientific one, but a military operational question." He asserted that the intercontinental strategic bombardment aircraft was a variety of military aviation which "may very well become less important and disappear ... possibly within the decade."[159]

After he had conducted a review in DOD and had obtained President Kennedy's personal approval, Secretary McNamara informed Congress on 27 October 1961 that the B-70 would continue as a prototype development program.[160] McNamara also impounded the additional funds which Congress had appropriated for the procurement of an additional wing of B-52s. He reasoned that procurement of another wing of B-52s would increase the operational inventory of that aircraft by only 7 percent. For what it would cost to produce a wing of B-52s with tankers and Skybolt missiles and to operate it for five years, DOD could buy and operate 250 hardened and dispersed Minuteman missiles, or about 6 Polaris submarines. McNamara concluded:

> Manned bombers present soft and concentrated targets and they depend upon warning and quick response for their survival under nuclear attack. This is a less reliable means of protection than hardening, dispersal, and mobility. Moreover, reliance on warning and quick response means that bombers must be committed to attack very early in the war and cannot be held in reserve to be used in a controlled and deliberate way.[161]

Limited Mobilization for the Berlin Crisis

The immediate quick-fix amendments to the Department of Defense budget acted upon in the spring of 1961 left many larger decisions unmade, apparently because the evidence had not been completely sifted by defense studies that were still under way. At the same time that Secretary McNamara initiated his series of studies on critical requirements problems, he also ordered a detailed review and analysis of the Communist threat based on the latest and best intelligence information available.[162] In 1958 Soviet Premier Khrushchev had begun to threaten unilateral action that would jeopardize the West's position in Berlin, but it seemed to McNamara that the Soviet dictator became "much more categorical as to the actions he proposes to take" in the spring of 1961. McNamara related Khrushchev's actions to his endorsement of support for "wars of liberation" in his policy address of 6 January 1961.[163]

Khrushchev's announcements and actions appeared to "put flesh on the skeleton" of his January 1961 policy statement. On 18 April 1961 he charged that the Free Cuban invaders who had failed to overthrow Fidel Castro's Communist regime in Cuba in the ill-fated Bay of Pigs invasion had been "trained, equipped and armed in the United States of America." He added: "We shall render the Cuban people and their Government all necessary assistance in beating back the armed attack." During summit discussions held in Vienna on 3-4 June to exchange views on the German problem, Communist subversion in Laos, and other world problems, President Kennedy had what he described as a very "somber" meeting with Khrushchev. "He never gave way at all," Kennedy said. "I kept insisting that there could be no agreement between us as long as he supported Communist subversion all over the world, but he never gave way, never gave an inch." Speaking at the Kremlin on 8 July, Khrushchev announced that the Soviet Union was suspending its planned troop reductions and increasing its 1961 defense spending. He reiterated his determination to sign a separate peace treaty with East Germany by the end of 1961 if the West refused to sign treaties with both East and West Germany and to make West Berlin a demilitarized "free city," thus depriving the Western nations of their occupation responsibilities there.[164]

At the same time Khrushchev announced his bellicose intentions, the Kennedy administration continued its evaluations of US force capabilities. According to reports, the administration felt desperately short of conventional force capabilities when it considered the situations in Cuba and Laos. On 22 April President Kennedy appointed retired Gen Maxwell D. Taylor as presidential military adviser and directed him to investigate the Cuban affair, US counterinsurgency capabilities, and other aspects of defense policy. At a meeting with Rusk, McNamara, and Taylor on 8 July, Kennedy ordered an urgent review of United States military strength to determine if forces and planned expenditures were adequate in view of the Soviet threats to Berlin. Sometime in the spring of 1961 the Department of Defense's evaluation of the Soviet Union convinced McNamara that the United States and its allies had far larger conventional capabilities in relation to the Soviet Union than was commonly assumed. Speaking of the Soviets, McNamara observed: "They aren't 12-1/2 feet tall. They don't have 187 divisions. They don't have 175 divisions. A major portion of their divisions today are under strength... compared to the US division with its support forces."[165] The secretary's staff also started to question prevailing assumptions about Soviet tactical air power and soon concluded that the numbers of Soviet tactical fighters had been inflated and that the performance of their aircraft had been exaggerated.[166]

Appearing before Congress on 25 May 1961 in what he described as his second State of the Union message, President Kennedy among other things requested an additional $100 million to provide nonatomic weapons modernization for the Army and $60 million to enable the Marine Corps to expand its strength to 190,000 men, thus filling up its three existing divisions and air wings and organizing a cadre for a fourth division. The major response to the Berlin crisis, however, came on 25 July when Kennedy explained to the American people: "We cannot and will not permit the Communists to drive us out of Berlin — either gradually or by force." He had stated already that the nation must possess "a wider choice than humiliation or all-out nuclear action" and in a message to Congress on 26 July the president requested an additional appropriation of $3.247 million for the armed forces, an increase in the Army's strength from 875,000 to 1,008,000 men, and an increase of 29,000 and 63,000 men in the active duty strength of the Navy and the Air Force, respectively. Kennedy also asked Congress to enact a joint resolution that would authorize the president, until 1 July 1962, to order units and members of the Ready Reserve to active duty for not more than 12 consecutive months.[167]

When he began to explain President Kennedy's expanded defense program to Congress on 26 July 1961, Secretary McNamara prefaced his presentation with an assessment of the Soviet challenge and the indicated Western response to it.

> Believing that the Western World will be very reluctant to invoke the use of nuclear weapons in response to anything short of a direct threat to its survival, the Kremlin leaders hope to create divisive influences within the [NATO] alliance by carefully measured military threats in connection with the Berlin situation. In order to meet such threats with firmness and confidence and to provide us with a greater range of military alternatives, we will need more nonnuclear strength than we have today.[168]

He later added:

> We feel very strongly that the US Defense Establishment must have a greater degree of flexibility in responding to particular situations. We need to expand the range of military alternatives available to the President in meeting the kind of situation which may confront us in maintaining our position in Berlin.... What we are proposing now is not only to strengthen our nuclear capabilities, but also to increase our nonnuclear capabilities to provide a still greater degree of versatility to our military forces.[169]

Acting in an air of emergency, Congress approved President Kennedy's authority to order up to 250,000 members of the Ready Reserve for one year's active duty, and as finally enacted in August 1961 the national defense appropriation for fiscal year 1962 totaled $51 billion — an increase of $6.1 billion over the $44.9 billion recommended in the original Eisenhower budget. Since strategic forces were already in a high state of readiness, McNamara believed they required little augmentation for the Berlin crisis. He did, however, allocate funds and personnel to enable SAC to move more rapidly toward a 50-percent ground alert for both B-47s and B-52s, and he decided to retain in active service the six wings of B-47s scheduled for inactivation during the fiscal year. In the air defense field the emergency program hastened the preparation of manual backup facilities for the control of interceptor aircraft at radar sites, thus enabling the vulnerable semiautomatic ground environment (SAGE) facilities to be bypassed if this were necessary.

IDEAS, CONCEPTS, DOCTRINE

So far as the Air Force was concerned, McNamara's chief concern was with tactical air units and airlift. The Air Force received authority to retain the light bomber, tactical reconnaissance, tactical fighter, and C-118 air transport squadrons that were to be phased out during the fiscal year. In October and November 1961 the Air Force also called to active duty 36 squadrons from the Air National Guard and Air Force Reserve. These units included tactical fighters, tactical reconnaissance, and C-97 and C-124 transports. Seven Air National Guard fighter squadrons, one tactical reconnaissance squadron, and a tactical control group were deployed by air to European bases about a month after the October recall. Three Air National Guard F-104 air defense squadrons, which were recalled on 1 November, dismantled their aircraft for shipment overseas in C-124s, and were in place in Germany and Spain on 24 November. Largely as a result of the calls to active duty, Air Force strength rose from 88 wings to the equivalent of 97 wings (339 squadrons) in the year ending on 30 June 1962.[170]

As a part of its augmentation the Navy increased its amphibious lift and reactivated its troop transport ships. The Army received by far the largest force increase. Of the 14 Army divisions, 8 were overseas, 3 were assigned to the Strategic Army Command (STRAC) in the United States, and 3 were partly manned and employed in recruit training in the United States. As an initial response, the Army was authorized to increase the three training divisions to full strength and to assign them to STRAC; it also brought the Seventh Army and other units in Europe up to full strength. Heavier draft calls and mobilization of Army reservists filled existing units, and on 19 September two Army National Guard divisions were mobilized. In August the Berlin garrison was increased by 1,500 men, and in September some 40,000 troops were sent to Europe to increase the Seventh Army to full strength. By the end of 1961 the three former training divisions were ready for combat, and the two National Guard divisions completed their combat training in February 1962. SAC was accordingly expanded to two corps, each with four divisions. The expansion of the ground forces left the Marines programmed for three division-wing teams, plus a cadre organization for a fourth division. The refusal to expand the Marine Corps was justified by the fact that the type of divisions which might be required in Europe were Army divisions rather than Marine divisions, which were organized and equipped for independent assault operations.[171]

Of the $3.247 million requested to meet the Berlin crisis, $1.753 million was committed to the procurement of weapons, ammunition, and equipment to meet nonnuclear requirements. Even in the case of Nike Hercules batteries in Europe, Secretary McNamara foresaw "circumstances under which we would wish to utilize these batteries without nuclear warheads, avoiding if possible the immediate escalation to nuclear war that might well follow the use of nuclear warheads in these batteries."[172] Most of the large appropriations for conventional weapons, however, was justified to correct a situation which McNamara described as resultant from past tendencies "on the part of the services to base their planning and force structures on their own unilateral views of how a future war might be fought." McNamara said that the Air Force had planned primarily in terms of a short nuclear war, had not provided sufficient stocks of combat consumables for conventional limited war, and thus could not fight a conventional war as long as the Army. The Army had based its requirements on plans for a large-scale conventional war of long duration, but these requirements had been only partially used as the basis for annual procurement programs. As a result the Army had only about one-third of its so-called requirements in its inventories and specific items in the inventory were badly out of balance.[173]

The Joint Chiefs of Staff visualized the fundamental purposes of the Berlin crisis buildup as being to improve the credibility of United States national policies and the total deterrent posture and to place the United States "in a better position to implement military operations on whatever scale may be required."[174] What the effect of the conventional augmentation may have been on Soviet policy remained a matter of speculation. In a speech on 11 August, Khrushchev expressed doubt that the West would fight to preserve the freedom of the West Germans. Before dawn on 13 August the East German government closed access routes between East and West Berlin and shortly thereafter the Communists built a wall along most of the 25-mile border within Berlin, thus effectively although illegally ending free movement within Berlin and between Berlin and the East German territory. On 31 August the Soviet Union also announced that it was resuming nuclear weapon tests, allegedly because the West had threatened to unleash war as a countermeasure to the conclusion of a peace treaty with East Germany. As the Berlin crisis abated, Secretary McNamara stated: "We are convinced that the rapid buildup in our conventional forces made possible by the callup of the Reserves has done much to stabilize the Berlin situation." A little later McNamara described the mobilization of the reserves as being the thing that had called the hand of the Soviets. "I don't believe," he said, "there is any action that has been taken that more clearly demonstrated the strength, the will, and the firmness of purpose of this Nation than the callup of those units."[175]

Emerging Strategy: Flexible Response and Multiple Options

In the same months the Kennedy administration made quick-fix amendments to the original Eisenhower defense budget during 1961, Secretary McNamara commenced studies of a five-year projection of defense requirements which would in effect engraft strategy into the national defense budgets. In this task McNamara indicated that he expected to "start with the plan or the policy and translate it into quantitative terms." "I consider the budget nothing more than and nothing less than the quantitative expression of a plan or a policy," he added.[176] The five-year force projection involved the mission to be accomplished by military forces, the latest intelligence data on the capabilities of the Soviet Union and its satellites, and the cost-effectiveness relationships among the various alternative means of performing the defense mission.[177]

In his message to Congress on 28 March 1961 President Kennedy had already stated the basic mission to be accomplished by military forces, and this guidance was elaborated in continuing statements by both Kennedy and McNamara. In his State of the Union message of 11 January 1962 Kennedy explained: "We have rejected any all-or-nothing posture which would leave no choice but inglorious retreat or unlimited retaliation." As the military representative of the president, General Taylor explained that this statement meant that the administration had accepted a need for

> great flexibility in our present and future military policy, and in the military forces designed to sustain that policy. . . . Mindful of the awful dangers of atomic warfare, we require a military policy which takes as its primary purpose the deterrence of that disaster. At the same time . . . it must give due recognition to the need to cope with many situations short of general war — particularly para-war.[178]

From time to time President Kennedy reiterated the policy that the United States definitely would not "launch a preemptive attack, an act of aggression." There were at least two strong reasons for this policy. In the first place, Kennedy advanced the belief that no nation could win a nuclear war. He stated on 14 February 1962:

> Now, if someone thinks we should have a nuclear war in order to win, I can inform them that there will not be winners of the next nuclear war, if there is one, and this country and other countries would suffer very heavy blows. So we have to proceed with responsibility and with care in an age where the human race can obliterate itself.[179]

Several weeks later Kennedy pointed out a second reason for foreswearing a military initiative when he observed that "the basic problems facing the world today are not susceptible to a final military solution."

In a major policy address at the University of Michigan on 16 June 1962, Secretary McNamara added his own interpretation of the role of military forces in United States policy.

> I want to emphasize that we see our military strength not as the means of achieving the kind of world we seek, but as a shield to prevent any other nation from using its military strength, either directly or through threats and intimidation, to frustrate the aspirations we share with all the free peoples of the world.[180]

While the five-year force projection was being planned, DOD conducted a careful review of prospective Communist capabilities to endanger the United States. In President Kennedy's view the changing Communist military capabilities in themselves demanded changes in United States military policy. "As late as 1954," Kennedy explained in March 1962, "the balance in air power, in nuclear weapons, was all on our side. That change began about 1958 or 1959 with the missiles. Now we have got to realize that *both* sides have these annihilating weapons, and that changes the problem."[181] At the Tushino air show over Moscow in July 1961, the Soviets displayed three new supersonic bombers, two new Mach-2 fighters, a new jet seaplane, a flying crane helicopter, and a very large converti-plane. The new bombers included an exceptionally large delta-wing plane called the Bounder; an advanced swept-wing Mach-2.5 heavy bomber slightly larger than the B-58 and designated as the Beauty; and a Mach-2 swept-wing design called the Blinder that could apparently perform a dual role as a bomber or as an interceptor. The Bounder was almost as large as a B-36 and although it was powered by large jet engines it seemed capable of serving as a test vehicle for nuclear engines. Older Badger twin jet bombers carried air-to-surface missiles resembling the Hound Dog design, and the Beauty carried what appeared to be a ballistic missile similar to a Skybolt slung under its belly.[182]

Although the new Soviet aircraft demonstrated excellent progress in aerodynamics, Secretary McNamara received no evidence that the Soviets were producing any significant numbers of long-range bombers, and he could only estimate that the number of manned bombers the Soviets might send against the United States would not be very large. By November 1961 his study of Communist force projections caused him to conclude that "while the ICBM threat will be increasing during the next several years, present indications are that the manned bomber threat will be declining." A manned-bomber attack against the United States, moreover, assumably would follow an initial Soviet ICBM attack. In view of the vulnerability of the United States to intercontinental or submarine-launched ballistic missile attack, McNamara visualized that "the protection of our strategic offensive forces against surprise missile attack can be achieved only by warning, hardening, [and] mobility, rather than by an active defense." Similarly, since the main danger of hostile bomber attack would be in the wake of a missile attack, McNamara noted that "warning and dispersal and protection of our air defense forces are more important than mere numbers."[183] Even though McNamara recognized that the first-generation Soviet missile force would be vulnerable to attack on its exposed launching pads, he also predicted that "as the Soviet Union hardens and disperses its ICBM force and acquires a significant number of missile launching submarines . . . our problem will be further complicated."[184] "It will become increasingly difficult, regardless of the form of attack," he added a little later, "to destroy a sufficiently large proportion of the Soviet's strategic nuclear forces to preclude major damage to the United States, regardless of how large or what kind of strategic forces we build."[185]

In evaluating the Soviet threat to the United States, Secretary McNamara apparently continued to attach great importance to Premier Khrushchev's "For New Victories of the World Communist Movement" address of 6 January 1961. He told a congressional committee that this was "one of the most important speeches of 1961," and, in an address in Chicago on 17 February 1962, he suggested that "it may prove to be one of the most important statements made by a world leader in the decade of the 60s." Speaking of Khrushchev, McNamara said: "I have every reason to believe that he was outlining very clearly his objectives and his plans for accomplishing them." Although the Soviet chief had indicated that the free world would continue to face the cold war struggle for years to come, McNamara was confident that the United States could deter the Soviets from initiating general or limited war by maintaining "the kind of forces which would make global nuclear war, and even local wars, unprofitable for the Soviet Union." "We must continue to convince him," McNamara said, speaking of Khrushchev, "that thermonuclear wars would destroy the Soviet Union and therefore that he should refrain from actions that would bring on such wars."[186]

During these strategic evaluations, Secretary McNamara's staff redoubled its efforts to solve the riddle of Soviet ground strength. Although the evidence apparently was not conclusive in the winter of 1961–62, something seemed to be wrong with assessments of Soviet surface strengths. With a strength of a million men the US Army could field only 16 divisions, yet the Soviets were credited with being able to obtain something like 150 American-style divisions from about 2.2 million men. The Soviets possessed a heavily mechanized and armored force, but if they launched an attack in Western Europe the Soviet forces would be operating at the end of a very long supply line. As a result of the force augmentations incident to the Berlin crisis, NATO would soon have the equivalent of 26 divisions, including the 5 fully manned US divisions, and their supporting forces on its central front in Europe.[187]

At the start of preparation for making the fiscal year 1963 defense budget estimates in May 1961, McNamara asked the service secretaries and chiefs to make recommendations on the force levels and weapons they would require during fiscal years 1963 through 1967. Even though the services were asked to submit individual requirements with no budgetary limitations, they were directed to group recommended forces into "program packages" — such as "strategic retaliatory," "continental air and missile defense," and "general purpose forces" — that were related to the accomplishment of specific missions. From July through October 1961 Secretary McNamara and Deputy Secretary of Defense Roswell L. Gilpatric received and reviewed the service requirements. McNamara described the review process as essentially ensuring that "we are to attain the specific force levels necessary to support the political objectives at the lowest possible cost."[188] Gilpatric characterized the review as a "fusion of force structure to military strategy and, ultimately, the two of them to our larger national goals."[189] Had all the service recommendations been accepted, the fiscal year 1963 budget would have totaled about $63 billion, but by having in effect invited the services to bid freely against each other for the performance of mission responsibilities within program packages, McNamara was able to get cost-effectiveness evaluations of competing service proposals. Thus, on 4 August, the Navy presented its proposals in the presence of key Air Force officials, the Air Force presented its proposed program with key Navy men listening, and Army officials commented on both the Navy and Air Force proposals. Based upon this and other reviews, McNamara prepared and forwarded to the Joint Chiefs and service secretaries in mid-September a tentative program guidance for computing the fiscal year 1963 budget and for making program projections for the five-year period. When the service budgets were submitted beginning on 23 October, McNamara found that they still totaled about $54.5 billion. Working with the service secretaries and the chiefs, McNamara made some 620 separate decisions in the next month, some raising items and others lowering items in the service budgets. Upon reclama McNamara reversed himself on about 60 items but ended with about 560 changes, which reduced the total defense budget for fiscal year 1963 to the $51.6 billion President Kennedy asked Congress to appropriate in January 1962. As a result of the whole budgetary process, McNamara defended the proposed force structure as being necessary to meet military requirements without regard to arbitrary budget ceilings but calculated to be attainable at the lowest possible cost.[190]

Five-Year Military Force Projection

When he presented the fiscal year 1963 defense budget and the five-year force projections to Congress in January 1962, Secretary McNamara explained that they reflected "the conclusion that, while our nuclear forces are increasing, greater emphasis than in the past must be given, both by ourselves and our NATO allies, to our nonnuclear forces.... What is being proposed ... is not a reversal of our existing national policy but an increase in our nonnuclear capabilities to provide a greater degree of versatility to our limited-war forces."[191] When he was asked to cut across the program-package approach and rate the priority of separate items in terms of national importance, McNamara stated the following order of priority: (1) nuclear deterrent forces to include Air Force Minuteman and Navy Polaris missiles; (2) raising the Army to 16 regular combat-ready divisions; (3) proper equipment for the 16 Army divisions; (4) airlift and sealift capabilities to move the combat-ready forces; (5) nuclear attack submarines for antisubmarine warfare; (6) Air Force fighter aircraft for the support of ground forces; (7) increased procurement of Navy and Marine Corps aircraft; and (8) a new aircraft carrier. He further remarked that torpedoes for the Navy and iron bombs for the Air Force would rank high on the illustrative priority list.[192]

Unlike most other military requirements, Secretary McNamara considered that the requirement for strategic retaliatory forces—the program package that included long-range bombers with air-to-ground and decoy missiles and supporting tankers, land-based and submarine-based strategic missiles, and the system for command and control of the forces—lent itself "rather well to reasonably precise calculation." The major mission of these forces was to deter war by their capability to destroy the enemy's war-making potential. This was judged to be a reasonably finite problem, and the quantitative procurement of strategic retaliatory forces included allowances for losses incurred in a hostile first strike; the number, types, and locations of the aiming points in hostile target systems; the numbers and explosive yields of weapons that would be required to destroy specified targets; the degree of reliability of each weapon system; and the cost effectiveness of each weapon system in comparison with alternate systems. Assuming that the Soviet Union ultimately would build a large ICBM force, the United States had to develop the kind of strategic offensive forces which would "be able to ride out an all-out attack by nuclear-armed ICBMs in sufficient strength to strike back decisively."[193]

In the way of forces the defense budget for fiscal year 1963 visualized the completion of the 13-squadron Atlas and 12-squadron Titan missile programs, the funding of 4 additional squadrons of hardened Minuteman missiles (thus providing 17 squadrons and 800 missiles), and the addition of 6 Polaris submarines, with 6 more programmed for fiscal year 1964, making a total projection of 41 Polaris submarines in the five-year program. The development of the rail-mobile Minuteman missile was canceled, since McNamara was convinced the benefits from the system would not be worth the cost. A mobile Minuteman would cost "several times" as much as a fixed-base Minuteman; it would be more expensive to operate, less reliable, less accurate, more susceptible to sabotage, and fraught with difficult operational problems such as its protection from sabotage. As for strategic bombers, the five-year defense projection included the maintenance in the inventory of 14 wings of B-52s (many of which were supposed to be equipped with Skybolt missiles) and 2 wings of B-58s. As the missile forces were built up, the number of B-47 wings would be reduced. After additional study, McNamara still believed that "the B-70 will not provide enough of an increase in our offensive capabilities to justify its very high cost." He nevertheless wished to continue the B-70 in the limited-development program, which would "preserve the option of developing a manned bomber if we should later determine that such a system is required."[194]

Under the program-package budgeting arrangement, continental air and missile defense forces included the weapon systems, warning and communications networks, and ancillary equipment required to detect, identify, and track unfriendly forces approaching the North American continent and to destroy them. Viewing the threat to the United States as rapidly changing from manned bombers to the ICBM and submarine-launched missiles, McNamara envisioned the defensive task as being (1) to reduce the vulnerability of the existing bomber defense system to ballistic missile attack; (2) to improve the certainty and the timeliness of warning against ballistic missile attack; (3) to provide for an active defense against ballistic and submarine-launched missiles; (4) to develop a defense system against unfriendly satellites; and (5) to provide fallout protection for the population of the United States. Concluding that the air defense system against hostile aircraft was already "very extensive and sophisticated," McNamara proposed to continue the system in being over the next several years with few improvements other than continuing to provide manual backup for the SAGE system and more dispersal for existing air defense fighters. Most new air and missile defense expenditures would have to be programmed in the research and development of antiballistic missile systems, including continuing development of the Nike Zeus terminal defense system. "We must bear in mind that no matter how much we spend, we simply cannot in this day and age provide an absolute defense for the continental United States," McNamara observed.[195]

The defense budget for fiscal year 1963 included most of the Army's combat and combat support units, virtually all of the Navy's units, all Marine Corps units, and the tactical air warfare units of the Air Force under the general-purpose forces program package. McNamara explained: "These are the forces on which we would depend in any conflict short of general nuclear war. . . . It is the limited war mission which primarily shapes the size and character of the general purpose forces." To McNamara the general-purpose forces were intended for the support of United States allies around the world, and the great diversity of units and weapons in this package, the wide variety of possible contingencies that had to be contemplated, the role that the reserve forces might play, and the relationship of United States and allied general-purpose forces made it most difficult for DOD to determine precisely the specific requirements for general-purpose forces. As Secretary McNamara looked at the problem, however, United States general-purpose forces either had to be stationed in potential trouble areas or had to be highly mobile and readily deployable from a central reserve in the United States. If the forces were retained in a central reserve, the United States had to have adequate airlift and sealift capabilities to move them promptly to trouble areas. Since there was a practical limit on the volume of material that could be shipped overseas in a short period of time, attention had to be given to prepositioning stocks for mobile forces in various parts of the world. Since no one could be sure where forces might have to fight, the general-purpose forces had to have a great deal of built-in versatility. Finally, since the general purpose forces would to a large extent complement similar allied forces, their size and character would be affected by the size and character of allied forces.[196]

In response to the Berlin crisis the Department of Defense had already increased the size of the general-purpose forces by the mobilization of National Guard and Reserve units for a year's service. On 3 January 1962 President Kennedy announced that the regular Army's strength would be increased from 14 to 16 divisions, and the activation of 2 new regular divisions in February 1962 brought the Army to a newly authorized strength of 960,000 military personnel. Where earlier planning had relied upon the expansion of Army units to meet war emergencies by the mobilization of reservist elements, McNamara sought immediate readiness for Army units and the maintenance of a capability to deploy rapidly up to six divisions to Europe, while simultaneously maintaining a reserve of other ready divisions for deployment to other parts of the world.[197]

During the Berlin crisis the Navy expanded its force level to 16 attack carriers and 10 air-sea warfare carriers. In determining force levels for fiscal year 1963, the Joint Chiefs of Staff agreed that 15 attack carriers and 9 antisubmarine warfare (ASW) carriers should be supported, with these levels to be subject to review in future years. In the course of budget review within DOD however, Gen Curtis E. LeMay, Air Force chief of staff, and George H. Decker, Army chief of staff, questioned the advisability of including the construction of a new *Forrestal*-class carrier in the fiscal year 1963 funding. General LeMay also wanted to place greater emphasis on antisubmarine carriers and less emphasis on attack carriers. On the other hand, Adm George W. Anderson, Jr., chief of naval operations, strongly pointed out that attack carriers were uniquely suited for limited-war employments and would be able to survive under general war conditions. General Lemnitzer agreed with Admiral Anderson. "I think," Lemnitzer said, "the attack carrier is as important today as it was during World War II." In the end McNamara accepted the value of the attack carrier in the limited-war role, although he reasoned that the value of the attack carrier would gradually diminish in the general war role as larger forces of strategic missiles became available. He stated:

> There are many potential trouble spots in the world where the attack carrier is and will continue to be the only practical means of bringing our air striking power to bear. Carrier airpower can be employed without involving third parties, without invoking treaties, agreements, or overflight rights. And ... the carrier task force is a most effective means for presenting a show of force or establishing a military presence, which often has helped to maintain the peace and discourage hostilities.[198]

Admiral Anderson maintained that the Navy required a nuclear-powered aircraft carrier, but McNamara's studies indicated that a nuclear-powered carrier would cost about one-third to one-half more to construct and operate than an equivalent conventionally powered carrier. "The operational benefits to be derived from the nuclear-powered carrier, particularly in limited-war operations," he observed, "do not, in our judgment, justify the higher cost."[199]

Reflecting the mobilization of Air National Guard and Air Force Reserve units in the autumn of 1961, the strength of worldwide tactical air forces—including tactical fighters, bombers, and reconnaissance, Matador and Mace missiles, troop carrier planes, and overseas-based fighter-interceptors—rose sharply from 32 wings to 43 wings. Anticipating the release of reservist personnel in spite of an augmentation of tactical air forces, the Air Force secured McNamara's approval in November 1961 for an expansion of the regular tactical fighter force from 16 wings to 21 wings.[200] The temporary equipment of the five additional fighter wings would be managed by retention of old F-84 fighters in the regular inventory when Air National Guard squadrons were released from the federal service. In the future the TFX (F-111) was expected to be developed for use by both the Air Force and the Navy. In the interim some new fighters were required for the modernization of the tactical fighter wings. Taking an active interest in the matter, McNamara worked closely with LeMay in an examination of the prospects for Air Force procurement of either additional F-105s or of Navy-developed A-4Ds or F-4Hs. At first McNamara ruled that the Air Force would procure A-4Ds since they would cost only about one-third as much as the F-4Hs. The Air Force preferred the F-4H since it was newer, carried more ordnance, and was operationally superior, and, on the basis of these arguments, McNamara reversed his order. The Air Force nevertheless continued to pose some reservations about the F-4H in comparison with the F-105. Because of stresses placed upon fighter bombers during maneuvers, the Air Force had long required these planes to have a built-in strength capable of withstanding 8.67 G loadings. The F-105 had been designed with these characteristics, but the McDonnell F-4A had a designed strength of 6.5 Gs. The Navy maintained that a modern fighter, which employed guided missiles from greater ranges, would not be subjected to tight high-G maneuvers, and after studying the statistics the Air Force ultimately agreed that it could accept the design capabilities of the F-4H. Other than for slight reservations about the stress loading, Air Force tests showed the F-4H to be superior in many ways to the older F-105. In February 1962 DOD accordingly authorized the Air Force to reduce F-105 procurement and order substantial numbers of F-4Hs, which were subsequently designated F-110As and finally F-4Cs. The Air Force also changed its plan to procure RF-105 aircraft in favor of RF-4Cs. Somewhat later, McNamara described the F-105 and F-4 experience as a "perfect illustration" of opportunities for major savings.

> It was not until after the completion of development and the start of procurement that we standardized on the F-4H for both services. This is very wasteful, because we had duplicate development and, to a considerable degree, duplicate production facilities prepared for these aircraft. We did ... achieve ... savings ... in spare parts procurement and certain maintenance functions as a result of the standardization. We are better off than if we had not standardized, but we standardized too late.[201]

From the start of his administration, President Kennedy emphasized the need to expand national military airlift capabilities, and Secretary McNamara was confident that the establishment of the separate planning, programming, and budgeting package for airlift/sealift forces would bring these forces into balance with forces, equipment, and supplies that would require deployment.[202] In the mobilization of 1961 five Air Force Reserve C-124 squadrons reported to the Tactical Air Command, and six Air National Guard C-97 squadrons joined the Military Air Transport. Made available by diverting production from tankers to transport planes, 45 C-135s became available to MATS, which assigned them to 3 squadrons, 1 of which was a converted C-118 squadron.[203] Except for the C-133s and C-135s, however, airlift aircraft in service early in 1962 were more than 10 years old, and the expansion of airborne mobility was still more a matter of promise than of actuality. Although the C-135s proved useful for quick movements of troops over long distances, they had no airdrop capability and only a limited-cargo capacity. In making the fiscal year 1963 budget, McNamara considered procurement of more C-135s, but he ultimately decided that these planes could not be delivered until better aircraft could be manufactured.[204] The better plane would be the C-141 Starlifter, an aircraft selected for development during 1961 in what General LeMay described as "the best coordinated project that we have had up to date." This plane was configured to carry 98 percent of the equipment items of an airborne division for distances up to 5,500 nautical miles at a speed of more than 440 knots. The fiscal year 1963 budget contained funds for the initiation of production of the C-141 and for the purchase of a test and evaluation quantity of the plane. As of January 1962 Secretary McNamara nevertheless confessed that he had found "no simple black or white solution" for calculating military airlift requirements.

> We estimate that our current capability is sufficiently great to permit the deployment of significant forces to any remote area in a relatively short time. This capability, while impressive, is nevertheless less than what we feel we ought to have to meet a full range of contingencies.[205]

General LeMay Fears for Strategic Superiority

As a matter of fact, General LeMay, who had become Air Force chief of staff on 30 June 1961, agreed "with the administration's policy of trying to build up a little more conventional power that could take care of limited wars in a little better manner than we might have been able to do it in the past." He also contended that the total amount of defense money requested in the fiscal year 1963 budget was generous. "When you get an increase in the overall Department of Defense budget of the size contemplated this year," he remarked, "I do not think any reasonable man will say we should have more." General LeMay was nevertheless greatly concerned that the 1963 budget and the five-year force projection would not continue to build strategic superiority. The total obligational authority allocated to strategic retaliatory forces in fiscal year 1963 ($8.5 billion) was a lesser amount than in 1962 ($9.1 billion), and according to the five-year program the commitment of funds to strategic forces would trend downward from about 18 percent to 20 percent of the total defense budget to about 8 percent.

> I think that your strategic forces must come first. . . . I worry about the trend as established by this year's budget. . . . I do not think you can maintain superiority in this field with that sort of a program.[206]

LeMay feared the loss of strategic superiority because experience indicated that a nation could counter limited aggression only if it maintained its strategic initiative. "I point out," he said, "that you cannot fight a limited war except under the umbrella of strategic superiority. For example, we would not have dared to go into Lebanon . . . without strategic superiority which kept the enemy air force off."[207] Speaking as Air Force director of plans, Maj Gen David A. Burchinal further developed the relationship of strategic capability to the handling of lesser conflicts. He explained:

> If you have a strategic capability which is clearly superior . . . then you have in fact established your ability to control . . . escalation in the lower levels. In other words, if two conventional forces in a limited engagement come together, the fact we could win at the higher level would make it unprofitable for the enemy to let it expand, and we would therefore control the intensity and be able to keep it at that [lower level].[208]

In public speeches and in testimony in the winter of 1961-62, Gen Frederic H. Smith, Jr., Air Force vice chief of staff, emphasized that strategic superiority was a prerequisite of counterforce. Smith pointed out:

> The gravest risk an aggressor faces is the loss of his military forces. Without these forces, he is helpless. Aggression is no longer possible. Worst for him, without forces an aggressor can't even control the people he has already conquered. Thus the capability to defeat an enemy's forces is the only rational objective of military preparedness.[209]

Smith determined that the maintenance of strategic superiority was imperative both to keep ahead of Soviet technological challenge and to permit the United States to enjoy a wide variety of counterforce options in target selection. Speaking of a Soviet commander, Smith rationalized:

> He will realize his range of options as we realize ours, and if he determines that regardless of how he attacks we are going to end up with a clear advantage, then I do not think he will come. And certainly he would decide that if he does not concentrate on our military force, then we have an overwhelming force to go back at him, and I don't think he would be illogical. . . . By having two or more options we might well better our situation if war comes, over that which it would be if we just had a complete all-out phase destruction without any application of logical reasoning.[210]

General Smith also presented the epitome of Air Force strategic thinking to the Armed Services and Appropriations Committees of the Senate and House of Representatives in February 1962. His statement read:

> At the outset, we should be quite clear that of the various levels of international conflict — from troubled peace through cold, limited, and general war — general war and local wars that can escalate to general war pose the primary military threat to the security of the free world.
>
> This will remain true for the foreseeable future. It is our conviction, therefore, that the core of our security planning lies in the maintenance of an effective capability to prosecute successfully a general war. Only with this capability can we insure national survival if general war occurs. Only if we have, in fact, the shield of this capability can we support our commitments worldwide — either in the cold war or in limited conflict.
>
> Accordingly, ours must be a posture based upon strategic force capabilities which provide confidence in winning a general war if one is forced upon us. All of our other capabilities depend upon this fundamental one. Such a posture will provide the basis for an effective deterrent to a Soviet decision to attack the United States or its allies. With lesser capabilities, the Nation might ultimately reach a position of strategic inferiority marked or repeated, potentially disastrous incursions against our security, and finally, against our very survival.
>
> The foregoing is fundamental to our strategic concept. This concept requires a war waging capability — our primary goal is to deter war, but, if deterrence fails, we must have the capability to fight and prevail.
>
> In assessing the types of forces required to maintain this strategic posture we must first determine the tasks to be performed and under what conditions they must be accomplished. Simply stated, our forces must possess the ability to survive an enemy attack, penetrate enemy defenses, and attack with weapons of sufficient yield and accuracy to assure the destruction of targets that remain to threaten the United States

and our allies. At the same time, we must obtain the essential facts concerning the course of the conflict during and after our attacks. This requires reconnaissance of enemy territory for both targeting and retargeting as well as for damage assessment.

Our strategic capabilities must include a secure means for sustained command and control of the strategic force. The decision making process must be geared to the quick reaction and flexibility which is built into the strategic weapon systems.

In our strategy, we must continue to cover with a high assurance factor all targets representing long-range enemy strategic forces. This requires warheads and bombs of adequate yields, and missiles and aircraft of sufficient range and accuracy to do the job. In the event of war, an important part of the overall task is to determine the degree of success we have achieved in destroying targets, and the capability to restrike those targets which we have not yet destroyed.

Essential to continued strategic superiority is a diversification of the force to include both manned and unmanned vehicles, since no single weapon system can do the entire job. In general, diversification provides four advantages: First, it gives us a flexible or versatile capability, so that if one method of attack is rendered ineffective because of enemy defenses, we have other methods available. Second, it forces the enemy to expend effort and resources in his attempt to defend against all methods of our attack. Third, it compounds the enemy attack problem, both in types and numbers of weapons, which in turn enhances the survivability of each of our systems. And, fourth, the manned systems give us a capability to observe and report the physical evidence of an enemy's situation. This information is a vital requirement for the conduct of war. For, without it, it would be impossible to make controlled responses or even to find bases for negotiations, were the enemy to indicate his desires to negotiate.

Since the enemy capability is by no means static, there is a requirement for continuous modernization—improving existing weapon systems and introducing new ones. As the enemy develops new defenses, we must develop new means to penetrate those defenses.

A trend that is obvious from continuous study of the changing threat and analysis of our force requirements is that all weapons sooner or later are overtaken by events. We do not believe there is such a thing as an ultimate weapon and certainly nothing in our present or projected inventory can claim that distinction. Therefore we believe we must continue to take full advantage of the broadening horizons of technology both to meet the threats posed by our adversaries and, where possible, present those adversaries with technological surprise.

Strategic offensive forces and continental defense forces have a complementary role in providing a deterrent posture or in providing for survival of the Nation should general war occur. A nation whose national philosophy is not to strike the first blow must have.... overwhelming offensive forces—and by "overwhelming"... I mean forces of sufficient character, hardness, and size, as to endure a first strike by an enemy and have the resultant strength necessary to destroy any residual capability which he has, to enable us to achieve our objectives and prevail.[211]

Against the backdrop of these summarizations of the importance of strategic superiority, General LeMay and Air Staff officers made known their specific objections to the fiscal year 1963 budget. LeMay maintained that in addition to the

200 Minuteman missiles authorized for procurement at least 100 more should be purchased and that the budget should include money for the long lead time items for about 150 additional Minuteman missiles. Given a choice of systems, however, General LeMay admitted a preference for a manned system, though he suggested that both could be acquired by arranging rather than increasing Air Force budget allocations.[212] Even though the Air Force was confident that the B-52H, equipped with Skybolt missiles (which were being funded for initial procurement in the fiscal year 1963 budget), would be able to penetrate hostile defenses, Secretary McNamara's refusal to release the $525 million that Congress already had appropriated for additional B-52s made it evident that continuation of this plane in production was impossible. The Air Force accordingly placed all its efforts behind getting approval for the B-70 as a strategic weapon system.[213]

Even in its original concept the B-70 had included many features that fitted it for service as a reconnaissance/strike aircraft as well as a bomber. With the passing of time the role and reliability of ballistic missiles could be seen more clearly, and many state-of-the-art advances were achieved in reconnaissance sensors and air-to-ground missiles. Thus by the summer of 1961 the B-70 system was increasingly referred to as the RS-70, and, as a result of new studies, the Air Force submitted to Secretary McNamara on 5 October 1961 a proposal for the development of the RS-70 as a weapon system capable of performing reconnaissance, strike, damage assessment, and intelligence collection missions. The Air Force was confident that suitable air-to-ground missiles could be developed to replace gravity bombs as the armament for the RS-70, and since the RS-70 would not have to fly directly over highly defended target areas defensive subsystems could be simplified. In its submission, the Air Force asked that six RS-70 aircraft should be built (including the three B-70s) to develop and test the full reconnaissance-strike concept. After a review of the proposal the Office of the Secretary of Defense ruled that the state of the art was not adequate to support the system development outlined by the Air Force. It asserted that technical development programs should be conducted for a year or two on radar sensors, strike missiles, and communications equipment prior to a decision on the RS-70 weapon system. Except for LeMay, the Joint Chiefs agreed with Secretary McNamara's decision to proceed with a limited development program designed to provide three flyable B-70s without weapon system components.[214]

In an appearance before the House Appropriations Subcommittee in January 1962, Secretary McNamara accepted the possibility that a reconnaissance-strike aircraft might be useful, but he considered that the RS-70 proposal would require a great deal more study to determine whether the advantages of such an aircraft would be worth the great costs involved.[215] McNamara's presentation to the House Armed Services Committee proposed to continue the B-70 program in a developmental stage, both to realize benefits from past expenditures of funds and to maintain an option to introduce the vehicle into the operating force.[216] Both Secretary Eugene M. Zuckert and General LeMay disagreed with the secretary of defense's position on the RS-70. Zuckert told the Senate Subcommittee on Appropriations on 27 February:

> Our recommendation was that we should proceed with the B-70 as a full weapons system rather than the limited development program which was approved.... I think that the judgment as to whether or not you go ahead is determined by your judgment as to the effectiveness of the weapons system. On this, the Secretary of Defense and the Air Force quite obviously do not agree.[217]

General LeMay was equally positive. He said, "I do feel that we must go on with the manned systems development—the RS-70 and the full weapons system."[218]

At the invitation of the House Subcommittee on Appropriations, an Air Force officer, Col David C. Jones, made a special presentation on the RS-70 on 15 March. "We in the Air Force," Jones remarked, "are firmly convinced that the capabilities ascribed to the RS-70 are well within the current state of the art. We have had this problem reviewed in detail by highly qualified personnel who have confirmed the technical feasibility." Jones wanted to enjoy the RS-70 to complement the future ballistic missile force. He strongly emphasized the reconnaissance aspects of the manned system: such on-the-spot reconnaissance could not be provided by a reconnaissance satellite that would have to orbit far above the banks of cloud cover that lay over the Soviet Union and China a large part of the day. In summary, Jones said the RS-70 would accomplish essential tasks:

> First, observe and report the condition of the enemy during and after the initial strikes.... Second task. Increase assurance of destruction of primary targets.... Third task. Seek out and destroy unique targets—the extremely hard, the mobile, and imprecisely located, and fourth, provide the prevision, discrimination, and flexibility which must be an inherent part of our strategic capability.[219]

Jones submitted the RS-70 "will find a serious void in the planned force structure by providing on-the-spot judgment, force management visibility of the entire force, and the extremely accurate delivery of weapons of appropriate yield. It is ideally suited for employment in a strategy of flexible response."[220]

Secretary McNamara acknowledged that either Zuckert or LeMay had the right to appear before a congressional committee and to express personal opinions (not official Air Force positions), but he considered it inappropriate that a representative of the Air Force should present what purported to be an official Air Force position that was distinct from the president's position as represented by the administration's budget.[221] On 13 March McNamara requested the secretary of the Air Force to establish a study group to reassess the RS-70 weapon system.[222] At a press conference on 15 March, McNamara delivered a long statement in which he described the B-70 as "a more technically complex vehicle than any of the ICBMs" and the RS-70 as introducing even more complicated subsystems that "may well lie beyond what can be done on the basis of present scientific knowledge." He insisted: "Until we know much more about the proposed system—its technical feasibility, its military effectiveness and its cost—we have no rational basis for committing this aircraft to weapon system development or production." McNamara saw no reason why B-52s or B-58s, which would arrive in the hostile target area after ICBMs had suppressed the enemy's defenses, could not perform necessary reconnaissance functions.[223]

Already on record with the belief that DOD was prematurely discarding manned bombers in favor of missiles, the House Armed Services Committee readily accepted the Air Force proposals for the RS-70. "As our missile force grows," the committee reported in March, "the role for manned strategic aircraft shifts more toward observing, reporting, evaluating and exercising on-the-spot judgment and action." Referring to the Defense Department's refusal to spend the additional money Congress had voted in 1961 for long-range bombers, Chairman Vinson thought that the time had come to determine whether Congress could "exercise a positive authority" by requiring that funds be spent for appropriated purposes. The report of the House Armed Services Committee therefore "directed, ordered, mandated and required" the spending of $491 million authorized for the RS-70, this being the amount necessary for the six-plane program that the Air Force recommended. "If this language constitutes a test as to whether Congress has the power to so mandate," the report read, "let the test be made and let this important weapon system be the field of trial."[224] On 14 March a presentation which McNamara gave to Vinson in the Pentagon left the House Armed Services Committee apparently unmoved. Vinson declared that he and his committee would "fight for legislation on the floor of the House in the exact form that we recommended it."[225] Although he did not change his mind on the need for the RS-70, Vinson later remarked that he knew that Congress could not "compel" the president to do its bidding. On 20 March, moreover, McNamara informed Vinson that DOD would restudy the matter in the light of congressional recommendations. Writing on this same day, President Kennedy declared that it was "incumbent upon the Executive [Branch] to give every possible consideration . . . to the views of Congress." Late that afternoon in the Rose Garden at the White House, Kennedy discussed the RS-70 with Vinson, and, on the morning of 21 March, the House Armed Services Committee unanimously voted to move an amendment to its earlier report, deleting the word "directed" and adding "authorized" in the mandate for action on the RS-70. Later in the day the House passed the appropriations bill with such wording, thereby authorizing $491 million for the RS-70. Vinson assured his colleagues from the floor that "authorized" in this particular instance meant more than ever before and promised that "we are going to watch this new study by the department every step of the way from this point on."[226]

After he had carefully studied the material with Secretary Zuckert, Secretary McNamara permitted Colonel Jones to present the Air Force briefing on the RS-70 to the Senate Subcommittee on Appropriations on 2 April. The revised presentation maintained a more cautious tone on the technical side of the story.[227] Sentiment in the Senate, however, ran in favor of an expanded RS-70 program. Speaking on 11 April, Chairman Richard B. Russell of the Armed Services

Committee conceded that Secretary McNamara probably would not spend any additional money that Congress appropriated for the RS-70, but he nevertheless wished to raise the RS-70 appropriation to $363.7 million, thus financing the three B-70s and two additional RS-70 aircraft. "It would be worthwhile for the United States to have some of the RS-70s going around the world and landing at airfields, where the people of various countries could see them," Russell said. "The long-range missiles could be placed in silos all over the United States, and we could have 1,000 or 10,000 of them, but that would not impress people all over the world and lead them to believe that we are still the most powerful nation on earth."[228]

Before the Senate Subcommittee on Appropriations on 18 May, LeMay again expressed his reservations about the amount of funds allocated to strategic forces in the fiscal year 1963 budget and called for additional Minuteman missiles as well as an acceleration of the RS-70 program. To LeMay the RS-70 was a "low-risk program" that would be "a tremendous weapon system." He emphasized that he had confidence in the RS-70 because of its capabilities rather than just because it was a bomber. "I object," he said, "to having the term 'bomberman' applied to me. I use the weapon system that will do the job. If kiddie cars will do the job I will use those." "If we lose our strategic superiority," he concluded, "we are losing a considerable proportion of our security, if not all of it, because without the strategic umbrella, you can do nothing else."[229]

Although LeMay asked the Senate to approve the $491 million amount requested for three XB-70s and three RS-70s to prevent the dismantling of subcontractor facilities that were being used to build the stainless steel aircraft, the final budget voted by Congress in August 1962 followed the Senate's recommendations that $363 million be committed to the RS-70 program to finance the completion of the three XB-70s and the construction of two additional RS-70s with necessary weapon subsystems. By raising the amount for the RS-70 from the $171 million requested in the administration budget, Congress had apparently voted the funds that DOD would need to move rapidly ahead with the RS-70 program, providing reviews of the program justified such action.[230]

According to his later recollections on the subject, Secretary McNamara had told the Air Force and Congress as early as February 1962 that he would proceed with a three-aircraft test program for the B-70 but that he was "absolutely and unequivocally opposed to the deployment of the airplane."[231] Following his directive for the establishment of a study group to reassess the RS-70 weapon system, Secretary McNamara further directed Zuckert on 31 March to have the study group broaden its work to a review of the possible usefulness of an RS-70 force in a nonnuclear or limited war environment. Headed by Dr Joseph V. Charyk, under secretary of the Air Force for research and development, the RS-70 ad hoc group submitted a total of 11 documents on the system during June 1962. In August General LeMay and Secretary Zuckert made program change recommendations, and, according to LeMay, on 29 September the chairman and the members of the Joint Chiefs of Staff agreed that the XB-70 program should be reoriented to the armed reconnaissance concept and recommended approval of those portions of the proposal necessary to accomplish the reorientation required to demonstrate the feasibility of the aircraft and the associated subsystems in a timely manner. In explaining his support for the RS-70, Gen Earle G. Wheeler, Army chief of staff, described his opinion as a "purely military" judgment. Admiral Anderson recommended the continuation of RS-70 development because it represented "a considerable advance" in the development of high-speed aircraft and related subsystems for reconnaissance purposes and because we wanted fully to capitalize on the already great investment in the B-70.[232]

At the same time the Joint Chiefs of Staff provided Secretary McNamara with a military judgment in favor of developing the RS-70, Dr Harold Brown, who had become director of defense research and engineering, provided McNamara with his "views on the technical feasibility of doing some of the things that the RS-70 was supposed to do."[233] Doctor Brown concluded that "so far as vulnerability is concerned, speed and altitude are not great advantages." He asserted that the Nike Hercules missile was probably capable of knocking down a B-70 and that by the time the airplane could become operational, missile defenses would be even more sophisticated. Brown also argued that the recallability of manned aircraft, which might be dispatched in critical junctures on "fail-safe" missions, did not give additional time for decisionmaking. Even in an all-missile force, he demonstrated, "human judgment is present in deciding which missiles to fire, how to change the war plan ... during the war and so on. The judgment goes in before you press the button. Once you press the button the equipment takes over just as it takes over after you drop the bomb out of the airplane." Rather than the RS-70 — which would fly higher and faster — Brown suggested that study should be given to an airplane "designed to fly low and as fast as it can comfortably fly low."[234] He specifically determined that the RS-70 probably could not in its operational time period attain the attack accuracy claimed for it and that its capability to penetrate undegraded defenses at high altitudes would not be "very large."[235]

Possibly as a result of Doctor Brown's reasoning, Secretary McNamara directed the Air Force on 15 October to study the possible development of a long endurance aircraft — called the Dromedary — which might serve as a mobile platform for certain types of missiles and which might be added to the strategic force.[236] As a result of the continuing studies of the RS-70, McNamara was not able to make a final decision on the matter until 20 November 1962, by which time the DOD review of the fiscal year 1964 budget was already under way. At this time McNamara ruled that the program would be limited to the development of the three prototype B-70s but that $50 million of the additional funds voted by Congress for the RS-70s would be used to develop selected sensor components for such aircraft. President Kennedy subsequently approved McNamara's decision on the matter.[237] When he explained the administration's decision, McNamara related it not to the future of manned weapon systems but to the question of "whether this particular aircraft, in either of its configurations, could add enough to our already programmed capabilities to make it worth its very high cost." The Air Force had justified the RS-70 as necessary for transattack reconnaissance (reconnaissance during or after a missile attack) and for the ability to examine targets and to attack them immediately with strike missiles. If a target were known to be somewhere within a relatively small area, McNamara believed that its location eventually could be established with enough precision to permit an attack by a missile. As for postattack reconnaissance, he suggested that "other means are expected to be available to determine whether targets previously attacked by ICBMs have been destroyed." In summary, McNamara said:

> The RS-70, by carrying air-to-surface missiles, would provide only a very small increase in overall effectiveness. In my judgment this increase is not worth the large additional outlay of funds estimated at more than $10 billion above the $1.35 billion already approved.[238]

Air Force Thinking on Limited War

In his commentaries on the Department of Defense budget for fiscal year 1963, General LeMay was chiefly concerned with the reduction in emphasis accorded to strategic forces within it. As early as the autumn of 1961, however, the Air Force evidently viewed the new program-package budgeting approach as providing for undesirable divisions of air power which would deny air power its inherent flexibility in operations. In the course of a major address in Philadelphia on 21 September 1961, General LeMay reminded his audience that aerospace power was indivisible and offered the ultimate in flexibility.

> Our problem then, as I see it, as we reach higher and farther, is that we must maintain our unity of mission and unity as an organization. . . . To be a credible deterrent, aerospace power must consist of flexible and diversified forces that have a war-waging and war-winning capability. . . . We need to restate firmly that the United States Air Force is an entity. Its elements all contribute to the aerospace power that is vital for our defense.[239]

Presented on 24 April 1962 by Brig Gen Jerry D. Page, Air Force deputy director of plans for aerospace plans, and subsequently circulated as an Air Force position paper, "The USAF Concept for Limited War," engrossed many of the old doctrines about air power and new ideas that had been developed during the strategic debates earlier in 1962. The paper visualized war "in terms of the well-known 'spectrum of conflict,' with cold war at one extreme, general war at the opposite extreme, and limited war, with its numerous gradations, in between." It postulated:

> The military base for successful deterrence at any level is overall force superiority; that is, a capability to fight successfully at whatever level of intensity necessary to win our objectives. Overall force superiority means maintaining control of the conflict by fighting on our terms, and its *sine qua non* is a war-winning ability to disarm the enemy even if the highest threshold of war is crossed. . . . Since limited war against Communist forces is not a separate entity from general war, our strategy and forces for limited war should not be separated from our overall strategy and force structure. The artificial

distinction of limited war forces for this war and general war forces for that war destroys the inter-acting strength of our forces that will provide force superiority and continuous deterrence at any level of conflict.[240]

The paper provided a set of maxims and offered them as a guide for national strategy, military force posture, and for planning "in the real world of the 1960s and 70s." These maxims were as follows:

1. The deterrence of limited war is directly proportional to the risk assessed by the potential aggressor. Policies which appear to lower the risk in the eyes of the aggressor will encourage his aggressive acts.

2. One risk that is always unacceptable to any Communist state is the threatened loss or neutralization of its military capabilities.

3. If deterrence has failed and the US is involved in a limited war, the primary objective will be to attain the political ends for which the US entered the conflict — normally involving the ending of hostilities as soon as possible, on favorable terms and at the lowest practicable level of intensity.

4. Success in limited war is contingent upon maintaining a superior general war capability.

5. Escalation must be feared most by the power with the weaker general war capability.

6. With general war superiority, a nation should respond to limited war aggression with the timely application of whatever forces are necessary, but no more, to achieve its objectives.

7. A nation's resources for defense are not unlimited. Within these resources the required general war forces demand the highest priority; expenditures for forces capable of fighting less than general war must not infringe on the maintenance of a superior general war capability.

8. A nation with technological superiority should use this asset to produce the most effective weapons and delivery systems, and thereby offset any deficiencies in defense resources, such as total manpower, conventional armaments, etc.

9. In limited war, control of the course of the conflict is paramount. The conflict should be conducted to take advantage of our best capabilities, to provide us with maximum choices rather than have the choices forced upon us by the enemy.

10. Insofar as practicable, military forces should be designed with the range, mobility, flexibility, speed, penetrative ability, and firepower delivery that can perform in cold, limited and general war situations.[241]

In his explanations of the program-package budgeting approach, Secretary McNamara carefully pointed out that "we would use certain elements of the strategic retaliatory forces and continental air and missile defense forces for particular limited war tasks and, of course, all our forces would be employed in a general war."[242] Mindful that the Air Force possessed bomb-rack kits that enabled the B-47s and B-52s to be converted into conventional bomb carriers, McNamara was willing to admit that these planes had a limited capability for conventional bombing in small wars, but he remarked that the RS-70 would have no conventional bomb-carrying capability. When considering a conventional bomb war, moreover, McNamara considered it important to remember that the new F-4 tactical fighters and the experimental TFX would have "very substantial conventional bombing capabilities."[243]

Emergence of the McNamara Strategy

Since the Kennedy-McNamara administration was unwilling to provide a neat package description of national strategy, the full dimensions of the new US defense policy and strategic outlook emerged only gradually during 1962. McNamara accepted a part of the Air Force counterforce strategy that called for the maintenance of particularized weapons, hardened weapons deployment, and secure command and control systems that would permit measured attacks against hostile military forces rather than all-out "spasm" strikes against cities and population centers. Speaking in Ann Arbor, Michigan, on 16 June 1962, McNamara stated:

> The United States has come to the conclusion that to the extent feasible basic military strategy in a possible nuclear war should be approached in much the same way that more conventional military operations have been regarded in the past. That is to say, principal military objectives, in the event of a nuclear war stemming from a major attack on the Alliance, should be the destruction of the enemy's military forces, not of his civilian population.... In other words, we are giving a possible opponent the strongest incentive to refrain from striking our cities.[244]

Apparently discounting minimum deterrence in this same address, McNamara judged that

> relatively weak national nuclear forces with enemy cities as their targets are not likely to be sufficient to perform even the function of deterrence. If they are small, and perhaps vulnerable on the ground or in the air, or inaccurate, a major antagonist can take a variety of measures to counter them. Indeed, if a major antagonist came to believe there was a substantial likelihood of it being used independently, this force would be inviting a pre-emptive first strike against it.[245]

Even though Secretary McNamara favored a counterforce posture as presenting a favorable option, he was not entirely sure that the posture would divert initial Soviet attacks away from American cities. He replied: "I can imagine such a situation, yes. I am not suggesting that I think it highly probable but I think that this higher requirement for survivability is a requirement that we should consider."[246] After an interview late in 1962, McNamara was quoted as having stated:

> I believe myself that a counterforce strategy is most likely to apply in circumstances in which *both* sides have the capability of surviving a first strike and retaliating selectively. This is a highly unpredictable business, of course. But today, following a surprise attack on us, we would still have the power to respond with overwhelming force, and they would not then have the capability of a further strike. In this situation, given the highly irrational act of an attempted first strike against us, such a strike seems most likely to take the form of an all-out attack on both military targets and population centers. This is why a nuclear exchange confined to military targets seems more possible, not less, when both sides have a sure second-strike capability. Then you might have a more stable "balance of terror." This may seem a rather subtle point, but from where I'm sitting it seems a point worth thinking about.[247]

Many commentators interpreted McNamara's Ann Arbor address as a conceptual acceptance of the doctrine of counterforce which seemed logically to demand "acceptance of its *sine qua non* — the ability to locate, seek out, and destroy enemy forces wherever and in whatever manner they may be deployed."[248] To correct this misinterpretation, McNamara explained that he had carefully refrained from using the word *counterforce* because it meant different things to different people. He wanted to say no more than

> that our total force requirement is determined on an assumption that we must have sufficient strategic forces to absorb a full Soviet strike, and survive with sufficient strength to absolutely destroy the Soviet Union. We consider the possibility, but it is only a possibility, that we may wish to launch that force in waves, if you will. Now the fact that it is launched in waves means that certain portions of it are exposed to potential further destruction during the period it is withheld prior to launch. This, in turn, increases our requirement for secure communications, secure command and control centers, and invulnerable forces.[249]

Far from posing a requirement for a first-strike preemptive force, McNamara stressed that "our second-strike capability is so sure that there would be no rational basis on which to launch a preemptive strike."[250] He continued:

> The [Ann Arbor] conference included the point that weak nuclear forces operating individually under the control of a single nation were dangerous, obsolete, and costly. It has been the policy of this government, and will continue to be the policy, to deter the proliferation of national nuclear forces.[251]

As time passed the commentators who assumed that McNamara had endorsed a transcendent counterforce in his Ann Arbor address began to report that he had instead visualized a "stalemate" in the employment of nuclear weapons. When General Taylor was questioned on this matter on 9 August 1962 — the day the Senate confirmed his appointment as chairman of the Joint Chiefs of Staff — he responded: "I am not sure what is meant by 'stalemate.' If that means a reluctance to resort to general atomic war, of course that is the mutual deterrence we are talking about, that is what we are seeking now. We are in a stalemate in that sense."[252] Early in 1962 Secretary McNamara pointed out that the destruction of Soviet missile forces would be further complicated as the Soviets hardened and dispersed their missiles and acquired missile-launching submarines. During 1962 there was evidence that the Soviets followed both courses.

> A very large increase in the number of fully hard Soviet ICBMs and nuclear-powered ballistic missile launching submarines would considerably detract from our ability to destroy completely the Soviet strategic nuclear forces. It would become increasingly difficult, regardless of the form of the attack, to destroy a sufficiently large proportion of the Soviets' strategic nuclear forces to preclude major damage to the United States, regardless of how large or what kind of strategic forces we build. Even if we were to double and triple our forces we would not be able to destroy quickly all or almost all of the hardened ICBM sites. And even if we could do that, we know no way to destroy the enemy's missile launching submarines at the same time. We do not anticipate that either the United States or the Soviet Union will acquire that capability in the foreseeable future.[253]

The prospects of a stable strategic balance of nuclear terror and a fear that employing tactical nuclear weapons could lead to an escalation of a small conflict were thus affecting the defense strategy of the United States. At the same time, the same factors — plus a new appreciation of Western Europe's growing economic strength and a desire to prevent a proliferation of nuclear weapons — caused the Kennedy administration to reassess the strategy of the North Atlantic Treaty Organization. Looking for a follow-on to the tactical Matador and Mace missiles, the Air Force had issued a special operational requirement for a mobile medium-range ballistic missile (MMRBM) which would be small enough to be deployed on a mobile van or truck but would have a high degree of accuracy. Although nuclear weapons for employment on allied tactical fighters were increasingly augmented in Europe after 1958, Gen Lauris Norstad, the NATO commander, was fearful of the vulnerability of NATO aircraft to Soviet IRBM attack and pressed strongly for the development of the MMRBM and its assignment to American forces.[254] Following DOD's approval of the development of the AGM-87 Skybolt in February 1960, arrangements were made in June 1960 to permit the British to participate in the development of this air-launched ballistic missile. It also was agreed that the British would be able to procure the developed missile for employment by the Royal Air Force V-bomber force.[255] By fitting a British nuclear warhead on the Skybolt, the Royal Air Force would be able to prolong the usefulness of its Vulcan bombers, and the British also would have an independence of action that was not possible with the Thor intermediate-range missiles, which were jointly controlled by United States and British personnel.

Under President Kennedy's administration, the United States' defense policy began to shift away from the assumption that nuclear weapons would be almost automatically employed in a defense of Western Europe. Deputy Secretary of Defense Gilpatric told a press conference on 6 June 1961, "I, for one, have never believed in a so-called limited nuclear war. I just don't know how you build a limit into it once you start using any kind of nuclear bang."[256] The United States also began to fear the consequences of proliferations of nuclear capabilities within national forces. Under President Charles de Gaulle the French were creating their own nuclear capability. In Ottawa on 17 May 1961, President Kennedy offered to "commit to NATO . . . five — and subsequently still more — Polaris submarines . . . subject to any agreed NATO guidelines on their control and use" and also expressed willingness to consider the development of "a NATO sea-borne force, which would be truly multilateral in ownership and control."[257] In Chicago in February 1962 Secretary McNamara insisted that in a general war the United States' strategic forces would be sufficient to perform any needed nuclear mission. "Allowing for losses from an initial enemy attack," he pointed out, "we calculate that our forces would destroy virtually all Soviet targets without any help from deployed tactical air units or carrier task forces which, of course, have the capability of attacking these targets with nuclear weapons."[258] In view of the sufficiency of US strategic forces, independent nuclear forces in Europe appeared to be superfluous and wasteful. McNamara developed this theme in an address to the NATO ministerial meeting in Athens, Greece, on 6 May 1962 and repeated it in his Ann Arbor address the following month. In Athens McNamara reminded his audience that the United States had committed five Polaris submarines to NATO, with more to come, and suggested that "if the French and British [nuclear air] forces were used independently of other Western forces . . . they would have to be deployed against Soviet population centers, and this certainly would invite retaliation, immediate retaliation." In both the Athens and Ann Arbor speeches McNamara called upon the NATO allies to strengthen their nonnuclear general-purpose forces, thereby complementing the US nuclear deterrent.[259]

In his initial survey of defense projects after he took office, Secretary McNamara gave attention to the Skybolt missile, and this survey convinced him that the "cost history" of Skybolt was "particularly poor." Early in 1960 the Air Force had estimated that Skybolt would cost $214 million to develop and $679 million to procure, but in its July 1962 program submission the Air Force increased the estimated procurement cost to $1.771 billion. Hoping to give the Skybolt system a fair chance to establish its worth, McNamara supported an additional $50 million for Skybolt in the fiscal year 1962 budget, and the fiscal year 1963 budget carried funds for the first procurement of the air-to-ground missile. By late 1962, however, the Air Force was estimating that the cost to develop and procure Skybolt would run to $2.263 billion, and McNamara accordingly ordered an extensive Department of Defense review of the whole program, which was conducted between September and November 1962. In this review, the Air Force strongly supported the air-to-ground ballistic missile. "It has been our view that this was a good weapons system, and it would have enhanced the capability of the manned force considerably, and in all probability would have extended the life of the B-52 beyond what we see now," LeMay stated.[260] Lt Gen James Ferguson, Air Force deputy chief of staff for research and development, saw no special technical problems outstanding in the Skybolt development effort. "I would go further to say that in the opinion of people who have gone through many of these growing pains of introducing some new weapon, that this program was at least as healthy if not healthier than some others that reached fruition and that went into inventory."[261]

IDEAS, CONCEPTS, DOCTRINE

In Joint Chiefs of Staff deliberations, Generals Wheeler and LeMay and Admiral Anderson recommended the continuation of Skybolt in the defense program.

> I favored the Skybolt because, first of all, we are in a period of transition, of technical change, and I have some doubts as to the reliability of missiles in the period we are talking about. I do not have the same confidence in any of the missile systems as do some of the technicians who attest to the performance of the missiles.[262]

Gen David M. Shoup, commandant of the Marine Corps, apparently did not formally act with the Joint Chiefs on the Skybolt matter, but he agreed with Admiral Anderson. "I feel we should never, never eliminate the possibilities that our bombers have until we are absolutely sure of the reliability of missiles," Shoup said.[263]

After considering the guidance laid before him, Secretary McNamara made his own decision to cancel the development of the Skybolt missile. Doctor Brown offered the technical advice that the Skybolt "could be made to work" but that it would cost well over the amounts estimated and that, even when perfected, Skybolt's accuracy would be "considerably worse than fixed missiles or missiles on Polaris submarines." Secretary McNamara himself believed that "the Skybolt would very likely have become nearly a $3 billion program, not counting the additional costs of warheads. And even then, there was no assurance that the Skybolt development would result in a reliable and accurate missile." He further reasoned that Skybolt also would "combine the disadvantages of being soft and concentrated and relatively vulnerable on the ground and the bomber's slow time to the target."

> On the one hand, Skybolt would not have been a good weapon to use against Soviet strategic airbases, missile sites, or other high priority military targets because it would take hours to reach its target, while a Minuteman could reach it in 30 minutes. On the other hand, Skybolt would not have been a good weapon for controlled, countercity retaliation. Aside from its relative vulnerability to antiballistic missile defense, it has the important disadvantage that its carrier, the B-52, must be committed to its targets, if at all, early in the war because it would be vulnerable on the ground to enemy missile attack. Common sense requires that we not let ourselves be inflexibly locked in on such a matter. And being "locked in" is unnecessary when we have systems like Polaris whose missiles can be withheld for days, if desired, and used at times and against targets chosen by the President.[264]

In lieu of the capability that would have been provided by the 1,012 Skybolt missiles the Air Force had expected to procure, Secretary McNamara added 100 Minuteman missiles to the Air Force program, with the understanding that these missiles and already existing Hound Dog missiles would be used for the suppression of hostile defense targets.[265] "I am perfectly happy with abandoning the Skybolt," McNamara said, "As a matter of fact, I think it is very much in our national interest to do so, and I do not believe it has any effect whatsoever on the life of the B-52."[266]

In that the United Kingdom had expected to purchase 100 Skybolt missiles to extend the usefulness of their Vulcan bombers into the late 1960s and early 1970s, the Kennedy administration's decision to cancel development of the missiles had important repercussions within the NATO alliance. As the decision to cancel Skybolt was being made in the late autumn of 1962, the maturing DOD study of Soviet ground capabilities indicated there was a good possibility for a conventional NATO response to Soviet aggression on the central front in Western Europe.[267] In an address before the NATO Parliamentarians Conference on 16 November, Under Secretary of State George W. Ball emphasized that there was no reason NATO could not maintain conventional forces that were at least equal to those in Eastern Europe.[268] During the following month while en route to the NATO Ministers Conference, Secretary McNamara discussed Skybolt in London with British Defense Minister Peter Thorneycroft, who reportedly stated that a US abandonment of the missile would lead to an agonizing reappraisal of Anglo-American defense plans. To reach a common understanding, President Kennedy and Prime Minister Harold Macmillan met at Nassau between 18–21 December. During their meeting, President Kennedy offered either to continue Skybolt, with the British to bear half of the cost of completing its development, or to make Hound Dog missiles available for British procurement. It was finally agreed, however, that the United States would permit the British to purchase Polaris missiles. The British would build their own submarines and would provide warheads for the missiles. These British submarines and other similar American forces would be assigned to a NATO nuclear force and would get their targeting in accordance with NATO plans. Except where supreme national interests were at stake, these forces would be used solely for international defense. Kennedy and Macmillan also agreed that the ultimate purpose was to develop a NATO multilateral nuclear force and that the United States would invite France to participate on terms similar to those offered Great Britain. In the final paragraph of the Nassau communiqué the two leaders announced a reversal of the atomic "sword" and conventional "shield" strategy that had prevailed in Europe. They agreed that "in addition to having a nuclear shield it is important to have a non-nuclear sword."[269] For this purpose they agreed on the importance of increasing the effectiveness of their conventional forces on a worldwide basis.

During the late autumn of 1962 the decisions made on the strategic systems — including the prototype development of the B-70 and the cancellation of the Skybolt missile — tended to be obscured by public concern about the Cuban missile crisis. In February 1963, however, a writer in *Air Force/Space Digest* bluntly charged: "Skybolt was killed because it did not conform to the new defense policy. . . . Much the same can be said for the RS-70 Mach 3 airplane."[270] General LeMay viewed the changing strategy with more reserve.

> I am concerned . . . about the trend about phasing out bombers and depending too much on missiles. . . . I have spent a lot of my time . . . trying to convince the Secretary of Defense on the subject of manned bombers. I have not been able to convince him or the President. I think I have convinced a lot of other people, but they make the decisions.

IDEAS, CONCEPTS, DOCTRINE

And I have no other choice except to be a good soldier and carry them out and that is what I am doing.[271]

NOTES

1. John F. Kennedy, "Book in the News, B. H. Liddell Hart, *Deterrent or Defense*," *Saturday Review*, 3 September 1960, 17.
2. Senate, *Major Defense Matters: Hearings before the Preparedness Investigating Subcommittee of the Committee on Armed Services*, 86th Cong., 1st sess., 1959, 3.
3. House, *Department of Defense Appropriations for 1964: Hearings before a Subcommittee of the Committee on Appropriations*, 88th Cong., 1st sess., 1963, pt. 1:261 (hereafter cited as *1964 DOD Appropriations*).
4. Gen Maxwell D. Taylor, *Uncertain Trumpet* (New York: Harper & Bros., 1959), 54, 158–64.
5. Lt Gen James M. Gavin, *War and Peace in the Space Age* (New York: Harper & Bros., 1958), 238.
6. Charles J. Hitch and R. N. McKean, *The Economics of Defense in the Nuclear Age* (Cambridge: Harvard University Press, 1960); Senate, *Organizing for National Security: Hearings before the Subcommittee on National Policy Machinery of the Committee on Government Operations*, 86th Cong., 2d sess., and 87th Cong., 1st sess., 1960–1961, pt. 1:1005–6.
7. Taylor, *Uncertain Trumpet*, 82.
8. Paul H. Nitze, "Organization for National Policy Planning in the United States," prepared for delivery at the 1959 annual meeting of the American Political Science Association, 10–12 September 1959, in Senate, *Organizing for National Security*, 2:285.
9. Henry M. Jackson, "Organizing for Survival," *Foreign Affairs*, April 1960, 451.
10. Senate, *Organizing for National Security*, 1:1068, 1075.
11. House, *Sundry Legislation Affecting the Naval and Military Establishments for 1959: Hearings before the Committee on Armed Services*, 86th Cong., 1st sess., 1959, 905, 907 (hereafter cited *Sundry Legislation for 1959*).
12. Senate, *Missiles, Space, and Other Major Defense Matters: Hearings before the Preparedness Investigating Subcommittee of the Committee on Armed Services in Conjunction with the Committee on Aeronautical and Space Sciences*, 86th Cong., 2d sess., 1960, 447–48.
13. House, *Department of Defense Appropriations for 1961: Hearings before the Subcommittee of the Committee on Appropriations*, 86th Cong., 2d sess., 1960, pt. 4:634 (hereafter cited as *1961 DOD Appropriations*).
14. Senate, *Organizing for National Security*, 1:1066, 1074.
15. *Congressional Record*, vol. 106, pt. 2:1373.
16. Gavin, *War and Peace in the Space Age*, 5.
17. William W. Kaufmann, *The McNamara Strategy* (New York: Harper & Row, 1964), 253–54; Gavin, *War and Peace in the Space Age*, 5; "The USSR and the NATO Powers," *Air Force Magazine*, March 1960, 38–40; Kenneth R. Whiting, *Soviet Reactions to Changes in American Military Strategy* (Maxwell AFB, Ala.: Aerospace Studies Institute, 1965), 8–14.
18. Senate, *Fiscal Year 1963 Military Procurement Authorization: Hearings before the Committee on Armed Services*, 87th Cong., 2d sess., 1962, 49–50 (hereafter cited as *FY 1963 Military Procurement*); House, *Department of Defense Appropriations for 1960: Hearings before the Subcommittee of the Committee on Appropriations*, 86th Cong., 1st sess., 1959, 177 (hereafter cited as *1960 DOD Appropriations*); *Congressional Record*, vol. 106, pt. 2:1373; Kaufmann, *The McNamara Strategy*, 40–41; Stuart Symington, "Where the Missile Gap Went," *The Reporter*, 15 February 1962, 21–23.
19. Max Rosenberg, *USAF Ballistic Missiles, 1958–1959*, USAF Historical Division Liaison Office, 1960, 14–17; House, *Supplemental Defense Appropriations for 1958*, 85th Cong., 2d sess., 1958, 45;

Ernest G. Schwiebert, *A History of the U.S. Air Force Ballistic Missiles* (New York: Praeger, 1965), 221–23.

20. Senate, *Inquiry into Satellite and Missile Programs: Hearings before the Preparedness Investigating Subcommittee of the Committee on Armed Services*, 85th Cong., 1st and 2d sess., 1957–1958, 2318–19.

21. Ibid., 2318.

22. House, *1964 DOD Appropriations*, pt. 5: 974–76; Maj Gen Osmond J. Ritland, "Concurrency," *Air University Quarterly Review* 12, nos. 3 and 4 (Winter and Spring 1960–1961), 245.

23. Rosenberg, *AF Ballistic Missiles, 1958–1959*, 18; House, *Hearings on Military Posture and H. R. 2440 before the Committee on Armed Services*, 88th Cong., 1st sess., 1963, 277–80, 282–83; House, *1964 DOD Appropriations*, pt. 5:974–96; Senate, *Fiscal Year 1964 Military Procurement Authorization: Hearings before the Committee on Armed Services*, 88th Cong., 1st sess., 1963 (hereafter cited as *FY 1964 Military Procurement*), 7–8.

24. House, *1960 DOD Appropriations*, pt. 1:55; Senate, *Missile and Space Activities: Joint Hearings before the Preparedness Investigating Subcommittee of the Committee on Armed Services and the Committee on Aeronautical and Space Sciences*, 86th Cong., 1st sess., 1959, 5–8; House, *Sundry Legislation for 1959*, 792, 818–20, 840, 888–89, 904–7, 914–15.

25. House, *1960 DOD Appropriations*, pt. 1:55.

26. Taylor, *Uncertain Trumpet*, 72–73; House, *1960 DOD Appropriations*, pt. 1:378–79.

27. House, *1960 DOD Appropriations*, pt. 1:594.

28. Senate, *Major Defense Matters*, 124–25.

29. House, *1960 DOD Appropriations*, pt. 2:389–90.

30. House, *Missile Development and Space Sciences: Hearings before the Committee on Science and Astronautics*, 86th Cong., 1st sess., 1959, 137; House, *1960 DOD Appropriations*, pt. 5:681–83, 704–25, 731; Senate, *Investigation of Governmental Organization for Space Activities: Hearings before the Subcommittee on Governmental Activities of the Committee on Aeronautical and Space Sciences*, 86th Cong., 1st sess., 1959, 438, 446–48.

31. Gen Thomas S. Power, commander in chief, Strategic Air Command, to Gen Thomas D. White, letter, December 1959; Dwight D. Eisenhower, *Waging Peace, 1956–1961, The White House Years* (Garden City, N.Y.: Doubleday & Co., 1965), 547n.

32. House, *1960 DOD Appropriations*, pt. 1:863; Senate, *Missiles, Space, and Other Major Defense Matters*, 122–23.

33. House, *1960 DOD Appropriations*, pt. 2:380–81.

34. Ibid., pt. 6:42–43; Senate, *Department of Defense Appropriations for Fiscal Year 1960: Hearings before a Subcommittee of the Committee on Appropriations*, 86th Cong., 1st sess., 1959, 238–41, 1424–25, 1489, 1566 (hereafter cited as *FY 1960 DOD Appropriations*); Rosenberg, *USAF Ballistic Missiles, 1958–1959*, 26–28; Senate, *Missiles, Space, and Other Major Defense Matters*, 122–23.

35. Senate, *FY 1960 DOD Appropriations*, 1656; Jacob Van Staaveren, *USAF Intercontinental Ballistic Missiles, Fiscal Years 1960–1961*, USAF Historical Division Liaison Office, January 1964, 2.

36. Senate, *1960 DOD Appropriations*, 1424–25, 1489, 1567.

37. House, *1961 DOD Appropriations*, pt. 1:57–59, 159; pt. 2:331–32, 374–75; House, *Review of the Space Program: Hearings before the Committee on Science and Astronautics*, 86th Cong., 2d sess., 1960, pt. 1:79.

38. House, *1961 DOD Appropriations*, pt. 1:9, 71; pt. 2:293; pt. 5:471–72; pt. 7:65–66, 77–78, 109–10; House, *Department of Defense Appropriations for 1961: Reappraisal of Air Defense Programs*, 86th Cong., 2d sess., 37; Senate, *Missiles, Space, and Other Major Defense Matters*, 13–14, 41–44, 111–12, 122–24, 132, 138, 144–45, 268, 297, 316, 359, 386, 387, 424–25, 429, 463–64; Power to White, letter, 10 December 1959.

39. House, *1961 DOD Appropriations*, pt. 1:4.

40. Van Staaveren, *USAF Intercontinental Ballistic Missiles*, 5; Senate, *FY 1963 Military Procurement*, 49–50.

41. Taylor, *Uncertain Trumpet*, 131.

IDEAS, CONCEPTS, DOCTRINE

42. Address by Gen Thomas S. Power, commander in chief, Strategic Air Command, at the Economics Club of New York City, 19 January 1960, in House, *1961 DOD Appropriations*, pt. 2:174–79.

43. *Congressional Record*, vol. 106, pt. 2:1373.

44. Senate, *Department of Defense Appropriations for Fiscal Year 1961: Hearings before a Subcommittee of the Committee on Appropriations*, 86th Cong., 1st sess., 1959, pt. 2:1363–69 (hereafter cited as *FY 1961 DOD Appropriations*).

45. House, *1961 DOD Appropriations*, pt. 1:135–36.

46. Ibid., pt. 2:271, 374–75.

47. Samuel P. Huntington, *Common Defense: Strategic Programs in National Politics* (New York: Columbia University Press, 1961), 263–64.

48. Kaufmann, *The McNamara Strategy*, 40–44.

49. Taylor, *Uncertain Trumpet*, 130–64.

50. Brig Gen John A. Dunning, "USAF Doctrine, Roles, and Missions," lecture, Air War College, Maxwell AFB, Ala., 17 December 1959.

51. House, *1961 DOD Appropriations*, pt. 2:380–81.

52. History, Joint Air Transportation Board, 2 July 1951–3 March 1955, 30.

53. History, Tactical Air Command, January–June 1956, 29, and July–December 1956, 12–30, 31.

54. House, *Military Air Transportation: Hearings before a Subcommittee of the Committee on Government Operations*, 85th Cong., 2d sess., 1958, 498–99.

55. Senate, *Study of Air Power: Hearings before the Subcommittee on the Air Force of the Committee on Armed Services*, 84th Cong., 2d sess., 1956, 498–99.

56. Ibid., 840–46.

57. TSgt Harold L. Craven, "Hercules—A Legend Come True," *Airman Magazine*, June 1958, 14–15; House, *1960 DOD Appropriations*, pt. 2:432–33.

58. Senate, *Study of Air Power*, 976–77.

59. House, *Department of Defense Appropriations for 1958: Hearings before a Subcommittee of the Committee on Appropriations*, 85th Cong., 1st sess., 1957; House, *Hearings before the Special Subcommittee on National Military Airlift of the Committee on Armed Services*, 86th Cong., 2d sess., 1960, 4398–99.

60. House, *Sundry Legislation Affecting the Naval and Military Establishments for 1963: Hearings before the Committee on Armed Services*, 88th Cong., 1st sess., 1963, 3:5368, 6075 (hereafter cited as *Sundry Legislation for 1963*).

61. Maj Gen William H. Tunner, deputy commander, Air Materiel Command, "Air Transportation—Global Logistics for the Air Age," 23 February 1953; Lt Gen E. W. Rawlings, "Maintenance and Distribution of Logistics," lecture, Air War College, Maxwell AFB, Ala., 14 May 1953; Maj Gen George W. Mundy, "Air Force Logistics and Transportation," lecture, Air War College, Maxwell AFB, Ala., 3 December 1954; AFR 76-16, *Air Transportation: Policy on the Use of Air Transportation*, 30 March 1954.

62. House, *Department of Defense Appropriations for 1957: Hearings before a Subcommittee of the Committee on Appropriations*, 84th Cong., 2d sess., 1956, 160 (hereafter cited as *1957 DOD Appropriations*).

63. House, *Department of Defense Appropriations for 1959: Department of the Air Force: Hearings before the Subcommittee of a Committee on Appropriations*, 85th Cong., 2d sess., 1958, 437; House, *Investigation of National Defense Phase II: Hearings before Special Subcommittee on Armed Services*, 85th Cong., 2d sess., 1958, 73.

64. History, Air Materiel Command, January–June 1954, 1:165–75; House, *Military Posture Briefings: Hearings before the Committee on Armed Services*, 87th Cong., 1st sess., 1961, 1205.

65. House, *Hearings before the Special Subcommittee on National Military Airlift*, 4398–99.

66. House, *1957 DOD Appropriations*, 156.

67. House, *Investigation of National Defense Phase II*, 233.

68. House, *Department of Air Force Appropriations for 1957*, 84th Cong., 2d sess., 1956, 1469–70.

69. House, *Hearings before the Special Subcommittee on National Military Airlift*, 4060; History, Military Air Transport Service (MATS), January–July 1957, 90–110, and July–December 1958, 179–204.
70. House, *Military Air Transportation*, 498–99; History, MATS, July–December 1958, 179–204.
71. House, *Investigation of National Defense Phase II*, 209.
72. Senate, *Inquiry into Satellite and Missile Programs*, 2438.
73. House, *Investigation of National Defense Phase II*, 17–19.
74. House, *Military Air Transportation*, 502.
75. House, *Military Air Transportation: Report of the Committee on Government Operations*, 85th Cong., 2d sess., 1958, H. Rept. 2011, 5–7.
76. "Airways Say MATS Should Stick to Missiles," *Armed Forces Management*, July 1958, 29.
77. Assistant secretary of defense (Supply and Logistics), director of transportation policy, Air Transport Service in Peace and War, February 1960; House, *1960 DOD Appropriations*, pt. 1:101.
78. House, *Investigation of National Defense Phase II*, 223.
79. Ibid., 224; House, *1961 DOD Appropriations*, pt. 4:476; memorandum by Col Paul L. Steinle, assistant chief of staff, to deputy chiefs of staff and chiefs, Special Staff Agencies, Headquarters MATS, subject: MATS Position on 22 Recommendations in House Report No. 2011, 26 July 1958.
80. House, *1961 DOD Appropriations*, pt. 4:484; Bill Borklund, "MATS and the Mission," *Armed Forces Management*, August 1959, 15–17.
81. Senate, *Major Defense Matters*, 87–88.
82. Senate, *Inquiry into Satellite and Missile Programs*, 2043.
83. House, *United States Defense Policies in 1958*, 86th Cong., 1st sess., 1959, H. Doc. 227, 19.
84. House, *1961 DOD Appropriations*, pt. 2:425–26.
85. Senate, *Major Defense Matters*, 20–22, 40, 62.
86. House, *1960 DOD Appropriations*, pt. 1:101–2.
87. House, *1961 DOD Appropriations*, pt. 2:425–26.
88. House, *Investigation of National Defense Phase II*, 230; House, *1960 DOD Appropriations*, pt. 5:584–85, 653.
89. Senators A. S. Monroney and Stuart Symington to Secretary of Defense Neil H. McElroy, letter, 25 March 1959.
90. History, MATS, January–December 1958, 77; "The Role of Military Air Transport Service in Peace and War," 11–12.
91. House, *Military Air Transportation: Report of Committee on Government Operations*, 86th Cong., 1st sess., 1959, H. Rept. 1112, 9–10.
92. House, *Report of the Special Subcommittee on National Military Airlift of the Committee on Armed Services*, 86th Cong., 2d sess., 1960, 4029–34.
93. House, *1961 DOD Appropriations*, pt. 4:618.
94. Ibid., pt. 2:381.
95. House, *Hearings before the Special Subcommittee on National Military Airlift*, 4857.
96. History, Tactical Air Command, January–June 1960, 40–44; House, *Military Posture Briefings*, 1209; House, *Department of Defense Appropriations for 1962: Hearings before a Subcommittee of the Committee on Appropriations*, 87th Cong., 1st sess., 1961, pt. 2:1096 (hereafter cited as *1962 DOD Appropriations*).
97. House, *1961 DOD Appropriations*, pt. 2:380–81.
98. House, *Hearings before the Special Subcommittee on National Military Airlift*, 4350–51.
99. Department of Defense, "The Role of Military Air Transport Service in Peace and War," 1959, 2–3, 11–12.
100. House, *1961 DOD Appropriations*, pt. 4:458.
101. Senate, *FY 1961 DOD Appropriations*, 1538.
102. House, *Hearings before the Special Subcommittee on National Miltiary Airlift*, 4055–56.
103. House, *1961 DOD Appropriations*, pt. 4:457, 476–77, 524.
104. Ibid., pt. 7:330; House, *Sundry Legislation for 1963*, 5962.

IDEAS, CONCEPTS, DOCTRINE

105. House, *1961 DOD Appropriations*, pt. 7:332–33.
106. House, *Report of the Special Subcommittee on National Military Airlift of the Committee on Armed Services*, 4027–55.
107. Senate, *FY 1961 DOD Appropriations*, 1538; House, *Sundry Legislation for 1963*, 5962; House, *United States Defense Policies in 1960*, 87th Cong., 1st sess., 1961, H. Doc. 207, 26.
108. House, *Hearings before the Special Subcommittee on National Military Airlift*, 4885–86.
109. Huntington, *Common Defense*, 263–64; House, *1962 DOD Appropriations*, pt. 1:1–2; *Department of Defense Annual Report for Fiscal Year 1962* (Washington, D.C.: Government Printing Office, 1963), 6 (hereafter cited as *DOD Annual Report for FY 1962*).
110. House, *United States Defense Policies in 1960*, 5–6.
111. *Public Papers of the Presidents of the United States: Dwight D. Eisenhower, 1959–61* (Washington, D.C.: Government Printing Office, 1961), 1038; Kaufmann, *The McNamara Strategy*, 33.
112. House, *1962 DOD Appropriations*, pt. 3:122; Senate, *Department of Defense Appropriations for Fiscal Year 1962: Hearings before a Subcommittee of the Committee on Appropriations*, 87th Cong., 1st sess., 1961, 49 (hereafter cited as *FY 1962 DOD Appropriations*).
113. Senate, *1962 DOD Appropriations*, 49.
114. *Public Papers of the Presidents of the United States: John F. Kennedy, 1961* (Washington, D.C.: Government Printing Office, 1962), 24, 230–32 (hereafter cited as *Public Papers: Kennedy*).
115. House, *Military Posture Briefings*, 735–36.
116. Secretary of Defense Robert S. McNamara, "The Communist Design for World Conquest, Some Shift in Our Military Thinking Required," speech delivered before the Fellows of the American Bar Foundations, Chicago, Illinois, 17 February 1962, in *Vital Speeches of the Day*, 1 March 1962, 296–99; Stewart Alsop, "Kennedy's Grand Strategy," *Saturday Evening Post*, 31 March 1962, 12; House, *Hearings on Military Posture and H. R. 9637 before the Committee on Armed Services*, 88th Cong., 2d sess., 1964, 7001.
117. Senate, *FY 1963 Military Procurement*, 49.
118. House, *Hearings on Military Posture and H. R. 9637*, 6951.
119. House, *Military Posture Briefings*, 646–47.
120. Kaufmann, *The McNamara Strategy*, 49–50; Senate, *FY 1963 Military Procurement*, 49; *Public Papers: Kennedy*, 8–9.
121. John F. Loosbrock, "A Look Back—A Look Ahead: Interview with Gen Bernard A. Schriever," *Air Force/Space Digest*, May 1964, 44; "Space and National Security Symposium: Questions from the Audience and Answers from the Panel," *Air Force/Space Digest*, November 1962, 78.
122. Senate, *Organizing for National Security*, 1:1218.
123. House, *Recommendations Relating to Our Defense Budget, Message by the President of the United States*, 87th Cong., 1st sess., 1962, H. Doc. 123, 1–5; *Public Papers: Kennedy*, 24, 230–32; see also Theodore C. Sorensen, *Kennedy* (New York: Harper & Row, 1965), 604–5.
124. House, *Authorizing Appropriations for Aircraft, Missiles, and Naval Vessels for the Armed Forces: Hearings before the Committee on Armed Services*, 87th Cong., 1st sess., 1961, 1237; House, *1962 DOD Appropriations*, pt. 3:58, 101; Richard Fryklund, *100 Million Lives, Maximum Survival in a Nuclear War* (New York: Macmillan Co., 1962), 31.
125. Kaufmann, *The McNamara Strategy*, 276.
126. Senate, *Fiscal Year 1962 Military Procurement Authorization: Hearings before the Committee on Armed Services*, 87th Cong., 1st sess., 1961, 61 (hereafter cited as *FY 1962 Military Procurement*); House, *1962 DOD Appropriations*, pt. 3:104–5.
127. Fryklund, *100 Million Lives*, 31; Kaufmann, *The McNamara Strategy*, 52–53.
128. House, *Authorizing Appropriations for Aircraft, Missiles, and Naval Vessels for the Armed Forces*, 1297.
129. House, *1962 DOD Appropriations*, pt. 3:7–9; House, *Sundry Legislation Affecting the Naval and Military Establishments for 1961: Hearings before the Committee on Armed Services*, 87th Cong., 1st sess., 1961, 1239–44, 1283, 1292, 1302 (hereafter cited as *Sundry Legislation for 1961*); House, *Hearings*

on Military Posture and H. R. 9751 before the Committee on Armed Services, 87th Cong., 2d sess., 1962, 3175.

130. House, *Authorizing Appropriations for Aircraft, Missiles, and Naval Vessels for the Armed Forces*, 1286.

131. House, *1960 DOD Appropriations*, pt. 1:255; House, *1961 DOD Appropriations*, pt. 1:186, pt. 2:313; House, *Sundry Legislation for 1961*, 1591.

132. House, *Sundry Legislation for 1961*, 1244, 1654.

133. House, *1962 DOD Appropriations*, pt. 1:6–7, pt. 3:429; Senate, *FY 1962 DOD Appropriations*, 1683; House, *Military Posture Briefings*, 1160–61.

134. House, *1962 DOD Appropriations*, pt. 3:463–65; House, *Sundry Legislation for 1961*, 1588, 1593, 1595.

135. House, *Authorizing Appropriations for Aircraft, Missiles, and Naval Vessels for the Armed Forces*, 138.

136. House, *1962 DOD Appropriations*, pt. 3:10–12.

137. Ibid., 12–13, 40; Senate, *FY 1962 DOD Appropriations*, 1683.

138. House, *Sundry Legislation for 1961*, 1244.

139. House, *1962 DOD Appropriations*, pt. 3:176.

140. Ibid.

141. Ibid., 18–23.

142. Ibid., 75, 79.

143. Ibid., 136; pt. 6:197.

144. House, *Military Posture Briefings*, 1077, 1137.

145. Ibid., 1140.

146. Senate, *FY 1962 Military Procurement*, 408.

147. Ibid., 409.

148. Ibid., 486; see also "Air Force Explanation of Counterforce," in *Air Force Information Policy Letter for Commanders: Supplement*, no. 111, 15 September 1962, 8–9.

149. House, *1962 DOD Appropriations*, pt. 3:406–7.

150. House, *Military Posture Briefings*, 1086–87, 1095, 1140, 1146.

151. Ibid.

152. Ibid.

153. Ibid., 1562; House, *1962 DOD Appropriations*, pt. 3:429–31.

154. House, *1962 DOD Appropriations*, pt. 3:429–31.

155. House, *Military Posture Briefings*, 1170–72; Senate, *FY 1962 DOD Appropriations*, 275–76; House, *1962 DOD Appropriations*, pt. 3:434–39, 461, 474, 495; House, *Sundry Legislation for 1961*, 1593–96.

156. House, *Sundry Legislation for 1961*, 1598, 1681–82; House, *1962 DOD Appropriations*, pt. 3:454–56, pt. 5:463–65; Senate, *Department of Defense Appropriations for Fiscal Year 1963: Hearings before a Subcommittee of the Committee on Appropriations*, 87th Cong., 2d sess., 1962, 184–85 (hereafter cited as *FY 1963 DOD Appropriations*).

157. House, *1962 DOD Appropriations*, pt. 5:465; pt. 6:195–96.

158. Senate, *FY 1962 DOD Appropriations*, 1682.

159. House, *1962 DOD Appropriations*, pt. 4:29–32, 35.

160. Letter of Secretary of Defense Robert S. McNamara to Hon Dennis Chavez, chairman, Senate Subcommittee on Department of Defense Appropriations, 27 October 1961, in Senate, *FY 1963 DOD Appropriations*, 185.

161. House, *Hearings on Military Posture and H. R. 9751*, 3174.

162. House, *Department of Defense Appropriations for 1963: Hearings before a Subcommittee of the Committee on Appropriations*, 87th Cong., 2d sess., 1962, pt. 2:4 (hereafter cited as *1963 DOD Appropriations*).

163. House, *Sundry Legislation for 1961*, 2474.

164. Ibid.; Alsop, "Kennedy's Grand Strategy," 12.

IDEAS, CONCEPTS, DOCTRINE

165. Kaufmann, *The McNamara Strategy*, 269; Alsop, "Kennedy's Grand Strategy," 12; House, *Sundry Legislation for 1961*, 3478–79.
166. Kaufmann, *The McNamara Strategy*, 83.
167. House, *Sundry Legislation for 1961*, 2243–53.
168. Senate, *FY 1962 DOD Appropriations*, 1625.
169. House, *Sundry Legislation for 1961*, 2444–45.
170. Ibid., 2243–44, 2248; *DOD Annual Report for FY 1962*, 6, 294, 316–17.
171. House, *Sundry Legislation for 1961*, 2444–46; *DOD Annual Report for FY 1962*, 18–19; House, *1963 DOD Appropriations*, pt. 2:86.
172. Senate, *FY 1962 DOD Appropriations*, 1631, 1667–68.
173. House, *1963 DOD Appropriations*, pt. 2:50–52.
174. House, *Sundry Legislation for 1961*, 2459.
175. House, *1963 DOD Appropriations*, pt. 2:10; Senate, *FY 1963 DOD Appropriations*, 85.
176. Senate, *Organizing for National Security*, 1:1218.
177. House, *1963 DOD Appropriations*, pt. 2:4–5.
178. Gen Maxwell D. Taylor, military representative of President Kennedy, "Our Changing Military Policy, Greater Flexibility," in *Vital Speeches of the Day*, 15 March 1962, 347–49.
179. Quoted in George E. Lowe, *The Age of Deterrence* (Boston: Little, Brown & Co., 1964), 232.
180. Remarks of Secretary of Defense Robert S. McNamara, DOD news release of the commencement address, University of Michigan, Ann Arbor, 16 June 1962.
181. Alsop, "Kennedy's Grand Strategy," 11.
182. Cecil Brownlow, "Tushino Stresses USSR Aircraft Priority," *Aviation Week*, 17 July 1961, 31–34.
183. Letter of Secretary of Defense McNamara to Congressman Bob Miller, 3 November 1961; House, *Sundry Legislation for 1963*, 2729–30.
184. House, *Hearings on Military Posture and H. R. 2440 before the Committee on Armed Services*, 88th Cong., 1st sess., 1963, 308.
185. Ibid., 309.
186. Senate, *FY 1963 Military Procurement*, 85–86; House, *1963 DOD Appropriations*, pt. 2:20, 27; McNamara, "The Communist Design for World Conquest."
187. Kaufmann, *The McNamara Strategy*, 83–84; House, *1963 DOD Appropriations*, pt. 2:49.
188. Senate, *Organizing for National Security*, 1:1194.
189. Roswell L. Gilpatric, deputy secretary of defense, "Matching DOD Capabilities and Objectives," talk before the Electronic Industrial Association, Washington, D.C., 15 March 1962, in *Air Force Information Policy Letter for Commanders: Supplement*, no. 104, May 1962, 20.
190. Senate, *Organizing for National Security*, 1:1203–4; House, *Hearings on Military Posture and H. R. 9751*, 3193–94; House, *1963 DOD Appropriations*, pt. 2:5–6.
191. House, *1963 DOD Appropriations*, pt. 2:8–9.
192. Ibid., 172.
193. Ibid., 13–14.
194. Ibid., 14–19.
195. Ibid., 42–47.
196. Ibid., 47–48.
197. Ibid., 53–54; *DOD Annual Report for FY 1962*, 18.
198. House, *1963 DOD Appropriations*, pt. 2:66–67, 167–71, 385–86; Senate, *FY 1963 Military Procurement*, 454; House, *1964 DOD Appropriations*, pt. 2:328.
199. House, *1964 DOD Appropriations*, pt. 2:328.
200. House, *1963 DOD Appropriations*, pt. 2:73–75, pt. 4:320–21; *DOD Annual Report for FY 1962*, 300.
201. House, *Hearings on Military Posture and H. R. 9751*, 3343–45, 3732–34, 3859; House, *1963 DOD Appropriations*, pt. 2:73–75, 133–34, 141, 320–21; House, *1964 DOD Appropriations*, pt. 1:471.
202. House, *Sundry Legislation for 1963*, 5965.

203. *DOD Annual Report for FY 1962*, 303; History, MATS, July–December 1961, 1:37.
204. House, *1963 DOD Appropriations*, pt. 2:105–6.
205. Ibid., 103, 106; Senate, *Department of Defense Appropriations for Fiscal Year 1965: Hearings before the Subcommittee on Department of Defense of the Committee on Appropriations and the Committee on Armed Services*, 88th Cong., 2d sess., pt. 1:730–31 (hereafter cited as *FY 1965 DOD Appropriations*).
206. Senate, *FY 1963 DOD Appropriations*, 185–86, 188.
207. Ibid., 177–78, 186.
208. House, *1963 DOD Appropriations*, pt. 2:525.
209. Address by Gen Frederic H. Smith, Jr., vice chief of staff, US Air Force, before the Joint Training Assembly Armed Services Reserves, Washington, D.C., 12 October 1961, in *Air Force Information Policy Letter for Commanders: Supplement*, 15 November 1961, 17.
210. House, *1963 DOD Appropriations*, pt. 2:491, 494.
211. Ibid., 469–70; Senate, *FY 1963 Military Procurement*, 507–8; House, *Hearings on Military Posture and H. R. 9751*, 3706–8.
212. Senate, *FY 1963 DOD Appropriations*, 185, 192–93.
213. Ibid., 1050.
214. Ibid., 166, 193, 954, 1029–31, 1045–47.
215. House, *1963 DOD Appropriations*, pt. 2:18–19.
216. House, *Hearings on Military Posture and H. R. 9751*, 3187.
217. Ibid., 166.
218. Ibid., 185.
219. House, *1963 DOD Appropriations*, pt. 5:370–85.
220. Ibid.
221. Senate, *FY 1963 DOD Appropriations*, 1011.
222. House, *Hearings on Military Posture and H. R. 2440*, 340.
223. Statement of Secretary McNamara on the RS-70, 15 March 1962, in House, *1963 DOD Appropriations*, pt. 5:63–67.
224. "House Unit Orders Use of B-70 Funds," *Aviation Week*, 12 March 1962, 310.
225. Katherine Johnsen, "Vinson Refuses to Drop Fight for B-70," *Aviation Week*, 19 March 1962, 28.
226. *Congressional Record*, vol. 108, pt. 4:4691–723; Katherine Johnsen, "Restudy of RS-70 Is Ordered; Vinson-McNamara Clash Averted," *Aviation Week*, 26 March 1962, 17–18; Claude Witze, "Trial by Press Conference," *Air Force/Space Digest*, April 1962, 16, 19–20.
227. Senate, *FY 1963 DOD Appropriations*, 1007, 1009, 1011.
228. "Senate Votes $363.7 Million Extra for RS-70," *Aviation Week*, 22 April 1963, 26.
229. Senate, *FY 1963 DOD Appropriations*, 1356–71.
230. Ibid., 1358–59; House, *1964 DOD Appropriations*, pt. 1:114; *DOD Annual Report for FY 1962*, 361–62.
231. House, *Department of Defense Appropriations for 1965: Hearings before a Subcommittee of the Committee on Appropriations*, 88th Cong., 2d sess., 1964, 4:61.
232. House, *Hearings on Military Posture and H. R. 2440*, 340, 1174–75; House, *1964 DOD Appropriations*, pt. 2:129–30, 313–14.
233. House, *Hearings on Military Posture and H. R. 2440*, 614.
234. House, *1963 DOD Appropriations*, pt. 5:73; Senate, *FY 1963 DOD Appropriations*, 972, 976.
235. House, *Hearings on Military Posture and H. R. 2440*, 611–12.
236. House, *1964 DOD Appropriations*, pt. 1:358.
237. Ibid., 114–16; Kaufmann, *The McNamara Strategy*, 125.
238. House, *1964 DOD Appropriations*, pt. 1:113–14.
239. Address by Gen Curtis E. LeMay, chief of staff, US Air Force, to the Air Force Association Convention, Philadelphia, Pennsylvania, 21 September 1961, in *Air Force Information Policy Letter for Commanders: Supplement*, 15 November 1961, 1–6.

240. Brig Gen Jerry D. Page, deputy director, Plans for Aerospace Plans, US Air Force, presentation to the Scientific Advisory Board on the USAF Concept for Limited War, 24 April 1962.
241. Ibid.
242. House, *1963 DOD Appropriations*, pt. 2:48.
243. Senate, *FY 1964 Military Procurement*, 79.
244. Remarks of Secretary of Defense McNamara, Ann Arbor, Michigan, 16 June 1962.
245. Ibid.
246. House, *1963 DOD Appropriations*, pt. 2:250.
247. Stewart Alsop, "Our New Strategy, The Alternatives to Total War," *Saturday Evening Post*, 1 December 1962, 18.
248. John F. Loosbrock, "History and Mr. McNamara," *Air Force/Space Digest*, October 1962, 33.
249. Senate, *FY 1964 Military Procurement*, 317.
250. Alsop, "Our New Strategy, The Alternatives to Total War," 18.
251. Kaufmann, *The McNamara Strategy*, 148–49.
252. Senate, *Nominations of Gen Maxwell D. Taylor and Gen Earle G. Wheeler: Hearing before the Committee on Armed Services*, 87th Cong., 2d sess., 1962, 14.
253. House, *Hearings on Military Posture and H. R. 2440*, 308–9; House, *1964 DOD Appropriations*, pt. 1:110–11.
254. House, *1963 DOD Appropriations*, pt. 5:352–54.
255. Department of Defense, *Annual Report of the Secretary of Defense and Annual Reports of the Secretary of the Army, Secretary of the Navy, and Secretary of the Air Force, July 1, 1959 to June 30, 1960* (Washington, D.C.: Government Printing Office, 1961), 90, 360.
256. "Nuclear Reply to Red Attack Declared U.S. Policy in Europe," *New York Times*, 7 June 1961, 9.
257. Raymond Daniell, "Kennedy Bids Canada Joins Hemispheric Role," *New York Times*, 18 May 1961, 1, 12.
258. "McNamara Warns Soviets to Beware of Limited Wars," *New York Times*, 18 February 1962.
259. "Text of Ministerial Council Communiqué on NATO Meeting," *New York Times*, 7 May 1962, 12; Senate, *FY 1964 Military Procurement*, 85, 106, 317.
260. House, *1964 DOD Appropriations*, pt. 1:114–16, 526; pt. 2:549; Senate, *FY 1964 Military Procurement*, 923.
261. Senate, *FY 1964 Military Procurement*, 1029.
262. Ibid.
263. House, *Hearings on Military Posture and H. R. 2440*, 1174–76; House, *1964 DOD Appropriations*, pt. 2:129–30, 313–14, 337.
264. House, *Hearings on Military Posture and H. R. 2440*, 612; House, *1964 DOD Appropriations*, pt. 1:114–16.
265. House, *1964 DOD Appropriations*, pt. 1:319.
266. Senate, *FY 1964 Military Procurement*, 77.
267. Kaufmann, *The McNamara Strategy*, 120–21.
268. Under Secretary of State George W. Ball, "NATO and the Cuban Crisis," *Department of State Bulletin*, 3 December 1962, 831–35.
269. House, *Hearings on Military Posture and H. R. 2440*, 399–400; House, *1964 DOD Appropriations*, pt. 1:98–102, 250–51, 256–57; Kaufmann, *The McNamara Strategy*, 121–28; House, *A Compilation of Material Relating to United States Defense Policies in 1962*, 88th Cong., 1st sess., 1963, H. Doc. 155, 64; *Public Papers of the Presidents of the United States: John F. Kennedy, 1962* (Washington, D.C.: Government Printing Office, 1963), 908–10.
270. Claude Witze, "Farewell to Counterforce," *Air Force/Space Digest*, February 1963, 28.
271. House, *Hearings on Military Posture and H. R. 2440*, 1191–96.

Lt Gen James Ferguson, deputy chief of staff for research and development.

Gen Curtis E. LeMay, Air Force chief of staff.

Dean Rusk, secretary of state.

Christian A. Herter, secretary of state.

Gen Earle G. Wheeler, Army chief of staff.

Eugene M. Zuckert, secretary of the Air Force.

A Titan missile ignites during an attempted launch.

CHAPTER 2

THE NEW FRONTIER:
MATURITY OF FLEXIBLE RESPONSE

The confrontation between the United States and the Soviet Union, arising from the emplacement of Soviet missiles in Cuba in October 1962, appeared to many knowledgeable Americans to mark a watershed in history. Writing in the aftermath of the missile crisis, Walter Lippman observed:

> It had become plain by the summer of 1963 . . . that the postwar period had ended. Europe had recovered and the danger of a great war in Europe had subsided with the Kremlin's acceptance of a balance of power in which it acknowledged American superiority and we acknowledged that we were not supreme and omnipotent.[1]

Although the complete record of the Cuban missile crisis remained closed to the public, participants in the confrontation freely published their experiences and reported the lessons they had learned. These "lessons" soon became determinants of the maturing defense strategy of the Kennedy-McNamara administration.

Shortly after the Cuban Missile Crisis of 1962, the ill-fated Bay of Pigs invasion, the Soviet Union began to supply Premier Fidel Castro's revolutionary government with large quantities of conventional local-defense weapons, including MiG-15, -17, and -19 aircraft, motor torpedo boats, and coastal patrol vessels. In July and August 1962 an unusually large number of Soviet vessels landed cargo and passengers at Cuban ports, and the cargoes were unloaded by Soviet military personnel. On 29 August a high-altitude U-2 reconnaissance pilot took photographs which revealed that SA-2 surface-to-air antiaircraft missiles had been installed at several locations. Successive flights disclosed additional SA-2 emplacements, as well as a growing number of short-range coastal defense missile installations. Citing the need for an ability to respond to challenges in any part of the free world, President Kennedy asked Congress on 7 September to renew his authority to order units and individuals of the Ready Reserve to not more than 12 months' active duty. This legislation was voted and approved on 3 October.[2] In an official statement the Soviet government asserted on 11 September that armaments and military equipment being sent to Cuba were "designed extensively for defensive purposes" and that the Soviet Union had "no need . . . to shift its weapons . . . for a retaliatory blow, to any other country, for instance Cuba."[3] Speaking of the movement of Soviet arms to Cuba at a news conference on 13 September, President Kennedy maintained that the "new shipments do not constitute a threat to any other part of this hemisphere." If continuing surveillance indicate that Cuba should possess a capacity to carry out offensive actions against the United States, Kennedy promised, "the United States would act."[4]

According to later evidence the first Soviet medium-range ballistic missiles began to arrive in Cuba on about 10 September. A reconnaissance photograph taken on 28 September showed crates on a freighter's deck that could have held fuselages of twin-jet Ilyushin-28 bombers. Early on the morning of 14 October, after cloud cover from Hurricane Ella had delayed aerial surveillance for a week, photographs taken by a U-2 aircraft of the 4080th Strategic Reconnaissance Wing revealed Soviet medium-range ballistic missile units being deployed in the San Cristobal area. Three days later other high-altitude photography positively disclosed an intermediate-range ballistic missile installation near Quanajay, and other such installations were soon located near Remedios.[5] Quite unlike the local defense weapons that had been sent to Cuba earlier, the Soviet missiles and the Il-28 bombers were clearly offensive weapons.

In a televised interview a few weeks after the missile crisis, President Kennedy suggested that neither the United States nor Premier Khrushchev had made correct evaluations during the period leading up to the confrontation.

> I don't think that we expected that he would put the missiles in Cuba, because it would have seemed such an imprudent action for him to take.... Now, he obviously must have thought that he could do it in secret and that the United States would accept it.[6]

Kennedy speculated that the Soviets had intended to establish the missiles in Cuba secretly and were planning to disclose them during November. Since the Soviets had ICBMs at home, Kennedy did not conceive that the Soviets needed other missiles in Cuba to redress the military balance of power, but he observed that the Cuban missiles nevertheless "would have politically changed the balance of power."[7] Admitting that his opinion was speculation, Secretary of Defense McNamara suggested that Khrushchev intended to disclose "the introduction of offensive weapons systems directed against the Nation at some time appropriate to him, perhaps in conjunction with the renewed pressure upon Berlin, and endeavor, thereby, to weaken the negotiating position of the Western World."[8] In an official explanation to the Supreme Soviet on 12 December 1962, Khrushchev stated that strategic weapons were deployed to Cuba solely to defend Cuba against United States attack and that once President Kennedy had removed the threat of such an attack the weapons had served their purpose and could be removed. On 28 October the official Soviet newspaper *Izvestiya* positively denied that the Soviets had undertaken the Cuban venture preparatory to a trade whereby they would remove their missiles from Cuba in exchange for the removal of NATO missiles from Turkey.[9] At the height of the crisis on 27 October, however, Khrushchev did propose that the Soviet Union would agree to remove its missiles and that the United States would "evacuate its analogous weapons from Turkey."[10]

Even though Kennedy and McNamara emphasized the political rather than the military effect of the Soviet missions in Cuba, Rand analyst Arnold L. Horelick advanced the hypothesis that the deployment of strategic weapons in Cuba "may have recommended itself to the Soviet leaders as a 'quick fix' measure to achieve a substantial, though far from optimal improvement in Soviet strike capabilities against the United States."[11] The American fear of a missile gap had dissipated, and the Soviets rather than the United States had a deficit in intercontinental ballistic missiles. According to the British Institute for Strategic Studies, the Soviets had 75 ICBMs and 700 MRBMs operational in October 1962. The medium-range missiles threatened the United States. During this same month the United States had 8 Polaris submarines with 128 missiles at sea, and it would appear from later congressional testimony that 170 Air Force ICBMs also were operational. The US strategic missile order of battle was rapidly increasing: according to Secretary McNamara, the United States would have 144 Polaris and 210 Atlas, Titan, and Minuteman missiles operational on 30 January 1963.[12] By establishing a missile base in Cuba the Communists would be able to employ cheaper and more plentiful medium-range missiles against the United States. Even though their deployment was cut short (five large-hatch ships turned back after the American quarantine began) the Soviets had 42 medium- and intermediate-range missiles in Cuba, and they were deploying them at 6 MRBM and 3 IRBM sites.[13] When added to the estimated 75 ICBMs that the Soviets possessed, the Cuban missiles might well have provided an immediate counterpopulation capability against the 130 American cities with population in excess of 100,000.

Without seeking to know Khrushchev's exact motives, Kennedy assembled a selected group of his advisers at 1145 hours on the morning of 16 October to determine a course of action relative to the emplacement of Soviet offensive weapons in Cuba. The group elected to intensify air reconnaissance, to preserve the tightest secrecy, and not to disclose knowledge of the bases until the United States was prepared to act. As the crisis continued, the small group of men, variously referring to themselves as the "Think Tank," the "War Council," and the "Excom," provided a steady flow of advice to President Kennedy. This group included Secretary McNamara, Secretary of State Dean Rusk, Attorney General Robert F. Kennedy, Under Secretary of State George Ball, and Deputy Under Secretary of State U. Alexis Johnson. There appeared to be three possible courses of action: the destruction of the missile sites by air attack, the surface invasion of Cuba, or a blockade or quarantine of the island. The practicability of surface invasion was soon ruled out: it would take too long to mount, would negate surprise, and might alienate world opinion. The group ultimately accepted what Ball described as "the wisdom — indeed the necessity — of the measured response." Presidential assistant Theodore C. Sorensen described the executive reasoning process:

> An air strike on military installations in Cuba, without any advance warning, was rejected as a "Pearl Harbor in reverse" — and no one could devise a form of advance warning (other than the quarantine itself, which was a type of warning) that would not leave this nation vulnerable to either endless discussion and delay (while work on the missiles went forward) or to harsh indictment in the opinion and history of the world.[14]

After 16 October high-altitude air surveillance flown by the Strategic Air Command was greatly intensified by presidential order, and the entire Department of Defense was ordered "to prepare for any eventualities." As it finally developed, command of the general-purpose forces readied for employment in the Cuban crisis was assigned to the commander in chief, Atlantic, and under the unified commander the Continental Army Forces were designated as Army Forces, Atlantic, and the Tactical Air Command was designated as Air Forces, Atlantic. The commander of the XVIII Army Airborne Corps was designated joint task force commander to plan any joint operations that might become necessary. The president and the secretary of defense exercised overall control through the Joint Chiefs of Staff, who named the chief of naval operations as their representative for the quarantine. Under the operational control of the North American Air Defense Command (NORAD), fighter-interceptors and Hawk and Nike Hercules antiaircraft battalions were moved to the southeastern United States to support local air defense forces. Starting on 20 October SAC began dispersing its bombers to continental and overseas bases and placing all aircraft on an upgraded alert — ready to take off, fully equipped, within 15 minutes. ICBM crews assumed a comparable alert posture, and Polaris submarines went to preassigned stations at sea.[15]

President Kennedy first informed the American people of the Soviet offensive arms buildup in Cuba and of the steps that would be taken to counter it in a radio and television address early on the evening of 22 October. Kennedy explained that the United States would initiate a strict quarantine on the movement of all offensive military equipment to Cuba. It would increase close surveillance of Cuba and its military buildup. The US naval base at Guantánamo Bay, Cuba, had been reinforced and all dependents were being evacuated. Kennedy also stated that the United States was calling an immediate meeting of the Organization of Consultation under the Organization of American States (OAS) and of the Security Council of the United Nations. Kennedy announced:

> It shall be the policy of this Nation to regard any nuclear missile launched from Cuba against any nation in the Western Hemisphere as an attack by the Soviet Union on the United States, requiring a full retaliatory response upon the Soviet Union.[16]

Finally Kennedy called upon Khrushchev to withdraw the missiles from Cuba. Coincident with the president's address, NORAD air defense interceptor units went either on patrol missions or on a 5-to-15 minute alert, and the Strategic Air Command started its B-52 bombers on a continuous air alert. Some 67 B-52s, carrying a total of about 300 thermonuclear bombs or missiles, appear to have been continuously airborne within striking distance of the Soviet Union between 22 October and 21 November 1962.[17]

As the crisis unfolded President Kennedy's strategy of providing a spectrum of possible graduated responses became clear. At each threshold of action, possibilities for negotiation were provided. Announced as impending on the evening of 22 October, implementation of the quarantine against further shipment of offensive arms—bombers as well as missiles—awaited approval of the Organization of American States on 23 October, and later that day Kennedy announced that it would begin at 1400 hours Greenwich time on 24 October.[18] Even though Khrushchev protested the illegality of the quarantine, he had the option of either attempting to force through it or to order the vessels carrying war materials to return to the Soviet Union. Work on the missile sites continued at a very rapid rate, but 16 dry cargo ships en route to Cuba returned to the Soviet Union.[19] In his policy statement Kennedy studiously ignored Castro and informed the Soviet Union that "full retaliatory response" would be visited upon the USSR if a Cuban-based missile were fired (thus eliminating the possibility of the Soviets using Castro as a proxy), but US news releases underplayed the strategic nuclear response and emphasized the concentration of general purpose forces in a position of readiness to invade Cuba.[20]

Khrushchev was keenly aware of the danger of nuclear war. In an unusual letter to Lord Bertrand Russell of Great Britain on 25 October, Khrushchev stated, "We are fully aware that if this war is unleashed, from the very first hour it will become a thermonuclear and world war."[21] On the evening of 26 October (27 October in Moscow), President Kennedy received a personal message from Premier Khrushchev that was not released to the public but was described in general terms. Stated Roger Hilsman, then director of intelligence and research in the State Department, "It contained no specific proposal on conditions but showed throughout an appreciation of the risk of nuclear war and the need for reaching an agreement."[22] Khrushchev's personal message greatly relieved the anxiety of Washington officials. "Remember when you report this," Secretary Rusk told a newspaper reporter, "that, eyeball to eyeball, they blinked first."[23]

In an explanation to the Supreme Soviet on 12 December, Khrushchev pointed out the danger posed by the concentration of United States general-purpose forces in Florida. He stated that several paratroop, infantry, tank, and armored divisions—numbering about 100,000 men—were detailed for an attack on Cuba alone.

> On the morning of October 27 we received information from our Cuban comrades and from other sources which directly stated that this attack would be carried out within the next two or three days. We regarded the telegrams received as a signal of utmost alarm, and this alarm was justified. Immediate actions were required in order to prevent an attack against Cuba and preserve peace.[24]

Putting himself in Khrushchev's position at this critical juncture, Secretary McNamara rationalized that

> we had a force of several hundred thousand men ready to invade Cuba.... Had we invaded Cuba, we would have been confronted with the Soviets ..., had we been confronted with the Soviets, we would have killed thousands of them [and] the Soviets would probably have had to respond.... They might have had nuclear delivery weapons ... and they might have been launched.... In any event,... Khrushchev knew without any question whatsoever that he faced the full military power of the United

States, including its nuclear weapons. That might be difficult to understand for some, but it is not difficult for me to understand, because we faced . . . the possibility of launching nuclear weapons and Khrushchev knew it, and that is the reason, and the only reason, why he withdrew those weapons.[25]

Although Premier Khrushchev's nerve appears to have broken during the night of 26–27 October, a second Soviet letter to President Kennedy—signed by Khrushchev but not written in his personal style and received in Washington during the day on 27 October—indicated that Soviet policy might be hardening. This communication proposed that NATO missiles be removed from Turkey in exchange for the removal of Soviet missiles from Cuba.[26] On 27 October work at the Cuban missile sites continued, and while on a high-altitude U-2 flight over the island Maj Rudolph Anderson, Jr., was shot down and killed. During the afternoon of 27 October (28 October in Siberia) another U-2 pilot, who was flying a routine upper air sampling mission from Alaska, wandered 800 miles deep into the Chukotski peninsula of Siberia. The Soviets dispatched interceptors, but American planes moved out of Alaska and escorted the U-2 to safety.[27] In a statement to the press issued during the day, the White House postponed any consideration of the Soviet proposal to remove NATO missiles from Turkey,* and on the evening of 27 October Secretary McNamara ordered 24 Air Force Reserve troop carrier squadrons to active duty. That same evening, Kennedy and his advisers composed and dispatched a letter to Khrushchev which informed him that his proposals of 26 October seemed generally acceptable. These proposals included removal of offensive weapon systems from Cuba under United Nations supervision and a Soviet agreement to halt further introduction of such weapons into Cuba. Following establishment of adequate United Nations safeguards, the United States would remove its quarantine and give assurances against invasion of Cuba.[28]

When he was told about the wandering U-2 pilot on the afternoon of 27 October, President Kennedy was reported to have laughed and said: "There is always some so-and-so, who doesn't get the word."[29] The Soviet leaders, however, manifested extreme apprehension about the Strategic Air Command's airborne alert and the danger that some accident might set off a general war. In his speech to the Supreme Soviet on 12 December, Khrushchev emphasized "the direct menace of a world thermonuclear war, a menace that arose in connection with the crisis in the Caribbean." He specifically mentioned the SAC airborne alert. "About 20 percent of all US Strategic Air Command planes, carrying atomic and hydrogen bombs were kept aloft around the clock," he said.[30] On the morning of 28 October, when

---

* In a conversation with Soviet Ambassador Anatoly Dobrynin on the evening of 27 October, Attorney General Robert Kennedy explained that President Kennedy had wanted to remove the missiles from Turkey and Italy for a long time. Even though the United States would not remove the missiles under pressure or without NATO's consent, Robert Kennedy told Dobrynin that in his judgment the missiles "would be gone" within a short time after the crisis was over. (Robert F. Kennedy, "Thirteen Days, The Story About How the World Almost Ended," *McCall's*, November 1968, 170.)

Khrushchev accepted Kennedy's propositions for resolving the conflict, the Soviet Premier apparently referred to the previous day's U-2 overflight with great apprehension.

> Is it not a fact that an intruding American plane could be easily taken for a nuclear bomber, which might push us in a fateful step; all the more since the US Government and Pentagon long ago declared that you are maintaining a continuous nuclear bomber patrol?[31]

In the main portion of this message, Khrushchev accepted Kennedy's assurance that the United States would not invade Cuba as a sufficient reason to remove the arms which had been described as offensive. Khrushchev revealed that he had instructed the Soviet officers in Cuba to discontinue construction of sites, to dismantle the weapons, and to return them to the Soviet Union. He was prepared to accept a United Nations verification of the removal of the weapons.[32]

During the crisis, however, Fidel Castro had been virtually ignored by both the Soviet Union and the United States, and he would refuse in the end to permit a UN inspection and verification of the removal of the Soviet offensive weapons from Cuba, thus technically relieving President Kennedy of his pledge not to invade Cuba. Based on aerial inspection, however, the Soviets lived up to their agreement to remove the missiles and the Il-28 bombers from Cuba. They also dismantled and destroyed the missile installations. In view of the Soviet actions, Kennedy instructed Secretary McNamara on 20 November to lift the quarantine, and shortly afterward the special alert activities of the armed forces were gradually reduced.[33] Secretary McNamara emphasized "without any qualifications whatsoever there was absolutely no deal . . . between the Soviet Union and the United States regarding the removal of the Jupiter weapons from either Italy or Turkey."[34]

But in the aftermath of Cuba, the United States took immediate steps to remove its vulnerable IRBMs from Europe and to replace them with Polaris submarines. According to Gen Curtis E. LeMay, the British had never been very enthusiastic about the Thor missile as a weapon system, and they readily agreed to dispense with such missiles. The first Thor squadron was taken out of operation early in 1963 and the last was apparently dismantled in August 1963.[35] During the NATO ministerial meeting in December 1962, McNamara discussed the removal of the Jupiter missiles with the ministers of defense of Italy and Turkey. Aside from the vulnerability of the Jupiters, McNamara remarked: "It costs us roughly $1 million per year per missile simply to maintain the missile in Turkey . . . and we see no need to continue that expenditure for such an ineffective weapon."[36] The Jupiters were taken out of operation and dismantled by April 1963, and an equivalent number of Polaris submarines was assigned to the supreme allied commander, Europe, to replace the land-based missiles.[37]

Evaluations of the Cuban Missile Crisis

Efforts to assess the meaning of the Cuban missile crisis and to determine its lessons closely followed the successful resolution of the confrontation. President Kennedy observed on 17 December 1962, "I think, looking back on Cuba, what is of concern is the fact that both governments were so far out of contact, really." Extending his remarks, Kennedy suggested that World War I, World War II, and the Korean War had been brought on by "misjudgments" that in many ways were similar to the Soviet misjudgment of the effect that the installation of the offensive missiles in Cuba would have on the United States.[38] Although it was only a part of the problem, Kennedy noted that slow diplomatic communications had hampered the resolution of the Cuban crisis. He accordingly welcomed Soviet acceptance on 20 June 1963 of his proposal to establish a direct telecommunications link between Washington and Moscow. "This age of fast-moving events, requires quick dependable communications for use in time of emergency," he said.[39]

At the NATO Parliamentarians Conference in Paris early in November 1962, Under Secretary of State Ball used the Cuban crisis to illustrate the requirement for conventional military forces.

> Why were we able to modulate and attune our responses so closely to the degree of our need? Surely it was because we had the ability to deploy as required a very large variety of land, sea, and air forces in the fashion necessary to accomplish the task at hand. Because we had clear superiority of conventional forces, we were never confronted with the awful dilemma of having to utilize major nuclear weapons or to retreat from our objective.[40]

In another State Department assessment, Secretary Rusk emphasized that a major lesson to be drawn from the missile crisis was a requirement for international arms limitations.

> There are many things which can and will, in due course, be said about the Cuban crisis. One of them is that Cuba has provided a dramatic example of the deadly dangers of a spiraling arms race. It is not easy to see how far-reaching disarmament can occur.... Nevertheless, it is also obvious, as we have seen in recent weeks, that modern weapons systems are themselves a source of high tension and that we must take an urgent and earnest effort to bring the arms race under control and to try to turn it downward if we possibly can.[41]

In his public assessments of the lessons of the Cuban crisis, Secretary McNamara usually prefaced his remarks with the conclusion that Premier Khrushchev had been confronted and defeated.

> I think that throughout the world today, both in the Communist bloc and in the non-Communist bloc there is a clear recognition that Khrushchev capitulated.... My own strong personal belief is that we did not sucker for a play by Khrushchev, that he has been defeated, and that our position in the world today is far stronger as a result of the action.[42]

On another occasion, he remarked: "The Soviets suffered a serious defeat when they attempted to introduce ballistic missiles into Cuba . . . and were forced to reverse their plans by the threat of the application of military pressure by this country. It was one of the most serious defeats of this decade."[43]

In assessing the reasons Khrushchev had capitulated in the Cuban crisis, McNamara believed that

> he backed down . . . because we had both a nuclear superiority and a conventional superiority in that particular instance. . . . If there was a single decisive factor, it was the US determination to use force on the Cuban issue, if necessary. The improvement in our general purpose forces was an element which helped make that determination credible to the Soviets.[44]

At the NATO ministerial meeting in December 1962, McNamara referred to the Cuban crisis and pointed out that "perhaps most significantly, the forces that were the cutting edge of the action were the nonnuclear ones. Nuclear force was not irrelevant but it was in the background. Nonnuclear forces were our sword, our nuclear forces were our shield."[45] As has been seen, this same idea found its way into the Kennedy-MacMillan communiqué that closed the Nassau conference. Speaking for the Army, Maj Gen Earle G. Wheeler agreed "wholeheartedly" with McNamara's conclusions.

> In my opinion, the major lesson for the Army in the Cuban situation lies in the demonstrated value of maintaining ready Army forces at a high state of alert in order to equip national security policy with the military power to make a direct confrontation of Soviet power.[46]

When asked about the role of the Strategic Air Command in the Cuban crisis, McNamara responded: "SAC's principal role during the crisis was to help to lend credibility to our determination to take whatever actions were necessary to achieve the removal of Soviet offensive weapons from Cuba."[47] General Wheeler also apparently agreed with this finding. Placing SAC on airborne alert "put the Soviets on notice that we were serious, and it put them on notice we were ready to carry through, prepared to carry through," he said.[48]

Even though Secretary McNamara was unwilling to draw "just one single lesson from Cuba," he nevertheless stated that the improvements made in general-purpose forces during the first two years of the Kennedy administration had been "an important determinant when the showdown came."[49] But he still found deficiencies in the general-purpose forces during the crisis. To effect the quarantine, the United States had to employ Air Force and Navy planes to locate every Soviet ship moving toward the Western Hemisphere, and there were not enough planes available to accomplish this objective. McNamara also noted that the Navy lacked sufficient patrol craft and escort vessels. There had been shortages in transport aircraft.

> We needed transport aircraft, because of the invasion that we were prepared for and were ready to undertake. We were so short of transport aircraft that... I called up 14,000 citizens and put them into the Air Force and brought 400 transport aircraft that were obsolete into active duty in order that they might be used to fly over Cuba 36 hours later.[50]

McNamara also disclosed that the Cuban crisis had revealed a shortage of Air Force fighter aircraft.

> We were terribly short of fighter aircraft. We moved them from all over the country into the southeast area and we were still short.... We needed air defense for the southern area. We stripped air defense from other parts of the country to put down there.[51]

The Air Force agreed with McNamara's findings regarding the shortage of tactical air capabilities. During the crisis the Air Force was compelled to cancel rotation of Tactical Air Command squadrons to NATO, and to draw upon supply stocks as far away as the Philippines. In the process of laying down limited war contingency supplies overseas, the Air Force had shorted itself in the zone of interior. As a result of the events in Cuba, the Air Force also began to emphasize the need for the development of more modern tactical air reconnaissance systems, especially systems that could pierce cloud cover and detect hostile activities by sensing emitted or reflected energy.[52]

Although the Air Force agreed that the Cuban crisis had disclosed deficiencies in tactical air capabilities, General LeMay was unwilling to accept many of the other conclusions that were offered. To LeMay the Cuban missile crisis demonstrated that the Soviet Union would "take advantage of any technical breakthrough or make any strategic move which they believed might swing the balance of power in their favor without undue risk."[53] In assessing why Khrushchev had capitulated, LeMay asserted:

> I am convinced that superior US strategic power, coupled with the obvious will and ability to apply this power, was the major factor that forced the Soviets to back down. Under the shelter of strategic power, which the Soviets did not dare challenge, the other elements of military power were free to exercise their full potential.[54]

LeMay believed that Khrushchev had gone into Cuba with the full knowledge that he could not support conventional action in such a remote spot. "It was a matter of bluff then, whether we would stand up to this or not," LeMay said. "We did stand up. It was the strategic power that ran the ball. When we indicated we were willing to use that [strategic power], he lost the game."[55]

On the philosophical level the Cuban crisis provided General LeMay with another example of the capabilities of superior strategic power, coupled with a manifest willingness to employ it, to deter both general and limited war — an idea which he developed in 1963-64. He argued in February 1963 that we had the conventional forces to go in and take care of the missiles in Cuba or any other conventional Russian forces that were there. Our strategic superiority gave us the option of whether we would go or not. The choice was made that it was not necessary to go because the Russians removed the missiles.[56]

Recalling the often-repeated assertion that superior United States strategic power had not prevented limited war in Korea, LeMay pointed out:

> As far as strategic superiority not preventing limited wars, it did not prevent the limited war in Korea because we did not exercise it like we did in Cuba. In Korea we did not say there will be no limited war. We just said there will be no general war or we will use our nuclear weapons. I think if we had said that there will be no limited war or there will be no war in Korea or we will use our nuclear weapons, there would not have been any.[57]

In February 1964, LeMay suggested additional thoughts on Korea, saying:

> Korea, I think, was brought on because we practically publicly stated we were getting out of Korea and were no longer interested. So they came in and then they felt they were doublecrossed because we then changed our minds and went into Korea and fought under artificial restrictions with their having a sanctuary north of the Yalu. We fought this with conventional weapons, TNT only, no nuclear weapons considered. . . . Furthermore, with artificial barriers, we had to wait until the enemy came into Korea before we could do anything about them. We could not destroy the Chinese and the North Korean strength at its source, which was on the other side of the Yalu.[58]

In concluding his 1963 summary, LeMay had said: "It was not until the armistice period at the end of the Korean War that we stated, if it ever started up again, then we would use whatever weapons were necessary in places of our own choosing." In summary, LeMay concluded that the Korean War had resulted from the failure of the United States to announce in advance a policy of employing strategic superiority to prevent such a type of conflict. "Once a war starts and we are attacked, as in the case of Korea, where we were in there fighting I think that could have been stopped by the threat of using nuclear weapons."[59]

In a continuation of his discussion of the capability of strategic power to deter limited war, LeMay suggested that President Eisenhower's statement that ground forces would not be relied upon to defend Berlin had deterred the Soviets from action in 1958. LeMay described the Lebanon experience of 1958 as "another classic example of what you can do if you have strategic superiority and then are able to exploit any situation with your conventional force without interference. Without nuclear and strategic superiority, I do not think we would have dared go into Lebanon." In the Cuban crisis, LeMay considered that the United States had shown "a will to use all our power to force the Russians to move their missiles." He was confident that the same lesson would apply in the future: "If you have the power to stop a big war, certainly the same power ought to be capable of stopping a small war."[60]

In a summary of his views, General LeMay pointed out that the nation's investment in airpower "positively proved its worth in the . . . Cuban crisis."

Manned systems had demonstrated an ability "to make swift and clearly recognizable moves to evidence US resolve in the face of provocation." Although ballistic missiles had remained fixed in their silos, the movement of tactical aircraft to the southeastern United States, the worldwide deployment of other aircraft, and the SAC's airborne alert had provided visible evidence of the national resolution and determination to prevail in Cuba. "Admittedly I suffer from some bias," LeMay observed, "but I believe the investment in airpower is the best dollar value on the market today." To LeMay the Cuban operation "once more proved the value of military airpower, designed and operated by dedicated professionals who are experienced in operating airpower as an entity."[61]

Politico-Military Effects of the Cuban Crisis

In the United States and also in the Soviet Union the enormity of the possibilities that the Cuban crisis might escalate into all-out war had a sobering effect upon national leaders. In an impromptu toast at a Kremlin reception on 7 November 1962, Premier Khrushchev declared that during the Cuban crisis "we were very close — very, very close — to a thermonuclear war.... If there had not been reason, then we would not be here tonight, and there might not have been elections in the United States."[62] Speaking of the Cuban confrontation Secretary Rusk regarded it important to remember

> that something new in history happened ... and that is that nuclear powers had to look actually and operationally at what nuclear exchange could mean and ... this was an experience that those who carried responsibility on all sides recognized that one does not go through as a weekend avocation.[63]

One of the most important results of the Cuban crisis was the emphasis given at the top level of United States leadership to a need for ever closer political and military relationships in the determination of national strategy. Shortly after he had assumed office, President Kennedy had told the Joint Chiefs of Staff that he expected them to take both military and political factors into consideration in solving their problems.[64] This instruction required a reorientation of the Joint Chiefs of Staff since under the Eisenhower administration they had regarded themselves as the military advisers to the president and had attempted to advise him based upon military factors that Adm Arleigh Burke had described as a "minimum of economic and political factors."[65] Under the Kennedy mandate, General LeMay noted that the Joint Chiefs felt compelled to give political considerations to the problems they approached but that they nevertheless attached primary importance to the military considerations affecting the problems. In other words, the Joint Chiefs undertook to weigh the political aspects of problems in the same manner that the State Department could not avoid considering the military aspects of problems although State was primarily concerned with the political aspect.[66] After Cuba, however, Secretary McNamara observed: "To the best of my knowledge there has never been since World War II a closer relationship between the State Department [and] the Defense Department at all echelons than exists today."[67] McNamara reasoned that strategy must be made by the State Department and the Defense Department working in close association and must represent a proper appreciation of the national objectives of the United States, the nature of the hostile challenge, and the real and potential capabilities of military forces.[68]

Strategic Debates of 1963

Since he conceived that national strategic policies had a direct impact upon the congressional constitutional mandate to raise and maintain military forces, Secretary McNamara attempted, beginning in January 1963, to discuss strategy with Congress even more fully than he had done in the past. In his appearances before congressional committees, he prefaced his discussion of military strategy with a new assessment of the capabilities and threats presented by Communist nations. He pointed out that during 1962 the Soviet Union had attempted to extend its offensive military power into Cuba, had continued to exert pressure on Berlin, and had sought to make inroads into the Arabian peninsula and the Congo. The Chinese Communists led the drive to subvert Southeast Asia and had launched overt military aggression against India. McNamara concluded, "All these crises or probing actions are simply the more obvious manifestations of the communist drive toward their basic objective of world domination." Although the basic Communist objective did not change, McNamara noted that the Soviet Union was becoming a "have" nation with a great deal to lose in a nuclear war—material wealth as well as human life. The Red Chinese, on the other hand, were economically impoverished, held human life in little value, and appeared more willing to run the risk of nuclear war. From these observations, McNamara concluded that "the apparent monolithic structure of world communism has been fractured, perhaps irreparably."[69]

When he again assessed the Communist menace for the benefit of Congress early in 1964, Secretary McNamara maintained that the basic trends he had anticipated early in the preceding year had materialized. He said, "Indeed as far as the Soviet Union is concerned, the Cuban crisis of October 1962 seems to have marked the crest of the latest in the series of crisis cycles.... We now appear to be on the downward slope of this latest cycle and tensions in our relations with the Soviet Union are easing." He believed that the substantial increase in the military strength of the United States, its demonstrated willingness to use force in defense of its vital interests, and its continuing efforts to assist free nations, together with economic difficulties and agricultural failures within the Communist nations, had caused the Soviet Union and Communist China to abstain from military provocations during 1963. Although the Communists had changed their tactics, McNamara nevertheless warned that their objectives had not changed.

> I do not believe we can reasonably assume that these manifestations of a change in policy reflect a change in the ultimate objective of the Soviet leadership, which is to extend the sway of communism over the rest of the world.... Expansionism is so deeply engrained in Communist doctrine that it would be naive for us to expect any Communist leadership to repudiate it.[70]

Early in 1963 Secretary McNamara asserted that national strategic intelligence estimates of Soviet forces and force capabilities bore out his commentary on the changing nature of Soviet tactics. In February 1963 McNamara emphasized that the Soviets actually possessed a "very limited ... manned bomber capability."[71] The Soviet intercontinental and submarine-based ballistic missile force was the principal danger to the United States. The Soviets were continuing to harden their ICBM sites, and they had kept submarines "a fair distance off the coast" of the United States during the Cuban crisis.[72] The Soviets held the option to produce ICBMs in sufficient numbers to support a counterforce strategy, or they could procure only enough of the missiles to destroy population centers. Since intelligence indicated the USSR would have far fewer intercontinental missiles than the 1,000 land-based missiles the United States would possess by 1 July 1965, McNamara could only conclude that the Soviet strategy was what Khrushchev said it was – "a strategy directed primarily against our cities and our urban society."[73]

Nothing occurred during 1963 to make McNamara revise his force estimates. On the contrary, in December 1963 Khrushchev announced another 4 percent reduction in the Soviet defense budget and a slowdown in foreign aid and space programs. Whereas McNamara had earlier concluded that NATO possessed ground forces equivalent to those of the Soviets, he stated in January 1964 that "in total terms, NATO forces have more ground forces than the Soviet bloc." The major difficulty confronting NATO was no longer one of numbers, but the fact that the "NATO forces are not located, in certain cases, as effectively as the Soviet bloc forces, and can't be reinforced as quickly as the Soviet bloc forces."[74] McNamara now considered Red China as the most aggressive Communist nation and "a threat to the security of the Asian land mass." He assumed there was a "very substantial" possibility that China could become a "military threat" to the United States, but that such eventuality was "years away" in the normal sense of the term.[75]

In speaking about nuclear war in an interview published in December 1962, McNamara referred to a "balance of terror."[76] In his prepared statement presented to congressional committees in January 1963, he stated:

> More armaments, whether offensive or defensive, cannot solve this dilemma. We are approaching an era when it will become increasingly improbable that either side could destroy a sufficiently large portion of the other's strategic nuclear force, either by surprise or otherwise, to preclude a devastating retaliatory blow.[77]

Although the United States would continue to invest large sums of money in research and development in the fields of air-sea warfare and antiballistic missile defense, McNamara reported that the "best minds and best brains" in the

Department of Defense and in the scientific community had assured him that neither the United States nor the Soviet Union would score a breakthrough in these areas in the next several years.[78] "I don't believe that either the Soviets or we could take action to so protect our population that a nuclear strike would result in a low level of fatalities," he summarized.[79] Under such circumstances, McNamara urged that the United States could not "win a nuclear war, a strategic nuclear war in the normal meaning of the word 'win'." Even if the United States did "win" over the Soviets, McNamara visualized, "we would win in the sense that their way of life would change more than ours because we would destroy a greater percentage of their industrial potential and probably destroy a greater percentage of their population than they destroyed of ours." But the United States would sustain such severe damage "that our way of life would change, and change in an undesirable direction. Therefore, I would say that we had not won."[80]

Even though the transcendence of nuclear missile offense over defense ruled out the utility of military force in terms of the old Clausewitzian theory that war was the continuation of state policy by different means, Secretary McNamara nevertheless maintained that the United States, in any reasonable sense of the word, was "winning" because its "program to win was broader than the application of strategic military forces."[81] Speaking of the overall objectives of the United States, McNamara said:

> The basic objective is to ... protect our national security and our vital interests. ... To be more explicit, it is to prevent, in association with other Government policies, the advancement of communism to the control of areas not now controlled by it. ... The long-range objective is ... the spread of freedom throughout the world.[82]

Still on the relationship of military force to the national objectives, McNamara observed:

> As to our objective, I think ... it is to advance the cause of freedom throughout the world and to do this in a way that protects our own national security, which means we are not to destroy our Nation in the process of attempting to advance freedom elsewhere in the world. ... I do not believe we should embark on a course that is almost certain to destroy our Nation when that course of action can be avoided without substantial penalty to us.[83]

As a matter of fact, McNamara did not believe that the objective of spreading freedom throughout the world could "be achieved primarily through the development of military forces or the application of military forces," but he thought that

> it is quite clear that we as a nation ... have standards of values, standards of behavior, economic power, and a record of accomplishment such that, given the opportunity to exist in a peaceful world, the advancement of our forms of society is almost certain to occur over a long period of time.[84]

IDEAS, CONCEPTS, DOCTRINE

Because of his belief that Communist nations must not be allowed to mistake the military capabilities of the United States, Secretary McNamara outlined the force requirements represented in the Department of Defense budget for fiscal year 1964 in precise detail.[85] In the strategic retaliatory program package, McNamara proposed to continue to keep half of the 650 bomber force on a 15-minute ground alert and to retain a capability for flying one-eighth of the force on air alert for one year. He further proposed to phase out gradually two wings of B-58 bombers, to complete the three-aircraft B-70 program at a cost of $1.3 billion, and to expend an additional $50 million of the extra $190 million voted by Congress for the development of selected sensor components. In the Air Force, 13 Atlas squadrons with 126 missiles were already operational and would continue in place pending a decision to phase out some of the older, softer missiles. All 6 squadrons of Titan I missiles, aggregating 54 missiles, were in place, and 6 additional squadrons of improved Titan IIs (54 missiles) were expected to be operational by December 1963. The fiscal year 1964 budget included funds for 150 Minuteman II missiles, raising the total force of Minuteman to 950. It also funded the completion of the 41-boat Polaris submarine force, which would have a total of 656 missiles.[86]

In the continental air and missile defense forces package, the fiscal year 1964 national defense budget planned to install a semiautomatic backup intercept control system to supplement semiautomatic ground environment system (SAGE), to keep existing all-weather fighter, Bomarc, and Nike Hercules units operating, and to reserve decisions about the modernization of the weapon systems. The major defense problem was to develop systems effective against intercontinental and submarine-launched ballistic missiles. Tests had shown that the Nike Zeus would not be effective against a sophisticated threat in the late 1960s; accordingly, over $450 million was included in the fiscal year 1964 budget to initiate development of an improved Nike X and to continue tests with the Nike Zeus. The budget also provided increased developmental funds for systems that would provide possible defense against submarine-launched missiles.[87]

In the general-purpose forces package, the fiscal year 1964 budget recognized that the Army had reached its proposed five-year strength, but it would be allowed to expand its active strength to 975,000, thus adding 15,000 men and permitting the testing of an airmobility concept. A total of $3.3 billion was allocated to the procurement of Army weapons and materiel. The Air Force general-purpose forces would continue at 21 wings of tactical fighters, which would be equipped by increased procurement of F-4C fighters. The tactical reconnaissance forces would be expanded and would be equipped with RF-4Cs. In the airlift and sealift forces category the budget proposed to acquire several additional squadrons of C-130E aircraft and to phase out the old C-124s. Substantial funds also were committed to purchase new C-141s. Originally scheduled to be phased out in fiscal year 1964, the C-123 assault transport had proved useful in support of counterinsurgency operations in Vietnam and would be continued in the force program for the time being.[88]

In presenting the fiscal year 1964 budget request, Secretary McNamara pointed out that $7.3 billion in total obligational authority was committed to strategic retaliatory forces, $2 billion to continental air and missile defense forces, $19 billion to general-purpose forces, and $1.4 billion to airlift and sealift forces. Looking backward at the trend in obligational authority in the Kennedy years, the amounts committed to strategic retaliatory forces had declined each year, the funds for the continental air and missile defense forces had held steady, and the funding for general purpose and airlift and sealift forces had increased sharply.[89] In explaining the force levels, Secretary McNamara pointedly refused to be "tied down to any rigid doctrine about when and how the different types of forces should be employed."[90] He preferred to say that the primary objective of DOD was national security—not economy—and that he saw no reason the nation could not continue indefinitely the larger levels of military spending of the Kennedy administration. Having determined force levels, he meant to procure and operate those forces at the lowest possible cost.[91] During discussions in the spring of 1963, however, McNamara revealed his perspectives on defense requirements. Wrote William W. Kaufmann, "he wanted to have the capabilities for all modern types of warfare and, if forced to commit himself, he wanted to place main but not sole reliance on non-nuclear weapons."[92] In essence, the Kennedy administration, confronted by the dilemma of "humiliation or holocaust," wanted to increase its options, hoping that nuclear weapons might not have to be used.

Air Force Questions about the McNamara Strategy

Implications—some real and some imagined—of the emerging defense policy of the Kennedy-McNamara administration gravely concerned a number of defense commentators and the leaders of the Air Force. In January 1963 John F. Loosbrock, editor of *Air Force/Space Digest*, charged:

> The doctrine of nuclear deterrence is being replaced by a doctrine of nuclear stalemate. The strategic umbrella, under shelter of which major Soviet aggression has been deterred or repulsed at many times and in many places since the end of World War II, is being replaced by a strategic ceiling—rigid, immovable, and possibly brittle.[93]

Loosbrock pointed out that possession of strategic superiority had permitted the nation to control the escalation of small wars and had enabled the United States to shelter NATO against Soviet aggression. He suggested that lack of faith in the US nuclear deterrent was causing President Charles de Gaulle to build an independent French nuclear deterrent. "Today," Loosbrock wrote, "the argument over conventional vs. nuclear weapons may prove to be the reef on which NATO founders."[94]

During the late 1950s Gen James M. Gavin had maintained a keen interest in preparedness for limited warfare, and President Kennedy had named him United States ambassador to France. Despite his interest in limited war, Gavin had been careful to point out in his writing that "a limited-war theory is only valid when one has a massive strategic strike capability, and it is only within the framework of a significant strategic capability that one may indulge in the solution of problems involving lesser force." After reading Loosbrock's analysis, Gavin wrote that he was "just about in complete agreement" with it. Gavin agreed with the assertion that there was no "absolute" weapon system, and he suggested that an alert enemy might achieve technological surprise in such areas as antisubmarine warfare, ballistic missile defense, space, or biological and chemical warfare.[95]

In justifying his action relative to the RS-70 and Skybolt, Secretary McNamara cited considerations of cost effectiveness of manned systems as compared with intercontinental missiles in performing the strategic mission. Other officials developed an additional concept that hardened intercontinental missiles were better suited to the maintenance of a stable strategic deterrent than were aircraft. While attending an international conference of scientists held in Moscow from 27 November to 5 December 1960, Dr Jerome B. Wiesner, who would become presidential scientific adviser, and Walt W. Rostow, who would head the State Department's Policy Planning Council, found high-ranking Soviet delegates gravely concerned with the prospect that an accident might provoke an unwanted nuclear war between the United States and the Soviet Union. Such an accident might occur because of misjudgments of radar warning, a frustrated major power's escalation of a small war, or the spread of nuclear weapons to smaller and perhaps less responsible nations that might be allied with either the United States or the Soviet Union. At the conference, Wiesner presented a paper in which he suggested that "a limited deterrent force might be used as a basis for comprehensive disarmament." He also pointed out that the development of highly secure deterrent forces by both sides—desirably as small as feasible, since larger forces increased the dangers of accidental war—would relieve much of the incentive for an unlimited arms race, which if undertaken could not result in either side attaining an overwhelming military position in the foreseeable future. While in Moscow, Wiesner and Rostow were invited to discuss security matters with Soviet Deputy Foreign Minister Vasilyevich Kuznetsov, who expressed apprehension that a major US missile buildup would force the Soviet Union to respond, thus setting off a highly competitive missile race. Wiesner and Rostow emphasized in reply that the Kennedy rearmament program would be designed to provide a more secure deterrent posture, thus contributing to the cause of world peace. In an article published in 1961 Wiesner offered a short analysis of manned bombers as viewed from the new calculus of stable deterrence:

> Because of the vulnerability to missile attack of bomber bases and because air defense systems make the effectiveness of manned bombers somewhat uncertain, they may not be an attractive component of a stable deterrent system. It is hard to visualize building a bomber force as secure from attack as missile forces can become (unless it is kept in the air).[96]

In the United States during 1961 and 1962 more than 300 books and articles were published on arms control, and many of the arms control advocates described manned strategic weapon systems as first-strike, destabilizing weapons. Writing of the Soviets, for example, civilian strategist Thomas C. Schelling, reasoned: "Too great a capacity to strike him by surprise may induce him to strike first." In December 1962, Gen Dale O. Smith, special assistant for arms control to the Joint Chiefs of Staff, suggested that the arms control rationale might have been responsible for the curtailment of the B-70 and the Air Force space programs. Smith opposed the arms control argument that bombers are first-strike surprise weapons rather than second-strike retaliatory weapons. "Wars, do not occur like magic or from a whim. There must be some sort of strategic buildup, and many bombers would be launched when war seems probable," he wrote. Launched on the basis of reliable warning and held on air alert, bombers would be "well-nigh invulnerable." They could reach and destroy enemy launching pads long before a second enemy missile could be wheeled into place; and "fail-safe" controls that regulated the actions of bomber crews were fully as secure as those that governed missile crews. Smith also warned that the explosion of a 100-megaton Soviet warhead could do incalculable damage to Minuteman emplacement, but would not affect airborne bombers that were being held on air alert.[97]

In his presentations to congressional committees in the spring of 1963, General LeMay viewed the Soviet threat to the peace as changing in character and aspect but unchanging in its objectives. He pointed out that the Soviet Union was proceeding with great determination in areas of space, missiles, and high-yield nuclear weapons. It was continuing to apply science and technology to military purposes with impressive research and development programs, the result being a rapid progression of military systems from invention to operational inventory.[98] LeMay was willing to concede that a condition which could be described as "mutual deterrence" could conceptually exist for a short period of time, but the status of deterrence would change from day to day. He definitely did not consider that the United States and the Soviet Union had reached a period of mutual deterrence.[99] LeMay thought accepting mutual deterrence would "inevitably lead to defeat. In other words, if we stop trying, we certainly are not going to succeed in defending ourselves."[100]

Secretary Eugene M. Zuckert generally agreed with LeMay on the subject of mutual deterrence and chose to emphasize its transitory duration in an era of rapid technological change.[101] Speaking more openly than either Zuckert or LeMay, Gen Thomas S. Power described the United States as being in an arms race with the Soviet Union.

> We are running at a certain speed and he is running at a certain speed. If we slow our pace down or stop, it is obvious that he is going to get as strong as we are some day and get stronger. So this depends on how fast we run. You are in an arms race. And the name of the game is to stay ahead of him....[102]

Power continued his remarks in another off-the-cuff summation:

IDEAS, CONCEPTS, DOCTRINE

> I just feel that the surest way to prevent war — and that is my goal, and I feel very strongly about it — is to have overwhelming strength so that it is ridiculous for anybody to even think of attacking the United States. That is what it has been in the past, and that is what it is today.... I think our science, our economy, and everything else can help us win this race.... But it takes the will to do it.[103]

In a summary of his general position, General LeMay believed that the United States faced an enemy that would take advantage of any real or apparent technical development. In this situation, LeMay thought:

> There are certain precautions we can take.... We must retain our flexibility of action in the event of an enemy technological breakthrough ... by exploring every feasible weapon system.... We must also continue this exploration because we cannot accept the premise that since there is no known counter to a particular threat there is nothing we can do. If we accept this premise ... we invite the Soviets to vigorously probe our determination to resist.[104]

LeMay rejected any notion that the United States could accept parity with the Soviet Union in a dynamic situation, and he argued that the United States had to possess strategic superiority to remain secure. He pointed out that since World War II, the United States had allowed "the Russians to catch up in some fields and perhaps even surpass us in some."[105] LeMay was unwilling to

> accept the principle that it now appears impossible to build enough weapons ... or the kind of weapons that could knock out every single one of the Russian weapons.... This is an idealistic goal, and I doubt that it can ever be achieved. But that is no reason for not trying to achieve it. At least, let us get as close to it as we can, so if war should descend upon us, we will be in the best possible position.[106]

As the final comment preliminary to a discussion of exact Air Force requirements in his congressional presentations, LeMay stated the capabilities that a deterrent force had to possess to be credible to an enemy. These were:

> First, a capability to acquire that information necessary to attack effectively selected elements of enemy strength. For this, we rely on reconnaissance and comprehensive intelligence efforts.
> Secondly, a capability to survive. For this, we rely on diversity, numbers, hardening, dispersal, ground and airborne alerts, early warning systems, and constant training.
> Third, rapid response to an order to execute operational plans. For this, we rely on a high state of alert; and rapid, dependable, and survivable command and control.
> Fourth, immediate response in full strength or with selectivity under continuous control. Alert manned aircraft and missile forces provide this capability.
> Fifth, sustained effectiveness in portions of the force which may be withheld from initial attacks as uncommitted reserve, or for contingencies. Missiles which are dispersed, hardened, and mobile and manned systems which are dispersible on the ground and in the air — as well as recoverable and reusable — give these capabilities.
> Sixth, the ability in a portion of our forces to make swift and clearly recognizable moves to evidence US resolve in the face of provocation. Manned systems provide this capability.[107]

Following this statement of capabilities, LeMay described several other characteristics of a deterrent force:

> To maintain an effective deterrent, the posture of the strategic force must be updated continuously. At the same time, we must have the capability to meet requirements for conflicts of lesser magnitude than general war. In this portion of the conflict spectrum, military force is required for show of force, counter-insurgency and conventional war. As these needs are met, we broaden the available options of response so that escalation up to the most serious threat—general war—is but one of many options, and one which we, not the enemy, must control.
>
> Development and maintenance of the "many option" strategy requires forces to support the options. In acquiring these forces, we must maintain a credible general war force so that lesser options may be exercised under the protection of this general war deterrent. It is the general war strength of aircraft and missile forces which place an upper limit on the risks an aggressor is willing to take, and which deter escalation into all-out conflict.[108]

When they explained Air Force budgetary requests for fiscal year 1964, Secretary Zuckert and General LeMay disclosed to congressional committees that the Air Force had submitted requests of $25,521.9 million to DOD, had sustained an initial downward adjustment of $4,989.7 million, and had subsequently received a restoration of $119.1 million, making a total recommended Air Force program of $20,651.3 million. In response to Air Force reclama, President Kennedy had restored funds to provide for the procurement of additional C-130E transports, but two other desired items had been turned down. The first of these was the Air Force requirement for a long-range fighter interceptor with at least Mach-3 speed, an airborne radar capability, and a capability to intercept hostile targets from the surface to 100,000 feet without any assistance from a ground radar station. Secretary McNamara had refused this request because the declining Soviet bomber threat did not justify initiation of a $3-to-$5 billion program. He was also doubtful about the effectiveness of such an interceptor and wanted additional time to study aircraft that seemed likely prospects for the function. Believing that the tactical fighter force ought to be expanded from 21 to 25 wings and rapidly modernized, the Air Force had asked for a second production source for F-4C/RF-4C aircraft. Even though McNamara had conceded that 25 tactical fighter wings might be required in the late 1960s, he wished to postpone the decision because his cost-effectiveness analyses indicated that modernization of the existing 21 tactical fighter wings would give the greatest increase in combat effectiveness and that an expansion of the single F-4C/RF-4C production source could obviate the need for a second source.[109]

At the same time that he was concerned about the fact that the last manned interceptor for the Air Defense Command had been delivered in March 1961 and about the indefinite response to the requirement for a long-range interceptor, General LeMay was even more disturbed about deficiencies in projected strategic forces.[110] In brief, LeMay reported that he had "asked for more missiles by far than the secretary of defense has seen fit to give me." He also noted: "I want the best manned system I can get.... I want the RS-70 very badly.... When something faster comes along I want it."[111] LeMay thought that one of his basic differences with Secretary McNamara was on the size of an effective strategic deterrent force. LeMay said, "He thinks it can be done with something less than I think it can be done." When he viewed strategic superiority over the Soviet enemy, LeMay wanted "sufficient military power to knock out all of the targets that we know he has, or all the weapons that we know he has, and ... a little cushion to take care of some that we might not know he had."[112] LeMay wanted "clear superiority and flexibility" in the strategic force because he could not visualize the set of conditions under which a future war might begin. "I want to get a force and a combat capability that will cover anything you can think of," he said, "because I don't believe you can forecast how the next war is going to start and what conditions are going to be."[113] He continued, "I firmly believe that it is the duty of all of us who have responsibility for defending the United States to take whatever measures may be necessary under the circumstances, to do the best possible job of defending the country."[114]

General LeMay recognized that once the United States was committed to war, there were many tasks that could be performed better by missiles than by a manned weapon system, but Air Force war gaming had demonstrated to him that "the most efficient campaign can be fought with a mixture of the two, so you can use the strong points of each of the weapon systems and get a net result greater than the sum of each one of them if you use them separately."[115] In arguing for an advanced manned strategic weapon system in the spring of 1963, LeMay emphasized the value of such a system for show of force, as a safeguard against the uncertain reliability and unexplored vulnerability of missiles, and as insurance against the possibility that the Soviets might develop effective antimissile defenses. He additionally pointed out that it would cost the Soviet Union far more to defend against a mixed-force strategic capability than it would cost the United States to produce the weapon systems. This would be to the advantage of the United States. "If we don't diversify and don't force them to spend those resources on defense, then they would probably put a substantial portion of them on offensive weapon systems that would be an additional danger to us," he said.[116]

In his discussions of a manned strategic weapon system, LeMay expressed confidence that with proper tactics and proper penetration aids attack aircraft would be able to reach their assigned targets. He said, "I do not think, that we can predict the outcome of future engagements before we have the engagement. But based on my past experience and my knowledge of the defenses and how we have operated against them—and we have operated against all of the defenses of the world—I believe we will penetrate." Speaking of the future, LeMay noted that aircrews were going to fight hostile defenses rather than ignore them.

> We now have the capability of taking a portion of the penetrating force and putting it on the defense system and destroying it so you can go in without opposition. We have the weapons to do this. And we plan on doing it. I sometimes think that we have given the defense system too much credit. And we are taking too great a percentage of our

force and putting it on this task. But there is no doubt in my mind that proper tactics—proper execution of the mission—will produce the results we are looking for.... Experience, I think, is more important than some of the assumptions that you make.[117]

The Air Force was positively committed to the urgent need to develop and maintain a mixed strategic force, to include both missiles and a manned reconnaissance strike capability, but there was beginning to be less agreement on what the follow-on manned aircraft should be. LeMay still wanted the RS-70; he believed that it would continue in active inventory up until 1980 when it would probably be replaced by an aerospace plane. The RS-70 program, however, had encountered many delays, leading LeMay to comment that "even if we get a favorable decision . . . you cannot buy back that time."[118] Established in 1962 in response to Secretary McNamara's request for a look at alternate possibilities to the RS-70, the Air Force Manned Aircraft Systems Steering Group headed by Lt Gen James Ferguson, the Air Force deputy chief of staff for research and development, examined the prospects for the development of three different types of aircraft that could be had without straining the state of the art and would be a replacement for the old B-52s. Because it was especially interesting to McNamara, the Ferguson group carefully examined a plane that was variously called "Camel," "Dromedary," or the "multi-purpose, long-endurance airplane" (MPLE). This was conceived to be a large, low-speed, turboprop airplane that would have long endurance and would keep well outside enemy defenses and launch missiles into target areas. Although it would not have reconnaissance-strike capabilities, the long-endurance plane might additionally serve as an airborne weapon system for air defense, as a very large transport, or as a tactical command and control vehicle that could be used by tactical air units in advanced areas.[119] The second prospect was to develop a low-altitude manned penetration (LAMP) aircraft which would enter defended areas at high speed and at low altitudes, where hostile defenses would be ineffective. The third potential candidate was a Mach 3, very high altitude, advanced manned precision strike system (AMPSS). Similar in concept to the RS-70 this plane would take advantage of the state-of-the-art developments and would probably be only half the size of the RS-70.[120]

Although the Air Force thus began in-house studies of alternate follow-on strategic aircraft programs, it still hoped that the RS-70 might win approval for weapon system development since it could enter the operating inventory three to four years before any of the alternate systems. The Ferguson group accordingly did not begin detailed studies of the advanced manned strategic system until April 1963.[121] Noting that he might well have a "parochial viewpoint" as commander of SAC, General Power informed the House Committee on Armed Services in May 1963 that some arrangements positively ought to be made to keep SAC's future strength high. He favored the maintenance of a proper ratio that would weight proven aircraft against unproven missiles.[122] Power wanted the RS-70, but if it was not to be, he was willing to accept "the premise that anything is better than nothing." Thus he indicated in August 1963 that he would be willing to get more

B-52s if production lines could be rebuilt, and he seriously recommended procurement of additional B-58s to serve as interim bombers until a follow-on aircraft could be developed. Speaking of the need for an advanced manned strategic weapon system, Power called for rapid decisions: "I think time is a matter of great urgency. I would say that this fall or before this year is over they should make up our minds, because we have waited too long."[123]

Rebuttal to Air Force Questions

Although General LeMay and other senior Air Force officers presented the case for counterforce as a war-winning, damage-limiting strategy to generally sympathetic congressional committees during the spring of 1963, they were unable to sway either President Kennedy or the Department of Defense. On 17 December 1962 Kennedy already had stated: "There is just a limit to how much we need, as well as how much we can afford to have a successful deterrent.... I would say when we start to talk about the megatonnage we could bring into a nuclear war, we are talking about annihilation."[124] In an address to the American people on 26 July 1963, he noted: "A full-scale nuclear exchange, lasting less than 60 minutes, with weapons now in existence, could wipe out more than 300 million Americans, Europeans, and Russians, as well as untold numbers elsewhere."[125] In remarks to a press conference in January 1963, President Kennedy was willing to agree that there might "be a good many struggles in the globe in the late sixties or early seventies which are not subject to solution by missiles... where manned bombers may be very useful," but it was perhaps significant that he visualized a utility of manned bombers in what he described as "more limited war."[126]

Almost in rebuttal to Air Force positions offered in the strategic debates of 1963, secretaries Rusk and McNamara presented a concept of strategic aerospace power as being essential but much less versatile throughout a spectrum of conflict than Air Force leaders conceived. Stated Rusk, "I believe that the United States must maintain in its own security interests a very large over-all nuclear superiority with respect to the Soviet Union." But he immediately added: "This involves primarily the capacity to demonstrate that regardless of who strikes first, the United States will be in a position effectively to destroy an aggressor."[127] Secretary McNamara wanted a strategic nuclear force large enough and secure enough to give the United States an option to attack hostile forces rather than enemy cities, but he placed himself on the record in agreement with the president's statements that the United States had almost reached the point in the strategic level where "enough is enough." McNamara said, "I am not a believer in unlimited arms spending, not in the 'more the better' school of thinking."[128] At the same time that he described a "cities only" strategic retaliatory posture as being "dangerously inadequate," McNamara wrote off the theory of a "full first strike force" as being "simply unattainable." Such a "full first strike" capability would have to be accompanied by vast programs of antimissile, antibomber, and civil defense, and even then fatalities would run into tens of millions. McNamara therefore concluded:

> Thus a "damage limiting" strategy appears to be the most practical and effective course for us to follow. Such a strategy requires a force considerably larger than would be needed for a limited "cities only" strategy. While there are still some differences of judgment on just how large such a force should be there is general agreement that it should be large enough to ensure the destruction, singly or in combination, of the Soviet Union, Communist China, and the Communist satellites as national societies, under the worst possible circumstances of war outbreak that can reasonably be postulated, and, in addition, to destroy their warmaking capability so as to limit, to the extent practicable, damage to this country and to our allies.[129]

When closely questioned by members of the House and Senate Armed Services Committees early in 1963, Secretary McNamara revealed little patience with many of the charges that had been made against the "McNamara strategy." His program provided for maintaining nuclear superiority, including the capability to destroy any aggressor. Speaking with some heat, he described journalists' charges that a nuclear deterrent strategy required manned bombers and that a nuclear stalemate strategy was predicated upon missiles as "irresponsible" and "irrational" and retorted that it was "a disgrace that the American public was being fed this type of material."[130] He did not agree that the situation which he described as "mutual deterrence" comprised a "nuclear stalemate." Quite the contrary, he considered that the United States would emphasize research and development to ensure that it maintained a full deterrent capability and superiority in numbers and effectiveness of weapons.[131] He did not agree that nuclear superiority could be a "universal deterrent" against Soviet aggression; nuclear superiority, for example, had not prevented the Korean conflict.[132] He was unwilling to accept unreservedly the Air Force concept that a nation that possessed superior strategic power could control the escalation of conflict. Escalation had to do with the mental attitude of belligerents. "I think in many cases an inferior power acting in desperation has escalated the conflict," he said.[133]

Even though McNamara was in favor of maintaining "a mix of strategic systems," he did not necessarily believe that such a force would include a mix of missiles and gravity bombers. A future strategic-system mix could well include surface-based and air-launched missile systems. He added, "As a matter of fact, I believe it will have to be a mix of missile systems . . . , each system with characteristics different from the other systems and, therefore, adding in total to the problem of defense."[134] McNamara answered fears that missiles might not be reliable:

> If the missiles do not come through, we will presume for the minute that the Soviets have the same problems we do, and in that sense we will not be at any competitive disadvantage. At any rate, it would be impossible for the United States to continue to rely upon free-fall strategic bombing since by the end of the 1960s Soviet air defense would make it nearly impossible for an aircraft to penetrate into the Soviet Union and launch its weapons over a target.[135]

In the final analysis, the manned strategic weapon system that McNamara could visualize for the 1970s would be "an aircraft that is used to launch a very complicated missile system, a missile system more complex, more costly, less reliable, probably less accurate, than the missile systems we are now planning to have on hand at that time."[136]

Vicissitudes of a Strategic Bomber Program

Sympathetic to the Air Force statement of requirements for a manned strategic weapon system, Chairman Carl Vinson and the House Armed Services Committee in February 1963 added $363.7 million to the fiscal year 1964 defense budget, to be used solely for research, development, and test of the RS-70. After additional hearings, the Senate Armed Services Committee concurred in the increased appropriation.[137] Even though these powerful congressional committees endorsed the requirement for manned weapons, various technological factors began to work against the manned systems and in favor of missiles.

Funded from prior year appropriations, substantial numbers of intercontinental missiles became operational in the winter of 1962-63 and the missile programs progressed rapidly throughout 1963. The six-squadron Titan I missile force became operational in September 1962, and the entire 13-squadron Atlas force was operational by December 1962. Despite a worrisome technical problem, the six-squadron Titan II force would be operational on 27 December 1963.[138] By early 1963 a Minuteman missile silo was being completed almost every day. At Malmstrom AFB, Montana, the 3 squadrons of the 341st Strategic Missile Wing, each with 50 Minuteman missiles, became operational in February, May, and July 1963. At Ellsworth AFB, South Dakota, the 44th Strategic Missile Wing began to occupy its silos: its first Minuteman squadron would become operational in September and its second and third squadron in October 1963. The 455th Strategic Missile Wing at Minot AFB, North Dakota, would have its first Minuteman squadron in operation in January 1964, and its other two squadrons were expected to be operational shortly thereafter.[139] By the winter of 1963-64 construction of a base for the 351st Strategic Missile Wing would be nearly complete at Whiteman AFB, Missouri, and the Air Force expected to have a total of 4 wings of Minuteman missiles with 600 of the three-stage, solid propellant ICBMs in place by 30 June 1964.[140] The Air Force would locate the 90th Strategic Missile Wing with 4 Minuteman squadrons (200 missiles) at Francis E. Warren AFB, Wyoming, where a contract for necessary construction had been awarded in October 1962 and where the base would be nearing completion by early 1964.[141] To accommodate the additional 150 Minuteman II missiles authorized for procurement in fiscal year 1962, the Air Force would commence construction of a sixth Minuteman wing base at Grand Forks AFB, North Dakota, in the spring of 1964.[142]

In the same months that Titan, Atlas, and Minuteman missiles were coming into the Air Force operating inventory, the development of the B-70 encountered a maze of difficulties. In October 1962 the North American Aviation Company experienced a technical problem having to do with the welding of the plane's stainless steel honeycomb wings (which were hollow inside for use as fuel tanks) to the stainless steel fuselage. The best weld that could be made developed small pin holes, which allowed fuel to escape. Although a small amount of escaping fuel would not have been a problem in a subsonic aircraft, the wings of the Mach-3 XB-70 would heat to 600 degrees in flight and any escaping fuel would be hazardous. Some new synthetic fuel-tank sealant would have to be developed that could withstand very high temperatures. The North American Aviation Company promptly contacted sealant manufacturers in the United States and Europe, but none of these companies wanted to undertake an expensive developmental program when only three aircraft were involved. As a result of these delays, the XB-70A could not meet its initial flight schedule in December 1962, and each month's delay added to the production overrun costs.[143] On 24 April 1963 Secretary McNamara wrote Chairman Carl Vinson that the additional funds authorized by the House and Senate Armed Services Committees for the RS-70 would not be needed, and in a rare revolt against Vinson's leadership the House of Representatives refused to vote additional funds for the RS-70 when it passed the defense appropriation measure in late June 1963. In the Senate, committee chairman Richard Russell told his colleagues that it would be a "serious mistake" to forsake manned strategic aircraft and rely upon unproven missiles, but in September 1963 the Senate went along with the House's decision not to vote any additional money for an RS-70 weapon system.[144]

Under existing directives the Air Force continued to be responsible for the development and flight-testing of three prototype B-70 aircraft at a cost of not more than $1.5 billion (nearly all of which had already been expended), but General LeMay observed that up and down financing and fluctuating interest had killed the B-70 program. He said, "I feel the B-70 program is dead."[145] Production overrun costs mounted when the North American Aviation Company, with assistance from Air Force laboratories, developed a new fuel-tank sealant; but as funds ran short the third plane in the program, which would have had a bombing and navigation system, had to be canceled on 7 March 1964 when work was limited to two XB-70As. The sealant problem was solved in February, and the prototype XB-70 would make its maiden flight on 21 September 1964, but by this time weapon system development for the plane was no longer appropriate.[146] Looking backward at the B-70 program during his tenure as director of defense research and engineering, Dr Harold Brown observed that the designers had pressed the state of the art too much and had run into bad luck.

> Since I have been here, and I think since before I came, the Department of Defense has taken the attitude that until the technology is developed you shouldn't go into a big system with all the expense that that entails unless you can show an overriding need, unless you can show that the security of the country depends in a real way on having that system.[147]

Arms Control and Limited Nuclear Test Ban

In much the same manner that the Cuban missile crisis affected the military strategy and force composition of the United States, the nuclear confrontation about Cuba had—in the words of Secretary Rusk—"a very real bearing" on the consummation of a limited nuclear test ban treaty between the United States, Great Britain, and the Soviet Union during the summer of 1963.[148] Specific negotiations on a nuclear test ban treaty can be traced directly to 4 April 1958, when the Soviets completed a series of nuclear tests of unprecedented intensity and proposed that the United States and the Soviet Union immediately suspend nuclear testing. After the United States and the United Kingdom concluded scheduled test programs during the summer of 1958, President Eisenhower announced on 31 October 1958 a voluntary suspension of tests pending negotiations of an effectively controlled nuclear test agreement. The United Kingdom and the Soviet Union followed this lead and also suspended testing.[149] According to Gen Nathan F. Twining the United States held a substantial lead in nuclear technology in 1958, but as the moratorium dragged on without a positive agreement the Joint Chiefs of Staff pointed out many times that from a military point of view continual testing was required.[150] For one thing, the Air Force had commenced its missile hardening program late in 1957, and there had been no time to test the effect of a nuclear explosion atop a missile silo before the moratorium went into effect. Even though the Air Force used hardness criteria extrapolated by scientific advisers in the design of its hardened missile sites, it was unable to test the ability of an installation to withstand the earth shock and electromagnetic pulse of an atomic burst.[151] Although the Atomic Energy Commission attempted to maintain laboratories and a readiness-to-test capability during the moratorium, this capability declined materially since the standby program proved unable to retain competent scientists.[152] Summing up the situation, General Twining remarked: "We all but allowed our testing capability to go to seed."[153]

To provide a military capability in support of the lagging disarmament negotiations at Geneva, the Joint Chiefs of Staff established a special assistant for arms control outside the Joint Staff in December 1959.[154] The Geneva negotiations progressed poorly, and on 1 September 1961 the Soviet Union suddenly broke the test moratorium and ran off in rapid order a very comprehensive series of tests that involved the detonation of more than 300 megatons. The Soviets demonstrated very sophisticated nuclear weapon technology, made very complex high-altitude-effects tests, and detonated one 58-megaton weapon. The nuclear test series begun by the United States on 25 April 1962 and concluded on 4 November 1962 was mostly limited to low-yield devices, and the testing was greatly inhibited by efforts made to minimize fallout.[155]

To get an understanding of nuclear test ban proposals, General LeMay asked General Twining to return from retirement in December 1961 to head a study group to consider the military effect of a test ban. This group filed its first report on 5 January 1962 and updated the report on 4 March 1963. "A test ban would involve greater risks to the national security than perhaps have been realized," the committee warned.[156] After studying the results of United States and Soviet tests, General Taylor said that the Joint Chiefs of Staff concluded that the Soviets were ahead of the United States in high-yield nuclear technology, in weapons effects knowledge derived from high-yield nuclear explosions, in the field of yield/weight ratios of high-yield devices, and in the antiballistic-missile field. The Soviet Union was judged to be about even with the United States in intermediate-range weapons technology and to be behind in low-yield weapons. In the field of tactical nuclear weapons, particularly in very low-yield weapons, the United States appeared to be ahead in the quality and diversity of systems, although the superiority in quality was open to question since the Soviets could have conducted very low-yield tests that would have remained unknown to the United States.[157]

The Department of Defense gave close attention to arms control negotiations, especially after 27 August 1962 when the United States and the United Kingdom submitted a proposal to the 18-Nation Disarmament Conference in Geneva to ban nuclear tests in the atmosphere, outer space, and underwater. In February 1963 Secretary McNamara announced support for a nuclear test ban treaty that would maintain what he described as "our favorable differential balance of power." As a nation,

> I personally believe we will be far less secure 15 years from now or 10 years from now if nations not now possessing independent nuclear arms do then possess them. One of the major objectives of the test ban in my opinion should be to deter the further proliferation of independent nuclear forces.[158]

The Joint Chiefs of Staff recommended three cardinal principles to govern any test ban treaty: that the treaty should incorporate a detection, identification, and inspection system adequate to ensure the highest feasible probability of discovering treaty violations; that testing which could not be detected by the control system should not be prohibited by the treaty; and that withdrawal procedures should be simple.[159] General LeMay agreed with the JCS criteria and he also wanted to conduct some additional tests before a test ban went into effect. He specifically suggested that the United States detonate an antimissile warhead in the vicinity of a live missile warhead to determine the kill radius of an explosion and detonate a nuclear warhead over an actual Minuteman missile silo to determine the effects of such an explosion on the missile emplacement.[160]

In a speech at the American University on 10 June 1963, President Kennedy maintained that a treaty to outlaw nuclear tests "would place the nuclear powers in a position to deal more effectively with one of the greatest hazards which man faces in 1963 – the further spread of nuclear arms." President Kennedy revealed that he, Premier Khrushchev, and British Prime Minister Harold Macmillan had agreed to make a fresh start on test ban negotiations and to transfer the discussions from Geneva to Moscow.[161] Renewed negotiations began on 15 July, and the three negotiators initialed an agreed draft of a limited nuclear test ban treaty on 25 July. Officially signed on 5 August 1963, the limited test ban treaty prohibited tests in the atmosphere, underwater, or in outer space, but did not prohibit underground nuclear explosions as long as all fallout was contained within the country where the test or explosion was conducted. Since the treaty permitted tests that easily could be detected, no provision was made for on-site inspections or an international verification agency. Any signatory nation which decided that its supreme interest had become jeopardized would be permitted to withdraw from the treaty with three months' advance notice.[162]

When he forwarded the text of the nuclear test ban treaty to the Senate on 8 August 1963, President Kennedy declared that its prompt ratification was in the national interest. During hearings before the Senate Committee on Foreign Relations, Secretary of State Rusk argued that the treaty would slow the spiral toward bigger and more destructive weapons without damaging the relative strength of the United States and the Soviet Union, would help contain the spread of nuclear weapons by making it more difficult and expensive for nations to develop them, and would help reduce radioactive pollution of the planet.[163] Secretary McNamara testified:

> The Soviet Union's acceptance of the US proposal for a three-environment test ban offers some evidence . . . that its leadership has at last grasped an essential fact — that the sheer multiplication of a nation's destructive nuclear capability does not necessarily produce a net increase in its security.[164]

Responding to a question about the military advantages of the limited test ban treaty, McNamara said:

> I believe that the effect of the treaty to retard . . . the proliferation of nuclear weapons is very much in our interest, and increases our national security. Furthermore . . . I believe that the treaty will delay the Soviet developments in certain areas in which we presently have . . . a technological advantage, and that this will be to our interest as well.[165]

In a conference with General LeMay on 19 July and in a meeting with all of the Joint Chiefs of Staff on 24 July, President Kennedy urged the military leaders to take all factors into consideration as they examined the limited test ban treaty. He asked them to examine the political aspects of the matter as well as the military aspects. Setting aside all of their previous positions, the Joint Chiefs made a new assessment of the new treaty. They determined that the Soviet Union was ahead in high-yield nuclear technology, that the United States and the Soviet Union were about even in intermediate-range yields, and that although the United States was ahead in low-yield technology, the Soviet Union easily could conduct underground tests to develop low-yield weapons. LeMay thought that the United States should develop a 100-megaton bomb, but he was willing to accept the assurance that the Atomic Energy Commission could develop a 50-megaton weapon without testing. Under the treaty, the Joint Chiefs believed that the United States and the Soviet Union could make about the same rate of progress in developing an antiballistic missile, but they agreed that the Soviets possessed nuclear blackout information that was not available to the United States. The chief fear of the Joint Chiefs was that the treaty might breed euphoria, and they urged that the United States must maintain an active underground testing program, facilities and resources necessary to institute atmospheric testing in case the Soviets abrogated the treaty, and capabilities to monitor compliance with the treaty. General LeMay believed that the treaty contained military disadvantages, but he was willing to accept it because of the political advantages it appeared to offer. "I think it might be to our political disadvantage if we did not ratify it," he said.[166]

Well before the Moscow conference drafted the limited nuclear test ban treaty, Dr Edward Teller, the nuclear physicist who had developed the American H-bomb, had voiced his belief that a nuclear war ought not to be considered "unthinkable." Although such a war might be catastrophic, Teller urged that the United States could save up to 90 percent of its people by implementing a proper shelter program. Teller also was confident that an effective antimissile defense program could be developed. He warned, "If we listen to those who wrongly state that a next war will necessarily be lost, we might easily end up living on our knees and perhaps later dying in a war that others fight over our impotent bodies."[167] In appearances before the Senate Preparedness Investigating Subcommittee and the Senate Foreign Relations Committee during August 1963, Teller offered numerous reasons for opposing the ratification of the limited test ban treaty, his most telling argument being his belief that the treaty would hinder United States antimissile development programs while the Soviets might have acquired the information they needed to develop antimissile defenses.[168] General Power also opposed the ratification of the treaty. Based on his own interpretation of history, Power believed that

> disarmament is a proven concept to get you into a war. ... In other words, you have an aggressor, and he never attacks unless he has a victim, somebody whom he can attack and get a profit out of it. He looks for a weak nation, a nation that disarms itself. And the surest way to cause a war, nuclear war or any war, is to disarm.[169]

Both General Twining and Admiral Burke also agreed that the nuclear test ban treaty had such serious military defects that it should not be ratified. Twining warned that the Soviets might have made a breakthrough in nuclear technology that was unknown to the United States. He added that the treaty

> creates an artificial restriction on our ability to acquire and use increased knowledge of nuclear weaponry. Artificial ceilings on man's acquisition of knowledge are unnatural. The uncertainty of not knowing whether or not one is behind or losing superiority could create great international instability.[170]

While he conceded that the treaty would probably be ratified, Admiral Burke voiced his opposition to any test ban arrangement that did not permit some positive inspection authority.[171]

At a press conference on 20 August, President Kennedy noted Dr Teller's opposition to the limited nuclear test ban treaty and released the information that his own scientific advisory committee assured him that the test ban "is a source of strength to us." Four days later, the White House released an exact statement from the president's scientific advisory committee, which read: "The Committee believes that the continued unrestricted development and exploitation of military technology by both the Soviet Union and the United States would in time lead to a net decrease in our real security." After weighing all the evidence, the Senate approved the limited nuclear test ban treaty on 24 September. It was formally signed by President Kennedy on 7 October, and was formally proclaimed by the United States on 10 October 1963.[172]

During the winter of 1962-63 disarmament efforts of the United States focused on the limited nuclear test ban negotiations, even though another activity that would be described as "arms restraint" or "nonnegotiated arms control" techniques drew much less public notice. In an address on 5 September 1962, Under Secretary of Defense Gilpatric was reported to have said that the United States had not placed any weapons of mass destruction in orbit and had no program to do so.[173] At a disarmament symposium at the University of Michigan in mid-December, Assistant Secretary of Defense John T. McNaughton stated that decisions on the improvement of national security through the use of "nonnegotiated techniques" were "being made today, and every day, to a large extent by the Defense Department in the fields of strategic doctrine."[174] When asked to explain the meaning of "nonnegotiated arms control techniques," Dr Harold Brown said that he considered this to be "mostly hypothetical" but added that "there are situations in which tacit agreements, maybe not expressed even privately but just signaled by actions, can improve our security and improve Soviet security at the same time."[175]

When asked about orbiting nuclear weapons in February 1963, Secretary McNamara noted: "We haven't found any requirements for such weapons yet. We might find them, but we haven't found any weapons to put into space that offer greater potential than a weapon that is land-based, sea-based, or airborne."[176] Later that month the commander of the Soviet missile forces stated that the Soviets could launch rockets from satellites at a command from earth, and this statement caused careful evaluation in the Department of Defense.[177] Doctor Brown thought it was technically feasible for the Soviets and for the United States to place satellites in orbit and to launch missiles from them at earth targets, but he did not consider that this would be militarily useful. The cost in thrust of launching a large missile carrier into orbit would greatly exceed the cost of launching a payload from surface to surface; moreover, the accuracy of a space-based missile against an earth target would be even less than the accuracy that the Skybolt missile would have possessed.[178]

In a statement in March 1963 President Kennedy not only questioned the military necessity of placing nuclear weapons in orbit, but also observed that "it is a good thing to keep them out of the atmosphere." Rather than attempting to get a bilateral agreement with the Soviets, Kennedy preferred that the United Nations General Assembly should handle the problem, because "other countries may someday have the same capability, and I think every country should declare that they are not going to put atomic weapons in the atmosphere."[179] In subsequent actions in the General Assembly both the United States and the Soviet Union individually stated that they would not put nuclear weapons into outer space, and on 17 October 1963 the General Assembly adopted a resolution by acclamation that welcomed the intent of the United States and the Soviet Union not to station objects carrying nuclear or other mass-destruction weapons in outer space. The resolution additionally called upon all nations to refrain from orbiting weapons of mass destruction, installing them on celestial bodies, stationing them in outer space, and causing, encouraging, or participating in the conduct of such activities.[180]

In the spring of 1963 Doctor Brown described the decision of the United States and the Soviet Union not to place nuclear weapons in orbiting space vehicles as a clear illustration of nonnegotiated arms restraint.[181] In a later continuation of the discussion of "the arms restraint philosophy," Brown pointed out that "unilateral restraint really has to have a quid pro quo. We do not do something and they must respond by not doing something, even though it was not explicitly arranged. Otherwise, we do not proceed and not do the next thing." Brown considered that the decision by the DOD not to procure as many Minuteman missiles as the Air Force recommended recognized that there would be no advantage in deploying more missiles. He added that this might be considered to be an arms restraint decision which sought to prevent a Soviet reaction that would negate the United States action. He described arms restraint as being "the difference between a rational arms race and an irrational arms race."[182]

Maturity of the Strategy of "Controlled Flexible Response"

During the summer of 1963, while the United States was—in Secretary McNamara's words—presenting the Soviet Union "an alternative to the cold war [by] holding the door wide open to proposals for lessening world tensions, for reaching agreements on nuclear tests, and for bringing the armaments race to a halt,"[183] the Department of Defense was engaging in studies that were necessary background to the preparation of the fiscal year 1965 defense budget that President Lyndon B. Johnson would submit to Congress in January 1964. Within the Air Force a good many of these background studies would not be complete by January 1964, and as a result Air Force requirements and force levels would be actively debated in congressional subcommittee hearings.

To Secretary Zuckert one of the major meanings of the strategic debates and the arms limitation agreements of 1963 was that "arms control is now a military requirement in itself." Zuckert believed that the nations of the world had found themselves "caught in the bind of feeling on the one hand that they must have military power to defend themselves and enforce peace, while on the other, they recognize that uncontrolled use of that power totally defeats its purposes." He conceived that

> current military planning must provide for forces not dependent upon nuclear testing or any other type of restrictions to which nations may agree. They must be forces which are stabilizing in effect and not provocative either through vulnerability or other characteristics. These forces must have built-in assurance against accidental, unauthorized, or premature employment, and the force structure must be adaptable to monitoring and inspection roles as they may emerge.[184]

A quality which Zuckert described as "crisis management" was closely related to arms control, and Zuckert described it as "the ability to keep even an intense and long-lasting international crisis from exploding into war, or a low-intensity conflict from escalating into higher dimensions of war."[185]

In putting together the Air Force's force requirements, Secretary Zuckert considered deterrence of war — general or otherwise — to be the primary national objective. He thought that the importance of the deterrent capability at any level of intensity was directly proportional to the damage to be expected at that level. Thus, the deterrence of general war was of primary importance, but the Air Force nevertheless had to avoid being "caught with no choice but all-out nuclear response." "This is what was wrong with the massive retaliation theory," he said. Other capabilities or qualities had to be built into the deterrent force to defend and to preserve the United States. These included flexibility, controlled response, multiple options, survivability, damage limitation, maintenance of a threshold of negotiation, and a war-termination capability. The maintenance of a threshold of negotiation reflected a determination to stop war at the lowest point of intensity on favorable terms, a clear understanding of what those terms should be, acknowledgment that destruction of an enemy was not an objective, and recognition that unrestrained warfare would be unfavorable to all belligerents. The war-termination capability implied a need for forces to be able to return to an attack in a degraded environment, counter escalation with increased power at each higher level of intensity, control forces at all times, and maintain an intelligence capability that would permit an initiative in timing. Secretary Zuckert stated that the 10 characteristics that he enumerated would be the objective criteria for designing the most economical Air Force structure for the future.[186]

McNamara and LeMay Dispute Strategic Requirements

In his initial look at the planned and existing status of the nation's strategic retaliatory forces preliminary to the making of the fiscal year 1965 budget request, Secretary McNamara was almost willing to admit that the planned combined total of Air Force bombers and intercontinental missiles and of the Navy's Polaris missiles had nearly reached a point of overkill.[187] Where earlier thinking had visualized a continuing of Minuteman missiles, and the Air Force recommended further expansions of the Minuteman force level, the prospects of the Minuteman

II missile for force modernization caused major revisions in the Minuteman program. Essentially the choice in the fiscal year 1965 program was whether to make a faster Minuteman buildup with a slower rate of retrofit of the older Minuteman I models or to follow a slower rate of buildup with the more powerful and more accurate Minuteman II missiles. McNamara accepted the latter alternative, and the fiscal year 1965 budget request proposed to add only one additional Minuteman squadron (50 missiles) to the existing force levels. This additional squadron brought Minuteman authorizations to a force of 1,000 missiles, and McNamara indicated that, although Minuteman II retrofitting modernizations would continue, any further increases in the size of the force would depend upon world conditions.[188] With the increase in the Minuteman force it was increasingly inefficient to retain first-generation, liquid-fueled Atlas and Titan I missiles in the Air Force's operating inventory. The yearly cost of maintaining the liquid-fueled missiles was about $1 million per missile in comparison with about $100,000 per missile for the Minuteman. The defense program for fiscal year 1965 therefore sought to phase out Atlas D missiles at Warren and Offutt AFBs during the year and to phase out Atlas E and Titan I missiles later.[189]

Except that the Air Force had recommended the procurement of more Minuteman missiles than the secretary of defense was willing to buy, General LeMay was satisfied with the missile program as represented in the fiscal year 1965 defense budget requests. Like other new weapon systems, the reliability of the missiles was low, but LeMay assumed that enough of them had been scheduled against war plan targets to take care of any unknown low-reliability factor. Some unknowns in the missile program nevertheless continued to trouble LeMay. Except for the firing of a single Polaris missile under less than full operating conditions, no intercontinental ballistic missile (ICBM) replete with its nuclear warhead had ever been tested. Missiles could not be test-fired from their operational silos, even without their warheads. Any missile to be test-fired had to be removed from its silo, transported to Vandenberg AFB, placed in another silo, and fired on the Pacific range. LeMay did not believe that such a test program provided a realistic and adequate operational test. General Power additionally was concerned about whether the Minuteman silos were as resistant to a hostile nuclear blast as the scientists had predicted; because of the limited nuclear test ban treaty, no actual test of the matter could be undertaken.[190]

Despite these uncertainties General LeMay was willing to accept missiles as a component of the strategic retaliatory forces, but he was unwilling to accept them as the sole strategic capability.[191] With the death of the B-70 program no replacement existed for the B-52s. Unlike General Power, General LeMay saw no benefit from resuming expensive B-52 production. As a matter of urgency, General LeMay maintained that the Air Force had to get the authority to develop an acceptable advanced manned strategic system and drive it on through. "Otherwise," he warned, "I am afraid the B-52 is going to fall apart on us before we can get a replacement for it."[192] To find an alternative to the B-70, the Air Force Manned Aircraft Systems Steering Group had set in motion study contracts that were to be completed in March 1964. In its initial budget recommendations on 3 July 1963, the Air Force anticipated the study contracts and requested that $25 million be included in fiscal year 1965 funds to initiate development, including program definition, of an advanced manned strategic system. On 3 September the Office of the Secretary of Defense approved $15 million for the program definition phase. By October General LeMay perceived that there was a "good enough feel" on the problem to warrant submission of a memorandum to the secretary of defense stating the general type of system desired. The aircraft proposed was the advanced manned precision strike system (AMPSS). This plane would be smaller than the B-70, built of aluminum rather than stainless steel, capable of operating from short airfields, and able to fly approximately half of its range at high altitudes and supersonic speeds and then, when it reached the fringe of enemy radar detection, to descend to an altitude just above the terrain from which it would make attacks at high-subsonic or low-supersonic speeds. The primary armament of the plane would be highly accurate air-to-surface missiles, but it was to have a capability to deliver laydown weapons—both nuclear and conventional—of all types.[193]

Since he had approved a strategic retaliatory force level to include 1,000 Minuteman missiles, 656 Polaris missiles, 630 B-52s, and 80 B-58s, Secretary McNamara could see no pressing requirement for an advanced manned strategic system. He said, "Now what is the role of a bomber after you place 1,000 to 2,000 missiles on the Soviet Union? What have you left to mop up? . . . If it is not a mop up operation what is the role of the bomber?" He suggested that missiles were advantageous because:

> First, there is the matter of time to target. The quicker our retaliatory force can reach the opponent, the more chance we have of catching a substantial part of his force on the ground . . . and the more difficult we make it for him to plan and mount a full surprise attack. . . . Secondly, the missile has, because of the possibility of hardening it, a much greater potential for surviving an enemy attack and surviving with a capability to apply force against enemy targets. And thirdly, at least for the foreseeable future, the missile has much greater penetration capability.[194]

Until the Air Force could make a case for the AMPSS, McNamara was unwilling to program money for a project definition phase. Instead of the $15 million originally approved by the Office of the Secretary of Defense, $5 million was put in the fiscal year 1965 budget request so that the Air Force could define an operational role for the plane that would be acceptable to the Joint Chiefs of Staff.[195] In an immediate reclama the Air Force offered to fund the fiscal year 1965 AMPSS effort by reducing some other part of its activity. When the Joint Chiefs had discussed the proposed fiscal year 1965 budget with President Johnson in December 1963, LeMay again had stated that he felt such a strong need for the AMPSS that he would be willing to reprogram Air Force money to do the job.[196]

As the Air Force studies on the advanced manned precision strike system progressed, the Air Force was able to specify that it required $52 million for the project in fiscal year 1965, $15 million for program definition, and the remainder to begin the development of propulsion and avionics subsystems. On 20 January 1964 service members of the Joint Chiefs of Staff recommended approval of the Air Force proposal, but the chairman recommended funding of only the program definition phase and withheld approval of any subsystem development until more data was available. As soon as it could get three studies from Boeing, North American, and General Dynamics, the Air Force submitted the additional data on 15 February. After viewing this data, the Joint Chiefs of Staff, except the chairman, reaffirmed their previous recommendations. The chairman held to his previous view in support of only the program definition phase.[197] At the same time that the studies went forward to the Joint Chiefs of Staff, copies of them were also submitted to Secretary Zuckert for his study, conclusions, and submission to Secretary McNamara. After a preliminary review, Secretary Zuckert had a number of serious questions about the operational concept for the system. He specifically questioned what he described as General LeMay's tendency to downgrade the effect of hostile defenses on the ability of the proposed aircraft to penetrate to a target.[198]

Although he apparently did not share the full support of the secretary of the Air Force, General LeMay nevertheless believed that it was vital for the Air Force to go ahead with the advanced manned precision strike system — "to leapfrog a bit" — and avoid having to wait on the fiscal year 1966 budget cycle. He accordingly asked Congress to increase the appropriation request for a follow-on strategic aircraft from the $5 million specified in the fiscal year 1965 budget to the $52 million needed for program definition and advanced development. As presented to the House Military Appropriations Subcommittee, LeMay's expanded views on the need for a strategic manned weapon system left little more to be unsaid on the subject:

> The environment in which future war may be initiated, the method of opening hostilities, the basic character of war, the length and scope of war, and the conditions and procedures by which the war may be terminated are all factors which will determine the weapons systems actually needed in a future conflict. But forecast of war, or of the events constituting a preamble to war, have rarely proven to be accurate. Accordingly, any analysis of the potential contributions of a weapon system which is based upon a single concept of war is far from reliable. When a large number of possible circumstances indicate the necessity for a follow-on strategic aircraft system, as is the case in our studies, I consider that timely action is warranted to provide the required capability. Otherwise we will be placing our sole reliance upon ballistic missile forces that have never reacted to the conditions of actual war or even to conditions which constitutes a peacetime simulation to the wartime environment.
>
> I am in complete agreement with the need for a modern, effective ballistic missile force as an important element of our deterrent posture. Additionally, a secure ballistic missile force, in concert with other survivable strategic forces provides the strongest possible incentives to the USSR to abstain from attacks on the population centers of the United States, either in an initial attack or as a rational option during conflicts of lower intensity.
>
> It is important to recognize, however, that the ICBM and SLBM (submarine launched ballistic missile) forces represent both the United States and Soviet potential

for strategic nuclear warfare at the highest, most indiscriminate level. The employment of such weapons in a crisis or lower level conflict would be an inappropriate response and would immediately escalate the situation uncontrollably to an intensity which could be vastly disproportionate to the original aggravation.

In my judgment, a strategic force posture which placed sole or principal reliance on ballistic missiles would deny to the future national leadership the ability to respond in a flexible yet unambiguous manner to a wide range of lesser provocations. To the extent that in fact it would not be credible for the United States to employ a total ballistic missile response to peripheral aggression, such enemy calculations and subsequent aggressions ultimately could result in Communist domination of major segments of the free world. On the other hand, a strategic aircraft would provide the national leadership with a capability to retain the initiative at all levels of confrontation of conflict, thereby decreasing the dangers of enemy miscalculation and insuring that we can in fact control or contest a given situation without high risk of a missile exchange and the unnecessary losses in American lives which would result. This ability to respond under closely controlled conditions by use of discriminate force in a fashion which clearly transmits with it our intent to prevail requires characteristics available only in a mixed force. For this reason, I consider that a mix of ballistic missiles and manned strategic aircraft, in numbers appropriate to their respective tasks, will remain the only appropriate basis for general war planning for the foreseeable future.

A complementary mix of manned aircraft and ballistic missiles will continue to be essential to the national security for other important reasons as well. In any future conflict, we will need forces which can respond quickly under careful national direction to a wide variety of unforeseen and rapidly changing circumstances. Ballistic missiles inherently were designed to be—and remain—a single shot, irrevocably committed weapon system. In this regard, the manned element of the force, with its unique capability to react immediately to redirection, to exploit fleeting advantages, and to execute a broad range of missions, provides an effective complement to the ballistic missile forces.

While we are reasonably confident that we will demonstrate satisfactory reliability with our ballistic missile force, at best this will be based on relatively small statistical samples, without any substantial opportunity to test the force in its operational environment.

Manned aircraft and ballistic missiles also complement one another in the manner in which they compound the offensive and defensive problems of the enemy. Since the alert aircraft can be launched under the positive control in conditions of ambiguous warning, the enemy is unable to achieve a high confidence that he can attack successfully a major portion of our strategic force. Similarly, so long as he is faced by a mixed strategic force, the enemy cannot concentrate his resources either on ABM (Antiballistic Missile) or Air Defense; he must dilute and divide his efforts between the two. Thus, a mix of US strategic forces and attack options provides strong incentive for the enemy to spend a large portion of his military budget on the defensive environment, thereby reducing the funds which otherwise would be available for offensive systems to be employed against the United States.

As a final point, I consider it important that the Nation have a long range, strategic system which can support war operations against the Soviet Union or engage in lesser conflicts at our determination without the necessity for forward basing. In addition, this capability can be exploited over and over again; it is not a single shot weapon system. The flexibility inherent in a manned aircraft system gives us the opportunity to provide visible evidence of national resolve and determination—as we did in the case of Cuba—to employ such forces in initial or follow-on operations which are designed to achieve an early conflict termination at the lowest practicable level of conflict, and to provide a means of policing or enforcing the truce, once it has been achieved.[199]

In his appearances before congressional committees to discuss the fiscal year 1965 budget, Secretary McNamara was willing to allocate $5 million so that the Air Force could study an advanced bomber that he thought would never be built, but he strongly recommended against the addition of any more funds to the project. When the House Armed Services Committee recommended the addition of approximately $50 million for the study and development of a manned strategic weapon system, McNamara asked the House Appropriations Committee not to authorize the money. He emphasized that the Air Force had not presented him with any statement of concept or operational plan or specifications of such a bomber that would indicate a need for it. In a future war, missiles would have to be employed against "time-sensitive" targets; other types of targets—troop concentrations, transportation centers, battlefield targets—could be handled by new aircraft under development, such as the TFX fighter-bomber.[200] In rebuttal to the suggestion that the TFX might serve as an advanced strategic system, LeMay argued that the advanced fighter was designed as a tactical weapon, which meant that it would not be able to penetrate sophisticated defenses. It did not have enough space within it to carry the electronic countermeasures and other things that had to be employed by a strategic aircraft.[201] LeMay's reasoning was accepted in Congress. Stated Rep George H. Mahon, chairman of the House Defense Appropriations Subcommittee, "I believe most members of Congress feel as I, that we cannot with prudence abandon strategic manned systems in the foreseeable future. This is a risk we are not willing to take at this time."[202]

Continental Air and Missile Defenses

In stating the requirements for continental air and missile defense forces during fiscal year 1965, the Department of Defense assumed that the weight of the hostile strategic threat to the United States would continue to shift from manned aircraft to intercontinental and submarine-launched ballistic missiles and that, as Secretary McNamara said, "the main thrust of ... defensive efforts in the years ahead should be directed to meet this rising threat." As long as the Soviet Union continued to possess bombers that could reach the United States, however, McNamara believed that the United States must continue to maintain some air defenses. He also reasoned that the Soviet Union would make initial attacks with missiles and then follow up with manned bombers.[203]

Despite Premier Khrushchev's boast that bombers were good only for museums, General LeMay and other Air Force officers doubted that the Soviets would abandon strategic aircraft. Published in 1962 under the editorship of Marshal V. D. Sokolovsky, *Military Strategy*, an open review of Soviet military thinking, indicated that the communists saw values in aviation for military operations. This book acknowledged that long-range bombers were "rapidly giving way" to intercontinental and intermediate-range ballistic missiles, but it noted:

> Of course, this replacement process can take a long time, and in the event of war, bombers and rockets will be used simultaneously for attacking objectives located in the enemy zone of interior and in theaters of military operations. It is all the more likely that aviation has still not lost its combat possibilities. The arming of bombers with various classes of missiles, which are able to strike blows at great distances, makes it possible, in a number of cases, for them to operate beyond the range of air-defense weapons and to perform combat missions with reasonable effectiveness. In addition, certain specific missions (for example, attacks against moving targets) can be performed more successfully by the air force than by missiles.[204]

During their 1963 air show, the Soviets displayed four new aircraft, and General LeMay urged that the United States must recognize that the Soviets "are now building good airplanes, good strategic airplanes" and that they had "the capability of going forward with a strong aeronautical program." The Soviet long-range air force was also equipping its bombers with standoff missiles. "Our predictions are that the Russians are going to continue on with a mixed force. We can be wrong, but we just believe that they will continue on," LeMay concluded.[205]

At the direction of Secretary McNamara, an Air Force continental air defense study group made a comprehensive survey of the problem of modernizing the Air Defense Command's interceptor force and submitted its final report on 10 May 1963. This study examined the possibility of developing a new improved manned interceptor (IMI) and of adapting other aircraft to an interceptor role, including the F-111 (TFX) and the C-135B, the latter to be an air-to-air missile platform. According to Secretary McNamara the study showed that any one of the alternative systems would provide roughly comparable defenses against a fairly wide range of possible bomber threats for about the same total program costs. Confident that there were a number of good choices for a follow-on interceptor if it proved to be needed, McNamara ruled that the Department of Defense would proceed with the production and improvement of existing fighters, the F-111, and a number of subsystems that might be needed for a new interceptor. He approved a commitment of $5 million in the fiscal year 1965 budget for studies of an improved manned interceptor, but he considered that it would be "premature to make the choice" in air defense fighters until the character of the hostile manned bomber threat became more apparent. Having provided the funds that would permit a dispersal of Air Defense Command fighter interceptors during 1964, McNamara planned no change in the manned interceptor force.

> We believe that this force is appropriate for defense against what we presently foresee as a declining Soviet manned bomber threat. However, if the Soviets should deploy a new long-range bomber, which does not seem likely, we would have to reevaluate the size and character of our interceptor force, and particularly the need for modernization.[206]

Other air and missile defense requirements were also affected by the changing nature of the hostile threat. Where SAGE had included 12 direction centers at its maximum planned development, 2 SAGE centers, 16 heavy radars, and 10 gap-filler radars were to be closed in October 1963. In fiscal year 1965 it was planned to close still more SAGE centers in favor of an expansion of semiautomatic backup interceptor control centers at prime radar stations. Where the Air Force possessed 195 Bomarc A and 188 Bomarc B missiles on launchers, Secretary McNamara proposed to phase out all the "A" missiles during 1965, thus effecting a saving of $10 million in annual operating costs. Since Nike Hercules antiaircraft missiles could operate independently of SAGE, the Department of Defense planned to continue them but to transfer some of the batteries to the Army National Guard to replace older Nike Ajax missiles manned by the Guard. The program for fiscal year 1965 generally emphasized antimissile warning facilities, including the ballistic missile early warning system (BMEWS), over-the-horizon radars, and a more sophisticated bomb alarm system to be called nuclear detonation detection and reporting system (NUCDETS). McNamara planned to keep the Nike X antimissile system under development, but he suggested once again that an antimissile defense deployment would be meaningless without a strong civil defense fallout shelter program.[207] Because of the changed nature of the Soviet aircraft threat to one of supersonic aircraft armed with stand-off missiles, the Air Force agreed that the short-range Bomarc A missiles should be deleted from the Air Defense Command inventory. The Air Force wanted to keep the Bomarc B until some decision was made on an improved manned interceptor, but even the Bomarc B, which had seemed to have so many advantages a few years earlier, now was seen to be less desirable than a new manned interceptor. With the advantage of hindsight, Maj Gen R. J. Friedman, Air Force director of aerospace programs, remarked that if the Air Force had to do it over again it would seek a more flexible manned interceptor rather than the relatively inflexible unmanned missile interceptors that had been developed during the 1950s.[208]

At the time the Department of Defense's budget estimates for fiscal year 1965 were nearing completion, Secretary Zuckert informed Secretary McNamara that progress was being made with the studies of an improved manned interceptor and that the Air Force would need a sizable sum of money in addition to the $5-million study appropriation request if it was to proceed with the development of an improved manned interceptor. Since Zuckert did not consider that the Air Force had provided an adequate substantiation of the need for an operating concept of a new interceptor, he was not willing to approve an official program change request in favor of it. General LeMay, however, held much stronger views on the subject. When he appeared before Secretary McNamara seeking authority to readjust Air Force research and development funds to include a follow-on manned strategic aircraft, LeMay also proposed to use $40 million of research and development money for the development of an improved manned interceptor. His proposal was also submitted to the Joint Chiefs of Staff, who agreed that the Air Force should proceed to develop the improved manned interceptor aircraft.[209] In his appearances before congressional committees in February 1964, LeMay testified that the second most important requirement of the Air Force after the manned strategic aircraft was the development of a manned interceptor with greatly increased speed and range. He stated that neither the F-4C nor the TFX would be as good an interceptor as an especially designed IMI, and he asked Congress for about $40 million for engine development and to continue development of the fire-control system work that had been carried over when the F-108 was canceled. LeMay told Congress:

> The improved manned interceptor has dominated possible weapon systems in recent comprehensive studies of air defense against the aerodynamic threat through the early seventies. The flexibility afforded an air battle commander by this weapon, as opposed to current systems, is greatly enhanced because of the IMI's inherent speed, range, and weapon capabilities.[210]

When they appeared together before the House Armed Services Committee, Secretary Zuckert did not support LeMay's request for the improved manned interceptor but instead agreed with Secretary McNamara's position that Congress did not have enough evidence that the Soviets were building a supersonic bomber to warrant the immediate development of the new interceptor.[211]

When the House Armed Services Committee reported out the military authorization bill for fiscal year 1965, it included funds requested by General LeMay for starting the development of the improved manned interceptor.[212] In a surprise announcement on 29 February 1964, however, President Johnson for the first time revealed the existence of the long-range, Mach-3 aircraft being developed by the Lockheed Aircraft Corporation under Lockheed's designation as the A-11. He said the A-11 already was undergoing tests to determine its capabilities as a very long range, 2,000-mile-an-hour manned interceptor. According to later aviation reports, Lockheed had secretly begun to develop the A-11 at Burbank, California, in 1959 for the Central Intelligence Agency. Profiting from X-15 technology, the A-11 was ready to begin secret flight-tests at an airfield in Nevada in 1961.

Members of the House Armed Services Committee revealed that they had known about the A-11 when they had authorized funds for the IMI, but late in February the Senate Armed Services Committee accepted the assurance that the A-11 would meet Air Force requirements for an improved interceptor and refused to authorize development of the IMI. At a press conference on 5 March Secretary McNamara said that "the A-11 is an interceptor, it is being developed as such, and beyond that I have nothing further to say on its use." Accepting such assurance, a Senate-House joint conference committee eliminated the House recommendation for $40 million for the development of an improved interceptor aircraft from the fiscal year 1965 military authorization bill.[213] As secrecy gradually gave way, the new plane was officially designated as the YF-12A interceptor weapon system, and comprehensive Air Force test programs during 1964-65 showed that the prototype YF-12A was "an air defense interceptor of the first order." Whether the plane would be procured and taken into the Air Defense Command active operating inventory depended on the possibility that the Soviet Union might deploy a force of new supersonic aircraft.[214]

Although cuts were made in the appropriation bills for defense they were passed, both the House and Senate included the $52 million that LeMay requested for beginning the follow-on strategic weapon system in their bills. As the House-Senate joint conference committee was beginning to resolve differences in the two versions of the Defense Appropriations Act for fiscal year 1965, President Johnson in another surprise announcement made on 24 July 1964 revealed the successful development of a major new strategic aircraft system, which he said would be employed by the Strategic Air Command. He described the system as the SR-71, stated that the development program had begun in February 1963, and predicted that flight-testing of the first operational aircraft would begin early in 1965. He claimed that the SR-71 would "provide the strategic forces of the United States with an outstanding long-range reconnaissance capability" that would be "used during periods of military hostilities and in other situations in which military forces may be confronting foreign military forces." Once again it was subsequently revealed that the SR-71 was an outgrowth of the Lockheed A-11 aircraft. It would include a reconnaissance pod and would incorporate aerodynamic and power plant improvements. The first test-flight of the SR-71 was made at Palmdale, California, in December 1964.[215]

President Johnson's announcement concerning the SR-71 apparently reduced congressional pressure on the administration to proceed with the development of an advanced manned strategic system. As passed by Congress on 4 August the Department of Defense Appropriations Act for fiscal year 1965 contained the $52 million appropriation for a manned strategic aircraft, but the matter of using the money was left to the discretion of the secretary of defense.[216] Late in August DOD noted that its forward planning intended to keep substantial numbers of bombers in operation as far as 1972. Beyond 1972 decisions had not been made but the department was making advance provisions for possible strategic uses of manned systems already in production. "We will have manned bombers, and plenty of them just as long as they are needed," the DOD statement reported.[217] After a meeting with President Johnson, Secretary McNamara announced on 10 November 1964 that the president had agreed that there was no immediate requirement to begin the development of a strategic system to follow the B-52 but that DOD would continue to pursue research projects which would, if the need arose, permit the United States to follow any one of three designs in producing a new manned strategic weapon system.[218]

General-Purpose Forces Projections

With a few exceptions, the augmentation of United States general-purpose forces — including most of the Army's combat and support units, virtually all of the Navy units, all of the Marine Corps units, and the tactical wings of the Air

Force—appeared to be reaching maturity during 1963. In view of the expansion of United States general-purpose forces, the buildup of forces by the NATO allies, and the announced reductions in Soviet ground forces, Secretary McNamara could conclude in early 1964 that "the forces envisioned in NATO plans for the end of 1966, fully manned, trained, equipped, and properly positioned, could hold an initial Soviet attack on the central front, using nonnuclear means alone." Until the 1966 planning goals were realized, however, the defense of Europe against an all-out Soviet attack—even if the attacking forces used nonnuclear weapons—would require NATO forces to respond with tactical nuclear weapons.

> In summary our requirements studies indicate that except in the case of a massive attack by the Soviet Union or Communist China, we, together with our allies, have sufficient active forces for the initial stages of a conflict, without immediately resorting to nuclear weapons. It would, however, be necessary to mobilize Reserve component units rapidly at the start of a conflict in order to provide the additional forces needed to sustain combat and to reconstitute the strategic reserve. And, in all case, it is clear that ultimate allied success would be heavily dependent upon achieving early air superiority and upon having adequate air and sea lift.[219]

Even though McNamara believed that US general-purpose forces had to be designed to support allied nations around the world, he also held to the policy that it was "in the interest of the entire free world for nations threatened by Communist attack or subversion to defend themselves insofar as possible without direct intervention by US military forces."[220] At the NATO Council of Ministers meeting in December 1963, he pointedly stated that the US contribution of five M-day divisions and three separate regiments was a fair share of the total western Europe defense requirement, considering the responsibilities of the United States "for furnishing the strategic nuclear forces for NATO and for supporting allies in other parts of the world."[221] At the Nassau conference the United States had agreed to support and participate in a NATO multilateral nuclear force, but McNamara indicated that "we are not trying to sell it." Although the strategic forces of the United States provided essential amounts of deterrent force, he said that there was "no urgent military requirement" for the multilateral force. "The force, as it is conceived of and being discussed, would have a clear military utility but its purpose would be primarily, in my mind, to increase the political unity among the members of NATO," he noted on 29 January 1964.[222]

In a discussion of the fiscal year 1965 budget from the point of view of the Army chief of staff, General Wheeler stated that limited-war contingency planning studies demonstrated that 18 divisions—rather than the existing 16—would be the optimum figure for the strength of the Army. Wheeler made it clear to his superiors that with only 16 divisions the Army would have to call up reserves sooner than would otherwise be the case, but he was willing to accept the force level of 16 active and 6 reserve divisions, with standby equipment sufficient to supply the reserve divisions and with enough consumables to maintain 16 divisions and their supporting forces in combat between D-day and the time when production lines would be able to catch up with the rate of combat consumption.[223] In addition to this Army strength, DOD appropriation request for fiscal year 1965 envisioned that the Marine Corps would continue to maintain three combat divisions-air wings.[224]

In putting together the defense budget for fiscal year 1965 Secretary McNamara took a hard look at the future of the Navy's attack aircraft carriers. After July 1965 a sufficient number of strategic missiles would be in place to permit the carriers to be relieved of responsibilities for strategic alert retaliatory missions. Since some carrier aircraft could not operate at night, others could not get off in bad weather, and none of them could reach their targets unless their carriers were in a precise operating location, Secretary McNamara believed that removal of carrier aircraft from the single integrated operation plan would be beneficial. When the carriers were relieved from strategic retaliatory responsibilities, they would augment the limited-war forces. There was little doubt about the utility of aircraft carriers in a limited-war mission, but carrier task forces were enormously expensive, and four were needed to keep two on station, one in the Mediterranean, and one in the Far East. A task force, comprising 2 attack carriers with about 200 aircraft aboard, required protection and support by more than 50 ships.

The entire initial cost of the force amounted to as much as $6 billion, and the operating costs to about $1 billion per year. Moreover, the increasing range of land-based tactical aircraft promised to reduce requirements for forward-based air power. Thus with in-flight refueling, F-4s and F-105s could be flown from the United States to Europe and to the western Pacific. The F-111 (TFX) would be able to deploy to Europe without any in-flight refueling.[225]

Based upon the consideration of the increasing ranges of land-based tactical aircraft and their ability to operate from relatively unprepared airstrips, as well as the increased effectiveness of *Forrestal*-class carriers and of modern naval aircraft, Secretary McNamara informed Congress in January 1964 that Navy programs were going to be readjusted to reflect some reduction in the total number of attack aircraft carriers that would be in operation in the early 1970s. Although the Navy would continue to operate 15 attack carriers for the next several years, it would begin to readjust its aircraft procurement to emphasize a nonnuclear limited war mission.[226] McNamara accordingly eliminated the attack aircraft carrier that the Navy had requested funding for in fiscal year 1965 at a cost of $410 million, and he added seven escort ships and four attack cargo ships to the Navy's budget at a cost of $340 million.[227]

In a candid discussion of DOD's projection for reducing the strength of attack aircraft carriers, Adm David L. McDonald, the new chief of naval operations, stated early in 1964 that such "might be the Secretary of Defense's plan" but that it was "not the Navy plan today."[228] McDonald judged that a force of 15 attack carriers — with 9 in the Pacific and 6 in the Atlantic — was a "best estimate of naval requirements for force deployments in support of limited war contingency plans." While McDonald agreed that the attack carriers should be released from a general-war alert, he urged that carrier aircraft should continue to possess general-war capabilities for employment in a possible emergency.

> The post-initial strike potential of the carrier is of vital national importance in general war. Follow-on precision air strikes, based on reconnaissance, requests for support from beleaguered ground forces, and prevention of third force usurpation following an initial exchange in general war are the types of general war tasks for which the attack carrier is suited. Survivability considerations indicate that carrier decks may be the most secure means of providing for follow-on general war offensive and reconnaissance requirements.[229]

While the Navy apparently questioned the Department of Defense's plan to reduce its number of attack aircraft carriers, it began to make plans to revamp the aircraft carrier complement to accomplish a limited war role. A Navy study completed in May 1963 indicated that existing attack aircraft that had been conceived in the late 1940s and designed to carry single nuclear weapons would not meet the demands of limited nonnuclear war. It accordingly recommended the development of a new visual light-attack (VAL) aircraft that would be subsonic but would have a long loiter time and would carry a large conventional bomb load. Since the VAL would cost only about one-third as much as the TFX, it could be purchased in larger numbers. It would be able to penetrate strong enemy defenses, but the Navy concept of operations visualized that a task force would move in on an objective area and roll back hostile defenses with preliminary air strikes.[230] Requests for proposals on the development of the VAL were released to contractors on 29 June 1963, and, without addressing the Joint Chiefs of Staff on the matter, the Navy secured approval from DOD for a reprogramming action for the development of the VAL (which would subsequently be designated as the A-7 Corsair II) with fiscal year 1965 budget funds.[231]

At the start of the VAL project, when Secretary McNamara asked if the Air Force wanted to participate in it, General LeMay examined the concept of the specialized aircraft and concluded that the Air Force would not advance its capabilities by buying a new aircraft with reduced performance characteristics. "We feel the TFX is the best airplane to buy in this category in this time period by far; by any criteria you want to measure, cost effectiveness, performance, capability, everything, it is a better airplane," LeMay said.[232] General Wheeler also initially announced that he could not support the VAL, or "a specific and optimized close support aircraft." Even though VAL would doubtless cost less per individual item and would be a better close-air-support vehicle, it would not be versatile for the performance of air superiority and long-range interdiction missions. According to General Wheeler, an Army staff study showed that in terms of specialized tactical air squadrons the employment of an optimized close-support aircraft would be extremely costly. Wheeler therefore held "the position that the Army would stick with the Air Force in regard to using high-performance aircraft in the Tactical Air Command."[233] In a justification of the Department of Defense's position on VAL, however, Dr Harold Brown pointed out:

> One will always want a large number of cheaper aircraft as well as a small number of expensive aircraft to do more difficult roles. The TFX could do more difficult things than the VAL, but in many cases one will not want to use it, because the requirement doesn't demand either that high a performance aircraft or that expensive an aircraft.[234]

With the passing of time the Air Force accepted this logic. It also began to participate in the development of the Ling-Temco-Vought A-7A in 1965, and the aircraft would be programmed for procurement as a TAC replacement.

As foreshadowed by planning for the fiscal year 1965 budget, the shape of the future tactical air forces was related to the characteristics of new tactical fighters, the basing concepts to be used by tactical air units, and the capabilities of airlift forces to support rapid worldwide deployments. Concerned with building adequate air support if the Army were to engage in a sustained nonnuclear conflict, the Air Force pressed during interdepartmental hearings on the fiscal year 1965 budget for an expansion from 21 to 25 tactical air wings. McNamara authorized 24 tactical air wings, but he indicated that there would be no overall expansion of tactical air strength. Thus the Air Force would have to build up its tactical fighter resources with personnel from inactivated B-57 and KB-50 squadrons and from F-102 air defense squadrons that would be withdrawn from Japan and from Europe. As for aircraft, the tactical fighter wing expansion would be managed initially by retaining F-100 fighters in the active force longer than had been planned. The Air Force already had bought all the F-105s it would procure, and orders of F-4 aircraft in fiscal year 1965 would be stretched out to attain the most modern modifications of this plane. Given initial procurement of the F-111A during fiscal year 1965, the Air Force eventually planned to convert the squadrons equipped with F-100, F-101, and F-105 aircraft to F-111A units. Although the planned conversion of the 14-squadron RF-101 and RB-66 tactical reconnaissance force to RF-4Cs had lagged, the Air Force planned to continue this program and to expand the tactical reconnaissance force as it might be authorized by acquiring RF-111s.[235] The tactical air force level also included five Mace A and one Mace B tactical missile squadrons in Europe and two Mace B squadrons on Okinawa. These squadrons were admittedly vulnerable to surprise attack, but they would continue in the tactical air inventory.[236]

In "Jet Age," a study published in November 1956, TAC had proposed that all tactical air wings be returned from overseas bases to stations in the United States and that rotational squadrons from the redeployed wings should serve six-month tours at overseas bases. This forward-looking concept had been only partly accepted because it placed heavy demands upon scarce air-refueling capabilities and because some tactical aircraft were not suited for aerial refueling. The F-102 interceptors, for example, had to be stationed overseas because they lacked aerial-refueling capabilities.[237] Early in 1963 the Air Force was better able to update its overseas deployment planning. All-purpose F-105 tactical fighters could be rapidly deployed overseas, and conversion of other wings to versatile F-4C aircraft would begin during the year. Because of both increasing allied air defense capabilities and of the growing ability of TAC to reinforce threatened areas rapidly, it would be possible to redeploy F-102 interceptor squadrons from Japan and Europe during 1964. In February 1963 General LeMay directed the preparation of a study designated Clearwater, which envisioned a dual-forward and rear-basing concept for tactical air wings. Rotational tactical fighter squadrons would operate from dispersed and moderately hardened airfields in Europe and in the Far East, while rear bases in the United States would accommodate the main bodies of the wings. The consolidation of expensive and vulnerable heavy maintenance facilities at rearward bases would add to security. Secretary McNamara also hoped that the concept would "result in manpower, spare parts, and foreign exchange savings."[238]

The feasibility of the Clearwater concept and the possibility that both Army and Air Force units might be held in the United States and rapidly deployed overseas were closely related to the capabilities of the airlift and sealift program package. In a test of the United States Strike Command's ability to reinforce NATO rapidly with an armored division and tactical air units, the Military Air Transport Command lifted the 2d Armored Division from Texas to Rhein-Main Air Base, West Germany, in a period of 63 hours beginning on the morning of 22 October 1963. As a part of the same Big Lift exercise, TAC deployed three squadrons of fighter aircraft and a composite tactical air reconnaissance force to Europe with an average deployment time of seven hours per aircraft.[239] In an informal comment on Big Lift, General LeMay pointed out: "Our ability to deploy such forces rapidly will permit us to reduce some of our overseas tactical units without lessening our ability to meet our commitments in those areas."[240] In an implementation of the Clearwater concept during 1964, the Air Force redeployed F-102 interceptor squadrons from Japan and from Europe, and it also applied the concept to troop carrier activity in Europe. Effective on 1 April 1964 the United States Air Forces in Europe transferred its 322d Air Division and the management of the theater tactical airlift force to the Military Air Transport Service (MATS). Concurrently the 317th Troop Carrier Wing and its three C-130 squadrons were reassigned to TAC and were redeployed from Europe to Lockbourne AFB, Ohio, during May and June 1964.[241]

At the same time that Big Lift provided a test for the Clearwater concept it also provided a check upon the progress being made in modernizing the airlift portion of the DOD airlift and sealift forces. Within MATS the major development during 1963 was the factory rollout of the first turbofan-powered C-141A in August and its successful maiden flight on 17 December 1963. Able to span any ocean nonstop at high-subsonic cruise speeds, this heavy cargo plane promised to be a great enhancement of the MATS capability. Thus in flying Big Lift, MATS employed 202 transport aircraft, and even though the accomplishment of the deployment was substantial Maj Gen Glenn R. Birchard, vice commander of MATS, pointed out that 100 new C-141 Starlifters can accomplish a movement comparable to Big Lift in only 20 hours.[242] In an airlift program change reflecting the successful development of the C-141, decisions were made in the fiscal year 1965 defense budget to cut off two late-program C-130 squadrons committed to MATS, to divert the 40 C-135s that MATS had been given for interim modernization to other uses, and to add C-141s to the MATS inventory. When MATS was equipped with C-141s, all C-130 aircraft would be transferred to the Tactical Air Command, thus providing TAC with a modern four-engine troop carrier aircraft that would have ocean-spanning abilities. To compensate for the loss of airlift capacity resulting from the cancellation of the two squadrons of C-130s and the phase-out of the C-135s, old C-124 aircraft would be held in the MATS inventory longer than had been previously planned.[243]

In its design phase the C-141 had been well conceived, but with the passing of time it was evident that a still larger "outsized" cargo transport would have to be developed. When the Army and the Air Force had laid out the design criteria for the C-141, the Army had been planning on limiting most of its requirements for airmobility to the characteristics of the equipment possessed by an airborne division. By 1963 the Army wished to be able to transport all types of divisions by air, but a large proportion of Army equipment would not fit within the cargo hatch of the C-141. By 1970, moreover, the Air Force also would require an outsized cargo plane that would replace the old C-124s and C-133s. To meet both requirements the Air Force declared the need for the development of a new cargo experimental heavy logistics support (CX-HLS) aircraft, but in the winter of 1963–64 Secretary McNamara was unwilling to endorse the project until all possible solutions for the problem had been explored. He wished to examine various alternative actions such as modifying of the C-141, dismantling large cargo items, prepositioning equipment, or redesigning items of equipment that would have to be transported by air. By February 1964 the Air Force had almost convinced McNamara that none of the alternatives was practical, but he still wanted more study. He therefore committed about $10 million from his fiscal year 1964 emergency fund to a CX-HLS study project.[244] After a very complete program definition study, the Department of Defense accepted the case for a very large transport aircraft, and in 1965 the Lockheed-Georgia Company won the C-5A development contract. The C-5A would have about three times the work capacity of the C-141, and it would be able to move heavy mechanized infantry and armored divisions, complete with tanks, trucks, artillery, and combat supplies.[245]

Deputy Secretary Gilpatric Views the Future

With the completion of the fiscal year 1965 national defense budget, the Kennedy-Johnson (McNamara) administration had effected the fourth successive revision of the military force levels of the United States, and the shape of these force levels was indicative of the kind of military strategy the New Frontier meant to continue. Writing unofficially in *Foreign Affairs* in April 1964, shortly after he had left the post of deputy secretary of defense, Roswell L. Gilpatric outlined the proportions and characteristics of the military program he conceived would meet the defense needs of the United States in the decade of the 1970s. Based upon the assumption that the détente between the United States and the Soviet Union would continue, Gilpatric predicted that the military forces of the United States would be shaped as follows by 1970:

> *Strategic retaliatory forces.* A deterrent force, consisting only of hardened and dispersed land-based and sea-based missiles, with all of the vulnerable, earlier-generation missiles deactivated and all manned bombers retired from active deployment. Such a force, comprised of weapons systems invulnerable to surprise attack, would be capable of destroying the centers of Soviet and Chinese Communist society.
>
> *Continental air and missile defense forces.* Only warning systems, such as the big ballistic missile detection and tracking radars in Alaska, Greenland and Scotland, and the current generation of surface-to-air missiles systems for tactical deployment would be maintained. Manned interceptors with their ground-control counterparts and all other bomber defense and warning systems would be phased out unless the Soviets changed their presently indicated intention of concentrating their strategic power in missiles. There would be no production or deployment of anti-ballistic-missile systems in the absence of Soviet moves to proceed beyond experimental installations of such systems.
>
> *Reconnaissance forces.* Both aircraft and satellite-based reconnaissance systems would be retained and improved to take full advantage of state-of-the-art developments, so as to provide the United States at all times with a world-wide capability for the collection of both strategic and tactical intelligence.
>
> *General-purpose forces.* No significant changes would take place in this category except for a reduction of Army divisions that might be withdrawn at some stage from Korea or from Europe (if a decline in the Soviet threat allowed). The remaining army ground forces and the existing Marine divisions, with presently planned air support and airlift (consisting of all the Tactical Air and Military Air Transport units, plus the Marine Air Wings), would be needed to deter or counter threats of aggression not directly inspired or supported by the USSR. The bulk of the US forces now assigned to the Pacific Command are there primarily to meet the threat from Communist China and her satellites, plus Indonesia. Hence, in the event of a détente with the Soviet Union alone, it would not be safe to reduce US force levels in the Pacific.[246]

Although Gilpatric had played an important role in the reshaping of United States defense posture after 1961, his views in April 1964 could not fairly be said to be precisely synonymous with the forward planning within DOD. In August 1964, however, Secretary McNamara reflected on the record of the Kennedy-Johnson administration and provided a brief analysis of the defense strategy that had come into being.

> We believed in a strategy of controlled flexible response, where the military force of the United States would become a finely tuned instrument of national policy, versatile enough to meet with appropriate force the full spectrum of possible threats to our national security from guerrilla subversion to all out nuclear war.... Development of the greatest military power in human history—with a capability to respond to every level of conflict—is beyond question the most significant achievement in the defense establishment during our years in office.[247]

NOTES

1. Walter Lippman, "The Intermission Is Over," *Newsweek*, 9 November 1964, 23.
2. House, *Hearings on Military Posture and H. R. 2440 before the Committee on Armed Services*, 88th Cong., 1st sess., 1963, 235–36 (hereafter cited as *Hearings on Military Posture and H. R. 2440*); letters of John F. Kennedy to President of the Senate and Speaker of the House, 7 September 1962, in *Public Papers of the Presidents of the United States: John F. Kennedy, 1962* (Washington, D.C.: Government Printing Office, 1963), 665.
3. *New York Times*, 12 September 1962, 16.
4. "The President's News Conference of September 13, 1962," in *Public Papers: Kennedy, 1962*, 674–75.
5. House, *Hearings on Military Posture and H. R. 2440*, 237–41.
6. "Television and Radio Interview: After Two Years—A Conversation with the President," 17 December 1962, in *Public Papers: Kennedy, 1962*, 898.
7. Ibid.
8. House, *Department of Defense Appropriations for 1964: Hearings before a Subcommittee of the Committee on Appropriations*, 88th Cong., 1st sess., 1963, pt. 1:23, 36 (hereafter cited as *1964 DOD Appropriations*).
9. Arnold L. Horelick, *The Cuban Missile Crisis: An Analysis of Soviet Calculations and Behavior*, Memorandum RM-3779-PR (Santa Monica, Calif.: Rand Corp., 1963), 12.
10. Letter of Khrushchev to Kennedy, 27 October 1962, in *Department of State Bulletin*, 12 November 1962, 741–43.
11. Horelick, *The Cuban Missile Crisis*, 27–28.
12. House, *A Compilation of Material Relating to United States Defense Policies in 1962*, 88th Cong., 1st sess., 1963, H. Doc. 155, 17; Lt Col Walter B. Kamp, "Deterrence in Action, An Analysis of the Deterrent Effectiveness of the SAC Expanded Airborne Alert during the Cuban Missile Crisis of October 1962," thesis no. 2523 (Maxwell AFB, Ala.: Air War College, 1964), 41–42; House, *Hearings on Military Posture and H. R. 2440*, 316.
13. House, *Hearings on Military Posture and H. R. 2440*, 239–49.
14. "A Step by Step Review of the Cuban Crisis," in *The "Cuban Crisis" of 1962*, ed. David L. Larson (Boston: Houghton Mifflin Co., 1962), 223–30; Roger Hilsman, "The Cuban Crisis: How Close We Were to War," *Look*, 25 August 1964, 17–21; Theodore C. Sorensen, *Decision Making in the White House, The Olive Branch or the Arrows* (New York: Columbia University Press, 1963), 35.
15. *Department of Defense Annual Report for Fiscal Year 1963* (Washington, D.C.: Government Printing Office, 1964), 4–5 (hereafter cited as *DOD Annual Report for FY 1963*).
16. "Radio and Television Report to the American People on the Soviet Arms Buildup in Cuba," 22 October 1962, in *Public Papers: Kennedy, 1962*, 806–9.
17. *DOD Annual Report for FY 1963*, 5; Kamp, "Deterrence in Action," 41–42, 59–60.
18. "Resolution Adopted by OAS," 23 October 1962, *Department of State Bulletin*, 12 November 1962, 722–23; Proclamation 3504: Interdiction of the Delivery of Offensive Weapons to Cuba, 23 October 1962, in *Public Papers: Kennedy, 1962*, 809–11.
19. House, *1964 DOD Appropriations*, pt. 1:13.
20. Horelick, *The Cuban Missile Crisis*, 54–55; Kamp, "Deterrence in Action," 34.
21. Letter of Khrushchev to Lord Bertrand Russell, 25 October 1962, in Larson, *The "Cuban Crisis" of 1962*, 126.
22. Elie Abel, *The Missile Crisis* (Philadelphia: J. B. Lippincott Co., 1966), 178–81; Hilsman, "The Cuban Crisis," 21.
23. Hilsman, "The Cuban Crisis," 20.
24. *Current Digest of the Soviet Press* 14, no. 51 (18–24 December 1962).
25. House, *1964 DOD Appropriations*, pt. 1:31.
26. Letter of Khrushchev to Kennedy, 741–43.

27. Hilsman, "The Cuban Crisis," 17; Pierre Salinger, *With Kennedy* (Garden City, N.Y.: Doubleday & Co., 1966), 301.
28. "White House Statement on Soviet Proposals Relating to International Security," 27 October 1962, and "Message to Chairman Khrushchev Calling for Removal of Soviet Missiles from Cuba," 27 October 1962, in *Public Papers: Kennedy, 1962*, 813–14; *DOD Annual Report for FY 1963*, 6.
29. Hilsman, "The Cuban Crisis," 17.
30. *Current Digest of the Soviet Press* 19, no. 51 (18–24 December 1962).
31. Ibid.
32. Letter of Khrushchev to Kennedy, 743–45.
33. House, *1964 DOD Appropriations*, pt. 1:12–21; *DOD Annual Report for FY 1963*, 7.
34. House, *1964 DOD Appropriations*, pt. 1:57.
35. Ibid., pt. 2:29, pt. 5:973.
36. House, *Hearings on Military Posture and H. R. 2440*, 277; Senate, *Fiscal Year Authorization for Military Procurement: Hearings before the Committee on Armed Services*, 88th Cong., 1st sess., 1963, 313 (hereafter cited as *FY 1964 Military Procurement*).
37. House, *1964 DOD Appropriations*, pt. 5:973; House, *Hearings on Military Posture and H. R. 2440*, 277; *DOD Annual Report for FY 1963*, 51.
38. "Television and Radio Interview," 17 December 1962, in *Public Papers: Kennedy, 1962*, 898.
39. "White House Announcement of Agreement to Link Washington and Moscow by Direct Telecommunications Link," 20 June 1963, in *Public Papers: Kennedy, 1963*, 405.
40. Ball, "NATO and the Cuban Crisis," 835.
41. Secretary of State Dean Rusk, "Basic Issues Underlying the Cuban Crisis," *Department of State Bulletin*, 10 December 1962, 869.
42. House, *Hearings on Military Posture and H. R. 2440*, 271–72; House, *Department of Defense Appropriations for 1965: Hearings before a Subcommittee of the Committee on Appropriations*, 88th Cong., 2d sess., 1964, pt. 4:83 (hereafter cited as *1965 DOD Appropriations*).
43. Ibid.
44. Senate, *FY 1964 Military Procurement*, 84.
45. Ibid.
46. *New York Times*, 15 December 1962, 1; House, *1964 DOD Appropriations*, pt. 2:117.
47. Senate, *1964 DOD Military Procurement*, 85.
48. Ibid., 585.
49. Ibid., 84.
50. Ibid.
51. House, *1965 DOD Appropriations*, pt. 4:84–86.
52. Senate, *FY 1964 Military Procurement*, 905, 983, 988.
53. House, *1964 DOD Appropriations*, pt. 2:428.
54. House, *Hearings on Military Posture and H. R. 2440*, 1172.
55. House, *1964 DOD Appropriations*, pt. 2:445.
56. Ibid., 503.
57. Ibid.
58. Ibid.
59. Ibid., 503–4; House, *1965 DOD Appropriations*, pt. 4: 466–67.
60. House, *1964 DOD Appropriations*, pt. 2:448–51, 503–4; Senate, *Military Aspects and Implications of Nuclear Test Ban Proposals and Related Matters: Hearings before the Preparedness Investigating Subcommittee of the Committee on Armed Services*, 88th Cong., 1st sess., 1964, pt. 1:361.
61. House, *1964 DOD Appropriations*, pt. 2:427, 429; House, *1964 DOD Appropriations*, pt. 4:498.
62. *Facts on File*, 1962, 387/1B.
63. Senate, *Nuclear Test Ban Treaty: Hearings before the Committee on Foreign Relations*, 88th Cong., 1st sess., 1963, 67.
64. Senate, *Military Aspects and Implications of Nuclear Test Ban Proposals and Related Matters*, 733.

65. Ibid., 963.
66. Senate, *Nuclear Test Ban Treaty*, 409.
67. Senate, *FY 1964 Military Procurement*, 4.
68. Ibid.; Senate, *Organizing for National Security: Hearings before the Committee on National Policy Machinery of the Committee on Government Operations*, 86th Cong., 2d sess., and 87th Cong., 1st sess., 1960–61, 1:1184–85, 1215–16, 1281.
69. House, *Hearings on Military Posture and H. R. 2440*, 288–90, 421; House, *1964 DOD Appropriations*, pt. 1:90–91.
70. Senate, *Department of Defense Appropriations for Fiscal Year 1965: Hearings before a Subcommittee on Department of Defense of the Committee on Appropriations and the Committee on Armed Services*, 88th Cong., 2d sess., 1964, pt. 1:8–9 (hereafter cited as *FY 1965 DOD Appropriations*).
71. House, *Hearings on Military Posture and H. R. 2440*, 411.
72. Ibid., 308; House, *1964 DOD Appropriations*, pt. 1:332.
73. House, *Hearings on Military Posture and H. R. 2440*, 332, 572; House, *1964 DOD Appropriations*, pt. 1:232–33; Senate, *FY 1964 Military Procurement*, 125.
74. Senate, *FY 1965 DOD Appropriations*, pt. 1:8–9; House, *Hearings on Military Posture and H. R. 9637 before the Committee on Armed Services*, 88th Cong., 2d sess., 1964, 6943–44.
75. House, *Hearings on Military Posture and H. R. 2440*, 421.
76. Stewart Alsop, "Our New Strategy, The Alternatives to Total War," *Saturday Evening Post*, 1 December 1962, 18.
77. House, *1964 DOD Appropriations*, pt. 1:311.
78. House, *Hearings on Military Posture and H. R. 2440*, 308, 310; House, *1964 DOD Appropriations*, pt. 1:313.
79. House, *Hearings on Military Posture and H. R. 2440*, 581.
80. House, *1964 DOD Appropriations*, pt. 1:340.
81. Ibid., 316.
82. Ibid., 330.
83. Ibid.
84. Ibid., 330–32.
85. House, *Hearings on Military Posture and H. R. 2440*, 384.
86. Ibid., 308–18.
87. Ibid., 321–26.
88. Ibid., 432–57.
89. Ibid., 320, 326, 454, 458.
90. William W. Kaufmann, *The McNamara Strategy* (New York: Harper & Row, 1964), 88.
91. House, *1964 DOD Appropriations*, pt. 1:316; Congress, *Impact of Military Supply and Service Activities on the Economy: Hearings before a Subcommittee on Defense Procurement of the Joint Economic Committee*, 88th Cong., 1st sess., 1963, 13.
92. Kaufmann, *The McNamara Strategy*, 88.
93. John F. Loosbrock, "Strategic Retreat from Reality," *Air Force/Space Digest*, January 1963, 28–31.
94. Ibid.
95. Senate, *Inquiry into Satellite and Missile Programs: Hearings before the Preparedness Investigating Subcommittee of the Committee on Armed Services*, 85th Cong., 1st and 2d sess., 1957–1958, 1488; letter of Lt Gen James M. Gavin, US Army, Retired, to editor, *Air Force/Space Digest*, April 1963, 10.
96. "Report from Moscow on Disarmament and World Security," 3 January 1961, in Senate, *The Pugwash Conferences: A Staff Analysis Prepared for the Subcommittee to Investigate the Administration of the Internal Security Laws . . . of the Committee on the Judiciary*, 87th Cong., 1st sess., 1961, appendix 5; Jerome B. Wiesner, *Where Science and Politics Meet* (New York: McGraw-Hill Book Co., 1965), 109, 215, 226, 263; Arthur M. Schlesinger, Jr., *A Thousand Days, John F. Kennedy in the White House*

IDEAS, CONCEPTS, DOCTRINE

(Boston: Houghton Mifflin Co., 1965), 301; Everett S. Allen, *New Bedford* (Mass.) *Standard Times*, staff writer, "Missile Gap . . . A Significant Myth?" reprinted in *Alabama Journal*, 27 January 1965.

97. Maj Gen Dale O. Smith, "How Arms-Control Doctrine Can Affect U.S. Strategy," *Air Force/Space Digest*, December 1962, 71–76.

98. House, *1964 DOD Appropriations*, pt. 2:427–28.

99. Ibid., pt. 2:439.

100. Ibid., pt. 2:581.

101. Ibid., pt. 2:440.

102. House, *Fiscal Year 1964 Military Construction Authorization: Hearings before the Committee on Armed Services*, 88th Cong., 1st sess., 1963, 2470 (hereafter cited as *FY 1964 Military Construction*).

103. Senate, *Military Aspects and Implications of Nuclear Test Ban Proposals and Related Matters*, pt. 2:782.

104. House, *Hearings on Military Posture and H. R. 2440*, 1164.

105. Senate, *Nuclear Test Ban Treaty*, 363–64.

106. House, *1964 DOD Appropriations*, pt. 2:447–48.

107. House, *Hearings on Military Posture and H. R. 2440*, 1162–63; House, *1964 DOD Appropriations*, pt. 2:428–29.

108. House, *1964 DOD Appropriations*, pt. 2:429.

109. Ibid., 506–7, 575; House, *Hearings on Military Posture and H. R. 2440*, 451, 1189–90.

110. House, *Hearings on Military Posture and H. R. 2440*, 434.

111. Senate, *FY 1964 DOD Military Procurement*, 954.

112. House, *Hearings on Military Posture and H. R. 2440*, 1226.

113. Ibid., 1225, 1230.

114. House, *1964 DOD Appropriations*, pt. 2:481, 588–89.

115. Ibid., 526.

116. Ibid., 526–27, 578–79; House, *Hearings on Military Posture and H. R. 2440*, 1233–34.

117. House, *Hearings on Military Posture and H. R. 2440*, 1185–86; House, *1964 DOD Appropriations*, pt. 2:521–22; Senate, *FY 1964 DOD Military Procurement*, 948–49.

118. House, *Hearings on Military Posture and H. R. 2440*, 1178–79; House, *1964 DOD Appropriations*, pt. 2:470, 575.

119. House, *1964 DOD Appropriations*, pt. 2:530; House, *Hearings on Military Posture and H. R. 9637*, 7892.

120. House, *Hearings on Military Posture and H. R. 2440*, 1215; House, *1964 DOD Appropriations*, pt. 6:514.

121. House, *1965 DOD Appropriations*, pt. 5:399.

122. House, *FY 1964 Military Construction*, 2457.

123. Senate, *Military Aspects and Implications of Nuclear Test Ban Proposals and Related Matters*, pt. 2:784.

124. "Television and Radio Interview," 17 December 1962, in *Public Papers: Kennedy, 1962*, 551.

125. "Radio and Television Address to the American People on the Nuclear Test Ban Treaty," 26 July 1963, in *Public Papers: Kennedy, 1963*, 603.

126. "The President's News Conference of January 24, 1963," in *Public Papers: Kennedy, 1963*, 98.

127. Senate, *Nuclear Test Ban Treaty*, 45.

128. Ibid., 150–51.

129. House, *Hearings on Military Posture and H. R. 9637*, 6918–20; House, *1965 DOD Appropriations*, pt. 4:25–28.

130. House, *Hearings on Military Posture and H. R. 2440*, 415.

131. House, *1964 DOD Appropriations*, pt. 2:311, 333, 491; Senate, *FY 1964 Military Procurement*, 88.

132. House, *1964 DOD Appropriations*, pt. 1:227–28.

133. Ibid., 337.

134. Ibid., 317.

135. Senate, *FY 1964 Military Procurement*, 93.
136. House, *1964 DOD Appropriations*, pt. 1:523–24.
137. House, *Hearings on Military Posture and H. R. 2440*, 1305–6, 1310; House, *1965 DOD Appropriations*, pt. 1:713–14.
138. House, *1965 DOD Appropriations*, pt. 2:96, pt. 4:442.
139. House, *Hearings on Military Posture and H. R. 9637*, 6949.
140. House, *1965 DOD Appropriations*, pt. 4:442; House, *Fiscal Year 1965 Military Construction Authorization: Hearings before the Committee on Armed Services*, 88th Cong., 2d sess., 1964, pt. 1:8390 (hereafter cited as *FY 1965 Military Construction*).
141. House, *FY 1964 Military Construction*, 2317.
142. House, *FY 1965 Military Construction*, pt. 1:8390.
143. House, *1965 DOD Appropriations*, 477.
144. *Aviation Week & Space Technology*, 13 May 1963, 25; 1 July 1963, 25; 23 September 1963, 28.
145. Senate, *FY 1965 DOD Appropriations*, pt. 1:736, 743; House, *Hearings on Military Posture and H. R. 9637*, 7439.
146. House, *1965 DOD Appropriations*, pt. 5:396–97; C. M. Plattner, "Systems Tests Begin XB-70A Checkout for First Flight," *Aviation Week & Space Technology*, 1 June 1964, 84–91.
147. House, *Hearings on Military Posture and H. R. 9637*, 7559.
148. Senate, *Nuclear Test Ban Treaty*, 67.
149. Ibid., 4–5.
150. Senate, *Military Aspects and Implications of Nuclear Test Ban Proposals and Related Matters*, pt. 2:970, 973.
151. Ibid., 818–19.
152. Ibid., pt. 1:352–53.
153. Ibid., pt. 2:972.
154. House, *1965 DOD Appropriations*, pt. 2:611.
155. Senate, *Military Aspects and Implications of Nuclear Test Ban Proposals and Related Matters*, pt. 1:353–55.
156. Ibid., 978–80.
157. Ibid., 588–89.
158. Senate, *FY 1964 Military Procurement*, 132.
159. House, *1964 DOD Appropriations*, pt. 2:315.
160. Senate, *Military Aspects and Implications of Nuclear Test Ban Proposals and Related Matters*, 352–58, 363, 376.
161. "Commencement Address at American University in Washington," 10 June 1963, in *Public Papers: Kennedy, 1963*, 463.
162. Senate, *Nuclear Test Ban Treaty*, 4–5; "Joint Statement by the Heads of Delegations to the Moscow Nuclear Test Ban Meeting," 25 July 1963, in *Public Papers: Kennedy, 1963*, 599–600.
163. "Special Message to the Senate on the Nuclear Test Ban Treaty," 8 August 1963, in *Public Papers: Kennedy, 1963*, 622–24.
164. Ibid.
165. Senate, *Nuclear Test Ban Treaty*, 109, 150.
166. Ibid., 275, 306, 355–73; Senate, *Military Aspects and Implications of Nuclear Test Ban Proposals and Related Matters*, 587–91, 719–24, 761.
167. House, *Consideration of H. R. 3516, Civil Defense, Fallout Shelter Program: Hearings before the Committee on Armed Services, Subcommittee no. 3*, 88th Cong., 1st sess., 1963, pt. 2:4911–12.
168. Senate, *Military Aspects and Implications of Nuclear Test Ban Proposals and Related Matters*, 545–46; Senate, *Nuclear Test Ban Treaty*, 422–23, 457.
169. Senate, *Military Aspects and Implications of Nuclear Test Ban Proposals and Related Matters*, 779–810.
170. Ibid., 978–79.
171. Ibid., 941–46.

172. "The President's News Conference of August 20, 1963," and "Remarks at the Signing of the Nuclear Test Ban Treaty," 7 October 1963, in *Public Papers: Kennedy, 1963*, 635–36, 765–66.
173. Senate, *FY 1964 Military Procurement*, 321; House, *Hearings on Military Posture and H. R. 2440*, 382.
174. House, *1965 DOD Appropriations*, pt. 5:56.
175. Ibid., 56, 61.
176. Senate, *FY 1964 Military Procurement*, 321; House, *Hearings on Military Posture and H. R. 2440*, 382.
177. Senate, *FY 1964 Military Procurement*, 347.
178. Ibid., 428–29.
179. "The President's News Conference of March 21, 1963," and "The President's News Conference of October 9, 1963," in *Public Papers: Kennedy, 1963*, 277, 769.
180. United Nations Resolution 1884 (XVIII), 17 October 1963.
181. House, *1965 DOD Appropriations*, pt. 5:56, 61.
182. Ibid., 60–62.
183. Senate, *FY 1965 DOD Appropriations*, pt. 1:8–9.
184. Excerpts from an address by Hon Eugene M. Zuckert, secretary of the Air Force, before the Harvard Business School of Washington, Washington, D.C., 8 January 1964.
185. Ibid.
186. Ibid.
187. Senate, *FY 1965 DOD Appropriations*, pt. 1:42.
188. House, *1965 DOD Appropriations*, pt. 4:30, pt. 3:110–11; House, *Hearings on Military Posture and H. R. 9637*, 6979.
189. House, *1965 DOD Appropriations*, pt. 2:420, pt. 4:29; House, *Hearings on Military Posture and H. R. 9637*, 6946–47.
190. House, *1965 DOD Appropriations*, pt. 4:514–15.
191. Ibid., 735.
192. Senate, *FY 1965 DOD Appropriations*, 742.
193. House, *1965 DOD Appropriations*, pt. 4:484–85, 534–36; pt. 5:400–3.
194. Senate, *FY 1965 DOD Appropriations*, pt. 1:57–58; House, *Hearings on Military Posture and H. R. 9637*, 6934–35.
195. Senate, *FY 1965 DOD Appropriations*, pt. 1:57–58.
196. House, *1965 DOD Appropriations*, pt. 4:492, 535.
197. Ibid., 534–36.
198. Ibid., 485–86, 499–500, 516–17.
199. Ibid., 497–98.
200. House, *Hearings on Military Posture and H. R. 9637*, 6934–35; Senate, *FY 1965 DOD Appropriations*, pt. 1:52–61; House, *1965 DOD Appropriations*, pt. 4:49–50, 308–9.
201. House, *1965 DOD Appropriations*, pt. 4:487.
202. Ibid., pt. 5:50–51.
203. Ibid., pt. 4:180–82.
204. V. D. Sokolovsky, ed., *Military Strategy* (Wright-Patterson AFB, Ohio: Foreign Technology Division, Air Force Systems Command translation, 1962), 356–57.
205. Senate, *FY 1965 DOD Appropriations*, 716, 724–26.
206. House, *1965 DOD Appropriations*, pt. 4:184–85.
207. Ibid., 180–90.
208. Ibid., pt. 2:481.
209. Ibid., pt. 4:138; House, *Hearings on Military Posture and H. R. 9637*, 7477–79.
210. House, *Hearings on Military Posture and H. R. 9637*, 7477–79; House, *1965 DOD Appropriations*, pt. 4:455; Senate, *FY 1965 DOD Appropriations*, pt. 1:716.
211. House, *Hearings on Military Posture and H. R. 9637*, 7477–79.

212. "President Affirms A-11 Surveillance Role," *Aviation Week & Space Technology*, 3 August 1964, 16–17.

213. Senate, *FY 1965 DOD Appropriations*, pt. 1:713–14; Katherine Johnsen, "New Bomber Funds Win Early Approval," *Aviation Week & Space Technology*, 24 February 1964, 26–27; George C. Wilson, "McNamara, Congress Differ on A-11 Role," *Aviation Week & Space Technology*, 9 March 1964, 18–19.

214. Col Allen K. McDonald, "The YF-12A Interceptor Weapon System," *Air University Review* 16, no. 3 (March-April 1965):13–17; House, *Department of Defense Appropriations for 1966: Hearings before a Subcommittee of the Committee on Appropriations*, 89th Cong., 1st sess., 1965, pt. 3:266 (hereafter cited as *1966 DOD Appropriations*).

215. "President Affirms A-11 Surveillance Role," *Aviation Week & Space Technology*, 3 August 1964, 16–17; House, *1966 DOD Appropriations*, pt. 5:103, 113.

216. "Senate Votes DOD $46.8 Billion; Most House Cuts Are Confirmed," *Aviation Week & Space Technology*, 3 August 1964, 27.

217. *Aviation Week & Space Technology*, 31 August 1964, 19.

218. Allan R. Scholin, "Aerospace World," *Air Force/Space Digest*, December 1964, 21.

219. House, *1965 DOD Appropriations*, pt. 4:197.

220. Ibid., 197; Senate, *FY 1964 Military Procurement*, 178.

221. House, *1965 DOD Appropriations*, pt. 4:196.

222. House, *Hearings on Military Posture and H. R. 9637*, 6937–39, 6977.

223. House, *1965 DOD Appropriations*, pt. 4:198–201, 602–3.

224. Ibid., 212.

225. Ibid., 206; Kaufmann, *The McNamara Strategy*, 286–87; House, *Hearings on Military Posture and H. R. 9637*, 6952.

226. House, *1965 DOD Appropriations*, pt. 4:206–7.

227. Ibid., 134.

228. Ibid., 719.

229. Ibid., 705–6, 719–20.

230. Ibid., 207; pt. 5:20, 104–5; House, *Hearings on Military Posture and H. R. 9637*, 7220–21.

231. Senate, *FY 1965 DOD Appropriations*, pt. 1:738–40; House, *Hearings on Military Posture and H. R. 9637*, 7514–15.

232. Senate, *FY 1965 DOD Appropriations*, pt. 1:739; House, *Hearings on Military Posture and H. R. 9637*, 7514–15.

233. House, *1965 DOD Appropriations*, pt. 4:579.

234. Ibid., pt. 5:104–5.

235. Ibid., pt. 2:420–22, 530; pt. 3:7, 69–70; pt. 4:216–20.

236. Ibid., pt. 4:218.

237. History, Tactical Air Command, July–December 1957, 1:81–93.

238. House, *1965 DOD Appropriations*, pt. 2:429, pt. 4:220.

239. Maj Gen Glen R. Birchard, "Anatomy of an Airlift," *Air University Review* 15, no. 4 (May–June 1964):17–34; House, *1965 DOD Appropriations*, pt. 4:452.

240. House, *1965 DOD Appropriations*, pt. 4:452.

241. History, US Air Forces in Europe, January–June 1964, 11.

242. Birchard, "Anatomy of an Airlift," 17–34.

243. House, *1965 DOD Appropriations*, pt. 2:422, pt. 3:7, pt. 4:222–26.

244. Ibid., pt. 4:222–26, 526.

245. J. S. Butz, Jr., "C-54 — Even More than Meets the Eye," *Air Force/Space Digest*, December 1965, 33–36, 39–40.

246. Roswell L. Gilpatric, "Our Defense Needs — The Long View," *Foreign Affairs*, April 1964, 373–74.

247. Robert S. McNamara, "US Defense Policy, A Balanced Military Force," delivered before the Democratic Platform Committee, Washington, D.C., 17 August 1967, in *Vital Speeches*, 15 September 1964, 710, 712.

Harold Brown,
secretary of defense.

James M. Gavin, President Kennedy's
ambassador to France.

Adm David L. McDonald, Retired,
former chief of naval operations.

Rep George H. Mahon of Texas,
chairman of House Defense
Appropriations Subcommittee.

Maj Gen Dale O. Smith, special assistant
for arms control to the
Joint Chiefs of Staff.

CHAPTER 3

THE AIR FORCE IN A CHANGING DEFENSE ENVIRONMENT

"We must improve the administration of our defense agencies, and we must do so without delay," stated Sen John F. Kennedy on 14 September 1960.[1] During his successful presidential campaign, Senator Kennedy and the men who would occupy key positions in his administration voiced concern about delays in missile and space programs which were attributable to an inability of the existing organizational structure of the national government to provide quick and definite decisions on matters of critical importance. One of these men, Secretary of State Dean Rusk, would later explain, "Over a period of time . . . we had felt that much of the committee machinery left dangling and hidden vetoes all over town and that this tended to slow down operations rather considerably."[2] While the presidential campaign was still under way, Senator Kennedy asked Sen Stuart Symington to dispatch a committee report to him regarding legislative and executive measures that should be taken to obtain an adequate national defense, and a few days after his election, Kennedy requested Dr Jerome B. Wiesner to head an ad hoc committee on national space requirements.[3] Doctor Wiesner was the second of the two men who would assume key roles in the Kennedy administration. Shortly after assuming office in January 1961, President Kennedy's administration undertook changes within the National Security Council (NSC), within the national organization for space exploitation, and within the Department of Defense.

Centralization of National Security Management

Even though it was established by the National Security Act of 1947 the National Security Council was, in the words of Robert Cutler, "a vehicle for the President to use in accordance with its suitability to his plans for conducting his great office."[4] Brought into being by Cutler while he served as special assistant to President Eisenhower for National Security Affairs, the NSC Planning Board was composed of representatives of the National Security Council and served as the principal body for formulating and transmitting policy recommendations to the council. Established by executive order in September 1953, the NSC Operations Coordinating Board was composed of deputies to the principal members of the National Security Council and had the responsibility of translating approved NSC policies into operational directives.[5]

IDEAS, CONCEPTS, DOCTRINE

In the late 1950s the institutional framework of the National Security Council was the subject of criticism. As has been seen, Gen Maxwell Taylor charged: "The National Security Council has not come to grips with the fundamental defense problems and has failed to produce clear-cut guidance for the armed forces."[6] Speaking as a defense analyst in September 1959, Paul H. Nitze suggested that President Eisenhower's dependence upon the National Security Council for policy formulation as well as for advice in making decisions may have been "wrong in theory and abortive in practice." Nitze said the NSC Planning Board worked under the "full pressures of interservice and interdepartmental rivalries" and made compromises even in the gathering of information. The concentration of responsibility for formulating new national policy ideas in the National Security Council, moreover, relieved the executive departments of a full sense of their responsibility for such work and tended "to cut off cross-fertilization of ideas between departments and the services."[7] On 12 December 1960 Sen Henry M. Jackson's Subcommittee on National Policy Machinery, a part of the Senate Committee on Government Operations, recommended that steps be taken to "deinstitutionalize" and "humanize" the National Security Council process. The subcommittee charged that the NSC Planning Board tended to overshadow the NSC and usually provided a means only for negotiating "agreed positions." The subcommittee found good reason for abolishing the NSC Operations Coordinating Board and assigning the responsibility for implementing policies cutting across departmental lines to a particular department or to a particular action officer, possibly assisted by an informal interdepartmental group.[8]

In conversations before they took office, Secretaries Robert S. McNamara and Rusk agreed to foster and sponsor a close relationship of all echelons within the Department of Defense and State Department. Although the program was not intended to replace informal day-to-day contacts at working levels, Rusk and McNamara soon expanded a state-defense exchange program whereby Foreign Service officers were detailed to politico-military offices in the Defense Department, and an equal number of military officers and defense civilians were assigned to tours in various offices of the State Department. "There are not curtains, iron curtains," McNamara announced in August 1961, "between the Departments of any echelon. On a day-to-day basis, this results in expeditious action, and I believe an entirely satisfactory working relationship at all echelons."[9]

Acting within his executive prerogative, President Kennedy named McGeorge Bundy as his special assistant for national security affairs, but he preferred to rely mainly upon personal contacts with his cabinet officers and upon task forces to accomplish interdepartmental policy planning and coordinating. To rid the National Security Council of its formalized institutionalism, Kennedy abolished the NSC Operations Coordinating Board effective 19 February 1961. Where the National Security Council had held weekly meetings under President Eisenhower, President Kennedy preferred to call NSC meetings only after determining that a particular issue was ready for discussion in such a forum. Much of the policy business that formerly flowed through the weekly NSC meetings was settled in other ways—by separate meetings with the president, by letters or memoranda, and at levels below that of the presidency. A weekly meeting in the Executive Office of the President, attended by the under secretary of state and the deputy secretary of defense among others, served as a regular point of contact, which kept officials of the two departments in close touch. When specific national security problems arose, the president assigned the responsibility for preparing a plan of action to a particular department or individual who became responsible for obtaining the views of all interested agencies. When common views were not forthcoming, no effort was made to find a common denominator but the divergent positions were submitted to the president.[10]

When Kennedy approved policy guidance, he also assigned responsibility for its implementation to a specific department or individual, and used the NSC staff or the White House staff to check the follow-up action. Most frequently, the departments or individuals vested with responsibility for handling problems assembled intergovernmental teams or task forces, usually on a short-term basis. Both McNamara and Rusk considered that the new procedures were advantageous. Speaking of the president, McNamara said: "It is my belief, under this new system, he is confronted with more alternatives and more differences in point of view than under the old."[11] Rusk pointed out: "Since the authority for the task force stems directly from the President or other high officials, there usually results added urgency and a more thorough consideration of the problem than would otherwise have been possible."[12]

When he took office Secretary McNamara considered that one of his "first objectives was to establish a close relationship both personally with Secretary Rusk, and also formally and officially at all levels of the Defense Department, with corresponding levels in the State Department," but he emphasized that "I feel that my channel of authority runs directly to the President. And I wouldn't accept from the State Department . . . advice which I didn't feel was good advice."[13] The new policymaking procedures nevertheless met the criteria that McNamara believed essential for national defense decisions. Stated Deputy Secretary of Defense Roswell L. Gilpatric:

> Secretary McNamara and I believe that it is imperative, if we are to have a defense adequate to meet the needs of this nuclear and space age, that decisions be made as promptly as possible. We do not feel that important decisions affecting the national security of the United States can be deferred pending attempts to work out a *modus vivendi* which will be satisfactory to everyone. Once you try to compromise the positions of competing interests, you water down the solution to a point where we believe it cannot be as effective as it should be.[14]

Speaking for himself, Secretary McNamara described his basic management philosophy.

> It is a philosophy based on a decision pyramid and a system of administration in which all possible decisions are pushed to the bottom of that pyramid. But for intelligent

> decisions to be made at the bottom of the pyramid there must be a framework within which those decisions can be made. Basic policies must be established against which a decision maker in the lower levels can compare his decision and gain some confidence that he is acting in accordance with a pattern of decisions elsewhere in the organization. This will lead to unity and strength, rather than an imbalance, which can only lead to weakness. And it is the establishment of these policies that can only be done at the top.[15]

The reorientation of the machinery for making national security decisions promised closer relationships between the foreign and military policies of the United States, but it also caused some concern. Thus some senators questioned the wisdom of President Kennedy's personal instruction that the members of the Joint Chiefs of Staff would consider political as well as military aspects of national problems. The Joint Chiefs, however, apparently accepted the realism of the instruction. "It is impossible," Adm George W. Anderson, Jr., noted, "for us in the world in which we live, the environment in which the Joint Chiefs of Staff live, completely to divorce themselves from the political and the psychological factors."[16] In the spring of 1961, *Fortune* magazine editorially feared the influence of the cross-department group within the New Frontier: the magazine was alarmed at the prospect that this group — which it called the *Technipols* — would fix strategy and monopolize the direction of military concepts, thereby reducing the influence of the Joint Chiefs of Staff.[17]

The fear that the National Security Council and the Joint Chiefs of Staff would lose their influence over national military policy was further aggravated on 26 June 1961, when President Kennedy, in the wake of the Bay of Pigs incident, announced that he was recalling Maxwell Taylor to active duty as military representative of the president. A White House statement emphasized that General Taylor would have no command authority but would advise the president on military and intelligence matters. Speaking of his relationships with the Joint Chiefs of Staff and of his duties, Taylor subsequently said:

> I am definitely not over the Chairman, I am not over any of the Chiefs. I am an individual adviser to the President outside of the channel of command, and so far as I know, the only person I can issue orders to is the aide who sits outside of my office.[18]

Both Secretary McNamara and Secretary Rusk minimized the effect of the Taylor appointment. Rusk explained:

> General Taylor is a personal adviser to the President on military and intelligence matters and he effects a close liaison with the two agencies principally engaged in those two fields. . . . The chief role which the advisers in the White House play is that of liaison and assistance in the preparation of papers and agenda of meetings. They do not operate as independent policymakers.[19]

Effective on 1 October 1962, President Kennedy named General Taylor to succeed Gen Lyman L. Lemnitzer as chairman of the Joint Chiefs of Staff and allowed the position of military representative of the president to lapse. Although it was difficult to question the prerogative of the president to name his own personal advisers, Brig Gen J. D. Hittle, USMC, Retired, and an expert on military staff procedures, nevertheless challenged the need for a presidential military adviser.

> It is conceivable that there is a constructive role for one to perform in the position ... but I could visualize ... that ... it could develop into an agency of defense planning, strategic authority, and military advice, completely outside of and in contradiction to the Joint Chiefs of Staff system which is established, and deliberately so, by Congress in law.[20]

Under the Eisenhower administration the annually issued "Basic National Security Policy" paper provided the guidance for the preparation of national defense budgets, but the Kennedy administration reportedly arrived in office with the belief that these papers had represented such generalized and compromised viewpoints as to be inadequate as statements of strategic concept.[21]

Secretary Rusk also questioned the worth of generalized planning.

> We felt that general planning was not of too great utility. It was important in terms of the education of those who were to make policy decisions, and for the background, alternatives, and general orientation of policy. The most effective planning, however, is that focused rather particularly on a situation or on a developing crisis or any idea on foreign policy.[22]

In May 1961 the Department of Defense indicated that a basic national security policy paper would be prepared for guidance in the preparation of the five-year force package projections, but the paper was not completed and, in the end, Department of Defense directives about force structure and the concept of multiple operations ultimately provided guidance for forward planning.[23] In the absence of a policy paper, presidential addresses—particularly Kennedy's message to Congress on 28 March 1961—and other statements by key administration officials provided guidance on national security policy.[24]

Providing a NASA-Defense Interface

During his campaign for the presidency in 1960, Senator Kennedy promised to move the United States into a position of prominence in space, but he urged that the immediate national objective in space was to achieve an adequate deterrent missile force. He expressed the belief that at least a part of the difficulty in the management of defense missile programs stemmed from distractions caused by vast new space programs, and he accordingly announced that he would make good use of the National Aeronautics and Space Council for advice on the implementation of plans and for coordinating government space activities.[25]

At Kennedy's request the Wiesner Ad Hoc Committee on Space provided an analysis of the national space situation as well as recommendations for the future in a report which President-elect Kennedy released on 11 January 1961. The Wiesner committee pointed out that the new National Aeronautics and Space

Administration (NASA) wished to establish a potentially duplicative in-house research committee and asserted the general belief in aviation circles that NASA's preoccupation with space development had all but halted experimental work in the theory and technology of aerodynamic flight. The Wiesner committee also stated that the Army, Navy, and Air Force were competing in space research and development, since under a DOD directive of 18 September 1959 the services were permitted to undertake study efforts and laboratory experiments at moderate costs without the approval of the director of defense research and engineering. Thus in December 1960 the Navy made the uncoordinated announcement that it was initiating a series of new communications and reconnaissance satellite programs. Uncoordinated speeches and press releases relating to preliminary study projects generated industry-sponsored activity and frequently caused NASA to believe that the Department of Defense was not abiding by existing agreements.[26]

After pointing up the areas of weakness in the national space organization, the Wiesner committee based its recommendations on its belief that there were five principal motivations for a vital, effective, national space program:

> First, there is the factor of national prestige.
>
> Second, we believe that some space developments in addition to missiles, can contribute much to our national security—both in terms of military systems and of arms-limitation inspection and control systems.
>
> Third, the development of space vehicles affords new opportunities for scientific observation and experiment....
>
> Fourth, there are a number of important practical nonmilitary applications of space technology....
>
> Finally, space activities particularly in the fields of communications and in the exploration of our solar system, offer exciting possibilities for international cooperation with all the nations of the world.[27]

Believing that the United States was lagging in the development of missiles and space technology, the Wiesner committee stated an urgent requirement for more effective management and coordination. It specifically recommended that the National Aeronautics and Space Council be made an effective agency for managing the national space program; that a single responsibility be established within DOD for managing the military portion of the space program; that a vigorous, imaginative, and technically competent top management be provided to NASA; that the national space program should be reviewed and redefined in terms of two years of experience in booster programs, manned space flight, the military uses of space, and the application of space technology to civilian activities; and that organizational machinery be established within the government to administer an industry-government-civilian space program.[28]

As Secretary McNamara began to examine management organization within the Department of Defense, he determined that studies made of broad administrative, organizational, and management problems had generally been accomplished by ad hoc boards. Believing that some single Department of Defense activity should to be concerned with continuous responsibility for organizational and managerial planning, McNamara established an office of organizational and management planning studies under the general council to conduct systematic research on such problems. This small office was immediately directed to review the military organization for research and development in space, and after consultations with the director of defense research and engineering and officials in the individual military services it drew up a new defense directive on the subject. Secretary McNamara circulated the draft directive to the nonmilitary departments and to other interested agencies in the Department of Defense, including the chairman of the Joint Chiefs of Staff. He gave them a week to file their comments. This deadline ran out on 2 March 1961, and on 6 March McNamara issued a memorandum on the development of military space systems. Deputy Secretary Gilpatric acknowledged that the decision on the matter was made in "less time than has customarily been the practice," but he considered that he and McNamara had personally evaluated all the points of view that had been presented before they arrived at their final decision.[29]

In the Department of Defense directive of 6 March, Secretary McNamara authorized each military department to conduct preliminary research for the development of new ways of using space technology to accomplish assigned functions. All proposals for research and development beyond preliminary research were to be submitted to the director of defense engineering for review and later to the secretary of defense for approval. Research, development, test, and engineering of approved Department of Defense space development programs or projects would be (except in unusual circumstances when the secretary or deputy secretary of defense made a specific exception) the responsibility of the Department of the Air Force.[30] In explaining the directive, Gilpatric pointed out that the Wiesner committee had recommended that a single military space program manager be designated; that the Air Force already was responsible for over 90 percent of the total defense effort in space; that the directive permitted the secretary of defense to make a case-by-case determination of space projects; and, where peculiar talents were involved, to authorize deviations from development by the Air Force.[31] The directive did not affect space research and development projects already assigned to the military departments, such as the Army's Advent communications satellite program and the Navy's Transit navigation system, but on 28 March McNamara acted under the new directive and assigned to the Air Force the responsibility for research, development, and operation of all defense reconnaissance satellite systems and for research and development of all instrumentation and equipment for processing reconnaissance data from satellite sources.[32]

In considering the establishment of effective relations between DOD and NASA, Secretary McNamara began with the premise that the president and Congress desired that there would be two agencies developing projects for operations in space but that there ought to be a well-coordinated national space program. At a meeting with NASA administrator James E. Webb in February 1961, McNamara emphasized that DOD would expect to develop the techniques and technology that it might require for future military operations in space but that both agencies should ensure that their activities did not overlap, duplicate, or cause unnecessary expenditures to the nation.[33] A little later McNamara stated that any defense space program would have to meet the criteria: "First, it must mesh with the efforts of the NASA in all vital areas. . . . Second, projects supported by the Defense Department must promise, insofar as possible, to enhance our military power and effectiveness."[34] In their initial discussions McNamara and Webb agreed to continue to use the Aeronautics and Astronautics Coordinating Board (AACB), and on 23 February 1961 Webb and Gilpatric jointly signed a letter of agreement establishing a national launch vehicle program. The AACB was given the responsibility for interagency planning of launch vehicles, and neither NASA nor DOD would initiate the development of a launch vehicle or booster without the written acknowledgment of the other that such a new development would be consistent with proper objectives of the composite space program.[35]

As he had promised in his campaign, President Kennedy undertook to revitalize the National Aeronautics and Space Council (NASC). He appointed Dr Edward C. Welsh as executive secretary of the council on 23 March, and on 10 April he asked Congress to amend existing legislation to establish the council in the Executive Office of the President and to designate the vice president, the secretary of state, the secretary of defense, the NASA administrator, and the chairman of the Atomic Energy Commission as its members. The vice president would serve as chairman of the council, and the council would advise and assist the president with respect to the performance of functions in the aeronautics and space field. This amendment to the National Aeronautics and Space Act was approved by Congress and signed into law on 25 April.[36] On 13 May NASA additionally asked Congress to repeal the statutory requirement for the superseded Civilian-Military Liaison Committee, and in hearings on the proposal both NASA and Defense Department spokesmen maintained that the Aeronautics and Astronautics Coordinating Board could serve as an effective interagency coordinating authority without being established by law. Apparently because the deletion of the Civilian-Military Liaison Committee section of the Space Act would have eliminated the legal admonition that the Department of Defense would have interests in space, Congress refused to approve this requested amendment.[37]

Under the emerging management concept for the national space program, the National Aeronautics and Space Council was charged to advise and assist the president, to fix the responsibilities of government agencies engaged in aeronautical and space activities, and to develop a comprehensive program for such activities. The Aeronautics and Astronautics Coordinating Board, with six working panels, was designed to "facilitate the planning of aeronautical and space activities of NASA and DOD to avoid undesirable duplication and to achieve efficient utilization of available resources; to coordinate activities in areas of common interest; [and] to identify problem areas and exchange information."[38] The AACB was not intended to be a managerial group in a collective sense, and actions based on the board's consideration could be taken by individual members only by using the authority vested in them by their respective agencies.[39] Working under this management structure, Deputy Director of Defense Research and Engineering John H. Rubel told the Senate Aeronautical and Space Committee on 5 March 1962 that "we've been successful in making policy and dividing responsibility, but we have had a little more difficulty coming down to specifics."[40] Most important decisions—such as the national launch vehicle program and the national launch center agreement whereby the Department of Defense undertook to support NASA at the Cape Canaveral and the Pacific Missile Range—had to be thrust upward for decisions by Secretary McNamara and Administrator Webb.[41]

By early 1962 NASA and the Department of Defense had achieved a meeting of minds on broad policy matters, but there was a need for specific decisions. "We are coming to the point where broad policy is not as important as making detailed decisions and working out arrangements in which the military research capability can be made available to the space agency," Deputy Director Rubel said.[42] Gen Bernard Schriever, now in command of the Air Force Systems Command, additionally pointed out that the space agency would make increasing contributions to national security, where in the past the Department of Defense had largely supported NASA. In conversations with NASA officials, Schriever urged that the time had come to establish interaction arrangements or "interface" between the Air Force Systems Command and NASA, first in Washington and then on down to the working levels of both organizations.[43] To ensure a closer meshing of military and civilian space programs, Secretary McNamara issued a policy directive on 24 February 1962 declaring:

> It is in the national interest for the Department of Defense, to the extent compatible with its primary mission, to make its resources available to NASA, in the form of facilities and organizations, in order to comply effectively the nation's total resources for the achievement of common civil and military space objectives.[44]

Except for such special arrangements as the secretary of defense might make, the directive assigned responsibility to the secretary of the Air Force "for the research, development, test, and engineering of satellites, boosters, space probes, and associated systems necessary to support specific NASA projects and programs arising under basic agreements between NASA and DOD."[45]

Although the Department of Defense would continue to exercise close patrol over space research and development, the McNamara directive of 24 February 1962 was a manifestation of a trend toward the centralization of defense space activities under the Air Force and its subordinate Air Force Systems Command. On 11 June 1962 the Department of Defense canceled the Army's Advent project and assigned the Air Force responsibility for the development, production, and launching of defense satellite communications devices. The Army also was charged to develop and operate ground communications stations, and the Defense Communications Agency was asked to assure the effective integration of ground and space components.[46] Acting under the new directive of 24 February, the Air Force moved into closer cooperation with NASA. On 26 April 1962 General Schriever named Maj Gen O. J. Ritland as deputy commander of the Air Force Systems Command for Manned Space Flight, provided him with a staff of 28 officers (5 of whom were physically located with NASA), and charged him to effect a close association and coordination between the Systems Command and NASA. Although the Air Force was not authorized to present military requirements to NASA, General Ritland was charged to participate in NASA's programming and planning activities and was able to make the Air Force's requirements known.[47]

By the end of 1962 some 50 arrangements and agreements were outstanding between the DOD and NASA, and during the year the Department of Defense performed more than $550 million worth of work for NASA. Most of the defense effort continued to support NASA, and late in 1962 Secretary McNamara faced the prospect that the Department of Defense should make more use of NASA.[48] He was especially concerned about the prospect that NASA's Gemini program, which had been approved on 7 December 1961 and visualized extended-duration, two-man orbital space flights, had advanced beyond the Air Force's Dyna-Soar project "in technique and technology and potential."[49] If this were true, Dyna-Soar could be canceled, provided that Gemini could be made responsive to Air Force technological requirements.[50] Even though the Air Force did not agree that Dyna-Soar duplicated Gemini, Assistant Secretary of the Air Force Brockway McMillan maintained that "the potential joint value of the NASA and Defense Department programs can be more fully realized by closer collaboration in the early conceptual phases, to insure that the objectives of each agency are clearly recognized at each successive stage of program evolution."[51]

Believing that there was a real possibility that the national manned space programs would develop out of Gemini and Dyna-Soar, Secretary McNamara and Administrator Webb jointly signed a letter of agreement to ensure the most effective utilization of the Gemini program in the national interest. The agreement sought to ensure that the scientific and operational experiments undertaken during the Gemini program would be directed at objectives and requirements of both the DOD and NASA. To this end, McNamara and Webb established a Gemini program planning board, under the cochairmanship of the associate administrator of NASA and the assistant secretary of the Air Force for research and development. This board was to delineate requirements and program monitoring procedures to ascertain what mutual objectives would be met in planning requirements, in the actual conduct of flight and in-flight tests, and in the analysis and dissemination of the results. NASA would continue to manage Gemini, and DOD would contribute funds to assist in the attainment of program objectives. As a policy for additional programs of the future, McNamara and Webb concluded: "It is further agreed that the DOD and NASA will initiate major new programs or projects in the field of manned space flight aimed chiefly at the attainment of experimental or other capabilities in near-Earth orbit only by mutual agreement."[52] On 22 January Webb and McNamara also announced an agreement setting forth the management responsibilities for operations in the Cape Canaveral range area. This agreement specified that the Air Force would continue as the single manager of the Atlantic Missile Range and as host agency at the existing Cape Canaveral launch area. Through its Launch Operations Center, NASA would manage and serve as host agency at the 87,000-acre Merritt Island launch area, which it had purchased and was developing north and west of Cape Canaveral. DOD and NASA would be responsible for their own logistics and administrative functions in their respective launch areas, but the Department of Defense would continue to be responsible for scheduling launches, flight safety, range search, and sea recovery over the Atlantic Missile Range.[53]

Secretary McNamara considered the precedent of the Gemini program planning board to be a major step forward, and he refused to question the military-civilian space organizational structure that Congress had established. "Without regard to whether or not some other alternative might not be better," he said, "I am satisfied we can operate effectively with the present organization within the Government; that is to say, specifically with NASA and the Defense Department both participating in developments in this field."[54] As a matter of fact, the Gemini program planning board would discover that what it had been initially constituted for would either be very expensive or impossible to attain at such a late date.[55] For its own part, the Air Force was far from satisfied that NASA's Gemini program and its subsequent Apollo moonflight program would provide the technological knowledge needed for future military operations in space. During fiscal year 1964 budget negotiations, the Air Force accordingly proposed that about $177 million should be provided for a separately manned military space flight project referred to as Blue Gemini and for the development of a manned space station called the manned orbital development system (MODS). Secretary McNamara, however, considered these projects as duplicative and excluded them from the budget requests submitted to Congress in January 1963.[56]

During 1963 the DOD sought to cooperate harmoniously with NASA to attain national space objectives. At Houston, Texas, where NASA was building its manned spacecraft center, the Air Force temporarily hosted NASA personnel at Ellington AFB, Texas, and the Air Force Systems Command opened a field office in Houston to manage military experiments during the Gemini program. In continued support for NASA, the Air Force made Brig Gen Samuel C. Phillips, who had been serving as vice commander, Air Force Ballistics Systems Division, available for appointment as deputy director of NASA's Apollo project. Prior to

General Phillips's assignment to this position on 31 December 1963, General Schriever emphasized to Phillips that "he was going to work for NASA and be loyal to NASA."[57] During the autumn of 1963, NASA was a partner in the deliberations within the DOD that culminated in December when the Dyna-Soar program was terminated and a new program for the development of a manned orbital laboratory (MOL) was initiated in the Air Force. Where the Air Force had previously supported NASA, General Schriever now indicated that he intended to ask NASA for personnel to participate in the MOL project.[58] NASA would provide extensive technical support to the project.[59]

When the Air Force was directed in June 1962 to assume responsibility for military communications satellites (a program that would have to be developed in context with the civil project to be controlled by the Communications Satellite Corporation),[60] the Air Force was in effect charged with all military space research and development efforts except for the Navy's Transit navigational satellite system. Management of Department of Defense missile test ranges and flight-test facilities, however, continued to be divided between the Air Force and the Navy. In April 1963 Secretary McNamara asked the director of defense research and engineering to make a study of these range and test facilities looking toward the elimination of duplication and establishment of a national system. This study was completed in June 1963. The Air Force was directed to assume responsibility for managing and operating a worldwide satellite tracking and control facility for all defense space programs except for Transit and a limited number of other projects that might be exempt in the future. The Air Force was also directed to provide a central authority for the management of launch area range instrumentation and on-orbit satellite control facilities at both the Atlantic and Pacific missile ranges as well as at remote worldwide control and tracking stations. The Air Force already controlled the Atlantic Missile Range, and it would begin to take over the Navy's installations at Point Arguello and Point Pillar, California, in July 1965. To handle the new tasks, the Air Force established the National Range Division under the Air Force Systems Command at Patrick AFB, Florida, on 2 January 1964. Becoming fully operational at Andrews AFB, Maryland, on 1 July 1965, the National Range Division began to exercise command over the Air Force Eastern Test Region at Patrick AFB and the Air Force Western Test Region at Vandenberg AFB, California. With the completion of the reorganization, the Department of Defense would have centralized control under one service to support the worldwide operations of satellites, the space programs of NASA, and other programs that tied in with the Atlantic and Pacific ranges.[61] Where the Air Force and the Navy had engaged in an active controversy over the control of California range facilities in 1957–58, Secretary McNamara's decision to transfer the Pacific Missile Range to the Air Force drew only mild comment from the Navy spokesman, who observed: "We were not enthusiastic about it, I would say."[62]

Secretary McNamara and Defense Management

The Democratic party platform of 1960 called for a complete examination of the organization of the armed forces of the United States as a first order of business in a new administration, and during the summer of 1960 Senator Kennedy asked Senator Symington to head a study committee that would provide a concrete program with specific proposals for needed national defense reorganization. On 14 September 1960, Kennedy announced that Symington would head this Committee on the Defense Establishment and that the members would be Clark M. Clifford, Thomas K. Finletter, Roswell L. Gilpatric, Fowler Hamilton, and Marx Leva. Dr Edward C. Welsh would serve as executive director. Kennedy expected the committee without conducting "another sweeping investigation," to study existing informed opinion and to make its recommendations known by 31 December so that the new administration could take steps "to remedy present basic weaknesses in the administration and management of our national defense establishments."[63]

In preparing a unanimous report that was handed to President-elect Kennedy on 5 December 1960, the Symington committee depended on existing defense studies for source materials and avoided discussions with members of the defense establishment. The committee found that the existing structure of the Department of Defense was "still patterned primarily on a design conceived in the light of lessons learned in World War II, which are now largely obsolete."[64] To the committee, time had become an "unprecedented strategic value."[65] In World War II the United States had used 18 months to build and mobilize its forces; in a World War III the United States "would be fortunate to have 18 minutes to react."[66] The crucial element of time also entered into defense preparedness; there was a need for earlier selection among alternative weapon systems and for a shorter time between the conception of weapon systems and their availability for use. Time could not be bought; it could only be saved by reduction in duplication, wasted effort, and elimination of multilayered decisionmaking structures. The committee concluded that three major objectives were to be sought in modernizing the DOD. The first objective was to shorten the time factor in bringing new weapon systems from conception to utilization. This could be handled by eliminating multilayered decisionmaking. In view of the concept of concurrency in weapon systems management, the committee suggested that there was "no longer any validity in separating the development and production cycle into two parts."[67] The second objective was to correct the predominance of service influence in the Joint Chiefs of Staff, which resulted in defense planning becoming a series of compromised positions. The third objective was to make the defense establishment a flexible organization under the clear authority of the secretary of defense.[68]

To implement the general objectives, the Symington committee made specific recommendations looking toward a strengthening of civilian authority, new procedures for the command of military operations, and a centralization of budgetary controls. To strengthen civilian authority, the committee recommended that the secretary of defense, the deputy secretary of defense, and two new under secretaries of defense—one for administration and the other for weapons systems—would be made statutory officers; the seven existing assistant secretaries of defense should be abolished and their functions should be absorbed by staff directories working with the new under secretaries. The committee proposed a sweeping reorganization of the military services:

> The military services would be retained, but the present departmental structure of the Army, Navy, and Air Forces would be eliminated. This in turn would do away with the present positions of Service Secretaries. The Services would remain separate organic units, albeit within a single department (as in the case today with the Marines) and subject to the direction, authority, and control of the Secretary of Defense.[69]

For the command of military operations, the committee recommended that the chairman of the Joint Chiefs of Staff should be redesignated as the chairman of the Joint Staff and made the principal military adviser to the president and the secretary of defense. The chairman would direct an enlarged Joint Staff and would preside over a military advisory council, comprised of presidentially appointed senior officers who would no longer retain service identities. Each of the military services would continue to have a chief who would report directly to the secretary of defense. Three unified commands—Strategic, Tactical, and Defense—plus other regional or area specified commands would report directly to the chairman of the Joint Staff and would include all personnel, equipment, and weapon systems required for the performance of their respective missions. The committee recommended that all defense funds should be appropriated to the Department of Defense under the control of the secretary of defense and that research and development funds and long lead time procurement appropriations should be voted on multiyear schedules.[70]

The Air Force already was on record in support of increased defense unification. At a conference held by the secretary of defense at Quantico on 18 June 1960, General White stated:

> Unity is the watchword—unity in concept, in our objectives, in our planning and in our operational effort—unity is the guiding principle for the reorganized defense establishment. In my opinion, our progress in this direction falls short of the technological progress which is being made in the environment in which the Department of Defense must operate.[71]

In an interview during July 1960, General White pointed out that the atomic bomb and the advent of missiles had totally changed the science of warfare. He said that scientists had told him "that the rate of advance in space is not going to suddenly reach a plateau and level off, but we're going to keep right on, on this asymptotic curve."[72] Speaking of his philosophy of military organization he said that "the answer to my mind is unification at the top."[73]

What the Army thought about the Symington committee's recommendations was not read into the public record, but the Navy was quite opposed to them.

Several weeks before the Symington report was made public, the Navy prepared a 17-point declaration entitled "What the Navy Is For." This declaration argued for a continued maintenance of the existing defense organization, at least until the full effect of the Defense Reorganization Act of 1958 could be realized. When the Symington report became available, Adm Arleigh Burke directed that packets be made up including the Symington report, the Navy declaration, and a number of press comments on the Symington committee report. These packets were mailed to Navy attachés and other interested persons on 27 December 1960. Speaking to Symington a few weeks later, Burke stated positively: "I do not agree with the conclusions you drew in the report."[74] Key congressional leaders also were cool to sweeping proposals for defense unification. "I am not," explained Sen Richard Russell, "a rampant advocate of complete unification, a monolithic command, and, as a matter of fact, I am opposed to it."[75] Senator Russell, however, favored unification in fields of activity such as intelligence and communications, and in some phases of training.[76] Congressman Carl Vinson commented:

> One of the basic reasons why we have four services and four separate Chiefs who are responsible for their service and for their viewpoints as members of the Joint Chiefs of Staff is to be very sure that we do not have one single type of thinking. We want, and the law expects, divergent views of defense planning.[77]

By April 1961 Senator Symington noted that Congress was of the opinion that new organizational legislation ought not to be considered until the DOD "uses the authority it has to straighten out some of these cans of worms so far as efficient organization is concerned."[78]

As soon as he assumed office on 20 January 1961, Secretary McNamara revealed that he had decided views about his role as the top manager in the Department of Defense. "My strong belief is," he would say, "a manager should be an aggressive leader, an active leader, asking questions, suggesting alternatives, proposing objectives, stimulating progress."[79] As has been seen, McNamara immediately implemented President Kennedy's mandate that he reappraise the adequacy of the entire defense structure and provide preliminary conclusions without delay by demanding answers to 96 sweeping questions. Most of these questions (as well as an additional number of queries added to the list) were assigned from study and report to special task groups, each headed by a senior official. Nearly 35 of the most important questions were assigned to the Joint Chiefs and the Joint Staff for study and analysis.[80] Secretary Thomas S. Gates had followed a procedure of meeting weekly with the Joint Chiefs, and Secretary McNamara continued the practice. He believed that "by personally raising issues for discussion with the Joint Chiefs of Staff, I have been able to expedite the decision-making process."[81] Although McNamara was willing to accord "primary responsibility" to the Joint Chiefs of Staff in making normal day-to-day decisions with respect to combat operation, he nevertheless considered that the secretary of defense had to play a major role in establishing the future force levels, since these levels had to be established in relation to the total objectives of the nation, particularly its foreign objectives.[82]

As McNamara studied the National Security Act of 1947 and its amendments, he became convinced that the secretary of defense legally possessed many powers which had never been used, possibly because the organization of national defense had never really been studied under the auspices of the Office of the Secretary of Defense. To handle such studies, McNamara organized the Office of Organizational and Management Planning Studies. Even though he acted quickly on this office's first recommendation and concentrated space research and development within the Air Force, McNamara stated that any general review of the basic organizational structure of the Department of Defense—which would answer such questions as whether unification of the services was required—would take many months. In the meanwhile he promised that "we should do everything that we can, that is within our legal power to do, to streamline the decision making process, to avoid duplication, to eliminate waste, and to strengthen the lines of authority and responsibility, and this we are doing on a daily basis as opportunity presents itself."[83] As time passed, the Office of Secretary of Defense continued to pursue the evolutionary approach to defense reorganization. Deputy Secretary Gilpatric further explained the matter in May 1962, when he said:

> Whether ultimately a major restructuring of the Defense Department must take place remains to be seen. I thought so once and favored such an approach but as of now the more gradual evolutionary process of change makes more sense to me and that is the approach we are going to take in the coming year.[84]

Under existing legislation the power of appointment and the power of the purse were at the disposal of the secretary of defense, and the control of the budget would be a major force for evolutionary change within the DOD. At the beginning of the Kennedy administration, McNamara brought Charles J. Hitch from the Rand Corporation, where he had served as chief of the Economics Division since 1948, to Washington as assistant secretary of defense for comptroller. While at Rand in 1960, Hitch had coauthored a book, *The Economics of Defense in the Nuclear Age*, which had advanced a plan whereby defense budgets would be arranged in categories corresponding to end-product defense missions and whereby defense packages could be costed out for five years in the future.[85] Working with the Joint Staff and the military departments, Hitch devised nine budget program packages: (1) Strategic Retaliatory Forces, (2) Continental Air and Missile Defense Forces, (3) General Purpose Forces, (4) Airlift and Sealift Forces, (5) Reserve and National Guard Forces, (6) Research and Development, (7) Servicewide Support, (8) Classified Projects, and (9) Department of Defense. In May 1961 Hitch instructed the military departments to submit their 1963 budget requests in terms of these program packages and to project the requests into costs that would run five years into the future. At the completion of the basic five-year program review, Hitch visualized that annual budgets would be more easily made up in terms of the phased accomplishment of the five-year program and such program changes as might be approved. As the program package budget was being put into effect, Hitch reasoned that "the existence of the services . . . raises problems." He also suggested that the functional budget procedure "may add something to the argument for changing the organization in the direction of greater responsibility for specified and unified commands."[86] Speaking tentatively at first, McNamara suggested that the program package budget "can serve as a substitute for a change in the organizational structure."[87] By January 1962 he had begun to see the functional budget as a possible substitute for increased defense unification. "I think," he explained, "it would make it more difficult to prove that a single service was desirable or necessary because some of the advantages attributed to a single service are being accomplished without a single service by this so-called programming approach."[88]

When the Department of Defense program package budget was being set up in August 1961, Secretary McNamara predicted that it would permit the military departments to "play a fuller role" in defense planning.[89] During the preparation of the fiscal year 1963 budget and the initial five-year projection, the Office of the Assistant Secretary of Defense (Comptroller) assembled and organized the data submitted by the military departments and specifically viewed the estimates from a standpoint of cost effectiveness. Other agencies of the Office of the Secretary of Defense also were called upon to review the departmental submissions and to advise the secretary on aspects of the programs within the areas of functional responsibility.[90] Beginning with the preparation of the fiscal year 1964 budget—which included program changes in the five-year plan—Secretary McNamara employed a somewhat different review process. Having anticipated controversial issues among the program changes, he asked the chairman of the Joint Chiefs of Staff to have a series of special studies prepared on them. Where necessary McNamara also discussed the issues with the Joint Chiefs, and he submitted his recommendations to the president, giving both sides of the arguments bearing on the issues.[91] In a memorandum on 31 May 1963 looking toward the fiscal year 1965 budget, McNamara enumerated major proposed program changes and designated specific individuals within the Office of the Secretary of Defense to prepare coordinated recommendations on them—thus passing major program review from the Office of the Comptroller to offices of the assistant secretaries.[92]

As the Department of Defense program-package budgeting became perfected, both McNamara and Gilpatric looked upon the new management practice as an adequate substitute for organizational change. On 16 October 1963 Gilpatric said, "I would not recommend any basic changes in our national security legislation."[93] When asked about interservice rivalry on 19 February 1964 McNamara replied:

> I think the answer depends entirely upon the decisiveness of the Secretary of Defense. The Secretary has the power and the authority to recommend to the President, and by that means to the Congress, the budget he considers necessary regardless of service pressure reflecting a more parochial point of view. If the Secretary exercises that power and authority, there need not be waste introduced in the budget by the fact that interservice rivalry may exist.[94]

McNamara regarded "careful cost-effectiveness analyses" and the relationship of programs to missions rather than to the military services as the major contributions to the new system of management. In a prepared statement in February 1964, McNamara used a hypothetical example to illustrate cost-effectiveness analysis.

> Suppose we have two tactical fighter aircraft which are identical in every important measure of performance, except one—aircraft A can fly 10 miles per hour faster than aircraft B. However, aircraft A costs $10,000 more per unit than aircraft B. Thus, if we need about 1,000 aircraft, the total additional cost would be $10 million. . . . If we approach this problem from the viewpoint of a given amount of reasons, the additional combat effectiveness represented by the greater speed of aircraft A would have to be weighed against the additional combat effectiveness which the same $10 million could produce if applied to other defense purposes—more aircraft B, more or better aircraft munitions, or more ships, or even more military housing. . . . Thus, the fact that aircraft A flies 10 miles per hour faster than aircraft B is not conclusive. We still have to determine whether the greater speed is worth the greater cost. This kind of determination is the heart of the planning-programming-budgeting, or resources allocation problem within the Defense Department.[95]

To streamline the upper echelon of the Department of Defense, Secretary McNamara eliminated two of the seven assistant secretaries of defense at the outset of his administration, but he soon established a new Office of Assistant Secretary of Defense for Civil Defense. Additional prestige was given to the Office of the Director of Defense Research and Engineering by making its deputy director an assistant secretary of defense.[96] Several additional actions consolidated similar military departmental activities within the Office of the Secretary of Defense. In 1961 contact between Congress and the military departments was centralized in the Office of the Special Assistant of the Secretary of Defense for Legislative Affairs. Early in 1964 separate service book and magazine branches and community and industrial relations functions were merged under the assistant secretary of defense for public affairs.[97] When he first explained the program-package budget procedure, Comptroller Hitch suggested that it would concentrate authority within the Office of Secretary of Defense. "Program decisions," he said, "will be required. . . . They are the decisions of the sort which can only be made by the Secretary, and, therefore, the role of the Secretary's advisers will be greater."[98]

This prediction apparently came true. Thus in 1962 the report of a Special Subcommittee on Defense Agencies of the House Committee on Defense Agencies of the House Committee on Armed Services noted that the implementation of the program package defense budgets had given the assistant secretary of defense (comptroller) and later the assistant secretaries of defense and the director of defense engineering (when the primary responsibility for program integration was shifted from the comptroller to appropriate assistant secretaries) an enormous control over the military departments. The special subcommittee pointed out that the agency that prepared cost analyses of program changes became the primary control mechanism over the program category.[99] On the basis of evidence such as this a student of defense management could conclude in 1964 that "the Secretary of Defense has chosen to use his civilian staff as his primary agents of policy control within the department."[100]

During its consideration of the Defense Reorganization Act of 1958, Congress approved an amendment offered by Rep John McCormack which authorized the secretary of defense, when he deemed it advantageous in terms of effectiveness, economy, or efficiency, to arrange to have any supply or service activity common to two or more military departments conducted by a single agency. Acting under authority of the amendment of 2 May 1958, Secretary Gates established the Defense Communications Agency under the direction, authority, and control of the secretary of defense through the Joint Chiefs of Staff, and charged it to exercise a centralized control over all long-haul and point-to-point communications.[101] Shortly after taking office, Secretary McNamara also began to exercise authority given to him by the McCormack amendment. "One of the most productive fields of the economic application of centralized management," he said, "is in the provision of common supplies and related services to all the military departments."[102] On 31 August 1961 he accordingly announced the establishment of the Defense Supply Agency (DSA), which reported directly to the secretary of defense (rather than through the Joint Chiefs of Staff) and gradually assumed management responsibility over eight common supply categories previously exercised by the secretaries of the Army and Navy—subsistence, clothing-textiles, medical supplies, petroleum, general supplies, industrial supplies, construction supplies, and automotive supplies. The DSA also assumed control of the Military Traffic Management Agency (MTMA).[103] As he took office McNamara also noted that a number of intelligence agencies had been performing similar, if not parallel, work with no unified direction of the total defense intelligence activity. "To obtain unity of effort among all components of the Department of Defense in developing military intelligence and to achieve a strengthened overall capacity in the department for the collection, production, and dissemination of defense intelligence information," Secretary McNamara accordingly established the Defense Intelligence Agency (DIA) on 2 August 1961 and directed it to report to the secretary of defense through the Joint Chiefs of Staff. To the extent that the military services had intelligence requirements unique to their own operations (technical intelligence, for example, was essential for research and development functions), they were permitted to maintain certain limited intelligence activities.[104] Under the new arrangement the Intelligence Directorate (J-2) of the Joint Staff continued in being until 15 May 1963, at which time it was disestablished and its functions and personnel spaces were transferred to the Defense Intelligence Agency.[105]

In his list of study questions directed to the Joint Chiefs of Staff and the Joint Staff, McNamara asked whether a unified command should be established to control limited-war forces. Both Gen Thomas D. White and General Taylor had earlier recommended such a command, and Senator Symington's Committee on the Defense Establishment had endorsed these recommendations.[106] On 24 July 1961, both Gen Frank F. Everest, commander of the Tactical Air Command (TAC), and Gen Herbert B. Powell, commanding general of the Continental Army Command (CAC), jointly recommended the immediate establishment of a unified tactical command as a joint headquarters with Army, Navy, and Air Force component commands. They visualized that this command would be built around a relatively small, unified command headquarters, which would possess great mobility and would be capable of rapidly deploying fully effective command elements to areas of crisis.[107] With general agreement that the action should be taken, Secretary McNamara announced the establishment of the US Strike Command (STRICOM) on 19 September 1961 with its headquarters at MacDill AFB, Florida. Gen Paul D. Adams, who had commanded the US ground forces in the Lebanon operation, was named commander in chief and Lt Gen Bruce K. Holloway, US Air Force, was designated as deputy commander in chief.[108]

According to its mission assignment as a unified command, STRICOM was to provide an integrated, mobile, highly combat-ready force that would be trained as a unit and would be instantly available to augment forces existing under unified theater commanders or would be prepared to serve as a primary force in the event of conflict in the Middle East or Africa. STRICOM's six specific functional responsibilities required it to provide a general reserve of combat-ready forces, to provide forces to reinforce unified theater commands, to conduct planning for contingency operations, to develop joint doctrine for the employment of assigned forces, and to conduct joint training exercises to ensure a high level of combat readiness and effectiveness. The commanders of the Tactical Air Command (TAC) and the CAC were additionally designated as commanders in chief, Air Force Strike and Army Strike, and the two commands were charged to furnish combat-ready forces to serve under the operational control of CINCSTRIKE. At MacDill, General Adams established a headquarters with typical joint staff divisions, which were manned almost half and half with Army and Air Force personnel. Except for the assignment of one Marine Corps and four Navy officers to the headquarters, no naval forces were assigned to STRICOM. In the event he was given a contingency mission requiring Navy or Marine forces, Adams envisioned that he would ask the chief of naval operations to assign an appropriate naval component to work with his headquarters. On 28 December 1961 Adams reported to the Joint Chiefs of Staff (JCS) that STRICOM was operationally ready.[109]

In its mission assignment STRICOM was charged with the principal tasks of reinforcing unified theater commands and of maintaining a preparedness for independent operations in crisis areas that were not within existing unified theater command boundaries. Some 200 contingency plans were drawn up looking toward the reinforcement actions in specific emergencies.[110] In accordance with the supporting mission, STRICOM made combat-ready tactical air wings and ground divisions available to the commander in chief, Atlantic Command, during the Cuban missile crisis.[111] If STRICOM were directed to deploy to a remote trouble spot, General Adams planned that with the approval of the JCS he would draw boundaries around the crisis area, establish a small theater of operations, and move into Headquarters STRICOM, or a smaller joint task force headquarters into the area to command necessary operations.[112] In its initial months of operations, STRICOM had no clear mandate as to the area of the world in which it might be required to undertake independent operations, and the US Army was responsible for controlling military assistance to newly independent African nations. With dissenting opinions from the Navy and Marine Corps members, the majority of the Joint Chiefs of Staff recommended phasing out the Naval forces in the eastern Atlantic Ocean and the Mediterranean Sea and making CINCSTRIKE responsible for all United States defense activities in the Middle East, Southern Asia, and sub-Saharan Africa. Under its new responsibility CINCSTRIKE would be additionally designated CINCMEAFSA on 1 December 1963.[113] In the subsequent transfer of the responsibility, CINCMEAFSA gained some 1,000 military personnel overseas, mostly in military assistance advisory groups. CINCMEAFSA also assumed operational control over the small naval task force stationed in the Red Sea-Persian Gulf area, which was known as the US Middle East Force.[114]

Among the questions he presented to the Joint Chiefs of Staff early in 1961, Secretary McNamara called for a study and a report on national military command and control systems. Subsequently acting on advice from the JCS, McNamara appointed Gen Earle E. Partridge, USAF, Retired, as the head of a National Command and Control Task Force and directed the force to make a very exhaustive study of such matters. Completed on 14 November 1961, the Partridge report was a highly classified document, but some of the conclusions in the report were subjected to public discussion. For example, to serve both cold and hot war requirements a National Military Command System had to be able to provide indications that a critical situation could occur; to be able to assess and analyze the dangers the situation could present; to develop a spectrum of military alternatives available to comprehend the situation; to arrive at decisions; and to be able to direct the execution of actions implicit in the situation. General Partridge's task force was reported to have recommended the establishment of a supreme United States military commander over the several unified and specified commands. Speaking in reference to the Partridge report, McNamara stated: "Among its recommendations, it did include a recommendation for a certain consolidation of control either within the Joint Chiefs of Staff or relating to the unified commands." He added that he was unwilling to consider this recommendation.[115]

To provide continuing study the Joint Command and Control Requirements Group was established in May 1962 under the Joint Chiefs of Staff but outside the Joint Staff. Early in the following October, Secretary McNamara issued a directive that established the concepts of operation of the National Military Command

System, including the National Military Command Center at the Pentagon, the Alternate National Military Command Center, the National Emergency Airborne Command Post, and the National Emergency Command Post Afloat, together with various survivable communications networks linking the command facilities, the unified and specified commands, and the military service headquarters. In the directive the director of operations (J-3) of the Joint Staff was responsible as the manager of the National Military Command Center, but the National Military Command Center was initially established outside the Joint Staff. Such a location was advantageous from the standpoint of personnel spaces, since the strength of the Joint Staff was legally established at 400 officers. In 1962, moreover, the Special Subcommittee on Defense Agencies of the House Committee on Armed Services had expressed a fear that the command and control system might be headed by an "assistant for operations" in the Department of Defense or a "director of operations" on a Joint Staff.[116]

The National Military Command System directive had not been fully implemented at the time of the Cuban crisis, but the National Military Command Center was in operation under the supervision of the director of the Joint Staff, and it was able to serve the national command authorities—the president and the secretary of defense. As a result of the experience during the Cuban crisis and of an additional exercise in February 1963 when American forces shadowed a Venezuelan ship that had been hijacked in the South Atlantic, the director of operations of the Joint Staff insisted that since he was responsible as the manager of the command and control system he had to exercise a right over the direction of the system's resources. Accordingly on 6 June 1963 the Joint Staff Operations Directorate (J-3) was reorganized to include the National Military Command Center (NMCC) under a deputy director for the National Military Command System. New Department of Defense directives confirmed the National Military Command Center as the Senior Military Command Center, established rules for interaction between key government agencies, and, as described by Brig Gen Paul W. Tibbets, who served as the first deputy director for the National Military Command System, "in general, indicated that all political/military matters would be directed to the NMCC where top level judgment could be exercised to determine actions to be taken."[117]

Although the scheduled completion of a fully automated National Military Command System promised by 1967 to permit top United States leaders to communicate with a frontline infantry commander or a tactical aircraft in flight in some overseas theater,[118] the command and control system did not provide for a unity of military command in Washington other than the president. The line of command over the unified and specified commands continued to run through the Joint Chiefs of Staff collectively to the secretary of defense and to the president. In March 1964 former Deputy Secretary of Defense Gilpatric offered an opinion that the Joint Chiefs of Staff should be taken out of the military line of command. "Too often, in critical conflict situations," he wrote, "the President and his other policy advisers are confronted with a fractured military position reflecting divergent service positions rather than differing military judgments."[119] Since there was no existing law that required the Joint Chiefs to be brought into the line of authority over tactical operations, Gilpatric proposed that the chain of command over military operations could extend down from the president through the secretary of defense and the chairman of the Joint Chiefs of Staff to the commanders of the unified and specified commands. He urged:

> If the United States is to hold or regain initiative in international security affairs, and if its military establishment is to be responsive to the need for almost split-second reaction in crisis situations, the President and his assistants must be able to receive, clearly and speedily, miliary advice of a range and depth that will not always be forthcoming under the present J.C.S. system.[120]

Changing Air Force Views on Defense Unification

In hearty agreement with President Eisenhower's statement that the day of separate ground, sea, and air warfare was gone forever, General White and other Air Force leaders had given strong support for the Defense Reorganization Act of 1958. General White believed that transcendant aerospace weapon systems had rendered the old land, sea, and air modes of operations an invalid determinant for service roles and missions. Committed traditionally to a doctrine of unity of command, the Air Force leaders appeared to have assumed that a centralization of defense authority would provide unity of command. Viewed in retrospect, the Air Force leaders of the late 1950s wanted a national defense reorganization along the lines that Secretary of War Elihu Root had instituted in the United States Army in 1903. At that time the General Staff Act had provided for an Army chief of staff to the president, who, acting under the direction of the president or the secretary of war and with the assistance of the War Department General Staff, had supervision not only of all troops of the line but also of the special staff and supply departments that had formerly reported directly to the secretary of war. The Root organization had ended the separate status of the great administrative departments, whose activities outside the line of military command had almost brought chaos to the Army during the Spanish-American War.[121] As the McNamara reorganization of the Department of Defense progressed, Air Force thinkers began to discover that centralization of defense authority would not necessarily provide the unity of command they had desired.

Some change in Air Force attitudes toward national defense organization became apparent when Secretary Zuckert and General LeMay took over Air Force leadership in 1961. "Our problem . . . as I see it," LeMay stated in September 1961, "is that we must maintain our unity of mission and unity as an organization as we approach our operational tasks in space."[122] Zuckert observed in February 1962, "We do have a sufficiently focused area of activity to keep the Air Force a cohesive organization with a clearly apparent personality and spirit."[123] In the summer of

1961 when he established the Defense Supply Agency (DSA), Secretary McNamara stated that he would continue to look to the military departments for management of their respective weapon systems. Air Force spokesmen were nevertheless troubled that the DSA was established outside the line of military command and was additionally authorized to make studies as to whether it should assume responsibilities over the common procurement and distribution of aeronautical spare parts, chemical supplies, and industrial production equipment. During hearings before the Special Subcommittee on Defense Agencies of the House Armed Services Committee in mid-1962, Gen Frederic H. Smith, Jr., speaking as Air Force vice chief of staff, strongly opposed any addition of authority that would result in the DSA becoming "a fourth service of supply or a Ministry of Supply."[124] As a result of these hearings, the Special Subcommittee on Defense Agencies found that "the new Department of Defense agencies, although perhaps conceived as coordinating agencies, are in fact operational and directional in nature."[125] The subcommittee warned that "in time of emergencies requiring flexibility, responsiveness, and speedy resolution of issues at hand, the overcentralized system will be largely ineffectual, perhaps to the point of endangering our national security."[126] In an examination of defense organization in the years from 1898 to 1960, the Concepts Division of Air University's Aerospace Studies Institute concluded in May 1963 that the establishment of the Defense Communications Agency had introduced a possible trend toward the establishment of defense agencies (such as the Defense Supply Agency). These agencies would be composed of functional service elements placed outside fixed military channels and directly responsible to the secretary of defense. If located outside of military channels, these defense agencies would bear a striking resemblance to the independent War Department bureaus that had existed prior to the Root reorganization of 1903.[127]

At the same time that the independent defense agencies were being examined, other studies noted the concentration of defense authority within the Office of the Secretary of Defense. Even though General White had been an outspoken proponent of armed service unification, he questioned in an article published on 11 July 1962 what he described as a concentration of general staff authority in the civilian staff of the Office of the Secretary of Defense.[128] After its investigations, the Special Subcommittee on Defense Agencies concluded on 13 August 1962 that, despite the fact that Congress had repeatedly opposed merger of the military services and the establishment of a single chief of staff and general staff, "the groundwork is being laid for the very thing that Congress has repeatedly expressed concern about and attempted to prevent." The subcommittee was "convinced of the rapid growth of a system which moves the decision making process higher and higher on the scale of centralized authority and into the hands of a few people."[129] It warned of the adverse effect of such centralization of authority in the civilian staff at the Office of the Secretary of Defense:

> As time goes on, with all decisions being made at the Secretary of Defense level, lower echelons will develop a "no decision" or indecisive philosophy.... Those entrusted to make decisions with the accompanying authority and responsibility will increasingly turn to the next higher authority until ultimately all decisions, large and small, will be crowding in at the top and awaiting resolution.... Obviously such a system is ponderous and slow and unresponsive to the immediate needs of subordinate levels.[130]

Except for expressing their opposition to any action which might establish a fourth service for supply or a ministry of supply, the Joint Chiefs of Staff did not discuss the evolving pattern of defense management when they appeared before the House Subcommittee on Defense Agencies during the summer of 1962.[131] When asked in February 1963 whether military officers wielded sufficient influence in the establishment of military policy, General Taylor responded:

> I would say that we military people have ample opportunity to exert influence on military policy. The question is, are we persuasive enough, are we able to bring forward a case that carries conviction? I always complain to my own staff and to all the staffs I have ever had, that we have lots of brave soldiers, sailors, and airmen, but too few men who can write a good paper, or properly present the message orally or in writing.... The serious answer... is that we have ample opportunity to influence policy. We in the Joint Chiefs of Staff always are queried as a body, and ... I have often been queried as an individual. That does not mean necessarily our advice is always followed. Obviously it is not.[132]

Although he had kept silent earlier, General LeMay began to speak quite freely about the frustrations he felt as chief of staff of the Air Force and as a member of the Joint Chiefs of Staff in the early months of 1964. As a service chief, LeMay knew the difficulty of pushing a program through the secretary of the Air Force, the secretary of defense, the bureau of the budget, the president, and finally through the armed services committees and the appropriations committees of Congress.[133] LeMay also stated that the corporate Joint Chiefs did not play as fundamental a part as in the past in making major decisions on overall programs and policies. The five-year force projection, for example, had become the controlling factor in budgeting; to secure modifications in the five-year plan, the services presented program changes to the secretary of defense, who might or might not send them to the corporate Joint Chiefs for comment. The Navy's visual light-attack (VAL) aircraft program change incorporated in the fiscal year 1965 budget, for example, was not submitted to the Joint Chiefs, although LeMay considered that the program change was highly important and that the completion of the program would cost nearly $1.5 billion. Even when they were asked to make comments on program change proposals, the Joint Chiefs looked "at these items piecemeal" and said we [JCS] will "never have an opportunity to get together and look at everything we have done and say this is more money than we can afford, what is the order of priority of these things."[134] "We would like," LeMay said, "to take a look at the overall budget at the end, after we have approved these individual items as they come along to see what we have done, to establish some of priority, and try to get in balance."[135] LeMay considered cost-analysis to be "very useful to know exactly what you are getting and what you have to pay for it when you are proposing new weapons systems," but he was fearful of an analysis which "tends to put an emphasis on the cost differential rather than the performance differential."[136] "Generally speaking, particularly at the working level," LeMay concluded, "it is becoming more and more difficult to get experience and judgement ground into the solution of problems. We have to try to translate experience and judgement into cold hard facts to win a case. Sometimes this is very difficult to do."[137]

Early in his tenure of office Secretary Zuckert was willing to believe that the Air Force would have a cohesive mission for the future, and his continuing studies of the matter convinced him that the trend in weapons development would not end the requirement for the Air Force. To penetrate through the "technological shock" engendered by the development of missiles, Zuckert established Project Forecast in the spring of 1963. This project, conducted under the direction of General Schriever, sought to provide a blueprint of technological possibilities in the 1965–75 time period. Available by February 1964 but kept highly classified, the Project Forecast report represented "a new, hard look at the fundamentals of airpower employment."[138] Among other things, Project Forecast demonstrated that while technological possibilities for advanced weapon systems appeared relatively unlimited, the cost and complexity of all weapons had increased so much that there was no possibility that any military service could have everything it would like.[139] Relating the problem of weapon systems to defense organization in September 1964, Zuckert outlined three fundamental facts. There was "no indication that the weapons we now have or those which can be foreseen will destroy the identity of any of the three general categories of warfare—land, sea, and aerospace."[140] Although this was true, Zuckert believed that it was "almost impossible to conceive of substantial military action carried out by one service alone. Any war of the future will be a joint action. Hence we must deter or fight war jointly, as a thoroughly coordinated action, with all forces—aerospace, land, and sea—acting under unified control."[141] As a third considered judgment, he believed that "many of the weapons of war will continue to increase in complexity, sophistication, and cost. The proper allocation of defense resources will remain a central problem."[142]

As he assessed the relationship of military technology, national strategy, tactics, force levels, and doctrine to national defense organization in September 1964, Secretary Zuckert noted that the pattern of centralized national defense organization which had developed since 1947 was "working well" in the areas of planning, budgeting, and operational commands. "A loose confederation of forces such as we had seventeen years ago," he said, "simply is not adapted to the defense needs of the nation."[143] But when he responded to the rhetorical question: Should the United States go all the way to a single service? Zuckert stated an emphatic "No." The developing national defense organization had achieved centralized planning and operational control and a balance of forces appropriate to the threat without destroying the identities of the three services. Four reasons were paramount for maintaining separate departments of Army, Navy, and Air Force. There was a constantly increasing requirement for military professionalism. In an era of complex weapons, soldiers, sailors, and airmen could no longer easily move from one service to another or intelligently serve a single service. The separate services were needed to train professionals and funnel many of them upward to serve the unified commanders, Joint Chiefs of Staff, and the secretary of defense. Providing military equipment, military doctrine, and effective military forces for aerospace, land, and sea warfare was the task of the military departments. "If we did not have them," Zuckert said, "we would have to invent a substitute for the purpose."[144] Zuckert also noted that interservice competition — controlled enough to create positive contributions to national defense — "provides an effective system of checks and balances" and "assures that a full range of alternatives and new ideas will be examined before major decisions are taken." The individual services also were required to provide for efficient management. "Military administration, training, logistic support, and research and development," Zuckert asserted, "can be managed most efficiently on the basis of three military departments, each of which is relatively homogeneous in terms of the type of warfare on which it focuses. We should not disturb this arrangement."[145] Finally, there was the intangible element of esprit de corps which was at the heart of a true fighting force. "The people who operate and maintain SAC's weapons and the people of the Logistics Command who supply them," Zuckert pointed out, "are all in the same uniform. . . . They are part of a team and their working relations are quite different from the impersonal relations that might exist between loosely related organizations which worked for different bosses."[146]

In the summation of his address on national defense organization, Secretary Zuckert warned: "The purists in organization sometimes want to carry their work to extremes which appear logical on paper but which in practice may lose more than is gained."[147] He believed that the evolving organizational structure had centralized overall planning, budgeting, and operational control within the Office of the Secretary of Defense, but that it had decentralized the development and support of combat forces and the formulation of doctrine along environmental lines. Zuckert concluded:

> This careful weaving of functional unification and environmental decision permits both to be effectively exploited. . . . That which is wise, natural and efficient is not likely to disappear in the continuing process of evolving the best possible defense organization. The three separate military departments of Army, Navy (with its Marine Corps), and Air Force make an indispensable contribution to the defense of this nation and will continue to do so. I predict that they are here to stay.[148]

Where the Air Force had in the past customarily provided the strongest support for national defense unification, Secretary Zuckert's landmark address in September 1964 indicated that the Air Force was reevaluating the requirement for defense unification in the light of new ideas of technological possibilities and strategic requirements.

Air Force Organizational Adjustments to Defense Reorganization

Except for the establishment of the Air Research and Development Command in 1951, the internal organization of the Air Force in 1957–58 was markedly similar to the management structure set up in the immediate post-World War II years when the new Air Force was loosely federated with the Army and the Navy in the Department of Defense. The impact of the Soviet Sputnik and the Department of Defense reorganization of 1958 stimulated a ferment of introspective studies looking toward the internal reorganization of the Air Force. "We are standing at the crossroads of Air Force history," General Schriever exclaimed in one planning paper. "It would seem fortuitous indeed, if an organization conceived for 1950's problems were the best for changed needs of 1960–1970."[149]

With the accomplishment of the Department of Defense reorganization of 1958, the departments of Army, Navy, and Air Force lost command over military combat forces and were restricted to the principal task of creating combat-ready forces for employment by the unified commanders in the field. With only partial guidance from the Department of Defense, each of the military departments managed its internal reorganizations in a manner that represented necessary readjustments to the new defense organizational requirements and to projected trends in defense activity. The effectiveness of each service's internal organization would depend in a large measure upon the accuracy with which the services predicted future trends. Within the Air Force these estimates of future trends were manifested in the form of assumptions, and these assumptions were often more apparent from the statements of key individuals than from formal Air Force documents.

Air Force Reorganization of Doctrinal Pursuit

Reflecting the belief of its founding commander Gen Muir S. Fairchild that a university not only disseminated knowledge but also sought to develop knowledge through research, Air University from 1946 onward had been charged to study Air Force responsibilities for national security and to develop recommendations as to long-range Air Force objectives. Air University also was charged to prepare doctrinal manuals in fields of Air Force strategy, procedures, and techniques.[150] After an early incandescence in the early 1950s, the flame of research began to flicker at the Air University by 1956. In that year, Air War College students no longer were expected to contribute solutions to problems of Air Force and defense interest in their student theses.[151] When reductions in force and other manpower reductions had to be made within the command in the autumn of 1957, Air University commander ruled that cuts would not be made across the board but in research areas that did not support the educational mission. The manner in which the personnel reduction was accomplished left no doubt that the training mission of the Air University had a higher priority than research.[152] In the spring of 1958 Air University's Board of Visitors noted and criticized the fact that the Air Force appeared reluctant to assign sufficiently high-quality personnel to the Air War College's evaluation staff.[153]

At the same time the Air University was reducing its research capabilities, a group of officers in Headquarters Air Research and Development Command, under the leadership of Col Taylor Drysdale, was impressed with the conclusion that nothing was being done in the Air Force to develop the science of warfare, although billions of dollars were being spent each year on the research and development of weapon systems. Weapon systems were being conceived, developed, and produced without consideration of the manner in which they might or might not affect the enemy and without regard to the nature of the military influence they were expected to wage. The Rand Corporation, operations analysis functions, the Weapon Systems Evaluation Group, the Lincoln Laboratory, the Air University, and a host of other agencies were engaged in random and piecemeal studies, but "nowhere," Drysdale said, "is there a rational program for research and development of military science as a whole to learn the still unknown, fundamental principles of military power which, governing the outcome of real military actions, are at least important as the tools they call forth."[154] On 8 April 1957 Drysdale briefed Gen Thomas S. Power, who was then in command of the Air Research and Development Command, on this thinking and received instructions to form a study group, to make a survey of the military science function, and to prepare a development planning note describing a program for action. After five months' work, the Drysdale group completed an extended study that was summarized in a United States Air Force Directorate of Development Planning note published on 17 February 1958. This note proposed a gradual establishment of a military science research and development organization to include 1,621 military and professional persons by the end of fiscal year 1967.[155]

When briefed on the Drysdale study shortly after becoming Air Force vice chief of staff, General LeMay acknowledged that the objective was important and worth pursuing. He pointed out that studies of defense matters by outsiders and observers generally lacked utility, and he emphasized that the only men who could provide the product that Drysdale was seeking would be persons who bore the responsibility for military action and who understood the nature of combat and the price that might have to be paid for the achievement of a necessary military end.[156] At Air University, where he was completing a four-year tour as commandant of the Air Command and Staff College, Maj Gen Lloyd P. Hopwood proposed on 6 January 1958 that vigorous efforts ought to be made by Air University to provide "conceptual R&D" for the Air Force through the rejuvenation of an Air Force board-type function. Somewhat more cautiously, Maj Gen Robert F. Tate, the commander of the Air War College, pointed out that the Air Force had changed since Air University had been established. The Air Staff had been expanded, the major air commands had undertaken their own conceptual planning, and a large number of study groups in industry and civilian institutions were studying a wide range of Air Force problems. An Air University organizational study committee, nevertheless, recommended that the Air University create a warfare institute that would combine the talents still available in the Air University Research Studies Institute and the Air War College's evaluation staff.[157] Despite agreement that the Air University ought to invigorate its research organization, the Drysdale proposal for a military science research and development organization met a skeptical reception at Air University. One senior evaluation staff officer called it a "panacea" and suggested that the development planning note had "fallen into the trap of believing that properly qualified and organized people, with adequate resources, can eventually resolve the basically irresolvable conflicts we are faced with today in the field of national security."[158] Another note:

> Our studies on new weapon systems foreseen during the next 15 years have concluded that the present strategy of deterrence will continue essentially unchanged and so will the basic tasks of our military forces.... The key to changes in future strategy will rest with scientific development; for the nation which can gain a clear ascendancy over all the rest in adequate numbers of more highly effective weapons, whether offensive or defensive, will be in a position to dominate other nations in all forms of military conflict.[159]

In his discussion of the requirement for research and development in military sciences, Colonel Drysdale emphasized that the task of developing future knowledge could not be entrusted to Air Force planners or operations analysts, who were accustomed only to applying and analyzing already existing knowledge. "A truly professional approach to a profession," he argued, "must admit to the essential difference between the generation of knowledge and the application of that knowledge whether for the present actions or for the future actions."[160] Possibly because of this thinking, the Air Research and Development Command organized a small Science of Warfare Office under its deputy commander for research and development on 2 January 1958.[161] The Air Staff, however, equated conceptual research with long-range planning. An increasing recognition that the Air Force ought to look ahead led to the establishment of the deputy chief of staff, plans and programs, as a separate Air Staff office early in 1957. In an internal reorganization on 15 July 1958, the Office of the Deputy Director for Policy (formerly the Policy Division) was established under the director of plans. At the same time, the Air Doctrine Branch was established under the Air Policy Division.[162] Hearing of this action, General Tate was skeptical of the decision to place Air Doctrine Branch under the deputy director of policy, Directorate of Plans, since this placed Air Force doctrine in a subordinate position to Air Force policy. "The Air University," he urged, "is in a position to develop doctrine free from day to day policy considerations. This is as it should be and is a major reason for retaining the basic doctrinal responsibility within the Air University."[163]

At its establishment in July 1958 within the Air Staff, the Air Doctrine Branch was designated as the single point of reference for the review of basic air doctrine prepared at Air University and for operational doctrine prepared in the major air commands. For a time the Air Doctrine Branch merely attempted to keep current on Air Force doctrine, but changes caused by the implementation of the Defense Reorganization Act of 1958 indicated that the Air Doctrine Branch might be expected to perform an enlarged role. Under new defense directives, the Joint Chiefs of Staff were given responsibility for prescribing doctrine for the conduct of unified operations. Each of the Joint Chiefs, as a service chief, would have an input into unified doctrine, and the Air Force chief of staff would require close assistance and advice from the Air Staff to formulate his doctrinal input to Joint Chiefs of Staff discussion.[164] On 1 December 1958 the Air Force Directorate of Plans recommended that the Air Doctrine Branch be given the responsibility for preparing basic air doctrine. After lengthy discussions within the Air Staff, the Air Force announced on 6 March 1959 that responsibility for the preparation of Air Force basic doctrine would be retained at Headquarters USAF.[165] That same month, the Air Research and Development Command inactivated its Science of Warfare Office,[166] but the Air Staff wished Air University to revitalize its research activities by the establishment of an institute of strategy.[167] After studying the matter during the spring of 1959, Air University consolidated the Air War College's evaluation staff into the Research Studies Institute on 1 July. Even though the mission of the Research Studies Institute (subsequently renamed the Aerospace Studies Institute) was broadened to require it to function as a doctrinal center for developing sound concepts concerning elements of military influence and aerospace, it was expected to operate without increases in its relatively small staff.[168]

Air Force Systems Command/ Logistics Command Reorganization

Although the Air Staff did not ignore the problem of conceptual research in military science, the major interest of the Air Force was clearly centered on the development and procurement of advanced weapon systems. Established at the request of General White, the Ad Hoc Committee on Research and Development of the Air Force Scientific Advisory Board, chaired by H. Guyford Stever, prefaced its report of a survey of the Air Force research and development organization on 20 June 1958 with a broad statement of concept:

> In all of its activities the Air Force will continue to experience at a growing rate the impact of advancing technology. The research and development phases will enlarge and become of greater importance. Though in the past the Air Force has introduced major changes to adjust to this increasing role of research and development, it has not kept pace with the need.[169]

According to the division of responsibility specified in 1950–51, the Air Research and Development Command (ARDC) developed weapon systems and the Air Materiel Command (AMC) procured the developed systems and provided continuing logistical support for them as long as they remained in the operational inventory. To provide command coordination each major weapon system was managed by a weapon system project office, staffed jointly by ARDC and AMC personnel. To speed the development of ballistic missiles, the ARDC Ballistic Missiles Division and the AMC Ballistic Missile Center were located together in Inglewood-Los Angeles.[170] By melding together personnel and responsibilities in a concurrency concept, the Air Force was able to field operationally ready ballistic missiles in a much shorter time than would have been possible with a "fly-before-buy" concept. Other instances of expedited development were less satisfactory. The F-106 interceptor was put into procurement on the basis of a contractor's assurance that its missile and fire control system would be flyable in 1953. The missile and missile control system were not completed until 1956, and the F-106 weapon system, which was expected to be operational in 1954, did not enter the active force inventory until 1959.[171]

To keep pace with technological progress, the Air Force had superimposed weapon system management procedures on top of the existing Air Materiel Command and the Air Research and Development Command without inquiring whether some more sweeping reorganization might not be more appropriate. While the system was working, it appeared to be full of delays. Seeking some new thought on the matter, General White told Air Force Council on 30 April 1959 that the Air Force must abandon old step-by-step progressions in development and seek to make a "quantum jump" toward the best possible weapons for the future. This approach involved risk, for combat strength might be weakened while advanced weapon systems were under development, but White thought that the potential gain would be worth the risk.[172] To review policies and procedures for the management of weapon and support systems throughout their life cycles, General LeMay established a weapon systems study group on 29 May 1959. He named Gen S. E. Anderson, commander of the Air Materiel Command, as the group chairman and included General Schriever, commander of the Air Research and Development Command, and Maj Gen Mark E. Bradley, acting Air Force deputy chief of staff for materiel, as members of the group.[173] After studies had been made, the majority of the group favored a plan of organization offered by General Bradley at a meeting on 11 March 1960. In essence Bradley proposed that other AMC centers/ARDC divisions should be organized and should pattern their operations after those of the Ballistic Missile Center/Ballistic Missiles Division concept, thereby extending the dual-responsibility approach to aeronautical and electronics systems. He also proposed that scattered responsibilities for weapon systems in the Air Staff should be collected into joint program and project offices. General Anderson was unwilling to continue the "piecemeal, patchwork approach" and proposed to reintegrate the AMC and ARDC into one aerospace weapons command. General Schriever accepted the Bradley plan, but he thought it did not go far enough. He proposed a single operating agency for the acquisition phase — a weapon acquisition command — and an aerospace support command for logistical support.[174]

At a meeting in the Pentagon on 2 June 1960 General White heard arguments from Anderson and Schriever and provided new guidance to the Weapon Systems Study Group. He said that there would be no recombination of ARDC and AMC because this would be a step backward. Schriever's proposal also was unacceptable because any shift of procurement and production into the ARDC would dilute its efforts and hinder research and development. White generally accepted the Bradley plan, and he cautioned that organization of programs along with weapon system concept should be selective since not all systems were suited to expedited program development.[175] At its last meeting with General White on 16 August 1960, the group proposed and White endorsed the view that "the present functional organization of the Air Force and Air Staff is sound and best suited to the over-all Air Force management problem."[176] White also agreed that "product or weapon systems oriented management should be employed to integrate the functional activities of the Air Force."[177] General LeMay approved the report of the Weapon Systems Study Group on 30 August, and the new alignment began to be put into effect. To complete the parallel field organizations that already included the Ballistic Missile Center/Ballistic Missile Division on the West Coast and the Aeronautical Systems Center/Wright-Patterson Air Development Center at Dayton, Ohio, the Air Materiel Command activated an electronics systems center parallel to the Command and Control Development Division at Bedford, Massachusetts. In November 1950 General White announced that B-70, F/RF-105, Dyna-Soar, Skybolt, Atlas, Titan, Minuteman, Midas, Saint, Samos, SAC Control (465L), and the Air Weapon Control (412L) systems would be given expedited development.[178] To accomplish a completely functional organization, the Air Research and Development Command planned to divide its strength into four major divisions: one dedicated to ballistic missile and space systems in California; one dedicated to the development of aeronautical systems in Dayton; one dedicated to command and control systems at Bedford; and the fourth devoted to basic research in Washington. Integration of Air Force activities was to be attained by restructuring weapon system project offices into system program offices, which would have representatives of the ARDC, AMC, ATC, and the using command. These offices would remain in being as long as their weapon systems continued in the operating inventory: they would handle responsibilities for the weapon systems from inception to final disposition.[179]

Although the Air Force had determined that no major changes should be made in the organizational structure of the Air Materiel Command and the Air Research and Development Command, General Schriever was not entirely satisfied with the outcome of the Weapon Systems Study Group. For one thing, the two commands tended to compete with each other for technologically trained personnel as well

IDEAS, CONCEPTS, DOCTRINE

as skilled management people.[180] During the latter half of 1960, General White refused to accept Schriever's objections, but early in 1961 Schriever's proposals for reorganization began to look more logical. Shortly after the Kennedy administration took office, Deputy Secretary of Defense Gilpatric apparently indicated to Secretary Zuckert that the military mission in space might well be centered in the Air Force, provided this service would "put its house in order."[181] Gilpatric apparently believed that the Air Force could not handle the military space mission unless the machinery for performing research and development, tests, and procurement was centralized in one command.[182] Early in March Secretary McNamara called Zuckert and LeMay to his office and informed them that the major military responsibility for the space program would be assigned to the Air Force, and immediately thereafter Zuckert assembled White, Bradley, and Schriever to decide the basic outline of the reorganization that had to be made. It was now agreed that Schriever's recommendations to the Weapon Systems Study Group would be accepted, and that Schriever, who would be promoted to full general and given command of a new Air Force Systems Command, would also be given the responsibilities for activating ballistic missile sites. Secretary McNamara approved the proposals, and Zuckert negotiated an agreement with the secretary of the Army whereby the Army Corps of Engineers would make a general officer available for assignment as deputy commander for site activation in the Ballistic Systems Division.[183]

That the Air Materiel Command would be reorganized was not generally known at the Air Staff level until the plan for the reorganization was announced by Secretary McNamara on 17 March 1961. This announcement and official orders issued on 20 March provided that the Air Materiel Command and the Air Research and Development Command would be redesignated on 1 April 1961 as the Air Force Logistics Command and the Air Force Systems Command. The Research Division of the Air Research and Development Command was redesignated as the Office of Aerospace Research and assigned directly to Headquarters USAF, as a separate operating agency. The Air Force Systems Command took over the Air Materiel Command functions and personnel at the parallel operating locations and organized its forces into a Ballistic Missiles Systems Division, Space Systems Division, Aeronautical Systems Division, Electronic Systems Division, and a Foreign Technology Division. To complete its internal organization, the Air Force Systems Command subsequently established an Aerospace Medical Division at Brooks AFB, Texas, on 1 January 1962. Provisionally organized at Bolling AFB in April 1962, the Research and Technology Division was made permanent on 1 July 1962. The Aerospace Medical Division was intended to improve the military "interface" with NASA since it provided "one focal point in the Air Force for the bioastronautics, life sciences activity."[184] The Research and Technology Division provided centralized management for the Air Force Rocket Propulsion Laboratory at Edwards AFB, California, the Weapons Laboratory at Kirtland AFB, New Mexico, the Aero-Propulsion, Materials and Flight Propulsion

Laboratories at Wright-Patterson AFB, Ohio, and the Electromagnetics Laboratory at Griffiss AFB, New York. As its mission after the 1 July 1961 reorganization, the Air Force Logistics Command was charged with the operation and control of the worldwide logistics system for the support of the Air Force.[185]

In a press conference held on the afternoon of 17 March 1961, Secretary Zuckert explained that the Air Force Systems Command-Air Force Logistics Command reorganization was designed to improve management. "When you have a clear line of authority," he said, "you are going to have better management."[186] In a schematic diagram of the cycle of weapon system acquisition, principal responsibility for basic research lay in the Air Force Office of Aerospace Research; the Air Force Systems Command was responsible for development, procurement, and production; and the Air Force Logistics Command remained responsible for logistic support of operational systems, including spares and maintenance equipment.[187] Speaking of the climate of thinking that lay behind the reorganization, Gen R. J. Friedman said: "I think that the day of the short development period and long run production is over, and I think we are talking about practically — apart from basic and applied research — practically concurrent development."[188] To avoid misunderstanding, Zuckert emphasized that the Air Force had not been reorganized into a weapon systems structure, but he nevertheless demonstrated the manner in which the new structure would expedite all of the myriad actions involved in bringing the 12 systems that the Air Force had selected for expedited management decisions into operational use quickly.[189] In explanation of the establishment of the Air Force Systems Command, General White predicted that the action would

> provide more rapid decisions and accelerated actions on ballistic missile and other designated system programs . . . insure efficient, responsive management of the . . . space development mission . . . provide for the close integration and participation of the Army Corps of Engineers in the ballistic missile site activation task [and] provide for effective liaison and active participation by the Army, Navy, and the National Aeronautics and Space Administration in projects being developed for those agencies by the Air Force.[190]

As a follow-on to the field reorganization of the Air Force Systems Command and the Air Force Logistics Command, the major Air Staff offices of Headquarters USAF, were realigned effective on 1 July 1961. Under the old Air Staff organization, the deputy chief of staff for materiel and the deputy chief of staff for development had provided a parallel Air Staff organization to the Air Materiel Command and the Air Research and Development Command. Under the 1 July 1961 reorganization, however, the new deputy chief of staff for systems and logistics assumed responsibility for system development functions. The new deputy chief of staff for research and technology became the Air Force point of contact for the entire scientific community and was given staff cognizance over basic research and all applied research that was not a part of a system.[191] The top-level Air Staff reorganization, together with revised management procedures, sought to extend to all designated systems the same type of expeditious handling previously accorded to ballistic missile and space systems. On 25 July 1961 Zuckert established the Designated Systems Management Group as an expansion of the former Air Force Ballistic Missile and Space Committee. Chaired by the secretary and including the highest statutory civilian and military officials, this group assisted the secretary in discharging his responsibilities toward programs that were designated to be of highest priority. The former Weapons Board was redesignated as the Systems Review Board; headed by the director of operational requirements, the Systems Review Board continued to function as a cross-function board at the Air Staff directorate level, and it was provided with committees, panels, and working groups that were designed to monitor programs and ensure that all Air Staff elements received the information they required to guarantee adequate systems management. The Designated Systems Management Group and the Systems Review Board shared a common secretariat, thus ensuring continuity of action from all levels of the Air Staff through to the secretary of the Air Force.[192] The Office of Deputy Chief of Staff for Systems and Logistics included project offices for certain component and equipment programs that were of lesser scope than a system and for 11 designated systems offices (systos) which were designed to provide up-to-the-minute status data for all matters pertaining to individual specified systems. Systos provided the chairmen of the working groups of the Systems Review Board. Under the new management concept there was to be no intermediate-level review or disapproval authority between responsible Air Force Systems Command system program directors in the field and the Designated Systems Management Group/Systems Review Board in the Pentagon. Employing a "red-line" technique, the system program directors of designated systems were able, in the words of General Schriever, "to go quickly to the top for fast decisions on their programs."[193] Schriever further explained: "Under 'Red Line' procedures a Director goes to the Air Staff and the Secretary of Defense. Thus when a matter demands immediate attention, the Director can present it to the decision-maker in the course of a single day."[194]

The organization of the Air Force Systems Command and the new system management concept were expected to provide an environment wherein quantum jumps in technology could be quickly translated into operational weapon systems by concurrency programming. Based on his experience with ballistic missiles, Schriever was completely convinced of the value of concurrency. "If you find that you have a fundamentally sound weapon," he said in 1959, "you actually save money by [using] this technique because you do not stretch out the program so long. With time as important as it is in our day and age of thermonuclear weapons and ballistic missiles, I see no other choice but to do our jobs in this manner."[195] The establishment of the designated system management procedures in 1961, Schriever said, was "based on the premise that streamlined channels, as originally provided for in the ballistic missile program, are sound in principle and can be applied to many important programs in today's environment."[196] General Schriever's belief in the concurrency concept and in centralized management was not completely shared by some Air Force leaders. Early in 1961 Lt Gen Roscoe C. Wilson, who would soon retire from his post as deputy chief of staff for research and technology, suggested:

> We have always felt in the Air Force that the real genius lay among the people of the United States at large and just could not be cooped up in any bureaucracy at all, and all of our efforts have been aimed at reaching out to these people rather than trying to pull them in to us.[197]

In a private interview just prior to his retirement, Wilson described the concurrency concept as "useful but very wasteful."[198] He thought that a service could stand the cost of one or two concurrency programs, but the Air Force had far more programs under way than it would be able to afford. Wilson further predicted that the new red-line management procedures would fail because too much responsibility was being concentrated at the top of the management structure.[199] Speaking as director of defense research and engineering, Dr Harold Brown also pointed out that excessive concurrency could delay rather than hasten the operational availability of a weapon system. "Premature commitment of subsystems before you know how they will interact with everything else and, indeed, before you have the subsystem worked out, can produce an actual delay," Brown maintained.[200]

During 1961–62 the Department of Defense severely reduced the number of concurrent development programs which the Air Force was attempting to maintain, chiefly because the Air Force was unable to show a proper interaction requirement for the systems in a future environment. By the winter of 1962–63, moveover, General Schriever frankly admitted that the red-line management review concept between the Air Staff and the responsible system program offices had not worked very well. The full effect of the procedure was to force the management of programs in greater and greater detail up into the Air Staff and the Department of Defense. The recommendations made by the system programs offices and systos dealt with individual problems and lacked total program relationships when viewed in terms of the whole Air Force program. The number and types of reviews at levels above the Air Force Systems Command increased greatly, and these reviews necessarily involved complex technical evaluations as well as functional considerations. "Thus," Schriever wrote, "the attempt to eliminate levels of review has actually resulted in an increase in detailed data required at the top and a decrease – in the name of urgency – in the quality of the review."[201] From this experience Schriever drew the basic lesson that the "unique short-circuit management techniques and administrative procedures" that had worked for programs involving "extreme national urgency or risk" could not "be extended beyond a relatively few programs without some deleterious effect on the normal management structure and on the portion of the system program that does not fall within the highest priority category."[202] To add more and more systems to a specialized management list merely diluted the amount of special management emphasis that might be applied in priority areas and degraded the normal management emphasis available for lesser priority systems.[203]

During the summer of 1962, following the retirement of Gen Frederic H. Smith, Jr., General LeMay brought Gen William F. McKee from his assignment as commander of the Air Force Logistics Command and named him Air Force vice commander. Early in the 1950s McKee had provided guidance for the reorganization of the Air Staff, and his first task as Air Force vice commander was to superintend a major realignment of the Air Staff. One objective of the reorganization was to comply with Secretary McNamara's directive that headquarters staffs be reduced and management should be decentralized. Another objective provided by Secretary Zuckert was to "increase responsiveness to the stringent demands of modern 'command and control'."[204] As announced on 1 February 1963 the new Air Staff organization included the deputy chief of staff, plans and operations, as a consolidation of the former deputy chief of staff for plans and programs, and the Directorate of Operations from the now-disestablished deputy chief of staff, programs and requirements, included elements from the former deputy chief of staff for operations. A new deputy chief of staff, program and requirements, included elements from the former deputy chief of staff for operations, such as the Directorate of Operational Requirements and a new Directorate of Aerospace Programs. The functions of the deputy chief of staff, systems and logistics, and the deputy chief of staff, research and development, were made to parallel the field organization of the Air Force Logistics Command and the Air Force Systems Command. The deputy chief of staff, systems and logistics, generally would be concerned with production: its former Directorate of Systems Acquisition and Directorate of Systems Services and the 12 designated systems offices were combined into a Directorate of Production. Concurrent with the elimination of the systems offices, the Air Force Systems Command took over the responsibility of providing technical expertise and systems advocacy before the Air Staff and the Office of the Secretary of Defense. Within the Office of the Chief of Staff, the Air Force Council remained as the senior organ for study and recommendation. The Designated Systems Management Group also continued in being, but other boards, including the Systems Review Board, were combined into a new Air Staff Board. Headed by the director of operational requirements, the Air Staff Board was organized into two committees—one on force structure and the other on program review—and eight working panels. The Air Force Council and the Air Staff Board were charged to make recommendations to speed decisions: they did not make decisions.[205]

"What it amounts to," said Secretary Zuckert in reference to the Air Staff reorganization of 1 February 1963, "is we're learning to go to the doctor before we really get sick."[206] The new organization for systems research and development sought to correct the difficulties that had arisen from the July 1961 organization. Although the Designated Systems Management Group remained in being, the Air Force reevaluated its list of designated systems to ensure that only a minimum number of highly important projects would be accorded special management procedures.[207] Lt Gen James Ferguson, Air Force deputy chief of staff for research and development, conceived his responsibilities to be "those related to policy, to broad general direction, to major programing. . . . We identify what needs to be done, we get the work started, issue the instructions to the field, we review what is done, we sponsor it to the Department of Defense, we issue policy guidance."[208] Within the Air Force Systems Command, General Schriever sought to make program study and review meaningful at every echelon. Thus the project level — laboratory or system project office — was to be recognized as the last word technically within the command. The project level, however, could not evaluate the relative importance of individual projects in a whole Air Force program. This evaluation had to be the contribution of Headquarters Air Force Systems Command, employed collectively as a central command review group on a continuing basis, since it was the only agency with a broad enough knowledge of the entire command program to evaluate new proposals or changes in existing proposals. To strengthen functional review, Schriever organized an Air Force Systems Command Council — comparable to the Air Force Council — and charged it to maintain a review of the research and development programs recommended to the Air Staff. "These actions," Schriever believed, "promise to bring a significant improvement in the management capability that is the pacing element in achieving technological superiority."[209]

Continued Thinking about Air Doctrine

Whether aerospace power was to be known as "military science" or "doctrine" the task of rationalizing and enunciating the fundamental beliefs that were to underlie its development, deployment, and employment in peace or war did not appear to progress well following the assumption of the mission by the Air Force deputy chief of staff for plans and programs on 6 March 1959. Located under the Aerospace Policy Division of the Plans Directorate, the Doctrine Branch initially attempted to maintain in its possession a current statement of Air Force basic doctrine. It sought to keep a working draft of Air Force Manual (AFM) 1-2, *United States Air Force Basic Doctrine*, current by revising portions of the 1955 manual that had been affected by the development of new weapons and by the Defense Reorganization Act of 1958. As previously noted, a revised edition of AFM 1-2 was issued on 1 December 1959, but the revisions consisted principally of changes of terminology rather than of substance. One of the major functions of the Aerospace Policy Division was to provide Air Force "positions" on subjects of defense interest, and many of these position papers became the basis of speeches and statements by Air Force leaders. Published by the Secretary of the Air Force Office of Information, the *Air Force Information Policy Letter for Commanders* and the monthly *Supplement to the Information Policy Letter for Commanders* contained excerpts or full texts of statements by national leaders on matters of special interest and value to Air Force personnel. In September 1961, the Air Force directed that the *Policy Letter* "provides concepts, doctrine, facts, references, and suggestions for all Air Force commanders and their staffs in meeting their responsibility to advance understanding inside and outside the Air Force."[210] In the aftermath of the Air Staff reorganization of 1 July 1961, an internal reorganization within the Office of the Deputy Chief of Staff for Plans and Programs made Brig Gen Jerry D. Page the deputy director of plans for aerospace plans and established the Aerospace Doctrine Division and the Long-Range Plans Division under him.[211]

In the autumn of 1961 it became evident to General LeMay that even knowledgeable persons were no longer sure of what the Air Force stood for in the way of concepts and doctrine. Attempting to clear up some of the confusion, LeMay asserted: "I think we have been consistent in our concepts since the formation for the GHQ Air Force in 1935. Our basic doctrine has remained generally unchanged since that time."[212] At least by implication, LeMay endorsed extant statements of Air Force doctrine and stated that the Air Force must "act with vision and daring to exploit technology to achieve distinct strategic advantages."[213] In an address in February 1962, however, General Page attempted to place science and technology in perspective with strategy.

> Although science is a search for new knowledge and is essentially unpredictable, technology is another story; it goes essentially where it is directed to go. . . . For the future the military planner must spend more time applying his professional judgment to determine what is needed from technology for meaningful improvements in strategy, and less time listening to predictions of ways in which strategy must be influenced by hypothetical trends in technology.[214]

In the course of the revolution in national military strategy that took place during 1961–62, the Air Force found it very difficult to justify many of its forward-looking weapon systems because of its failure in predicting the future operational environment in which the weapon systems would have to be employed. At Air University in April 1963, the Board of Visitors of Air University recommended that, both for instructional and planning purposes as well as for the benefit of the total national defense effort, there was "a need for clear, long-range thinking on such matters as doctrine and the role of the Air Force and its programs in relationship to other defense agencies."[215] In the Pentagon, after some conversations with General Page, Maj Gen Dale O. Smith prepared and submitted to General McKee on 15 April 1963 a scathing indictment of Air Force failures to keep its doctrine dynamic. "The deplorable condition of aerospace power today," Smith wrote, "is to a large extent the result of allowing Air Force doctrine to stagnate and become inapplicable to modern conditions." Smith urged that the Air Force must devote substantial resources to "in-service, blue-suit, research on matters of Air Force doctrine."[216] "The idea of letting our doctrine drift from the whim of one operational leader to another, or from one *ad hoc* measure to the next," he warned, "will never provide us with the comprehensive, dynamic understandable, and salable doctrine necessary to save the Air Force."[217] Smith pointed out that the Army, through intellectual activity and organizational structure, had adapted its mission and capabilities to changing national strategy in the years after 1954. "The Army," he noted, "suffered by the front-running Air Force doctrine of massive retaliation during the early 1950s, yet they have recovered in less than a decade."[218] The Air Force, on the other hand, had become a victim "of 'hardening of the categories' by avoiding full consideration of national military doctrine, national and foreign policy, as well as arms control philosophies," and had not "appropriately related or influenced developments in these fields to pure Air Force doctrine nor anticipated their impact."[219]

Challenges of Army Doctrinal Development

Although General Smith possibly overemphasized the role of the Army in the changing national military strategy, it was nonetheless true that the Army had built a visualizing, planning, testing, and developmental organization that was extremely productive of new concepts for the employment of ground forces in a future military environment. In the immediate post-World War II years, Generals Eisenhower and Bradley had been hesitant to authorize the reopening of an Army war college because they believed that the National War College could better serve a purpose of unifying military thought. In January 1950, however, Gen J. Lawton Collins decided to reopen the Army War College, and, after a first year at Fort Leavenworth, Kansas, the senior institution relocated its permanent home at Carlisle Barracks, Pennsylvania.[220] The Army War College sought to prepare Army officers with a knowledge of the capabilities and limitations of their own service. Although a consideration of joint operations was included, primary emphasis in the curriculum was placed on Army problems associated with military doctrine, national strategy, and supporting military programs.[221] The Army Command and Staff College at Fort Leavenworth continued to be a principal center for the formulation of Army doctrine,[222] but reportedly because of the recommendation of Dean Rusk, who was then serving as the chairman of the Army War College's Board of Visitors, the Army created an advanced study group at Carlisle Barracks in 1954. This group apparently received strong support from its parent service, and it ultimately propounded many of the basic concepts of the strategy of flexible response. "It was here at the Army War College," commented Brig Gen Noel F. Parrish, director of the Air University Research Studies Institute, "that the Army concentrated its new emphasis on brains and foresight, while the Air Force emphasized the 'big operator'."[223]

During the 1950s the Army found itself in almost the same situation of adversity that the Army Air Corps had known in the 1930s, and in a pattern of action remarkably parallel to those earlier days, Army thinkers at Fort Leavenworth and Carlisle Barracks funneled new ideas and concepts up through the Continental Army Command to the Department of the Army. The new ideas and concepts were designed to provide an understanding of the role of warfare in a land environment.

While the Army actively challenged existing doctrine, the Air Force found itself increasingly defending the old doctrines that had been proven in World War II.

Many of the Army proposals for change in air-ground doctrines related to a basic contention that the principle of unity of command demanded that local ground commanders should have command control over the air units that supported them.[224] To guarantee adequate air support, the Army stated a requirement that the Air Force should provide approximately two tactical reconnaissance wings for each field army and one wing of tactical fighter aircraft for each army division committed to combat. It further stipulated that close-support fighter wings should be under the control of division commanders in order that they would be immediately responsive to ground requirements. Arguing from past experience, the Air Force urged that the national economy could not support duplicative and specialized air units and that the centralized control of tactical air units under an air commander was vital to a proper accomplishment of a theater commander's mission. The Air Force also noted that its tactical air units had to be prepared to support both United States ground forces and the friendly foreign forces in the North Atlantic and Southeast Asia Treaty Organizations.[225]

Another point in controversy throughout the 1950s was the Army's belief that the advancing speeds of tactical fighter aircraft would prevent Air Force pilots from accomplishing effective close-support missions. "The Army recommends," General Lemnitzer stated in 1960, "the development of an inexpensive tactical fighter capable of operating off semi-improved fields. This aircraft should be specifically designed for accomplishment of the close support mission."[226] In the early 1950s, Air Force leaders remembered the fate of the Nazi Stuka close-support aircraft and opposed the development of a vulnerable single-purpose plane that would have little expectation of defending itself in the air. By 1956–57, however, the Air Force position showed some signs of change as Gen Lauris Norstad, thinking as supreme commander Europe, foresaw a requirement for a relatively inexpensive, light-weight, easily maintained tactical strike aircraft that could operate from short, relatively unprepared runways. As a result of studies conducted by NATO's advisory group for aeronautical research and development (AGARD), Fiat of Italy designed and built the G.91, a lightweight strike and reconnaissance aircraft. When it became available in 1959, the G.91's price of approximately $300,000 appealed to the smaller NATO nations.[227] Both in response to Norstad's requirement and in the belief that a less expensive aircraft might be obtained for military assistance pact procurement, the Air Force expressed substantial interest in 1957 in the Northrop Aviation Corporation's proposal to develop a lightweight tactical fighter from its T-38 jet trainer. This plane failed in key competitions in 1958–59, when the F-104 became the new standard fighter for the Netherlands, Norway, Japan, Canada, and West Germany, but the Air Force nevertheless awarded Northrop a contract for the development of three N-156 aircraft. In April 1962 the Air Force would place substantial orders for this plane, now designated as the F-5, for service as a replacement fighter in the inventories of many military assistance pact nations. The F-5 was retrogressive in speed and altitude capabilities, but it promised advantages in range and maneuverability and had cost-effectiveness advantages for nations with fewer resources than the United States.[228]

To settle the lingering controversy over the type of close-support fighter that the Air Force would expect to possess in the future, General White proposed to Gen George H. Decker in January 1960 that the Army could have the decisive voice in the selection of interim modernization aircraft for 11 squadrons that were to be kept in the Air Force inventory for the special purpose of supporting ground forces. In mid-April at Nellis AFB, senior Army and Air Force officers viewed all currently inventoried planes that appeared suitable for selection as an interim close-support plane. After a study of the matter, General Decker decided that he did not wish to make the choice of the aircraft that would be employed for close support. The Army would instead prefer to express its requirements for tactical support in terms of the type of support to be provided rather than in terms of the specifics of the delivery vehicles.[229] As has been seen, Gen Earle G. Wheeler later agreed with the prevailing Air Force position that Air Force tactical fighters ought to be high-performance planes that would perform all tactical air warfare missions with a high degree of versatility.

Possibly because the subject involved a projection of developing surface-to-air missile weapon systems into a future operational environment, the Army and the Air Force had more difficulty arriving at procedures for the control of the air over an overseas battle area. Early in the 1950s, the Army and Air Force operated in accordance with the Vandenberg-Collins agreement which provided that an Air Force air defense commander in an overseas combat zone would exercise operational control over antiaircraft artillery "insofar as engagement and disengagement of fire is concerned."[230] Based on its interpretation of Secretary Wilson's roles and missions memorandum of November 1956, however, the Continental Army Command asserted in 1957 that an Army field commander would be solely responsible for the air defense of his combat area and would not only control all air defense units but would also regulate all air operations through the air space above his combat area.[231] The Army believed that surface-to-air missiles would eventually become so effective that it would be able positively to control the air space over its ground armies. Unable to arrive at any mutually acceptable agreement, the Tactical Air Command and the Continental Army Command ultimately noted that the unified commanders in Europe and in the Pacific had already effected command control arrangements for battle area air space in their theaters. In the summer of 1960 the two commands began to employ these theater command control arrangements in their joint maneuvers.[232] After months of study Generals LeMay and Decker signed a statement of agreement on a doctrine for overseas area air defense on 12 July 1962. This agreement accepted the basic principle that a coordinated and integrated air defense system under a single commander would be essential to successful theater operations and that this single commander would be expected to ensure that the mix of weapon systems available to him would be effectively organized and employed. A unified theater commander normally would appoint his air component commander as the area air defense commander, but where another service contributed a significant portion of the air defense weapons, a senior officer from that service would be appointed to serve as deputy in air defense matters to the area air defense commander. All commanders were to ensure that surface-to-air missiles, manned interceptors, and command and control systems were integrated into a single air defense system. Since the LeMay-Decker agreement was not officially promulgated as joint doctrine, it affected Army and Air Force relationships but was not mandatory upon theater commanders.[233]

At the same time that the Army maintained an active interest in the air support that it would obtain from the Air Force, Army thinkers also put together a visionary plan to increase the Army's ground mobility by the employment of organic Army aviation. The concept was first publicized in an article published by Gen James M. Gavin in April 1954 under the title "Cavalry, and I Don't Mean Horses."[234] Gavin asserted that the Army should develop helicopter-borne troop units that could operate in old-fashioned cavalry missions.[235] Another Army aviation enthusiast, Maj Gen Hamilton H. Howze, expanded Army requirements for organic aviation during his period of service as director of Army Aviation. In May 1956 Howze emphasized that the Army required simple and rugged aircraft capable of providing observation, lifting troop units within the combat zone, performing cargo lift, serving liaison and communications purposes, and evacuating casualties from frontline positions. He also envisioned that Army units equipped with helicopters would perform reconnaissance, screening, security of open flanks, seizure of critical areas, pursuit, and limited-exploitation missions.[236] To Army planners the prospects of a nuclear battlefield—where troop units would be widely dispersed and targets would be fleeting and elusive—dictated a clear requirement for air cavalry units that would be able to cover advance, flanking, or rearguard actions; to control or deny terrain that was remote or inaccessible to ground vehicles; to secure areas against enemy airborne, guerrilla, or infiltrating units; and to cross or enter areas of nuclear contamination. "Army aerial vehicles, far more mobile than surface transport," General Lemnitzer observed, "provide the best means of accomplishing these reconnaissance missions."[237]

As it was issued in November 1956 Secretary Wilson's roles and missions directive appeared at first to pose a check to the development of the visionary plans for Army aviation. The directive limited fixed-wing Army planes to an empty weight of 5,000 pounds and Army rotary-wing aircraft to an empty weight of 20,000 pounds. Although the directive authorized the Army to develop a limited-airlift capability, it stipulated:

> Provision of this limited airlift capability will apply only to small combat units and limited quantities of material to improve local mobility, and not to the provision of an airlift

capability sufficient for large-scale movement to sizeable Army combat units which would infringe on the mission of the Air Force.[238]

In the directive Wilson promised to make specific exceptions to the weight limits placed on Army aviation after a consideration of Army requirements and the capabilities of the other services to meet them. Almost immediately he authorized the Army to procure five de Havilland DHC-4 Twin Otter aircraft for test and evaluation. Subsequently, the Office of the Secretary of Defense permitted the Army to procure limited numbers of 15,000-pound Caribou transport planes and 9,000-pound Mohawk turboprop observation aircraft. Despite these exceptions, General Lemnitzer was opposed to any weight limitations on Army aircraft. He said:

> The Army does not consider it advisable or desirable to have weight limitations imposed on any Army aircraft.... Despite the fact that two exceptions to the aircraft have been authorized by the Secretary of Defense ... the weight limitations have inhibited the thinking of Army planners and the initiative of the aircraft industry to produce new aircraft for the Army.[239]

In the late 1950s the Army began tests of the basic air cavalry concept at Fort Stewart, Georgia, where it organized an aerial reconnaissance and security troop. This troop employed 16 observation helicopters and 11 larger helicopters, some of which were armed with machine guns and rockets. Discovery of the enemy was said to be the primary function of the air cavalry; it was not described as an organization that would engage in a sustained firefight.[240] Other Army spokesmen developed more ambitious concepts. Maj Gen Robert J. Wood, deputy chief of staff of Army research and development, stated in 1958: "We have to be able to move over the battlefield and to reconnoiter with what our sky troopers now call 'zero foot pressure' on the terrain, which means moving in the nap of the earth just above the battlefield."[241] In the scenario for an exercise prepared by the Continental Army Command for cooperative play with the Tactical Air Command in 1960, Army officers visualized a helicopter-mounted airborne assault of six battle groups into an area 30 miles beyond the forward edge of the battle area. As commander of the Tactical Air Command, Gen F. F. Everest had difficulty conceiving that the movement of six airborne battle groups could be considered a small-unit action, and he thought that such an operation would clearly duplicate the Air Force's assigned responsibility for airborne assault operations. Rather than to allow doctrinal differences to interfere with training, however, the Tactical Air Command participated in the planned maneuver.[242]

When President Kennedy took office in January 1961, the Army began to find a favorable climate of opinion for effecting the far-reaching organizational and operational concepts that had been maturing during the 1950s. President Kennedy spoke of a need for reorganizing and modernizing the Army, for improving the Army's tactical mobility in any environment, and for improving the national ability to deal with guerrilla forces, insurrections, and subversion in emerging free nations

IDEAS, CONCEPTS, DOCTRINE

of the world. Secretary McNamara stated that the Department of Defense would not apply weight limitations to the development of Army aircraft, and the Department of Defense program-package budgeting procedure in effect minimized the old roles and missions and invited the services to bid against each other in terms of cost-effectiveness comparisons for the performance of outlined military tasks.[243] In a very long range strategic forecast issued on 21 February 1961, the Army's Strategic Studies Group at Carlisle Barracks posed an optimistic outlook for the Army:

> Although service roles and missions will change with the advent of a greater degree of centralization at Department of Defense level vital responsibilities will remain with the services. . . . The Army will be responsible for developing doctrine and for providing forces and weapons required for successful conduct of warfare in the land environment plus that portion of the air and water space adjacent to the land in which its forces and weapons will be employed.[244]

Beginnings of an Army Aviation Challenge

During the 1950s the Tactical Air Command and the Continental Army Command had provided an interface for the development of air-ground doctrine, and the Army and Air Force chose to continue the relationship as they established counterinsurgency programs. During the spring of 1961 the Army raised the status of its Special Warfare Center at Fort Bragg, North Carolina, and substantially increased the strength of its special forces. In April 1961 the Tactical Air Command established the 4400th Combat Application Crew Training at Eglin AFB. The 4400th was soon redesignated 1st Air Commando Wing and given the twofold mission of furnishing the air power needed to support US Army Special Forces and of training foreign air forces for the conduct of special air warfare operations. In April 1962 the Tactical Air Command expanded the Eglin AFB establishment into the Air Force Special Air Warfare Center (SAWC) under the command of Brig Gen Gilbert L. Pritchard. SAWC included the 1st Air Commando Wing and the 1st Combat Applications Group, the latter organization being designed to provide a quick response to field requirements and to develop doctrine, tactics, techniques, and equipment required in the field on short notice. In July 1962 the Air University also introduced a two-week course on counterinsurgency, which was available to officers assigned to foreign missions and military assistance advisory groups, and to select staff and operational personnel.[245]

Although the essential relationships of TAC and CAC were continued in the counterinsurgency field, the establishment of the United States Strike Command (STRICOM) in the autumn of 1961 promised to make marked changes in the old relationships. Under its terms of reference, CINCSTRIKE was authorized to develop joint doctrine for the employment of the forces assigned to him. CINCSTRIKE was to be guided by the provisions of the Unified Action Armed Forces publication, but in the interest of developing rapid reaction capabilities and joint-striking power he was authorized to develop new ideas and concepts, to test and prove them in the field, and to recommend them to the Joint Chiefs of Staff for issuance as revisions or additions to the Unified Action Armed Forces papers. In this endeavor, CINCSTRIKE was cautioned to give careful consideration to the specific doctrinal requirements of the unified commands to which STRICOM augmentation forces might be committed.[246] As soon as STRICOM became operational, the Office of Defense General Counsel recommended to Secretary McNamara on 19 March 1962 that a STRICOM Combat Developments Test Center should be established to conduct select combat developments study projects and materiel test and evaluation projects, which would be of joint concern and which would be relevant to the organization, equipment, and concepts of employment of land-air forces. The recommendation provided that the scope of Combat Developments Test Center projects would

> include deployment of forces to theaters of operation and employment of forces under the entire range of possible conditions, namely from large-scale operations of regular forces, both nuclear and nonnuclear, on the one hand, to counter guerilla operations, support of indigenous forces in counterinsurgency operations, and other cold war actions on the other.[247]

When asked about this recommendation in June 1962, Secretary McNamara showed no intention of establishing such a combat developments test center, at least not in the near future. He said in regard to STRICOM:

> I wouldn't believe it wise to assign to that command any responsibility for the tactical doctrine or development that could properly be handled by one of the military departments separate from the activity of the other military departments. But such a doctrine ... as that relating to the use of tactical air in close coordination with tactical ground forces ... are quite proper subjects for review with and assignment to the Strike Command.[248]

In his list of projects which he assigned for study early in 1961, Secretary McNamara directed the general counsel of the Department of Defense to report on the organization of the Army, emphasizing the technical services and recommending such organizational changes as might be appropriate. This study was completed within the Army in October 1961 and, as approved by the secretaries of the Army and of Defense, it became the basis for the Army reorganization plan that President Kennedy submitted to Congress on 16 January 1962. In headquarters of the Army, operational functions were removed from the old chiefs of the arms and services. Almost all individual and unit training responsibilities were assigned to the Continental Army Command. The Army Combat Developments Command, activated on 20 June 1962, was charged to develop organizational and developmental doctrine, materiel objectives and quantitative requirements, wargaming and field experimentation, and cost-effectiveness studies. The Army Materiel Command became operational on 1 August 1962 and was assigned all operating responsibilities for research, development, testing, production procurement, storage, maintenance, and

IDEAS, CONCEPTS, DOCTRINE

distribution of materiel on a wholesale basis.[249] With its headquarters at Fort Belvoir, Virginia, the US Army Combat Developments Command was expected to provide continuing study and answers to the questions: How should the Army be organized? How should it fight? Its mission required it to formulate and document current doctrine for the Army, and, in anticipation of the nature of land warfare in the future, to determine the types of forces that would be required and how they would be employed. Where these functions had previously been performed in some 30 different combat developments sections, boards, and agencies, they were now given a command focal point. The Combat Developments Command had 6,400 people assigned in subcommands and activities throughout the United States. Its activities could range from studies, estimates, and assessments that would extend 20 years into the future and were made at the Institute of Advanced Studies at Carlisle Barracks to the actual testing of ideas, concepts, equipment, and organization under field conditions by a 4,000-man Combat Development Experimentation Center at Fort Ord, California. After developing doctrine, the Combat Developments Command was the primary agency for translating it into usable media such as doctrinal manuals, detailed requirements for equipment, and tables of organization and equipment.[250]

Without awaiting the completion of the Army reorganization, Secretary McNamara requested the secretary of the Army on 19 April 1962 to provide him with an imaginative study on the future role of Army aviation without regard to traditional military doctrine. To handle the study the Continental Army Command established the US Army Tactical Mobility Requirements Board, under the presidency of Lt Gen Hamilton H. Howze, commanding general, XVIII Airborne Corps. The Howze Board's principal activities were centered at Fort Bragg, and a number of Army aviation units were temporarily moved there for field tests and maneuvers. The unclassified version of the board's directive required it to "conduct an extensive program of analyses, exercises and field tests to evaluate new concepts of battlefield mobility in terms of cost-effectiveness and transport-effectiveness factors." It also was charged to determine "the extent to which air vehicles, operating in the environment of the ground soldier, can be substituted for conventional military surface systems, both tactically and logistically."[251] After some 18 weeks of study, the Howze Board published its final report on 20 August 1962.[252] To evaluate the Howze Board's report, General LeMay established the US Air Force Tactical Air Support Requirements Board, under the presidency of Lt Gen Gabriel P. Disosway, Air Force director of programs and requirements. The Disosway Board completed its analysis and evaluation on 14 September, and Secretary Zuckert forwarded this report to Secretary McNamara with some added comments.[253] The reports of the Howze and Disosway boards were not released to the public, but many of their salient recommendations were apparently discussed before congressional committees during the spring of 1963.

When he presented the substance of the Howze Board's report to Congress in February 1963, Secretary McNamara noted:

AF IN A CHANGING ENVIRONMENT

> I asked that the Howze Board be established. I am very pleased with the depth of its work, the imagination it showed during the period of its work, and the intensity of its work. I think many of the recommendations are very beneficial and will greatly strengthen the total military establishment . . . but there are a number of recommendations . . . which I question at the present time.[254]

The Howze Board recommended the organization of two new types of completely airmobile Army units. These would be air assault divisions, each with 459 organic aircraft, and air cavalry combat brigades, each with 316 aircraft. It also stated a requirement for two new types of special purpose Army air units; air transport brigades, each with 134 aircraft, and corps aviation brigades, each with 207 aircraft. The board visualized that the air assault division would employ air-transportable weapons together with armed helicopters and fixed-wing aircraft as a substitute for conventional ground artillery. The air assault division also would be allotted 24 Mohawk aircraft to perform a "very close" support mission for its own troops. Possessing a very high degree of tactical mobility, the air assault division would be able to make deep penetrations into enemy territory, to outflank an enemy by moving over inaccessible terrain and executing quick-strike delaying actions, or to serve as a highly mobile combat reserve for other more conventional divisions. Even though the air assault division probably would be able to perform most of the missions expected of airborne divisions, it would be particularly valuable for conflicts outside of Europe. The air cavalry brigade would be equipped with a large number of helicopters, and the brigade would be useful for attacks against an enemy's flanks, rear areas, and armored penetrations, since it would have large numbers of antitank weapons—including missiles—mounted on its helicopters. Each air assault division would be supported by an air transport brigade, which would have 54 helicopters and 80 AC-1 Caribou light-transport aircraft. The brigade would pick up cargo delivered by Air Force aircraft and carry it forward to the ground troops. Under this concept the Air Force would provide "wholesale" distribution of cargo, and the Army air transport brigade would "retail" the cargo to frontline units.[255] Both General Wheeler and Secretary Vance emphasized that the Army would continue to look to the other services for a continued performance of air transport, air supremacy, and air support missions.[256]

In his testimony before the House Committee on Armed Services, General LeMay stated:

> What the Howze Board report is advocating, I think is in effect building another Air Force for the Army. . . . I think the Air Force is capable and has the capability now of performing these tasks for the Army, and I think this should be done rather than build the duplicating capability in another service.[257]

LeMay pointed out sound reasons for centralizing the command of tactical aviation. In theaters of operations tactical air forces always had been employed under theater commanders, who had been Army officers. Under these circumstances, tactical air squadrons could have been assigned to local ground commanders, but experience had shown that tactical aircraft had to be centrally controlled and employed for the performance of priority missions determined by the theater commanders.[258] Both LeMay and the Disosway Board emphasized that the Howze Board had not considered the ability of the Air Force to perform the functions that were recommended for Army aviation. "We can perform anything that the Army wants done with airplanes," LeMay asserted.[259] In hearings before the House Subcommittee on Defense Appropriations, Gen David M. Shoup, commandant of the Marine Corps, expressed a fear that helicopters were too vulnerable for the work of active combat. He stated that Marine Corps experiments had shown that helicopters could not penetrate into well-fortified areas. The Marines depended on attack aircraft, rather than helicopters, for fire support. LeMay agreed with the Marine Corps position: "Anybody can shoot down a chopper. It is a poor platform from which to deliver munitions."[260]

After studying the reports of the Howze Board and the Disosway Board, the Joint Chiefs of Staff recommended on 17 January 1963 that the US Strike Command should be directed to test and evaluate the Army's airmobility concept and that the test and evaluation should include the suitability of Air Force capabilities and procedures for the enhancement of the mobility of Army units. Although he was generally convinced that the new type units recommended by the Howze Board would significantly increase the Army's capabilities, Secretary McNamara agreed that the proposals were "so revolutionary in character and so closely related to the Air Force Mission" as to demand thorough testing. McNamara thought it possible that the Air Force could use new C-130 and C-141 transport aircraft to lay down cargoes very close to frontline units, thus eliminating the Army's need for many of the Caribou light transports. The Howze Board, moreover, had not clearly indicated how proposed increases in Army airmobility would reduce requirements for lines-of-communication forces, such as trucks, pipelines, and depots. McNamara therefore accepted the Joint Chiefs of Staff recommendation that the Army concept should be tested by Strike Command. In a separate but related action, he requested on 16 February the Army and the Air Force to examine jointly the problem of improving Air Force close air support for ground operations. In support of the proposed airmobility tests, McNamara and the Joint Chiefs of Staff recommended that the Army be authorized to add 15,000 men to its fiscal year 1964 strength to form a provisional air assault division.[261]

Strike Command Tests of Army and Air Force Concepts

Within the Air Staff there was considerable dismay that the Howze Board report could be having such a major impact on DOD.[262] As the Air Staff started to effect an Air Force organization for conducting extensive tactical air warfare tests, however, it began to recognize—as General Smith pointed out—that the Army, through intellectual activity and organizational structure, had brought itself forward while the Air Force had failed to give full considerations to the development of national military doctrine and had become a victim of a "hardening of the categories."[263] In the implementation of its share of the tests that would be drawn up by Strike Command, the Army would be able to use the concentrated resources of its new Combat Developments Command and its Continental Army Forces. General LeMay on 28 February chartered the Air Force Tactical Air Support Evaluation Board (TASEB) under the presidency of Maj Gen Fred M. Dean, vice commander of the Twelfth Air Force, and instructed it to make recommendations regarding Air Force organization and methods of operation necessary to test and evaluate a STRICOM joint test plan. On 27 April General Dean reported that the Air Force possessed no single organization that could carry out the air-ground test and development program. Air Force regulations divided bits and pieces of the necessary capabilities between the Tactical Air Force, Systems Command, the Pacific Air Forces, and the US Air Forces in Europe. The Dean Board recommended that the Air Force take steps to handle the immediate testing problems, but that it should look toward the establishment of a permanent organization that would be able to give continued attention to the development of doctrines, tactics and techniques, and equipment in the field of tactical air warfare.[264]

To prepare the study Secretary McNamara desired on the subject of improving Air Force close air support for ground forces, the Army established an Army Close-Air-Support Board, headed by Lt Gen John S. Upham, Jr., and the Air Force established an Air Force Close-Air-Support Board, headed by General Dean. The two boards assembled at Fort Meade, Maryland, in May 1963 and prepared a final report that was filed on 15 August. An unclassified appendix in the final report contained conclusions and recommendations regarding the development of tactics, procedures, and techniques of close air support. The boards pointed out that the Joint Chiefs of Staff never had approved a doctrine for air-ground operations or for the utilization of air space over a combat area and that no joint Army-Air Force agency had a continuing mission of examining doctrine and evaluating equipment for close air support. They accordingly recommended that the departments of Army and Air Force establish a bilateral air-support center to evaluate and test equipment, to examine doctrine, to develop new tactics and techniques for close air support, and to provide a continuous review of system testing. Although Strike Command had specified responsibilities relating to the development of joint doctrine, the boards believed that this command would have to continue to depend on the services to develop their respective doctrine, tactics, and techniques. "The Services," the boards concluded, "are charged with those responsibilities and rightly so as they are intertwined with logistical and developmental functions, which are also responsibilities of the Services."[265]

During 1963 Air Force officers at the Air Staff level also gave close attention to the problems of developing doctrine. In the 1 February 1963 Air Staff reorganization, the Directorate of the Plans for Aerospace Plans remained unchanged, but the establishment of the Directorate of Plans and the Directorate of Operations affected the procedures for developing and monitoring the development of Air Force doctrine. Under the new system, the director of plans was responsible for formulating, coordinating, and reviewing the Air Force basic doctrine and for preparing and disseminating basic Air Force doctrinal manuals. The director of operations was made responsible for monitoring and reviewing operational Air Force doctrine, and the responsibility for developing and submitting operational doctrine was assigned to the Tactical Air Command (tactical air operations), the Strategic Air Command (strategic operations), the Military Air Transport Service (strategic airlift operations), the Air Force Communications Service (communications operations), the Air Weather Service (weather operations), and the Air Rescue Service (search and rescue operations). Operational doctrine was defined as "rules, tactics, techniques, and procedures employed by an organization in carrying out a specific function."[266] The responsibility for the performance of Air Force actions looking toward the promulgation of unified doctrine for joint operations by the Joint Chiefs of Staff also was divided between the Directorate of Plans and the Directorate of Operations. Plans was responsible for monitoring Air Force doctrinal projects to the Joint Chiefs and for attempting to resolve service divergencies before projects were submitted to the Joint Chiefs. Operations was responsible for determining the appropriate Air Force organization or command to develop doctrine required by the Joint Chiefs, for the direct supervision of the preparation of such doctrines, and for providing Plans with necessary assistance during the formal process of obtaining JCS approval of doctrinal projects.[267]

At the same time that Air Staff responsibilities in doctrinal matters were given clarification, Col J. M. Hill, assistant chief of the Aerospace Doctrine Division, Air Force Directorate of Plans, was charged to prepare a study looking toward the accomplishment of the Dean Board's recommendation for an organization that would give continuing attention to the development of doctrine, tactics and techniques, and equipment for air warfare. This study determined that within the Air Force there was no "organization, agency or activity with the resources to think and plan ahead in terms of concept and doctrine; to study, evaluate, war game and if necessary physically test new concepts and doctrine."[268] It also proposed that any course of action which the Air Force might take to improve its system for developing doctrine should have the capabilities to initiate basic ideas and concepts; to evaluate, test, and coordinate them before presenting them to the Air Staff; and to be free from the press of daily priority work that inevitably would detract from the primary mission. If the function were assigned to an office in the Pentagon, it would have an advantage in that it would be close to sources of information on national policy and technological development, but such an assignment "would almost certainly result in a gradual involvement in Air Staff activities with a resultant decrease in the ability to develop doctrine."[269]

As Gen William F. McKee began to attack the Air Force organizational problem of providing a test and development establishment, he initially indicated that he intended to form an interim organization that could later be expanded into a separate major air command that would be able to serve as a single agency for the development of concepts and doctrine as well as for long-range, Air Force-wide tactical employment testing.[270] Under existing regulations, the Tactical Air Command had the mission of developing air-ground doctrines and procedures, and the Air Force Systems Command was charged to perform testing and evaluation to establish the technical adequacy and qualitative characteristics of materiel. Making a beginning of the interim organization, Gen Walter C. Sweeney, Jr., commander of the Tactical Air Command, organized, effective on 1 February 1963, the Air Force Tactical Air Reconnaissance Center at Shaw AFB, South Carolina, and on 7 May 1963 the Air Force charged the Tactical Air Reconnaissance Center to develop, coordinate, validate, and test tactical air reconnaissance requirements, concepts, doctrine, tactics, and procedures; to test airborne and ground tactical air reconnaissance equipment; and to train aircrews.[271] On 26 July General McKee informed the Air Force Systems Command that he intended to use the command's resources to establish the 1106th Tactical Test Group at Eglin AFB, Florida, under the command of a general officer and with immediate responsibility to Headquarters USAF. The 1106th would provide Air Force support to STRICOM tests, and it would later be expanded into a major air command.[272] General Schriever promptly protested what he referred to as a preemption of Air Force Systems Command responsibilities. He urged that the establishment of the 1106th from AFSC personnel resources as a separate Air Force organization would disrupt the interface between the Air Force Systems Command and the Tactical Air Command.[273] As a result of Schriever's thinking, the Air Force Systems Command designated and organized the 3209th Tactical Test Group at Eglin AFB on 15 August with assignment to its Air Proving Ground Center.[274] On 16 September, however, the Air Force charged the Tactical Air Command with responsibility for Air Force support of the STRICOM tests, and, accordingly, effective on the following day, the Tactical Air Command established the 4475th Tactical Air Warfare Group at Eglin AFB and the Air Force Systems Command concurrently discontinued the 3209th Group.[275] On 10 October the Air Force accepted the Tactical Air Command's proposal that the 4475th Group be expanded into the Air Force Tactical Air Warfare Center — which would be done on 1 November 1963 — but at the same time it called upon the Tactical Air Command to make plans for an eventual consolidation of the Special Air Warfare Center and the Tactical Air Warfare Center into a single establishment to handle testing, develop concepts, and conduct training.[276]

In preparation for the tests, Strike Command organized a Joint Test and Evaluation Task Force in September 1963, manned by Army and Air Force personnel and headed by Maj Gen William B. Rosson, as director, and Brig Gen Andrew S. Low, Jr., as deputy director.[277] As approved by the Joint Chiefs of Staff, the STRICOM test plan sought to establish conditions under which a comparative evaluation of the Army and Air Force concepts for improving Army tactical mobility could be measured. Both services refined and defined their concepts; Air Force concepts were set forth on 8 December 1963, and Army concepts were expressed in another publication on 12 December 1963. Both the Army and the Air Force were allotted several months to prepare test forces. Taking advantage of additional personnel spaces authorized to it, the Army formed the 11th Air Assault Division (Test) and the 10th Air Transport Brigade (Test) at Fort Benning, Georgia, in February 1964. It also organized an Army Test, Evaluation, and Control Group at Fort Benning under the Army Infantry Center commander. This group was charged to monitor the control test activities and to provide reports and recommendations up through the Combat Developments Command to the Department of the Army.[278] Since the Air Force was allowed no additional strength for the tests, the Tactical Air Command had to accept some reductions in its war-plan commitments. TAC nevertheless organized and assigned the 4485th Test Wing to the Tactical Air Warfare Center effective on 1 February 1964. The wing organized troop carrier and reconnaissance test squadrons, and it took control over detachments of a tactical fighter wing and a communications and control group that were attached to it. Effective on 1 March the Air Force Fighter Weapons School at Nellis AFB, Nevada, was also attached to the Tactical Air Warfare Center.[279]

After making a comparison of the Air Force and Army concepts papers for the tests, General LeMay pointed out that there seemed to be a general agreement that the tasks of tactical air power included counterair, interdiction, ground support, and reconnaissance. One point of difference in the concepts was that the Air Force believed that air war requirements would necessitate the use of increasingly sophisticated aircraft which would be able to live in a hostile environment. LeMay remarked that the Army wanted all the support it could get from the Air Force, but it wanted the support "farther back behind the front lines and farther back into the rear areas." "Now, the Army's position," he said, "is that they want to outline the battlefield and say this is the Army's task. . . . In other words we haul everything by air from the United States right up to the rear of the battle zone, dump it out there. Then the Army will take it and distribute it with their airplanes. Then they say we will do all the interdicting and everything outside the battle zone deep in the enemy territory, and they will do everything over the battle zone."[280] LeMay maintained that the Army concept would involve the building of two tactical air forces—one Army and one Air Force—at enormous expense, with duplicate training establishments, logistic support, and procurement organizations. He was confident that there would always be more requirements for aircraft than money to buy them, that it would be wasteful of the nation's resources to build another air force, and that the Air Force could perform required tasks much cheaper than the Army could create, man, and equip a specialized battle-area air force.[281] LeMay's remarks summarized the Air Force's concepts paper that had been submitted to Strike Command. In this paper the Air Force agreed that the Army should be provided with increased mobility and combat effectiveness, but it urged that the armed services had to be mutually supporting and that flexible Air Force capabilities could perform required air-ground tasks without the need for the duplication of effort inherent in Army proposals.[282] Speaking at a public meeting on 25 May 1964, Maj Gen Gilbert L. Myers, commander of the Tactical Air Warfare Center, described the basic Air Force concept on tactical air warfare as being quite simple.

> This concept is that current Army divisions with their full complement of combat equipment, teamed with Air Force units with first-line aircraft, provide the optimum in combat strength and staying power, significant increases in mobility, and the ability to engage the most capable of potential enemies. By tailoring weapons, equipment and forces, this flexible combat team can handle threats from enemies of lesser capability.[283]

In a series of field exercises called "Indian River" held on the Eglin AFB reservation from June through September 1964, the Tactical Air Warfare Center worked with elements of the 1st Infantry Division, a standard reorganization objective army division (ROAD), to plan, perfect, and train in new ground support techniques. These exercises prepared the air-ground forces for the major STRICOM text exercise, called "Gold Fire I," which was conducted in the Fort Leonard Wood-Camp Crowder area of Missouri between 25 October and 11 November 1964. In these exercises, a joint task force commander and joint task force headquarters exercised command and control over the ground and air forces through respective component commanders. Using more than $20 million worth of newly developed experimental equipment, the Tactical Air Warfare Center tested some 40 new concepts, items of equipment, and procedures. To speed the transportation of close-support requests from the front lines, Air Force forward air controllers radioed the air strike requests directly to a direct air support center (DASC) at corps level; intermediate Army unit headquarters monitored the request net, and if they did not cancel the request, the DASC ordered it flown. This procedure had been used by the Ninth Air Force during World War II, but it had not been incorporated in postwar air-ground procedures because the Army had undertaken to provide its own organic tactical air request communications facilities. Employed for the first time in field tests, F-4C Phantom II jets of the 557th Tactical Fighter Squadron proved able to operate from new aluminum matting forward airstrips. Although not functioning to the complete satisfaction of the Army, these world's fastest tactical fighters were able to provide fighter cover for helicopters: four F-4Cs were able to fly a generally circular "pork-chop" pattern over the helicopters at holding speeds of 400 knots, and in this pattern one of the fighters was always in a position to attack a hostile target within 14 seconds. When a fifth F-4C was added to the pattern, the attack reaction time could be reduced to eight seconds.[284]

During Indian River and Gold Fire I the Tactical Air Warfare Center tested the ability of RF-101 and RB-66 aircraft to perform battlefield reconnaissance. Each of the exercises also provided extensive tests of the capabilities of C-130 troop carrier planes. In fact, Gold Fire I was a test of the concept that some 10,000 men and equipment of a standard ROAD division could be moved a distance of 2,200 nautical miles and landed ready to fight on 2,000-foot dirt strips in a combat area. While the troops were in action, a new movement control center concept was evaluated. In this concept a forward-assault airlift coordinating officer was assigned to battalion-sized Army units to relay mission planning information back to the airlift task force control center at the same time that the battalion was clearing its request for emergency resupply through Army channels. As was the case with the DASC close-support procedure, the airlift force was able to prepare for a resupply mission while Army channels were determining whether it needed to be flown. The C-130s also tested new supply delivery techniques. In a low-altitude parachute extraction system (LAPES), cargo pallets were snapped out of C-130s as they skimmed across a cleared zone. In a parachute low-altitude delivery system (PLADS), loads were discharged into very small clearings from 200-foot altitudes. A ground proximity extraction system (GPES) permitted C-130s to discharge their cargoes by flying low and engaging a trailing hook in a cable stretched across a drop zone. A new rough-terrain loader (RTL) hastened unloading of C-130s that landed in forward airstrips. In a brief summary of Gold Fire I, General Myers stated: "We effectively utilized the C-130 in forward operating areas and have demonstrated we can fly escort missions for assault helicopters flying in combat zones."[285]

At the same time that the Air Force was testing its concepts, the Army commenced brigade-size tests of its 11th Air Assault Division and 10th Air Transport Brigade in May 1964. As was the case with Indian River, the Army's Air Assault 1 tests were unilateral exercises conducted by the Army Test, Evaluation, and Control Group under the review of the Army Combat Developments Command. Between 20 September and 15 November, the Army additionally tested the 11th Air Division in field exercises called Air Assault 2 in the Fort Jackson-Fort Bragg areas of North and South Carolina. Even though STRICOM observers were present at Air Assault 2, the Army Test, Evaluation, and Control Group and the Combat Developments Command maintained control of the tests because of a reasoning that the Army was not certain whether its concepts were sound, how far it might want to go with them, or what form of organization and types of air vehicles it might ultimately need.[286] Under these circumstances STRICOM made the official report and recommendations on Gold Fire I to the Joint Chiefs of Staff, and the Army's Combat Developments Command reported results of Air Assault 2 to the Army chief of staff who made the information available to the Joint Chiefs of Staff. Although joint tests of the Army and Air Force concepts were to have been made in March 1965, the Army recommended that sufficient data had been accumulated on the airmobile concept and that plans for further tests should be canceled.[287]

Even though he had considered the Howze Board's report fresh and challenging, Secretary McNamara had not agreed that the Army should be given a combat area air force. He had demanded cost-effectiveness comparisons between the Army Caribou and the Air Force C-130 and also between the Army Mohawk surveillance aircraft and the Air Force tactical reconnaissance system. These comparisons went against the Army: the Mohawk was deleted from the Army's fiscal year 1965 budget and proposed purchases of Caribou I light transports were severely reduced.[288] While he was sympathetic to the idea that increased numbers of helicopters could improve the Army's tactical mobility, General Wheeler appeared skeptical of the Howze Board's willingness to substitute aerial firepower for all-weather artillery support. He also suggested that the Army probably would not require many air assault divisions; such units would be much more useful against relatively unsophisticated defense environments such as might be found in Southeast Asia than against the sophisticated air and missile defenses that existed in Europe.[289]

Early in 1965 the Joint Chiefs of Staff agreed that sufficient data was at hand to permit an evaluation of the airmobility concept and canceled further tests. Early in 1965 Secretary McNamara also directed the Army to make a comprehensive review of its future requirements for aircraft, and on 19 February the Army released contracts for the program definition phase of an advanced aerial fire support system, which was conceived to be an armed helicopter that would have a speed in excess of 200 knots. As late as February 1965, the 11th Air Assault Division was scheduled to be phased out at the end of the fiscal year, but in March the Joint Chiefs of Staff — now including Gen John P. McConnell as the new chief of staff of the Air Force — completed their analysis of the field test results, and in June of the same year Secretary McNamara, on the basis of JCS recommendations, authorized the reorganization of an existing infantry division at Fort Benning, Georgia, as the 1st Cavalry Division (Airmobile). Shortly after it was formed, the new division was deployed to Vietnam. In comparison with the 3,200 ground vehicles and 101 aircraft in a standard 15,500-man ROAD division, the airmobile division would have 15,700 men, 1,750 ground vehicles, and 434 aircraft, including 283 UM-1 Iroquois utility helicopters, 95 light observation helicopters, 50 CH-47 Chinook transport helicopters, and 6 OV-1C Mohawk fixed-wing observation aircraft. The Army also planned that the new advanced aerial fire support helicopters would be incorporated into the airmobile division if they proved practical for production. With the 434 organic aircraft, the new airmobile division marked a rapid expansion of Army air power, which had grown from the 10 aircraft in World War II triangular divisions, to 16 aircraft in Korean War divisions, to 49 in Pentomic divisions, and to 101 in the standard ROAD divisions.[290]

Clarification of Responsibilities for Doctrine

One of the results of the studies of the Air Force and Army plans for enhancing the mobility and fire support for ground troops was a direction of attention to the roles and missions definitions included in JCS Publication 2, *Unified Action Armed Forces*, to the category of military thinking described as "doctrine," and to the status of existing joint doctrine. The Army offered a consistent position that the augmentation of its organic aircraft would not change the assigned roles and missions. Lt Gen Dwight D. Beach, commanding general of the Army Combat Developments Command, stated that army aviation

> is part of land power. It provides us with a better means to do what armies have always had to do since time immemorial — close with and destroy the enemy, or break his will and force his surrender. Army aviation is not air power in any sense of the word, since air power involves air-to-air combat, the gaining of air superiority, air strikes deep in the enemy rear with strategic objectives, interdiction of the battle area, close air support by high speed tactical aircraft, strategic airlift of Army and other forces. Army aviation is not any of these.[291]

The Air Force, on the other hand, saw the buildup of Army aviation — particularly the armed helicopters, the battlefield surveillance capabilities, and the very heavy cargo helicopters — as both a violation of assigned roles and missions and as a costly duplication of Air Force capabilities.

To play a role as a mediator, General Adams at Strike Command proposed that both the Army and the Air Force were tending to infringe on each other's assigned missions. Adams admitted that the arming of Army aircraft contravened existing unified doctrine, but he acted under Secretary McNamara's instructions and authorized that such aircraft should be tested. Where the unified doctrine did not clearly comprehend other points that might be at issue, General Adams proposed that Strike Command would make tests and devise findings that would be forwarded to the Joint Chiefs of Staff for consideration as joint doctrine. In a definition of joint terms appended to its Army Mobility Test Plan, Strike Command defined "doctrine" as

> that which evolves from a series of actions, tests, or studies which are repeated, revised, modified, or rerun in sufficient numbers and over a sufficient period of time to prove the validity of the thinking which forms the basis of the doctrine.[292]

Adams organized a Doctrine and Requirements Division within the STRICOM J-5 Plans Directorate and charged it to develop "joint doctrine and operating procedures with the objective of bringing doctrines of the several services consonance for deployment and employment of land, sea and air forces assigned to the USSTRICOM."[293] In an interview, Adams maintained that readying a doctrine involved preparing preliminary papers by a "thoroughly integrated staff"; soliciting service views on the preliminary papers; testing proposed doctrine in field exercises; and finally submitting the proposed doctrine to the Joint Chiefs of Staff for approval as joint doctrine. He concluded his remarks with the observation that doctrine was "not the outpouring of a genius," but rather the consensus of a number of individual opinions and talents.[294]

Even though the US Strike Command was empowered to recommend joint doctrine to the Joint Chiefs of Staff, the Air Force conceived that joint doctrine would be an outgrowth of basic service doctrine that would be prepared within the several services. As issued on 20 March 1963, Air Force Regulation (AFR) 1-1, *Aerospace Doctrine: Responsibilities for Doctrine Development*, described Air Force basic doctrine, operational doctrine, and unified doctrine. As already shown, the Air Force delegated its responsibility for negotiating doctrine in most joint fields to the Tactical Air Command. In coordinating doctrine with interface agencies in the other services, however, the Air Force developing commands were instructed not to accept any proposals that would conflict with basic Air Force doctrine.[295]

As it was charged under Air Force Regulation 1-1, the Tactical Air Command undertook to work in coordination with the Army Combat Developments Command to develop mutually agreeable joint doctrinal manuals for submission to the Joint Chiefs of Staff. Toward the end TAC completed the draft of a proposed joint airborne operations manual and circulated it to interested commands for comments and recommendations. When he received a copy, General Adams recognized the need for the manual but he informed General Sweeney on 13 June 1963 that STRICOM would have to serve as the focal point for all jointly developed doctrine pertaining to joint airborne operations. He requested Sweeney to forward the working papers on the draft manual to STRICOM. "To take full advantage of the effort expended in preparing the draft manual," Adams wrote, "it is logical that US Strike Command assume responsibility for the review, editing, joint testing and evaluation, preparation for final draft and submission to the Joint Chiefs of Staff for approval."[296] In separate letters to General Adams, the commanders of the Tactical Air Command and the Combat Developments Command (CDC) pointed out their service responsibilities for developing joint doctrine. General Sweeney also forwarded the correspondence to General LeMay with a recommendation that he secure a clarification of CINCSTRIKE's doctrinal responsibilities.[297]

In the clarification of doctrinal responsibilities, the military services retained the primary responsibility for the development of proposed joint doctrines, but STRICOM was charged to develop and forward appropriate recommendations to the Joint Chiefs regarding doctrines and techniques for the joint employment of forces assigned to it. As a result of the changed terms of reference, Strike Command modified its methodology for making doctrinal recommendations, providing that perfected doctrinal positions would be circulated to the services and to the unified commands as a last step before they were submitted to the Joint Chiefs of Staff.[298] In considering changes to existing doctrine or in the development of new joint doctrinal recommendations, the Strike Command additionally proposed that it would adhere to three basic principles; joint doctrines would attain a maximum integration of combat power, would dictate a maximum freedom of action for service components, and would employ joint command and control to attain unity of effort, to facilitate operations of components, and to affect economies of force.[299]

When the responsibilities of the military services for recommending joint doctrines were clarified, the Tactical Air Command and the Combat

IDEAS, CONCEPTS, DOCTRINE

Developments Command seriously addressed themselves to efforts to secure agreements that would be mutually acceptable.[300] Since the Air Force was the responsible service for coordinated development of a unified doctrine for air defense of overseas combat areas, the Tactical Air Command's Directorate of Plans drew upon the basic guidance of the LeMay-Decker agreement for the formulation of a doctrinal paper. As reviewed and amended by the other services and the unified commands, this paper was accepted by the Joint Chiefs of Staff who issued it in official print as JCS Publication 8, *Doctrine for Air Defense from Overseas Land Areas* (FOUO), on 23 May 1964.[301] Also active in the doctrinal field, the Air Defense Command, in coordination with the Army Air Defense Command and the Navy Forces for Continental Air Defense, polished a doctrinal statement that was subsequently published as JCS Publication 9, *Doctrine for the United Defense of the United States against Air Attack* (FOUO), on 9 September 1964.[302]

As the Air Force moved toward a recapturing of initiative in its areas of military responsibility, General Page realized that eight Air Force doctrinal manuals were nine years old and that the basic Air Force doctrinal manual was four years old. The Army's equivalent basic doctrinal manual was one year old and the Navy's equivalent publication was one and one half years old.[303] As will be shown, a number of false starts were made to revise the Air Force doctrinal manuals after 1959, and in each case the work was delayed pending clarifications of DOD policy and strategy. In the spring of 1963, the Air Force Directorate of Plans again undertook work designed to consolidate and revise the Air Force's nine doctrinal manuals into a single volume. This plan, however, soon gave way to another project which involved the preparation of an entirely new basic doctrinal manual, reflecting changing considerations of national policy and the characteristics of military aerospace forces that had been incorporated in the report of Project Forecast. A draft of this manual was completed in the winter of 1963-64, and Air Force Manual 1-1, *United States Air Force Basic Doctrine*, was published on 14 August 1964.[304] Citing the fact that the basic Air Force doctrinal manual was in preparation, the Air Force Directorate of Operations listed a companion series of Air Force operational doctrine manuals that would be prepared by the major commands.[305]

More convinced than ever on 8 July 1963 that one of the central problems facing the Air Force was its need for an organization similar to the Army's Combat Developments Command, Maj Gen Dale O. Smith commented: "I suspect that people in the Air Staff will say that Project Forecast will solve the doctrinal problem."[306] Smith could not agree that any ad hoc solution could solve a problem or provide the novel, dynamic, and well-presented studies that the Air Force required as a basis for its forward projections.[307] Although the challenge of the Army's airmobility concept caused the Air Force to review lessons on the unity of air power, both the Air Staff and the TAC elected to make interim responses to the organizational problem. In its Combat Developments Command, on the other hand, the Army appeared to have established an organization that could think and plan ahead in concepts and doctrine; that could study, evaluate, wargame, and physically test new concepts and doctrines; and that could prepare novel, dynamic, and well-presented studies.[308] Reported Assistant Secretary of the Army W. M. Hawkins in March 1964, "The Army has done, I think a really good thing in creating their Combat Developments Command. . . . I believe it is just now coming to full fruition."[309]

Defense Rationale on Science and Technology

"I think all of us fully realize," observed Lt Gen Donald L. Putt, Air Force deputy chief of staff for development, in May 1956, "that we are living today in an era of vigorous scientific and technological revolution unprecedented in the history of mankind."[310] Confronted with a "ruthless and determined aggressor foe," who understood the importance of technological superiority, the United States faced the difficult and costly necessity, as Putt saw it, of simultaneously performing research and development work on at least four generations of weapons:

> First, model improvements of weapons in production and in inventory; second, scheduled development of the next weapon system to go into production; third, pursuit of those technical developments of new equipment and techniques which will form the building blocks for the next succeeding generation of weapons; and, finally, basic or fundamental research to acquire new knowledge to push back the scientific frontiers, and remove the barriers to still more advanced and effective weapons.[311]

The views expressed by General Putt were generally shared within the Department of Defense. In 1958 and again in 1959, Secretary Neil H. McElroy pointed out that the United States, the Soviet Union, and the world were "moving rapidly into a period of increasing danger."[312] "It is the inevitable consequence," McElroy said, "of the explosive progress in science and technology which is making available a succession of weapons of ever-increasing destructiveness and speed of delivery."[313] Faced with the critical threat that the Soviets had shortened lead time in the development of new weapons and appeared willing to afford duplicate prototypes of new weapons, General White wished to see an acceleration of research and development in the United States. "We in the Air Force, and I think all of the military services," he stated, "always want to see technology move faster because we realize that it is from the area of new developments that our lifeblood stems."[314] Writing anonymously in 1961, two Air Force military analysts asserted:

> Technology wins wars. . . . Technology paces strategy and determines its nature. Strategy can place demands on technology in order to meet momentary requirements. But over the long haul, changes in strategy come primarily from technology.[315]

Even though a nation might have the greatest technology in the world, such a capability would be useless for military purposes unless it was translated into useful weapon systems. These processes demanded an increasingly close association between science, industry, and the Air Force. General Putt observed:

> An alliance, or marriage, has occurred between science and arms, between the scientists and the military. New weapons devised by science are bringing about significant changes in tactics and strategy. Conversely, changes in tactics and strategy required by changing world conditions generate demands for new weapons to meet new strategies. The interaction between science and strategy is continuous.[316]

Although the Air Force always had relied heavily upon industry for research and development, the Air Force had built up a very substantial in-house organization that was able to evaluate and manage research and development in the aeronautical field. After World War II, however, the Air Force faced tremendous requirements in new fields – ballistic missiles, and space electronics – areas where it had few in-house technical capabilities.[317] In the era of technological explosion and cold war conflict, new organizations for scientific engineering and technical management were brought into being in the form of nonprofit corporations.

The oldest of the nonprofit companies was the Research and Development (Rand) Corporation, which was initiated in 1945 with five people to provide the Air Force with a full-time, competent, and objective group to analyze advanced technology; wargame and evaluate new systems that were possible from advanced technology; determine the effects upon the Air Force; and recommend the introduction of new systems into research and development. From the five original people, the Rand "think factory" grew to some 900 people by 1960 and continued to provide conceptual studies to the Air Force and other defense agencies.[318] Requiring a similar though smaller scientific advisory organization closer at hand in July 1958, the Air Force deputy chief of staff for development sponsored the establishment of Analytic Services Inc. (Anser) in Alexandria, Virginia. With a professional staff of approximately 40 people, Anser was able to provide quick evaluations of proposed weapon systems or proposed solutions to immediate technical problems involved in developmental planning.[319]

In view of its internal aeronautical knowledge, the Air Research and Development Command's Aeronautical Systems Division at Wright AFB, Ohio was able to provide sound planning, evaluation, and management in the aeronautical field of systems acquisition. As an unprecedented organizational approach to the revolutionary challenge of ballistic missile technology, the Air Force in 1954 drew upon a special technical support contractor – the Guided Missile Research Division at San Bernardino, California. The search for a long-term management organization for military space led to the establishment of the Aerospace Corporation in June 1960 in proximity to the Air Force Space Systems Division in Los Angeles. The MITRE Corporation had its beginning in 1957 when the Air Defense Systems Integration Division (ADSID) was established at Hanscom AFB, Massachusetts, and contracted with the Massachusetts Institute of Technology's Lincoln Laboratory for electronic technical assistance. When the university contract proved unsuitable, MITRE Corporation was established in 1958, and it supported ADSID's successor, Electronics Systems Division.[320]

By relying on nonprofit corporations for the engineering and technical direction of certain systems development, the Air Force was able to accelerate the translation of technology into aerospace weapon systems. The procedure also reduced the need for defense contractors to build up and maintain self-sufficient scientific management capabilities, thus overbidding and fractionating scarce national technical manpower. As a general rule, however, industrial corporations received contracts but did not appreciate the fact that nonprofit corporations received contracts as prime weapon system contractors; and Congress suspected that the corporations provided a means of evasion of the classified civil service salary schedules. Despite these criticisms, General Schriever believed the nonprofit corporations to be very effective. "From where I sit as Commander of the Systems Command," he stated, "I would not know what I would do if I did not have this capability. I just could not get the job done. It is that simple."[321]

Especially in aeronautical fields the Air Force relied strongly on proposals from industry to provide the most feasible concepts for new weapons.[322] Some corporations, such as Lockheed Aircraft (which spent over $1.5 million on studies and testing of a supersonic transport and another half-million dollars on an airborne early warning plane), used company funds for research and development in the expectation of developing an item that would be bought by the armed services, but the costs were so high and the frequency with which they had to enter competitions to maintain volume business was so great that few corporations could tie up their own funds for prolonged periods. Recognizing this problem, the armed services usually contracted for feasibility studies and even design proposals. To remain solvent, however, aviation corporations had to achieve repeated successes in design competitions, and the most successful corporations had their engineering staffs to invent devices or discover articles that would be useful in filling a military role.[323] When asked about the organization of ideas for new weapon systems, Dr Herbert F. York, while serving as director of defense research and engineering in 1959, recognized that the individual armed services probably got many of their new ideas from industrial organizations.[324] General Schriever noted that Air Force general operational requirements were established by a combination of operational need and technological opportunities. "I might say ... in terms of our inputs," Schriever said, "that we constantly have industry studying and making proposals to the Air Force and these are part of the inputs and the establishment of general operational requirements."[325]

At the same time the pressure of the Soviet technological threat brought increasingly close relationships between scientists and the military, the Eisenhower administration maintained a favorable attitude toward the pursuit of parallel lines of development. Established in 1955 to determine means of reducing lead time in the weapon systems cycle, an ad hoc committee headed by Deputy Secretary of Defense Reuben B. Robertson, Jr., recommended in July 1956 that parallel development should be accepted among other things as a definite policy for accelerating development.[326] Parallel development and production of projects and systems designed for the same general mission was recognized as being very costly. Not only were there duplicative development costs, but duplicative production lines had to be set up and tooled, and the economies of large-scale, repetitive production were lost, thus significantly increasing the cost per unit. Duplicative pipelines of spares and unique support equipment had to be established in the logistics systems, and, finally, duplicative sets of obsolete spares and support equipment had to be disposed of when the weapon systems were phased out of the operational inventory. In the 1955–58 time period, however, the Air Force and the Navy each had two tactical fighters under development. Even though special requirements appeared to necessitate different aircraft, the House Appropriations Committee noted in its report on the 1958 appropriation bill that the Navy's F-4H-1 and F-8U-3 aircraft had approximately the same characteristics and demanded that the Navy take prompt action to determine which aircraft should be placed in production. The Navy eventually chose the F-4H-1, but by the time the F-8U-3 development was terminated it had cost over $136 million. The Air Force simultaneously developed the F-105 and the F-100B (redesignated as the F-107A) and ultimately terminated the latter at a cost of $85 million.[327] As has been seen, President Eisenhower and Secretary of Defense Charles E. Wilson relied on budgetary ceilings that kept the armed services "running a little hungry" to ensure that lesser priority projects would be discontinued. Nevertheless, the need to select between two prospective systems often made for an agonizing experience. "It is the hardest thing in the world," commented Lt Gen C. S. Irvine, Air Force deputy chief of staff for materiel in 1959, "to stop a program."[328]

Secretary McNamara Revises Research and Development Priorities

When the Kennedy administration was taking office early in 1961, the Air Force expressed its views on the future and its future requirements in some detail. On several occasions, Secretary Zuckert stated the basic conception that "for every weapon in the inventory another must be in development and a third in idea."[329] "Future technological growth," wrote Maj Gen Bruce K. Holloway, Air Force director of operational requirements, "will continue to accelerate at an exponential rate."[330] In the development of new weapon systems, General LeMay stated that the Air Force believed that "we must push the state of the art right up to the limit; that we cannot go into battle with anything less than that."[331] Making a philosophical approach to the phenomenon of technological breakthrough, Col Francis X. Kane, special assistant to the Air Force deputy chief of staff for development, demonstrated that the "onrush of technology" did not spontaneously produce technological breakthroughs. Instead, revolutionary advances had progressed in recognizable steps: first, the intellectual breakthrough and the identification of theory; second, the invention which translated theory into devices; third, the policy breakthrough which involved the decision to translate an invention into materially useful products; and, fourth, the engineering breakthrough, which was the step wherein the intervention chosen by management was produced in numbers. Colonel Kane believed that the key step was the policy breakthrough, which involved the problem of evaluating—in terms of costs and ultimate utility—the interrelationships of a growing number of inventions.[332] Under the Defense Reorganization Act of 1958, the secretary of defense and the director of defense research and engineering had been given responsibility for the supervision of all research and development programs in the Department of Defense and were thus the agents who would determine policy breakthroughs. By the 1958 act, the secretary of defense was additionally empowered "to assign, or reassign, to one or more departments or services, the development and operational use of new weapons or weapons systems."[333] In the words of Congressman Carl Vinson, Congress intended the Defense Reorganization Act of 1958 "to place defense research and engineering under one responsible official with the power to stop unnecessary duplication, speed up essential work, and eliminate unnecessary competition or rivalry."[334] In the preparation of the defense budget for fiscal year 1960, Secretary McElroy directed the shifting of funds for test and evaluation that had formerly been included in the procurement appropriations to the research and development budget.[335]

In his initial submission of questions requiring answers in March 1961 and in his subsequent expansion of the questions into projects which required investigation, Secretary McNamara gave much attention both to defense organization for research, development, test, and engineering and to specific projects that were under way. In his search for rational explanations of why things were being done as they were, McNamara brought many civilian analysts from nonprofit corporations into the Department of Defense, and the analysts, who had formerly advised military leadership, now assumed basic positions of responsibility. Within a few months, Secretary McNamara, Deputy Secretary Gilpatric, and Dr Harold Brown, who became director of defense research and engineering, put together a new rationale toward research and development which was markedly different from that of the Eisenhower administration.

The new Department of Defense thinking on the organization of research and development began to become evident on 6 March 1961 when Secretary McNamara assigned primary responsibility for the development of military space projects to the Department of the Air Force. In regard to this action, Deputy Secretary Gilpatric explained that it was "the policy of the Department of Defense to make use of unique technical capabilities within the Department of Defense wherever they exist."[336] In the past, the using service had been charged to conduct the research and development on a weapon system; this practice would be continued in cases in which only one service had a unique requirement, but where projects were of triservice interest there would be an integration of responsibilities in one service to avoid the emergence of large, multiple-management organizations.[337] Speaking personally rather than as chairman of the Joint Chiefs of Staff, General Lemnitzer opposed the policy. He urged that the service that would use a weapon system should develop it in order that it might concurrently organize and train units to employ the operational system.[338]

In the past the Air Force also had maintained that the service that would employ weapons should develop them, but it was willing to see a reevaluation of the concept. In the infancy of aviation, for example, the centralization of aircraft research and developments in either the War Department or the Department of the Navy might have been valid from an economic standpoint, but it had been impossible because there was no central executive control of the two departments below the president. In World War II mass production of aircraft would have swamped one management establishment. In 1961, however, a new situation might well have existed because the science of aeronautics was relatively mature, and the role of pure aeronautics in military affairs was firmly established. The airframe and airbreathing industries were in the descendant, and the unit and dollar volumes of military aircraft development were waning. Development costs nevertheless constituted an increasing portion of total aircraft program costs, due in some measure to the limited numbers of modern aircraft that were being procured and the continued large investments in departmental development organizations. The Air Force pointed out:

> Careful study might determine that many advantages would accrue from consolidation of Department of Defense aircraft development when the unit or dollar volume of such reaches a level which would no longer justify the continuation of separate departmental organizations for such tasks.[339]

Based on careful study of the text and legislative history of the Defense Reorganization Act of 1958, Secretary McNamara reached his own conclusions as to how defense research and development should be managed. Congress clearly intended that the military services and departments should not be merged. McNamara asked himself, "What is essential—what is the essence of a military department?" And he concluded: "The essence of a military department is the major actions it is taking to prepare forces for its specified mission."[340] Although research and development of new weapons was a major action looking toward the preparation of forces to accomplish a specified mission, Congress clearly expected the secretary of defense to eliminate duplication in research and development. Where a new weapon might be used by two departments, the law thus provided that the secretary of defense could choose between the departments and make either of them responsible for the development of the new weapon. In regard to the development of a new aircraft, Secretary McNamara reasoned:

> I feel I have the authority to assign the research and development responsibility for that weapon to either the Air Force or the Navy, but not to the Army, because to assign the

responsibility for research and development to the Army is a move away from a separate Air Force, and this seems to me to be contrary to the intent of Congress.[341]

Before 1961 the Air Force and the Navy had used as many as 50 versions of the same common aircraft, especially reconnaissance, transport, training, utility, and rotary-wing aircraft. Among combat types, the Navy had bought the FJ-Fury, a version of the F-86 Sabre, and the Air Force had procured the B-66 as a version of the Navy A3D. The chief difficulty in commonality was the fact that the Air Force, operating from land bases, could employ higher performance planes that were generally too heavy to operate from the Navy's aircraft carriers.[342] Despite this problem, McNamara made sustained efforts to eliminate parallel development projects and systems that he considered designed for the same general mission. He reasoned that parallel development and production of weapon systems was a major source of waste, involving duplicate development costs and duplicate stocks of spares and support equipment. After some 1961 studies, which have been noted, McNamara directed the Air Force to terminate its F-105 procurement and to buy F-4H (later F-4CZ) tactical fighters, which would become the basic tactical fighter for both the Navy and the Air Force. He assigned supply management responsibilities for all spare parts and components peculiar to the F-4H to the Department of the Air Force, and required the Air Force and the Navy to develop joint plans for the maintenance of the aircraft.[343]

In response to a Tactical Air Command requirement for a follow-on tactical fighter put forward in 1959, the Air Force had begun to design the Tactical Fighter-X, or the TFX, during the last year of the Eisenhower administration. The system development requirement called for a short take-off and landing aircraft that would have an extended unrefueled ferrying range, high speed at high and low altitudes, and an ability to penetrate heavily defended enemy environments. Early in 1961 the TFX project was taken under review by the Office of the Secretary of Defense, and on 14 February Dr Herbert F. York, who was then director of defense research and engineering, ruled that the TFX would be developed by the Air Force as a triservice tactical fighter, specifically designed to meet the requirements of the Army, Navy, Air Force, and Marine Corps. The Air Force already planned to use a variable-sweep or a variable-geometry wing on the TFX, which would permit the plane to fly at top supersonic speeds or to fly at low speeds with the wing extended. In addition the Department of Defense concluded that new developments in aerodynamics and engine performance would permit the development of a tactical fighter which could operate from aircraft carriers as well as from shorter and rougher runways than normal and still carry the heavy conventional ordnance loads that would be needed in limited wars. At McNamara's direction the Army, Navy, and Air Force listed their requirements for such a tactical fighter, and a committee of defense and service representatives undertook to reconcile differences.[344]

The Army and the Air Force reached an agreement on desired aircraft characteristics fairly easily, but the Navy was pessimistic about the prospect of a triservice fighter. Fundamentally, the Air Force wanted to press the state of the art

IDEAS, CONCEPTS, DOCTRINE

in developing the advanced fighter and visualized a longer and heavier plane than the Navy could accept for carrier-based employment. Even though the negotiations dragged on through the summer of 1961, McNamara was encouraged by the Air Force's success in using the Navy F-4 in place of the F-105. After reviewing final proposals, which showed that a TFX could be developed in two versions but with a high percentage of common parts, McNamara expressed his opinion on 1 September 1961 that the development of a single aircraft of genuine tactical utility to both services was technically feasible. He therefore directed the Air Force, in collaboration with the Navy (to include Navy participation on the source selection board), to develop plans for the management and funding of the TFX program. He further ordered that changes to the basic Air Force tactical version of the aircraft needed to accommodate it to Navy use would be held to a minimum.[345]

At the same time that the triservice fighter was in its predevelopment stage, Secretary McNamara was evaluating other outstanding research and development projects. Beginning with a Bell Telephone Laboratories study in 1955, the Navy had brought forward the concept of a fleet air defense system designated Eagle-Missileer, which included a large, subsonic, long-endurance, radar-equipped Missileer aircraft that would be armed with high-performance, air-to-air, long-range Eagle missiles. The system had originally been conceived for fleet air defense, but the Navy broadened the concept of Eagle-Missileer to include its use in the defense of a Marine amphibious objective area, especially in the early phase of such an operation before ground control for other type air superiority systems could be brought ashore. The Eisenhower budget for fiscal year 1962 did not include funds for the whole system, but $57.7 million was included for continuing development of the Eagle missile in the expectation that it could be employed on some other aircraft. In his review of Eagle-Missileer, McNamara concluded that the system would ultimately cost $3.5 billion, that the Navy was developing the Typhoon ship-to-air defense missile, and that the triservice fighter would be more profitably developed to meet the air defense needs of the Navy and the Marines. He accordingly canceled the development of the Eagle, thus ending the Eagle-Missileer.[346]

The Office of the Secretary of Defense also gave close attention to the Air Force's aircraft nuclear propulsion (ANP) program. This program had begun in 1945 when the Army Air Forces had directed the old Air Technical Service Command to investigate all possible military applications of nuclear energy, but study projects in cooperation with the Atomic Energy Commission were very modest until 1950. Even then, ANP was subject to fluctuating support. As has been seen, early planning for the B-70 visualized it as an aircraft with long-endurance nuclear-cruise power and a chemically fueled supersonic dash capability. In 1957, the Air Force had recognized that such a weapon system was beyond the current state of the art and that the effort to set up ANP "requirements" that were apparently beyond the realm of technological possibility had in fact resulted in opposition within the scientific community.[347] ANP was continued as an experimental project, and it received close scrutiny in 1959. At this time General White visualized that a very long endurance aircraft with consequent very long range, which would be equipped with air-to-surface missiles, would vastly complicate hostile defenses since it would compel an enemy to guard against attack from any direction. As a result of the long study, two types of nuclear power plants showed technical feasibility; the first was a direct cycle which would provide direct heat to a turbojet engine; the other would be an indirect cycle that would transfer heat to an engine through pipes filled with liquid metal. Either installation would require heavy shielding to protect the crew against radiation. The direct air-cycle system could have produced a flyable aircraft, but it would not have been a very good plane, and the system also would have exhausted some small amounts of radioactive matter into the atmosphere.

After studying ANP in 1959, the Joint Chiefs of Staff took the position that there was no specific military requirement for a nuclear-powered aircraft, but they noted that they would like to see a research project continued in the hope that a militarily useful aircraft could be developed. General White agreed that a nuclear aircraft was not "vital" and that he was not ready for full weapon system development. Looking back at the ANP program in March 1960, Lt Gen R. C. Wilson, Air Force deputy chief of staff for development, maintained that the Air Force probably should have concentrated earlier on the direct-cycle engine that could have provided a not-very-good but nonetheless flyable aircraft. By this time, however, the Air Force had missed the chance to have an early flying nuclear-powered plane, and General Wilson reasoned that it would be just as well to try for what would be a more useful plane.[348]

Air Force research and development expenditures on ANP were never very high in any one year, but through fiscal year 1961, it had expended $511.6 million on the project, and the Atomic Energy Commission had invested a further amount which brought the total expended on ANP to approximately $1 billion. On the basis of a study provided to him by the director of defense research and engineering on 20 March 1961, Secretary McNamara judged that the ANP project had suffered from "chronic optimism," that it would cost an additional $750 million to $1 billion to complete, and "that there appeared to be little military potential to the present development." "While it is true," McNamara stated, "that with an even larger effort some kind of nuclear-powered flight could have been accomplished by now, the aircraft involved would have had little or no military value. It almost inevitably would have been subsonic and limited to an altitude of about 35,000 feet."[349] McNamara was unwilling to accept the proposition that the nation which first achieved nuclear-powered flight would attain considerable world prestige. "In any event there is a real question as to whether defense projects should be pursued solely to provide strategic value," he added.[350] Based on McNamara's recommendation, President Kennedy announced on 28 March 1961 that the military ANP project would be canceled and that work on the nuclear power plant and airframe would be abandoned. The Atomic Energy Commission would continue to carry on scientific research in the fields of high-temperature materials and high-performance reactors.[351]

The Air Force was shocked by the sudden cancellation of the ANP project and gave a good amount of attention to what had gone wrong. In his assessment of ANP in May 1961, Under Secretary of the Air Force Joseph V. Charyk noted that the Air Force had felt it necessary to attain support for the project to spell out detailed military requirements which really did not make too much sense in terms of the state of the art. Charyk said:

> I believe that some of our major errors have been in attempting to hold back development until we could completely spell out a military requirement. This has led to two difficulties. On the one hand ... we have been very late in starting because we could not completely spell out the details of a potential military system so that when we began the actual development, we were behind. We had to accelerate the program. We had to conduct the program on a high concurrency, expensive basis. At the other end of the spectrum in order to permit development to proceed we have attempted to create a military requirement.... As a result we brought into being a fairly massive, expensive program which ... we were not in a position to exploit as a full-scale weapon system development.[352]

Later on, in 1963, General LeMay stated that the Air Force had "not lost faith in atomic power." He continued:

> The trouble is that while we can build an atomic powerplant that will power an airplane ... the power we are going to get out of the powerplant is not competitive with what we can do with chemical fuel, and if they are not competitive against the enemy threat, you are just not in business.[353]

As has been seen, the Air Force generally agreed with Secretary McNamara's decisions to defer development of the mobile Minuteman mission in the spring of 1961 and his later decision to cancel its development. The mobile Minuteman cost substantially more than the silo-based model, and the concept of the mobile Minuteman had had more validity when it had seemed that the Soviets might have fielded far more intercontinental missiles than the United States.[354] The Air Force was less prepared to accept McNamara's opinion that the ANP project had suffered from "chronic overoptimism." As previously noted, General LeMay took abrupt objection to McNamara's conclusion that many of the subsystems planned for the RS-70 were technically infeasible and certainly beyond the state of the art. During 1962 McNamara also became convinced that the "cost history" of the Skybolt missile was "particularly poor."[355] Each of these case histories evidently added to McNamara's assessment of failings in the research and development effort of the Defense Department. By early 1962 McNamara concluded that the old traditions of cost-plus-fixed-fee contracts had created a psychological situation wherein neither the services nor their contractors had paid much attention to costs or cost estimating. He believed that if sufficient attention were given to the design of a weapon system it could become a low-risk, realistically costed undertaking that could be developed on a fixed-price, incentive-type contract.[356] Each of these assessments began to manifest itself in DOD research and development programs, particularly in the handling of the research and development contract of the TFX aircraft.

When Secretary McNamara directed the Air Force to submit requests for development proposals for the TFX in the autumn of 1961, he recognized that the Air Force and the Navy had not completely reconciled their divergent thinking on the aircraft's characteristics, but he was hopeful that contractor proposals could bring a further refinement of work requirements. As directed, the Air Force sent out requests for development proposals in September 1961 and additionally established a TFX system source selection board with representatives from the Air Force Systems Command, the Air Force Logistics Command, the Tactical Air Command, and the Navy. A senior Navy admiral also sat with the Air Force Council after 24 January 1962, when it considered recommendations from the TFX selection board. After preliminary evaluations of proposals from interested companies, Boeing and General Dynamics were awarded 90-day design contracts, which were evaluated in April and June 1962. After the June 1962 evaluation Secretary Zuckert and Secretary of the Navy Fred Korth remanded the proposals to the system source selection board with a directive that the board would work with both competitors as if each of them had been chosen as the prime contractor. In a fourth evaluation made on 8 November 1962 the Air Force council, with the concurrence of the Navy representative, found both the Boeing and General Dynamics proposals to be acceptable but voted unanimously that the Boeing design proposal had "clear and substantial advantage."[357] The Boeing proposal included thrust reversers and a location of air-intake scoops at a high level to minimize the ingestion of foreign objects into the engines. The Air Force Council and the Navy representative believed that these features would make the Boeing design more suited for employment in austere operating conditions. Admiral Anderson and General LeMay endorsed the recommendation that Boeing be selected as the TFX contractor.[358]

In reviewing the TFX recommendation on 21 November 1962, Secretaries McNamara, Zuckert, and Korth agreed that both the Boeing and General Dynamics proposals were acceptable and that either would offer a capability far beyond that of contemporary fighters. The three secretaries nevertheless directed that the General Dynamics proposal would be accepted because it proposed the greatest degree of commonness in Air Force and Navy versions, contemplated the use of conventional materials, provided a higher confidence in structural design, and offered a better possibility of providing the aircraft desired on schedule and within programmed dollar costs. On 24 November, the Department of Defense announced that the General Dynamics Corporation, with Grumman Aircraft as an associate, had been selected as the prime contractor for the development of the F-111A for the Air Force and the F-111B for the Navy.[359] In an interview in which he justified this decision on 16 April 1963, Secretary McNamara called attention to the Air Force's earlier inability to provide "realistic cost estimates" for Skybolt and stated that his own calculations led him to believe that Boeing's predicted costs were less realistic than those of General Dynamics. McNamara also believed that Boeing's planned use of titanium, thrust reversers, and top-mounted inlet ducts, as well as its proposal to hollow out certain structural parts to reduce the weight of the Navy version, would add elements of risk to the development of the TFX. In short, Boeing's proposal pushed the state of the art, thereby posing greater developmental risks and promising greater costs. McNamara thought that the greatest risk in the TFX program lay in the variable-sweep wing that was common to both proposals and that it would be unwise to incur the additional peripheral risks in Boeing's proposal. Secretary Zuckert favored the General Dynamics proposal for these same reasons, and he emphasized that General Dynamics had a distinct edge over Boeing in the higher degree of commonness promised for the Air Force F-111A and the Navy F-111B.[360] Zuckert maintained that the careful definition of the program that preceded the Department of Defense's decision to purchase a test quantity of 23 F-111 (TFX) aircraft would permit a reasonably constructive degree of optimism that the program would proceed within estimated costs and on schedule.[361]

In the course of Senate investigations of the TFX contract negotiations held by the permanent Subcommittee on Investigations of the Committee on Government Operations, a civilian aviation consultant testified that many "old pros" in the Navy and Air Force still believed that interservice competition tended to generate more effective weapons.[362] High-ranking Air Force officers, however, expressed great faith in the TFX. In his best professional judgment, General LeMay had concluded that the Boeing proposal would provide the most advanced aircraft (and he had attempted to convince Secretary Zuckert of this belief), but he defended the right of the civilian secretaries to make the final decision on the matter.[363] He said in regard to the TFX, "Now it is true that we could have done a little bit better on our side of the fence, as the Navy could have done a little better on their side, if we had gone our separate ways. But the money that we are saving in doing it this way more than offsets that."[364] Speaking as Air Force director of operational requirements, Maj Gen William W. Momyer enthusiastically described the TFX as an aircraft with characteristics that would make it suitable for the gamut of war running from counterinsurgency to general conflict. Argued Momyer, "When you consider that within this tactical fighter we will be doing all the jobs that in World War II we did with B-17s, B-24s, B-26s, P-51s, and P-47s and you look at this machine in terms of this kind of flexibility, I think the state-of-the-art has come a long way in enhancing our tactical ability."[365] Since all subsystems identified for the General Dynamics TFX were essentially in being, the plane was considered to be a very low-risk weapon system and the development of it could be contracted on a fixed-price basis. To General Schriever this procedure had obvious advantages, but he cautioned that it also had some disadvantages. Under the fixed-price contract it would be difficult to incorporate improvements in subsystems that might be made simultaneously with the development of the TFX airframe. The plane which would enter the operating inventory four or five years in the future would thus represent the state of the art that had existed when its design was frozen at the beginning of its development.[366] As a matter of fact, however, the development of the TFX would not be completely frozen in its original design stage. Even though the development of the F-111A was kept on schedule and the first flight of the F-111A was completed ahead of schedule in December 1964, it proved possible to make a reconfiguration of the plane to add external fuel capacity to it, thus enhancing its range and providing a possibility that the plane later could be developed in an FB-111A bomber configuration. In addition, the F-111B development program was extended to allow more time for the development of a Phoenix fire control missile system.[367]

The McNamara Rationale on Research and Development

From the handling of research and development projects during his first two years in office, Secretary McNamara evolved new rationale, organization, and procedures for defense research and development which was explained and put into effect in 1963–64. In explaining the new rationale early in 1963, McNamara pointed out that the Kennedy administration had markedly reduced the Soviet threat to the United States by building nuclear and nonnuclear forces. As a general rule, he was willing to observe that most developmental work "would add only marginally to our combat strength."[368] In the past, developments such as the A- and H-bombs and the ICBM had added new and unique dimensions to military capabilities and had justified great costs and risks. McNamara stated on 7 February 1963:

> When the potential payoff is extremely great, correspondingly great costs and risks are justified. But developments which meet this test are rare. The typical development promises, if successful, to achieve a capability that can also be achieved in other ways, usually including the more extensive or imaginative use of existing weapons. In such cases, the urgency is not as great. We believe that the substantial increase in the defense program initiated during the last two years has put us in a position where we can now afford to move more carefully in the initiation of new major weapon system developments.[369]

Based on this rationale and observations of past mistakes, Secretary McNamara and Doctor Brown effected management changes in the defense research and development area. McNamara recounted:

> Poor planning, unrealistic schedules, unnecessary design changes and enormous cost increases over original estimates have continuously disrupted the efficient operation of our research and development program. Most of these difficulties have resulted from inadequate prior planning and unwarranted haste in undertaking large-scale development, and even production, before we have clearly defined what is wanted and before we have clearly determined that a suitable technological basis has been developed on which to build the system. We have often paid too little attention to how

a proposed weapon system would be used and what it would cost, and, finally, whether the contribution the development could make to our forces would be worth the cost.[370]

In McNamara's view, the actual costs of weapon systems had commonly increased from 300 to 500 percent over the original estimated costs because original cost estimates were unrealistically optimistic, because of insistence that weapon systems meet performance standards that went far beyond essential military requirements, because of insufficient definition at the outset of what a contractor was being tasked to develop, because inadequate and unsatisfactory procedures had often been employed in selecting major contractors, and because of reliance on cost-plus contracts that provided no incentives to a contractor to reduce costs.[371]

Within the Department of Defense the phases of research and development were restructured in a manner believed to represent a logical progression from ideas to the development of military hardware for operational employment. Research and development was broken down into sequential steps: (1) Research (basic and applied), where effort was directed toward expansion of knowledge in physical and environmental sciences; (2) exploratory development, where work was directed toward the solution of specific military problems short of actual development of experimental hardware; (3) advanced development, where experimental hardware for technical or operational testing was produced; (4) engineering development, where developments were engineered for service used prior to receiving approval for production and deployment; and (5) operational systems development, which involved continued development, test, evaluation, and design improvement of projects which already had entered a production-deployment stage.[372] McNamara looked upon the first three steps as being designed to provide in an orderly manner "the basic technical building blocks" that would permit large-scale systems developments to be undertaken as they were identified and without a need to engage in costly and inefficient crash programs. "By planning the nonsystem part of our defense research and engineering effort in the large, without tying it to a particular systems development we should be able to effect some degree of standardization which, through repeated use of the same components, should increase reliability and reduce costs," McNamara suggested.[373]

As ideas progressed toward the development of hardware for experimental tests in the advanced development step of research and development, Secretary McNamara directed that no large system development project would be undertaken before the completion of a program definition phase. This activity involved in-house or contractor studies whose purpose was to define a program, develop designs, and determine costs and potential military worth. McNamara emphasized that "to the greatest extent possible we want to do our thinking and planning before we start 'bending metal.' Pencils and paper, and even the feasibility testing of 'pacing' components, are a lot cheaper than the termination of programs."[374] McNamara was quite willing that the program definition phase of an important project would run as long as a year and cost anywhere from $2 to $5 million. Only by careful program definition could the Department of Defense ensure that necessary programs could be accomplished expeditiously or less worthwhile programs rejected. Although the time consumed by program definition might seem a delay, McNamara reasoned that this was not necessarily true. "I have observed that in most cases careful and comprehensive prior planning actually saves time as well as money and results in more effective and more dependable weapons," asserted McNamara.[375]

In the aftermath of the TFX source selection controversy, Deputy Director of Defense Research and Engineering John H. Rubel proposed that military source selection boards should be changed into military evaluation boards and that the secretary of defense and the secretaries of the military departments should be authorized to make decisions on source selection, which, of course, they did anyway.[376] This suggestion was not accepted, but the new Department of Defense rationale and procedures on research and development nevertheless greatly increased the role of the Office of the Secretary of Defense in the field. Acting closely together, Secretary McNamara and Doctor Brown exercised close scrutiny over the defense research, development, test, and engineering budget. Brown explained:

> When we make our reductions we go quite far down on the marginal utility curve. We cut out all the programs that we think do not make very much sense. Then we cut a little more. We cut to the point where we feel that one can argue convincingly on either side of a question, that one should do it or one should not do it. Further cuts, of course, get more and more painful because they are cutting into things that we feel there is no question should be done.[377]

As director of defense research and engineering, Doctor Brown not only had much to say about the initiation of projects, but he also maintained close supervision over what was being done in the research and development efforts under way in the services. He provided guidelines for the implementation of programs and controlled the rate and direction of activity by releasing funds in incremental authorizations. In response to a question in February 1964, General Ferguson, Air Force deputy chief of staff for research and development, testified that there was more concentration of authority in Doctor Brown's office than in the past.[378]

Something of the new concentration of authority in the Office of the Director of Defense Research and Engineering was revealed in the quest for a counterinsurgency (COIN) aircraft during 1963–64. The Air Force response to the problem of providing an aircraft that could operate in a primitive area was to use obsolescent aircraft and converted trainer aircraft; it accordingly requested and received authority to modify T-37 and T-28 training planes for COIN employment. The Army, however, wanted a COIN aircraft that could perform helicopter escort, limited close air support, armed surveillance, and light logistics duty, and could carry and drop four to six fully equipped paratroopers. The chairman of the Joint Chiefs of Staff strongly supported the requirement for a special COIN aircraft, and

Department of Defense studies indicated what were described as significant cost advantages in developing a new COIN aircraft. As Doctor Brown described the problem, the major decision was to determine whether the plane should be developed by the Air Force, the Army, the Navy, or the Advanced Research Projects Agency. Although ARPA was quite anxious to get the task, Brown did not want to put the small agency in the airplane development business. He noted that the Air Force did not want to develop the plane since it would duplicate obsolescent aircraft that could be used for COIN work, although possibly not as efficiently as a specially designed plane. Brown reasoned that the Army ought not to develop a plane that was "at least marginal in terms of the agreement on what size aircraft can be managed by the Army."[379] Except for the Marines, the Navy did not have any large use for a COIN aircraft, but since the choice resolved down to it, the Department of Defense placed the request for development funds for the COIN aircraft in the Navy's budget and directed that the Navy's Bureau of Weapons would develop the plane.[380] After testing modified T-28 and T-37 planes, the Air Force decided that these planes did not possess advantages for counterinsurgency tasks that were better than the A-1 planes already in use. The Navy program, however, developed a counterinsurgency/light armed reconnaissance aircraft (COIN/LARA), and in October 1964 the North American Aviation Company was awarded a contract to provide seven prototype planes for operational evaluation.[381]

At times during the 1950s the Air Force research and development program had included five or six fighter projects, three or four ballistic missiles, three cruise missiles, and a couple of transport aircraft — all progressing simultaneously toward weapon systems. By the early 1960s, however, the majority of these projects were completed and emphasis in Air Force research and development had shifted from weapon systems to exploratory development.[382] Although editorials and articles decried "the Topsy-like, uncontrolled growth of R&D," General Ferguson pointed out that the apparent funding increase in research, development, test, and engineering (RDT&E) funds had come when test and engineering accounts (previously a part of production appropriations) had been included within research and development funds. Taking into account a 12-percent increase in the cost of living, Ferguson demonstrated that research and development funds actually had increased only 6 percent in the 1957–65 time period. In fiscal year 1961 RDT&E funds amounted to 15 percent of the total defense budget; in the departmental requests for fiscal year 1965, the ratio of RDT&E funds to the total budget was 13 percent, and not all of the requested funds would be approved by Congress. "The real 6 percent increase in R&D funds in the last nine years," Ferguson warned, "provides little flexibility to cope with the complexity of choice we have today."[383] Although Ferguson was unwilling to accept the glib assumption that the nation's research and development effort had reached what was being described as a "technological plateau," he noted: "If I could identify a quantum jump, I am sure that we would jump right into it."[384] Apparently more impatient than Ferguson, General LeMay described the Air Force's research and development funding for fiscal year 1965 as "skimpy." He said, "I think we are going to keep on moving, maybe not at the same rate, but in a lot of things we are just scratching the surface."[385]

In February 1963, Secretary Zuckert could not conceive that an arms stalemate could exist in the world "with technology moving as fast as it has moved and, presumably, will move in the years to come."[386] A year later he called the idea of a "technological plateau" an "oversimplification," and added:

> I think at the moment we are in a little bit of what might be called technological shock because the missile development has come upon us and come to fruition so quickly the people have not really had the time to digest the situation, nor has there been the fermentation of ideas so that we can be at all precise about what the next generation of weapon systems will be like.[387]

At least two prominent scientists, however, not only apparently accepted the concept of a "technological plateau" but projected it even further. Wrote Dr Jerome B. Wiesner and Dr Herbert F. York in an article published in October 1964:

> Both sides in the arms race are thus confronted by the dilemma of steadily increasing military power and steadily decreasing national security. *It is our considered professional judgment that this dilemma has no technical solution.* If the great powers continue to look for solutions in the area of science and technology only, the result will be to worsen the situation. The clearly predictable course of the arms race is a steady open spiral downward into oblivion.[388]

Something of the difficulty that had begun to affect a research and development program that promised to be expensive was illustrated by the story of the mobile medium-range ballistic missile (MMRBM). In 1957 the Air Force had faced the prospect that by 1963–65 Soviet forces would possess SS-3 (700-mile range), SS-4 (1,100-mile range), and SS-5 (2,200-mile range) transportable tactical missiles that would possess relatively high accuracy and would be able to react rapidly against tactical targets in Europe and the Pacific. The Air Force's Matador and Mace tactical missiles were obsolescent, cruise-type vehicles that were tied to fixed positions, and the Army's 385-mile range Pershing missile was outranged by the Soviet tactical missiles. Under these circumstances, the Air Force issued a special operational requirement for a follow-on missile to the Mace that would possess high accuracy under all weather conditions, and exceptional mobility. It was planned that the new tactical missile would be employed primarily against the kinds of targets that might appropriately be attacked by fighter-bombers.[389]

Speaking before a NATO parliamentarians' conference in November 1960, General Norstad stated that midrange ballistic missiles with great mobility should be made available to the North Atlantic Treaty Organization, and at the NATO Council meeting the following month the United States asked for consideration of the concept that a multilateral force might be established with the medium-range ballistic missiles. On 3 October 1961, the Department of Defense directed the Air Force to assume responsibility for the MMRBM system.[390] Secretary McNamara envisioned that the weapon system could be deployed on trucks or ships, would be capable of quick reaction and great accuracy, and would not require extensive ground-support equipment.[391] The Air Force envisioned that the MMRBM would be a relatively small solid-fuel missile that could be mounted in a vehicle about the size of a furniture van. The missile was to be capable of being fired within a matter of minutes, and the vehicle that transported it could be kept moving about at random over the highways of Europe.[392] The range of the MMRBM would be between the 385 miles of the Pershing and the 2,500 miles of the A-3 Polaris. Where the problem of safetying the MMRBM had delayed its earlier acceptance, a new nuclear-lock command and control system would prevent its accidental or irresponsible employment. At the time that the MMRBM was authorized, the Air Force already had a program under way looking toward the development of a stellar inertial guidance system for missiles, and the bulk of the effort under this contract was committed to the MMRBM development effort. Where the old Snark cruise missile had been able to direct its slow-moving course by observing the stars, the envisioned system would be able to locate the position of the ballistic missile and navigate it on course even in its boost phase.[393]

On 29 March 1962 Secretary McNamara authorized the Air Force to proceed with a program definition phase of an MMRBM that was capable of employment either from land vehicles or surface ships. In fiscal year 1963 DOD asked for $100 million for the MMRBM, and Congress appropriated $80 million. In fiscal year 1964 the DOD asked for $143 million for the missile, and speaking in support of the request Secretary McNamara gave it strong backing. He said:

> I personally am anxious to see us pursue this development as an insurance program, assuming that there is evidence which leads us to believe we can accomplish the objectives we have outlined, that is . . . the high degree of mobility, the low weight, and the high accuracy.[394]

Once again, however, Congress did not approve the full amount of money requested for the missile. Since only a part of the fiscal year 1963 appropriations for the MMRBM had been allocated, Congress doubted that the full amount requested for fiscal year 1964 could be spent and reduced the appropriation to $73 million. McNamara did not reclama this reduction because other more important things also had been reduced and because he sensed the mood of Congress was shifting away from generous research and development appropriations.[395] A member of the House Armed Services Committee who visited Paris in September 1963 nevertheless reported that members of the NATO staff seemed intent on impressing him with the fact that the development of the MMRBM was a vital requirement.[396]

Early in 1964 Secretary McNamara still could not tell congressional committees of any definite plans for the deployment of the MMRBM missiles, but he urged that it would be important to proceed with their development because the missile would be capable of very rapid deployment and would fill a range gap, and because there was the possibility that they might be deployed "in lieu of certain of our other strategic weapons."[397] Alleging its inability to discover any plan for the deployment of the MMRBM, the House Armed Services Committee cut the requested authorization for its development from $110 million to $40 million, thus in effect deleting the missile but continuing the development of the stellar inertial guidance system.[398] In the Senate Committee on Armed Services, both Chairman Russell and Senator Symington observed that the MMRBM left them "very, very cold."[399] Speaking to Doctor Brown about the missile, Russell said: "I think it will go up in smoke before it is developed along with the $700 to $800 million you are going to spend on R&D."[400] Sen Allen J. Ellender was even sharper with Brown: "You scientists are having a heyday there at the Pentagon. It strikes me that some stop ought to be put to it."[401] Secretary Zuckert subsequently testified that the Air Force was "strongly behind the MMRBM" because of its promised flexibility, and General LeMay pointed out that both General Norstad and General Lemnitzer had pressed for the development of the missile.[402] In the end, however, the fiscal year 1965 budget voted by Congress carried only $40 million for a continued development of the guidance system that would have been used by the MMRBM. In the autumn of 1964, the Air Force accordingly notified the MMRBM contractors that their development contracts would not be renewed.[403]

The case of the MMRBM marked the beginnings of what appeared to be a new congressional attitude toward defense research and development. Speaking of Congress and its actions toward the mobile missile in 1963, Secretary McNamara observed that "all of a sudden the mood of Congress shifted from one of giving me more money than I wanted to spend to one of giving me less money than I felt essential."[404] On the other hand, influential congressmen blamed the Department of Defense and the Air Force for not providing an adequate plan of employment for the MMRBM. In the dialogue on Capitol Hill early in 1964, Doctor Brown defended the MMRBM by stating that McNamara had "a visceral feeling that this is a very important program."[405] But Rep Daniel Flood replied that such a "visceral feeling" was not enough.[406] Some members of Congress—including Senators Russell and Symington—associated the MMRBM with NATO requirements and with the multilateral force proposal that had made little headway in attaining political acceptance in Europe. Other members of Congress noted that serious people in authority were stating that world tensions appeared to be lessening. To General LeMay this latter belief promised eventually disaster. Cautioned the general:

> The Russians have told us over and over again... that they expect to take over the world, and they are going to do it by any way they can see to do it. The thing that worries me more than anything else is that they will act peaceful and act like decent and ordinary people until we get lulled into sleep, and get off balance, and then we will get hit....
> The more world tensions decrease, the more alert we should be.[407]

Threats and Opportunities in Space

Stated General White in April 1958:

> The United States must win and maintain the capability to control space in order to assure the progress and preeminence of the free nations.... This is necessary because until other ironclad methods are devised, only through our military capability to control space will we be able to use space for peaceful purposes. I visualize the control of space as the late twentieth century parallel to the age-old need to control the seas and the midtwentieth century requirement to control the air.[408]

That same month General Putt made the same plea: "We have always strived to try to fly higher and higher. One could control the atmosphere by just being able to fly a little bit higher than the other fellow. So I think the same thing will occur in space."[409] Answering a rhetorical question regarding the military advantage of space power, Brig Gen H. A. Boushey, Air Force deputy director of research and development, stated:

> For years our job has been to achieve, and at times to exercise, a dominant capability to deliver firepower against an enemy by military operations above the surface of the earth. In doing this job we have been, and still are, guided by one major premise, that a decisive margin of advantage goes to the nation whose delivery vehicles can attain the greatest speed, the greatest range, and the greatest altitude.[410]

At the dawn of the space age, Air Force visionaries evidently found it difficult to conceive the precise applications through which a control of space might be exercised. "To control space," noted General White, "we must not only be able to go through it with vehicles that travel from point to point, but we must stay in space with human beings who can carry out jobs efficiently."[411] General Boushey added, "First of all I do not believe that machines alone, controlled from the earth, can establish a capability to dominate space.... On the spot exercise of human intelligence, judgment, and discrimination will be needed for effective control of space."[412] Boushey additionally urged that the moon would be the ultimate "high ground" both for launching further explorations of the solar system and for dispatching missiles against an aggressor on earth.

> As regards the moon, I personally believe it could, at some future date, be used as a secure base to deter aggression. Lunar landing sites, perhaps located on the far side of the moon, which could never be viewed directly from the earth, could launch missiles earthward. They could be guided accurately during flight and to impact, and thus might serve peaceful ends by deterring any would-be aggressor.[413]

The visionary moon-based proposal was promptly attacked by Dr Lee A. DuBridge, president of the California Institute of Technology, who dismissed lunar-based deterrence as a "Buck Rogers" stunt.[414]

In a more conservative vein General Putt suggested in April 1958 that "control of space could start initially at a relatively short distance away from the surface of the earth."[415] As has been seen, General White early in 1959 introduced the new concept of "aerospace," or the concept that "air and space comprise a single continuous operational field in which the Air Force must continue to function."[416] Even though the *aerospace* term seemed strange at first, it gained increasing acceptance. By February 1960, Congressman Overton Brooks, chairman of the House Committee on Science and Astronautics, accepted it. "Frankly," he said, "I think we are straining at a gnat when we question the word 'aerospace.' If we can come up with a better word, that is something else."[417] Shortly after this, the Joint Chiefs of Staff accepted "aerospace" as a word for joint usage and defined it as: "Of, or pertaining to, the earth's envelope or atmosphere and the space above it; two separate entities considered as a single realm of activity in launching, guidance, and control of vehicles which will travel in both realms."[418]

During 1959 the Air Force began to bridle its thinking about space. In April, General Schriever defended "in-the-blue" thinking, but he asserted that the value of a base on the moon, assuming that it was technologically possible, would have to be determined in relation to other ways in which some other weapon system might be able to do the same job at perhaps lesser costs. In an address before the National Press Club on 11 January 1960, General White agreed that there had been "excessive talk about manned expeditions to the Moon, Venus, Mars, and beyond — as though these ventures were well within our present capability."[419] On 4 February, in answer to his own question as to how far manned vehicles would be sent into space, General White said:

> The answer, as I see it, is — as far as they need to go in regular operations. I feel that initially our systematic missions will operate at rather shallow altitudes — relatively speaking — within a few hundred miles of the earth. Our immediate operational concern is events which may occur on earth and in the zone immediately above it. We don't provide anything by operating farther away than we need to go.[420]

Based on these ideas, the Air Force logically accepted the concept that space systems "should complement or replace current inventory systems and should be employed within existing concepts."[421] The Air Force's position on the relationship of space to military potential was that "space systems should be developed when required to perform an essential military mission if they will provide a unique, more effective or more economical means for performing the mission."[422] Both in testimony before a congressional committee in February and in an April 1960 article, Lt Gen R. C. Wilson explained that an Air Force space system had to be judged by the criterion of its relative effectiveness and could not be developed to perform particular function unless "it offers the only means of doing the job; or . . . it is the best way to do the job and is not excessively expensive (for example, very early warning of hostile ICBM launchings); or . . . it offers a more economical way of doing a job (as may well be true of a communications satellite system)."[423]

Since the Air Force did not compartmentalize its development program into astronautics and aeronautics, or space and nonspace, it could not logically develop a space plan as a separate plan. Certain programs nevertheless met the "relative-effectiveness" criteria: missiles, navigation and communications satellites, and the Discoverer, Midas, and Samos missile programs that were aimed at the exploitation of early warning and reconnaissance capabilities. In this respect, the Air Force did envision development objectives both generally and in terms of growth potential of programs under way in 1960. The development objectives included reduction of costs and time required for launchings, improvement of guidance systems, increases in component reliability, and extension of the effective lifetimes of orbital satellites.[424] Even though the Air Force did not have a long-range space plan similar to NASA's 10-year plan, Doctor York noted in March 1960: "We do have some ideas about how various of these programs might develop in the future, but we don't believe that considering our mission we can develop a plan for space-related programs independently of the overall defense program."[425] In supporting the Eisenhower defense budgets for fiscal year 1960 and fiscal year 1961, Doctor York stressed that the objectives of defense efforts in space were

> the development, production, and operation of space systems where it can be demonstrated with reasonable certainty that the use of space flight will enable us to accomplish our basic defense mission, and ... the development of components which will be needed in systems which cannot be clearly defined at this time but which will develop as the future unfolds in this new sphere of activity.[426]

Two days before the launching of the first Soviet Sputnik in October 1957, Soviet Maj Gen G. I. Pokrovsky had predicted: "The struggle in and for outer space will have tremendous significance in the armed conflict of the near future."[427] By mid-1959 Lt Gen R. C. Wilson was willing to speak in public of "a growing Soviet potential to wage war from an environment in space—possibly from satellite vehicles circling the earth at various altitudes, from space stations on the so-called stationary orbits, or perhaps eventually from a military lunar base."[428] At the height of his presidential campaign on 10 October 1960, Senator Kennedy also gave voice to fears that the Soviets might be winning the space race. He declared:

> We are in a strategic space race with the Russians, and we have been losing. Control of space will be decided in the next decade. If the Soviets control space they can control earth, as in past centuries the nations that controlled the seas dominated the continents.[429]

Contending that opportunities and threats in space were beginning to come into focus, General Schriever asked Trevor Gardner on 11 October 1960 to assemble a group of the nation's leading scientists and executives, similar to the John von Neumann committee of 1954, that would study and recommend a space development program for the future. Acting without delay, Gardner assembled the Air Force Space Study Committee that same month, and the committee (whose members included Dr Harold Brown) submitted its unclassified report on 20 March 1961. The report provided assessments of the Soviet space threat, recommendations on Air Force organization, and requirements for Air Force space activities. Among its findings, the committee asserted that the Air Force role in space was "envisioned too narrowly" and that a "dogma" prevailed within the Air Force "that technical developments, particularly those involving any substantial application of resources, must be justified by a specific weapon system which in turn is tied to a close military requirement."[430] By committing itself to systems development, the committee reasoned that the Air Force was treating space systems requirements as if it knew the framework of strategy and space technical boundary conditions that would exist in the future. The committee emphasized:

> The development of urgently needed technical capabilities such as boost, rendezvous, maneuverability, and communications are essential to the speedy attainment of effective military use of space. The premature initiation of "systems" produces inefficiencies and may severely limit or foreclose the opportunity for the full development of such fundamental capabilities.[431]

When he appeared before the Senate Committee on Armed Services on 11 April 1961, Secretary Zuckert voiced official concern that the Soviets, who had established a superior space capability which gave them the promise of machines to work in space, might attain mastery and dominance of space. He warned that "the lesson is that through and from space, earth can be dominated.... This Nation and her allies have no choice but to extend our influence into space to the end that no nation shall be disfranchised in space, and no nation shall be disfranchised on earth through dominance of space by another."[432] At the time Zuckert was speaking, there were rumors from Moscow that the Soviets had put the world's first human cosmonaut into orbit, and on 12 April the Soviet Union announced that air force Maj Yuri Gagarin had encircled the earth in a five-ton Vostok satellite. "This first manned orbital flight bears out the Air Force's previous estimates of the extremely high priority of Soviet space efforts and their concentration on the near-earth region as the logical area for the near-term expansion of military aerospace power," General White stated.[433] In remarks at his retirement ceremony on 30 June 1961, White reminded his listeners that in the course of history the people who had controlled the land had controlled the world; then the people who had controlled the seas had controlled the world; and then the people who had controlled the air had controlled the world. "I make this prediction," he concluded "in the future the people who control space will control the world."[434]

On numerous occasions after he became Air Force chief of staff, General LeMay anticipated that the entry of the United States into space would follow the same parallel that had occurred with the air program. In 1961 LeMay said that the United States was "at about the same position ... in regard to space technology as we were in aerodynamics along about 1908, 1910, or 1911, along in there."[435] In a parallel to the experience in aeronautics, the Air Force had developed the first satellites for a primarily passive, peaceful, and defensive employment designed to enhance command and control and to reduce the danger of surprise attack. But just as had been the case with the aviation experience in World War I, LeMay anticipated that an enemy would not be able to countenance a loss of surprise and security and anticipated that "an aggressor will seek ways and means to eliminate our defensive systems."[436] He concluded: "A nation that has maneuverable space vehicles and revolutionary armaments can indeed control the world. For peace or for aggression."[437] Continued Soviet space spectaculars added weight to LeMay's warning. On 6–7 August 1961, Soviet air force Maj G. S. Titov orbited the earth 17 times in 25 hours. In December 1961, Premier Khrushchev told the world, "We have bombs stronger than 100 megatons. We placed Gagarin and Titov in space and we can replace them with other loads that can be directed to any place on earth."[438]

Spurred on by President Kennedy's statement to Congress on 25 May 1961 that the United States would take "a clearly leading role in space achievement" and by an appreciation of the Soviet threat in space, the Air Force undertook preparation of a 10-year plan which attempted to identify, as best as could be done based on careful analysis, what could and should be done to meet military requirements in space with a commitment of limited resources.[439] As issued in September 1961, the Air Force Space Plan represented the best thought within the Air Staff and was intended to provide basic guidance to the research and development community. General Ferguson described the general concepts of the plan in congressional testimony. The plan described Air Force space policy as a part of the national space policy but characterized it as being more specifically designed to ensure that space remained free for mankind. It recognized that space systems would have to be considered in relation to all other weapon systems. The space plan noted that space systems for geodetic mapping, target identification and location, warning of ballistic missile attack, navigation, and weather surveillance had already been justified, and it posed an urgent requirement for the development of a satellite inspection system and for a broad range of space technology of military interest. Space systems, for example, promised a breakthrough in defense against ballistic missile attack, a means of deployment of command and control systems in deep space, and fast retaliation strikes from space bombers in low orbits. In a summary of desired military characteristics of space technology, the plan pointed out the need for more powerful, cheaper, and quicker reacting space boosters, for rendezvous, docking, and transfer capabilities in space, and for the development of reusable space vehicles which would be able to make aerodynamic landings within specified geographical areas after performing space missions. Finally, all evidence pointed to a role for man in space. Said General Ferguson:

> Man has certain qualitative capabilities which machines cannot duplicate. He is unique in his ability to make on-the-spot judgments. He can discriminate and select from alternatives which have not been anticipated. He is adaptable to rapidly changing situations. Thus, by including man in military space systems, we significantly increase the flexibility of the systems, as well as increase the probability of mission success.[440]

The plan noted that cooperative arrangements between the Air Force and NASA mutually were advantageous, but it pointed out that simultaneous research on "purely military aspects" of space technology was essential because "some operational and technical needs are not common to both the civil and military effort."[441]

The preparation of the Air Force Space Plan also may have been intended to reassure Congress that the Air Force was not dragging its feet in regard to space. Early in 1961 the House Appropriations Committee criticized the Air Force's Dyna-Soar program as lacking in imagination and boldness. As has been seen, this program was designed to test the concept of a manned space glider in orbit, but pending the availability of a more powerful booster, the Air Force planned to test the vehicle in a number of short launches down the Atlantic missile range. The House committee specifically recommended development of a higher thrust booster. In its appropriations for fiscal year 1962, Congress voted $185.8 million specifically for Dyna-Soar—$85.8 million more than had been requested by the executive branch.[442] Even though Secretary McNamara was not going to allow the expenditure of the additional Dyna-Soar funds, the maturity of a launch-vehicle agreement between the Department of Defense and NASA nevertheless promised to permit a more imaginative Dyna-Soar program. Extending over a period of three to four months, representatives of Defense and NASA debated requirements of a new booster that would provide military thrust capabilities and also would serve to back up the Saturn booster that NASA was developing to use in manned orbital programs.[443]

At the end of this prolonged study and discussion, the Department of Defense gained authority in December 1961 to proceed with the development of a thrust-augmented Titan rocket that would be known as Titan III. Where the Saturn was a relatively complicated, liquid-fueled rocket, the Titan III would employ solid and storable fuels, thus permitting shorter reaction time, and would afford a means of launching loads weighing up to 25,000 pounds. The first flight of the Titan IIIA—a modified Titan missile plus an upper stage—was expected in 1965, and the Titan IIIC—the Titan IIIA with two, 120-inch strap-on solid motors—was scheduled to fly in 1966.[444] Since the Titan III would be powerful enough to put Dyna-Soar into orbit, the Air Force requested and received authority in December 1961 to reorient the Dyna-Soar program. Although unmanned Dyna-Soar flights were planned earlier, the first manned Dyna-Soar flight was visualized for July 1966.[445] From the Air Force point of view, the Dyna-Soar would be a useful experimental vehicle. Its aerodynamic characteristics would allow a pilot great flexibility in selecting the time at which he might choose to deorbit and where he would land. Although Dyna-Soar could lead to the development of a vehicle with military applications, it would initially complement the NASA Mercury and Gemini vehicles, which would have the ballistic type of reentry.[446]

The Air Force was confident that its space plan, issued in September 1961, represented "a comprehensive study of the potential Soviet threat, the status of our technology relative to space applications, and the long-range objectives and needs of the Air Force . . . derived from a national viewpoint."[447] Secretary

IDEAS, CONCEPTS, DOCTRINE

McNamara and Doctor Brown did not accept the Air Force thinking. McNamara said on 29 January 1962, "The requirement for military operations in outer space is not at all clear at the present time."[448] Although he saw some rather limited requirements for warning, navigation, and communications satellites, the military purpose of other space operations was not yet clear. McNamara concluded:

> Therefore, our program is directed to (a) achieving a technology which will permit us to engage in military operations in outer space if the requirement does develop in the future, and (b) developing certain of the basic equipment required for such military operations, specifically boosters for launch vehicles sufficiently large to place into outer space equipment of the size we might possibly require.[449]

Speaking as director of defense research and engineering, Brown explained:

> At this stage of development, it is difficult to define accurately the specific characteristics that future military operational systems of many kinds ought to have. We must, therefore, engage in a broad program covering basic building blocks which will develop technological capabilities to meet many possible contingencies. In this way, we will provide necessary insurance against military surprise in space by advancing our knowledge on a systematic basis so as to permit the shortest possible time lag in undertaking fullscale development programs as specific needs are identified.[450]

In testimony before congressional committees early in 1962, Air Force spokesmen viewed the Soviet military threat and the military potential of space with a higher degree of urgency than did the Office of the Secretary of Defense. Secretary Zuckert stated:

> Every time we have made a significant advance, we seem to have found a way for using it for a military purpose. I think it is important to take seriously the space capability the Russians have developed in such a short period of time and to realize after this period of time military possibilities seem to be opening up. As the years move on, these military possibilities could well become a reality.[451]

The Air Force chiefly feared that the Soviets might exploit their technological lead to establish a control over space. General Ferguson explained one way in which control might be exercised in space by discussing in open congressional testimony the Bambi (ballistic missile boost intercept) concept of a satellite system for antiballistic missile defense. When launched, ballistic missiles emitted tremendous heat which could be detected by infrared sensors, and Bambi contemplated the maintenance on station of a number of orbital vehicles that would search for, home on, and destroy hostile missiles in their vulnerable boost phase. If an unfriendly nation ventured into space with the Bambi concept, it could obviously establish an effective space blockade.[452]

In an address on 28 March 1962, General LeMay expressed an opinion that "beam-directed energy weapons" would be able to transmit energy across space with the speed of light, thus effecting a technological disarmament of nuclear weapons. He warned, "Whatever we do, the Soviets already have recognized the importance of these new developments and they are moving at full speed for a decisive capability in space. If they are successful, they can deny space to us."[453] On 29 March, General Schriever described the basic capabilities fundamental to potential military space weapon systems as:

> The ability to orbit, maneuver, rendezvous, deorbit, reenter, and land on a routine basis; the ability to support manned space flight; the ability to transfer men and materiel between spacecraft in orbit; the ability to guide, navigate, and communicate in deep space operations.[454]

Even though an Air Force spokesman explained the requirements for space operational capabilities, Secretary McNamara in defining the limits of the Department of Defense space program in his statement on 29 January 1962, maintained that the program would seek "to achieve a technology which will permit us to engage in military operations in outer space if the requirement does develop in the future."[455] On 23 February 1962 McNamara wrote a long classified memorandum to Zuckert specifying desirable features of military systems to be investigated in space and setting down ground rules under which he felt the Air Force ought to consider experiments with both manned and unmanned space flight for military purposes.[456]

To provide an acceptable, integrated Air Force space program as envisioned by Secretary McNamara, the Air Force drew heavily upon its own resources, those of the scientific community, and those of the not-for-profit contractors. As a result of these studies, the Air Force assembled an Air Force space program, which General Ferguson described early in 1963 as a "bound book" that spelled out "in quite readable English" two basic objectives: "(1) To augment, by use of space systems, the existing military capabilities of US terrestrial forces; (2) To develop a military patrol capability for the protection of US interests in space." "The various elements of the proposed Air Force space program," he stated, "would combine to form a stream of advance toward useful military capabilities in space, some of which can be realized almost immediately, others being dependent upon further technological progress."[457] He pointed out that key elements in the program—the Titan III launching system and the Dyna-Soar—were already approved. An additional key element which was recommended for the program would be the development of a military orbital development system (MODS), which would include a military test station that would be put into low orbit and to which men would shuttle back and forth to explore problems of sustained operations in space. This concept had been proposed in the 1961 space plan, but it was programmed in terms of technology in the 1962 program. Beginning in fiscal year 1964, the Air Force proposed to allocate $177 million to the beginning of the development of the MODS space station and for the acquisition of Blue Gemini vehicles—an Air Force acquisition of NASA-developed technology—which would permit an early beginning of Air Force training in space flight.[458]

Although the Air Force was drawing up its space program, the Soviets continued to display an interest in expanding their military technology into space. On 11–12

August 1962 the Soviet Union placed two astronauts into orbit within a 24-hour period, the orbits of the two Vostok vehicles being so carefully calculated that they approached to within three miles of each other. Appearing in public print, Marshal V. D. Sokolovsky's *Military Strategy* portrayed Soviet activities in space as peaceful and reactive to the American space threat, but the volume noted: "An important problem now is warfare with artificial earth satellites, which can be launched for diverse reasons, even as carriers of nuclear weapons."[459] It also stated:

> Soviet military strategy takes into account the need for studying questions on the use of outer space and aerospace vehicles to strengthen the defense of the socialist countries.... It would be a mistake to allow the imperialist camp to achieve superiority in this field. We must oppose the imperialists with more effective means and methods for the use of space for defense purposes.[460]

Under a Moscow dateline of 23 February 1963, Marshal S. S. Biryuzov announced: "It has now become possible at a command from earth to launch rockets from satellites at any desirable time and point of the satellite's trajectory."[461] Biryuzov added that the Soviet Union had a superiority in rockets and in nuclear weapons over the Western nations.[462]

Accepting the fact that the United States was behind in space technology, General Ferguson defended the Air Force space program as "a prudent one in a dangerous world."[463] The Air Force program, however, was based on guidance provided in January 1962, and new Department of Defense thinking began to appear even before the program books were printed. In a speech on 5 September 1962, Deputy Secretary of Defense Gilpatric stated: "An arms race in space will not contribute to our security. I can think of no greater stimulus for a Soviet thermonuclear arms effort in space than a United States commitment to such a program. This we will not do."[464] In another address on 9 October 1962, Deputy Director of Defense Research and Engineering John H. Rubel reminded his audience that the Department of Defense was not a "Department of Space" and that defense space projects must further a basic defense mission. Even though defense expenditures for space technology had been very large, Rubel noted that "we have not evolved any very new ideas for military operations in space during the past several years."[465] Such ideas might be forthcoming, but Rubel emphasized that technical and policy decisions concerning the development of systems for military use were not being made on general or philosophical grounds "or in furtherance of abstract doctrinal concepts."[466]

> Polaris does not augment America's "sea power" in the Mahan sense, nor was it started and supported because anyone thought it would. Minuteman does not augment America's "air power" in the conventional sense any more or any less than Polaris does, nor is it either supported or opposed because it is essentially a "land" system, owing its survival to dispersal and hardening under ground. Doctrinal abstractions such as "sea power" or "air power" or "aerospace power" are often useful for analysis and discussion of the patterns as history reveals them. But these doctrinal abstractions do not translate

well into new programs and projects. Here technology takes over, and technology . . . tends to obsolete such concepts and abstractions rather than the reverse.[467]

In conclusion, Rubel stated the considerations that affected defense research and engineering: systems must meet clear-cut military requirements; decisions must be governed "by what we ought to do, not just what we can do, although new developments often affect both";[468] developments must be feasible and worthwhile in relation to urgency and effectiveness; and decision must ensure technological growth in all fields of military interest and concern.[469]

Commenting to a journalist on Rubel's address, an unidentified officer who was said to be very familiar with military space affairs maintained that the size of the defense space research and development program was not the issue but rather the lack of doctrinal concepts which could "guide the men charged with the responsibility for weapons development and procurement in properly selecting what is needed."[470] In this officer's view doctrinal concepts were not abstract; they were courses of actions and of the conduct of operations; and they were "the blueprints for the use of certain environments in a certain way."[471] When Secretary McNamara was asked to explain what Rubel meant by his references to "doctrinal abstractions," he replied:

> I interpret the quote . . . to mean that Mr Rubel believes that if we develop weapons systems for space, they are likely to be new weapons systems, not merely extensions of current weapons systems designed primarily for earth-bound use, and to that extent . . . I fully share Mr Rubel's view.[472]

When asked to comment on General White's assertion that "those who control space will control the world," McNamara responded: "I don't understand what it means. . . . I have heard of no space weapon in concept form or otherwise which offers potential greater than other weapons in our inventory."[473] In reply to another specific question, McNamara described the Bambi antimissile satellite as "nothing more than a paper study of a very esoteric system."[474] A little later, Doctor Brown also was asked about White's contention that the world could be controlled from space, and he replied:

> I would not subscribe to that statement partly because I am not quite sure what control of space means. I do not see that it is really feasible to control space because a country will always have an advantage in space over its own territory because it can easily operate from the ground up into space. I do not see a way, for example, in which space can be controlled to the extent that one can prevent ballistic missiles from being fired here from going through space and coming down there. If a country could do that it would indeed be in a fair way to control the world, and we continue to work on ideas that might have that effect. But I think in the end it is not going to be feasible.[475]

Brown also reasoned that it was "conceivable but not likely" that space might become an area in which armed conflict might take place: it might be possible to knock out a hostile space vehicle with "another thing based in space."[476] He added,

"I believe that is not very likely because you can probably do it better than the ground...."[477]

In the preparation of the Department of Defense budget requests for fiscal year 1964, which took place during calendar year 1962, Secretary McNamara demanded that any space project undertaken for military purposes would mesh with the efforts of NASA in all vital areas and would "promise, insofar as possible, to enhance our military power and effectiveness." The defense space program thus was divided into three categories of projects: projects for which there was a clear military requirement such as satellites for mapping, communications, navigation, detection of nuclear testing, and weather forecasting; projects related to developmental work on probable future military requirements such as missile warning systems and additional communications; and research and development work related "to the development of certain capabilities which would be required were we subsequently to find it necessary to put man into space in conjunction with some military requirement that might arise in the future."[478]

As previously noted, McNamara refused to accept the Air Force requirement for the manned orbital development system and the Blue Gemini, both because they did not mesh with the NASA program and because they would duplicate Gemini and Dyna-Soar. In the Department of Defense budget request for fiscal year 1964, which was submitted to Congress in January 1963, McNamara estimated that $1,650 million was for space and that the military space program amounted to more than 20 percent of the total research and development budget.[479] Although McNamara followed normal usage in referring to a "military space program," Dr Lawrence L. Kavanau, special assistant for space in the Office of the Director of Defense Research and Engineering, subsequently explained that a military "space program" actually could not exist as a separate entity under McNamara's criteria, since most space projects had to compete with other systems on a functional and cost basis within the total defense program structure.[480]

In presenting the Air Force's position on space to congressional committees early in 1963, General Ferguson pointed out that even though the Soviets faced formidable free-world air, sea, and land defenses "the advent of human space activity exposes an open flank" in which "the Soviet strategist may well hope to attain strategic ascendancy."[481] Dr I. A. Getting, president of the Aerospace Corporation, was even more fearful of the space race. "In the exploitation of space," he was quoted as saying, "we appear to be risking unilateral disarmament."[482] In rebuttal, Secretary McNamara insisted that he knew of many things in space that the United States was doing, that he had no information the Soviets were doing, and that, on the other hand, he knew of nothing that the Soviets were doing that the United States was not undertaking. He further observed: "I do not believe the Soviets are utilizing space for military purposes to nearly the extent that we are today. I say that because our operations in space for military purposes are truly quite extensive."[483] Secretary McNamara could find no logical reason for placing weapons of mass destruction in orbit. "I haven't had recommended to me the introduction into space of any weapon that I can recall, nor am I aware that we have developed a weapon which offers sufficient potential to warrant being placed in space," he said.[484] Both LeMay and Ferguson accepted the viewpoint that the employment of orbital weapons against earth targets appeared to have no immediate tactical advantages in comparison with intercontinental ballistic missiles, but they were not willing to rule out a future possibility that such weapons might not prove practicable. The main advantage of orbital weapon systems would be the reduction of the time that a missile thus launched would require to strike a target.[485]

In his presentations about space, General Ferguson also placed great emphasis upon the importance of man as an essential element of future space systems. He stated early in 1963:

> The Air Force is convinced that man will have an important place in aeronautical and space systems of the future.... We firmly believe that manned operations provide more assurance of mission success because of the proven ability of man to reliably cope with unanticipated military problems. In addition, military equipment gains in flexibility and capability and at the same time is less complex with a human operator aboard. Finally, we can think of no way to build into automated military equipment the determination of a military man to perform his missions in spite of unforeseen obstacles or national deficiencies.[486]

Although a manned orbital military space station would be an "important building block" in the Air Force space program,[487] Ferguson submitted that the program had even more important objectives:

> The goal of manned military space operations is the ability to launch into orbit with minimum delay, to perform the required mission, and quickly return to a secure area, preferably in the United States. Such operations, to be effective, must not be limited by restrictive recovery plans such as are used by Mercury and Gemini. Reliable and routine recovery of the pilot and his reusable spacecraft with its special equipment is a must.[488]

Based on this concept, the Air Force judged that the experimental Dyna-Soar was "a most critical part of the national space program."[489]

From his public statements, Doctor Brown was known to have personal doubts about the usefulness of man in space.[490] Early in 1963, Secretary McNamara also began to express doubts on the subject:

> As for the requirement for a manned military operation in space, it is not clear to me what we gain by putting a man in space for military purposes. I do not see the future clearly. It may be that certain of our requirements in space cannot be met without a man there. It may be that in order to inspect properly unidentified satellites we might have to have a man in a US satellite in space. I think it is rather unlikely we would require a man for those purposes, in part because a man greatly complicates the operation in space. You have to put so much in space just to allow a man to exist that it greatly adds to the complexity of the operation. Today it appears to us we can achieve military capabilities in space more quickly without a man than with a man. But as our knowledge of space operations advances this conclusion may prove false and I believe, therefore,

IDEAS, CONCEPTS, DOCTRINE

> we should have boosters with a sufficient capability to put into space satellites that will allow men to operate within them and we should have an understanding of the strains on the man and the extent of his capability in that space environment.[491]

At the very least, Doctor Kavanau reported that the subject of man's usefulness in space was controversial within the Office of the Director of Defense Research and Engineering.[492] To Rubel the question resolved down to a matter of taking first steps first:

> We could not define a mission in space until we had done the very first things necessary to put the man up there and find out what his functional capabilities were, what his functional limitations were, what the relative costs and advantages of having him there are . . . so that the first step in any program, even if we could define with the greatest precision right now exactly what military mission he would perform . . . would be . . . to do the bioastronautic work and perform the tests and experiments necessary to get the fellows up there and find out their capabilities.[493]

Moved by an uncertainty as to the worth of man in space and by a belief that NASA's Gemini program had outstripped the Air Force's Dyna-Soar program, McNamara began to question the advisability of continuing with Dyna-Soar. In view of the NASA-DOD agreement permitting defense representatives to sit on the Gemini planning committee, McNamara asked the Air Force on 18 January 1963 to consider the possibility of cutting back the Dyna-Soar program and proceeding with Gemini.[494] To Rubel a close examination of Dyna-Soar made much sense: the program was laid out to cost $800 million and probably would cost more; the X-20 vehicle of the Dyna-Soar project was of a "very advanced character" and "technically far out"; and, finally, answers were needed to the question of why—considering Gemini—the Air Force ought "to support such a large effort at the same time you have another one going to put man in a near space orbit at very great expense when we know so little about what is involved in the support of life and the limitations and capabilities of man in space."[495]

During the Department of Defense's examination of Dyna-Soar in the summer and autumn of 1963, the Air Force submitted that the X-20's lifting maneuver and radiative cooling design made it substantially different from the ballistic characteristics of Mercury and Gemini. The X-20 would explore regimes of flight from Mach 5 to Mach 25, and its flexibility in orbital recovery would open a wide recovery "window" (the time-space when a deorbit decision had to be made). Its ability to maneuver would permit it to land at a selected point within an area in excess of 10,000 square miles, as compared with a few thousand square miles for the Gemini. Since the X-20 would not require the great numbers of naval vessels and as many as 20,000 people required to recover the Gemini, it promised a substantial saving in recovery forces. General LeMay stated, "We feel that if we are ever going to do anything useful out in space, we must be able to get out there cheaply and be able to return at a precise time and spot on the globe, which means controlled reentry."[496] In essence, the Air Force assumed that the X-20 Dyna-Soar was going to be an initial step into what would become a large, manned military mission in space, and Secretary McNamara refused to accept this assumption until he could get some hard evidence. At a briefing given by the X-20 systems program office in Denver on 23 October, McNamara asked many more questions about the manned space mission than about the Dyna-Soar, and he subsequently justified the decision to terminate Dyna-Soar by describing the X-20 as "a narrowly defined program, limited primarily to developing the techniques of controlled reentry at a time when the broader question of 'Do we need to operate in near-orbit orbit?' has not yet been answered."[497] Although maneuverability was admittedly of great interest, McNamara felt that the maneuverability of the X-20 would not be needed until man's capabilities in space had been demonstrated and were actually being used in a semiroutine manner. By such a time — if such a time eventuated — a much more capable vehicle than the X-20, which could carry only one person and had very limited flight endurance and payload capacity (75 cubic feet/1,000 pounds), would obviously be required. Speaking of Dyna-Soar, McNamara said: "I think this is a good illustration of what happens when we start on a program with a poor definition of our end objective."[498]

Believing that Dyna-Soar should be terminated but that national security demanded the development of manned military space flight technology, the Office of the Secretary of Defense worked closely with NASA officials to devise a substitute program. When Secretary McNamara announced the cancellation of Dyna-Soar on 10 December 1963, he simultaneously proposed the initiation of a manned orbital laboratory (MOL) study and expansion of an unmanned aerothermodynamic structural systems environmental test (ASSET) project. The MOL project was to be directed specifically to determine one's utility in performing military functions in space. This system would be made up of a modified Gemini capsule coupled to a pressurized cylinder that would be equipped as an orbiting laboratory. It would be launched by a Titan IIIC. Viewed in concept, a two-man MOL crew would be seated in the Gemini B capsule during launch; would move back into the laboratory section after the vehicle was in orbit; and would reenter the Gemini, detach it from the laboratory section, and employ the capsule as the reentry vehicle for return to earth. With provisions for about 30 days' stay in orbit and ample working space, MOL promised to provide a much more comprehensive test of military man in space than either Gemini or Dyna-Soar, but ASSET would lack maneuvering capability, orbital capability, and horizontal landing capability.[499]

In justifying the cancellation of Dyna-Soar early in 1964, Secretary McNamara estimated that the cost of the canceled program would be about $400 million, including termination charges, and he further estimated that about $100 million of the cost could be considered salvageable in the form of added knowledge about reentry controls. He confessed that he had been remiss in not having canceled the project earlier. To his way of thinking, Dyna-Soar was another example of "the problem that we have had in this space age, when there has been tremendous pressure on all parties to initiate large projects with rather ill-defined purposes."[500]

Neither Secretary Zuckert nor General LeMay concurred in the cancellation of Dyna-Soar. LeMay admitted that the MOL and ASSET programs would be "of great significance."[501] Zuckert said that the idea of a military orbital laboratory had been "an important cornerstone" of the Air Force's space program. He also recognized the finality of McNamara's decision on Dyna-Soar. But he insisted for the record that approximately an additional $373 million would have financed Dyna-Soar through its initial flight in July 1966.[502] Since half of the Dyna-Soar project already had been funded, LeMay thought that the cancellation of the project would not represent a realistic saving. He explained:

> The capability of returning from space in a precise, maneuverable, pilot-controlled manner is of fundamental importance to the conduct of practical and routine manned military space operations. Dyna-Soar was vigorously supported by the Air Force because it provided the most promising approach to such a capability. It is our considered judgement that the problem of precision return will some day have to be resolved.[503]

Reflections on Military Space Requirements

The Kennedy administration had come into office with the evident belief that the United States was in danger of losing a space weapons race with the Soviet Union, but much of the fear of Soviet technological superiority evidently disappeared in 1962 and 1963. Senator Russell observed, "When Khrushchev pulled out of Cuba it settled any issue in my mind as to where superiority is today." Secretary McNamara agreed: "I think all of Khrushchev's actions indicate the conclusion that he knows we can completely destroy his society today should he attack us from the ground, the sea, the atmosphere, or space."[504]

Even though DOD policy in regard to space research and development appeared to be changing early in 1963, Secretary McNamara flatly denied the allegation that the United States was unilaterally foregoing the development of offensive space systems in the hope that the Soviets would do likewise. He also was sure that the Soviets were not exercising voluntary restraint on military space programs. He stated in February 1963: "I don't believe they are exercising voluntary restraint on anything. They are seeking every possible form of power that will give them an advantage over us."[505] As already noted, however, both the United States and the Soviet Union accepted the United Nations resolution of 17 October 1963 that called upon all nations to refrain from orbiting weapons of mass destruction in space. This resolution did not prevent research and development of orbital weapons, but Dr Brown subsequently stated that no more than three or four people in one of the contract organizations were studying the matter in the United States during fiscal year 1964. Brown expected similarly small efforts in fiscal year 1965 for two reasons: "First, it is not a very good idea.... Second, there now is a U.N. resolution ... not to put bombs in orbit."[506] In Brown's judgment orbital weapons "are not very great threats to us in the near future, and ... they are unlikely ever to be. Such weapons would be largely antipopulation in nature and would not appear to alter Soviet military posture sufficiently to justify several obvious difficulties in their deployment."[507] In summation on an orbital weapon system, Brown observed that "apparently neither the Russians nor we believe it is a very important strategic weapon or a very valuable strategic weapon considering how much it would cost and how little it would do beyond what can be done by ballistic missiles."[508]

When he explained the defense research and development budget request for fiscal year 1965 to congressional committees early in 1964, Secretary McNamara repeated his belief that the Soviets did not have any precedence over the United States in defense space efforts. He said, "I believe our military space program is at least as extensive as theirs today."[509] In this budget McNamara continued to emphasize the requirement that military space projects must mesh with NASA efforts and must hold "the distinct promise of enhancing our military power and effectiveness."[510] About half of the defense space research and development effort was directly related to relatively well-recognized and understood military requirements, such as satellite communications and navigation systems. The balance of the defense space effort was "aimed at creating a broad base of new technology, devices, and in some cases systems for possible future application."[511] The policy of creating a broad base of space technology without necessarily developing military systems was reminiscent of policies of the 1930s and 1940s which had sought to maintain an aeronautical potential in being for use in a mobilization effort. Based on the availability of the Titan IIIC large-thrust military booster and the building-block approach to space technology, General Ferguson ventured a "horseback guess" that a required space weapon system probably could be developed with an absolute minimum lead time of three years.[512] The demonstration of a satellite intercept capability "in just about a year" of work in 1963–64 provided an illustration of how the broader space technological base might permit the United States to respond to requirements. The satellite interceptor was put together to include a Thor booster and guidance components that had been developed for other purposes.[513]

Although they accepted the evolutionary approach to military space technology, Air Force leaders continued to give credence to Soviet space threats to the security of the United States. Noted General Ferguson in March 1963:

> History records that an acceptable peace in any medium has been maintained only through the existence of ready military strength applicable to that medium. Unfortunately, it also records that every medium affording military possibilities has been used for military purposes.[514]

General LeMay stated that the United States certainly should be thinking about a strategic space force, even if the time was not right for it. "A military capability for defense is the product not only of technology, but also of training and operational experience," he warned.[515] Emphasizing "the factor of time by which space threats and counterthreats are governed," LeMay pointed out that "if an unforeseen threat emerges in the new medium of space, months or years will be required to devise, develop, and render operational the necessary defense against the new threat."[516] Unlike the divided civil and military space programs in the United States, LeMay reasoned that the Soviet space program was "entirely military."[517] In one of his first public addresses following his retirement from the Air Force in February 1965, LeMay emphasized that the ability of the United States to evaluate Soviet intentions had never been outstanding. Very nearly all Soviet acts of aggression had been accompanied by an element of surprise. "It is in the area of space that Soviet technological developments are most likely to bypass this generation of US weapon systems," he concluded.[518]

Future in Prospect: Project Forecast and Air Force Manual 1-1

Secretary Zuckert remarked in February 1963:

> Beyond the immediate future the picture is not as clear as we would like it to be. The natural uncertainties inherent in forward planning are complicated by such imponderable factors as the life expectancy of today's manned strategic bombing systems, the complications in the planning and employment of an all-missile strategic system, the question of an appropriate defense structure, and the uncertainties as to the nature of development of military activity in space.[519]

Both Zuckert and LeMay evidently recognized that the time had come for the Air Force to take stock of its capabilities and to look to its future potential. In March 1963, LeMay directed General Schriever, as commander of the Air Force Systems Command, to make "a comprehensive study and analysis of the Air Force structure projected into the 1965–1975 time period."[520]

The LeMay directive set in motion a major Air Force study that came to be known as Project Forecast. To escape the disruptions of the Pentagon, Schriever concentrated the study of future Air Force technological opportunities and requirements in the Air Force Systems Command's Space Systems Division complex at Los Angeles, California. In a period of some nine months of sustained effort, representatives of some 40 government activities, including 27 Air Force organizations, the Army, Navy, and Marine Corps, and 10 other federal agencies, participated in Project Forecast. Twenty-six universities and colleges provided members from their faculties and research staffs. Seventy corporations and 10 nonprofit research agencies also provided a strong civilian technical input and consultant services to the investigation.[521] Between 400 and 500 individuals were engaged at various times and in some capacity in the study.[522]

In its organization, Project Forecast sought to provide an orderly screening of the widest range of technological possibilities provided by 12 technology panels in terms of the estimate of the hostile threat provided by a threat panel and of the present and future national policies of the United States as identified by a policy panel. These screened inputs were used by five capability panels that synthesized them into military weapons and support systems which promised to provide a military capability to service in a future conflict environment. After all potential weapon and support systems were identified, an analysis, evaluation, and synthesis panel selected preferred systems after a consideration of their cost-effectiveness characteristics. A special cost panel provided cost-estimate data to all panels and participated heavily in the work of analysis, evaluation, and synthesis. A special personnel resources panel was established to examine human skill requirements that would be required by advanced weapons and support systems.[523] Drawing upon top technical imagination, the study process sought to examine every technological possibility that might exist in the post-1970 time period and to determine the enhancement of military capabilities that might be derived from it for employment in general war, limited war, continental defense, intelligence and reconnaissance, or supporting functions.[524]

One of the first findings of Project Forecast was that technology was just as dynamic as it had been since World War II and that a "technological plateau" did not exist. One Project Forecast panel identified more than 40 different future aircraft systems that could be developed. But while technology was dynamic, new weapons would be extremely costly to develop. Secretary Zuckert observed after hearing Project Forecast briefings: "I do not think there is going to be any dearth of ideas about new weapon systems of the future. I think . . . that the problem will be a matter of selecting the ideas we can afford to pursue."[525] Even before the project was completed the Air Force began to feed Forecast findings into its planning. Thus the requirements for the CS-heavy logistics support aircraft included in Air Force development planning for fiscal year 1965 were shaped by Project Forecast data.[526] Forecast also pointed out that with improvement of local enemy defenses, particularly short-range surface-to-air missiles, both strategic and tactical delivery systems would require a standoff strike capability to survive in a future general or limited-war environment. During 1964 the Air Force developed the requirement for a short-range attack missile (SRAM) that would be much smaller than the discontinued Skybolt and could be employed either to suppress hostile defenses or to attack primary targets. The fiscal year 1966 research and development budget included funds for a project definition phase research on the short-range attack missile.[527]

In the process of trying military systems capabilities against stated national policy goals, Project Forecast spotlighted deficiencies in the capabilities and stated attendant requirements. Current intercontinental ballistic missiles were not well suited to destroy military targets while limiting collateral damage to a surrounding area. A worldwide pattern of potential conflict demanded a degree of global air mobility that did not exist. The Air Force was not as well prepared as current technology could provide to participate in low levels of limited war, particularly in underdeveloped areas. An anti-ICBM capability would be essential to ensure the maintenance of strategic deterrence. A manned strategic aircraft system would be required throughout the spectrum of conflict in situations where ballistic missiles would not be used. Members of Project Forecast also examined a number of potential new systems which might be employed against a submarine-launched missile threat, and they stated their belief that the United States should build forces capable of coping with the problem of potentially hostile space satellites.[528]

In addition to the identification of special weapon and support system opportunities and requirements, Project Forecast drew attention to five areas of technology in which progressive research and development could promise what General Schriever described as a "potentially enormous payoff."[529] Over the years the Air Force had made reasonable investments in the development of aluminum compounds, titanium, columbium, and other advanced materials that had been tested in the X-15, but Project Forecast recommended that even greater sustained efforts be made to pursue technical advances in the fields of oxide-dispersion-strengthened metals, metal and metalloid-fiber techniques, and new families of organic and inorganic polymers. This work could yield a virtual breakthrough in materials that would be light in weight, possess a very high tensile strength, and withstand very high temperatures. The application of these new materials, as well as a new technique in jet propulsion, promised to provide a whole new era of air-breathing propulsion technology. The keystone to the development of a useful vertical takeoff and landing aircraft, for example, had long been recognized as the development of engines with greater propulsive efficiency, and the new materials and propulsion techniques recommended by Forecast promised to hasten the development of an operationally effective vertical takeoff and landing (VTOL) aircraft.[530]

By the process of examining individual advances in separate technical fields as a whole, Project Forecast was able to foresee a "cascading" effect of various collective gains in the fields of flight dynamics and flight vehicle design. Thus proper combinations of individual advances could provide new generations of flight vehicles with virtually any operational capability that could be desired by a military or a civil air planner. Other significant developments could spring from forward projections of guidance and computer technology. As an unclassified example of possibilities in these fields, Forecast visualized the development of a new generation of computers that could be employed by a user in terms of the system's requirements without a vast commitment of hours necessary to program them. Although the full description of the technological possibilities foreseen by Forecast remained classified, General Schriever summed them up by saying: "In a number of technical areas, such as materials, propulsion, flight dynamics, guidance, and computer technology, we identified many promising technological opportunities."[531]

Secretary Zuckert Describes Air Doctrine Guidelines

Looking backward at his service as Air Force secretary, which had begun in January 1961, Eugene Zuckert observed: "It took some time for some of our old attitudes and outlooks to change; adjusting to new hardware still seems easier than adjusting to new ideas and new methods."[532] As a matter of fact, Zuckert suggested: "New hardware was welcomed with more enthusiasm than were new ideas in the realms of strategy, concepts, and doctrine." Especially in 1961, Zuckert asserted that some Air Force leaders

> were still approaching top-level problems of national security in terms of the concepts, doctrine, and study methods of the early 1950s. There were too many who took a parochial view of the big problems of planning, programming, and budgeting; who refused to believe that national policy and strategy were what the administration said they were — not what an element of the armed forces thought they ought to be. I suppose this was a hangover from the ten or more years when we had been the principal guarantor of Free World security and in many ways the favored service. In those years our nuclear superiority had made the issues of strategy more clear-cut than they were after the U.S.S.R. achieved nuclear parity.[533]

On the basis of this commentary, Zuckert evidently conceived that Air Force doctrine should be designed to support national policy and strategy, which was a somewhat different concept from a pure aerospace power doctrine based on the absolute capabilities and limitations of aerospace forces in peace and in war. Reflecting aspects of pure aerospace doctrine, the Air Force basic doctrinal manuals of the 1950s described the military effects that any military force might produce upon another nation as being deterrence, persuasion, neutralization, denial, destruction, and capture. The predominant characteristics of aerospace forces had been proven to be range, mobility, speed, penetration, firepower, and flexibility.[534] In the aftermath of the Defense Reorganization Act of 1958, the Air Force recognized that it needed to provide new doctrines and procedures for organizing, equipping, training, and employing its forces, but the task proved to be by no means easy. As it was published on 1 December 1959, Air Force Manual (AFM) 1-2, *United States Air Force Basic Doctrine*, represented a minor revision of the older manual on the same subject to include *aerospace* terminology. With the publication of the revision of the basic doctrine manual, the Air Force director of plans determined that the corollary Air Force Manuals 1-3 through 1-11 would be reorganized into four manuals on the subjects of offensive functions, defensive functions, air support functions, and organization, training, and equipping of forces to fulfill specified combatant functions. The responsibility for preparing the four new corollary manuals was assigned respectively to Strategic Air Command, Air Defense Command, Tactical Air Command, and Air University. In 1960 the Air Force Directorate of Plans, in cooperation with the Air Photographic and Charting Service and Air University, also undertook to prepare a training film on Air Force basic doctrine. In 1960–61 the responsible commands prepared drafts of the specified manuals and a scenario was written for the training film, but in the latter half of 1961 the Air Force Plans Directorate suspended action on all of the projects pending a maturity of the New Frontier strategy. In terms of the developing New Frontier strategy, AFM 1-2 appeared to place excessive emphasis upon massive retaliation and mass destruction and did not give adequate emphasis to the application of precisely measured power in limited or general war.[535]

During Project Forecast Maj Gen Jerry D. Page headed the policy panel that sought specifically to identify the goals of national policy that would influence development decisions within the Air Force. The panel did not attempt to determine what national policy should be, but it sought to define and interpret the meaning of policy as deterrence of war, general or otherwise, and that the importance of a deterrent capability at any level of intensity would be directly proportional to the damage an aggressor could expect to sustain at that level. Maintenance of superficial strategic forces could deter a general nuclear war, but at levels of conflict below nuclear holocaust — limited wars, insurgency wars, insurrections, civil unrest — other objectives would become important. The policy panel stated that these objectives would be the maintenance of multiple options and flexibility of forces for crisis management under varying lesser conflict situations; maintenance of the survivability of forces against uncertainties; realistic arms control measures that would not leave the United States vulnerable; controlled response and damage limitation in order that an enemy would not mistake the intent of prescribed military action; and the maintenance of thresholds of negotiation and war termination capabilities that would ensure the accomplishment of US objectives. Some of these goals would be factors in preventing the outbreak of hostilities; others would be applicable in wartime, when the overriding objective would be to control the hostilities and to conclude them successfully at the lowest level of intensity. The main thrust of United States military policy appeared to be the creation of a stable military environment.[536]

The thinking of Project Forecast's policy panel permitted a clarification of Air Force basic doctrine. Secretary Zuckert accepted the Forecast checklist of policy objectives and stated on 10 February 1964 that they would be employed in the design of the Air Force structure for the future.[537] Working under the direction of General Page during the winter of 1963–64, Lt Col Richard C. Bowman, Lt Col George H. Sylvester, and Maj William E. Simons shared authorship of the draft of the new basic Air Force manual that was coordinated through the Air Staff and published as Air Force Manual 1-1, *United States Air Force Basic Doctrine*, on 14 August 1964.[538] The authors of the new manual had served on the Project Forecast policy panel, and the thinking in the manual generally followed Forecast findings. As described in the manual the nature of modern conflict was related to the 10-point checklist of characteristics of forces which had been set forth in Project Forecast. The general characteristics and requirements of aerospace forces were specified as being flexibility (derived from range, mobility, responsiveness, and tactical versatility), survivability, central direction of command and control, penetration ability, selective target destruction capability, and recovering and recycling ability. Separate chapters described the employment of aerospace forces in general war, in tactical nuclear operations, in conventional air operations, and in counterinsurgency. In its conclusion, the new manual stated a correction on national security:

> Since the United States seeks a world free from aggression, its military forces must develop capabilities which clearly signal to a potential enemy that war at any level cannot produce a meaningful advantage. However, the nature of modern war has altered the use of force to the extent that total victory in some situations would be an unreasonable goal. Where enemies with capabilities to destroy our urban centers are involved, we should seek military objectives more realistic than total defeat of the enemy.[539]

With the publication of AFM 1-1, the Air Force had adapted its doctrine to the concept of national security that had emerged from the new strategic situation in which thermonuclear weapons and an assured delivery capability in the hands of potential enemies had altered the use of total military power. In an additional exposition of the new rationale, the Air Force Deputy Directorate of Advance Planning published a statement on "National Policy and Conflict Management" in November 1964.[540] In categorizing future conflict this statement distinguished between all-out thermonuclear holocaust in which national annihilation would be the apparent objective and all other conflicts of lesser intensity. All-out counter-city thermonuclear war would be the least likely form of conflict between the United States and the Soviet Union, since it was inconceivable that either nation would rationally and deliberately embark on a course of national suicide. All-out thermonuclear war could be deterred as long as the United States maintained a retaliatory capability that could survive a surprise attack with certainty, an ability to penetrate whatever defenses the Soviets might have or might build, and warheads large enough to assure damage levels of a very high order of magnitude. Under this condition no surprise attack could possibly look attractive to Kremlin planners. And it would be equally inconceivable that the United States would initiate such a war.[541]

Although all-out counter-city nuclear holocaust would be unlikely if the United States maintained necessary deterrent capabilities, a wide spectrum of lesser conflict remained available to the Communists, who had pledged that they would use military force to attain their objectives in cases in which potential gains would exceed risks that would be involved. One distinctive characteristic of the lesser forms of conflict would be that in each case hostile military forces would be the legitimate objective of military action. Since the sole purpose of these military actions would be to achieve a particular political end, the United States would seek to use its military force to gain military advantage over the enemy's military force and thereby facilitate the attainment of its political goals. To deter lesser conflicts, the United States would require a capability and a determination to present an enemy with a confrontation in which the risks would be greater than the gains he might expect to achieve through a particular act of aggression. To maintain this capability the United States would require forces that would permit it the option of escalating any lesser conflict all the way to the top of the upper end of the spectrum of conflict. Thus, even though military capabilities would have to be keyed to the concept of providing military advantage at the upper end of the spectrum of conflict, the United States could not permit any significant gaps to exist in its capability to handle lesser conflicts. The maintenance of this force posture would prevent an enemy from escalating a conflict to a portion of the spectrum of conflict where the vital interests of the United States or its survival might be at stake.[542]

When viewed against the spectrum of future conflict, the Deputy Directorate of Advance Planning suggested that the Air Force's checklist of 10 national policy objectives assumed understandable meaning. Deterrence was the credible capability to discourage and thereby prevent aggression and was the number one national objective. Survivability of forces and weapon systems had to be evident for deterrence to be credible. Crisis management involved the ability to endure periodic and even prolonged international crises without either relinquishing the political objectives or allowing the situation to deteriorate into open conflict. It would require excellent intelligence, superior military forces capable of demonstrating enduring survivability, and strong nerves without actually being employed in a hostile sense. Realistic arms control suggested that future forces would be designed with an eye to their stabilizing effect, their immunity to accidental or premature employment, and their possible role in monitoring and inspecting functions. Next to deterrence, controlled response was probably the most important item on the checklist. It prescribed the kind of military action required in the event that deterrence should fail. It ensured that military objectives would be kept in tune with political objectives and that exactly the right amounts of force would be employed to win political objectives. It suggested that there were responses other than spastic ones which would be more in the interest of national security. The subject of multiple options would seek to provide a national decisionmaker with a number of choices for responding to any particular contingency. Such options would be available when the national military posture had sufficient flexibility to permit alternative targeting plans, incremental applications of force, employments of force in both strategic and tactical missions, and responses to unforeseen contingencies. The damage-limitation objective involved the employment of military action in pursuit of political objectives without bringing destruction to the things that the nation was trying to preserve by going to war. Enemy capabilities which were threats to the United States or its allies would be targeted for precise priority counterforce attacks. By intentionally avoiding widespread collateral destruction of the enemy, the United States would provide the enemy with a strong incentive to avoid deliberate attack on its own population centers. If hostilities occurred, the United States would be interested in attaining negotiation thresholds that would be advantageous points on the ladder of conflict escalation. To prevent the expansion of a lesser conflict to a level of unrestrained conflict, the United States would seek to terminate a conflict at the lowest threshold at which it could attain its political objectives. The objective of war termination imposed requirements for intelligence capabilities, forces that could recover and recycle for a continuing employment in a degraded environment, reliable command and control, and continuing military capabilities for a posthostilities period. The Deputy Directorate of Advance Planning stated that the 10-point checklist was being used by the Air Force to analyze its future weapon system requirements and further predicted that it would become "a well-thumbed reference to Air Force planners in the years ahead."[543]

August 1964: New Thoughts in Basic Air Doctrine

In many ways the retirement of Gen Curtis E. LeMay as Air Force chief of staff on 1 February 1965 marked the end of an era in the Air Force. General LeMay was the last major commander of World War II to retire from active duty. Witnessed Secretary Zuckert:

> Our country owes a debt of gratitude to Curt LeMay. He has been one of the great leaders of our time — in war and in peace. The Strategic Air Command ... stands as a testimony to his genius as an organizer, manager, and leader. For seven years, he served as Vice Chief of Staff and Chief of Staff of the Air Force. During those years, the precision which he had created in SAC was infused into all of our operating and support commands. That precision was accompanied by growing flexibility, by new ideas, and new ways of thinking about military problems.... With his retirement, we enter a new era in which we will owe much to the many foundations of our strength for which he was responsible.[544]

As it was published in August 1964, AFM 1-1, *United States Air Force Basic Doctrine*, manifested an intention to look forward. The older basic doctrine manuals had stated: "Basic doctrine evolves from experience and from analysis of the continuing impact of new developments."[545] The new manual held: "Basic doctrine evolves through the continuing analysis and testing of military operations in the light of national objective and the changing military environment."[546] The older manuals had taught that the United States Air Force was "the primary aerospace arm of the United States" and that "of the various types of military forces, those which conduct operations in the aerospace are most capable of decisive results."[547] The new manual stated: "Aerospace Forces are one part of a national military establishment maintained to support national policy objectives in our relations with foreign powers."[548] As Secretary Zuckert viewed the matter, Air Force leaders were willing to abandon their old disbelief that "there was any war which couldn't be won by air power alone," but they rightly knew that air power was "the supreme deterrent to general war" and "that there was no war which could be won without air power."[549]

IDEAS, CONCEPTS, DOCTRINE

NOTES

1. "Committee on the Defense Establishment, Release by Senator Kennedy, St. Louis, September 14, 1960," in Senate, *Fiscal Year 1962 Military Procurement Authorization: Hearings before the Committee on Armed Services*, 87th Cong., 1st sess., 1961, 284 (hereafter cited as *FY 1962 Military Procurement*).
2. Senate, *Organizing for National Security: Hearings before the Committee on National Policy Machinery of the Committee on Government Operations*, 86th Cong., 2d sess., and 87th Cong., 1st sess., 1960–1961, 1:1324.
3. Senate, *FY 1962 Military Procurement*, 183.
4. Robert Cutler, "The Department of National Security Policy," *Foreign Affairs*, April 1956, 441–58.
5. Ibid.; George A. Wyeth, Jr., "The Pattern of Formulating Security Policy at the Highest Governmental Level," lecture, Air War College, 27 October 1955.
6. Gen Maxwell D. Taylor, *The Uncertain Trumpet* (New York: Harper & Bros., 1959), 87.
7. Paul H. Nitze, "Organization for National Policy Planning in the United States," in Senate, *Organizing for National Security*, 2:285.
8. Senate, Subcommittee on National Policy Machinery, "The National Security Council," in Senate, *Organizing for National Security*, 3:38–39.
9. Senate, *Organizing for National Security*, 1:1184–85, 1215–16, 1282.
10. Ibid.
11. Ibid.
12. Ibid., 1217–19, 1281, 1290, 1324–25, 1336.
13. House, *Hearings on Military Posture and H.R. 9751 before the Committee on Armed Services*, 87th Cong., 2d sess., 1962, 3205–7.
14. House, *Defense Space Interests: Hearings before the Committee on Science and Astronautics*, 87th Cong., 1st sess., 1961, 15.
15. House, *Hearings on Military Posture and H. R. 2440 before the Committee on Armed Services*, 88th Cong., 1st sess., 1963, 373–74.
16. Senate, *Military Aspects and Implications of Nuclear Test Ban Proposals and Related Matters: Hearings before the Preparedness Investigating Subcommittee of the Committee on Armed Services*, 88th Cong., 1st sess., 1963, pt. 2:915.
17. "Air Power in the News," *Air Force/Space Digest*, June 1961, 21.
18. Senate, *Nominations of Gen Maxwell D. Taylor and Gen Earle G. Wheeler: Hearings before the Committee on Armed Services*, 87th Cong., 2d sess., 1962, 8–9.
19. Senate, *Organizing for National Security*, 1:1226, 1326.
20. House, *Sundry Legislation Affecting the Naval and Military Establishments for 1963: Hearings before the Committee on Armed Services*, 88th Cong., 1st sess., 1963, 3:6246 (hereafter cited as *Sundry Legislation for 1963*).
21. William W. Kaufmann, *The McNamara Strategy* (New York: Harper & Row, 1964), 24.
22. Senate, *Organizing for National Security*, 1:1325.
23. Ibid., 1037; Kaufmann, *The McNamara Strategy*, 87–88.
24. Kaufmann, *The McNamara Strategy*, 87–88; *Air Force Policy Letter for Commanders: Supplement*, November 1968, 8.
25. Sen John F. Kennedy, "If the Soviets Control Space They Can Control Earth," *Missiles and Rockets*, 10 October 1960, 12–13; "Mr Kennedy and National Defense," *Air Force/Space Digest*, December 1960, 5–6.
26. Dr Jerome B. Wiesner, chairman, Report to the President Elect of the Ad Hoc Committee on Space, 12 January 1961, in House, *Defense Space Interests*, 18, 85–86.
27. Ibid.
28. Ibid.
29. Ibid., 17–23.

30. Senate, *Organizing for National Security*, 1:1186; House, *Military Astronautics: Report of the Committee on Science and Astronautics*, 87th Cong., 1st sess., 1961, H. Rept. 360, 8; House, *Defense Space Interests*, 11–12, 14–15.

31. Department of Defense Directive (DODD) 5160.32, subject: Development of Space Systems, 6 March 1961; memorandum by Robert S. McNamara to the secretaries of the military departments et al., subject: Development of Space Systems, 6 March 1961, in House, *Military Astronautics*, 8–10.

31. House, *Military Astronautics*, 11; House, *Defense Space Interests*, 82–83.

32. DODD 5160.34, subject: Reconnaissance, Mapping and Geodetic Programs, 28 March 1961, in House, *Defense Space Interests*, 113–14.

33. House, *Department of Defense Appropriations for 1963: Hearings before a Subcommittee of the Committee on Appropriations*, 87th Cong., 2d sess., 1962, pt. 2:143–44 (hereafter cited as *1963 DOD Appropriations*).

34. House, *Department of Defense Appropriations for 1964: Hearings before a Subcommittee of the Committee on Appropriations*, 88th Cong., 2d sess., 1963, pt. 1:174 (hereafter cited as *1964 DOD Appropriations*).

35. Roswell L. Gilpatric, deputy secretary of defense, to James E. Webb, administrator NASA, letter, 23 February 1961, in House, *Defense Space Interests*, 23–24.

36. House, *H.R. 6169—A Bill to Amend the National Aeronautics and Space Act of 1958: Hearings before the Committee on Science and Astronautics*, 87th Cong., 1st sess., 1961, 1–8.

37. Senate, *Amending Various Sections of the NASA Act of 1958: Hearings before the Committee on Aeronautical and Space Sciences*, 87th Cong., 1st sess., 1961, 4–61; House, *Amending the National Aeronautics and Space Act of 1958*, 87th Cong., 1st sess., 1961, H. Rept. 747, 7.

38. House, *1963 NASA Authorization: Hearings before the Subcommittee on Manned Space Flight of the Committee on Science and Astronautics*, 87th Cong., 2d sess., 1962, 583–86.

39. Ibid.; House, *Posture of the National Space Program: Report of the Committee on Science and Astronautics*, 88th Cong., 1st sess., 1963, 36–39.

40. "AF Support Role Grows, NASA Still in Charge," *Missiles and Rockets*, 26 March 1962, 52–53; House, *1963 DOD Appropriations*, pt. 2:143–45.

41. House, *1963 DOD Appropriations*, pt. 2:143–45.

42. "AF Support Role Grows, NASA Still in Charge," 53.

43. House, *1963 NASA Authorization*, pt. 2:660, 668.

44. DOD Directive, subject: Department of Defense Support of National Aeronautics and Space Administration (NASA), 24 February 1962; House, *1964 DOD Appropriations*, pt. 1:174–75.

45. House, *1964 DOD Appropriations*, pt. 1:174–75.

46. Department of Defense Release 906-62, 11 June 1962; *Department of Defense Annual Report for Fiscal Year 1962*, 25 (hereafter cited as *DOD Annual Report for FY 1962*).

47. House, *Posture of the National Space Program*, 39; "Space and National Security Symposium," *Air Force/Space Digest*, November 1962, 82.

48. House, *1964 DOD Appropriations*, pt. 1:173–75.

49. Ibid.

50. Ibid., 258.

51. Under Secretary of the Air Force Brockway McMillan to Sen Clinton P. Anderson, chairman, Senate Committee on Aeronautical and Space Sciences, letter, 7 August 1963, in *Congressional Record*, 88th Cong., 2d sess., 109:13900.

52. "Agreement between the National Aeronautics and Space Administration and the Department of Defense Concerning the Gemini Program, January 1963," in House, *1964 NASA Authorization: Hearings before the Subcommittee on Manned Space Flight of the Committee on Science and Astronautics*, 88th Cong., 1st sess., 1963, pt. 2(a):407.

53. House, *Posture of the National Space Program*, 37; *NASA, Astronautics and Aeronautics, 1963, Chronology on Science, Technology, and Policy* (Washington, D.C.: National Aeronautics and Space Administration, 1964), 21.

54. House, *1964 DOD Appropriations*, pt. 1:371.

IDEAS, CONCEPTS, DOCTRINE

55. McMillan to Anderson, letter, 7 August 1963.
56. House, *1964 DOD Appropriations*, pt. 1:375.
57. House, *Department of Defense Appropriations for 1965*, 88th Cong., 2d sess., pt. 4:235–39 (hereafter cited as *1965 DOD Appropriations*).
58. Ibid.; Senate, *Fiscal Year 1965 NASA Authorization: Hearings before the Committee on Aeronautical and Space Sciences*, 88th Cong., 2d sess., 1964, pt. 2:441–44, 450, 459.
59. House, *1965 DOD Appropriations*, pt. 4:237.
60. Ibid., 317.
61. Ibid., pt. 2:307–8, pt. 4:248, pt. 5:409; "Davis Heads Range Division," *Missiles and Rockets*, 13 January 1964, 10.
62. House, *1965 DOD Appropriations*, pt. 2:308.
63. Senate, *FY 1962 Military Procurement*, 262, 283–84.
64. Ibid.
65. Ibid.
66. Ibid.
67. Ibid.
68. Ibid., 277–79.
69. Ibid., 280–81.
70. Ibid.
71. Address by Gen Thomas D. White, chief of staff, USAF, "Air Force Outlook," Secretary of Defense Conference, Quantico, Va., 18 June 1960.
72. *American Heritage* interview with Gen Thomas D. White, July 1960.
73. Ibid.
74. Senate, *FY 1962 Military Procurement*, 263–85.
75. Ibid., 120.
76. Ibid.
77. House, *Hearings on Military Posture and H.R. 9751*, 3307–8.
78. Senate, *FY 1962 Military Procurement*, 54.
79. Kaufmann, *The McNamara Strategy*, 296.
80. House, *United States Defense Policies in 1961*, 87th Cong., 2d sess., 1962, 76–77; Senate, *Organizing for National Security*, 1:1187.
81. Senate, *Organizing for National Security*, 1:1187.
82. House, *Hearings on Military Posture and H.R. 2440*, 373–74, 408.
83. Senate, *Organizing for National Security*, 1:1186; Senate, *FY 1962 Military Procurement*, 54.
84. House, *Report of Special Subcommittee on Defense Agencies: Committee on Armed Services*, 87th Cong., 2d sess., 1962, 6625.
85. Charles J. Hitch and Roland N. McKean, *The Economics of Defense in the Nuclear Age* (Cambridge: Harvard University Press, 1961), 52–59.
86. Senate, *Organizing for National Security*, 1:1004–12, 1026, 1031.
87. Ibid., 1192.
88. House, *Hearings on Military Posture and H.R. 9751*, 3328.
89. Senate, *Organizing for National Security*, 1:1196, 1204.
90. Ibid., 1010–11.
91. House, *Hearings on Military Posture and H.R. 2440*, 334–35.
92. Memorandum by Secretary McNamara to the secretaries of the military departments et al., subject: Designation of OSD Offices as Points of Contact for the Selective Review of Major Proposed Program Changes, 31 May 1962, in House, *Report of Special Subcommittee on Defense Agencies*, 6629–30.
93. House, *Sundry Legislation for 1963*, 3:6225.
94. House, *1965 DOD Appropriations*, pt. 4:302.
95. Senate, *Department of Defense Appropriations for Fiscal Year 1965*, 88th Cong., 2d sess., 1964, 5–6 (hereafter cited as *FY 1965 DOD Appropriations*); House, *1965 DOD Appropriations*, pt. 4:305.

96. Senate, *FY 1962 Military Procurement*, 54; House, *United States Defense Policies in 1961*, 78.
97. John C. Ries, *The Management of Defense* (Baltimore: Johns Hopkins University Press, 1964), 189n.
98. Senate, *Organizing for National Security*, 1:301.
99. House, *Report of Special Subcommittee on Defense Agencies*, 6629–30; Ries, *The Management of Defense*, 189–90.
100. Ries, *The Management of Defense*, 190.
101. House, *Report of Special Subcommittee on Defense Agencies*, 6623; DODD 4600.2, *Defense Communications System*; and DODD 5105.19, *Defense Communications Agency*, 12 May 1960.
102. House, *1963 DOD Appropriations*, pt. 2:153.
103. Ibid.; *DOD Annual Report for FY 1962*, 29; DODD 5105.22, *Defense Supply Agency*, 6 November 1961.
104. Senate, *Organizing for National Security*, 1:1187, 1199, 1222, 1223; House, *1963 DOD Appropriations*, pt. 2:153; House, *Report of Special Subcommittee on Defense Agencies*, 6620.
105. House, *1965 DOD Appropriations*, pt. 2:611–13.
106. House, *Department of Defense Appropriations for 1962*, 87th Cong., 1st sess., 1961, pt. 2:479 (hereafter cited as *1962 DOD Appropriations*); House, *1963 DOD Appropriations*, pt. 2:41; Senate, *Organizing for National Security*, 1:783.
107. Gen F. F. Everest, commander, Tactical Air Command, and Gen Herbert B. Powell, commanding general, US Continental Army Command, letter, subject: USCONARC-TAC Proposal for a Unified Tactical Command, 24 July 1961.
108. House, *United States Defense Policies in 1961*, 38–39.
109. Ibid.; House, *1963 DOD Appropriations*, pt. 2:41, 151; pt. 3:463; House, *Sundry Legislation for 1963*, 3:6103–6; Allan R. Scholin, "'STRIKE' Newest Unified Command," *Air Force/Space Digest*, May 1962, 33–34, 38, 41; "U.S. Strike Command," *Airman Magazine*, May 1962, 27–32; Maj Gen Clyde Box, "United States Strike Command, Stateside and Global," *Air University Review* 15, no. 6 (September–October 1964): 4–14.
110. Box, "United States Strike Command," 8.
111. House, *1964 DOD Appropriations*, pt. 1:452.
112. "U.S. Strike Command," *Airman Magazine*, May 1962, 29.
113. House, *1965 DOD Appropriations*, pt. 2:464, pt. 4:316; House, *Hearings on Military Posture and H.R. 9637*, 88th Cong., 2d sess., 7004–5; Box, "United States Strike Command," 4, 10.
114. Box, "United States Strike Command," 11.
115. "Partridge Report," *Aviation Week & Space Technology*, 18 December 1961, 25; James Baar, "New U.S. Command System Coming," *Missiles and Rockets*, 4 December 1961, 12; House, *Hearings before Special Subcommittee on Defense Agencies*, 87th Cong., 2d sess., 6960–61.
116. Brig Gen Paul W. Tibbets, "About Our Working National Military Command System," *Armed Forces Management*, July 1964, 26; House, *1965 DOD Appropriations*, pt. 2:611–13, pt. 4:258–59; House, *Hearings before Special Subcommittee on Defense Agencies*, 6946–47.
117. House, *1964 DOD Appropriations*, pt. 2:611–13; Tibbets, "About Our Working National Military Command System," 26.
118. J. S. Butz, Jr., "White House Command Post – 1966," *Air Force/Space Digest*, April 1964, 73.
119. Roswell L. Gilpatric, "An Expert Looks at the Joint Chiefs," *New York Times Magazine*, 29 March 1964, 11, 71–72.
120. Ibid.
121. Concepts Division, Aerospace Studies Institute, *Development of Organization for National Defense* (Maxwell AFB, Ala.: Aerospace Studies Institute, June 1963), 1–10.
122. Address by Gen Curtis E. LeMay to Air Force Association Convention, 21 September 1961.
123. Senate, *Fiscal Year 1963 Military Procurement Authorization*, 87th Cong., 2d sess., 1962, 501.
124. House, *Hearings before Special Subcommittee on Defense Agencies*, 6824–25, 6845, 6974.
125. Ibid.; AFLC Historical Study 338, "The Trend Leading Toward the DSA Decision, 1958–1961," November 1962, passim.

126. House, *Report of Special Subcommittee on Defense Agencies*, 6631–35.
127. Aerospace Studies Institute, *Development of Organization for National Defense*, 209–10.
128. Quoted in *Report of Special Subcommittee of Defense Agencies*, 6626.
129. Ibid.
130. Ibid., 6631–35.
131. House, *Hearings before Special Subcommittee on Defense Agencies*, 6824–25.
132. House, *1964 DOD Appropriations*, pt. 2:5.
133. House, *Hearings on Military Posture and H.R. 9637*, 7508–9.
134. Ibid.
135. Ibid., 7447; House, *1965 DOD Appropriations*, pt. 4:509–10.
136. House, *Hearings on Military Posture and H.R. 9637*, 7447.
137. House, *1965 DOD Appropriations*, pt. 4:512-13.
138. House, *Hearings on Military Posture and H.R. 9637*, 7814; House, *1965 DOD Appropriations*, pt. 4:479–80, 527; Hon Eugene M. Zuckert, "An Appraisal of U.S. Aerospace Power, 1964," *Air Force Information Policy Letter for Commanders: Supplement*, 8 January 1964.
139. "Schriever Disputes 'Plateau' Theory," *Aviation Week & Space Technology*, 11 November 1963, 31; Zuckert, "An Appraisal of U.S. Aerospace Power, 1964."
140. Zuckert, "An Appraisal of U.S. Aerospace Power, 1964."
141. Ibid.
142. Hon Eugene M. Zuckert, "Keeping the Organizational Engine in Tune," *Air Force/Space Digest*, October 1964, 37.
143. Ibid.
144. Ibid.
145. Ibid.
146. Ibid., 39–40.
147. Ibid.
148. Ibid., 40.
149. Lt Gen B. A. Schriever, commander, ARDC, to Gen S. E. Anderson, commander, AMC, letter, subject: Weapon Systems Management, 26 April 1960, quoted in Air Force Systems Command History Study, "The Genesis of the Air Force Systems Command," 10.
150. History, Air University, July–December 1956, I:106–8.
151. AWC briefing for AU commander and staff by Col P. R. Hawes, 13 September 1956, 4.
152. History, Air University, July–December 1957, I:12, 13.
153. Ibid., I:40.
154. Col Taylor Drysdale briefing to Air University staff, 28 April 1958; Directorate of Development Planning USAF, Development Planning Note 58-DAP-2, A Program for Coherent Research and Development of Military Science, 17 February 1958.
155. Ibid.
156. USAF Development Planning Note 58-DAP-2, 29.
157. Maj Gen Lloyd P. Hopwood, commandant, ACSS, to commander, AU, letter, subject: Evaluation Staff, 6 January 1958; 1st wrapper ind., Maj Gen Robert F. Tate, commandant, AWC, to commander, AU, 24 January 1958; Disposition form, Col Loring F. Stetson, Jr., DCS Operations, AU, to commander, AU, subject: Warfare Systems Institute, 26 February 1958.
158. Memorandum for Col H. C. Dorney, assistant deputy for evaluation, AWC, from Col Allen F. Herzberg, chief, Employment Division, AWC Evaluation Staff, subject: Comments on "A Program for Coherent Research and Development of Military Science" (58-DAP-2), 30 March 1959.
159. Col H. C. Dorney, comments on 58-DAP-2, 25 March 1959.
160. Drysdale briefing for AU staff, 28 April 1958, 18.
161. Col Frank J. Seiler, Science of Warfare Office, ARDC, to commander, AU, letter, subject: Joint Effort in Research and Development in the Science of Warfare, 11 July 1958; *USAF Research and Development Quarterly Review*, Winter 1957–1958, 14.

162. Department of Defense, *Semiannual Report of the Secretary of Defense . . . January 1 to June 30, 1957*, 296; History, director of plans, DCS, Plans and Programs, USAF, July–December 1958, 114.

163. Robert F. Tate to commander, AU, letter, subject: Reorganization of Air University, 3 April 1959.

164. Dunning, "USAF Doctrine, Roles and Missions," vol. 1, no. 229, 17 December 1959, 487.

165. History, director of plans, DCS Plans and Programs, July–December 1958, 163–64; Lt Gen W. E. Todd, commander, AU, to Lt Gen John K. Gerhart, deputy chief of staff, Plans and Programs, USAF, letter, 27 October 1959.

166. History, Headquarters ARDC, January–June 1959, I:8.

167. Maj Gen L. P. Hopwood, director, Personnel Procurement and Training, DCS, Personnel, USAF, to Todd, letter, 23 December 1958; Lt Gen John K. Gerhart, DCS, Plans and Programs, USAF, to Todd, 4 March 1959.

168. History, AU, January–June 1959, I:33–34; History, Research Studies Institute, July–December 1959, 1.

169. H. Guyford Stever, chairman for the Ad Hoc Committee on Research and Development, to Dr James H. Doolittle, chairman, USAF Scientific Advisory Board, letter, 20 June 1958, in *Air University Quarterly Review*, vol. X, no. 3 (Fall 1958), 44.

170. House, *Missile Development and Space Sciences*, 86th Cong., 1st sess., 95; 86th Cong., 1st sess., *Investigation of Governmental Organization for Space Activities*, 427–28; "The Air Research and Development Command," *Air Force/Space Digest*, September 1959, 170–71.

171. House, *1963 DOD Appropriations*, pt. 5:59.

172. Arthur K. Marmor, "The Search for New USAF Weapons, 1958–1959" (USAF History Division Liaison Office, April 1961), 2–3.

173. LeMay to commander, AMC, letter, subject: Weapon Systems Management, 29 May 1959.

174. History, AMC/AFLC, July 1960–June 1961, I:36–39; Gen S. E. Anderson, commander, AMC, to LeMay, letter, 29 April 1960.

175. History, AMC/AFLC, July 1960–June 1961, 40.

176. Anderson to LeMay, letter, 26 August 1960.

177. Ibid.

178. History, AMC/AFLC, July 1960–June 1961, 45.

179. House, *Department of Defense Appropriations for 1961: Hearings before a Subcommittee of the Committee on Appropriations*, 86th Cong., 2d sess., pt. 6:508–9 (hereafter cited as *1961 DOD Appropriations*).

180. Schriever to White, letter, 1 September 1960; White to Schriever, letter, 12 September 1960.

181. AFSC History Study, "The Genesis of the Air Force Systems Command," 30.

182. Ibid.

183. History, AMC/AFLC, July 1960–June 1961, 54–55.

184. Ibid.

185. Department of Defense Press Release, 17 March 1961; AFOMO 590m, letter, subject: Redesignation and Reorganization of the Air Materiel Command and the Air Research and Development Command, and Certain Other USAF Unit Actions, 20 March 1961; Senate, *FY 1963 DOD Appropriations*, 158–59; House, *1963 NASA Authorization*, pt. 3:1503; Lt Col George Zinnemann, "Aerospace Medicine and Bioastronautics," *Air University Quarterly Review*, vol. XIV, nos. 1 and 2 (Winter/Spring 1962–1963), 218–19; Maj Gen Marvin C. Demler, "Research and Technology Management," *Air University Quarterly Review*, vol. XIV, nos. 1 and 2 (Winter/Spring 1962–1963), 102–5.

186. Zuckert and White, press conference, 17 March 1961.

187. Secretary of the Air Force Office of Information, Air Force Information Fact Sheet, Systems and Logistics Management, April 1963.

188. Senate, *FY 1962 Military Procurement*, 490.

189. House, *FY 1963 DOD Appropriations*, 158–59.

190. House, *1962 DOD Appropriations*, pt. 3:410.

191. House, *1963 DOD Appropriations*, pt. 2:459; USAF History Division, Liaison Office, interview with Wilson, 13 October 1961.

192. SAF Order No. 117.1, Designated System Management Group, 25 July 1961, 103; Gen F. H. Smith to deputies and directors, Headquarters USAF, letter, subject: Designated Systems Management Group, 1 August 1961; John J. McLaughlin, "Organization of the Air Force, A Revolution in Management," *Air University Quarterly Review*, vol. XIII, no. 3 (Spring 1962): 12–13; Joseph H. Imrie, assistant SAF (Materiel), "Management in the Aerospace Age" (Address before the National Security Industrial Association, 12 October 1961), in *Air Force Information Policy Letter for Commanders: Supplement*, 15 November 1961, 7–15.

193. House, *1963 DOD Appropriations*, pt. 2:459; Gen B. A. Schriever, "The Role of Management in Technological Conflict," *Air University Quarterly Review*, vol. XIV, nos. 1 and 2 (Winter/Spring 1962–1963): 24–25.

194. Schriever, "The Real Challenge to Military Management," *Armed Forces Management*, February 1962, 41.

195. House, *Missile Development and Space Sciences*, 131.

196. Schriever, "The Role of Management in the Technological Conflict," 24.

197. Interview with Wilson, 13 October 1961.

198. House, *1962 DOD Appropriations*, pt. 4:437.

199. Interview with Wilson, 13 October 1961.

200. House, *1963 DOD Appropriations*, pt. 5:59–61, 69–70.

201. Schriever, "Management in Technological Conflict," 24–27.

202. Ibid.

203. Ibid.

204. House, *1964 DOD Appropriations*, pt. 2:421–22.

205. Ibid.; House, *Posture of the National Space Program*, 236; Claude Witze, "New Look in the Air Staff Organization," *Air Force/Space Digest*, March 1963, 34, 36–37; Larry Booda, "Development, Procurement Roles Split in USAF Headquarters Shift," *Aviation Week & Space Technology*, 11 February 1963, 34.

206. "The Military Departments: Secretary of the Air Force," *Armed Forces Management*, November 1963, 35.

207. Schriever, "Management in Technological Conflict," 27.

208. House, *Posture of the National Space Program*, 236.

209. Schriever, "Management in Technological Conflict," 25–26, 28.

210. Air Force Regulation 190–18, *Information Activities: Air Force Internal Information Program*, 8 September 1961.

211. Organizational Chart, DCS, Plans and Programs USAF, July 1961.

212. Address by LeMay to Air Force Association Convention, 21 September 1961.

213. Ibid.

214. Brig Gen Jerry D. Page, deputy director for plans, Aerospace Plans USAF, "A Strategy for the Future and Air Force Support of the Land Battle: 1975–1980," lecture, Army War College, 27 February 1962.

215. Board of Visitors to Air University, "Report of the Nineteenth Meeting," 19 April 1963, 7.

216. Ibid.

217. Ibid.

218. Ibid.

219. Maj Gen Dale O. Smith, special assistant to the JCS for Arms Control, Development of Air Force Doctrine, 15 April 1963; Smith to Lt Gen Troup Miller, Jr., commander, AU, letter, 24 May 1963.

220. John W. Masland and Laurence I. Radway, *Soldiers and Scholars: National Education and Military Policy* (Princeton: Princeton University Press, 1957), 145–48.

221. Harold F. Clark and Harold S. Sloan, *Classrooms in the Military* (New York: Institute for Instructional Improvement, 1964), 61.

222. Masland and Radway, *Soldiers and Scholars*, 287.

223. Ibid., 439; Brig Gen Noel F. Parrish, D/Research Studies Institute, to commander, AU, letter, subject: Report on the Army War College National Strategy Seminar, 5–8 June 1962, 2 August 1962.

224. Senate, *Study of Air Power: Hearings before the Subcommittee on the Air Force of the Committee on Armed Services*, 84th Cong., 2d sess., 1956, 794–97.

225. "Report Submitted by the Department of the Air Force on the Air Force Concept of Close Air Support," ca. 19 March 1957, in House, *Sundry Legislation Affecting the Naval and Military Establishment for 1957: Hearings before the Committee on Armed Services*, 85th Cong., 1st sess., vol. 1:537–41; House, *1961 DOD Appropriations*, pt. 4:618–19.

226. House, *Department of Defense Appropriations for 1957*, 84th Cong., 2d sess., 612; *United States Defense Policies in 1960*, 28–29.

227. John F. Loosbrock, "Little Plane with a Big Mission, G. 91-NATO Lightweight," *Air Force/Space Digest*, December 1959, 42–43.

228. House, *Department of Defense Appropriations for 1958*, 85th Cong., 1st sess., 1074–75; Hal Bamford, "Is Cost Effectiveness Really Efficient?" *Armed Forces Management*, August 1964, 35–36; J. S. Butz, Jr., "F-5: Little Plane with a Big Future," *Air Force/Space Digest*, December 1964, 34–36, 39, 40.

229. Senate, *FY 1962 Military Procurement Authorization*, 379–81, 488–89; House, *Military Posture Briefings*, 87th Cong., 1st sess., 1961, 837–38, 1208–9, 1216; House, *DOD 1962 Appropriations*, pt. 3:164, 170, 219–20, 250, 404–6; pt. 4:295; pt. 5:109; Senate, *Department of Defense Appropriations for FY 1962*, 87th Cong., 1st sess., 1553, 1555.

230. Division Historian Service, Air Defense commander, History Study No. 4: Army Antiaircraft in Air Defense, 1946–1954, 1–33.

231. History, Tactical Air Command, January–June 1957, I:255.

232. Everest to Gen Bruce C. Clarke, commanding general, Continental Army Command, letters, 8 and 25 July 1960; History, Tactical Air Command, July–December 1960, I:36, 396.

233. Maj Gen C. H. Childre, acting deputy chief of staff, Plans and Programs, USAF, to USAFE, PACAF, TAC, letter, subject: Resolution of Army-Air Force Divergencies, 23 June 1961; Gen C. E. LeMay and Gen George H. Decker, Doctrine for Area (Overseas) Air Defense, 12 July 1962.

234. Maj Gen James M. Gavin, "Cavalry, and I Don't Mean Horses," *Harper's Magazine*, 26 April 1954, 54–60.

235. Ibid.

236. *Study of Air Power*, 794–99.

237. House, *1961 DOD Appropriations*, pt. 2:482.

238. Memorandum for members of the Armed Forces Policy Council from Wilson, subject: Clarification of Roles and Missions to Improve the Effectiveness of Operation of the Department of Defense, 26 November 1956.

239. House, *United States Defense Policies in 1960*, 87th Cong., 1st sess., 1961, 27–28.

240. House, *1961 DOD Appropriations*, pt. 2:482.

241. Senate, *Department of Defense Appropriations for FY 1959*, 85th Cong., 2d sess., 513.

242. Everest to Clarke, letter, 25 July 1950.

243. House, *United States Defense Policies in 1961*, 82–87.

244. US Army Institute of Advanced Studies, Strategic Studies Group, Very Long Range Strategic Forecast, 20 November 1962, 13–14.

245. House, *United States Defense Policies in 1961*, 87; House, *1965 DOD Appropriations*, pt. 2:487; *DOD Annual Report for FY 1962*, 314.

246. Gen Paul D. Adams, commander in chief, US Strike Command, to Joint Chiefs of Staff et al., letter, subject: Command Relationships, 22 November 1961; House, *Sundry Legislation for 1963*, 3:6103.

247. Draft memorandum for the chairman, Joint Chiefs of Staff, subject: Establishment of Combat Developments and Test Center—STRICOM, 29 March 1962, in *Report of Special Subcommittee on Defense Agencies*, 6615–16.

IDEAS, CONCEPTS, DOCTRINE

248. House, *Hearings before Special Subcommittee on Defense Agencies*, 6903–7.
249. *A Compilation of Material Relating to United States Defense Policies in 1962*, 88th Cong., 1st sess., 1963, 91–94; Senate, *FY 1963 Military Procurement*, 390.
250. Senate, *FY 1963 Military Procurement*, 383; Lt Col Joseph D. Bailey, "Does the Air Force Need a Combat Developments Command?" thesis no. 2669 (Maxwell AFB, Ala.: Air War College, April 1965), 4–17.
251. *A Compilation of Material Relating to United States Defense Policies in 1962*, 42; *DOD Annual Report for FY 1962*, 118–19.
252. House, *1964 DOD Appropriations*, pt. 2:123–24; US Army, Tactical Mobility Requirements Board, Final Report, 20 August 1962.
253. Headquarters USAF, Tactical Air Support Requirements Board, comments on report by US Army, Tactical Mobility Requirements Board, 4 vols., preliminary report, 14 August 1962; Tactical Air Support Evaluation Board, Reference Library Listing (unclassified), 22 March 1963; Larry Booda, "McNamara Pushing USAF-Army Rivalry," *Aviation Week & Space Technology*, 14 January 1963, 26–27.
254. House, *1964 DOD Appropriations*, pt. 1:415.
255. Ibid., 132–33; Senate, *Fiscal Year 1964 Military Procurement Authorization*, 88th Cong., 1st sess., 1963, 570.
256. House, *1964 DOD Appropriations*, pt. 2:100, 125.
257. House, *Sundry Legislation for 1963*, 3:6072.
258. House, *1964 DOD Appropriations*, pt. 2:472, 495–96; Senate, *FY 1964 Military Procurement*, 918, 933–34.
259. Senate, *FY 1964 Military Procurement*, 918.
260. House, *1964 DOD Appropriations*, pt. 2:380–81, 483–86.
261. Ibid., pt. 1:132–33, 221n, 415.
262. Brig Gen Noel F. Parrish, director, Aerospace Studies Institute, to commander, AU, letter, subject: Development of Air Force Doctrine in Air University, 2 August 1963, w/incl.: Staff Study by Headquarters USAF/XPD Recommending a System for Doctrine Development Best Suited to the Needs of the Air Force.
263. Maj Gen Dale O. Smith, Development of Air Force Doctrine, 15 April 1963.
264. Headquarters USAF, Tactical Air Support Evaluation Board, Final Report, 27 April 1963, tab 3, as summarized in "Does the Air Force Need a Combat Developments Command?" Bailey, 31–36.
265. US Army–US Air Force Close Air Support Boards, Final Report, August 1963, appendix 3 to annex H.
266. AFM 1-1, *Aerospace Doctrine: Responsibilities for Doctrine Development*, 20 March 1963.
267. Ibid.
268. Parrish to commander, AU, August 1963, w/incl.: Staff Study by Headquarters USAF/XPD Recommending a System for Doctrine Development Best Suited to the Needs of the Air Force.
269. Ibid.
270. Gen W. F. McKee, vice chief of staff, to AFSC, letter, subject: Weapons Effectiveness Testing, 26 July 1963.
271. Headquarters Tactical Air Command, Special Order G-14, 31 January 1963; AFR 23-24, subject: Tactical Air Reconnaissance Center, 1 July 1963 to 30 June 1964.
272. McKee to AFSC, letter, 26 July 1963.
273. Schriever to Headquarters USAF (AFCCS), letter, subject: Weapons Effectiveness Testing, 5 August 1963.
274. Headquarters AFSC, Special Order G-96, 14 August 1963.
275. Maj Gen John K. Hester, assistant vice chief of staff, USAF, to TAC and AFSC, letter, subject: Air Force Support of the CINCSTRIKE Test and Evaluation Plan, 16 September 1963; Headquarters Tactical Air Command, Special Order G-129, 16 September 1963; Headquarters AFSC, Special Order G-112, 17 September 1963.

276. T-763, Headquarters USAF to TAC, message, 10 October 1963; Headquarters Tactical Air Command, Special Order G-147, 31 October 1963; History, USAF Tactical Air Warfare Center, 1 November 1963 to 30 June 1964.

277. Box, "United States Strike Command," 10; House, *1965 DOD Appropriations*, pt. 2:453.

278. Cecil Brownlow, "Army, USAF Testing Air Support Roles," *Aviation Week & Space Technology*, 21 September 1964, 83; House, *1965 DOD Appropriations*, pt. 2:89–90.

279. History, USAF Tactical Air Warfare Center, 1 November 1963 to 30 June 1964, 7–11.

280. Senate, *FY 1965 DOD Appropriations*, pt. 1:727–34.

281. Ibid.

282. Headquarters Tactical Air Command, USAF Tactical Air Concepts for Test and Evaluation, 6 December 1963, 1-1 and 1-2.

283. Maj Gen Gilbert L. Meyers, "USAF Tactical Air Warfare Center Concepts," briefing to Aviation/Space Writers Association Meeting, Miami Beach, Florida, 25 May 1964.

284. Brownlow, "Army, USAF Testing Air Support Roles," 77-84, 87; Maj Robert G. Sparkman, "Exercise Gold Fire I," *Air University Review* 16, no. 3 (March–April 1965): 22–24.

285. Brownlow, "Army, USAF Testing Air Support Roles," 84, 87; Sparkman, "Exercise Gold Fire I," 24–25, 30–31; Capt Brian Sheehan, "Tailored by TAWC," *Airman Magazine*, March 1965, 7–11.

286. Brownlow, "Army, USAF Testing Air Support Roles," 83; Sheridan Stuart, "Air Concepts on a Collision Course?" *Air Force/Space Digest*, August 1964, 35; House, *Hearings on Military Posture and H.R. 9637*, 7131, 7146.

287. "Washington Roundup," *Aviation Week & Space Technology*, 25 January 1965, 21; House, *Department of Defense Appropriations for 1966: Hearings before a Subcommittee of the Committee on Appropriations*, 89th Cong., 1st sess., 1965, pt. 3:557 (hereafter cited as *1966 DOD Appropriations*).

288. House, *Hearings on Military Posture and H.R. 9637*, 352–53, 7140–41, 7144; House, *1966 DOD Appropriations*, pt. 3:342.

289. Senate, *FY 1964 Military Procurement*, 513–15.

290. George C. Wilson, "DOD Approves Army Air Assault Concept," *Aviation Week & Space Technology*, 26 April 1965, 32; Senate, *Department of Defense Appropriations for Fiscal Year 1966: Hearings before a Subcommittee of the Committee on Appropriations*, 89th Cong., 1st sess., 1965, pt. 2:128–29, 831; House, *1966 DOD Appropriations*, pt. 3:383–84, 557; House, *Department of Defense Appropriations for 1967: Hearings before a Subcommittee of the Committee on Appropriations*, 89th Cong., 2d sess., 1966, pt. 1:141.

291. Quoted in George Wilson, "Detailed Analysis to Affect Selection of Army Aircraft," *Aviation Week & Space Technology*, 15 March 1965, 80.

292. USSTRICOM to commander, Tactical Air Command, and commanding general, US Army Combat Development Command, letter, subject: Roles and Missions of the Armed Forces as Related to Joint Tests and Evaluation of Army Air Mobility Concepts, 20 January 1964; USSTRICOM Army Mobility Board Test Plan, 1963, annex C, "Joint Terms."

293. Headquarters US Strike Command, *Organization and Functions Manual*, 1 June 1964, 57.

294. Quoted in Brownlow, "Strike Command to Test Air Support Plan," *Aviation Week & Space Technology*, 26 October 1964, 63.

295. AFR 1-1, *Aerospace Doctrine: Responsibilities for Doctrine Development*, 20 March 1963.

296. Gen Paul D. Adams, commander in chief, USSTRICOM, to commander, Tactical Air Command, letter, subject: Draft Joint Airborne Operations Manual, dated May 1963, 13 June 1963.

297. Gen Walter C. Sweeney, Jr., commander, Tactical Air Command, to USAF (AFCCS), letter, subject: Doctrine for Joint Airborne Operations, 31 July 1963.

298. Outline of STRICOM Procedures at USAF Representatives Conference, Maxwell AFB, Alabama, 17 February 1965.

299. Box, "United States Strike Command," 9–10.

300. History, Tactical Air Command, January–June 1964, 1:182–84.

301. Interview with Lt Col George G. Loving, Jr., 24 May 1965; JCS Pub 8, *Doctrine for Air Defense from Overseas Land Areas* (FOUO), 23 May 1964.

IDEAS, CONCEPTS, DOCTRINE

302. JCS Pub 9, *Doctrine for the United Defense of the United States against Air Attack* (FOUO), 9 September 1964.
303. Parrish to commander, Air University, 2 August 1963, w/incl.: Headquarters USAF/XPD Staff Study.
304. *Air Force/Space Digest*, January 1965, 34; AFM 1-1, *United States Air Force Doctrine*, 14 August 1964.
305. Message, Brig Gen Pinkham Smith, Directorate of Operations, USAF, to TAC, ADC, MATS, AFSC, AU, SAC, AWS, ARS, 28 January 1964.
306. Smith to Maj Gen C. H. Pottinger, vice commander, Air University, letter, 8 July 1963.
307. Ibid.
308. Parrish to commander, Air University, 2 August 1963, letter, w/incl.: Headquarters USAF/XPD Staff Study.
309. House, *1965 DOD Appropriations*, pt. 5:168.
310. Senate, *Study of Air Power*, 533–37.
311. Ibid.
312. House, *Department of Defense Appropriations for 1960*, 86th Cong., 1st sess., 1959, pt. 1:69 (hereafter cited as *1960 DOD Appropriations*).
313. Ibid.
314. House, *Missile Development and Space Sciences*, 76.
315. "Are We Using or Abusing Technology?" *Air Force/Space Digest*, October 1961, 45–48.
316. Senate, *Study of Air Power*, 533–35.
317. House, *1964 DOD Appropriations*, pt. 6:658.
318. Senate, *Investigation of Governmental Organization for Space Activities*, 86th Cong., 1st sess., 462–63; House, *1961 DOD Appropriations*, pt. 7:183–84.
319. House, *1961 DOD Appropriations*, pt. 6:454–55, pt. 7:181.
320. House, *1964 DOD Appropriations*, pt. 6:598–606.
321. House, *1963 DOD Appropriations*, pt. 5:338–39.
322. *Organization and Management of Missile Programs*, 86th Cong., 1st sess., 1959, 3–4.
323. House, *Weapon System Management and Team System Concept in Government Contracting: Hearings before the Subcommittee for Special Investigation of the Committee on Armed Services*, 86th Cong., 1st sess., 1959, 125–26.
324. *Organization and Management of Missile Programs*, 493.
325. *Investigation of Governmental Organization for Space Activities*, 427–28.
326. House, *1961 DOD Appropriations*, pt. 6:338; Richard D. Thomas, *History of the Aeronautical Systems Center*, Study in the Evolution of Weapon Systems Management, September 1958–June 1960, 7–9.
327. Congress, *Impact of Military Supply and Service Activities on the Economy: Hearings before the Subcommittee on Defense Procurement of the Joint Economic Committee*, 88th Cong., 1st sess., 1963, 11.
328. House, *1960 DOD Appropriations*, pt. 5:622.
329. "Statement of Eugene M. Zuckert, Secretary of the Air Force, before Committee on Armed Services, United States Senate, 11 April 1961," in *Air Force Information Policy Letter for Commanders: Supplement*, April 1961, 6.
330. Maj Gen Bruce K. Holloway, "Requirements for Aerospace Weapon Systems," *Air University Quarterly Review* 12, nos. 3 and 4 (Winter/Spring 1960–1961): 213.
331. Senate, *Department of Defense Appropriations for Fiscal Year 1962*, 87th Cong., 1st sess., 1961 (hereafter cited as *FY 1962 DOD Appropriations*).
332. Col Francis X. Kane, "Technical Breakthrough," *Air University Quarterly Review* 12, nos. 3 and 4 (Winter/Spring 1960–1961): 264–75.
333. Public Law 85–599 75 Stat. 514, Department of Defense Reorganization Act of 1958.
334. House, *Sundry Legislation Affecting the Naval and Military Establishments for 1958*, 85th Cong., 2d sess., 6809.

335. House, *Sundry Legislation Affecting the Naval and Military Establishments for 1959*, 86th Cong., 1st sess., 801.
336. *Defense Space Interests*, 86.
337. Ibid.
338. Ibid., 207.
339. Ibid., 110.
340. House, *Hearings before Special Subcommittee on Defense Agencies*, 6894–95.
341. Ibid.
342. Senate, *TFX Contract Investigation: Hearings before the Permanent Subcommittee on Investigations of the Committee on Government Operations*, 88th Cong., 1st sess., 1963, pt. 3:776.
343. *Impact of Military Supply and Service Activities on the Economy*, 9, 11.
344. House, *Authorizing Appropriations for Aircraft, Missiles, and Naval Vessels for the Armed Forces*, 87th Cong., 1st sess., 1961, 1252–53, 1264–65; History, Aeronautical Systems Division, AFSC, January–June 1963, 1:43–51.
345. House, *1962 DOD Appropriations*, pt. 3:266–67; Senate, *FY 1962 DOD Appropriations*, 87th Cong., 1st sess., 1961, 1553; memorandum by Secretary McNamara to the secretary of the Air Force and secretary of the Navy, subject: TFX, 2 September 1961, in *TFX Contract Investigation*, pt. 2:333–34.
346. House, *Authorizing Appropriations for Aircraft, Missiles, and Naval Vessels for the Armed Forces*, 1265; House, *1962 DOD Appropriations*, pt. 4:362–64, 1377; House, *Department of Defense Appropriations for 1964*, 88th Cong., 1st sess., 1963, pt. 1:445.
347. Robert D. Little, *Nuclear Propulsion for Manned Aircraft: The End of the Program* (USAF Historical Division Liaison Office, April 1963); House, *1961 DOD Appropriations*, pt. 7:90; "Are We Using or Abusing Technology?" *Air Force/Space Digest*, October 1961, 45–48; *Aircraft Nuclear Propulsion Program: Hearings before the Subcommittee on Research and Development of the Joint Committee on Atomic Energy*, 86th Cong., 1st sess., 1959, passim.
348. *Aircraft Nuclear Propulsion Program*, 39–40, 40–42; *Major Defense Matters*, 86th Cong., 1st sess., 1959, 95; House, *1961 DOD Appropriations*, pt. 6:469–70.
349. House, *1962 DOD Appropriations*, pt. 3:14–15.
350. House, *Authorizing Appropriations for Aircraft, Missiles, and Naval Vessels for the Armed Forces*, 1245–46.
351. Ibid.; Senate, *FY 1965 DOD Appropriations*, pt. 1:178; *US Defense Policies in 1961*, 97–98.
352. House, *1962 DOD Appropriations*, pt. 4:515–16.
353. House, *Hearings on Military Posture and H.R. 2440*, 1200–1.
354. *Military Posture Briefings*, 87th Cong., 1st sess., 1146; Senate, *FY 1962 Military Procurement*, 401; House, *1963 DOD Appropriations*, pt. 4:425.
355. House, *1964 DOD Appropriations*, pt. 1:115.
356. *TFX Contract Investigation*, pt. 3:901–3.
357. Ibid., 757–60, 901–3.
358. Ibid.
359. Ibid., 757–58; memorandum for the record by Zuckert, Korth, and McNamara, 21 November 1962, in ibid., pt. 4:1031–34; DOD News Release No. 1907–62, 24 November 1962.
360. *TFX Contract Investigation*, pt. 3:901–3, pt. 8:1910.
361. Ibid., pt. 9:2412.
362. Ibid., pt. 5:1203.
363. Ibid., pt. 3:698.
364. Ibid., 711; House, *Hearings on Military Posture and H.R. 2440*, 1205.
365. House, *1964 DOD Appropriations*, pt. 6:521–22, 524.
366. Ibid., 655.
367. House, *1966 DOD Appropriations*, pt. 5:16.
368. House, *1964 DOD Appropriations*, pt. 1:161–62.
369. Ibid.
370. Ibid., 161.

IDEAS, CONCEPTS, DOCTRINE

371. *TFX Contract Investigation*, pt. 2:375–76.
372. *Impact of Military Supply and Service Activities on the Economy*, 6.
373. House, *1964 DOD Appropriations*, pt. 1:162–63.
374. Ibid., 161–62.
375. *Impact of Military Supply and Service Activities on the Economy*, 8–9; Senate, *FY 1965 DOD Appropriations*, pt. 1:179.
376. *TFX Contract Investigation*, pt. 5:1291–1332.
377. House, *1964 DOD Appropriations*, pt. 5:124.
378. Senate, *FY 1965 DOD Appropriations*, pt. 1:815–16.
379. House, *1965 DOD Appropriations*, pt. 5:21, 65–68.
380. Ibid.
381. House, *1966 DOD Appropriations*, pt. 5:18.
382. House, *1965 DOD Appropriations*, pt. 5:354.
383. Senate, *FY 1965 DOD Appropriations*, pt. 1:821; House, *1965 DOD Appropriations*, pt. 5:2.
384. House, *1965 DOD Appropriations*, pt. 5:355.
385. Ibid., pt. 4:474–75.
386. House, *1964 DOD Appropriations*, pt. 2:443.
387. House, *1965 DOD Appropriations*, pt. 4:479.
388. Jerome B. Wiesner and Herbert F. York, "National Security and the Nuclear Test Ban," *Scientific American*, October 1964, 35; *Nuclear Test Ban Treaty*, 88th Cong., 1st sess., 1963, 762.
389. House, *1963 DOD Appropriations*, pt. 5:352–54.
390. *A Compilation of Material Relating to U.S. Defense Policies in 1962*, 30; *DOD Annual Report for FY 1962*, 333.
391. House, *1963 DOD Appropriations*, pt. 2:117.
392. Ibid., pt. 2:499, 532–33; pt. 5:352–53.
393. House, *1964 DOD Appropriations*, pt. 6:567–68.
394. Ibid., pt. 1:254–55, pt. 6:561; *DOD Annual Report for FY 1962*, 333.
395. House, *1965 DOD Appropriations*, pt. 4:70–74.
396. House, *Hearings on Military Posture and H.R. 9637*, 6955.
397. House, *1965 DOD Appropriations*, pt. 4:71, pt. 5:353.
398. Ibid.
399. Senate, *FY 1965 DOD Appropriations*, pt. 1:357–58.
400. Ibid.
401. Ibid.
402. House, *1965 DOD Appropriations*, pt. 4:528.
403. "MMRBM Has Quiet Funeral," *Missiles and Rockets*, 31 August 1964, 8–9.
404. House, *1965 DOD Appropriations*, pt. 4:73–74.
405. William J. Caughlin, "That Visceral Feeling," an editorial, *Missiles and Rockets*, 31 August 1964, 46.
406. Ibid.
407. Senate, *FY 1965 DOD Appropriations*, pt. 1:359–60.
408. House, *1965 DOD Appropriations*, pt. 4:529.
409. Gen Thomas D. White, "Space Control and National Security," *Air Force Magazine*, April 1958, 80.
410. *Astronautics and Space Exploration*, 85th Cong., 2d sess., 110.
411. Ibid., 522.
412. White, "Space Control and National Security," 83.
413. Ibid.
414. Ibid.
415. *Astronautics and Space Exploration*, 525; Lt Col S. E. Singer, "The Military Potential of the Moon," *Air Force/Space Digest*, January 1960, 63–65.
416. *Astronautics and Space Exploration*, 110.

417. Ibid.
418. *Review of the Space Program*, 86th Cong., 2d sess., 492.
419. JCS Pub 1, *Dictionary of United States Military Terms for Joint Usage*, 1 February 1952.
420. Ibid.
421. *Investigation of Governmental Organization for Space Activities*, 483.
422. Ibid.; *Review of the Space Program*, 461–64.
423. House, *1961 DOD Appropriations*, pt. 3:781.
424. *Review of the Space Program*, pt. 1:480; Lt Gen R. C. Wilson, deputy chief of staff, Development, USAF, "Research and Development Today for Military Space Systems Tomorrow," *Air Force/Space Digest*, April 1960, 52–57.
425. House, *1961 NASA Authorization*, pt. 1:545–46; House, *1961 DOD Appropriations*, pt. 6:421–22.
426. House, *1961 NASA Authorization*, pt. 1:508.
427. House, *1962 DOD Appropriations*, pt. 4:16.
428. House, *1963 NASA Authorization*, pt. 2:656–57.
429. House, *1960 DOD Appropriations*, pt. 6:161.
430. Sen John F. Kennedy, "If the Soviets Control Space They Can Control Earth," *Missiles and Rockets*, 10 October 1960, 12.
431. Lt Gen B. A. Schriever, commander, ARDC, to Trevor Gardner, letter, 11 October 1960; Report of the Air Force Space Study Committee, 20 March 1961.
432. Senate, *FY 1962 Military Procurement*, 315; *Air Force Information Policy Letter for Commanders: Supplement*, April 1961, 7–8.
433. House, *1962 DOD Appropriations*, pt. 3:403.
434. Senate, *Department of Defense Appropriations for Fiscal Year 1963*, 87th Cong., 2d sess., 1962, 1039.
435. House, *Hearings on Military Posture and H.R. 9637*, 7431.
436. "Address by LeMay before the Michigan Post, American Ordnance Association, Detroit, Michigan, 26 October 1961," *Air Force Information Policy Letter for Commanders: Supplement*, January 1962, 12, 14.
437. Ibid.
438. House, *1963 NASA Authorization*, pt. 2:627.
439. House, *Space Posture: Hearings before the Committee on Science and Astronautics*, 88th Cong., 1st sess., 1963, 230.
440. House, *1963 DOD Appropriations*, pt. 2:477–88.
441. Ibid.; House, *Hearings on Military Posture and H.R. 9751*, 3766–74.
442. *U.S. Defense Policies in 1961*, 97.
443. Ibid.
444. House, *1963 DOD Appropriations*, pt. 2:144; House, *Space Posture*, 184; Senate, *Fiscal Year 1965 NASA Authorization: Hearings before the Committee on Aeronautical and Space Sciences*, 446, 452–53.
445. *Hearings on Military Posture and H.R. 9751*, 3789; House, *1965 DOD Appropriations*, pt. 4:522.
446. House, *1963 NASA Authorization*, pt. 3:1510.
447. House, *1963 DOD Appropriations*, pt. 2:477.
448. House, *1963 DOD Appropriations*, pt. 2:28.
449. Ibid.
450. Senate, *Fiscal Year 1963 NASA Authorization: Hearings before the Committee on Aeronautical and Space Sciences*, 87th Cong., 2d sess., 1962, 335.
451. House, *1963 DOD Appropriations*, pt. 2:539.
452. House, *Hearings on Military Posture and H.R. 9751*, 3781, 3788–89; "Bambi Study Program," *Aviation Week*, 16 January 1961, 26.
453. House, *1963 NASA Authorization*, pt. 2:1056.
454. Ibid., 657.

455. House, *1963 DOD Appropriations*, pt. 2:28.
456. House, *1964 NASA Authorization*, pt. 2(a):411.
457. House, *Space Posture*, 224–30.
458. House, *1964 DOD Appropriations*, pt. 1:479; pt. 6:579–80.
459. Sokolovsky, ed., *Military Strategy*, 466–73.
460. Ibid.; House, *Space Posture*, 225.
461. Senate, *FY 1964 Military Procurement*, 347.
462. Ibid.
463. House, *Space Posture*, 229.
464. *A Compilation of Material Relating to U.S. Defense Policies in 1962*, 77.
465. Ibid., 76–77; "Rubel Spells Out Space Philosophy," *Missiles and Rockets*, 22 October 1962, 37–38.
466. "Rubel Spells Out Space Philosophy," 37–38.
467. Ibid.
468. Ibid.
469. Ibid.
470. James J. Haggerty, Jr., "A Close Look at the Rubel Doctrine," *Army-Navy-Air Force Journal and Register*, 10 November 1962, 16, 22.
471. Ibid.
472. Ibid.
473. House, *1964 DOD Appropriations*, pt. 1:481; Senate, *FY 1964 Military Procurement*, 328.
474. House, *1964 DOD Authorizations*, pt. 1:430.
475. Senate, *FY 1964 Military Procurement*, 477.
476. Ibid., 476.
477. Ibid.
478. Ibid.
479. House, *1964 DOD Appropriations*, pt. 1:173–75, 368–69, 479.
480. House, *Space Posture*, 174–75.
481. Ibid., 225.
482. House, *1964 DOD Appropriations*, pt. 1:480.
483. Ibid., 476–77, 480.
484. Senate, *FY 1964 Military Procurement*, 321–22, 327.
485. Ibid., 1025–26; House, *1964 DOD Appropriations*, pt. 2:478; House, *Space Posture*, 236–37.
486. Senate, *FY 1964 Military Procurement*, 1028.
487. House, *Space Posture*, 230.
488. Senate, *FY 1964 Military Procurement*, 1027.
489. House, *Space Posture*, 231.
490. Senate, *FY 1964 Military Procurement*, 1031.
491. House, *1964 DOD Authorizations*, pt. 1:386.
492. House, *Space Posture*, 180.
493. House, *1964 NASA Authorization*, pt. 2(a):625.
494. House, *1964 DOD Appropriations*, pt. 1:258; House, *Hearings on Military Posture and H.R. 2440*, 589.
495. House, *1964 NASA Authorization*, pt. 2(a):629–30.
496. House, *1965 DOD Appropriations*, pt. 5:14–15, 413; House, *Hearings on Military Posture and H.R. 9637*, 7431.
497. House, *1965 DOD Appropriations*, pt. 4:235–36.
498. Ibid.; Senate, *FY 1965 DOD Appropriations*, pt. 1:173–74.
499. House, *1965 DOD Appropriations*, pt. 4:236–37; Senate, *FY 1965 NASA Authorization*, 441–44.
500. Senate, *FY 1965 DOD Appropriations*, pt. 1:173–74, 177.
501. House, *1965 DOD Appropriations*, pt. 4:520–25.

502. Ibid.; History, Aeronautical Systems Division, AFSC, July–December 1963, vol. 3, *Termination of the X-20A Dyna-Soar*.
503. History, Aeronautical Systems Division, AFSC, July–December 1963.
504. Senate, *FY 1964 Military Procurement*, 347.
505. Ibid., 322.
506. House, *1965 DOD Appropriations*, pt. 5:12, 101–2.
507. Ibid.
508. Ibid.
509. Ibid., pt. 4:325.
510. Ibid.
511. Ibid., 235.
512. Senate, *FY 1964 Military Procurement*, 1026.
513. House, *1966 DOD Appropriations*, pt. 5:150.
514. House, *Space Posture*, 227.
515. House, *Hearings on Military Posture and H.R. 2440*, 1201–2; Curtis E. LeMay, "Keeping Space Free," *Air Force/Space Digest*, April 1963, 41.
516. Ibid.
517. Ibid.
518. "Airpower in the News," *Air Force/Space Digest*, May 1965, 15.
519. House, *1964 DOD Appropriations*, pt. 2:412.
520. Gen B. A. Schriever, "Forecast," *Air University Review* 16, no. 3 (March–April 1965): 3.
521. Ibid., 4; Schriever, "Basic Aims and Some Findings of Project Forecast," *Air Force Policy Letter for Commanders: Supplement*, August 1964, 20.
522. House, *1965 DOD Appropriations*, pt. 5:355.
523. Schriever, "Forecast," 4–6.
524. Ibid., 4–6; Schriever, "Basic Aims and Some Findings of Project Forecast," 20.
525. "Schriever Disputes Plateau Theory," *Aviation Week & Space Technology*, 11 November 1963, 31; House, *1965 DOD Appropriations*, pt. 4:479.
526. House, *Hearings on Military Posture and H.R. 9637*, 7814.
527. Schriever, "Forecast," 7; House, *1966 DOD Appropriations*, pt. 5:112.
528. Schriever, "Forecast," 7.
529. Ibid.
530. Ibid., 7–10; House, *1966 DOD Appropriations*, pt. 5:355.
531. Schriever, "Forecast," 10–12; Schriever, "Basic Aims and Some Findings of Project Forecast," 20.
532. Eugene M. Zuckert, "Some Reflections on the Military Profession," *Air University Review* 17, no. 1 (November–December 1965): 5–6.
533. Ibid.
534. AFM 1-2, *United States Air Force Basic Doctrine*, 1 December 1959; Concepts Division, Research Studies Institute Project No. AU-501-60-RSI, Revision of SFP, "USAF Basic Doctrine," 16 March 1962.
535. Maj Gen Hewitt T. Wheless, Directorate of Plans, deputy chief of staff, Plans and Programs, USAF, to commander, Air University, letter, subject: Preparation of Air Force Doctrine, 6 March 1959; Lt Gen John K. Gerhart, deputy chief of staff, Plans and Programs, USAF, to Lt Gen W. E. Todd, commander, Air University, letter; USAF message, Headquarters USAF/XPD-96702, 14 December 1959; Concepts Division, Research Studies Institute, Air University, Project Files, Project No. AU-500-59-RSI; AFM 1-6, *Aerospace Doctrine-Combat Development*, December 1960; "USAF Basic Doctrine," March 1960.
536. Schriever, "Forecast," 5–7.
537. Zuckert, "An Appraisal of U.S. Aerospace Power, 1964," 28 January 1964; message, CSAF to TAC et al., 28 January 1964.

538. *Air Force/Space Digest*, January 1985, 34; AFM 1-1, *United States Air Force Basic Doctrine*, 1964. Under the old Air Force manual system, AFM 1-1 had been *Joint Action Armed Forces*. Since the subject matter of this JAAF manual had been included in a JCS Publication, the new Air Force basic doctrine manual was renumbered 1-1.

539. Ibid.

540. Deputy Director of Advance Planning, Directorate of Plans, deputy chief of staff, Plans and Operations, USAF, "National Policy and Conflict Management," *Air Force Information Letter for Commanders: Supplement*, November 1944, 26–29.

541. Ibid., 27–28.

542. Ibid., 26–29.

543. Ibid., 26–27.

544. Senate, *Fiscal Year 1966 Military Procurement Authorization: Hearings before the Committee on Armed Services and the Subcommittee on Department of Defense of the Committee on Appropriations*, 89th Cong., 1st sess., 1965, pt. 1:956.

545. AFM 1-2, 1 December 1959, i.

546. AFM 1-2, 14 August 1964, i.

547. AFM 1-2, 1 December 1959, i, 13.

548. AFM 1-1, 14 August 1964, 7–1.

549. Zuckert, "Some Reflections on the Military Profession," 4.

Lt Gen Bruce K. Holloway, deputy commander in chief of the United States Strike Command.

Gen Gabriel P. Disosway, Air Force director of programs and requirements.

Gen Lyman L. Lemnitzer, chairman of the Joint Chiefs of Staff.

X-20 Dyna-Soar.

Adm George W. Anderson, Jr., chief of naval operations.

Maj Gen Fred M. Dean, vice commander of the Twelfth Air Force.

Brig Gen Gilbert L. Pritchard, commander of the Air Force Special Air Warfare Center.

Maj Gen Richard C. Bowman, director of NATO and Eurpoean Affairs in the Office of the Assistant Secretary of Defense for International Security Affairs.

CHAPTER 4

INSURGENCY AND WAR IN SOUTHEAST ASIA

The war in Southeast Asia has captured the imagination of military historians and military theoreticians alike. These groups have shown an intense fascination for the part insurgency has played in making the conflict in Southeast Asia a memorable one.

Objectives and Strategy

The adherence of the United States to the Southeast Asian Treaty Organization (SEATO) in September 1954 quite shortly involved strategic requirements for diplomatic and military assistance to South Vietnam, Laos, and Cambodia. Providing the military assistance was complicated by the Geneva Agreement on Indochina which banned reinforcements of military personnel or equipment into both North and South Vietnam. This provision limited US support for South Vietnam, but it was virtually ignored by the aggressive Communist regime of Ho Chi Minh in Hanoi. The US objective in Indochina was steady: five presidential administrations attempted to get North Vietnam to allow South Vietnam, Laos, and Cambodia to determine their own futures.

Although the objective remained unchanged, the strategy and military means employed to achieve the objective frequently changed, offending a successful accomplishment of principles of strategy described by Maj Gen Robert N. Ginsburgh:

> A good strategist seeks to preserve maximum freedom of action to cope with the enemy while restricting the choices available to his opponent. To achieve this objective, he should devise a strategy that will take maximum advantage of his own military strengths, minimize the adverse effect of his own military weaknesses, and restrict the enemy's ability to do the same. An associated principle is that the manner in which conventional military power is used in a conflict like that waged in Southeast Asia should be based on consideration of the degree of commitments, so that national objectives and costs are balanced.[1]

In regard to Ginsburgh's "costs," Maj Gen Richard A. Yudkin, an experienced Air Force planner and student of military/political strategy, has concluded that "to define objectives without a concurrent understanding on price, seems to me to be at best an incomplete action." Yudkin further equated price as not only dollars and cents, but positive and negative effects on international relationships and degrees of diversion of effort and support from domestic programs.[2]

In the deepest analysis of strategy in the Vietnam War, Col Harry G. Summers, Jr., US Army, focused intensely on what he considered a neglect of strategy by professional military officers in the post-World War II nuclear era. The professional military had become "merely a logistics and management system to organize, train, and equip active duty and reserve forces." "The quintessential 'strategic lesson learned' from the Vietnam War is that we must once again become masters of the profession of arms," Summers urged. He postulated the additional criterion that an effective strategy must enjoy the support of the American people; this being so essential that "popular support" could be added to the old principles of war.[3] Gen George J. Eade, USAF, deputy chief of staff for plans and operations, reminded his listeners that a long war is deleterious to popular support and military effectiveness:

> Militarily, and any other way a long war is disadvantageous. If we allow the war to continue over an extended period, it is due to self-imposed restrictions on the forces we employ. . . . This is not to say that military forces can achieve an objective only when unconstrained and given a free rein; but, rather a balance must be reached in the decision-making process between political constraints and force limitations so that the ability to achieve a desired objective is optimized.[4]

Each of the foregoing commentators agreed that US strategy in Southeast Asia was defective in failing to permit the most effective employment of military power—particularly air power—and that in the end the "cost" or "price" of the defective strategy was too large for the attainment of the objective. In the view of General Eade, effective use of air power, or any type of military power, required a precise and realistic understanding of its capabilities *and* limitations by those who are empowered to call it into action. As for air power, it was given roles that it could not possibly carry out effectively, and it was shackled in the very areas where it was most effective.[5] In his foreword to Summers's *On Strategy*, Maj Gen Jack N. Merritt, commandant of the Army War College, wrote that lack of appreciation of the relationship of military strategy to national policy resulted in the exhaustion of the US Army against a secondary guerrilla force and an ultimate failure of military strategy to support the national policy of containment of Communist expansionism.[6] After leaving duty as deputy secretary of defense, David Packard recalled thinking a great deal about why the United States did not win the war in Vietnam:

> I think in large part it was the fact that we did not have any coherent strategy. Nobody had really thought through the problem to know how to deal with that kind of a situation, so we had a whole bunch of people out there, each trying to do their own thing.[7]

Advisory Assistance to South Vietnam

Immediately after the Geneva Conference, Ho Chi Minh revealed his bitterness by calling for a "long and arduous struggle" to win "North, Central, and South Vietnam," which he described as "territories of ours."[8] During the massive deterrence years of the mid-1950s, Hanoi received little support for its campaign from either Red China or the Soviet Union. In this period the SEATO defense strategy envisioned an indigenous army defense buildup against external aggression to defend the 17th parallel demarcation line. The buildup of indigenous air forces was not emphasized, one reason being the plan to provide US air support in the event of overt North Vietnamese attack. Air Force studies suggested that Southeast Asian countries were building conventional army forces when the major threat was by internal subversive groups with covert external support. Counterinsurgency capabilities such as development of air surveillance, rapid airmobility for light infantry, and programs for air/ground strikes against guerrilla forces, camp sites, supply routes, and base areas were recommended. As military assistance plan programs progressed, however, the main threat continued to be envisioned as external aggression. Air facilities in Laos and Vietnam were developing so slowly that it was evident to Lt Gen Frederic H. Smith, Jr., Fifth Air Force commander, that they could not support mobile US air strike forces required to fight with conventional weapons. A study was prepared envisioning employment of small-yield nuclear bombs against unpopulated bottlenecks on probable invasion routes.[9]

During 1958, Ho Chi Minh was able to take advantage of Red China's increased belligerency as well as the beginnings of the Sino-Soviet split, which enabled him to extort support from both Peking and Moscow. During the summer of 1959, North Vietnamese army troops moved into the panhandle of Laos and began to refurbish the network of jungle roads into South Vietnam, later collectively known as the Ho Chi Minh trail. In 1960 the Soviets airlifted military supplies and equipment into Laos to Communist Pathet Lao and Neutralist forces, and as has been seen, on 6 January 1961 Soviet Premier Nikita Khrushchev announced his support of subversion, guerrilla warfare, and insurgency wars to hasten the historical inevitability of world communism. This speech proclaiming "wars of liberation" and President Kennedy's confrontation with Khrushchev at Vienna led to vigorous reexamination of US military strategy. In Washington, Kennedy directed an expeditious development of US forces with special skills in the conduct of counterinsurgency or sublimited wars. The Army's response was to reorient its Special Forces (Green Berets), and the Air Force established air commando training at Eglin AFB, Florida. In May, the US Joint Chiefs of Staff recommended the movement of US combat ground and air forces into South Vietnam. President Kennedy decided against an open and substantial commitment of conventional US combat troops and favored increased assistance to South Vietnam.[10] At Eglin AFB, the 4400th Combat Crew Training Squadron—code-named Jungle Jim—assembled highly motivated volunteers who were rapidly qualified to perform covert air commando operations and train airmen of emerging nations. On 11 October, President Kennedy authorized deployment of a detachment of the 4400th to South Vietnam, initially for training and not for combat.[11]

On the same day (11 October 1961) that he authorized the air commando detachment — code-named Farm Gate — to deploy, President Kennedy sent his personally selected military adviser, Gen Maxwell D. Taylor, and his national security adviser, Walt W. Rostow, to Saigon to find out how best to help South Vietnam. Maj Gen T. R. Milton, commander of the Thirteenth Air Force and as such responsible for Air Force activities in Southeast Asia, joined the mission in the Philippines. In a six-day visit, General Milton recalled:

> The Taylor mission went at its job diligently. Each of us focused on things he knew best, and each of us also, it must be admitted, tried to see to it that his client's interest — whether CIA, the Army, Navy, Marines, Air Force, AID, wherever his allegiance lay — were advanced. If Vietnam was where the action was going to be, then everybody wanted a piece of the action.[12]

Back in Washington, the Joint Chiefs of Staff did not care for the Taylor-Rostow reports. They wanted a positive American commitment to a clear objective of preventing the fall of South Vietnam, even if it meant US military forces must fight. According to President Kennedy, however, the war could be won only as long as it remained Vietnam's war. He authorized an expansion of American military advisory effort to include Army helicopter companies, an Air Force transport squadron, the Farm Gate squadron, an air reconnaissance detachment, and a tactical air control system.[13]

Toward the end of the Taylor mission visit, General Milton was requested to arrange a flight over Laos. General Taylor and adviser Rostow stood in the cockpit of an old C-54 transport during a cautious 10-minute foray over the Mekong River and above the plains near Savannakhet. Rostow then announced with satisfaction that he had seen Laos: this was important, he said, because President Kennedy had told him that he could never approve a US policy toward Laos until someone he knew and trusted had seen the country with his own eyes. In General Milton's recollection no one in the Taylor mission raised any question about the probable difficulty, if not impossibility, of dealing with an enemy who moved freely in Laos and Cambodia while US efforts would stay strictly inside the borders of South Vietnam. Through the spring of 1962, Milton recalled that Laos was off-limits when discussing the problems of Vietnam, even though there were photos of a Soviet supply drop at Tchepone in Laos.[14] In regard to Laos, Secretary of State Dean Rusk continued to hope that the Soviet Union would enforce genuine neutrality of the country on Vietnam's flanks. In May 1962, creeping Communist aggression in Laos suddenly flashed into an all-out attack, and President Kennedy reluctantly directed an Air Force-Marine deployment to Thailand. The show of force was influential: on 23 July 1963 delegates at Geneva agreed to neutrality for Laos. Quite shortly, Hanoi was patently continuing to violate Laos neutrality, but in the US State Department Roger Hilsman was sanguine that the international agreement would hold infiltration into South Vietnam down to "a guerrilla warfare level," which the South Vietnamese could handle.[15]

As a matter of fact, Communist activity in South Vietnam at the close of 1961 had progressed from insurgency into at least "sublimited war." American military advisers — through necessity, natural inclination, and an approved policy of using Vietnam as a "laboratory" for development of counterinsurgency techniques — did not limit themselves to training South Vietnamese forces but rather sought combat, thus distorting their proper purpose to build indigenous strength.[16] By mid-1962 many senior air officers in Washington maintained that air strikes against North Vietnam would be necessary if the war in South Vietnam were to be ended. Most senior US commanders to whom Gen William W. Momyer talked in 1963 "felt sure that the war was rapidly expanding into a conventional conflict." But the OSD view continued to be that the problem was counterinsurgency; and Secretary McNamara was on record with the assessment that the Army would play the "important role" in counterinsurgency. He said: "While naval and air support operations are desirable, they won't be too effective, and we should not think they will win the war." In 1964, the Joint Chiefs of Staff agreed that the United States would have to intervene if South Vietnam were to be saved, but they differed on how the intervention should be done. Gen Earle G. Wheeler, Army chief of staff, maintained that US Army troops should take more of a combat role. An air campaign should be directed at lines of communication in Laos and North Vietnam near the South Vietnamese borders; most senior Army officers believed that the war would be won in South Vietnam and the main requirement would be for air support. Secretary McNamara essentially agreed with the Army's view. General LeMay argued that a minimum number of troops should be deployed to South Vietnam to secure the main airfields and other strategic areas. Then there should be concentrated air attacks against targets in the heart of North Vietnam. Indirect attacks against jungle-covered lines of infiltration were not apt to be decisive.[17]

Air Attacks against North Vietnam

When initial "tit-for-tat" air strikes in response to Communist attacks against Americans failed to get results, President Lyndon B. Johnson in December 1964 was willing to authorize air attacks against lines of communication in Laos and just above the demilitarized zone (DMZ) in North Vietnam, the former to begin in December and the latter when and if the North Vietnamese continued their aggressive activities. In February 1965 Flaming Dart reprisals were flown just north of the DMZ; on 2 March 1965 a continuing, systematic air campaign termed *Rolling Thunder* began against North Vietnam, at first in the area south of the 19th parallel. Shortly after becoming the Air Force chief of staff on 1 February 1965, Gen John P. McConnell proposed to make Rolling Thunder a "fast/full squeeze," hard-hitting campaign against 94 air targets grouped into basic categories of airfields, lines of communication, military installations, industrial installations, and armed reconnaissance routes.[18] In gross summary of Rolling Thunder as a strategic undertaking, President Johnson was going to follow a strategy of graduation with only limited expectations of the possible accomplishments of bombing. Secretary Rusk was determined to avoid giving the USSR or China what he frequently described as "an orgasm of decision making."[19] On equally numerous occasions, Secretary McNamara asserted and reasserted that air power alone would not eliminate the capability of the north to supply the south; that there were no military targets in the north of fundamental consequence to the carrying on of Communist operations in South Vietnam. The purpose of the attacks was to raise South Vietnamese morale, reduce the flow of men and materiel southward, and raise the political price to Hanoi.[20] Although air target zones were grudgingly moved north from the 20th parallel, the final decisions on targets to be authorized, the number of sorties to be flown, and in many instances the tactics to be used by pilots were made at Tuesday luncheons attended by the president and his civilian advisers. Not until late in 1967 was General Wheeler, by then chairman of the Joint Chiefs of Staff, invited to attend the Tuesday meetings.[21] From time to time in efforts to influence Hanoi to agree to truce discussions, frequent bombing pauses were ordered by President Johnson; and on 31 October 1968, when Johnson concluded that Hanoi had agreed to participate in ongoing truce talks in Paris, restrain military action in the DMZ, and forego attacks on South Vietnamese cities, he halted the Rolling Thunder bombing.[22]

Americans Join the In-Country Ground War

In the McNamara strategy, the bombing of the North was always "intended as a supplement to and not a substitute for the military operations in the South."[23] Gen William C. Westmoreland, commander US Military Assistance Command, Vietnam (COMUSMACV), had first claim in all locally available Seventh Air Force and US Seventh Fleet strength for ground support. On 18 June 1945 Strategic Air Command B-52s flying from Guam also commenced ground-supporting Arc Light strikes. The first Marine and Army combat troops were ordered to Vietnam for airfield protection: the 9th Marine Expeditionary Brigade to Da Nang in March 1965 and the 173d Airborne Brigade to Vung Tau and then Bien Hoa. From these beginnings, Westmoreland requested and began to receive an inflow of US Army divisions, initially including the experimental 1st Cavalry Division (Airmobile), formed up after Strike Command tests at Fort Benning, Georgia.

Westmoreland had the alternatives of employing the arriving US forces in defense of areas where US bases were being established (the "enclave" strategy described and strongly recommended by Lt Gen James M. Gavin, US Army, Retired) or of meeting and gaining an initiative over the Communist attack anticipated for the autumn of 1965. From base areas established in Cambodia, the North Vietnamese, as was anticipated, planned to destroy special forces camps in the central highlands of South Vietnam, capture Pleiku, and cut South Vietnam in half. To combat this, Westmoreland ordered a "search-and-destroy" strategy whereby US forces would search out and destroy enemy main force units, at first in spoiling attacks and later in deliberate operations against base areas. The Communist forces lost hope for quick victory in unsuccessful campaigning during the November 1965 to May 1966 dry season in South Vietnam, and General Westmoreland accomplished Phase I of his strategy plan — the buildup and preparation of forces.[24]

In mid-1966 General Westmoreland was ready to begin Phase II planned offensives. Since American forces had the greater mobility and firepower, they would be used in the bulk of the offensive against Vietcong southern forces and North Vietnam units. South Vietnamese forces would be employed in pacification efforts, while also in preparation for active field service. The Communist strategy appeared to be designed to fight main force units from sanctuary areas where they could hope to wear down US and South Vietnamese forces without risking a full response of American air and ground firepower. The main thrust of Communist infiltration went down the Ho Chi Minh trail through Laos and Cambodia. And in February 1966, North Vietnam's astute military commander — Gen Vo Nguyen Giap — opened a second front at the DMZ. Since it was important to counter the enemy threat without diverting too many ground troops to the DMZ, General Momyer, as MACV deputy for air operations, planned and laid on Operation Neutralize beginning on 12 September. Under a seeking, locating, annihilating, and monitoring concept (SLAM), reconnaissance aircraft and intelligence agencies located targets; heavy bomber strikes by B-52s usually triggered the attack; and tactical air strikes and coordinated artillery followed. At the completion of Operation Neutralize on 30 October, General Westmoreland judged that SLAM was one of his most valuable and responsive tools. "During the 49 days of the SLAM operation in support of Con Thien we dislodged a firmly entrenched enemy, destroyed his prepositioned supplies, and forced him to withdraw at great loss — with massed firepower alone," Westmoreland wrote. In November, west of Dak To in Kontum province, the North Vietnamese 1st Division was badly defeated and driven back into Cambodia. Westmoreland called the battle for Dak To "the beginning of a great defeat" for the enemy. "I am absolutely certain that whereas in 1965 the enemy was winning, today he is certainly losing," he told newsmen.[25]

In Saigon in the summer of 1967, many experts forecast that the Communists would return to protracted guerrilla warfare, but General Giap evidently sold the Hanoi politburo on the idea of a "go-for-broke" strategy. Phase I involved set-piece battles mounted from sanctuaries with concentrated (rather than dispersed) main force units to draw American troops away from populous areas. Phase II would see large numbers of Communist attacks all over South Vietnam during which it was expected that the Republic of Vietnam's armed forces would disintegrate and the civilian population would rise in revolt. Phase III would culminate in a great conjoined fixed battle at a place most favorable for a major Communist victory. The "go-for-broke" strategy included a negotiational ploy whereby Hanoi would hold out hope for a political settlement of the conflict.[26]

IDEAS, CONCEPTS, DOCTRINE

Early in January 1968, the North Vietnam 325C and 304th Divisions began to concentrate in the vicinity of a US Marine defense position at Khe Sanh, the western anchor of the US defense line at the DMZ. To defend Khe Sanh the Marine commander wanted all the air strikes he could get, preferring air to artillery because this would reduce ammunition resupply problems and give greater flexibility. Westmoreland visualized bombs flowing around Khe Sanh like water pouring over Niagara Falls, and he chose the name Operation Niagara for the air effort to be flown in Khe Sanh's defense. While the preparations were afoot at Khe Sanh, the North Vietnamese and the southern Vietcong in a Tet offensive on 29 January unleashed some 84,000 troops in surprise attacks against major cities, towns, and military installations. The pattern indicated an expectation that the South Vietnamese armed forces would collapse and the population would rise in revolt. But South Vietnam did not collapse, and between 29 January and 11 February the Communists lost some 32,000 men killed and 5,800 captured. By 5 February, Khe Sanh was under an attack that would not be broken off until 23 March. In this battle air power and the Marine defenses tore the heart out of crack North Vietnamese divisions. A senior US Army general called Khe Sanh "probably the first major ground action won entirely or almost entirely by air power."[27]

"The reality of the 1968 Tet offensive was that Hanoi had taken a big gamble and had lost on the battlefield, but they had won a solid psychological victory in the United States," Adm Ulysses S. Grant Sharp, commander in chief, Pacific Command, wrote in summary. Hard after the Communist defeat in Tet, Admiral Sharp would have liked to have seen air assault against every war-making facility in North Vietnam, but this was not possible.[28] According to Under Secretary of the Air Force Townsend Hoopes, "a growing segment of the foreign-military bureaucracy" was already disenchanted with Westmoreland's attrition strategy: at Hill 875 near Dak To, for example, US paratroopers had lost 135 dead and 150 wounded and since the hill had no intrinsic value it was immediately abandoned.[29] On 1 March 1968 Clark Clifford succeeded McNamara as secretary of defense. He had been a strong supporter of the war, but when he visited Saigon in July General Momyer noted that he had changed. Lacking any concrete evidence that the war could be won by military means by any specific date in the near future, Clifford now proposed to recommend to the president that bombing of North Vietnam be stopped and that US ground forces begin to withdraw, leaving the South Vietnamese responsible for the war.[30] That same month President Johnson instructed the new COMUSMACV, Gen Creighton W. Abrams, to implement "spoiling operations" — intensive small-unit patrolling that would hopefully incur fewer casualties than earlier multibattalion undertakings. At this juncture, the Communists had lost most control over the countryside because of casualties sustained in the Tet assaults: main force units forced back into sanctuary base areas required supplies from outside South Vietnam. There was hope that a new interdiction effort to be called Command Hunt could be more effective than had been the case with previous aerial interdictions. In April 1968 President Johnson directed a cessation of bombing north of 19 degrees north, and at meetings on

13–16 October, he secured assent on a complete bombing halt of North Vietnam, provided the North Vietnamese held to supposed understandings. President Johnson also briefed the Joint Chiefs of Staff and General Momyer, who in August had yielded command in Saigon to Gen George S. Brown and had assumed command of the Tactical Air Command. He solicited their individual views, and in Momyer's recollection:

> Each of us assured the President that the North Vietnamese would take advantage of the bombing halt to improve their position for a future offensive. Furthermore, we said, it would be unrealistic to suppose that airpower could control the enemy's flow of supplies into South Vietnam by striking the LOCs in Laos if all the alternative routes in North Vietnam were immune to attack. Each of us advised that if the President were convinced that the North Vietnamese sincerely wanted substantive negotiations he might try a brief bombing halt without unduly jeopardizing our forces in South Vietnam. But if the North Vietnamese made no prompt, visible efforts to stop the fighting in South Vietnam, if they continued the infiltration of troops, if they failed to begin the withdrawal of regular divisions, and if they showed no serious interest in the negotiations, then the bombing campaign should be resumed against all military targets throughout North Vietnam, and such a campaign should continue with no let-up until our demands for a cease-fire were satisfied.[31]

On 31 October President Johnson announced his decision to stop all bombing of North Vietnam but to continue reconnaissance flights and interdiction of enemy traffic through Laos.

President Nixon and Vietnamization

In negotiating sessions at Paris, the North Vietnamese remained obstructive, and in Indochina they continued to prepare for renewed military operations. They continued to use Laos as a conduit for supplies, and Cambodia became a major base not only for rice and medicine supplies as had been the case as far back as 1966 but now for ammunition and guns. General Abrams cabled General Wheeler that human and photointelligence showed that the location of the Communist headquarters for all of South Vietnam was immediately across the Cambodian border. The US military command in Saigon was convinced (rightly as it later turned out) that large shipments of arms were coming in through the port of Sihanoukville, but the Central Intelligence Agency (CIA) and the State Department urged that the Communists could secure all the support they needed over the Ho Chi Minh trail through Laos.[32]

In his victorious campaign for the presidency, Richard M. Nixon charged that far too little had been done to train and equip the South Vietnamese to fight their own war. On a visit to South Vietnam early in March 1969, new Secretary of Defense Melvin Laird accordingly advised military commanders that the combat burden had to be shifted to the Republic of Vietnam's armed forces "promptly and methodically." Laird coined the word Vietnamization, and his principal objective was to let nothing interfere with an expedited US withdrawal from Vietnam.[33]

During a visit to Southeast Asia in July 1969, Nixon drew a broad outline of long-range policy that became known as the Nixon Doctrine. In brief, the president promised that the United States would keep its treaty commitments, would provide a shield if a nuclear power threatened an allied nation or one whose survival was vital to US security, and would furnish military and economic assistance in accordance with treaty commitments. But the United States would look to the nation directly threatened to assume primary responsibility of providing manpower for its defense.[34]

In the earlier years of war, when the Communist guerrillas and North Vietnamese army units had relatively free access to supplies in South Vietnam, US policy had accepted enemy use of Cambodia rather than risk expansion of the war. In preparation for the withdrawal of US troops, it became more critical that supply centers in Cambodia and Laos be reduced; moreover, supply was becoming a potential limitation to the North Vietnamese army's conventional field operations which by now had to be supported by large numbers of trucks and armed vehicles. Although President Nixon instructed General Abrams to keep American casualties to a minimum, the United States was losing about 250 men a week. As the North Vietnamese continued to expand their supply system, the Joint Chiefs pressed for a resumption of bombing of North Vietnam below the 20th parallel. When Secretary Laird doubted that this was politically supportable, General Wheeler proposed, as an alternative, attacks on the North Vietnamese bases across the border in Cambodia.[35] In 1967, Prince Norodom Sihanouk had authorized bombing of the North Vietnamese base areas in his country providing there was no public announcement. In early March 1969, the Vietnamese Communists increased attacks which raised American casualties from 300 to 400 a week and also fired rockets into Saigon. President Nixon ordered an immediate B-52 attack on the Cambodian sanctuaries, and the first strike was flown against Base Area 353, three miles inside the Cambodian border, on 18 March. Code-named Menu, these B-52 strikes were conducted against six enemy base sanctuary areas along the South Vietnamese/Cambodian border under special security procedures whereby the strikes were bureaucratically reported as having taken place against targets in South Vietnam. In the following year a total of 3,875 B-52 sorties dropped 108,823 tons of bombs in the Menu areas. In periodic reviews of the effectiveness of these strikes, General Abrams credited them with disrupting enemy logistics, aborting several enemy offensives, and reducing the threat to Saigon. As combat action developed during ground operations in Cambodia in early May and June 1970 the requirement for special security procedures was lifted; the last Menu strike was on 26 May 1970.[36]

On 18 March 1970, when Sihanouk was out of Cambodia, Gen Lon Nol, the Royal Khmer chief of staff, deposed the prince from his long-held position as head of state. Sihanouk promptly sought North Vietnamese support, and the North Vietnamese began plunging deep into Cambodia with the obvious intention of overthrowing the government and taking territory that would vastly improve their logistics base. On 30 April, President Nixon declared that Communist activity in

Cambodia clearly endangered the lives of Americans who were in the process of withdrawing from Vietnam. He authorized US air support for South Vietnamese divisions moving to assist the Cambodian government, and he also directed a limited penetration by US forces to a depth of 21.7 miles into Cambodia to destroy Communist staging, logistical, and control centers. Unless there were a subsequent congressional authorization, Nixon promised that US ground combat troops would not remain in Cambodia more than eight weeks. The Cambodian incursion set off bitter student demonstrations in the United States. All US ground combat troops were removed within the promised time, but Congress found such employment unacceptable. On 30 June and routinely thereafter Congress approved amendments to various legislation barring the introduction of US ground combat forces into Cambodia, Laos, or Thailand.[37]

The loss of stored equipment and supplies in Cambodia, together with the closing of the port of Kompong Som (formerly Sihanoukville) to Communist traffic, caused a very large reduction of the North Vietnamese capability to threaten the Saigon area. After the Cambodian incursion, the war virtually ended in the southern half of South Vietnam and never regained full force after 1972. With Hanoi almost completely dependent upon the Ho Chi Minh trail through Laos for logistic support in South Vietnam, General Abrams was convinced that if the Ho Chi Minh trail could be denied or substantially disrupted for even one dry season, Hanoi's ability to conduct major offensives would be curtailed for some time. Abrams accordingly conceived of an operation whereby American forces would establish support positions along Route 9 and Khe Sanh, and the South Vietnamese 1st Division would make airmobile and armored attacks that would seize the town of Tchepone, at the hub of many of the roads comprising the Ho Chi Minh trail. No American ground troops could cross into Laos, but American air power would support the operation to be called Lam Son 719. The Seventh Air Force collocated a direct air support center (DASC) with the US XXIV Corps forward command post at Quang Tri. English-speaking Vietnamese flew with Air Force forward air control (FAC) pilots and aboard C-130 aerial command posts to bridge language difficulties. Based on experience in South Vietnam, the XXIV Corps did not estimate that the antiaircraft fire would be as heavy as the Seventh Air Force predicted and decided that most of the fire support for troop-carrying helicopters would be provided by Army helicopter gunships.[38]

Lam Son 719 was launched on 8 February 1971 when a mechanized unit crossed the border and other troops were airlifted to a landing zone near Tchepone. The Communists reacted strongly, eventually bringing 24,000 combat troops, supported by antiaircraft guns, artillery, and tanks, to bear against the South Vietnamese. The South Vietnamese armor bogged down some 20 kilometers inside Laos and most of the South Vietnamese fire-support bases came under attack. Even with support from B-52s and extensive fighter support, the situation deteriorated rapidly. Only through the effort of the FACs, who brought in a stream of fighters, was the North Vietnamese tank force stopped just short of engaging South Vietnamese armor retreating to the border. The plan was to stay in Laos

IDEAS, CONCEPTS, DOCTRINE

until the wet season in late April and destroy the large stocks of North Vietnamese supplies. Instead, the South Vietnamese commander ordered a hasty withdrawal that took place with not a little accompanying panic. Both sides lost heavily in men and equipment. American helicopter liftships proved particularly vulnerable to Communist "hugging tactics," which permitted the enemy to get rockets and automatic weapons in very close to fire bases. The US Army reported a total of 94 helicopters shot down between 5 February and 11 March but other reports put the loss for the Laos incursion at 219 helicopters. From Lam Son 719 General Momyer drew a lesson that heliborne assaults had the same limitations as earlier airborne operations. He wrote:

> The employment of such forces requires almost complete air superiority and the ability to maintain a stream of fighters overhead throughout the initial phases and until such forces can link up with an advancing column on the ground. Until such a link-up, the force is vulnerable to an armor attack. For airborne troops to survive such an assault, airpower must provide the heavy firepower until the soldier again has his own organic support.[39]

Air Power and the 1972 Spring Invasion

In President Nixon's assessment, it was no longer necessary in March 1971 to use American ground combat forces in active battle. This meant that the American withdrawal would continue, hopefully even ahead of schedule. On the other hand, he promised to use air power against the North in response to cause:

> One, . . . we would attack these missile sites that fired at our planes. . . . Second, . . . if I determined that increased infiltration from North Vietnam endangered our remaining forces in South Vietnam at a time we were withdrawing I would order attacks on the supply routes, on the infiltration routes, on the military complexes, and I have done that in the past. And I shall do so again if I determine that such activities by North Vietnam may endanger our remaining forces in South Vietnam, particularly as we are withdrawing.[40]

Since 1968, however, North Vietnam had been relatively free from air attack. The rules of engagement authorized escorted reconnaissance and if the enemy hazarded the reconnaissance plane either by ground fire or aerial interception or illumination by a missile-director radar, the escorts were expected to respond with active force.[41]

In late 1971 reconnaissance and intelligence reports indicated that the North Vietnamese were undertaking unusual logistic preparations. There were 7,000 to 8,000, mostly Soviet-built, trucks in North Vietnamese motor parks, apparently loaded with military supplies. Road repair and rebuilding was intensive southward from Hanoi and Haiphong. Two fuel lines reached from Haiphong toward the DMZ. The North Vietnamese began to make incursions into Laos with their MiGs; they shot down an F-4 and posed a decided hazard to B-52 bombing. Surface-to-air (SAM) missile sites were being pushed down the DMZ, and from time to time

SAMs were fired at American aircraft in Laos. In late December, aircrews were reporting that missiles were being fired at them with no indication of activity on Fan Song missile direction radars: apparently the Communists were netting early warning radars into the missile sites and using data from them to direct missile fire. The MiGs that were appearing in Laos seemed to be staging quickly through forward airfields at Bai Phong, Quang Lang, Vinh, or Dong Hoi. It was easy to see how SAMs were getting into Laos: photoreconnaissance along Route 137 down the North Vietnamese panhandle into Laos frequently showed parked radar vans and SAMs on transporters waiting for bad weather to slip across into Laos. On another occasion a reconnaissance plane photographed 60 tanks parked in the open at Bat Lake, about eight or nine miles north of the DMZ.[42]

In Saigon, Gen John D. Lavelle had assumed command of the Seventh Air Force on 1 August 1971, and he anxiously viewed the North Vietnamese activities, most of which were not subject to air attack under the rule of returning fire only. Under exceptional circumstances, Washington could authorize attacks: this was done during Operation Proud Deep from 26 to 30 December 1971 when the Joint Chiefs of Staff directed maximum effort strikes in North Vietnam up to 20 degrees and on 16–17 February 1972 when air strikes were authorized against newly designed Communist 130-mm artillery guns sited to fire across the DMZ. On the other hand, the tank aggregation at Bat Lake could not be attacked because the tanks posed no threat to aircraft. In Washington, Secretary Laird turned aside a congressman's query about the tremendous buildup of trucks in North Vietnam by saying that they were not approved targets under the protective reaction rule. In Saigon, General Lavelle requested authority from Laird to strike MiGs in the southern airfields, and, as Lavelle remembered, Laird told him that it was an inopportune time to come in to Washington requesting any new authorities but to make maximum use of the authorities he had. A conference in Honolulu held to discuss what to do about the MiG hazard brought instructions that field commanders should be more aggressive and schedule larger numbers of fighter escorts to ensure adequate damage on protective reaction flights. Believing that he was being encouraged to be more aggressive and more flexible, General Lavelle issued orders that all missions over North Vietnam would be assumed to be under fire and that all operations reports would show hostile reaction. News of Lavelle's activity soon reached the press and provoked controversy. On 6 April 1972 General Lavelle was relieved as Seventh Air Force commander; he subsequently retired from active duty with a reduction to his permanent rank.[43]

In February 1972 Secretary Laird was assured that the North Vietnamese had a capability for no more than limited actions, and he expected to continue to withdraw Americans at an average rate of 23,500 a month.[44] Whereas the US Seventh Air Force had mustered 41 squadrons in 1968, it was down to 15 tactical air squadrons in March 1972. B-52 sortie allocations were cut from 1,700 per month in 1968 to 1,400 in early 1972. But whereas the South Vietnamese Air Force had had only 17 squadrons at the time of Tet, it now had 44 squadrons, including such tactical fighters as F-5s, A-37s, and A-1s.[45] Allied air strikes within South Vietnam totaled 4,000 during February 1972, of which 3,300 were flown by the Vietnamese air force.[46]

The Communists may well have been concerned about the progress of Vietnamization. At any rate, Gen Vo Nguyen Giap's battle plan for 1972 was to be an enormous effort, gambling North Vietnam's regular army forces and modern tanks, artillery, and antiaircraft missiles—including a first commitment of SA-7 Strela handheld, infrared, heat-seeking antiaircraft missiles. There were to be three thrusts. The chief one was frontally across the DMZ, seeking to capture Quang Tri and Thua Thien provinces. A second effort would forge into Kontum province to An Khe to cut South Vietnam in half. The third would be directed down the Loc Ninh-Saigon axis. If the offensives progressed moderately Hanoi would be in a good position to call for a cease-fire. If they were very successful the Republic of Vietnam could collapse. The Communist Easter offensive was launched soon after midnight on Good Friday, 30 March, in massed attack across the DMZ. For the next several days rain, thick overcasts, and low ceilings sheltered the tank-led attacks that stormed southward to Quang Tri City. The North Vietnamese also captured the key town of Dak To in Kontum province. The town of Loc Ninh soon fell to the North Vietnamese, but to the south the South Vietnamese defenses held at An Loc. By all accounts the Vietnamese air force acquitted itself well; in the low-ceiling weather, the relatively slow moving aircraft flown by the Vietnamese were able to operate low enough to give close air support. But before long, the SA-7s, forced low-performing aircraft out of their vicinity and made it necessary for high-performance fighters to take over.[47]

The major factor that influenced the Easter offensive was the decision by President Nixon to provide United States tactical and strategic air assistance. By the end of May, Air Force forces in South Vietnam and Thailand included nearly 400 F-4s and F-105s—almost double the strength of tactical fighters present at the start of the offensive. B-52 strength in the Pacific was 171, whereas 83 B-52s had earlier been positioned at bases on Guam and in Thailand. Through the late spring, six American aircraft carriers were in the Far East and at least four were in position for air operations each day. There was no question about the effectiveness of air power against the Communists' mechanized and armored forces, which were difficult to conceal on the flatland of eastern Quang Tri. The North Vietnamese also bared a logistic tail that was vulnerable to air attack. B-52 firepower was very effective against the massing Communist forces: one ground general commented that the B-52s "were decisive in stopping the advance of the North Vietnamese toward Hue and permitted us to retake Quang Tri."[48]

But early in May, the Communist offensive was still forging ahead, and following the Communist capture of Quang Tri City, President Nixon on 8 May directed that Hanoi must be denied the weapons and supplies it needed to continue the aggression. Therefore all entrances to North Vietnamese ports would be mined. Rail and all other communication would be cut off to the maximum extent possible. The objectives of the Linebacker I air campaign were (1) to reduce the flow of supplies into North Vietnam from external sources; (2) to destroy the existing stockpiles of supplies already in North Vietnam; and (3) to reduce the flow of supplies from North Vietnam to units in the South. US Navy and Marine airmen mined Haiphong harbor in an "almost textbook operation" — quickly and without casualties. The other aspects of interdiction were done equally well. After Washington authorities approved and validated a master target list, US senior commanders in the field secured the authority to make the important day-to-day decisions. Introduction of a new generation of precision-guided munitions, so-called smart bombs, made for highly effective strikes against key targets or in politically sensitive areas. By way of comparison, 120 Rolling Thunder sorties with 600,000 pounds of bombs had been flown against the Thanh Hoa combination rail and highway bridge, a key link on the Route 1 highway down the North Vietnamese panhandle, but the bridge was never successfully neutralized. On 13 May F-4s carrying laser-guided bombs and conventional 500-pound bombs struck the bridge and left it unserviceable. Both the northeast and northwest rail lines from Hanoi to China were cut within a few days. Some 15 bridges on each of them were taken down and kept down as fast as they were repaired. All but one of the enemy's major power plants were rapidly put out of operations; far different from the dribbling approach of Rolling Thunder. The North Vietnamese pipeline down to the DMZ was reportedly a "lousy target," but strikes against major storage areas, pumping stations, and similar key chokepoints got results.[49]

By the end of May, the bombing and air interdiction of the north were limiting the ability of the Communists to fight in the south, and concurrently, the heavy expenditures and losses of supplies by the Communists in the south increased the effectiveness of aerial interdiction, intensifying shortages and forcing the enemy to make hazardous daylight movements.[50] The Easter offensive had ground to a complete halt by October. In this effort the North Vietnamese had lost as many as 75,000 dead and 700 tanks destroyed — 70 percent of the tanks killed by air and most of them by the South Vietnamese air force. South Vietnamese forces had held, but at a cost of perhaps 30,000 killed. As had been true at Tet, when the Communists had lost but had won a psychological victory, Communist troops in October 1972 were geographical winners since the forthcoming military truce agreement would allow them to leave forces at existing battle positions inside South Vietnam.[51]

When truce negotiations in Paris appeared to take a turn for the better, the United States again ceased bombing above the 20th parallel, effective 23 October 1972.[52] But before very long, the Communist delegates once again stopped constructive negotiations, possibly because they awaited the outcome of the US presidential election, which returned President Nixon to office. At this same time, South Vietnamese President Nguyen Van Thieu was gravely concerned about provisions in the draft agreement that would allow North Vietnamese troops to remain within South Vietnam. To speed negotiations, President Nixon, in consultation with Adm Thomas H. Moorer, JCS chairman, and Presidential Adviser Henry Kissinger (but with opposition from Secretary of Defense Laird), ordered very heavy air strikes against previously unattacked military targets in

IDEAS, CONCEPTS, DOCTRINE

Hanoi and Haiphong. This was a bad weather period over North Vietnam, making visual bombing attacks usually impossible. It was therefore decided to use Strategic Air Command B-52s which were the best all-weather bombers. Since Hanoi and Haiphong probably had the heaviest concentrated air defenses in the world and the B-52s would have to make repetitive strikes from high attitudes where they would be most vulnerable to SA-2 missiles, the decision to use the strategic bombers was not made lightly. When General McConnell had been the Air Force chief of staff he had estimated that half of any B-52 force sent to Hanoi-Haiphong would be lost, but counterdefense capabilities had increased, and it was now estimated that only 2 percent of the B-52 sorties flown would be lost. All-weather Air Force F-111s and Navy A-6s supplemented the B-52s, and Air Force and Navy tactical fighters would bomb through the overcast. (In one 12-hour break in the weather, some important targets would be attacked with "smart bombs.")[53]

The first warning order for Linebacker II was issued on 15 December 1972, and the 11-day air campaign ran from 18 to 29 December, with a brief pause for Christmas Day. The attacks were relentless, around-the-clock, despite the monsoon weather. Targeting emphasis was on transportation-related targets and military supply storage; only valid military objectives were hit, and unmanned photoreconnaissance aircraft revealed that bombing accuracy was extremely good. During Linebacker II, 15 B-52s, 2 F-4s, 2 F-111s, and 1 A-7 were lost by the Air Force, and the US Navy lost 6 aircraft. The loss rate for all aircraft was a little less than 2 percent and well under the 3 percent that had been expected. The loss of 15 B-52s in 729 sorties over targets came out to just about the predicted 2-percent loss rate. The Communists fired 1,242 SAMs, and many of these missiles had to be launched in barrage fire when missile-detector radars were jammed. Toward the end of the strikes, the Communists appeared to have virtually exhausted their supply of antiaircraft missiles. The high degree of professionalism manifest in the raids doubtless contributed toward low-loss rates. Admiral Moorer summed this up:

> The 11-day air campaign of December 1972 will, I am certain, go down in history as a testimonial to the efficacy of airpower the way it should be used — it constituted the use of joint forces in a skillfully coordinated effort the way they should be used. Its success was due to our airmen's qualities of professionalism, skill, dedication, and raw courage in their highest tradition.[54]

The missions also demonstrated outstanding total force participation. Each day's support figures varied, based on weight of B-52 effort, target area, axes of attack and withdrawal, threat analysis, and so forth. The overall ratio of support to bombers averaged out as 1.3 to 1. In a maximum compressed attack effort on 26 December, 116 B-52s and some 300-plus tactical aircraft were over North Vietnam in 30 minutes, each giving support to the others in a general diminution of enemy defenses.[55]

While Linebacker II was in progress, President Nixon stated that the bombing would end when Hanoi indicated it would negotiate in a constructive attitude.

Technical negotiation in Paris resumed on 2 January; and on 8 January the principals began meetings that resulted in final truce agreements on 27 January 1973. In this period as Linebacker II was ended, B-52 aircrews were quoted as wondering why their operation was standing down when North Vietnam's defenses were in shambles and they could strike with impunity. The British expert on war in Southeast Asia, Sir Robert Thompson, would state:

> In my view, on December 30, 1972, after eleven days of those B-52 attacks on the Hanoi area, *you had won the war. It was over!* . . . They and their whole rear base at that point were at your mercy. They would have taken any terms. And that is why, of course, you actually got a peace agreement in January, which you had not been able to get in October.[56]

As a matter of fact, however, the terms of the cease-fire were not notably better for the United States and South Vietnam than those stated in October. They were an in-place cease-fire; the United States withdrawal in 60 days; the release of prisoners of war; the establishment of an International Commission of Control and Supervision to handle disagreements; and the provisions for general election looking toward national unification at a later date.[57] In retrospect it would become apparent that erosion of congressional support for military employments in Southeast Asia largely vitiated the realization of political advantages that might otherwise have been attained from Linebacker II.

Epitaph for the Republic of Vietnam

If the pressure of Linebacker II persuaded North Vietnam to sign the Paris Agreement, it was equally true that the assurance of this powerful military stroke, plus promises of future armed retaliation, was probably decisive in securing the Republic of Vietnam's agreement to generally unfavorable truce terms. When President Thieu balked at agreeing to an in-place cease-fire that would permit 149,000 regular North Vietnamese troops to remain within South Vietnam, President Nixon—according to correspondence subsequently released by a South Vietnamese official—wrote Thieu on 14 November 1972: "You have my absolute assurance that if Hanoi fails to abide by the terms of this agreement it is my intention to take swift and severe retaliatory action." A second letter on 5 January 1973 stated, "You have my assurance of continued assistance in the post-settlement period and that we will respond with full force should the settlement be violated by North Vietnam."[58]

In the aftermath of the signing of the Paris Agreement, the government of Cambodia immediately announced a cease-fire, but in Cambodia the North Vietnamese continued to be active. They mushroomed support for the Communist Khmer Rouge, who were expected to close the line of support to Phnom Penh, the Cambodian capital. They also brought large quantities of supplies down to North Vietnamese forces in South Vietnam through eastern Cambodia. American air strikes, including B-52 strikes, continued against Communist supply caches and routes, but the situation was very fluid, making it very difficult to find really effective and worthwhile targets. In answer to congressional queries, Admiral Moorer defended the bombing as being in the national interest, since the North Vietnamese were using the lines of communication in Cambodia to supply their forces deep down in South Vietnam. In addition, if the North Vietnamese regained use of the port of Kompong Som, they would use it to enhance their capabilities and thereby destabilize the peace. As for the legality of this, new Secretary of Defense Elliot L. Richardson urged that the president had "authority as Commander-in-Chief to use U.S. airpower and potentially other forces in Southeast Asia, so long as he is following-up on something that we are already doing, and he is trying to bring it to a close."[59] The administration's position was that the Paris Agreements were not effective until they accomplished their goals. This was decidedly not the case in Cambodia, where the president continued to have authority to use military, political, and diplomatic means to terminate the conflict.[60]

In the spring of 1973 the removal of American combat forces from Vietnam and the return of American prisoners of war reduced congressional support for any continuation of US participation in hostilities in Indochina. Simultaneously, the burgeoning scandal about abuses of presidential power incident to the Watergate scandal quickly undermined President Nixon's influence over events in the year remaining before his resignation. On 1 July 1973 Nixon was forced to accept a bargain whereby the defense supplemental appropriation bill passed by Congress terminated, effective on 15 August 1973, any US combat activities in or over Cambodia, Laos, North Vietnam, and South Vietnam or off the shores of those countries. On 7 November 1973 Congress overrode Nixon's veto of a War Powers Resolution which further restricted the president's authority to introduce US armed forces into hostilities. The cutoff of American combat assistance implicit in these congressional measures allowed Hanoi to know that any renewed hostilities would not be approved by the United States.[61] Nixon would point out:

> Vietnam was lost not because of a lack of power, but because of a failure of skill and determination at using power. Those failures caused a breach in public trust and led to a collapse of our national will. Finally, the presidency was weakened by the restrictions Congress placed on the President's war-making powers and by the debilitating effects of the Watergate crisis.[62]

When the Paris Agreement cease-fire took effect in January 1973, Hanoi regained complete security for its rear bases in North Vietnam, in Laos, in Cambodia, and in the parts of South Vietnam that its forces held. The United States even undertook the responsibility for removing its blockade of naval mines which had dried up North Vietnam's inflow of war materiel and had caused grave civilian food shortages. After a very short rehabilitation of its domestic situation, Hanoi commenced a major road improvement and building program down through the Laotian panhandle into the central reaches of South Vietnam's Military Region III. Where it had once required 70 days for a North Vietnamese battalion to go by foot down the Ho Chi Minh trail—taking casualties from air attack and malaria en route — a battalion in 1974 could make the trip in three weeks, riding in trucks most of the way and without encountering any hazards.

The Communists built 340 miles of pipeline from the Chinese border to the former DMZ (which was now occupied by North Vietnamese troops). By January 1975, within South Vietnam or immediately adjacent thereto, the Communists had built their combat troops up from 149,000 to 185,000; in armor, they had gone from 150 to 600 tanks; and in field artillery, from 225 to 400 pieces. The Communists were especially alert to antiaircraft defenses. They deployed four battalions of surface-to-air missiles — SA-2 type — just south of the old DMZ stretching on a line from the Cua Viet River to Khe Sanh. MiG aircraft were deployed on repaired airfields in the southern part of North Vietnam so that they could expect to attack as far southward as Da Nang. They increased from 13 to 23 regiments of antiaircraft artillery in the south, and introduced SA-7 Strelas into each South Vietnamese military region. Finally, the North Vietnamese stored enough military supplies in forward areas to support 15 to 20 months of all-out offensives.[63]

In the annual appropriations for South Vietnamese security assistance after the Geneva Agreements, Congress showed less and less inclination to support Vietnam. Despite relentless North Vietnamese probing, the South Vietnamese were compelled to cannibalize equipment, defer maintenance, and hoard ammunition and petroleum, oil and lubricants (POL).[64] At first the South Vietnamese continued their old strategy of attempting to hold all real estate and to keep the enemy at bay by extensive use of artillery and air strikes. By April 1974 President Thieu warned his military commanders that the lavish days of American support were over. He specifically advised: "Use helicopters only in cases of absolute necessity; don't be tied to Air Force or artillery support."[65] In late 1974 Thieu held a meeting of his top military commanders at Da Nang, where he stated that defense lines must be shortened, since military assistance from the United States was under strenuous attack in Congress. It was the general understanding that South Vietnamese ground troops would give up South Vietnam's northern province and most of the central highlands, falling back to a defense line running from Qui Ninh through Da Lat to Qui Ninh City. The commander of the Vietnamese air force was not aware of these discussions, nor was the Vietnamese Joint General Staff brought into the planning for such a withdrawal. In this and other matters after the American departure, Thieu became increasingly rigid in controlling an increasingly politicized military force. Where control of the Vietnamese air force had been centrally managed through a tactical air control center, thus allowing its forces to be fragged to the military region where they were most needed, Thieu gave the four individual military region commanders control of all units — including air units — in their regions. The Vietnamese air force was thus divided into small packets that were employed by local commanders with limited vision.[66]

One of the important factors in convincing President Thieu to go along with the cease-fire in January 1973 was the fact that the United States honored requests for extremely large amounts of Air Force equipment regardless of their validity. In

October, November, and December, high-level decisions in Washington dictated a transfer of a large number of miscellaneous aircraft obtained from many sources around the world to South Vietnam. It was not possible to provide adequate training or support for the volume and variety of equipment so suddenly introduced. Nevertheless on 27 January 1973, the Vietnamese air force had a strength of 65 squadrons, 61,147 people, and 2,073 aircraft of 25 different types. Several thousand contract supply and maintenance personnel were brought in from the United States, and 224 aircraft were put in flyable storage because there were no spare parts or petroleum products available to fly them. Just before the cease-fire, 32 old C-130A transports were passed to Vietnamese control with no prior provisioning. Arrangements were made for depot maintenance in Singapore, but even with this help, the operational readiness rate for Saigon's only air transport capability averaged only 30 percent. After the Da Nang meeting in late 1974, Vietnamese air force flying hours were cut by one-half, and tactical fighter bomb loads were reduced from four to two. In late November 1974, however, these figures were modified: the tactical fighters again carried four bombs, but flew still fewer sorties—a change designed to make Vietnamese ground commanders more certain of the value of the targets they wanted attacked. Probably the greatest weakness of the South Vietnamese air force was not logistical but was attributable to the relatively low-performance aircraft it had been assigned under the supposition that the operational environment would be as permissive as it had been before the Communists introduced major antiaircraft weapons, beginning with the Easter offensive in 1972. Since the Vietnamese airmen had no electronic countermeasures (ECM), any operation into the Communist-held areas was hazardous and ultimately not undertaken. Even so, Vietnamese air strength declined from combat and operational causes from 2,073 authorized aircraft to 1,479 possessed aircraft at the end of 1974. These losses were not replaced by the United States, though this was permissible under the Paris Agreement.[67]

On the eve of the North Vietnamese spring offensive of 1975, the government of South Vietnam still possessed in South Vietnam about a 2 to 1 advantage in total combat troops and a 3 to 1 advantage in artillery. These figures, however, were somewhat deceptive since the South Vietnamese had to defend lines of communication and populated areas whereas the Communists could gather their forces and strike where they chose. They chose to strike first out of Cambodia into the Military Region (MR) III area north of Saigon, and by 6 January 1975 they had captured the provincial capital of Phuoc Long province. In this offensive heavy antiaircraft fire and heat-seeking SA-7s forced Vietnamese air-support planes too high for effectiveness and drove airborne forward air controllers out of the area. Two C-130s were destroyed while the Communists were taking Duc Phong airfield. On the night of 9 March the North Vietnamese opened a major attack against the road communications hub city of Ban Me Thuot, in Military Region II. President Thieu ordered the city held at all costs, but the tank and infantry attack easily prevailed. Some years later, Lt Gen Tran Van Minh, last chief of the Vietnamese Air Force, was asked to contrast the successful defense of An Loc in 1972 with the defeats in 1975. Minh concluded that the Communists' ground forces were stronger in 1975 and the allied air response much weaker. He pointed out that at An Loc in 1972, the battle had turned on B-52 and C-130 support. At Ban Me Thuot and in Phuoc Long, the Vietnamese simply did not have the massive bombing and airlift capabilities provided by the Air Force in 1972.[68]

News of the execution of several Vietnamese airlift contract technicians at Ban Me Thuot caused a rumor of an impending Communist bloodbath to spread through South Vietnam like wildfire. The capture of Ban Me Thuot, moreover, opened the way for the Communists to advance to the sea and bisect South Vietnam. At a meeting at Cam Ranh Bay on 14 March, President Thieu ordered abandonment of the old defense strongholds at Pleiku and Kontum to provide forces for a counterattack against Ban Me Thuot. As had usually been true in the case of Thieu's conferences, there were no Vietnamese air force representatives at the Cam Ranh Bay meeting, and General Minh knew nothing about the decision to abandon the major airfield at Pleiku until the commander of the 6th Air Division was given 48 hours to evacuate. It appears also that the Vietnamese army commander of MR-II hurriedly departed the area, leading a stream of fleeing troops and civilians in a rout hastened by Communist harassing artillery fire. Some measure of air force evacuation was managed, but 64 aircraft were abandoned, and there were contradictory reports of the degree of destruction of fuel and ammunition. At this same juncture, the Military Region I commander ordered a fallback from Quang Tri and Hue in the north of Da Nang, and concurrently Thieu directed the movement of South Vietnam's airborne division from Da Nang to augment the defenses of Saigon. Pandemonium spread rapidly in Da Nang. The 1st Air Division was not adequately employed, and after 27 March approximately 180 aircraft, including 33 A-37s, were abandoned because of confusion and breakdown of security at Da Nang airfield. Once Da Nang fell, the Communists continued down the east coast, and the major coastal cities fell like dominoes. Hanoi now committed all its divisions, including those held on defense reserve in North Vietnam, giving it a force of more than 19 divisions, with 325,000 troops knifing their way into South Vietnam. The enemy moved as rapidly as possible, bumper to bumper, down coastal Highway 1. Tanks and artillery were jammed up for miles.[69]

At the direction of President Gerald Ford, Army Chief of Staff Frederick C. Weyand was on a special mission to Vietnam and expressed hope that a truncated Republic of Vietnam (the remainder of Military Regions III and IV) could survive with emergency military assistance deliveries. Congress was adamant against additional appropriations for a lost cause, but the charade — if this was the case, as administration supporters later intimated — that additional aid could be forthcoming at least fostered an environment permitting an evacuation from Vietnam and Cambodia.[70] Military assistance materiel still remaining on account from earlier appropriations was rushed to Vietnam by Military Airlift Command planes, and the empty transports became a readily available means to carry out evacuees at the beginning of what later became an all-out evacuation. By another

IDEAS, CONCEPTS, DOCTRINE

stroke of remarkable foresight a satellite communications unit was airlifted to Tan Son Nhut airfield and was ready for action on 30 March, several days before the Communists cut the out-of-country cablehead to the Philippines at Nha Trang. On 12 April, President Ford closed the US Embassy in Phnom Penh, and all Americans were evacuated in an operation called Eagle Pull. Eagle Pull was in many respects a dress rehearsal for the Talon Vise/Frequent Wind evacuation of Saigon, since similar rules of engagement were used and a great many of the same covering forces were involved. The evacuation began with initial efforts from 1 to 4 April; quickened in pace with a fixed-wing aircraft buildup from 5 to 19 April; reached a massive fixed-wing flood tide from 20 to 28 April; and concluded with a last minute helicopter phase on 29 to 30 April, as Saigon surrendered. In this largest aerial evacuation in history, 99 percent of the Americans evacuated from South Vietnam came out by air. Fixed-wing aircraft carried out 50,493 people including 2,678 orphans. Tactical fighters were active over the evacuation area. The US Navy flew 173 carrier-based sorties in A-7s, A-6s, and F-14s; the Air Force flew 127 missions in F-4s, A-7s, AC-130s, and F-111s from bases in Thailand. In addition, Air Force KC-135 tankers and radio-relay planes, electronic countermeasure and rescue planes, and C-130 airborne battlefield command and control aircraft flew 85 sorties in support of the covering aircraft.[71]

Viewed in retrospect, it becomes obvious that the Vietnamese armed forces always believed that the United States would employ its air forces against a North Vietnamese invasion in 1975 as it had done in 1972.[72] Had the United States responded as it did in 1972, the results would have been very damaging to the grossly exposed military strength of North Vietnam. Wrote one commentator of military affairs, "In 1975 the USAF could have destroyed the North Vietnamese Army as a fighting force for the next five or ten years. They did not because of the political atmosphere in the United States."[73] In his analysis of the Vietnamese air force, General Momyer concluded that the VNAF as a whole fought better than any other element of the Republic of Vietnam's armed forces. In the last days of the conflict, three apparently disaffected A-37 pilots dive-bombed the VNAF parking area at Tan Son Nhut, but other more valiant Vietnamese pilots continued air strikes from Binh Thuy Air Base in the South Vietnamese delta against Communist tanks as they entered Saigon. These airmen then stripped down their A-37s and flew to U-Tapao Royal Thai Air Force Base, most planes carrying three pilots and some four. As the Republic of Vietnam surrendered on 30 April 1975, 26 F-5s and 27 A-37s had made it to Thailand.[74] A number of years after the event, US Secretary of Defense Caspar W. Weinberger offered a final critique of the war in Southeast Asia:

> The problem was we didn't want to win that war. We never intended to win that war. And that is what infuriates me so much about hearing how America lost that war. . . .
>
> No matter what firepower superiority we assembled, we were never able or in effect allowed to use it, because there was no intention ever to win that war. And that is the

worst kind of situation you could ever get into.... If it isn't important enough to win, it is not important enough to be there.[75]

Organization and Operations

Through experience in World War II, the Air Force was committed to the principle that a warfighting organization was a joint team of land, sea, and air forces operating together, integrated by organization and plans, as a coherent force – optimizing power. Forces were deployed and employed in an operational chain by supreme allied commanders, commanders in chief, or joint commanders. In turn, the land, sea, and air forces were directed by ground, naval, and air component commanders. The components supported each other operationally, as effectuated through plans and tasking orders, as component commanders provided the supreme allied commander, commander in chief, or joint commander with advice on appropriate employment of component forces. The combined commanders' decision then drove component action, with all forces directed toward theater objectives. By their nature, aerospace forces had demonstrated broader perspectives than surface bound forces, and this perspective of necessity had to be viewed from a theater entity.[76]

Command Organization Affecting Air Power

In the view of General Momyer, the National Security Act of 1947 and the Reorganization Act of 1958 had properly assigned "divisions of labor" along the lines of expertise into the three environmental areas of land, sea, and air. Moreover, Momyer said:

> The decision to have one commander of theater air forces was forged in the most severe combat conditions we have experienced – World War II. If we choose to turn our back on this experience, we will again suffer the defeat experienced in the early days of North Africa unless we expend enormous resources to provide adequate forces for each service to carry out its war in isolation to the others.[77]

In reflection regarding US military organization in Southeast Asia, Lt Gen Elwood R. Quesada ruefully observed that official doctrine – even at the national defense level – was not necessarily binding.

> Doctrine is awfully fine but doctrine is nothing more than a whole group of words. A lot depends on the personality of the people who are implementing doctrine.... You can have all the doctrine you want, but unless you have people, commanders, to implement those doctrines, you might as well throw your doctrines away.[78]

Under the Defense Reorganization Act of 1958, as has been seen, the authority of the new commander in chief, Pacific (CINCPAC), Adm Harry D. Felt, in common with other US unified commanders, was markedly broadened to "full operational command" of assigned Army, Navy, and Air Force forces. Himself an experienced though somewhat autocratic naval aviator whose exceptionally long tenure as CINCPAC would stretch from July 1958 through June 1964, Admiral Felt issued contingency plans that provided the origins of a Southeast Asia command structure which grew by ad hoc and skip-echelon arrangements into an organization that violated sound principles of unity and was inefficient and costly. As a result of the command organizations, the United States fragmented its assets for limited war over four "theaters," while Hanoi fought a total war in a single Southeast Asian theater.[79]

In event of a general war in the Pacific, Admiral Felt indicated his intention to exercise his operational command through his major component commands — US Army Pacific (ARPAC), US Pacific Fleet (PACFLT), and US Pacific Air Forces (PACAF). In other circumstances, Felt would employ a US Navy-style joint task force-subunified command arrangement. In the event of Chinese Communist aggression, a commander of the US Southeast Asia (COMUSSEASIA) would have directed operations from a headquarters located at Korat in Thailand. Otherwise, US Marine Corps forces from Okinawa were to comprise the nucleus of a standing-order Joint Task Force 116 that would be airlifted to meet emergencies in individual countries. The initial commander would be a Marine officer, but when preponderant Army reinforcements arrived, command would pass to an Army officer. In the PACAF organization, the Air Force units were divided between the Fifth Air Force in Japan and the Thirteenth Air Force in the Philippines: PACAF therefore designated the commander, Thirteenth Air Force, to head any air component assigned to JTF-116. Admiral Felt expected his military assistance advisory groups (MAAGs) in each country to be developing indigenous forces that would be supplemented by JTF-116.[80]

In case of the commitment of US combat forces to South Vietnam, Felt intended to name the Saigon MAAG chief as commander of US forces in Vietnam, and to expect him to function under CINCPAC control. The command structure that emerged in Vietnam also was affected by practices used in the US Strike Command (STRICOM) in maneuvers in the United States. STRICOM exercises featured a usual employment of joint task force headquarters for the detailed direction of subordinate forces. By increasing Joint Staff controls, the STRICOM field exercises tended to override the authority of component commanders. The Joint Staffs employed in the field exercises, moreover, were never large enough to perform the air missions that an air component commander should direct in a theater of war. But the impact of these exercises carried over into the contingency planning for force organization in Southeast Asia.[81]

A pervasive belief that the mission in Southeast Asia was chiefly an Army mission also affected command organization. Secretary McNamara for one argued that the Army must be predominant:

> If you have two or three men engaged in an operation one has to be primary. The Army has to be primary in land war. The Air Force is there to serve the Army in the airlift role and the close support role, and the Air Force must tailor its activities to the Army.[82]

In Saigon US military organization sprang from a beginning as a military assistance advisory group, and in November 1960, President Eisenhower had strengthened the role of American ambassadors in all countries to include "affirmative responsibilities" for all US activities. In May 1961 President Kennedy reiterated this instruction, and although he exempted military forces in the field from an ambassador's direct authority, the ambassador was specified to be chief of mission and expected to work hand in glove with a military commander in the formulation of policy and the coordination of programs.[83] General Westmoreland would refer not too jocularly to the American ambassadors in Thailand and Laos as "field marshals."[84] As matters worked out, the US ambassador in Thailand exercised no control over the operations of US forces in that country, although he had to be kept informed of all military activities. In Laos, however, the US ambassador, as the senior US official, was responsible for all US military activities. All air operations came under the detailed surveillance and control of the embassy, and, in effect, the Air Force air attaché in the embassy served as the country's air commander, since he could act through the authority of the ambassador.[85] When President Johnson sent Gen Maxwell D. Taylor to Saigon as US ambassador in July 1964, he reminded Taylor of President Kennedy's earlier instruction to all ambassadors, adding, "I wish it clearly understood that this overall responsibility includes the whole military effort in South Vietnam and authorizes the degree of command and control that you consider appropriate." This letter of instruction could have been construed to eliminate Adm U.S. Grant Sharp, newly installed as CINCPAC, from the command chain in South Vietnam. But Ambassador Taylor saw fit voluntarily to limit his degree of control to overall policy and did not seek to interfere in the day-to-day business of the military effort. To increase coordination of action between the US embassies and military commands in Southeast Asia, Ambassador Taylor established and General Westmoreland continued an informal Southeast Asia coordinating committee (SEACOORD), composed of heads of mission in South Vietnam, Laos, and Thailand. The ad hoc oversight group met at irregular intervals and, in Taylor's estimation, failed to yield any great results.[86]

The decision of President Kennedy to expand US combat advisers in Vietnam in November–December 1961 dictated that the Saigon MAAG be reorganized and augmented. At the outset, the Joint Chiefs of Staff recommended a new subordinate unified command under CINCPAC to be designated US Forces Vietnam and provided in Saigon with Army, Navy, and Air Force component commands. This recommendation was a compromise, since the Army and Air Force had maintained that the new command should be independent of CINCPAC and report directly to the Joint Chiefs. The senior Navy spokesman supported CINCPAC in a view that the initial organization should be a subunified command and that a later evaluation should determine whether a separate theater command reporting to the Joint Chiefs was needed. And in Washington, US Secretary of State Dean Rusk did not want the United States to get too deeply committed in Southeast Asia. Compromise between Secretaries Rusk and McNamara resulted on 8 February 1962 in the activation in Saigon of the US Military Assistance Command, Vietnam (MACV), under Gen Paul D. Harkins.[87]

While the command structure for MACV was under study, Gen Jacob E. Smart, CINCPACAF, and the Air Staff in Washington were working to establish an appropriate air structure. The basic assumption was that the main threat in the Far East was the escalation of hostilities into a war with Communist China and that PACAF's command structure should be kept prepared to meet the threat by keeping the main element of the Pacific Air Forces under a single air command structure. If many air units were assigned to MACV solely for in-country use, the forces available to CINCPACAF for a larger air campaign would be limited, since assigned forces would be difficult to withdraw. It would be better to keep air units in Southeast Asia assigned to the Thirteenth Air Force and placed in support of MACV as needed for specific periods of time. In line with these conceptions, the Thirteenth Air Force established an anomalous 2d ADVON in Saigon under command of Brig Gen Rollen H. Anthis as an advanced echelon of its headquarters on 15 November 1961, and this anomalous unit served as the air component to MACV. This arrangement was still new when in response to a crisis in Laos, President Kennedy directed Admiral Felt to move JTF-116 into Thailand on 12 May 1962. At this time, General Harkins sought control of all forces in both Vietnam and Thailand, but Admiral Felt secured approval for an arrangement whereby Harkins would be given two subordinate headquarters—MACV and Military Assistance Command, Thailand (MACTHAI). Shortly afterward, effective 8 October 1962, PACAF secured a long-delayed authority to activate a legitimate 2d Air Division in Saigon, which from the outset served as component of MACV and forward command of the Thirteenth Air Force for the control of any air operations outside Vietnam. If the war should expand against China, it was understood that the Thirteenth Air Force would become the air component of COMUSSEASIA, and the 2d Air Division would be dissolved.[88]

The establishment of MACV immediately engendered two doctrinal issues. Joint doctrine provided that staffing of a joint headquarters should be reasonably balanced to reflect service composition of assigned forces. The MACV staff, however, was dominated by US Army and US Marine Corps officers, the allegation being that the conflict in Vietnam was primarily a ground insurgency. The second doctrinal controversy concerned the fact that General Harkins chose to serve both as subunified commander and as commander of the US Army forces, an undertaking forbidden by joint doctrine. Since there was no substantial US Navy activity in Southeast Asia, a naval component command was not established.[89] While on a visit to South Vietnam in April 1962, General LeMay got the impression that air activities were "depreciated ... rather than appreciated." More air officers were needed on the MACV staff to create a better understanding of air power capabilities. LeMay believed that making an air officer deputy commander of MACV would lead to a clearer understanding and a better employment of air power. General Harkins was unwilling to accept an air officer as his deputy commander, although he was willing to name the commander of the 2d Air Division to added duty as deputy commander, MACV, for air operations. LeMay rejected this proposal, feeling that it would be largely meaningless. The Joint Chiefs were divided on the issue and were still considering it when Secretary McNamara arrived in Saigon in December 1963 and agreed with Harkins — who was facing retirement because of age in mid-1964 — that an Army officer should be named his deputy. Lt Gen William C. Westmoreland arrived in Saigon as deputy commander, MACV, on 27 January 1964.[90]

In personal instruction, Gen Earle G. Wheeler, Army chief of staff who would soon become chairman of the Joint Chiefs, told General Westmoreland "to get the air missions straightened out." If Army doctrine got in the way of the war effort, Wheeler said he could and would change doctrine with a stroke of his pen. At the end of January 1964, Maj Gen Joseph H. Moore, a close friend of Westmoreland since boyhood, was assigned to replace General Anthis as commander of the 2d Air Division.[91] Quite soon, commander US Military Assistance Command Vietnam (COMUSMACV), recommended that MACV should be made a specified command directly responsible to the Joint Chiefs. As a specified command, MACV would have a "joint" staff principally of Army personnel, as was appropriate, it was maintained, since counterinsurgency was said to be an Army function. CINCPAC should be removed from the chain of command since he was only a reviewing authority and could only slow down the decision process between Washington and Saigon. Adm U. S. Grant Sharp, who assumed duty as CINCPAC in February 1964, promptly rejected these recommendations, saying that a unified effort in Vietnam needed to be strengthened, not diluted. The Joint Chiefs did not accept the divorcement from PACOM or the proposal for a specified command, but they approved melding the old Military Assistance Advisory Group into a MACV organization that would continue to be heavily staffed with Army personnel. When Westmoreland moved up to COMUSMACV on 20 June 1964, there was still hope for an Air Force officer as deputy. At this time and again a year later, Westmoreland wanted an Army deputy and urged that the 2d Air Division commander be named to additional duty as deputy COMUSMACV for air operations. In mid-1964, General LeMay would not go along with this, but in mid-1965 a new Air Force chief of staff, Gen John P. McConnell, agreed with Westmoreland, and the Joint Chiefs approved the air deputy position on 25 June 1965. As it turned out the deputy for air had no staff support in MACV and precious little authority except to advise.[92]

In a summary description of the grave command decisions required in 1965, Admiral Sharp as CINCPAC elected to manage air strikes against North Vietnam and allow General Westmoreland as COMUSMACV a relatively free hand in South Vietnam, plus an "expanded battlefield" lapping over into the southern panhandles of Laos and North Vietnam. At the same time these decisions were being made, Thailand was dissatisfied with the combined COMUSMACV-COMUSMACTHAI. The Thai government also wanted a commander of all Air Force units based in Thailand to be located in Thailand. To meet the Thai request and yet keep all Air Force air power under a single commander, General

IDEAS, CONCEPTS, DOCTRINE

McConnell effected a unique arrangement. He appointed a single commander of the 2d Air Division and for that part of the Thirteenth Air Force in Thailand, where a deputy commander 2d Air Division/Thirteenth Air Force had logistical and administrative responsibility. These added responsibilities, as well as an increase in air units in both South Vietnam and Thailand, strained the capabilities of an air division staff. Accordingly, on 14 March 1966 the 2d Air Division was inactivated and the Seventh Air Force established. The headquarters in Thailand was redesignated deputy commander, Seventh/Thirteenth Air Forces. On 1 July 1966 Gen William W. "Spike" Momyer—the most knowledgeable Air Force tactical airman—received command of the Seventh Air Force.[93] Other manifestations of expansion belatedly converted Army and Navy logistical support services into component subunified commands. The US Army, Vietnam, was designated in July 1965 with General Westmoreland serving as its commander. This was done after progressive expansion from Army Support Group to Army Support Command. In April 1966 US Naval Forces, Vietnam, was established as the Navy Component Command.[94]

As set forth in MACV Directive 95-4 issued 6 May 1965, the deputy commander MACV for air operations had operational control over Air Force and US Navy Task Force 77 carrier air operating in South Vietnam and the extended battlefield. Under such circumstances, naval aircraft were controlled like other aircraft under Air Force jurisdiction. The directive excluded any reference to the air deputy controlling Army helicopters. His authority also was restricted by an initial exclusion of authority over US Marine Corps aviation. The directive noted that Marine Corps aviation was organic to the Marine Amphibious Force that had come ashore and established itself in Military Region I and provided that the Marine air wing was to be commanded and directed in support of tactical operations as designated by the commander of the Marine Amphibious Force. The Marine Corps tactical air control system was to exercise positive control over all Marine Corps aircraft in support of Marine Corps operations and over other aircraft as might be in support of such operations. Only in the event of a major emergency, and then only at the specific direction of COMUSMACV, would the 2d Air Division exercise control over Marine Corps aviation in Military Region I.

The control and employment arrangements for B-52 conventional strikes into South Vietnam, first worked out in June 1965, were sensitive to the fact that B-52s had a nuclear attack mission and should remain under the control of the Strategic Air Command. There also was some fear at high levels that a B-52 might be lost to the Communists, thus reducing the credibility of the B-52's role in nuclear deterrence. As a result, COMUSMACV nominated targets which if approved were struck by the B-52s. As the strikes became routine, a SAC advanced echelon (ADVON) was attached to the MACV air deputy on 10 January 1967 to furnish interface and expertise for bomber employment.[95]

As early as 1966 General Westmoreland studied the possibility of giving his deputy for air operational control of the Marine Air Wing in Military Region I. Under MACV Directive 95-4, however, control of air power in MR-I was inefficiently fragmented into two separate tactical air forces, one controlled by the theater air component commander and the other by the equivalent of a corps commander. Each day the 1st Marine Air Wing scheduled its in-commission aircraft in a flow into the areas of the 1st and 3d Marine Divisions just as if an amphibious assault were continuously in progress. Any sorties not used to support the Marine divisions were made available daily to the Seventh Air Force, the Marine Air Wing deciding how many sorties could be provided. This arrangement went on from month to month, since Westmoreland perceived that any major change "would arouse a violent and emotional opposition on the part of the Marines at every echelon from Vietnam to the White House." The problem of divided air command in MR-I nevertheless came to a head early in 1968, incident to the Khe Sanh-Tet offensive. With the buildup of enemy forces in MR-I, it was necessary to reinforce the Marine Amphibious Force (MAF) with Army divisions, including the movement of the 1st Cavalry Division to Thua Thien province. When the cavalry division was moving, Westmoreland personally admonished the commander of the 1st Marine Air Wing, Maj Gen Norman J. Anderson, in the presence of the III MAF commander, Lt Gen Robert E. Cushman, Jr., to make certain that the Army divisions received air support. But when Westmoreland subsequently visited the cavalry division he found that the Marine command had not established contact with the Army division or arranged communications for expeditious air support. By this time, the North Vietnamese were closing around Khe Sanh, and to provide support for the beleaguered garrison, it would be necessary to concentrate all available air power, since Westmoreland judged the situation as "too conducive to error." As he noted to General Wheeler, "it was a 'dog's breakfast'."[96]

In a message to Admiral Sharp on 18 January 1968, Westmoreland stated that it was "no longer feasible nor prudent to restrict the employment of the total tactical air resources to given areas. I feel the utmost need for a more flexible posture to shift my air effort where it can best be used in the coming battles." Consequently, Westmoreland proposed to give the MACV deputy for air "operational control of the 1st Marine Air Wing, less its helicopters."[97] Westmoreland was hopeful initially that Generals Cushman and Anderson would see the need for this move, but when he explained his intention to them, it was reported that "Anderson became rather 'emotional,' declaring that the Marine air wing belongs to the Marines and no one else."[98] The commandant of the US Marine Corps, Gen Leonard Chapman, Jr., stated that the proposal was not doctrinally or functionally suited to Marine requirements, and Admiral Sharp both cautioned against any change that would trigger an interservice debate and declined to approve any radical alteration in the status of Marine aviation in Vietnam. A temporary arrangement agreed to on 22 January between Momyer-Cushman representatives linked Seventh Air Force and Marine tactical air control networks, using an orbiting Air Force airborne battlefield command and control center (ABCCC) to achieve coordination of the massive air support laid on at Khe Sanh. General Momyer pointed out as discussions dragged on during

February, "The question was not whether there should be one man responsible for all air operations but how best to accomplish this arrangement while preserving the principle of Marine air units supporting Marine ground units whenever the tactical situation permitted." At this time the number of Army forces in MR-I (I Corps Tactical Zone) was exceeding those of the Marine Corps. On 2 March Admiral Sharp took this into consideration when he approved a single manager plan. "I didn't think the single manager concept necessary as long as Marines were the only troops in I Corps," he explained, but as Army numbers increased, "it got to be a reasonable thing to do." On 8 March Westmoreland announced the establishment of a US Army Provisional Corps, Vietnam (later XXIV Corps), to control American forces in the two northernmost South Vietnamese provinces of Quang Tri and Thua Thien, and on the same day Westmoreland designated his deputy for air operations as the single manager for tactical combat aviation in all of South Vietnam to include the extended battlefield. General Cushman was instructed to place his fighter bombers, attack planes, and reconnaissance aircraft and the Marine air control system under the "mission direction" of Momyer.[99]

In approving the single manager plan, Admiral Sharp provided that General Cushman had a right to appeal to higher authority; in Washington, General Chapman took his concerns to General Wheeler, now chairman of the Joint Chiefs. In a handwritten note to General Wheeler on 4 March, General McConnell voiced Air Force disagreement with Chapman: "Westy has now done something he should have done a long time ago. He should also, in my opinion, place Navy air into the same structure. Also I consider that Westy has the authority to do what he has done." During April 1968, the Joint Chiefs of Staff considered General Chapman's concern, and, to the dismay of General Westmoreland, Army Chief of Staff Gen Harold K. Johnson failed to support Westmoreland's position, possibly because of a concern that some precedent be established leading to a loss of control over Army helicopters. While the Joint Chiefs debated, Westmoreland assured Admiral Sharp that his efforts were designed "to bring to bear the maximum fire power on the enemy. This is not an Air Force maneuver designed to change roles and missions. The exercise is on my initiative as a Joint Commander." As Westmoreland recalled, this was the only issue to occur during his service in Vietnam to prompt him to consider resigning. General Wheeler forwarded the split JCS paper to the secretary of defense for resolution, and in May 1968 Deputy Secretary of Defense Paul Nitze provided a compromise decision. He endorsed Westmoreland's action saying that the unified commander "on the scene should be the best judge of how the combat forces assigned to him are to be organized, commanded, and deployed." Nitze, however, did not believe that "the assignment of Marine air units under the single management of the Deputy COMUSMACV for Air should constitute a precedent for centralized control of air operations under other combat conditions, or need pose a threat to the integrity of the Marine air/ground team." He said that General Westmoreland ought to "revert to normal command arrangements for III MAF when the tactical situation permits." During June, General Chapman continued to assert that the single manager plan was not acceptable, even though modifications were gradually shifting more "control" back to the Marines. In response, the Joint Chiefs required CINCPAC and COMUSMACV to keep the single manager concept under evaluation.[100]

Although the single manager system was in the process of establishment while much of the heaviest air support was in progress at Khe Sanh, the assurance of his unitary control enabled General Momyer to deliver on his promise that all air power was available for the support of the besieged Marine garrison. Later, when asked what was the turning point at Khe Sanh, General Momyer replied, "The MACV decision to have a single manager for air power."[101] By September 1968, all evaluations were concluded, and General Wheeler reported to the secretary of defense that the single manager system was providing the best overall use of tactical air and that the system should be permitted to continue as long as COMUSMACV deemed it necessary. On 22 November General Wheeler — with General Chapman nonconcurring — so informed the secretary of defense, and secured Deputy Secretary Nitze's agreement to continue the system in operation.[102] As time passed, the Marines in Vietnam lost their worry that single management would take operational control of Marine air resources away from the commanding general of III MAF. Marine Lt Gen Keith B. McCutcheon, who was commanding general of III MAF after February 1970, endorsed the system, writing:

> There is no doubt about whether single management was an overall improvement as far as MACV as a whole was concerned. It was. And there is no denying the fact that, when three Army divisions were assigned to I Corps and interspersed between the two Marine divisions, a higher order of coordination and cooperation was required than previously.[103]

Gen Creighton W. Abrams, who commanded MACV from July 1968 to June 1972, not only made no changes in the single manager for air but ultimately provided an exceptionally strong endorsement of the value of centrally controlling tactical air power. With control centralized he was able to focus the sheer hitting power of high performance fixed-wing aircraft very quickly:

> I don't mean from the first brigade to the second brigade. I am talking about going anywhere, instead of putting it in MR-4, you go to MR-1. You switch the whole faucet, and you do it in about 45 minutes. The whole control system and base system that supports that, there is nothing in the Army like it. There is nothing anywhere in the world like it.[104]

During consideration of formal command arrangements looking toward control of Rolling Thunder air strikes against North Vietnam early in 1965, the Air Force recommendation was to put Task Force 77's carrier air strikes under the control of CINCPACAF as the theater air component commander. PACAF would delegate this operational control to the 2d Air Division in Saigon, and the unity of air power would be ensured. Instead, at the insistence of the CINCPACFLT, Admiral Sharp used the same terminology that was followed in the Korean War and made CINCPACAF the "coordinating authority" for Rolling Thunder. Issued during March 1965, CINCPAC's charter also called for establishment of a Rolling Thunder Coordinating Committee to coordinate and resolve items of mutual concern to the Navy and Air Force. The 2d Air Division formed a working committee with Task Force 77 to decide upon methods of coordinating force employment. Several schemes were analyzed, later ultimately dividing North Korea into six "Route Packages," with Route Package VI being divided into VIA (Air Force) and VIB (Navy). Three packages were given to the Air Force and four to the Navy. After assuming command of the Seventh Air Force, General Momyer noted: "The route package system was a compromise approach to a tough command and control decision, an approach which, however understandable, inevitably prevented a unified, concentrated air effort." Momyer ultimately concluded: "Coordinating authority is simply inadequate when operations must be changed rapidly and when intricate details must be quickly resolved."[105]

Several times during the 1965–68 air offensive, General Momyer proposed changes in the Rolling Thunder command arrangement, and in May 1972 Gen Lucius D. Clay, Jr., CINCPACAF, expressed the same view held by the Seventh Air Force commanders: that operational control of naval air by the air component commander was the only sound arrangement; and that combat was not an appropriate place for coordinating committee decisions. Admiral Sharp and his successor, Adm John S. McCain, Jr., remained committed to coordination, but Adm Noel Gayler, who became CINCPAC on 6 October 1972, agreed that CINCPACAF and CINCPACFLT must each be authorized to schedule strike missions into the vital "integrated strike zone," including the North Vietnamese Northeast/Northwest rail line and the Hanoi environ. This arrangement was not adequately tested in the remaining weeks of air strikes, but final experience in handling Strategic Air Command Linebacker II B-52s in the 11-day air campaign of December 1972 rather clearly demonstrated that complicated mission planning could not be adequately handled by coordination. In the first three days of this campaign, Gen John C. Meyer, CINCSAC, used his specified command authority and coordinated targets directly with the Joint Chiefs of Staff. After this, he discussed support arrangements with Admiral Gayler and Gen John W. Vogt, Jr., deputy MACV for air and commander, Seventh Air Force. As chairman of the coordinating group, Vogt was responsible for detailed coordination with representatives from Task Force 77 and SACADVON. Vogt had his own priority mission of laying on and supporting laser strikes into the Hanoi area, and he was additionally responsible for planning and flying fighter cover, electronics countermeasures (ECM), and Wild Weasel antiradar support for the B-52s. He needed 18 hours of advance notice to coordinate a SAC mission, and SAC was presenting targets so late that he did not have adequate time for detailed planning. On 21 December, Admiral Gayler changed the arrangement, making SAC and PACOM jointly responsible for target determination within JCS guidance. After the Christmas recess, PACOM took sole responsibility for air operations over North Vietnam, and SAC, Task Force 77, and Seventh Air Force nominated targets for CINCPAC approval. Under both arrangements, all mission details were worked out by the coordinating committee in Saigon, since Admiral Gayler agreed that those matters had to be dealt with by people close to the scene of combat. Once again, the ad hoc arrangement worked, but the fundamental requirement for unity of air power was unfulfilled.[106]

As an eventuality of the Vietnamization program, plans for the dissolution of the US Military Assistance Command began to be seriously conceived in October 1972. Following the Paris Agreements, MACV was inactivated on 29 March 1973 and concurrently replaced by the unified Headquarters, US Support Activities Group/Seventh Air Force, located at Nakhon Phanom Royal Thai Air Force Base. The Seventh Air Force took operational control of supporting Air Force activities and also supported the Joint Casualty Resolution Center. As commander of USSAG/Seventh Air Force, General Vogt continued to control about 200 tactical air sorties flown each day into Cambodia until the bombing halt there took effect on 15 August 1973. Effective with the disestablishment of MACV, a defense attaché office began to function in the old MACV compound at Tan Son Nhut Air Base with an initial manning authority of 50 military, 1,200 US civilian, and 3,500 Vietnamese spaces countrywide. The defense attaché reported to the US ambassador for political, economic, and psychological matters and at first to the commander of USSAG/Seventh Air Force and later directly to CINCPAC for military matters — this arrangement being something of a violation of the principle of unity of command. At Udorn Royal Thai Air Force Base, a small Thirteenth Air Force advanced echelon (formerly deputy commander Seventh/Thirteenth Air Forces) handled matters which were a unilateral Air Force responsibility such as logistic support and training for Air Force units in Thailand.[107] This command organization was exercised during the emergency evacuations from South Vietnam and Cambodia and provided local control of force employment during the recapture of the American vessel *Mayaguez* in May 1975. By mid-1976, the USSAG/Seventh Air Force was inactivated — as was the entire Seventh Air Force — and all US air combat units had departed from Southeast Asia.[108]

Counterair Battles Maintained Air Superiority

To informed observers it was ironic that the importance of air-to-air, eyeball-to-eyeball combat in aerial maneuvering as a primary function of gaining and maintaining air superiority was so soon discounted after both World War II and the Korean conflict. In the mid-1950s, maneuver experience simulating the employment of tactical nuclear weapons clearly demonstrated that the way to gain aerial superiority was to destroy hostile air forces by attacks against enemy air bases. In these years, the Air Force Air Staff was heavily inclined toward bombardment expertise rather than fighter operations, and the Tactical Air Command was oriented toward overseas rotation postures and nuclear strike training. In Tactical Air Command the idea that enemy aircraft would be destroyed on the ground worked against any development of an air-to-air fighter while the idea of flexibility of air power mitigated against the idea of single-purpose fighters.

In this era, the F-105 Thunderchief (later called the "Thud") was designed as a nuclear fighter-bomber which would attack at high speed from low levels. Despite Air Force misgivings, Secretary McNamara dictated Air Force procurement of the F-4C Phantom as the standard tactical fighter. This aircraft was a development from the basic US Navy A-4D fleet air defense missile-equipped aircraft; like the Navy plane, the F-4C did not have guns or cannon for close air-to-air combat. It was expected to engage enemy aircraft with missiles while standing off from them. In making this decision, McNamara had the cost-effectiveness support of his assistant secretary of defense for systems analysis, Dr Alain C. Enthoven. Enthoven would continue to insist, "I think, given the mission for which we envision our tactical fighters, and given our view of the total air battle, that we made a good choice with the F-4."[109]

The Tactical Air Command by the late 1950s was configured as a training base amounting to approximately 12 percent of the force, a modest training resource capable of accomplishing a tactical nuclear alert commitment worldwide, but too small for conventional fighting of protracted duration. Where training in air combat tactics had been stressed during the Korean War, the Air Force went away from such training in the 1950s, much more so than did the Navy, which continued to stress aerial combat for fleet defense. As a consequence, Navy pilots were at first better prepared than the average Air Force pilot when going into combat over North Vietnam.[110] In World War II and Korea, electronic countermeasures and chaff had been employed extensively by bombers; but most fighter commanders believed that they ought not to trade performance for protection, and that speed and maneuverability could defeat antiaircraft artillery and surface-to-air missile fire. A research and development program for fighter ECM was not started until 1961, and then the decision was to put the ECM into a pod so that the equipment could be carried or not, depending on the threat.[111] Another reason the Air Force gave low priority to electronic warfare was the policy of preparing for a nuclear war where attrition would not have the serious effect that it would have in a conventional war, where aircrews would go back into the same areas, day after day, with a great number of missions.[112] One other result of the preoccupation with preparations for nuclear war affected the air campaign in North Vietnam. Tactical fighter crews were drilled in low-level dash and pop-up bombing, appropriate to nuclear delivery. When bombing began in North Vietnam, bombing accuracies were not good. The circular error probable (CEP) was on the order of 750 feet and several years were required to get combat circular error probable down to 365 feet. Technology for guided bombs had been known since World War II, but had not been grasped by Air Force research and development — one reason being that precise bombing accuracy was not needed for nuclear bombs.[113]

It was tragic irony that the air war in Southeast Asia would necessitate an agonizing relearning process and a hurried adaptation of weapon systems back into an arena thought to have been eliminated. In the early days of 1965, Air Force aircraft flying from Thailand and Da Nang and Navy planes from Task Force 77 aircraft carriers in the Gulf of Tonkin could have destroyed the embryonic North

Vietnamese air defense system with near impunity. Gen Hunter Harris, CINCPACAF, recommended that the first Rolling Thunder air strike include a B-52 attack with tactical fighter follow-up against Phuc Yen airfield near Hanoi where 30 MiG-15/17 jet fighters were located. This was disapproved by higher authority. An argument frequently advanced for not striking airfields was that US aircraft losses would be too great in comparison with damage that could be done by not-too-accurate bombing. In the beginning it was also said that airfield attacks would be more provocative to Hanoi than desired. Gia Lam airfield in Hanoi was never attacked because it was thought politically desirable not to end transport traffic to and from the Communist capital. And in mid-1967, when airfield attacks were belatedly approved, MiGs easily and quickly dispersed across the nearby border to Chinese sanctuaries. Under these circumstances, the concept of gaining air superiority by airfield attacks proved impractical because of unforeseeable political strictures. Early in 1965 Generals Westmoreland and Moore sought approval to knock out SA-2 missile sites being built around Hanoi and Haiphong. This was not agreeable to Washington. On a visit to Saigon, Assistant Secretary of Defense John McNaughton ridiculed the request as unnecessary. He observed, "You don't think the North Vietnamese are going to use them! Putting them in is just a political ploy by the Russians to appease Hanoi."[114]

In the earliest US air strikes against North Vietnamese targets, Air Force crews flew low-altitude, pop-up attacks, frequently making multiple passes in train in their anxiety to do a good job. Enemy automatic weapons and small caliber fire soon caused losses, forcing attacks to roll in for dive-bombing from about 20,000 feet with pull-out at about 4,500 feet. At these higher altitudes, chances of surprise were lost, since the North Vietnamese were building a Soviet-style internetted radar complex of some 200 installations, cross-telling into three or four major ground control intercept (GCI) sites. With the GCI in operation, Communist ground controllers dictated virtually every action of MiG interceptor pilots from takeoff to landing. On 4 April 1965 a flight of MiG-17s which was working under GCI control evaded MiG combat air patrol (CAP) F-100s and pounced on heavily loaded F-105s orbiting while waiting turns to attack; the MiGs shot down two F-105s with cannon fire and escaped at high speed. It was obvious that enemy jet pilots under GCI control had substantial advantages over bomb-laden F-105s which lacked warning of impending attacks. Because of distances and terrain shielding, the US ground-based radar system in Thailand and South Vietnam did not have the capability to control air operations much above the 19th parallel. The Navy's early warning ship, *Piraz*, in the vicinity of the 18th parallel and operating under the call sign Crown, could not see more than about 50 miles inland; in the Hanoi area, traffic had to be higher than 10,000 feet to be in view of Crown. To fill in the radar gaps, a detachment of Air Defense Command EC-121 aircraft came to Southeast Asia where one of them (code-named College Eye) kept station over the Gulf of Tonkin during all operations above the 20th parallel. This plane served as an airborne command and control center and handled the execution of orders from the special advanced headquarters of the Seventh Air Force known as the

Tactical Air Control Center (TACC) North, code-named Motel, and located on Monkey Mountain near Da Nang. The EC-121 had excellent radar coverage over water, but it could not "look down" over land, because ground clutter obscured the radar return. Another Air Force deployment brought EB-66C Brown Cradle radar jamming ECM aircraft to Thailand; when one of these aircraft was shot down in February 1966, the remainder were compelled to pull back their orbits to safe areas over Laos and the Gulf of Tonkin where they were too remote to be notably effective in standoff jamming of enemy fire control radars. With so many radars in a small area, moreover, it was useless to try to jam anything but specific radars that were actively working against American planes.[115]

Except for the success against F-105s in early April 1965, the North Vietnamese Air Force appeared to be in training and made only sporadic challenges, usually against F-105s. On 17 June two Navy F-4Bs downed two MiG-17s with Sparrow missiles, and on 10 July two Air Force F-4Cs covering the tail of a strike force downed two other MiG-17s with Sidewinder missiles. These were the only two Air Force aerial victories during 1965, since after July 1965 and through March 1966 MiG pilots largely limited themselves to extensive training. In any event, there was a noticeable reluctance on the part of the Communists to engage Phantom jets — either Navy or Air Force.[116] Unhappily, however, SA-2 surface-to-air missiles were thrown into the breach. On 24 July two SA-2s were fired at a flight of four F-4C strike aircraft, causing the loss of one plane and damage to the others. After that, SAM defenses, initially circling 30 to 40 miles out around Hanoi, grew rapidly to about 200 sites, which would be the approximate total peak strength. The SA-2 was not a mobile missile, but it could be readily transported from place to place, and it was very difficult to tell from reconnaissance which sites might be occupied in advance of a given mission. In all of 1965 the enemy fired 180 SAMs and destroyed 11 aircraft. The immediate response was to return to low-profile missions in SAM-defended areas, but the cure was worse than the disease, since by the summer of 1966 General Momyer was describing the Communist antiaircraft artillery defenses as "formidable." They had as many as 7,000 guns of all calibers, with the heaviest concentration around Hanoi and Haiphong. Once again attack altitudes had to be finally adjusted to start a dive to target from about 12,000 feet and pull out above 4,500 feet. At medium altitudes, strike aircraft were still vulnerable to antiaircraft artillery — particularly the 57-mm gun — but a SAM was still accelerating at this altitude. If a pilot sighted an SA-2 in time, he could outmaneuver it by turning into it with a hard diving turn, then making an abrupt four-G rolling pull-up, which the SAM was not able to follow. For several years radar homing and warning (RHAW) equipment for fighters had been in preparation, and General Momyer got all planes used against North Vietnam equipped with it. This electronic equipment gave a pilot indication that a SAM guidance radar was activated, and a strobe told him the direction from which the SAM would be launched. From the intensity of the signal, he could determine whether the SAM was within range of his aircraft. This equipment greatly decreased pilots' vulnerability to SAMs and gave them greater freedom of action.[117]

Later in 1965 another device began to counter SAMs: F-100F two-seat fighters were modified with special electronic gear that enabled a backseat operator to give directions to a frontseat pilot to position the aircraft to launch air-to-ground missiles that would home in on the beam emitted by a SAM radar. Two-place F-105G aircraft soon replaced the too-vulnerable F-100s in this role, which was affectionately code-named Wild Weasel. In practice an Iron Hand flight comprised two Wild Weasels equipped with air-to-ground missiles (four Strike missiles at first and later nine Standard Arm antiradiation missiles to each plane) and two wingmen flying strike fighters loaded with conventional bombs. The Iron Hand flights preceded a strike mission to a target by about five minutes, got the SAM site to activate its radar, and suppressed it with missiles or bombs. They also covered the egress of strike fighters along homeward-bound routes and caught many SAM launches. Once introduced in late 1965, these tactics became standard in 1965–68 and again in 1972. In response to the Wild Weasels, North Vietnamese instituted "emission control," a practice of not turning on the SAM terminal guidance radar until 10 to 15 seconds prior to the launch. This safeguarded the radar against Iron Hand discovery, degraded the capability of antiradiation missiles, and, in some instances, denied the RHAW equipment the time to give warning to aircrews to sight and avoid missiles. But if a SAM site radar was kept from functioning, the SA-2 missile was effectively suppressed, and thus the Iron Hand flights were considered eminently successful.[118]

In 1965 North Vietnam was rather clearly relying on SA-2 defenses while building its combat air forces. In the spring of 1966, the picture changed, possibly because electronic countermeasures were becoming more effective and air strikes were shifting into the Hanoi area, where most MiG airfields were clustered. The North Vietnamese put their MiG-17s back into combat and introduced later model MiG-21s, the latter being a small Mach 2.3 specially designed interceptor armed with an internal cannon and later with Atoll heat-seeking air-to-air missiles. MiGs were destructive: MiG-17s attempted to engage at lower altitudes, where they had superior turning characteristics at slower speed; MiG-21s worked at higher altitudes, where they were positioned by GCI controllers for Mach 1.4-plus high-speed 6 o'clock hit-and-run Atoll missile passes through Seventh Air Force formations. The operational situation forced upon the Seventh Air Force tactical fighters in 1966 made it difficult to deal with MiGs. Since the MiG threat had been relatively slight in 1965, and since the Washington authorization to hit particular targets was often withdrawn after very short intervals, it was necessary to have maximum strike loadings on aircraft. Accordingly, all strike aircraft were fragged to carry bombs and, if formations were attacked, F-4s were expected to jettison their bombs and escort the attacking F-105s. Because of fuel limitations, even with in-flight refueling over Laos as standard procedure, the Thailand-based strike forces could not do much better than 480 knots en route to targets. This meant that it was very difficult for an F-4C to jettison and then get up speed to overtake an attacking MiG-21. To make it even more difficult, all American crews had to make visual identification of an aircraft as hostile before firing an air-to-air missile. The F-4Cs smoked badly and were easily distinguishable at altitude; the little MiG-21s were visually acquirable normally at two miles, at which distance they were already within their missile range. MiG pilots also discovered that they could successfully outmaneuver US air-to-air missiles with a rapid turning descent, since the Navy's Sparrow (AIM-7) and the Air Force's Sidewinder (AIM-9) were designed to down bombers, and the missiles could not maneuver fast enough for a fighter engagement. As a consequence, Air Force pilots asked that guns be installed on their F-4s for close-in combat. External 20-mm gun pods received expedited development and were first used in combat in May 1967.[119]

During 1966, the increasing numbers of MiG engagements yielded larger MiG kills, Air Force pilots scoring confirmed kills of 12 MiG-17s and 5 MiG-21s; but the purpose of the Rolling Thunder air campaign was to put bombs on targets. When MiGs appeared, American strike aircraft jettisoned and failed to accomplish their mission. It appeared that the initiative was being lost to MiG interceptors. The Joint Chiefs of Staff once again recommended that North Vietnamese airfields be cleared for attack, but Secretary McNamara judged that the hostile air threat was not yet sufficiently large to interfere with strikes. Nevertheless, something dynamic was needed to restore the initiative, and this turned out to be a fighter sweep flown on 2 January 1967 by the 8th Tactical Fighter Wing. In the sweep — called Operation Bolo — what happened quite simply was that F-4s, loaded with air-to-air munitions, used F-105s' ground attack call signs, routes, and formations. A substantial MiG-21 force, quite possibly manned by Vietnamese fresh from training in the Soviet Union, challenged what looked to be F-105s only to be met by F-4s. In 12 minutes of combat, seven MiGs were shot down, with no damage to Air Force aircraft. On 6 January F-4Cs simulated a weather reconnaissance mission, and this lure resulted in the destruction of two more MiG-21s. Stunned by these losses, the North Vietnamese air force stood down for training, which extended to February 1967. Operation Bolo also indicated to the Seventh Air Force that some F-4s ought to be devoted to combat air patrol. The F-4C and MiG-21 had about the same top speed, but when the MiG came in at supersonic dash, a combat-loaded F-4 could not jettison and accelerate fast enough to engage. Beginning in February 1967, F-4s were fragged for combat air cover, a favorite formation consisting of 16 F-105s and two flights of F-4 escorts, one flight ahead of the lead strike flight and the other at the immediate rear of the force.[120]

The phase of Rolling Thunder operations conducted between 14 February and 24 December 1967 reached a new peak of intensity into the high terminal threat density areas in the vicinity of Hanoi and Haiphong. The success of American airmen in dealing with hostile defenses reduced casualties; it also may have influenced Washington decisionmakers to allow attacks against previously proscribed targets. In any event, General Momyer emphasized that any excessive losses of aircrews could very well have led Washington to reduce or terminate the operations. Beginning with F-105 strike wings in October 1966 and continuing with

F-4 wings early in 1967, all tactical fighters were equipped with external ECM pods that provided a fighter formation with a capability to jam hostile GCI, AAA director, and SAM tracking and director radars. Fighter formations thus were able to provide the same en route ECM jamming that the EB-66s could no longer expect to furnish. SAMs fired per kill went from 10 early in 1966 to 50 to 70 fired per aircraft kill through 1967. Although the ECM pods had a profound effect on vulnerability to SAMs, it was necessary that tactical fighters maintain a flight of four planes for mutual support. Invariably, if a formation of four aircraft broke up while in a SAM belt, missiles became accurate and losses went up.[121]

By April 1967 it must have become evident to the North Vietnamese that MiGs would bear the brunt of defense of their key military facilities. In April–June, their airmen tried a great variety of tactics. Once again F-105s were forced to jettison ordnance and some were lost to MiGs. In April Washington authorized attacks against Hoa Lac, Kep, and Kien An airfields. During the first six months of 1967 – but primarily in April–June – US aircrews scored 54 confirmed MiG kills at a cost of 11 US aircraft. In airfield strikes, 9 MiGs were destroyed on the ground in April and 15 more in May. When MiG activity diminished in July, escort F-4s were again used to carry bombs. They also carried missiles and performed combat air cover after bombing.

During the spring of 1967, when the North Vietnamese were having difficulty with US air forces, they perfected a very well-integrated GCI network in North Vietnam after the Soviet radar model. In addition to GCI sites, all redundant radars, including terminal threat radars, were netted very carefully with redundant communications. The logic of this was that as airplanes encroached, all available radars, whether acquisition or early warning, fed into filter centers. The filter centers, in turn, passed information on the ingressing aircraft to fire control radars, and, in cases where the latter might be jammed, the filter centers could furnish tracking information for antiaircraft artillery or SAMs.[122] As has been seen, this capability would be still further developed by the winter of 1971–72, but in August 1967 the Communists were mastering the intricacies of soft point intercepts. MiG-21s, flown by elite pilots, took off in pairs from either Phuc Yen or Gia Lam and flew at low level, keeping within radar ground clutter until they were abeam of an inbound Air Force force. Once they were behind the American formation, MiG-21 pilots fired their afterburners to climb to a high perch from which, with GCI vectoring, they launched down at speeds in excess of Mach 1, fired their Atoll missiles, and either zoomed back to altitude or passed through the Air Force formation. After one firing pass, MiGs would separate and head for an airfield either in North Vietnam or China. These slashing attacks were very successful: from August 1967 through the end of February 1968, 18 US aircraft were lost to MiGs, although only 5 MiGs were confirmed as destroyed. The only immediate Air Force response was to return F-4s to combat air patrol to guard the rear quadrants of strike forces. Other requirements were identified: to get warning of MiGs which were in launch range before they could be visually acquired and identified; and to provide more acceleration for F-4Cs, thus giving them a better

IDEAS, CONCEPTS, DOCTRINE

chance to overtake attacking MiG-15s. Other responses were directed against enemy ground defenses: when direction radars could not be jammed, old-fashioned flak suppression put barrage fire on some SAM sites to keep the missile crews down while strike forces were inside on heavily defended targets. Another program was the modification of strike aircraft designed to reduce their vulnerability to fuel fire and hydraulic system damage, which ranked one and two as causes of aircraft combat losses in Southeast Asia.[123]

When President Johnson halted all air attacks north of the 19th parallel on 1 April 1968, US air strikes were localized in the panhandle of North Vietnam, where MiGs had no GCI support and proved unable to operate without it. The Vietnamese seemed to have recognized this, and the MiG threat dwindled even before 1 November 1968, when President Johnson halted all air and naval attacks against North Vietnam, except in instances when reconnaissance aircraft were hazarded, whereupon armed escort fighters could return fire. The Vietnamese were quick to seize the advantage of the cease-fire. They extended radar control down the panhandle of North Vietnam and moved in SAMs and AAA, which they fired both across the DMZ and across the border into Laos. Between 1 November 1971 and 31 January 1972, there were 57 MiG incursions into the panhandle of Laos, mostly at night and probably with the hope of shooting down a B-52 or AC-130 gunship engaged in air interdiction strikes. As a consequence, Air Force strike aircraft were dispatched to fly combat air patrols and escort B-52s. Additional EC-121Ts, code-named Disco, were stationed over Laos to provide both warning and control. Special F-4D crews were designated and authorized to intercept MiGs, identified either by Disco or the Navy's Red Crown radar warning and control vessel in the Gulf of Tonkin. These actions checked MiG activity. In February and March 1972, there were only 10 enemy penetrations, and in 13 air-to-air engagements, the United States lost one aircraft while Communists lost more than five AIM-7 Sparrow missiles fired by specially modified F-4Ds. The Disco EC-121Ts were equipped with improved radar, but like the earlier College Eye radar, it could not look down into ground clutter and was dependent upon other sources of information to fill out their knowledge of the air situation.[124]

The strength of the North Vietnamese air force was greatly increased by early 1972. The fighter inventory included 93 MiG-21s (some of them the latest Soviet Fishbed-J models), 33 MiG-19s (probably provided by the Chinese), and 120 MiG-15/17s. During the Easter offensive of 1972, the Communists were compelled to rely very heavily upon the MiG force, since on 6 April American airmen were authorized to resume attacks (code-named Freedom Train) as far north as 20 degrees. This operation was expanded into Linebacker I on 8 May, when President Nixon authorized mining of North Vietnamese ports and resumption of air and naval strikes throughout North Vietnam. At this juncture, laser-guided bombs were devastating Communist lines of communication; and, with the ports closed by mines, the North Vietnamese had to make maximum use of what logistics they could to support their conventional armored attack. American defense suppression had largely negated the SAM threat, leaving the MiG force as the main hope for the defense of North Vietnam, and it advanced more engagements now than in any period of the war. During May, the Communists introduced MiG-19s in large numbers, and when these older jets were not an effective air defense, they went again to the very capable tactic of using MiG-21s under close control and supersonic attack with Atoll missiles. These interceptions were especially hazardous to F-4s that for the first time used chaff (aluminum reflective material dropped to mask aircraft from radar direction) in an effort to lay down safe passage corridors into target areas. The chaff aircraft were thus out ahead of strike forces and quite vulnerable; later, chaff would be dispensed from high altitudes in "clouds" over targets virtually at the same time that strike planes and escorts appeared. In June and July Seventh Air Force pilots suffered more casualties than they scored aerial victories.[125]

The Seventh Air Force had to find some way to alleviate the unfavorable loss ratio of aircraft. One possibility was to add more escort for strike planes, and this was important since only a few F-4s were equipped for laser-guidance bombing. During Linebacker I the rate of support aircraft (chaff, escort, combat air patrol, SAM/flak suppression, ECM, and search and rescue standby cover) was not infrequently as high as 5 to 1. The Air Force already had effected several actions. Air-to-air combat training was in progress at the Fighter Weapons School, Nellis AFB, Nevada; and it was found that during Linebackers I and II most MiG kills were scored by more experienced pilots, especially former fighter weapons instructor pilots.[126] The Air Force also had developed the new and improved model F-4E, with the Rivet Haste modification, including leading-edge wing slats to give it improved maneuverability and speed and yield a more stable gun platform. The lead-computing sight was improved, switches in the cockpit for guns and missiles were made easier to see, and the E-model was equipped with target identification system electro-optical (TISEO) equipment, essentially a binocular telescope in the left wing of the aircraft that greatly increased a pilot's visual acuity.[127] Both the Air Force and the Navy stated a common requirement for the development of a new highly maneuverable dogfighting missile, but past experience showed that it took 8 to 10 years to develop new missiles, and it was necessary to make quicker evolutionary improvements. The Air Force introduced the AIM-9J, an improved version of the Sidewinder heat-seeking missile, and began extensively to use the AIM-7E2 dogfight version of the radar-guided Sparrow missile. The Seventh Air Force also examined what the US Seventh Fleet was doing, because the Navy was not suffering the same type of loss ratios. Operating generally in the vicinity of Haiphong under cover of the Red Crown radar, the Navy aircraft could get quick warnings of impending MiG attack, and barrier combat air patrol aircraft could be directed against the planes. Air Force planes could and did avail themselves of Red Crown when they could, but the Seventh Air Force area of responsibility was Route Packages V and VIA, generally north and west of Hanoi, where its pilots were not getting the required information needed for MiG warning and for vectoring CAP aircraft. In the split-second jet air combat, getting advance warning was vitally important. One jet pilot summed it up:

IDEAS, CONCEPTS, DOCTRINE

> I think that history bears us out that the vast majority of kills in the air combat arena have been achieved by an unforeseen bogey or enemy fighter. A man who is shot down very seldom sees the man who shoots him down. And as that first tallyho, that first sighting is extremely critical.[128]

Had the Seventh Air Force possessed an airborne warning and control system (AWACS) which could have provided "look-down" radar coverage and positive control over counterair fighters, it is probable that three-quarters of the Air Force air-to-air losses could have been avoided in Vietnam. As it was, General Vogt, Seventh Air Force commander, put together Teaball at advanced headquarters at Nakhon Phanom (NKP) RTAFB, Thailand. Teaball utilized the complexities of communications and computers at NKP and voiced its control through the Disco airborne command and control aircraft orbiting over Laos in the 1972 campaign, much as Motel had done in 1965–68. The major difference was that Teaball integrated all radar plots and other intelligence information into a single facility and was able—through Disco or Red Crown relay—to provide voice warnings of impending MiG attacks and vector CAP forces against MiGs before they could strike. All these refined capabilities turned the air battle around: between 1 August and 15 October, Air Force pilots had a 4-to-1 kill ratio over MiGs.[129] Capt Richard S. "Steve" Ritchie, whose fifth confirmed victory on 28 August 1972 made him the first Air Force jet ace of the Vietnam War, credited radar control with his success:

> In every mission in the Hanoi area that I have participated in where I was successful, we had good AWACS type information from Red Crown and Disco. It was not enough, but it was that type of information. Every mission which was unsuccessful, we did not get that information. So I can tell you with great certainty I would not have five MiG-21s without the information we have received from the two sources.[130]

By 22 October, when Linebacker I ended because of the belief that Hanoi was willing to come to terms on a truce, two other Air Force weapon systems officers had become jet aces: Capt Charles B. De Bellevue, with six MiGs as of 9 September, and Capt Jeffrey S. Feinstein, with five MiGs by 13 October.

Although B-52 strategic bombers had long been committed to single-integrated operational plan (SIOP), general war strikes against route and terminal air defenses in the Soviet Union, the problem confronting them in the Linebacker II strikes against Hanoi and Haiphong to be undertaken on the night of 18 December 1972 was immensely more complex. In the case of the Soviet Union, the number of potential targets was very large, and the air defenses had to be spread over a vast area. Moreover, Air Force bombers were to be penetrating at low altitudes and using short-range air missiles (SRAMs) to suppress SAM defenses. They were to be using nuclear weapons, so that only a single bomber would need to penetrate to destroy the target and probably much of its defenses.[131] Over North Vietnam, in view of the political-military concern to avoid damage of stray bombing to population centers surrounding strategic targets, Gen John C. Meyer, CINCSAC, required flight crews to be doubly sure they held to the planned course and in-trail formation with cells of three aircraft. On the first raids, bombers also were required to stabilize flight for approximately four minutes prior to bomb-release, so as to avoid midair collisions, enhance mutual ECM jamming support, and increase bombing accuracy. The Seventh Air Force was programmed to support B-52s as well as daytime "smart bomb" attacks. Both missions required support often by the same aircraft (and sometimes the same tired crews), which flew both day and night missions. B-52s and newly arrived F-111s, which were entering combat for the first time, attacked at night: the F-111s struck every MiG airfield (except Gia Lam International Airport) every night of Linebacker II in the 30 minutes prior to B-52s going in. F-111s also used their precision-bombing techniques to attack the Hanoi dock area, where bomb damage assessment revealed all bombs were laid on the long, narrow dock and warehouse area, with no damage to adjacent civil structures. On the last two nights of Linebacker II, F-111s hit six SAM sites in the 30-minute time period before B-52s went in. In the earlier days of Linebacker II, F-4s attempted to lay chaff corridors, but this was difficult because no one could precisely predict upper air winds and the chaff corridors began to blow away before the fighters or bomber stream arrived. In a change, F-4s laid chaff clouds over the terminal threat areas. F-4s also flew escort and combat air patrols; on the three days that weather permitted visual bombing, F-4s equipped for laser bombing struck high-priority targets. On other days, F-4 Pathfinders employed LORAN positioning for other F-4s and also for A-7Ds which were being introduced to combat. F-4 and F-105 hunter-killer teams provided Wild Weasel flak and SAM suppression; EB-66s degraded surveillance radars from a distance; US Navy EA-6Bs used a very high power ALQ-99 jammer that was able to degrade not only surveillance but also terminal threat radars. Throughout the campaign each day's support for B-52s varied, based on weight of B-52 target effort, target area, and axes of attack and withdrawal, but the overall ratio of tactical support to bombers averaged out to 1.3 to 1.[132]

The intensity of Linebacker II disrupted North Vietnam's air defenses and allowed the Communists no time to recover during the campaign. The few MiG fighters that were airborne at night flew through B-52 formations apparently aimlessly; two were shot down by B-52 tail gunners. SAMs did more damage but still less than expected; an estimated 884 SAMs were fired at B-52s, but only 24 achieved hits and only 15 resulted in downed aircraft — one of which almost made it safely to U-Tapao. This was a 1.7-percent kill rate for the number of SAMs launched; and 15 B-52s lost during 729 sorties flown resulted in a 2.06-percent loss rate overall. In addition to the B-52 sorties, the Seventh Air Force flew 613 tactical strike sorties and 2,066 support sorties. One SAM downed a tactical aircraft; three other tactical aircraft were lost to AAA and two to MiGs. The fact that few MiGs were out and about was very favorable to the B-52s, since maintaining an integral formation was an essential element in negating the SAM director radars. Another circumstance occurred at the SAC staff level in Omaha when it was noted that current photography examined on day three indicated no spare missiles at firing sites; SAC requested and secured JCS approval to start hitting all but one storage area beginning on 26 December, and the SAC staff came to believe that successful bombing of the storage sites essentially disarmed the North Vietnamese by the end of the 11 days of Linebacker II.[133]

General Momyer pointed out, "Given the advanced fighter weapons available to us in Vietnam we might have expected to achieve a much higher air-to-air kill ratio than we had in World War II and Korea."[134] Instead in these earlier wars, employing .50-caliber machine guns, US airmen had substantially better shoot-down records. In Korea, enemy air-to-air losses were 874 compared to 122 US fighter losses, or a ratio of 7.2 to 1 because of Air Force fighter shoot-down. In Europe, the best available figures show that the enemy lost 7,422 fighters in World War II in fighter-versus-fighter combat, as compared to 1,691 US fighters, for a 4.4 to 1 ratio. The total air-to-air losses for the Vietnamese was 195 (139 to the Air Force, 56 to the Navy), while the United States lost 77 (61 by the Air Force, 16 by the Navy), for a ratio of 2.53 to 1.[135] In the air-to-air combat, the Communist airmen had the advantage of positive GCI radar control, whereas Air Force and Navy pilots who had neither precise GCI control nor permission to fire missiles "in the blind" using onboard radar, regularly conceded the initiative—probably the most important factor in split-second engagement, the average Air force-MiG engagement in Southeast Asia taking about 60 seconds. After August 1972, with the special Teaball facility being created to provide warnings of impending MiG attack, Air Force and Navy airmen were favored with a 5 to 1 win ratio and were at last able to dominate the air-to-air war.[136] Based on combat experience in a sophisticated high-threat environment with large quantities and diversities of SAMs, AAA, and fighters, combat survivability was factored out first as a function of aerodynamic performance (especially sustained speed and G capabilities), then as a function of designed-in survivability features, especially adequate ECM (passive and active, including chaff). But the lesson learned in Vietnam was that aerodynamic performance was the most important factor in combat survivability.[137]

Aerial Interdiction and Close Air Support

In World War II and Korea, ground combat took place along fairly distinct lines of contact between friendly and enemy forces. Once control of the air was maintained, air interdiction of enemy forces in his territory behind the lines of contact was the most effective mission for tactical air power. As a beginning for his systematic study of aerial interdiction in Southeast Asia, Col Herman L. Gilster defined air interdiction as

> the systematic attack of an enemy's logistics network for the purpose of destroying, neutralizing, or delaying his military potential (manpower and material) before it can be brought to bear effectively against friendly ground forces. The range of interdiction strikes may span a distance from the immediate battlefield up to, and sometimes including, the enemy's heartland. Normally, these attacks are made at such a distance

to the enemy's rear that detailed coordination with friendly ground forces is unnecessary.[138]

When an enemy comes into close proximity to friendly ground forces, air attacks must be coordinated and integrated with the efforts of the ground commanders. As defined by the Joint Chiefs of Staff, close air support comprises

> air attacks against hostile targets which are in close proximity to friendly forces and which require detailed integration of each air mission with the fire and movement of those forces.[139]

Since these air targets are in direct support of the friendly ground units, the ground commander has the responsibility of determining when support is required, what target is to be struck, and what effect is desired. The air commander is responsible for determining what size force and type of munitions are required to produce the effect desired by the ground commander. At the highest command level, the unified or joint commander controls the apportionment of total air resources between aerial interdiction and close air support and the requirements for close air support among various ground commands—all in context with the unified or joint commander's plans for combat.[140]

Although it was evident that North Vietnam was actively supporting Communist insurgency in South Vietnam and was controlling and using lines of communication through Laos and Cambodia, the Taylor mission of November 1961, which provided the conceptual basis for the beginning of US involvement in Vietnam, conceived the major problem to be local Communist insurgency rather than external aggression. There were no front lines; ground contacts occurred in unpredictable patterns over a wide area. Food was plentiful in South Vietnam, and the insurgents could limit their requirements for munitions by picking and choosing the times and places of their attacks. Taylor recommended and President Kennedy accepted a policy of support for South Vietnamese counterinsurgency inside South Vietnam. The chief purpose of aviation would be close support for ground forces in localized ground operations.[141]

In South Vietnam the Pacific Air Forces insisted that close air support organization should follow the time-honored Air Force principle of centralized control and decentralized operations. Central control would allow the small Vietnamese air force to be employed as necessary. In the Vietnamese armed forces, however, there was no overall commander, since each of the four Army of Vietnam corps commanders was practically autonomous. The corps commanders—later called military region commanders—had little respect for the Vietnamese air force and also considered that all military units of any kind in their areas belonged to them. At this same juncture, Lt Gen Thomas S. Moorman, vice CINCPACAF, would recall: "I heard Army Generals in Vietnam state that Vietnam was to be the proving ground for the 'Howze' concept of an airborne Army—and that the Army could and would provide their own support."[142] In World War II and Korea, there had been little decentralization of authority below the tactical air force/field army level, although an air liaison officer was assigned at corps level. But in Vietnam, an air support operations center (ASOC) was established in each ARVN corps (military region), with operational responsibility for employment of air sorties allocated by the VNAF/2d Air Division Air Operations Center (AOC) in Saigon. When ARVN communications proved incapable of flashing immediate requests for air support up through channels, VNAF/2d AD took the responsibility to the Air Force, which established radio communications for the purpose. The US Army established a tactical air support element (TASE) in Headquarters 2d Air Division to receive all requests for preplanned air support, place them in priorities, and pass them to the air operations center for execution. After some months of frequently uncoordinated helicopter assaults, COMUSMACV directed that a US Army aviation operations center be collocated with the VNAF/US Air Force AOC and that the commander of Army aviation would coordinate all helicopter assault operations. The operational requirements in Vietnam also demanded larger numbers of forward air controllers (FACs) than had been the case in earlier wars: to prevent civilian casualties air strikes required approval by Vietnamese authorities and positive FAC direction, usually by an airborne FAC who was also — operating in an area day after day — a prime source of intelligence about the enemy.[143]

These arrangements were made locally in Vietnam to provide close air support as a matter of urgency. In the United States in June 1962, the United States Strike Command began tests to devise means to facilitate air support. After four USSTRICOM joint exercises (Three Pairs, Coulee Crest, Swift Strike III, and Desert Strike), Air Force Chief of Staff Gen John P. McConnell (on 19 March) and Army Chief of Staff Gen Harold K. Johnson (on 28 April 1965) signed approval of a "Concept for Improved Joint Air-Ground Coordination." The tactical air force's operational facility that planned and coordinated employment of total tactical air effort was to be designated the Tactical Air Control Center (TACC), and thus VNAF/US Air Force AOC became the 2d Air Divison (Seventh Air Force) Combat Operations TACC; and with the beginning of out-country strikes, there would be an in-country TACC and an out-country TACC. At Corps levels, ASOCs were redesignated direct air support centers (DASCs). DASCs were subordinate to TACC, and their prime function was to provide fast reaction with sorties allocated to them by TACC for immediate close air support and tactical air reconnaissance. Air Force tactical air control parties (TACPs) forwarded requests for immediate air support to DASC over an Air Force request net, with TACPs at progressively higher levels monitoring the requests and having authority to disapprove if the Army fire support coordination center or tactical operations center considered the request inappropriate. Preplanned requests for air support continued to be forwarded over Army communications systems.[144]

Under the new US Army/US Air Force concept for joint air-ground coordination, the unified/joint commander would decide on a day-to-day basis the proportion of the air effort he wanted applied to counterair, interdiction, and close-air-support tasks. At the end of April 1965, General Westmoreland announced that air missions within South Vietnam would have highest call on air power. First priority would go to supporting ground troops who were engaged with the enemy. Then, air power would be used for preparatory strikes and air cover for units carrying out major ground operations. Escorts for trains and convoys came next. Interdiction outside South Vietnam could come only after close-air-support needs inside South Vietnam were met.[145] Under this mandate, General Momyer recalled:

> I considered all the forces that I operated in South Vietnam day in and day out were close support. . . . As you know, the forces that I operated against the lines of communications primarily were based in Thailand, and I did use the one wing of F-4s that were based up at Da Nang . . . both in and out of the country. But the F-100s, the A-37s, and the A-1s rarely went out of the country; this effort was totally committed, in my judgment, to close support because there wasn't an interdiction campaign within South Vietnam.[146]

The air wings flying close air support were fragged to fly at rates that would permit some escalation. During the Tet and Khe Sanh offensives, for example, the sortie rate jumped from a standard 1.2 sorties per day per aircraft to 1.8. Under the single manager system General Momyer required the 1st Marine Air Wing to identify its total sortie capability available to the countrywide air support system at 1.0 sorties per jet aircraft. At these rates on a given day within South Vietnam, Seventh Air Force flew about 300 preplanned sorties, the 1st Marine Air Wing another 200, and the VNAF 100. On an average, 40 aircraft were held on alert and were scrambled for immediate air support three to four times a day. In addition to alert aircraft, fighters proceeding to relatively lower priority preplanned support could be diverted in the air to immediate targets. Ground alert aircraft normally took 35 to 40 minutes to put ordnance on targets; diverts required 15 to 20 minutes to get into an area and in contact with FACs.[147]

As has been seen, General Westmoreland, as COMUSMACV, controlled the ordnance delivery of the B-52 Arc Light forces. In 1968-69 (fiscal year 1969), the B-52 squadrons, divided between Guam and Thailand, numbered five squadrons and were programmed for 1,800 sorties per month, or as many as 30 B-52 sorties a day. COMUSMACV selected B-52 targets, using recommendations by the two US Army field forces and the Seventh Air Force, and supplied the B-52 effort on a priority basis to close-air-support targets within South Vietnam. General Momyer wrote, "This departure from fundamental air doctrine reflected the primary interest of COMUSMACV in the ground war and the Secretary of Defense's guidance that gave priority to the war in South Vietnam."[148]

In South Vietnam General Momyer pointed out that the Army controlled the planning and request process for air support:

> The unified or joint commander controls the apportionment of the total in resources. . . . The ground commander controls close air support resources in that he selects the targets to be attacked; establishes the time of attack; and establishes his own priority among the total requests which have been submitted. . . . Each Army unit

IDEAS, CONCEPTS, DOCTRINE

> commander and his staff plans and requests his own air support along with other fire support. . . . Within this context, the ground commander controls and is responsible for the efficient utilization of CAS resources allocated.[149]

In all earlier wars in which the Air Force had participated, the Air Force had been directly involved in the daily development of a data base of enemy activities fraught with Air Force interest. This was not the case in Southeast Asia since, as concerned close air support, the role of the air component commander was to provide control of "mission execution in response to Army approved request." In a reflection about such matters, Maj Gen George Keegan, Jr., Seventh Air Force deputy chief of staff for intelligence in 1968–69, recalled that he had been suddenly faced at the time of Khe Sanh with a recognition that the Air Force—overnight and by ad hoc means—had to set up an intelligence-gathering and targeting structure for the most effective use of air assets. This ad hoc structure was highly effective in the defense of Khe Sanh, but it was thereafter abandoned, and, as Keegan said, the Air Force was again limited to providing fire on call to the Army in South Vietnam.[150]

Since the Seventh Air Force played next to no part in planning and selecting targets for air strikes within the close-air-support parameters applied to South Vietnam, the Air Force was actually unable to establish the effectiveness of close air support, although there were numerous ground commanders on record in favor of the very heavy application of aerial firepower. According to Secretary McNamara, General Westmoreland on a number of occasions emphasized his great satisfaction with the results of B-52 strikes. "The key to our success at Khe Sanh was firepower," Westmoreland emphasized, "principally aerial firepower. The B-52s . . . were instrumental in preventing the enemy from assembling in large formations."[151] One respondent from among 173 Army general officers queried about the outcome of the war in Southeast Asia volunteered that B-52s were decisive in enabling South Vietnamese forces to stop the North Vietnamese advance toward Hue and to retake Quang Tri in 1972. It also would appear that Army formation commanders—recognizing that a conscript army in an unpopular war must minimize casualties to sustain even marginal public support—substituted both air and artillery firepower for maneuver in close encounters with the enemy. In fighting in the Central Highlands in 1968, for example, the US Fourth Infantry Division reported 13 to 1 casualties inflicted when search and clear tactics were abandoned in favor of small reconnaissance patrols that found the enemy, pulled back, and called in air strikes and division artillery support.[152] Although the conclusion is inescapable that the Air Force delivered the air support desired by the Army, there were questions as to whether such heavy expenditures of munitions were warranted or even generally beneficial. One OSD system analysis study estimated that in 1966 some 65 percent of the total tonnage of bombs and artillery rounds used in Vietnam was expended against places where the enemy might be, without reliable information that he was there.[153] On a visit to Vietnam early in 1966, Gen Elwood R. Quesada drew an unusually candid observation: "Our effort in Vietnam . . . to me as far as air power was concerned was a little bit of what I used to refer to as operational masturbation. I have always felt the B-52s were to a large extent bombing forests . . . it was just clear to me that tactical air power as being exercised in that theater was the product of the Army and Army thinking."[154] Maj Gen Theodore R. Milton, also writing from retirement like Quesada, was equally critical: "The Army became over-dependent on air support, and air support of a kind highly vulnerable against a modern force."[155] Brig Gen Douglas Kinnard (US Army, Retired) made much the same point but about the South Vietnamese army: "Another side effect [of heavy firepower] was the bad habit acquired by the South Vietnamese forces: they learned the expensive habit of employing vast amounts of munitions—a habit that in the final years could not be sustained as US support was gradually reduced."[156]

During 1965, Secretary McNamara explained the air attacks against North Vietnam in terms of aerial interdiction subsumed to support for military defense of South Vietnam. The objectives of air strikes outside South Vietnam were never changed. They remained (1) to reduce the flow and/or increase the cost of infiltration of men and supplies from North Vietnam to South Vietnam, (2) to make it clear to Hanoi that the Communists would have to pay a price in the North for aggression in the South, and (3) to raise the morale of the South Vietnamese people.[157] In 1965, Air Force Chief of Staff Gen John P. McConnell viewed the air strikes into North Vietnam as possibly more psychological than military:

> These strikes have actually a dual purpose. First, they are designed to assist our aerial interdiction effort in impeding the flow of supplies and reinforcements to the Viet Cong from the North because that is where the supplies are coming from. Second, our only hope of stopping these supplies is to discourage the North Vietnamese from supporting the Viet Cong by making such support too costly to them. This strategy, which is best described as "strategic persuasion," gives the President a highly flexible tool in inducing North Vietnam eventually to accept his offer of unconditional discussions.[158]

"We have stated before and I wish to repeat today," Secretary NcNamara reiterated in January 1967, "that the bombing of the North is intended as a supplement to and not a substitute for the military operations in the South."[159]

In conceptualizing the most effective aerial interdiction program for Vietnam shortly after its inception, Generals Wheeler, McConnell, and Ryan—with support from Admiral Sharp—argued that the main focus of interdiction strikes should be in the Hanoi-Haiphong area where rail lines and the ports employed in bringing in military supplies from China and the Soviet Union centered as it were at a narrow aperture that spread out southward into a maze of rail lines, roads, and trails into route packages around and into the periphery of South Vietnam. General Momyer also believed that a Linebacker-type air action in 1967 would have forced the North Vietnamese to negotiate.[160] Maj Gen George Keegan, who became Air Force assistant chief of staff, intelligence, was even more positive, at least in his rhetoric:

> Contrary to the judgments held by 99 percent of our defense analysts and political leaders, I for one came out of that war convinced that a bombing campaign like

IDEAS, CONCEPTS, DOCTRINE

> Linebacker II... could have brought the war to a close as early as 1965. North Vietnam could have been isolated from the battlefield in a matter of weeks and North Vietnam's wherewithal to fight in the South would have been reduced to such proportions that the ground defenders could have managed far more easily than they did. I continue to believe that North Vietnam since 1965 has been nothing more than a transmission belt for Soviet and some Chinese military material to which the North Vietnamese have added human cannon fodder.[161]

General Keegan, an experienced air intelligence officer, attributed some of the shortcomings to the Air Force:

> I would like to observe that the Air Force long since had lost the ability to plan and support, with intelligence, interdiction operations. Years ago, the mission of targeting was taken away from the Department of the Air Force and passed to the Defense Intelligence Agency, where it simply died. The assessment analysis of enemy logistics (economic impact) has fallen to the CIA by default. So the Air Force entered this war with very limited tools for assessing logistics flow in depth, and yet one of the Air Force's principal missions is to impede the flow of logistics into the battlefield.[162]

In the Wheeler-Sharp-McConnell-Ryan-and-Momyer assessment, mining and blockade of Haiphong was essential to put maximum stress on the North Vietnamese logistical system through interdiction. Secretary McNamara and his staff, however, considered that concentrating interdiction efforts farther south would have adequate effect on the enemy.[163]

In April 1965, Laos was divided into zones primarily to establish interdiction responsibilities. Barrel Roll was far to the north and of interest to defense of the Royal Lao government until 1971, when the Communists began a sustained attack against the Plain of Jars. The area of Laos south from the Mu Gia pass to the 17th parallel was called Steel Tiger, while the remainder of the Laos panhandle from Tchepone south to Cambodia was designated Tiger Hound. In 1966 a 30-mile zone above the DMZ was made a special interdiction zone called Tally Ho. Interdiction in the border zones was affected both by terrain and weather. The southwest summer monsoon season prevails west of the Annam Mountain Range in Laos; the jungle becomes soaked and trails and roads are flooded bogs. The winter monsoon brings adverse weather to north and central South Vietnam, which are east of the Annam Range. In Laos there were entries into North Vietnam through the mountain passes: Mu Gia, Ban Karai, and Ban Raving. The Ho Chi Minh trail was a maze of trails and roads long used for clandestine movements in colonial Indochina. In Laos interdicting air strikes were bound by stringent rules of engagement designed to protect nonmilitary structures, noncombatants, and friendly Lao road patrols, the latter of such questionable worth as to be more of a detriment to effective air attack than a source of intelligence. The rules prohibited air attacks on any active village, defined as any building, hut, or group of huts not validated by the American embassy in Vientiane for an air strike. The US ambassador also limited attacks to 200 yards on either side of roads unless the strike forces were under control of an airborne forward air controller (FAC) and had approval from a Laotian controller. These rules prevailed through the years of conflict, and the best way to live with them proved to be the assignment of a Laotian officer to an ABCCC aircraft assigned to an area. This officer could either validate targets or get them validated from Vientiane. In the Tally Ho area immediately north of the DMZ, FACs flying little O-1 observation aircraft were the primary source of enemy information; they located targets and marked them for tactical fighters called in to attack. By the summer and autumn of 1967, however, a buildup of antiaircraft weapons was preventing the O-1 from covering principal roads; accordingly, the Seventh Air Force put FACs in the backseats of F-100F aircraft (and later F-4s) and employed these two-seat high-speed planes as "Misty FACs." These planes patrolled specified areas below the 18th parallel day after day, uncovering targets of opportunity for attack fighters.[164]

In the dry monsoon winter season months of 1965-66, a Seventh Air Force Tiger Hound task force stalked North Vietnamese trucks on the Ho Chi Minh trail. When summer floods curtailed enemy transit in Laos, another special Tally Ho task force worked in the dry season north of the DMZ. These task forces were effective in employing tactical fighter strikes against hostile road traffic in daylight hours. The North Vietnamese, however, stopped moving logistics in daylight unless flying weather was bad, in which case they would run convoys under cloud cover. After the initial seasonal employment, Tiger Hound and Steel Tiger were no longer treated as separate task force entities when the 1966 dry season began, and Tally Ho was discontinued as a separate entity by the winter of 1967. Interdictory activity in Laos and Route Package I was incorporated into Seventh Air Force out-country strike activity. Quite frequently, strike fighters, weathered out of targets in North Vietnam, were diverted to drop their ordnance in Laos, usually on selected chokepoints on lines of communication. As had been true in earlier wars, roads were poor interdiction objectives since the North Vietnamese road gangs quickly filled craters or bypassed them. The repair of the roads and their defense nevertheless required the commitment of as many as 40,000 to 50,000 personnel organized in Laos into Binh Trams. These roads had the necessary transportation, engineer, and AAA battalions to ensure movement and security of materiel in their sectors. Including the route packages in North Vietnam in addition to Laos, some 300,000 to 500,000 troops and civilian militia were committed to road maintenance, substantially reducing the availability of enemy manpower that could have been used for aggressive military purposes.[165]

Early in 1966, when it was becoming evident that Rolling Thunder attacks had not influenced Hanoi to cease infiltration of men and materiel into South Vietnam, Secretary McNamara became interested in the suggestion of Assistant Secretary of Defense John T. McNaughton that the United States and South Vietnam adopt the concept of physically cutting off North Vietnamese support for infiltration by erecting an on-the-ground barrier, roughly along Route 9 from the sea to the Mekong, 180 miles across South Vietnam and Laos. The germ of this barrier idea was conveyed by McNamara to the Jason committee, a collection of distinguished civilian scientists mustered into summer study by the Institute of Defense Analysis. At the end of August, the Jason committee presented a series of four studies; they concluded that the bombing of North Vietnam was ineffective and proposed a concept for inhibiting enemy troop and supply infiltration by means of an air-supported barrier system of electronic sensors to detect enemy activity and the use of tactical aircraft, mines, and other munitions to counter enemy incursions thus detected. The Joint Chiefs of Staff were not enthusiastic about the barrier project—they questioned its expense and doubted if it would meet the scientists' expectations. Nevertheless, on 15 September 1966 McNamara appointed Lt Gen Alfred Starbird to head Joint Task Force 728 within the OSD Directorate of Defense Research and Engineering, charged with implementing the infiltration system as conceived by the Jason committee. The joint task force was given the cover name of Defense Communications Planning Group (DCPG).[166]

By July 1967 a little more than 90 percent of approximately 173,000 Rolling Thunder sorties had been directed at North Vietnam's lines of communication, with the heaviest concentration in Route Package I, where panhandle roads led into Laos and the DMZ. In these forward areas the North Vietnamese depended principally upon Soviet-built six-wheel-drive Zil 157 trucks. Of the estimated 9,000 trucks possessed by North Vietnam in February 1965, US aircrews claimed to have destroyed or damaged approximately 8,100; yet, in July 1967, the North Vietnamese truck inventory stood at some 10,000 to 12,000 vehicles, indicating either that Hanoi's allies were delivering trucks faster than they were being destroyed or that our estimates were wrong. In August 1967 Washington intelligence statistics, based on the observation that Communist battalions in South Vietnam were drawing their food from local sources and were fighting on an average of only one day a month, showed that Vietcong/NVA forces in South Vietnam required only 15 tons per day of externally supplied materiel, chiefly weapons and other ordnance. At this juncture, General Momyer pointed out that a classical air-interdiction campaign included attacks against productive sources of enemy supplies and equipment, interdiction of movement between the enemy's heartland and his forward field forces, and formalized ground combat that caused the enemy to consume logistics faster than he could replenish them. In Southeast Asia, the first and third elements of classical interdiction were lacking, since supplies delivered to North Vietnam could not be attacked at ports of entry, and the Vietcong/NVA had the option of giving or refusing combat. In the summer of 1967 the Joint Chiefs of Staff were on record as advocating the closing of North Vietnam's major ports and opposing proposals to limit Rolling Thunder strikes to the area south of the 20th parallel. "In conducting an interdiction campaign of the type that we are conducting, I think it is a matter of arithmetic that the more of the enemy's area and the more of his forces that are exposed to your offensive action, the greater the result is going to be," General Wheeler explained. While these arguments and assessments were waging in Washington, the North Vietnamese greatly expanded the road routes available in Laos during the summer monsoon season of 1967. Important roads received gravel surfacing, and substantial numbers of 37-mm antiaircraft weapons were brought in. Almost as if by signal with the drying weather in October 1967, North Vietnamese trucks flooded through the Mu

Gia and Ban Karai passes and down Laotian Route 922, where supplies went into South Vietnam in the vicinity of the A Shau valley.[167]

Early in its research and development effort, the Defense Communications Planning Group veered away from the so-called McNamara wall conventional barrier system in favor of the development or adaptation of technology for an air-supported, anti-infiltration system. Installation of this Igloo White electronic detection and interdiction system began in mid-1967. The basic system elements were air-delivered acoustic and seismic sensors strung along Laos roads, and aircraft that airdropped the sensors, a readout-relay aircraft that retransmitted sensor signals from the sensors, and a large computerized ground assessment center at Nakhon Phanom RTAFB that received, analyzed, and reported enemy logistic flow activities for air strikes managed by the airborne battlefield command and control center (ABCCC) over Laos. As an evolution of the AC-47 "Spooky" side-firing gunship used in permissive environment inside South Vietnam, an AC-130A arrived in July 1967. The transport C-130A was modified with a low-light television, an infrared sensor, and a radar, plus side-firing batteries of 20-mm cannon and 7.62-mm miniguns. Later versions of the AC-130 carried 40-mm guns. Later models also were equipped with a laser-designator. General Momyer was at first quite skeptical about the advertised capability of the AC-130 to kill trucks, but he ultimately concluded that it "became the best truck-killing weapon in the war."[168] In early operations, Igloo White was able to locate truck parks for B-52 Arc Light strikes; F-4s provided cover and flak suppression for gunships and attacked targets that could be illuminated or marked by flares. At first the US Navy VO-67 Squadron laid and monitored the Igloo White sensors, but in June 1968 the Air Force was equipped to drop sensors from F-4s and it monitored them with an EC-121R aircraft, thus releasing VO-67 from the operational control of Seventh Air Force to return to the United States.[169]

The Tet offensive of February 1968 both caused a diversion of many of the Igloo White electronics assets to the defense of Khe Sanh and demonstrated that the Communists, despite interdiction attacks against North Vietnam and Laos, were able to field a substantial force for an intensive, albeit short, campaign. Air Staff analysis made under immediate direction of Air Force Vice Chief of Staff Gen Bruce K. Holloway on 1–4 March 1968 predicted that as long as the Communist Vietnamese received large quantities of military supplies from the Soviet Union and China and controlled the tempo of fighting, it was virtually impossible to prevent them from building stockpiles in sanctuaries near prospective battlefields. The number one alternative was thus to attack the Haiphong docks and railway equipment on the main northeast rail line to China. If this were impossible to get approved, the number two alternative was to concentrate more effort against truck routes and supply trails in the panhandle of North Vietnam and Laos, including the shifting of approximately half of the daily sorties away from Hanoi-Haiphong areas to southern transport routes. The new Igloo White system, new AC-130 gunships, and new time-delay munitions promised in theory a fourfold increase in the effectiveness of interdiction, lending hope that intensive air interdiction could cut into the minimal 50-150 tons daily required by enemy field forces.[170] The second alternative became a basis for President Johnson's announced decision on 31 March to eliminate bombing above the 20th parallel (which was actually to be a cessation of air attack above the 19th parallel). In anticipation of still further bombing limitations, Headquarters Pacific Air Forces developed a plan—code-named Commando Hunt—for intensified interdiction with the option to include North Vietnam up to 19 degrees north latitude. As approved by headquarters in succession up to the Joint Chiefs of Staff, the plan called for emphasis on truck destruction during the winter (October to April) dry season. The cessation of bombing in North Vietnam on 1 November 1968 caused Commando Hunt I to be limited to southern Laos when it was initiated on 15 November 1968. The objective was to reduce the flow of supplies by destroying vehicles and interdicting vulnerable road segments and water crossings. The nature of the terrain actually focused primary operations into a small segment of southeastern Laos, roughly from Mu Gia pass on the north to the road junctions at Tchepone on the south, the emphasis being on denial to the enemy of free access to the expanding system of roads in southern Laos.[171]

During 1965–68 Communist capabilities inside South Vietnam had been based on an active main force of Vietcong guerrillas and a politically organized base infrastructure. In the Tet offensive, Hanoi perhaps purposefully sacrificed the indigenous Vietcong infrastructure and the Communist hold on the food-producing countryside. In the changed situation, NVA and some Vietcong remnants enjoyed much reduced local support and were dependent on lines of communication to North Vietnam. In short, the "people's war" was conventionalized, and Communist forces in Vietnam had to be supplied through the Ho Chi Minh trail, through the port of Kompong Som in Cambodia, and over the DMZ. With the closing of the port of Kompong Som in 1970, Communist forces in Military Regions II and III were limited to support transiting the Ho Chi Minh trail, but in the north, in Military Region I, the Communists were successful in leaking supplies through the DMZ. Thus some 400 to 800 tons of supplies used to support the Easter invasion of 1972 were leaked through the DMZ. As General McConnell had predicted earlier, stopping logistics movement across the DMZ became very difficult, considering frequent bad weather and the buildups of enemy supplies immediately north of the border. From November 1968 through March 1972, Air Force and Navy pilots flew four dry season Commando Hunt campaigns against Communist logistical activity on the Ho Chi Minh trail, with the following statistical results:

	Commando Hunt I	Commando Hunt III	Commando Hunt V	Commando Hunt VII
Inclusive dates	1 November 1968– 30 April 1969	1 November 1960– 30 April 1970	10 October 1970– 30 April 1971	1 November 1971– 30 March 1972
US strike sorties (daily average)				
Fighter-attack	399	288	203	182
Gunship	2	8	11	13
B-52	22	23	30	21
Enemy resupply				
Input (tons)	45,000	54,000	61,000	31,000
Throughput (tons)	8,500	19,000	7,000	5,000
Ratio (TP/IP)	1/5	1/3	1/9	1/6
Enemy trucks Destroyed or Damaged	6,000	10,000	20,000	10,000

When the enemy initiated the Easter offensive in 1972, the last Commando Hunt VIII was immediately terminated, and the air resources committed to the trail were used for air support and tactical interdiction roles within South Vietnam.[172]

The Commando Hunt interdiction program provided a first test of an "electronic battlefield" represented by Igloo White. As a summary evolution, the multimillion-dollar Infiltration Surveillance Center built at Nakhon Phanom RTAFB in Thailand proved more able to perform an intelligence mission than a real-time operational function, at least as far as enemy road movements in Laos were concerned. The airdropped strings of sensors were seldom useful for real-time location of targets, but their activations provided a basic index of enemy truck activity. This information was useful for positioning the interdiction force and on a longer time basis for making input throughput output models of enemy logistics activity. Almost all Communist movement was at night and by trucks whose drivers made short shuttles over the same routes, generally starting shortly after nightfall and tailing off about 3:00 A.M. to unload, disperse, and conceal cargo. An estimated 2,500 to 3,000 trucks were in Laos in the 1970 and 1971 dry seasons, with 500 to 1,000 moving at night, each carrying about four tons of supplies. Replacement trucks were drawn from large inventories at Hanoi and Haiphong. At peak deployment, 600 to 700 antiaircraft guns were along the trail. In the Commando Hunt planning stage, it was hoped that a munitions package concept would cut the road for extended periods. The road would be first cut by laser-guided bombs at a point difficult to bypass. Next, antimateriel land mines would be emplaced, powerful enough to destroy a truck. Third, antipersonnel land mines were emplaced to deter mine clearing. Finally, sensors on both sides of the munitions package would determine if truck traffic was getting through. The road-busting and aerial-mining plans were attempted but did little to constrain the Communists. There were very few ideal interdiction points, and a vast network of interlinking routes provided numerous options for continuing movement of supplies, while interdiction packages were quickly cleared out. The Communists similarly quickly repaired even massive B-52 bomb damages in the roads through Mu Gia and the other passes.[173] The large bomb load of B-52s was exploited to attack truck parks, but the Communists seldom displayed such concentrated truck parks or supply dumps. AC-130s and similarly outfitted old AC-119s had the best truck-killing rate during the early stages of Commando Hunt; with the buildup of hostile AAA, each of these gunships had to be covered by three F-4s, which suppressed flak for them. Laser bombs were excellent against hostile AAA, but two F-4s were shot down while attempting to cover gunships. In the 1971–72 dry season, the Communists also slipped SAMs into Laos; they launched more than 160 of them, causing the loss of 10 US aircraft. On 29 March 1972 the first AC-130 was shot down by a SAM located southwest of Tchepone. In General Momyer's analysis: "The AC-130 had been an exceptional weapon system in a semi-permissive defense environment, but it had to give way or become extinct when the enemy brought the full weight of his best defensive weapons against it."[174]

During the Vietnam conflict and thereafter, the role of serial interdiction was the subject of intense debate in civilian and military circles. Secretary McNamara's chief analyst, Alain C. Enthoven, concluded early on:

> One of the important lessons of the Vietnam war, we believe, is that deep-interdiction bombing appears far less effective in this kind of war than its advocates claim. Although there was much complaint about them, the bombing restrictions under which US forces operated in 1967 were reasonable and of small significance for the military effectiveness of the operation.[175]

The original purpose of Rolling Thunder, however, was more psychological than military: to make Hanoi pay an increasingly greater and ultimately unacceptable cost for aggression. Because of heavy assistance from the Soviet Union and China, Hanoi may have received more income than loss from Rolling Thunder strikes. In the protracted war, moreover, the Communists had minimum pressure from the timeliness of replacements, a factor of otherwise critical importance in intense, large-scale confrontations between opposing forces in more conventional conflict. The early interdiction campaigns thus failed to increase the cost of aggression to a level unacceptable to Hanoi. And with the advantage of time, the Communists were able in the protracted war to accumulate materiel to support offensives: at least six months of military inactivity and supply conservation were necessary to accumulate supplies for the 1972 Easter offensive. As this offensive got under way, tactical interdiction almost immediately overwhelmed the enemy's forward supply distribution, while deep-in interdiction denied replacement receipts through

Hanoi and Haiphong. The main offensive in Quang Tri province ground to a halt after less than 30 days, even before the throughput of supplies via the DMZ and Ho Chi Minh trail was unacceptably drawn down, leading Colonel Gilster to conclude: "Mobility denial, rather than supply denial, had been the key to the Allied success. Supply denial has seldom, if ever, proved to be a viable objective, and the experience in Southeast Asia tends to substantiate the validity of this premise."[176]

Airmobility: US Air Force Transports and Army Helicopters

The ground war in Southeast Asia was an airlift engaged war, and it could not have been fought as it was fought without Air Force fixed-wing transport and Army helicopters. In the definitive history of the Air Force tactical airlift in the conflict, Col Ray L. Bowers notes:

> Air transportation gave the allies in Vietnam a powerful tool for mobility and supply, permitting major operations in remote areas on short notice. Airlift also made it possible to economize on defensive forces by affording a fast means of reinforcing threatened regions, either from off shore or from other parts of Vietnam. Transports routinely sustained isolated garrisons, when necessary by parachute. Finally, the transport force conducted a countryside passenger and logistics service and made immediate delivery of spare parts to repair grounded aircraft.[177]

The payloads lifted by Air Force transports, Bowers points out, far exceeded the combined payloads airlifted in the Korean War, the Berlin airlift, and in the China-Burma-India theater of World War II.[178] In 1966 alone, Air Force transports lifted 730,000 tons of cargo and 1,524,000 passengers within Vietnam, or more than the intratheater airlift for the three years of the Korean War.[179]

In the US Army there was a prevalent belief that the use of rotary-wing aircraft helicopters was the greatest single innovation in the whole conflict in Vietnam.[180] The Korean War experience of the Army with helicopters, and the Army's desire for aircraft that could perform observation, liaison, command and control, supply, and limited troop movement with the Army in the field, caused the increase of the number of aircraft in an infantry division from 10 to 50, and in 1962 the standard army divisions were authorized 101 aircraft, many of them helicopters. The vast expansion of Army helicopters had its beginnings in 1962, with the US Army Tactical Mobility Requirements Board (Howze Board), which recommended, as has been seen, that the Army form very mobile units with large numbers of helicopters for direct assault, firepower, transportation, and supply. Secretary McNamara authorized the Army to form an 11th Air Assault Division which received tests by the US Strike Command (STRICOM) for comparative evaluations with the Air Force transport and strike support. Before tests were completed, McNamara authorized the formation of the 1st Cavalry Division (Airmobile) and its deployment with 434 organic aircraft to Vietnam in August 1965. In addition to the helicopters of the airmobile division, many Army helicopter

IDEAS, CONCEPTS, DOCTRINE

companies were used for general support. The Army also developed an attack helicopter to support assault landings and provide immediately available fire support. During the peak war years, the Army had well over 3,000 helicopters in Vietnam, some 2,200 of them centrally assigned to the 1st Aviation Brigade and allocated to various ground units for specified operations in accordance with previously approved operation plans.[181]

In the view of General LeMay as Air Force chief of staff, the Army's aviation programs surfacing in 1964 contravened the pertinent Department of Defense directive of 18 March 1957 that made it clear that the Air Force included "among its primary responsibilities those of furnishing close combat and logistical air support for the US Army." It also spelled out the Army aviation program in some detail and contained a specific statement that the US Army aviation program would not provide for aircraft to perform the function of close combat air support. Despite this directive, the Army almost immediately obtained secretary of defense authorization to procure limited numbers of Caribou transport aircraft and Mohawk turboprop observation planes, as well as growing numbers of helicopters. Said LeMay in February 1964:

> Now, the Army's position is that they want to outline the battlefield and say this is the Army's task.... In other words we haul everything by air from the United States right up to the rear of the battle zone, dump it out there. Then the Army will take it and distribute it with their airplanes. Then they say we will do all of the interdicting and everything outside of the battle zone deep into enemy territory, and they will do everything over the battle zone. Now that is their concept.[182]

The Army's position, as expressed somewhat later by Lt Gen Robert R. Williams, US Army assistant chief of staff for force development, was:

> Primary does not connote totally. The Air Force has many responsibilities, and I certainly hope that primary among those responsibilities will always be close air support. I certainly hope it never becomes a secondary and a second-class role for the Air Force. It has a primary responsibility providing close air support but it does not give the Air Force the total role or the exclusive role.[183]

Although General LeMay actively attacked the "overlap, duplication, and so forth" inherent in the US Army's aviation buildup, he had great respect for Army Gen Paul D. Adams, commander in chief, Strike Command, and was sure that General Adams and his staff would come up with the proper solution to get the most out of Army and Air Force forces.[184] Secretary of the Air Force Eugene Zuckert, moreover, was entirely sympathetic to the Army's desire "to try to find greater mobility" and thought the Howze Board had "made the Air Force take a great deal more active interest in the problems of ground support."[185] In a memo to McNamara in March 1965, Zuckert requested that the Air Force be authorized six heavy cargo helicopter squadrons to provide forward transport support for the Army in the field until vertical-flight transport became available. This was not agreeable to Secretary of the Army Cyrus Vance, and the new airlift system largely represented the US Strike Command's maneuver experience already noted. General Adams concluded that Air Force transports should deliver supplies as far forward as possible and that further distribution should be made by Army helicopters. The STRICOM tests also showed the value of an airlift control center (ALCC) that was subordinate to the tactical air control center, tactical airlift liaison officers (TALOs) who were attached to tactical air control parties at brigade and lower levels, and airlift control elements (ALCEs) that were positioned at forward airheads. The new Air Force chief of staff, General McConnell, began his tenure determined to do something about service differences on tactical aviation, and Army Chief of Staff General Harold Johnson was said to be less of a partisan of Army aviation than some of his subordinates. He was said to be particularly tired of defending armed Army Mohawk aircraft.[186] Convinced that the lack of an agreement would injure operations in Vietnam, McConnell and Johnson conferred privately for six months before agreeing upon a handwritten draft decision on pragmatic rather than theoretical grounds. As signed on 6 April 1966, the Army transferred the operational CV-2 Caribou and test quantity CV-7 Buffalo fixed-wing transports to the Air Force, the latter becoming responsible for intratheater fixed-wing tactical transports, with the provision that Caribous and C-123s could be attached to subordinate field army echelons as thought necessary by joint/unified commanders. The Army became responsible for all helicopter support for intratheater movement, fire support, and supply and resupply of Army forces and Air Force tactical air control elements in the field. The Air Force became responsible for rotary-wing aircraft for search and rescue, administrative, and other limited functions.[187]

"Upon my assumption of command of 7AF, there was no organization for the control and direction of the airlift force, yet the daily airlift requirement was going up with each new ground unit that was brought into the theater," General Momyer recalled.[188] In October 1966 the 834th Air Division was formed under Seventh Air Force at Tan Son Nhut Air Base, with Brig Gen William G. Moore, Jr., an experienced tactical airlifter, as its commander. The 834th ALCC at Tan Son Nhut was an element of the Seventh Air Force TACC, although the two units were each too large to be collocated and were accordingly physically separate. The ALCC exercised its command and control responsibilities through ALCEs at 14 operating locations, each of which had a collocated aerial port squadron or detachment. In addition, small aerial port detachments, sometimes only a forklift and a few men, were at some 40 locations around the country. Tactical airlift officers were at division or independent brigade level and above, and these men, in addition to providing airlift expertise and planning assistance to Army units, also advised the DASC and ALCC of emergency resupply mission requirements being processed upward through Army channels. In this way the ALCC was able to accomplish forewarned coordination with affected Air Force units and prealert all concerned before the MACV combat operations center (COC) gave final approval to the emergency request. In the airlift reorganization, the Air Force C-123 transport aircraft were assigned to the 834th Air Division, as were the six squadrons of the

Army Caribou transport (which the Air Force designated C-7As). C-123s continued to serve in common service airlift, and as agreed between Generals McConnell and Johnson, the C-7 Caribous remained largely under a "dedicated-user" system whereby the MACV COC/834th AD ALCC issued daily orders allocating the small transports to specified users. There were C-130 operating location beddowns at Cam Ranh Bay and Tan Son Nhut. C-130s were the airlift workhorses in Southeast Asia, but they and their aircrews remained assigned to PACAF's 315th Air Division and worked on temporary duty in Vietnam from bases on Okinawa, Taiwan, and the Philippines. This ferrying arrangement appeared ineffective and wasteful to General Momyer, who continued to press for assignment of a reinforced tactical airlift wing to the 834th Air Division for stationing at Cam Ranh Bay.[189]

The Military Airlift Command (MAC) was responsible for the air portion of the line of communication to Southeast Asia. MAC also had good capabilities for airborne operations — the delivery of combat forces into an objective area both during and subsequent to an assault. Thus in a 27-day airlift begun on 27 December 1965, MAC flew Operation Blue Light, lifting 3,000 men and 4,600 tons of equipment of the 3d Brigade, 25th Infantry Division, directly from Hawaii to Pleiku. On 12–29 December 1967, MAC C-141 and C-133 aircraft in Operation Eagle Thrust flew 10,356 men and 5,118 tons of equipment (including 37 helicopters) of the 101st Airborne Division from Fort Campbell, Kentucky, to Bien Hoa. MAC C-133s were not infrequently pressed into service to lift outsize equipment within Vietnam, and Brig Gen Burl W. McLaughlin, who commanded the 834th Air Division in 1967–69, received routine authority to reschedule C-141s that unloaded in Vietnam for second in-country stops. In November 1970 the Air Force made a decision that up to 42 C-141s should be made available for Vietnam to meet temporary abnormal in-country demands. These C-141s and several C-133s were used in Vietnam during the Lam Son 719 campaign.[190]

In Vietnam logistical airlift operations — the air line of communication — stood out as the primary task of Air Force tactical airlift. Normally, logistic requirements were met through airlanded operations that comprised some 95 to 97 percent of the cargo and personnel moved through the airlift system. The remaining 3 to 5 percent was provided by aerial delivery, which provided additional force flexibility by offering — as at Khe Sanh in 1968 — an important option when airlanding resupply became too hazardous for sustained operations. During the height of the battle at Khe Sanh, Air Force transports were delivering over 300,000 pounds of cargo each day, the limiting factor on the tonnage being the ability of the people on the ground to remove it from the drop zone. Direct delivery of air supply in small retail quantities to Army battalions and separate companies was not great in magnitude but a valid and essential requirement nevertheless. In Vietnam fixed-wing paratroop assaults proved generally disappointing; battalion jumps ceased after early 1967, and the applicability of paratroops in future conflicts seemed limited and generally unable to compete successfully with more flexible helicopter assault. On the other hand, battlefield mobility such as the incursions into Cambodia and Laos were quite dependent upon fixed-wing transport air movements into forward bases and upon air transport resupply, especially "bladder bird" deliveries of fuel for Army helicopters.[191] Maintaining battlefield mobility was one of the essential tasks of airborne operations. To maintain mobility, Army units in Vietnam frequently had only one or two days of basic supplies. The responsiveness of tactical airlift was thus of paramount importance, with 1,600 tons every day being a reasonable figure for the daily requirements of a normal Army division in combat. The airmobile division required 20 percent more, mostly in fuel and oil for its helicopters.[192]

On all occasions in the past, the Tactical Air Command had vigorously insisted that tactical airlift was distinctly different from strategic airlift since it operated in a medium which demanded association and integration with other tactical forces and had to be directed and controlled by a theater air commander. In short, tactical airlift, or the old troop carrier aviation, was an integral function of the Tactical Air Command. In his end-of-tour report, General Momyer strongly emphasized that the "one major lesson which stands out above all others with respect to airlift" was that tactical and strategic airlift were different:

> Whereas the strategic airlift task can, in an ultimate sense, be handled by a commercial carrier, the theater airlift task is rooted in combat which requires emphasis on entirely different factors such as short, relatively unprepared fields, exposure to ground fire, coordination with escorting fighters and integration into the tactical control system for direction, assistance and redirection.[193]

In the Air Force Corona Harvest evaluation process, however, a team of officers prepared an initial four-volume evaluation of tactical airlift that was refined into a single volume by a panel chaired by Col Louis P. Lindsay, the experienced airlift officer whose assignments had included service as the 834th Air Division director of operations. The Corona Harvest report recommended that the tactical air control center and the airlift control center continue to be separate, as they had been in Vietnam due to physical circumstances. Further, the Lindsay committee cited duplications in control, aerial port, and support elements in Southeast Asia and made a unanimous recommendation "that steps be taken to achieve a single airlift command as soon as possible." General McLaughlin, who had commanded the 834th, called the Lindsay recommendation "just great." After some internal Air Force debating, Secretary of Defense James R. Schlesinger in the summer of 1974 directed that "the worldwide airlift mission, roles, resources, and responsibilities" be consolidated under the Military Airlift Command. Tactical Air Command C-130s in the United States were transferred to the Military Airlift Command in late 1974, overseas units in early 1975.[194]

Without generous tactical airlift, large numbers of helicopters, and a generally permissive hostile environment, the American campaigns in South Vietnam in 1965–68 could not have been conducted as they were, a fact that became suggestive in 1972 and starkly apparent in 1975. With the buildup of SA-7s, AAAs, and toward the end truck-borne SA-2 missiles, helicopters and tactical transports would not operate into areas where North Vietnamese troops were deployed. In American practice, when a unit set up a leapfrogging fire-support base, it helio-lifted in 105-mm howitzers very quickly, lowered the tubes, and blew away the vegetation and any enemy that might be lurking nearby. In Lam Son 719, the South Vietnamese did not do this, with the result that the enemy got in extremely close, and the helicopter liftships going in and out proved extremely vulnerable.[195] In General Momyer's analysis, the Vietnamization programming assigned VNAF too many helicopters (929 at the time of the Paris Agreement cease-fire), which could not be effectively used to shift ground units between military regions, both because of the density of enemy defenses and the lack of range, speed, and payload. "From a strategic viewpoint," Momyer concluded, "it is better to have fewer ground forces and have a fully developed tactical airlift force than it is to have an inadequate tactical airlift force that is unable to move ground units as the combat threat unfolds."[196] As the final collapse came in 1975, Col Le Minh Hoang, the last VNAF intelligence chief, pointed out that the "mobility balance" of the war had shifted sides — allied forces had lost their heliborne mobility while North Vietnamese moved openly on the roads in trucks.[197] What the effect of relatively cheap, portable surface-to-air missilery would be on fixed-wing airlift was not proven in the 1972 and 1975 experience. General Momyer contended that C-130 landings forward of a division base could well prove too dangerous. In the final evacuations from South Vietnam, however, C-5s and C-141s operated into Saigon and Da Nang under SAM threat, and the C-130s and C-141s that flew into Tan Son Nhut were outfitted with antiradiation devices to warn them against surface-to-air missiles. In the words of Gen Paul K. Carlton, Military Airlift Command's commander, MAC did not intend to expose the mammoth C-5 unless the risk was worth it: "We treat it very carefully and conservatively, but . . . if the risk is worth taking to win the battle, we will take it. . . . The answer . . . is, how much is it worth to us to do it? The JCS makes the decision on the use of the C-5 under almost all circumstances of risk."[198]

Evaluations of the Air War

In a message to Washington on 3 March 1962, Lt Gen Thomas S. Moorman, vice CINCPACAF, recommended that the time had come to secure an appropriate documentation of Air Force actions in Southeast Asia, both for support of immediate ongoing requirements and for eventual historical purposes. As a result of this recommendation, Pacific Air Forces on 30 June 1962 was directed to organize Project CHECO (Current Historical Evaluation of Counterinsurgency Operations) for the purpose of preparing a "continuing history of USAF operations in SE Asia." The Air Force allocated three personnel spaces (one lieutenant colonel, one major, and one civilian historian), and in this manning Lt Col Donald F. Martin went to the theater as chief of the project. On 1 May 1964 CHECO published a voluminous six-part *History of the War in Vietnam, October 1961–December 1963*.[199]

The initial CHECO report established the organization's importance and credibility at the same juncture that the escalation of operations in Southeast Asia made it advisable to Gen Hunter Harris, CINCPACAF, to expand evaluation efforts. Headed by Col Edward C. Burtenshaw, a CHECO division was established in 1965 under the Directorate of Tactical Evaluation, DCS Plans and Operations, PACAF; in Saigon a civilian historian, Kenneth Sams, headed the CHECO field establishment. In May 1965 *USAF Terms of Reference* expanded CINCPACAF responsibility for specialized historical documentation by Project CHECO to include reporting on all US Air Force combat operations, with the result that in the acronym CHECO the word *combat* replaced *counterinsurgency*. In the 1965 organizational change CHECO was reassigned from the PACAF Office of Information to the Directorate of Plans and Operations, a move Sams considered beneficial to the status of the project's work. In Washington, the Air Force's director of plans monitored CHECO, receiving and assigning Air Staff requests for special one-time reports and for other continuing reports prepared on a regular basis. Under normal circumstances, two-man field teams prepared special reports in about two months; on one study a team of four men prepared a study in less than three weeks. CHECO reports thus had immediate value, and Sams was quick to admit that they might lack historical perspective. He explained, "But we don't pretend to be historians. That's why our title specifically states 'contemporary historical evaluation.' Yet we do collect and study everything we can get and I think our studies are valuable in that they provide the 'feel' for an operation at the time it takes place. We literally become a part of an operation." In the summer of 1968 the CHECO staff in Saigon included five civilians, three officers, and two airmen research writers. These men were advantageously augmented during the summer months by instructors from the Air Force Academy who served on temporary duty with CHECO. In August 1968 the Air Force vice chief of staff designated CHECO as the single Air Force agency in the Pacific for the collection of documents, data, materials, and recordings of personal interviews in Southeast Asia. Once again the wording of the acronym CHECO was changed, becoming Contemporary Historical Examination of Current Operations.[200]

The major Air Force evaluation of air operations in Southeast Asia had its inception in a report in which Dr Charles Herzfeld, director of the Advanced Research Projects Agency, and Maj Gen Edward G. Lansdale, USAF, Retired, the special assistant to the US ambassador in Saigon, had discussed the feasibility of a major tactical bombing and firepower survey applicable to Southeast Asia, along the lines of the US Strategic Bombing Survey of World War II. Col Kemper N. Baker, chief of the ARPA Research and Development Field Unit, sat in on the discussion and on 24 November 1965 recommended that the Air Force initiate action, suggesting also that Lt Gen John W. Carpenter and the Air University ought to be called on for rules, framework, and guidance.[201] Although General Carpenter agreed that the Air University was in an "excellent position" to prepare an evaluation of air power in Southeast Asia, the staffing of the matter consumed almost a year. In Washington, Gen Bruce K. Holloway, Air Force vice chief of staff, wished to retain supervision of such an evaluation in his office and ultimately named a steering committee composed of senior officers from the Air Staff and headed by the vice chief to undertake this function. The Air University was determined to have certain advantages as a working agency: ideal facility and environment, students and faculty immediately available and qualified to assist in the task, historical documentation (already an assigned Air University function), and the likelihood that evaluation would enhance and complement the professional military education program. On 23 November 1966 General Holloway charged the Air University with the task of evaluating air power in Southeast Asia, the major objectives being to evaluate the effectiveness of air power; identify and define air power lessons learned; assess the validity of current concepts and doctrine in the light of the air power operations; recommend modifications of existing concepts and doctrine to ensure more effective applications of air power; and record US air power accomplishments for historical purpose. The Air Force steering committee would ensure integrated support of the evaluation by all Air Force agencies and provide broad policy guidance and direction to the Air University evaluation group to be organized in the Air University Aerospace Studies Institute. General Holloway further directed the Air Force's major commands to name project officers to support the objectives of the evaluation.[202]

In the Aerospace Studies Institute, Project Loyal Look—the code-name Loyal being the designator for the Air University—undertook to provide a plan for the evaluation to be implemented by 1 June 1967. The first step in the overall procedure naturally was the establishment of a data base. This was done initially by screening resources locally available at Maxwell AFB and then by requiring major command project officers to fill in and forward data base inventory (DABIN) sheets identifying pertinent documents. In the Air War College student research projects prepared papers on the politico-military situation in Southeast Asia; Air Command and Staff College seminars developed outlines of various applications of air power; and the Academic Instructor and Allied Officer School followed oral history procedures gotten from Columbia University and began an oral history program drawing information from men returned from combat. In their studies Air War College students met difficulties, since they lacked high-level classified information that was available only in Washington. Air Command and Staff students lacked enemy information: they could, for example, evaluate the efficiency of Arc Light B-52 strikes, but their information ended when bombs were dropped. The name Loyal Look seemed increasingly parochial. The steering committee stepped up to some of these problems. In the summer of 1967 an Aerospace Studies Institute group spent three months researching National Security Council and Joint Chiefs of Staff papers in Washington. This effort yielded a highly classified study of national policy which, as it turned out, was quite small in comparison with the many-volume OSD study of US-Vietnam relations. That study was in progress at the same time and would be leaked to the press as the "Pentagon Papers." The name Loyal Look was changed to Corona Harvest on 13 April 1967, Corona being the code name of the Air Force chief of staff and Harvest the particularized project code name. The Air Force made efforts to get MACV to send scout teams into target areas for the B-52s immediately following Arc Light strikes, but such evaluations more often than not yielded no firm evidence permitting any analysis of B-52 effectiveness.[203]

"One of the major problems the [Corona Harvest] project has encountered is how to measure the effectiveness of airpower as viewed by the enemy.... We need to assess our weapons and our strategy and tactics through the eyes, mind, and history of the enemy if the CORONA HARVEST evaluation is to be complete," noted Brig Gen Roger E. Phelan on 21 March 1968. A year before this, Rand analyst Amron H. Katz had pointed out that the Air Force could evaluate the "efficiency" of air operations but not the "effectiveness," since only the enemy—Ho Chi Minh and his cohorts—could tell the effect of air power on *their* plans and operations. Katz pointed out the need for a group of experts who could devote their efforts to thinking "full time like Ho Chi Minh and the VC."* Phelan asked that the Rand Corporation organize such a "Red Team," but Rand declined in view of a lack of qualified personnel and an inability to get delivery of needed high-level intelligence information.[204] Working on contract for Corona Harvest, the Battelle Memorial Institute prepared a chronological compendium, *Communist Policy Towards Southeast Asia, 1954–1969*, which was published with full recognition that public statements did not necessarily reflect true governmental intent or policy.[205] In addition to the problems of the enemy as the real source of evaluation, it was obvious early in the Corona Harvest project that evaluations of the effectiveness of air power in World War II had been largely the product of intensely personal experiences and views of the participants in the conflict. These varied views and experiences had permitted different interpretations.[206]

There had been earlier intimations that the Air University would use faculty and students to accomplish Corona Harvest evaluations, but this expectation collapsed when the steering committee decided to hold the work to "Air Force eyes only." Students at the Air University included officers from all services as well as friendly foreign officers. The ongoing plan, begun in mid-1967 and continued when Brig Gen Robert N. Ginsburgh took command of the Aerospace Studies Institute in May 1969, emphasized personal expertise to be drawn from throughout the Air Force. First, major commands and staff agencies would follow a standard format and prepare inputs on selected subjects covering the years 1965–68. This was soon expanded to include a second input from each command or agency covering mid-1968 through 1969. At the completion of the 1965–68 inputs, nine writing panels of experienced field grade officers would come to the Air University and

---

* Along these same lines but years earlier, the historian Douglas Southall Freeman had pointed out that Confederate Gen Robert E. Lee had required one of his staff officers to identify with and "think like" whichever Union Commander Lee was opposing at the time. This was made more simple in those days since many generals—North and South—had known each other as cadets at the Military Academy and later on active duty in the US Army.

IDEAS, CONCEPTS, DOCTRINE

prepare reports. As it turned out there would be activity inputs from 19 commands and agencies covering 47 functional areas grouped into tasks, hardware, personnel, support activities, and plans, concepts, and doctrine. After laying on this task, the steering committee decided that the years 1954–61 and 1961–64 should be covered and that this work would be done by persons assigned "in-house" to Corona Harvest. There would be command and agency activity reports for mid-1968 through 1969, and since it turned out that there were few new lessons or recommendations in this period, short reports were assembled by the Corona Harvest staff. The periods were designated as Phases I and II, 1954 to 1964; Phase III, 1964 to mid-1968; Phase IV, mid-1968 through 1969; and Phase V, 1970 to termination in 1973. Each Corona Harvest report was to be reviewed individually first by a verification panel of tactical and technical experts who would examine conclusions and lessons and then by a final review board of high-ranking officers. The steering committee dropped the plan for the final review board, inasmuch as it intended to make a final review of each report's lessons and recommendations. Here the vice chief of staff, sitting with the steering committee, would accept or reject the recommendations prior to appropriate staffing action by the Air Staff.[207]

In the beginning the Air Force and major commands gave generally unqualified support and cooperation to the Air University for Corona Harvest, but the continuation of the hostilities and Air Force manpower reductions made the mission in its broad-scale application quite burdensome. The Corona Harvest Steering Committee elected to continue to require staff and command inputs in Phase IV, mid-1968 through 1969, but Gen John C. Meyer, who had become vice chief of staff, raised a query as to what should be done after January 1970. After taking command of the Tactical Air Command, General Momyer considered that he had given strong support to Corona Harvest, including from July 1969 to December 1970 a minimum of 10,300 man-days in providing activity inputs and over 3,500 man-days in evaluation proceedings. In his view, the command inputs for Phase IV had findings that were substantially unchanged from previous periods, leading him to feel that Corona Harvest inputs should be terminated and further investigations narrowed to individual case studies, such as examinations of new hardware, tactics, or techniques not covered in adequate depth in previous reports or introduced during later time periods. In January 1971 General Meyer announced that the steering committee had decided to phase the Air University out of Corona Harvest but to continue to levy special individualized reports on interested major commands. These reports—which would be prepared mostly by the PACAF Directorate of Tactical Evaluation—would replace the across-the-board Corona Harvest coverage.[208]

The Corona Harvest Steering Committee began its consideration of the lessons learned and recommendations in the individual reports at almost the same juncture that the nation was wracked by the clandestine leak of the highly classified volumes subsequently known as the "Pentagon Papers." The temporary duty writing panels brought to the Air University had been encouraged to "tell it like it was," recognizing no "sacred cows." The resulting reports sometimes contained intemperate comments about people and policies and often took narrow views hardly representative of Air Force judgment. The verification panels clarified and cleaned up lessons learned and recommendations as needed, but the final reports were planned to be layered documents with the initial reports, verification actions, and steering committee reviews bound together. Alarmed lest some narrowly conceived comment should be somehow released to the public as an Air Force evaluation, General Meyer directed the Air University to rewrite the Corona Harvest reports in succinct language appropriately avoiding bombast. This project was completed by in-house Corona Harvest personnel in the year prior to mid-1973. As a result, the Air University Corona Harvest output numbered 11 final reports and 45 miscellaneous backup "working papers," these last items containing judgments and information not necessarily endorsed by the Air Force. Between 1970 and 1973, PACAF completed 12 working papers on subjects specified by the Corona Harvest Steering Committee.[209]

Since much of the basic work on the Corona Harvest reports had been done by Air Force staff and major commands, the burden of their findings had some early influence, as, for example, the airlift report's recommendations for a single airlift command, which were accepted in 1974. As was the case with General Meyer, Gen Horace M. Wade, Meyer's successor as vice chief of staff, was fearful that some unfortunate assertion in a working paper would be leaked and publicized as an Air Force finding. He also noticed parochial views of the Air Force commands that caused inconsistencies in different reports: Strategic Air Command versus Tactical Air Command biases, for example.[210] But Gen Richard H. Ellis, who followed Wade as vice chief, told the 4 June 1974 meeting of the Corona Harvest Steering Committee that he wanted the Air Force to use the lessons and recommendations from the reports. To this end he brought in General Momyer from retirement as his special consultant and charged him to review and appraise the lessons learned/recommendations of each Corona Harvest report from a senior commander's perspective. At the same time, Ellis directed Lt Gen Felix M. Rogers, Air University commander, to use three senior colonels as a review committee to read and recommend reductions of security classifications (many were top secret) of the Corona Harvest working papers. General Momyer's evaluations went fairly rapidly, and they were passed in packages by the Directorate of Doctrine, Concepts, and Objectives to the Air Staff for appropriate staffing.[211] With the passing of time, the Corona Harvest reports were also particularly valuable to General Momyer in preparing his book, *Airpower in Three Wars*.[212]

Although Corona Harvest developed and disseminated approximately 800 lessons learned/recommendations relevant to the Air Force in Southeast Asia, the project was — in the view of its two principal directors, Col John E. Van Duyn and Col Robert L. Gleason — unable to accomplish its principal purpose: a meaningful evaluation of overall air power effectiveness.[213] There were several contributing reasons, beginning with the failure of the Air Force reporting systems to provide meaningful data for evaluation. For the 1954–64 time phases, Colonel Gleason pointed out that the US Military Assistance Activity was generally outside Air

Force cognizance and no reasonable records existed about the buildup of the Vietnamese air force. Colonel Van Duyn described CHECO as the "best approach" for gathering data during the initial stages of Corona Harvest but said "there were problems connected with the combination of 'history' (which is concerned with gathering and recording data on a broad scale) and 'evaluation' (which focuses on narrower subjects) with CHECO. In the field, the CHECO organization was not capable of performing any high degree of definitive evaluation."[214] With the Air Force reporting system increasingly computerized, Van Duyn and Gleason both spoke of a need to define the kind of information that would be needed for broad evaluation efforts. In this regard, Gleason said that considerable enemy materiel was available to the Air Force during the Vietnam conflict but "was never conscientiously pursued or specifically gathered for the purpose of judging airpower effectiveness." Gleason concluded that "what is suggested here is that standard Air Force reporting procedures should be revised to ensure that we, the Air Force, will go out of our way to gather material and data customized to support effectiveness studies."[215]

To Colonel Gleason one of the "stark realities" of Corona Harvest was the identification of the fact that "airpower effectiveness and airpower efficiency were two different things." The old standards for measuring air power's effectiveness—sortie rates, number of bombs dropped, supplies airlanded, how quickly or how economically air power could perform tasks—had actually been standards of "efficiency," whereas "effectiveness" was measurable only in terms of impact of the performance of a task "on the enemy or the enemy's will to operate. Halting 90 percent of an enemy truck LOC would be less than 90 percent effective if the enemy only needed 5 percent of those trucks to sustain his operations."[216] Early in the Corona Harvest program, Lt Gen Albert P. Clarke, then commanding Air University, had argued that identification of lessons learned in Air Force staff and command inputs was not true evaluation looking toward an overall evaluation of air power. The identification of lessons learned concerned efficiency—not effectiveness. In Gleason's remembrance, the steering committee put Clarke's remonstrance on "the back burner," and each meeting passed the problem on to the next meeting so that the evaluation system "just sort of evolved." Both Gleason and Van Duyn agreed that the identification of "lesson learned" was well done. These lessons, however, were usually concerned with weak areas that were easily spotted. Making a recommendation about what to do about a lesson learned deficiency was another matter, since there might be several solutions to a particular problem, and the selection of a solution to one problem could well impact other problems. Van Duyn's solution was to divide identification from suggested solutions. He proposed that future Corona Harvest-type evaluations should concentrate on developing good, sound lessons learned. A higher order authority should take the lessons learned and develop recommendations from them.[217]

Probably the fundamental problem of evaluating the effectiveness of air power—or military power of any kind—in Southeast Asia was the lack of any precedence for such evaluation. Essentially, the conflict spectrum of a modern time includes, first, total nuclear war, second, conventional war, and third, guerrilla war or low-level conflict. In a nuclear age, in terms of total annihilation where there was no military experience, systems analysis of cost-effectiveness promised one method of evaluation but all efforts to quantify military effectiveness in countable aspects (enemy body count, for example) in Southeast Asia were failures. Similarly, conventional military experience derived from years of war in Europe from the Napoleonic Wars through World War II, between metropolitan equals, with people using the same conceptions of "victory" and "defeat," was not applicable to the fighting in Vietnam. As General Momyer ultimately concluded: "The nature of the terrain, character of the fighting, and lack of conventional battle lines prevented the traditional measures of effectiveness of tactical air."[218] Under these circumstances the evaluation of the effectiveness of air power was necessarily subjective, Momyer continued:

> The measure of effectiveness must be sought in subjective assessments of the effects air attack had on the ability of the enemy to sustain combat and what would have been the results if our own ground forces did not have air support.... I think we can measure how well our weapons perform, how well our pilots do and how good our doctrine is, but how effective we are remains a subjective matter.[219]

When all things were considered, judgments of effectiveness were "gut" feelings based on professional observations of enemy actions. Momyer concluded:

> I think the most fundamental accomplishment of airpower in the Vietnam war... was the restraint put on the level of forces the North Vietnamese could maintain in South Vietnam and the intensity and direction that these forces could sustain in battle. The combination of the interdiction campaign and the close air support prevented the enemy from deploying and maintaining a higher level of activity.... The North could have used much more sophisticated equipment in South Vietnam which later appeared in I Corps with the Easter offensive of 1972 if they could have supported those mechanized forces, SAMs and AAA. The stopping of the bombing in North Vietnam on October 31, 1968 permitted the North Vietnamese to move these more sophisticated forces in complete security to the DMZ where they were staged for the invasion of South Vietnam. The cessation of the interdiction campaign permitted this to happen.[220]

NOTES

1. Maj Gen Robert N. Ginsburgh, "Strategy and Airpower: The Lessons of Southeast Asia," *Strategic Review* 1 (Summer 1973): 19.

2. Maj Gen Richard A. Yudkin, "Vietnam: Policy, Strategy and Airpower," *Air Force* 56 (February 1973): 32.

3. Col Harry G. Summers, Jr., *On Strategy: A Critical Analysis of the Vietnam War* (Novato, Calif.: Presidio Press, 1982), passim; see also A. G. B. Metcalf, "Clausewitz Revisited, On Strategy: A Critical Analysis of the Vietnam War," in *Strategic Review*, Summer 1982, 65-67.

4. *Air Force Policy Letter for Commanders*, 1 May 1973; Gen George J. Eade, "Reflections on Air Power in the Vietnam War," *Air University Review*, November–December 1973, 8-9.

5. Gen George J. Eade, "USAF Prepares for Future Contingencies—The Lessons of Vietnam," *Air Force* 56 (June 1973): 34.

IDEAS, CONCEPTS, DOCTRINE

6. Summers, *On Strategy*, Foreword.
7. House, *Reorganization Proposals for the Joint Chiefs of Staff: Hearings before the Investigations Subcommittee of the Committee on Armed Services*, 97th Cong., 2d sess., 1982, 135.
8. See "Working Paper on the North Vietnamese Role in the War in South Vietnam," *Congressional Record*, 9 May 1968, 12614-20. See also Battelle Memorial Institute, *Communist Policy Towards Southeast Asia, 1954–1969, A Chronological Compendium* (Maxwell AFB, Ala.: Project Corona Harvest, 1970).
9. Robert F. Futrell, *The United States Air Force in Southeast Asia: The Advisory Years to 1965* (Washington, D.C.: Office of Air Force History, 1981), 37-38; Gen Frederic H. Smith, Jr., "Nuclear Weapons and Limited War," *Air University Quarterly Review*, Spring 1962, 3-27.
10. Futrell, *US Air Force in Southeast Asia*, 68-69.
11. Ibid., 76.
12. Gen T. R. Milton, USAF, Retired, "How We Backed into Vietnam," *Air Force*, May 1978, 33.
13. Futrell, *US Air Force in Southeast Asia*, 88-90.
14. Gen T. R. Milton, USAF, Retired, "Dissent and the Soldier," *Strategic Review*, Spring 1979, 19; Milton, "How We Backed into Vietnam," 33.
15. Robert F. Futrell, "Air Power against Insurgency in Southeast Asia, 1950–1965," in *A Quarter Century of Air Power*, ed., John H. Scrivner, Jr. (Maxwell AFB, Ala.: Air Force ROTC, 1973), 125-26; Gen William W. Momyer, USAF, Retired, *Airpower in Three Wars* (Washington, D.C.: Department of Air Force, 1978), 11-12.
16. Momyer, *Airpower in Three Wars*, 11; Col Robert L. Gleason, "Quo Vadis? — The Nixon Doctrine and Air Power," *Air University Review*, July–August 1972, 46-56.
17. Momyer, *Airpower in Three Wars*, 12-14; Futrell, *US Air Force in Southeast Asia*, 119.
18. Momyer, *Airpower in Three Wars*, 19.
19. Henry F. Graff, *The Tuesday Cabinet: Deliberation and Decision on Peace and War under Lyndon B. Johnson* (Englewood Cliffs, N.J.: Prentice-Hall Inc., 1970), 87.
20. Senate, *Supplemental Defense Appropriations for Fiscal Year 1966: Hearings before the Committee on Appropriations and the Committee on Armed Services*, 89th Cong., 2d sess., 1966, 151-54, 157, 178-79.
21. Adm U. S. Grant Sharp, *Strategy for Defeat, Vietnam in Retrospect* (San Rafael, Calif.: Presidio Press, 1976), 86-87.
22. Lyndon Baines Johnson, *The Vantage Point, Perspectives of the Presidency, 1963–1969* (New York: Holt, Rinehart, and Winston, 1971), 518-28.
23. Senate, *Supplemental Defense Appropriations and Authorizations, Fiscal Year 1967: Hearings before the Subcommittee on Department of Defense of the Committee on Appropriations and Committee on Armed Services*, 90th Cong., 1st sess., 1967, 13, 20.
24. Unless otherwise cited the description of the ground campaign is based on Adm U. S. Grant Sharp and Gen William C. Westmoreland, *Report on the War in Vietnam (as of 30 June 1968)* (Washington, D.C.: Government Printing Office, 1969), sec. 2.
25. *U.S. Department of State Bulletin*, vol. 57:785-88.
26. Douglas Pike, *War, Peace, and the Viet Cong* (Cambridge: Massachusetts Institute of Technology Press, 1969), 124-26; Patrick J. McGarvey, *Visions of Victory* (Stanford, Calif.: Stanford University, 1969), 40-46, 199-251; Dave Richard Palmer, *Summons of the Trumpet, U.S.–Vietnam in Perspective* (Novato, Calif.: Presidio Press, 1978), 163-81.
27. History Section Republic of Vietnam Armed Forces, *The Vietnam Cong "Tet" Offensive (1968)* (Saigon: RVNAF Printing and Publications Center, ca. July 1969); Capt Moyers S. Sho II, *The Battle for Khe Sanh* (Washington, D.C.: Historical Branch, US Marine Corps, 1969); William H. Greenhalgh, Sr., *AOK, Air Power over Khe Sanh* (Maxwell AFB, Ala.: Aerospace Studies Institute, 1970); Bernard C. Nalty, *Air Power and the Fight for Khe Sanh* (Washington, D.C.: Office of Air Force History, 1973).
28. Sharp, *Strategy for Defeat*, 214-18.
29. Townsend Hoopes, *The Limits of Intervention* (New York: David McKay Co., Inc., 1969), 65-66.
30. Momyer, *Airpower in Three Wars*, 28.

31. Ibid., 28-29; Johnson, *Vantage Point*, 516; Graff, *The Tuesday Cabinet*, 164.

32. Senate, *Fiscal Year 1970 Military Procurement Authorization, Research and Development, and Reserve Strength: Hearings before the Committee on Armed Services*, 91st Cong., 1st sess., 1969, 336-37; Henry Kissinger, *White House Years* (Boston: Little, Brown & Co., 1970), 241.

33. Senate, *Bombing in Cambodia: Hearings before the Committee on Armed Services*, 93d Cong., 1st sess., 1973, 445-46.

34. Senate, *Briefing on Vietnam: Hearings before the Committee on Foreign Relations, with Secretary of State William P. Rogers and Secretary of Defense Melvin R. Laird*, 91st Cong., 1st sess., 1969, passim.

35. Momyer, *Airpower in Three Wars*, 29-30; Kissinger, *White House Years*, 241.

36. Kissinger, *White House Years*, 239-54; "Department of Defense Report on Selected Air and Ground Operations in Cambodia and Laos," in Senate, *Bombing in Cambodia*, 481-94.

37. Kissinger, *White House Years*, 505-9; Futrell, "Air Power against Insurgency in Southeast Asia, 1950–1965," 185–86.

38. Kissinger, *White House Years*, 990-1010; Momyer, *Airpower in Three Wars*, 321-24.

39. Momyer, *Airpower in Three Wars*, 323-24; Senate, *Close Air Support: Hearings before the Special Subcommittee on Close Air Support of the Preparedness Investigating Subcommittee of the Committee on Armed Services*, 92d Cong., 1st sess., 1971, 143-45.

40. "The President's News Conference on Foreign Policy, March 4, 1971," in *Public Papers of the Presidents of the United States: Richard Nixon, 1971* (Washington, D.C.: Government Printing Office, 1971), 388.

41. Senate, *Nomination of John D. Lavelle, General Creighton W. Abrams, and Admiral John S. McCain: Hearings before the Committee on Armed Services*, 92d Cong., 2d sess., 1972, 443.

42. Ibid., 294-95, 451-52; Maj A. J. C. Lavalle, ed., *Airpower and the 1972 Spring Invasion*, USAF Southeast Asia Monograph Series, vol. 2, monograph 3 (Washington, D.C.: Government Printing Office), 3.

43. Senate, *Nomination of John D. Lavelle, General Creighton W. Abrams, and Admiral John S. McCain*, 23-99; Senate, *Certain Nominations in the Air Force and the Navy: Hearings before the Committee on Armed Services*, 93d Cong., 1st sess., 1973, 2, 17, 33; House, *Department of Defense Appropriations for 1973: Hearings before a Subcommittee of the Committee on Appropriations*, 92d Cong., 2d sess., 1972, pt. 2:3-6 (hereafter cited as *1973 DOD Appropriations*).

44. House, *1973 DOD Appropriations*, pt. 3:377.

45. Gen William W. Momyer, *The Vietnamese Air Force, 1951–1975, An Analysis of Its Role in Combat*, USAF Southeast Asia Monograph Series, vol. 3, monograph 4 (Washington, D.C.: Government Printing Office), 42; W. Scott Thompson and Donaldson D. Frizzell, eds., *The Lessons of Vietnam* (New York: Crane, Russak & Co., 1977), 161.

46. Lavalle, *Airpower and the 1972 Spring Invasion*, 1.

47. Ibid., 4-14; Momyer, *The Vietnamese Air Force*, 45-50.

48. Lavalle, *Airpower and the 1972 Spring Invasion*, 15-30; Douglas Kinnard, *The War Managers* (Hanover, N.H.: University of Vermont, 1977), 150; Momyer, *Airpower in Three Wars*, 326-33.

49. Elmo R. Zumwalt, Jr., *On Watch, A Memoir* (New York: Quadrangle/New York Time Book Co., 1976), 383-89; Edgar Ulsamer, "Airpower Halts an Invasion," *Air Force Magazine*, September 1972, 60-71; Gen Richard H. Ellis and Lt Col Frank B. Horton III, "Flexibility—A State of Mind," *Strategic Review* 4 (Winter 1976): 28-30; Thompson and Frizzell, *The Lessons of Vietnam*, 164-66; House, *Department of Defense Appropriations for 1950: Hearings before a Subcommittee of the Committee on Appropriations*, pt. 1:315.

50. Lavalle, *Airpower and the 1972 Spring Invasion*, 106.

51. Kinnard, *The War Managers*, 150-51; "Airpower Is Proving Itself," *Air Force Policy Letter for Commanders*, 1 September 1972.

52. Momyer, *Airpower in Three Wars*, 333.

53. Sharp, *Strategy for Defeat*, 251-52; Senate, *Fiscal Year 1974 Military Procurement Authorization, Research and Development, Construction Authorization for the Safeguard ABM, and Active Duty and*

IDEAS, CONCEPTS, DOCTRINE

Selected Reserve Strengths: Hearings before the Committee on Armed Services, 93d Cong., 1st sess., 1973, pt. 6:499 (hereafter cited as *FY 1974 Military Procurement*).

54. Brig Gen James R. McCarthy and Lt Col George B. Allison, *Linebacker II: A View from the Rock* (Maxwell AFB, Ala.: Airpower Research Institute, 1979), passim, 139.

55. Ibid.; Eade, "USAF Prepares for Future Contingencies – The Lessons of Vietnam," 35; Sharp, *Strategy for Defeat*, 254; *Air Force Policy Letter for Commanders*, 6-9 November 1973, 9; Senate, *FY 1974 Military Procurement*, pt. 1:373.

56. McCarthy and Allison, *Linebacker II: A View from the Rock*, 172-73.

57. Kinnard, *The War Managers*, 152; Daniel S. Papp, *Vietnam: The View from Moscow, Peking, and Washington* (Jefferson, N.C.: McFarland & Co., 1981), 142-45.

58. Copies of these letters were released in Saigon by Nguyen Tien Hung, former minister of planning, and were printed in the *New York Times*, 1 May 1975, 16.

59. House, *Department of Defense Appropriations for 1974: Hearings before a Subcommittee of the Committee on Appropriations*, 93d Cong., 1st sess., 1973, pt. 1:153, 159, 171 (hereafter cited as *1974 DOD Appropriations*).

60. Ibid., pt. 2:208, 210.

61. P. Edward Haley, *Congress and the Fall of South Vietnam and Cambodia* (Rutherford, N.J.: Fairleigh Dickinson University Press, 1982), passim; Sharp, *Strategy for Defeat*, 262-64.

62. Richard Nixon, *The Real War* (New York: Warner Books, 1980), 123.

63. House, *Department of Defense Appropriations for 1975: Hearings before a Subcommittee of the Committee on Appropriations*, 94th Cong., 1st sess., 1975, 9 (hereafter cited as *1975 DOD Appropriations*).

64. Ibid., 5-8.

65. Kinnard, *The War Managers*, 154-55.

66. Ibid., 155-56; Momyer, *The Vietnamese Air Force*, 58-59, 68-69; *Air Force Policy Letter for Commanders*, August 1975, 18.

67. Momyer, *The Vietnamese Air Force*, 60-69; House, *1974 DOD Appropriations*, pt. 2:49; House, *1975 DOD Appropriations*, 95-96, 86, 92, 105.

68. Momyer, *The Vietnamese Air Force*, 70-73; House, *1975 DOD Appropriations*, 9-13; House, *Department of Defense Appropriations for 1976: Hearings before a Subcommittee of the Committee on Appropriations*, 94th Cong., 1st sess., 1975, pt. 1:61-62, 77-78; Lavalle, *Airpower and the 1972 Spring Invasion*, 104.

69. Momyer, *The Vietnamese Air Force*, 74-78; Lt Cols Thomas G. Tobin, Arthur E. Laehr, and John F. Hilgenberg, *Last Flight from Saigon*, USAF Southeast Asia Monograph Series, vol. 4, monograph 6 (Washington, D.C.: Government Printing Office, 1978), 14-19.

70. Haley, *Congress and the Fall of South Vietnam and Cambodia*, 151-52.

71. Tobin et al., *Last Flight from Saigon*, passim.

72. Ibid., 7.

73. Adrian Hill, "Air War Over Vietnam," *Royal United Services Institute for Defence Studies*, December 1976, 30.

74. Momyer, *The Vietnamese Air Force*, 79-81; Tobin et al., *Last Flight from Saigon*, 70, 116-17.

75. House, *Department of Defense Appropriations for 1982: Hearings before a Subcommittee of the Committee on Appropriations*, 94th Cong., 1st sess., 1981, pt. 1:355.

76. Department of the Air Force, Doctrine Information Publication 10: Background Information on Air Force Perspective for Coherent Plans (Command and Control of TACAIR), April 1981, atch. 2: Background Paper on Joint Organizations in Plans by Col D. R. McNabb, Headquarters USAF/XOXID, 27 March 1981.

77. Senate, *Close Air Support*, 249.

78. Richard H. Kohn and Joseph P. Harahan, eds., *Air Superiority in World War II and Korea: An Interview with Gen James Ferguson, Gen Robert M. Lee, Gen William Momyer, and Lt Gen Elwood R. Quesada* (Washington, D.C.: Office of Air Force History, 1983), 69-72.

79. BMD Corporation, *A Study of Strategic Lessons Learned in Vietnam*, vol. 4, *Conduct of the War*, book 2, "Functional Analyses," rev. ed. (McLean, Va.: BMD Corporation, 1981), 11-46.

80. Futrell, *US Air Force in Southeast Asia*, 46-47. These matters are more fully developed in the draft manuscript of this published history which was greatly truncated before publication.

81. Momyer, *Airpower in Three Wars*, 65-66.

82. House, *Military Posture Briefings: Hearings before the Committee on Armed Services*, 89th Cong., 2d sess., 1966, 7609-10.

83. Futrell, *US Air Force in Southeast Asia*, 65-66.

84. Gen William C. Westmoreland, *A Soldier Reports* (Garden City, N.Y.: Doubleday & Co., 1976), 76-77.

85. Momyer, *Airpower in Three Wars*, 84-85.

86. Sharp, *Strategy for Defeat*, 36-38; Westmoreland, *A Soldier Reports*, 77; Gen Maxwell D. Taylor, *Swords and Plowshares* (New York: W. W. Norton & Co., 1972).

87. Momyer, *Airpower in Three Wars*, 66-70; Futrell, *US Air Force in Southeast Asia*, 94-97.

88. Momyer, *Airpower in Three Wars*, 71-73.

89. Maj Gen George S. Eckhardt, *Vietnam Studies: Command and Control, 1950–1969* (Washington, D.C.: Department of the Army, 1974), 25-37; Lt Col John J. Lane, Jr., *Command and Control and Communications Structures in Southeast Asia* (Maxwell AFB, Ala.: Air University, 1981), 39-44.

90. Momyer, *Airpower in Three Wars*, 73-75.

91. Futrell, *US Air Force in Southeast Asia*, 208.

92. Eckhardt, *Vietnam Studies*, 38-42; Momyer, *Airpower in Three Wars*, 76-81.

93. Momyer, *Airpower in Three Wars*, 81-84.

94. Lane, *Command and Control*, 42-46.

95. Momyer, *Airpower in Three Wars*, 81-82, 88-106.

96. Ibid., 284-87, 309; Westmoreland, *A Soldier Reports*, 342-43; Kinnard, *The War Managers*, 61-62.

97. Momyer, *Airpower in Three Wars*, 309.

98. Westmoreland, *A Soldier Reports*, 343; Kinnard, *The War Managers*, 62.

99. Momyer, *Airpower in Three Wars*, 316-17; Nalty, *Air Power and the Fight for Khe Sanh*, 68-81.

100. Nalty, *Air Power and the Fight for Khe Sanh*, 68-81; Westmoreland, *A Soldier Reports*, 343-44; Department of the Air Force, Doctrine Information Publication 10, April 1981, atch. 2.

101. George Weiss, "TAC Air: Present and Future Lessons, Problems, and Needs," *Armed Forces Journal*, September 1971, 36.

102. Department of the Air Force, Doctrine Information Publication 10, April 1981, atch. 2.

103. Lt Gen K. B. McCutcheon, USMC, "Marine Aviation in Vietnam, 1962–1970," *US Naval Institute Proceedings*, May 1971, 137.

104. Momyer, *Airpower in Three Wars*, 274-75; *Air Force Policy Letter for Commanders: Supplement*, December 1975, 29-30.

105. Momyer, *Airpower in Three Wars*, 89-98.

106. Ibid., 98-107.

107. Tobin et al., *Last Flight from Saigon*, 3-5; House, *Department of Defense Appropriation for 1975: Hearings before a Subcommittee of the Committee on Appropriations*, 93d Cong., 2d sess., 1974, pt. 2:323-24.

108. Tobin et al., *Last Flight from Saigon*, passim; Capt Thomas D. Des Brisay, *Fourteen Hours at Koh Tang*, USAF Southeast Asia Monograph Series, vol. 3, monograph 5 (Washington, D.C.: Government Printing Office, 1977), passim; "Pacific Air Forces," *Air Force*, May 1976, 72-73.

109. Senate, *U.S. Tactical Air Power Program: Hearings before the Preparedness Investigating Subcommittee of the Committee on Armed Services*, 90th Cong., 2d sess., 1968, 190-93; Senate, *FY 1974 Military Procurement*, pt. 6:4076-77.

110. Senate, *Department of Defense Appropriations for Fiscal Year 1967: Hearings before a Subcommittee of the Committee on Appropriations*, 89th Cong., 2d sess., 1966, pt. 2:355; Senate, *Fiscal Year 1977 Military Procurement Authorization, Research and Development, Construction: Hearings*

IDEAS, CONCEPTS, DOCTRINE

before the Committee on Armed Services, Authorization for the Safeguard ABM, and Active Duty and Selected Reserve Strengths, 94th Cong., 2d sess., 1976, 4916 (hereafter cited as *FY 1977 Military Procurement*).

111. Momyer, *Airpower in Three Wars*, 125-26.

112. House, *Department of Defense Appropriations for 1972: Hearings before a Subcommittee of the Committee on Appropriations*, 92d Cong., 1st sess., 1971, pt. 5:1095.

113. Weiss, "TAC Air," 31.

114. Unless otherwise indicated the summary of air activity over North Vietnam in this section is based on the first chapter of *Aces and Aerial Victories: The United States Air Force in Southeast Asia, 1965–1973* (Washington, D.C.: Office of Air Force History, 1976), 1-17; Momyer, *Airpower in Three Wars*, 118, 140; Westmoreland, *A Soldier Reports*, 120.

115. Momyer, *Airpower in Three Wars*, 118-19, 154-55.

116. Senate, *FY 1974 Military Procurement*, pt. 6:4077.

117. Momyer, *Airpower in Three Wars*, 127-29; Senate, *FY 1974 Military Procurement*, 4576-77.

118. Momyer, *Airpower in Three Wars*, 130-32; Senate, *FY 1974 Military Procurement*, 4577.

119. Senate, *FY 1974 Military Procurement*, 4391-92; Momyer, "Tactical Air Power," *Ordnance*, November–December 1969, 302; Momyer, *Airpower in Three Wars*, 142-45.

120. Momyer, *Airpower in Three Wars*, 145-47; Senate, *FY 1974 Military Procurement*, 4392-93.

121. Momyer, *Airpower in Three Wars*, 126-27; Senate, *FY 1974 Military Procurement*, pt. 6:4579.

122. Senate, *FY 1974 Military Procurement*, pt. 6:4579.

123. Ibid., 4579, 4393; Senate, *U.S. Tactical Airpower Program: Hearings before the Preparedness Investigating Subcommittee of the Committee on Armed Services*, 90th Cong., 2d sess., 1968, 78.

124. Senate, *FY 1974 Military Procurement*, 4393; Momyer, *Airpower in Three Wars*, 154-55.

125. Senate, *FY 1974 Military Procurement*, 4393-94; Momyer, *Airpower in Three Wars*, 127-30.

126. Senate, *FY 1974 Military Procurement*, 4402-3.

127. Ibid., 4408-13.

128. Ibid., 4393; Senate, *Fiscal Year 1975 Military Procurement, Authorization, Research and Development, and Active Duty, Selected Reserve and Civilian Personnel Strengths: Hearings before the Committee on Armed Services*, 93d Cong., 2d sess., 1974, pt. 8:4154 (hereafter cited as *FY 1975 Military Procurement*).

129. Senate, *FY 1974 Military Procurement*, 4394; Momyer, *Airpower in Three Wars*, 155.

130. Senate, *FY 1975 Military Procurement*, 4153.

131. Senate, *Department of Defense Appropriations for Fiscal Year 1975: Hearings before a Subcommittee of the Committee on Appropriations*, 93d Cong., 2d sess., 1974, pt. 1:101.

132. McCarthy and Allison, *Linebacker II: A View from the Rock*, passim; Senate, *FY 1974 Military Procurement*, 4580-81, 4702-4, 4670-73.

133. McCarthy and Allison, *Linebacker II: A View from the Rock*, 97-98, 151, 171-72.

134. Momyer, *Airpower in Three Wars*, 155.

135. Senate, *FY 1974 Military Procurement*, 4389.

136. Ibid., 4394-95.

137. House, *Department of Defense Appropriations for 1978: Hearings before a Subcommittee of the Committee on Appropriations*, 95th Cong., 1st sess., 1977, pt. 3:603.

138. Col Herman L. Gilster, "Air Interdiction in Protracted War," *Air University Review*, May–June 1977, 3.

139. Senate, *Close Air Support*, 174-75, 224. Pages 173-249 of these hearings are the statement and testimony of Gen W. W. Momyer, USAF, commander, Tactical Air Command.

140. Ibid.

141. Milton, "How We Backed into Vietnam," *US Air Force*, 33; Futrell, *US Air Force in Southeast Asia*, 85-91.

142. Lt Gen Thomas S. Moorman, USAF, Retired, to chief, Histories Division, Office of Air Force History, 22 June 1972.

143. Momyer, *Airpower in Three Wars*, 258-70.

144. "Concept for Improved Joint Air-Ground Coordination," in *Air Force Policy Letter for Commanders: Supplement*, June 1965, 27-32.

145. Col John Schlight, "USAF in Southeast Asia: South Vietnam, 1965–1968," history manuscript, Office of Air Force History, 64.

146. Senate, *Close Air Support*, 199.

147. Momyer, *Airpower in Three Wars*, 278; McCutcheon, "Marine Aviation in Vietnam," 137.

148. Senate, *Department of Defense Appropriations for Fiscal Year 1970: Hearings before a Subcommittee of the Committee on Appropriations*, 91st Cong., 1st sess., 1969, pt. 6:63; Momyer, *Airpower in Three Wars*, 283.

149. Senate, *Close Air Support*, 224-25.

150. W. Scott Thompson and Donaldson D. Frizzell, eds., *The Lessons of Vietnam* (New York: Crane, Russak & Co., 1977), 137-39.

151. House, *Department of Defense Appropriations for 1968: Hearings before a Subcommittee of the Committee on Appropriations*, 90th Cong., 1st sess., 1967, pt. 2:43; Sharp and Westmoreland, *Report on the War in Vietnam*, 171.

152. Kinnard, *The War Managers*, 46-49; *Air Force Policy Letter for Commanders*, 15 January 1969.

153. Alain C. Enthoven and K. Wayne Smith, *How Much Is Enough? Shaping the Defense Program, 1961–1969* (New York: Harper & Row, 1971), 305.

154. Kohn and Harahan, eds., *Air Superiority in World War II and Korea*, 69-70.

155. Bruce Palmer, ed., *Grand Strategy for the 1980s* (Washington, D.C.: American Enterprise Institute for Public Policy Research, 1978), 67.

156. Kinnard, *The War Managers*, 46.

157. Senate, *Supplemental Defense Appropriations for Fiscal Year 1966*, 84-85; Momyer, *Airpower in Three Wars*, 173.

158. Address of Gen John P. McConnell, chief of staff, US Air Force, to Detroit Economics Club, 6 December 1965, *Air Force Policy Letter for Commanders: Supplement*, January 1966, 3-4.

159. Senate, *Supplemental Defense Appropriations and Authorizations for Fiscal Year 1967*, 13-95.

160. Momyer, *Airpower in Three Wars*, 237.

161. Thompson and Frizzell, eds., *The Lessons of Vietnam*, 141-43.

162. Ibid.

163. Momyer, *Airpower in Three Wars*, 237.

164. Ibid., 85-86, 175-77, 217-18; House, *1973 DOD Appropriations*, pt. 1:54.

165. Momyer, *Airpower in Three Wars*, 190, 199-200.

166. House, Committee on Armed Services, *United States-Vietnam Relations*, book 6, vol. 1, Committee Print, 149-80; Senate, *Investigation into Electronic Battlefield Program: Hearings before the Electronic Battlefield Subcommittee of the Preparedness Investigating Subcommittee of the Committee on Armed Services*, 91st Cong., 2d sess., 1970, 3-6.

167. Robert F. Futrell, "Air Power against North Vietnamese Aggression, 1965–1971," in *A Quarter Century of Air Power*, Scrivner, 176-77; Senate, *Air War against North Vietnam: Hearings before the Preparedness Investigating Subcommittee of the Committee on Armed Services*, 90th Cong., 1st sess., 1967, pt. 2:124-28, 130, 132-33, 136, 139-40, 143-44, 166, 168, 192-93.

168. Senate, *Investigation into Electronic Battlefield Program*, 8-11; Momyer, *Airpower in Three Wars*, 211-12. See also Jack S. Ballard, *Development and Employment of Fixed-Wing Gunships, 1962–1972: The United States Air Force in Southeast Asia* (Washington, D.C.: Office of Air Force History, 1982), passim.

169. Futrell, "Air Power against North Vietnamese Aggression," 177.

170. Ibid., 177-78; Hoopes, *The Limits of Intervention*, 176-77.

171. Senate, *Investigation into Electronic Battlefield Program*, 106-7.

172. Col Herman L. Gilster, "Air Interdiction in Protracted War, An Economic Evaluation," *Air University Review*, May–June 1977, 3-18.

173. Ibid., 11; Gilster, "The Commando Hunt V Interdiction Campaign: A Case Study in Constrained Optimization," *Air University Review*, January–February 1978, 25.

IDEAS, CONCEPTS, DOCTRINE

174. Momyer, *Airpower in Three Wars*, 214.
175. Enthoven and Smith, *How Much Is Enough?*, 304-5.
176. Gilster, "Air Interdiction in Protracted War," 16.
177. Ray L. Bowers, *Tactical Airlift: The United States Air Force in Southeast Asia* (Washington, D.C.: Office of Air Force History, 1983), vii-viii.
178. Ibid.
179. Senate, *Department of Defense Appropriations for Fiscal Year 1968: Hearings before a Subcommittee of the Committee on Appropriations*, 90th Cong., 1st sess., 1967, 825.
180. Jac Weller, "Lessons from Vietnam," *National Guardsman*, April 1973, 7.
181. Senate, *Close Air Support*, 51-52, 240.
182. Senate, *Department of Defense Appropriations for FY 1965: Hearings before the Subcommittee on Department of Defense of the Committee on Appropriations and the Committee on Armed Services*, 88th Cong., 2d sess., 1964, pt. 1:729 (hereafter cited as *FY 1965 DOD Appropriations*).
183. Senate, *Close Air Support*, 136.
184. Senate, *FY 1965 DOD Appropriations*, 729.
185. House, *Department of Defense Appropriations for 1966: Hearings before a Subcommittee of the Committee on Appropriations*, 89th Cong., 1st sess., 1965, pt. 3:846.
186. Bowers, *Tactical Airlift*, 23-39; Frederic A. Bergerson, *The Army Gets an Air Force* (Baltimore: Johns Hopkins University Press, 1980), 117-20.
187. Momyer, *Airpower in Three Wars*, 214; Schlight, "USAF in Southeast Asia: South Vietnam, 1965–1968," 223-27.
188. Momyer, "Observations of the Vietnam War," quoted in Lt Col Jimmy L. Jay, "Evolution of Airlift Doctrine," Report 93 (Maxwell AFB, Ala.: Air War College, March 1977), 60-61.
189. Ibid., 61; House, *Military Airlift: Hearings before the Subcommittee on Military Airlift of the Committee on Armed Services*, 91st Cong., 2d sess., 1970, 6366-81; Bowers, *Tactical Airlift*, 241-67.
190. Bowers, *Tactical Airlift*, 383-85.
191. Ibid., 654.
192. House, *Military Airlift*, 6388.
193. Momyer, "Observations of the Vietnam War," 59-60.
194. Bowers, *Tactical Airlift*, 649-50.
195. Weller, "Lessons from Vietnam," 7; Senate, *Close Air Support*, 144.
196. Momyer, *The Vietnamese Air Force*, 65; Bowers, *Tactical Airlift*, 639.
197. Bowers, *Tactical Airlift*, 640.
198. Ibid., 652; House, *Hearings on the Posture of Military Airlift before the Research and Development Subcommittee of the Committee on Armed Services*, 94th Cong., 1st sess., 1975, 88.
199. Col Edward C. Burtenshaw, chief, Project CHECO, to Col Thomas B. Kennedy, Pacific Air Forces, Tactical Evaluation Center, 16 November 1965; Edward T. Russell, *Research Guide to the Published Project CHECO Reports, 1964–1976* (Maxwell AFB, Ala.: Historical Research Center, July 1976), 1.
200. Gen John C. Meyer, vice chief of staff, US Air Force, to commander in chief, Pacific Air Forces, letter, subject: Update of Project CHECO Terms of Reference, 30 August 1969; Lt Col William L. Brantley, "CHECO Is Its Name," *Airman Magazine*, July 1968, 32-35; Sgt Richard Liefer, "CHECO, War History Recorded as Combat Continues," *Air Force Times*, 8 April 1970, 30.
201. Col Kemper W. Baker, commander, Advance Research Project Agency, R&D Field Unit, to Maj Gen Andrew Kinney, assistant deputy chief of staff, Research and Development, US Air Force, letter, subject: USAF Tactical Bombing and Firepower Survey, Vietnam, 24 November 1965.
202. Lt Gen John W. Carpenter, commander, Air University, to Headquarters USAF/XDC, Lt Gen K. K. Compton, letter, subject: Evaluation of the Effectiveness of Airpower in Southeast Asia, 4 February 1966; Brig Gen Richard A. Yudkin, director, Doctrine, Concepts, and Objectives, Deputy Chief of Staff, Plans and Operations, to Lt Gen K. K. Compton, Headquarters USAF/XDC, letter, 18 August 1966; Col B. P. Gibson, Headquarters USAF/XODI to Headquarters USAF/XDO, letter, subject: Visit of Colonel Gibson and Maj Van Cleave to Air University, 14 November 1966; General

Bruce Holloway to Air Staff, letter, subject: Evaluation of Airpower in SEA, 23 November 1966; Holloway to TAC et al., letter, subject: Evaluation of Effectiveness of Airpower in SEA, 23 November 1966; Holloway to Air University, letter, subject: Evaluation of the Effectiveness of Airpower in Southeast Asia, 23 November 1966.

203. Minutes, Third Meeting of USAF Steering Committee, 28 March 1967; Brig Gen Richard A. Yudkin, director, Doctrine, Concepts, and Objectives, to General Holloway, Headquarters USAF/CVC, letter, subject: Nickname to Replace Loyal Look, 3 April 1967; Corona Harvest Newsletter, 30 April 1968; memorandum by Leslie H. Gelb, chairman, Office of Secretary of Defense, to secretary of defense, Task Force, subject: Final Report, OSD Vietnam Task Force, 15 January 1969, in *United States Vietnam Relations, 1945–1967*, study prepared by the Department of Defense, printed for the House, Committee on Armed Services (Washington, D.C.: Government Printing Office, 1971), 12 vols.

204. Brig Gen Roger E. Phelan, commander, Aerospace Studies Institute, to Headquarters USAF/RDQ, letter, subject: Project RAND Support for Project CORONA HARVEST, 21 March 1968; Maj Gen William G. Moore, Jr., director, Operational Requirements and Development Plans, Deputy Chief of Staff, Research and Development, to Henry S. Rowen, Jr., Project RAND, letter, 29 March 1968; Rowen to Moore, letter, 29 April 1968.

205. *Communist Policy Towards Southeast Asia, 1954–1969, A Chronological Compendium*, iii.

206. Commentary by Robert F. Futrell on Noble Frankland, "The Combined Bomber Offensive: Classical and Revolutionary, Combined and Divided, Planned and Fortuitous," in *Command and Commanders in Modern Military History* (Washington, D.C.: Office of Air Force History, US Air Force Academy, 1968), 284–86.

207. Corona Harvest Newsletter, 30 April 1968; "SEA Airpower's Effectiveness Weighed," *Air Force Times*, 9 June 1971, 21; memorandum by Col Vernon K. Cammack, vice commander, Aerospace Studies Institute, to Lt Gen Albert P. Clark, commander, Air University, 22 September 1969.

208. Gen William W. Momyer, commander, Tactical Air Command, to Gen John C. Meyer, Air Force vice chief of staff, 31 December 1970; Gen John C. Meyer to commander in chief, Pacific Air Forces, letter, subject: Project Corona Harvest, 26 January 1971.

209. Robert L. Gleason, commander, Corona Harvest project office, End of Mission Report (The Anatomy of an Airpower Evaluation), July 1973; Lt Col E. J. Wakham, Headquarters USAF/XODD, Point Paper on Corona Harvest Consultant, 31 May 1974; Maj A. J. C. Lavalle, Headquarters USAF/XODDD, Point Paper on Corona Harvest Documentation, 20 February 1975.

210. Oral History, Gen Horace M. Wade, Office of Air Force History, 10–12 October 1978.

211. History, Directorate of Doctrine, Concepts, and Objectives, January–June 1964, 51; point papers by Wakham and Lavalle in note 209.

212. Momyer, *Airpower in Three Wars*.

213. Col John E. Van Duyn, chief, Project Corona Harvest, to commander, Air University, letter, subject: End of Tour Report, 16 March 1972; Robert L. Gleason, chief, Project Corona Harvest, to commander, AU, letter, subject: End of Mission Report (The Anatomy of an Airpower Evaluation), July 1973.

214. Van Duyn, Corona Harvest.

215. Gleason, Corona Harvest.

216. Ibid.

217. Van Duyn, Corona Harvest.

218. Memorandum by Gen W. W. Momyer, USAF, Retired, to General Ellis, subject: CORONA HARVEST (In-Country Air Strike Operation, Southeast Asia, 1 January 1965–31 March 1968), 1 July 1974.

219. Ibid.

220. Ibid.

Townsend Hoopes,
under secretary of the Air Force.

Melvin Laird,
secretary of defense.

James R. Schlesinger,
secretary of defense.

Gen William C. Westmoreland,
commander of the United States
Military Assistance Command.

Gen Creighton W. Abrams, Jr.,
commander of the United States
Military Assistance Command.

Gen George J. Eade, Air Force
deputy chief of staff
for plans and operations.

Vice Adm Ulysses S. Grant Sharp,
Jr., commander in chief of the
Pacific Command.

CHAPTER 5

STRATEGIC CHALLENGES TO AIR POWER 1970–83

"You know, we really don't design our weapons systems, the Russians design our weapons systems for us," Adm Thomas H. Moorer told a gathering of senior officers in 1973. What the chairman of the Joint Chiefs of Staff (JCS) was saying was substantially the same as Gen Bruce K. Holloway, commander in chief, Strategic Air Command (CINCSAC), had told the Senate Armed Services Committee on 30 April 1971:

> I would like to touch on the growing Soviet threat . . . since this is really the generic determinant of all defense programs. . . . To begin with, I would emphasize that the main concern now is the threat from the Soviet Union. We are quite familiar with the situation in the Warsaw Pact countries, the Mid-East, and China, North Korea and North Vietnam in the Pacific. . . . However, in my judgment, the only real immediate threat to the United States today is the Soviet Union, and it is continuing to grow. Therefore, I submit that extraordinary emphasis and attention today must be focused upon the USSR.[1]

Early Military Analysis of the Soviet Missile Threat

Looking backward to the course of events following the Cuban missile crisis of 1962 from the vantage point of 1980, Gen Richard H. Ellis, CINCSAC and JCS director of strategic target planning, laid the blame for the shift of the strategic balance of power in favor of the Soviet Union basically to "bad intelligence; in other words, intelligence estimates that did not prove out."[2] Again in retrospect, Paul H. Nitze has described how President Kennedy after having run for the presidency in the 1960s' election campaign on a missile gap issue learned from U-2 photography in 1961 that the Soviet Union in the late 1950s had given first priority to the production and deployment of intermediate-range nuclear missiles rather than intercontinental missiles. There was no intercontinental ballistic missile (ICBM) gap; rather, during the Cuban missile crisis, the United States possessed substantial strategic superiority.[3] Hard on the heels of the missile crisis of 1962, the Soviets evidently resolved not to get caught short again but to get a position of superiority over the strategic forces of the free world, something like the United States had over them in 1962. In Nitze's view, the United States gave inadequate attention to the wargaming Soviet armament program, because U-2 photographs showed the Soviet missiles to be "big, inaccurate, liquid fueled, and based on soft pads. . . .

They looked like deterrent weapons, not the kind of weapons one would want if one actually contemplated fighting."[4] Gen Russell E. Dougherty, who closed out his Air Force career as CINCSAC, also has remembered that US underestimation was caused in part because "we were preoccupied with Vietnam (a tragic perturbation to our entire policy of deterrence) and deflected by myriad pulls and tugs from the essential decision making and investment needed to keep our strategic offensive and defensive focus relevant...."[5] In a public interview in April 1965 Defense Secretary Robert S. McNamara said, "The Soviets have decided that they have lost the quantitative race, and they are not seeking to engage us in that contest. It means there is no indication that the Soviets are seeking to develop a nuclear force as large as ours."[6]

According to Gen John D. Ryan, Air Force chief of staff, one of the requisites of "adequate deterrence" is an ability to project thinking 10-20 years into the future, this because of the long lead time involved with developing and deploying new weapons to combat new and totally unanticipated enemy capabilities that appear.[7] In the arms race, the Soviets got some immediate advantages, partly through accident and partly from US defense management innovations. Early in their missile development the Soviets built massive missiles and large warheads to compensate for lesser accuracies; they needed and built large silo defenses. These permanent silos were put to use by new generations of missiles which mastered massive throw weight.[8] Gen David C. Jones, Air Force chief of staff in 1975, stressed on several occasions a belief that the five-year defense plan of the Department of Defense gave the Soviets a "very precise road map ... as to what we were going to do." Moreover, the five-year plan broadcast the moderating trend in strategic focus, a shift in emphasis from strategic to general-purpose forces. In Jones's words to a Senate committee:

> In the early 1960s there was a large strategic program, B-52 high production rate buildup, B-58s coming in, and the start of the F-111. We also had the B-70 and Skybolt in development. We had the Atlas in development, the Titan, the Minuteman coming on, and the Polaris submarines. But from year to year, as succeeding 5-year defense programs were published, the projections for the strategic force kept coming down and down.
>
> Minuteman started in the program at 2,000 missiles. Then it went down to 1,600 and finally down to 1,000. So, if somebody was comparing last year's program with this year they would say, well, their objectives had diminished.
>
> I believe we had an objective of 56 nuclear powered Polaris submarines originally. That came down to 41. The B-70 was canceled. The Skybolt was canceled. We were starting to phase down our bombers.
>
> Also, when the force projection showed only 54 Titan IIs it was clear to the Soviets and to the world that we were not developing large missiles with large throw weight; we were going for the smaller Minuteman and Polaris missiles which have relatively low throw weights.[9]

Where Jones believed that the strong US strategic response to Sputnik gave the Soviets faint hope of arms competition, the five-year defense plan inaugurated by Secretary McNamara allowed them to calculate what it would take to achieve parity with the United States and they embarked on very ambitious programs.[10]

During the late 1950s when Nikita Khrushchev was apparently engaged in a Soviet version of the "New Look" with a good deal of emphasis on pure bluff and nuclear threats, the US defense effort was larger than the Soviet effort. After 1964, when Leonid I. Brezhnev succeeded Khrushchev, Soviet military expenditures grew steadily and consistently year by year increasing roughly in line with the growth of the Soviet gross national product, whereas US baseline military budgets (with military retired pay and incremental costs of the war in Southeast Asia excluded) declined in real terms.[11] There was absolutely no indication that the Brezhnev defense budget was reactive to US defense expenditures. Said Dr Malcolm R. Currie, OSD director of defense research and engineering, "I see a program there that has its own set of goals, its own ultimate reasons for being whatever, and it is relatively insensitive to what we do."[12] The Soviets nationalized and controlled aerospace industries appeared to Lt Gen Otto J. Glasser, the Air Force deputy chief of staff for research and development, to "operate at a level of effort regardless of what they produce.... Occasionally, as things come out of there that seem to be attractive, they put them into production." In the United States by contrast defense industries geared up for space undertakings, and when these specifics were accomplished the capacity was dissipated.[13] To Deputy Secretary of Defense for Research and Engineering William J. Perry, the Soviet defense industry seemed to have a momentum of its own. He said, "We rarely see a program being terminated in the sense that we terminate programs ... and we rarely see a design group being terminated." Perry was critical of the Soviet practice of building in duplicate — as was his example in 1978 of multiple ICBM versions — as being an "enormous waste of money on their part."[14]

But from a user's viewpoint, Secretary of Air Force Robert C. Seamans, Jr., and General Ryan agreed that Soviet prototype development was very useful:

> In the field of fighter and interceptor type aircraft, they have been carrying out a very active series of developments. They have a number of what might be thought of as competing development teams turning out about one new prototype per year. They are then in a position from time to time to pick out one of these aircraft on the basis of its performance and put it in their production and in their inventory.... It is what we here sometimes call in the colloquial, "fly before you buy." We would like to do this.[15]

Seamans assumed that the Soviets could follow such a course of military research and development because they were sacrificing in other areas. "I would say at this particular time, this country [the United States] would not be prepared to make that type sacrifice," he concluded.[16]

As early as 1962 the US government became aware of a monster SS-9 missile, and in 1964 the Soviets paraded the SS-9 in the streets of Moscow, enabling the United States to get pictures of this continental missile. Initially, the United States also had fielded very large missiles such as the Atlas and Titan because warheads were large, but ways had been found to reduce the weight of the warhead so that a mission of assured destruction could be performed with a much smaller missile like the Minuteman. At first it seemed that the Soviets must be doing the same thing with the SS-9 that the United States had done with the Atlas and Titan. The SS-9, however, had a warhead capability of 20 to 25 megatons, and it was possible that the Soviets might intend it to be a city-destruction weapon. This conception collapsed when the Soviets displayed in excess of 100 SS-9s, since there were not enough US cities of a size to justify such a number of missiles. The second reason for increasing concern for the SS-9 came when it was flown with three multiple reentry vehicle (MRV) warheads. A third concern was the demonstration that the SS-9 was more accurate than any other missile then in the Soviet inventory. In the same season that the SS-9 was deployed the Soviets fielded large numbers of new solid-fuel SS-11s similar to the US Minuteman missiles. All assessments now began to point to the SS-9 not as a retaliatory or assured destruction weapon but as a counterforce warfighting missile zeroing in on the US Minuteman fields.[17]

After the development of the new missiles, the Soviet program proceeded rapidly. According to estimates accepted by Gen John P. McConnell, Soviet operational ICBM launchers totaled some 720 missiles in October 1967, more than double the 340 of a year earlier.[18] By October 1969 the Soviets had achieved parity in strategic missiles with the United States. They had more ICBM launchers in place than the 1,000 Minuteman and 54 Titans in the United States strategic forces, and more than 230 of their missiles were the mammoth SS-9s. In the same year, the Soviets also had started deployment of seven or eight new missile launcher submarines, each with 16 missiles believed to have a range of 1,500 nautical miles. The weapon, operated in a depressed trajectory mode from about 400 miles offshore, could reach US coastal strategic air bases in a flight time too short to allow adequate time to "flush" an alert bomber force. Secretary Seamans noted that "with the ICBM launchers now under construction and their existing submarine launched ballistic missiles, they will have over twice as much total missile payload as the entire US land and sea based missile force. This payload advantage could present a serious threat to the United States."[19]

From the end of World War II onward, the Soviet Union built and maintained the world's largest strategic defense force as a matter of highest national policy. So, for example, when the United States put the B-70 into full-scale development, the Soviets immediately laid on two programs which resulted in the high-technology MiG-25 Foxbat interceptor aircraft and the SA-5 medium-to-high-altitude, surface-to-air missile. Both were fielded in time to counter the B-70, had it been produced.[20] In the Moscow parade of November 1964, the Soviets revealed for the first time a missile in a transportable cannister which they described as a new antiballistic missile, subsequently nicknamed the Galosh. Khrushchev's boast that "you can say our rocket hits a fly in outerspace," plus what was known about Soviet nuclear tests at high attitude in 1961 and 1962, led to a belief that a Soviet antiballistic missile (ABM) was technically feasible. The Soviets began to deploy a Galosh ABM complex around Moscow, beginning with emplacements for missiles that might still be in development. It was also possible that the Tallinn system designed to cope with manned aircraft or air-to-surface missiles might be adaptable to ABM purposes. As expressed by Secretary McNamara and Secretary of the Air Force Harold Brown, the administration's viewpoint was that the Soviets were just wasting money building ABM defenses which US missiles would penetrate. Secretary McNamara said of the Soviets that "they have this almost religious fanaticism toward the subject of defense, and I think that is what has led them to deploy an antiballistic missile defense, although it will be as wasteful and ineffective in my opinion as their bomber defenses." In both the US Navy and the US Air Force the technical response to the likelihood of a Soviet ABM development was the multiple independently targetable reentry vehicle (MIRV) programs gotten under way in 1962–64 to permit Poseidon and Minuteman missiles to carry multiple warheads, including some decoys to confuse antimissile defenses.[21] The development of the Poseidon MIRV was approved in the autumn of 1964; its deployment was approved in 1966, and the first loading was deployed at sea in the *James Madison* SSBN on 1 April 1971. The first flight of 10 Minuteman III missiles with MIRV was turned over to the Strategic Air Command on 19 June 1970.[22]

Search for a United States Nuclear Strategy

When Robert McNamara took office as secretary of defense in January 1961 he was briefed at length on strategic matters by William W. Kaufmann, a Rand analyst who was familiar with the thinking in Air Force circles about the "no cities" approach to nuclear targeting that was popularly known as counterforce. As has been seen, McNamara appeared to endorse counterforce as a second-strike US alternative to countervalue city bombing. In a much quoted speech at Ann Arbor, Michigan, in June 1962, he said that "nuclear war should be approached in much the same way that more conventional military operations have been regarded in the past."[23] A second-strike counterforce strategy would have required many more large nuclear warheads than McNamara was willing to afford; moreover, as revealed many years later by Sen Henry M. Jackson, "the decision to go the Minuteman route could only represent one course of conduct and that was to have solely a retaliatory capability." Jackson said that "by design and premeditation," the Joint Committee on Atomic Energy and especially his subcommittee on Military Application of Atomic Energy had ensured that the United States abjured counterforce.[24] Writing in long retrospect in 1983, Secretary McNamara recalled that in the early 1960s, his view was — or came to be — "*that nuclear weapons serve no military purpose whatsoever. They are totally useless — except only to deter one's opponent from using them.* . . . This is my view today. It was my view in the early 1960s."[25] In February 1964 McNamara said:

> While a cities-only strategic retaliatory force would, in our judgment, be dangerously inadequate, a full-first-strike force ... is ... simply unattainable. Moreover, I know of no responsible Pentagon official, certainly or of the Joint Chiefs of Staff, who proposes such a force.[26]

In 1964 McNamara recommended a "damage-limiting strategy" as the "most practical and effective course for us to follow." He continued:

> While there are still some differences of judgment on just how large such a force should be, there is general agreement that it should be large enough to insure the destruction, singly or in combination, of the Soviet Union, Communist China, and the Communist satellites as national societies, under the worst possible circumstances of war outbreak that can reasonably be postulated, and, in addition, to destroy their war-making capability so as to limit, to the extent practicable, damage to this country and to our allied.[27]

Already suggested in 1964, McNamara presented Congress in February 1965 with a well-thought-out strategic requirement for general nuclear war forces to accomplish "assured destruction" and "damage limitation." "Assured destruction" would be "the capability to destroy the aggressors as viable societies, even after a well planned and executed surprise attack on our forces." "Damage limitation" was "the capability to reduce the weight of the enemy attack by both offensive and defensive measures and to provide a degree of protection for our population against the effects of nuclear detonations." When applied to the USSR, assured destruction was initially qualified as being the destruction of about 25 percent of the Soviet population and two-thirds of its industrial capacity. By 1968 a decline in the assured-destruction criterion ranged from one-fifth to one-fourth of the Soviet population and to one-half of the Soviet industry. When the criterion was used to measure force requirements, Secretary of the Air Force Brown remarked that assured destruction if one planned it well was feasible, whereas damage limiting was "much less feasible, or more chancy." Damage limiting depended on actions that the other side would take during a war. Assured destruction was something that could be used to structure a force, but damage limiting had to be a sort of faceout from assured destruction as far as the purchase of hardware was concerned.[28]

After taking office in 1961, Secretary McNamara had weighed the pros and cons of deploying a Nike Zeus ABM system that had been under development and had concluded that development of a still more advanced system was advisable. In March 1967 McNamara still was opposed to a US ABM system, rationalizing:

> We believe the Soviet Union has essentially the same requirement for a deterrent or "assured destruction" force as the United States. Therefore, deployment by the United States of an ABM defense which would degrade the destruction capability of the Soviets' offensive force to an acceptable level would lead to expansion of that force. This would leave us no better off than we were before.[29]

Both in 1966 and 1967 the Joint Chiefs of Staff disagreed with Secretary McNamara and agreed among themselves that the United States needed a measure of strategic defense within its military posture. They did not consider that increasing their missiles might be the only course of action open to the Soviets for reasons stated by Gen Earle G. Wheeler:

> One, they do place great weight on defense, they always have historically, and it has served them well. They conceivably, instead of increasing their offensive forces could increase their defensive forces to further compound our problem. They could increase offensive forces and defensive forces, which probably would be more logical from their point of view. Two, we must take into account the competition for resources in the Soviet Union. Whether they would be able and willing to pay the sum to increase their defense forces to the degree necessary to offset our offense is a question in my mind, particularly if we had a defense.[30]

In rebuttal to General Wheeler, McNamara insisted that US offensive increases — Poseidon, Minuteman III, MIRV warheads, and penetration aids (pen aids) — would more than offset the Soviet ABM. He said:

> We will get more weapons through to the Soviet Union as a result of their deploying an ABM than we would if they had not. We presented ... a program that with a high degree of probability will more than offset their ABM. That simply means that more weapons would detonate on their soil than would have been the case had they not started an ABM defense.[31]

When President Kennedy had refused the single integrated operational plan (SIOP) I that was in effect when he took office because it proposed firing the US nuclear arsenal "in one flush" in the event of Soviet attack, the McNamara-Johnson strategy of assured destruction looked more and more like old concepts of massive retaliation against Soviet cities. As a matter of fact, SIOP II, developed in response to President Kennedy's demand for flexible response, was described as having four options, reflecting escalating applications of force against expanding target lists. The first option was said to exclude the Soviet decisionmaking apparatus in Moscow from attack, but each option would be very damaging to the Soviet Union, and the fourth option was the old all-out attack.[32] In McNamara's strategy, "damage limiting" shared billing with "assured destruction," but McNamara appeared to have doubts about the feasibility of targeting nuclear strikes against Soviet military targets. In 1965 he shrugged off a query as to whether it might not be possible in the strike plan to maximize strikes on military targets and to limit incidental mass destruction of civilians with the response that a Soviet first strike would "be most likely to attack cities as well as military targets and do so simultaneously."[33] And in 1966 McNamara said that "massive retaliation" could be appropriate depending on

> what you are retaliating to. Massive retaliation to a Soviet nuclear strike against us is in my opinion the only proper response. And it is the clear recognition by the Soviets that

> we have that capability in terms of survivable weapons and delivery vehicles and of the will that will deter such a Soviet attack against us.[34]

In 1967 Air Force Secretary Harold Brown pointed out that the United States and the Soviet Union had both lost a first-strike capability since both countries now possessed the ability to weather a nuclear strike and respond with unacceptable destruction to the other. Brown incidentally defined a first-strike capability as "the situation that prevails if one side can strike first and destroy the other without itself being destroyed."[35] In 1968 McNamara stated that the era predicted by such experts as Gen Henry H. Arnold, Secretary Charles E. Wilson, Deputy Secretary Donald A. Quarles, and the James R. Killian committee had arrived: "an era when it would become impossible for either side to destroy a sufficiently large portion of the other strategic nuclear force to preclude a devastating retaliatory blow." Neither the United States nor the Soviet Union could hope to limit damage through offensive or defensive means. "Under these circumstances, surely it makes sense for us both to try to halt the momentum of the arms race which is causing vast expenditures on both sides and promises no increase in security," he reasoned.[36]

The increasing emphasis on "assured destruction" in the McNamara-Johnson strategy and reduced emphasis upon "damage limiting" was in part inevitable since the Soviets in the 1960s followed the US initiative and did things four or five years after the United States. Said Secretary Brown:

> They dispersed their silos, they hardened them, they put in the equivalent of a BMEWS [ballistic missile early warning system] to warn their bombers. They built nuclear submarines, with ballistic missile launch capability. All of these things made their forces more survivable and, therefore, reduced our capability to limit damage—just as our previous actions had greatly reduced their ability to limit damage to them.[37]

There were now not only a great number of military targets in the Soviet Union, but they were increasingly hardened so that missile warheads had to be either increased in megatonnage or greatly increased in circular error probable (CEP) accuracy.

> The principal value for a very accurate ICBM, or very accurate MIRV, is actually in the destruction of hard military targets, which, of course, is connected with damage limitation. And, so, to the extent that we work on very small CEPs, if we do, it is a sign we have not abandoned completely damage limitation as a role of our forces.[38]

Early in the McNamara administration, General LeMay had urged the development of large nuclear bombs to be delivered against hard targets by B-70 bombers, thus striking objectives that could not be handled by missiles. But Secretary McNamara refused to move in this direction because he chose to emphasize accuracy, survivability, penetrability, and greater numbers of separately targetable warheads in place of megatonnage.[39] MIRV warheads reduced the megatonnage of Minuteman individual reentry vehicles, and in this program the Department of Defense elected to emphasize assured destruction qualifications over hard-target-kill requirements, apparently because of cost effectiveness. As Dr John S. Foster, Jr., director of defense research and engineering, explained: "The essence of our guiding philosophy in meeting the requirement for an assured destruction capability can be understood by discussing two terms: survivability and penetration." A Mark-17 (MK-17) MIRV warhead development emphasizing optimized accuracy for hard target attacks was canceled in 1968, ostensibly to save money.[40] Within the US military high command there was a recognition that Soviet defenses were steadily decreasing the US counterforce – now described as damage limiting – capability, but there was a decided reluctance to base national strategic planning on the accomplishment of assured destruction. This reluctance was revealed in testimony before the Preparedness Investigating Subcommittee of the Senate Armed Services Committee early in 1968 when General Wheeler, JCS chairman, said:

> Yes, you attack the urban industrial base that is the population base and industry, but we also have always held to the view that we must attack those forces of the Soviet Union which are able to inflict destruction on ourselves and our allies.[41]

Adm Thomas Moorer, chief of naval operations, testified that in his judgment the United States needed "to retain the capability to kill a hard target." When asked what weapon would be the most effective for the purpose, he added: "The aircraft would provide the best means of killing a hard target, simply because it can carry a larger warhead." General McConnell emphatically favored damage limiting as much as feasible. He stated:

> I do not believe we should give up the damage limiting part of the scenario, and we should continue to apply all that we can against damage limiting targets while at the same time, shall I say, guarantee our assured destruction capability.... I do not think we should give up on damage limiting. It should be a corollary. But I do not believe under any circumstances that we should just take our forces and say, "all we need to do now is to be certain that we can destroy 50 percent of their people," without paying any attention to their weapon systems.[42]

In January 1967 President Johnson informed Congress that if discussions with the Soviet Union were not successful in limiting ABM defenses, he would reconsider earlier decisions to keep the US Nike X ABM system that had been held so long in development and allow its deployment. In the first half of 1967 several developments bore on this problem: The Soviet Union had accelerated deployment of hard ICBMs; the Chinese Communists had launched a nuclear-armed medium-range ballistic missile; the Nike X had reached a state of development where the start of concurrent production and deployment was feasible; and the Joint Chiefs of Staff strongly urged a prompt decision to deploy the system. In an address in San Francisco, Secretary McNamara on 18 September 1967 announced the Johnson administration's decision to move forward with a deployment of an antimissile defense primarily against the potential threat of a small-scale Chinese Communist ICBM attack in the mid-1970s. McNamara still held his original viewpoint that the Soviet Union (like the United States) could overcome ICBM defenses by committing large numbers of missiles, but a thin defense close to major cities would provide area defense against a smaller-scale Chinese ICBM threat, protect against an accidental ICBM launch, and provide an option for a later defense of Minuteman sites against Soviet attack so that "at a modest cost we would in fact be adding even greater effectiveness to our offensive force and avoiding a much more costly expansion of that force." With congressional approval the Sentinel ABM system was under way in 1968, and completion of the entire system was scheduled for January 1975.[43]

President Nixon Demands Selectivity and Flexibility in Targeting

Immediately after President Richard M. Nixon assumed office in January 1969, he requested Secretary of Defense Melvin R. Laird to review the Sentinel ABM system. President Nixon also requested the National Security Council to obtain a broader exposure to facts looking toward presidential decisions. In this review, the secretary of defense, the service secretaries, and the Joint Chiefs of Staff submitted agreed-on conclusions and recommendations that were discussed at two meetings of the National Security Council. The review took cognizance of the fact that in the two years since Sentinel was planned, the Soviets had deployed an offensive missile capability at a very fast rate, including the big SS-9 missiles with multiple warheads. "Now," concluded Deputy Secretary of Defense David Packard, "I am afraid that the Soviets are looking toward a first strike capability." On 14 March 1969 President Nixon stated that the Sentinel system would be reoriented into a Safeguard program, principally structured to protect the US land-based retaliatory forces against a direct attack by the Soviet Union and incidentally to defend the American people against a small-scale Chinese Communist missile attack or an accidental attack from any other source. The president and his spokesman emphasized that Safeguard should not be considered provocative to the Soviet Union and that dismantling of Soviet and US ABM defenses would "certainly be negotiable."[44]

During the Nixon administration's presentation of recommendations for Safeguard to the Senate Committee on Armed Services, Sen Edward W. Brooke of Massachusetts was very critical of the "destabilizing effects" of the US work on MIRV and now the ABM. Brooke insisted that the United States should avoid moving "toward a first strike counterforce capability."[45] Testifying before a House of Representatives' Appropriations Subcommittee on 7 October 1969, Secretary of Air Force Robert C. Seamans and Gen John D. Ryan, now Air Force chief of staff, endorsed the Safeguard plan to provide protection to the two Minuteman fields at Grand Forks AFB, North Dakota, and Malmstrom AFB, Montana. Seamans additionally called for a hardening of the Minuteman vehicle and the beginning of a new manned-bomber system. General Ryan agreed and added an afterthought: "We have a program we are pushing to increase the yield of our warheads and decrease the circular error probable so that we have what we call a hard target killer which we do not have in the inventory at the present time."[46] This statement caused Senator Brooke to query President Nixon about the matter, and on 29 December 1969 Nixon was said to have written Brooke that he had abandoned any attempt to obtain "pinpoint accuracies" with Minuteman III because he thought that might raise the spectre of a first-strike capability. Apparently because of this letter, the Department of Defense did not request hard-targeting funds in the fiscal year 1971 budget, and in the annual posture statement on 3 March 1970 Secretary Laird said that the US MIRV system was designed "to attack the essential soft urban/industrial targets in the Soviet Union." On 22 September 1970, however, General Ryan reopened the controversy in the course of an address to the Air Force Association when he mentioned that Minuteman III would be "our best means of destroying time-urgent targets like the long-range weapons of the enemy." He also referred to the MIRV in a damage-limiting role, of attacking "the remaining strategic weapons which the enemy would no doubt hold in reserve." Senator Brooke now went public in a letter to Secretary Laird protesting that Ryan's comments would "undercut the Administration's assurances that the United States was pursuing an exclusively second-strike deterrent strategy." And Laird reassured Brooke that: "We have not developed, and are not seeking to develop a weapon system having, or which could reasonably be construed as having, a first-strike potential."[47]

Although General Ryan was said to have been personally discouraged by being "beaten around the ears" by Senator Brooke, the Air Force continued to support a concept of increased accuracy for Minuteman, and, as CINC Strategic Air Command, Gen Bruce K. Holloway made improved accuracy for Minuteman the top priority in his listing of desirable activities.[48] In testimony before congressional committees in March and April 1971, Holloway emphasized a need for accuracy:

> The probability of inflicting damage on a target depends on three basic factors: target hardness, weapon yield, and the accuracy of weapon delivery. The most important of these factors is accuracy — and I really think this is the least understood.[49]

Accuracy was necessary as a fundamental economy of force: to permit one weapon to do the work of three. It was necessary to avoid collateral damage: in North Vietnam a demand for precise bombing to reduce civilian damage was at an all-time high. Holloway said:

> I think it is very unrealistic to think that if in fact we become involved in nuclear conflict, we would never have a situation in which we were not concerned with limiting collateral damage. With such terrible weapons it is difficult — and without hope — for me to think that the only way they would possibly be used is in Armageddon proportions accentuating a maximum number of deaths.[50]

Accuracy was vital to defense suppression: Holloway pointed out that in all nuclear attack options a large proportion of ICBM force was targeted for an "effective defense suppression laydown" to clear the way for "follow-on objective sorties." Missiles could be made markedly more accurate with improved guidance and control systems—essentially electronics and redesigned gyroscopes—that could be developed for about $155 million and added to existing Minuteman III missiles for about $300,000 per copy, and this in about four years.[51]

After the winter and spring of 1971, Adm Elmo R. Zumwalt, Jr., chief of naval operations, reminisced that the Joint Chiefs of Staff were in some measure kept informed of the status of strategic arms limitation talks between the United States and the Soviet Union, but he reflected that the real negotiations were "back channel" between Presidential Assistant for National Security Affairs Henry Kissinger and Soviet Ambassador Anatoly F. Dobrynin.[52] These negotiations culminated in May 1972 with the conclusion in Moscow on the 26th of a treaty on the limitations of ABM systems and an interim agreement on the limitation of strategic arms. The ABM treaty limited each side to one ABM site for the defense of its national capital (Moscow and Washington) and one site for each side for defense of an ICBM field. To be effective for five years while negotiations for a permanent agreement were to continue, the interim SALT I agreement limited ICBMs on each side of those under construction or deployed on 1 July 1972—1,618 ICBMs for the USSR and 1,054 for the United States. Modernization of missiles was permitted.[53] Secretary of Defense Laird supported the arms limitation agreements as "essential to apply the brakes to the crushing strategic weapons momentum." The objective of the agreement, in Admiral Moorer's words as JCS chairman, was "to stop the momentum that the Soviets already had under way and which would continue during this interim period." After the agreements were signed, the Joint Chiefs went forward with three assurances required to prevent Soviet developments from putting the United States in a position of inferiority. These were: a strong and vigorous development program in missile fields; construction of new equipment such as the B-1 bomber and the Trident submarine; and improvement in verification capability and intelligence collection capability associated with strategic forces. Speaking for the Air Force, General Ryan pointed out that the United States had agreed to an ICBM launcher ceiling favoring the Soviet Union by 3 to 2. He argued that the United States should pursue every reasonable opportunity to maintain and increase the quality of its strategic forces. Air Force programs required were dispersed basing of strategic bomber and tanker forces, acceleration of an advanced ballistic reentry system (ABRES), further development of military satellites for early warning and communications, and expansion of Strategic Air Command communications. The B-1 remained one of the Air Force's highest priorities, and Ryan once again plugged for acceptance of increased missile accuracy. He said:

> We could improve the capabilities of our ICBMs through a relatively inexpensive option which could be implemented in the near future. This option would continue the modernization of the Minuteman force beyond the current plan and attain a force of 1,000 Minuteman III[s] at the earliest practical date. This would give us additional reentry vehicles and substantially increase our force effectiveness.[54]

In the Senate, Sen Henry M. Jackson disliked the quantitative edge accorded the Soviet Union; he obtained Senate approval of a proviso in the ratification resolution that the United States should negotiate future agreements on the basis of rough numerical parity. Senator Brooke noted that funds were in the defense appropriation bill to give hard-target accuracy to the MK-19 reentry vehicle. In a successful action on the Senate floor, Brooke got approval of a sense-of-Congress provision affirming the "long-standing United States policy that neither the Soviet Union or the United States should seek unilateral advantage by developing counterforce weapons which might be construed as having a first-strike potential."[55]

When the Nixon administration was considering new approaches to military strategy in June 1969, presidential adviser Kissinger had pointed out to President Nixon the dilemma he would face in response to a possible limited Soviet nuclear attack if assured destruction continued to be the accepted strategy. In addresses in 1970 and 1972, Nixon expressed his dissatisfaction with a lack of a flexible range of strategic options. "No president," he informed Congress on 9 February 1972, "should be left with only one strategic course of action, particularly that of ordering the mass destruction of enemy civilians and facilities.... We must be able to respond at levels appropriate to the situation."[56] Studies of this matter were in progress during the administrations of Secretary of Defense Laird and his successor, Elliot L. Richardson. The approach to the problem was to make strategic forces more flexible by improving the warning system (with an interim capability satellite early warning system), deploying an advanced airborne command post, adding protection for the national command authorities, improving the hardness of Minuteman vehicles and silos, developing a command data buffer system permitting more rapid retargeting of missiles, and developing quieter submarines.[57] These actions sought to add some credibility to the likelihood that a president could respond in a more limited way to a more limited attack by the other side.

When James R. Schlesinger took office as secretary of defense on 2 July 1973, he brought a new appreciation of nuclear strategy based in part on work that he had done for the Rand Corporation in the area of strategic nuclear weapons. In Schlesinger's view the concept of assured destruction of Soviet cities had emerged as a means of preparing computer models by which it was possible to program nuclear forces sufficient to ensure that, whatever the circumstances, it would be possible to have enough capability left to destroy the urban industrial base of the Soviet society. Schlesinger thought that the "women and children first" implication of assured destruction city bombing was a rather crude doctrine at best and that it was inapplicable to a weapons balance when the Soviets would be able to respond by killing 90 million Americans and destroying the US urban industrial base. Schlesinger said:

> One must have the ability to threaten credibly the use of US strategic nuclear forces if great national interests are involved. And unless that occurs, then the deterrent is

worthless for deterring anything other than the very limited likelihood threat which is represented by an initial first strike at American cities.[58]

In the spring of 1973 a study group headed by Dr John S. Foster, Jr., director of defense research and engineering, provided the basis for a changed approach to strategy signed in January 1974 by President Nixon as National Security Decision Memorandum (NSDM) 242. The first purpose of nuclear weapons was deterrence of nuclear attack on American territory or forces, of nuclear or conventional attack on American allies, and of "coercion" of the United States or its allies by nuclear threats. If deterrence failed, the second purpose of nuclear forces was to conduct "selected nuclear operations to seek early war termination . . . at the lowest level of conflict feasible."[59]

It was Secretary Schlesinger's view that under the "assured destruction notions" nuclear weapons "were regarded by some as a *deux ex machina*, as a substitute for thinking the [ICBM] program." As the chief architect and certainly the principal exponent of the new strategy, Schlesinger stated often that he was attempting to "deal very precisely with the calculus involved in nuclear war" and thereby seeking to strengthen the overall effects of deterrence. He explained:

> I might add that for deterrence one has got to have an implementable threat. If one says that a deterrent is based upon a nonimplementable threat, such as both sides going after each other's cities, what one is saying is that the deterrent is logically unsound. Now, it may be psychologically sound at the same time it is logically unsound, but I would like to have deterrence based upon a logically sound notion.[60]

At the outset of his presentation of the new strategy, Schlesinger emphasized that instruction for the preparation of a new single integrated operations plan required "target packages" to give the president a "selectivity and flexibility" across an entire spectrum of conflict. Although population bombing was to be avoided, the new target strategy could not necessarily be described as "counterforce," since the target spectrum would include many different categories of targets. It was important that these target packages be devised in advance as response options and not hurriedly devised in the heat of combat. Since the new strategy was not counterforce, it did not require changes in the US forces: increased weapons use against hard targets was not required by the change in targets, although increased accuracy would, of course, improve missile performance.[61]

When asked about Pentagon support for the National Security Council study that generated NSDM 242, Admiral Moorer said that the Joint Chiefs of Staff unanimously supported the change in strategy in its general thrust, although there might have been some "divergences about details." An Air Force spokesman testified favorably to the change, both because of its inevitability and its possible utility. Secretary of Air Force John L. McLucas reasoned that the change merely capitalized a technological work that had been done in the past. "So I do not see this as a dramatic change other than in the statements that are being made about it," he said. McLucas suggested that the new strategy might well hinge for its success on whether there were command and control systems in such a condition as would permit a flexible and selective employment of nuclear weapons. Air Force Chief of Staff Gen George S. Brown thought that assured destruction had been a useful deterrent strategy as long as the United States had possessed a predominance of nuclear power but that when the Soviet Union got about the same power, it was no longer credible "to think we will shoot everything and destroy as much of the Soviet Union, their weapons, production base, over every conceivable contingency with which we might face the Russians."[62] General Brown added that Secretary Schlesinger wanted a "range of options," and the Air Force was generating one. He remarked, "The condition under which an option would be selected, I think, depends on how those conditions are interpreted by the National Command Authority at the time."[63] Gen John C. Meyer, who had recently become commander in chief, Strategic Air Command, also attested that

> the time has come where the assured destruction as the only measure of deterrence or the *sine qua non* of deterrence has passed us by.... The time has come now when not only Soviet and US strategic forces are in parity, but it is understood by the world to be so, or nearly so.... That raises a question of credibility of the United States['s ability] to respond to a major adventurism on the part of the Soviets—less than an all-out strategic attack on the United States in any nuclear way—to respond in a way that means a choice of either killing large numbers of Soviets with the certainty of losing great numbers of American lives, or not responding at all.[64]

Under the new strategy, Meyer visualized that

> we could select some targets on the periphery or within the Soviet Union that we could attack with nuclear weapons and that these targets would be targets of high value, something that the Soviets would cherish, and our capability to do that in a selective way would become apparent before we would in fact do so, the Soviets then, recognizing that we do have such a capability to respond to their possible use of nuclear weapons, may perceive more readily a challenge by US nuclear response if all out retaliation is not our only option.[65]

In visualizing how selective strikes would be managed, Meyer said that it would be important to destroy the selected target with assurance and without significant collateral damage. Since Minuteman and Poseidon force missiles were insufficiently accurate, he envisioned using the bombing accuracy of aircraft for precision targeting: F-4s off carriers for peripheral targets, FB-111s for deeper targets, and the still to be developed B-1s for far interior objectives. Meyer strongly supported proposals to increase ICBM accuracy:

> It is just more efficient to have missiles that are just more accurate. You can do more things, more damage, with less collateral damage—in the lesser intense strategic action. Or, you could destroy hard targets with much less expenditure of missile force. It doesn't really matter whether it is a missile or not. If you have the right combination of accuracy and yield, you can do whatever you want with a lot less.[66]

At the time of the signing of the SALT I agreements in May 1972, the United States was considered to have distinct qualitative advantages in terms of MIRVs, guidance, weapons technology, and reentry vehicle technology, and these advantages were thought to compensate for gross advantages of the Soviet Union in terms of numbers and warhead throw weight. In his foreign policy address of 1973, President Nixon spoke of the necessity to maintain "essential equivalence" — not matching Soviet forces in mirror image but in gross characteristics of forces. Secretary Schlesinger defined equivalence:

> I think for equivalence... we need three elements: One is the traditional second strike capability.... Secondly, ... we must not allow a great asymmetry with regard to counter-force capability such that they may think they have an advantage.... And, thirdly, there should be perceived equality.[67]

It was also hoped that SALT I would break the momentum of the Soviet missile buildup, but immediately after the agreement was signed the Soviets started testing four new ICBMs the size of which portended dramatic importance for the United States if the Soviets married the numbers and throw weight to advancing technologies. Three of the four missiles — the SS-17, SS-18, and SS-19 — demonstrated MIRV capability; each had on-board computers; and the new missiles promised to give the Soviets 10 to 12 million pounds of throw weight, whereas the United States had approximately 2 million pounds. Within the bounds of "essential equivalence" Secretary Schlesinger noted that the United States could countenance a discrepancy of perhaps 3 to 2 in throw weight, but 6 to 1 could not be construed as essential equivalence.[68]

At the outset of his advocacy of the new strategy, Secretary Schlesinger had emphasized that it did not necessarily require increased missile accuracy. Similarly, he said, "there is no desire on the part of the United States to develop a counterforce capability." But the new Soviet missile development looked like a grab for counterforce capabilities since in a real-world nuclear exchange throw weight could compensate in limited but adequate degree for accuracy degradation. In Schlesinger's assessment, there was "no possibility, as far ahead as we can see, of either the US or the USSR acquiring a disarming first-strike capability."[69] He nevertheless requested congressional approval of research and development funding since improved accuracy would be "helpful to improve our capabilities for more discriminate targeting and minimization of unintended collateral damage, thus to aid in control of escalation."[70] In addition:

> Accuracy improvements could well be necessary to maintain essential equivalence with the Soviet Union. If the Soviets proceed to exploit fully their great advantage in missile numbers and throw-weight by MIRVing and improving the accuracy of their ICBMs, as their present development program portends, they will have a very substantial and greatly asymmetrical hard-target kill capability compared with the United States. Under these circumstances, in order to maintain essential equivalence, we would have to put more stress on improved accuracy because of the constraints in payload and yields which have resulted from our lower missile throw-weights.[71]

The nuclear weapons employment policy guidance which Secretary Schlesinger provided to the Joint Chiefs of Staff in April 1974 for transmission to the Joint Strategic Target Planning Staff required a general revision of strategic targeting that would be continuing through much of the administration of President Gerald R. Ford, in which time Donald H. Rumsfeld succeeded as secretary of defense. In the guidance the objective of US national policy was deterrence. If this failed, the next objective was to control escalation if possible to limit the conflict. Should it prove impossible to control escalation, the goal could be to assure a position of US power and influence superior to the Soviet Union. The basic objectives of the strategic nuclear forces were stated by Secretary Rumsfeld as being:

- To have a well-protected, second-strike force to deter attacks on our cities and people, at all times.
- To provide a capability for more controlled and measured responses, to deter less than all-out attacks.
- To ensure essential equivalence with the USSR both now and in the future so there can be no misunderstandings or lack of appreciation of the strategic nuclear balance; and
- To maintain stability in the strategic nuclear competition, forsaking the option of a disarming first-strike capability and seeking to achieve equitable arms control agreements where possible. According to this description, the three elements of US strategic deterrence were defined as "assumed destruction" plus "options" plus "essential equivalence."[72]

Where the first four of the single integrated operational plans laid out by the Joint Strategic Target Planning Staff (JSTPS) since inception in 1960 had changed only slightly in response to new weapons entering the inventory or modest changes in the target base, the Schlesinger limited counterforce doctrine introduced a much broader range of targets. The exact classification of enemy installations targeted was highly secret, but Air Force Chief of Staff Gen David C. Jones said in 1975 that the nuclear targeting packages were

> structured to be militarily and politically effective when used in conjunction with appropriate conventional forces and mutually supporting political measures. Within these essential guidelines, targeting packages are being developed that discriminate with respect to number, type, and location of targets, number and types of weapons employed, types of delivery systems utilized, and timing of weapons delivery. An especially critical feature of these packages is the avoidance of designated nontargets, particularly urban areas.[73]

The national policy of deterrence specified to the JSTPS for implementation included a first step of "control[ling] escalation to limit conflict while assuring US position of power and influence," and a final outcome if deterrence failed would be to "maximize position of political, economic, and military power relative to the enemy in the postwar period to preclude enemy domination."[74] In Omaha the task of the JSTPS in reprogramming against many and scattered targets was quite time consuming. With the command data buffer system in Minuteman III, missiles could be retargeted in 36 minutes, whereas retargeting had previously required about nine hours. But many new target trajectories had to be computed, and it ultimately required about 18 months to develop the flexible response SIOP. According to the Strategic Air Command's vice commander, Lt Gen J. M. Keck, the US Triad of bombers, ICBMs, and submarine-launched ballistic missiles (SLBMs) could cover about three-fourths of the targets on the new SIOP.[75] According to Secretary Rumsfeld's criteria, an important outcome of assured retaliation was to be able to retard the ability of the USSR to recover from a nuclear exchange and regain the status of a twentieth-century military and industrial power more rapidly than the United States. The question of what degree of destruction was to be required was difficult to answer. One senator said that the Pentagon told him that this would require destroying 70 percent of the Soviet industry needed to achieve economic recovery. Other extrapolations attempted to compute how long under specific circumstances would it take to reach 80 percent of prewar activity. If the military structure in Eastern European satellites was not destroyed it was possible that Soviet recovery could draw on this economic structure. "The validity of the[se] calculations," observed John B. Walsh, deputy director of defense research and engineering in 1977, "is well recognized to be questionable. It is a very flaky area of endeavor."[76] Asked about such matters, General Jones refused to speculate but stated:

> Credible deterrence ... cannot be reduced to some explicit type and minimum number of targets. ... In general, we must maintain the capability to destroy a large enough portion of an enemy's economic, political, and military infrastructure that he will be continuously deferred from initiating strategic nuclear war.[77]

Explaining the change in US strategic doctrine in 1974, Secretary Schlesinger stated and repeated that "a first strike disarming capability is, for better or worse, beyond the reach of either side."[78] Two years later, Secretary Rumsfeld wanted to keep a stable deterrence in which neither side could see advantages in nuclear war. "We seek a situation in which neither side will see any advantage in initiating the use of strategic forces," Rumsfeld stated.[79] Quite shortly, however, Gen George S. Brown, new chairman of the Joint Chiefs of Staff, noted that the Soviets were marching to a different drumbeat:

> The Soviet military strategy has been to acquire equal or greater forces than the United States to insure their defense as well as provide strong psychological backing for expansion of Soviet influence. ... From the Soviet point of view, perceived strategic superiority has a direct application to the deterrence of strategic nuclear war. It implies maintenance of strategic forces capable of inflicting unacceptable damage on the United States, limiting damage to the Soviet Union, and successfully waging a nuclear war. Their programs are designed not only for deterring nuclear war, but to fight and win as well.[80]

A secretary of defense survey of Soviet military doctrine publications concluded that Soviet doctrine writers had not abandoned a traditional view that war was a final instrument of policy, the dawning of the nuclear age notwithstanding. Belief in the possibility of a prolonged nuclear war remained consistent in open literature, this perhaps stemming from a belief that a militarily well-prepared modern state might prove resilient to even a nuclear attack. With the passing of the 1970s, Harold Brown, secretary of defense in 1979, was forced to conclude:

> The Soviet Union's approach to war is different from that of the US. They desire and are seeking capabilities which would enable them to fight, win, and survive a nuclear exchange. In the Soviet view, it is the existence of an effective and credible warwaging capability, with its attendant potential of achieving victory, which serves to deter an attack. The principal difference between this Soviet view of deterrence and that of Western concepts is that the Soviets stress the requirements for responding effectively and achieving victory in the event war occurs rather than stressing measures required primarily to prevent war in the first place.[81]

At the time of SALT I Soviet missile accuracy appeared to be substantially less than that of the US Minuteman. Secretary Schlesinger argued that Soviet missile throw-weight superiority in part compensated for lesser missile accuracy, but he was skeptical that combat missile accuracy would even measure up to test-range accuracy. Since neither US nor Soviet missile systems had been tested in transpolar operational trajectories there were many uncertainties in the potential accuracies of inertial-guidance systems that would result from gravitational anomalies, weather conditions, and biases which could not be exactly predetermined. Even a small deviation could have a significant impact on damage probabilities, especially against a US or Soviet missile silo. Observations of Soviet tests from southern Russia near the Aral Sea, at targets in Siberia, the Kamchatka Peninsula, or into the Pacific Ocean, indicated that Soviet ICBMs were not accurate enough to get a high probability of kill (PK) against a Minuteman silo; two missiles so aimed promised better theoretical results, but the tendency of exploding nuclear warheads to destroy those following closely behind — an effect called "fratricide" — would hinder such a strike against a silo. The 1975 national intelligence estimate pointed out that the most accurate Soviet missiles — the SS-18s and SS-19s — had a circular error probable (CEP) of almost a quarter of a mile and thus were not accurate enough to jeopardize Minuteman silos.[82]

Beginning in the 1961–63 period when Air Force missile and space men were studying requirements for the future, Air Force intelligence appreciations of Soviet actions were different. The Soviets were following consistent test programs for missiles that indicated they were developing their technology quite independently of US actions. This assessment was counter to the accepted OSD threat analysis culture which rationalized that weapon systems were procured on the basis of analysis of the threat, the technology available, and as a reaction to enemy actions. The OSD-CIA assessment was that the Soviets were not procuring new weapons in a continuing program. According to an experienced Air Force space systems planner, Col Francis X. Kane, Air Force projections of Soviet missile activities were always closer to actuality than official estimates, but the Air Force was accused of self-serving by scaring Congress as to the rate of the buildup of the Soviet threat.[83]

In 1974 and 1975, Air Force Intelligence, headed by Maj Gen George Keegan, Jr., gathered evidence that the Soviets were spending large sums to build deep shelters for Soviet leaders — 75 within the Moscow ring road alone, some hardened to withstand blast pressures of 1,000 psi. When CIA analysts discounted this intelligence, Keegan charged that the 1975 national intelligence estimate (NIE) totally ignored Soviet civil defense and thus "illustrated one more gross intelligence failure." In 1976 a mammoth CIA civil-defense study of the Soviet Union supported Keegan's conclusions. During the same year, it was also becoming evident that the 1975 NIE estimate of Soviet missile accuracy was erroneous inasmuch as SS-18s and SS-19s would likely attain an accuracy of a tenth of a nautical mile — about 600 feet. Ironically, this increased accuracy would be possible much earlier than could have been predicted because of a Soviet purchase of key American machines — the Centalign B — for the manufacture of miniature precision ball bearings that were vital to the production of miniaturized guidance and control systems for missiles. First Soviet efforts to purchase machines for the production of these small, finely ground bearings were blocked by Department of Defense objections, but in the euphoria of 1972 the Soviets purchased and received delivery of 164 Centalign B machines, more than twice the number in use in the United States.[84] Secretary of Defense Caspar Weinberger would say of the Soviets in 1982:

> The accuracy of their reentry vehicles has been essentially attained by technology taken from us, some of it transferred legally, some of it stolen.... The one item that has helped them the most ... was the ability to turn out very small, finely ground ball bearing systems, which they took as part of a contract ... that ... did not have the proper scrutiny to demonstrate that it had a high military capability.[85]

President Carter's Countervailing Strategy

When President Jimmy Carter took office in the White House in January 1977 he was said to have believed that the use of nuclear weapons was to deter war, not to fight one. At a preinaugural briefing he astounded the Joint Chiefs of Staff with a suggestion that the United States could make do with a retaliation force of 200 nuclear weapons — the old figure used by US Navy advocates of "finite deterrence" in 1959. President Carter selected the experienced Dr Harold Brown to be his secretary of defense, and Brown's visceral feeling expressed in February 1977 was that "once one starts to use nuclear weapons, even in a tactical way, it is quite likely it will escalate." Brown nevertheless emphasized that the Carter administration's policy would continue to be to maintain rough equivalence or essential parity with the Soviet Union in strategic arms. By essential equivalence, Brown meant the maintenance conditions that:

- Soviet strategic nuclear forces do not become usable instruments of political leverage, diplomatic coercion, or military advantage.
- Nuclear stability, especially in a crisis, is maintained.
- Any advantages in force characteristics enjoyed by the Soviets are offset by US advantages in other characteristics.
- The US posture is not in fact, and is not seen as, inferior in performance to the strategic nuclear forces of the Soviet Union.

Brown believed it necessary that the United States not allow any "perceived imbalance" in strategic forces to exist since this would have "severe political consequences, both here in the United States and with our allies, and with neutrals, and on the actions of the Soviet Union. Insistence on essential equivalence guards against any danger that the Soviets might be seen as superior even if the perception is not technically or militarily justified."[86] At the same time the Carter administration was taking office, General Keegan retired from active duty with a statement to journalists that the Soviet Union had attained military superiority over the United States. Asked for comments, Gen George S. Brown said that Keegan, although a "superb fellow" had "always seen things in a more dramatic light than his contemporaries or his associates." Brown nevertheless got a short statement from the Joint Chiefs of Staff:

> The Joint Chiefs of Staff do not agree that the Soviet Union has achieved military superiority over the United States. The available evidence suggests the U.S.S.R. is engaged in a program designed to achieve such superiority but they have not attained this goal. The Joint Chiefs are concerned, however, that the recent US and Soviet trend in military programs and civil defense could permit the U.S.S.R. to obtain superiority. The Joint Chiefs of Staff will continue to advocate [that] the United States do what is necessary to maintain strategic nuclear equivalence. Central to this position is continued JCS support of SALT negotiations heading to an equitable agreement, which will assure the strategic balance.[87]

In February 1977 the Carter administration did not have any new plans or doctrines respecting employment of strategic nuclear forces. Secretary Brown endorsed neither countercity retaliation (assured destruction) nor disarming counterforce. "Rather," he said, "we seek to deter any strategic exchange by insuring the required overall survivability of our own strategic forces, together with the maximum possible flexibility in their use."[88] President Carter started his administration with numerous requests for studies which were called presidential review memoranda (PRMs, pronounced Prims) and one of them was PRM-10, "Comprehensive Net Assessment and Military Force Posture Review." This was to be an interagency study on national security policy with special emphasis on strategic doctrine. Prepared under the direction of Lynn Etheridge Davis who had been appointed deputy assistant secretary of defense for policy planning, the strategic forces study of PRM-10 ended up as Annex C and turned out to be an effort to establish criteria for the number of weapons that would be required to effect possibly 70 percent destruction to four basic categories of targets—Soviet nuclear forces, other Soviet military forces, command and control centers, and urban and industrial targets. The study was said to have shown that the United States had more than enough weapons to destroy categories of Soviet targets, but at a high-level review in August 1977, Presidential Adviser for National Security Affairs Zbigniew Brzezinski complained that Annex C did not yield any information about how to wage a nuclear war. He wanted to know why the Great Russians—or the Russian Russians—who ran the Soviet Union were not targeted as a group since killing them would speed the disintegration of the Soviet empire. The main result of the abortive PRM-10 was to generate a new presidential directive (PD) 18 calling for a follow-on study on national targeting policy review.[89]

As it happened the Carter administration made decisions on strategic weapons well before a final codification of the new strategic targeting concept called for in PD-18. In the election year of 1976 Congress had come to a conclusion that the next president should determine whether the prototype B-1 bomber should be produced, and President Carter had come into the office with the opinion that it should not, provided he could make a convincing case. Secretary Brown provided the reasons the B-1 should not be built on the basis of the four prototypes at hand: B-52s carrying still-to-be-developed, air-launched cruise missiles (ALCMs) would be more effective and cheaper than B-1s. There was also a promise of new "stealth" technology that would permit another follow-on strategic bomber to minimize the visibility of suitably designed air vehicles to hostile radar. On 30 June 1977 President Carter announced his decision to cancel production of the B-1 bomber and, instead, to develop and produce long-range cruise missiles for B-52s and perhaps other air-launch aircraft.[90] On 15 September 1977 Secretary Brown presented the Carter amendments to the fiscal year 1978 defense appropriation to Congress, prefacing his remarks with a strategic assessment:

> Our primary measure of strategic capability is our ability to retaliate after a Soviet first strike on our forces. Our analyses show that, over a range of wartime events, our current forces could ride out such a massive Soviet first strike and retaliate with devastating effect.[91]

Nevertheless, Brown urged that it would be wise to "hedge against unexpected developments or overlooked factors, and the impact of comparative capabilities with the Soviet Union on international perceptions (Soviet, third party, and our own)." As this hedge, Brown strongly supported a B-52/cruise missile combination, saying: "I am certain that the cruise missile will improve the world's perception of the potency of our forces." Among other strategic programs, he expected to continue development of the Mark-12A warhead for the Minuteman III, backfitting of a long-range and more accurate C-4 (Trident I) missile into Poseidon submarines and production of Trident submarines with C-4 missiles. Brown mentioned a possible need for an advanced land-based force deployment in the mid-1980s to assure strategic equivalence, and he promised to review the possibility of developing a new mobile MX intercontinental missile when reviewing the fiscal year 1979 defense budget.[92]

In December 1977 the Soviet Union served notice that on the last 10 days of the month it would run missile tests into the North Pacific. Up until this time the SS-18 was a large missile—about 4 times as large as the Minuteman—with 8 to 10 independently targeted warheads, but it had a relatively crude and inaccurate guidance system and presented no significant threat to Minuteman silos. But the missiles tested at the end of December had new guidance systems, evidently including new ball-bearing technology obtained from the United States. After analysis of the tests it was clear by the middle of 1978 that the Soviets had succeeded in developing a guidance system which gave the SS-18 and later the SS-19 sufficient accuracy to destroy Minuteman silos. A defense analyst, James P. Wade, Jr., drew a graph of Minuteman survival rates after a hypothetical Soviet attack with two missiles per silo. He concluded that the Soviets beginning in 1981 or 1982 would be able to effect 80 to 90 percent PK on Minuteman silos; the downward plunge could not begin to improve before the late 1980s and then only if the MX missile still on the drawing board was developed and produced. Wade described the dip of his graph line as "the window of vulnerability."[93]

The immediate effect of the enhanced Soviet hard-target kill capability was to serve notice that the Soviets were seriously presenting the establishment of a nuclear warfighting capability as the sine qua non of nuclear deterrence. Technical improvements in nuclear weapons portended their use in a traditional military manner. During 1978 the follow-on strategic targeting study required by PD-18 progressed to completion in the Department of Defense, and Secretary Brown sent it to the White House in December 1978. The study was said to have presented three principal conclusions. First, Soviet targets were growing steadily in number and being made harder to destroy, meaning that strategic forces should have greater flexibility in targeting and that more options should be available. Second, that both the US strategic forces and the command, control, communications, and intelligence (C^3I) that controlled the forces should have much greater endurance. Third, greater attention should be directed toward improving the effectiveness of US attacks against military targets.[94] Secretary Brown moved to implement the basic precepts of the follow-on strategic study, outlining the precepts as a new "countervailing strategy" in his Department of Defense annual report for fiscal year 1980. He submitted it to Congress on 25 January 1979. Brown described the countervailing strategy as a response "in such a way that the enemy could have no expectation of achieving any rational objective, no illusion of making any gain without offsetting losses."[95]

The Soviets hard-target, missile kill capability spurred US strategic weapons activities that had long been delayed by opponents who, in the description of Dr William J. Perry, under secretary of defense for research and engineering, long had used a tactic which could be called "paralysis by analysis." When the Carter administration was presented the MX as an ongoing research and development program in 1977 the program was regarded with some skepticism. The first question that President Carter asked when briefed on the MX was whether the vulnerability of the Minuteman force was "strictly theoretical" or "practical." If it was theoretical why spend as much money for the MX? Carter also was intensely interested in the president's decision handbook, explaining procedures for national command authorities (NCA) in the event of nuclear attack. When he learned that Minuteman silos were indeed vulnerable, he asked, "Why could I not simply put my forces on a launch under attack?" The ICBM flight time from the Soviet Union was about 30 minutes with ballistic missile early warning system (BMEWS), perimeter acquisition radar (PAR), and satellite early warning detection system providing warning. With warning it was possible for national command authorities to launch the Minuteman force on warning of a nuclear attack or during such an attack. When this matter was beginning to be discussed in September 1977, Secretary Brown personally was inclined to believe that any nuclear attack would not come "out of the blue" but was much more likely to follow a period of tension where there had been "a generated alert." Thus the NCA could be "close to the trigger" and launch under attack could always be a viable option. Brown said about launch under attack, "I think that it is not our doctrine to do so — neither is it doctrine that under no circumstances would we ever do so." Launch under warning was a different matter, and it was soon agreed that this was too hazardous. Warning systems were inherently soft targets admitting easy and early destruction; they were in part located in remote places in the world and had long and tenuous links back to the NCA. Warning systems could malfunction. President Carter accepted the OSD recommendation that launch on warning would not be appropriate and that launch under attack was, as Secretary Brown said, "something that could be considered only with the greatest caution."[96] Launch under attack continued to be talked about and Gen Lew Allen, Jr., Air Force chief of staff, stated Air Force views:

> It is the Air Force's responsibility to ensure that the warning systems are as reliable as they can be in order to provide data with regard to an incoming attack that is sufficiently precise and of unquestionable confidence to be made. . . . Similarly, the command and control must be sufficient so that the National Command Authorities have the opportunity to exercise control and react. . . . Nevertheless, as a matter of US philosophy and as a policy alternative to a survivable force, it is, in my personal opinion, a totally unacceptable approach. It requires a decision — the most critical ever faced by mankind — in an extremely short period in order to save money, which doesn't seem to me to be an appropriate thing to do.[97]

In view of projected vulnerability of land-based ICBMs, President Carter considered a proposition that this leg of the strategic triad (ICBMs, SLBMs, and bombers/ALCMs) should be abandoned in favor of a dyad (SLBMs and bombers/ALCMs) and that all strategic missiles should be sent to sea in submarines, rather than about half of them as was then the case. Carter rejected this plan not because of technical reasons but because there was a possibility that in 10 or 20 years the Soviets would develop a way to detect and destroy submarines at sea. There was no indication that detection was likely, but if all missiles were at sea, all the eggs would be in one basket. Secretary Brown also provided a chart showing that ICBMs had more of the desired strategic force characteristics than SLBMs or bombers/ALCMs, as follows:

Current Strategic Force Characteristics

	ICBMs	*SLBMs*	*Bombers/ALCMs*
Secure and Reliable C^3	yes	?**	?
Flexibility/Responsiveness	yes	?**	no
Assured Penetration	yes	yes	?
Prompt Counterforce Capability	yes	?**	no
Sovereign Basing	yes	no	yes
Enduring Survivability	*	yes	?
Survives Without Tactical Warning	*	yes	no

* May be "yes" with multiple-protective structures (MPS) and some survivable basing modes.
**Would require new programs and/or changes to SSBN operational practices.

Brown also pointed out that failure to modernize the ICBM force was likely to be taken by the Soviets and perhaps other countries as an indication that the United States was not going to be competitive in strategic weapons and might be willing to accept inferiority.[98]

From the early 1960s the Air Force had devoted a large effort in studying basing options to reduce eventual vulnerability of ICBM silos. In 1964 under Project 75 the Air Force examined options such as the acquisition of many small missiles, off-road mobile systems, water mobile systems, and a superhard arsenal that would be buried deep underground and house several missiles with multiple-launch exits to the surface. In 1967 under Project STRAT-X the Air Force examined some multiple-protective structure systems such as missiles deployed among many silos buried in rock or soft soil and missiles deployed in rock or soft soil tunnels. It also examined underwater basing in canals. In 1970 the Air Force began the Minuteman Rebasing Study. It considered upgrading the existing silos' hardness and burying silos in hard rock, as well as three mobile concepts: a dash-to-shelter, on-warning mobile system and two off-road mobile concepts employing either an all-terrain or an air-cushion vehicle. At this time it was determined that upgrading the hardness of existing silos would be an effective near-term solution to ICBM survivability. In 1973–74 the Air Force examined an airmobile concept employing wide-bodied commercial-type aircraft. The airmobility concept was dropped because of the susceptibility of aircraft to potential Soviet nuclear missile barrage attack blanketing an airfield and its vicinity and the very great expense that would have been required to make aircraft sufficiently superhard to live through such a barrage. In 1973–76 the Air Force also examined other MPS concepts, including a trench in which missiles would be shuttled along to changing locations and horizontal and vertical shelters in large numbers into which missiles could be inserted and removed to confuse Soviet targeting. Most of all these concepts were rejected without detailed cost analysis simply because they did not preserve the desired characteristics of the ICBM force, which were:

- Different preattack survival mode than aircraft or SLBMs and a different penetration to target mode than aircraft.
- Independence from strategic or tactical warning for prelaunch survival.
- Exceptionally reliable command, control, and communications (C^3) for positive control.
- Unique military capability as embodied in the ICBM's rapid response capability, prompt retargeting ability, short flight time to target, hard target capability, high alert rate, and range.
- Enduring survivability in an extended nuclear conflict.
- Low domestic profile, but large international perception.
- High confidence in nuclear weapon safety and security.
- Relatively low operating cost and personnel requirements.
- Independence from concealment for survival.
- Straightforward SALT verification concept.

For example, most of the road mobile concepts were highly dependent on warning. Mobile systems not so heavily dependent on warning required continuous movement involving high operations and support costs as well as security problems. Other concepts such as the buried arsenal were rejected because of operational problems (subterranean basing of crews and equipment) and high-technical risks. All the major flaws in pure hardness and mobility concepts forced acceptance of some MPS systems, which meant that the solution to the problem would be to hide a relatively small number of missiles in a relatively large number of shelters. Since the missiles could not be hidden forever, there was a need for a transporter to move missiles from shelter to shelter. The dimension of the MX could not be finally specified until basing arrangements were made, and in 1978 it was becoming essential to get moving along with the missile development. In December 1978 the Air Force's recommendations to the second Defense Systems Acquisition Review Council (DSARC-II) favored going ahead with full-scale engineering development of a MX missile to be deployed in a vertical MPS mode, with many vertical shelters to shield 200 MX missiles in random and changing deployments. At this time President Carter and several of his senior advisers expressed a great deal of reservation about the whole concept of survivability of land-based missiles, and the DSARC directed additional studies, including use of a new short takeoff and landing (advanced medium STOL aircraft—AMSA) aircraft that the Air Force was developing as an airborne MX missile carrier. Another problem involved the SALT discussions, in which each side was going to expect to verify by its own surveillance the numbers of fixed ICBMs of the other side, which would be difficult for the Soviets to manage in a vertical MPS deployment.[99]

In August 1977, shortly before Gen Richard H. Ellis assumed command of SAC and directorship of the JSTPS, he was called to testify before a subcommittee of the Senate Committee on Armed Services. At that time he found that sufficient strategic forces were available "to carry out national level guidance." In his first year at SAC, however, Ellis found the balance with the Soviets getting tighter. He found, for example, that the number of potential Soviet targets had been increasing by about 10 percent each year for several years. This increase was caused by Soviet construction of new installations, intelligence discovery of previously undiscovered installations, and additions of targets caused by changes in national targeting policy. Ellis was said to have argued against any revision of the SIOP contemplated in the strategic follow-on study called for in PD-18 on the grounds that he did not have enough force to do his present job. In December 1978 Gen Lew Allen, Jr., Air Force chief of staff, convened a board of Air Force general officers at SAC headquarters to explore possible alternatives to the shortfall of US strategic capabilities in the early 1980s. The board noted that some capability would be regained with the deployment of 300 Mark-12A warheads on Minuteman III missiles starting in 1980, deployment of the first squadron of cruise missiles in 1982, and production of Trident SSBNs and C-4 backfit in some Poseidon submarines. No single option, however, promised to redress the shortfall. The most promising option appeared to be in the manned-bomber projection. The Air Force F-111s in the operating inventory could be given new engines, stretched fuselages to accommodate weapons, sharply increased range capabilities, and assignment to SAC to supplement B-52s. Or else the B-1 could be put back into development. In a return visit to the Senate Armed Services Committee in February 1979, Ellis recommended that first priority be given to development of MX, that attention be given to modification of F-111s as FB-111s, and that C^3 systems conceived in the 1950s and affected in the 1960s be renovated to admit communications and connectivity to continue during nuclear war.[100]

The DSARC-II review of MX was on hold in the early months of 1979 while the Air Force summed up alternatives for basing the new missiles. In May 1979 President Carter received five options for MX basing and MX engineering development. One was to do nothing, one was to go ahead with MPS, and the other three were to go mobile. The first of these was road mobile, which was rejected because of its dependence on strategic warning. The AMSA airmobile concept involved deploying transport aircraft carrying airmobile MXs to small dispersed airfields on strategic warning, but this idea was rejected for cost reasons and also because it had the same vulnerabilities and limitations as a bomber force. Finally, there was an option (the enhanced Triad) to accelerate the cruise missile program, build more cruise missile carriers, accelerate the Trident program, build more submarines, and procure a new large sea-based missile. The National Security Council debated the options and ultimately selected MPS, which was the great favorite of the Air Force.

IDEAS, CONCEPTS, DOCTRINE

DSARC-II was completed on 21 July 1979 and that summer President Carter approved the full-scale engineering development of the larger of the two MX variations offered him. Carter approved an MPS deployment concept but he wanted some assurance that the concept would still be viable in the year 2010. Toward this end he did not like a vertical deployment but favored a horizontal concept, saying: "I will be willing to pay a premium on the order of 10 percent to put in a horizontal mode where, in addition to concealment[,] I will be able to move it rather rapidly."[101] Full-scale engineering development was initiated on 7 September 1979, with the understanding on Gen Lew Allen's part that there would be more refinements. Essentially what was basically planned was to devise a complex that could survive an attack of 6,000 to 7,000 Soviet warheads, each of which would carry a one-megaton bomb, and each capable of being directed within 600 to 700 feet of a target. In the horizontal mode 200 MX missiles, each lifting 10 MK-12A warheads, would be dispersed in 4,600 shelters, and the MXs would be moved from place to place in large transporters covering over 8,000 to 10,000 miles of gravel-surface roads. It was assumed that the Soviets would have to use 2.3 warheads to destroy each shelter, which would expend their entire ICBM force potentially to destroy 200 MXs. It was planned that the MX missile complexes would be located on federal lands in Utah and Nevada and would have a minimal ecological effect on these desert areas.[102]

As indicated in congressional testimony over a considerable period of time, Gen David C. Jones, the Air Force chief of staff who became chairman of the Joint Chiefs of Staff, reasoned that

> the principal foundation of Soviet influence in the world derives from their military power. As this power and the capability to project that power grow in relation to the US and allied capability to counter it, the Soviet leadership will inevitably perceive a wider range of options in pursuing their national and ideological objectives.[103]

In December 1979 Soviet troops invaded Afghanistan, marking in Secretary Brown's assessment a new pattern of aggression, different from the earlier invasions into Czechoslovakia or Hungary, since these countries were members of the Warsaw Pact and could be considered Soviet-bloc countries. Afghanistan was a traditional buffer state and had not been part of a Soviet sphere of control.[104] After the Soviet invasion of Afghanistan, President Carter asked the Senate to delay consideration of a ratification of the SALT II treaty so that Congress and the executive branch could devote full attention to a response to the invasion of Afghanistan.[105]

Where Gen Richard H. Ellis had accepted an assessment in February 1979 that the United States stood essentially equivalent with the Soviet Union, his presentation to House and Senate appropriations subcommittees as CINCSAC in February 1980 stressed a new assessment that the United States no longer possessed the comparative force capabilities with the Soviet Union that had been specified in 1977 to be "essential equivalence." The accelerated rate of Soviet modernization, compounded with cancellations and slippages of major US programs, had altered the strategic relationship from that of 1977.

> Ellis told members of the House Subcommittee on Appropriations on 5 March; I would like to begin by saying that the strategic balance as we measure it has shifted in favor of the Soviet Union. Now there are several reasons for this . . . but basically it relates to bad intelligence; in other words, intelligence estimates that did not prove out. . . . It relates to the Soviet momentum and the deployment of their new ICBM systems, SLBM systems, and the accuracy they have been able to achieve with these systems. . . . Of course, shippage and cancellations of US programs also have played a major role. . . . Recent Soviet activity in Africa and South Asia can be traced, not to a change in our overall conventional force capabilities, but rather to a shift in our strategic balance . . . their increased adventurism is a result of the changing strategic nuclear balance.[106]

General Ellis's charges opened a disputation in Washington that demonstrated that it was extremely complex to attempt to measure relative strategic balances of force. Gen Lew Allen pointed out that General Ellis had established a quantitative baseline for strategic equivalence as being late 1977/early 1978 because national guidance to him had specified that "parity" or "equivalence" existed then and was to be maintained in the future. Ellis viewed degradation of US capabilities as a loss of essential equivalence. General Allen agreed with Ellis that US capability relative to that of the Soviets was declining and that the trend should be reversed, but he described the relative relationship as being one of "rough equivalence."[107] When asked to comment on Ellis's testimony about "adverse strategic imbalance" in nuclear forces, Secretary Brown responded that analytical approaches to such matters inevitably provided a variety of conclusions because of differences in number and kind of underlying assumptions. Brown concluded:

> In the end, assessment of the strategic balance is a matter of judgment. . . . It is our present judgment that Soviet and American strategic forces currently possess a roughly comparable capability to survive a surprise attack and to retaliate with roughly comparable effectiveness. Because of this, we now have a situation of essential equivalence.[108]

Brown also differed with Ellis on the relationship of strategic nuclear imbalance to Soviet peripheral adventurism, saying:

> We have recognized for many years that strategic nuclear forces, by themselves, could credibly deter only a narrow range of contingencies. For peripheral political and military actions in particular, it is our conventional forces that are the primary military deterrent to possible Soviet adventurisms. . . . Nuclear forces may contribute, however, through justifiable concern about escalation, to the deterrence of nonnuclear military actions. The nuclear balance can also affect perceptions of US willingness and ability to protect its interests in general, and thereby enter into the considerations of the Soviets, our allies, and others in a variety of situations. This is one reason we are determined not to allow an imbalance in strategic nuclear capabilities.[109]

In his final report to Congress, Secretary Brown concluded that the era of US nuclear superiority had been overtaken by "parity" and that the United States and the Soviet Union were roughly equal in strategic nuclear power. He offered four conditions as a valid description of "essential equivalence," namely:

1. Soviet strategic nuclear forces do not become usable instruments of political leverage, diplomatic coercion, or military advantage;
2. nuclear stability, especially in a crisis, is maintained;
3. any advantages in strategic force characteristics enjoyed by the Soviets are affected by US advantages in other characteristics; and
4. the US strategic posture is not in fact, and is not seen as, inferior to that of the Soviet Union.

Using these four conditions as his basis for judgment as he was going out of office, Brown stated: "I conclude that the strategic nuclear forces of our two countries remain essentially equivalent."[110]

In his appearances before a congressional committee as the year turned into 1980, Secretary Brown said that the Soviets were getting a payoff from their military efforts not because the United States had not been matching the Soviets but because "we have been on the wrong side of the relative momentum." It was necessary to show the Soviets that they could not prevail by a buildup of military capability. He continued:

> In order to strengthen deterrence—and in order to provide a range of options in the event deterrence fails—we have adopted a countervailing strategy designed to make a Soviet victory as improbable (seen through *Soviet* eyes) as we can make it over the broadest plausible range of scenarios.... In support of the countervailing strategy we must have plans to attack Soviet military force structure, industry, and political control structure, and in addition to hold an assured destruction force in reserve. Thus, we are not self-deterred, for our strategy, the forces deployed in support of that strategy, and the employment plans for those forces simultaneously enhance deterrence of a Soviet attack *and* provide a range of options appropriate to the type and scale of any Soviet attack in the event deterrence fails. If in the Soviets' view, however, our ability to mount an effective response is evident, that very assessment should deter them from providing the occasion for such a response.[111]

Secretary Brown explained his idea of a countervailing strategy in the *Department of Defense, Annual Report, Fiscal Year 1981*, released on 29 January 1980.[112] In June 1980 Secretary Brown explained the general nature of the countervailing strategy to a NATO nuclear planning group meeting in Norway, saying that the strategy was under consideration and that there would be a presidential decision.[113]

According to an apparently informed source, Secretary Brown reasoned that explanations of the new countervailing strategy in his annual defense reports should make it sufficiently authoritative, but presidential adviser Brzezinski argued the need for President Carter to issue a directive that would prod Washington agencies inside and outside the Pentagon. In addition to this, NSDM 242 did not require the necessary hard-target accuracy and yield of the MK-12A warheads being retrofitted into Minuteman III and planned for the MX. How could the administration persuade Congress to fund hard-target killers without an official strategic doctrine to justify them? On 25 July 1980 President Carter signed an implementing directive—Presidential Directive No. 59—codifying the restated strategic doctrine and giving guidance for further planning and systems acquisition. Although PD-59 was closely held for security reasons, Secretary Brown received the task of explaining it in an address at the Naval War College on 20 August 1980 and at a top-secret hearing of the Senate Foreign Relations Committee on 16 September 1980. After a few months PD-59 was sanitized and published. At the outset of his explanatory remarks, Secretary Brown emphasized that PD-59 was not a new strategic doctrine, not a radical departure of strategic policy, but a refinement, a codification of previous statements of strategic policy. Nuclear weapons programs required for a countervailing strategy had already been approved. The big difference in procurement that PD-59 would likely make would be in command, control, and communications. This difference was to ensure what was being called "connectivity" between national command authorities, unified and specified commanders, and the actual forces themselves. The strategy sought to deter nuclear conflict by shaping Soviet views. The Soviet system, for example, placed a high value on political and military control structures. The new strategy required targeting of systems and smaller "sets," including counterpolitical and countermilitary objectives. Overall there was emphasis on force flexibility—the ability to respond at an appropriate level to Soviet actions on any level.[114]

In his final secretary of defense report to Congress filed on 19 January 1981, Harold Brown described and explained the Carter administration's countervailing strategy at great length. He wrote in summation:

> To the Soviet Union, our strategy makes clear that no course of aggression by them that led to use of nuclear weapons, or any scale of attack and at any stage of conflict, would lead to victory, however they may define victory. Besides our power to devastate the full target system of the USSR, the United States would have the option for more selective, lesser retaliatory attacks that would exact a prohibitively high price from the things the Soviet leadership prizes most—political and military control, nuclear and conventional military force, and the economic base needed to sustain war.[115]

Five basic elements of force employment policy served to achieve the objectives of the countervailing strategy: flexibility; escalation control; survivability and endurance; ability to destroy four general categories of Soviet targets (strategic nuclear forces, other military forces, leadership and control, industrial and economic base; and survivable and enduring reserve forces and C^3I system). For the deterrence of the countervailing strategy to remain credible, the overall capability of strategic nuclear forces had to be "essentially equivalent" both in appearance and in fact to those of the Soviet Union. Brown stated:

> Maintenance of a strategic balance characterized by essentially equivalent forces strengthens deterrence by dispelling any illusion on either side that the outcome of a nuclear war could be advantageous. . . . For these reasons, we pursue essential

IDEAS, CONCEPTS, DOCTRINE

equivalence and stability as objectives in their own right, inasmuch as both conditions reduce the likelihood of nuclear war.[116]

President Reagan Opts for Both Offense and Defense

From the start of the 1980 presidential campaign Republican Ronald W. Reagan emphasized the need for increased US defenses. "America's defense strength," Reagan said when accepting his party's nomination, "is at its lowest ebb in a generation, while the Soviet Union is vastly outspending us in both strategic and conventional arms." In the words of the new secretary of defense, Caspar W. Weinberger, Reagan's victory at the polls gave his administration a "mandate [that] emphasized the strengthening of America."[117] In Weinberger's initial appearance in Congress in March 1981 he expressed two highest priorities:

> One is to redress the strategic balance which I think has been allowed to fall into serious imbalance, and the second is to do all we can to improve the readiness of what we have, using the term in the broadest sense of the word. It does include pay increases for servicemen who were leaving the Service in too great numbers. . . . It does involve a strengthening of missiles because we feel the missiles we have do not have the degree of survivability they should. It does involve a new manned bomber. . . . We have no interest whatever in allowing any unnecessary expenditures. . . . It is just that after years of neglect and after encountering an enormous increase on the Russian side, we do need to do many things all at once. . . . I think we will start to sort it out.[118]

In the case of the MX missile and the manned bomber, Weinberger asked Congress to provide necessary project funds with formal policy decisions to be submitted after further study — in the case of the MX, its basing mode and of the manned bomber, which of three alternatives would ultimately be decided upon.[119]

In presenting the Reagan rearmament requests to the House Military Appropriations Subcommittee on 19 March 1981, Weinberger noted his appreciation of the fact that Congress wanted him to relate his requests to "a very explicit policy and strategy." He was not yet prepared to do this but he was in process of establishing a "new sense of direction." "The principal shortcoming of the budget we inherited was that it failed to provide full funding for many programs the previous administration conceded were necessary, but felt unable to afford." When asked how his defense policy was different, Weinberger replied that the new policy differed from the policy of previous administrations which "was driven too much by whether or not it would appeal to domestic political constituencies, and on an improper assessment of Soviet intentions and on a feeling that we should not take actions that would in any way provoke activities against us."[120] At this same hearing, Weinberger provided a written response to a question as to whether mutually assured destruction or essential equivalence constituted "a workable policy."

> Answer. Mutual assured destruction and essential equivalence are concepts that have been used to describe strategic force capabilities and balances. They have been

used—and misused—so often that they have acquired the connotation of a grand strategy or panacea. As abstract concepts, they have a simplistic appeal. They suggest that if our cities and Soviet cities remain vulnerable to attack, or if we have as many warheads as the Soviets, or if we can do as much damage as they can, nuclear war will be averted.

Those are big "ifs" and there is little evidence from their actions that the Soviets intend to accept vulnerability or anything less than military superiority and the international political leverage that such superiority provides. Nor is it clear that either concept has provided the kind of guidance that has allowed us to build a force structure that has caused them to abandon their efforts to expand their influence throughout the world.

Wars break out over irreconcilable conflicts in vital interests. To cope with that situation requires a far more comprehensive doctrine, strategy and policy. Neither mutual assured destruction nor essential equivalence is sufficient for this purpose.

There is a difference between an overall national policy and strategy for safeguarding all of our vital interests throughout the world, and policies and strategies for the design, acquisition and employment of the military forces needed to support such an overall grand design.

In terms of strategic nuclear war, for example, we do have a doctrine of needs and objectives, and a policy for achieving them. That policy has as its objective deterrence of Soviet nuclear attack upon the United States, its allies, and friends, through acquisition of countervailing retaliatory forces credibly capable of denying the Soviets achievement of any meaningful objective or of exacting costs that exceed any possible gain regardless of the scale of Soviet aggression—forces that hold at risk all of the things that the Soviets value most. Obviously, this policy and strategy transcends the limited scope of essential equivalence or mutual assured destruction. But it falls short of a grand design.

Integration of this policy and strategy with other policies and strategies aimed at defeating other forms of Soviet adventurism is a far more complex task, and one that will require much more work before we can confidently say that we have a coherent doctrine, strategy and policy capable of safeguarding all of our interests.[121]

Weinberger further explained how the MX missile and the new manned bomber fitted into strategic nuclear policy:

Answer. It is the objective of the Defense Department to prevent war—particularly nuclear war. But it is the mission of the Defense Department to prepare to wage war, if necessary—including nuclear war. The conduct of war, at all times has to serve national policy; that is to say, it must serve political objectives and be clearly guided by a plan for terminating the war in a manner that enhances these objectives.

The primary role of US strategic nuclear forces is deterrence of attack on the US, its forces, and its allies and friends. US forces must be capable of absorbing a Soviet first strike and still retaliating with devastating effect. Force planning should seek to redress the current strategic imbalance through an aggressive and comprehensive modernization program for both forces and supporting C^3I.

> Deterrence is served by increasing our capabilities to implement counter-military attacks against the Soviets, with a posture that will make Soviet assessments of war outcomes sufficiently uncertain and unfavorable so as to deter them from launching attacks on the US, our forces, or upon our allies. Because of the Soviet emphasis on warfighting, we must increase our capabilities to attack military targets in different wartime situations, in order to deprive them of any confidence that they could outlast us or reach a situation in which they could maintain significant nuclear capabilities while our own would either be eliminated or could no longer endure or be effectively employed.
>
> Emphasis on matching static indicators of Soviet forces, particularly preattack measures of Soviet forces, will be decreased. Greater emphasis will be placed on the multiplicity of strategic systems and basing modes to strengthen the benefits of the Triad. The purpose of the Triad (and additional arrangements for multiplicity of strategic offensive forces) is to complicate Soviet defense and attack planning, to create a synergism among the strategic force elements in our own attack planning and execution, and to hedge against unforeseen degradations in individual force elements.
>
> The MX missile and the new manned bomber are integral elements of the modernization program needed to develop a military posture credibly capable of supporting attainment of these goals.[122]

Although the Reagan administration favored a decentralization of decisionmaking within the Department of Defense and allowed force increases to be budgeted by the separate services, the Department of Defense maintained an active interest in the planning for strategic augmentation — particularly the manned bomber and the MX. As CINCSAC and thus the commander responsible for two of the legs of the strategic Triad, Gen Richard H. Ellis appeared in February 1981 with a very clear statement of needs:

- MX must be our first priority.
- The strategic manned penetrator remains critical for an effective Triad.
- The immediacy of the near term threat demands an interim bomber.
- We need an advanced technology bomber for the 1990s, and
- Without an effective C^3I network — strategic modernization does not regain needed capability.[123]

Ellis would have preferred to go directly to the advanced technology bomber and have it fielded by the mid-to-late 1980s, in which case an interim bomber would not be needed, but Air Force technology programming could not visualize a sound planning date for the first operational squadron of advanced technology bombers before 1990. Ellis therefore wanted an interim bomber: either a version of the B-1 that had not been produced or a modified FB-111. Ellis favored the FB-111 bomber modification because he thought it would be cheaper and would be available sooner than a B-1 bomber.[124] Gen Lew Allen differed with Ellis and believed that a B-1B could well be a more advantageous interim bomber than an FB-111.[125] To gather facts, the secretary of defense put to work a joint OSD/Air Force bomber alternatives study group. One group evaluated six missions for the bomber — now becoming known as the long-range combat aircraft (LRCA): SIOP (both in initial and protracted phases), worldwide extension (counterinterdiction, theater nonnuclear, and maritime support), and theater nuclear. For these six missions the LRCA would have to maximize payload and range, and have the ability to deliver nuclear weapons, air-launched cruise missiles, and conventional weapons in both tactical and strategic roles. Comparative analysis soon projected that considering range and payload, 100 B-1s would be equivalent to 250 FB-111s; however, as a matter of fact, only 130 to 140 FB-111B/C aircraft were available for potential modification.[126]

In February 1981 General Allen was all out in support of the development and deployment of the MX in the multiple-protective shelter mode. He ended his prepared statement on the subject to the Senate Armed Services Committee with a strong plea to move forward:

> I want to restate the conviction of the Air Force and the Joint Chiefs of Staff that a survivable land-based ICBM is critically needed to redress the strategic balance and maintain a stable deterrent. Based on many years of detailed study we are convinced that the MPS concept offers the best solution.[127]

On the other hand, Secretary Weinberger was doubtful about MPS; he mentioned that 4,600 shelters for 200 MX missiles would cost $34 billion and probably more and that the Soviets could negate the shelter program by adding warheads to their strike force. A poll of citizens in a number of counties to be affected in Nevada was overwhelmingly opposed to the deployment, as was the governor of Nevada and the Church of Jesus Christ of Latter Day Saints.

Lt Gen Daniel Graham, US Army, Retired, who had been a director of the Defense Intelligence Agency and an adviser to President Reagan during his campaign, decried the MX, saying:

> The problem is [that] the MX is the grotesque child of bad strategy. It's grotesque to take a missile that's designed for counterforce — that is, to hit certain of the most dangerous Soviet weapons before they can hit you — and then deploy it in a system that is supposed to absorb all of the effects of those weapons before you fire. That's a grotesquery, from a military standpoint.[128]

During his campaign, President Reagan also made statements to the effect that he was not sold on the MPS deployment. In March 1981, Secretary Weinberger set up a committee headed by Prof Charles Townes and consisting of scientists and the like from outside the Department of Defense to advise him on basing the MX — not on the MX itself, for its need was agreed on. The Air Force was required to provide information on "all alternative basing modes that can be conceived as being sensible." But Secretary of Air Force Verne Orr still insisted:

> The Air Force position is simply this: Having studied some 30 or 35 different modes over a 7-year period covering three administrations, it seems that the multiple protective shelters in the areas of Nevada and Utah appear to be the most acceptable option.[129]

The Strategic Air Command statement of requirements presented by General Ellis in February 1981 pointed out that the full potential of strategic weapon system required corresponding improvements in command, control, communications, and intelligence (C^3I) systems that supported them. The Joint Chiefs had highlighted the fragile nature of C^3I in a connectivity study; the soft, fragile, peacetime systems conceived in the 1950s and put into operation in the 1960s depended on ground communications terminals at fixed sites that were highly vulnerable to attack. One of the pressing areas of concern was the high stress on the C^3I posed by Soviet submarines that patrolled off the east and west coasts. Because of their closeness to Washington and coastal military installations the submarines greatly decreased the amount of warning and decision time available to national command authority. General Ellis reminded Congress that although PD-59 addressed a general requirement for national security telecommunications, it did not provide for any single high organization that would have capability and responsibility to lay out a comprehensive C^3I plan for the future. Ellis concluded:

> With the full understanding that considerable study and evaluation are still required, I recommend creation of a national security communications organization with the authority to pull together the military C^3I network throughout the executive branch. Such an organization could implement the spirit, as well as the letter, of PD-59.[130]

Secretary Orr and General Allen labeled C^3I upgrading as "of equal importance" to modernization of weapons. They described requisite characteristics:

> Our command, control, and communications systems should be capable of providing unambiguous warning and attack assessment information to the president or his designated successors—the National Command Authorities. These links should be two-way so that force status information can be passed to the National Command Authorities, and command and execution decisions can be passed to the appropriate forces.[131]

The Air Force Satellite Communications System had become operational in 1979 and was slated for full deployment in 1983, but the Orr-Allen statement called for a follow-on space-based system to provide improved hardening and jam resistance.[132]

On 2 October 1981 President Reagan announced a comprehensive plan to revitalize US strategic forces. He said:

> Our plan is a comprehensive one. It will strengthen and modernize the strategic triad of land-based missiles, sea-based missiles, and bombers. It will end longstanding delays in some of these programs and introduce new elements into others. And just as important, it will improve communications and control systems that are vital to these strategic forces.[133]

There were five main features to the program:

First, I have directed the Secretary of Defense to revitalize our bomber forces by constructing and deploying some 100 B-1 bombers as soon as possible, while continuing to deploy cruise missiles on existing bombers. We will also develop an advanced bomber with "stealth" characteristics for the 1990s.

Second, I have ordered the strengthening and expansion of our sea-based forces. We will continue the construction of Trident submarines at a steady rate. We will develop a larger and more accurate sea-based ballistic missile. We will also deploy nuclear cruise missiles in some existing submarines.

Third, I've ordered completion of the MX missiles. We have decided, however, not to deploy the MX in the racetrack shelters proposed by the previous administration or in any other scheme for multiple protective shelters. We will not deploy 200 missiles in 4,600 holes, nor will we deploy 100 missiles in 1,000 holes.

We have concluded that these basing schemes would be just as vulnerable as the existing Minuteman silos. The operative factor here is this: No matter how many shelters we might build, the Soviets can build more missiles, more quickly, and just as cheaply.

Instead, we will complete the MX missile which is much more powerful and accurate than our current Minuteman missiles, and we will deploy a limited number of the MX missiles in existing silos as soon as possible.

At the same time, we will pursue three promising long-term options for basing the MX missile and choose among them by 1984, so that we can proceed promptly with full deployment.

Fourth, I have directed the Secretary of Defense to strengthen and rebuild our communications and control system, a much neglected factor in our strategic deterrent. I consider this decision to improve our communications and control system as important as any of the other decisions announced today. This system must be foolproof in case of any foreign attack.

Finally, I have directed that we end our long neglect of strategic defenses. This will include cooperation with Canada on improving North American air surveillance and defense, and as part of this effort, I've also directed that we devote greater resources to improving our civil defenses.[134]

Explaining his decision not to proceed with the Carter administration's plan to use the MPS mode for MX basing, President Reagan referred to the Townes panel study, which reasoned that the Soviets would only have to increase the number of warheads targeted against a particular area to take it out. In Reagan's assessment the MPS would thus not provide invulnerable missile basing.[135]

Unlike earlier presidents from Eisenhower through Carter, President Reagan was slow to state a military strategy or policy in his first year of office. "We knew little was to be gained," Secretary Weinberger said, "by an early enunciation of some elaborate 'conceptual structure,' a full fledged Reagan strategy." On the other hand, Prof Samuel P. Huntington, who had served as coordinator of security planning for the National Security Council in 1977–78, suggested that the Reagan administration was merely hesitant to admit, at least at first, that it was following the basic approach of Carter's PD-59, with the exception that the Reagan administration far more than the Carter administration was attempting to make the strategy a reality by hard programs of systems acquisition.[136] During the first six months of 1982 three major statements began to spell out the Reagan administration's policy and strategy: Secretary Weinberger's annual report to Congress on 8 February, the 125-page "Fiscal Year 1984–88 Defense Guidance," completed in late March and leaked to the press in late May, and an eight-page National Security Division Directive (NSDD) on national strategy approved by the president on 21 May and described by his national security adviser, William P. Clark, and other officials shortly thereafter. In his report, Secretary Weinberger spoke of the need for defense policy to shape means but of the difficulty of reshaping policy when means on hand were inherited from previous administrations. There was, of necessity, a continuity of strategy and policy between administrations because of the 8 to 12 years required to conceive and field weapon systems. Weinberger said, "Thus, the means available during the next few years have largely been shaped by past policies and strategies and by past expectations about our adversaries and the threats we will face. We are, to a greater extent than we would like, the prisoners of our immediate past."[137] The five-year overall defense plan was described as the "first complete defense guidance of this administration." The document's basic theme was that the United States must be prepared for a protracted conflict, as opposed to a concentrated all-out exchange. It was said that US nuclear capabilities "must prevail even under the conditions of a prolonged war." Another section emphasized that American nuclear forces "must prevail and be able to force the Soviet Union to seek earliest termination of hostilities on terms favorable to the United States." The nuclear strategy emphasized communications so that the president and NCA could control a nuclear exchange, including ad hoc plans subsequent to attacks. In nuclear targeting there was to be an emphasis on "decapitation strikes" against Soviet political and military leadership and communication lines. But the nuclear forces would have to maintain very high levels of damage to Soviet industry.[138] The National Security Division Directive resulted from President Reagan's order in February for a National Security Council review of overall strategy which he said was "a collection of departmental policies" that had been developed during the first year of his administration. The National Security Council led the effort, with the defense five-year plan providing the foundation for the military portion of the study. The text of the NSDD was not released to the public, but presidential adviser Clark said that it provided a coordinated marching order for "diplomatic, political, economic, [and] need informational components built on a foundation of military strength." Clark said that the ultimate objective was to "convince the leadership of the Soviet Union to turn their intention inward," thereby ameliorating external Soviet threats.[139]

Although the Reagan strategic policy required the United States to have a capability for a survivable and enduring response to demonstrate that its strategic forces could survive Soviet strikes over an extended period, Secretary Weinberger took pains to disarm press reports that the administration was planning to wage a protracted nuclear war, or was seeking to acquire a nuclear "warfighting" capability, or believed it possible for anyone to "win" a nuclear war. On the other hand, the Soviets were designing hard-targeting weapons in such a way and in sufficient numbers to indicate that they believed they could begin, endure, and win a nuclear war. It was unavoidably necessary for the United States to respond to the Soviet challenge through the establishment of capabilities that promised first to deter Soviet use of nuclear weapons and, if deterrence failed, to survive a first strike; to limit the scope of the conflict, to the extent possible and practicable; and to retaliate in a way that would, according to variations in statements, "[to] permit the United States to achieve its objectives," or "[to] restore peace on favorable terms," or "to deny the enemy his objectives and bring a rapid end to the conflict in terms favorable to our interests."[140] Secretary Weinberger iterated these ideas and discussed them at some length in a series of letters to Sen Claiborne Pell in August and September 1982.[141] The under secretary of defense for policy, Dr Fred C. Iklé, found four purposes for US nuclear forces:

> (1) to deter nuclear attack on the United States or its allies; (2) to help deter major conventional attack against US forces and our allies, especially in NATO; (3) to impose termination of a major war on terms favorable to the United States and our allies, even if nuclear weapons have been used — and in particular to deter escalation in the level of hostilities; and (4) to negate possible Soviet nuclear blackmail.[142]

In December 1982 Secretary Weinberger was called upon to compare the Reagan nuclear strategy with the Carter-Brown "countervailing" strategy. The new strategy, he said, "does not change substantially or materially the policy set out in Presidential Decision Paper 59. It refines it a bit. It takes into consideration some of the new and growing capabilities. But the essential strategic doctrine set out in PD 59 remains." But when pressed to explain *any* differences, Weinberger responded in writing that the Reagan nuclear guidance stressed the acquisition of weapon systems suited for employment if deterrence failed. It placed greater need for diversity in force structure since this strengthened flexibility, survivability, and endurance which, in turn, strengthened deterrence, complicated Soviet attack and defense planning, and hedged against the possibility of Soviet technological breakthrough. The current guidance also gave a better recognition of the importance of command, control, and communications as a contribution to stable deterrence. The guidance also ensured that all national capabilities as well as military capabilities deterred Soviet aggression.[143] These comments may have been reflective of a General Accounting Office report entitled "Countervailing Strategy Demands Revision of Strategic Force Acquisition Plans," issued on 5 August 1951. This report concluded that none of the existing strategic Triad weapon systems had been designed for — nor had — a proper combination of timeliness and hard-target kill capability needed to implement the countervailing strategy. The report read:

> Existing ICBMs have no meaningful single-shot capability for destroying Soviet targets that have been substantially hardened (possible command bunkers and certain ICBM silos), even though countervailing strategy increased the emphasis on striking those targets. The low single-shot probability of damage of Minuteman III against these targets would require the use of several warheads against each target. However, the limited number of US warheads currently available effectively precludes multiple targets (i.e., missile silos, nuclear storage sites, and C^3 facilities).[144]

Where the strategy outlined in Carter administration state papers seemed often to have gone unrealized in practice,[145] the Reagan force modernization program sought through synergistic advances to provide a capability to hold at risk the full range of assets the Soviets considered important to their war effort, including those that were hardened. President Reagan's commitment that C^3I be accorded the same high priority as weapon systems not only reflected the long lag in adopting communications to nuclear war scenarios but also marked a recognition that C^3I had a tradeoff value in increasing weapons capability. The effective C^3I system would ensure that detailed, unambiguous warning and accurate attack assessment information was made available to decisionmaking authorities, and provide an enduring capability for command and control of forces worldwide through all phases of conflict. In earlier days it was only necessary for command and control to launch nuclear forces in a massive strike—to get an initial message out without further concern for the survival of the system. The changed nuclear strategy required an enduring capability that could last for an indefinite period, exercise control over reconstituted strike forces after perhaps several nuclear exchanges and also provide nuclear damage assessment information against both the United States and an enemy. In the words of General Ellis, "The ultimate, of course, is to recognize that we are under attack, to characterize that attack, get a decision from the president, and to disseminate the decision to the forces prior to the first weapon impacting on the United States."[146] Although the risk of a surprise attack "out of the blue" imposed severe requirements on C^3I systems, Under Secretary Iklé pointed out that enhanced warning and C^3I systems could reduce the vulnerability of strategic forces through increased readiness, dispersal, airborne alert, and other measures. This could be very meaningful during periods of heightened danger—in particular the increased tensions during conventional military operations.[147]

In the Air Force assessment the Reagan administration's acceptance of the requirement for manned bombers was very important since for some years bombers would possess the main hard-target kill capability in the Triad. General Ellis remarked, "If we are, in fact, serious about warfighting (as a critical underwriting aspect of our overall attitude about deterrence), then there is a real and solid future for penetrating aircraft."[148] With the Reagan program, General Allen projected that the bomber leg of the Triad would remain "at more or less the same effectiveness . . . during a decade in which the Soviets are going to be improving their defenses." The first ALCM-equipped B-52G achieved alert status in September 1981, and the continuing addition of cruise missiles to the bomber force would increase the number of weapons available against the Soviet Union until about 1985, and then the Air Force would start moving the old B-52s into an all-standoff role. As the result of a congressional approval of a 100 B-1B bomber program in the autumn of 1981, General Allen projected that the first B-1B squadron would enter operational service on schedule in 1986. In the development of the B-1B the Air Force would accord a very high priority to what was now being called "base safe escape time," or the ability to get airborne in time to survive a possible submarine-launched ballistic missile strike. It also included advances in design to reduce its radar cross section and latest electronic countermeasures. The Air Force was confident that the B-1B would be able to penetrate air defenses and strike targets throughout the Soviet Union well into the 1990s, by which time the still-to-be developed advanced technology bomber (ATB) should be on-line and operational. Gen Bennie L. Davis, who became CINCSAC in 1981, noted, "It is my firm belief that sequential deployment of the B-1B and the ATB will retain for us that much-needed bomber penetration capability in the next century."[149]

Although manned bombers were effective against hard targets, they of necessity lacked the quick response of ballistic missiles. In December 1982 Secretary Weinberger pointed out the serious consequences of the Soviet monopoly of prompt hard-target kill capability:

> From the beginning, Soviet nuclear doctrine has been fundamentally different from US doctrine in that it sees nuclear conflict as merely a more destructive form of conventional conflict. Put another way, Soviet doctrine has always asserted the possibility of fighting and winning a nuclear war by preemptively destroying opposing strategic nuclear capability and limiting damage to the Soviet Union. During the years of American nuclear superiority, this Soviet sentiment was more an expression of ambition than a reflection of a policy that was in harmony with actual strategic capability. Unfortunately, this policy is no longer just a hollow ambition. Today it serves as the guiding hand for a powerful strategic force that is the result of a massive strategic build-up that began in the 1960s, reached full stride in the 1970s, and continues unabated to this day. Specifically, the Soviet Union has devoted and widely deployed large, highly accurate, and survivable intercontinental nuclear weapons and has hardened and proliferated its strategic command, control and communications facilities. These two developments have dramatically increased the vulnerability of US strategic forces — especially ICBMs — to Soviet attack while reducing the vulnerability of Soviet forces to US retaliation.
>
> The central characteristic of this Soviet strategic force is an enormous and destabilizing prompt hard target capability. The United States today has no such capability. This one-sided advantage in one of the most important measures of strategic capability is at the core of the current United States-Soviet strategic force imbalance. The Soviet monopoly in this capability provides them a two-fold advantage over US forces. First, it enables them to threaten the survivability of our entire land-based ICBM force in a first-strike attack while expending only a small proportion of their strategic ICBM force in the process. This large store of remaining ICBMs would enable them to divert weapons to other essential targets in a first-strike attack and still maintain a large and effective reserve force to conduct follow-on attacks and quickly deal with unforeseen contingencies. Second, the absence of an adequate United States prompt hard target capability affords Soviet war planners the luxury of knowing that for the crucial first few

> hours of a nuclear conflict, the bulk of their ICBM force and supporting command and control structure would remain largely immune to US retaliation. This virtual immunity would eliminate one of the major sources of uncertainty that is so important to deterrence—the unpredictable effects of US retaliation on Soviet war plans. Without this crucial uncertainty exerting an influence on Soviet war planning, their confidence in their ability to limit escalation and force an early termination of hostilities on terms favorable to Soviet interests is reinforced.
>
> The development is too dangerous to be allowed to continue unchallenged. If we do nothing, we will face the very real danger that Soviets could at some point come to believe that they could use, or threaten to use, nuclear forces in a limited manner to suppress military opposition and thereby gain military and political ends while limiting retaliation.[150]

The Reagan rearmament program proposed two responses to the Soviet monopoly on prompt hard-target kill. One was a new and improved nuclear submarine fleet equipped with longer-range, more powerful, and more accurate SLBMs. The 31 Poseidon ballistic missile submarines of the US Navy were secure at sea, as about half of them were at all times. Each submarine carried 16 Poseidon C-3 missiles with MIRV warheads, and by virtue of their numbers the SLBMs contributed most to damage expectancy against softer targets. The Reagan program provided orderly replacement of the Poseidon submarines with larger Trident submarines that would be armed with Trident II (D-5) missiles. The D-5s would be powerful and effectively accurate against hardened targets.[151] The Trident program, however, had been delayed early on and the Trident II (D-5) missile was not projected for operational use until December 1989. This was three years later than the Air Force MX—now being called the "Peacekeeper"—could be operational, with the result that the Peacekeeper option presented the Reagan administration with the best possibility of eliminating the Soviet hard-targeting monopoly. Although President Reagan announced that the MX would not be deployed in multiple-protective shelters, he nevertheless wanted the missile kept in development and some other way found to give it a protected deployment. The MX program was reduced from 200 to 100 missiles, each to have 10 MIRV warheads. As a supposedly temporary expedient the first 40 MX production missiles were to be placed either in Minuteman silos or silos that had sheltered the old Air Force Titan missiles which were to be withdrawn from service incrementally. As a matter of record Air Force leaders were disappointed that President Reagan did not approve the MPS basing mode since it was thought after many years' study to be the best plan. Several basing concepts were nevertheless brought back for more study: deep underground basing; a new long-endurance "Big Bird" aircraft platform; and defended, deceptive silo basing eventually called "dense pack" or the "closely spaced basing" (CSB) mode. Secretary Weinberger was said to favor Big Bird; the Townes panel recommended more attention be given to the nuclear fratricide phenomenon whereby an incoming nuclear warhead's explosion would be expected to neutralize closely following warheads. On 8 November 1982 the Joint Chiefs of Staff told the president that they unanimously favored going ahead with MX development and production and basing MX in Minuteman silos while searching for a better mode. They also said that they felt that the president was being forced into a final basing decision prematurely; at this time Gen John W. Vessey, Jr., chairman of the Joint Chiefs of Staff, and Gen Charles A. Gabriel, chief of staff of the Air Force, recommended going ahead with closely spaced basing and the other three chiefs disagreed, two thinking that the technological and cost uncertainties were too great. On 14 December 1982 Secretary Weinberger urged Congress

> to act swiftly in approving Peacekeeper/CSB. Deployed in an attack-resistant CSB mode, the Peacekeeper... will restore the viability of our land-based ICBMs which have a number of attributes that make them crucial to our strategic deterrent. They are flexible, respond quickly, enjoy reliable, real-time communications with command authorities, offer alert rates approaching 100 percent and can be maintained at low operating cost. No other single strategic system possesses all these important qualities.[152]

Even before this, Congress had been demanding definite basing plans, ensuring reduced MX vulnerability, and on 20 December 1982 it voted to hold up MX funding until an acceptable basing plan was in hand. In December President Reagan asked the Joint Chiefs of Staff to review the strategic forces modernization program and report back to him. On 3 January 1983 Reagan established an 11-man Commission on Strategic Forces, headed by retired Air Force Lt Gen Brent Scowcroft, who had been President Ford's military assistant, and including such distinguished men as former secretaries of defense Brown and Laird and former Secretary of the Air Force Thomas C. Reed. The Joint Chiefs of Staff briefed the president on the results of their study on 11 February 1983, and the Commission on Strategic Forces filed its report in April 1983. The major findings in both efforts were fundamentally the same, so similar in fact that on 4 April the Joint Chiefs informed President Reagan that they were unanimously in support of the commission report. Remarked General Vessey, "We came up with a set of recommendations... that were so parallel to the Commission's recommendations you could put them both under the same umbrella and nobody would get wet." The prepared statement of the JCS summarized the recommendations as calling for:

> • Continued strong support for the TRIAD, and continued support to modernize the TRIAD. We believe that the combination of land-based ICBMs, sea-based ballistic missiles, and bombers with air-launched cruise missiles provide a broad range of capabilities whose synergism complicates the Soviet planning, provides us flexibility and provides an important hedge against technological surprise by the Soviets in neutralizing any particular leg of the TRIAD.
>
> • Continued highest priority support for improvements in command, control, communications and warning. Because our strategy is one that does not include a first-strike, the ability of the command and control and intelligence system to survive an attack and provide the wherewithal to retaliate is key to deterrence.

- Field MX in MINUTEMAN silos. The accurate, prompt, hard-target attack capability of the MX is needed now and will add greatly to our deterrent strength.

- Continued research and development for survivable land-based ICBM systems, to include research on small mobile ICBMs.

- Continued research to resolve the uncertainties about hardness of fixed bases for ICBMs.

- We also recommended that the president set a new direction for the future and announce increased research for active defense against ballistic missiles. We pointed out our recognition that there was no near-term solution for defense against ballistic missiles, but that technological developments on the horizon could give hope to our own people and to our allies that we could use our technology to provide defenses which, when supplemented with arms control agreements, could move us away from sole dependence on the threat of retaliation.[153]

In a nationally televised address on 23 March 1983, President Reagan called for long-term development of imaginative military technology presumably employing lasers, microwave devices, and particle beams. This technology would be based either on the ground or in space, would render nuclear missiles "impotent and obsolete," and would hold "the promise of changing human history." "I am taking an important first step," Reagan said, "I am directing a comprehensive and intensive effort to define a long-term research and development program to begin to achieve our ultimate goal of eliminating the threat posed by strategic ballistic missiles."[154] On 19 April President Reagan wrote Congress requesting authority to procure 100 MX Peacekeeper missiles to be sited in Minuteman silos in Wyoming and Nebraska. He also recommended the design and development of a small, single-warhead, more mobile missile soon to be popularly called "Midgetman."[155]

The Scowcroft-Joint Chiefs of Staff recommendations were received skeptically in Congress, particularly so in view of earlier dialogue about a "window of vulnerability" and statements about the vulnerability of Minuteman silos to destruction by Soviet missiles. In the course of congressional hearings, General Scowcroft, Secretary Weinberger, and the Joint Chiefs were questioned closely. In lead testimony, General Scowcroft spoke of "very uncertain times" and of "groping for ways to improve the system." He continued:

> We are talking about systems which will come to fruition over two to three different presidential terms. One of the things we would hope [to come] out of this — we don't have ideal recommendations. We could not find any ideal ones. What we hoped for was a kind of package which was minimally acceptable across philosophical views and party views [and] which could establish a sufficient consensus in this country to move forward with some confidence into this very uncertain future.[156]

Other witnesses supported Scowcroft's testimony. The MX was needed to break the Soviet monopoly in hard-target kill; as long as the Soviets had such a monopoly they had no incentive to negotiate arms control agreements. Existing Minuteman silos could be superhardened by new construction techniques; by locating MX missiles in existing complexes in Wyoming and Nebraska rather than in the scattered Titan silos, there might be possible means of ABM defense or of taking some advantage of fratricide, a phenomenon still not well understood. Admitted General Gabriel, "Peacekeepers in Minuteman silos is not the most survivable solution. You probably cannot build a land-based system that is totally invulnerable, but its high accuracy, its alert rate, reliability, and command and control, these are the reasons that make a land-based system so important to the TRIAD."[157] The MX promised the most rapid means to provide prompt hard-target kill: the first Peacekeeper was projected to be operational in October 1986, the tenth in December 1986, and the one hundredth in December 1989. Several congressmen were concerned about a report on Capitol Hill that the Air Force was dragging its feet on the Midgetman and would ultimately renege on this program in favor of, at some future date, making a plea to keep the MX production line open. General Gabriel called this "a gross misunderstanding." After three years of research and development, beginning at once, he would be committed to full-scale engineering development on the small missile. "I will take the MX today, [I] need a small missile in a survivable mode when I can get it.... We don't have the option today to take one or the other," General Gabriel said.[158]

After hard battles in the Senate and the House, Congress voted approval for the beginning of MX production in July 1983. Before the votes were tallied, however, the discussions of the Reagan rearmament projections and the Scowcroft report brought a fuller national appreciation of nuclear arms. Former Secretary of Defense McNamara and former Secretary of State Cyrus R. Vance stated on 16 May, "We are convinced [that] we can have equivalent security for a smaller investment, and that is the main thesis we put before you today." McNamara argued that in the 1950s President Eisenhower had "fallen into" the Triad because his objective was to field "a sufficiently strong nuclear force to absorb a first strike by the Soviets, with such remaining power as to force upon the Soviets unacceptable damage." After this beginning, McNamara said, the Triad had become "a function of rivalry among the services." The existing Triad was adequate to deter the Soviets without additional strategic weapons. McNamara asserted, "Today we have in total in our strategic forces in the Triad about 9,700 warheads. Of those ... about 3,300 would survive a Soviet first strike today." With the addition of scheduled cruise missiles on B-52s the United States would have 12,900 strategic warheads in 1988, of which some 4,600 "would almost certainly survive a Soviet first strike." The United States thus had deterrent capability and would continue to have it. McNamara accordingly proposed canceling the MX while retaining funds for research on a single-warhead missile. He would cancel the B-1 and move from the B-52/ALCM combination to a yet-to-be developed advanced-technology stealth bomber. Both Vance and McNamara endorsed the main thrust of the Scowcroft recommendation, as Vance put it, "to move away from missile systems which present what in the jargon are called high value multiwarhead cargoes." They did not agree with the commission's proposal to deploy MX missiles in Minuteman silos.[159] McNamara was asked why he favored the mobile minimissile when he had vetoed the mobile Minuteman in 1962; he explained that the mobile configuration was much more expensive than a silo-based Minuteman force and that at this time silos provided adequate protection. McNamara also said that his support for MIRV warheads—where he now favored single-warhead launchers—had been because of a perceived necessity to overcome Soviet antiballistic missile defenses which appeared to be likely to extend across the Soviet Union. And, as has been seen, McNamara published articles in 1982 and 1983 waging the themes: *"Nuclear weapons serve no military purpose whatsoever. They are totally useless—except to deter one's opponent from using them. This is my view today. It was my view in the early 1960s."*[160] And even though Secretary Weinberger staunchly supported the MX missile, he saw something of a paradox in replying to a question as to how the Reagan administration would expect to use it in a war scenario. He said:

> The administration would plan to use the MX by never using it. It is our hope and our belief that if we can deploy this new, stronger, more accurate missile with a hardened target kill capability the chances of our having to use it or the Minuteman diminish very sharply. And that is the whole purpose of putting it in the ground. That is a part of the paradox.... I have to keep asking for these very expensive things that we never want to use at all, and if we are completely successful we will never have to use them.[161]

In summary evaluations of the search for a nuclear strategy in the years after 1960, two retired Air Force officers with substantial technological planning authority were constructively critical about what happened. Col Francis X. Kane, who had served as director of advanced planning in the Air Force Space Systems Division, in articles in 1974 and 1979, demonstrated a failure of OSD appreciations of Soviet strategic missile projections. By 1960–62 Air Force space planners had watched Soviet missile tests long enough to observe predictable patterns that were in no way related to US "threats" but made it evident that the Soviets were advancing technology as "the keystone of Soviet power." Kane recalled that OSD would not accept this. He wrote:

> This approach was counter to the accepted culture of threat analysis. Our method "was not rational." Weapon systems, according to the DOD philosophy then current, were not procured on the basis of a continuing program. They were procured on the basis of an analysis of the threat, the technology available, and the program which the United States would institute in reaction to those conditions. Inasmuch as that "rational" method was used in US weapon system procurement, it followed that the Soviets pursued a similar technological strategy.[162]

At this time, some analysts were asserting that the Soviets would not build more than 800 ICBMs. Neither projection was correct, but the Soviets gained years of time advantage because their research and development activities were not appreciated by the United States. The first visible indicators of new Soviet ICBMs came with flight tests of the booster and reentry vehicles, followed by construction of launch pads and bases. By this stage of the program, the Soviets were only a few years from having a new ICBM in their arsenal. In reactions to visible evidences of Soviet deployments, the United States required two to three years to modify its budget and additional years to field a new system. According to Colonel Kane, forecasts were made in the early 1960s that technological change would result in the vulnerability of hard silos, but it was difficult to say when this would occur. The prediction that the Soviets would not build more than 800 ICBMs and the assertion that Soviet technology was too primitive to attain missile accuracy resulted in the lack of a US program to cope with ICBM vulnerability, thus opening a significant gap in the balance of strategic power. To prevent this sort of thing, Kane urged that the United States must pursue an aggressive research and development program to develop subsystems and prototypes and potential "quick fixes" for use when needed after assessment of physical evidence from Soviet tests. Kane wrote, "This technological strategy requires acceptance of the basic approach that the role of R&D is to give the US time to respond without panic and the resulting high cost solutions if Soviet programs threaten basic American objectives."[163]

On 17 May 1983 the day following the appearance of former secretaries Vance and McNamara before the subcommittee of the House Committee on Appropriations, Brig Gen Robert C. Richardson, USAF, Retired, presented testimony with the major thrust that after 1960 the United States had sacrificed its military capabilities by self-imposed restraints assumed for nonmilitary reasons. Richardson said, "In my judgment, the additional costs and loss of military effectiveness have resulted from a search for an optimum or ideal nonmilitary or political solution to essentially military problems." How costs were driven up by nonmilitary decisions could be found in the MX program:

> First, the basing schemes have all been aimed at solving the survivability problem, while ignoring the traditional role that active defense has played in providing survivability.... Second, the size of the MX — now criticized due to the limits it imposes on mobility and the lightning rod effect that its ten warheads creates for Soviet offensive weapons — was the by-product of planned limitations on numbers of launchers established in the interest of arms control. None of the basing modes that have been proposed may be said to have been motivated by a search for the best military solution to a basically military problem.[164]

Richardson added to this charge in oral testimony:

> The cost of the MX missile program, very basically, was driven up by the nonmilitary arms control aspirations that dictated sole attention to survivability through passive measures. If you are denied the right to use active measures, you have to come up with the next best solution, and the next best solution is going to be a multibillion dollar Dense Pack or MPS, or some other solution, when in the real world, had that constraint not been there, had the president's decision of March 23rd been implemented 15 or 20 years ago, an appropriate mix of active and passive defenses would have provided for survivability and in all probability the problem that we are familiar with would not have come about.[165]

In regard to the time-consuming development of US weapon systems, General Richardson was even more severely critical than Colonel Kane. He pointed out that acquisition time had gone from an average of 6 years in the 1950s to 11 to 12 years in 1983. Every year added to an acquisition cycle added about 30 percent to the cost. The lengthy acquisition cycle was not only costly but it had three adverse consequences: (1) The Soviets could now see what the United States planned to build (for example, the stealth bomber), and they had the time to steal or copy the building-block technique and build and deploy systems as good or better before the United States could. (2) No president, given two terms in the White House, could ever again change US strategy to meet a new threat if such a change required new hardware while he was in office. (3) Public and congressional enthusiasm for lengthy weapons programs was hard to maintain. "Projects launched with enthusiasm tend to be laughed at when the Department of Defense finally returns after, say, ten years of R&D to ask for the necessary megabucks to go into production," recounted Richardson. He had three suggestions for shortening the acquisition process:

> One is in the front-end decision process. We sit around and study to death what we are going to buy from the time we decide until we make the decision to let the first contract for the first development.
>
> Now, I would point out, for instance, that the Polaris submarine went to sea 3.8 years after the decision was made, the first contract was let, to go. Now it takes six years, according to the DOD studies, merely to get up to the first development contract. . . .
>
> This I believe to be a function of overcentralization of authority, each decision has to be referred to many study groups for a Gallup-poll, trade-off type approach, and that process can be greatly shortened by the appointment for special weapons systems of a von Neumann type committee which is what General Eisenhower used, where he in effect took three or four top people and made their decision his decision and said, let us go on the basis of that.
>
> The second major area has become a way of life, and that was introduced by Secretary Robert McNamara, who in the 1960s, introduced the so-called low-risk, building-block, fly-before-buy, all technology-in-hand approach. It precludes concurrency in many weapon systems. . . .
>
> There is some 40 months' loss in the cycle by virtue of the fly-before-buy-and-test and low-risk approach. This is a major area.
>
> And the third major area lies in lack of dedication to the end product from the onset. . . . We need congressional multiyear funding, so that we can move forward without having to rejustify on a yearly basis all the component activities.[166]

When assembled early in the 1970s to study the need for and performance to be required from a follow-on strategic missile to Minuteman, Air Force Project Blue Lance, according to Colonel Kane, expressed dissatisfaction with the assured-destruction strategy. The use of projections of killing Soviet civilians as a criterion of success was offensive. Colonel Kane remembered, "The use of this criterion . . . challenged our belief in the basic purpose of military forces. . . . Our view of our role was that we should create forces which could destroy Soviet forces and thus protect our own population from annihilation."[167] The thrust of Blue Lance was directed toward a hard-target killer missile but in its same time frame Maj Gen Haywood S. Hansell, USAF, Retired, frequently advanced his assessment that no offensive military strategy such as assured destruction would be acceptable to the American people unless there also was a highly effective antimissile defense system for the United States. He urged that the national ABM system must have "first priority" to lend credence to deterrence. As long as US urban centers "stand naked, it is not likely that our threats of strategic response to aggression abroad will be credible to anyone," Hansell wrote. He continued:

> An effective system to defend cities is likely to be some radical new approach, probably totally or partially space based, and possibly using weapons effects and control systems that lasers may make feasible. Or it might involve integration of several systems, some space based, some air based, some surface based. It is certain to be expensive. However, that is the *sine qua non* of any extended military option.[168]

Under the antiballistic missile treaty with the Soviet Union, the United States was authorized to continue ABM research and development, and it did so as a contingency program in case the Soviets abrogated the treaty or the Soviet threat to US missile silos became so serious that site defense would be a protective option. Although Congress discontinued money for the prototype development of site defense in 1974–75, one experimental radar at the Kwajalein Missile Range was kept in use in tests of the radar and the associated data system against a large number of ICBMs fired sporadically into Kwajalein from Vandenberg AFB. The tests were "extremely successful," according to Maj Gen Grayson D. Tate, Jr., US Army, commanding general of the Ballistic Missile Defense Systems Command and ballistic missile defense program manager. Also, in December 1979 the secretary of defense approved a generic development of a low-altitude defense system (LOAD) by General Tate's command. When President Reagan eliminated the MPS basing option for the MX in October 1971, the BMD program had to be redesigned to develop a "common" defense concept to accommodate whichever MX basing plan ultimately would be accepted. The growth pattern broadened into what was called endoatmospheric nonnuclear kill (ENNK) or terminal defenses with nonnuclear interceptors and exoatmospheric defense (an outside-the-atmosphere layered defense, or overlay, with a second tier, or underlay to engage penetrating reentry vehicles missed by the overlay defenses).[169] Thinking about exoatmospheric defense sparked a return to the old 1962 Air Force Bambi space defense concept already noted, which had been brusquely dismissed by Secretary McNamara as "a paper study of a very esoteric system." Strong privately funded support for an expanded ABM defense came from Project High Frontier, headed by Lt Gen Daniel O. Graham, US Army, Retired, a former head of the Defense Intelligence Agency and a preelection adviser to President Reagan. The project advocated an outer layer of exoatmospheric orbiting Bambi-type "space trucks" loaded with nonnuclear, heat-seeking missiles that would home on the firetails of Soviet ICBMs in the first eight minutes of their trajectories. A second layer would add infrared sensors to pick out "cold" ICBM missiles against the backdrop of space up until their reentry into the atmosphere. The LOAD defense would provide defense of Minuteman-MX silos as a third layer defense. "The High Frontier concepts constitute first and foremost a change of US strategy—from the bankrupt and basically immoral precepts of mutual assured destruction to a stable and morally defensible strategy of assured survival," General Graham stated. He also spoke fluently of the strategic situation demanding change from assured destruction as a strategy:

> Those of us who undertook the High Frontier study, as a public service effort outside the bureaucratic constraints, have recognized all along that Western strategic thinking is set in concrete, that mind-sets formed over the last 2 decades have convinced many—including most of those in this congressional generation—that there is no feasible alternative to a balance of terror with horrendous nuclear casualties if that balance fails to deter. Such thinking leads to never-ending demand for more and more offensive weapons and more and more destructive power at rapidly escalating costs, as we see only too clearly today.
>
> Something has to give. We hope that it will be the concrete mind-sets which blind us to other more feasible and effective ways to keep the Soviet leadership sober and responsible at a cost we can afford even in these difficult times.
>
> As a nation, we fell into the mental rut of ever more offensive and destructive capability to keep the peace because we ignored the technology of defense and its implications for affecting the strategic balance. For example, we assumed 20 years ago—falsely, as it turns out—that defense against a nuclear missile attack is hopeless and technically infeasible.
>
> We forgot that throughout all of history technology advances across the board. At one point it favors the defense, as when the castle walls of Europe were impregnable. At another time it favors the offense, as when gunpowder and cannon broke down those castle walls and changed the entire structure of European society.
>
> In modern times and over the past 20 years, technology of defense has again made great advances. It is indeed possible to hit a bullet with a bullet and kill it today. While we cannot hit and kill all nuclear bullets with our defending bullets, we can hit and kill enough to produce chaos in the offensive planners' minds—and that uncertainty is the essence of deterrence.
>
> This is what deterrence really means—creating crucial uncertainties in the Soviet mind as to what would happen if they launched a missile attack against us and say 20, or 30, or 40 percent of those missiles failed to reach their targets. In fact, the High Frontier systems would prevent 95 percent of those missiles reaching their targets. . . .
>
> But High Frontier is not a mere military strategy, it is a true national strategy addressing the legitimate economic and political aspirations of this Nation and those of our allies, as well as our security needs.

> The High Frontier study set[s] out to seek technology that would support a new strategy, and not the other way around. Fortunately, the United States—at least for the moment—has a technological lead over the Soviet Union, especially in space. This advantage has been dramatically demonstrated by the Space Shuttle, which gives us the capability of delivering men and material into space to do some of the key things High Frontier is recommending.[170]

Graham blamed the strategy of mutually assured destruction—which had cut through both Republican and Democratic administrations—for the lag in defense strategy:

> I think basically the reason why we are not farther along with the space-born defense is because mutual assured destruction says safety lies in vulnerability, that we should remain vulnerable so as to maintain this balance of terror. It is militarily idiotic but it is the prevailing view and the reason why we have no defenses and the reason we have gotten rid of such defenses as we once had.[171]

Without endorsing the High Frontier concept, Adm Thomas H. Moorer, retired JCS chairman, agreed that mutual assured destruction had hindered military technology.

> It has been my experience—and I have been present when actions of this kind have been taken—that we have imposed self-restraint on the technological improvements of our systems on the grounds that not to do so would provoke the Russians and it would be destabilizing. The programs to improve the accuracy of our missile warheads have been deliberately cancelled or deferred on conceptual or philosophical grounds rather than on technical grounds.[172]

General Richardson was highly supportive of strategic defense or "assured survival." He reasoned, "The American people want to be defended. It makes military sense, because the role of the military for years has been to defend the country, not merely to be able to retaliate in the event of an attack."[173] Both in October 1981 and in October 1983 President Reagan called for stepped-up ABM defense, but the Scowcroft Commission was more pessimistic. Regarding ballistic missile defense, the commission reported, "No ABM technologies appear to combine practicality, survivability, low cost and technical effectiveness sufficiently to justify proceeding beyond the stage of technology development." The Joint Chiefs of Staff responded collectively in writing when asked on 3 May 1983 whether they agreed:

> Yes, the Joint Chiefs of Staff understand the Commission's concern over the technical difficulties associated with defense against ballistic missiles in the immediate future. For this reason, we believe that for the near term, deterrence must continue to depend on strong offensive forces.[174]

IDEAS, CONCEPTS, DOCTRINE

Articulation of the Strategic Triad Concept

The threefold strategic deterrent force of manned bombers, land-based ICBMs, and submarine-launched ballistic missiles (SLBM) grew from the restructuring of US strategic forces in the post-Sputnik years of the Eisenhower administration. Dr Herbert F. York, director of defense, research and engineering at that time, later attributed the birth of the strategic Triad concept to "technological turmoil."

> In those days no ICBM had ever been flown, and no large missile had ever been launched from under water. We were worried about whether the second stage of the TITAN could be ignited successfully in outer space under conditions of vacuum and free-fall. We didn't know whether the POLARIS missile could achieve enough range to be useful. We did not know how well we could determine the position of a submarine, and we did not know how well we could determine the direction and distance to a target. We did not even know the shape of the earth with sufficient accuracy. The press carried flamboyant stories of how hard it was to design an ICBM warhead capable of reentering the atmosphere at meteoric speeds. It made good sense then to have several parallel approaches to an objective when we could not be certain that any particular one would work at all.[175]

In requesting fiscal year 1966 defense appropriations in February 1965 Secretary McNamara grouped strategic offensive forces, continental air and missile defense forces, and civil defense under a heading of nuclear war forces. He explained,

> It was clear last year that because of the close interrelationship and, indeed, the interaction of the three major components of our general nuclear posture, the only practical way to deal with this problem was to incorporate all three components in a single analytical framework.[176]

McNamara's strategic offensive forces included manned bombers, ICBMs, and SLBMs, and in March 1967 Dr John S. Foster, Jr., director of defense, research and engineering, urged that it was "absolutely essential that we not rely on any single system . . . that we plan to rely for the foreseeable future on land-based missiles, sea-based systems, and on aircraft." This was true because "any system we might build is potentially subject to being negated if the Soviets spend enough money and if technology advances in some possibly unforeseen way to adversely affect our system vulnerability."[177]

Although former Secretary McNamara would eventually assert in 1983 that the fielding of the three elements — aircraft, ICBMs, SLBMs — strategic force grew out of "rivalry among the services."[178] The Joint Chiefs of Staff agreed in 1968 that strategic forces must "(1) be designed to operate over a broad spectrum of possible conditions, (2) contain a mix of land and sea launched missiles and manned aircraft, and (3) contain both active and passive defenses in depth."[179] During his tenure as chief of naval operations, Adm Elmo R. Zumwalt, Jr., stated that the era of "major battles over service roles and missions had passed" and that only mild parochialism surfaced during the SALT ABM discussions. Then the Air Force was more willing to limit the Army's ABM than its bombers or ICBMs; the Navy felt that if strategic offensive power was to be limited it had better be Air Force bombers and missiles rather than Polaris and Poseidon submarines; and the Army tended to advocate stressing limiting offense rather than its ABM defenses.[180] With the conclusion of the ABM treaty with the Soviet Union and Secretary Schlesinger's decision to minimize continental air defense, air and missile defenses were much reduced during the 1970s.

The term *Triad* was seized upon in the early 1960s by Air Force Brig Gen Glenn A. Kent who needed a means to describe mixed strategic forces, and it came into vogue in 1969–71 as a method of emphasizing the synergy of ICBMs, SLBMs, and bombers. "Unless people recognize the fundamental nature of the Triad," remarked Lt Gen Otto J. Glasser, Air Force deputy chief of staff for R&D, "it is very difficult to sell the new [B-1] bomber."[181] In a full-blown article in January 1971 three Strategic Air Command general officers described the Triad of strategic forces as offering maximum deterrence because:

> (1) No aggressor nation could afford to concentrate its attack on a single system.
>
> (2) More of the aggressor's resources must be committed to multiple defensive measures.
>
> (3) A technological breakthrough countering any one element could multiply the deterrence of only a part of the Triad.
>
> (4) No attack could eliminate all elements simultaneously.
>
> (5) A combination of strategic forces provides flexibility to the United States.[182]

In a presentation in Congress in the spring of 1971, Gen Bruce K. Holloway, CINCSAC, used the term *trilateral force* to describe land-launched missiles, sea-launched missiles, and manned bombers. In his testimony he zeroed in on his opposition to a proposal by unidentified "people" to discard the Minuteman force and move all missiles to sea to increase survivability. Holloway stated,

> Land-launched missiles collectively have a number of important attributes with regard to accuracy, range, payload, readiness, penetration aids, command and control reliability, and mission flexibility — many of which are not attributable to sea-launched missiles.[183]

Gen John C. Meyer pointed out in the fall of 1971 that the combination of the bombers, ICBMs, and SLBMs provided "synergy in the Triad which adds value beyond costs." Multiple-independent approaches added reliability since unforeseen vulnerability of any one system would not put the United States out of business. Each system had individual advantages. The three systems, operating in concert, implicated an enemy's defense problems and limited his offensive strategies since, Meyer said,

> a simultaneous surprise attack on all elements of the Triad is virtually impossible, and a strike on any one element gives warning to the others. Thus ... the advantage of a first-strike surprise attack is largely foreclosed by the Triad of strategic forces.[184]

Lt Gen Otto J. Glasser, Air Force deputy chief of staff for research and development, said in March 1972, "We are on record ... as being firmly in support of the TRIAD." At this juncture, Glasser nevertheless figured that the Air Force and more particularly the Strategic Air Command was providing the preponderance of force to the Triad. "Something like three-quarters of all the delivery vehicles ... the bombers, the silos, and the tubes in the submarines, something like three-quarters of those are Air Force elements of the TRIAD," Glasser said. He extended his comments to additional advantages inherent in land-based forces:

> The operating cost per alert Minuteman is far less than that of the other elements of the TRIAD.... Another important feature of the Minuteman force is its responsiveness to command and control by the National Command Authorities (NCA).

> Among other important advantages, the B-52 provides essential insurance against presently unanticipated, but possible, gross failure in our missile systems.... The B-52 can carry a greater payload, and deliver the payload with greater precision, than any other of our strategic systems.... The bomber is also particularly useful in third area conflicts both in a nuclear and a conventional bombing role.[185]

Glasser suggested that vulnerability of land-based bombers and missiles was somewhat overstated; in any event, with satellite missile warning systems—although not a part of the Triad—it would be possible to have advanced notice of incoming Soviet ICBMs or SLBMs.

> Indeed, if you work your way through that equation of what is the launch posture of the bombers and of the missiles, with that warning up there, it is virtually impossible for the Soviets to generate a plan which they can rely upon with confidence and that they can execute without resulting in a massive response from this country.[186]

In discussing the Triad, General Glasser demonstrated that with 12–30 hours' advance warning, the Strategic Air Command land-based legs of the Triad would be expected to generate from 82 to 85 percent of the strategic nuclear striking power. In the strategic equation, striking power depended on the degree and status of nuclear alert forces. In the 1970s, 50 to 60 percent of US nuclear submarines were continuously at sea, on station, or in transit; the remainder were in port where they were vulnerable to attack and somewhat difficult to return to sea duty even with substantial warning. The Strategic Air Command counted on 98 percent of its ICBMs on day-to-day alert, and as ICBMs were programmed into service in the 1960s and 1970s, SAC reduced the status of alert of its bomber forces. In 1964 and 1965, as SAC B-47 bombers were retired, "reflex" operations that shuttled aircraft to alert postures were discontinued, the mission of quick time-over-the-target being taken on by Minuteman missiles and tactical fighters on quick reaction alert

(QRA) in West Germany.[187] In the late 1950s when it was believed that the Soviets were bringing in missiles very fast, the SAC B-52 force observed a 50-53 percent rate of 15-minute ground alert, this being the expected BMEWS warning time. In 1967 Secretary McNamara passed down his decision to reduce the B-52 ground alert to 40 percent, indicating that he would have accepted a still lower figure except that he believed it necessary to maintain a crew ratio against a possible requirement for large-scale conventional bombing.[188] After a B-52 with four nuclear weapons aboard crashed and burned while attempting an emergency landing at Thule, Greenland, on 22 January 1968, General McConnell on his own initiative ended the old practice whereby alert B-52s flew airborne alerts with nuclear weapons aboard.[189] In July 1968 SAC instituted a new bomber alert called selective employment of air and ground alert (SEAGA) whereby in times of international tension B-52s and tankers would disperse into a number of satellite-basing and air-alert postures, thus reducing the time required to launch the force and compounding enemy targeting problems.[190] In 1975 the secretary of defense judged that a Soviet surprise attack out of the blue was quite unlikely and that any nuclear attack likely would be preceded by a sharp deterioration of relations with the Soviet Union in a series of crises. Accordingly, the SAC B-52, FB-111, and tanker crew allocations were cut back, permitting only about 30 percent of the bomber/tanker force to be maintained on day-to-day alert. SAC calculated that if warning permitted all aircraft would be generated into alert before Soviet ICMBs hit; otherwise, if the bombers had to ride out a first attack, only the 30 percent on alert would be expected to survive.[191]

In the more than 20 years during which the conception of the Triad was the central tenet of the design and acquisition of the US strategic deterrent, it was recognized that Triad's diversity protected the United States against technological failures within one system or an unexpected technological breakthrough by the Soviets that allowed them substantially to threaten one of the elements of the Triad. To Gen Lew Allen, Jr., the fact that the United States stood in danger of losing up to 90 percent of the Minuteman force—what General Ellis at SAC called the "centerpiece" of the US deterrent—"vividly demonstrated the wisdom of developing a Triad." General Allen agreed:

> While our overall retaliatory capability is diminished, it has not been reduced to the point where the Soviets could prevent a devastating US nuclear response. Thus the positive side of our predicament has been its reaffirmation of the value and indeed the necessity of maintaining a strategic nuclear Triad.[192]

The threatened vulnerability of Minuteman silos and the prospective cost of ICBM modernization generated OSD studies of the feasibility of a substitute for the Triad in the form of what was called a Splendid Diad, namely a large SLBM force paired with a large cruise missile force. In this circumstance, one would not attempt to build a penetrating bomber or have a land-based ICBM system. It has been seen in the consideration of developing nuclear strategy that President Carter rejected a diad because of the prospect that an all-out Soviet R&D effort might develop a technique of pinpointing submarines at sea. But there were other findings: notably, that a diad could do the work of the Triad but would not be less expensive. Since there were no overriding cost issues, the Triad had clear advantages of flexibility and resiliency to the Soviet theater.[193]

Another review of the concept of the Triad was appropriate in view of President Reagan's veto of the MPS basing for the MX. At this time General Allen reviewed and "violently disagreed" with what General Graham appeared to endorse, namely minimizing the requirement for force survivability by providing exoatmospheric ABM defense: "I disagree with General Graham's views. . . . I believe he has notions of castles in the sky for his final solutions, and I think it unwise to bet the security of the country on such ideas."[194] The new CINCSAC, General Davis, agreed that the first priority should be to develop strategic offensive systems capable of deterring nuclear attack and prosecuting war should deterrence fail, but he observed:

> A reasonable level of defensive capability creates uncertainty and strengthens deterrence. The defensive element in the deterrent equation has suffered from neglect, and the fiscal year 1983 steps are appreciated.[195]

Acceptance of the Triad remained fundamental in President Reagan's strategic defense policy. It was endorsed by the Scowcroft Commission on Strategic Forces, and on 3 May 1983, Secretary Weinberger gave an appropriate summation of the Triad's significance:

> To deter Soviet aggression, we have maintained over the last two decades a strong and independent combination of strategic forces known as the Triad which consists of the land-based intercontinental ballistic missiles, the sea-based ballistic missiles, and manned strategic bombers. This multiplicity of forces provides three significant benefits:
>
> Each of the strategic components of the Triad acts in concert with the others to complicate Soviet planning, making it more difficult for the Soviets not only to plan and execute a successful attack but also to defend against retaliation.
>
> Each of the legs of the Triad acts as a hedge against a possible technological break-through that could threaten the viability of any single strategic system. By maintaining a Triad we force the Soviet Union to disperse their resources among three components, preventing them from concentrating their considerable resources on defeating two or perhaps only one US strategic system.
>
> Finally, only a Triad of three unique systems can provide us with all the elements necessary to provide a strong, secure deterrent. The strengths of each system not only complement the strengths of the other two but also compensate for their weaknesses. To deter successfully all types of nuclear attack, our forces as a whole must possess a number of characteristics and capabilities—including survivability, . . . prompt response, mission flexibility, and sufficient accuracy and warhead yield to retaliate against hardened Soviet military targets. No single weapons system can incorporate all of these capabilities. Submarines are less vulnerable, thus they are more survivable,

however they are less accurate, they don't have the yield and at times it is difficult to communicate with them.

Bombers are accurate, and retrievable, but they are much slower. ICBMs are easier to command and control, faster and more accurate, but they are more vulnerable than submarines and once launched, they are irretrievable.

All three systems together, however, can incorporate all of those elements necessary to deter against all types of attacks.

For many years it was our good fortune to possess a Triad whose effectiveness could be assured well into the future. Unhappily, due to the massive, and largely unmatched, strategic buildup that the Soviets have sustained since the 1960s, those days are gone.

That buildup has created substantial vulnerability in our strategic Triad which in turn has altered the strategic balance and reduced the effectiveness of the retaliatory forces, thus weakening our ability to deter war.

In recognition of this fact, the President instituted, and the Congress supported, over the past two years, a number of programs designed to restore the strategic balance and improve the effectiveness of our forces.

We have begun and are continuing to modernize and improve the sea and air based legs of the Triad and the Scowcroft Commission very significantly has recommended that we continue this without any change.[196]

Struggle for a Long-Range Combat Aircraft

"I want you to understand that the Strategic Air Command and the B-1 had a love affair for ten years. We have a lot of blood and tender loving care that went into the development of that program," remarked CINCSAC Gen Richard Ellis in a 1980 retrospective statement.[197] As General Ellis indicated, the Air Force from the early 1960s gave deep thought to the requirement for and characteristics of a follow-on advanced manned strategic aircraft (AMSA) and quite frequently this forward thinking involved backward looks at the B-70/RS-70 programs of the 1950s that were scotched by Secretary McNamara at the insistence of the Kennedy administration.

When the statement of requirements that led to the B-70 was published, Gen James Ferguson was Air Force director of operational requirements and as such was responsible for the matter. The B-70, XB-70, and RS-70, Ferguson remembered, was "a follow-on to the philosophy that we followed for many, many years. For many years we wanted to go higher and faster whenever we could, and as fast and as high as the state of the art would permit."[198] To Lt Gen Otto J. Glasser, Air Force chief of staff for research and development in 1971, the B-70 "was designed as the last and faster approach to improved manned aircraft systems. The B-70 was capable only of operating very high, very fast, and when the SAM missiles came into operational use, the B-70 found it could not operate in its design regimen, and it had little residual capability to operate in other regimes."[199] The fault usually described of the B-70/RS-70 was its design limitation to high speed and high altitude, but a more mature reflection demonstrated that this was not entirely true or at least was not true in all cases. Gen David C. Jones, Air Force chief of staff in 1976, noted that "the predictions of the mid-1960s that no aircraft could penetrate at high altitude, high speed had been proven to be wrong."[200] Jones continued to believe, "At high altitudes, we think supersonic speed is important to test the Soviets. They will have to develop a capability against it." Both as director of defense research and engineering and as secretary of the Air Force during the McNamara days, Harold Brown opposed the B-70:

> The extreme speed of the B-70, mach 3, proved not to be of particular use, because the B-70 was limited to the high altitudes, high speed regime — it could not perform well at all at low altitude. Between the time the B-70 was designed and the time it was cancelled, it became clear that . . . low altitude was the best way to escape being destroyed by ground defenses. . . . As I make clear . . . , however, in the extended air defense area, where there are no ground defenses, but there can be airborne defenses, supersonic speed at high altitude could well be the best means of penetrating that part of the defenses. . . . Therefore, I want to build into the aircraft the flexibility to be able to penetrate supersonic[ally] if high is the best way or to be able to penetrate subsonically at low altitude in circumstances where that's the best way to penetrate.[201]

Another technical problem of the B-70/RS-70 was a conscious decision at its inception to accept risks in pressing forward in every key technical area. Said General Glasser: "The B-70 development essentially involved risk in every key technical area. Its very high speed and altitude necessitates a large, heavy airframe requiring engine and airframe manufacturing techniques which were then beyond the known state-of-the-art."[202] General LeMay ultimately despaired of the B-70 when it was limited to a three-aircraft program since it was impossible to get any technical assistance from industry to handle technical problems that arose when so few aircraft were being built in a dead-end project. LeMay was adamant that some follow-on bomber was essential. "I am afraid the B-52 is going to fall apart on us before we can get a replacement for it. There is a serious danger that this may happen to us," he said in February 1964.[203] On the contrary, Gen George S. Brown, who would become Air Force chief of staff but was on Secretary McNamara's staff and saw things from the OSD side of the fence during the B-70 controversy, disagreed:

> At the time the B-70 work was going on, it was not a follow-on bomber, it was to be added to the B-52 force. . . . At the time the B-70 development program was under way, there was not a general consensus of opinion that we needed a manned bomber then. In other words, we had the B-52; it had considerable life left in it. The judgement was that you could improve some of its penetration aids and it had lots of life left in it.[204]

In a recapitulation of the problems of the B-70, Gen David Jones, as chief of staff, had "a vivid memory" of the adverse ultimate effect when some Air Force leaders made an "end run" to Congress and got a mandate drafted to overturn President Kennedy's decision to cancel the B-70. According to General Jones this "left a great deal of ill will in its aftermath and set back attempts by the Air Force to move on to a new bomber program."*[205] The B-70 program of three experimental aircraft — one of which was lost in an aerial collision — cost $1,468.1 million. Of the B-70/RS-70 General McConnell said:

> As far as inventory of the Air Force is concerned, it is a dead duck.... As far as having the RS-70 in the Air Force inventory, I am not in favor of it.... We tried to go too far out. We had to develop the things that went into it as we went along. We just did not have the state of the art, in my opinion.[206]

Secretary McNamara said in February 1966,

> Today there isn't a single senior military or civilian official in the Department of Defense who believes it would be wise to have that B-70 in operation. And, "today," is still a year or two away from the time it would have been in operation had the decision been made to deploy it in 1961 or 1962. This simply indicates we would have wasted many billions of dollars if we had gone ahead at that time.... The problem is to define a suitable role for a strategic bomber in the missile era, and to determine what specifications will give that bomber sufficient effectiveness to make it worth developing and deploying.[207]

When he became secretary of the Air Force, Harold Brown noted one other adverse effect of the B-70 affair, saying:

> There is, I believe, in some parts of the Office of the Secretary of Defense a concern either that the Air Force does not know what it wants ... or that it has previously made mistaken statements about ... aircraft it desired. You all remember the B-70, about which the Air Force said it knew what it wanted; and then when we got it, it turned out to be designed for the wrong mission....[208]

In considering the matter of an advanced manned strategic aircraft, Secretary McNamara demanded that the Air Force must develop a "clear concept for utilizing this bomber."

> It is difficult to envisage how to use a strategic bomber in an era of missiles. I think everybody agrees that the primary weapon must be the missile. Once you accept that ... it is extremely difficult to figure out how and for what purpose to use a bomber.... Until you do that you do not know what kind of bomber to develop.[209]

Early in 1963 when it was obvious that the B-70 program was defunct, General LeMay had charged his staff to examine various alternatives for a follow-on to the B-52. A research and development study began in April 1963 and resolved into a

---

* In part because of this happening General Jones refused to make an attempt to get Congress to override President Carter's cancellation of B-1 production in 1977. He said: "I was not, have not been, and will not be in the future, a party to an attempt to undermine a decision by my commander. If asked in Congress what I think, I'll give my candid views. But I will not go out and make speeches, nor will I go backdoor with Congress or anyone else, to undermine the President. Neither I nor any other military commander wants subordinates to work to undermine our decisions. But we can only expect that kind of discipline in the military if we observe it ourselves with respect to the Commander-in-Chief."

consideration of a very large airplane in four configurations to serve as an airborne missile launcher for SAC, an airborne weapon system for air defense purposes, a very large transport, and a command and control plane for TAC use in advanced areas.[210] Early in 1964 General LeMay gave his personal view of what the new bomber should be:

> Long range was paramount; there was no use in having it if it couldn't reach the target. It had to be able to penetrate to the target, meaning that the plane had to be large enough to carry necessary penetration aids. It would be advantageous for it to carry missiles that could take care of defenses, and it should have the capability to lay down large-yield weapons required by hard targets.[211]

LeMay ruled out a proposal that was going round that the TFX or F-111 should be accepted as a SAC bomber: "The main trouble with the TFX is that it is a small airplane, and it will not carry the things you need to penetrate modern defenses and still have long enough range to do it."[212] In 1963–64 the AMSA conception of the Air Force was described as a large 200,000–350,000 pound plane that would require the development of new engines and new avionics. Speaking of the plane and the Air Force designers, Harold Brown, then director of defense research and engineering, said: "I think what they want is a new airplane . . . and they are going to write down a mission performance at some point that they think . . . will give them an airplane different from the one we have."[213]

In March 1965 Secretary McNamara's projection of the general war problem into the 1970s clearly demonstrated to him that the missile force would be a persuasive deterrent to a deliberate attack on the United States. Nevertheless, he believed it wise to keep a continuing option for manned strategic bombers. McNamara pointed out that SAC had 630 B-52s, plus 80 B-58s: "The 52s and 58s appear to have a life expectancy extending into the early to mid-1970s. So there is no pressing need for a follow-on bomber to be developed earlier than the early to mid-1970s."[214] Accordingly, McNamara wanted to continue to develop advanced avionics and propulsion but to postpone development of the AMSA. In this same season, speaking as director of defense research and engineering, Doctor Brown proposed that the F-111 production line at General Dynamics turn out 200 FB-111 aircraft models for the Strategic Air Command, which would be possible in five years. At this same time, General McConnell had become chief of staff and was actively concerned with the state of the B-52 force. B-52A/F models had been delivered to the Air Force between 1954 and 1959 and, because of their wing structure, were going to reach the end of their estimated service life in fiscal year 1967. The B-52G/H models had been built with a very rugged wing and should have remained sound until the early 1970s. In McConnell's assessment FB-111s could not do the job he had in mind for AMSAs because they were range-limited, couldn't carry the same amount of ordnance, and would require overseas recovery bases. But they could very well cover the gap of the loss of the early model B-52s, and McConnell proposed to McNamara that still operational B-52Cs/Fs be replaced on a 2 to 3 basis with FB-111s; this to provide SAC with a force of 14 operational squadrons (210 unit equipment FB-111s). In April 1965, General McConnell made an informal replacement proposal to Secretary McNamara, and in June the Air Force formally proposed to procure 210 UE FB-111s as replacements for 345 B-52Cs/Fs. The Joint Chiefs concurred in August, and Secretary McNamara recommended the proposition to President Johnson who approved development and procurement of the FB-111s, which were to be little changed from the basic F-111. FB-111s were programmed into the SAC inventory beginning in fiscal year 1969 and scheduled for completion in fiscal year 1971. The phaseout of the C through F series of B-52s was scheduled to begin in fiscal year 1967 and to be completed in fiscal year 1971.[215] At the end of fiscal year 1971 Secretary McNamara intended that the old B-58s also would have been phased out, all the actions resulting in "giving us a modernized force of 465 manned bombers (210 FB-111s and 255 B-52Gs/Hs) by the end of that fiscal year and at less than the cost which would result from the maintenance of the older B-52s and the B-58s in the force."[216]

In the aftermath of the FB-111 commitment, Secretary McNamara strongly emphasized that this was not an "interim bomber" as far as he was concerned but "a true 'dual purpose bomber'." It was to be used either for a strategic nuclear operation or strategic conventional operation or for a tactical air operation. Except as a dual-purpose bomber, he said he would not have recommended the FB-111. He thought it would be very difficult to see a use for the FB-111 in conjunction with a 1,000-nuclear missile strike.[217] After Doctor Brown became secretary of the Air Force in October 1965, he agreed with General McConnell on the requirement for continuing a mixed force of nuclear missiles and manned bombers, which implied that a follow-on bomber would be needed at some point. Since the B-52G/H range and payload were far beyond the FB-111A, an alternative to the latter would be needed. This replacement would require careful judgment of the uses of a follow-on bomber, and Brown's immediate reaction was that Air Force thinking about the follow-on bomber was almost entirely for nuclear conflict whereas he wanted more attention to be given to thoughts about a versatility for employment either in a nuclear environment or in a nonnuclear conflict in a remote area. "Statistics of the use of the B-52 in Vietnam and the many laudatory comments of ground force commanders give convincing evidence that our strategic bombers are very effective for limited war, in some circumstances, even against tactical targets," Brown pointed out in February 1966.[218] Brown also stated that the exact timing of a need for a follow-on bomber would depend upon the threat of Communist air defenses: as long as they did not markedly improve, the B-52Gs/Hs could expect to penetrate. In a hearing before a House of Representatives appropriations subcommittee in February 1966, both Brown and McConnell agreed that the fielding of a mixed force of missiles and manned aircraft was advantageous because it prevented an enemy from concentrating all his resources to a single missile or air defense system. During these same hearings, General McConnell said that Brown's only disagreement with the AMSA design was that he had not looked at its conventional as well as nuclear role; he expected that more study could shortly remedy this deficiency.[219]

With added study during the summer of 1966, the Air Force completed design configuration of an AMSA that would have significant conventional as well as nuclear bomb capabilities. In November the Air Force formally issued the specifications desired for the AMSA. The specifications would feature a variable sweep wing, and four medium bypass-ratio engines would provide continuous supersonic speeds at high altitudes and supersonic dash speeds at low-altitude penetrations. The AMSA also would carry a large payload of short-range attack missiles and an internal payload of nonnuclear ordnance nearly double that of the B-52. The power of the AMSA would permit it to take off from 6,000-foot runways, thus making it possible to increase survivability by wide dispersion and quick takeoffs. For some time Dr John S. Foster, Jr., director of defense research and engineering, had been reviewing Air Force AMSA plans submissions in terms of criteria of penetrability, survivability, and flexibility. He considered the November specifications suitable in terms of survivability and flexibility, but he thought that penetration capability would become critical for a bomber that would have to be operational at least 20 years from 1966. He remanded the AMSA plan for more study of penetration aid payloads and their possible influence in aircraft size, configuration, and crew requirements.[220]

Early in 1967 the Soviets had begun deployment of an antiballistic missile defense, but there was as yet no indication as to what the Soviet antiaircraft defense would be in the 1970s. Air Force cost effectiveness studies showed that a new AMSA would be an optimum solution over B-52s and FB-111s if Soviet defenses increased, this being true because the advanced manned bomber was bigger and cost less per pound of payload.[221] If the Soviets deployed a greater-than-expected defense, such as advanced surface-to-air missiles, advanced interceptors with airborne warning and control systems, or advanced ABM defenses with high effectiveness, then Secretary Brown said that an advanced bomber would be cost effective, but since it was not yet evident what the Soviet air defense would be, the United States had time to decide what to do about AMSA. General McConnell disagreed; he urged that Secretary McNamara should permit contract definition of the AMSA since the Soviets could substantially improve their defenses so suddenly that the United States would have little time to react. McConnell also argued that the bomber portion of the US assured destruction force would become more vital as the Soviets developed their ABM capabilities.[222] Secretary McNamara would not accept these arguments. In view of the Soviet ABM the "first order of business in the strategic offensive forces" was to provide missile penetration aids and produce and deploy the Poseidon SLBM. McNamara asserted:

> These are relatively expensive programs, particularly Poseidon, but they are far more important to our future assured destruction capability than a new manned bomber. Indeed, if the Soviets were to deploy a full scale and highly sophisticated ABM system

and enhance their strategic missile capability, I believe the requirement for a highly survivable ICBM would have a far higher priority than a new manned bomber.[223]

In 1968 Secretary Brown and General McConnell both agreed that the secretary of defense ought to approve a contract definition for the AMSA. Secretary Brown continued to believe that production of the AMSA would depend on the development of Soviet air defenses, but he believed that the design for the AMSA was flexible enough to handle any changes in tactics that might occur in the next 15 years. He also recognized that Secretary McNamara probably did not want to approve contract definition because the Air Force had made mistakes about the B-70, and McNamara was reluctant to get "locked into" support for the AMSA. But Brown was confident that the Air Force could and should begin contract definition with no commitment for eventual AMSA production. Early in 1968 the Joint Chiefs of Staff also agreed that it was important to protect an option for an advanced-bomber initial operational capability (IOC) of mid-1976, and this could only be done by initiating some form of contract definition during 1968.[224]

The proposal to undertake contract definition failed to gain acceptance from Secretary McNamara or from his successor as secretary of defense, Clark M. Clifford, although the latter started changes in the strategic bomber force. During 1968 the continuing OSD strategic bomber studies reinforced a view that a principal problem was in penetration capability and that new penetration aids were required. The SRAM already was in development and a new subsonic cruise armed decoy (SCAD) was accepted for development in fiscal year 1970. Because of its smallness, the FB-111 could not carry the kind of penetration payload to cope with increased Soviet defenses; moreover, the costs of FB-111s had soared. Where the cost of a force of 14 operational squadrons (210 UE aircraft) was estimated originally at $1.9 billion, excluding SRAM, only 6 operational squadrons (90 UE aircraft plus 16 for support, training, and attrition) could now be purchased for an estimated $1.8 billion, excluding SRAM. In the light of these developments, Secretary Clifford elected to reduce the FB-111 program to 6 operational squadrons; to extend the phaseout of equivalent B-52 C-F squadrons to provide a conventional bombing capability on the order of the B-52Ds that had been optimized to carry 108 500-pound bombs against targets in Southeast Asia; and to keep the B-58s until SCAD became available for the B-52s.[225]

The presidential inauguration of Richard M. Nixon at the beginning of 1969 brought into authority Secretary of Defense Melvin R. Laird and Secretary of the Air Force Robert C. Seamans, Jr. Secretary Laird was familiar with military affairs from his long years of service in Congress. In a colloquy with Secretary McNamara in 1966, Laird had argued that McNamara was putting "all our strike payload as far as the strategic forces [were concerned] into the missile basket." He continued: "I am not sure that it is not nice to have something around in the time period of 1975 to 1980 that is not completely automated such as the missile."[226] Secretary Seamans also thought highly of manned aircraft because of their flexibility:

> We tend to think of what I will call scenarios, and then people begin to believe that is exactly what is going to happen. The truth of the matter is we never know exactly what is going to happen. Nothing provides much better flexibility, in my mind, than some human beings in an airplane that can range around the surface of the earth. A good case in point it seems to me is the use of a plane which we designed as a strategic bomber, which is now one of the most valuable weapons systems that we have in Vietnam, and I think it would be a great mistake not to continue with manned systems.[227]

In his examination of the strategic balance of power with the Soviet Union, Secretary Laird was concerned with the vastly superior throw weight of Soviet missiles.

> In order to keep up with them in megatonnage, because of missile developments we have had in this country the only way we can come close, and we are behind them now as far as megatonnage delivery is concerned, is through the use of B-52s. . . . If we didn't have this B-52 bomber . . . we would be in a very bad position as far as delivery of nuclear megatonnage in the Soviet Union is concerned.[228]

One of the first decisions in which secretaries Laird and Seamans were involved was the decision to stop the procurement of the long-questioned FB-111 at the number in production at the moment and to proceed with the more advanced AMSA, which OSD now named the B-1. "The FB-111 will not meet the requirements for a true intercontinental bomber and the cost per unit has reached a point where the AMSA must be considered to fill the void," Laird explained.[229] And Seamans agreed: "Against a typical target system it would take six times as many FB-111s as B-1s and require six times the tanker support. And due to its relatively small size, there is little growth potential for penetration aids in the FB-111."[230] In Laird's revision of the Clifford fiscal year 1970 defense budget, the FB-111 program was cut back to 2 wings with 60 UE aircraft, plus 16 for command support. Production was terminated at the 76th FB-111, and others on the line were to be finished as F-111 tactical fighters. In Senate budget hearings General Wheeler revealed that the Joint Chiefs of Staff, in addressing termination of the FB-111 procurement, had recommended that the original procurement of 14 combat squadrons be maintained. Laird explained, however, that he had felt for eight years that the Air Force should go directly from the B-52 to the AMSA, without the FB-111 "interim bomber."[231] Although General McConnell initially favored the Clifford budget's proposed retention of the 78 SAC B-58s, the B-58s lacked needed electronic countermeasures and low-altitude terrain equipment and had only a limited capability for conventional bombing. Important savings also could be secured by phasing out the entire B-58 structure in fiscal year 1970, and this was acceptable to both the Air Force and the Joint Chiefs of Staff, provided additional B-52s were kept in operation to compensate for the reduction in the planned FB-111 wings and the actual B-58 wings. As a result of phasing out some older B-52C/F bombers during fiscal year 1969, the Strategic Air Command during mid-1969 had 17 squadrons (255 UE) of B-52G/H series aircraft and 13 squadrons (195 UE) of C/F models. The Air Force got approval to keep the 13 C/F squadrons through fiscal year 1970, 6 squadrons being assigned to the strategic nuclear mission, 5 to Southeast Asia operations, and 2 to training and rotation.[232]

The approval for the Air Force to proceed with the development of the AMSA — now the B-1 — specially stipulated that there would be no binding commitment to its production. Benefiting from five years in which AMSA had been studied from virtually every angle, the Air Force requested proposals for full-scale engineering development of the B-1 on 3 November 1969, and on 5 June 1970 Secretary Seamans announced the two winners — North American Rockwell for the airframe and General Electric for the engines. The initial contract with Rockwell called for seven prototype airframes, five for flight tests, one for static tests, and one for fatigue tests. Flight-tests were expected to begin in mid-1974. The Air Force estimated the total research and development, test and evaluation (RDT&E) cost for the B-1 would be about $2.3 billion. The cost for a buy of 200-plus aircraft would be about $7 billion. Operation and maintenance (O&M) costs for 10 years was estimated at $3.7 billion. All these costs totalled approximately $13 billion over some 18 years.[233] It was planned that a production decision would not be made until a year after the first flight in 1974.[234] The B-1 development program was planned on a basis that there should be required in no single year more than approximately a half-billion dollars of development funds. Inasmuch as the program plan for fiscal year 1972 called for significantly more money than this, the Air Force deliberately excised from the program everything that could be removed that was not fundamental to reaching a decision to go further. In February 1971 the number of flight-test aircraft was reduced from five to three. One notable tradeoff for cost reduction was the elimination of requirement for supersonic velocity at low altitude, which was analyzed and determined not to contribute enough to operational capability to justify the cost. Provisions in the form of space cubage, electrical power, and cooling capacity were put in, but decisions about the B-1 avionics system were deferred: this money saver had some utility since there was no really good way to project avionics requirements when the aircraft would be operational.[235] Some congressmen, however, were skeptical that down the road the Air Force would be coming in with a large request for avionics money.

At the initiation of the B-1 program and when it was cut back in 1971, the Air Force laid great emphasis on the fact it was emphasizing research and development rather than eventual production. Asked to explain this approach, Secretary McLucas said: "You are talking about a climate when there wasn't all that much support, in our minds, for the B-1. . . . At that time, what we were trying to do was to take out insurance in case there might be a need, so we wanted to pay as small a premium for that insurance as we could." The shift in nuclear strategy from assured destruction to selective response, in McLucas's view brought a real need for the B-1. He remarked, "It seems to me now we are in a period where it looks as though we probably will want the B-1, and if that is true, then you should do all those things that a prudent man would do to put himself in a best position to go into production."²³⁶ When Doctor Seamans and General Ryan were in charge of the Air Force, they reported B-1 development on schedule, but Secretary McLucas and Gen George Brown had another view and found indications that the program manager could not live up to schedule. In August 1973, McLucas appointed a special committee, headed by Dr Raymond Lewis Bisplinghoff, the deputy director of the National Science Foundation, to undertake an independent review of the B-1 program. The committee reported back in November 1973. It found no technical problems, but identified a number of management difficulties arising from the austere program funding. The committee also pointed out that a three-aircraft contract was not adequate to permit Rockwell to keep a competent staff at the plant properly employed and available to begin production during the time between the beginning and completion of flight-tests. To rectify this, the committee recommended that two additional airplanes should be added to the R&D program so that the production line could be kept open during an adequate test period. The number 4 and 5 airplanes would be close enough to a final production configuration so that they would probably enter the operational inventory. After reviewing the Bisplinghoff committee report, the Air Force in its fiscal year 1975 budget request made to Congress in February 1974 requested funding of $499 million for a restructured B-1 program including a fourth and possibly a fifth air vehicle as preproduction aircraft to provide a better basis for transition into production. Congress approved $445 million for the B-1 program, $54 million below the Air Force request. Congress stated that after a successful first B-1 flight and with congressional approval, the Air Force could start aircraft number 4 with such funds as it might have on hand. This first B-1 test flight was successfully flown on 23 December 1974.²³⁷

"The B-1 bomber has become one of the most controversial programs in the Department of Defense," Congressman George H. Mahon, chairman of the House Appropriations Subcommittee on the Department of Defense, told Secretary McLucas and Gen David Jones, early in 1975.

> There are a lot of people who would like to be against it. A lot of people voted for it rather than join in the opposition, feeling they did not want to be associated with anything that smacked of a slowdown in our defense at a time when the Soviet Union is moving forward rather aggressively and ambitiously to acquire greater power and exceed the United States in military strength.²³⁸

Mahon said that Congress wanted answers to issues: What was the role of a B-1 in the strategic Triad; What were the cost-effectiveness alternatives to the B-1; and What were the 240 production bombers going to cost.²³⁹

The question of whether the B-1 AMSA was an anachronism in a missile era had been asked in many wordings for many years, and the answers yield an assessment of the distinctive utility of manned aerospace vehicles. In November 1969 Mahon had asked Secretary Laird to say how AMSA would enhance national security and to quantify its contribution. Laird replied:

In all candor, Mr. Chairman, this is a question which is difficult to answer in quantifiable terms since the answer depends so completely upon the underlying assumptions. I have already made clear that we have sought to achieve our objective of deterrence by maintaining an ability to penetrate enemy defenses by attacking from all altitudes and azimuths with a mix of ICBMs, SLBMs, and bombers. AMSA would enhance our security by helping to maintain a bomber force which is capable of surviving and penetrating increased enemy defenses in the future.

I am sure you realize the difficulty in assessing, in definite terms, the future viability of these systems. Essentially, AMSA would help to provide insurance against unanticipated failures in our missiles, or unforeseen developments in weapons which might counter our missiles. I firmly believe that bombers materially contribute to the viability of the missile systems by forcing the Soviets to allocate their resources to defense against bombers as well as missiles, rather than simply against missiles alone. But this factor is not meaningfully quantifiable.

I should note that bombers have one distinctive feature, which could someday be of immeasurable value, and which is not possessed by missiles.

This is the ability to be launched upon warning and yet still be recallable after launch. During a time of crisis we might even keep our bombers on continuous airborne alert. I believe this is a significant and desirable feature, although I am still unable to quantify it. It is my intention to do all I can to insure the continued viability of our missile systems—which is equivalent to saying I shall attempt to insure we would not be helpless without a bomber force. But I believe, for reasons such as I have just mentioned, that we need to continue our development of AMSA in order to keep the deployment option open.[240]

In July 1969 Sen Richard Russell had asked General McConnell to tell him why the flexibility of a manned bomber was of value to national command authorities and planners. McConnell explained:

The primary advantage derived from the inherent flexibility of manned aircraft is the increased number of options available. The following are examples of bomber capabilities that can be exploited by military planner and command authorities to provide these options:

1. Bombers can be used in a show of force during periods of tension.
2. Bombers can be returned to base prior to commitment of the force thus enabling authorities to cease military operations if political decisions require.
3. Bombers can be assigned multiple targets releasing weapons on preplanned or alternate targets as dictated by the tactical situation.
4. Bombers are more accurate than missiles and can be used to accomplish selective strikes under conditions of rigid constraint.
5. Bombers can be recovered and reconstituted subsequent to an initial nuclear exchange and used to strike additional targets detected by our reconnaissance and surveillance systems or to strike those targets not struck initially.
6. Bombers provide capabilities in nonnuclear environments that are not available from other systems. These include long-range and large-payload capacity.
7. Bomber tactics can be altered to decrease the effectiveness of enemy defenses.
8. In summary, the reusability of bombers—including launch under positive control, show of force, nonnuclear options, and recovery and reconstitution following nuclear

strikes—demonstrates their flexibility to provide multiple options to military planners and national authorities over the full range of military operations.[241]

And in April 1974, General Allen spoke about the role of the manned bomber in a selective employment.

> QUESTION: General Allen, you state, "And if deterrence should fail, the TRIAD gives the Nation the capability to respond selectively and thereby reduce the chances of uncontrolled escalation to a general nuclear war."
>
> If deterrence fails, under what circumstances do you visualize a selective response?
>
> GENERAL ALLEN: I would hope, . . . and I personally have always thought about it this way, the basic mission of the military forces of the United States are the defense of our country, our population, our society and so forth.
>
> It is not possible for us to know precisely what type of an attack we would receive should deterrence fail.
>
> Certainly we hope that it never does, and our basic efforts are to make sure that we have a good deterrent capability.
>
> If deterrence should fail, it is possible that it could fail in a manner in which the United States received a limited attack as opposed to an all-out assault against our population centers as well as our military forces.
>
> It could be a selective attack against the United States. It could be the type of attack we have discussed a little bit this morning against our bomber bases, for example. It could be an attack against our missile bases. It could be an attack against our submarine bases.
>
> If we received a limited attack of that nature, it would seem to me very important that our response be a response that was at least as controlled as the attack which we received.
>
> If we had received a limited attack, and if we responded, for example, against Soviet population centers, I think all we would be assuring would be another response by the Soviet Union against our population centers and assuring the destruction of New York and Chicago and Washington and all the other major population centers of the United States.
>
> We would want to make a controlled response which could be against a small segment of the target system. It could be against an individual target. There are myriad possibilities. It could be a target or series of targets within range of tactical aircraft as was suggested by the chairman earlier this morning.
>
> QUESTION: That is the point I wanted to get into. It is not that the TRIAD provides the total selectivity for response, there are other forces that we have that also provide the ability to make a selective response, that is, the tactical forces.
>
> Would you agree to that?
>
> GENERAL ALLEN: If the objective of your selective response was within range of the tactical forces, yes, sir.

QUESTION: Do you believe a selective response is feasible with the Minuteman or Poseidon force?

GENERAL ALLEN: Yes, sir. I believe it is feasible with the Minuteman or Poseidon force. However, I believe the use of the missile force in a selective response could incur some disadvantages. Those disadvantages are in two areas primarily.

First, it is very important in a selective response that the enemy know that you are indeed executing a limited selective response.

When he sees ballistic missile warheads coming through his radar screen, he is going to have to make a very, very fast judgment as to whether this is a small number or a small number that are preceding a large attack, and so forth, and he is going to have to make a very, very fast judgment in terms of what he does.

This can be contrasted with his decisionmaking process, if he sees a few, three, four, six bombers coming intermittently through his radar screen, as he sees, and then loses them through the terrain masking. He knows for a fact that his country is not about to get destroyed by those handful of bombers coming. He knows he has got some time to think the thing over. He has some time to get on the hot line with Washington and discuss the situation and he is not faced with a fast, immediate instinctive reaction which could go the wrong way with that type of response.

That is one aspect.

The other aspect is, in a selective response, it would seem to me it could be critically important for the national command authority to know how well that response went. Did it do what it was supposed to do?

Did it do more than it was supposed to do, or less than it was supposed to do?

If it was supposed to be a discriminate response, did it miss and hit downtown in the city someplace in the area or not?

Did it destroy the targets it was intended to destroy?

With a Polaris or Poseidon response, you are not going to have a very good idea of the answers to those questions.

With a manned aircraft response, you get immediate reports back on how well it did.[242]

The question of cost-effectiveness alternatives to the B-1 was the subject of a monumental study effort initiated at the direction of Secretary Schlesinger in August 1973. The study was referred to as the Joint Strategic Bomber Study because it was conducted by three groups acting in concert: the Offices of the Director of Defense Research and Engineering, the Assistant Secretary of Defense for Program Analysis and Evaluation, and the Air Force Assistant Chief of Staff for Studies and Analysis. For comparative purposes the study group analyzed the cost and capability of a modified and refurbished B-52 known as the B-52I, a stretched FB-111 known as the FB-111G, and a B-1. In terms of a 10-year system cost to deliver a weapon on target, the B-1 and B-52 showed a significant advantage over the FB-111. The B-1 was the most cost-effective primarily because of greater penetration capability and weapon-carrying capacity, in spite of additional costs for procurement. Only if the B-1 procurement costs, not including inflation, rose by over 50 percent would the B-1 not be the most cost-effective.

The Air Force had an air-launched cruise missile in research and development for use by B-52s and B-1s in defense suppression, and the Joint Strategic Bomber Study group entertained an alternative whereby wide-body cargo aircraft would carry and launch the cruise missiles in a standoff mode. The study concluded:

> The third alternative, air-launched cruise missiles (ALCM) employed from standoff, wide-body transports, is less effective than the B-1 in both the launch and penetration phases.
>
> During takeoff, the wide-body cargo aircraft would be more vulnerable to SLBM attacks than B-1s. Transports are slower flying out to a safe distance and are difficult to harden against nuclear effects. The relatively few transports, each with many ALCMs—up to 100 in some concepts—would be lucrative targets, inviting attack by long-range interceptors before their cruise missiles could be launched. During the penetration phase, the ALCM itself will not have the potential capability of the manned bomber in ECM, range, accuracy, or ability to evade enemy defenses. ALCMs could be expected to incur heavy attrition in attacking targets protected by low-altitude capable SAMs. Bombers can attack fixed SAMs with short-range attack missiles and can use information from their warning receivers to evade mobile SAMs, but ALCMs cannot. This is a major weakness in an ALCM-only attack. Further, the DOD supplementary analyses showed that a "precursor" attack by our ICBM/SLBMs on these low-altitude SAMs would not make the ALCM attack cost-effective.
>
> The DOD study found that a force of primarily B-1s will place about twice as many weapons on target as will an equal-cost, all standoff cruise missile force. Moreover, a purely standoff force greatly simplifies an enemy's defense problems. He would be able to concentrate his defensive efforts on low-altitude SAMs around targets, and perhaps, long-range interceptors on the periphery. Such a concentration would severely attrite an all-ALCM force.[243]

To summarize the alternatives, the Joint Strategic Bomber Study's two major observations were that (1) the low-flying, fast, nuclear-hardened B-1 with its high-quality ECM outperformed all other nuclear vehicles examined by a wide margin, and (2) of the various equal-cost forces examined, those consisting principally of B-1s performed substantially better. Based on these observations, the study reaffirmed the conviction that the B-1 has the most cost-effective way to modernize the strategic bomber force.[244]

In response to what he recognized as "considerable criticism about the inflated cost of the B-1," General Allen defended the B-1 program as being very cost conscious and well managed. In 1975, the Air Force was describing the B-1 program as being a $20.6-billion program over its complete procurement life span. The difficulty was the inflation that was gripping the national economy. In original cost estimates in 1970 the Air Force had allowed $1.3 billion for inflation; in 1975, the program was showing $9.6 billion for inflation. Since the complete buy out of the B-1 program was not until 1985, General Allen was unable to make a realistic guess about ultimate program costs because he did not know what the inflation rate would be in 1985.[245] But the Senate Appropriations Committee called for cost reductions in the B-1 program, and the Air Force substituted ejection seats for a planned crew module, made changes in avionics, deleted the requirement for an external pylon to carry external weapons, and agreed to relax somewhat the high-altitude requirements for speed and range by changing the engine inlet design from a variable to a fixed configuration. If the higher speed capability at high altitude should be required later by changes in the Soviet threat, it was proposed that controls and actuations for the variable engine inlets could be procured and installed without major redesign.[246] In 1976 Congress was awash with conflicting cost estimates on the B-1. There was general agreement that 244 B-1s would cost more than $20 billion. One calculation cited was that the price tag had risen from $41 million a plane in 1970 to $100 million a plane in 1976.[247]

Early in 1976 two analysts at the Brookings Institution published *Modernizing the Strategic Bomber Force: Why and How*. This study concluded that "the effectiveness of the current bomber force is more than adequate now and, with minor force modifications, will remain so in the future under foreseeable conditions. . . . There appear to be no significant military advantages to be gained by deploying a new penetrating bomber such as the B-1." The study also recommended development of a standoff cruise missile carrying attack force, the objective of the force being to deliver 400 one-megaton weapons and destroy 50 Soviet cities with three-fourths of the industrial capacity and about one-third of the Soviet population.[248] Both Air Force Secretary Thomas C. Reed and General Jones strongly opposed the Brookings study, pointing out that it was in no way equal to the Joint Strategic Bomber Study and highlighted two major points of bias. Where the Joint Strategic Bomber Study's target base had included government controls (national, civil, and political), industrial-economic installation, and military installations, the Brookings analysts—in General Jones's words—"changed the strategy which reduced the numbers, and then claimed we could save money." The formal Air Force response to the Brookings study also pointed out that the study's conclusions were predicated on "simplified analytical methods that biased the case against the [B-1] penetrating force. . . . By using a formula in which only mass could overwhelm the air defenses, forces containing large numbers of penetrating objects had to be the most effective." Secretary Reed reasoned that people tended to "lean too heavily one way or the other" in discussing penetrating bombers versus cruise missiles. The Department of Defense supported a "middle view," namely:

> The DOD views cruise missiles as being useful to strike lightly defended targets, while allowing more flexible bomber routing and a proliferated attack. Where Soviet defenses are strongest—SAMs protecting their highest value targets—is where a penetrating manned bomber with ECM and supersonic SRAMs, is required. A mix of B-1 aircraft with SRAMs plus B-52s utilizing first generation cruise missile technology is clearly the most threat insensitive force for the rest of the century.[249]

IDEAS, CONCEPTS, DOCTRINE

Anticipating that the B-1 will "again be a big issue in the Congress in 1976," Sen Barry Goldwater asked Gen Russell E. Dougherty, CINCSAC, to give his views. General Dougherty's literate and comprehensive reply of 23 February 1976 is listed in the appendix.

Appendix*

General Dougherty's Reply

I appreciate the opportunity to be heard on these important issues and am pleased to provide my views as requested—views that you should feel free to use as you and your colleagues in the Senate see fit.

If you would indulge me in a reordering of the questions you have posed, I would first like to address the "value of keeping a manned system as part of the strategic equation"—for I consider the "requirement for the B-1" as subordinate to (and flowing from) a more generic and fundamental *US Strategic Requirement for a fully modern manned penetrating bomber:*

If deterrence of attempted coercion, intimidation, or direct attack on the sovereignty of the United States (and those allies we choose to associate with our vital national interests) is to remain the basic tenet of our national security policy, US authorities must continue to have the assurance of a panoply of relevant and diversified military capabilities that can support them in any and all actions necessary to preserve that sovereignty . . . no matter what the circumstances of confrontation.

A hardened, long-range, manned penetrating bomber offers a uniquely capable and dependable strategic delivery system that spreads itself reliably and capably across the broadest possible spectrum of those required military capabilities. When completely modernized and manned with skilled, ingenious military crews, such a penetrating bomber offers the United States an overall flexibility of choice and application that is unmatched by an[y] other weapons system. It can:

Carry a larger number of weapons (conventional or nuclear) than any other strategic delivery system—to any fixed targets, anywhere, under a wide variety of circumstances.

Achieve unequalled accuracies in long-range delivery under all circumstances; and, through self-contained sensors, offers our only long-range capability against mobile or imprecisely located targets.

Provide a highly visible deterrent force, one that can be used as a recognizable expression of national determination and resolve in either pre-planned or ad hoc contingency situations.

Accommodate (or readily be adapted to) the delivery of multiple types of conventional and nuclear weapons—highly accurate gravity delivered, standoff-

---

*Source: Senate, *FY 1977 Military Procurement*, 2830–34.

STRATEGIC CHALLENGES TO AIR POWER

launched cruise, ballistic, semi-ballistic or defensive weapons — in large quantities, for multiple or selective delivery.

Through design growth characteristics, adapt rapidly in tactics and/or avionics to negate or avoid unanticipated defenses and other threats.

Drive an enemy requirement for extensive diversion of his resources to defensive (vice offensive) systems — but still can be designed with the flexibility to penetrate those defenses if penetration is required for assurance.

Provide us the most effective and economical way to redress the already serious (and worsening) imbalance in deliverable megatonnage vis-à-vis the Soviet Union.

Provide a simultaneous capability for long-range, real (or near real) time strike assessment deep within enemy territory with the flexibility of striking alternate planned targets or withholding unnecessary attacks and retaining weapons.

Be launched as a visible expression of active deterrence, yet be recalled without expenditure of ordnance, even after launch, should the deterrent objectives be achieved.

Provide our nation an assured capability to extract severe penalties on an enemy society, regardless of any unexpected degradation or blunting of our SLBM or ICBM force; thus providing insurance against unexpected defenses or failure of any aspect of our strategic ballistic missile systems.

Be used repeatedly. Depending on the nature of conflict, substantial recovery can be anticipated — thus enabling rearming and reuse for any required strategic purpose in subsequent warfighting or war terminating activities.

Exploit superior US technology and capability; for we can build, maintain and operate a flexible, modern delivery system of this type better than any potential adversary.

Be applied across the spectrum of military capabilities — and is uniquely useful for an infinite number of lesser contingency missions; without loss of ultimate capability as a major delivery system for large nuclear payloads.

Survive blunting attacks and reliably be protected from destruction on the ground through tried, proven launch procedures of Strategic Air Command adapted to reasonable expectations of our modern detection and warning systems.

We know what we can do with a manned delivery system. With a modernized manned penetrating delivery system in our mix of major strategic weapons systems, we are confident of our ability to continue to provide our National Authorities assurance of a viable deterrent posture, *under all circumstances of threat or attack.* Without it, we are not confident that we can provide such assurances in the future.

Turning now to my views on the requirement for the B-1 (and I will not repeat the statistics and details of program characteristics, costs, etc. which are matters of record with the Congress):

Simply stated, I view the B-1 as the best candidate vehicle reasonably available to satisfy the future requirement for a modern manned penetrating bomber — and to provide the

US with the diversified characteristics that are and will be needed in our complementary mix of strategic delivery systems. Not only do I view it as the best, I do not see any other comparable system that can reasonably be expected to do this job as I think it must be done for assurance — or for long-term economics.

We are satisfied that the B-1, as it has evolved, will provide our nation with the most efficient and effective manned penetrating weapons system ever conceived. It will accomplish the varied missions that could be required of it with an assurance we do not believe possible in other alternatives that have been proposed and considered.

Strategic weapons planning is dynamic, complex, and demanding. In the thirty year experience of Strategic Air Command with such planning and with the analyses of the plans for efficiency and completeness, SAC achieved a measure of expertise in applying strategic weapons systems to the jobs to be done that is unparalleled. When that expertise is applied to the future problems of maintaining a credible strategic deterrent force, the performance characteristics of such a force containing the B-1 clearly exceed those of a force mix of other, alternative weapons systems. These expert analyses support our individual judgments that no other system reasonably available to us will do the job as well, as efficiently, or as long into the future as will the B-1.

As we now have it, the B-1 development represents a careful blend of operational requirements, modern technological feasibility, fiscal constraints and life-cycle support considerations. It is a *real thing* — a modern manned penetrating bomber that has been conceived, developed and tested to the point that we are confident that it will perform the future requirements for such a delivery system and give us a viable weapon system mix. It is not a paper study or a theoretical analysis of what *might be* or what *might satisfy* future requirements. The B-1 is here, it is timely, and it is competent — postulated alternatives meet none of those criteria.

Your third question is *"Why Strategic Air Command does not support the various alternatives to the B-1 that have been suggested?"* You are correct, we have not supported those alternatives for the overall reason that none of them has stood the tests of long-term sufficiency, cost effectiveness, or supportability over the years ahead. They may have superficial or analytical appeal to some, but they don't measure up with those of us who must maintain and operate our deterrent forces.

To some degree, all the alternatives suggested are either an upgrading of existing equipment that offers expensive short-term improvement without long-term sufficiency, or inadequate performance to remain viable under anticipated high threat situations.

The various models of the B-52 have provided us a magnificent penetrating bomber: its design has given us the inherent growth potential to adapt to changed penetration tactics, offensive and defensive avionics enhancement, and to accommodate to improved types of air-launched missiles and bombs. But the operational B-52 has carried a primary deterrent load for over 20 years, and its ability to adapt to change and modification is not infinite — regardless of its sterling performance throughout those two decades. The basic B-52 technology is that of the 1950s. The aircraft is soft to blast effects; its launch and escape time is relatively long; its radar reflectivity is great; it has no supersonic capability; it cannot penetrate at extremely low altitudes; it is expensive to man and maintain; its design characteristics preclude flexibility in dispersal and deployment. Importantly, even though modified and upgraded, it would be perceived as "nothing new" in the dynamics of deterrence.

Our serious study of the major B-52 modifications proposed as an alternative to the B-1 procurement (e.g., larger engines, redesigned wing, fuselage extension, etc.) leads us to the reasoned conclusion that these improvements will not provide the modern characteristics needed for the future and are, in sum, expensive stopgap measures that would provide neither an adequate nor a cost effective, long-term vehicle to do what we see as required. While I could support these B-52 modifications as desirable to upgrade its viability during the remaining time it is part of our strategic force, they do not offset or obviate the requirement for the B-1. Also, such an extensive modification program would cause a protracted reduction in our operational bomber inventory when the need for these delivery systems is increasing.

One of the principal alternatives that has been advanced is an improved and enlarged version of the FB-111. This alternative has the initial appeal of offering a more modern and higher performance penetrator since the FB-111 is basically a hard and fast aircraft with low radar reflectivity. However, our continuing analysis of the various proposals for FB-111 upgrade has led to the conclusion that the extensive modification required to make the FB-111 comparable to the B-1 would be, in effect, an entirely new aircraft with all the expense, time, and testing required. The basic FB-111 design is already an adaptation of a fighter/bomber aircraft; and it does not have the growth potential to compete, efficiently, with the B-1 without such a major redesign that, in effect, it is a new aircraft.

In our view, the redesign suggestions that have been advanced leave us with an aircraft that lacks growth potential, does not have the desired low-level range and payload characteristics; and, in order to do the job required, would have to be procured, manned, and supported in such large numbers that it is neither an economical nor efficient long-term alternative to the proposed B-1 force.

As respected as the FB-111 is within Strategic Air Command's manned penetrating bomber force, we have a pragmatic recognition of its limitations in size and range, neither of which can adequately be overcome by modification. In fact, and in perception, such an alternative is considered inadequate for the future requirements of our manned bomber force.

The other alternative that seems to have attracted the attention and support of some analysts is a large, "stand-off" aircraft armed with air launched cruise missiles. Standing alone as an alternative for the B-1, I think this approach to solving our complex future problems of deterrence would be extremely dangerous, if not ineffective and grossly deficient. The concept of an air launched cruise missile does have appeal to us, however, as a secondary and lesser included mode of attack for use within our overall strategic force mix. This weapons development offers the possibility in the future for compensating an inability to attack an expanding enemy target system with the limited number of delivery vehicles through the extended use of obsolescing penetrating bombers (e.g., the early models of the B-52) that in future years may no longer have a high probability of being able successfully to penetrate in depth. Such weapons could be useful in low threat areas and contingency situations to degrade peripheral defenses and attack shallow targets, provide interdiction support in land or sea areas, thereby augmenting the potential firepower of our primary manned penetrating forces.

As an alternative for the B-1, the concept suffers from serious inflexibility since the stand-off aircraft are, by design, unable to penetrate under any circumstances; the result is a serious erosion of flexibility and overall capability in our manned bomber force. A penetrating bomber can always be adapted to utilize and exploit any advantages of a stand-off air launched cruise missile, while still retaining the important advantage of not being limited to a stand-off role and being able to extract high levels of damage against deep targets, including those requiring a high order of accuracy and yield to achieve reasonable damage levels.

The question of vulnerability of a large stand-off missile launching aircraft is, in itself, sufficient for us to discount this as a primary weapons delivery mode for our strategic forces. Its patent lack of credibility in future years would seriously (if not totally) degrade its deterrent value.

The air launched cruise missile is viewed by us as a potentially valuable adjunct to our total force flexibility to handle a constantly expanding threat and target system and, possibly, as an economical, efficient way to challenge an enemy to maintain expensive area and terminal defenses—thus diverting resource allocation from his offensive capabilities against us. It is not yet tested; its operational utility, accuracy, cost and efficiency stand as important unknowns.

I would advise those in positions of responsibility for our overall deterrent and defensive capabilities not to pursue this alternative except as an additive capability for possible use in future years—it is not adequate as a primary weapons system for deterrence.

You have courteously offered me an opportunity to present *"any other comments"* that I consider relevant to you and your colleagues' determinations on the B-1 issue. I would like to accept this invitation to address the issue of *relative cost of the B-1*; for I, as any responsible American, recognize the impact of such an expensive weapons system on our national budget and our nation's fiscal resources.

At the outset, I am reminded that much of the cost of this long-term production program will be returned to our nation's economy (and our Treasury) in the form of wages, goods, services and tax receipts generated through classic economic multiplier effects. Notwithstanding these economic realities, however, I think the overall cost of the program, which is the rallying cry of many opponents, must be placed in perspective in order to be understood; i.e.

In describing the critical role of our nation's strategic forces, Secretary Rumsfeld said (in his 1977 Defense Report): "Without the foundation of adequate strategic nuclear forces, the United States and its Allies cannot hope to deter aggression and contribute to some semblance of international stability. . . ." Within the context of that critical, central role for our strategic forces, the cost of those forces (Air Force, Navy, Army—offensive and defensive—procurement, O&M, personnel, RDT&E, and military construction) is seen in perspective as but a small fraction of our present and projected total obligational authority (in constant FY77 dollars) in the DOD budgets for 1977-1980 (i.e., 1977—9.1%; 1978—9.5%; 1979—9.5%; 1980—10.5%). These projections include the anticipated B-1 procurement requests.

In my view, there is no weapons delivery system program that is more important, more critical, or offers more deterrent utility within the total mix of our strategic forces than the B-1. Without such a capable, flexible, and visible strategic weapons delivery system, our deterrent forces would be seriously deficient across the potential spectrum of confrontation and/or conflict. Yet, the widely publicized "20 billion dollar" B-1 program appears in far better perspective if it is viewed as a percentage of the DOD budget requests in those years: i.e., 1977—1.4%; 1978—1.7%; 1979—2.1%; 1980—2.6%.

In the context of its central importance to our nation's future security—and as an average of 1.95% of our expected DOD budget requests during these years—the "20 billion dollar B-1 program" appears far more understandable to me... and, I hope, to the Congress and the nation.

In sum, I see no real alternative to the B-1 from among the suggestions that have been advanced. If we are denied timely production of this aircraft and rapid introduction of the B-1 into our operational inventory, it is my opinion that the nation's deterrent force mix soon will be seriously deficient in its ability to maintain an essential balance—real or perceived—with the strategic forces of the Soviet Union.

In summary of the Air Force's case for the B-1, Gen David Jones's briefing to the Senate Committee or Armed Services concluded:

> In our judgment, the airplane is ready for production. . . . In our judgment, there is a valid need for the B-1. . . . The program is going well. . . . There is a great need for the aircraft. We think now is the time to make a decision to move ahead.[250]

The contract for the first three production copies of the B-1 was scheduled to be signed in November 1976, and the opponents of the B-1 program in Congress arrived at a shrewd plan to circumvent Congress's reluctance to challenge the White House on a major weapons decision in an election year. The Senate Appropriations Committee added a provision in the defense appropriations bill blocking a production contract until February 1977, thus allowing the winner of the 1976 presidential election to review the decision.[251]

In his 1976 presidential campaign, Jimmy Carter had mentioned the B-1 bomber as an example of an unnecessary weapon that should not be built. In President Gerald Ford's budget request submitted to Congress in February, however, there was an item for production of eight B-1s, and the Carter amendments only reduced the number from eight to five. In his memoirs, President Carter recalled that his studies of what to do about the B-1, made with the help of Secretary of Defense Harold Brown and the Joint Chiefs of Staff, were necessary in his view not to determine the merits of the case but to build a case that would prevail against powerful supporters of the B-1. In February 1977, Secretary Brown stated that he remained to be convinced one way or another about the B-1.

> I came to the examination of the B-1 with a belief that a bomber component is an important part of our strategic capability, particularly when fixed land-based missiles are likely to become more vulnerable in the future. But that is not a doctrinal matter with me; it doesn't mean that I cannot decide that we didn't need bombers and so recommend to the president, nor does it mean that I cannot decide that we need bombers but don't need the B-1.[252]

IDEAS, CONCEPTS, DOCTRINE

According to President Carter, Secretary Brown proved extremely helpful on 24 June 1977 when he recommended that the B-1 not be built. On 12 July 1977, as has been seen, Carter originally informed Congress that he was halting production of the B-1 due to recent evolution of the air-launched cruise missile as an effective weapon system and the continued ability to use B-52 bombers well into the 1980s. Where Secretary Brown, when serving as Air Force secretary in 1966, had advocated a need to replace the B-52Gs/Hs in the 1975 time period with the AMSA that became the B-1, he explained his change in posture in 1977 by saying: "That was indeed my view. My view has been changed more than anything else by the development of the cruise missile."[253] Over the next several years and eventually rather fully in August 1980, the public would learn details of a new stealth technology that was said to have affected President Carter's decision to opt for cruise missiles, but the immediate effect of Carter's decision on 12 July 1977 was to focus the attention of the Department of Defense on newer applications of what had been the earliest form of guided missile activity.

Early on in the 1950s in the search for guided missiles, the US Air Force developed and fielded a generation of subsonic cruise missiles capable of operating as unmanned aircraft in atmospheric flight. These included the Snark intercontinental cruise missile and the tactical Matador and the improved Mace cruise missiles, five squadrons of the Mace being deployed to Europe and two to Okinawa. In these same years, the US Navy developed a Regulus cruise missile. In the 1960s these old cruise missiles were phased out because they were vulnerable to surprise attack and were thought not to be "terribly useful" in view of the emergence of the US Army's Pershing ballistic missile and long-range Polaris and Minuteman missiles. In 1964–65 Secretary McNamara accepted a requirement for an Air Force mobile midrange ballistic missile (MMRBM), but Congress did not approve development of this missile which would have replaced the Mace, especially in a deployment to Okinawa.[254] Whereas the United States discontinued cruise missiles in favor of ballistic missiles, the Soviets continued to field a wide selection of naval cruise missiles for tactical use, the longest range missile normally being able to reach out 500 to 600 miles.[255] For employment by B-52s, the Air Force developed and made operational air-to-ground missile (AGM-28) Hound Dog turbojet-powered air-to-surface missiles, to be used for rolling back enemy defenses by attacking airfields; and the Quail missile, which could be launched at high altitude as a decoy to simulate a B-52. A B-52 could carry only two of the large and heavy Hound Dogs in wing pylons; the missiles, moreover, had relatively poor accuracy and imposed substantial aerodynamic drag. Its nuclear warhead was counted to be unnecessarily large, but this warhead was all that was available when the Hound Dog was developed. The Quail decoy, when employed at low altitudes, was deficient in range, flight profile flexibility, and basic ability to simulate a bomber's radar signatures. In 1964 Project Forecast had advocated emphasis be put on standoff weapons to negate hostile local defenses, and the Air Force fiscal 1966 budget included funds for a short-range attack missile (SRAM) to be carried by B-52s and FB-111s. The Air Force programmed the 17 B-52G/H squadrons and all FB-111s for SRAM, even though the need to redesign the small ballistic missile's solid rocket motor delayed its development. A B-52G/H could carry a maximum loading of 20 nuclear-tipped SRAMs—8 internally on a rotary rack and 12 on external pylons. The first SRAMs entered the operating inventory in 1972; Hound Dogs were phased out incrementally as the B-52G/H squadrons were fitted with SRAMs.[256]

The Air Force requirement for an improved decoy to replace the obsolete Quail recognized that Soviet defenses were expanding in both quantity and sophistication while the number of Air Force bombers was being significantly reduced, thus greatly diminishing the ability to dilute air defenses by mass attack.[257] The original decoy the Air Force proposed to develop to replace Quail was to be an unarmed vehicle, sized to be carried either internally on B-52 rotary racks or pylons in place of SRAMs, a feature which limited the design size of the vehicle. The decoy would have an electronics package that would provide a radar simulation of a B-52. The design criteria of the decoy were expanded to provide a nuclear warhead because someone reasoned that sooner or later the Soviets would discover how to differentiate between a bomber and the decoy and to disregard the latter. But if some of the decoys were armed, the Soviets would have to assume that all were armed and have to go after them all, thereby diluting their defenses. OSD approved the initiation of advanced development of the subsonic cruise armed decoy (SCAD) on 15 July 1970. Development contracts for SCAD were awarded in July 1972, and one year of real effort by the Williams Research Company yielded a design for an airframe and the development of a small and highly efficient turbofan engine.[258] Although the SCAD airframe was designed to be capable of accepting a nuclear warhead, the Air Force position was that the important concern was to get on with the development of a decoy and let the armed version wait. General Ryan explained:

> SCAD would not be a very good attack missile because it is being optimized for all the wrong characteristics desired for an effective attack missile. For example, to perform as a decoy it is being optimized to be seen on a threat radar as a B-52, whereas an attack missile would be optimized to have a very low probability of detection.[259]

Air Force studies showed that SCAD was not essential to the penetration capabilities of the B-1 but would be helpful to the B-52s.[260] While the Air Force was working on SCAD, the US Navy in 1971 initiated a concept of a submarine-launched cruise missile (SLCM) which would make use of unused torpedo tubes on nuclear submarines. It would be cost-effective to use submarines: The cruise missiles would be developed in two versions, a long-range item for inland attacks and a short-range item for attacking hostile naval vessels.[261]

In 1971, when the Subcommittee of the Committee on Appropriations of the House of Representatives was studying the annual defense appropriations act, opponents of the B-1 bomber argued that the aircraft should be terminated since an armed SCAD carried on an aircraft of lesser performance could be a satisfactory substitute weapon. There also were reports that the Air Force was hesitant to develop an armed version of the SCAD because such an armed standoff weapon might be attractive enough to degrade the requirement for the B-1. In 1972 a study made by the President's Scientific Advisory Committee recommended that a harder look should be given to standoff missiles, and further suggested that the B-1 would be the best missile carrier because of its quick start-up from the ground and various other flight characteristics. In the Air Force the Saber Penetrator IV Study, completed in November 1972, compared the effectiveness of bombers penetrating enemy defenses using short-range attack missiles, SCADs, and gravity weapons to long-range strategic cruise missiles launched from aircraft standing off beyond enemy defenses.[262] After a review of the SCAD program validated the Air Force criticisms of it, Secretary of Defense Schlesinger directed the decoy's termination on 30 June 1973 and its replacement with a program to employ SCAD technology in the development of an air-launched cruise missile (ALCM). The Air Force and the Navy were directed to get together on a cruise missile with as much design compatibility as practicable. OSD also envisioned that the cruise missile would be suited for launching from a ground base.[263]

The Navy and the Air Force formed a joint cruise missile systems project office to attain a high degree of commonality in the ALCM and SLCM development, but a single design for both Air Force and Navy proved impossible. The missiles employed a common nuclear warhead, the efficient Williams turbofan engine, and an inertial-guidance system that was updated at selected en route checkpoints by a self-contained terrain contour matching (TERCOM) navigation system. The ALCM employed the airframe that had been designed for the SCAD. This airframe was interchangeable with a SRAM on B-52/B-1 rotary racks on wing pylons, but it was not suited to carriage and ejection through submarine torpedo tubes, the fact that of necessity made for the difference between the ALCM and SLCM. In the Air Force the ALCM was a low-risk program since much development already had been done on the SCAD airframe and engine. The first powered flight of the ALCM from a B-52 was successful on 5 March 1976, and on 14 January 1977 the deputy secretary of defense directed the Air Force to proceed into full-scale development of the AGM-86 air-launched cruise missile with a projected initial operation capability of July 1980.[264]

Although the Air Force agreed that the ALCM was a useful adjunct to a manned bomber, it did not agree that an automated missile could be a substitute for a manned bomber. In 1972 General Glasser expressed this view:

> The efficacy of the manned bomber is not its penetration capability. The penetration capability is not for the purpose of doing it the hard way. It is to get the man in the loop, in there in the target area, to see what is going on and to make intelligent decisions, and to evade and counteract enemy tactics.[265]

In 1974 Secretary McLucas said:

> Our feeling is that even though you could simulate many of the characteristics of the manned bomber by putting various features into missiles, eventually you get to a point where it is not cost-effective. There are simply some things that men can do better than programmed automated defenses of one kind or another. The most obvious one is dealing with unexpected situations.[266]

In April 1974 Dr Walter B. LaBerge, assistant secretary of the Air Force for research and development, pointed out that a 2,000-mile-range cruise missile would need to be supersonic and contain a heavy cargo of electronic countermeasures. LaBerge added,

> I don't personally know how to design a 2,000-mile cruise missile that is supersonic without having it be essentially of the size of a manned airplane. . . . We emphasize that the current ALCM program is to develop a subsonic cruise missile for deployment with penetrating bombers. Thus, conceptually the ALCM would have some of the mutual support advantages of the bomber's Electronic Countermeasures (ECM) and real time intelligence-derived Electronic Counter-Countermeasures (ECCM), launch point flexibility, and defense suppression by SRAM. It would also benefit from the overall expected degradation to enemy defenses caused by a proliferated ALCM and manned bomber attack. The character of this type ALCM attack is far different from the pure standoff attack where the ALCM would be uniformly appearing threat to the defense and would have to "go it alone" through area, as well as terminal, defense.[267]

Secretary McLucas repeated many of the findings of the Joint Strategic Bomber Study regarding ALCMs as an alternative to the B-1 and added:

> While all the alternatives are still paper proposals, the basic FB-111 and B-52 designs are well-tested in the existing models. On the ALCM, however, we still must accomplish considerable R&D to validate its design.
>
> The analyses show the ALCM not as an alternative to the B-1, but rather as a complement because it could help dilute the enemy's defenses. Similarly, we see the present FB-111s as a complement to the heavy bombers. The FB-111 is a very good aircraft for its limited role of striking peripheral targets, but it would not be suitable as our primary strategic bomber. The B-52 also is an extremely capable aircraft today, and we have modified it so that it will remain effective against the Soviet air defense we expect throughout the seventies. However, it is getting old and both the bomber study and the GAO review reaffirmed that for the threats postulated for the 1980s and beyond, B-1 forces become more cost-effective than even the proposed B-52Is.[268]

In March 1976, Sen John C. Stennis, chairman of the Senate Committee on Armed Services, told Secretary of the Air Force Thomas C. Reed and General Jones that senators and everyone else wanted to know about the role, value, and prospective future use of the cruise missile.

> I know there is no such thing as certainty in your profession. I wish you would give the committee the benefit of a written memorandum . . . in which you undertake, professionally and officially to estimate the role, value, and prospective future use of this cruise missile from the sea or from the air. . . . There has to be more known about it.[269]

IDEAS, CONCEPTS, DOCTRINE

In a letter dated 22 March 1976, Jones and Reed described what was known about the ALCM:

DEPARTMENT OF THE AIR FORCE
HEADQUARTERS UNITED STATES AIR FORCE
Washington, D.C., March 22, 1976

HON. JOHN C. STENNIS,
Chairman, Committee on Armed Services, U.S. Senate

DEAR MR. CHAIRMAN: This letter is provided in response to your request for information concerning the role, value and future use of cruise missiles.

The technology incorporated in the current generation of cruise missiles opens up very broad applications across the entire spectrum of conflict. However, since the thrust of the discussions which raised your question was principally in the strategic nuclear area, the following discussion will be confined to our projections on the Air Launched Cruise Missile (ALCM). The Air Force has had cruise missiles in the inventory for several years. The Hound Dog, phased out last year because of obsolescence, was a long range nuclear armed cruise missile carried by the B-52 force. The Quail, which could be considered a cruise missile, is an unarmed decoy presently carried by the B-52 force.

The ALCM, currently in advanced development, is being designed to provide increased capability both in attacking targets and in countering defenses.

The ALCM flew its first powered flight on March 10. The first guided flight is scheduled for September of this year. Based on the results of development testing and proof of concept, the ALCM full-scale development decision will be made in January 1977. Production and procurement decisions, including the number required by the Air Force, will also be based on development and test results.

We envision ALCM employment as an adjunct to the strategic bomber force in the 1980s. Assuming design specifications are achieved the ALCM will have utility in both the SIOP role and in limited nuclear options. It could enhance bomber effectiveness in a number of areas:

Dilution of Area Defenses. By adding to the penetrating force, ALCM would compound the enemy's defensive problems. Identification would be required once ALCMs were detected by enemy radar and, therefore, would require the air defender to commit additional resources.

Increased Flexibility in Bomber Routing. The ALCM could be employed against isolated undefended targets, eliminating the need to route bombers against those targets. The ALCM would provide, in effect, an increase in bomber range. Such routing flexibility reduces exposure and thus losses.

Added Stress to Enemy Defense System. ALCM deployment would force the Soviets to deploy an extensive low altitude SAM network in order to defend against it. These defenses would require resources which could be used for offensive systems. Moreover, such defenses would be relatively ineffective against SRAMs employed by the penetrating bomber.

While these are some of the capabilities gained by ALCM employment, it must be stressed that the ALCM has limitations as well. It has limited utility, for example, against terminally defended targets since its speed makes it vulnerable to sophisticated SAM defenses. These targets could most effectively be covered by other weapon systems. ALCMs are limited in their capability to penetrate perimeter defenses and would be better carried through these defenses by the manned bomber using detection, evaluation, avoidance, and countermeasure techniques. Additionally, when launched outside perimeter defenses, the ALCM is limited by its range capability. Large concentrations of cruise missiles in standoff carriers would be lucrative, relatively vulnerable targets.

Given our assessment today of the ALCMs potential capabilities and limitations, we see no value in replacing SRAMs or gravity bombs on the B-1 with ALCMs. We seriously doubt the viability and cost-effectiveness of a pure standoff force, and see no need to pursue development of a wide-bodied carrier for that role.

We believe the most effective use of ALCM would be as a mixed load with SRAM and gravity bombs on the B-52G/H force. Such an employment concept takes maximum advantage of the capabilities of both the ALCM and the manned bomber. The B-52 with ALCM would be most effective in a penetrating role, against shallow and moderately well defended targets. If the threat and target base were to evolve in such a way that a standoff capability became useful, the B-52 would be a cost-effective resource for that role.

The ALCM does represent a new technology meriting the word "breakthrough." It offers a tenfold improvement in accuracy over earlier cruise missiles such as the Hound Dog at a projected *decrease* in cost in constant dollars.

Because the technology is new, employment doctrine is still emerging. While we have discussed the most immediate use of ALCM as a nuclear standoff weapon, there are other distinct employment options. By 1990 the ALCM may prove useful as a decoy and/or a nuclear or conventional armed weapon for use in tactical warfare.

For now, the ALCM is a bomber-carried weapon which would add a new dimension of flexibility in penetrating tactics, targeting and force employment options.

Sincerely,

DAVID C. JONES,
General, USAF Chief of Staff,

THOMAS C. REED,
Secretary of the Air Force[270]

One other fact not talked about much because of security reasons was that the small ALCM was range-limited in terms of the vastness of the Soviet landmass. Neither the basic ALCM-A nor a stretched, extended-range ALCM-B mandated for emphasis in development in fiscal year 1978 could reach all important targets in the USSR from standoff; some air vehicle would have to launch them after penetrating Soviet airspace.[271]

At the outset of the Carter administration in January 1977, Secretary Harold Brown reasoned that the ALCM was "potentially a very effective weapon system" but what its role was to be "depends on our arriving at a clearer concept than I, at least now, have on where it fits into the strategic picture."[272] As the Carter administration zeroed in on the B-1 early in 1977, the Joint Chiefs of Staff prepared a memorandum recommending that the strategic forces of the United States needed the B-1 and that the United States should go ahead with its production. Secretary

IDEAS, CONCEPTS, DOCTRINE

Brown noted the memo and sent it forward without his concurrence. An OSD study of the B-1 was described by Gen George S. Brown as complete, fair, and evenhanded, even though it went against his own recommendation that the B-1 be produced.[273] On numerous colloquies after July 1977 Secretary Brown explained his preference for the B-52/ALCM over the B-1. He showed that the B-1 was a penetrating bomber and that the ALCM was never really an important part of the B-1 fleet. On the other hand, B-52s could carry 20 ALCMs and Secretary Brown's guidance to the Air Force was to convert the B-52G fleet to ALCM carriage, thereby providing an operating inventory of over 3,000 ALCMs. He did not doubt that B-52s, even without cruise missiles, would be able to penetrate and survive, say through 1985, and he believed that cruise missiles would allow the combined systems to penetrate through the rest of the 1980s and probably well into the 1990s. Even though the B-1 fleet could have been modified to carry 3,000 ALCMs, Secretary Brown rationalized that there was not much point in using B-1s to launch ALCMs since the great expense in the plane was in giving it the ability to penetrate and this money would be wasted if the B-1s were used as ALCM "freight carriers." Brown insisted that the B-52/cruise missile combination was a better choice than the B-1 on grounds of expected cost and effectiveness.

> The judgement was made that while the B-1 would probably be an effective penetrator there was more confidence in the ability of cruise missiles to penetrate on fundamental physical considerations than there was in the ability of B-1s to penetrate aided by ECM. This combined with the fact that an equally effective cruise missile force would be about 40 percent cheaper than the B-1 force led to the decision on the B-1 program.[274]

When President Carter announced his decision to terminate B-1 production in favor of development of air-launched cruise missiles, he said: "Our triad concept of retaining three basic delivery systems will be continued: the submarine launched ballistic missiles, intercontinental ballistic missiles, and a bomber fleet including cruise missiles as one of its elements."[275] Gen Richard H. Ellis, CINCSAC, took this statement by the president to convey an intent to support some kind of manned penetrator; especially since both Carter and Secretary Brown had gone on record expressing a desire for a follow-on manned penetrating bomber as a hedge against an uncertain future.

> Ellis believed that "facts and logic" indicated continued life for a manned penetrating bomber force and that "rigorous analysis and thoughtful consideration" firmly supported that belief.[276]

"The prospects of the air launched cruise missile are exciting," Ellis added, "To me, it represents one of the things we Americans do best—the application of advanced technology to provide for defense needs." But the Strategic Air Command needed time for planning, Ellis said:

> We have done a lot of work on cruise missiles at SAC but we are really in the horse-and-buggy days in terms of our planning and the application of this weapon system. We have an intensive effort underway and it will be a continuing thing with the best brains we have in SAC.[277]

The Air Force did not delay to provide President Carter and Secretary Brown with recommended options for a follow-on penetrating bomber to the B-1. As an indication that they wanted to keep their options open, Carter and Brown asked for continued research and development appropriations for the B-1 as a way to keep a slender bomber production option open. Air Force Chief of Staff Gen David Jones—long an advocate of the B-1—now approached any prospect of spending three quarters of a billion dollars for the number 5 and number 6 B-1s when he could not conceive that there was any possibility that B-1 production would ever be picked up.[278] Both the Air Force and the Strategic Air Command sought an acceptable bomber option, and General Ellis's criteria were stated as follows:

> Provide real and perceived deterrence across the widest possible spectrum of conflict—including conventional; maximize damage against the SIOP target base; be cost effective; hedge against SALT uncertainties—here we are concerned with the question of how cruise missile carriers will be counted and with the range limitations to be imposed on the missiles; hedge against cruise missile reliability and capability shortfall; and maximize Soviet expenditures on defensive systems.[279]

One of the first bomber options was to rebuild B-52s and include new wings and engines as a B-52X. Secretary Brown considered this and concluded that it would cost as much as the B-1 production program and would ultimately pinch off, as the number of B-52 airframes was used up. General Ellis had no hope for the B-52X, and he estimated that his B-52Gs/Hs and FB-111s could "continue to be effective penetrators until 1987—and probably to 1990 or even beyond." Secretary Brown seemed pleased with this estimate of the prospective long life of the B-52s and FB-111s, but he judged differently about penetration:

> The B-52 is going to run out of its ability to do that in probably late 1980s, not because it is old, but because it is too easy [for radar] to see. The Soviet air defenses are improving and we are working on possible successors (to the B-52), not the B-1, because the B-1 is not that hard to see, but on possible other successors, and when we will come up with something, we don't really know.[280]

A year after the decision not to produce the B-1, Secretary Brown was more sure of the B-52/cruise missile combination than ever, saying in May 1978:

> The more I look at it, the surer I am that cruise missiles are going to be a very important, perhaps the most important, part of our bomber force for the next decade. We need to move forward full speed on that. That includes keeping open the option for a cruise missile carrier.[281]

During 1977 and early 1978 Secretary Brown looked with increasing favor on a prospective use of wide-bodied commercial transport planes as cruise missile carriers (CMCs). Bomb bays probably would have to be cut out of the bottom of the transports; the CMCs would carry three times more missiles than B-52s; they would be quite attractive if deployed along with a large number of penetrating bombers or with a smaller aircraft carrying cruise missiles. Brown said the CMC "is the most effective way to get a very large number of cruise missiles into the force. It is ... the only way by which we can add ... warheads to our strategic inventory in a short time."[282]

In August 1977, the prospect of a commercial CMC was under study at both Air Force and SAC, and General Ellis could see some possible advantages in them, particularly economy and possibly a synergism of a combined CMC and manned penetrator force attack. In February 1979, however, Ellis was pointing out the weakness of a CMC. For preplanned survival a nuclear-hardened and relatively fast aircraft was required for successful base escape; commercial- or military transport-type aircraft do not inherently possess these characteristics. In launch areas, CMC aircraft defense systems would be required. Generally, it was easier to equip a bomber-type aircraft with defense capabilities than similarly to equip a commercial wide-body aircraft. Finally, a nonpenetrating CMC aircraft would permit an enemy to optimize his defenses, concentrating long-range interceptors and airborne warning and control systems (AWACS) against the CMC launch vehicle.[283] During 1979, the Air Force had an intensive program of studies in progress on a cruise missile carrier aircraft. The more the matter was studied, the steadier it was concluded that a CMC should be a bomber. Out of the studies, Lt Gen Kelly H. Burke, Air Force deputy chief of staff for research, development, and acquisition, reported the B-52s could serve as cruise missile carriers as long as they could fly, and then

> if you were going to build a new cruise missile carrier from scratch it would tend to look a lot like a B-1, because the thing you are after is fast base escape—a hard, fast airplane.... The transport versions did not turn out to be very good choices. If one assumed very low levels of threats, they are okay, but I do not think a prudent man would make that assumption, if he is embarking in a new large-scale program. All of which led us to the conclusion that there was ample evidence and data to pick the B-1 variant cruise missile carrier as the right choice if we needed one, which we did not think we need at this time. We find ourselves in a somewhat anomalous position for the Air Force to be arguing against buying airplanes. But we think that the evidence to date argues rather persuasively that the B-52 will be perfectly adequate well into the 1990s. But we agree that we ought to hedge that a little bit, because we are not absolutely sure.[284]

Accordingly, the Air Force requested funding in fiscal year 1981 to permit it to take one of the four B-1s that it had and modify it to be a cruise missile carrier to see how it would perform in that role.[285]

When President Carter announced his decision against production of the B-1 in mid-1977, the Air Force assumed that the B-1 program was ended. "We thought about this a long time and had many long hours of study and concluded beyond a shadow of a doubt in our mind that the B-1 is dead," recalled Lt Gen Alton D. Slay, deputy chief of staff of R&D, in 1977. He continued, "We need an effective penetrating bomber. . . . We understand why the President made his decision. We support that decision. Having said all that, we still feel that we need an option for a manned penetrating bomber." The Air Force accordingly submitted to OSD a program for research and development of a stretched FB-111H with B-1 engines, all amounting to a substantial change in design. President Carter had said he wanted an option. General Slay said:

> Given that the Air Force has told the Secretary of Defense, "We don't believe the B-1 poses a viable option, because we cannot conceive of the eventuality of production being picked up. Now we can give you an option for roughly one third the cost. That is the FB-111H, and you can either pick it up or not, the same as you could the B-1; but for a longer period of time and at less cost."[286]

According to Dr William J. Perry, deputy director for defense research and engineering, either he nor Secretary Brown liked the FB-111H other than as a potential way of maintaining a production option for a follow-on penetrating bomber which the president wanted.

> Our studies show that small aircraft such as the FB-111H are not a cost effective solution to providing a bomber force. The FB-111H is inadequate to carry the avionics required to penetrate the projected threat. Size also limits its flexibility and potential for change in a dynamic environment as well as severely limiting the weapon load and target coverage potential.[287]

The Strategic Air Command worked closely with the Air Staff in visualizing the FB-111 modifications, and General Ellis soon stoutly supported the FB-111H. Early in 1979 Ellis submitted the continuing SAC proposals to the Air Staff. They visualized committing the operational B-52G/H fleet to standoff missile employment, thereby planning for delivery of almost 5,000 cruise missiles; discontinuing plans for early cruise missile carrier development; and modifying the SAC FB-111s and the Tactical Air Command's FB-111 fighters as FB-111B/C penetration bombers. The FB-111B/C would be a scaled-down modification from the FB-111H by reduction of a lot of sophisticated ECM. Ellis pointed out that the money saved by giving up the continuing modifications of B-52s for penetration, plus discontinuing CMC research and development, would pay for the conversion of FB-111s, FB-111As, and F-111Ds (155 in all) to FB-111B/Cs and also for a "new technology bomber." The FB-111B/C modification was, in Ellis's explanation, strictly a near-term solution and would not replace Doctor Perry's long-term solution. The modified F/FB-111s would provide

> a comparatively modern aircraft with excellent prelaunch survivability and extremely accurate weapons delivery to help redress our strategic deficiencies in the eighties. Because of its smaller size and radar cross section, greater maneuverability and penetration speed, the modified F/FB-111 would provide us with a usable penetrator for several years longer than the B-52.[288]

After an evaluation of the stretched FB-111B/C proposed by SAC, the Air Staff concluded that the Air Force FY 1979 and FY 1980 budgets would not accommodate the larger reprogramming required to fund such a highly concurrent program. The Air Staff also examined a slightly less concurrent program with major investment to commence in fiscal year 1981. The evaluation of this option indicated that it would not solve the near-term strategic deficiency confronting the United States and would severely impact other critical Air Force programs.[289] Speaking of the SAC FB-111B/C proposal in February 1980, Air Force Chief of Staff Gen Lew Allen said it was "a sound technical program which provides an airplane of good characteristics" that would put airplanes in the strategic inventory as quickly as possible to cover the critical period between 1980 and the time when the air-launched cruise missiles and the MX missiles came on line. Allen said that in the Air Force assessments the FB-111B/C simply could not be given a priority as high as other things that were needed. In fact, in view of the Soviet invasion of Afghanistan, Allen thought that the FB-111B/C program could not be offered even if several more percentages of available money were voted in the Air Force budget.[290]

The issue of providing an interim penetration bomber for SAC came into focus in Congress in 1980. At first the issue related to the Air Force's request for fiscal year 1981 funds to develop one of the B-1s as a cruise missile carrier and its failure to request funds for the FB-111B/C. When asked in February whether he favored the B-1 or the FB-111B/C for warfighting, General Ellis said:

> SAC considers the B-1 to be the best penetrator available in the world today. If both the FB-111B/C and the B-1 were available in the same time frame—and at the same cost—SAC would opt for the B-1. However, faced with both the deficiencies of strategic forces in the early eighties and the paucity of funds, we have recommended modification of the FB-111 aircraft as rapidly as possible.[291]

In a 5 March hearing, Ellis came down very hard on the serious strategic imbalance facing the United States:

> This country has never faced a situation like this before. Since we have had nuclear weapons we have always had at least essential equivalence or superiority or supremacy. We do not have that now, if our measurements are right, and nobody has told us they are wrong yet in a substantive way. So, time to me means an early fix, at the earliest possible fix.[292]

The two options available were the B-1 or the FB-111B/C. Ellis said that the Air Force Systems Command projected that with a production go-ahead in October 1980 a force of 100 B-1s could be available in 1987. On the other hand, 155 FB-111A and F-111D aircraft could be modified with B-1 engines, have enlarged weapons capacity and greatly increased range, and be available in 1986. Ellis said:

> Based on an earlier operational date and a favorable cost factor of approximately 2.5 to 1 for an equivalent force, SAC believes the better alternative is the FB-111B/C. However, should the President change his mind regarding production of the B-1 as a result of the

drastic deterioration of relations with the Soviets, SAC would certainly welcome this initiative.[293]

The House Armed Services Committee apparently accepted General Ellis's assessment of the seriousness of the strategic situation rather than his aircraft request. It added $600 million to the fiscal year 1981 defense authorization bill to prepare for production of a simplified version of the B-1 as an ALCM launcher. The House approved this on 14 May by a margin of nearly three to one.[294] At this juncture the rank and file of Congress and the public at large suddenly became acquainted with a third strategic provisioning option—the stealth bomber that had been about for some years but had been kept highly secret as far as techniques went.

When the Carter administration took office in 1977, research on the stealth program had advanced to the technology exploration phase. According to President Carter, his understanding about stealth—basically development of technology in a combination of applications to negate the effectiveness of air defense systems in detection of manned and unmanned air vehicles—contributed to his decision not to produce the B-1. After reviewing the stealth technology and deciding to increase greatly its funding and rate of development, Secretary Brown decided to place the entire effort under even greater security, including a new step of classifying the fact of the existence of the stealth program. Brown hoped to keep the program secret for two years.[295] From time to time in the next three years there were references to stealth and the stealth characteristics of a follow-on bomber that would be developed in an appropriate future time frame. Under Secretary of Defense Perry frequently applied the stealth description to cruise missiles, and he emphasized that the B-1 was deficient in that it depended upon ECM for assistance in penetration rather than stealth:

> In the case of our bomber penetration, with the advent of the new look-down shoot-down precision guidance systems, we are going to cruise missiles. Basically we are introducing stealth. I use that term to mean that the cruise missiles are very much more difficult for ground systems to detect them than is a bomber. They can fly right through an air defense system without being seen. That is a technique that is being used there.[296]

On separate occasions in 1978 and 1979 Perry referred to the need to make a new manned bomber as undetectable to radar as possible:

> The features which I think would have to predominate would be the same features we are counting on in the cruise missile; namely, low detectability. What remains to be determined—and it is a very important factor—is whether we could build an airplane as large as a bomber with the same low detectability features which we have incorporated in the cruise missiles. The direction of our R&D is to investigate the extent to which we could do that using a variety of techniques.[297]

In February 1980 General Ellis envisioned a new bomber to be available in the 1990s. It would have significant advantages:

IDEAS, CONCEPTS, DOCTRINE

> A new bomber should offer significant advantages over an improved FB-111 or a B-1. It would include improvements in terms of lighter aircraft structure and economy of operation. This translates into a new manned bomber of larger range and endurance with less dependence upon air refueling support. The major difference, however, would be in observables; that is, low radar cross section and reduced infrared emissions. By decreasing such observables, penetration aids would be more effective, thus enhancing bomber survivability. Of course, it should be capable of both nuclear and conventional roles.
>
> The Nation vitally needs a new penetrating bomber. We have studied proposals for over 20 years, but have yet to deploy a replacement for the B-52. We need to stop studying and start building that replacement.[298]

Because of the increasing size and scope of the stealth program, as the Department of Defense was beginning preparation of the fiscal year 1982 budget, Secretary Brown foresaw that more people would have to be aware of the program and that maintaining security would be difficult. In June 1980, while the Senate had not yet approved the House of Representatives' action on the B-1, the story of the development of a new secret bomber that could be made invisible to enemy radar was leaked to a Washington newspaper and printed on 28 June. Other stories in other publications immediately added details about stealth, leading Secretary Brown to acknowledge publicly the existence of the stealth program on 16 August 1980. In testimony to the House Armed Services Committee on 4 September, General Ellis now stated that SAC would prefer the B-1 over the FB-111B/C as an interim bomber if it did not jeopardize the new technology bomber. When the House bill, approved on 14 May, reached the Senate floor, several members offered an amendment earmarking $91 million to develop a bomber that could be ready by 1987 to carry out multiple roles in both tactical and strategic employment. This multiple role was fully specified as being SIOP (both in the initial and protracted phases), worldwide extension (counterinterdiction, theater, nonnuclear, and maritime support), and theater nuclear. To accomplish these six missions, the new aircraft would have to maximize payload and range and have the ability to deliver nuclear weapons, air-launched cruise missiles, and conventional weapons in both tactical and strategic roles. As a result of Senate floor action and an authorization conference report, Congress finally authorized $300 million for the development of a multiple-role manned bomber to be in the field as soon as possible but no later than 1987. Candidate aircraft were the B-1, B-1 variants, the stretched FB-111B/C, and the advanced technology bomber (ATB) options. The president who would take office after the 1980 elections was to be directed to make recommendations on the strategic bomber matter and report back to Congress by 15 March 1981.[299]

The Joint OSD/Air Force Bomber Alternatives Study was chaired by the Office of the Under Secretary of Defense for Research and Engineering and included representatives from all of the important Air Force operating groups that had responsibility in bomber matters. It was decided that the Air Force would solicit proposals from industry and actually go through negotiations, so that on the day the study was approved a program could start with final costs and a confident schedule. President Reagan's expanded defense budget for fiscal year 1982 asked $2.4 billion for a new manned bomber. At the outset of the bomber study it was generally accepted that the long-range ATB stealth bomber was going to be put into research and development for attainment of an initial operational capability in the early 1990s. In this matter, the Air Force leadership all agreed that advanced technology was extremely promising and ought to be pursued vigorously. The leadership also agreed that the availability of the advanced technology was sufficiently uncertain that a nearer-term solution also was needed. The contest thus was between the stretch FB-111B/C and the resurrected B-1. General Ellis at SAC, who would retire in June 1981, supported the FB-111B/C, and General Allen, Air Force chief of staff, wanted a B-1 variant. General Allen spoke about this matter in March 1981:

> General Ellis believes—and I agree—that the Soviet air defense of the homeland in the, let's say, mid-1990s, looking well ahead, will be a very effective defense, one that will be very difficult to penetrate consistently and effectively; and, therefore, we must not allow ourselves to be deterred from pushing ahead with new technology wherever there are real opportunities to prepare ourselves to meet that very serious threat.... He and I have similar data on the effectiveness of an FB-111 and the B-1. He has tended in his testimony to say that he is concerned that fund limitations would be such that one might have to defer too long on the advanced technology, unless he pursued the least expensive of the nearer term options, which would be the FB-111. So, he tends to favor that.... At that point I do not support that pre-judgment because we are working that problem right now.... The B-1 is, by far, the better machine. There is no doubt about that.[300]

Where Congress had specified 15 March 1981 as the date it expected a decision on the new bomber, Secretary Weinberger asked for and got authorization to submit an interim status report on that day and a final report with firm negotiated contracts on the aircraft that was now being called the long-range combat aircraft (LRCA), as distinguished from the advanced technology bomber. In early April 1981 the Department of Defense forwarded an interim report to Congress that fairly well indicated that the FB-111B/C candidate did not contain the attributes to satisfy all the multiple-role missions that Congress had specified that the new bomber would be able to fill. The stretched F-111, for example, could be rigged to carry 6 to 10 ALCMs on external pylons, but there would be significant aerodynamic drag and only 4 to 6 inches ground clearance. Pilots asked: "What would you do if you had a flat tire?" Another aspect of the problem was that the withdrawal of F-111D fighters from the tactical air forces would necessitate replacement of planes that were needed for all-environment, low-level, and high-speed penetration capabilities, most feasibly with air-to-surface missionized F-15s at an estimated cost of $2.9 to $3.5 billion.[301]

When the B-1 was obviously about to become the basic LRCA, the Air Force Strategic Systems Program Office sent separate requests for proposals soliciting prices on what would become the B-1 variant or the B-1B, the idea being to streamline the acquisition process and reduce program cost inflation in the outyears to come. There were major improvements in the B-1B over the basic B-1 that had been designed with 1977 technology, especially in stealth techniques to aid penetration. The radar cross section of the B-1B was reduced substantially over the original B-1 to reduce radar detection. Where the B-1A had an offensive avionics system taken largely from the 1970 design for the FB-111 system, the B-1B avionics was to be the best and most modern electronics. The ECM suite above the B-1B was upgraded to handle the latest Soviet threats, particularly the look-down, shoot-down interceptor. One of the most important changes was that the B-1B was to have an internal and an external cruise missile capability and also a conventional weapons capability. The aircraft could go supersonic but that was not planned since the B-1B was intended to penetrate at low altitude with high subsonic speed. This provided decreased fuel consumption, and a simplified engine air intake reduced radar reflection surfaces, thereby reducing the plane's radar cross section.[302]

Lt Gen Kelly H. Burke, Air Force deputy chief of staff for research and development, said that General Ellis continued to maintain his position that it was vital not to compromise the vigor with which the Air Force would work to get the advanced technology bomber by taking the more expensive B-1 interim bomber rather than the FB-111B/C, but the Air Force's position recommended to Secretary Weinberger on 21 May 1981 was that the B-1 was the most capable aircraft, with good growth potential and versatility, and would ultimately be the cruise missile carrier when the ATB came in and the B-52s gave up the ghost. Both the Air Force Advisory Board and the Defense Study Group agreed that the Air Force should move forward with the B-1. Dr Richard D. DeLauer, under secretary of defense for research and engineering, advised Secretary Weinberger that because of the need to modernize the force as quickly as possible he would recommend that the United States go after the B-1 to start with, simultaneously undertaking research and development on the ATB "with every intention in the world to put it into production." Doctor DeLauer rationalized, "As a threat comes and as our capability develops, I think it is a distinct advantage for us to have two programs going at the same time—if something happens to one program over another, and also from the competitive standpoint."[303] The Air Force's recommendation was that it be authorized to buy 100 B-1Bs ($20.5 billion in fiscal year 1982 dollars) which would enter service in 1986–87 and 110 stealth ATB bombers (estimated cost $30 billion), beginning in the early 1990s.[304]

On 2 October 1981 President Reagan announced that his strategic modernization program would need to depend heavily on bombers (and sea-based forces) in the 1980s while the United States took steps to strengthen its land-based missiles. Therefore, the United States should develop and procure 100 B-1Bs, with the first squadron to be operational in 1986, while continuing to pursue a vigorous R&D on the ATB stealth bomber which was planned to be deployed in the 1990s. B-52Gs/Hs would be modernized with cruise missiles; older B-52Ds would be retired in 1982–83. Over 3,000 ALCMs would be deployed on B-52Gs/Hs and ultimately on

B-1Bs. KC-135 tankers needed to support the expanded strategic force would be modernized with new engines.[305] More exact Air Force planning details for the B-52s already projected earlier in 1981 included a deployment concept whereby B-52Gs would load 12 ALCMs externally while retaining their internal load of gravity bombs and sort-range attack missiles. This configuration would support a tactic of shoot and penetrate, help prevent the Soviets from concentrating their defense against either the bomber or the cruise missile, and provide maximum delivery of megatonnage during the ALCM transition period. The IOC of the first squadron of ALCM-equipped B-52Gs was scheduled for December 1982. By 1985–86, B-52G modifications would permit eight additional cruise missiles to be carried internally in place of gravity bombs and short-range attack missiles. Procurement of 3,418 ALCMs would permit all B-52Gs to be equipped with 20 cruise missiles each. The decision to retire B-52Ds presented some difficulty since these aircraft had been modified to carry 108 general-purpose bombs. They were, however, expensive to maintain and had not been updated with terrain following and other modernization. The Air Force programmed inactivation of three of the five B-52D squadrons in calendar year 1982 or 1983. The Strategic Air Command had been flying round-robin B-52H show-of-force missions from Guam into the Persian Gulf. These very long missions were a way of demonstrating that the United States could project force into this vital area, but the B-52H could transport only 27 MK-82 general-purpose bombs. As B-52Ds retired, SAC's proposal was to take 61 of its B-52Hs, equip them with external racks to carry 27 additional 750-pound bombs and designate them as a B-52H strategic projection force.[306]

In the 1981 Defense Authorization Act, Congress had instructed the secretary of defense to field a new multiple-role bomber no later than 1987. In even greater retrospect, Congress traditionally had supported manned bombers: Assistant Secretary of Defense for International Security Policy Richard N. Perle remarked in March 1982 that without congressional committee action "we would have gotten out of the manned bomber business long ago."[307] Under the presidential and congressional mandate, the Air force in the fall of 1981 entered into contracts with Northrop to make a preliminary contractor study looking toward the ATB and with Rockwell as the prime contractor for the B-1B. But Congress was by no means unanimous in its acceptance of the strategic modernization program. There were numerous questions about the timing of various shifts within the strategic bomber force. In the Congressional Conference Report on the fiscal year 1982 DOD Appropriations Act, the conferees argued that B-52Ds ought to be continued in operation until such time as the B-1B or other new strategic bombers became available. In this matter the Air Force went ahead with the inactivation of three B-52D squadrons as planned in 1983 because it had to free critical resources for higher-priority programs, but to assuage Congress the Air Force programmed an additional 67 B-52Gs for modification for external bomb carriage; these were to transition into a conventional role as the B-1B was operational and the final two

IDEAS, CONCEPTS, DOCTRINE

B-52D squadrons were disbanded.[308] Air Force officials were called upon to respond to charges that the stealth ATB could be in service almost as quickly as the B-1B, and that expenditure of funds for the B-1B delayed the ATB and MX programs. Here, Secretary Weinberger assured Congress that the ATB program was receiving the funds necessary to develop bombers as fast as technology would allow:

> By committing to a B-1B, the Air Force reduces the risk of a high technology program. The ATB contractors are fully aware that if either the advanced technologies do not develop as desired or if these programs are mismanaged, the Air Force will have the option of producing more B-1Bs from an active assembly line. . . . On the other hand, should Rockwell encounter problems of program delays, etc., and the ATB advances at the expected pace, the Air Force has the option of buying less than 100 B-1Bs.[309]

This rationale did not convince Joseph P. Addabbo, chairman of the House Defense Appropriations Subcommittee and a longtime opponent of building the B-1, who retorted: "There simply is not enough money to build both."[310]

In April 1982, as congressional critics sparred with the Pentagon, Chairman Addabbo directed a pointed question at Dr James P. Wade, principal deputy under secretary of defense for research and engineering, and General Burke and elicited a prescient response about the continuing role of manned bombers expected in the years to come. "Are we placing too much emphasis on the manned bomber portion of the Triad?" Addabbo asked, and received these responses:

> Doctor Wade. No, sir. First the bomber force gives us an enhancement in the sense of the ability to present, react on early warning with a counter to a Soviet potential first strike. That is, you can launch the bombers in a crisis. You can move it on alert. Once launched, you can control it, by recalling it.
>
> It is a weapon system that has the capability of being controlled in real time, in the sense of being able to attack imprecisely located C^3 and military targets and deliver high megatonnage. It can be brought back and reloaded, once employed.
>
> In my personal opinion, the bomber force is certainly of equal importance to the other two legs of the Triad. I would not want to indicate here that it is any less unimportant.
>
> General Burke. I might just add a sentence or two, Mr Chairman. That is that the bombers, unlike the ICBMs, or SLBMs, or air-launched cruise missiles have another dimension. That is, they are available and applicable across lesser conflict circumstances than the all-out nuclear war. They have in the past, and will in the future, play a major role in non-nuclear military operations. Bombers have a unique and outstanding ability to project power at great distances rapidly and if necessary to bring that power to bear.
>
> So we get double duty out of bombers, not just sitting there solely for nuclear deterrence or war fighting.
>
> Perhaps an even more important consideration is that if we look down this long road of strategic competition with the Soviet Union, which I think even the most optimistic would expect will last for decades, if not centuries, we should carefully consider the action-reaction process that takes place between the two. An interesting anomaly in the

way we look at military investment is the Soviets have a much greater inclination to invest in their air defenses than do we.

Historically, for every dollar that we have spent for a bomber, the Soviets have spent somewhere between three and five dollars to defend against that bomber. That is a very desirable circumstance.

I think we ought to encourage that in the future because the defensive systems they buy to deal with our bomber force are not otherwise threatening to us by and large.[311]

Denigration and Re-creation of Strategic Defenses

When the North American Air Defense Command (NORAD) was organized officially in September 1957, its mission was simply an injunction: "defend the continental United States, Canada and Alaska against air attack." The defense of the North American continent against Soviet long-range bomber attack probably from over the North Pole was viewed as a single, indivisible problem shared by the United States and Canada. Substantial forces from both nations were assigned to NORAD's operational control, including eight NORAD regions, each equipped with a combat center of the semiautomatic ground environment (SAGE) type; 22 air divisions, each equipped with a SAGE direction center; 65 regular US and Canadian fighter-interceptor squadrons; 14 air defense artillery gun batteries; 244 Nike missile batteries; 9 Bomarc missile squadrons; 193 long-range radar sites; 105 gap-filler radars; 57 distant early warning (DEW) live stations; 11 airborne early warning and control stations off the US coasts; and 90 mid-Canada line stations. The SAGE system used electronic digital computers in place of the usual manual controllers to link together early warning and tracking radars, the DW system, the air defense missiles, and a variety of fighter aircraft. CINCNORAD was responsible to the president of the United States and the prime minister of Canada through the Joint Chiefs of Staff and the secretary of defense and Canadian chief of defense staff and minister of defense. Should US forces assigned to NORAD be committed to a unilateral action, US personnel would operate under the Continental Air Defense Command (CONAD). Otherwise, the binational NORAD was assigned operational control of three component commands: the Air Force Air Defense Command, the Canadian Forces Air Defence Command, and the US Army Air Defense Command. The system was designed and equipped to identify, intercept, and destroy medium- to high-altitude subsonic to slightly supersonic Soviet bombing planes. The system also provided a great amount of data about high-powered radar, defensive missiles and rockets, and the use of computers in real-time military situations.[312] Since the anticipated Soviet bomber threat to the United States did not materialize, Dr Jerome B. Wiesner, who had been President Kennedy's influential special assistant for science and technology from 1962 to 1964, retrospectively viewed the air defense system established in the latter 1950s as mostly a learning process. "So this all was in part a very expensive education, for those involved . . . in defense technology," he said.[313]

As has been seen, the major threat to the United States eventually came to be seen as ICBMs and soon afterward ICBMs plus SLBMs. The SAGE system made principal use of early developed vacuum-tube technology with one result being that the huge SAGE blockhouse installations were "soft" targets to even moderately accurate Soviet missile blasts. In the years 1958 to 1961, Director of Defense Research and Engineering John S. Foster, Jr., would recall that "a large segment of the informed technical opinion in the country did not believe it was at all reasonable to be able to build a ballistic missile defense."[314] This belief led to a US national policy of reliance on deterrence to prevent an enemy attack. The importance of defense against enemy attacks was thus reduced, with Secretary McNamara arguing in early 1965 that the arrival of Soviet missiles would in itself signal an attack long before Soviet bombers could reach NORAD warning lines. He said, "As a result, large portions of existing surveillance warning and control systems constructed during the 1950s are either obsolete or are of marginal value to our defense."[315]

Each year the Defense Intelligence Agency and other national intelligence activities projected that the Soviets would start phasing down their heavy-bomber force of 200 aircraft, including about 50 tankers, and engaged in debate as to whether the Soviets would be able to employ their approximately 700 medium bombers against the United States. But the Soviet manned-bomber force did not decrease in size coincident with the great buildup of Soviet missiles; rather, it was modernized with standoff missiles, development of low-altitude penetration tactics, and entry into service in the mid-1970s of the swing-wing Tupolev Backfire long-range bomber. The national intelligence estimates conceded that the Soviet heavy-bomber force was targeted against the United States, and from time to time after early 1968, Soviet Bison and Bear heavy bombers probed US air defense identification zones (ADIZs) in close vicinity to Newfoundland, Labrador, Greenland, and all over Alaska's waters. General McConnell rationalized that they were not keeping bombers only for harassment: "I believe they are doing it for the same reason we do, for the purpose of being able to use a bomber force in actual application of firepower in time of war."[316]

In 1961 Secretary McNamara revealed his assessment that the North American air defenses in a missile age could be destroyed rather quickly. As the decade was ending, he remarked: "I think there are serious doubts as to whether we should maintain our current air defense system, unless we are maintaining it as a foundation on which to build the new system which we are proposing."[317] At the end of the 1960s Secretary Seamans and Gen Seth J. McKee, CINCNORAD, suggested that there had been a second reason for the drawdown of continental air defenses, namely a conception among high-level decisionmakers that the Soviets did not *intend* to use bombers against the United States even though they maintained the capability. McKee said, "Some people just do not believe there is a credible threat. . . ."[318] In Air Force wargaming of the 1969–71 time frame, Soviet bombers were very significant because the total payload carried by them was quite high (more than a third of the total Soviet strategic firepower as late as 1975). The most likely attack scenario was one in which Soviet submarines would launch missiles to destroy US bombers on the ground; then there would be a follow-up wave of ICBMs; and the bombers would either be programmed against US withheld forces or urban/industrial areas which were not time-sensitive. If the Soviets knew that their bombers were going to be unopposed by an effective atmospheric defense, they would feel quite free to apply the full weight of their missiles to an attack against US strategic forces and to use their bombers against nontime-urgent urban/industrial targets in the continental United States (CONUS).[319] In 1968 when he was Air Force secretary, Doctor Brown thought that air defense should not be counted on for damage-limitation: "I don't think it can accomplish a high degree of damage limitation; that is, defense of our cities. I think it can do a better job of defending our offensive forces, which are harder for the enemy to knock out." He elaborated:

> Therefore, the criterion in the various defensive forces which I have indicated here is to avoid giving the enemy a free ride with bombers—in the same way that SENTINEL actually avoids giving him a free ride with missiles, even though in the end SENTINEL is unable to stop a Soviet attack, or defend against a Soviet attack. It forces the other side to put some of its payload into penetration aids and so on.
>
> The corresponding thing for air defense is the No. 1 priority—avoid giving them a free ride.
>
> Two, force them to go to air-to-surface missiles, thereby giving up some of their payload. And three, prevent them from making attacks on our land-based missiles with their bombers with impunity—otherwise they would at a low cost be able to knock out most of our land-based missiles, because bomber accuracy is at present better than missile accuracy.
>
> There is one other factor. We must prevent them from flying bombers around and over the United States with impunity. This is one thing that they cannot really do with missiles. They have got missiles, and they sit there. There is no easy way to intimidate us by making them more threatening to us. With bombers, by flying them around our coastline, they may make some of our citizens pretty nervous, and with reason.
>
> And finally, I think that air defenses, like missile defenses, will have some damage-limiting capability, but not enough to make any substantial difference in my opinion.[320]

In a 1969 Air Force statement of the impact of air defense on a Soviet bomber force, it was said that an air defense system in being effected "actual attrition" resulting from the air battle and "virtual attrition" by forcing an offensive force to make tactical modifications that reduced its effectiveness. For example, the quantities of ECM carried on board reduced the amount of ordnance that could be carried; operating at low altitude to avoid high- and medium-altitude defenses increased fuel consumption; and carrying external standoff missiles increased aerodynamic drag, reducing range and payload. "Thus, the existence alone of a credible air defense which is accepted as effective by the Soviet Union forces him [the enemy] to adapt tactics which will considerably reduce the size of the bomber attack he can mount—in terms of warhead payload."[321]

The drawdown of North American Air Defense Command strength progressed along a broad outline of yearly undertakings. The SAGE system was gradually replaced by backup interceptor control (BUIC) at prime radars, then the number of radars was progressively reduced, and finally arrangements were prosecuted to combine the military air defense and Civil Aeronautics Authority (CAA) air traffic control, first in the control portion of the United States and then on the periphery. The eastern and western approaches to the United States were to be guarded by over-the-horizon backscatter (OTH-B) radars that used a scatter radar technique which in effect bounced electronic signals between the earth and ionosphere out to the 1,500 mile range. The concept for this technique had originated at the Air Force Cambridge Research Laboratories in 1946 and was being developed into functional equipment that would guard high-threat corridors into the northeastern and northwestern United States.[322] In 1964–65, the Air Force withdrew its all-weather interceptor squadrons from Japan, Spain, Okinawa, and the Philippines, leaving this mission to indigenous forces and in the case of Okinawa and the Philippines to rotational F-4C tactical fighter squadrons. In 1965, Secretary Zuckert announced that the Air Force would place increasing dependence upon Air National Guard squadrons for continental air defense and would begin replacing their F-86, F-89, and F-100 aircraft at first with F-102 interceptors that would deal with a Soviet subsonic conventional bomber threat.[323] In 1964 the secretly developed Lockheed A-11 airplane was developed as the SR-71 reconnaissance plane and also as the YF-12A improved manned interceptor (IMI) that the Air Force had wanted for some years. General McConnell described the F-12A at the beginning of 1965, saying: "I do not think we could have come up with a better aircraft if we had started from scratch. It is the most sophisticated interceptor aircraft there is in the world today, assuming we do a little more work on it." The F-12A had a combat radius of 1,200 nautical miles and a Mach-3-plus speed, but each would cost between $15 and $18 million. The Joint Chiefs of Staff supported the requirement for an IMI, but not necessarily the F-12A since it was possible that the F-111 could serve the purpose.[324] But Secretary McNamara stated and reiterated from year to year the assessment that

> the elaborate defenses which we erected against the Soviet bomber threat during the decade of the 1950s no longer retain their original importance. Today, with no defense against the major threat of Soviet ICBMs, or antibomber defenses alone would contribute very little to our damage limiting objective and their residual effectiveness after a major ICBM attack is highly problematical.[325]

He was willing only to allow the Air Force to continue to test the F-12A and to seek to develop an airborne radar for it. Any decision to produce it and deploy it would depend upon whether the Soviets developed supersonic attack bombers; even then, the missile threat ought to be taken care of first through fallout shelters, antimissile defense deployment, and ultimate surface-to-air missile defenses against the bomber threat.[326]

Both the Air Force EC-121 airborne early warning and control aircraft and the Navy E-2A fleet air defense aircraft had moving target identification radars that worked well over water where they were intended to be used but lacked a capability to extract information on moving targets flying over land clutter. This capability was critically needed to support air operations over North Vietnam, where the North Vietnamese radars were able to see the entire situation and control their forces, but the United States could not do so. In 1963, the Air Force issued a specific operational requirement for an aircraft warning and control system (AWACS) that would be equipped with overland radar that could look down and detect aircraft in flight. The overland radar program developed improved antenna designs, improved circuitry coming from solid-state electronic components, improved computer methods of handling and displaying radar data, and dozens of exploratory, advanced, and engineering development programs. The AWACS installed in an air transport aircraft—a modified Boeing 707 airframe—would be an extremely complex system, but critical experiments with look-down overland apparatus in 1967 convinced the Air Force and OSD that AWACS was surely feasible. At this same juncture, the airborne radar for the F-12 had not advanced to the point where the Air Force and OSD could be assured that it would be effective.[327]

Early in 1967 Secretary McNamara was willing to entertain a modernization of air defenses if it could be financed out of operating cost savings achieved by replacing the existing force. During the year, as the feasibility of the AWACS was established, the Air Force opted for a modernized integration of over-the-horizon warning radars and an airborne mobile control AWACS fleet in exchange for the SAGE and ground radar systems that were expensive to operate and vulnerable to missile attack. In November 1967 OSD ordered the development of the AWACS but discontinued development of the F-12 interceptor in favor of converting some other available aircraft to work with AWACS. General McConnell opposed closing out the F-12 and hoped the decision would eventually be reconsidered, but under the circumstances he said he could accept a modernized F-106X aircraft—the F-106 being the most advanced interceptor already in operation. Secretary Brown explained that on an airplane-for-airplane basis, the F-12 was a much better aircraft than an F-106X, but it would have cost about 10 times as much as the F-106 modernization. Moreover, a number of F-12s would have been required to defend the continental United States, and the cost of the program was difficult to justify when the United States, after all, could not be defended against Soviet ICBMs. The defense modernization was elaborately briefed to Senate and House committees; the OTH-B radar and AWACS programs were approved for development, but Congress did not accept the F-106X program which would have retrofitted F-106s with look-down tracking radars at a cost altogether of some three quarters of a billion dollars.[328]

IDEAS, CONCEPTS, DOCTRINE

In the waning months of President Johnson's administration in response to the 1968 draft presidential memorandum (DPM) on strategic offensive and defensive forces, the Air Force recommended a mixed air defense force with a small number of F-12s and more F-106Xs. The record of decision DPM, dated 9 January 1969, did not approve the F-12s but accepted the F-106X force for continuation in the program. The main justification for not approving the small force of F-12s was the absence of any hard evidence that the Soviets were developing either a new long-range air-to-surface missile (ASM) or an intercontinental supersonic bomber, and therefore the AWACS/F-106X force was selected. Since Congress had already failed to authorize funds for the F-106X, the Air Force elected not to pursue this less attractive option for air defense.[329] As General McConnell saw the situation, the Air Force had been promised modernization of bomber defenses, including AWACS and new interceptors, in return for phasing down existing defenses; the phasedown had occurred, but the modernization was continually postponed with the result that the Aerospace Defense Command would have "only marginal capability throughout the 1970-74 time period to respond to all demands both in the United States and for overseas contingencies."[330]

In the first year of the Nixon administration, Secretary Laird assessed the continental US air defenses as being "fairly effective against high altitude bombers dropping gravity bombs, but would be less effective against low-altitude attacks or attacks by bombers launching air-to-surface missiles." But, because of budget limits, Laird elected not only to continue but to hasten air defense reductions both by phaseouts and transfers of F-101 aircraft to the Air National Guard. AWACS and OTH-B remained in research and development, and by March 1970, the Air Force had given up on the F-106X as being unacceptable to Congress and the F-12 as no longer being a reasonable alternative since the tooling for it had been abandoned.[331] In March 1971 Secretary Seamans made the development of the airborne warning and control system the "number one priority for air defense." This system, working with prior-positioned F-106s, could provide some air defense in the light and thin defense perimeters along the eastern, western, and northern borders. In response to a question put to him in the Senate Armed Services Committee, Seamans strongly supported a reawakening of air defense:

Question. Mr Secretary, do you fully support the modernization of our air defense against Soviet bombers which will cost the Air Force $4.1 billion over the next few years?

Answer. I fully support the modernization of our air defenses against Soviet bombers, as a vital element of realistic deterrence. In view of the evident Soviet commitment to a mixed strike force, and especially in view of the latest evidence of Soviet emphasis on all elements of their strategic forces, we must be prepared to deal with Soviet bomber options which are clearly within their capabilities. The known capabilities of Soviet Long Range Aviation, the value to the Soviets in both a damage-limiting and assured-destruction role of a bomber attack on CONUS, and the risks to the US of an uninhibited Soviet bomber capability, all argue that the Soviet bomber threat to the US is real and must be addressed. Now, regarding costs, beginning with the initial approval of the air defense modernization

> program in 1967, our studies have consistently shown that modernized air defenses will correct major deficiencies in the existing system, will improve system survivability, will increase effectiveness and will reduce air defense operating costs.
>
> To help amortize the costs of modernization we have reduced air defense annual operating costs each year since 1966, the year prior to approval of modernization. Last year, for example, we experienced an annual operating cost for air defense which was approximately $500M below the 1966 level. This year will show a further reduction. We estimate that the modernized air defense system, once costs have leveled off, will provide the advantages I have outlined at an annual operating cost some $600M below 1966 costs. Our most recent cost exercise indicates that we can acquire the modernized system and still attain a net reduction of over $6B in air defense costs, FY 66 through FY 83, the level off year for modernization.
>
> I must point out that we are moving conservatively in our progress toward modernization. We will demonstrate, with hardware, the fact that required technical capabilities have been attained before large sums are committed to these program elements. At the same time, as these efforts take place, we will have ample opportunity to assess the threat on a continuing basis and to adjust the modernization program to respond intelligently.[332]

At these same hearings the Air Force was provided statistical tables on the drawdown of air defense forces in the decade 1961–71.

In their strategic assessment for fiscal year 1973, the Joint Chiefs of Staff recommended to Secretary Laird that the United States should emphasize air defense modernization since the extant system was old and that the country had to recognize that the Soviets could overfly the United States and were known to be building the modern Backfire bomber. Admiral Moorer said:

> I do think it is important, however, that we have a capability for protecting the air sovereignty of the United States so that we can't have unidentified aircraft flying anyplace over our country.... In this connection... we are taking steps to permit the National Guard to participate more in the interceptor role of the air defense system.[333]

Secretary Laird agreed, saying: "The Soviet bomber force is not as great a threat when compared to the strategic submarine and land-based missile forces which the Soviet Union has." Laird wanted to press on with modernization: "This effort keeps open the option of deploying an air defense system which would be effective against sophisticated bombers and less vulnerable to ballistic missile attacks than the existing air defense system."[334] The fiscal year 1973 program kept the AWACS in development with three test aircraft to be procured and the OTH-B radar in development for an initial deployment on the coast of Maine. There was no money for an IMI, but the program retained all 486 existing interceptors, with the provision that the number of interceptors on alert would be reduced by one-half. Two additional active Air Force squadrons were to be transferred to the Air National Guard; the remaining five Bomarc squadrons were phased out as were most of the backup radar control centers.[335] General Ryan, who had become Air Force chief of staff, spoke about these reductions in April 1973:

TABLE 1

STRATEGIC DEFENSIVE FORCES

Interceptor Forces—Active

Aircraft, end fiscal year:	1961	1962	1963	1964	1965	1966	1967	1968	1969	1970	1971
F-101:											
Squadrons	17	17	17	16	15	15	15	13	6	3	0
Aircraft	384	312	312	312	270	270	270	234	108	54	0
F-102:											
Squadrons	11	11	10	9	9	3	1	1	1	—	0
Aircraft	293	293	255	235	235	85	34	26	26	—	0
F-104:											
Squadrons	—	—	2	2	2	2	1	1	1	—	0
Aircraft	—	—	42	42	36	36	24	24	24	—	0
F-106:											
Squadrons	14	14	13	13	13	13	13	11	11	11	11
Aircraft	270	276	240	240	234	228	216	210	210	198	198
TOTAL:											
Squadrons	42	42	42	40	39	33	30	26	19	14	11
Aircraft	947	881	849	829	775	619	544	494	368	252	198

Source: Senate, *Fiscal Year 1972 Authorization for Military Procurement, Research and Development, Construction and Real Estate Acquisition for the Safeguard ABM, and Reserve Strength: Hearings before the Committee on Armed Services*, 92d Cong., 1st sess., 1971, pt. 5:3530, pt. 2:1269.

TABLE 1 (Continued)

Interceptor Forces—Air National Guard

		Fiscal Years									
Aircraft, end fiscal year:	1961	1962	1963	1964	1965	1966	1967	1968	1969	1970	1971
F-86:											
Squadrons	10	8	6	4	—	—	—	—	—	—	—
Aircraft	250	200	150	100	—	—	—	—	—	—	—
F-89:											
Squadrons	10	10	9	9	9	5	2	2	2	—	—
Aircraft	250	250	225	225	180	100	36	36	36	—	—
F-100:											
Squadrons	3	3	3	2	—	—	—	—	—	—	—
Aircraft	66	67	72	42	—	—	—	—	—	—	—
F-102:											
Squadrons	7	7	9	9	13	17	20	20	20	14	10
Aircraft	130	127	152	191	208	313	367	367	367	259	180
F-104:											
Squadrons	3	—	—	—	—	—	—	—	—	—	—
Aircraft	61	—	—	—	—	—	—	—	—	—	—
F-101:											
Squadrons	—	—	—	—	—	—	—	—	—	3	6
Aircraft	—	—	—	—	—	—	—	—	—	54	108
TOTAL:											
Squadrons	33	28	27	24	22	22	22	22	22	17	16
Aircraft	757	644	599	558	388	413	403	403	403	313	288

TABLE 1 (Continued)

Surface-to-Air Missiles—Active

	\multicolumn{11}{c}{Fiscal Years}										
	1961	1962	1963	1964	1965	1966	1967	1968	1969	1970	1971
Bomarc:											
Squadrons	—	8	8	8	6	6	6	6	6	5	5
Missile	—	307	383	200	180	180	172	164	156	140	140
Hercules:											
Battery	—	139	127	107	95	73	73	73	52	44	28
Missile	—	2,502	2,316	1,926	1,500	1,194	1,194	1,194	891	730	485
Hawk:											
Battery	—	—	8	8	8	8	8	8	8	8	8
Missile	—	—	288	288	288	288	288	288	288	288	288

Surface-to-Air Missiles—Army National Guard

	1961	1962	1963	1964	1965	1966	1967	1968	1969	1970	1971
Ajax:											
Battery	—	69	34	—	—	—	—	—	—	—	—
Missile	—	1,440	720	—	—	—	—	—	—	—	—
Hercules:											
Battery	—	—	16	36	48	48	48	48	44	38	27
Missile	—	—	648	649	726	726	726	726	669	609	540

TABLE 1 (Continued)

Control and Surveillance

	\multicolumn{11}{c|}{Fiscal Years}										
	1961	1962	1963	1964	1965	1966	1967	1968	1969	1970	1971
NORAD COC	1	1	1	1	1	1	1	1	1	1	1
Combat centers	8	8	8	7	7	6	6	6	5	0	0
Direction centers	20	21	18	16	16	14	14	14	13	0	0
Regional control centers	—	—	—	—	—	—	—	—	—	8	8
NORAD manual control center	3	3	4	4	4	4	4	4	4	5	4
BUIC II	0	0	0	0	0	13	13	9	0	0	0
BUIC III	0	0	0	0	0	0	0	0	12	14	14
EC121 (UE)	60	67	67	67	67	67	67	67	67	46	18
Search radars	182	179	179	168	162	158	154	141	128	101	99
Gap-filler radars	112	103	96	100	100	91	88	17	17	17	0
ANG radars	6	6	6	6	6	6	3	3	3	3	3
DEW radars	67	67	67	39	39	39	39	39	39	33	32
Radar ships	31	32	22	22	19	0	0	0	0	0	0
SAM fire-coordination centers	10	28	28	26	25	19	22	22	22	14	10

IDEAS, CONCEPTS, DOCTRINE

> Our air defense system continues to be a matter of concern. In the mid-sixties, we began a sharp phasedown of our relatively obsolescent air defense system to provide resources for modernization. Unfortunately, these resources were diverted to other pressing needs, and we now find ourselves with a greatly reduced capability with little progress toward modernization. . . . Until the modernized air defense force, consisting of OTH-B, AWACS, and IMI, becomes fully operational, the deficiencies of the present system will continue to exist, and any delays in deploying the new system will result in prolonging that risk.[336]

In the same years that continental US atmospheric defense was being drawn down, the United States developed and implemented Sentinel and Safeguard ABM programs and in effect terminated them with the signing of the US-USSR Antiballistic Missile Treaty on 26 May 1972. The ABM programs drew R&D funds that could have been applied to other defense efforts, and the ABM treaty's aftermath brought a near disestablishment of continental air defense. The genealogy of the ABM began at least in 1945 when the US Army fostered development through the years of Nike surface-to-air missiles: Nike Ajax deployed in 1953, Nike Hercules deployed 1958, Nike Zeus development started 1956, and Nike X development started 1963. The Nike Hercules and Zeus had ABM potentials, but President Eisenhower did not favor their production for deployment. Army hopes that the new Kennedy administration would be more receptive were ill founded: both Secretary McNamara and Director of Defense Research and Engineering Harold Brown were sympathetic to continuing research, but concerned that the Nike Zeus could be easily saturated and could not protect populated areas. The Nike X sought to provide a better area defense against many incoming missiles. This system combined a long-range Spartan interceptor, short-range, high-acceleration Sprint, and a phased array radar. Doctor Brown continued to be sympathetic to the Nike X as a worthwhile experiment, but both he and Secretary McNamara made the point that it could not protect area populations unless there were fallout shelters. As Air Force secretary in 1966, Doctor Brown still wanted Nike X held in development as an experiment that, among other things, would yield information that would help the development of US missile penetration aids. Brown said, "I think defense is unlikely ever to catch up with offense, and I think that is a good reason for not putting most of our expenditures into strategic defensive systems." General McConnell had added on views: "I think I lean a little further toward establishing a real ABM system in the United States. . . . I think we ought to have the system." McConnell's view which was to go ahead with the development and deployment of the system over a period of years since it was a complicated system coincided with that of the Joint Chiefs.[337]

In 1962, the Advanced Research Projects Agency (ARPA) of the Department of Defense Research and Engineering commissioned the Rand Corporation to examine scenarios involving ABM options other than against all-out attack, which was the usual option stressed by Secretary McNamara. These studies suggested the possibility of defense against thin, unsophisticated missile strikes. In ARPA, Dr

Charles M. Herzfeld was responsible for ABM research and viewed the Rand findings as being "somewhat of a solution in search of a problem." He mentioned this to McNamara rather casually, and about a year later in 1963 McNamara directed ARPA to establish four contractual study groups to explore further the concept of a thin ABM defense. These studies yielded a clearer insight that there were situations in which it would be useful to have a thin ABM defense which could comprehend a reduced problem even if "a really thick defense against a really big attack was a pretty 'iffy' thing, if at all possible."[338] In 1964 Communist China exploded its first nuclear device, and in formulating recommendations for the 1965 draft presidential memorandum in the summer of 1964, OSD Systems Analysis included a suggestion that the United States seriously consider deployment of a small ABM defense against unsophisticated threats.[339]

In response to increasing demands for ABM defense, Secretary McNamara continued to assert that all that the Soviets would do would be to build more ICBMs to subvert the defense. A US ABM employment would spur a dangerous and costly arms race. In 1965 and 1966, satellite photos revealed that the Soviets appeared to be building an ABM defense around Moscow. Here again, McNamara said the proper response would be to upgrade US offensive missile forces rather than erect an ABM. Some of McNamara's scientific support now began to waver: Dr John S. Foster, Jr., director of defense research and engineering, testified in March 1966 that the Nike X-Sprint combination was technically feasible and that a thin defense could be designed to "destroy with high probability a few missiles launched from another country." As it happened, Congress displayed disagreement with McNamara in 1966 by appropriating an unasked for $167.9 million to begin ABM procurement. The Joint Chiefs of Staff were unanimously in support of an area defense of much of the country with augmented defenses of the highest density populated areas, recommending this for two reasons: they had watched the growing ability of the Soviets to destroy US population and industry, and they considered that the research and development program of Nike X had reached a point where Nike X was ready for deployment. At a meeting with President Johnson on 8 December 1966, with the Joint Chiefs in attendance, McNamara offered a compromise that was acceptable, whereby the administration would ask Congress for $375 million for "possible" ABM deployment of an unspecified sort pending exploration of an arms control agreement with the Soviet Union. In Senate hearings in January 1967, McNamara continued to express apprehension that a US ABM would fuel an arms race. He said, however, that if the Soviets did not put a limit on their antiballistic missile deployment and arrived at a very heavy defense, then the United States would have no choice but to expand its offensive capability, either by more Poseidons or something of that kind or alternatively protecting its offensive forces. An ABM system would be "well worth considering" to protect Minuteman missiles. In the course of the congressional hearings, Secretary Brown thought the thin ABM system—now called Sentinel—would be "at least technically feasible and probably practical as well." He supported the thin system to protect the United States against "a potential and, indeed, expected Chinese [missile] capability of the mid-1970s." He did not support a large ABM deployment aimed at the Soviet Union because "the offense can penetrate the defense at a substantially lower cost than the defense expends." He reasoned that at some point it would be desirable to deploy point defenses for land-based ballistic missiles, but he did not think the United States had reached that point. General McConnell was asked to speak about the relationship of offense and defense and replied:

> I think, of course, that if I could have only one, either a strong offense or a supposedly impenetrable defense, I would take the offense. Therefore, I think the improvement of our offensive systems to act as a deterrent to the Soviets is the most important single item for the United States to engage in. The improvement of our offensive capability in itself may continue to deter.
>
> However, it is my opinion that we should also have a reasonable defense against their offensive capability. And I mean by that the deployment of a reasonable amount of antiballistic-missile capability, sufficient to be sure that we are not going to be subject to blackmail by their threat to throw a few missiles over to see what our reaction would be. We need a sufficient number of antiballistic missiles to protect to some degree, at least, a portion of our own land-based offensive missile force. In my opinion, then, that must be augmented with the deployment of the advanced interceptor systems and their survivable control system to counteract any bomber threat which the enemy has now and which he might develop in the future.[340]

At a meeting with Soviet Premier Aleksey Kosygin at Glassboro, New Jersey, in June 1967, Johnson and McNamara could not get the Soviets to agree that the ABMs were more than purely defensive weapons and entirely unobjectionable. On 18 September 1967 Secretary McNamara announced the Johnson administration's decision to deploy a Sentinel ABM system to protect US population centers from Chinese attack, to intercept accidental launches, and give some protection with Sprints to the Minuteman sites against an all-out Soviet attack. Preliminary estimates indicated an investment of approximately $5 billion.[341]

The Sentinel systems management was established directly under the chief of staff and secretary of the Army, and the program was expected to require five years to accomplish, beginning with the establishment of test capabilities on Meck Island, Kwajalein Atoll, in the Pacific Ocean. The five major subsystems were the perimeter acquisition radars (a very long-range phased-array surveillance/tracking radar to be housed in five-story above-ground buildings), the long-range Spartan missile, the shorter-range very rapidly accelerating Sprint missile, missile site radars to direct Sprints, and a data-processing subsystem. In the first year of Sentinel, fiscal year 1968, the activity was primarily that of surveying, planning, and early tests. The system was to be directed against transpolar enemy missiles, and residents of cities near designated Sentinel sites grew anxious about the dangers to them of missile intercepts with nuclear interceptor warheads. There were growing criticisms that the perimeter acquisition radar (PAR) and the missile site radars (MSRs) were very soft and would be easily destroyed by a single Soviet missile.[342]

When President Nixon assumed office in January 1969, he recognized the fragility of support for the Sentinel ABM, but he nevertheless wished to proceed with the ABM system because of campaign promises, the need for a bargaining chip for SALT negotiations with the Soviets, and the very real and growing Soviet MIRV missile threat to Minuteman silos. In the interest of a quick decision, Nixon elected to get the matter studied outside the National Security Council system he was restructuring, and on 6 February 1969 Secretary Laird announced a halt in Sentinel, pending a month-long review. A study group soon offered four options to Nixon, the most feasible and the one ultimately accepted being a modified 12-site deployment plan called I-69. Under this plan, all sites would be moved away from cities, thus emphasizing the protection of Minuteman but also providing a thin area of defense for the population. On 14 March 1969 Nixon publicly announced his decision to convert the ABM effort to a Safeguard program with the primary object being protection of US land-based retaliatory forces against direct attack by the Soviet Union. He promised that the program would be reviewed and phased annually from the point of view of (a) technical developments, (b) the threat, and (c) the diplomatic context, including any arms-limitations talks. In the fiscal year 1970 budget, following the Safeguard decision, the president proposed to move forward with the deployment of an initial phase, looking toward 12 sites. Congress approved only four specified sites, including authority to begin work at only two of them: one near Grand Forks AFB, North Dakota, and the other near Malmstrom AFB, Montana. The full Senate approved these first two sites by only one vote. The administration's fiscal year 1971 proposal, made in 1970, was to go forward with the Grand Forks and Malmstrom sites; commence deployment near Whiteman AFB, Missouri; provide additional Sprints at Grand Forks and Malmstrom AFBs; and undertake advanced preparation for deployment at five other sites. Congress limited authorization for advanced preparation to a single site near Francis E. Warren AFB, Wyoming. In the fiscal year 1972 budget request, made in 1971, the president's proposal recommended continued deployment at Grand Forks and Malmstrom AFBs, initiation of construction at Whiteman AFB, and authorization for deployment of a fourth site at Warren or in the Washington, D.C., area. Congress approved continued deployment at Grand Forks and Malstrom AFBs, limited activity at Whiteman and Warren AFBs to advanced preparations only, and eliminated consideration of predeployment activities in the Washington, D.C., area. For fiscal year 1973, presented in 1972, the defense budget included proceeding with the planned deployment at the four Minuteman sites; initiating advance preparation for Safeguard defense of the national command authorities (NCA) in Washington, D.C.; and planning for longer-term continuation of Safeguard to the 12 sites.[343] In the view of Sen Henry Jackson, the Senate Armed Services Committee expressed its reservations—or even opposition—to Safeguard by making cuts in requested appropriation. In 1971, Senator Symington placed in the record several protests of the ABM sites from Boston, Chicago, and Seattle, saying, "Don't put it around here." In his home state of Missouri, Symington protested the site at Whiteman AFB, which was only 25 miles from Kansas City. The Joint Chiefs of Staff always recommended an ABM system in the Washington, D.C., area because they assessed it as essential to protect the national command authorities. Said Admiral Moorer, "We are not talking in terms of protecting industry or population per se, but rather the nerve center . . . of the command system which issues the instructions to the operating forces." In this matter, however, Senator Jackson retorted that it clearly was not the intention of Congress to appear to be protecting itself when the remainder of the country was not similarly protected.[344]

Where the Soviet leaders had been unwilling to bargain at Glassboro in mid-1967, strategic arms limitation talks yielded on 26 May 1972 a US-USSR Antiballistic Missile Treaty and an Interim Agreement on Strategic Offensive Arms. The Treaty on the Limitation of Antiballistic Missile Systems limited each party to no more than 200 ABM missiles and 200 ABM launchers—100 each for the defense of the national capital and 100 each for the defense of an ICBM area. There were other limits on radar complexes and other aspects of missile defense, but development and testing could continue. In a final reckoning, the United States had from 1968–73 expended $5,070,400,000 in support of the Grand Forks Safeguard deployment. After the ABM treaty, a new secretary of defense terminated all work at Malstrom AFB but requested an additional $402 million to work to the completion of the Grand Forks installation with 100 missiles on launchers (30 Spartan and 70 Sprint), one missile site radar, and one perimeter acquisition radar. The site was expected to be operational before mid-1975, and the completed site would give experience with a deployed ballistic defense system. Defense Secretary Elliot L. Richardson also asked for funds to develop site defenses for Minuteman silos so that they could include a new phased array radar, a commercial data processor, and an improved version of Sprint. He did not propose to establish ABM defenses for Washington without more study of the matter. In March 1974 Secretary of Defense James R. Schlesinger also urged Congress to give strong support to ABM development in fiscal year 1975. Schlesinger warned:

> If we fail to advance our ABM technology while the Soviet Union continues to pursue its on-going ABM development programs, which are clearly permitted by the treaty, the Soviet Union might achieve a position where, by abrogating the treaty, it could shift the strategic balance drastically in its favor before we could react.[345]

Viewing the ABM treaty in retrospect, Air Force Chief of Staff David Jones suggested that the Soviets agreed to freeze ballistic missile defense (BMD) because they were far behind in technology. Jones pointed out:

In 1972, the United States was clearly ahead of the Soviet Union in all aspects of BMD capability. We were spending more on BMD R&D testing and deploying a superior system; at that time we were capable of exceeding any Soviet deployment initiatives.[346]

After the 1972 treaty the Department of Defense sought to maintain a strong ABM R&D effort, but Congress was reluctant. Congressional action in 1975 terminated operation of the Safeguard system. The site at Grand Forks AFB was accordingly dismantled except for the phased-array radar, actually located 75 miles northwest of Grand Forks and looking northward. The Defense Department kept PAR on the condition that it surveyed the Northern Hemisphere, would recognize incoming missiles, and would provide immediate calculations of missile origins and intended aiming points—this being sensed as "attack characterization." Although the Air Force was at first reluctant to take on the expense of this radar's operation (and a congressional committee recommended its abandonment), the Army modified it to provide coverage of possible SLBM attacks from the Arctic, and the Air Force took over responsibility for its operation. One reason ultimately suggested for congressional reluctance to continue to support an ABM program was the pervading opinion of many observers that missile defense was not cost-effective: that it would cost the Soviets less to build enough missiles to swamp any ABM defense than it would cost the United States to field such ABM systems. In the aftermath of the 1972 treaty, however, the Soviets—unlike the United States—continued to operate the Moscow ABM defenses and to upgrade them. This led Richard N. Perle, assistant secretary of defense for internal security policy, to draw a significant lesson from the 1972 treaty. He said in 1982:

You enter into a treaty and it prohibits deployment or permits research and development, and as time passes the Congress and the public grow weary of funding research and development on a system when the deployment of those forces are prohibited. . . . One of the things that has happened in recent years is that the Soviets, uninhibited by public concern, have vastly increased their investment in ABM research and development to the point where the advantage we possessed at the time the treaty went into effect has been significantly eroded.[347]

In March 1971 Gen Seth J. McKee, CINCNORAD, although regretful about the tardiness of bomber defense modernization, was confident that the mission of NORAD would see little change in the years to come, other than assumption of control over Safeguard. McKee said, "I feel . . . that we will have a continuing requirement for a defensive system incorporating surveillance, command and control, air-to-air combat capability, i.e., interceptors and surface-to-air missiles in the foreseeable future."[348] But in early 1974, in the aftermath of the US-USSR ABM treaty, Secretary of Defense Schlesinger accepted as a reality the "cruel" fact that "there is not protection for American cities against a coordinated strike by the strategic forces of the Soviet Union. Since we cannot defend our cities against strategic missiles, there is nothing to be gained by trying to defend them against a relatively small force of Soviet bombers." The new circumstances changed the air defense mission from a primary role of defense against air attack to peacetime surveillance and control to ensure sovereignty of US air space, plus maintenance of a mobile air defense capability which could be deployed promptly overseas. Gen Lucius D. Clay, CINCNORAD in 1974, explained:

> We no longer have as our primary mission the air defense of the North American continent. We have, instead, a three-part mission with the elements set down in a descending order of importance: (1) provide global airspace surveillance, warning and assessment of ballistic missile attack; (2) control sovereign airspace of the United States and Canada; (3) provide limited defense against bomber attack in the event of hostilities. . . .[349]

In allocating forces for continental air defense, Schlesinger said there was need for "a limited capability, so that nobody has a free ride over the United States . . . and we do not want anybody to feel that he can overfly the United States or the North American continent without paying a significant attrition." This mission required only "a thin area-type defense plus a high quality surveillance capability."[350] Accordingly, the OSD proposed to phase out all strategic Nike Hercules batteries which were located around nine urban areas and eventually to reduce the interceptor force to 12 squadrons, 6 active Air Force and 6 Air National Guard (ANG), all to be equipped with F-106s. In addition, there would continue to be one F-4 air defense squadron and three active Army Nike Hercules batteries in Alaska, and one ANG air defense squadron (F-102s converting to F-4s) in Hawaii. The ANG interceptor units standing down would be converted to general-purpose force units that would be more relevant to the requirements of national defense in the 1970s than air defense units. A CONUS air defense system structured primarily for peacetime surveillance would not require a dedicated AWACS force, the principal purpose of which would be to provide a survivable means to control air defense aircraft in a nuclear war environment. However, a mobile air defense force which could be employed quickly as a package would be extremely useful to support general-purpose forces overseas. Accordingly, OSD continued to program for AWACS (or E-3As, as it was being called) as a part of general purpose forces rather than air defense.[351] To improve surveillance, Schlesinger proposed to continue to consolidate military with Federal Aviation Administration civilian radars so that by the late 1970s jointly used radars located around the US perimeter would replace all military surveillance radars in CONUS. Over-the-horizon backscatter (OTH-B) radars on the East Coast and West Coast, and possibly looking north and south, would be developed to enhance surveillance capabilities for the 1980s.[352]

There was philosophical agreement in the top-level Air Force command with Schlesinger's announced rationale for reducing air defense but there was little support for a general disestablishment of the mission. Said Secretary McLucas:

> My own view is that philosophically I would agree with the Secretary of Defense, that given the limitations on missile defense, this sort of sets the ceiling on air defense, but we should not go below the point where we can protect our territory against overflight, or defend against an attack by a limited number of bombers.[353]

According to CINCNORAD at the time, Gen Lucius Clay, only the efforts of Air Force Chief of Staff Gen George S. Brown prevented air defense from going down the drain. Clay stated, a good many people in the Pentagon wanted to inactivate NORAD and either eliminate its forces or put them all in the Air National Guard. According to Clay, General Brown said: "I'll accept the Guard buildup; that makes sense to me, but I'm going to maintain some element of a regular force in the air defense business to provide standardization, supervision, and guidance on tactical doctrine and techniques." Clay recalled that he and Brown "felt it was proper and appropriate to keep at least a thin line of direct interceptor control for the unknown . . . a thin line and perhaps some day move into some form of space defense."[354] Speaking for himself in April 1974, General Brown said he had had his day in court about air defense, had been able to prevail to some extent, and would see some hope that Schlesinger had "left the door open a crack" so that the debate on air defense would continue. Both McLucas and Brown wanted to hold on to as many of the Air National Guard F-101 squadrons slated for inactivation as possible, since they had highly motivated and accomplished people.[355]

In view of the reduction in continental air defense efforts, the Air Force began studies of changes that should be made in the organization of the North American Air Defense Command establishment in 1973, even before the full impact of Secretary Schlesinger's slashes was evident. NORAD itself was the top-level headquarters jointly manned by the United States and Canada, and changes in it required international negotiation. The US Continental Air Defense Command was a US unified command superior to the US Army Air Defense Command (ARADCOM) and the Air Force's Aerospace Defense Command (ADC). To reduce headquarters manpower spaces, the Air Force in 1973 studied proposals to combine ADC with SAC or TAC but instead decided effective on 28 June 1973 to consolidate Headquarters ADC with Headquarters CONAD, allowing for a single CINCNORAD/CONAD with staffs that functioned as an entity in dual-hatted status.[356] Following deactivation of the majority of the US Army's surface-to-air missile Nike Hercules forces in the US air defenses, the Army disestablished ARADCOM on 4 January 1975. Since CONAD could no longer lay claim to unified command status (i.e., an organization composed of significant assigned forces of two or more services), OSD disestablished CONAD and recognized the Air Force's Aerospace Defense Command (ADCOM) as a specified command (i.e., composed principally of major forces from one service). After this reorganization in 1975, NORAD contained the Air Defense Group of the Canadian Forces Air Command (CFADG) and ADCOM, the latter specifically tasked to provide forces to NORAD for ballistic missile warning, space defense, and air defense.[357]

In the 1975 renewal of their NORAD agreement, the United States and Canada specified that the mission of NORAD would be

- aerospace warning and attack assessment,

- surveillance and control of US and Canadian airspace, and

- defense against air attack.[358]

In Secretary of Defense Donald H. Rumsfeld's requests for fiscal year 1977 defense appropriations, made early in 1976, the strategic defense mission was specified as being to

- perform surveillance and peacetime control of US airspace;
- provide warning and assessment of a bomber, missile, or space attack;
- defend threatened areas overseas, including air and sea LOCs [lines of communication], in time of crisis;
- be in a position to deploy an ABM or space defense, if needed; and
- reinforce the credibility of the flexible response strategy; enhance survival of the US population, and assist in national recovery in the aftermath of a nuclear war.[359]

The NORAD/ADCOM mission of providing warning and surveillance remained predominant: Said Gen James V. Hartinger, in March 1981, "My key mission as CINCNORAD is to support our country's flexible targeting strategy with unambiguous, reliable missile warning and precise attack assessment information—in a pre-, trans-, and post-attack environment."[360] Because of the ABM treaty, the Department of Defense continued to reduce its emphasis on defending the United States actively. Antibomber defenses were programmed to maintain a capability for limited day-to-day control of US airspace in peacetime as well as forces that could be surged in times of crisis to defend against limited attacks, raise the uncertainty that had to be considered by offensive planners, and deny any intruder a free ride in CONUS airspace. The problem of providing a follow-on interceptor (FOI) to replace attrition of the aging F-106s troubled the Air Force and eventually dictated a reorganization of the Air Defense Command.[361] In February 1975 Gen David Jones stated that it was Air Force policy to take advantage of all air defense capable assets, in part by augmenting the dedicated interceptor force with tactical fighters.[362] The F-106, as it turned out, was a very well-built aircraft. Lt Gen Alton D. Slay, deputy chief of staff for R&D, said of it, "The 106 evidently was built like a tank. It just doesn't have a problem on life."[363] After the Schlesinger cutbacks, the air defense force mustered six active and six ANG squadrons equipped with F-106s, plus four other ANG squadrons equipped with F-101s which the Air Force managed to keep. Because of attrition during a 20-year lifespan, the National Guard F-106 squadrons could be provided with only 15 aircraft per squadron instead of 18, and there were no nonoperating active (NOA) plans to support scheduled periodic maintenance and modifications. As of 1977 the Air Force and the Air Defense Command were putting together a requirement for either an F-14, F-15, or F-16 interceptor version to replace the old F-106s. These new planes would have look-down, shoot-down capabilities needed to oppose low-altitude gravity and cruise missile bombers. All these new fighters, however, were expensive and to replace the 331 interceptors in the United States would cost several billion dollars. The Ford administration requested $26 million for fiscal year 1978, looking toward a buy in 1979 of F-15s configured as FOIs "to retain the option to deploy follow-on interceptors beginning in fiscal year 1980."[364] This also would keep the F-15 production line open. Quite soon after the Carter administration took office, Defense Secretary Harold Brown reported on 22 February 1977 that the administration was deleting funding for the follow-on interceptor program. He said: "This defers commitment to the F-15 while further con- sideration is given to the potential bomber threat, other candidate systems, the possible use of tactical aircraft based in the United States, and the total future need for manned interceptors."[365] In the fiscal year 1978 budget requests, one F-101 ANG squadron was scheduled to convert to F-4s and transition to the tactical fighter force; Secretary Brown instead continued the commitment of this new F-4 squadron to the Air Defense Command, even though F-4s did not have the characteristics needed for an FOI.[366]

Since the Air Force could not get authority to procure F-15s as follow-on interceptors, Air Force Secretary John C. Stetson and General Allen realized no recourse but to shift the burden of air defense interception to the Air Force Tactical Air Command, which already owned the AWACS E-3B airborne control planes and now would increasingly use some of its tactical fighters for continental air defense. Secretary Stetson went so far as to recommend to Secretary Brown that maintenance of ADCOM as a separate Air Force command to organize, man, train, equip, and administer air defense resources was no longer justified or required. Stetson further recommended that positive benefits would derive from centralizing the development of doctrine, training, and procedures for all air defense aircraft in TAC and from placing all active force fighters, including those dedicated to air defense, under the control management of TAC.

The considerations about disestablishing ADCOM which were running very strong in 1978 were affected by two moderating influences. Canada was reported to have objected to a reorganization that would place the air defense mission in an offensive command (the Tactical Air Command). In 1978, moreover, the Air Force was considering whether it required a control management organization for space missions (space shuttle, space reconnaissance and intelligence, threat assessment and warning systems, etc.) or whether the mission should continue under decentralized management modes. If management were centralized, the Air Force element at NORAD/ADCOM could most feasibly become the nucleus of the space mission organization.[367] In the completion of the studies in progress in 1978, the Air Force concluded that management of space defense ought to be vested in ADCOM for operational employment purposes. In the reorganization of atmospheric defense effected on 1 October 1979, resource management responsibility for atmospheric defense forces was transferred to the Tactical Air Command, which was charged to organize, train, equip, administer, and maintain combat ready air defense forces to CINCNORAD/CINCAD operational control. The responsibility for the strategic air defense of the United States and North America remained with CINCNORAD/CINCAD and was not relegated to TAC as an ancillary mission.[368]

When asked to comment on the status of strategic air defenses in 1981, Gen Richard Ellis characterized them as "Very weak to poor. They are very limited and could only begin to act in response to very light attacks."[369] Air Force analysis revealed that 6 F-15 squadrons (108 unit equipment aircraft) when complemented by other aircraft and combined with modernized warning and surveillance and AWACS would provide an effective defense against a Soviet long-range aviation threat including the Backfire bomber in the 1980s. Concluded an Air Force statement in 1980, "The Air Force views an air defense dedicated force of four to six squadrons of F-15s, complemented by other aircraft, as a prudent level for the North American air defense role. The total number of air defense dedicated aircraft would remain essentially what it is today." This rrecommended air defense modernization was costed at an estimated $4 billion excluding AWACS, which was separately funded. The Air Force, however, could not specifically program the procurement of F-15s for air defense in its five-year defense plan beginning with fiscal year 1981. Nevertheless, the Tactical Air Command was authorized to organize one F-15 air defense squadron at Langley AFB, Virginia, using aircraft programmed as attrition reserve resources for its F-15 tactical fighter wings.[370]

Early in 1982 the DOD North American Air Defense Master Plan submitted to Congress on 9 March identified a continued Soviet air threat to North America, and an unacceptable risk of threat was not countered. General Allen expected the Soviet Backfire to become an intercontinental bomber, and the Soviets were beginning the production of a Blackjack bomber comparable to a B-1. Both Backfire and Blackjack had standoff mission-delivery capabilities. Allen said:

> We have not taken [air defense] very seriously, and we should now provide a plan which takes it more seriously and gradually increases the capabilities we would have. . . . We have a technical capability to do that for the first time. That is, with the over-the-horizon backscatter radars, and the look-down, shoot-down airborne radars, and fighters, we can build equipment with a good capability against low-flying aircraft, if we choose to do so. . . . In my mind the most hopeful new thing on the scene is that those airborne radars and look-down, shoot-down interceptors need not be specifically designed to the air defense mission; that is, there is no difference between an AWACS that is assigned to do a job in the United States, and an AWACS that you would send to Europe for a war. An F-15 is an F-15 and the pilot can be trained simultaneously in both missions. We have not had that situation in the past. . . . We have an advantage now that we can exploit by deploying dual purpose aircraft. Thus, it is a little bit easier to justify some improvement in continental air defense since we could reassign many of these systems to theater roles if we need to.[371]

After so many years of neglect, the DOD North American Air Defense Master Plan made significant recommendations for an effective atmospheric defense. Significant improvements included tactical warning capabilities: the tests of the OTH-B radar on the eastern coast had worked well, and two additional OTH-Bs were planned to cover the northwestern and southern approaches to the United States. Because of the polar aurora, the backscatter principle had not worked looking northward; accordingly, it was planned to refurbish the old Arctic DEW line with man-saving unattended radars. The five-year air defense projection called for 15 squadrons of air defense fighters; the 5 active squadrons were to be equipped with F-15s, and the 10 ANG squadrons were to receive F-16s, the plan being that all F-106s would be replaced by fiscal year 1986. These squadrons were equipped in 1982 with a few F-15s, F-4s, and mostly F-106s, and maintained ground alerts at sites around the periphery of the continental United States, in Alaska, and in Canada. In a crisis, Air Force, Navy, and Marine Corps fighters would be available. In a nuclear air attack scenario, the Joint Surveillance System (JSS), operated by the Federal Aviation Administration and Air Force, was not expected to survive, and the AWACS would have to take over and provide survivable command and control independently of ground-based systems. Beginning in fiscal year 1985 the Air Force hoped to buy 12 additional AWACS aircraft for North American air defense at a rate of 3 aircraft per year. These planned aircraft and others already possessed would fly random surveillance and warning patrols over coastal and northern approaches to CONUS in the critical years while the radar defense warning systems still were vulnerable. After ground-based radars were deployed, AWACS would augment and support them.[372]

As the aerial air defense of the United States was refurbished, space defense became feasible. Hard after the launching of the Soviet Sputnik in October 1957, the United States and Great Britain opened three ballistic missile early warning system (BMEWS) stations, at Clear, Alaska; Thule, Greenland; and Fylingsdale Moor in the United Kingdom. Becoming fully operational in 1962, BMEWS provided warning of a missile attack on the United Kingdom as well as North America. NORAD personnel operated the sites at Clear and Thule; Royal Air Force personnel operated at Fylingsdale Moor. In addition to BMEWS, the United States after about 1971 was exploiting satellite platforms for early warning; these satellites, deployed in synchronous equatorial orbit, transmitted data to ground stations which was immediately processed and sent to SAC, NORAD, and National Military Command System (NMCS). To supplement satellite coverage for detection of SLBMs launched from waters off the East Coast and West Coast of the United States, six existing Air Force height-finder radars (FSS-7) were pressed into service; their accuracy, however, was not sufficient to provide credible impact predictions, and long-range Soviet SLBMs would overfly their coverage. These radars were replaced by phased array radars at Otis AFB, Massachusetts, and Beale AFB, California, while a large experimental phased array radar at Eglin AFB, Florida, provided coverage for SLBM launches to the southward. In addition to surveillance and warning, space satellite system provided important global communications and navigation reckoning. By 1974, Maj Gen Lee M. Paschall, Air Force director of command, control, and communications, could point out the relevancy of space to détente and deterrence:

> We have become, since 1971, rather heavily dependent on early warning from satellite platforms. They are our principal means of warning. The whole détente is based upon, I

> believe, a mutual understanding on the part of the Soviet Union and the United States that a nuclear war is a very, very dangerous kind of thing. One of the reasons that that attitude has come to be accepted is the fact that neither side can be surprised and destroyed. The extent, then, that one endangers warning of surprise attack, one also endangers the deterrent, itself.[373]

Viewed in retrospect of Col Francis X. Kane, the American response to Sputnik was "not a full-scale military program to exploit space, but rather a highly constrained, incremental effort, with specific steps taken only as Soviet advances were clearly demonstrated." After initial US study of a satellite inspection and negation (SAINT), the United States lost interest in programs to develop an antisatellite system in the 1960s and early 1970s. Most US satellites moreover were designed in "soft" configurations as weight-saving required. Despite a continuous propaganda barrage to the effect that space should be kept peaceful, the Soviets ran test programs revealing constantly improving ASAT systems that ultimately were able to intercept targets on first orbits.[374] Maintaining the US space tracking system was an Air Force responsibility, and it was exercised by NORAD in a facility hewn out of the Cheyenne Mountain at Colorado Springs, Colorado. By 1977, when the NASA-DOD space shuttle was in the offing, it was becoming evident that the development and continued testing by the Soviets of an ASAT together with the termination of similar US programs had created a strategic asymmetry. Noted Colonel Kane, "In effect, Soviet satellites operate in a sanctuary, while those of the United States are vulnerable."[375] In 1968 the question of reorganization of the Air Force Aerospace Defense Command was tied up with studies within the Air Force as to which operating command ought to be given responsibility for a space defense mission. Also tied up was the consideration of the relative merits of centralizing versus leaving decentralized the management of space mission resources.[376] As part of his comprehensive strategic force modernization program, President Reagan announced on 2 October 1981 that the ASAT program would be accelerated, and Air Force Secretary Verne Orr expressed strong views that space was emerging as a fourth medium for military operations. Secretary Orr and General Allen asserted:

> The United States is becoming increasingly dependent on space based assets to conduct effective and efficient military operations. It is difficult to imagine how we would operate on a modern battlefield or conduct effective strategic defense without surveillance, warning, communications, meteorologies and navigation support from satellites. . . . Transition to the space shuttle will profoundly change the way we operate in space. In view of this, the Air Force must take the necessary steps to develop both the military doctrine and the operational capability to exploit this new technology.[377]

Space not only offered a realm for ballistic missile defense as conceived by President Reagan, but an enduring antisatellite element that would deny the Soviets a follow-on surveillance access to the United States after a first strike—a surveillance access that would allow them to know what military assets remained and would need a second strike—would compel them to lay down a second strike equivalent to the first, thus multiplying the relative force level that the Soviets would require. Dr James P. Wade, Jr., principal deputy under secretary of defense for research and engineering, spoke of the Soviets:

> If we could prevent him from having the eyes needed to achieve that type of [follow-on] information, then in effect we would double his requirements to provide in order to perform a second battle. That way we would increase the effectiveness of our total force without any additional weapons or additional bombs.[378]

The concept that space was a place made advisable new organizational and operational equipment to operate in and defend space. In 1981 the Colorado Springs area close to the NORAD complex was selected as the site for a consolidated space operations center (CSOC), the objective of the CSOC being to provide a secure Department of Defense space control facility that would eliminate dependence on single modes and provide a required control system capability for both satellite and space shuttle operations.[379] In 1981–82 the Air Force used an F-15 air defense fighter at Langley AFB as the bed for a prototype antisatellite weapon that consisted of a SRAM motor as a first-stage and an Altair rocket motor as a second-stage booster for a lethal system guided by a homing device. The F-15 flew to a high altitude, pulled up, and fired the rocket into normal satellite operating heights. The advantage of using an F-15 was that it could go to whatever area was advantageous to intercept a satellite target. Both OSD and the Air Force also redoubled efforts to investigate potential for developing high-energy-directed beam laser weapons for space applications.[380] On 21 June 1982 the Air Force announced the impending formation on 1 September 1983 of an Air Force Space Command (SPACECOM) with headquarters in the Colorado Springs area. The CINCNORAD/CINCAD additionally was named commander of SPACECOM, and the incumbent in the CINC position, Gen James V. Hartinger, USAF, assumed the command. The mission of SPACECOM was specified:

- Serve as the Air Force MAJCOM [major command] focal point for the strategic defense mission area.

- Manage and operate assigned USAF strategic defense assets in support of NORAD and unilateral requirements.

- Manage and operate assigned command, control, and communications assets associated with strategic defense.

- Provide air defense requirements, in coordination with TAC and on behalf of NORAD and ADCOM to Headquarters USAF.[381]

In an address in January 1983, General Hartinger asked the rhetorical question "Why a Space Command?" He answered:

> Our conception of space has changed. It is now seen that space is a place—like the land, and the sea and the air—another dimension. And it was just a matter of time until we started treating it as such. Our view is that this move will substantially contribute to deterrence, and thus international stability, by reducing uncertainty.[382]

IDEAS, CONCEPTS, DOCTRINE

NOTES

1. Senate, *Fiscal Year 1975 Authorization for Military Procurement, Research and Development, and Active Duty, Selected Reserve and Civilian Personnel Strengths: Hearings before the Committee on Armed Services,* 93d Cong., 2d sess., 1974, pt. 6:2933 (hereafter cited as *FY 1975 Military Procurement*); Senate, *Fiscal Year 1972 Authorization for Military Procurement, Research and Development, Construction and Real Estate Acquisition for the Safeguard ABM, and Reserve Strength: Hearings before the Committee on Armed Services,* 92d Cong., 1st sess., 1971, pt. 2:1644 (hereafter cited as *FY 1972 Military Procurement*).

2. House, *Department of Defense Appropriations for 1981: Hearings before a Subcommittee of the Committee on Appropriations,* 96th Cong., 2d sess., 1980, pt. 4:76 (hereafter cited as *1981 DOD Appropriations*).

3. House, *Department of Defense Appropriations for 1983: Hearings before a Subcommittee of the Committee on Appropriations,* 97th Cong., 2d sess., 1982, pt. 4:810 (hereafter cited as *1983 DOD Appropriations*).

4. Ibid.; House, *Department of Defense Appropriations for 1972: Hearings before a Subcommittee of the Committee on Appropriations,* 92d Cong., 1st sess., 1971, pt. 2:280 (hereafter cited as *1972 DOD Appropriations*).

5. "Deterrence Is Everybody's Business," *Air Force Magazine,* January 1982, 35. These are extracts from Dougherty's testimony before the Senate Foreign Relations Committee.

6. "Interview with Robert S. McNamara: Is Russia Slowing Down the Arms Race?" *U.S. News & World Report,* 12 April 1965, 52.

7. Senate, *Fiscal Year 1974 Authorization for Military Procurement, Research and Development, Construction Authorization for the Safeguard ABM, and Active Duty and Selected Reserve Strengths: Hearings before the Committee on Armed Services,* 93d Cong., 1st sess., 1973, pt. 2:1170 (hereafter cited as *FY 1974 Military Procurement*).

8. Senate, *U.S.-U.S.S.R. Strategic Policies: Hearings before a Subcommittee on Arms Control, International Law and Organization of the Committee on Foreign Relations,* 93d Cong., 2d sess., 1974, 41.

9. Senate, *Department of Defense Appropriations for Fiscal Year 1974: Hearings before a Subcommittee of the Committee on Appropriations,* 93d Cong., 1st sess., 1973, pt., 4:120 (hereafter cited as *FY 1974 DOD Appropriations*).

10. Ibid.

11. Senate, *Department of Defense Appropriations for Fiscal Year 1979: Hearings before a Subcommittee of the Committee on Appropriations,* 95th Cong., 2d sess., 1978, pt. 1:7, 314–17 (hereafter cited as *FY 1979 DOD Appropriations*); Senate, *Department of Defense Authorization for Appropriations for Fiscal Year 1980: Hearings before the Committee on Armed Services,* 96th Cong., 1st sess., 1979, pt. 1:12–15 (hereafter cited as *FY 1980 DOD Authorization*).

12. House, *Department of Defense Appropriations for 1977: Hearings before a Subcommittee of the Committee on Appropriations,* 94th Cong., 2d sess., 1976, pt. 3:41 (hereafter cited as *1977 DOD Appropriations*).

13. Senate, *Fiscal Year 1973 Authorization for Military Procurement, Research and Development, Construction Authorization for the Safeguard ABM, and Active Duty and Selected Reserve Strengths: Hearings before the Committee on Armed Services,* 92d Cong., 2d sess., 1972, pt. 3:1441–42 (hereafter cited as *FY 1973 Military Procurement*).

14. House, *Department of Defense Appropriations for 1979: Hearings before a Subcommittee of the Committee on Appropriations,* 95th Cong., 2d sess., 1978, pt. 3:647 (hereafter cited as *1979 DOD Appropriations*).

15. House, *Department of Defense Appropriations for 1971: Hearings before a Subcommittee of the Committee on Appropriations,* 91st Cong., 2d sess., 1970, pt. 1:572–73 (hereafter cited as *1971 DOD Appropriations*).

16. Ibid.

17. Senate, *Department of Defense Appropriations for Fiscal Year 1971: Hearings before a Subcommittee of the Committee on Appropriations,* 91st Cong., 2d sess., 1970, pt. 1:608–9 (hereafter cited as *FY 1971 DOD Appropriations*).
18. Senate, *Status of U.S. Strategic Power: Hearings before the Preparedness Investigating Subcommittee of the Committee on Armed Services,* 90th Cong., 2d sess., 1968, pt. 2:172–73.
19. Senate, *Department of Defense Appropriations for Fiscal Year 1970: Hearings before a Subcommittee of the Committee on Appropriations,* 91st Cong., 1st sess., 1969, pt. 1:244; pt. 4:8, 10–11 (hereafter cited as *FY 1970 DOD Appropriations*).
20. House, *Leaks of Classified National Defense Information—Stealth Aircraft: Hearings before the Investigations Subcommittee of the Committee on Armed Services,* 96th Cong., 2d sess., 1980, 104.
21. House, *Department of Defense Appropriations for 1966: Hearings before a Subcommittee of the Committee on Appropriations,* 89th Cong., 1st sess., 1965, pt. 3:815 (hereafter cited as *1966 DOD Appropriations*); Senate, *Department of Defense Appropriations for Fiscal Year 1968: Hearings before a Subcommittee of the Committee on Appropriations,* 90th Cong., 1st sess., 1967, pt. 1:284–85, 899 (hereafter cited as *FY 1968 DOD Appropriations*); Senate, *FY 1974 Military Procurement,* pt. 2:940–41.
22. Herbert F. York, "The Origins of MIRV," *The Dynamics of the Arms Race,* ed. David Carlton and Carlo Schaerf (New York: John Wiley and Sons, 1975), 31–32.
23. Thomas Powers, "Choosing a Strategy for World War III," *The Atlantic,* November 1982, 93–94.
24. Senate, *Military Implications of the Treaty on the Limitations of Anti-Ballistic Missile Systems and the Interim Agreement on Limitation of Strategic Offensive Arms: Hearings before the Committee on Armed Services,* 92d Cong., 2d sess., 1972, 267.
25. Robert S. McNamara, "The Military Role of Nuclear Weapons: Perceptions and Misperceptions," *Foreign Affairs,* Fall 1983, 79.
26. Senate, *Department of Defense Appropriations for Fiscal Year 1965: Hearings before a Subcommittee of the Committee on Appropriations and the Committee on Armed Services,* 88th Cong., 2d sess., 1964, pt. 1:31 (hereafter cited as *FY 1965 DOD Appropriations*).
27. Ibid., 32.
28. House, *1966 DOD Appropriations,* pt. 2:370; Senate, *Department of Defense Appropriations for Fiscal Year 1966: Hearings before a Subcommittee of the Committee on Appropriations and the Committee on Armed Services,* 89th Cong., 1st sess., 1965, pt. 1:214–33 (hereafter cited as *FY 1966 DOD Appropriations*); Henry Kissinger, *White House Years* (Boston: Little, Brown and Co., 1979), 215; Senate, *Status of U.S. Strategic Power: Hearings before the Preparedness Investigating Subcommittee of the Committee on Armed Services,* 90th Cong., 2d sess., 1968, pt. 2:238–39, 127.
29. Robert S. McNamara, *The Essence of Security, Reflections in Office* (New York: Harper & Row, 1968), 74; House, *Department of Defense Appropriations for 1968: Hearings before a Subcommittee of the Committee on Appropriations,* 90th Cong., 1st sess., 1967, pt. 2:159–67, 197–214 (hereafter cited as *1968 DOD Appropriations*).
30. House, *1968 DOD Appropriations.*
31. Ibid.
32. Powers, "Choosing a Strategy for a World War III," 8.
33. Senate, *FY 1966 DOD Appropriations,* 355.
34. House, *Department of Defense Appropriations for 1967: Hearings before a Subcommittee of the Committee on Appropriations,* 89th Cong., 2d sess., 1966, pt. 1:85 (hereafter cited as *1967 DOD Appropriations*).
35. Senate, *FY 1968 DOD Appropriations,* pt. 1:900.
36. House, *Department of Defense Appropriations for 1969: Hearings before a Subcommittee of the Committee on Appropriations,* 90th Cong., 2d sess., 1968, 243 (hereafter cited as *1969 DOD Appropriations*); Secretary of Defense Robert S. McNamara, *Fiscal Year 1969 to 1973 Defense Program and Defense Budget for Fiscal Year 1969* (Washington, D.C.: Government Printing Office, 1968), 53.
37. Senate, *Status of U.S. Strategic Power,* 238–39.
38. Ibid., 219.

IDEAS, CONCEPTS, DOCTRINE

39. House, *1969 DOD Appropriations,* 264; Senate, *Military Applications of the Treaty on the Limitations of Anti-Ballistic Missile Systems,* 383.
40. House, *1968 DOD Appropriations,* pt. 3:5; Ted Greenwood, *Making the MIRV: A Study of Defense Decision Making* (Cambridge, Mass.: Ballinger Publishing Co., 1975), 70.
41. Senate, *Status of U.S. Strategic Power,* pt. 2:7, 334, 220–21.
42. Ibid.
43. Senate, *FY 1970 DOD Appropriations,* pt. 1:468–69.
44. *Public Papers of the Presidents of the United States, Richard Nixon, 1969* (Washington, D.C.: Government Printing Office), 216–19; Senate, *Fiscal Year 1970 Authorization for Military Procurement, Research and Development, and Reserve Strength: Hearings before the Committee on Armed Services,* 91st Cong., 1st sess., 1969, pt. 1:148–49, 96–100; pt. 2:1700, 1709a–1709b (hereafter cited as *FY 1970 Military Procurement*); Senate, *FY 1970 DOD Appropriations,* pt. 1:453–89.
45. Senate, *FY 1970 Military Procurement,* pt. 7:45.
46. House, *Department of Defense Appropriations for 1970: Hearings before a Subcommittee of the Committee on Appropriations,* 91st Cong., 1st sess., 1969, pt. 7:45 (hereafter cited as *1970 DOD Appropriations*).
47. Ronald L. Tammen, *MIRV and the Arms Race: An Interpretation of Defense Strategy* (New York: Praeger Publishers, 1973), 115–19; Senate, *FY 1972 Military Procurement,* pt. 5:3769–70.
48. USAF Oral History Interview 955, Gen Bruce K. Holloway, 16–18 August 1977.
49. Ibid.
50. Ibid.
51. House, *1972 DOD Appropriations,* pt. 2:250, 268; Senate, *FY 1972 Military Procurement,* pt. 2:1644–58.
52. Elmo R. Zumwalt, Jr., *On Watch, A Memoir* (New York: Quadrangle/New York Times Book Co., Inc. 1976), 348–49.
53. Senate, *Military Implications of the Treaty on the Limitations of Anti-Ballistic Missile Systems,* 9–17.
54. Ibid., 160–61, 169–70, 424.
55. Tammen, *MIRV and the Arms Race,* 123–25.
56. Ibid., 125.
57. House, *Department of Defense Appropriations for 1974: Hearings before a Subcommittee of the Committee on Appropriations,* 93d Cong., 1st sess., 1973, pt. 1:461 (hereafter cited as *1974 DOD Appropriations*).
58. House, *Department of Defense Appropriations for 1975: Hearings before a Subcommittee of the Committee on Appropriations,* 93d Cong., 2d sess., 1974, pt. 1:456–57, 459–62, 499 (hereafter cited as *1975 DOD Appropriations*).
59. Ibid.; Powers, "Choosing a Strategy for World War III," 106–7.
60. Senate, *FY 1975 Military Procurement,* pt. 1:10–11, 254, 265.
61. Ibid.; House, *1975 DOD Appropriations,* pt. 1:338–39, 344–45; Senate, *Department of Defense Appropriations for Fiscal Year 1975: Hearings before a Subcommittee of the Committee on Appropriations,* 93d Cong., 2d sess., 1974, pt. 1:41–45, 123–31 (hereafter cited as *FY 1975 DOD Appropriations*); Senate, *U.S.-U.S.S.R. Strategic Policies,* 7–19, 42, 54–55.
62. House, *1975 DOD Appropriations,* pt. 1:499, pt. 2:336–41.
63. Ibid.
64. Senate, *FY 1975 Military Procurement,* pt. 7:4105–7.
65. Ibid.
66. Ibid.
67. House, *1975 DOD Appropriations,* pt. 1:308–9; Senate, *U.S.-U.S.S.R. Strategic Policies,* 41–42, 56.
68. House, *1975 DOD Appropriations,* pt. 1:308–9.
69. Senate, *FY 1975 DOD Appropriations,* pt. 1:41–45.
70. Ibid.

71. Ibid.

72. House, *Department of Defense Appropriations for Fiscal Year 1976: Hearings before a Subcommittee of the Committee on Appropriations,* 94th Cong., 1st sess., 1975, pt. 1:282 (hereafter cited as *1976 DOD Appropriations*); Senate, *Department of Defense Appropriations for Fiscal Year 1976: Hearings before a Subcommittee of the Committee on Appropriations,* 94th Cong., 2d sess., 1976, pt. 1:9 (hereafter cited as *FY 1976 DOD Appropriations*); House, *Department of Defense Appropriations for Fiscal Year 1978: Hearings before a Subcommittee of the Committee on Appropriations,* 95th Cong., 1st sess., 1977, pt. 2:210 (hereafter cited as *1978 DOD Appropriations*).

73. Senate, *FY 1976 DOD Appropriations,* pt. 4:213–14.

74. Ibid; Senate, *Fiscal Year 1978 Supplemental Military Authorization: Hearings before the Subcommittee on Research and Development of the Committee on Armed Services,* 95th Cong., 1st sess., 1977, 195–96 (hereafter cited as *FY 1978 Supplemental Military Authorization*).

75. "Targeting Flexibility Emphasized by SAC," *Aviation Week & Space Technology,* 10 May 1976, 29–34.

76. House, *1978 DOD Appropriations,* pt. 2:193, 242.

77. Ibid., 289.

78. Senate, *FY 1975 Military Procurement,* pt. 1:254.

79. Ibid; Senate, *Department of Defense Appropriations for Fiscal Year 1977: Hearings before a Subcommittee of the Committee on Appropriations,* 94th Cong., 2d sess., 1976, pt. 1:58 (hereafter cited as *FY 1977 DOD Appropriations*).

80. Senate, *FY 1977 DOD Appropriations,* pt. 1:525.

81. Senate, *Nuclear War Strategy: Hearings before the Committee on Foreign Relations,* 96th Cong., 2d sess., 1980, 38–40; Senate, *FY 1980 DOD Authorization,* pt. 1:105.

82. Senate, *FY 1975 DOD Appropriations,* pt. 5:221–31; Senate, *FY 1976 DOD Appropriations,* pt. 1:284–86.

83. Dr Francis X. Kane, "Criteria for Strategic Weapons," *Strategic Review,* Spring 1974, 44–53.

84. Powers, "Choosing a Strategy for World War III," 101–2; Mark E. Miller, *Soviet Strategic Power and Doctrine: The Quest for Superiority* (Miami: Advanced International Studies Institute, 1982), 231–32.

85. Senate, *U.S. Strategic Doctrine: Hearings before the Committee on Foreign Relations,* 97th Cong., 2d sess., 1982, 93.

86. Power, "Choosing a Strategy for World War III," 83–84; Senate, *Department of Defense Appropriations for Fiscal Year 1978: Hearings before a Subcommittee of the Committee on Appropriations,* 95th Cong., 1st sess., 1977, pt. 1:8–13, 247–48 (hereafter cited as *FY 1978 DOD Appropriations*); House, *1979 DOD Appropriations,* pt. 2:676, 712.

87. Senate, *FY 1978 DOD Appropriations,* pt. 1:196–97.

88. House, *1978 DOD Appropriations,* pt. 2:108–9.

89. Powers, "Choosing a Strategy for World War III," 85–86; Senate, *FY 1978 Supplemental Military Authorization,* 181.

90. Jimmy Carter, *Keeping Faith: Memoirs of a President* (New York: Bantam Books, 1982), 81–83.

91. House, *1978 DOD Appropriations,* pt. 7:142–59.

92. Ibid.

93. House, *Status of the MX Missile System: Hearings before the Committee on Armed Services,* 5; Powers, "Choosing a Strategy for World War III," 15.

94. Powers, "Choosing a Strategy for World War III," 96; Senate, *FY 1980 DOD Authorization,* pt. 1:74, 100, 101, 298–99, 407.

95. *Report of Secretary of Defense Harold Brown to the Congress on the FY 1980 Budge, FY 1981 Authorization Request and FY 1980–1984 Defense Programs* (Washington, D.C.: Government Printing Office, 1979), 77.

96. House, *Status of the MX Missile System*, 5–6; House, *1978 DOD Appropriations*, pt. 7:154–61; House, *1979 DOD Appropriations*, pt. 2:292, 795; pt. 3:59, 630.

97. House, *Department of Defense Appropriations for 1980: Hearings before a Subcommittee of the Committee on Appropriations*. pt. 2:385–86 (hereafter cited as *1980 DOD Appropriations*).

98. House, *Status of the MX Missile System*, 6–7; *Report of Secretary of Defense Harold Brown to the Congress on the FY 1980 Budget*, 118.

99. House, *1980 DOD Appropriations*, pt. 3:277, 289–97; Senate, *Department of Defense Authorization for Appropriations for Fiscal Year 1981: Hearings before the Committee on Armed Services*, 97th Cong., 1st sess., 1981, pt. 7:3940–41 (hereafter cited as *FY 1981 DOD Authorization*).

100. Senate, *FY 1981 DOD Authorization*, pt. 1:546; Senate, *FY 1981 DOD Authorization*, pt. 1:393–98, 318–20; Powers, "Choosing a Strategy for World War III," 96.

101. House, *Status of the MX Missile System*, passim; Senate, *FY 1981 DOD Authorization*, pt. 7:3937–84.

102. Ibid.

103. Senate, *Department of Defense Appropriations for Fiscal Year 1981: Hearings before a Subcommittee of the Committee on Appropriations*, 96th Cong., 2d sess., pt. 1:421 (hereafter cited as *FY 1981 DOD Appropriations*).

104. House, *1981 DOD Appropriations*, pt. 1:600.

105. Senate, *FY 1981 DOD Appropriations*, pt. 1:436.

106. Senate, *FY 1980 DOD Authorization, pt. 1:318–20*; Senate, *FY 1981 DOD Authorization*, pt. 1:504–5, 529–31, 534–38, 546–59; House, *1981 DOD Appropriations*, pt. 4:76–77, 80, 163.

107. Senate, *FY 1981 DOD Authorization*, pt. 2:969–70.

108. Ibid., pt. 1:424–26.

109. Ibid.

110. *Report of Secretary of Defense Harold Brown to the Congress on the FY 1982 Budget, FY 1983 Authorization Request and FY 1982–1986 Defense Programs*, 9 January 1981, 43–44.

111. House, *1981 DOD Appropriations*, pt. 1:621–22.

112. *Report of Secretary of Defense Harold Brown to the Congress on the FY 1981 Budget, FY 1982 Authorization Request and FY 1981–1985 Defense Programs* (Washington, D.C.: Government Printing Office, 1980), 5–6, 65–70.

113. Senate, *Nuclear War Strategy: Hearings before the Committee on Foreign Relations on Presidential Directive 59* (Washington, D.C.: Government Printing Office, 1981), 5–23.

114. Ibid., passim; address, "U.S. Strategic Nuclear Policy," presented by Harold Brown, Secretary of Defense at the Convocation Ceremonies for the 97th Naval War College Class, Navel War College, Newport, R.I., 20 August 1980, in *Air Force Policy Letter for Commanders: Supplement*, October 1980, 2–8.

115. *Report of Secretary of Defense Harold Brown to the Congress on the FY 1982 Budget, FY 1983 Authorization Request and FY 1982–1986 Defense Program*, 38–45.

116. Ibid.

117. *Report of Secretary of Defense Caspar W. Weinberger to the Congress on the FY 1983 Budget, FY 1984 Authorization Request and FY 1983–1987 Defense Programs* (Washington, D.C.: Government Printing Office, 1982), I–3.

118. Senate, *Department of Defense Appropriations for Fiscal Year 1982: Hearings before a Subcommittee of the Committee on Appropriations*, 97th Cong., 1st sess., 1981, pt. 1:73–74 (hereafter cited as *FY 1982 DOD Appropriations*).

119. Ibid., 4.

120. House, *Department of Defense Appropriations for 1982: Hearings before a Subcommittee of the Committee on Appropriations, H.R.*, 97th Cong., 1st sess., pt. 1:160 (hereafter cited as *1982 DOD Appropriations*).

121. Ibid., 385–87.

122. Ibid.

123. Senate, *Department of Defense Authorization for Appropriations for Fiscal Year 1982: Hearings before the Committee on Armed Services*, 97th Cong., 1st sess., pt. 7:3786 (hereafter cited as *FY 1982 DOD Authorization*).

124. Ibid.

125. Ibid., 4327–28.

126. House, *1982 DOD Appropriations*, pt. 1:319–21.

127. Senate, *FY 1981 DOD Authorization*, pt. 7:3919–20.

128. Ibid., pt. 1:78–79, 561; House, *1982 DOD Appropriations*, pt. 2:126–34, 151–55, 254–55.

129. House, *1982 DOD Appropriations*, pt. 2:126–34, 151–55, 254–55.

130. Senate, *FY 1982 DOD Authorization*, pt. 7:3874–85.

131. Ibid., pt. 2:24; Senate, *FY 1982 DOD Appropriations*, pt. 1:524–25.

132. Senate, *FY 1982 DOD Appropriations*, pt. 1:524–25.

133. *Public Papers of the Presidents of the United States: Ronald Reagan, 1981* (Washington, D.C.: Government Printing Office, 1982), 878–80.

134. Ibid.

135. Ibid.

136. Samuel P. Huntington, "The Defense Policy of the Reagan Administration, 1981–1982," in *The Reagan Presidency: An Early Assessment*, ed. Fred I. Grunstein (Baltimore, Md.: Johns Hopkins University Press, 1983), 89–90.

137. *The Annual Report of Secretary of Defense to the Congress on the FY 1983 Budget*, 8 February 1982, I–9.

138. Richard Holloran, "Pentagon Draws Up First Strategy for Fighting a Long Nuclear War," *New York Times*, 30 May 1982, 1.

139. Richard Holloran, "Reagan Aide Tells of New Strategy on Soviet Threat," *New York Times*, 22 May 1982; Thomas C. Reed, "Details of National Security Strategy; Prevailing with Pride," *Vital Speeches of the Day*, 15 August 1982, 642–45.

140. Senate, *U.S. Strategic Doctrine*, pt. 2:79; Senate, *Department of Defense Authorization for Appropriations for Fiscal Year 1984: Hearings before the Committee on Armed Services*, 98th Cong., 1st sess., 1983, pt. 1:22–24 (hereafter cited as *FY 1984 DOD Authorization*).

141. Senate, *FY 1984 DOD Authorization*, pt. 1:22–24.

142. Fred Charles Iklé, "The Reagan Defense Program: A Focus on the Strategic Imperatives," in *Strategic Review*, Spring 1982, 17.

143. Senate, *U.S. Strategic Doctrine*, 99–100.

144. Senate, *Department of Defense Appropriations for Fiscal Year 1983: Hearings before a Subcommittee of the Committee on Appropriations*, 97th Cong., 2d sess., pt. 2:78–79 (hereafter cited as *FY 1983 DOD Appropriations*).

145. Huntington, "The Defense Policy of the Reagan Administration, 1981–1982," 90.

146. Senate, *FY 1982 DOD Authorization*, pt. 7:4213.

147. Iklé, "The Reagan Defense Program."

148. Senate, *FY 1982 DOD Authorization*, pt. 7:3789.

149. House, *1982 DOD Appropriations*, pt. 2:245–46; Senate, *Department of Defense Authorization for Appropriations for Fiscal Year 1983: Hearings before the Committee on Armed Services*, 97th Cong., 2d sess., 1982, pt. 7:4180–81, 4152–53 (hereafter cited as *FY 1983 DOD Authorization*); House, *1983 DOD Appropriations*, pt. 4:290–91, 478–81.

150. Senate, *U.S. Strategic Doctrine*, 14–15.

151. *The Annual Report of Secretary of Defense, FY 1983*, III–59.

152. Senate, *FY 1983 DOD Authorization*, pt. 7:4150–58, 4168–69, 4982–85; Senate, *U.S. Strategic Doctrine*, 15–16; House, *Department of Defense Appropriations for 1984: Hearings before a Subcommittee of the Committee on Appropriations*, 98th Cong., 1st sess., 1983, pt. 8:246–47 (hereafter cited as *1984 DOD Appropriations*).

153. House, *1984 DOD Appropriations*, pt. 8:124–298, passim.

IDEAS, CONCEPTS, DOCTRINE

154. Ibid.
155. Ibid.
156. Ibid.
157. Ibid.
158. Ibid., passim, and 167–68, 291, 280.
159. Ibid., pt. 9:19–35; House, *Defense Department Authorization and Oversight Hearings, Department of Defense Authorization of Appropriations for Fiscal Year 1984, and Oversight of Previously Authorized Programs before the Committee on Armed Services*, pt. 2:231–32.
160. House, *Defense Department Authorization and Oversight Hearings, Department of Defense Authorization of Appropriations for Fiscal Year 1984, and Oversight of Previously Authorized Programs before the Committee on Armed Services*, 22–23; McNamara, *The Military Role of Nuclear Weapons*, 79.
161. House, *1984 DOD Appropriations*, pt. 8:234–35.
162. Kane, "Criteria for Strategic Weapons," 44–53; Kane, "Safeguards from SALT: U.S. Technological Strategy in an Era of Arms Control," in *The Fateful Ends and Shades of SALT*, Paul H. Nitze, James E. Dougherty, and Francis X. Kane (New York: Crane, Russak & Co., 1979), 90–132.
163. Kane, "Safeguards from SALT," 90–132.
164. House, *1984 DOD Appropriations*, pt. 9:60–62, 88.
165. Ibid.
166. Ibid., 95.
167. Kane, "Criteria for Strategic Weapons," 47.
168. Maj Gen Haywood S. Hansell, USAF, Retired, "What Kind of Posture for What Kind of Commitment," *Air Force Magazine*, March 1970, 58.
169. Senate, *FY 1983 DOD Authorization*, pt. 7:4431–33, 4442–44, 4478–80.
170. Ibid., pt. 8:4880–4906; Senate, *MX Missile Basing Mode: Hearings before a Subcommittee of the Committee on Appropriations*, 195–215.
171. Senate, *MX Missile Basing Mode*, 195–215.
172. Ibid., 214.
173. House, *1984 DOD Appropriations*, pt. 9:94.
174. Ibid., pt. 8:297–98.
175. Senate, *FY 1972 Military Procurement*. pt. 2:1598–99.
176. Senate, *FY 1966 DOD Appropriations*, pt. 1:214.
177. House, *1968 DOD Appropriations*, pt. 3:49.
178. House, *Defense Department Authorization and Oversight Hearings*, pt. 2:231–32.
179. Senate, *Status of U.S. Strategic Power*, pt. 2:312.
180. Zumwalt, *On Watch, A Memoir*, 284.
181. Pave Schratz, "The Triad—A Three Gunned Cowboy," *Shipmate*, May 1983, 5; House, *1972 DOD Appropriations*, pt. 6:295.
182. May Gen G. W. Johnson, Lt Gen D. C. Jones, and Lt Gen P. K. Carlton, "The Strategic Triad," *Ordnance*, January–February 1971, 343–46.
183. Senate, *FY 1972 Military Procurement*, pt. 1:1644–58.
184. Gen John C. Meyer, "The Synergy of the Trian," *Air University Review*, September–October 1971, 22–23.
185. Senate, *FY 1972 Military Procurement*, pt. 3:1434–38.
186. Ibid.
187. Senate, *FY 1973 Military Procurement*, pt. 3:1434; House, *1966 DOD Appropriations* pt. 3:872.
188. House, *1968 DOD Appropriations*, pt. 1:761, pt. 2:171.
189. Senate, *FY 1970 Military Procurement*, pt. 1:1024; *Office of Historian SAC, The Development of Strategic Air Command, 1946–1981*, 1 July 1982, 151.
190. Senate, *FY 1970 DOD Appropriations*, pt. 4:53.
191. House, *1976 DOD Appropriations*, pt. 1:372–73; pt. 7:809; House, *1981 DOD Appropriations*, pt. 4:83, 113.

192. Senate, *FY 1981 DOD Appropriations*, pt. 7:3918.
193. House, *1980 DOD Appropriations*, pt. 3:320; House, *1982 DOD Appropriations*, pt. 2:130–31.
194. House, *FY 1982 DOD Appropriations*, pt. 2:130–31.
195. Senate, *FY 1983 DOD Appropriations*, pt. 7:4174.
196. House, *1984 DOD Appropriations*, pt. 8:205.
197. House, *1981 DOD Appropriations*, pt. 4:149.
198. Senate, *FY 1965 DOD Appropriations*, pt. 1:837.
199. House, *1972 DOD Appropriations*, pt. 6:286.
200. Senate, *Fiscal Year 1977 Authorization for Military Procurement: Hearings before the Committee on Armed Services*, 1976, pt. 5:2884–87 (hereafter cited as *FY 1977 Military Procurement*).
201. Senate, *Status of U.S. Strategic Power*, pt. 2:253.
202. House, *1972 DOD Appropriations*, pt. 6:288.
203. Senate, *FY 1965 DOD Appropriations*, pt. 1:742–43.
204. House, *1975 DOD Appropriations*, pt. 2:315–16.
205. Senate, *FY 1982 DOD Appropriations*, pt. 1:70–71.
206. House, *1967 DOD Appropriations*, pt. 1:524–25.
207. Senate, *Department of Defense Appropriations for Fiscal Year 1967: Hearings before a Subcommittee of the Committee on Appropriations and the Committee on Armed Services*, 89th Cong., 2d sess., 1966, pt. 1:274 (hereafter cited as *FY 1967 DOD Appropriations*).
208. House, *1969 DOD Appropriations*, pt. 1:735.
209. House, *1967 DOD Appropriations*, pt. 1:290.
210. House, *Department of Defense Appropriations for 1965: Hearings before a Subcommittee of the Committee on Appropriations*, 88th Cong., 2d sess., 1964, pt. 5:399–400 (hereafter cited as *1965 DOD Appropriations*).
211. Ibid.
212. Senate, *FY 1965 DOD Appropriations*, pt. 1:712–15.
213. Senate, *FY 1966 DOD Appropriations*, pt. 1:446.
214. House, *1966 DOD Appropriations*, pt. 1:44–46, 133–39.
215. Ibid., 973; House, *1967 DOD Appropriations*, pt. 1:476, 484, pt. 3:459; Senate, *FY 1967 DOD Appropriations*, pt. 1:244.
216. Senate, *FY 1967 DOD Appropriations*, pt. 1:244.
217. Ibid., 306; House, *1970 DOD Appropriations*, pt. 1:289.
218. House, *1967 DOD Appropriations*, pt. 1:289.
219. Ibid., 477, 540–45.
220. House, *1968 DOD Appropriations*, pt. 3:35; Senate, *FY 1968 DOD Appropriations*, pt. 1:439, 857–59.
221. Senate, *FY 1968 DOD Appropriations*, 882–83; House, *1968 DOD Appropriations*, pt. 2:673.
222. House, *1968 DOD Appropriations*, pt. 2:723–24.
223. Ibid., 171.
224. House, *1969 DOD Appropriations*, pt. 1:675, 733–35; Senate, *Department of Defense Appropriations for Fiscal Year 1969: Hearings before the Subcommittee of the Committee on Appropriations*, 90th Cong., 2d sess., 1968, 7, 114 (hereafter cited as *FY 1969 DOD Appropriations*).
225. *The 1970 Defense Budget and Defense Program for Fiscal Years 1970–74, A Statement by Secretary of Defense Clark M. Clifford*, 15 January 1969, 58–60; House, *1969 DOD Appropriations*, pt. 6:271–72.
226. House, *1967 DOD Appropriations*, pt. 1:290.
227. Senate, *FY 1970 Military Procurement*, pt. 1:1024.
228. Senate, *FY 1970 DOD Appropriations*, pt. 1:55–56.
229. Senate, *FY 1970 Military Procurement*, 1:100.

230. Senate, *Department of Defense Appropriations for Fiscal Year 1973: Hearings before a Subcommittee of the Committee on Appropriations,* 92d Cong., 2d sess., 1972, pt. 4:69 (hereafter cited as *FY 1973 DOD Appropriations*).
231. Senate, *FY 1970 DOD Appropriations,* pt. 1:39–54.
232. Ibid., pt. 4:53; pt. 6:63; House, *1970 DOD Appropriations,* pt. 7:364.
233. House, *1971 DOD Appropriations,* pt. 6:691.
234. Senate, *Department of Defense Appropriations for Fiscal Year 1972: Hearings before a Subcommittee of the Committee on Appropriations,* 92d Cong., 2 sess., 1970, pt. 4:42–3 (hereafter cited as *FY 1972 DOD Appropriations*).
235. House, *1972 DOD Appropriations,* pt. 6:288–91 House, *Department of Defense Appropriations for 1973: Hearings before a Subcommittee of the Committee on Appropriations,* pt. 4:589–90.
236. Senate, *Department of Defense Appropriations for Fiscal Year 1967: Hearings before a Subcommittee of the Committee on Appropriations and the Committee on Armed Services,* 89th Cong., 2d sess., 1966, pt. 1:274 (hereafter cited as *FY 1967 DOD Appropriations*).
237. Ibid., pt. 6:2914–21, 3873–77, pt. 7:4105; House, *1975 DOD Appropriations,* pt. 1:129, pt. 2:254.
238. House, *1976 DOD Appropriations,* pt. 9:118.
239. Ibid.
240. House, *1970 DOD Appropriations,* pt. 7:376–77.
241. Senate, *FY 1970 DOD Appropriations,* pt. 4:142–43.
242. Senate, *FY 1975 Military Procurement,* pt. 7:3933–35.
243. House, *1976 DOD Appropriations,* pt. 9:118–24.
244. Ibid.
245. Ibid., 127.
246. Senate, *FY 1976 DOD Appropriations,* pt. 4:230.
247. *U.S. Defense Policy,* 3d ed. (Washington, D.C.: Congressional Quarterly, Inc., 1983), 100, 102.
248. Alton H. Quanbeck and Archie L. Wood, *Modernizing the Strategic Bomber Force: Why and How* (Washington, D.C.: Brookings Institute, 1976); Thomas C. Reed, secretary of the Air Force, to Sen Howard W. Cannon, letter, 9 March 1976; Senate, *FY 1977 Military Procurement,* pt. 5:2912–17, 2921–53; pt 2:936–43.
249. Senate, *FY 1977 Military Procurement,* pt. 2:885–87.
250. Ibid.
251. *U.S. Defense Policy,* 102.
252. Ibid; Carter, *Keeping Faith,* 80–81; House, *1978 DOD Appropriations,* pt. 2:43.
253. House, *1978 DOD Appropriations,* pt. 7:80, 166; Carter, *Keeping Faith,* 82.
254. Senate, *FY 1965 DOD Appropriations,* pt. 1:140, 357–61; House, *1978 DOD Appropriations,* pt. 7.
255. Ibid., 261; House, *1977 DOD Appropriations,* pt. 3:49.
256. House, *1966 DOD Appropriations,* pt. 3:72; Senate, *FY 1970 Military Procurement,* pt. 1:1056–57; House, *1975 DOD Appropriations,* pt. 1:130; House, *1976 DOD Appropriations,* pt. 2:173.
257. Senate, *FY 1974 DOD Appropriations,* pt. 4:712.
258. House, *1970 DOD Appropriations,* pt. 4:555–56; Senate, *FY 1974 DOD Appropriations,* pt. 4:712–13; Senate, *FY 1976 DOD Appropriations,* pt. 1:294.
259. Ibid.
260. House, *Department of Defense Appropriations for 1973: Hearings before a Subcommittee of the Committee on Appropriations,* H.R., 92d Cong., 2d sess., 1972, pt. 4:630 (hereafter cited as *1973 DOD Appropriations*); Senate, FY 1974 *Military Procurement,* pt. 2:1172.
261. Senate, *Military Implications of the Treaty on the Limitations of Anti-Ballistic Missile Systems,* 182–83; Senate, *FY 1974 DOD Appropriations,* pt. 1:71–72.
262. House, *1973 DOD Appropriations,* pt. 4:630; Senate, *FY 1975 Military Procurement,* pt. 7:3706.

263. Senate, *FY 1976 DOD Appropriations*, pt. 1:294–95; House, *1974 DOD Appropriations*, pt. 7:489–90, 1018.
264. Senate, *FY 1975 DOD Appropriations*, pt 1:510; Senate, *FY 1977 DOD Appropriations*, pt. 4:1246, 1324; Senate, *FY 1978 DOD Appropriations*, pt. 1:1022, pt. 7:262–63.
265. House, *1973 DOD Appropriations*, pt. 4:630; House, *1975 DOD Appropriations*, pt. 2:318.
266. Ibid.
267. Senate, *FY 1975 Military Procurement*, pt. 7:3838–39.
268. House, *1976 DOD Appropriations*, pt. 9:121.
269. Ibid.
270. Senate, *FY 1977 Military Procurement*, pt. 5:3001–2.
271. Senate, *FY 1978 DOD Appropriations*, pt. 7:382; House, *1978 DOD Appropriations*, pt. 2:314–15.
272. Senate, *FY 1978 DOD Appropriations*, pt. 1:212.
273. House, *1979 DOD Appropriations*, pt. 2:771–72.
272. House, *1978 DOD Appropriations*, pt. 7:65, 155, 164–65; Senate, *FY 1979 DOD Appropriations*, pt. 1:91–95; House, *1979 DOD Appropriations*, pt. 2:811–12.
275. *Public Papers of the Presidents of the United States: Jimmy Carter, 1977*, Book II (Washington, D.C.: Government Printing Office, 1978), 1197.
276. Senate, *FY 1978 Supplemental Military Authorization*, 187–88, 213.
277. Ibid.
278. House, *1978 DOD Appropriations*, pt. 7:198, 332; House, *1979 DOD Appropriations*, pt. 4:362–63.
279. House, *1979 DOD Appropriations*, pt. 4:362–63.
280. Senate, *FY 1978 Supplemental Military Authorization*, 190–91; House, *1981 DOD Appropriations*, pt. 1:45.
281. House, *1979 DOD Appropriations*, pt. 8:961.
282. House, *1978 DOD Appropriations*, pt. 7:159; Senate, *FY 1979 DOD Appropriations*, pt. 1:91, pt. 2:706–7, pt. 8:961–95.
283. Senate, *FY 1978 Supplemental Military Authorization*, 213; Senate, *FY 1980 DOD Authorization*, pt. 1:373.
284. Senate, *FY 1981 DOD Authorization*, pt. 1:496; House, *1981 DOD Appropriations*, pt. 3:1038.
285. Ibid.
286. House, *1978 DOD Appropriations*, pt. 7:157, 167, 312–13, 332; House, *1980 DOD Appropriations*, pt. 3:69.
287. House, *1980 DOD Appropriations*, pt. 3:69.
288. Senate, *FY 1980 DOD Authorization*, pt. 1:370, 373, 389.
289. House, *1980 DOD Appropriations*, pt. 1:696.
290. House, *1981 DOD Appropriations*, pt. 2:345.
291. Senate, *FY 1981 DOD Authorization*, pt. 2:615; House, *1981 DOD Appropriations*, pt. 4:88–91, 149.
292. House, *1981 DOD Appropriations*, pt. 4:88–91, 149.
293. Ibid.
294. Ibid.
295. Carter, *Keeping Faith*, 83; Howard Brown, secretary of defense, to Samuel S. Stratton, chairman, Investigations Subcommittee, House Committee on Armed Services, 19 September 1980, in House, *Leaks of Classified National Defense Information—Stealth Aircraft*, 192–93.
296. House, *1979 DOD Appropriations*, pt. 3:650; Senate, *Department of Defense Appropriations for Fiscal Year 1980: Hearings before a Subcommittee of the Committee on Appropriations*, pt. 4:203 (hereafter cited as *FY 1980 DOD Appropriations*); House, *1980 DOD Appropriations*, pt. 3:33.
297. House, *1979 DOD Appropriations*, pt. 3:650; House, *1980 DOD Appropriations*, pt. 3:33; Senate, *FY 1980 DOD Appropriations*, pt. 4:203.
298. Senate, *FY 1981 DOD Authorization*, pt. 2:615.

IDEAS, CONCEPTS, DOCTRINE

299. Brown to Stratton, letter, 19 September 1980; *U.S. Defense Policy*, 105; House, *1982 DOD Appropriations*, pt. 1:319–20; Senate, *FY 1981 DOD Authorization*, pt. 7:4274.
300. Senate, *FY 1982 DOD Authorization*, pt 7:4305–6; House, *1982 DOD Appropriations*, pt. 2:143.
301. House, *1983 DOD Appropriations*, pt. 1:825; Senate, *FY 1982 DOD Appropriations*, pt. 4:747–48; Pave Mann, "Springtime for a B–1? Choosing a New Long Range Combat Aircraft," *Military Electronics/Countermeasures*, April 1981, 28–34.
302. House, *1982 DOD Appropriations*, pt. 6:1081; Senate, *FY 1982 DOD Appropriations*, pt. 5:412–13, pt. 4:748–49; Senate, *FY 1983 DOD Authorization*, pt. 7:4560–61.
303. House, *1982 DOD Appropriations*, pt. 6:1094.
304. *U.S. Defense Policy*, 105–6.
305. "Background Statement by White House," 2 October 1981, in *New York Times*, 3 October 1981, 12.
306. House, *1982 DOD Appropriations*, pt. 2:23, 267–68; Senate, *FY 1981 DOD Authorization*, pt. 7:4596–602.
307. Senate, *FY 1981 DOD Authorization*, pt. 7:4596–602.
308. Ibid.
309. Senate, *FY 1982 DOD Appropriations*, pt. 5:480–81; Senate, *FY 1984 DOD Authorization*, pt. 1:105; *U.S. Defense Policy*, 3d ed., 106.
310. Senate, *FY 1982 DOD Appropriations*, pt. 5:480–81; *U.S. Defense Policy*, 3d ed., 106.
311. House, *1983 DOD Appropriations*, pt. 4:540.
312. Senate, *FY 1972 Military Procurement*, pt. 5:3638–39.
313. House, *Strategy and Science: Toward a National Security Policy for the 1970s; Hearings before the Subcommittee on National Security Policy and Scientific Developments of the Committee on Foreign Affairs*, H.R. (Washington, D.C.: Government Printing Office), 4–5.
314. Senate, *FY 1968 DOD Appropriations*, pt. 1:488.
315. Senate, *FY 1975 DOD Appropriations*, pt. 1:513; Senate, *FY 1966 DOD Appropriations*, pt. 1:366, 1021.
316. Senate, *FY 1970 Military Procurement*, pt. 1:991; House, *1971 DOD Appropriations*, pt. 6:105.
317. House, *1969 DOD Appropriations*, 328.
318. Senate, *FY 1972 Military Procurement*, pt. 5:3662; House, *1973 DOD Appropriations*, pt. 1:94.
319. House, *1970 DOD Appropriations*, 852; Senate, *FY 1972 Military Procurement*, pt. 2:1288–89; House, *1976 DOD Appropriations*, pt. 2:174.
320. Senate, *Status of U.S. Strategic Power*, pt. 2:210–11.
321. Senate, *FY 1970 Military Procurement*, pt. 1:1076.
323. House, *1966 DOD Appropriations*, pt. 2:372; House, *1970 DOD Appropriations*, pt. 4:339–40.
323. Senate, *FY 1966 DOD Appropriations*, pt. 1:1007; House, *1966 DOD Appropriations*, pt. 3:823.
324. House, *1966 DOD Appropriations*, pt. 3:826, 830–31.
325. Ibid., pt. 1:378, 513; House, *1967 DOD Appropriations*, pt. 1:58–65, 113, 107, 460.
326. House, *1967 DOD Appropriations*, pt. 1:58–65, 113, 107, 460.
327. House, *1969 DOD Appropriations*, pt. 2:219–20; Senate, *FY 1970 Military Procurement*, pt. 2:1809–10; Senate, *FY 1972 Military Procurement*, pt. 2:1285–86; Senate, *FY 1969 DOD Appropriations*, pt. 1:116; Senate, *FY 1968 DOD Appropriations*, pt. 1:271.
328. Senate, *FY 1968 DOD Appropriations*, pt. 1:271, 282–83; House, *1969 DOD Appropriations*, pt. 1:676–77, 732, 785, pt. 2:458; Senate, *FY 1969 DOD Appropriations*, pt. 1:90–97; Senate, *Status of U.S. Strategic Power*, 182–84, 247–52, 304–5; Senate, *FY 1970 Military Procurement*, pt. 1:987–88, 996.
329. Senate, *FY 1970 Military Procurement*, pt. 1:1070–71.
330. Senate, *FY 1970 DOD Appropriations*, pt. 4:141.
331. House, *1970 DOD Appropriations*, pt. 7:414–15; Senate, *FY 1971 DOD Appropriations*, pt. 1:70–73; Senate, *Fiscal Year 1971 Authorization for Military Procurement: Hearings before the*

Committee on Armed Services, 91st Cong., 2d sess., 1970, pt. 2:1138–39 (hereafter cited as *FY 1971 Military Procurement*).

332. Senate, *FY 1971 Military Procurement*, pt. 2:1138–39.
333. Senate, *FY 1973 Military Procurement*, pt. 2:671–73.
334. Ibid.
335. Ibid.
336. Senate, *FY 1974 DOD Appropriations*, pt. 4:66–67.
337. Frederick A. Mossir, "ABM," in *Commission in the Organization of the Government for the Conduct of Foreign Policy*, June 1975, appendixes, 4:161–65; House, *1965 DOD Appropriations*, pt. 4:48; House, *1966 DOD Appropriations*, pt. 3:355–59; House, *1967 DOD Appropriations*, pt. 186–91, 529–31.
338. Morris, "ABM" 164–67; House, *Strategy and Science*, 25–27.
339. House, *Strategy and Science*, 25–27.
340. Morris, "ABM," 167–68; Senate, *FY 1967 DOD Appropriations*, pt. 1:454–55; Senate, *FY 1968 DOD Appropriations*, pt. 1:249–53, 261, 196–97, 904–5; House, *1969 DOD Appropriations*, pt. 1:748.
341. House, *1969 DOD Appropriations*, pt. 1:7480.
342. Morris, "ABM," 168; House, *1969 DOD Appropriations*, pt. 3:4–11; Senate, *FY 1970 DOD Appropriations*, pt.1:248–53.
343. Morris, "ABM," 168–69; Senate, *FY 1973 Military Procurement*, pt. 3:1808–24.
344. Senate, *FY 1972 Military Procurement*, pt. 2:1526–32; Senate, *Military Implications of the Treaty on the Limitations of Anti-Ballistic Missile Systems*, 23, 192–93, 349.
345. Senate, *Military Implications of the Treaty on the Limitations of Anti-Ballistic Missile Systems*, 23, 192–93, 349.
346. Ibid.
347. Senate, *FY 1974 DOD Appropriations*, pt. 1:30–34, 59–62, 87; Senate, *FY 1975 DOD Appropriations*, pt. 1:115–16; Senate, *FY 1977 DOD Appropriations*, pt. 1:538, 409; Senate, *FY 1978 DOD Appropriations*, pt. 7:351–52; House, *1978 DOD Appropriations*, pt. 2:457–58, 443–50; House, *Department of Defense Appropriation Bill 1979*, 95th Cong., 2d sess., H.R. 95–1398 (Washington, D.C.: Government Printing Office, 1978), 204; Senate, *FY 1982 DOD Appropriations*, pt. 5:437; Senate, *FY 1983 DOD Authorization*, pt. 7:5000–5003.
348. Senate, *FY 1972 Military Procurement*, pt. 5:3703.
349. Senate, *FY 1975 Military Procurement*, pt. 1:9, 72–74; *Air Force Policy Letter for Commanders*, 15 April 1974 and 1 January 1975.
350. Senate, *FY 1975 Military Procurement*, pt. 1:73, 219.
351. Ibid.
352. Senate, *FY 1975 DOD Appropriations*, pt. 5:194–95.
353. House, *1975 DOD Appropriations*, pt. 2:277–78, 366; Edgar Puryear, Jr., *George S. Brown, General, U.S. Air Force: Destined for Stars* (Novato, Calif.: Presidio Press, 1983), 215.
354. Puryear, *George S. Brown*, 215.
355. Ibid.
356. House, *1974 DOD Appropriations*, pt. 2:163.
357. House, *1976 DOD Appropriations*, pt. 2:166–67; House, *1978 DOD Appropriations*, pt. 2:381–83.
358. Ibid., 382.
359. Senate, *FY 1977 DOD Appropriations*, pt. 1:82.
360. Senate, *FY 1982 DOD Authorization*, pt. 7:4223.
361. Senate, *FY 1977 DOD Appropriations*, pt. 1:82–85
362. Senate, *FY 1976 DOD Military Procurement*, pt. 4:101.
363. Senate, *FY 1977 DOD Military Procurement*, pt. 9:4892.
364. House, *1978 DOD Appropriations*, pt. 2:472–73.
365. Ibid., pt. 1:531–32; pt. 2:15, 472–73, 107.

366. Ibid., pt. 4:346; House, *1980 DOD Appropriations*, pt. 2:555–58.
367. House, *1980 DOD Appropriations*, pt. 1:726; Senate, *FY 1982 DOD Authorization*, pt. 7:3837–38.
368. Senate, *FY 1982 DOD Authorization*, pt. 7:3824.
369. Senate, *FY 1980 DOD Appropriations*, pt. 1:547; Senate, *FY 1981 DOD Authorization*, 576–77, 582; House, *1980 DOD Appropriations*, 670–72; Senate, *FY 1981 DOD Appropriations*, pt. 1:574.
370. House, *1983 DOD Appropriations*, pt. 2:397.
371. Senate, *FY 1980 DOD Appropriations*, pt. 1:547; House, *1983 DOD Appropriations*, pt. 2:397; Senate, *FY 1983 DOD Appropriations*, pt. 1:371, 388, pt. 4:108–9.
372. House, *1974 DOD Appropriations*, pt. 1:86; House, *1975 DOD Appropriations*, pt. 7:305–306; House, *1978 DOD Appropriations*, pt. 2:387–91.
373. Francis X. Kane. "Anti-Satellite Systems and U.S. Options," *Strategic Review*, Winter 1982, 56–64.
374. Ibid., 56.
375. House, *Department of Defense Resources for 1980: Hearings before a Subcommittee of the Committee on Appropriations*, pt. 2:557.
376. House, *1982 DOD Appropriations*, pt. 2:33.
377. House, *1983 DOD Appropriations*, pt. 4:579.
378. House, *1982 DOD Appropriations*, pt. 2:33, 270; Senate, *FY 1982 DOD Appropriations*, pt. 4:736.
379. House, *1982 DOD Appropriations*, pt. 2:33; Senate, *FY 1983 DOD Appropriations*, pt. 4:109.
380. Edgar Ulsamer, "Space Command: Setting the Course for the Future," *Air Force Magazine*, August 1982, 48–55; AFR 23–51, *Space Command*, 25 July 1983; Gen James V. Hartinger, "The New Space Command," *Signal*, March 1983, 23–26.
381. Hartinger, "Space Command," 23–26.
382. Ibid.

Gen Lucius D. Clay, commander in chief of the North American Air Defense Command.

Col (later Gen) David C. Jones, Air Force chief of staff.

Elliott L. Richardson, secretary of defense.

Gen Charles A. Gabriel, Air Force chief of staff.

Adm Elmo R. Zumwalt, Jr., chief of naval operations.

Gen Richard H. Ellis, Joint Chiefs of Staff director of strategic target planning.

Lt Gen Otto J. Glasser, Air Force deputy chief of staff for research and development.

CHAPTER 6

TWO DECADES OF TACTICAL AIR COMMAND DEVELOPMENT, 1964-84

"If we had asked the Congress in 1961 for $3 billion to buy iron bombs, I am sure we would not have gotten it," opined Gen John P. McConnell, Air Force chief of staff, in 1965. "Before that time ... the national strategy was that we would use nuclear weapons in places of our own choosing and whenever we wanted to." In line with this judgment, General McConnell was willing to accept a proposition that the dependence upon a nuclear "trip-wire" strategy for the defense of Western Europe had led to a neglect in fielding conventional military capabilities, including tactical air power.[1]

Early Emphasis on a European Nuclear Defense

When the North Atlantic Treaty Organization (NATO) allies could not meet the Lisbon Conference goals set in February 1952 for 96 divisions, of which 40 would be available from M-day through M-plus seven, further studies at the Supreme Headquarters Allied Powers Europe (SHAPE) recognized that there was danger that the allied structure would crumble before it could even take shape. It was recognized that greater reliance would need to be placed upon the use of nuclear weapons at the outset of Soviet aggression. This deterrent strategy was formally stated in Military Committee Document 14/2 (MC14/2). Adm Thomas J. Moorer, chairman of the Joint Chiefs of Staff, reminded a Senate committee that "up to the mid-1960s, the NATO strategy could be described as a 'trip-wire' strategy. The concept was that the first Soviet tank that came across from East Germany to West Germany would bring about an attack of nuclear weapons in Western Europe."[2]

Noted Lt Gen James Ferguson, Air Force deputy chief of staff for research and development:

> When the national policy dictated reliance on massive retaliation, Air Force development became heavily concentrated in the strategic/defense area. In fact, nearly all of the available resources were consumed in satisfying these overwhelming requirements. These were "lean years" for tactical developments, and particularly conventional weapons.[3]

At the end of fiscal year 1961 the worldwide Air Force tactical fighter force bottomed out at 16 wings; only 3 basic fighter types were developed after 1957, namely the F-106 interceptor, the F-4, and the F-111.⁴ Of these times in the late 1950s, Lt Gen Arthur C. Agan recalled that General LeMay as Air Force chief of staff wanted bombers, not fighters, and, whether knowingly or not, had loaded the Air Staff with SAC people who were not well acquainted with things like "air superiority." The going idea was that hostile air forces could best be destroyed on the ground by bombing attacks at their airfields.⁵

At the outset of the Kennedy administration in 1961 Secretary McNamara formalized and codified a need for a shift of strategy both in NATO and US defense away from principal reliance on nuclear weapons to the development of more nonnuclear strength. This shift in strategy was prompted by an awareness of Soviet nuclear strength and an absence of "low level" military capability to respond to minor provocations.⁶ McNamara pressed two major themes on the NATO allies:

> The first was realism—the need to match NATO's strategic assumptions and plans with its *de facto* budgets and forces. The second was the need for a balance in NATO's and the Warsaw Pact's over-all capabilities. We argued that only the existence of a balanced force could convince an aggressor beyond doubt that whatever effort he might make—would be matched by the Alliance. We emphasized that only under these conditions would it become obvious to the Soviet Union that military force of any kind or at any level would be useless as a means to secure political ends.⁷

Ironically, in 1961–66 when he was considering increases in conventional military capabilities, McNamara also increased the number of US nuclear weapons stored and available for use in Western Europe by about 85 percent. In the early 1960s the largest NATO-wide reequipment was the Lockheed F-104 Starfighter, adopted with a nuclear strike capability by the air forces of Belgium, Canada, West Germany, Italy, Holland, and Turkey. The Mirage IVAs of the French *Force de Frappé* and the Royal Air Force's Victor and Vulcan bombers were operational by 1965. McNamara said in early 1966:

> As far as Europe is concerned, it has always been recognized that a massive Soviet conventional attack on Western Europe by large numbers of Soviet divisions might require the use of nuclear weapons—tactical nuclear weapons, for example. We are prepared to do that insofar as having the capability is concerned.⁸

In the Berlin crisis of 1961 President Kennedy immediately augmented US general purpose forces by mobilizing National Guard and Reserve forces. After this crisis, apparently as an informal and certainly unpublicized planning objective, President Kennedy accepted the objective of preparing forces for a "two-and-one-half-war" strategy sufficient to mount an initial 90-day defense of Western Europe against a Soviet attack, make a sustained defense against an all-out Chinese attack on either Southeast Asia or Korea, and meet a contingency somewhere else, perhaps the Middle East. General Wheeler subsequently remarked that the "2-1/2-war" concept was only "loosely expressed" and was never budgetarily supported. For his own part, General McConnell said in 1968: "The military strategy calls for the capability to respond to simultaneous contingencies; for example, conflict in Vietnam and Korea plus maintaining an adequate capability for an initial defense of NATO."[9]

In the US augmentation of general purpose forces, Air Force tactical fighter wings increased in number from 16 at the end of fiscal year 1961 to 21 in fiscal year 1965. In the McNamara projection, 24 tactical fighter wings were authorized. General McConnell said that McNamara personally selected the number 24, saying, "That looks about right, 24 wings. . . . I do not know whether you need 24 wings. I cannot say whether you need 24 wings, whether you need 19 wings, or whether you need — wings. It is purely a matter of judgment." As a matter of fact, at the end of fiscal year 1966, the Air Force roster showed 27 tactical fighter wing numbered "flags," but the number of people and planes did not equate to this size flag force.[10] The expansion of the tactical fighter force was handled first by the retention of old F-100s that had been slated for retirement; the F-100s had a ground attack capability, and they could be refueled in the air, allowing them to be rapidly deployed overseas. Project Forecast had suggested that Air Force needs for an air superiority fighter in the 1970s would be met best by variants of the Navy-developed F-4, "optimized for the air superiority role." The Office of the Secretary of Defense and the Air Force in early 1962 agreed that the Air Force would purchase a number of F-4s to meet the requirements for an air superiority fighter and to fill a void left by the decision to discontinue procurement of F-105s.[11] Although the development of the F-111 (formerly the TFX) would be complete and the aircraft would enter the tactical fighter inventory, still more aircraft would need to be procured, and the decision as to their characteristics involved a substantial rethinking of the tactical air mission.

As a basic approach the Air Force had always argued that its fighters could perform the four tasks of counterair, air superiority, interdiction, and close air support. "If there is justification for specialization, it must be on the basis that it can perform the job more effectively than an aircraft that can do multimissions," said General Momyer, Air Force director of operational requirements. Momyer further argued that multipurpose fighters had been effective in World War II, in Korea, and in Southeast Asia, when F-4s had gone into North Vietnam and also provided close air support in South Vietnam.[12] As it happened, Secretary McNamara had been correct in his demands that the Air Force accept the Navy-developed F-4 instead of procuring more F-105 fighters, but from this he drew a belief that

> the basic premise . . . that one aircraft would serve the requirements of both Navy and Air Force is absolutely sound and ought to be adhered to in our future aircraft design to the greatest extent feasible. . . . The past belief is that the Navy required a different airplane than the Air Force, and, therefore, you should have the F-105 for the Air Force and the F-4 for the Navy. We have no doubt that to be absolutely wrong. We should never follow such a belief in the future.[13]

Secretary McNamara strongly supported the development of the missions of the F-111 with a high degree of commonality for both the Air Force (F-111A) and the Navy (F-111B). Admiral Moorer recalled: "During the time I was Chief of Naval Operations, we could get any amount of money put in the budget for that airplane even though it had a series of technical and performance difficulties from the Navy point of view."[14]

Although the Air Force's initial special operational requirement (SOR) looked toward a nuclear-capable F-111 suited for flexible employments with a variable sweep wing and afterburning turbofan power, the F-111A ultimately developed into a low-level, all-weather, tactical strike aircraft. At the same time, the Navy continued to want a multipurpose fighter optimized for a fleet air defense interceptor role, which the F-111B could not fulfill.[15] On the other hand, the Navy commenced development of a visual light-attack (VAL) aircraft which was optimized for close air support with new integrated bombing systems, subsonic speed, and large ordnance payload, and Secretary McNamara asked General LeMay to consider taking this aircraft—to be designated the A-7—as a close-air-support fighter. LeMay let it be known that he was "unenthusiastic" about the slow-flying A-7, and Lt Gen James Ferguson provided a rationale critical of an aircraft that could not fight:

> The airplane [providing close air support] must be able to exist in the air before it can conduct ground operations. If the airplane has no air-to-air fighting capability, it stays on the bench until air superiority has either been granted or won by some other means. In the last few years, we have not had to fight hostile air before we could attack on the ground; but nevertheless, we might—within a matter of minutes—do just that. In our opinion, we must be constantly prepared to do so.[16]

Although there was complete agreement within the Air Force on the need to get and maintain air superiority for successful air-to-ground operations, there was no universal agreement on the need for a specialized air superiority fighter. In 1965 parameters for an F-X tactical fighter were in work, and General McConnell remembered: "We had a very difficult time in satisfying all the people who had to be satisfied as to what the F-X was going to be.... There were a lot of people in the Air Force who wanted to make that F-X into another F-4 type aircraft." In Vietnam on an inspection visit, Senator Symington said that he "could not find a single pilot who was not pleading for a true air superiority fighter." Generals Ferguson and Momyer, however, were said to believe that the United States ought to have a multipurpose follow-on fighter. In the OSD Systems Analysis Office, Alain Enthoven argued for the effectiveness of cheaper airplanes in large numbers over high-cost specialized planes in scarce numbers. On 29 April 1965 the first Air Force letter on the F-X instructed the Air Force Systems Command to initiate studies on a low-cost, simple, visual air-to-ground attack aircraft with the capability of visual air-to-air combat in the 1970–75 time frame. On 23–25 June 1965 Gen Walter C. Sweeney, Jr., called together a Tactical Air Command Tactical Fighter Tactics and Weapons System Panel at Langley AFB and endorsed the twin ideas that enemy aircraft would best be destroyed on the ground and that what was needed was flexible air power rather than a single-purpose fighter.[17]

TWO DECADES OF TAC DEVELOPMENT

In Washington in 1964 as assistant deputy chief of staff for plans and operations at Headquarters USAF, Maj Gen Arthur C. Agan came to believe that the Air Staff was so dominated by Strategic Air Command experience that things like "air superiority" were not well known or stated. Agan assembled a colloquium of fighter aces who had each shot down more than 15 aircraft to discuss the need for a new air superiority fighter. He prepared a paper on "Air Force Doctrine on Air Superiority" which General McConnell sent out over his signature on 3 May 1965 to all major commands and operating agencies. The paper, among other points, bridged the hiatus between arguments for destruction of hostile air forces in the air or at base airfields, thusly:

> Enemy airpower is destroyed in two ways: in the air and on the surface. Both methods are essential parts of counterair operations and should be carried out concurrently. Regardless of the tactical air task or mode of attack, survival of the fighter aircraft we commit is at some time likely to hinge on air-to-air capability. Consequently, if *either* air-to-air or air-to-surface attacks are to succeed with attrition acceptable to us, we must provide aircraft, armament, and training which will succeed in air-to-air combat against the best enemy aircraft. For air-to-air combat we should *seek* advantages in such performance parameters as acceleration, climb, maximum speed, ceiling maneuverability, sighting equipment, and armament capability. Depending on what we actually achieve, we must adapt tactics to fight best against a given enemy.

The paper also pointed out what was resulting from the fact that the North Vietnamese MiG forces in Southeast Asia were operating in a political sanctuary:

> If political sanctuaries are permitted in the air battle, a large share of combat will be air-to-air—at times and places of the enemy's choosing. Thus, depending upon the effectiveness of air cover, aircraft on strike missions near a sanctuary will require the ability to drop their external ordnance and survive in air-to-air combat.

The paper concluded:

> Reconnaissance, close support, or interdiction may hold the key to a particular facet of tactical air operations; but if an enemy makes a determined bid for air superiority, the indispensable condition for success in joint operations will be our ability to seek out and destroy the enemy fighter forces.[18]

At the same time that Air Force thinking was turning toward a need for a specialized air-to-air fighter, Secretary McNamara and Doctor Brown, the latter then serving as director of defense research and engineering, demanded that the Air Force procure some less expensive aircraft specifically for ground attack support missions, and were particularly insistent that the Air Force look at the Navy's VAL—now designated the A-7A. The A-7 was to be a subsonic, single-seat, single-engine, relatively long-range plane that could carry a large bomb load. In Senate hearings, Senator Symington decried the news that the Air Force might receive A-7s: "Very sad, as I look at airplane development, the tactical situation, pretty soon we are going to have a plane that flies backwards so as to be sure to support ground troops properly."[19]

IDEAS, CONCEPTS, DOCTRINE

General McConnell would later tell how he came to agree to accept modified A-7As under an A-7D designation with changes including more powerful engines, albeit in a considerably lesser number of wings than the secretary of defense programmed for the Air Force:

> We were under considerable pressure by certain elements in the military and by certain elements in Congress because they said we had never provided a capability or a specialized airplane for close support of the Army. At that time, the Army was coming in with a strong close air support proposal which was the AH-56, the advanced helicopter. In order to demonstrate that we did want to give the Army every possible means of close support—and I know that we can do it better than they can, particularly with the AH-56—we opted for the A-7 in sufficient quantities to provide close air support for the Army in an environment that did not have intensive defenses. Close air support for the Army in an intensive defense environment would have to continue to be given by the F-4 and in some cases, the F-111. At that time we thought we could buy the A-7 airplane for less than half what an F-4 would cost, and for close air support of troops in a relatively permissive environment it is a good aircraft—was, and still is. It has two drawbacks: One is that it takes a long runway for takeoff, longer than the F-4E does. It has a longer loiter capability, so that it can be in the vicinity of the troops for a longer period of time. But in an environment of intensive defense you can't loiter anyhow. Now, when the price of this aircraft went up to $2.8 million, and in addition to that OSD wanted to start substituting these aircraft to the tune of . . . a 1-for-1 basis with the F-111 and in my opinion it was getting me in a corner.[20]

In November 1965 in the preparation of the fiscal year 1967 appropriations request, General McConnell personally recommended to the secretary of defense that the Air Force buy a limited number of A-7D aircraft to provide close air support in a permissive environment. The secretary of defense promptly programmed several more wings of A-7s than McConnell asked for or believed advisable. McConnell bought the A-7 because "it was supposed to be a reasonably cheap modification. . . . We bought it for one purpose, and that was to be able to supply heavy payloads with long loiter time in direct close air support of the ground forces." But the modification of the A-7 for Air Force use ran its cost up substantially, so that it was cost-competitive with the F-4E. The A-7 also turned out to need a longer hard-surfaced takeoff runway than the F-4. It thus cost too much and had to be based far back of front lines. When fiscal year 1970 appropriations requests were being put together, McConnell learned that he could have expected to buy 120 F-4E aircraft for the money programmed to buy 128 A-7s. At this time 74 A-7s were already in procurement, and McConnell attempted to "eat those 74 A-7s or otherwise dispose of them in some way" so that he could use the ongoing funds to secure F-4Es. He attempted to get Admiral Moorer to accept the Air Force A-7s, but the Navy could not use the planes without retrofitting them at a considerable expense. There was no way that the Air Force could support the logistical support and training costs for only 74 aircraft. And since McConnell could not find a taker for the planes he was compelled to seek a solution programming the Air Force for three wings of A-7s "as the best way out of a decision which, frankly, I wished we had never gotten into in the first place, but we were sort of forced into it by circumstances."[21]

In the view of Gen Gabriel P. Disosway, who assumed command of the Tactical Air Command in August 1965, the "philosophy that you are going to build one airplane to do everything" might have been "all right" in World War II but was no longer applicable in 1965.[22] The Air Force's decision to request procurement of the A-7—a specialized close-air-support aircraft—in November 1965 was referenced on 24 November when Headquarters USAF released a statement of work for parametric design studies for a more sophisticated higher performance aircraft as an air superiority replacement for the F-4. "If you are going to get into a fight with a sophisticated air force, then you have to have fighters to clean him out before you can use the A-7," General McConnell explained. On 8 February 1966 the commanders of the Tactical Air Command, Pacific Air Forces, and the United States Air Forces in Europe recommended to General McConnell that study for the new F-X fighter "must be optimized for the air-to-air role" and "that any attempt to configure the F-X for an air-to-ground mission will result in a second best aircraft, incapable of competing with modern hostile aircraft in aerial combat." On 23 March 1966 the Air Force awarded contracts to Lockheed, North American, and Boeing for parametric design of two classes of fighters, one for air superiority and one for air-to-ground attack.[23] In addition to the F-X air superiority fighter, the Air Force laid plans for an A-X close-air-support aircraft. In June 1966 General McConnell directed the Air Staff to make analyses of what areas of close air support were not being filled to the Army's satisfaction. When completed in August 1966, the analyses showed that the Army was generally satisfied with close air support in Vietnam but that there was a gap in Air Force capabilities that the Army was bridging with armed helicopters, namely the escorting of troop-carrying helicopters and the delivery of suppressive fire during airmobile assaults. There was a need for a follow-on Air Force close-air-support aircraft since it was already evident that the A-7 was too costly and lacked desired CAS performance capabilities. In September 1966 General McConnell directed immediate and positive action to obtain a specialized A-X air-support aircraft for the 1970s.[24]

Although the Air Force was moving toward increased tactical fighter aircraft specialization in 1966, the concept was not completely accepted. Dissatisfaction with the F-111B version caused the Navy to begin working out proposals for a new Navy VFAX fighter, which would desirably be a single plane that could accomplish both attack and fighter missions. On 3 May 1966 Secretary McNamara directed the establishment of a joint Air Force/Navy review team to set up commonality of the F-X and VFAX, and in General McConnell's words, "when you get two services, one of them wanting the same airplane to do something else, you have a hard time coming to agreement." Eventually, on 1 December 1967, a joint memorandum from the Air Force and Navy assistant secretaries for research and development reported that the requirements of the two services could not be met by one aircraft but that there could be a high degree of commonality in propulsion and avionics. McConnell also admitted that the "Air Force itself could not quite make up its mind about what exactly it wanted in the F-X.... Some people wanted it to have an overall capability, others wanted it to have only an air superiority capability."[25] McConnell wanted the F-X to have "a superiority capability only." In May and June 1968 he explained the need for increased specialization to the Preparedness Investigating Subcommittee of the Senate Committee on Armed Services:

> We believe that the basic requirement is for a balanced force consisting of a family of weapon systems, each designed to do one mission extremely well, and one or more other missions credibly well. To this extent, aircraft in the force will retain, to some extent, a multipurpose character designed to enhance flexibility in application to a variety of conflict situations. In view of this requirement, the force should include aircraft optimized for: (1) Air superiority and capable of operating in the enemy's defensive environment with superior performance against first-line enemy aircraft. (2) Close air support with capabilities for extended range or loiter, with heavy payloads, a high degree of weapons delivery accuracy, and high survivability. (3) Deep penetration and interdiction and capable of performing a variety of day, night, and all-weather attack missions.... There are a lot of people in the Air Force who wanted to make the F-X into another F-4 type of aircraft. We finally decided—and I hope there is no one who still disagrees—that this aircraft is going to be an air superiority fighter. Its purpose will be to gain air superiority over the enemy, and absolute air supremacy over the battlefield. We do not want to degrade it for anything else.[26]

The marked increase in US general purpose and tactical air forces had been sparked by the 1961 Berlin confrontation with the Soviet Union and was designed in no small part to reduce reliance on the old MC 14/2 nuclear trip-wire strategy defending NATO. After 1961 the Soviets relaxed tension in Europe and in 1964 made a cut of possibly 15,000 troops in East Germany. Impatient with American leadership, President Charles de Gaulle led the withdrawal in 1967 of French military forces from the unified NATO commands. At the request of the French, the NATO allies withdrew all forces from France, necessarily relocating NATO headquarters in Belgium and its forces principally in the United Kingdom and the Federal Republic of Germany. In December 1967 the United States recommended a new strategy to the NATO Council of Ministers. This strategy became known as Flexible and Appropriate Response or MC 14/3. Adoption of this strategy was one of the reasons given by France for withdrawing from the NATO integrated military structure. The flexible response strategy called for conventional and nuclear forces, doctrine, and planning which could deter Warsaw Pact aggression. If deterrence failed, NATO countries would seek to defeat aggression at any level of attack (conventional or nuclear). If direct defense failed, NATO allies would use deliberately increased military force as necessary to make the cost and risk disproportionate to the enemy's objectives and cause him to cease his aggression and to withdraw. In the event of general nuclear war, NATO countries would inflict extensive damage on the Soviet Union and other Warsaw Pact countries. This objective would be accomplished in conjunction with the strategic forces of the NATO nuclear powers.[27]

The announced decision in NATO to emphasize conventional aspects of defense placed a greater need for conventional forces on the NATO allies. For the United States 1967–68 became a time of force readjustments in Europe caused both by de Gaulle's demand that all US forces leave France by 1 April 1967 and a need to reduce the adverse US trade balance of international payments. Operation FRELOC got US forces out of France as scheduled but involved establishment of a new logistical support infrastructure running from the United Kingdom through the Benelux countries to Germany — a line of communications potentially vulnerable to a Warsaw Pact attack across the North German Plain.[28] During 1968 the US Army withdrew roughly 28,500 troops from Germany in Operation Reforger, the package including two-thirds of the 24th Division, an armored cavalry regiment, and combat support units — all remaining assigned to the US European Command and pledged to be returned quickly in the event of impending hostilities. Crested Cap was the Air Force's companion package, returning four tactical fighter squadrons (4,800 military spaces) from Germany to the United States for dual basing, and promising to return them when needed.[29]

In justification of the new NATO strategy and also the dual basing of Americans, Secretary McNamara believed that the most likely kind of conflict in Europe would be one arising from miscalculations during a period of tension rather than a deliberately preplanned Soviet attack. It was possible that the Soviets might attack following a concealed mobilization, but such a mobilization would need to be large and therefore would be difficult to conceal. As a result of political tension providing warning, McNamara concluded that the United States could deploy forces back to Europe in adequate time. The Joint Chiefs of Staff on the other hand held that in view of the Soviet threat there was no military basis for the redeployment of US forces from Europe to the United States. They also theorized that the period of warning would be less than McNamara believed. Some of the prospective confusion over warning surfaced in the spring and summer of 1968 prior to the Soviet march of a force, including five divisions, into Czechoslovakia. Remembered Gen David A. Burchinal, deputy commander of the US European Command:

> Now we had every political indicator and warning in the world that the Soviets might move into Czechoslovakia, no one said they would move, no one knew they were going to make the move, and so prior to that time we did not take any particular precautionary measures that that situation might have warranted. So while we say political warning could exist or the indicators would exist, there is a grave question in our minds whether that will serve as an adequate basis upon which the necessary political decisions could be taken to return, let us say, the dual based forces from the United States to Europe.[30]

Even though Air Force planning had to provide a capability to operate wherever directed by national authority, Maj Gen George S. Boylan, Jr., director of aerospace programs and deputy chief of staff for programs and resources, admitted that the planners he knew were very sensitive to NATO requirements:

> At all times ... I think every US military planner must keep right in front of him the capabilities of the Soviet Union, and it is against this highest threat that the US Air Force might ultimately be called on to perform. Certainly, through our NATO commitments, we face Soviet capabilities across Western Europe. Therefore, it is from this aspect of the threat that high performance capabilities must be acquired for weapon systems.[31]

In analyzing the European situation, however, Enthoven made the case for close air support of combat troops—or air capabilities contributing immediately to meeting a hostile attack in high-intensity conflict—as being of principal importance. This would be more valuable than deep interdiction that would make a contribution too late to affect short, high-intensity warfare. After the Air Force tactical air forces had initially expanded from 16 to 21 wings in 1961-62, Enthoven had recommended that the largest gains in tactical air capability could be managed by improving weapons effectiveness and delivery accuracy, and by reducing vulnerability rather than buying more aircraft. Enthoven was skeptical of the F-111 because it was expensive, apt to encounter heavy attrition in deep penetrations of enemy territory, and could be committed to deep interdiction in Europe. In August 1967 Secretary McNamara circulated a draft presidential memorandum (DPM) on Tactical Air Forces for fiscal year 1969 and for five years in the future. As a planning guide, McNamara wanted "to fight indefinitely in Asia while holding enough forces to fight in Europe" for a number of days that were not disclosed. Presidential Advisor Henry Kissinger subsequently wrote that the NATO strategy in 1969 was to stage a 90-day nonnuclear defense of Europe. In view of the promised bombing accuracy of the A-7D aircraft, OSD projected the reduction of Air Force tactical fighter wings worldwide from 24 to 23 wings. The Air Force made a reclama to this DPM without getting it changed. The DPM finalized on 4 January 1968 fixed the five-year Air Force tactical fighter wing strength at 23 wings, a strength which the Joint Chiefs of Staff subsequently noted might be adequate for the initial defense of NATO under optimum employment conditions but would leave a considerable risk that there would be inadequate tactical air forces available to assist any ally elsewhere or perform minor contingency operations. General McConnell strongly disagreed with the redirection:

> In terms of air-to-air combat against the Soviets, we clearly have to have superiority, because if you do not isolate the battlefield and gain air superiority, practically all over the theater, and air supremacy over any given segment of the battlefield at any one time, then you are not going to be able to fight. The ground forces are going to get chewed up by the enemy aircraft.[32]

Ordering TACAIR Resources for Realistic Deterrence

In Europe the Soviet-led invasion of Czechoslovakia in August 1968 seriously set back what had seemed to be a thawing of cold war relations and forced a reassessment of Soviet nations and their intentions. The occupation of

Czechoslovakia, as it turned out, marked the beginning of a gradual but sustained augmentation of Soviet and Warsaw Pact forces in Eastern Europe. Both manpower and new equipment — tanks, nuclear-capable rockets, and cannon and air defense missiles — were added.[33] On the worldwide scene, however, the Soviet invasion of Czechoslovakia brought a ray of hope to Henry Kissinger, who would become assistant for National Security Affairs to President Richard Nixon as the latter assumed office in 1969. In 1956 Communist China had supported the Soviet Union during upheavals in Poland and Hungary, but in 1968 China offered abusive condemnation of the Soviet Union. On the philosophical level, Kissinger asked through the National Security Council and got an interdepartmental group examination of the assumptions of the Kennedy-Johnson concept of preparations of general purpose forces for two and one-half wars. In his foreign policy report to Congress on 18 February 1970, Nixon stated that he would harmonize doctrine and capability by following a "1-1/2-war" strategy: maintaining general purpose forces adequate for simultaneously meeting a major Communist attack in either Europe or Asia, and contending with a contingency elsewhere. While returning from an Asian visit, Nixon first informally outlined the points of what would become known as the Nixon Doctrine at a press conference in Guam on 25 July 1969, and fully expounded the doctrine in an 18 February 1970 address to Congress. He said:

> The United States will keep all its treaty commitments. We shall provide a shield if a nuclear power threatens the freedom of a nation allied with us, or of a nation whose survival we consider vital to our security and the security of the region as a whole. In cases involving other types of aggression we shall furnish military and economic assistance when requested and as appropriate. But we shall look to the nation directly threatened to assume the primary responsibility of providing the manpower for its defense.[34]

In explaining the "1-1/2-war" concept, Secretary of Defense Melvin Laird and Gen Earle G. Wheeler, director of Army plans, stressed the fact that Secretary McNamara had demanded that the services prepare budget requests on the basis of preparation of general purpose forces for two major wars and a minor war. "They would prepare their budgets, and the budget figures they had worked long and hard on would mean very little because they weren't really in the ball park of what the country could support," Laird said. General Wheeler added: "The forces provided by the budget of past years could not support a 2-1/2-war concept, loosely expressed. We, in effect, were kidding ourselves by having a strategic concept which envisioned such a capability." Under the new initiatives to support what was called "A Strategy of Realistic Deterrence," Laird planned to indicate what the country could support in military expenditures: "If we price out where we are in our budget today, we are realistically in a position — if we discount the present Vietnam situation — where we could support one major war and one minor conflict." Now, he added, "The military departments and the Joint Chiefs of Staff will be asked to develop programs and forces under the total fiscal guidance, and to propose equal cost trade-offs which, in their judgement, will provide a more

IDEAS, CONCEPTS, DOCTRINE

balanced program within the total resources available." Whereas the Kennedy-Johnson administration had placed heavy reliance on the use of the draft to meet manpower needs, the Nixon administration expected to field an "all volunteer" military force, and Secretary Laird expected to place heavy reliance upon reserve forces as a part of what he described as a "total force" concept: "Members of the National Guard and Reserve, instead of draftees, will be the initial and primary source for augmentation of the active forces in any future emergency requiring a rapid and substantial expansion of the active forces."[35]

In March 1969 the Bureau of the Budget directed a $6-billion reduction in the federal budget, and the Defense Department and Air Force met substantial reductions. On the eve of his retirement at the end of July, General McConnell faced "a sobering conclusion" that he was leaving the Air Force with "less airpower than when I became its Chief of Staff 4-1/2 years ago." This in part was a result of the fact that the Air Force had been compelled to fight in Vietnam without increased appropriations. McConnell said:

> I want next to make a few observations about the management of the Vietnam war. Hopefully, this conflict can be resolved but the problems are grave; we face a determined enemy abroad and increasing impatience at home. When we are far enough downstream from this conflict, I believe that the evaluation by thoughtful students will produce the conclusion that:
>
> (1) It was by far the most closely managed war this country has ever fought. Secretary Seamans pointed out that our 1970 budget expressed in 1964 dollars is about the same as the 1964 budget. This means that we have fought the war to a considerable extent at the expense of modernization. Although we have carefully husbanded our resources in the process, I will make no pretense that waste cannot be found, but on the whole, I believe the effort in Vietnam and Southeast Asia has been well managed.
>
> (2) It will also be found that the professional military performed admirably under trying circumstances. They were again given limited objectives as in Korea—the only previous conflict in which they had been politically restrained from attempting to gain military victory. Under these restrictions our commanders in the field could not take advantage of some unanticipated tactical or strategic opportunities. While airpower in Vietnam has been used for close support more extensively than ever before, the overall limitations on its use have prevented its being decisive.... The success of airpower in achieving decisive results is predicated on proper employment to exploit its unique capabilities. These specific capabilities are range, mobility, responsiveness and tactical versatility. The results of these capabilities are manifest most decisively when offensive air forces strike at the source of enemy strength. In the case of North Vietnam, my preference would have [been] to destroy or neutralize his entire military, industrial and logistics base, rather than conducting selective and piecemeal attacks on road and rail nets, and certain power production and industrial facilities. Permission to conduct extensive operations against the complete military air defense environment of North Vietnam was never granted and [that factor] contributed to constant degradation of strike effectiveness. In the case of South Vietnam, our successes in supporting ground forces were realized in spite of procedures rather than because of them. Our air capabilities of responsiveness and versatility were generally minimized by the cumbersome, time-consuming, and redundant procedures for obtaining strike clearance through military and civilian officials even in remote and uninhabited areas.[36]

With reduced budgetary support, the Air Force envisioned an organization of which Secretary Seamans said: "The Air Force that I see will be leaner, more mobile, more streamlined, and . . . more volunteer oriented." The Air Force programs continued to muster 26 tactical fighter wing flags, but only 21 equipped tactical fighter wings—4 wings of F-111s, 3 wings of A-7s, and 14 wings of F-4s. Only 177 new planes in 1971 and 73 in 1972 were requested for purchase for the Air Force. These were the smallest numbers of annual purchase since the days of the Army Air Corps in 1935. The major factor in the sizing of the Air Force was "economic," but Secretary Seamans pointed out that there was very little ongoing aircraft production under way that could be bought: "We are going through an important aircraft development phase in the Air Force with the A-X, with the B-1, with the F-15, and with the AWACS, and feel it is not a time to procure large numbers of additional aircraft."[37] Although Secretary Seamans and Gen John Ryan were faced with maintaining a transitional holding action during their administration of the Air Force (1969–73), they witnessed the test in combat of F-111s and A-7s in Vietnam. And as they were going out of office in 1973, the Israeli-Arab Yom Kippur War provided new insight in tactical air warfare.

One of the first evaluations required of Secretary Seamans and General Ryan in mid-1969 was to determine the future of the F-111, which was described as probably "the most publicized airplane ever built." As has been seen, the F-111 was projected in 1961 as an all-purpose tactical fighter for the Air Force and Navy. Planning quantities of F-111s specified for procurement were 876 in October 1961, 1,726 in July 1962, 1,923 in May 1963, and 2,411 in March 1964. After this the planned quantities diminished each year, and in 1968 the Navy dropped its planned 705 F-111Bs out of the program, leaving the F-111 to the Air Force exclusively. The reduction in the planned quantity procurement caused large increases in the unit costs of F-111s. For the Air Force, however, the F-111's unique characteristics were vital to the tactical air mission. The F-111 was capable of sustained supersonic speeds, had an extended ferry range for worldwide deployment, could transport nuclear weapons or a 40,000-pound bombload with a high degree of accuracy in all-weather conditions, and was relatively inexpensive in maintenance costs (25 percent less than the F-105).[38] In April 1967 the commander in chief of Pacific Command requested an increased capability to deliver bombs against targets in North Vietnam during darkness and bad weather with accuracy. An Air Force test of available weapons revealed that the F-111A was superior in this regard. The first production F-111A was delivered to the Tactical Air Command at Nellis AFB, Nevada, on 16 October 1967, and 428th Tactical Fighter Squadron began qualifying a small group of pilots for a Combat Lancer evaluation of the plane in Southeast Asia. Detachment 1, 428th TFS, was deployed with six F-111As to Takhli Air Base, Thailand, on 15–16 March 1968. The aircraft demonstrated a clear ability to avoid ground fire by flying low, and they delivered their bombs more accurately in all weather and at night with their advanced radar and navigation system. But two F-111s disappeared while flying over Laos, and it was not known why the aircraft went down. F-111s were equipped with a terrain-following radar which allowed them to fly automatically over rough topography without colliding with the ground. There was a possibility in Laos, however, that the radar might have not shown the tops of jungle trees but rather set the altitude from the surface of the ground. The cause of these losses remained unknown, but a third F-111 went down at a location where the pilots survived and the plane was recovered. This crash was caused by a tube of sealant which was found to have been left in the pitch-roll control system when the plane was built. Before F-111s at Takhli could complete their shakedown flights, fatigue tests of an F-111 in the United States resulted in the premature failure of the plane's wing-box carry-through structure. All F-111s were restricted from flight pending evaluation of the malfunction. Although the restriction was in effect, the bombing of North Vietnam ceased, and there would not be any utility in keeping the F-111 detachment in the theater. Accordingly, the detachment was returned to the United States.[39]

At night against poorly defined targets in undeveloped areas of North Vietnam, the F-111A blind bombing system demonstrated high potential target destruction capabilities. In the offing was an F-111D model with a Mark II avionics system, including improved radar and navigation systems integrated with a versatile cockpit display. The question confronting Secretary Brown in his last months as Air Force secretary was what to do about the F-111 production line pending a fix on the wing-pivoting apparatus break under static testing. The decision in the secretary's office on 11 October 1968 was to continue acceptance of F-111As with unmodified wing boxes and to place flight performance limits on the planes pending eventual incorporations of a fix. In continuing evaluations of the F-111, Secretary Seamans and General Ryan wanted to go ahead with the plane. "I believe this plane, which has gone through a very tortuous life, is going to provide a very great capability for the Air Force," said Seamans. Ryan added: "I think the airplane is going to be a tremendous asset to us. It will give us a capability for night and all-weather interdiction which we do not have in the Air Force today in the tactical forces."[40]

In discussions of strengthening NATO conventional capabilities, the United States had been holding out the prospect of placing two wings of F-111s at bases in England. These rearward bases would be less vulnerable to Warsaw Pact attack than continental bases, and from them the long-range F-111s would be able to strike targets deep in Europe at night and in adverse weather. In the winter, flying weather over the North German Plain was almost always bad, adding to the advantage of the F-111. Secretary Laird explained the international significance of the F-111:

> The F-111A represents a vital part of our NATO deterrent in Europe.... We have made it clear to our allies for some time that this long range all-weather striking power would be part of the NATO forces both for nuclear and conventional operations. Deletion of the F-111 portion of the NATO force would weaken our military as well as political position, both in the eyes of our allies and the offspring Warsaw Pact nations.[41]

Even though Air Force leaders continued to insist that the F-111, in Secretary Seamans's words, "represents a major step in modernizing our interdiction and long range penetration capabilities," the aircraft continued to have structural problems. When the wing box difficulty was corrected, another F-111A crashed on 22 December 1969 because of a structural crack in a forged wing pivot fitting. All F-111s were immediately grounded pending inspections for forging cracks, and in the spring of 1970 many critics of the F-111 argued that the aircraft was a "lemon" and that the program should be terminated. In congressional hearings, Gen James Ferguson, commander, Air Force Systems Command, and Lt Gen Otto J. Glasser, deputy chief of staff for research and development, came strongly to the defense of the F-111, but, as a matter of interest, Glasser observed:

> We have learned through our F-111 experience . . . that aircraft that are built for too many purposes, that is too much of a multipurpose airplane is not a good thing. In many cases single purpose airplanes are best, and if an aircraft is to be built for more than one purpose, the purposes should be closely related.[42]

The expertise of the Air Force Scientific Advisory Board and the Air Force specialty teams were applied to the F-111, and all tests of wing pivot fittings failed to reveal any flaws, indicating that the crash in December was an anomaly. The F-111 program was nevertheless proving to be excessively expensive, and the Air Force was compelled to curtail the costs chiefly by reducing expenditures for avionics. The results were four models of F-111s. The F-111A was the basic, original TFX, and the F-111E was a refined "A" model with improved engine inlets and was used for the second tactical F-111 wing. The F-111D version incorporated an improved but expensive Mark II avionics system, which had moving target capabilities that significantly increased its air-to-ground effectiveness. The F-111D equipped the third F-111 tactical wing. The F-111F was fitted with higher thrust engines but equipped with less expensive avionics packages because of budgetary limitations. The F-111F equipped the fourth tactical F-111 wing.[43]

Demonstrating its capacity for nonstop flying early in 1971, an F-111A squadron proceeded without refueling to Upper Heyford, England. This base would receive a wing of F-111s in support of NATO. The first combat-ready F-111 wing, however, was the 474th Tactical Fighter Wing at Nellis AFB, Nevada, in February 1972. On 21 September 1972 the 474th was directed to deploy two squadrons of 48 F-111As to Takhli Air Base in Thailand for air operations against North Vietnam during darkness and adverse weather. The wing was initially committed to low-level operations into the high-threat areas of North Vietnam: it flew 806 single ship missions, of which 729 were successful, resulting in an overall success rate of 91 percent. During Linebacker II in December 1972, F-111s dropped the first bombs, striking MiG airfields and other key targets around Hanoi. On the last two nights of Linebacker II, the F-111s concentrated against SAM sites, and — although other planes were also hitting to cover the B-52s — on these nights the number of missiles fired at the strategic bombers was reduced from an average of over 200 to less than 20 each night. F-111s were also the only aircraft to attack the long, narrow docks and warehouse areas at Hanoi; bomb damage assessment showed 100 percent of bombs scoring on the docks and warehouses without collateral damage to surrounding civil structures. When operations were pulled back away from Hanoi, the 474th was fragged for medium-altitude bombing missions; 3,253 such sorties were flown, of which 89 led other planes to targets in pathfinder work. Nearly all of the medium-altitude strikes were successful. The wing had a total of six combat losses with one crew captured and later returned. F-111s normally required no aerial refueling on strike missions; in fact, only six missions, all against rail targets in far northeastern North Vietnam, ran short of fuel and had to hit tankers on the way back to Takhli. During the last weeks of combat in Laos, F-111s were counted to be highly successful in bombing at night and through clouds with offset aiming on beacons and allowing close air support for friendly ground troops. This ground beacon/radar offset bombing drew warm praise from General Vogt, commander in Southeast Asia, when he was attempting in the summer monsoon of 1973 to prop up the friendly Cambodian forces. F-111s were able both to bomb in proximity to friendly forces and to lead flights of less sophisticated aircraft to bomb enemy forces endangering friendlies. Early in 1974 Gen George Brown testified that the F-111 provided a "unique" capability to deliver conventional weapons accurately at night and in weather against the toughest targets in North Vietnam.[44]

Since the A-7D close-support fighter was a modified version of the already developed US Navy A-7A/A-7B attack aircraft, it was initially expected that the plane would be a well within the state-of-the-art program that would provide a relatively cheap subsonic aircraft, able to carry a heavy advance load, and with range enough to permit it to loiter leisurely while awaiting targets. Its secondary role was to be aerial interdiction. Designed originally for Navy carrier-based operations, the A-7 required time-consuming and expensive modifications to adapt it to land-based Air Force usage. The initial December 1965 decision to procure the A-7 did not envision the changes necessary to acquire a mission effective close-air-support aircraft, and Gen Otto J. Glasser, Air Force deputy chief of staff for research and development, expressed a later Air Force assessment that the procurement decision "might have been deemed premature from that point of view." After the configuration of the A-7D was determined and authorized, however, the program schedule was stabilized, and a very successful flight-test program was completed in August 1970. The original buy projection was for four wings of A-7Ds, but the projection was reduced to three wings when the tactical fighter force was cut from 23 to 21 wings. A combat crew training squadron for A-7Ds was opened at Luke AFB, Arizona, in the winter of 1970–71, and thereupon deliveries of A-7Ds began to equip the 354th Tactical Fighter Wing at Myrtle Beach, South Carolina.[45]

The 354th Tactical Fighter Wing received an execute order at Myrtle Beach on 3 October 1972 to deploy its three squadrons of A-7Ds to Korat Royal Thai Air Force Base, Thailand, for combat against the North Vietnamese. All 72 aircraft were in place at Korat on 16 October, the same day that the wing flew its first combat sorties. In the airlifted movement, nearly 1,600 people and 665 tons of equipment were moved by 43 C-141 sorties, 5 Boeing 707s, and 5 C-130s. In combat the daily frag rate built to a sustained 0.87 sortie rate, equating to 62 sorties a day. With its long range, the A-7D could strike from Korat to just about anywhere in Southeast Asia without aerial refueling. Almost from the first day's flying, the 354th began to get kudos from forward air controllers who directed close-support missions and who liked the long-loiter time that the A-7 could stay around and also their bombing accuracy. Col Thomas M. Knowles III, the 354th's commander, said that when the FACs "designate a target and say, 'hit my smoke,' we can hit the smoke." In combat employment, Colonel Knowles estimated the bombing accuracy of A-7s to have been about 10 meters, or at least this was a usual FAC evaluation. Early in November, A-7s took over the work of old A-1s in escorting search and rescue helicopters to pick up downed airmen. According to General Vogt, old A-1s were extremely vulnerable to Communist SA-7 hand-held infrared homing rockets—they were too slow and radiated too much heat, making it necessary to take them out of combat. Normally, an A-7 Sandy search and rescue mission lasted 4 to 5 hours, requiring the A-7 to tap a refueling tanker two or three times. In 12 days of Linebacker II the 354th Wing conducted 230 strike sorties; it was able to bomb visually on only three of the strike days and the remaining efforts were LORAN drops using F-4s as pathfinders. When Air Force air operations ceased in Laos on 23 February 1973, the wing had flown 5,796 strike/attack sorties, 542 Sandy SAR sorties, and 230 Linebacker sorties. Two aircraft and one pilot were lost in combat; the cause of the loss of one plane and pilot over Laos was unknown, but the other plane collided with a FAC, and the pilot was captured and later freed in a POW release. In summing up the wing's experience, Colonel Knowles stated that the A-7D was "the best [close-support aircraft] we have in the active inventory today.... We confirmed that our training in the Tactical Air Command provided us with a sound and effective wing team to conduct combat operations."[46]

Over North Vietnam American airmen had learned to live with the early generation SA-1 surface-to-air missiles chiefly by evading SAMs or by jamming missile radars. Efforts to attack Communist air defense were not reliable, one reason being that it was difficult to plot exact locations of electronic emitters. As will be seen, the Air Force at the end of the Southeast Asian war was working on a requirement to develop an advance location strike system (ALSS) employing novel distance measuring equipment for exact targeting and strike direction against electronic emitters.[47] Although the Soviet Union was generous in its support of the North Vietnamese, the major flow of the most modern Soviet weapons went to Egypt and Syria, who were being prepared to avenge their defeat by Israel in the war that had occurred in 1967. Many of the major weapon systems so provided had not been seen previously in combat. Since the land and air battles that were going to take place in the Middle East were fought with many newly developed weapons that would possibly be used in a war against NATO, and since the deployment of combatants in some areas was comparable to those expectable in Europe, the Arab-Israeli wars of June 1967 and the Yom Kippur War of October

1973 stimulated much thought in the United States, including evaluation and reaction that was perhaps keener than the evaluation and reaction to US experience in Southeast Asia.[48]

In the 1967 Middle East War the Israeli Air Force was able to destroy the Arab air forces on the first day with a lightning-fast, low-level air attack against airfields in a preemptive beginning to the conflict launched while the Arab adversaries were poised to attack. After this, the Israeli Air Force decimated Arab tank forces, permitting Israeli armor to wage blitzkrieg assault. In the months after 1967, Egypt and Syria built concrete shelters for their aircraft—chiefly MiG-21Js received from the Soviet Union. The Soviets provided the newly equipped Egyptian and Syrian T62 tank forces with an emplaced SA-2 and SA-3 surface-to-air missile antiaircraft umbrella and a rolling air umbrella of mobile SA-6 vehicle-mounted antiaircraft missiles. The Soviets also provided mobile 23-mm ZSU-23-4 radar-equipped, rapid-firing antiaircraft guns. The SA-6 was a technological surprise; its mobility permitted it to keep pace with advancing armored forces, and the SA-6 incorporated a continuous-wave, semi-actively guided Doppler technique against which existing US ECM jammers were impotent.[49]

The Israeli policy of maintaining a reserve army against a much larger Arab standing army was similar in some respects to the situation faced by the Free World in Europe with respect to the Warsaw Pact. The consequences of surprise attack in the Middle East were more serious, however, since the Israeli ground forces were maintained at only a fraction of their planned wartime manning and whereas NATO forces were held at nearer full strength. Although it was evident to the Israeli national command authority that Egypt and Syria were maneuvering and that attack was possible, the Israelis had been criticized in 1967 for preempting. Since the 6th of October was Yom Kippur, Israel did not mobilize. On this day a combined Arab force of over 2,000 tanks and 100,000 infantry swept simultaneously into the Golan Heights above Jerusalem and into the Sinai desert against a not-yet-mobilized Israeli force of about 400 tanks and 5,000 infantry. Maj Gen Benjamin Peled, Israeli Air Force (IAF) commander, would later say that if the Arabs started another war he felt that in the initial phases he would attempt to gain air superiority by attacking airfields and by locating and suppressing SAM sites, but with Syrian tanks coming down the Golan Heights and the strategic life of the country in jeopardy, his only choice was to throw his air units into the beach to delay the enemy and buy time to mobilize ground force reserves. These early Israeli close-air-support operations had to take place in a heavily defended area under very fluid and chaotic battlefield conditions. The Arabs' dense, overlapping, surface-to-air missile and antiaircraft artillery network, coupled with the Israeli army's initial lack of knowledge about their own and Arab troop locations, made IAF close air support particularly difficult. In a later recapitulation of these events in Washington, Maj Gen Harold E. Collins, Air Force assistant deputy chief of staff for research and development, said it appeared that the Israelis made a basic presumption that the SAM's were not going to bother them all that badly.... So they decided that they would go ahead in, and when they found that the SAM environment was pretty tough, and particularly the fact that that SA-6 had mobility, that drove them down to the deck and, of course, drove them into the AAA. That is where they got a devil of a lot of their losses.[50]

As chairman of the Joint Chiefs of Staff, Admiral Moorer drew several "lessons learned" from the initial war days:

First, ready, in-being, deployed forces are essential to maintaining the territorial integrity of any area whose defense is required.... Additionally, the classic doctrine that the priority of employment of air assets must be given to gaining and maintaining air superiority over the battlefield has been proven once again. Today, gaining air superiority includes defeating enemy SAMs in detail. Until enemy air defenses are degraded, any application of aerial firepower will be costly, but the losses will go down as air defenses are taken out.... In the interim, ground forces must be capable of fighting with reduced reliance upon close air support.[51]

Although the emergency commitment of the Israeli Air Force and the mobilization of ground forces successfully stalled Syrian and Egyptian thrusts, these forces had to be incautiously employed and losses were heavy. The Israeli Air Force was comprised principally of the US A-4 Skyhawk, the F-4E Phantom, and the French Mirage, the latter having little ground-attack capability but proving useful for aerial combat. According to Minister of Defense Moshe Dayan, the Israeli Air Force lost 102 aircraft, most of which were downed in the first three days of hectic fighting. During this time, Israeli armored forces were thrown at the enemy in tank columns which, unsupported by infantry and artillery, were easily picked off by Soviet-provided, infantry-operated antitank missiles of the AT-3 Sagger type. These early happenings engendered two false but widely spread conclusions: the one was that precision-guided defenses had rendered tanks practically obsolescent, the other that precision-guided missiles such as SA-6s and SA-7s rendered tactical aircraft obsolete. The true facts were that Israeli tanks, once they received combined arms support, rolled back the Syrians from the Golan Heights and ultimately surrounded the Egyptian Third Army on the southern front. As far as total losses of armor were concerned, a clear majority of the tanks on both sides were destroyed by other tanks. A sizable percentage of Arab armor was nevertheless destroyed as a result of Israeli air sorties. Destruction was particularly pronounced in the later stages of the conflict when antiaircraft missile defenses had been suppressed and the IAF brought into action urgently delivered US weapons, such as the electro-optically guided Maverick and the TV-guided Walleye glide bomb, which were reported to have recently achieved kill ratios in excess of 90 percent.[52]

Distorted misperceptions concerning the losses of aircraft in the Yom Kippur War failed to focus upon the fact that political considerations prevented the Israeli Air Force from preempting against Soviet missile defenses as it had intended and therefore it had to be recklessly employed in the opening days of combat. When both Israeli and Arab aircraft were counted, some 46 percent of all kills were scored in the air by other aircraft. Of the Arab losses of 480 to 514 aircraft, 55 percent were downed by Israeli fighters, while only 5 percent of 102 Israeli aircraft were lost in air-to-air fights. Of 222 Syrian aircraft lost in the war, 162, or 73 percent, were destroyed in aerial combat. The other Arab aircraft were shot down by Israeli AAA, US-provided Hawk missiles, except for 58 said to have been downed accidentally by friendly Egyptian and Syrian air defense missiles. Whereas 373 Arab aircraft were destroyed on the ground in the 1967 war, the Arabs' concrete hangarettes were extremely effective in the Yom Kippur action, and only 22 Arab planes were destroyed on the ground. Only 5 percent of Israeli aircraft were destroyed on the ground, possibly because the skies over Israeli airfields were kept "clean" throughout the war, and not one bomb fell on Israel. The successful maintenance of control of the air over Israel protected the IAF infrastructure. King Hussein of Jordan explained to the Arab world that he stayed out of the war and was unwilling to commit his forces because of Israel's control in the air over the potential battlefield. The training of Israeli pilots for air-to-air combat was described by Air Force observers as "outstanding" — far superior to Arab training. The Arab pilots were described as "no qualitative match for the Israeli pilots." Most air-to-air combat occurred in the immediate battle area. The Egyptians had a fairly good radar coverage, and their controllers could tell when the Israelis were coming, although not accurately enough to vector their airmen to long-range interceptions. Accordingly, the Egyptians used defensive orbiting patrols over point defenses that essentially were responsive to what the ground controller said, as was the custom in Soviet doctrine. Israeli pilots customarily penetrated to their targets at low level and high speed, popped up and lofted their ordnance; the Arab pilots were told to attack when they saw the Israeli pilots popping up, and by the time that they got in to attack, it was too late. With airplanes as dense as the F-4Es he was using for ground attack, General Peled insisted that speed was an absolute necessity for survival. A Joint Chiefs of Staff survey team agreed that a lesson to be learned from the Yom Kippur War was that a close-support airplane needed to attack at high speed needed excess thrust for maneuverability to avoid SAMs and sustain high speed, and needed a computer-aided bombing system for an accurate first-pass delivery. Another point raised by the JCS team was that airborne FACs in slow-moving planes could not have survived in such an intense air-defense environment.[53] The Air Force's response to these assertions was that there was a trade-off between speed and relative invulnerability (ability to take hits) in an aircraft. Speed made it more difficult for a pilot to acquire a target. Thus this trade-off was being reflected in the A-X (now the A-10) close-air-support plane. The finding on the survivability of an airborne FAC was additional support for the A-10, since it could — unlike a faster aircraft — find its own targets.[54]

According to one evaluation, if the Israeli Air Force had been able to strike immediately, it could have eliminated SAMs on both fronts in a period of between three to six hours, with an aircraft attrition of probably not much more than 1 percent. After the initial period of the war, the IAF in a brief concentration on defense suppression destroyed more than six-sevenths of all SAM sites, including four-fifths of the mobile SA-6s. The SA-2s and SA-3s were successfully jammed, and in the last stages of the war, Israeli drones sometimes attracted as many as three dozen SAMs per drone, depleting numerous sites of ammunition. SA-2s and SA-3s were relatively immobile, and thus the Egyptian armor on the Sinai front, after forging a bulge across the Suez, appeared to huddle under the antiair-missile defense umbrella and to lose its momentum of attack. When some armor lost patience and moved out, it was decimated by Israeli airmen. It was reported that SA-2s and SA-3s accounted for less than 40 percent of Israeli aircraft destroyed and that SA-6s and SA-7s accounted for only 10 and 4 percent respectively. More than 5,000 Strella firings were said to have downed only four Israeli planes. Arab antiaircraft (AA) accounted for over 40 percent of Israeli plane losses.[55] In a lecture to the Royal United Services Institute (RUSI) in England, Gen Chaim Herzog discussed air-to-ground action on the West Bank of the Suez Canal, saying: "The first mission of our armored force on the West Bank of the Suez Canal was to knock out the surface-to-air missile sites, which it did effectively. That force literally swept the area for the air force, and it was then free to attack at will." Based on this quotation, one Air Force officer inferred that prior to the elimination of SAM and AA defenses, the IAF was not free to attack at will. In a book written after his lecture to the RUSI, however, General Herzog stated:

> On the West Bank of the Suez Canal, an unusual example of mutual coordination emerged between the advancing ground forces and the Israeli Air Force. As the armored forces on the West Bank of the Canal destroyed one surface-to-air missile battery after another, the Israeli Air Force gained a freer hand and became a major factor in supporting the advancing Israeli forces.[56]

Elsewhere, Herzog was careful to point out, the IAF was successful in dealing with missiles on its own, thus contradicting a popular report that precision-guided Soviet missiles had rendered IAF aircraft almost obsolescent.[57]

"The effective use of airpower appears to me as the difference between destruction and survival for Israel," stated US Air Force Chief of Staff Gen George S. Brown on 21 March 1974.[58] As will be seen, the steady flow of US supplies to Israel by C-141 and C-5A airlift between 13 October–14 November was one of the decisive factors enabling Israel to continue to battle to a successful cease-fire, but the immediate focus of evaluation was on the tactical air aspect of the Yom Kippur War. A Royal Australian Air Force officer at Maxwell AFB, Alabama, Air War College, said the Yom Kippur War necessitated sweeping changes in air doctrine in addition to new equipment. "In the light of the lessons learned from the Yom Kippur War, defense suppression must now be elevated to rank with air superiority, interdiction, and close air support as one of the basic missions of tactical air forces," wrote Wing Commander Hans F. Roser.[59] But General Brown adopted a more measured cadence, namely that "air superiority" included "defense suppression": "You have to gain air superiority. That not only means against enemy fighters, it also means against enemy missiles. . . . We have just got to beat those defenses down. If you ignore the defenses, you are going to pay a terrific price."[60] Gen Robert J. Dixon, commander of the Tactical Air Command, expressed his insight into the Yom Kippur War in a rebuttal to the generalization that missile defenses brought an era where tactical aircraft could no longer survive over a battlefield. His judgment was "less startling but more credible." Tactical air power would need to "control the air-space, suppress the defenses, operate as a combined arms team."[61] In what might be described as a wrap-up of Air Force thoughts on Yom Kippur generalities, Maj Gen Robert P. Lukeman, assistant chief of staff for studies and analysis, responded to a question as to how the Air Force would fight October's Middle East War, as follows:

> Assuming USAF equipment and trained personnel were to be employed, and given the same general terrain, weather and military situation faced by the Israelis, the following general scenario may be constructed. First, a comprehensive counterair campaign would be launched to defend friendly air space, and to destroy and suppress enemy ground-based and airborne air defenses. The purpose of this campaign would be to obtain air superiority necessary to preclude enemy air attack of friendly ground forces and to permit freedom of action for USAF close air support, interdiction, reconnaissance and theater airlift activities. Simultaneous with the counterair campaign, large numbers of immediate and preplanned close air support sorties would be provided to friendly ground forces using the tactical air control system. An around-the-clock interdiction program would be initiated to destroy, delay, and harass the flow of enemy troops and materiel to the front and to destroy/disrupt his command and control elements. Tactical air reconnaissance, both day and night, would be accomplished and provided to the ground and air commanders on a timely basis. Tactical airlift would be employed to provide logistical air support as required. In support of all these missions, USAF tactical electronic warfare resources — self-screening electronic countermeasures, ECM, support ECM — chaff, flares to counter infrared weapons, and appropriate tactics, would be used to supplement direct suppression of defense and direct attack of hostile control elements. Finally, in order to insure optimum allocation of air resources to all missions to be performed and to obtain flexible, responsive command and control, all air activities would be centralized under the USAF component of the U.S. Army/Air Force/Navy joint task force.[62]

One of the more remarkable things about the Middle East War that deserved recording, according to Maj Gen Harold E. Collins, assistant deputy chief of staff for research and development, was the "capability of the Israeli Air Force, predominantly a fighter force, to achieve air superiority over the Arab forces with their emphasis on SAM defenses."[63] On the other hand, Dr Malcolm R. Currie, director of defense research and engineering, pointed out that new means must be found to protect close air support:

> A major lesson, reenforced by the Mideast War, is the necessity of countering enemy air defense systems which threaten our close air support aircraft. We rely on close air support much more heavily than the Soviet Union. We must be certain it can operate effectively. Many of our current developments are applicable to suppressing forward air defense. We need to explore some new approaches and we need to fill in gaps in our capability. Above all, we need to make certain that our total defense suppression capability will do the job.[64]

A still different forecast was offered by General Herzog:

> The proliferation of light, portable missile launchers in the front lines meant that close air support would be the exception to the rule in the future, with the air force being obliged to concentrate on isolating the field of battle, maintaining supremacy in the air, and destroying the forces in and near the field of battle.[65]

Already mindful that the Air Force would need to beat down hostile antiair defenses, General Brown on 2 November 1973 directed the Tactical Air Command and the Air Force Systems Command to review some 112 research and development items on the books that looked as if they would improve tactical strike capabilities, particularly at night and during adverse weather, with emphasis on defense suppression. As a result of this study an aggregate of 11 projects were collectively named Pave Strike ("Pave" being the AFSC code word and "Strike" the project) and mandated for special research and development management emphasis. The emphasis on night and all-weather capability was in recognition that military operations in the Middle East had generally ceased at night except for resupply movements and shifts of troops and armor. There was also a belated recognition that winter weather in Northern Europe was usually inhospitable to low-level air operations. There were three general categories of Pave Strike. First, to detect and target hostile emitters. Here the distance-measuring equipment techniques of the advanced location and strike system (ALSS) that had not gotten to Southeast Asia would be developed into an expanded precision emitter locator strike system (PELSS). Second, to provide strike force protection there would be a need to modify standard F-111As into EF-111As for electronics jamming ECM, to provide a coterie of Wild Weasel F-4Es that would strike hostile emitters, and to develop remotely piloted vehicle (RPV) modules to complement manned activity in ECM and reconnaissance and as precursors laying chaff corridors, saturating and diluting air defenses in advance of penetrating strike fighters. Third, to perfect many more guidance systems for bombs and rockets, especially laser and infrared sensors for the Maverick, which had been ordered for production in large numbers but whose electro-optical television guidance might not be too useful in northern European weather. In explanation of Pave Strike, General Collins emphasized that its programs would not be immediately fruitful since all the technology visualized had not yet been developed. Pave Strike would be evolutionary, not revolutionary, but it was important for long-term security to spark the technology it required.[66]

A group of congressmen who visited the Middle East in late November 1973 returned to Washington concerned that the conflict demonstrated that the Soviets achieved more effective military power by a proliferation of rugged, inexpensive devices rather than through the use of expensive, sophisticated technology. Congressman Joseph P. Addabbo of New York was especially concerned that in the fighting "we saw massive Soviet supplies used against our sophisticated type equipment." He said that the Israelis had lost heavily because they had met "a wall of steel." He also believed the Soviets stressed quantity rather than quality: "Russia

IDEAS, CONCEPTS, DOCTRINE

is not dealing with sophisticated weapons and would not put $60 million into one tank or plane. They would rather have 10 tanks or 10 planes of lesser quality."[67] In a colloquy early in 1974, Secretary McLucas argued that the Arabs had expended a great number of SAMs in comparison with the number of Israeli aircraft downed, but Sen Milton R. Young of North Dakota responded: "Yes, but they [the Arabs] can fire plenty of them. They are not too costly. The Israelis have lost three-quarters of a billion dollars worth of planes, and we paid for them. The ratio is too heavy."[68] As a matter of fact, the Soviets had provided Egypt and Syria with many items of expensive equipment. The Soviet-provided armored personnel carriers (APC), for example, were equipped for chemical-biological war and vastly exceeded the cost of US APCs. The mobile ZSU-23-4 was also extremely costly as compared to the US Vulcan. All systems had optical backup sighting to counter electronic jamming of radars. The SA-6 was not only modern and expensive but was a surprise entrant in the conflict. In the early phase of the war, however, both Arabs and Israelis used tremendous quantities of materiel and had very high rates of weapons expenditures. This trend toward rapid weapons expenditures placed a premium on plentiful, "affordable" weapons, but Director of Defense Research and Engineering Currie warned that the extent to which the performance of an individual weapon should be compromised to lower its cost demanded careful thought in each case.[69] For at least a year before the Yom Kippur War the Department of Defense had accepted an intention to go to a cost-quantity trade-off in weapons procurement to permit a "hi-lo" mix of costs of new weapons, the low end of the mix being designed to permit acquisition of larger numbers of weapons. In this regard, the Middle East War of 1973 gave impetus to the acquisition of more sophisticated weapons and also larger quantities of less costly but still usable weapons.

Response to the Soviet/Warsaw Pact Threat

After 1968, when the Soviet invasion of Czechoslovakia both ended an illusion of détente at the Elbe and marked a beginning of a clearly visible Soviet buildup of frontal attack forces endangering the North Atlantic Alliance, US national security policy gave the defense of Western Europe first priority after the defense of the United States. This policy not only meant that the Soviet/Warsaw Pact threat in large part dictated force sizing, but, in the case of the Air Force, the image of Soviet/Warsaw Pact attack generated characteristics of the new tactical fighter/attack forces. Thus when Lt Gen Alton D. Slay, Air Force deputy chief of staff for research and development, was asked whether the Air Force ought not to place greater emphasis outside Central Europe, and what the Air Force would do if it received additional funding, he responded:

> Our philosophy for a number of years has been if we prepare well enough for the big war, we have encompassed what is required for smaller wars. As an example, all of equipment that we have, with few exceptions, is equally applicable, say, for the Horn of

Africa as for Eastern Germany.... Now if we have a large war in Central Europe, quite obviously we can't handle much more, so to answer your second question, what would we do with extra money, we would buy more of the same.[70]

After the invasion of Czechoslovakia in 1968, the Soviets left behind 65,000 men, including five divisions. In this same time span, they began a change of emphasis in their military strength confronting NATO. Until this time Soviet/Warsaw Pact forces were principally defensive. Their air power was defensively oriented, trained, and equipped to intercept rather than to penetrate air defenses or bomb deep within NATO territory. They had a great proliferation of missile defenses, and their armies were disposed as occupation forces rather than in an attack posture.[71] Whereas the United States made force reductions under the Nixon strategy to those required for one and one-half wars, the Soviet Union moved up to a two-and-a-half war capability—expanding and modernizing the forces confronting NATO at the same time they were augmenting the forces in the east confronting China. By 1971 Gen David A. Burchinal, deputy commander in chief, European Command, said of the Soviets:

By almost any quantitative measure ... such as divisions, tanks, artillery, submarines, APCs—they have a significant quantitative edge. This is true. I think, however, that we are still retaining, overall, by and large, a qualitative edge and we do provide a very essential piece of this equation which is our tactical nuclear presence in Europe which only the United States can provide.[72]

At this time the Warsaw Pact was building a formidable armored force in the central region of Europe, defined in NATO as all of West Germany and the Benelux countries. The three most famous approaches into Western Europe were in the central region: the Fulda Gap in the north, the Meiningen Gap in the center, and the Hof/Cheb Gap in the south. Stated a US Army briefer,

It is evident that emphasis must be placed on countering the most apparent conventional threat in Europe—Warsaw Pact armor and ground mobility. The Russians are overweight in tanks. If you can stop their tanks, you can blunt their attack. Therefore, every means at our disposal must be used to kill his armored vehicles.[73]

In a formal statement in July 1973, Secretary Schlesinger described the pact forces opposite NATO as "indeed formidable," but he nevertheless maintained that the NATO force structure was sufficient to provide "a very limited temptation in the Warsaw Pact to move against Western Europe and thus there is now in Europe a fairly stable situation."[74] Schlesinger's evaluation discounted what he described as "a Pearl Harbor complex" or a belief that the Soviet/Warsaw Pact attack would come like a "bolt from the blue." He conceived that to make an attack, forces as far away as the three Soviet western military districts would need to be moved forward and that NATO intelligence sources would surely be forewarned by all this repositioning of Soviet/Warsaw Pact forces.[75]

The US national strategy guidance provided by President Nixon through the National Security Council in 1969 was predicated on the thesis that "within a period of 90 days after the initiation of a Warsaw Pact conventional attack on Europe, either a political settlement would be reached, or the Soviets would reach the limits of their conventional capability, or the war would have escalated to nuclear conflict."[76] In this period the Air Force's criterion for the sufficiency of the deterrent in Europe was to be able to sustain conventional conflict for 90 days while maintaining a capability to escalate to the use of nuclear weapons.

Remembering the air power lesson of the World War II Luftwaffe Stuka aircraft that was admirable for close air support but had no other capabilities, a generation of Air Force leaders had held to a doctrine that aircraft ought to be developed on a principle of multipurpose usage. Thus all fighters and attack aircraft should have varying capabilities for close air support. Ending his career as commander of the Tactical Air Command, General Momyer had earlier opposed specialized aircraft, but in 1971 he conceived that military requirements must be rationally developed from the future threat toward Europe. He said:

> We know from our recent experience over North Vietnam, and from the current situation in the Middle East, that the higher threat environments of the future will not be limited to Europe. But that is the principal threat, and the other threats in other areas will be reflection of it, on a smaller scale.[77]

In view of the "time limit" for a conventional conflict in Europe as well as the probability that any conventional conflict in Europe would probably be of higher intensity than any previous war in which the United States had been engaged, Momyer conceived that the United States and other NATO allies must be

> able to aggressively pursue air operations involving concurrent air superiority, counterair, interdiction, and close air support if deterrence fails. . . . In short, we will not be afforded the luxury of accomplishing tactical air missions one at a time if deterrence fails and we are thrust into a conventional war in Europe.[78]

The promised intensity of conflict in Europe, Momyer concluded, established "a requirement for a large number of airframes and tend[ed] to emphasize specialization."[79]

At the same time that the Air Force needed aircraft for high intensity and short-time-to-decision conflicts in Europe, Air Force leaders also faced a problem of balancing quality against quantity. In February 1972, Grant L. Hansen, assistant secretary of the Air Force for research and development, was called upon to speak to the subject of "goldplating," which he defined as "having features which are not absolutely necessary for the system to accomplish its intended mission." There had been some systems where this had been the case, Hansen said, but he added:

> The single driving fact in the acquisition of major weapons systems is that the capabilities required for survival in war present hard engineering problems that we have never faced before. . . . The history of the cost and complexity of fighter aircraft systems illustrates the problem. In World War I, a fighter aircraft cost about $5,000. By World War II, this rose to about $50,000. By the Korean War, the price had jumped to $500,000, and the cost of fighter aircraft systems of the 1970's [has] increased by roughly another factor

of 10. If one were to project these trends, by sometime in the 21st century we would be able to afford only one aircraft. Clearly, one aircraft, no matter how capable, will be inadequate for the simple reason that it cannot be more than one place at one time....

Obviously, we must compromise between the extremes of capability and numbers to develop new fighter aircraft systems that will have, first, an acceptable exchange ratio against enemy systems, and, second, a cost that will allow us to buy and operate enough to achieve and maintain air superiority for the United States if war should ever come.[80]

As deputy secretary of defense in the Laird tenure, David Packard received responsibility for reforming Department of Defense procurement procedures, and his studies convinced him that "by far the most important factor driving the cost [of weapons] up is the capability we ask for in new weapons."[81] Laird and Packard instituted new prototype development, "fly-before-buy," and "hi-lo" policies to drive down development and procurement costs, and Secretary Schlesinger agreed in 1974 that "in many situations, large numbers of relatively uncomplicated systems may prove more effective than equal cost but much smaller numbers of highly complex delivery vehicles." In 1975 Schlesinger stated that the Department of Defense was bound by the high-low mix principle to get a proper combination of sophistication and quantity. He informally defined the dividing line of aircraft cost between "high" and "low" as being a unit cost of about $6 million per copy—anything above that cost being "high" and anything below being "low."[82] With continued cost increases, some critics would argue that the low part of the mix had become so expensive that the "hi-lo" concept was violated, and Secretary of Defense Brown would argue that the last 5 to 10 percent of capability should be given up to secure the number of weapons needed.[83] Well acquainted with problems of the defense of Western Europe as a result of a tour as CINC, United States Air Forces in Europe (USAFE), immediately before becoming Air Force chief of staff in July 1974, Gen David C. Jones agreed with both high-low mix and mission optimization of aircraft:

The high-low mix and mission optimization go hand in hand. The planned mix of USAF tactical fighters emphasizes aircraft performance in specific mission areas. This mission optimization enhances proficiency and performance in each area while retaining inherent capabilities in the others. It results in significant cost savings when compared to the costs to develop, procure, and operate a force composed entirely of multipurpose aircraft.[84]

That the Air Force's concern for developing optimum tactical air capabilities was not academic in NATO was evidenced by a rapid modernization of Soviet/Warsaw Pact air forces. As late as the 1960s the Soviet Union continued to build large numbers of short-range defensive fighters, emphasizing quantity over quality. As a result, most observers credited NATO with technological superiority. The appearance of the high-altitude Foxbat/MiG-25 ended this trend, since this plane was equivalent to the US Air Force's never-procured F-12, and it was not only developed but procured in respectable numbers.[85] In the early 1970s and afterward, the Soviets vigorously modernized Soviet/Warsaw Pact frontal aviation, introducing MiG-21 Fishbed standard combat fighters, Su-17 Fitter swing-wing, ground support planes, and MiG-23 Floggers in all-weather counterair and ground attack versions, all in quantity. By 1975, in NATO's northern and central regions, 3,000 NATO tactical aircraft faced 5,000 Warsaw Pact planes. Soviet and Pact planes were dispersed at many fields under concrete shelters. Pact air defense and fighter control electronics were modernized. One weakness continued to be a Soviet doctrinal precept that air crews fought under ground controllers' directions, but Soviet fighter doctrine began to promote greater flexibility and became more offensively attuned.

As early as 1972 a Senate Armed Services Committee staff visit to NATO was said to have found all major Air Force officials thinking that it would be very difficult to achieve and maintain air superiority in a conventional war. An Air Force response to a congressional query in 1973 conceded that in an attack the Soviets would have the important advantage of initiative and would have a mobile target array, whereas NATO's airfields, ports, and lines of communications from outside Europe were "limited, well known, and susceptible to severe disruption or destruction."[86] Given the numerical superiority of in-theater Soviet/Warsaw Pact frontal aviation forces in 1975, General Brown, who had become chairman of the Joint Chiefs of Staff, was hopeful that between M + 3 and M + 30 day the Air Force could deploy sizable tactical air forces—both land based and carrier based—to NATO and so hold on to general air superiority:

> The loss of air superiority in a NATO conflict would have a severely adverse impact on the land battle. . . . Pact planners understand this. . . . Should they succeed, our reinforcements to Europe would be slowed or stopped, which would virtually render impossible our regaining air superiority. The choice would then be either relinquish major segments of NATO territory or resort to nuclear weapons.[87]

Early in 1975 General Jones made the case for the US Air Forces in Europe fighting as an integral part of the allied air forces under allied control with a US commander:

> In a war in Central Europe, the initial and principal task of Allied Air Forces must be to assist friendly forces in halting the Pact ground offensive. This requires that NATO air power become immediately and heavily engaged in close air support operations, while attaining local air superiority as necessary. Less immediate critical objectives, such as achieving theater-wide air superiority, must await a reduced need for close air support.[88]

In November 1975, Jones reiterated:

> There may be some documents that talk about air doctrines as to air superiority, interdiction and all of that, but we should recognize that as used in Europe, we operate as part of Allied Air Forces under Allied control with a U.S. commander. The plan is to use the air in Europe to stop a breakthrough with very, very limited operations deep in enemy territory or deep strikes for air superiority against his airfields. . . . I am not saying there will not be some of that. But, basically most of our air would be committed to battlefield support and battlefield air superiority.[89]

TWO DECADES OF TAC DEVELOPMENT

In response to another question, Jones expanded the same theme:

> There is some misinformation around as to what the Air Force's supposed objectives are [in a NATO war]. There are some who have said that we are not out to win an air battle and do deep interdiction, going deep into East Germany and into Poland. But that is incorrect.... The objective of NATO is to keep from losing NATO territory. Therefore, our primary requirements over there would be to help blunt an attack, particularly an armored breakthrough. In doing that we should be providing support to the Army both in attacking targets, and overhead in trying to provide some degree of local air superiority—to keep the enemy from attacking our forces, providing information, particularly in the area as to where possible breakthroughs would be, and hitting the enemy in the interdiction role but right over the hill, right behind his main forces as opposed to deep in his territory.... So we see our primary requirement is to prevent the loss of NATO territory, which is really the objective of the NATO alliance.[90]

When asked what proportion of the tactical air force would be used for air superiority, close air support, and then deep interdiction, General Jones responded,

> We do not break it out that way. We categorize it a little differently. We have our F-111s that are called deep interdiction airplanes by most people. We do not plan to use them for deep interdiction. It is the best all-weather tactical airplane we have. As a former commander of the 4th Allied Tactical Air Force in Europe, not only the U.S. Air Force but of our allies, I considered it to be the No. 1 plane we would use to blast a break-through at night and in bad weather.... We are extensively using it in radar beacon offset bombing and in other modes of employment near the front line. I do not say that under certain conditions we would not use it deeper behind the lines but primarily it would be used nights and/or all-weather in the forward areas in battlefield interdiction—not really close air support of a soldier in a foxhole but in the forward battle area.[91]

During his command in Europe, General Jones noted not only that the Soviets had begun to export their latest and very best equipment to the Warsaw Pact countries in quantity, but that these countries were changing their concepts of tactical air employment. Jones said in March 1975:

> We are reasonably certain that they have now developed a high speed, low altitude penetration capability and an all-weather ground attack capability; the Warsaw Pact forces are improving the overall versatility and flexibility of their fighter/attack aircraft. These developments form a marked departure from earlier austere Soviet aircraft capable of performing specialized missions with limited capability to perform secondary functions.[92]

In 1977, General Jones remarked:

> The Soviets have a new air force.... The significance of this is that for the first time in history, the U.S. Army and the U.S. Air Force are faced with an enemy who can put thousands of tons of weapons down on our air bases and on our supply lines in our rear areas.... In World War II, there were few cases of enemy air attacks on our troops, and none in Korea and Vietnam. Therefore, our task is much bigger; the task of air defense is much bigger. Our task of surviving—shelter for airplanes, being able to repair

airfields—is much bigger. Their aircraft, I would say, are today quite equal to ours from a technological standpoint.[93]

More thoughts about the air superiority situation were provided by Gen George S. Brown in 1978:

> It is our estimate that the Warsaw Pact forces opposite NATO would be able to gain and maintain air superiority over their own ground forces at least in the initial stages of a conflict.... The success of Warsaw Pact efforts to extend air superiority over NATO forces would depend on many factors not the least being the relative strength of opposing forces. Because of the larger number of SAM and AAA accompanying Warsaw Pact ground forces, many of the Pact aircraft could be released from defense counter air missions and launched against NATO forces. Because of this, the Warsaw Pact may be able to gain and maintain air superiority over some NATO forces at least for a limited time during the initial stages of the conflict.[94]

At its inception the NATO command organization arched over independent forces of 15 national entities, each of which continued logistical support for their own forces, which were most frequently kept in the owning country. US force locations continued to remain in southern Germany as a result of the historical location of these forces as World War II ended and occupation of Germany began. Under the nuclear response "trip-wire" strategy extant to 1967, command and control was sufficient if it provided surveillance and warning of Soviet/Warsaw Pact aggression. The flexible response strategy, emphasizing capabilities for sustained conventional defense, stressed a need for a command and control establishment far more versatile than required merely for warning. The steady improvement in Warsaw Pact capabilities in 1969 and thereafter, particularly in tactical aircraft able to attack at low altitudes, also demanded a knitting together of allied air capabilities. In acting against external military aggression, the NATO nations were pledged to work together in a common war effort; in peacetime, the only NATO function for which national forces were under NATO operational control was that of air defense. In the American establishment, the US European Command (USEUCOM) existed primarily to provide the US contribution to the Supreme Allied Commander Europe (SACEUR) used in wartime; in peacetime, the CINCEUCOM exercised operational command over assigned forces through US service components: CINC US Air Forces in Europe (USAFE), CINC US Army, Europe (USAREUR), and CINC US Navy, Europe (USNAVEUR). Although maintaining the integrity of NATO airspace and guarding it against attack were peacetime missions of NATO, General Jones, upon becoming CINCUSAFE in 1971, found West Germany divided between two tactical air forces—the Second Allied Tactical Air Force (2ATAF) in the north and the Fourth Allied Tactical Air Force (4ATAF) in the south. There were also six national air forces in NATO's central region. There was very little interoperability between the 2ATAF that supported the Northern Army Group (NORTHAG) with assigned British, German, Belgium, and Netherlands forces and the Four ATAF that supported the Central Army Group (CENTAG) with assigned US, German, and Canadian forces. With the concept of a short war almost immediately dominated by nuclear weapons, a coordinated application of air power between 2ATAF and 4ATAF had not warranted a great deal of priority. In 1961 the NATO Council had approved construction of an integrated ground control system for air defense called the NATO Air Defense Ground Environment (NADGE), comprising 84 sites in 9 NATO nations and including 2 sites in France. The NADGE system was under construction in 1973 but, like the SAGE system in the United States, it had been overtaken in its building by missiles and third-generation attack aircraft. The NADGE system included many radar sites that were very visible from the air and would be subject to destruction in the first minutes or hours of a war. Since NADGE was a ground-based system there were many terrain-shielded radar gaps through which low-level penetration could be made. The system, moreover, was primarily designed for warning rather than centralized control of aircraft.[95]

Under pressure both to reduce US military manpower in Europe for balance of trade reasons and to rationalize NATO forces for effective conventional defense, General Jones in 1971 conducted an in-depth review of USAFE and its subordinate headquarters, namely, Headquarters Third Air Force at South Ruislip on the outskirts of London, Headquarters Sixteenth Air Force at Torrejón AB, Spain, and Headquarters Seventeenth Air Force at Ramstein AB, West Germany. This study evidenced that USAFE was generously manned with support manpower in relationship to combat manpower because it had been visualized that Air Force commanders would have to receive in a war emergency dual-based rapid reaction and follow-on augmentation forces and make them operative soon after they arrived in Europe. In 1972–73 Headquarters USAFE took over most staff management functions and streamlined the headquarters of the Third, Sixteenth, and Seventeenth Air Forces as operational functions, the Third Air Force being moved to RAF Mildenhall, England, and the Seventeenth from Ramstein AB to Sembach AB, West Germany. The latter move permitted movement of Headquarters USAFE from Lindsey Air Station in the Wiesbaden area to Ramstein AB in mid-1973. At Ramstein, USAFE was collocated with 4ATAF, immediately facilitating closer working relations between US and allied air forces and breaking ground for a conversion of NATO air forces from a deterrent to a warfighting stance.[96]

In June 1974 NATO agreed to create Allied Air Forces Central Europe (AAFCE) and to establish a wartime operations center, effective on 28 June over 2ATAF and 4ATAF. These actions came in recognition of three things—the developing Warsaw Pact threat, the inherent flexibility of air power under unified command, and the need for a capability to commit effectively any of the central region air elements wherever needed in whatever strength throughout the whole region. In explanation of the action, an Air Force spokesman explained its doctrinal rationale:

> The requirement to establish a single air commander for an area of operations is based on sound principles and doctrine established and proven during World War II. These

IDEAS, CONCEPTS, DOCTRINE

principles have been further validated by combat experiences in every conflict since that time. The inherent flexibility and wide ranging capabilities of airpower demand that command and control be centralized to assure optimum employment of these assets and to assure a rapid capability to apply forces where and when they are most needed. To exercise effective command and control in modern warfare, the commander must have near real time information on the situation status of forces and the ability to direct and control his forces.[97]

Gen John W. Vogt, Jr., became CINCUSAFE in June 1974 and also assumed NATO command of Allied Air Forces Central Europe (AAFCE) at its establishment. General Vogt set up an initial peacetime AAFCE headquarters at Ramstein, and with US funds in a cooperative project the Federal Republic of Germany commenced building a secure underground bunker facility at Boerfink, West Germany, to shelter the Allied Forces Central Europe (AFCENT) and the Allied Air Forces Central Europe. Installation of US equipment started in 1976, and the facilities at Boerfink were officially transferred to NATO in June 1977. Headquarters 4ATAF was appropriately collocated with Headquarters Central Army Group at Heidelberg.[98] General Vogt, one of the most highly respected and experienced Air Force combat commanders and a World War II fighter ace, immediately began the work of standardizing and "rationalizing" NATO air power in Central Europe. Vogt first wished to come up with adequate command and control, then to standardize air doctrine, operating procedures, and as many facets of air materiel as possible.[99]

At the establishment of AAFCE General Vogt was tasked with

> the operational command of the assigned and earmarked air forces in the Central Region and the development of the policy required for the centralized direction of those air forces. This was to include the establishment of a common, or at least a fully compatible, air doctrine and procedures region-wide, improvements in interoperability and mutual support, and the tactical evaluation and standardization of training of the air forces.[100]

The background difficulty in rationalizing NATO air power lay both in dissimilar equipment and in dissimilar concepts of employment within the several NATO air forces. On the equipment side, airplanes from the south and central regions could not operate in NORTHAG and vice versa because of communications incompatibilities. American and British aircraft carried different bombs, with the result that bomb shackles and lugs were different and planes could not recover and rearm at each other's bases. The Dutch air force had no all-weather fighters capable of interceptions in extremely bad weather, but the Netherlands airplanes had a very fine ground attack capability. On the other hand, the Netherlands have a very small stretch of the forward edge of the battle area (FEBA). None of the NATO allies considered that they could afford to acquire aircraft designed for particularized missions like the US A-10. The United States stressed close air support much more than any of its allies. The Germans were next, and then the British. Some of the smaller allies were almost totally disinterested in close air support. With limited assets the allies wished to emphasize battlefield interdiction — concentrating where the enemy was massing to exploit a breakthrough — and to leave containment of a breakthrough to the ground forces. The United States and 4ATAF were heavily committed to centralization of TACAIR command and control; the 2ATAF believed that more decentralized methods of operations — especially two aircraft at very low quick-in-and-out — represented the probable realities of wartime. The Germans also liked quick-in-and-out at low altitude and high speed since they were going to be fighting over familiar territory when the crews were training. According to one report the Europeans did not want to be forced into the US mold. Dr Stephen L. Canby wrote about the NATO allies:

> They specifically contend that the U.S. experience in Vietnam is of limited relevance for the European context. In the European view, the nearly one-sided nature of that conflict in the air, the constraints of European weather, and insufficiently varied scheduling of U.S. sorties that unnecessarily exposed U.S. aircraft induced the USAF to prefer a task force mode of operations that may not be appropriate for Europe.[101]

Besieged by American persuasion in 1967, the NATO Council had accepted MC14/3, "Flexible and Appropriate Response," but there was a certain reluctance on the part of some of the allies to give up the trip-wire strategy. In July 1973 Secretary Schlesinger reasoned that the Federal Republic of Germany was most supportive of flexible response: "Others of our allies have been inclined toward the trip-wire strategy for reasons of budget savings, or the argument that if the American presence is there, the Russians will never start anything, so why spend the money."[102] After a visit to Europe in February 1974, Sen Sam Nunn of the Armed Services Committee described the allies as believing that NATO should be prepared to fight conventionally for a relatively short time — measured in weeks. The concept lying behind this plan was that NATO should not prepare to fight the Red Army in a long, conventional war that would destroy much of Western Europe, as in World War II. Rather, NATO should be prepared to fight very hard at the outset of a conflict to stop any conventional attack on the east/west before it penetrated very far. A strategy of initial forward defense at its eastern border was essential to the Federal Republic of Germany, and over the years of trip-wire nuclear planning, the strategy and posture of forward defense was accepted by NATO. The Americans maintained that the logical scenario for NATO to plan for would be a longer period of observed pact buildup for attack — measured in weeks. This plan would permit NATO mobilization and movement of American reinforcement to Europe. The Americans also believed that NATO should be prepared to fight for a longer period conventionally than the allies were willing to lay in logistics to support. Stated Senator Nunn, "These differences in strategic assumptions tend to weaken overall NATO conventional capability because they provide differing bases for force planning and resource allocation among the NATO Allies."[103] In 1975 Secretary Schlesinger agreed that the Warsaw Pact was inclining more and more toward a short war and a strong initial-attack strategy, dependent on a short mobilization and reinforcement. For this reason he ordered increased combat-to-support ratios in US combat forces in Germany with the increased combat strength to occur in forward deployment, in antitank weapons, and in a more rapid air and sea reinforcement capability. At the highest level the US national strategy guidance which had been predicated earlier on a 90-day conventional war scenario was changed to state: "In order to maintain a conventional deterrent, the United States must have the capability to conduct sustained conventional combat for as long as the Soviet Union and its allies are capable of fighting."[104] In January 1977 Senator Nunn nevertheless reported that the Department of Defense had continued to project a three-week's warning of attack against NATO followed by a conventional conflict of up to six months. Nunn said that there was still no common alliancewide agreement on these issues.[105]

One encouragement for a convergence of thought about air employments in the NATO alliance antedated Allied Air Forces Central Europe and was put in motion by the SACEUR, Gen Andrew J. Goodpaster, who in July 1970 requested the NATO Military Agency for Standardization to establish working parties on air, ground, and naval warfare doctrine. Subsequently, NATO defined doctrine as "fundamental principles by which military forces guide their actions in support of objectives." Doctrine covers a wide spectrum of affairs: at the highest level, "basic doctrine" set forth broad principles of warfare in specific media (land, sea, or air); the next lower level was "operational doctrine," which amplified basic doctrine in needed specific functional areas; finally, "operational tactics," the lowest level, dealt with employment of forces in specific combat undertakings, including how to stop attack by a specific enemy formation. The first meeting of the NATO air doctrine working party convened in Belgium on 21 June 1971. The draft of Allied Tactical Publication 33, "NATO Tactical Air Doctrine," was ratified by the NATO nations and promulgated by the NATO Military Agency for Standardization on 10 February 1975. This manual was designed as the doctrinal cornerstone for employment of air power by NATO air commanders. It accepted the Air Force concept of centralized control of air resources as its key principle, and it was considered particularly applicable to the organization of AAFCE, although employment principles set forth were valid throughout NATO. During 1976 ATF 40, "Doctrine and Procedures for Airspace Control in a Combat Zone," was drafted and circulated for allied approval; it became effective in September 1977.[106]

The mandatory US secretary of defense report to Congress on rationalization/standardization in NATO dated 28 January 1978, in the section on air warfare doctrinal development, ended with the statement: "US leadership in this field continues to drive NATO doctrine development programs."[107] The American effort to add commonality, where possible, to the NATO air effort probably led to assertions—including those of Dr Stephen Canby—that the Air Force was trying to force common tactics on the European allies, over their resistance.[108] General Vogt was quite clear on the fact that, "generally speaking, the American Air Force is way, way out ahead of the European air forces in the ECM business." He told a journalist, "And I think it's understandable because we've been the outfit that has been fighting in the missile environment, and we had to develop these things." Although the A-10 was scheduled to arrive in Europe, Vogt emphasized a need in NATO for dual-capability aircraft, an ability of a given plane to perform at least two missions. He wanted the new US lightweight fighter to have both an air-to-air and an air-to-ground capability. General Vogt was not at all opposed to specialization on the part of some of the smaller NATO nations, who might want to tailor their limited number of planes to special purposes. When asked to define the main role of the NATO air forces in combat, Vogt replied:

> I think the major, one of the major, if not the major role is going to be to provide a mass of fire power in support of the ground army to turn off heavy Soviet armor in great quantities. That to me is I think our main mission, our main challenge. But I want to be able to take on the air too, so that they can't interfere — that means neutralize him in the air at the right point in space and time above the battlefield.[109]

Vogt expected the air battle to be

> essentially one of maneuver, with a lot of airplanes mixing it up and very much getting back to the old World War I and World War II type of thing. Where you have to spot your enemy and identify him and get on his tail and shoot him down.... I expect in Europe very fluid battle situations, mobile units, Soviet armor which will be moving very fast . . . with the FEBA shifting back and forth, and with the air situation above the FEBA pretty much determining the outcome of what's happening on the ground. Because if he's able to get in with a lot of attack airplanes and work over our forces, the battle is apt to shift that way. On the other hand, if I can get local air superiority — not air superiority across the Central Front, but air superiority over the battlefield — then of course, we have achieved our objective. We can keep enemy air off the backs of our guys and put a lot of ground support in to destroy the heavy weapons and the armor of the enemy. And that's really what we're going to be doing.[110]

One of the problems in the rearmament of NATO air forces was the surge of Soviet/Warsaw Pact air forces in both quality and quantity of aircraft. By the same token, NATO needed modernization of its second generation jet fighters both in quality and quantity. In 1958-59 the Netherlands, Norway, Canada, and West Germany had selected the F-104 as the new standard fighter, and it needed replacement by a new fighter which General Vogt described as "an airplane that can do the close support mission, carry bombs and deliver them effectively, and do an air superiority job when required. In other words, it has to be able to take on Communist airplanes and cope with them, and outmaneuver them."[111] As Deputy Secretary of Defense Packard had recommended, the Air Force in 1972 instituted a lightweight-fighter prototype development program. In explaining what was afoot, Secretary Seamans suggested that some of the NATO countries might want such a plane since it would have utility in a European-type scenario where an enemy would bring the air battle to the FEBA. But from the outset Air Force spokesmen were reluctant to admit of a competitor for the F-15, which would be prepared to fight for air superiority deep in enemy territory.[112] In this prototyping the Air Force provided design goals for a lightweight, highly maneuverable, sustained supersonic aircraft and left specifics to contractor design teams. On 6 January 1972 the Air Force released proposals to industry, and five contractors submitted responses on 18 February 1972. After evaluation, two lightweight-fighter prototype development contracts, each to build two aircraft, were awarded on 14 April 1972: one with General Dynamics for a YF-16, and the other with Northrop Corporation for a YF-17. Both designs incorporated new technology that greatly increased maneuverability. In addition to maneuvering flaps, the YF-16 incorporated a blended wing/body design which increased lift and provided additional internal volume for equipment and fuel. The YF-16 used a single F-100 engine, which was developed for the F-15, whereas the YF-17 required two YJ-101 engines that were still in development. Both contractors understood that the average unit flyaway cost goal of the lightweight fighter would be held at $3 million in 1972 dollars based on a buy of 300 aircraft.[113]

Early in 1973 Lt Gen Otto J. Glasser was adamant that the lightweight fighter was "purely a technological endeavor." "We have no intention in the Air Force of going into production for this airplane, of asking for a force structure for this airplane," he said.[114] General Ryan said, "The lightweight fighter, as it is presently conceived, is not a weapon system. Instead, it is more of a technology effort so that you can try out these things to see if they do give you that increased performance." But Secretary Seamans was more sanguine, saying,

> Certainly we would not even go to the expense of building a prototype if there were not some chance of it being procured. As I visualize it, we could eventually end up with a mix of fighter aircraft, with the F-15 for all-weather air superiority, and with some kind of lightweight fighter that could be used under more visual conditions.[115]

In 1974 the Air Force added a line item to the fiscal year 1975 budget request that called for an "air combat fighter" which would allow continued improvements on the lightweight fighter if tests showed it interesting enough; but there were still no announced plans for its immediate procurement.[116] About this time, Secretary of Defense Schlesinger began to push for the development of the F-16, but General Brown, as Schlesinger recalled, was "very, very cautious in moving toward the F-16 ... preferring to stay with the F-15."[117] Brown nevertheless called a working group of fighter talent—the best talent from Europe, the Pacific, and the Tactical Air Command—to meet at Wright-Patterson AFB.[118] A key factor in the Air Force considerations was that F-4 fighters would need replacements in the 1980s and F-15s would be too expensive to buy in such great quantities. On 13 January 1975 the Air Force awarded a contract to General Dynamics to develop the F-16, one reason for this choice being that the F-16 had the same engine as the F-15. Air Force Secretary John L. McLucas said, "It is an engine that is already in our inventory, so we won't have to train technicians on the new engine."[119] Prodded by Congress to buy a cheaper fighter than its favored F-14, the US Navy would ultimately take the YF-17 prototype and develop it as the Navy F-18. The Navy liked the YF-17's two engines, among other features. The Air Force programmed a purchase of 650 F-16s to equip six wings. At the same time that the Air Force opted for development of the F-16, a four-nation NATO consortium team was also in Washington looking at this plane. Secretary McLucas hoped it would appeal to them, both because it would increase aircraft standardization in NATO and because quantity purchases would reduce the plane's ultimate costs. In June 1975 the Paris air show provided a fitting background for the NATO consortium of Belgium, Denmark, the Netherlands, and Norway to announce an intention to participate with the United States in coproduction of the F-16, and ultimately to purchase 348 of the planes, in addition to the 650. In the words of Secretary Schlesinger, the NATO allies recognized the happy circumstance wherein the lowest price aircraft had the best performance.[120]

General Jones commented:

> If fiscal constraints were not a driving factor in planning our fighter force, we would deploy the F-15 in sufficient numbers to meet the total threat. However, in the light of projected fiscal constraints, current plans include development and procurement of the less sophisticated, lower cost F-16 which will complement the F-15 in performing the air superiority role.[121]

The Air Force deliberately made the decision not to equip the F-16 for all-weather intercept and all-weather fighting, principally to get a cheaper airplane that would be supportable in the quantities needed. The F-16 would be more dependent on ground radar or AWACS control than the F-15, but it would be a superior fair-weather fighter that could arrest the gap in force size between NATO and the Warsaw Pact. It also was developed with good air-to-ground features. Said Lt Gen Alton D. Slay, Air Force deputy chief of staff for research and development:

> As far as the ground role is concerned, we view it as augmenting the F-111, the residual F-4 force, and the A-10, and it could cover the spectrum throughout that conflict. . . . It is not as survivable as the A-10 in the close air support environment; so we don't say the F-16 is principally a close-support airplane. It is a multimission, reasonably priced addition to our force. It just replaces a portion of the F-4 force, and it replaces a portion of the A-7D force. . . .
>
> We started out getting an air-to-air fighter. . . . And we found that the things that made the airplane good in an air-to-air role, such as power loading, low-wing loading, also were extremely good in air-to-ground context. . . . As an example of what the F-16 will do close to the ground, I almost had a heart attack watching the F-16 do a split "S" from 2,700 feet. It was fantastic as far as maneuverability is concerned. . . . So here we have a fighter that has the load carrying capability of an F-4, just due to its low-wing loading and high thrust, it has the turning capability . . . actually better than F-86, in an air-to-ground environment. And it just turned out that we got more than we paid for in having a multipurpose capable airplane. We aren't always that fortunate.[122]

In Central Europe the NATO air defense ground environment (NADGE) aircraft warning and control system was not even then completed in 1970 when perceptions first appeared that the Soviet/Warsaw Pact air forces were becoming potentially able to penetrate and attack at low level. Quite soon a large number of modern Soviet aircraft were being deployed to Warsaw Pact nations, and the Fitters and Floggers in particular were very capable of all-weather attack. Although NADGE control centers could be dug-in and hardened, ground-radar installations could not be so protected. Many of the radars had been in place for as many as 20 years, and it was inconceivable that the Soviets had not targeted them for immediate attack. In 1970–72 NATO examined various ways to counter the threat, which turned out to be adding more fixed radars to the system, deploying mobile radars, or going to an airborne early-warning stance. The last prospect was selected, and the issue was to make a choice between the Air Force's E-3A AWACS, the Navy's E-2, or Britain's Nimrod. The E-2 and the Nimrod were designed basically for fleet sea surveillance and warning, and the E-3A AWACS was the best prospect, but it would be very expensive in unit cost and would have to be financed with substantial sums of money above existing national defense programs. Moreover, the Air Force was taking its time developing a standard AWACS configuration. Maj Gen Richard C. Bowman, director of NATO and European Affairs in the Office of the Assistant Secretary of Defense for International Security Affairs, would recall:

> As you know, even in this country, even with it being our own people, we had trouble convincing many people [about the value of the AWACS]. The airplane doesn't drop bombs, it doesn't shoot machine guns and, therefore, if you haven't got a good understanding of the tactical air problem it is hard to picture just why a system that is this expensive should be part of the program.[123]

The major NATO problems affecting AWACS was the large cost of the program, but how to use the plane was a secondary concern. According to Gen Lew Allen, Jr., the NATO countries primarily focused on a need for AWACS as a provider of airborne early warning capability.[124] In American design, however, AWACS had the electronics for both warning and interceptor control, and there was good reason for the latter since the plane would be deployed as needed in many parts of the world. The ability of AWACS to look down in the ground clutter of Central Europe and put fighters on targets also would be a decided advantage. But airborne control of fighters in the European view would still provide more centralized direction that was distrusted — especially by the British, who believed that Allied Air Forces Central Europe should only be an overarching and a coordinating headquarters with minimum command and should leave real control (tasking) to 2ATAF and 4ATAF.[125]

In 1974 two Air Force officers voiced answers to why AWACS should not be limited to service as an austere NATO early-warning radar platform and leave data processing and interceptor control to ground-control centers which were hardened and presumably survivable. Lt Gen William J. Evans, deputy chief for research and development, admitted this as a possibility in Europe but argued that elimination of the surveillance and command and control capability of the AWACS would limit its usefulness "to only those areas which would have ... ground based capabilities, and would, therefore, restrict its use for worldwide contingencies."

Maj Gen Lee M. Paschall, director of command, control, and communications, and deputy chief of staff for programs and resources, pointed out that both AWACS and the Tactical Air Control System (TACS) would be used in Europe. The AWACS, for example, could not duplicate the large capacity for control existing in the ground TACS. Paschall said:

> When the two systems operate together, they complement each other. The AWACS provides continuity of control deep into enemy territory, warning friendly fighters of hostile actions and the ground system of hostile aircraft approaching friendly territory. The ground system is then better prepared to counter enemy actions and to defend and support ground forces and installations.[126]

Early in 1975 an experimental AWACS went to Europe and flew 21 sorties in a month, interoperating with the US Navy in the Mediterranean, the Royal Navy and Royal Air Force in England, and USAFE in Germany. All facets of AWACS were demonstrated in controlling aircraft and air strikes, running intercepts, and down-linking tracks and information to the NADGE and to the TACS to demonstrate what AWACS could accomplish in terms of providing detailed information to NATO commanders on the ground. In the demonstration AWACS was surprisingly able to pick up fast-moving automobiles on the speed-free autobahns of Germany.[127]

In March 1975 Secretary Schlesinger went on record with the statement: "We urgently need an AWACS capability in NATO Europe." But he added that the acquisition costs for AWACS would be much easier for the US taxpayer to understand if the NATO community paid a fair share of the total bill.[128] Under such circumstances the question of how many AWACS the Air Force would buy hinged in part on how many AWACS planes NATO would finance. The Air Force calculated AWACS requirements on a basis of two for each orbit—one in orbit and one on the ground preparing to relieve the one on station. Exclusive of NATO AWACS, the Joint Chiefs of Staff stated that the Air Force's "prudent risk" AWACS requirement worldwide was 53 E-3As, but its "fiscally constrained" objective was set at 34 aircraft. In 1975 the Air Force hoped that NATO would buy between 20 and 30 E-3As, or a force adequate for both of NATO's flanks as well as its center.[129] In late 1975 the NATO military committee declared that an airborne early warning (AEW) force was "the only feasible means, in the present state of technology, of providing the necessary enhancement of the defensive capability of the alliance against the growing threat posed by the Warsaw Pact's new and sophisticated weapons systems, particularly against NATO forces at low level." The NATO defense ministers recommended airborne early warning to their civilian superiors as a "priority one requirement." NATO asked for firm cost data on a buy of 20 to 32 NATO-configured AWACS.[130]

As the NATO defense ministers met in an unusual session on 25 March 1977, called solely to reach a final agreement on AWACS, there was an initial expectation that they would agree to recommend to their respective legislatures the procurement of 27 NATO-configured E-3As to be collectively purchased by the alliance. In the United States the Tactical Air Command had taken delivery of its first production model E-3A on 23 March 1977. Only Iceland, which had no military forces, had expressed no interest in buying into the AWACS force, but Iceland would accept basing effective in October 1978 of a US E-3A contingent to replace the EC-121s that had been covering the Greenland-Iceland-United Kingdom (GIUK) gap into the North Atlantic for the previous 25 years. At the meeting, however, the British were in a bad spot; they had put their Nimrod program on a hold status because AWACS was best for the alliance. In NATO armament programs each ally as a matter of practice always attempted to get the largest advantage for its industries, and AWACS was a program in which the greatest economic return from the NATO-AWACS procurement would remain in the United States. With unemployment running high in an economic downturn, the UK defense ministry was under tremendous political pressure to go for English production of the Nimrod rather than buy into AWACS. The British nevertheless emphasized that they would not opt out of the NATO program; they would put their Nimrods under NATO control, and it would do the same things that their part of the AWACS force would have done. This development sent the military planners back to their drawing boards, figuring out what the Nimrods would do, how many NATO E-3As would be required, and how the cost could be worked out. At a 5–6 December 1978 defense planning committee meeting in Brussels, the NATO defense ministers finally approved what was now called the NATO airborne early warning and control (AEW&C) program. The British contribution would be 11 Nimrods, NATO would procure 18 E-3A aircraft — both Nimrods and NATO E-3As to be interoperable with Air Force E-3As. The program called for modifications to make 52 ground sites interoperable with AWACS aircraft and the refurbishing of a main operating base (MOB) in Germany and some forward bases for the force. The modification of the ground sites was considered important since the procedure would be that the AWACS would send track information down to the hardened sites and they would control interceptions. This was necessary in a high-density attack environment since there would not be enough controllers in the E-3As to handle the entire region. As it was approved in December 1978, the NATO AEW&C program became the largest commonly funded project undertaken by the alliance.[131]

Although President Carter ordered in his Presidential Memoranda 10 a review of national security policy immediately after taking office, his view on NATO was best described as a reaffirmation of the long-standing strategy of US support for the Atlantic Alliance, with — in the words of Ambassador Robert W. Komer, who was bought in as adviser to the secretary of defense for NATO affairs — a few "new wrinkles." At a May 1977 NATO summit meeting in London, Carter stated that the United States would make the alliance the heart of American foreign policy. Carter told the Atlantic Treaty Association Conference in Reykjavík in August 1977, "The United States remains categorically committed to NATO's strategy of forward defense and flexible response." In the Carter view, the United States had let US capabilities to help defend Western Europe lag during a decade of primary focus on Southeast Asia and had "some catching up to do."[132] In assessing the situation in Europe, Secretary of Defense Harold Brown said:

> In recent years the Soviets, having first established divisional forces and supporting air units, filled them up to full strength and then, subsequently, upgraded their equipment. Although I think we probably still have an edge in some things, they are at least in the same ball park with respect to quality of equipment. Currently, they are ahead in numbers and close in quality of equipment.... To summarize the NATO situation, I think that we need to do more and our allies need to do more if we are to avoid a situation some years from now when the Soviets may feel themselves sufficiently ahead both in quality and quantity of materials to be encouraged either to make a military venture or, what I think is far more likely in those circumstances to start acting in a bullying, political way.[133]

Just as the Carter administration reaffirmed previous US policy toward the Atlantic Alliance, it also continued the strategy of preparing for one and one-half wars. In a response to a congressional question relevant to this strategy, the Office of the Secretary of Defense observed:

> It is true that Soviet non-nuclear capabilities have grown in size and sophistication, but US and Allied capabilities have changed as well. Most important, however, is the changed situation in Asia. While North Korea is no less a source of danger than it was a decade ago, the Sino-Soviet split and our changed relationship with the PRC [People's Republic of China] made it less likely that the North Koreans would receive any external encouragement or support for a major military adventure. Overall, it has become much more difficult than in the 1960's to imagine a large-scale conflict on the mainland of Asia requiring US forces more or less simultaneously with the demands of a major crisis or conflict in Europe.[134]

A harbinger of NATO emphasis under the Carter administration was reduction in the fiscal year 1979 budget requests originating in the preceding administration in favor of increases in tactical forces. The Department of Defense explained:

> The basic rationale for this modest shift in our priorities is our assessment (1) that an adequate U.S. strategic retaliatory posture can be achieved at some savings with our proposed bomber/ALCM force, vice the previously programmed B-1 force; (2) that a major, collective NATO effort, led by the United States, is necessary to counter the Warsaw Pact's growing capability to conduct a brief, intense conventional campaign in Central Europe, perhaps with only a few days advance warning to NATO; and (3) that improving our capability for such a conflict in the Central Region was sufficiently important at this time to justify some delays in modernization of our naval forces.[135]

To increase the strength of forward conventional defenses, the Carter administration's fiscal year 1979 defense budget included provisions for improved capabilities for rapid reinforcement. In 1977, in the first 10 days of war, the United States could expect to augment its 5-2/3 divisions and 28 tactical air squadrons in Europe by not much more than 1 division and 40 squadrons. The new plan was to be able by 1983 to add 5 divisions and 60 tactical air squadrons in the same amount of time; this by increased strategic airlift and repositioning of supplies in prepositioned overseas materiel configured to unit sets (POMCUS) stocks in Europe.[136] The Air Force also would modernize its forces in Europe and add additional units: a second wing of F-111s, a wing of F-15s in 1977, and the addition of A-10s which were going to begin to enter the inventory and would be sent to Europe soon.[137]

The Carter administration's priority to the Atlantic Alliance was reflected in the Air Force by activities that Gen Wilbur L. Creech, the assistant vice chief of staff who would become commander of the Tactical Air Command on 1 May 1978, described as full support for the requirements of coalition warfare. Creech said, "We are working hard to keep our people within the Air Force thinking about coalition warfare and its special demands and opportunities."[138] Lt Gen Howard Fish, who was serving as assistant vice chief of staff in 1978, summarized the Air Force needs relative to NATO as:

> Modernized forces, rapid deployment, adequate basing, high unit readiness, increased sortie rates, well-trained and motivated personnel, sufficient spares and munitions, improved airbase survivability and greater coalition warfighting capability through increased standardization and interoperability—all these will be needed to achieve a credible deterrent or war winning capability against the threat confronting us in Europe today.[139]

Under the press to "think NATO," already planned modernizations of US air forces in Europe were accelerated. The first F-15s of the 36th Tactical Fighter Wing were deployed to Bitburg Air Base, West Germany, in January 1977, and the wing (72 F-15s) completed the move in midsummer 1977. In March through midsummer 1977, an F-111F wing (84 F-111Fs) established itself at the Royal Air Force (RAF) base at Lakenheath in England. In 1978 the integrated air defense structure in the 2 ATAF area of responsibility was augmented by the movement of the 32d Tactical Fighter Squadron (18 F-15s) to Camp New Amsterdam, the Netherlands. This squadron gave the Royal Netherlands Air Force some familiarization with Air Force air defense procedures, and a second F-15 squadron was planned for the base in wartime. As already noted, the first operational employment of the E-3A AWACS of the Greenland-Iceland-United Kingdom (GIUK) gap commenced in October 1978, and 14 E-3As were operational by the end of the year. Production of A-10s ran ahead of projections, permitting the United States to notify NATO of the deployment of these close-air-support attack planes beginning in 1979 instead of 1981. RAF bases at Woodbridge and Bentwaters in England were approved as collocated operating bases (COBs) for a bed-down of six squadrons of A-10s, and the aircraft would be rotated to forward operating locations (FOLs) in Europe to train over territory where they would be expected to fight. The first A-10 squadron was activated at Myrtle Beach AFB, South Carolina, in July 1977 and became capable in October, three months ahead of schedule. During 1977 two A-10s made demonstration visits to Korea and six went to Germany. The bed-down of 108 A-10s at Bentwaters/Woodbridge began in January 1979, and the deployment of the last of two squadrons to Woodbridge was held up according to plan by the decision to begin to schedule A-10s and F-16s directly for the Air National Guard beginning in the summer of 1979. All of this happened before the last regular Air Force squadrons completed conversion.[140] In addition to these deployments to Europe, the Air Force was committed to very rapid reinforcement from the United States. In 1978 the Air Force made a major commitment to have active squadrons under way in less than 24 hours. Air National Guard and Air Reserve forces could be mobilized for deployment within 72 hours after notification. Flow plans and procedures were worked out to get these units overseas in a hurry and to bed them down smoothly and efficiently.[141]

In the Carter administration's emphasis upon the North Atlantic Alliance, the Air Force was committed to sharpen its capabilities to "deploy rapidly, beddown and fight immediately," but preparations for battle by a miscellany of allies continued to be difficult. In a spontaneous answer to a point-blank question put in June 1978, General Fish cited five key readiness deficiencies, in these words:

> I believe that one of the greatest of the deficiencies that we have is our command and control capabilities as far as being survivable and secure. Coupled with this is an insufficient capability to disrupt the enemy's command and control communications.... The second deficiency is, of course, our capability to fight under chemical warfare conditions.... Third, I would say is more realistic training on the ranges, particularly in Europe.... Our night and all-weather attack capability is deficient. I would put that high on the list. We are working on correcting this deficiency.... A fifth deficiency is our lack of capability to provide adequate airlift for our objectives to get the troops to Europe with their equipment.[142]

The prospect of operating effectively within a chemical warfare environment admitted no ready solution, since the best deterrent for chemical warfare was an offensive chemical capability, which the United States had foresworn. Provisioning of airlift, fighter training, all-weather air attack paraphernalia, and antielectronic attack capabilities were worldwide Air Force tactical air problems, and are considered later as such. The problems of developing a NATO command and control and base infrastructure, however, remained fraught with alliance divergencies. In 1978 Ambassador Komer pointed out that in his opinion nothing had been done to integrate alliance communications in the 30 years of NATO. He said, "It turns out, the telecommunication industry is a big operation in other countries besides the United States. Getting the various industrial barons together on some of these things is not exactly easy."[143] In response to a Soviet/Warsaw Pact threat, the Air Force was committed to a rapid, all-out movement of air units to Europe, where host nations would bed them down on collocated operating base (COB) facilities. The COB program thus made available for use by reinforcing US aircraft facilities excess to the needs of host nation at strategically located airfields. Although access to COBs provided a variety of otherwise unavailable facilities, these bases had little access to minimum essential facilities (MEF) — ammunition and fuel storage for initial operations plus adequate ramp space for dispersed aircraft parking. In March 1982 General Allen said that "great progress" had been made in identifying needed COBs and needed essential facilities but neither the host nations nor the US Congress had been willing to fund the construction. Gen Bernard W. Rogers, commander in chief, US European Command, reiterated: "Unfortunately, because of the limited NATO funding available and a U.S. reluctance to prefinance this effort, we are at present able to support with MEF only a small fraction of the U.S. air reinforcements that deploy to COB's."[144] The COB situation affected the potential of the US for sustained-duration operations in Europe as of 1982. Earlier—in 1980—General Allen and Secretary Hans Mark had pointed to another problem affecting sustained air operations with the newer models of aircraft, caused by a long-time, underfunding of operations and maintenance (O&M) accounts. Allen rationalized how this "inexcuseable" situation had come about:

> It was only a few years ago, that is in the early part of the mid-seventies when the US was still operating on a trip wire strategy against our major scenario of war in Europe.... In the 1973 time period that strategy began to change and it began to be clear that we wanted those aircraft to be able to fight for an extended period of time and not imagine that a nuclear war would start so quickly. Therefore, we set goals for ourselves—fifteen days, then thirty days, and later a longer time in terms of the sustainability of the force. These goals determine the war reserve spare kits, the base level sufficiency kits, and other war reserve material which we need. For various reasons in this period of time we have not taken the steps that should be taken to fill up those accounts. We have just never done it. As we introduced new aircraft, we were late filling those accounts because we wanted to develop good rates of consumption before we made a large investment in spares—that also put us behind. In other situations we just made compromises against those sustainability factors.... I think it is a case where we have not done the job of management that we should have done.[145]

At the insistence of the United States and over strenuous objections of some European governments, the Atlantic Alliance shifted away from reliance on a nuclear trip wire to an emphasis of a conventional response to Soviet/Warsaw Pact attack. Even so, there continued to be acknowledged reliance on what was described as the "NATO Triad," namely strong conventional forces, theater nuclear forces, and strategic force components. Secretary Brown justified the presence of nuclear warheads in Europe, stating:

> A sizeable continuing NATO theater nuclear force is certainly needed to offset Warsaw Pact forces.... The Alliance strategy is one of controlling escalation and terminating a conflict at the lowest level of violence possible, and the threat of escalation using forces held in reserve contributes to this strategy. The Warsaw Pact must perceive a high degree of risk and of uncertainty as to the NATO response. As long as theater nuclear forces are relatively survivable and can ride out attacks, and backed by highly survivable US strategic forces... the temptations to the other side to strike first are minimized.[146]

Although there were some 7,000 US tactical nuclear warheads in Europe in 1978, Gen Bruce K. Holloway, waiting after retirement, pointed out that there was no doctrine for their employment.

> Fortunately, since 1972 assured destruction has given way to a much wiser strategy of flexibility.... However, there are still large gaps in the strategy, and even larger gaps in the projected weapon and force structures that must match the strategy. The biggest gap is the lack of a doctrine for employment of tactical nuclear weapons.... We have long held that nukes are not "just another weapon." We have vigorously and self-righteously preached this notion on moral grounds, and not without logic. However, it is time to set aside this Sunday-school doctrine in favor of the kind of hard planning that amalgamates the entire spectrum of weaponry. The place to start is in Europe, in the European Command and in SHAPE. In Washington, this shift must be recognized as necessary and encouraged.[147]

In a similar tenor was an article by Col David L. Nichols, who pointed out that the concepts for the employment of nuclear TACAIR were "outdated." "The capabilities of TACAIR delivery systems have greatly benefited from advancing technology," he wrote, "but the mission concept has remained unchanged since 1952, when the first F-84 fighter-bomber was given a nuclear role in Europe."[148] The mission concept was typically nuclear alert, whereby tactical fighters were held ready for striking prebriefed quick-reaction alert (QRA) targets. Nichols agreed that in some instances QRA aircraft would have greater accuracy and inflict lower collateral damage than missile systems. Moreover, TACAIR on nuclear alert was the only means whereby some of the NATO allies could share in a nuclear strike role. But he urged that the QRA mission concept vitiated the potential flexibility of TACAIR, its advantages in mobility, range, responsiveness, tactical versatility, penetrating ability, firepower delivery, target acquisition/battlefield assessment, and recovery and recycling. Nichols argued, "TACAIR should continue with the alert role, particularly peacetime QRA; however, the overall alert concept needs to be modified to allow more flexibility."[149]

Early in 1961 photography by U-2 aircraft laid to rest President Kennedy's fears of a strategic nuclear missile gap with the Soviet Union by revealing that the Soviets had given first priority to the deployment of intermediate-range nuclear force (INF) missiles rather than intercontinental missiles.

Strategist Paul H. Nitze reminisced:

> For a long time, inadequate attention was given to the increasing deployment of the INF missiles by the USSR in part because they were big, inaccurate, liquid fueled and based on soft pads. They looked like deterrent weapons, not the kind of weapons one would want if one actually contemplated fighting.[150]

In the planning of the 1950s it was perceived that in Europe theater nuclear forces, by providing strong links between conventional forces and strategic forces and a wide range of targeting options, greatly strengthened deterrence. During the 1960s the Air Force operated Matador and Mace ground-launched cruise missiles, targeting them against fixed-enemy installations such as airfields. The Army fielded a short-range Pershing IA ballistic missile, targeting it against fixed, time-sensitive, and heavily defended objectives. As was seen earlier, NATO wanted and the Air Force requested development of a mobile, medium-range ballistic missile, but

Congress refused to fund its development. The US Army received approval for the development of an extended-range Pershing II missile in the mid-1970s. This missile was to be used in the eventuality of programmed nuclear strikes in support of SACEUR, after which it would revert to general support of the Army in the field. If based in West Germany, the range of the Pershing II would permit it to attack targets in the Soviet Union with very little warning time; it would have an earth-penetrator warhead option; its accuracy, combined with high-velocity, near-vertical trajectory, offered an assured, quick-reaction, all-weather capability for attacking enemy main operating bases (MOBs). The Pershing II was perceived to be a prime candidate for executing a "mousetrap" counterattack in which enemy MOBs would be knocked out while enemy aircraft were airborne during strikes against NATO, thus denying them a place to land or forcing their dispersal to other less-well-defended airfields where they would be easier to attack.

In 1977 the Army attempted to give the Pershing II to the Air Force but the Air Force did not want to pay for its development out of Air Force funding. The Air Force also preferred to proceed with the development of a less complex ground-launched cruise missile (GLCM) which would be fielded in a ready adaptation from a canister and booster launch design concept of the Tomahawk submarine-launched cruise missile (SLCM). General Jones conceived that the GLCM (soon popularly pronounced "glikkum") would take over the QRA nuclear alerts from tactical fighters and free them to fight conventionally. Although either GLCM or Pershing II could be used to attack many of the same all-weather fixed targets, each had unique capabilities to make both attractive. The GLCM, for example, had a stated range of 2,500 kilometers and could outdistance the Pershing. In 1977 General Jones got a small amount of money included in the fiscal year 1978 budget to work on a GLCM.[151] As development of an already nearly perfected submarine-launched cruise missile (slikkum) version of the nuclear-type GLCM got under way rather readily, the US Tactical Air Command could see nothing immediately better for defense emitter suppression than a GLCM with a conventional warhead. TAC asked that such be developed for a standoff defense suppression. Said Gen Robert J. Dixon, the TAC commander, "We have not found anything better . . . and we need a standoff capability desperately."[152]

Before 1977, Soviet theater-dedicated nuclear missiles were at vulnerable fixed sites, and each missile had only one warhead, but during the same year the USSR began deploying new mobile, solid-propellant, 5,000-kilometer range SS-20s. These missiles had three MIRV warheads, and each launcher was also provided with a refire missile, also with three warheads. Ambassador Nitze remarked, "They look like war fighting weapons. Unless they are limited or offset the entire Eurasian land mass would live under an intolerable threat."[153] The Backfire bomber and the Soviet/Warsaw Pact frontal aviation already threatened NATO, and in 1978 Gen Alexander Haig, CINCEUR, noted Europe's growing concern with the increasing imbalance in longer range theater nuclear systems represented by the SS-20. Haig regarded the increased survivability, accuracy, and affordability, "from the European perspective."[154] During the careful allied examination of longer range theater nuclear capabilities, the United States offered options of drawing on ongoing programs: Pershing II, GLCM, SLCM, air-launched cruise missile, a new medium-range ballistic missile (MRBM), and aircraft. In his analysis of the requirement for allied response to the Soviet threat, Secretary Brown rationalized:

> We do not plan our theater nuclear forces to defeat, by themselves, a determined Soviet attack in Europe, and we rely mainly on conventional forces to deter conventional attack.... It remains essential, nonetheless, for NATO to maintain, or as necessary acquire, the flexibility to leave the Soviets under no illusion that some way exists, by nuclear means, to gain military or political leverage on the Alliance. U.S. Central Systems, of course, remain the ultimate deterrent, and are inextricably linked to the defense of Europe. Augmentation of NATO's long-range theater nuclear forces based in Europe, however, would complete the Alliance's continuum of deterrence and defense, and strengthen the linkage of U.S. strategic forces to the defense of Europe. Indeed, increased NATO options for restrained and controlled nuclear responses reduce the risk that the Soviets might perceive—however incorrectly—that because NATO lacked credible theater military responses, they could use or threaten to use their own long-range theater nuclear forces to advantage.... We must also be able to counter the SS-20s and BACKFIREs from the theater, and place at risk Pact forces and assets deep in Eastern Europe and the western military districts of the USSR. As one example, we cannot permit a situation in which the SS-20 and BACKFIRE have the ability to disrupt and destroy the formation and movement of our operational reserves, while we cannot threaten comparable Soviet forces.[155]

In the Atlantic Alliance planning for the modernized theater missile undertaking, the Federal Republic of Germany was willing to accept Pershing II missiles, but it was unwilling to be the only continental country to accept a new long-range nuclear system. Consequently, longer-range GLCMs had to be accepted by the other NATO allies. On 12 December 1979 the foreign and defense ministers of the 14 NATO nations came to a two-track decision about what to do about the Soviet threat, namely to deploy offsetting Pershings and GLCMs; and also seek negotiations with the Soviets to limit such theater nuclear missile systems on both sides. In West Germany US Pershing IA missiles would be replaced one-for-one by Pershing II missiles, and 464 GLCMs would be procured and deployed in hard shelters in West Germany, the United Kingdom, Italy, the Netherlands, and Belgium, the latter two countries reserving the right to have additional time to consider whether to take the GLCMs allocated to them. Since the new theater nuclear systems would be deployed with US units in Europe, the United States agreed to assume most of their costs, except that there was a prospect that basing costs would be paid back from the NATO infrastructure program. The United States also undertook during 1980 to withdraw from Europe 1,000 nuclear warheads that could be released in the modernization effort. In outlining the agreement, Secretary Brown summarized:

> I should stress, in designing this response, that one of its purposes is to lay to rest any questions about the credibility of the US commitment to the defense of Europe.... Our strategic, theater nuclear, and conventional forces are and will remain capable of thwarting the purposes of any attacks on Europe and inflicting heavy costs on the

attacker. That is the essence of the flexible response embodied in NATO's military guidance (MC-14/3) and our countervailing strategy, and it is at the heart of credible deterrence.[156]

The NATO decision of 12 December 1979 to make a nuclear missile response to the growing Soviet theater-dedicated SS-20 nuclear missile threat was followed by a course of events, some of which do not appear to have been anticipated. The Soviet Union quickly increased the pace of its SS-20 buildup to a rate of one additional unit every five days. In February 1982, the US Department of Defense counted between 285–300 SS-20s in deployment, primarily directed toward Western Europe. Talks in Europe on intermediate-range arms, led on the American side by Ambassador Nitze, made no substantive progress. The Soviets made it apparent that they would not take part in serious arms control talks until they were thoroughly convinced that NATO was steadfast in its commitment to go forward with the GLCM and Pershing II. In March 1982, after the Soviets had fielded some 300 SS-20s with 900 warheads and 900 refire warheads, President Leonid I. Brezhnev announced a unilateral moratorium on the further deployment of SS-20s in the European Soviet Union in the absence of "practical preparations" for the deployment of GLCMs and Pershing IIs. Such a freeze was rejected because it would have locked NATO into a position of permanent inferiority as far as intermediate-range missiles was concerned, but the Brezhnev ploy further aggravated popular unrest in the form of antinuclear demonstrations in Western Europe. These burgeoning antinuclear groups tested the resolution of the Atlantic Alliance: the Federal Republic of Germany, United Kingdom, and Italy were unswayed, but Belgium and the Netherlands were willing to postpone receiving their share of the GLCMs.[157]

Because the Air Force GLCM was a variant of the Navy's Tomahawk and the Pershing II was in some respect an upgraded Pershing IA, the Department of Defense was optimistic about developmental problems. In March 1980 Secretary Brown projected that with procurement beginning in fiscal year 1981, GLCM would reach an initial operational capability in December 1983. The plan was to deploy 160 in Europe by September 1985 and have 464 of them in hard shelters in Europe by September 1988. All Pershing IAs were to have been replaced by Pershing IIs by September 1985. The total acquisition program cost at the inception of the GLCM program in fiscal year 1981 was projected to be $1.5 billion, but by fiscal year 1984, the cost was being quoted as being $3.6 billion. The Air Force's plan was that the Tactical Air Command would organize GLCM flights, each made up of four tractor-erector launchers and each with four missiles that would be assigned to Air Force units at NATO bases. The flights would go out into the field on direction and authorization from SACEUR; they would be subordinate to SACEUR through the Air Force component commander. As it happened, the ground equipment, especially the security for a launch control center and building of the transporter erector-launcher, was more complex and costly than first anticipated. These and other added costs concurrently needed to get an early IOC combined with inflation to cause the substantial increase of the GLCM program. In March 1981 General Allen could see no way to abandon the GLCM program, since the West German government would not receive Pershing IIs unless the other allies received GLCMs. The Air Force had accordingly not given any thought about what could be done better with the $3 billion plus to be spent for the GLCM program, but Allen added: "If the United States were to choose not to develop and deploy GLCM, the money currently programmed for GLCM would be spent on other priority Air Force programs not currently funded."[158] Another Air Force spokesman, however, had an alternate proposal for the GLCM. Lt Gen Kelly Burke, deputy chief of staff for research, development, and acquisition, in February 1981 called attention to the fact that Air Force F-111s were a very potent dual-capable asset, as were the tactical fighters belonging to West Germany, the Netherlands, Belgium, and Italy that were standing on QRA. The F-111s would remain on quick-reaction alert, and the NATO F-16s and Tornado tactical fighters that would be becoming operational would also be dual-capable fighters. New stockpiles of B-61 nuclear bombs with enhanced safety locks and security features were being stored in Europe. Combined with F-111 accuracy, Burke said, the B-61 "would be adequate for a hardened silo or would destroy a fair sized city.... The dual-capable airplane is really the most cost-effective way to add force, because the force is still available... for all manner of other missions; they are very flexible. You can put them against any target anywhere." Whereas the Air Force had earlier made the case for the GLCM relieving dual-capable fighters for conventional operations, General Burke now described the GLCM as "a very nice complement" to the dual-purpose plane, "particularly in the fact that it has very long range, it has very high en route survivability, and it is accurate."[159] "The modernization of LRTNF [Long-Range Theater Nuclear Forces] is my No. 1 priority, to follow through and get those GLCMs and Pershing IIs deployed," declared Gen Bernard W. Rogers, supreme allied commander Europe/CINC European Command, on 20 February 1981. He continued:

> Under current conditions with the status of our conventional forces, and particularly our lack of sustainability, we have built ourselves a short war. That is why the strategy which I can implement today... is the strategy of "delayed trip" wire, delayed by a certain number of days, depending upon warning time, timely decisions by political authorities ... and so on.... When D plus X day comes, we face two options in NATO under current conditions. We either have to escalate to theater nuclear weapons ... or we have to capitulate. Neither one of those is viable in my view and that is why our objective in Allied Command Europe is to get sufficient conventional forces to hold the initial thrust of the lead divisions of the lead armies until we can take under conventional attack the follow-on divisions of those lead armies that follow at about 70 to 200 kilometers behind.[160]

With hard commitments Rogers estimated that the Atlantic Alliance nations could develop the kind of conventional force he described by the end of the 1980s: "Then, if attacked conventionally, we can force the decision to the other side to escalate or withdraw." Meanwhile, the two nuclear legs of the NATO Triad — US strategic nuclear forces coupled with NATO nuclear defenses — would have to compensate for the third leg — NATO conventional power — in deterring Soviet/Warsaw Pact aggression.[161]

Fixed-Wing Air and Attack Helicopters in Controversy

The concept of US armed services roles and missions antedated the National Security Act of 1947, when the Air Force became a separate service. General Momyer recalled from years of study and experience,

> The Air Force position on this question is based on the promise that each service contributes the particular forces for which it is expert; and collectively, these forces form a unified, mutually supporting combat team. By each service specializing in its particular area of responsibility, economy is promoted, duplication is eliminated, and, most importantly, more effective combat power against the enemy is realized.[162]

Although the National Security Act of 1947 established the Department of the Air Force and the Air Force, it also provided that the Army, Navy, and Marine Corps would continue to possess "such aviation as may be organic therein."[163] In 1963 the OSD general council gave an opinion in regard to the aviation composition of the Army in terms of the National Security Act of 1947, stating that "Army aviation includes artillery spotters, observation and liaison aircraft and other similarly small aircraft which it is more efficient to place under the control of the Army, but not typical combat or significant transport aircraft."[164] A 26 November 1956 directive by Secretary of Defense Charles E. Wilson that was later republished as Department of Defense Directive 5160.22, dated 18 March 1957, made it clear that the Air Force included "among its primary responsibilities those of furnishing close combat and logistical air support for the US Army." The directive also contained a specific statement that US Army aviation would not provide an aircraft to perform the function of close combat air support. As has been seen, Secretary McNamara pressed the Army to give more attention to developing an organic airmobility capability and stated that he was not applying such limitations to the Army as the Wilson directive included. He said, however, that he would be sensitive to incipient "serious duplications" between the Army and Air Force. In March 1965 he said:

> The danger is, I think, that the Army will move beyond the procurement of aircraft directly related to its own mission and appropriately assigned to it, such as helicopters, into the procurement of aircraft to carry out functions such as close air support or transport of large quantities of materiel, which functions the Air Force would be better prepared to carry out. That is a danger. It is one we are sensitive to.[165]

Brig Gen William J. Maddox, Jr., US Army director of army aviation, explained the US Army interpretation of the language of the National Security Act of 1947:

> The primary function of the Army is . . . to organize, train, and equip land forces for operations on land. It is the Army's position that the aviation incorporated into its forces

and planned for the future is intended to further its mission and not to duplicate either the role or capability of any other service. This includes the role of close air support which the Army shares with all the services.... Under the Army's land force charter, it is logical to organize, train, and equip units for which a full-time need is apparent—for example, maneuver units, artillery, helicopter lift and support forces. It is reasonable to rely on other services for actions which are highly specialized or for which there is a nonrecurring need such as naval and air transport and tactical air support.[166]

In view of Secretary McNamara's expressed intention not to apply the rigid limits of DOD Directive 5160.22, the Army assumed that the directive was a dead letter. "The entire Howze Board—the air mobility concept," said Lt Gen Robert R. Williams, Army assistant chief of staff for force development, "was in direct violation of that directive." General Williams rationalized that weapon systems were allocated not by what "a piece of paper said 20 years ago" but by consideration in defense budgetary and programming and approval cycles and authorization cycles:

> If a ... service wants to develop a new system, any major system, it is required to go through a process in defense where a DCP [development concept paper] is written, all the services comment on it and finally at each step it goes before the [Defense Systems Acquisition Review] Council, of all the Assistant Secretaries, and has to be approved by the Deputy Secretary of Defense.[167]

After that the proposal had to be approved and funded by Congress.

The Marine Corps started the airmobility concept using H-19 helicopters for troop lift; but enjoying the support of Secretary McNamara and President Kennedy, who were interested in developing techniques to counterinsurgency, the Army added the attack helicopter as part and parcel of its helicopter airmobility program. Early in 1962 the Army deployed H-21 transport helicopters to Vietnam and used them to transport South Vietnamese troops. A unit of utility helicopters jury-rigged with weapons was soon sent to Vietnam, the original intent being for these aircraft to escort troop helicopters to landing zones. Fire support in the landing zone was still provided by US and South Vietnamese fixed-wing aircraft, but the Army shortly perceived a need for both armed helicopters and fixed-wing fire support in landing zones. The Cobra AH-1G gunship was built and deployed to Vietnam. The Army also began to field armed Mohawk fixed-wing aircraft for experimental fire support and sent Caribou transport aircraft to Vietnam to augment local air movement. In 1965 Secretary McNamara theorized that the Army might be moving beyond the procurement of aircraft directly related to its mission. For that reason, he said,

> I have overruled the Army in their request for purchase of what is known as the BUFFALO, as a successor to the CARIBOU to carry on a transport function that I believe the Air Force can properly carry with its C-130s and C-123s. Similarly I have refused the Army permission to buy the MOHAWKS and other aircraft which might be used for close air-support functions.[168]

IDEAS, CONCEPTS, DOCTRINE

Although the Army considered that DOD Directive 5160.22 was inactive, it officially differentiated between "close air support" and what was now called "direct aerial fire support." An Army statement explained the difference:

> Close air support (fixed wing mission) calls for penetration of a hostile environment, delivery of heavy munitions on relatively stationary targets, and protection of friendly forces against hostile air attack.... Direct aerial fire support is provided by the attack helicopter, which is one of a family of ground firepower systems. All its characteristics (weapons, target acquisition, nature of its targets, integration of fires, command and control) it shares in common with other Army weapons systems. Helicopter fires are typical of all fires that take place at the line of contact, the flanks, and within the battle position where a premium is placed on quick response, all weather capability, and a high order of accuracy in delivery of fires. There is a small area of overlap between close air support and direct aerial fire support on the battlefield. This overlap is considered necessary and desirable.[169]

From the beginning of his tenure as Air Force chief of staff, General McConnell sought solutions for roles and missions conflicts with the Army, and in the spring of 1965, the Army's Gen Harold Johnson was said to have been tired of defending armed Mohawks at great length with other members of the Joint Chiefs of Staff. The two generals conferred privately for six months before arriving at a meeting of minds. A new directive, "Concept for Improved Joint Air-Ground Coordination," signed by General McConnell on 19 March 1965 and by General Johnson on 28 April 1965 put into effect a revised tactical air-control system. This system provided continued centralized control of tactical aviation at Air Force component commander level, but allowed decentralized execution of allocated sorties by new direct air support centers (DASCs) at corps level. A year later on 6 April 1966, McConnell and Johnson signed another agreement personally worked out between them whereby the Army transferred the CV-2 Caribou and the CV-7 Buffalo to the Air Force which became responsible for intratheater fixed-wing tactical airlift. For his part, General McConnell agreed "to relinquish all claims for helicopters and follow-on rotary-wing aircraft which are designed and operated for intratheater movement, fire support — except Special Air Warfare — SAW — or Search and Rescue — SAR — forces and administration mission support aircraft."[170]

In the immediate aftermath of the 6 April 1966 McConnell-Johnson agreement, General McConnell directed immediate and positive action to obtain a specialized air-support aircraft for the 1970s. The US Army in 1966 started a development program for the AH-56A Cheyenne — an advanced aerial fire support system (AAFSS) that would be specifically tailored to future operational needs for higher intensities of combat. There were to be improvements in basic aircraft performance, including hover capabilities, payload, and endurance, and in equipment capabilities to provide more operational flexibility at night and in bad weather, in better navigation, and in longer standoff ranges for weapons firing.[171] In February 1966 General McConnell was asked what he thought about the AAFSS, and he responded:

> Of course, what the Army intends to do with the advanced helicopter that they are talking about is to use it for close support operations, which is traditionally a mission for the Air Force and [one] which the Air Force has always done very well. I have no problems with armed helicopters in their use by the Army in suppressing fire and moving people around. I do not think it is essential or necessary to build an armed helicopter with a capability for close support of Army forces, because this is already being done for them by the Air Force and in some instances the Navy. In the first place, it will not anywhere near stand up to the examination of cost effectiveness. In my opinion, it will cost too much to be able to stand up to cost effectiveness analysis.[172]

General Momyer later added that in the McConnell-Johnson agreement he was sure that General McConnell had not visualized that "the helicopter was going to be utilized and turned into the kind of firepower platform that we see in the Cobra and the Cheyenne." Speaking for himself, Momyer said:

> As I understand the functions assigned to the armed services, I consider the deployment of the helicopter gunship as performing close air support; and the close air support mission is assigned to the Air Force and, therefore, I concluded [sic] that it is a duplication of our mission.[173]

After their inception in 1966 neither the Cheyenne nor the A-X programs progressed rapidly. The Cheyenne development program encountered repeated technical problems, and the crash of a test aircraft during a high-speed run in 1969 caused the Army to terminate a fledgling production program. The Lockheed Corporation, which was developing the Cheyenne, identified and undertook to correct technical problems with the rotor system, but the development program remained at a slow pace while settlement of prospective costs of correcting the design failure was worked out.[174] The A-X program got under way with General McConnell's decision letter in September 1966. Contracted studies in 1967 established the feasibility of what was wanted in the program: a not-too-expensive airplane that could transport a heavy payload, could take off from an unimproved field with short runways, could be very rugged, and could take a beating from ordnance fired from the ground. The Army documented its close-air-support requirements, and the A-X design proposal met the requirements, but the Army did not request the A-X specifically. Gen William C. Westmoreland, Army chief of staff, said that the Army "would leave the development of detailed specifications of the airplane to the Air Force." In 1968 the proposed A-X was getting too big and too expensive and required more study before a supplemental concept formulation package of studies would be ready in September 1969.[175]

Even in its conceptual state, the A-X generated some roles and missions difficulties. At first, the Air Force circulated proposals that the A-X be especially dedicated to Army control, this by assigning A-X units to particular DASCs and allowing the air component commander/Tactical Air Control Center to use them elsewhere only in emergencies. Under these circumstances it was reasoned that the A-X should not be counted "above the line" in the Air Force tactical wing strength. Maj Gen George S. Boylan, Jr., director of Air Force aerospace programs, rationalized in April 1969:

> With the A-X, . . . I think the Air Force operational procedure and doctrine which will guide the employment of the aircraft will restrict it to close basing, to basing in close proximity to the ground forces, immediate response to the ground forces. I doubt that you would find the A-X, in this operational concept, forward of the main battle area, where the degree of exposure goes up.[176]

Oddly enough, Army spokesmen rebuffed the proposition, advocating the A-X or other fixed-wing, close-support aircraft to Army units as being contrary to long-standing Air Force doctrine. The proposition offended the flexibility of tactical air employment and the authority of the joint commander in a theater organization. An Army memo to the Air Force chief of staff on 13 January 1970 stated: "The joint commander should approve the apportionment of air effort on a daily basis. The apportionment should be changed only by the joint commander." Brig Gen William J. Maddox, Jr., director of Army aviation, elaborated:

> Viewed very simply, dedicating aircraft to close air support, and placing close air support strikes under Army control would make these aircraft more responsive to the ground force commander, but there are other factors which militate against this approach for conventional fixed-wing close air support aircraft—prime of which is that fixed-wing close air support aircraft are multi-capable. . . . For a full appreciation of close air support, responsiveness should be examined from the viewpoints of both the joint commander and the frontline soldier. These views will differ because the frontline soldier looks only for close air support against the targets to his immediate front. The joint commander, on the other hand, is concerned with a variety of missions which include air superiority, interdiction and reconnaissance, as well as close air support. The joint commander retains control of his fixed-wing close air support assets because they can contribute to other elements of his tactical air mission. For instance, the A-X and other fixed-wing aircraft have the inherent capability to perform interdiction as well as close air support. Under certain conditions, interdiction may take precedence over close air support. To assign these aircraft to the Army would reduce the responsiveness from the viewpoint of the joint force commander.[177]

In the words of Sen Howard W. Cannon, "The Marines apparently do not have a roles and mission problem since they provide their own close air support." In addition to F-4 Phantoms, A-4M Skyhawks, and A-6A Intruders, the Marines were in the post-Vietnam War years planning a buy of 114 AV-8A Harrier aircraft to be operated from Navy amphibious ships and austere forward-area strips ashore in a primary "ground loiter" close-air-support role. The Harrier had been developed in Britain and was operational in the Royal Air Force. It had swept-wing jet speeds, and it could be employed in a vertical takeoff and landing (VTOL) performance. But the Harrier's combat radius was only 50 miles with the VTOL mode of operation, and its combat time on station was very short. In addition, a typical Harrier sortie could require 8,000 pounds of fuel and ordnance so that the logistics requirements could be formidable for Harriers staging from short-expeditionary runways that could not accommodate logistical air transport supply.[178] From the

Air Force's point of view, General Ryan considered that in the VTOL mode the Harrier's payload capability became too small. Ryan said:

> We believe that it may provide satisfactory performance in the context of the Marine Corps concept of operations, which do not require as much range and payload capability as we do, but it does not appear to meet our close air support requirements.[179]

On 22 January 1970 Deputy Secretary of Defense David Packard requested Army Secretary Stanley R. Resor and Air Force Secretary Seamans to develop within 30 days a position paper on the A-X and the Cheyenne which would address their relationship in a close-air-support role. In turn, Lt Gen Robert R. Williams, assistant chief of staff for Army force development, and Maj Gen Glenn A. Kent, assistant chief of staff for Air Force studies and analyses, were tapped as action officers. In Joint Chiefs of Staff usage, close air support was defined as air attacks against hostile targets which are in close proximity to friendly forces and which require detailed integration of each mission with the fire and movement of those forces.[180] But to come to closer grips with the A-X versus Cheyenne comparison, it was necessary to elaborate. "I find," said Secretary Seamans, "that I certainly have learned a lot about close support lately. There are a lot of ramifications to it, and to really understand it, it is necessary to get into a large number of specific tasks, their locale on the battlefield, the method of command and control, et cetera." In a joint memorandum signed on 20 February 1970 the secretaries recommended continued research and development of both the A-X and the AH-56A through at least prototype development. The memorandum also addressed the complementary and competitive aspects of the two systems, and since complete agreement could not be reached, the memorandum outlined the individual service positions. The official Air Force position noted that DOD Directive 5160.22 and "Unified Action Armed Forces" both assigned the close air mission to the Air Force. Assistant Secretary of the Air Force (R&D) Grant L. Hansen said, "It is therefore the official position of the Air Force that it needs the A-X at the earliest possible date to provide improved capability for fulfilling its responsibility of providing that close air support for the Army."[181]

In the argumentation about the comparative values of the A-X and Cheyenne looking toward the preparation of a final memorandum from the Army and Air Force secretaries to Deputy Secretary Packard submitted on 26 March 1970, both the Army and the Air Force described the Cheyenne and A-X as both complementary or competitive, as the case might be. Lt Gen Otto J. Glasser, Air Force deputy chief of staff for research and development, asserted: "I am personally totally convinced, perhaps parochially so, that an A-X, which will do 80 to 90 percent of all the missions of the Cheyenne, and at one-third the cost, is the thing to do." If an attack helicopter were needed, Glasser recommended that "a Huey Cobra with an A-X is a much more cost effective solution to the problem."[182] In the final paper, the Army included a list of 17 "Tasks of Combat Air Support," many of which the Air Force pointed out were general tasks of tactical aviation — not close air support. In the end, the two secretaries agreed that the A-X and an advanced aerial fire support system (AAFSS) helicopter (not necessarily the Cheyenne) were complementary. The secretaries greatly expanded the JCS definition of close air support, breaking it out into eight separate tasks that were listed in an enclosure to their 26 March 1970 report. These were:

> *Task I:* — Support of Engaged Troops. This includes the delivery of supporting fires by air against enemy troops (and associated equipment and vehicles) out to the established fire coordination or safety line. Attacks are conducted during day, night and adverse weather conditions against such targets as weapon positions (both ground-to-ground and ground-to-air), bunkers and fortifications, enemy formations afoot, enemy formations of armored and mechanized vehicles, and suspected locations of enemy troops, vehicles, and weapon positions.
>
> *Task II:* — Support of Airborne/Heliborne Assaults. This includes:
>
> (1) attack of enemy targets in preparation of landing zones; and
>
> (2) supporting fire during landing and extraction.
>
> *Task III:* — Escort for protection of aircraft/helicopters (exclusive of those engaged in actual insertion/extraction operations) from attack — both air-to-air and ground-to-air.
>
> *Task IV:* — Provision of fire support for air cavalry operations.
>
> *Task V:* — Protection of Moving Formations of Troops (afoot or motorized not actively in contact with the enemy).
>
> *Task VII:* — Support of rescue missions, including extractions of troops on long-range ground patrols. This entails protection of air rescue aircraft from air-to-air ground-to-air enemy attacks and suppressive fire in support of those being rescued.
>
> *Task VIII:* — General Support of Battlefield Area. This entails attack of enemy targets beyond the established fire coordination or safety line and includes: Weapon positions (both ground-to-ground and ground-to-air); bunkers and fortifications; enemy formations afoot; enemy formations in armor and mechanized vehicles; enemy command and control facilities and positions; nuclear delivery systems; roads and bridges; combat support facilities; and suspected locations of enemy troops and supplies.[183]

These tasks were broader than the JCS definition of close air support, leading Deputy Secretary of Defense Packard to tell the Senate Special Subcommittee on Close Air Support,

> The degree to which any of the tasks identified by the Secretary of the Army and the Secretary of the Air Force in their memorandum fit the definition of close air support depends on the scenario. In final analysis, command and control procedures and joint doctrine must remain sufficiently flexible so that close air support sorties can be conducted in coordination with the fire and movement of friendly forces.[184]

Deputy Secretary Packard accepted the proposal for prototypes. At this juncture the Cheyenne helicopter was once again in a research and development phase, with the Lockheed Company confident that its rotor control problems were near solution. On 6 April 1970 Deputy Secretary Packard approved the development concept paper for the A-X to be for the construction by two aircraft companies of two prototype close-air-support aircraft each. When request for proposals went out on 7 May, six companies responded by 7 August, and on 18 December 1970 Secretary Seamans announced that the Fairchild Hiller Corporation and the Northrop Corporation were selected as the contractors for the competitive prototype phase of the A-X program.[185]

In 1970 in the course of House Appropriations Committee hearings on the fiscal year 1971 budget, committee members asked many pointed questions about close air support. In addition, Chairman George H. Mahon advised Secretary Laird that the Department of Defense should thoroughly evaluate available hardware options relative to close air support, including the Harrier, the Cheyenne, and the A-X, before proceeding with substantial procurement of any close-air-support aircraft. Early evaluations in OSD indicated to Deputy Secretary Packard that the issues affecting close air support were really wider than just three different aircraft, and warranted the personal attention of senior management. In February 1971 Secretary Laird established a high-level close-air-support review group with Packard as chairman and with representatives from OSD, JCS, Army, Air Force, and Marine Corps. Gen William W. Momyer, commander of TAC, represented the Air Force. On 8 March 1971 DOD Directive 5160.22, vesting close air support in the Air Force, was canceled. Packard explained the cancellation as being part of his "recent attempt to get rid of some directives that I consider unnecessary." He looked to the Joint Chiefs as advisers on roles and missions and said that there had been no discussions with them on mission changes. He did not see "any movement to change the roles and missions," but he also said that he was "willing and ready to make any adjustment that experience dictates advisable." What he wanted was to generate a better understanding of close air support essentially through the examination of the capabilities of current and candidate aircraft in a small number of scenarios that could represent the range of missions and threat environments. Referring to the A-X, the Cheyenne, and the Harrier as "systems," Packard said:

> The point I want to make is that I do not think the problem of close air support is related to which one of these systems is best, but to what is the best mix of these systems. It may turn out that we really should have all three — the A-X, the Cheyenne, and the Harrier. Maybe we do not need all three.... We are going to take a limited number of specific situations and analyze them and see if a more objective approach will give us some guidance as to which way we can go.[186]

From what Packard said, an Air Force doctrinal issues briefing concluded:

> The Deputy Secretary of Defense has made it very clear that decisions to procure new weapons and support systems are going to be made on their merits and not on the basis of any legalistic assignment of roles and missions. Further, the responsibilities of the

IDEAS, CONCEPTS, DOCTRINE

> services have become somewhat blurred by OSD policies for assigning weapon system development programs.[187]

Since it was already known that the consensus of the OSD hierarchy, both military and civilian, was that one type of aircraft would not meet diverse objectives, the Department of Defense Close Air Support Report submitted to Congress on 22 June 1971 contained few surprises, although its findings were based on a variety of analytical techniques and simulated approaches. Deputy Secretary Packard provided the conclusions and recommendations personally and allowed individual members to append their views. The conclusions noted that close air support was a complex mission. Interaction with ground elements and other weapons was one source of complexity. The diversity of probable scenarios, targets, tactical situations, terrain, and weather conditions also complicated the evaluation process. This complexity and diversity of close air support led to realistic requirements for different types of systems:

> One aircraft cannot do everything another aircraft can. The Cheyenne, Harrier, and A-X center their capabilities in important sectors of the CAS spectrum: Cheyenne in discrete, responsive, highly mobile fires operating as part of the ground maneuver force; Harrier in rapid response to urgent firepower requirements during amphibious operations; and A-X in concentrating heavy firepower, matching selected munitions to different targets, at threatened sectors from dispersed bases. There were four recommendations: 1. Continue the Harrier procurement plan. 2. Continue the A-X and Cheyenne development. 3. Execute tests to resolve uncertainties found during the study so that necessary information for Cheyenne and A-X production decisions and further Harrier procurement would be available. 4. Continue to refine the methodology for evaluating and comparing alternative close air support systems and arriving at procurement decisions.[188]

General Momyer agreed with the conclusions and recommendations, but he did not accept any intimation that the group was stating a need to procure all three systems for future force structures until such time as extensive field tests were concluded.

The Department of Defense Close Air Support Report had not been completed when the fiscal year 1972 defense budget was sent to Congress, but the recommendations of the report were included in the budgetary request. In view of the questions that had been raised about the three "duplicate" close-air-support planes, Sen John C. Stennis, chairman of the Senate Armed Services Committee, announced formation of a special subcommittee on close air support to be chaired by Sen Howard W. Cannon and to be charged to examine the total close-air-support program as well as specific hardware issues. Testimony on close air support commenced on 22 October 1971, and 21 witnesses were heard on seven hearing days before testimony concluded on 8 November. The subcommittee also had the advantage of testimony on the defense authorization and appropriations hearings in the first half of 1971, as well as the findings of the Packard study, whose findings the Cannon subcommittee concluded were based on inherently defective computerized systems analyses. In the Packard study, the Cannon subcommittee observed,

> the simulations basically were one-on-one studies; that is they pictured one airplane attacking one tank defended by one anti-tank gun.... Omitted were the effects of enemy fighter aircraft, suppression of enemy air defenses, SAM missiles, tactical electronic counter-measures, and the fact that many aircraft will be making multiple passes at a host of enemy targets, while flying through a barrage of anti-aircraft fire.[189]

In fiscal year 1972 authorization and appropriations hearings it was the Air Force's position that until the Cheyenne and the A-X were successful prototypes there was no way to compare their costs or capabilities. General Glasser noted:

> I think they are complementary and, of course, at the same time there is some overlap. Duplication is not always bad. Some duplication is highly desirable. Again I am not able to answer too explicitly in advance of completion of the development of the two aircraft.[190]

Testimony in the Cannon subcommittee hearings generally repeated existing Army and Air Force positions. But Admiral Moorer, speaking as JCS chairman, took a more detached view:

> In closing, I would like to reemphasize that under the current state of engineering knowledge, no single aircraft can provide the capabilities necessary to satisfy the close air support tasks that may be encountered in future operational environments.... For this reason, I believe that a mix of fixed wing aircraft and helicopters which permits a variety of operational and deployment alternatives to the spectrum of targets, tactical situations, terrain, and visibility conditions that will be encountered by U.S. forces is our best solution to the close air support problem.[191]

Admiral Moorer pointed out that the Joint Chiefs of Staff were responsible for the development of joint doctrine. Admiral Moorer further commented, "After service tests and the development of service employment concepts are completed as to new close air support equipment, it is anticipated that the JCS will require joint testing for refinement and further integration into close air support joint doctrine."[192] And Deputy Secretary of Defense Packard concluded that helicopters were necessary for air support under conditions of limited visibility. He said:

> One thing I have already alluded to is that under certain conditions of visibility and ceiling, you just can't use a supersonic aircraft unless you are going to use a radar bombing system which is not sufficiently accurate to be dependable. Under those conditions if you need close air support the only way you are going to be able to get it is with rotary-wing aircraft.[193]

Senator Cannon's Special Close Air Support Subcommittee completed hearings on 8 November 1971 and released its report on 18 April 1972, although a declassified version of its hearings had been published earlier. The report endorsed Air Force-Army and Navy-Marine command and control systems. It pointed out, however, that the Department of Defense "should redefine and assign the roles and missions of close air support." As the report was said to make clear, "in the twenty-four years since the Key West agreement of 1948, a series of interservice agreements and the evolution of helicopter technology have left the original definition and assignment ambiguous and unclear." The A-X program was judged "well worthy of prototyping," and the subcommittee recommended that an evaluation of the A-X should include a flyoff with existing close-air-support aircraft, especially the A-7D, and that the A-7D production line should be kept open until the flyoff tests determined whether the A-X would take the place of the A-7D. Senator Symington had long been a critic of the A-7D and disagreed with this recommendation. The subcommittee's recommendations regarding the Harrier and the lack of mention of the Cheyenne drew later clarification from Senator Cannon. The subcommittee did not believe duplication between the Harrier and the A-X "to be a valid issue," but it said that the Harrier was an experiment in V/STOL technology, resulting in a plane whose range and payload were so limited under VTOL conditions that no large procurements of it should be justified. The subcommittee's only mention of helicopters in its recommendations was: "Assuming that questions regarding helicopter vulnerability are resolved successfully, the subcommittee believes that there is a valid requirement for a more capable helicopter." Senator Cannon later said this sentence was not a specific recommendation for the Cheyenne.[194]

The Packard study report on close air support had recommended that the Cheyenne, Harrier, and A-X programs be continued until operational testing could be completed to resolve certain specified uncertainties about each. The Cannon subcommittee report called for flyoffs between the A-X and existing close-air-support aircraft. In December 1971, however, a General Accounting Office (GAO) report called attention to the fact that the Packard report did not focus on testing the Cheyenne, the Harrier, and the A-X against each other, but merely testing them against predecessors in their separate categories. The GAO also pointed out that there was no cohesive plan covering total defense requirements for close air support. Instead, the sizes and tactical concepts of close air support were proposed by the individual services planning independently. When asked about these concerns, Secretary of Defense Laird remarked that force planning integration was handled each year in the planning, programming, and budgeting cycle. "I think we are realistically working and attempting to define our CAS requirements and are carefully building our knowledge as we go to provide sound joint doctrine and operating procedures," Laird said. Although Laird considered that phase I of the Packard study provided "a good understanding of CAS environments, targets, concepts of operations, and CAS weapon systems required," he directed the study group to provide a phase II report on command, control, and logistics and basing requirements for providing close air support. Laird stated:

> It is entirely in keeping with the Total Force Concept that existing roles and missions be examined to determine which Service and which weapon system can contribute the greatest amount to a given task. It is also in keeping with the Total Force Concept to adjust existing roles and missions to better use our existing and planned resources.[195]

The way in which flyoff tests of close-air-support aircraft would be handled remained unsure in early 1972. Secretary of the Air Force Seamans told Senator Symington that tests would be run on the two A-X candidates to select one of them. Similar prescribed tests would be run on the Cheyenne. "On the basis of all these tests, the Department of Defense will then make a decision whether to proceed in production with the Cheyenne or with the A-X.... Not with both.... That is the understanding that we have in the Department of Defense."[196] General Westmoreland, Army chief of staff, dramatically disagreed:

> The Army considers the Cheyenne as an integral part of its ground combat forces, the same as a tank or a howitzer. In fact, when the decision was made to develop the Cheyenne, the Army traded off tanks and howitzers for the capability of raising part of its fire support means a few feet above the terrain and providing it with a significant increase in speed and maneuverability.... If any trade-offs exist, they are between the Cheyenne and other land combat fire support means... and between the A-X and other aircraft capable of performing the fixed wing close air support mission. There is no competition and no viable trade-off between the fixed wing and rotary wing capability. The Department of Defense has repeatedly testified before this and other committees that both capabilities are required and that they are complementary and not competitive.[197]

The Army's Cheyenne development program had been started specifically to meet the stringent requirements of a European-type war. The Cobra attack helicopter, while very effective in Southeast Asia, could not perform a full range of tasks required of the Cheyenne, although Cobras equipped with the tank-killing tube-launched, optically directed, wire-controlled (TOW) missiles could be deployed to Europe much earlier than the Cheyenne would be operational. There was no growth potential in the Cobra without a major redesign effort. Still, in 1971 some estimates of the projected costs of one Cheyenne had increased to well above $5 million, and the Army officially projected its cost to be $3.8 million. While the Cheyenne had lingered in development, alternative advanced gunship candidates were being developed privately by two helicopter companies. Sikorsky's Blackhawk started flying in August 1970, while Bell's King Cobra was flying in September 1971. Both were promised to be less costly than the Cheyenne. Because of the Cannon subcommittee's hearings, the Army had a flyoff between the Cheyenne, the Blackhawk, and the King Cobra, after which in August 1972 it announced the termination of the Cheyenne program and the initiation of a new program to develop an advanced armed helicopter less complex and less costly than the Cheyenne. Development contracts were awarded to two contractors each to fabricate two flying prototypes to be evaluated in a competitive flyoff. Testing of these two competitive prototypes was completed in September 1976, and

Hughes Helicopters of the Summa Corporation won a full-scale engineering development contract for the Army's antiarmor helicopter of the future.[198]

Unlike other Air Force aircraft the A-X was designed specifically for frontline close air support. The four basic characteristics of the A-X include lethality to targets, responsiveness, survivability, and simplicity. The two A-X prototypes — the Northrop A-9 and the Fairchild A-10 — had their first flights in May 1972, and from 10 October through 9 December 1973 there was a flyoff testing of the two planes at Edwards AFB, California. The A-10 was declared the winner. The question now became one of meeting the demands of the Senate Armed Services Committee that there be flyoff tests of the A-10 and the A-7D. During 1972 Maj Gen Robert P. Lukeman, assistant chief of staff for studies and analyses of the Air Force, commenced computer analyses of the A-7D and A-X. Saber Armor-Alpha, a study published in March 1972, projected the A-X as much more survivable than the A-7 against the same enemy defenses. The problem was then extended to a projected analysis of total force effectiveness of the A-7D and A-X in a study called Saber Armor-Charlie. The study team was led by an experienced fighter pilot, Col John R. Bode, and in preparation for it, a board of fighter officers was assembled to draw up operational concepts. After weeks of arguing about how each airplane would be used, the group identified the one fundamental concept intrinsic to the close-air-support mission. In the battle area, a very fluid, irregular line called the forward edge of the battle area (FEBA) divided friendlies from enemies. Colonel Bode demonstrated that the fixed targets behind the enemy lines could be systematically attacked with prior planning.

> We plan the ingress routes, and we often use non-visual systems. We try to make high speed, single pass attacks if we possibly can to hit those targets and keep moving. The FEBA is very fluid. It has the characteristics that our friendly forces are always close to it.... That requires very intimate integration with the fire and maneuver of the ground forces. That is not only the definition of the mission, but in my opinion that is the key concept of the close air support mission. . . . So that means that any airplane that is bought . . . to do the close air support mission has got to go through a visual acquisition phase, when the fighter pilot determines for himself where the friendlies are and where the enemy is. Besides that, the pilot has to specifically identify and locate a specific target and fly the airplane so as to aim at that target. That is particularly true of targets like tanks because for hard mobile targets like tanks, if you don't aim at it, you don't kill it. . . . This requirement for visual acquisition and this requirement for aiming the airplane at the target actually sets up the design of close air support aircraft. It comes out with different features from what you would get if you designed for the interdiction mission or the air superiority mission.[199]

Each of the computer simulations of the Saber Armor calculations favored the A-X over the A-7D, even though when there was a concern about how a factor should be weighed, it was weighed in favor of the A-7. The data was submitted for study by a Defense Systems Acquisition Review Council (DSARC) that met on 17 January 1973 and selected the Fairchild A-10 as the prototype winner. The Saber Armor studies were also briefed to the Senate Armed Services Committee, which in 1972 had recommended "a flyoff, a side-by-side flight comparison" between the

A-X and the existing close-air-support airplanes. In March 1973 General Glasser argued with Senator Cannon that there could be no meaningful flight test between the fully operational A-7D and the only partly fabricated A-10, but the Senate Armed Services Committee remained adamant and again in July 1973 recommended the flyoff. Senator Cannon insisted that the A-10 with its relatively slow speed could not have the survivability that the paper studies claimed. He had talked to many pilots back from Southeast Asia who told him that speed was necessary for survival in a high-intensity environment.[200] As a result of heavy Israeli aircraft losses in the Yom Kippur War, congressmen were intensely interested in hearing Secretary McLucas and General Brown relate the A-10 to such an intense missile-defense environment. Said McLucas:

> I think we can say that under the rubric of lessons learned in the Middle East, it did not change our views on the A-10. . . . Our feeling is that the activity in the Mideast demonstrates that weapon systems should not be considered in isolation from the rest of your force; we would employ our force in a combined action.[201]

General Brown pointed out that the A-10 was not going to hover over enemy defenses; its targets would be at the FEBA. Brown added:

> One thing that we do acknowledge is that the A-10 is built conceptually along the lines of the Stuka of World War II. It is a limited performance airplane for limited purpose. It is not an airplane that you would send deep into enemy territory to do interdiction, airfield attack, these sorts of things. It is not fast enough. . . . So you would go to the F-4 or the A-7. But to stay in the battle area and keep working, hammering right up there where the tanks are, is what the A-10 is built for.[202]

In April and May 1974, a flyoff between the A-7D and the A-X was held at Fort Riley/McConnell AFB, Kansas, where Army units were deployed in terrain and formations representing a Soviet deployment and active Hawk antiaircraft missile crews attempted to track the aircraft. Four pilots flew each aircraft an equal number of sorties, and the weapon systems evaluation group monitored the tests and analyzed the results under the aegis of the director of defense research and engineering. Following the competition DSARC IIIA was held in July 1974.[203] The A-10 entered production soon after the competition and Maj Gen Harold E. Collins, assistant deputy chief of staff for research and development, explained its characteristics, saying:

> The A-10 is specifically optimized to perform the close air support mission and has excellent maneuverability which will enable it to operate under low ceilings and to employ optimized attack profiles. . . . The aircraft will carry up to 16,000 pounds of ordnance for attacking ground units. Besides the Maverick missile and cluster munitions, the A-10 will be equipped with the GAU-8 30 mm gun for destroying hard targets such as tanks. The survivability features of the A-10 . . . will allow operation of the A-10 in a high threat environment. The simplicity of the aircraft will allow low maintenance and support requirements as well as high sortie rates. The A-10 can stage from austere forward bases and be very responsive to requests for air support.[204]

Dr John S. Foster, Jr., director of defense research and engineering, in April 1973 asserted that there was no "unwarranted duplication" between the A-X and the AAH. "Although there is some overlap in capabilities, they operate in different ways and perform best under different situations; thus, they present a much more difficult problem for the enemy to counter."[205] In August 1973 Maj Gen James J. Hill, director of programs and deputy chief of staff for programs and resources, advanced the idea that the role of the AAH was distinguishable from the role of the A-10, the latter being "clearly a close air support role as we have defined it within DoD." Hill explained:

> The AAH is being developed primarily to support airmobile operations and as a helicopter escort aircraft, providing light suppressive fires from positions over friendly territory against targets which threaten an air mobile assault at or very near the forward edge of the battle area. It will be capable of engaging armored targets which have penetrated the FEBA, but it is not envisioned as an aircraft that would survive if exposed to the dense enemy firepower expected to exist beyond the FEBA.[206]

As Air Force chief of staff, Gen George S. Brown fostered improving relations with Gen Creighton Abrams, his comrade in arms in Vietnam who became Army chief of staff. In fact just before Gen Robert J. Dixon took command of the Tactical Air Command in October 1973, Generals Abrams and Brown told him they wanted the agreements and good relations in Vietnam carried forward in peacetime.[207] Ending the controversy that had waged so many years, the Army and Air Force in mid-1975 agreed on the relationship of the attack helicopter and fixed-wing close air support, with this announcement:

> The *attack helicopter* is integral to the Army ground maneuver unit and is an *extension of organic firepower*. It is to be employed with, or to the rear of, ground forces along the *forward edge of the battle area* (FEBA) to provide helicopter escort and suppressive fire, to counter enemy armor at the FEBA, and to counter surprise enemy armor penetrations behind friendly lines.
>
> The Army and Air Force agree that the *attack helicopter does not perform CAS* but is intended to complement Air Force CAS capabilities. The attack helicopter and Air Force close air support offer the ground commander a complementary capability in terms of a wider spectrum of fire support, enhanced responsiveness, flexibility and capability. Because of the *limited range, speed and firepower of attack helicopters* as compared to Air Force fixed-wing CAS capabilities, the Air Force does not consider the attack helicopter as duplicating Air Force CAS.
>
> *Air Force CAS resources are centrally controlled by the Air Force component commander* and respond to the theater-wide CAS requirements of the ground commander—whereas *attack helicopter elements* are integral to the Army's combined arms team and are under control of, and employed directly by, the *various ground commanders* to which they are assigned. Through centralized control of Air Force resources, the Air Force provides a means to fully exploit the broader operational capabilities of tactical airpower.[208]

At Langley AFB, Virginia, where TAC headquarters was located, General Dixon quickly established amicable relations with Gen. William DePuy, commanding general of the the Army Training and Doctrine Command (TRADOC), whose headquarters was located at nearby Fort Monroe, Virginia. Dixon recalled: "We said at the beginning . . . that we think we have a tough job on our hands in the air-land battle, and we are setting out to do that job. We have not mentioned roles and missions yet."[209] The two generals agreed that the Army did not have a separate air force. General DePuy said:

> I find it very difficult to think about the Army's helicopters as another tactical air force. . . . We think about cavalry and we think about infantry, we think about communications, and we think about supply. . . . It just would not work to take Army Aviation out and put it in the Air Force any more than we want to take the Air Force and put it back in the Army.[210]

General Dixon agreed: "The Air Force does not consider Army helicopters an aviation force in the contest of a separate force. I think we have grown up. I think we understand each other. I think the overwhelming size of what we have to do takes first priority with us."[211]

US Navy and Marine Corps Tactical Air

During the hearings of the Senate Special Subcommittee on Close Air Support in 1971 Sen Barry Goldwater argued that the Air Force, Army, Navy, and Marine Corps were all operating tactical air forces despite soaring costs of tactical air weapons.[212] He thought it necessary to reiterate the purpose of the hearings: "It is not an effort to eliminate anything; it is an effort to answer the question of whether we need one, two, three or four tactical air forces. We started out with one; we have grown to four." Goldwater's remedy for the four duplicative tactical air forces, appended to the close-air-support subcommittee's report, was for the Department of Defense to clarify the basic roles and missions of the services. He said, "My concern is imbedded in duplication, a very costly duplication."[213] Over the years after 1971, senators frequently brought up the subject of the four tactical air forces, asking whether there was any plan in the Pentagon for their coordination and why could such common missions as air superiority and ground support be centralized under a single air force.[214]

During the Senate close-air-support hearings, Admiral Moorer had pointed out that development of joint doctrine for united operations was a JCS responsibility, and he had anticipated that joint testing would yield integration into close-air-support joint doctrine.[215] As a matter of fact on 13 February 1967 the Joint Chiefs of Staff had requested the Air Force to develop a joint doctrine for close air support in accordance with JCS Publication 2 and the chief of staff Army/Air Force agreement of April 1965. The Air Force assigned the project to the Tactical Air Command; by 1971 the undertaking had foundered after five drafts of a manual had been circulated among the services without arrival at unanimous

IDEAS, CONCEPTS, DOCTRINE

agreement.[216] In the aura of good feeling after the Army-Air Force accords on the AAH and fixed-wing A-10 operations, Gen David Jones took the position that there was some duplication in the tactical air forces fielded by the Air Force, Navy, and Marines but that when the size of the Soviet tactical air forces was considered there was a need for as large a total US force as possible. "We are coming closer together and I think in the next few years we will do better than we have in the past."[217] Gen George S. Brown in February 1976 responded to a question about the four tactical air forces by saying:

> Duplication between the tactical air elements of the four Services is more apparent than real. There is some overlap in capabilities among our various aircraft, but within the Department of Defense, the four Services establish and maintain separate air elements to perform their assigned roles and missions. The tactical air elements of each Service are tailored to meet specific Service mission requirements, some of which require very specialized tasks. They collectively contribute to the total U.S. aerial firepower available.[218]

Brown stated the purposes of the tactical air elements in some detail useful to an understanding of their separate taskings:

> The Air Force has structured its tactical air forces to meet its primary responsibilities, to include general air supremacy, air interdiction, air defense, close air support to ground forces, theater airlift, air reconnaissance, and to provide air forces for joint amphibious operations and airborne operations. In a theater of operations, the Air Force component commander (AFCC) centrally controls assigned or attached resources and integrates all TACAIR operations. Tactical airlift and tactical reconnaissance missions, as well as combat fighter operations are employed to meet the threat in concert with the overall land campaign. Navy tactical air forces are tailored to accomplish specialized operations, primarily oriented toward supporting the combat operations of a naval campaign. The responsibilities of Navy aviation include sea control, fleet defense, and local air superiority in an area of naval operations, and for sea projection operations, including support of amphibious assaults. Navy TACAIR will be used to strike opposing air, surface, and submarine forces at extended ranges, providing a defense in depth against missile and torpedo attacks.
>
> The primary mission of the Marine Corps is to provide Fleet Marine Forces of combined arms, including aviation components, with the ready capability to project combat power ashore against significant opposition. Such operations will include the seizure of defense of advanced naval bases and the conduct of such land operations as may be essential to the prosecution of a naval campaign. The Marine air arm is integral to the balanced air/ground team and is sized to Marine ground force requirements.
>
> Army aviation is dedicated to the Army's primary function of conducting prompt and sustained combat operations on land. The attack helicopter is organic to the Army ground maneuver unit and is an extension of organic firepower. The attack helicopter does not perform close air support, but is intended to complement close air support capabilities. The attack helicopter and Air Force fixed wing close air support offer the ground commander a complementary capability in terms of a wider spectrum of fire support, enhanced responsiveness, flexibility, and capability. In building tactical forces, we should base our judgements on the major threat — general war. That is the basis upon which the primary functions of our Services were developed and concomitantly how our

forces have been structured. The availability of naval aviation cannot be assured to support the air/land campaign in the advent of a major war in Europe. Each Service will be performing its primary functions and will probably have little opportunity to perform collateral functions in support of the other Services.[219]

Where General Brown's description of the separate service taskings held good during the 1970s, his prediction that there would be little opportunity for collateral functions was not entirely applicable. In fact as the 1970s progressed, the Joint Chiefs of Staff favored intermingling of collateral functions, as witness this statement filed in 1983:

Military Service capabilities have been tailored to unique service missions while contributing to the total military effort to support US national objectives. The Joint Chiefs of Staff have increased emphasis on integration of unique combat capabilities from other services into traditional single service missions, thereby expanding total combat capability. The war fighting perspectives of the unified and specified commanders in the field are strong influences in this process as the JCS develop more comprehensive joint doctrine and new weapons systems.[220]

The National Security Act of 1947 provided that the US Marine Corps, within the Department of the Navy, should be organized to include not less than three combat divisions and three combat air wings. This mandate recognized that the Marine Corps had continuously developed the art of amphibious warfare. The division/wing organization bespoke the fact that a forcible entry on a hostile shore in the face of a determined enemy was one of the most difficult of all military operations. Maj Gen H. S. Hill, Marine Corps deputy chief of staff for Air in 1971, explained:

The key to success of such an operation is the rapid buildup of combat power ashore, from an initial zero capability, to full coordinated striking power to defeat the enemy.... Initially, attack aircraft are provided from the aircraft carrier striking forces and subsequently from expeditionary airfields ashore supplemented with carrier aircraft. During the early phase of an operation, close air support and naval gunfire represent the only means of destroying targets that oppose the Marine Corps rifleman. Naval gunfire resources have been diminishing steadily since World War II and air support is the only remaining candidate available to fill the growing deficiency in firepower.[221]

The Marine Corps division/wing ground/air team was designed and practiced to provide immediately responsive air support to ground. As long as Navy carrier aircraft were present they provided air superiority and interdiction, and Marine aircraft were fully devoted to close air support.[222]

In a discussion of the Marine Corps in 1976, Gen George Brown pointed to its role and mission as being well beyond amphibious warfare. Its three active and one reserve divisions and wings were important parts of the nation's general purpose land and tactical air forces. Brown continued:

The Marine Corps' broader mission notwithstanding, our Marine amphibious forces constitute the only self-sustained, forcible-entry capability in the U.S. arsenal today. Our airlifted forces could deploy rapidly, but are not as readily sustainable as amphibious forces. In addition, the ability to forward deploy afloat amphibious forces will continue to be essential for meeting short-notice requirements for military power in distant areas.

> The U.S. cannot pre-position land and tactical air forces in every possible area where a crisis may threaten its interests, nor can it count on limitless base rights in overseas areas. Our capability to conduct amphibious operations with a force of combined arms offers the U.S. an advantage in a conflict, including a NATO-Warsaw Pact war where the availability of such forces provides defensive depth, resilience and capacity for opportune counterstrokes on the flanks of Europe, from the North Cape to the Eastern Mediterranean.[223]

As of 1978 in a NATO war, two Marine amphibious forces were earmarked by formal agreement for NATO, and when assigned to the Supreme Commander Europe would be the major element of his strategic reserve. There were no plans calling for the employment of Marines in NATO's Central Region; rather, plans called for a strategically mobile (preferably amphibious, although Marines could deploy by airlift) force in a variety of scenarios from the Arctic to the Mediterranean.[224] In the Marine Corps the accepted doctrine and practice was that there was a synergistic effect of the Marine Air-Ground Task Force (MAGTF) functioning together as an entity and that to fragment the team would violate a viable combat entity. As has been seen, the long-standing Air Force position was that—in General Momyer's words—"in a theater of operations it is absolutely essential that there be one air commander in order that the air can be employed where it is needed most; and you can't have areas within a theater that are under the various jurisdiction of different people." Momyer urged that once a MAGTF came into a theater, the Marine ground division should come under the theater air commander responsible for total close air support.[225] The Marine position on the inviolability of the MAGTF offered some difficulty in conceptualizing NATO reinforcement. Since there would be a serious shortfall of tactical air capability in NATO at a war's beginning and since the Marine air elements could be expected to arrive in advance of the ground division, would SACEUR have operational control over the air elements? Would SACEUR allow the Marine task force to continue to possess air elements once the MAGTF was ashore since the Marine air elements would be the only air assets in NATO that SACEUR did not own and control? When Lt Gen Andrew W. O'Donnell, deputy chief of staff for plans and policies, USMC, was called upon to answer these questions in 1978 he drew upon the stated policy of Gen Alexander Haig as SACEUR that "national forces are employed in a manner in which they are committed nationally or organized." O'Donnell was confident that Haig would support the Marine position. "He has recognized, as have all joint planners throughout the world, the entity that exists in the Marine air-ground team.... General Haig has stated that he would be remiss if he would reduce in essence, the capacity of what he views as a viable combat entity." Under these circumstances the Marine Corps's position on the command of air elements during and after a deployment to NATO was as follows:

> The Marine Corps considers organic aviation assets deployed in advance of other elements of a Marine Air-Ground Task Force (MAGTF) as advance combat elements of that force. Our employment concepts envision the simultaneous deployment of command elements of the MAGTF headquarters together with whatever combat elements—air or ground—are initially deployed. The MAGTF commander will report to the NATO commander to whom ordered and will employ his forces to accomplish missions as assigned him by that commander. Upon arrival of all elements of the force, the MAGTF will continue to carry out assigned missions as an integrated, combined arms team in accordance with approved NATO plans. Those plans provide explicitly for retention of the integrity of the MAGTF. We assume that formally approved Alliance plans constitute sufficient guarantees that Marine forces will be employed in consonance with those plans and with U.S. national doctrine for the employment of such forces.[226]

In joint service negotiations it would continue to be the USMC position that the MAGTF commander would retain ownership of his organic air assets both during and after amphibious operations. During joint operations the MAGTF air assets would normally be in support of the MAGTF mission, but the MAGTF commander would make sorties in excess of the MAGTF direct support requirements available to the joint force commander for tasking through the air component commander. Similarly, the MAGTF commander would make sorties for air defense, long-range interdiction, and long-range reconnaissance available to the joint force commander for tasking by the air component commander. But if the joint force commander considered it necessary as prescribed in JCS Publication 2, "Unified Action Armed Forces (UNAAF)," he could exercise other more direct methods of command and control over Marine air elements in his area of operations.[227]

In the Key West agreements of 1948 the Air Force had accepted collateral functions for maritime operations to include interdicting enemy sea power through air operations, conducting antisubmarine warfare and protecting shipping, and conducting aerial minelaying operations. But after 1948 the Air Force did little about these missions for several reasons noted by Maj Gen Robert N. Ginsburgh, USAF, Retired:

> First of all, the supremacy of the US Navy was so great that it neither needed nor wanted Air Force assistance in controlling the seas. At the same time, the Air Force was not interested in diverting its efforts from concentration on its primary functions. And finally, both Services questioned the capability of Air Force weapon systems to contribute significantly to the sea control mission.[228]

The first notable Air Force maritime employment occurred during the Cuban missile crisis, when Soviet freighters carrying missiles were en route to Cuba and their exact location was unknown. Then B-47 strategic aircraft were used in an Atlantic Ocean sea search to locate these vessels.[229] In 1968 Air Force EC-121s commenced patrol coverage of the Greenland-Iceland-United Kingdom (GIUK) gap into the North Atlantic, because the route was habituated by Soviet Bears and

Bisons from the Murmansk area and was the prime threat route for any penetration against North America.[230]

In 1970 when Admiral Zumwalt became chief of naval operations he judged that the United States had "just slightly better than an even chance . . . of winning a sea control war . . . with the Soviets." "After 1970," Zumwalt added, "our chances for success . . . diminished."[231] Zumwalt asked the Air Force to broaden its contingency plans to use B-52s for mining important waters, and this was approved in 1971. He proposed early in 1972 and brought it up again at an OSD breakfast in November 1972 that the Air Force's tactical air wings ought to be made carrier capable so that the United States could have optimal basing in instances where there was a lack of access to local airfields. Gen John Ryan, then Air Force chief of staff, had a study of the proposal made and declined to pursue it. Zumwalt later made this same proposal to Secretary Laird and Deputy Secretary Packard, and both declined to touch it because of its jurisdictional complications. Later on — in 1978 — another different proposal questioned why US Navy aircraft assigned to aircraft carriers that were withdrawn from sea duty during periodic port overhaul could not be detached to airfields in England. The Navy explained that its aircraft maintenance support equipment was permanently installed in its aircraft carriers and could not easily be put ashore; moreover, the Navy NATO commitment required that any ships in overhaul be returned to operations in 30 to 45 days. Removal of critical air-wing-support equipment and personnel would cause a considerable delay in meeting the NATO commitment.[232]

"We believe the Air Force can help the Navy control the seas," Secretary of Air Force McLucas said in a mid-1974 address. "Today, with longer-range aircraft, radar and other sensors in all our tactical aircraft, and guided weapons, we should be able to attack effectively even maneuvering enemy ships in virtually all of the major sea lanes."[233] Early in 1975 both Adm James L. Holloway III, now chief of naval operations, and Gen David Jones spoke favorably about the use of B-52s — probably B-52Ds — in augmenting Navy-sea control capability. Equipped with the Navy's Harpoon antiship missile, Holloway considered that B-52s would be a "beneficial adjunct" to the US Navy but not a completely dependable asset since the major role of the B-52s was in the SIOP.[234] On 2 September 1975 Holloway and Jones signed a Memorandum of Agreement (MOA) on "The Concept of Operations for USAF Forces Collateral Functions Training." This memorandum envisioned that Air Force capabilities might be employed to perform search and identification, electronic warfare, tactical deception, attack against surface and air units, and aerial minelaying. Air Force resources would be trained for these tasks that complemented and supplemented sea control operations and for which an inherent Air Force capability already existed. Since primary functions might necessarily preempt the availability of Air Force resources, the agreement recognized that a primary organic capability for sea control would have to be maintained. In the performance of the collateral tasks and training for them, Air Force forces would remain under the operational control of appropriate Air Force commanders and operate in support of naval commanders.[235] Under this agreement SAC, USAFE, PACAF, and TAC commenced training crews of B-52s, F-4s, and F-111s in conjunction with the US Navy. In the developing relationship, Navy spokesmen were careful to emphasize that any collateral support received should not influence the structuring of general purpose naval forces which were designed to carry out two principal missions: sea control (which included both subsurface and surface threats) and power projection. Thus, it was said:

> The rationale for use of Air Force assets for certain maritime functions is primarily one of providing an austere power projection in certain areas of the world where our naval forces do not normally deploy and which is capable of quick reaction to Soviet surface ship deployments during conditions of either crisis or sustained conflict.[236]

Admiral Holloway rationalized:

> I think aircraft have a number of advantages as an antisurface ship weapon system, in that they can move quickly to the scene of an encounter; they can search for targets.... The disadvantage is in lack of staying power of an airplane. It is good for sort of a one time shot and delivery of a weapon. You cannot keep long range aircraft on station, for example, in the Indian Ocean surveilling Soviet surface task forces in times of tension. That can much better be done by our own surface and subsurface fleet.[237]

In the late 1970s there was much favorable comment about the use of Air Force collateral resources for sea control, but there were actually some grave limitations on the Air Force side to the undertaking. Gen Russell E. Dougherty stated, "As commander in chief of SAC, I found that I had a lot of capabilities that I could share with other commanders that were very difficult to share." He and Adm Isaac C. Kidd, who was commander in chief, Atlantic (CINCLANT), recognized the potential long-range surveillance and sea-attack capability of SAC and began to exercise it. Dougherty said, however, that this was a "personality sensitive" matter because there was "no systemic opportunity to do this as a matter of routine." Dougherty continued:

> Also, because of the peculiar nature of the way we do things in the Department of Defense, I could use my capability in support of his [Admiral Kidd's] command, but if I got out there and found that I needed something to help me do that job better, I couldn't come back and ask for it because it was a collateral mission and could not generate a requirement. Collateral missions by definition inside the Department of Defense can't drive a requirement. So I had to use only the capabilities I had developed for other commands to be able to apply to his command, mine laying and long-range surveillance. If I could do it with what I had in hand, fine. If it required something new, something changed, something to be procured, I couldn't get it because it was a collateral mission.[238]

As a matter of fact, B-52s had very little antiship capability, mainly because neither gravity bombs nor limited-range glide bombs provided any standoff capability such as would be needed for an effective attack against any kind of defended group of combatants of the Soviet navy. Explained Gen Richard Ellis, CINCSAC, in 1981:

> SAC has been tasked by the Joint Chiefs of Staff Joint Strategic Capabilities Plan to perform three collateral missions: aerial minelaying, conducting antisubmarine warfare . . . and interdicting enemy sea power through air operations. . . . Given the proper tactical situation, our aerial minelaying can be a most effective deterrent. However, our sea power interdiction capability is severely limited by the lack of weapons with enough range to allow aircraft survivability. Most importantly, today we would have to remove forces from their SIOP commitments in order to accomplish these missions.[239]

In 1981 Adm John T. Hayward, chief of naval operations (CNO), was very concerned about the danger of Soviet Backfire land-based Navy bombers against US fleet units at sea, especially in the North Atlantic. He wanted to work with Gen Lew Allen to increase the number of AWACS aircraft to assure fleet protection, but he was skeptical about counting on the Air Force for assets not under Navy control. He was concerned that in a crisis, most available AWACS would be assigned to highest priority NATO missions in the Central Region. Similarly, the Navy was concerned about any proposal to augment antiship maritime support B-52 capabilities, since in an emergency the national command authorities would decide to generate a maximum nuclear SIOP force, and the B-52s would likely be withdrawn from an antiship role.[240]

During the Carter administration the emphasis laid upon strengthening NATO's Central Region had reduced funding for Navy and Marine Corps units worldwide. In the Reagan administration, Secretary of the Navy John Lehman, Jr., actively promoted a "maritime strategy" different from what he described as the "laid-back, Carter" strategy for protecting the sea lines of communication (SLOC) to Europe. Lehman's proposal was to protect the SLOC by offensively striking the Soviet Navy near its heavily defended fleet bases. In addition to a five-year plan to build to a 600-ship Navy including 15 carrier battlegroups, Secretary Weinberger in 1982 stated defense guidance that expanded the role of Air Force aircraft in defending the sea-lanes against Soviet long-range bombers armed with antiship missiles. Weinberger said, "Where geographically feasible, we plan to establish barriers composed of land-based interceptors, supported by long-range surveillance systems, to detect and engage Soviet bombers before they can threaten our naval forces transiting the sea lanes."[241] Staff preparation between the Navy and the Air Force developed areas of needed activity. The Navy essentially believed that it had sufficient assets to deal with antisurface warfare requirements and discouraged Air Force resource commitments to attacking ships, especially since B-52s lacked standoff munitions. The Air Force was planning on increasing mining capability in B-52H aircraft that were programmed for a new strategic projection force. The most pressing area where the Air Force could help the Navy was in antiair warfare. The new CNO, Adm James D. Watkins, considered the Backfire and Soviet submarine-launched cruise missiles to be the biggest threats to the

American aircraft carriers. Already Navy airmen were working very closely with Air Force AWACS controllers. "The AWACS aircraft has pulled the Air Force and the Navy closely together throughout the world. They are operating off Japan, Okinawa, and periodically Iceland," Watkins said. Even though he was favorably impressed with what was being described as Air Force-Navy "interoperability," Watkins sought formal memoranda of agreement (MOA) with Gen Charles Gabriel, who had taken over as Air Force chief of staff. Watkins noted: "I felt there was need to put teeth behind some of the rhetoric of interservice cooperation."[242] Gabriel and Watkins jointly signed a basic MOA on 9 September 1982, and on 25 October Secretaries Verne Orr and Lehman joined them in another endorsing MOA called, "Joint USN/USAF Efforts for Enhancement of the Joint Cooperation." In Gabriel's words:

> The memorandum of agreement with the Navy acknowledges that we can do the job better—together. Our first efforts will be directed toward sea lane air defense. We plan to have our skills for doing this through a joint training program and realistic joint exercises. Other areas in which the Air Force can help include indications and warnings; surveillance and targeting; command, control and communications; aerial minelaying; electronic warfare; delivery of Navy special operations force and aerial refueling.[243]

The top-down endorsement of the basic MOA on 25 October emphasized joint training and interoperability and agreed to establish a joint training center and "war at sea range" at Key West, Florida, that would develop joint tactical doctrine for maritime operations as well as combination air superiority, surface warfare, and undersea warfare training for both services. In February 1983, General Gabriel summarized the new Air Force-Navy relations:

> Let me say this—with the new CNO, Admiral Watkins, we are going to do everything we can to work closely together.... The F-15s and the AWACS will give cover to the Navy wherever they need it.... We practice it in the Pacific and in the Atlantic all the time now and in the Med[iterrean] and Indian Ocean. We can do that. We do have the crossover. We don't have the parochial blocks any longer.[244]

The Tactical Air Command – Training and Doctrine Command

In the aftermath of the roles and missions embroilment generated by often parochial assertions incident to the Cheyenne-AX programs, General Brown as Air Force chief of staff and General Abrams as Army chief of staff had hoped that the mutual understanding and common outlook they had shared in combat in Southeast Asia could be carried forward in peacetime, institutionalized, and expanded into a continual working process within and between the Army and the Air Force. Brown and Abrams personally impressed these thoughts on Gen Robert J. Dixon while he was on his way to take command of the Tactical Air Command on 1 October 1973. Four days later, on 5 October, General Abrams wrote Gen William E. DePuy, commander of the US Army Training and Doctrine Command

IDEAS, CONCEPTS, DOCTRINE

(TRADOC), with headquarters at Fort Monroe, Virginia, seven miles from Langley AFB, Virginia, of his desire for Army-Air Force cooperation:

> I have long believed that since there exists in the Army and Air Force a unique complementary relationship to conduct warfare on the landmass, it is absolutely essential that a close relationship exist, at all levels, between the two Services. The Army's recent experience in Southeast Asia has further reinforced my belief in the essentiality of close working ties with the Air Force.... The problem that George Brown and I both face, is how to carry over this commonality of purpose which existed so clearly in Vietnam, as it has in other operational settings, into the entire fabric of relationships between the two Services.[245]

On 16 October 1973 Dixon and DePuy met jointly and commenced a TAC/TRADOC relationship that matured from a dialogue to a partnership. The steady growth of Soviet/Warsaw Pact forces threatening NATO, already evident in number and capability in 1973, demanded that, in General Dixon's words, "the Army-Air Force air-land battle team get the most capability out of what we have and provide the most precise, analytical and coordinated information possible on our needs for added capabilities."[246] In view of the 1973 threat Dixon and DePuy decided first to focus improvements of existing joint combat capabilities on procedures to win the air-land battle. It was soon clear to Dixon and DePuy that the services in the past had tended to identify and present for DSARC review systems individually. Instead, the effectiveness of each individual system was often highly dependent on interface with other systems.[247] As a start, to begin to carry on daily work, the TAC deputy chief of staff for plans and the TRADOC deputy chief of staff for combat developments were made comanagers of a joint actions steering committee, and at their first meeting they established joint TAC/TRADOC working groups to devise procedures for airspace management and reconnaissance/surveillance. Soon, working groups on electronic warfare, air logistics, and remotely piloted vehicles (RPVs) were established. The working group arrangement did not provide a structure for continuous and detailed analysis. The air-land forces application (ALFA) directorate was accordingly formed with five Army and five Air Force officers, headed by a leader who rotated each year between services. Because ALFA was small it was authorized to form joint groups from TAC and TRADOC staffs to address particular problems related to the ALFA mission of developing concepts and procedures to win the air-land battle. By 1976 ALFA was working seven problem areas: airspace management, reconnaissance/surveillance (including RPVs and remote sensors), air defense suppression, electronic warfare, forward air controller/forward observer, air base defense, and air logistics.[248] The Langley AFB ALFA was actively supported by USAFE and USAREUR, and in 1976 these European commands organized their own joint directorate of air-land forces application (DALFA), located at Ramstein Air Base, West Germany, and charged to center on current problems of how best to generate maximum combat power. DALFA focused on more immediate concerns than the longer-range ALFA, getting some quick evidences of Army-Air Force cooperation in Europe.

Through a joint USAFE/USAREUR regulation, specific USAFE wings/squadrons were aligned with USAREUR divisions/regiments. Units so aligned cooperated with each other in daily planning and execution of close-air-support training and planning for effective support of Army war plans. Since Army general defense plans reflected expected enemy main axes of attack, a tactical air plan and exercise called Creek Braille was practicable. The concept of Creek Braille hinged on the ground commander identifying probable axes of attack; aircrews studied maps and area photography, and visually identified key terrain features, predesignated contact points, and preselected kill zones. Such preplanning, it was reasonable to expect, would result in a rapid response to a familiar target area, an increased possibility of effectiveness on a single ordnance pass, and an effective counter to hostile communications jamming, enhanced aircrew survivability through greater familiarity with the geographical environment, but decreased reliance on a command and control system that might be degraded by enemy action. Creek Braille was a technique and a prospective prudent response to chaotic conditions likely to exist in NATO's Central Region during the first few hours or days of a Soviet/Warsaw Pact attack.[249]

One of the first achievements of the TAC/TRADOC ALFA was the agreement on airspace management produced by an airspace management working group. The issue of Air Force overcontrol of low-altitude Army traffic was resolved by a flexible and simple establishment of a situation-dependent ceiling, where all air traffic above the ceiling operated under positive control of the Air Force tactical air control system and all Army traffic below the ceiling operated under procedures established by appropriate authority, such as operations orders for particular undertakings. Large-scale operations in the low-altitude regime were handled as exceptions to usual rules if need be. The altitude ceiling was set by joint force commanders, since terrain varied from place to place. The TAC/TRADOC arrangement for airspace management was accepted by both the Army and Air Force and was printed as a joint manual on 1 November 1976.[250]

The success of TAC/TRADOC in providing an agreeable system for aerospace management in a battle area was hailed by both General Jones, the JCS chairman, and Gen Fred C. Weyand, the later Army chief of staff, as a harbinger of the solution of air-land problems. General Weyand wrote:

> I have read the joint manual of aerospace management and believe it a major step toward insuring the integrated efforts of our air and land forces on the modern battlefield. Bill DePuy is very enthusiastic about the prospects for success in addressing other areas of mutual concern. The progress made in resolving our airspace management problem is proof that his enthusiasm is well founded.[251]

In projecting the TAC/TRADOC cooperative venture General Dixon expected to begin with procedures, expand to include current and future concepts, thence

IDEAS, CONCEPTS, DOCTRINE

joint requirements and priorities, and ultimately to address force structure. General DePuy gave more emphasis to developing common procedures:

> We are working on the procedures... for close air support, air defense suppression and a lot of other things. It is not that this has never happened before, but I submit to you it probably has not ever happened before with the intensity that it has right now. We are doing this because we have one objective. General Dixon and I are not in the R. & D. business, we are not in the force structure business. That is done by others. We have a mission which is to make the joint Air Force-Army team out there, the joint task force, as effective as we can by learning how to do these things together, the techniques, the tactics and the procedures.[252]

In General Dixon's view, the TAC/TRADOC "dialogue" developed into a "partnership," but it was nevertheless true that the partnership was better able to develop procedures than to handle resulting quantification of requirements. Analysis of systems, moreover, revealed that there were synergistic interrelations of prices adding to the complexity of quantification. For example, effectiveness in prices of reconnaissance/surveillance affected defense suppression. As work progressed, there were nevertheless desirable learning outcomes. In defense suppression, for example, the joint working group took 40 Army and Air Force systems that related to the defense suppression task and developed a picture of what could be done most effectively with existing capabilities, but could not immediately address what was needed or duplicative because the group lacked a means of systemic quantification. On the other hand, joint suppression of enemy air defenses (J-SEAD) procedures manuals were conceived and published, and specific bits and pieces of joint work were addressed and quantifiable. After the Yom Kippur War General Brown had directed that programs be looked at in defense suppression and that those with the most promise be brought forward as soon as possible. The existing Wild Weasel system used in Southeast Asia had many known deficiencies, and as a result an F-4G Wild Weasel optimized to detect, identify, locate, attack, and destroy enemy threat radars in Eastern Europe was put into development. The J-SEAD study essayed a rough, initial, joint quantification of the effect the programmed F-4G Wild Weasel would have. Before this could begin, however, the conferees discovered that there was no single source document that had the details on Warsaw Pact ground-based air defenses needed for analytical purposes. They therefore built and published a handbook on Warsaw Pact ground-based air defenses (code-named Hydra). The resulting study showed that the advanced F-4G Wild Weasel would effectively reduce total fighter losses in the US *V* and *VI* Corps areas of Central Europe by an undisclosed figure, simultaneously increasing the number of fighter sorties to be available at the end of the first three days of hostilities.[253]

The TAC/TRADOC examination of J-SEAD also yielded new thinking on the subject of the airborne forward air controller (FAC) and his survivability in a European defense environment. At Air Force level in 1976 there was thinking that a new, more-survivable FAC-X aircraft was quite possibly going to be a two-seat

A-10.[254] There was general agreement that the O-2 and OV-10 aircraft used by airborne FACs to find targets, identify them, mark them for attack, and to direct strike fighters would be grossly vulnerable in Europe. The TAC/TRADOC joint study proposed to address the problem by a new concept of operations that moved the airborne FAC to a rear position on the battlefield, changed his role to that of a coordinator of air strikes, and placed greater reliance on Army forward observers to acquire and designate targets. This concept was refined in concert with USAFE and USAREUR, and in November 1977 it was tested during more general maneuver exercises of Army attack helicopters and A-10s at Fort Hunter Liggett, in California. This joint air weapon system (JAWS) exercise used four Army scout helicopters, one of which lifted the Air Force ground FAC to an elevated view. The airborne Air Force FAC was in an OV-10 a number of kilometers back of the FEBA, where he acted as a communication link between the FAC in the scout helicopter and the four strike A-10s. The airborne FAC passed on target information, air defense locations, and the battle situation. In JAWS the abilities of Army strike helicopters and A-10s were demonstrated to be complementary in attack as well as a complication to the enemy air defense problem.[255]

The TAC/TRADOC joint reconnaissance/surveillance study group was called upon to perform a mission area analysis, quantifying joint capabilities and needs in 1980, 1984, and 1994. One past obstacle in quantifying reconnaissance/surveillance had been in defining analytically how to relate reconnaissance/surveillance to success in other mission areas and to determine precisely how reconnaissance/surveillance relates to the outcome of the air-land battle. To counter a Warsaw Pact offensive it would be necessary to destroy enemy forces before their contact with friendly forces, to have situation assessment and decisions in near real time, to identify elements posing the greatest threat, and to concentrate friendly firepower. The task was to get reconnaissance/surveillance to air and ground commanders who needed it to get their forces directed at the right place at the right time to stop an enemy advance. The existing 30 Air Force and Army systems could find and report groups of things, but with limited firepower there was a need for discriminate applications. The critical demand for reconnaissance/surveillance was thus to identify the enemy's combat momentum, which was essentially a combination of massed firepower and movement. The essential task of reconnaissance/surveillance was timely location and reporting of combat momentum.[256] In the European maneuver, NATO forces were outmanned and undergunned. They could not fight on a one-to-one basis and win. They had to maneuver effectively both on the ground and in the air. But to maneuver effectively, there was a need for information that was timely, useful, and given to the right commanders at all echelons. There was also a need to locate targets with essential timeliness and accuracy to bring Air Force or Army weapons to bear on them.[257]

As it happened, the main TAC/TRADOC contribution to the Air Force-Army reconnaissance/surveillance planning was the development of a joint mission element needs statement (MENS) since the reconnaissance programs undertaken

IDEAS, CONCEPTS, DOCTRINE

in the early 1970s strayed into some blind alleys, resulting in delays that eventually demanded expedited attention in 1977 at the Air Force-Army Washington staff level.[258] In Southeast Asia the Air Force had used remotely piloted vehicles (RPVs) for reconnaissance purposes basically to reduce manned aircraft attrition in high-threat environments. By using photographic RPVs over Hanoi, for example, the Air Force successfully reduced losses of photo aircraft and crews. The RPV equipment that was used in Southeast Asia was innovative and plagued with reliability and recovery problems, but it was made to fulfill an emerging combat mission by what was described as a Band-Aid approach—fixing defects and making improvements as needed. The Army and the Navy also experienced failures in RPV programs in the late 1960s that left them somewhat unenthusiastic about such techniques. The Air Force had some enthusiasm for RPVs, provided they could meet basic requirements of reducing manned aircraft in high-threat environments or of achieving significant cost advantages over comparably manned aircraft systems or providing a means of acceptable operation in politically sensitive areas or missions. In 1974 the main Air Force development RPV program was Compass Cope, or the twin prototype fabrication of two models of a high-altitude, long-endurance RPV that would be outfitted for signal intelligence (SIGINT), battlefield surveillance, precision emitter location strike system (PELSS), ocean surveillance, communications relay, or atmospheric sampling as needed. The Boeing Company fabricated a prototype YQM-94A and the Teledyne Ryan Company built a YQM-98A. The Air Force RPV program also included a tactical expendable drone system (TEDS) that would fly one-way missions to confuse, saturate, and degrade Soviet/Warsaw Pact defenses. A low-medium altitude multimission RPV (MMRPV), designated AQM-34, would be needed to fill reconnaissance, electronic warfare, and air-to-ground strike control requirements.[259] In addition to RPVs, the Air Force reconnaissance programs also included the upgrading of RF-4C aircraft to provide a quick-strike reconnaissance (QSR) capability that would be needed to counter a Warsaw Pact offensive.[260]

In September 1977 the Air Force realized that its ongoing reconnaissance programs were based on what was described as "a Vietnam War/Korean War/World War II mentality." There were problems in all-weather surveillance, getting the right information to the right user, and saturating communications lines. Under the direction of Gen Alton D. Slay, deputy chief of staff for research and development, Air Force and Army staff representatives undertook what they expected to be a "landmark effort which will have a long-term effect on the composition and employment of all reconnaissance resources of the United States." The study was approved by the Army and Air Force chiefs of staff on 1 December 1977 and was reflected in changes to the fiscal year 1979 budget and adjustments to the Army-Air Force five-year development plans. In addition, a coordinating committee was established at the general officer level within the staffs of the Departments of Army and Air Force to correlate reconnaissance programs of the two services. The resolution of reconnaissance/surveillance brought marked reductions in RPVs. General Dixon explained, "RPV technology and development has not matured to the point where RPVs can effectively perform all portions of the time sensitive reconnaissance mission. . . . Believe me, if we could get an efficient RPV – efficient in the overall sense – we'd press to have it produced."[261] Even before the reconnaissance study, the secretary of the Air Force canceled Compass Cope because it could not be justified as cost-effective: expected attrition in landing and takeoff posed excessive costs, and it could not be expected to have the lift capacity required for weight of the precision location strike system (PLSS). General Slay said, "I was never able . . . to make what I considered a real compelling case for our analysis on the cost effectiveness of Compass Cope."[262] The Air Force/Army Reconnaissance Force Study recommended that additional AQM-34 low-to-medium altitude remotely piloted vehicles not be procured, the rationale being based on the limited operational utility of the reconnaissance RPV and the high total cost and the complex recovery problems associated with current RPV operations. Additionally, the study concluded that the Air Force should look toward the Army, looking at a simple, cheap RPV for operation in and about the FEBA to save manned reconnaissance aircraft, rather than to continue to buy and operate bigger, more expensive RPVs.[263]

The major recommendation of the Air Force/Army Reconnaissance Force Study reflected a need for recce architecture conversant with the hostile threat to NATO and the prospective NATO strategy to deal with an enemy attack. "It is not feasible to match the Soviets man for man and tank for tank. However, it is possible to fight outnumbered and win provided you know when and where to employ your forces, and if they are employed against those elements of the threat, which if destroyed or degraded, reduced drastically the overall combat capability of the enemy," said Brig Gen Charles R. Canedy, deputy director of Army requirements and an Army aviation officer.[264] These were "critical modes," and they were command posts, communications centers, fire direction centers, weapons, prime movers, and jammers. The study proposed to reopen the U-2R production line at Palmdale, California, with stored tooling and produce 35 TR-1 high-altitude reconnaissance aircraft to be used as platforms for all-weather battlefield surveillance in the form of the precision location strike system. The PLSS was an advancement of the advanced location strike system (ALSS) being built for Southeast Asia requirements at the time US involvement in the war wound down. In the description of Maj Gen Richard C. Henry, director of development and acquisition and deputy chief of staff of Air Force research and development, the PLSS was admittedly complicated and expensive. "But every time we march up to the brink and address that system, we find that that is the only way that we know how to deliver weapons on target with execution accuracy."[265] The TR-1 and PLSS programs were strongly supported by both Army and Air Force, and procurement of the first two TR-1s started in fiscal year 1979. Produced at the Advanced Development Projects Division (Skunk Works) of the Lockheed California Company, the TR-1 program encountered an almost immediate cost overrun because its costs were shared with Lockheed's discontinued L-101 transport aircraft. The TR-1 was capable of long loiter standoff surveillance from altitudes above 60,000 feet; its modular payload changeable-mode concept permitted its use with a variety of reconnaissance sensors or to act as an airborne relay for the PLSS.[266]

Even though the PLSS was only partly in production and mostly still being designed in 1981–83, both the Air Force and the Army placed a high priority on the TR-1 and the PLSS. The Air Force planned to establish two TR-1 reconnaissance orbits and one PLSS Triad (three orbiting TR-1s) to cover the Central European borders. These orbits would provide critical indications and warning during peacetime and target detection and identification for battlefield management and strike execution during hostilities. The three sensor-equipped TR-1s would pick up any electronic radiation site from across the border, triangulate its location, and send the information back to the central processing ground station. The ground station, either in West Germany or England—and perhaps in both places, with the second station playing backup—would process the emitter location and provide the information to strike aircraft or friendly artillery for attack suppression. "It is our doctrine to key upon the command, control and communications elements of the Soviet-Warsaw Pact forces recognizing that they are highly centralized in their control," explained Brig Gen Richard D. Kenyon, the US Army aviation officer and the deputy chief of staff for operations and plans.[267] The TAC commander, Gen Wilbur L. Creech, described the PLSS:

> A critical element of our overall approach to defense suppression is the Precision Location Strike System (PLSS). Now, PLSS essentially is a system that provides . . . a precise location on each enemy threat emitter through electronic intercept by high-flying TR-1 aircraft. The great beauty of the system is that it allows us to keep track of those various threats in real time, and to develop the strategy for countering them. . . . Our strategy will call for us to kill some, disrupt others, and very importantly, to avoid the rest. . . . In this sense, PLSS is to the ground threats as AWACS is to the air threats.[268]

Second Echelon Attack/AirLand Battle

In 1972 Col Kenneth L. Moll of the Air Force Directorate of Doctrine, Concepts, and Objectives conceived of a project for putting together an Air Force future concepts workbook detailing where the Air Force should go and how to get there. Moll suggested among other things that criteria should be devised for measuring and comparing different concepts. When the project ran on without completion, Maj Gen Leslie W. Bray, Jr., who was the director of Doctrine, Concepts, and Objectives, suggested that a series of seminars like those used in the curriculum of the Air War College "back off and reexamine all of the concepts and doctrines for the employment of airpower that have been evolved and been handed down to us." The first week of the seminars concentrated on land and naval warfare, and from the discussions of the past emerged a new concept which General Bray was going to call "tactical counterforce."[269] Bray wrote:

> Tactical Counterforce has as its objective the destruction or disruption of major ground forces that threaten, but are not engaged with, friendly ground forces. The targets are enemy firepower elements located beyond the forward edge of the battle area. Because it strikes directly at enemy land forces rather than lines of communication, Tactical Counterforce differs from current perceptions and from the traditional emphasis of interdiction. . . . Isolation of the battlefield—interdiction, as it is commonly perceived today—would continue to be another essential function of tactical air. But Tactical Counterforce adds an enlarged dimension to current perceptions of interdiction.[270]

In the NATO Central Region, Bray pointed out, Warsaw Pact forces were poised on two fronts — designated "initial" and "reinforcing." The initial spearhead divisions were expected to break through NATO defenses and the reinforcing second echelon would exploit the breakthrough: this was the standard Soviet tactic of mass assault.

> It might be possible to use Tactical Counterforce against the fast-moving spearhead units before they came into contact with the friendly ground forces, but this is likely to be a brief, transitory phase. In the latter and continuing stages of the attack, the spearhead units would be operating within the reach of friendly ground forces; air attacks against these units would fall within the purview of close air support. But the bulk of the Warsaw Pact forces (the driving part of the wedge) would be deployed beyond the reach of friendly ground forces and outside the area covered by close air support. If a large number of these elements of enemy firepower (tanks, artillery, personnel carriers) could be rapidly attrited by Tactical Counterforce, the momentum of the attack would be blunted. Friendly ground forces, with close air support, could cope much more easily with the reduced pressures exerted by the spearhead and residual forces, thus significantly improving the prospects of halting the attack.[271]

On the basis of experience with aerial interdiction in Southeast Asia, it had been fashionable to demean the significance of air attack in any so-called choking off of enemy movement toward a ground front. On the basis of systems analysis, Alain C. Enthoven, for example, argued that deep interdiction in Europe would not be productive.

> It would be virtually impossible to disrupt the flow of essential war materiel from rear areas to the front by means of a conventional bombing campaign against railroad centers, bridges, and roads. Systems analysis studies indicated that even if flow capacity could be reduced by as much as 90 percent, the remaining capacity would be enough to reinforce and resupply an 80-division Warsaw Pact force. Moreover, an interdiction effort of this magnitude would require forces far in excess of even those recommended by the Services. This point is important, because half an interdiction campaign is not worth much.[272]

Possibly on the basis of such interpretations, Admiral Moorer, while JCS chairman, burst out:

> God forbid that we base our future on the total concept of operations as they have been conducted in South Vietnam. I think one of the unfortunate outcomes of this is that there has been placed in the minds of many people some question as to the utility, for

instance, of air interdiction in a combat environment. And here again it would be a grave mistake, I think, to draw conclusions with respect to the effectiveness of air interdiction solely on the basis of the way it has been conducted in Southeast Asia.[273]

In his exposition on tactical counterforce, General Bray noted that because of emphasis in Vietnam, Korea, and World War II, "interdiction today has come to be identified almost solely with reducing the flow of men and materials." Bray had in mind the use of new technology to track and destroy enemy forces. "Indeed, if airpower can find and strike enemy forces as effectively as is suggested by the new technology, this independent capacity should be given marked emphasis. It might well emerge as a significant and perhaps decisive factor for countering enemy land forces in the future."[274]

During the 1970–73 years the US Army was trying to restructure itself from the Vietnam experience, and the Army staff recognized that there was no well-articulated military policy. Of the possible wars of the future, a mechanized war in NATO Europe, although the least likely war, was the most important in terms of national survival and Western civilization. An analysis in TRADOC of more than 1,000 tank battles made it apparent that the smaller side did not necessarily lose to the numerically superior enemy. The 1973 Middle East War, moreover, demonstrated there was a "new lethality" in defense weaponry. Using terrain as a combat multiplier, the defender needed to see deep to find the following Soviet/Warsaw Pact echelon, move fast to concentrate forces, strike quickly before the enemy could break the defenses, and finish the fight quickly before the second echelon closed.[275] As the Army studies were progressing, the Air Force concept of interdiction as an attack against the Soviet/Warsaw Pact second-echelon forces fitted well. Lt Gen Robert R. Williams, US Army assistant chief of staff for force development, believes air superiority offers a deterrence to the enemy air force in Europe. With massive armor, he continues, the Army can drive back the enemy and hold them there.[276]

In 1976 General DePuy sequenced American responses to a massive Soviet attack.

> The first thing we really need to know is where is that attack going to take place. That is one of the first areas where we are dependent on the Air Force.... We need to see back where the second and third echelon are, and we need to see back there before it happens.[277]

While the US ground forces were racing to the scene of attack, DePuy continued,

> we would hope... that the US Air Force was working on his second echelon so that that particular problem did not arise on the battlefield. It is doubtful that the Air Force would eliminate the second or third echelon. It is highly desirable that they do it a lot of damage.[278]

On 1 July 1976 the Army issued a new version of Field Manual 100-5, *Operations*, that placed great emphasis on the concept of "fight outnumbered and win" by a combination of use of terrain as a defense multiplier and the "new lethality" of new antitank weapons. Emphasis was on winning the first battle — a firepower battle along the forward edge of the battle area. The 1976 version of FM 100-5 set in motion a pointed doctrinal debate by critics who insisted that it was based upon a conception of firepower/attrition and gave no real attention to a maneuver concept of war.[279]

In 1977 Gen Donn A. Starry replaced General DePuy as commanding general, TRADOC, and he brought a close interest in tactical doctrine sharpened by his most recent assignment as a US Army corps commander in West Germany. In Starry's eyes the focus of FM 100-5 on the central battle along the FEBA overlooked the enemy's massive second-echelon exploitation forces which, by Soviet doctrine, would roll through the first echelon and exploit any gains it had made. A Soviet/Warsaw Pact combined-arms army deployed in a depth of about 100 kilometers; its first-echelon divisions were about 30 kilometers deep, its second-echelon divisions about 50 to 60 kilometers back, and the reconnaissance elements of the second-echelon army were about 120 kilometers to the rear. Overall, Starry said, the enemy wanted a pre-attack preponderance of force of a minimum of 3 to 1 and preferably 6 to 1. On what he came to describe as the "extended battlefield," Starry demonstrated that a US Army corps commander would find it "essential for friendly air to keep enemy air off his back," would need "aerial reconnaissance and surveillance because he does not himself have the means to see the second echelon divisions or the second echelon army," and would have to depend on tactical air to interdict the movement forward of enemy second echelons since — except for the nonnuclear Lance missile — a corps commander's "organic fire support can reach only about as far as he can see." In the way of "observations" from the description of the extended battlefield, Starry said:

> Counterair, electronic warfare, and air defense operations must be carefully integrated and correctly employed in order to defeat the weight of airpower that the enemy can bring to bear on us. Finding the second echelon divisions and armies is so critical to the corps commanders that timeliness of response and responsiveness of coverage of the air reconnaissance system must be established and guaranteed beyond doubt. . . . Breaking up the mass and slowing the momentum of second echelon forces is critical to the ground commander fighting the first echelon. The air commander must concentrate on this task, for the ground commander hasn't the organic resources either to find or to fire at the second echelon. Forces fighting the first echelon must have the additional target servicing capability of aerial firepower to win against a breakthrough. Therefore, it is imperative that we completely integrate fixed and rotary wing antiarmor systems, and learn how to direct them in battle under command of a team leader, with whom they have trained extensively.[280]

To add clarity to the new Army fighting concept, General Starry chose "AirLand Battle" to describe it, since he conceived that the battlefield had a deeper dimension in time as well as distance, in air as well as on ground. A brigade commander looking beyond his forward line of own troops (FLOT) had to influence events up to 15 kilometers behind the enemy's rear, a division commander up to 70 kilometers, and a corps commander up to 150 kilometers. These distances translated into time from the FLOT to the onrushing enemy attack—12 hours for the brigade, 24 for the division, and 72 for the corps. In describing the new strategy, Gen Edward C. Meyer, Army chief of staff, talked of the old NATO defense strategy as fight and fall back, and said that as a change NATO forces would oppose an initial enemy attack, would not break away, would keep to the enemy's side, and would attack his flanks. Gen George Blanchard, commander in chief, US Army Forces, Europe, added:

> That still doesn't say that you don't have to move some battalions in front of penetrations. But the doctrine addresses that as well. And the great thing of the mobility of the battlefield, of the armored battlefield, is that you are allowed, if you will, to do that kind of activity, to attack, counterattack, in a somewhat different way than we think of from the traditional World War II counterattack involving a whole corps or a whole division. It is a counterattack even at the company level, throwing off balance, if you will.[281]

Blanchard agreed with a questioner's comment that intelligence requirements for the new strategy were higher than ever before. He said:

> I think your comment is a good one, because intelligence requirements which have always been high become even higher . . . and the ability to see across to the other side becomes essential. In fact, the total capability of NATO intelligence-wise, not just the United States, has to be integrated into the type of fusion capability that we are attempting to gain through our allied concept, as well as through our US concept. And the ability to perform what we refer to as target acquisition becomes extremely important on the battlefield, both to the Army and Air Force forces.[282]

Although the July 1976 edition of Army Field Manual 100-5, *Operations*, was able to encompass the incipient AirLand Battle concept, the 1976 manual continued to remain under attack, especially by the loose coterie of congressmen, civilian defense analysts, and mostly junior military personnel described as the military reform movement. One charge was that ever since the American Civil War the US military strategies were based upon attrition of the enemy rather than maneuver, and that the Soviet Union was obviously better able to endure a head-to-head war than the United States.[283] Under General Starry's initiatives, the air-land concept gradually took form in 1977–80. TRADOC presented the extended battlefield concept at the Army Commanders' Conference of October 1980, and General Meyer approved it at that time. After this, TRADOC developed briefings about AirLand Battle that were widely presented in Washington and throughout the Army. The congressional reform caucus was favorably impressed. At Fort Leavenworth, Kansas, work proceeded on revisions of FM 100-5, the principal author being Lt Col Huba Wass de Czega, an officer assigned to the Command and General Staff College. The draft revision was published in September 1981 and was subjected to an extended review in the Army prior to its publication in August 1982.[284] The codified doctrine placed primary emphasis on maneuver, counterattack, and the ability to keep the enemy off balance. Wass de Czega said that the purpose of second-echelon attack was not so much to whittle down the enemy troops before they reached the front as to throw off their timing. "The idea is to throw his timetable off so that we have a maneuver advantage," he said. "If you have the capability to make the long shots now and then, you loosen up the other side. But you can't count on those long shots, and they are not your bread and butter shots."[285]

The name AirLand Battle implied that there was cooperation and agreement between the Army and the Air Force, but in fact the doctrine was a unilateral development of the Army. Army leaders pointed to a memorandum of understanding between Generals Meyer and Gabriel signed in April 1983 as evidence of Air Force endorsement of the AirLand Battle, but to more critical viewers the official agreement merely committed the Army and Air Force to cooperate in "joint tactical training and field exercises based on AirLand Battle doctrine." One member of the AirLand Forces Application Agency, Maj James A. Machos, said of the Meyer-Gabriel MOU, "It does not acknowledge AirLand Battle doctrine as the sole governing principle for joint training and exercises, nor does it concede unequivocal primacy of AirLand Battle doctrine over established Air Force doctrine."[286] Another unnamed Air Force official said: "When we say we agree with the air-land battle concept, what we are saying is that we agree that the concept is a good concept for the Army."[287]

Both during the drawing of the concepts and later when appearing in the published field manual, the Army's AirLand Battle doctrine occasioned discussions of Air Force TACAIR. Because of the vast numerical superiority of the Soviet/Warsaw Pact forces, Edgar Ulsamer, an *Air Force Magazine* senior editor, pointed out, there would be a subtle change in air superiority doctrine:

> If intelligence is right, NATO ground forces could achieve local superiority against the first assault echelon. The second, equally decisive, "if" is whether US and other NATO tactical airpower would be able to deal with the Pact's second echelon before it could engage NATO ground forces at the forward edge of the battle area. This, then, leads to the third requirement for a successful defense by NATO forces—the rapid achievement of local air superiority over the main battle area to permit interdictions of Pact follow-on attacks.[288]

Elaborating on Ulsamer's diagnosis, Robert S. Dotson, an Air Force Reserve officer employed as a national security budget examiner in the Office of Management and Budget, added the prediction that the main air-ground battle would be against the Pact's second echelon and, in the exposition of this matter, coined a new term, *battlefield air interdiction* (BAI). In explaining the new term, Dotson noted that AFM 2-1, *Tactical Air Operations—Counter Air, Close Air Support, and Air Interdiction*, did "not differentiate within the air interdiction function relative to the forward edge of the battle area (FEBA)." He meant the term *battlefield interdiction* to refer to that portion of the air interdiction function in support of friendly ground forces beyond the range of weapons organic to those ground forces.[289]

At the Air War College, Col Robert D. Rasmussen almost immediately noted that the dividing line between close air support and interdiction had always been the fire support coordination line (FSCL) that had originally been called the bomb safety line. Detailed integration of air missions with the fire and movement of friendly forces was required for close air support within the FSCL for the safety of the friendly forces; detailed integration of air interdiction (AI) missions with the fire and movement of friendly forces outside the FSCL was not necessary because the safety of friendly forces was not involved. Rasmussen protested that fragmentation of the AI into battlefield air interdiction (BAI) and long-range interdiction ought to be stopped. "There is *no need* to fragment it, and the results could be degrading not only to the clarity of roles and missions but, more important, to combat effectiveness," he wrote. "There was no reason to subject interdiction strikes beyond the FSCL to cumbersome procedures necessary for friendly troop safety in the case of close air support."[290]

Rasmussen particularly objected to the fact that the draft of AFM 1-1, *Functions and Basic Doctrine of the United States Air Force,* in progress in 1978 had "broken off a piece of the interdiction mission, given it a separate title, and then essentially applied to it the definition of close air support in requiring it to be coordinated with the ground commander's fire and maneuver." Nevertheless, the 14 February 1979 edition of AFM 1-1 provided:

> That portion of the air interdiction mission which may have a direct or near-term effect upon surface operations—referred to by the term "battlefield air interdiction"—requires the air and surface commanders to coordinate their respective operations to insure the most effective support of the combined arms team.[291]

In NATO's Central Region, Army and Air Force organizations recognized a generic relationship of all operations in direct support of land forces as "offensive air support," the generic classification including close air support (CAS), BAI, and tactical air reconnaissance (TAR). Battlefield air interdiction was subject to joint Army/Air Force planning but did not require the detailed integration of CAS; it was flown beyond the FSCL and up to the reconnaissance and interdiction planning line—normally 80–100 kilometers beyond the FSCL. Published in 1980, Allied Tactical Publication 27(B), *Offensive Air Support,* highlighted the distinctions earlier accepted in the Central Region and gave international doctrinal status to BAI.[292] In December 1982, the US Army, US Readiness Command, and Tactical Air Command published a joint operational concept entitled "Joint Attack of the Second Echelon (JASK)."[293]

Upon the emergence of battlefield air interdiction as a viable concept, two Royal Air Force officers proposed in separate articles in 1979 and 1980 that BAI would be less risky and more productive and could fulfill the same role as close air support in helping to blunt and stop an armored thrust. They urged that the CAS mission had become too complex and had a disproportionate risk/reward ratio.[294]

In rebuttal, Maj Michael O. Beck, chief of the ALO/FAC Training Section, TAC, urged that both CAS and BAI were essential since TACAIR was in Beck's description a "force multiplier" in support of a ground army. Using AirLand Battle parlance whereby the capability to identify and deal with a Pact target was called "servicing" the target, Beck wrote:

> The value of TACAIR to the ground commander can be summarized by the term *a force multiplier*. CAS serves to reduce the stress on the battlefield by boosting the service rate of the engaged forces. BAI, on the other hand, serves two separate purposes: BAI decreases the enemy's arrival rate through disruption and dispersal, and it enhances the overall friendly service rate through in-depth attrition. Both missions are essential. If the enemy's arrival rate exceeds the combined friendly air/land service rate at the line of contact, the defender will be driven back or overrun. Likewise, if the service rate at the line of contact does not match or succeed [sic] that of the enemy, the enemy's arrival rate will be of little consequence; a breakthrough will occur anyway.... In summary, the effective use of air power is now, as it has been in the past, dependent on the dynamics of the battlefield. In order for TACAIR to make an effective contribution to this joint battle, the flexibility and capability to perform both CAS and BAI must be preserved and perfected.[295]

Although much of the discussion of BAI concerned destruction of enemy force capabilities, Gen Edward C. Meyer, Army chief of staff, pointed out another temporal aspect of Army-Air Force systems in second-echelon attack.

> Their mission is not just killing tanks. Their mission is also making certain that the reinforcing armored forces are either slowed or destroyed, and I say slowed, because slowed is equally important. If you are up in the front lines fighting and if you can keep the enemy from closing all of his forces on you at the same time, that is important to you.[296]

In the AirLand Battle focus, Army forces had vital interests not only on their immediate forward line of own troops but well out ahead of the FLOT. A US corps was expected to fight in an assigned area of influence and to get the necessary information to fight in the corps monitored area of interest out beyond the area of influence. The actual geographical size of these areas depended on situational factors (mission, enemy, terrain, troops, and time available) and the reaction time that a particular troop unit needed to counter battlefield developments. The corps in the AirLand Battle concept was the focal-point fighting unit, with any field army organization being available for logistics and support. The normal combat reaction time for a corps was 72 hours, a time guideline that translated into a distance guideline of 150 kilometers beyond the FLOT for the area of influence and 300 kilometers for the area of interest.[297]

In a theater the air commander had historically had the responsibility for interdicting air strikes against targets beyond the Army FSCL, being responsible for the location, identification, and attack of such targets. The ground force commander provided information from his sources and kept the air commander knowledgeable about Army interests in specific targets, but the air commander made decisions to attack, appraised results, and reported results. When asked for a background appraisal of the AirLand Battle concept of army corps as the focal points of operations with far-out areas of influence and interest, General Momyer suggested that:

> The Corps is seeking to be self-sufficient for any target array that has an influence on the Corps commander's strategy and tactical operations. If carried to its logical conclusion, it means the Corps commander is directly concerned with any enemy formation no matter how far away, if it could eventually impact on the operations of his Corps—an absurd idea, I think one would agree.[298]

Another air officer's appraisal demonstrated that the luxury of allowing each corps commander to "call his own shots" would fragment the *theater* air interdiction effort, replacing the theater perspective with several narrow, possibly conflicting, corps perspectives. Both General Momyer and Major Machos of the ALFA argued the case for a field army or army group over the multiple corps to provide overall guidance and continuity to ground operations. Momyer said:

> The Army doctrine is deficient in not having a headquarters, field army, above a multiple Corps deployment. These Corps cannot be directed out of the theater headquarters which has a full-time job of planning and directing the theater campaign as well as the day-to-day activities of coordinating the efforts of all the major forces.[299]

Although the April 1983 Air Force-Army memorandum of understanding did not mean that the Air Force was adopting completely the Army's AirLand Battle concept, senior Air Force officers concluded that the services working together under the MOU would improve the effectiveness of joint operations and help to iron out doctrinal differences between the Air Force and the Army. At a tactical air conference on 11–15 April General Creech wrapped up with the admonition that the Air Force should "take a positive approach" to the AirLand Battle concept and should welcome more Army input to the interdiction process. He insisted, however, that the AirLand Battle and its extended battlefield concept caused no change in the fundamental application of the principles of air power. The only reason for the detailed coordination of close air support was for the safety of friendly ground troops. BAI was a form of air interdiction; it implied a closer target, and the Army should have more interest and voice on BAI targets, but BAI should not be "mixed up" with CAS. Handling AI targets was an Air Force responsibility.[300] Earlier than this conference—in June 1981—General Creech had already expressed confidence in the ability of air-to-ground optimized F-16s being able to handle BAI as well as CAS, but he worried about what he considered to be relative inattention to long-range interdiction capabilities that were going to be needed. With the exception of the F-111s, the shortfall in long-range offensive interdiction appeared "very, very serious."[301]

In February 1983 Secretary Weinberger indicated that he was looking to the Joint Chiefs of Staff for an evaluation of "means for improving the development of joint doctrine which may be required as more sophisticated target acquisition and attack systems become available to field commanders."[302] Although the Joint Chiefs of Staff were kept briefed as a body, the initiatives for organizing, training, and equipping a compatible, complementary, and affordable total force that would maximize joint combat capabilities to execute air-land combat operations were worked out by six months of joint Army-Air Force effort and approved and issued in a Memorandum of Agreement by General Gabriel and Army Chief of Staff Gen John A. Wickam, Jr., on 22 May 1984. The MOA included 31 initiatives bearing on the air-land combat team and pledged the two services to an annual review/updating of the agreements to confirm their continued advisability, feasibility, and adequacy. The subjects handled as initiatives were (1) area surface-to-air missiles/air defense fighters, (2) point air defense, (3) countering heliborne assault threats, (4) tactical missile threats, (5) identification, friend or foe (IFF) systems, (6) rear area operations centers, (7) host nations support security equipment, (8) air base ground defense, (9) air base ground defense flight training, (10) rear area close air support, (11) mobile weapon systems, (12) ground-based electronic combat against enemy air attacks, (13) airborne radar jamming systems, (14) the precision location strike system (PLSS), (15) joint suppression of enemy air defenses (J-SEAD), (16) combat search and rescue, (17) rotary-wing support for special operations forces (SOF), (18) a joint tactical missile system, (19) Army and Air Force munitions RDT&E, (20) night combat, (21) battlefield air interdiction, (22) a joint target set, (23) theater air interdiction systems, (24) close air support, (25) air liaison officers and forward air controllers, (26) manned aircraft systems, (27) a joint surveillance and target attack radar system (J-STARS), (28) the TR-1 program, (29) manned tactical reconnaissance systems, (30) intratheater airlift, and (31) cross-service participation sister service programs essential to the joint conduct of air-land combat operations. In signing off on the MOA, Generals Wickam and Gabriel viewed their action "as the initial step in the establishment of a long-term, dynamic process whose objective will continue to be the fielding of the most affordable and effective airland combat forces."[303]

Electronics: Key to the Advancing Tactical Air Command Air Program

"The eighteenth century was the era of land wars, the nineteenth of the sea. The twentieth was the era of airpower, but war will be shaped in the twenty-first century by the electromagnetic combatants. The Air Force *must* be ready."[304] This was the prediction of Maj Gen Gerald J. Carey, Jr., in 1980, closing his career in command of the Air Force Tactical Air Warfare Center at Eglin AFB, Florida. In the deserts of the Yom Kippur War, Casey pointed out, the Israeli Air Force — "one of the finest air forces in the world" — was very nearly beaten by Egyptian ground forces moving under an umbrella of mobile air defense and surface-to-air missiles. He said, "The Israeli Air Force was devastated until Egyptian momentum stalled, and the Israeli ground forces were brought to bear against the SAMs."[305] Although the

IDEAS, CONCEPTS, DOCTRINE

Israelis lost 150 aircraft in the first three days of combat in 1973, they exploited electronic combat in 1982 in the destruction of Syrian SAM sites in the Bekáa Valley, followed by the wholesale devastation of Syrian MiG-21s and MiG-23s with minimal loss of Israeli F-15s and F-16s. In this textbook air battle, the Israelis used remotely piloted air vehicles to spoof and photograph Syrian SAM concentrations to provide real-time intelligence. An astute British defense expert who was very proud of Britain's successes in the Falkland Islands nevertheless commented: "We fought yesterday's war in the Falklands. The Israelis fought tomorrow's war in Lebanon."[306] Lt Gen Kelly H. Burke, USAF, Retired, added: "Lebanon was the war of the future — a war in which electronic combat was a central and dominant theme."[307] To Secretary of Defense Weinberger the British demonstration of new technology in the Falklands and the Israeli success in defeating the Syrian Air Force so easily demonstrated the "decisive effectiveness of high technology weapons."[308]

At the peak of its activity in Southeast Asia in fiscal year 1968, the US Air Force possessed 32 numbered tactical fighter wings. As US involvement in Southeast Asia wound down, the Air Force tactical air structure was programmed to include 23 regular wings of F-4s, F-111s, A-7s, F-100s, and F-105s in fiscal year 1971. For fiscal year 1972, however, the Air Force tactical force size was reduced to 21 active wings, this because of dollar and manpower constraints and adjustments in the national strategy which placed added emphasis on assistance to allies as opposed to direct use of American air power. The reduction in active tactical air wings also reflected Secretary Laird's "total force" policy of increased dependence on reserve forces. The rapid and smooth transition of Air National Guard and Air Force Reserve units into active service in 1968 had been, in the words of Gen John D. Ryan, "a proud chapter in Air Force history." Said Secretary Seamans in 1971, "The Air Force that I foresee will be leaner, more mobile, more streamlined, and ... more volunteer oriented."[309] Also in fiscal year 1972, Lt Gen George S. Boylan, Jr., Air Force deputy chief of staff for programs and resources, explained that the Air Force was moving away from the old concept of a single "fighter-bomber" to perform all combat missions and felt that "only specialized aircraft, such as the F-15 and A-X, can meet the critical demands of mission effectiveness at the extreme ends of the performance spectrum." Force structure limitations precluded specialization for every role. A year later Boylan asserted:

> If dollars were no restriction, manpower was no restriction, the optimum fighter structure probably would be basically three types of aircraft. One aircraft, in sufficient quantity, for air superiority ... unencumbered by any other equipment or mission, one for interdiction ... probably optimized along the lines of the F-111 having very sophisticated sensors, navigation equipment that would permit it to fly through bad weather or during night and perform precision attacks on targets relatively distant from the front lines. Then the third would be an aircraft designed or optimized for close air support. This aircraft ... would be unencumbered with the very sophisticated sensors, the equipment, the range and weight that is required in the interdiction mission.[310]

Although General Boylan reported that the Air Force favored specialized tactical aircraft, the limits on active tactical fighter wings, first at 23 wings and then at 21 wings, led to an effort to program the A-X "below the line"—that is, not among high-performance-capable tactical aircraft. In 1969 Boylan stated that it was the Air Force's position that the A-X should not be chargeable within a 23-wing strength. In 1970, however, the Air Force considered the A-X so important as to be included in the ongoing 23-wing active force. "One major advantage of the A-X is that because of its estimated low cost, it may give a well-sized force, even within tight fiscal constraints," it was said. In 1971 when the tactical active air structure was reduced to 21 wings, General Momyer was still hopeful that the A-X would be "additive" to the force structure.[311]

Although the Air Force was authorized only 21 active tactical fighter wings from fiscal year 1971 through 1975, it actually had 26 numbered tactical air wings on active duty, but each at reduced aircraft strength. Air Force studies had long revealed the desirability of according a tactical wing a unit equipment strength of 72 aircraft, divided into three squadrons each with 24 UE aircraft. With a 24 UE squadron, it was possible to put up 4 flights of 4 aircraft at an average use rate of between 0.9 and 1, which gave a daily capability to the squadron of some 16 combat sorties and at the same time provided a formation and total fighting force of optimum capability against an enemy. The 26-wing force structure was made fiscally possible by reducing squadrons to less than the desirable strengths.[312] Of the 26 tactical fighter wings, 15 were in the continental United States, 8 were in Europe, and 3 were in the Pacific. These actual peacetime deployments were driven largely by political agreements and understandings, the need to provide a credible in-place deterrent force, and finally by resource availability. Each year based on secretary of defense guidance the US unified commanders determined the force levels required to execute the national strategy in their theaters. US fighter force requirements to conduct close air support were calculated on the basis of providing five sorties per day per engaged maneuver battalion. On the basis of command inputs and their assessment, the Joint Chiefs' joint strategic operations plan (JSOP) each year reported "prudent risk" and "minimum risk" force requirements.[313] In 1974 the Air Force set a goal of 40 tactical fighter wings—26 active and 14 in reserves—with 2,880 aircraft (72 combat-coded per wing) by 1980.[314] Early in 1975 in consideration of the fiscal year 1976 budget, Secretary Schlesinger agreed to program a five-year growth of Air Force active tactical air wings to 26 wings, this through the "hi-lo" mix of less expensive A-10s and F-16s into the tactical air inventory that would hopefully allow these wings to be equipped with 72 UE aircraft each and still be within fiscal constraints. Ten reserve ANG and AFR wings would be supported, thus providing a modernized tactical force of 36 wings. The 26 active wings programmed were conceived as necessary to promote deterrence without mobilization, respond in crises, and blunt an initial thrust while awaiting mobilized reinforcements from reserve assets. The Air Force objective force was a larger number of wings than fiscally attainable, and the 26 active wing force contained greater risks than the objective force. It nevertheless represented to the Air Force the best balance between combat capability to pursue directed strategy and existing fiscal and manpower constraints.[315]

Although Secretary Schlesinger's "hi-lo" mix fiscal constraint cleared the way for the beginning of the Air Force tactical strike program toward 26 active and 10 reserve wings, it also locked the Air Force into a binding posture, one that was ill conceived in terms of Soviet challenges. The assumption had been that the TACAIR modernization would continue US technological superiority, but it began to be evident in the early 1970s that this advantage was fading. General Dixon said in 1978, "We are out-numbered. We have had the technical advantage over the years. I am told by experts, and I have my own view, that the technological advantage is vanishing."[316] Periods of darkness and bad weather had historically provided a sanctuary for resupply and reconstruction of combat elements, and winter weather in northern Europe had always been characterized by poor visibilities for aerial operations. In the north German plain region around Hanover, throughout January, there are only about 8.5 hours of daylight in each 24-hour day, and during those days the cloud ceiling is 1,000 feet or higher for only 6.3 hours with an average visibility of three miles. Therefore, the winter weather at low levels in Germany is almost always difficult. In the 1970s the Soviets and Warsaw Pact forces equipped and trained for night and all-weather combat and combat-support operations. Their tanks and helicopters were equipped with sensors and night-viewing devices. At first, Air Force Studies and Analysis took some comfort from its study of weather conditions and offered consolation that winter weather in northern Europe was cellular. Thus, in the words of Maj Gen James A. Welch, Jr., assistant chief of staff for studies and analysis,

> One can look at the very cellular nature of the bad weather and the good weather and find that the cells of bad weather are in fact somewhat smaller than the size of the large armored breakthrough. So that we can attack some part of the armored breakthrough most of the time even though you cannot attack all of it most of the time.[317]

This rationale was not too comforting. Since NATO had 900 kilometers of border to defend, the Soviet/Warsaw Pact nations could select their time, point of concentration, and choice of weapons, and would be less dependent on air support than the NATO forces, who would count on air support for mobile firepower. A joint analysis conducted by the Army TRADOC and the Air Force TAC in 1979 determined that the Air Force's most prominent deficiency in the close air support and battle interdiction mission area was its inability to detect, attack, and destroy hard mobile targets at night and in bad weather. "Everything we see about the Soviets indicates we had best be prepared to meet them under all weather conditions," Gen Lew Allen said in 1980.[318]

In the early 1970s the avionics in the F-111 and A-7 gave capabilities to deliver ordnance against fixed targets at night and in bad weather and combined with ground beacons to allow some capability to deliver conventional munitions on battlefield area targets. The Air Force, however, could not plan to send A-7s and F-111s against armored vehicles, and in the growing emergency in early 1978 it requested an appropriation to fund a night and adverse weather attack program. One question occurring in Congress at this time was that since everyone had known about Europe's weather for centuries, why had someone not laid night/all-weather attack requirements on the A-10 and F-16 programs? Dr William J. Perry, under secretary of defense for research and engineering, answered this question first.

> When the F-16 and A-10 aircraft were designed a night/weather attack requirement was uncertain, since the threat was not perceived to be so lethal nor was the threat perceived to be intent on promulgating a battle during night or poor weather conditions as it is today.[319]

Perry also mentioned the pressure to hold costs down on the F-16 and A-10. The F-16 had a ground-mapping radar and an accurate inertial navigation system (INS) which provided it with some night and adverse weather capability against fixed targets. It was also able to maneuver sharply within visual range of targets in marginal weather where higher performance airplanes would not be effective. Perry said later of the F-16:

> We kidded ourselves a little bit on the F-16 thinking we were buying an inexpensive airplane. What we were really building was an incomplete airplane. . . . One of the reasons this airplane is inexpensive is because we satisfied ourselves that we could operate it as a dogfight airplane in an air superiority role, which means it would deal with other airplanes either with a gun or with a short-range heat seeking air to air missile.[320]

The design of the A-10 was determined in the same era when there was pressure to keep cost moderate. "The A-10 was specifically designed for performing close air support," said General Dixon. "The concept was to keep the system as simple as possible for forward base operation and high sortie rates."[321] The A-10's maneuverability and weapons provided for close air support under adverse weather that would otherwise restrict such operations, but it had no autonomous navigation capability other than pilot dead reckoning to reach a target area. The Air Force had always considered that a self-contained navigation system would improve the aircraft effectiveness, but the improved capability—at the time the A-10 was decided upon—did not seem to justify the increase in cost. In March 1968, however, General Dixon reported a recent demonstration of an A-10 equipped with an INS and flown at England AFB, Louisiana. In low-level flight the INS significantly increased the A-10's first-pass effectiveness and substantially enhanced its ability to divert to a secondary target. Additionally, the INS allowed the pilot to devote more attention to external surroundings, which was advantageous for survivability in high-threat environments.[322] The A-10 was equipped with a 30-millimeter rapid-firing antitank GAU-8 cannon and electro-optical Maverick missiles. Although the television-guided Maverick got good results in tests against high-contrast targets at White Sands, New Mexico, and the Israelis used them to good effect in scoring 40 hits out of 49 firings in the Sinai desert in the Yom Kippur War, the requirement for optical guidance of the

Mavericks with TV heads did not work very well in the limited visibility circumstances of Europe. Deputy Secretary of Defense for Research and Engineering Robert A. Moorer admitted:

> Television Maverick does not work very well in Europe. I think that is one case where, in my opinion, R&D has failed and it failed because we did not test that weapon in a realistic environment.... That was a mistake, and from that, I think the lesson we should have learned is that we must test those sophisticated weapons in a realistic operational environment.[323]

Lt Gen Thomas H. McMullen, TAC vice commander, told a NASA Tactical Aircraft Research and Technology Conference in December 1980:

> As we are now equipped we fight the next war only part time.... Our night and bad weather capability is limited in both quality and quantity. As I see it, these two areas (and I note they are *two* areas), they rather than new speeds or altitudes, are the new frontiers for TACAIR.[324]

As it happened in 1978 and 1979, the Air Force had the need for night and all-weather attack of moving targets fully in mind but lacked substantial resources to handle them in a hurry. "It would be prohibitively expensive for us to build all, or even most, of our aircraft to operate all night or in bad weather," remarked Gen David Jones in 1978.[325] Of such night and all-weather capabilities for the A-10, General Dixon said: "If we had unlimited resources there would be a requirement now—as it is, we have to work on this and see whether we need and can manage to squeeze it into a force structure which is already budget limited."[326] Another reason for not rushing to a solution fix was that new technology that had not existed in the early 1970s was becoming available and needed proper evaluation.[327] In addition to the electro-optical television head Maverick, which was excellently accurate under conditions of high pilot visibility, the Air Force had under development an imaging infrared (IIR) head Maverick for use in low visibility and at night and a laser head Maverick that would home in on laser-illuminated targets. In 1978 the Air Force canceled its part of the laser Maverick and concentrated on development of the IIR Maverick as the weapon of choice for low-attack A-10s either by day or night. Despite adverse journalistic publicity regarding the Maverick program, this decision still held good in 1983.[328]

To fly to a target in bad weather, accomplish target acquisition, and determine weapons release points under such adverse conditions, attack aircraft would have to have sensors to provide for terrain avoidance, navigation to the target areas, and target acquisition, and night/adverse weather weapons that were effective. The mission, withal, was so complex that it appeared possible in 1978 that a two-man crew might be needed, one person to pilot and one to work the sensors and weapons. On the other hand, automatic techniques—some of them on-the-shelf—might be added to a single-seat airplane, taking the load off the pilot and allowing one man to perform night/all-weather attack. Industry saw an opportunity to come aboard with proposals, such as a two-seat A-10, a two-seat F-15, and, of course, the Navy's two-seat F-18. In fiscal year 1980 budget requests offered in early 1979, the Air Force asked for an appropriation to study an "Enhanced Tactical Fighter" (ETF) — the use of an existing aircraft with state-of-the-art avionics and munitions for night/all-weather attack. The two leading candidates were the F-15 that was already in a two-seat training version and the A-10, which Fairchild Aviation was plugging strongly. The precise mission element needs statement (MENS) for the ETF had no firm grasp of ultimate mission requirements or cost, however, with the result that Congress refused to fund the ETF.[329] Still hoping to keep the A-10 in production, Fairchild bailed back one of the planes from the Air Force and modified it with a second seat and sensors for tests at Edwards AFB, California, carried out by the Air Force Systems Command and Tactical Air Command. General Creech, the TAC commander, gave Fairchild "high marks" for using its own funds for the test plane, but he could not see putting it into production. The real need for the night/all-weather ETF was for second-echelon interdiction, and the A-10 continued to be too slow for penetration, best qualified even at night to operate along the FEBA in close air support. The tests did show, however, that an existing plane augmented with sensors would be affordable enough to be secured for clear nighttime or nighttime, under-the-weather operations. On the other hand, General Creech said that the development of an ETF for in-weather operations would not be soon "do-able" for reasons of costliness. Early in 1982 when speaking on the fiscal year 1983 Air Force budget request, General Allen would not be swayed from a decision to end A-10 production:

> The A-10 is an excellent weapon, and the GAU-8 is a super gun. We have never had a gun that has the effective accuracy that that gun has, nor the antiarmor kill capabilities that those munitions provide. Further than that, the A-10 armed with a Maverick, represents an addition to those capabilities which makes it one of the finest specialized aircraft for antiarmor kill that has ever been built. So, we are very pleased with the aircraft and we continue to be impressed with this armor-killing capability. However, we have met the basic inventory objectives. . . . It is a specialized aircraft, it is an antiarmor aircraft. It was designed largely for high-armor concentrations of the sort encountered in the central region of Europe, although it has application elsewhere. We have concluded that we have now met the inventory objectives and finished production with the 1983 requests.[330]

In one sense the enhanced tactical fighter seemed in 1979 to have been officially terminated by Congress, and Lt Gen Kelly Burke, deputy chief of staff for research and development, turned to an effort to meet the same requirement by a different approach, namely finding a means to take advantage of the large number of single-seat fighter aircraft that the Air Force was going to wind up owning. The Air Force was going to have to be more pragmatic, to attempt to do more with less. "Capability improvements to our aircraft, therefore, are to help redress existing aircraft inventory shortfalls rather than to allow reductions in future force structure," Burke explained.[331] One potential candidate for procurement was the LANTIRN (low-altitude navigation targeting infrared for night) system that could be used to provide a portion of the A-10s and F-16s with a night, under-the-weather capability in the 1983–85 period. Burke continued:

> It appears to us that the confluence of technology is such that we can, in fairly short order, develop this LANTIRN pod which will let those single place aircraft have a very good night/under the weather capability at low altitude with multiple kills per pass, and greatly add to our air to ground capability with those existing airplanes. . . . Not all weather, it is night/under the weather. We just don't know how to do that against mobile and imprecisely located targets. But night or under the weather, down to a few hundred foot ceiling, couple of miles visibility, we can do it.[332]

Another aspect of LANTIRN was that it increased day capabilities to find targets.[333] By 1981 the development contract for LANTIRN broke the system down into two pods: the LAN navigation pod enabled an aircraft to go in at very low altitude and come out the same way; the TIRN targeting pod enabled a pilot to deliver ordnance at night with essentially daytime accuracy. A given attack might require one or both of the pods, which being smaller at any rate had lower drag than a single pod. In 1981 General Creech ticked off advantages of operating A-10s and F-16s at night with LANTIRN. Operating at night provided more firepower with the same number of aircraft, denied the adversary the sanctuary of darkness, provided NATO ground forces the possibility of air support that they would need at night, provided a sanctuary for friendly air operations, and exploited a technological edge as an offset to quantity on the other side.[334] Some in Congress questioned the Air Force's move away from specialized aircraft: in 1982, Sen Alfonse M. D'Amato of New York complained:

> I should point out that the IIR Maverick . . . coupled with the LANTIRN pod capability, will change the A-10 from a day-only tank killer to a night and adverse weather tank killer. . . . We believe that will basically double the effectiveness of the A-10 in that it will permit it to operate during the night when, we believe, Soviet tactics require those tanks to move.[335]

The F-16 had started out to be good in the air-to-air role and the characteristics that made it good in this role, such as power loading and low-wing loading, also made it good in air-to-ground context. Lt Gen Alton Slay said in 1976, when speaking the praise of the F-16, "You need to be able to get well ahead of the power curve when you are delivering ordnance to get back up to make a re-attack, to turn fast, to be able to stay low."[336] Lt Gen Thomas Stafford, the 13th test pilot to fly the F-16, also marveled at it: "It is amazing, this little airplane that weighs half of an F-4 can carry the same bomb load as the F-4 twice as far using less fuel. It is the only airplane we have ever designed to pull nine G's. That is a lot of G's to pull."[337] As an interceptor, however, the F-16 could not compare with the F-15, the latter with long range, far more powerful radar, and medium-range radar-guided air-to-air AIM-7 Sparrow missile. The F-16 had a smaller radar and a short-range AIM-9 Sidewinder infrared heat-seeking missile; its lack of a radar-directed missile meant that it would yield first shot to an adversary with radar missiles. There was a limitation to the Sparrow in that the F-15 had to keep its radar pointed at the target until the missile reached it; in Red Flag training at Nellis AFB, Nevada, little inferior F-5 "aggressor" planes not infrequently came in behind F-15s intent on tracking other targets. In fiscal year 1977 Congress appropriated the first funds to finance development of a joint Air Force/Navy "Sparrow follow-on missile" that came to be called the AMRAAM or advanced medium-range air-to-air missile. Suited either for the F-16 or F-15, the AMRAAM had a fire-and-forget radar aboard the missile itself, and it allowed a pilot to engage two or three targets at a time and to fight successfully while outnumbered. With the AMRAAM an F-16 pilot could fire on, say, a MiG-23 before the MiG could intercept the F-16. If the F-16 got into a dogfight, it could easily turn the MiG inside out.[338] In fiscal year 1982 budget hearings, General Creech urged support for AMRAAM; and in 1983 hearings Maj Gen Robert Russ, deputy chief of staff, operational requirements, Air Force, declared the AMRAAM to be the "No. 1 priority air-to-air program for the TAC air forces."[339]

In the F-15 development and test phase the plane demonstrated a conventional weapons delivery air-to-ground superiority to both the F-4 and A-7 aircraft. In 1979 and 1980 both Generals Allen and Creech maintained that it was highly desirable to keep the McDonnell Douglas Corporation F-15 production line open with a buy of additional aircraft beyond the current program quantity of 729, to be procured prior to the program cutoff in fiscal year 1983. Whereas the focus of attention in the 1970s had been upon Western Europe, the Soviet invasion of Afghanistan and the beginning of the Iranian seizure of American hostages in Tehran in late 1979 made the Carter administration interested in the non-NATO world. General Creech was particularly impressed with the problem of distances in Southwest Asia and found the prospect of a "missionized F-15" particularly attractive in that regard.

> I think it [the F-15] is an outstanding airplane for the Rapid Deployment force and it is particularly attractive in the Persian Gulf and Middle East because of its range. In fact, range in the Persian Gulf area takes on a whole new importance that one does not feel in Central Europe, for example, although range is important there, because the distances are awesome. Saudi Arabia is bigger than the United States east of the Mississippi.[340]

Creech referred to the missionized F-15 as "an interesting case," but in 1980 he felt compelled to give all-out priority to getting LANTIRN for the F-16 and A-10.[341] This same year, the Air Force had also received funding for a mission analysis looking toward the development of an advanced tactical fighter (ATF) that was wanted for service in the 1990s. The "gestation period" of a new fighter program was conceived to be from 10 to 14 years, and the ATF was expected to be "next-generation" technology, not an upgraded version of an F-15 or F-16.[342]

In 1980 the Air Force projected a tactical fighter wing structure for the end of 1981 as being 12 reserve wings (10 in the Air National Guard and 2 in Air Force Reserve) and 26 active wings broken down with 1 in Alaska, 3 in the Pacific, 8 in

Europe, and 14 in TAC. It was still not expected that the Air Force would reach its full 26-wing goal of 1,872 aircraft until 1984, and considering assigned aircraft, General Creech figured worldwide TACAIR strength as being 34 wings (23 active and 11 reserves).[343] In view of the marked increase in the Soviet threat, Creech urged that the tactical air wing program should surely be increased to the 40 wings projected earlier and by the mid-1980s should include at least 5 additional active wings. Both Creech and Allen thought highly of the competency of the Air National Guard and Air Force Reserve units. Gen Lew Allen said that one of the "finest things" done in recent years was the formulation and enforcement of the total force concept, where, he said, "we fight together as Active and Reserve forces." But mobilization was always a serious dislocation to the nation and it was becoming "very difficult to respond to any conflict these days without mobilization."[344] Creech said in 1981:

> I would fully expect a Guard or Reserve unit going into combat, given the same kind of equipment, would fly better than an active squadron. This is because the pilots are much more experienced and, for that matter, the maintenance people are as well. They are first rate.[345]

Nevertheless, the active forces had to bear the burden of forward deployment and also had to be available in sufficient numbers in the continental United States to provide training and support to the forward-deployed forces.[346]

The revitalization of the American defense program by the Reagan administration commencing in 1981 faced some difficulty in regard to tactical forces. This was explained by Lt Gen Kelly Burke:

> Within our force planning we gave highest priority to strategic force modernization, followed by readiness and maintainability, and finally, to tactical force modernization and growth.... We recognize the overriding requirement for strategic force improvements, but we cannot ignore the global threat and very significant enhancements in Soviet conventional forces over the recent years.... In this regard, B-1 and MX are critical programs. At the same time, we cannot neglect tactical aircraft modernization and force expansion programs because of the evolving Soviet threat.[347]

Despite the priority to strategic forces, the Reagan administration also looked with favor on tactical power. The security guidance policy recognized that the Soviet threat was global and that the United States must be prepared to meet the threat globally in a sustained, conventional manner. Deputy Secretary of Defense Frank C. Carlucci emphasized the "vital interest" in Southeast Asia and the need for conventional US responses to Soviet activity there. "Unless we are prepared to put troops on the ground, I don't think the Soviets are going to believe we are credible," he said.[348]

Early in 1981 the Reagan administration announced that the Air Force had been forced to procure aircraft inefficiently and that the objective now would be to accelerate aircraft programs while reviewing force requirements. In the planning for aircraft procurement approved in 1981–82, the Air Force was authorized to increase to 40 tactical fighter wings (26 active and 14 reserve) in 1986 and then to 44 tactical fighter wings in 1990.[349] By early 1981 the McDonnell Douglas Corporation had turned out a demonstration missionized air-to-surface F-15 Strike Eagle that was very attractive to the Air Force. In thinking about possible employments in Southwest Asia, General Creech was attracted to the range and capabilities of a missionized F-15 which could be deployed there, initially performing in air-to-air combat, if necessary, and then serving in an air-to-ground attack mode. In a missionized configuration the F-15 would also be prepared to perform deep interdiction and counterair strikes against enemy airfields like an F-111 would do.[350] General Creech was especially enthusiastic about what he described as a dual-capable aircraft that could deliver either tactical nuclear or conventional munitions, and the Air Force asked funding in fiscal year 1982 for a derivative fighter based on the F-15. As it happened, however, General Dynamics had been working on an F-16XL with a redesigned "cranked arrow" wing that would provide substantially more internal fuel and payload lift. Congress would not approve funding of an enhanced F-15E in fiscal 1982 until such time as a derivative F-16E could also be tested.[351]

After give and take with Congress in 1981 in regard to fiscal year 1982 appropriations requests, the Air Force got a new perspective for the future requirements of tactical aviation. For fiscal year 1983, Lt Gen Kelly Burke explained:

> We have argued amongst ourselves, and in give and take with the Congress, to push back that new fighter quite distantly because the major changes that have come along in our business in the past few years have not been in airframe or aircraft engine improvements... but in electronics. There is a dramatic improvement in electronics. So, the trend—and I think it is a correct one—is to keep airplane designs longer and update the electronics portions of it to go with the older engine and old airframe. That basically is what we are doing. We are proposing to buy about 250 fighters a year. We are proposing to modernize them mostly in the electronic sense and not tactical development of the new airplane.[352]

The advanced tactical fighter (ATF) would be pushed back to the mid-1990s; it would be a "new technology fighter and a step ahead of the Russians."[353] In making a decision on the enhanced fighter, General Gabriel said he was going to look for "the most affordable and effective capability we can get at the cheapest price." Essentially he wanted the "E-model" F-15 or F-16, whichever chosen, to "get back in the second-echelon area... back before the follow-on [enemy] forces begin to fan out and come to the front, say, 200 kilometers back.... That is the area that right now, at nighttime, low-level, only the F-111 can handle. We can't get back there with anything else," he continued.[354] In comparison with the F-16E, the F-15E had a significant advantage in range that particularly fitted it for service in Southwest Asia or the Pacific. On 24 February 1984 General Gabriel announced that he had selected the F-15E as the new dual-role derivative fighter for air-to-air and deep-interdiction missions. It was going to be a two-seat aircraft, with provisions to employ AMRAAM and LANTIRN, plus a weapons load comparable

IDEAS, CONCEPTS, DOCTRINE

to that of an F-111. The Air Force planned on 392 F-15Es, enough to equip 12 squadrons and 2 training squadrons. In addition, new F-16s with improved air-to-air and air-to-ground capabilities would be bought, the program objective of the F-16 being increased from 1,388 to 2,651 to support a force modernization and equipment of 40 tactical wings. An advanced tactical fighter would remain in development for service in the mid-1990s. Air Force evaluation of the "cranked arrow" wing F-16XL would continue as a possible advanced version of the F-16 Fighting Falcon.[355]

In 1982–83 the US military services each undertook visionary efforts to foresee their individual and collective programs at the turn of the century, around the year 2000. The US Army led the way with "AirLand Battle 2000." It was a security classified future concept of the world environment during 1995–2015 and the requirements of battle that would drive Army training and equipping. AirLand Battle 2000 saw future battlefields becoming more fluid, shorter in duration, and more difficult for the commander to control. The study was said to urge a style of waging war in which agility, deception, maneuver, and tools of combat were used to face the enemy with a succession of dangerous and unexpected situations more rapidly than he could react to them.[356] Like the Army, the Air Force regularly reviewed its strategies and capabilities to meet an anticipated Soviet threat, and, conducted in 1982, Air Force 2000 envisioned the way that the Air Force should adapt itself to the world in two decades. After the Air Staff completed Air Force 2000, it began working with the Army Staff to meld the respective concepts in a new study called Focus 21.[357] These studies were classified, but Air Force leaders gave some public indication of the look of the future. In Europe, where the Soviet threat was most severe, the numerical superiority of Warsaw Pact air forces was expected to remain, and the Soviets were expected to continue to attempt to narrow the US technological lead in key areas. The main requirements of the tactical air forces would be to gain air superiority over the battle area and to provide offensive support to the land forces. The Air Force and the Army would need to work closely together to effect an organizational integration of combat capabilities. A joint AirLand Battle doctrine would be necessary as a first step in countering the threat from the Soviet and Soviet-surrogate forces. Priorities needed to be established for fighting battles, especially in the first hours. Success of a forward strategy for NATO depended upon the development of a rugged and common command, control, communications, computing/information and intelligence (C^4I^2) capability to aid in establishing the unity of effort and most effective application of force against the enemy. The whole question of antijam communications, General Lew Allen emphasized, had to be the focus of enormous attention in all plans for AirLand Battle.[358] As matters stood in mid-1964, General Creech, in context of six years as TAC commander, described planning relationships with the Army as "going magnificently" and "at an all-time high."[359] Keyed to the background year-2000 plans, an Air Force "Fighter Road map" existed on the lines sketched above and outlined the force size, mix, and capabilities needed into the future.[360]

NOTES

1. House, *Department of Defense Appropriations for 1967: Hearings before a Subcommittee of the Committee on Appropriations*, 89th Cong., 2d sess., 1966, pt. 1:532 (hereafter cited as *1967 DOD Appropriations*).
2. Senate, *Department of Defense Appropriations for Fiscal Year 1974: Hearings before a Subcommittee of the Committee on Appropriations*, 93d Cong., 1st sess., 1973, pt. 1:136 (hereafter cited as *FY 1974 DOD Appropriations*).
3. House, *1967 DOD Appropriations*, pt. 5:386.
4. Statement of Secretary of Defense Robert S. McNamara before the House, Armed Services Committee on the Fiscal Year 1965-69 Defense Program and 1965 Defense Budget, 27 January 1964, 84; Senate, *U.S. Tactical Air Power Program: Hearings before the Preparedness Investigating Subcommittee on Armed Services*, 90th Cong., 2d sess., 1968, 91.
5. Lt Gen Arthur C. Agan, USAF, Retired, US Air Force Oral History Program Interview 857, 2 October 1973, 15, 31.
6. M. J. Armitage and R. A. Mason, *Air Power in the Nuclear Age* (Urbana, Ill.: University of Illinois Press, 1983), 192-93.
7. Robert S. McNamara, *The Essence of Security, Reflections in Office* (New York: Harper & Row, 1968), 37.
8. Armitage and Mason, *Air Power in the Nuclear Age*, 191; House, *1967 DOD Appropriations*, pt. 1:84.
9. Henry Kissinger, *White House Years* (Boston: Little, Brown & Co., 1979), 220; House, *Department of Defense Appropriations for 1970: Hearings before a Subcommittee of the Committee on Appropriations*, 91st Cong., 1st sess., 1969, pt. 7:383 (hereafter cited as *1970 DOD Appropriations*); Senate, *U.S. Tactical Air Power Program*, 79.
10. Senate, *U.S. Tactical Air Power Program*, 117; Senate, *Fiscal Year 1977 Military Procurement Authorization: Hearings before the Committee on Armed Services*, 94th Cong., 2d sess., 1976, pt. 9:4899 (hereafter cited as *FY 1977 Military Procurement*).
11. Senate, *FY 1977 Military Procurement*, pt. 10:5698.
12. Senate, *Close Air Support: Hearings before the Special Subcommittee on Close Air Support of the Preparedness Investigating Subcommittee of the Committee on Armed Services*, 92d Cong., 1st sess., 1972, 192-93 (hereafter cited as *Close Air Support*).
13. House, *Department of Defense Appropriations for 1969: Hearings before a Subcommittee of the Committee on Appropriations*, 90th Cong., 2d sess., 1968, pt. 1:329 (hereafter cited as *1969 DOD Appropriations*).
14. Senate, *FY 1974 DOD Appropriations*, pt. 1:614.
15. Ibid.; House, *1969 DOD Appropriations*, pt. 6:262.
16. Senate, *Department of Defense Appropriations for Fiscal Year 1965: Hearings before the Subcommittee of the Committee on Appropriations and the Committee on Armed Services*, 88th Cong., 2d sess., 1964, pt. 1:738-40; Senate, *Department of Defense Appropriations for Fiscal Year 1966: Hearings before the Subcommittee of the Committee on Appropriations and the Committee on Armed Services*, 89th Cong., 1st sess., 1965, pt. 1:1140 (hereafter cited as *FY 1966 DOD Appropriations*).
17. Senate, *U.S. Tactical Air Power Program*, 92-93; Senate, *Department of Defense Appropriations for Fiscal Year 1970: Hearings before the Subcommittee of the Committee on Appropriations*, 91st Cong., 1st sess., 1969, pt. 4:664 (hereafter cited as *FY 1970 DOD Appropriations*); Maj Gen Edward A. McGough, Oral History Interview 860, 23 September 1973; Lt Gen Arthur C. Agan, Oral History Interview 857, 2 October 1979; Gen Louis C. Wilson, Jr., Oral History Interview 1178, 7-8 November 1979.
18. Agan interview; Gen John P. McConnell to all major commands and operating agencies, 3 May 1965; *Air Force Policy Letter for Commanders: Supplement*, 6 June 1965, 24-26.

IDEAS, CONCEPTS, DOCTRINE

19. House, *Department of Defense Appropriations for 1966: Hearings before a Subcommittee of the Committee on Appropriations*, 89th Cong., 1st sess., 1965, pt. 3:340, pt. 5:17; Senate, *FY 1966 DOD Appropriations*, pt. 1:419, 491, 1140, 1254.

20. Senate, *FY 1970 DOD Appropriations*, pt. 4:122–26.

21. Ibid., 124; Senate, *Fiscal Year 1970 Military Procurement Authorization, Research and Development, and Reserve Strength: Hearings before the Committee on Armed Services*, 91st Cong., 1st sess., 1969, pt. 1:1000–1 (hereafter cited as *FY 1970 Military Procurement*); Senate, *Department of Defense Appropriations for Fiscal Year 1971: Hearings before the Subcommittee of the Committee on Appropriations*, 91st Cong., 2d sess., 1970, pt. 4:308–15 (hereafter cited as *FY 1971 DOD Appropriations*).

22. Senate, *U.S. Tactical Air Power Program*, 112–13.

23. Senate, *Department of Defense Appropriations for Fiscal Year 1967: Hearings before the Subcommittee of the Committee on Appropriations and the Committee on Armed Services*, 89th Cong., 2d sess., 1966, pt. 1:931; Senate, *FY 1970 DOD Appropriations*, pt. 4:664.

24. Directorate of Doctrine, Concepts and Objectives, US Air Force, Doctrinal Divergencies Briefing, January–June 1968; Dr Edward C. Misher, *The A-X Specialized Close Air Support Aircraft: Origins and Concept Phase, 1961–1970*, Office of History, Headquarters Air Force Systems Command, vii–viii.

25. House, *Department of Defense Appropriations for 1968: Hearings before a Subcommittee of the Committee on Appropriations*, 90th Cong., 1st sess., 1967, pt. 3:395 (hereafter cited as *1968 DOD Appropriations*); House, *1969 DOD Appropriations*, pt. 2:123, pt. 3:205; Senate, *FY 1970 DOD Appropriations*, pt. 4:664.

26. "We Have to Maintain Superiority in Air-to-Air Combat Capability," *Air Force Policy Letter for Commanders*, 15 February 1969.

27. McNamara, *The Essence of Security*, 37–38; Armitage and Mason, *Air Power in the Nuclear Age*, 193; Theodore R. Milton, "Thoughts on Our National Strategy for the Future," in *Grand Strategy for the 1980s*, ed. Bruce Palmer, Jr. (Washington, D.C.: American Enterprise Institute for Public Policy Research, 1978), 59; Secretary of Defense James R. Schlesinger, *The Theater Nuclear Force Posture in Europe*, in House, *Department of Defense Appropriations for 1979: Hearings before a Subcommittee of the Committee on Appropriations*, 95th Cong., 2d sess., 1978, pt. 4 (hereafter cited as *1979 DOD Appropriations*).

28. House, *1969 DOD Appropriations*, pt. 1:531.

29. Ibid., pt. 1:532, pt. 4:970–71; Senate, *United States Security Agreements and Commitments Abroad, United States Forces in Europe: Hearing before the Subcommittee on United States Security Agreements and Commitments Abroad of the Committee on Foreign Relations*, 91st Cong., 2d sess., pt. 10:2061–64.

30. Senate, *United States Security Agreements and Commitments Abroad*, pt. 10:2061–65; McNamara, *The Essence of Security*, 81.

31. Senate, *FY 1970 Military Procurement*, pt. 2:1525.

32. Alain C. Enthoven and K. Wayne Smith, *How Much Is Enough? Shaping the Defense Program, 1961–1969* (New York: Harper & Row, 1978), 216–25; Kissinger, *White House Years*, 392; Senate, *U.S. Tactical Air Power Program*, 116–23, 130–33; Senate, *Department of Defense Appropriations for Fiscal Year 1972: Hearings before the Subcommittee of the Committee on Appropriations*, 92d Cong., 1st sess., 1971, pt. 4:69 (hereafter cited as *FY 1972 DOD Appropriations*).

33. Senate, *U.S. Forces in Europe: Hearings before the Subcommittee on Arms Control, International Law and Organization of the Committee on Foreign Relations*, 93d Cong., 1st sess., 1973, 104–5.

34. Kissinger, *White House Years*, 166–67, 220–25.

35. House, *1970 DOD Appropriations*, pt. 7:381–85; Senate, *FY 1972 DOD Appropriations*, pt. 1:47–75, 178–81.

36. Senate, *FY 1970 DOD Appropriations*, pt. 4:102–3.

37. Senate, *FY 1971 DOD Appropriations*, pt. 4:7; Senate, *FY 1972 DOD Appropriations*, pt. 4:13, 57–58; Senate, *Fiscal Year 1973 Military Procurement Authorization: Hearings before the Committee on*

Armed Services, 92d Cong., 2d sess., 1972, pt. 2:1131–41 (hereafter cited as *FY 1973 Military Procurement*); Senate, *Fiscal Year 1974 Military Procurement Authorization: Hearings before the Committee on Armed Services*, 93d Cong., 1st sess., 1973, pt. 6:4371 (hereafter cited as *FY 1974 Military Procurement*).

38. House, *1968 DOD Appropriations*, pt. 1:824; House, *1969 DOD Appropriations*, pt. 2:122; Senate, *FY 1970 DOD Appropriations*, pt. 4:34.

39. Senate, *Department of Defense Appropriations for Fiscal Year 1969: Hearings before a Subcommittee of the Committee on Appropriations*, 90th Cong., 2d sess., 1968, pt. 1:70–71; House, *1969 DOD Appropriations*, pt. 6:222–31, 256–60; House, *Department of Defense Appropriations for 1973: Hearings before a Subcommittee of the Committee on Appropriations*, 92d Cong., 2d sess., 1972, pt. 7:1155 (hereafter cited as *1973 DOD Appropriations*).

40. House, *1970 DOD Appropriations*, pt. 4:346–47, pt. 3:796–97.

41. Ibid., pt. 7:47–48; Senate, *FY 1971 DOD Appropriations*, pt. 1:43, 149–210.

42. Senate, *Fiscal Year 1971 Military Procurement Authorization, Research and Development: Hearings before the Committee on Armed Services*, 91st Cong., 2d sess., 1970, pt. 2:1136–37 (hereafter cited as *FY 1971 Military Procurement*); Senate, *FY 1971 DOD Appropriations*, pt. 4:10, pt. 5:584–85, 748–65.

43. House, *Department of Defense Appropriations for 1971: Hearings before a Subcommittee of the Committee on Appropriations*, 91st Cong., 2d sess., 1970, pt. 6:584–85 (hereafter cited as *1971 DOD Appropriations*); Senate, *FY 1972 DOD Appropriations*, pt. 4:23–26, 510–14; Senate, *Department of Defense Appropriations for Fiscal Year 1973: Hearings before a Subcommittee of the Committee on Appropriations*, 92d Cong., 2d sess., 1972, pt. 4:781–83 (hereafter cited as *FY 1973 DOD Appropriations*).

44. Senate, *FY 1972 DOD Appropriations*, pt. 4:23; Senate, *FY 1974 Military Procurement*, pt. 6:4689–4708; House, *Department of Defense Appropriations for 1975: Hearings before a Subcommittee of the Committee on Appropriations*, 93d Cong., 2d sess., pt. 7:1137 (hereafter cited as *1975 DOD Appropriations*).

45. Senate, *FY 1971 DOD Appropriations*, pt. 4:308–15; Senate, *FY 1972 DOD Appropriations*, pt. 4:20; House, *Department of Defense Appropriations for 1972: Hearings before a Subcommittee of the Committee on Appropriations*, 92d Cong., 1st sess., 1971, pt. 5:1010 (hereafter cited as *1972 DOD Appropriations*).

46. Senate, *FY 1974 Military Procurement*, pt. 6:4670–88; Gen John W. Vogt, Jr., "Implications of Modern Air Power in a Limited War," US Air Force Oral History Program Interview 723, 29 November 1973.

47. Senate, *Fiscal Year 1975 Military Procurement Authorization, Research and Development, and Active Duty, Selected Reserve and Civilian Personnel Strengths: Hearings before the Committee on Armed Services*, 93d Cong., 2d sess., 1974, pt. 8:4454–55 (hereafter cited as *FY 1975 Military Procurement*).

48. House, *1975 DOD Appropriations*, pt. 4:465–69.

49. Ibid., 4244–45; House, *Department of Defense Appropriations for 1976: Hearings before a Subcommittee of the Committee on Appropriations*, 94th Cong., 1st sess., 1975, pt. 4:370–71 (hereafter cited as *1976 DOD Appropriations*).

50. House, *1975 DOD Appropriations*, pt. 1:449–51; Senate, *FY 1975 Military Procurement*, pt. 8:4308–11.

51. Senate, *FY 1975 Military Procurement.*, pt. 8:4308–11.

52. Uri Ra'anan, "The New Technologies and the Middle East: 'Lessons' of the Yom Kippur War and Anticipated Developments," in *The Other Arms Race*, eds. Geoffrey Kemp, Robert L. Pfaltzgroff, Sr., Uri Ra'anan (Lexington, Mass.: Lexington Books, 1975), 79–81; Senate, *Department of Defense Appropriations for Fiscal Year 1975: Hearings before a Subcommittee of the Committee on Appropriations*, 93d Cong., 2d sess., 1974, pt. 5:183, 186 (hereafter cited as *FY 1975 DOD Appropriations*).

IDEAS, CONCEPTS, DOCTRINE

53. Uri Ra'anan, "The New Technologies and the Middle East," 83–84; Gen Chaim Herzog, *The Arab-Israeli Wars*, War and Peace in the Middle East (New York: Random House, 1982), 311; Senate, *FY 1975 Military Procurement*, pt. 8:4241–52, 4306–18.
54. Senate, *FY 1975 Military Procurement*, 4312–13.
55. Uri Ra'anan, "The New Technologies and the Middle East," 84–85.
56. Gen Chaim Herzog, "The Middle East War, 1973," *RUSI Journal*, March 1975, 15; Maj Donald J. Alberts, "A Call from the Wilderness," *Air University Review*, November–December 1976, 39; Gen Chaim Herzog, *The Arab-Israeli Wars, War and Peace in the Middle East* 310-11.
57. Herzog, *The Arab-Israeli Wars*, 310–11.
58. *Air Force Policy Letter for Commanders*, 1 April 1974.
59. Wing Comdr Hans F. Roser, RAAF, "Defense Suppression, Mission or Tactic?" *Air University Review*, July–August 1978, 26.
60. House, *1975 DOD Appropriations*, pt. 2:273.
61. Gen Robert J. Dixon, "The Range of Tactical Air Operations," *Strategic Review*, Spring 1974, 23–24.
62. House, *1975 DOD Appropriations*, pt. 9:285.
63. Senate, *FY 1975 DOD Appropriations*, pt. 4:585.
64. Ibid., pt. 1:520.
65. Herzog, *The Arab-Israeli Wars*, 311.
66. Senate, *FY 1975 DOD Appropriations*, pt. 4:6–8, 26, 51–53, 526, 578–79, 607–8; Senate, *FY 1975 Military Procurement*, pt. 8:4448–71.
67. House, *1976 DOD Appropriations*, pt. 1:65; House, *Department of Defense Appropriations for 1977: Hearings before a Subcommittee of the Committee on Appropriations*, 94th Cong., 2d sess., 1976, pt. 1:566 (hereafter cited as *1977 DOD Appropriations*).
68. Senate, *FY 1975 DOD Appropriations*, pt. 4:6.
69. Senate, *FY 1975 Military Procurement.*, pt. 3:791.
70. House, *Department of Defense Appropriations for 1979: Hearings before a Subcommittee of the Committee on Appropriations*, 95th Cong., 2d sess., 1978, pt. 5:99.
71. Senate, *U.S. Forces in Europe*, 105; Senate, *Department of Defense Appropriations for Fiscal Year 1977: Hearings before a Subcommittee of the Committee on Appropriations*, 94th Cong., 2d sess., 1976, pt. 1:407 (hereafter cited as *FY 1977 DOD Appropriations*).
72. House, *1972 DOD Appropriations*, pt. 9:33.
73. Senate, *Fiscal Year 1972 Military Procurement Authorization: Hearings before the Committee on Armed Services*, 92d Cong., 1st sess., 1971, pt. 5:4149 (hereafter cited as *FY 1972 Military Procurement*).
74. Senate, *U.S. Forces in Europe*, 60–61.
75. Ibid., 86; House, *1976 DOD Appropriations*, pt. 1:255.
76. Senate, *FY 1977 Military Procurement*, pt. 9:4854.
77. Senate, *Close Air Support*, 179.
78. Ibid.
79. Ibid.
80. Senate, *FY 1973 DOD Appropriations.*, pt. 4:691–93.
81. Report, David Packard to Melvin Laird in ibid., pt. 1:389.
82. Senate, *FY 1975 Military Procurement*, pt. 1:29; House, *1976 DOD Appropriations*, pt. 1:58–59, 65.
83. House, *1979 DOD Appropriations*, pt. 5:4; House, *Department of Defense Appropriations for 1982: Hearings before a Subcommittee of the Committee on Appropriations*, 97th Cong., 1st sess., 1981, pt. 6:313 (hereafter cited as *1982 DOD Appropriations*).
84. House, *1977 DOD Appropriations*, pt. 1:176.
85. Senate, *FY 1973 DOD Appropriations*, pt. 1:680–81.
86. Senate, *FY 1973 Military Procurement*, pt. 2:1123; Senate, *FY 1974 Military Procurement*, pt. 1:400; Senate, *FY 1977 Military Procurement*, pt. 9:4855.

87. Senate, *Department of Defense Appropriations for Fiscal Year 1976: Hearings before a Subcommittee of the Committee on Appropriations*, 94th Cong., 1st sess., 1975, pt. 1:355 (hereafter cited as *FY 1976 DOD Appropriations*).

88. Ibid., pt. 4:103; Senate, *Seminars, Service Chiefs on Defense Mission and Priorities, Task Force on Defense of the Committee on the Budget*, 94th Cong., 2d sess., 1976, 3:9, 23–24.

89. Senate, *Seminars, Service Chiefs on Defense Mission and Priorities, Task Force on Defense of the Committee on the Budget*, 94th Cong., 2d sess., 1976, 3:9, 23–24.

90. Ibid.

91. Ibid.

92. House, *1976 DOD Appropriations*, pt. 2:129; Senate, *Department of Defense Appropriations for Fiscal Year 1978: Hearings before a Subcommittee of the Committee on Appropriations*, 95th Cong., 2d sess., 1977, pt. 1:530, 968 (hereafter cited as *FY 1978 DOD Appropriations*).

93. Senate, *FY 1978 DOD Appropriations*, pt. 1:530–968.

94. Ibid.

95. Ibid., *FY 1978 DOD Appropriations*, pt. 1:969; House, *Department of Defense Appropriations for 1981: Hearings before a Subcommittee of the Committee on Appropriations*, 96th Cong., 2d sess., 1980, pt. 4:72–75 (hereafter cited as *1981 DOD Appropriations*); Senate, *FY 1974 Military Procurement*, pt. 1:176–77; House, *1977 DOD Appropriations*, pt. 3:61.

96. Senate, *FY 1973 Military Procurement*, pt. 2:1118–20; Senate, *FY 1974 Military Procurement*, pt. 1:179–80, pt. 2:1104.

97. House, *Department of Defense Appropriations: Hearings before a Committee of the Committee on Appropriations, H.R. Oversight of Fiscal Year 1975 Military Assistance to Vietnam*, 94th Cong., 1st sess., 1975, 718–19; House, *1976 DOD Appropriations*, pt. 2:164–65; House, *NATO Standardization, Interoperability and Readiness: Hearings before a Special Subcommittee on NATO Standardization, Interoperability, and Readiness of the Committee on Armed Services*, 95th Cong., 2d sess., 1978, 1094–98 (hereafter cited as *NATO Standardization, Interoperability, and Readiness*).

98. House, *NATO Standardization, Interoperability, and Readiness*, 1094–98.

99. Gen John W. Vogt, Jr., "Allied Air Power in Central Europe – The View from the Top," interview, *International Defense Review*, January 1975, 43–44.

100. Armitage and Mason, *Air Power in the Nuclear Age*, 198.

101. House, *1979 DOD Appropriations*, pt. 4:354, pt. 5:92–93; Dr Stephen L. Canby, "Tactical Air Power in Armored Warfare, The Divergence within NATO," *Air University Review*, May–June 1979, 14.

102. Senate, *U.S. Forces in Europe*, 79.

103. Senate, *Policy, Troops and the NATO Alliance, Report of Senator Sam Nunn to the Committee on Armed Services*, 93d Cong., 2d sess., 1974, 4–5.

104. House, *1976 DOD Appropriations*, pt. 1:255; Senate, *FY 1977 Military Procurement*, pt. 9:4855.

105. Senate, *NATO and the New Soviet Threat; Report of Senator Sam Nunn and Senator Dewey F. Bartlett to the Committee on Armed Services*, 95th Cong., 1st sess., 1977, 18.

106. History, Directorate of Doctrine, Concepts, and Objectivities USAF, January–June 1971, Aerospace Doctrine Division, n.p.; Senate, *FY 1978 DOD Appropriations*, pt. 1:238; House, *1979 DOD Appropriations*, pt. 4:137–38, 161–63.

107. House, *1979 DOD Appropriations*, 163.

108. Canby, "Tactical Air Power in Armored Warfare," 12; Maj Donald J. Alberts, "Tactical Air Power within NATO, A Growing Convergence of Views," *Air University Review*, March–April 1980, 60.

109. Vogt interview, "Allied Air Power in Central Europe – The View from the Top," 46.

110. Ibid.

111. Ibid., 45.

112. Senate, *FY 1973 DOD Appropriations*, 87–88; Senate, *FY 1973 Military Procurement*, pt. 6:3585.

113. Senate, *FY 1973 Military Procurement*, pt. 6:3574–83; Senate, *FY 1974 Military Procurement*, pt. 6:4465–73.

IDEAS, CONCEPTS, DOCTRINE

114. Senate, *FY 1974 Military Procurement*, pt. 6:4490.
115. House, *Department of Defense Appropriations for 1974: Hearings before a Subcommittee of the Committee on Appropriations*, 93d Cong., 2d sess., 1974, pt. 2:43 (hereafter cited as *1974 DOD Appropriations*).
116. Senate, *FY 1975 DOD Appropriations*, pt. 4:23.
117. Edgar F. Puryear, *George S. Brown, General, U.S. Air Force: Destined for Stars* (Novato, Calif.: Presidio Press, 1983), 220; Senate, *FY 1975 Military Procurement*, pt. 6:2876.
118. Senate, *FY 1975 Military Procurement*, pt. 6:2876.
119. Senate, *FY 1976 DOD Appropriations*, pt. 1:610–11, pt. 4:73–77, 464–67; Senate, *FY 1977 Military Procurement*, pt. 9:5098–99.
120. Senate, *FY 1977 Military Procurement*, pt. 9:5098–99.
121. Senate, *Seminars, Service Chiefs on Defense Missions and Priorities*, 3:66.
122. Senate, *FY 1977 Military Procurement*, pt. 9:4886, 4896–97.
123. Ibid., 4954–76, 4983–88; Senate, *Department of Defense Authorization for Appropriations for Fiscal Year 1979: Hearings before the Committee on Armed Services*, 95th Cong., 2d sess., 1978, pt. 6:4692–4705 (hereafter cited as *FY 1979 DOD Authorization*).
124. House, *Department of Defense Appropriations for 1980: Hearings before a Subcommittee of the Committee on Appropriations*, 96th Cong., 1st sess., 1979, pt. 2:517–18 (hereafter cited as *1980 DOD Appropriations*).
125. Canby, "Tactical Air Power in Armored Warfare," 6–7.
126. House, *1975 DOD Appropriations*, pt. 4:494, pt. 7:1318–19.
127. Senate, *FY 1977 Military Procurement*, pt. 9:4989.
128. House, *1976 DOD Appropriations*, pt. 1:4101, pt. 5:1266.
129. Ibid.
130. Senate, *FY 1977 Military Procurement*, pt. 9:4955; House, *1977 DOD Appropriations*, pt. 1:119, pt. 5:142.
131. House, *1979 DOD Appropriations*, pt. 4:79–81; Senate, *FY 1979 DOD Authorization*, pt. 6:4692–94; Senate, *Department of Defense Appropriations for Fiscal Year 1980: Hearings before a Subcommittee of the Committee on Appropriations*, 96th Cong., 1st sess., 1978, pt. 1:623, pt. 4:57 (hereafter cited as *FY 1980 DOD Appropriations*).
132. House, *1979 DOD Appropriations*, pt. 4:83, 135; House, *NATO Standardization, Interoperability and Readiness*, 497–98.
133. Senate, *FY 1978 DOD Appropriations*, pt. 1:185–86.
134. Senate, *Department of Defense Authorization for Appropriations for Fiscal Year 1980: Hearings before the Committee on Armed Services*, 96th Cong., 1st sess., 1979, pt. 1:173 (hereafter cited as *FY 1980 DOD Authorization*).
135. House, *1979 DOD Appropriations*, pt. 2:677; Senate, *Department of Defense Appropriations for Fiscal Year 1979: Hearings before a Subcommittee of the Committee on Appropriations*, 95th Cong., 2d sess., 1978, pt. 1:474–76 (hereafter cited as *FY 1979 DOD Appropriations*).
136. Senate, *FY 1979 DOD Appropriations*, pt. 1:474–76.
137. Senate, *FY 1978 DOD Appropriations*, pt. 1:236–38.
138. House, *1979 DOD Appropriations*, pt. 4:68; *Air Force Policy Letter for Commanders: Supplement*, May 1978, 18.
139. House, *NATO Standardization, Interoperability and Readiness*, 356.
140. House, *Department of Defense Appropriations for 1978: Hearings before a Subcommittee of the Committee on Appropriations*, 95th Cong., 1st sess., 1977, pt. 2:25 (hereafter cited as *1978 DOD Appropriations*); House, *1979 DOD Appropriations*, pt. 2:843, pt. 4:169–70, 246; Senate, *FY 1979 DOD Appropriations*, pt. 1:1096, pt. 6:4565–75, 4645–63; Senate, *FY 1980 DOD Appropriations*, pt. 1:139–52, pt. 4:1074–81; Senate, *Department of Defense Authorization for Appropriations for Fiscal Year 1981: Hearings before the Committee on Armed Services*, 96th Cong., 2d sess., 1980, pt. 4:2200–10 (hereafter cited as *FY 1981 DOD Authorization*).
141. House, *NATO Standardization, Interoperability and Readiness*, 339–57.

142. Ibid., 357.

143. House, *1979 DOD Appropriations*, pt. 4:86–87.

144. Senate, *Department of Defense Appropriations for Fiscal Year 1983: Hearings before a Subcommittee of the Committee on Appropriations*, 97th Cong., 2d sess., 1982, pt. 1:305, pt. 7:4363 (hereafter cited as *FY 1983 DOD Appropriations*).

145. House, *Department of Defense Appropriations for 1981: Hearings before a Subcommittee of the Committee on Appropriations*, 96th Cong., 2d sess., 1960, pt. 2:436–37 (hereafter cited as *1981 DOD Appropriations*).

146. Col David L. Nichols, "Who Needs Nuclear TACAIR?" *Air University Review*, March–April 1976, 16; House, *1979 DOD Appropriations*, pt. 2:787.

147. Gen Bruce K. Holloway, "United States Grand Strategy for the Next Ten Years," in *Grand Strategy for the 1980s*, ed. Bruce Palmer, Jr., 27–28.

148. Nichols, "Who Needs Nuclear TACAIR?" 19–20.

149. Ibid.

150. House, *Department of Defense Appropriations for 1983: Hearings before a Subcommittee of the Committee on Appropriations*, 97th Cong., 2d sess., 1982, pt. 4:810–11 (hereafter cited as *1983 DOD Appropriations*).

151. House, *1978 DOD Appropriations*, pt. 1:573, pt. 2:104–6, 288; pt. 3:339, 692; Senate, *FY 1978 DOD Appropriations*, pt. 1:964.

152. Senate, *FY 1979 DOD Authorization*, pt. 6:4481.

153. *Annual Report to the Congress, Caspar W. Weinberger, Secretary of Defense, Fiscal Year 1983* (Washington, D.C.: Government Printing Office, 1982), Soviet Military Power annex, 26–27; House, *1983 DOD Appropriations*, pt. 4:810–11.

154. House, *1979 DOD Appropriations*, pt. 4:21.

155. Senate, *FY 1980 DOD Authorization*, pt. 1:105; Senate, *Department of Defense Appropriations for Fiscal Year 1981: Hearings before a Subcommittee of the Committee on Appropriations*, 96th Cong., 2d sess., 1980, pt. 1:69–70 (hereafter cited as *FY 1981 DOD Appropriations*).

156. House, *1981 DOD Appropriations*, pt. 1:552–53, 618; Senate, *FY 1981 DOD Appropriations*, pt. 1:67–71; House, *1982 DOD Appropriations*, pt. 2:208.

157. House, *1983 DOD Appropriations*, pt. 1:3, pt. 4:380–81.

158. Senate, *FY 1981 DOD Appropriations*, pt. 1:71; House, *1982 DOD Appropriations*, pt. 2:207–8; House, *Department of Defense Appropriations for 1984: Hearings before a Subcommittee of the Committee on Appropriations*, 98th Cong., 1st sess., 1983, pt. 2:142–43 (hereafter cited as *1984 DOD Appropriations*).

159. Senate, *Department of Defense Authorization for Appropriations for Fiscal Year 1982: Hearings before the Committee on Armed Services*, 97th Cong., 1st sess., 1981, pt. 7:3891–92 (hereafter cited as *FY 1982 DOD Authorization*).

160. Ibid., 3849–50, 3861, 4328–37, 4362–63.

161. Ibid.

162. Senate, *Close Air Support*, 184.

163. Herman S. Wolk, *Planning and Organizing the Postwar Air Force 1943–1947* (Washington, D.C.: Office of Air Force History, 1984), appendix 9.

164. Senate, *Close Air Support*, 185.

165. Ibid., 12.

166. Senate, *FY 1966 DOD Appropriations*, 305.

167. Ibid.

168. Senate, *Close Air Support*, 76–77, 100–1, 136–37.

169. Ibid.; Senate, *FY 1966 DOD Appropriations*, 305.

170. House, *1971 DOD Appropriations*, pt. 5:64–65.

171. Frederic A. Bergerson, *The Army Gets an Air Force: Tactics of Insurgent Bureaucratic Politics* (Baltimore: Johns Hopkins University Press, 1980), 117–20; Col John Schlight, "USAF in Southeast Asia: South Vietnam, 1965–1968," history manuscript, Office of Air Force History, 223–27; "The

IDEAS, CONCEPTS, DOCTRINE

Forty-Year Split (evolution of land-air doctrine and practices in the U.S.)," *Army Magazine*, October 1965, 64; "Concept for Improved Joint Air-Ground Coordination," *Air Force Policy Letter for Commanders: Supplement*, June 1965, 27–32; Senate, *Close Air Support*, 86.

172. Senate, *Close Air Support: Report of the Special Subcommittee on Close Air Support of the Preparedness Investigating Subcommittee of the Committee on Armed Services*, 92d Cong., 1st sess., 1972, 23 (hereafter cited as *Close Air Support: Report*).

173. House, *1967 DOD Appropriations*, pt. 1:533.

174. Senate, *Close Air Support*, 188.

175. Senate, *Close Air Support: Report*, 23–24.

176. Senate, *FY 1970 Military Procurement*, pt. 1:1583, 1896–97; Senate, *FY 1972 Military Procurement*, pt. 5:3852.

177. Senate, *FY 1972 Military Procurement*, pt. 5:3852.

178. Senate, *FY 1970 Military Procurement*, pt. 2:1536–37; Senate, *Close Air Support*, 154, 85–86.

179. Senate, *Close Air Support*, 252–69; Senate, *Close Air Support: Report*, 22–23.

180. House, *1971 DOD Appropriations*, pt. 1:648.

181. Ibid.

182. Senate, *FY 1970 Military Procurement*, pt. 2:925–28, 948–49; House, *1971 DOD Appropriations*, pt. 6:678.

183. House, *1971 DOD Appropriations*, pt. 6:678.

184. Senate, *FY 1971 Military Procurement*, pt. 2:1140–44; Senate, *Close Air Support*, 99–100.

185. Senate, *Close Air Support*, 40.

186. Senate, *FY 1972 Military Procurement*, pt. 5:3852.

187. Ibid.

188. House, *1972 DOD Appropriations*, pt. 2:36–38; Senate, *Close Air Support*, 12–16; History, Directorate of Doctrine, Concepts and Objectives, US Air Force, July–December 1971, appended "Doctrinal Issues Briefing."

189. Senate, *Close Air Support*, appendix A: Department of Defense Close Air Support Report.

190. Senate, *Close Air Support: Report*, 1–6.

191. Ibid.

192. Senate, *FY 1972 Military Procurement*, pt. 2:1289, pt. 5:3872–73; Senate, *FY 1972 DOD Appropriations*, pt. 4:646.

193. Senate, *Close Air Support*, 7.

194. Ibid., 31.

195. Senate, *Close Air Support: Report*, 25–26; Senate, *FY 1974 Military Procurement*, pt. 1:190–92.

196. House, *Department of Defense Appropriations for 1973: Hearings before a Subcommittee of the Committee on Appropriations*, 93d Cong., 2d sess., 1972, pt. 3:529–30; Senate, *FY 1973 Military Procurement*, pt. 2:709.

197. Senate, *FY 1973 DOD Appropriations*, pt. 4:25, 83.

198. Senate, *FY 1973 Military Procurement*, pt. 2:1294.

199. Senate, *Close Air Support: Report*, 23–24; Bergerson, *The Army Gets an Air Force*, 122; Senate, *FY 1974 Military Procurement*, pt. 2:190–92; *Department of Defense Annual Report for Fiscal Year 1978*, 167; *Department of Defense Annual Report for Fiscal Year 1979*, 147.

200. Senate, *FY 1974 Military Procurement*, pt. 6:4526–74.

201. Ibid.

202. Ibid., pt. 2:954–56, pt. 6:4562, 4566; Dr George M. Watson, Jr., "The A-10 Close Support Aircraft, 1970–1976," *AFSC Historical Publication*, iv–v.

203. House, *1975 DOD Appropriations*, pt. 2:302–3.

204. Ibid., pt. 7:1098–99, pt. 9:225–26; Senate, *FY 1979 DOD Appropriations*, pt. 4:602–6.

205. Senate, *FY 1979 DOD Appropriations*, pt. 4:602.

206. Senate, *FY 1974 Military Procurement*, pt. 2:999.

207. House, *1974 DOD Appropriations*, pt. 5:1647.

208. Senate, *FY 1977 Military Procurement*, pt. 10:5639.

209. *Air Force Policy Letter for Commanders*, 1 September 1975.
210. Ibid.
211. Ibid.
212. Senate, *FY 1977 Military Procurement*, pt. 10:5639–40.
213. Senate, *Close Air Support*, 105.
214. Senate, *Close Air Support: Report*, 28–29.
215. Senate, *Seminars, Service Chiefs on Defense Mission and Priorities*, 3:7; Senate, *FY 1977 DOD Appropriations*, pt. 1:527.
216. Senate, *Close Air Support*, 7.
217. History, Directorate of Doctrine, Concepts, and Objectives, USAF, July–December 1967 and July–December 1971.
218. Ibid.
219. Senate, *Seminars, Service Chiefs on Defense Mission and Priorities*, 3:6–7.
220. Senate, *FY 1977 DOD Appropriations*, pt. 1:527–28.
221. Senate, *Department of Defense Authorization for Appropriations for Fiscal Year 1984: Hearings before the Committee on Armed Services*, 98th Cong., 1st sess., 1983, pt. 1:481 (hereafter cited as *FY 1984 DOD Authorization*).
222. Senate, *Close Air Support*, 252–69.
223. Senate, *FY 1977 DOD Appropriations*, 527.
224. House, *NATO Standardization, Interoperability and Readiness*, 435–36, 443–44.
225. Ibid., 435; Senate, *Close Air Support*, 209.
226. House, *NATO Standardization, Interoperability and Readiness*, 435–36, 443–44.
227. "Omnibus Agreement," Tactical Air Conference, Langley AFB, Va., 11–15 April 1983, appended to report, Col Arthur E. Ivins and Lt Col William Mack, Air War College, subject: Trip Report (HQ TAC/XPJ), 10–15 April 1983.
228. Maj Gen Robert N. Ginsburgh, USAF, Retired, "A New Look at Control of the Seas," *Strategic Review*, Winter 1976, 87.
229. Senate, *FY 1975 Military Procurement*, pt. 7:3918.
230. House, *1977 DOD Appropriations*, pt. 5:140.
231. Ginsburgh, "A New Look at Control of the Seas," 87; Elmo R. Zumwalt, Jr., *On Watch, A Memoir* (New York: Quadrangle/New York Times Book Co., 1976), 70–71; House, *1979 DOD Appropriations*, pt. 5:238.
232. Ginsburgh, "A New Look at Control of the Seas," 87; Zumwalt, *On Watch*, 70–71; House, *1979 DOD Appropriations*, pt. 5:238.
233. *Air Force Policy Letter for Commanders*, 1 July 1974.
234. House, *1976 DOD Appropriations*, pt. 2:42, 615.
235. *Air Force Policy Letter for Commanders: Supplement*, November 1975, 29–31.
236. *Air Force Policy Letter for Commanders*, 1 August 1976; House, *1977 DOD Appropriations*, pt. 1:797, 882, pt. 2:183.
237. *Air Force Policy Letter for Commanders*, 1 August 1976; House, *1977 DOD Appropriations*, pt. 1:797, 882, pt. 2:183.
238. House, *Reorganization Proposals for the Joint Chiefs of Staff: Hearings before the Investigation Subcommittee of the Committee on Armed Services*, 97th Cong., 2d sess., 1982, 476–78 (hereafter cited as *Reorganization Proposals for the JCS*).
239. Senate, *FY 1981 DOD Authorization*, 3844, 4328.
240. Ibid., 3925–27.
241. James D. Hessman, "Sea Power and the Control Front," *Air Force Magazine*, July 1983, 52; Senate, *Department of Defense Authorization for Appropriations for Fiscal Year 1983: Hearings before the Committee on Armed Services*, 97th Cong., 2d sess., 1982, pt. 7:4363 (hereafter cited as *FY 1983 DOD Authorization*); Senate, *FY 1984 DOD Authorization*, pt. 1:255.
242. Senate, *FY 1982 DOD Authorization*, pt. 3:1281–82; Tactical Air Conference, Langley AFB, Va., 11–15 April 1983; *Air Force Policy Letter for Commanders*, 15 November 1982; "Air Force and

IDEAS, CONCEPTS, DOCTRINE

Navy Agree to Closer Ties," *Air Force Magazine*, January 1983, 30; House, *1984 DOD Appropriations*, pt. 2:88, 430, 491.
243. "Air Force and Navy Agree to Closer Ties," 30.
244. Ibid.
245. Gen Robert J. Dixon, "TAC-TRADOC Dialogue," *Strategic Review*, Winter 1978, 46.
246. Senate, *FY 1979 DOD Authorization*, pt. 6:4423; Dixon, "The Future and Tactical Air Command," *Air Force Policy Letter for Commanders: Supplement*, February 1976, 19–20.
247. Dixon, "The Future and Tactical Air Command," 19–20.
248. Dixon, "TAC-TRADOC Dialogue," 47–48; Senate, *FY 1977 Military Procurement*, pt. 10:5615–16.
249. Senate, *FY 1977 Military Procurement*, pt. 10:5636–37; House, *1979 DOD Appropriations*, pt. 5:94; House, *NATO Standardization, Interoperability and Readiness*, 398–99.
250. Dixon, "TAC-TRADOC Dialogue," 48; Senate, *FY 1977 Military Procurement*, pt. 10:5617.
251. Dixon, "TAC-TRADOC Dialogue," 48.
252. Senate, *FY 1977 Military Procurement*, pt. 10:5613.
253. Ibid., 5628–29; Senate, *FY 1979 DOD Authorization*, pt. 6:4430–31, 4564, 4728–37.
254. Senate, *FY 1977 Military Procurement*, pt. 9:4887.
255. Ibid., pt. 10:5622; Senate, *FY 1979 DOD Authorization*, pt. 6:4432, 4482–89, 4494–95.
256. Senate, *FY 1979 DOD Authorization*, pt. 6:4440–41.
257. Ibid., 4894–95.
258. Ibid., 4908.
259. Senate, *FY 1975 Military Procurement*, pt. 6:3037, 3049–51, 3055; pt. 8:4393–4407.
260. Senate, *FY 1977 Military Procurement*, pt. 9:5164–75.
261. Senate, *FY 1979 DOD Authorization*, pt. 6:4498, 4889–4951; History, Directorate of Concepts, July–December 1977, 80.
262. History, Directorate of Concepts, 80.
263. Ibid.
264. Senate, *FY 1977 Military Procurement*, pt. 9:520–522; Senate, *FY 1979 DOD Authorization*, pt. 6:4738–57; House, *1979 DOD Appropriations*, pt. 5:52; House, *1983 DOD Appropriations*, pt. 2:671.
265. Senate, *FY 1979 DOD Authorization*, pt. 6:4738–57.
266. Ibid.
267. Senate, *FY 1983 DOD Authorization*, pt. 4:2636–37; House, *1983 DOD Appropriations*, pt. 2:671–73; House, *1982 DOD Appropriations*, pt. 6:4, 32–33, 345.
268. House, *1982 DOD Appropriations*, pt. 6:4, 32–33, 345.
269. History, Directorate of Doctrine, Concepts, and Objectives, US Air Force, July–December 1972, 122; January–June 1973, 113.
270. Ibid.
271. Speech by Maj Gen Leslie W. Bray, Jr., to National Security Industrial Association, 15 March 1973, in *Air Force Policy Letter for Commanders: Supplement*, June 1973, 31–38; Bray, "Tactical Counterforce" *Air Force*, June 1974, 36–40.
272. Enthoven and Smith, *How Much Is Enough?*, 222.
273. Senate, *Close Air Support*, 18.
274. Bray, "Tactical Counterforce," 38.
275. Gen Donn A. Starry, US Army, "A Tactical Evolution FM 100-5," *Military Review*, August 1978, 2.
276. Senate, *Close Air Support*, 113.
277. Senate, *FY 1977 Military Procurement*, pt. 10:5606–12.
278. Ibid.
279. William S. Lind, "Some Doctrinal Questions for the United States Army," *Military Review*, March 1977, 54–65; Lind, "Military Doctrine, Force Structure, and the Defense Decision Making Process," *Air University Review*, May–June 1979, 21–27.

280. John L. Romjue, "The Evolution of the AirLand Battle Concept," *Air University Review*, May–June 1984, 6; Senate, *FY 1979 DOD Authorization*, pt. 6:4444–54.

281. Romjue, "The Evolution of the AirLand Battle Concept," 7; House, *NATO Standardization, Interoperability and Readiness*, 1107.

282. Romjue, "The Evolution of the AirLand Battle Concept," 7.

283. Edward N. Luttwak, "The American Style of Warfare and the Military Balance," *Air Force Magazine*, August 1979, 86–88; Lt Col Walter Kross, "Military Reform: Past and Present," *Air University Review*, July–August 1981, 101–8.

284. Romjue, "The Evolution of the AirLand Battle Concept," 6–15.

285. Michael R. Gordon, "The Army's 'AirLand Battle' Doctrine Worries Allies, Upsets the Air Force," *National Journal*, 18 June 1983.

286. Ibid.; Maj James A. Machos, "TACAIR Support for AirLand Battle," *Air University Review*, May–June 1984, 16–24.

287. Gordon, "The Army's 'AirLand Battle' Doctrine Worries Allies, Upsets the Air Force."

288. Edgar Ulsamer, "TACAIR—History's Most Potent Fighting Machine," *Air Force Magazine*, February 1976, 22.

289. Robert S. Dotson, "Tactical Air Power and Environmental Imperatives," *Air University Review*, July–August 1977, 29.

290. Col Robert D. Rasmussen, "The Central European Battlefield, Doctrinal Implications for Counterair-Interdiction," *Air University Review*, July–August 1978, 12–13.

291. AFM 1-1, *Functions and Basic Doctrine of the United States Air Force*, 14 February 1979, 2:13.

292. Wing Comdr Jeremy G. Saye, "Close Air Support in Modern Warfare," *Air University Review*, January–February 1980, 6; Lt Col Donald L. Alberts, "An Alternate View of Interdiction," *Air University Review*, July–August 1981, 40.

293. Senate, *FY 1984 DOD Authorization*, pt. 1:122.

294. Group Capt Ian Madelin, Royal Air Force, "The Emperor's Close Air Support," *Air University Review*, November–December 1979, 82–86; Saye, "Close Air Support in Modern Warfare," 2–21.

295. Maj Michael O. Beck, "Close Air Support," *Air University Review*, September–October 1980, 100–1.

296. House, *1984 DOD Appropriations*, pt. 2:260.

297. Machos, "TACAIR Support for AirLand Battle," 19.

298. Ibid., 21; memorandum by Gen W. W. Momyer, USAF, Retired, to Col D. R. McNabb, Headquarters USAF/XOXID, subject: Background Paper on Theater Warfare Planning Boundaries, 1 April 1981, in Headquarters USAF/XOXID, Doctrine Information Publication no. 10, Background Information on Air Force Perspective for Coherent Plans (Command and Control of TACAIR), April 1981.

299. Memorandum by Gen W. W. Momyer, USAF, Retired, to Col D. R. McNabb.

300. Clifton Berry, Jr., "USAF Doctrine Comes Alive," *Air Force Magazine*, July 1983, 34–36; General Creech's discussion of AirLand Battle, Tactical Air Conference, Langley AFB, Va., 11–15 April 1983, appended to report, Ivins and Mack, subject: Trip Report (HQ TAC/XPJ, 10–15 April 1983).

301. House, *1982 DOD Appropriations*, pt. 6:9–10; Senate, *FY 1983 DOD Authorization*, pt. 4:2575.

302. Senate, *FY 1984 DOD Authorization*, pt. 1:122.

303. Department of the Army/Department of the Air Force, Memorandum of Agreement on US Army-US Air Force Joint Force Development Process, 22 May 1984.

304. Maj Gen Gerald J. Carey, Jr., "The Electronic Air Force: Electromagnetic Combat," *Air Force Magazine*, July 1980, 83–87.

305. Ibid.

306. Lt Gen Kelly H. Burke, USAF, Retired, "Electronic Combat: Warfare of the Future," *Jewish Institute for National Security Affairs Newsletter*, February 1983.

307. Ibid.

308. Senate, *FY 1984 DOD Authorization*, pt. 1:168.

IDEAS, CONCEPTS, DOCTRINE

309. House, *1971 DOD Appropriations*, pt. 1:274; Senate, *FY 1972 DOD Appropriations*, pt. 4:13, 57–58; Senate, *FY 1972 Military Procurement*, pt. 5:3781.

310. Senate, *FY 1972 Military Procurement*, pt. 5:3781; Senate, *FY 1973 Military Procurement*, pt. 6:3522.

311. Senate, *FY 1970 Military Procurement*, pt. 2:1536–37; Senate, *FY 1971 Military Procurement*, pt. 2:948–49; Senate, *Close Air Support*, 202.

312. Senate, *FY 1977 Military Procurement*, pt. 9:4894–95.

313. Ibid., 5691–92.

314. Senate, *FY 1983 DOD Appropriations*, pt. 4:146.

315. Senate, *FY 1977 Military Procurement*, pt. 9:4898–4900; House, *1976 DOD Appropriations*, pt. 1:333, pt. 2:128–29; Senate, *FY 1976 DOD Appropriations*, pt. 4:188–89.

316. Senate, *FY 1979 DOD Authorization*, pt. 6:4490.

317. Ibid.

318. House, *1979 DOD Appropriations*, pt. 4:306–7, pt. 5:17–18, 89; House, *1981 DOD Appropriations*, pt. 2:408; House, *1980 DOD Appropriations*, pt. 6:519; Senate, *FY 1981 DOD Authorization*, pt. 4:2249.

319. Senate, *FY 1981 DOD Authorization*, pt. 4:2249.

320. Senate, *FY 1979 DOD Appropriations*, pt. 5:232–33; House, *1981 DOD Appropriations*, pt. 5:379–80.

321. House, *1981 DOD Appropriations*, pt. 5:379–80.

322. Senate, *FY 1978 DOD Authorization*, pt. 6:4499.

323. House, *1981 DOD Appropriations*, pt. 7:667.

324. *Air Force Policy Letter for Commanders*, 15 December 1980.

325. Ibid.

326. Ibid.

327. Senate, *FY 1979 DOD Authorization*, pt. 6:4499; Senate, *FY 1979 DOD Appropriations*, pt. 1:1097; House, *1979 DOD Appropriations*, pt. 5:91.

328. House, *1979 DOD Appropriations*, pt. 5:91, 712; Senate, *FY 1980 DOD Appropriations*, pt. 1:687; House, *1980 DOD Appropriations*, pt. 7:390; House, *1984 DOD Appropriations*, pt. 2:187–94.

329. House, *1979 DOD Appropriations*, pt. 5:17–18; House, *1980 DOD Appropriations*, pt. 6:519; House, *1981 DOD Appropriations*, pt. 3:997.

330. House, *1980 DOD Appropriations*, pt. 7:510–11; House, *1981 DOD Appropriations*, pt. 2:408–9, 9:121; Senate, *FY 1983 DOD Appropriations*, 310–12.

331. House, *1980 DOD Appropriations*, pt. 7:510–11; House, *1981 DOD Appropriations*, pt. 2:408–9, 9:121; Senate, *FY 1983 DOD Appropriations*, 310–12.

332. House, *1981 DOD Appropriations*, pt. 2:408–9.

333. Ibid., 404, 407; pt. 3:1000.

334. House, *1982 DOD Appropriations*, pt. 6:5, 32.

335. Senate, *FY 1983 DOD Appropriations*, pt. 1:313.

336. Ibid.

337. Ibid.

338. Senate, *FY 1977 Military Procurement*, pt. 9:4896–97; Senate, *FY 1980 DOD Appropriations*, pt. 4:1627.

339. House, *1982 DOD Appropriations*, pt. 6:9; Senate, *FY 1983 DOD Authorization*, pt. 4:2593.

340. Senate, *FY 1983 DOD Authorization*, pt. 4:2593.

341. House, *1980 DOD Appropriations*, pt. 2:404, pt. 3:997, pt. 9:143, 144.

342. Ibid., pt. 3:1021, 1053; House, *1982 DOD Appropriations*, pt. 6:43.

343. Senate, *FY 1981 DOD Appropriations*, pt. 4:2200–10.

344. Ibid.

345. House, *1982 DOD Appropriations*, pt. 6:3-4, 8; House, *1983 DOD Appropriations*, pt. 2:364–65.

346. House, *1982 DOD Appropriations*, pt. 6:190; Senate, *FY 1983 DOD Appropriations*, pt. 1:313.

347. Senate, *FY 1983 DOD Appropriations*, pt. 4:146–47.

348. Ibid., pt. 3:292; House, *Reorganization Proposals for the JCS*, 837.
349. Senate, *FY 1983 DOD Appropriations*, pt. 1:315, 358, pt. 4:120–21, 146.
350. House, *1982 DOD Appropriations*, pt. 6:9, 23.
351. Senate, *FY 1982 DOD Authorization*, pt. 3:1271–76; Senate, *FY 1983 DOD Authorization*, pt. 4:150–53, 2597–99.
352. Senate, *FY 1983 DOD Authorization*, pt. 4:150–53, 2597–99.
353. Senate, *FY 1983 DOD Authorization*, pt. 4:2599; Senate, *FY 1983 DOD Appropriations*, pt. 4:143.
354. House, *1984 DOD Appropriations*, pt. 2:104–5.
355. *Air Force Magazine*, May 1984, 159–60.
356. House, *1984 DOD Appropriations*, pt. 2:335–36.
357. Brig Gen John A. Shaud, United States Air Force deputy director of plans, Deputy Chief of Staff/XPO, "Toward the Future," *Long Range Planning Conference, Theater Warfare 2003*, 12–13 April 1983; *Air Force Policy Letter for Commanders*, 15 February 1982.
358. House, *1983 DOD Appropriations*, pt. 2:392–93.
359. See John T. Correll, "Where TAC Is Heading," and Lt Gen Robert D. Russ, "The Fighter Roadmap," *Air Force Magazine*, June 1984, 50–63.
360. Ibid.

Lt Gen George S. Boylan, Jr., director of aerospace programs and deputy chief of staff for programs and resources.

Maj Gen Robert P. Lukeman, assistant chief of staff for studies and analysis.

Gen Wilbur L. Creech, commander of the Tactical Air Command.

Gen Alton D. Slay, Air Force deputy chief of staff for research and development.

Gen John W. Vogt, Jr., commander in chief of the United States Air Forces in Europe.

Lt Gen William J. Evans, deputy chief of staff for research and development.

Lt Gen Kelly H. Burke, deputy chief of staff for research, development, and acquisition.

C-5A.

Robert S. McNamara
secretary of defense.

Caspar W. Weinberger,
secretary of defense.

CHAPTER 7

THE AIR FORCE IN THE DEFENSE DEPARTMENT

Shortly after his retirement as chairman of the Joint Chiefs of Staff, Gen David C. Jones wrote:

> Although most history books glorify our military accomplishments, a close examination reveals a disconcerting pattern: unpreparedness at the start of a war; initial failures; reorganizing while fighting; cranking up our industrial base; and ultimately prevailing by wearing down the enemy—by being bigger, not smarter.... Although the current threat to our security is great, there is little likelihood that we will have the time to regroup if we do not meet the threat effectively at the outset of any major conflict. We can no longer afford the degradation of our defense capabilities that comes with less than effective organization.[1]

In April 1982, in his last weeks on active duty, General Jones did not feel that he could leave office in good conscience without speaking out strongly about defense organizational defects. Jones said in April 1982:

> Historically our military organization has tended to lag behind the changing demands of the defense environment. Organizational change has come more often than not in the aftermath of wartime failure than as a result of forward planning.... We got by in the past because of our industrial base and the factors of time and space which allowed us to mobilize that base. In the world wars we had the buffers of geography and of allies who could carry the fight until we mobilized and deployed. After World War II we depended largely on our nuclear superiority to cover imbalance in conventional capabilities and deter direct clashes with the Soviets.... Vietnam was perhaps our worst example of confused objectives and unclear responsibilities. The organizational arrangements were a nightmare; for example, each service fought its own air war. Since that time we have been concerned with how to react more effectively to contingencies, but have not as yet devised a way to integrate our efforts to achieve maximum joint effectiveness without undue regard to service doctrine, missions and command prerogatives.... Because of our past successes with superior resources in wars of attrition, our military institutions have not been forced to reexamine established doctrine or to break down the institutional barriers in the interests of achieving greater force effectiveness through imaginative combinations of the resources and doctrines of the separate services. We have bureaucratized our military institutions—and the great strength of a bureaucracy is its ability to protect and preserve institutional interests and self-image against the demands of a changing environment. We are comfortable with the past because it is the future, not the past, that challenges outmoded concepts, doctrines and organizational arrangements.[2]

General Jones's demands that the United States look to the organizational deficiencies that prevented combining the forces of the four armed services into the greatest possible joint warfighting capability kindled a lively interest in organizational complexities that generated perhaps more discourse than action.

Continuing Complexities of Defense Organization

In his address to Congress that contained the proposals enacted as the Defense Reorganization Act of 1958, President Eisenhower had defined a central issue: "Separate ground, sea, and air warfare is gone forever. If ever again we should be involved in war, we will fight in it all elements, with all services, as one single concentrated efforts."[3] As military assistant to President Eisenhower, Gen Andrew J. Goodpaster had participated in the preparation of Eisenhower's defense reorganization proposals that became law in 1958. Thinking back in 1982 to these times, General Goodpaster recalled that it had taken "the unique experience of an Eisenhower administration and the unique confidence of the American people in his military judgment to accomplish the reform measures of 1958, and even those did not go as far as he desired." Still speaking of Eisenhower, Goodpaster said:

> I think as President he said that on many, many, many occasions, the loss of effectiveness, and the effects of duplication came from over-concentration in the service role. When stung from time to time, he would deplore the parochialism that was being shown. Always his emphasis was on looking at these problems from the perspective of the national need, the provision of security against the overall threat that we were confronting. On the question of the integrated point of view, it was his hope, though he acknowledged some doubt, that through the changes that were put into effect in 1958, the emphasis on the corporate duties of the Joint Chiefs of Staff would become overriding.... I think that the system has not measured up to his hopes in that regard.[4]

It was General Goodpaster's opinion that the "corporate duties" of the Joint Chiefs of Staff visualized by President Eisenhower had not had priority and that the Joint Chiefs had not contributed to an effective US national security policy, strategy, and posture. The service chiefs had been heavily burdened with service responsibilities; their military advice and plans, he said, "lacks the timeliness and responsiveness it should have, reflects too much of 'weapons push' and service proponency rather than an 'operational requirements pull' based on overall strategy. Joint advice on budget formation and resource allocation, though a heavy burden to the whole organization, is not of such an order or of such a quality as to influence these decisions in a sufficiently major and useful way."[5] The 1958 reorganization act had vested "full operational command" of US forces assigned to unified or specified commanders, their line of command proceeding from the president, to the secretary of defense, through the Joint Chiefs of Staff to the unified or specified commander. In this function the Joint Chiefs of Staff did not initiate but transmitted the instructions of the national command authorities (the president/secretary of defense). The service departments and service chiefs did not possess command authority but were charged to train, organize, and support the force units assigned to the operational command of unified/specified commanders. It was General Goodpaster's opinion predicated upon his position as supreme allied commander in Europe in the 1970s that the information and recommendations of unified/specified operational commanders needed "to be strengthened and reflected in overall military planning and resource allocation."[6] Gen Russell E. Dougherty, who had served as chief of staff SHAPE and also CINCSAC shrewdly pointed out that even though the service departments and chiefs "provided, prepared, procured" and the unified/specified commands had "operational command" it was nonetheless true that "he who pays, controls," Dougherty said:

> That to me is one of the most serious weaknesses in our system. We have developed a system that is designed for bookkeepers and accountants and have lost a historical and strategic perspective on how to correlate forces to achieve objectives, either by defensing or by way of containing and defeating an enemy. We have abdicated to the bookkeepers; we think along that line.[7]

Making another point General Goodpaster said:

> If the services would . . . realign their forces to do the jobs in the field as seen by the people that bear the responsibility there, I think that this would be more efficient, a more effective directed pattern of programs and effort than if the impetus comes from the weapon systems themselves.[8]

When President Kennedy took office in 1961 his Democratic party platform had pledged him to make a complete examination of the organization of the US armed forces, and to this end in the summer of 1960 Kennedy asked Sen Stuart Symington to head a study committee looking toward national defense reorganization. The report of the Symington committee received by President-elect Kennedy called for a very high degree of centralization of authority in the Department of Defense, and in the years to follow both Symington and Roswell L. Gilpatric, who served on the committee, changed their opinions.[9] As deputy secretary of defense from 1961 to 1964, Gilpatric recalled that he concluded that there was "a value in having the senior service officers, the men who have risen to the head of their respective services, be in juxtaposition to the Secretary of Defense through bodies such as the Joint Chiefs." He believed and so wrote in 1964 that the Joint Chiefs ought to continue to be "a planning body." "When it came to issues of resources allocations, force strengths, missions," Gilpatric said, "I felt that the chiefs should not have any say in that process, nor should they be in the line of command from the President and Secretary of Defense down to the unified and specified commands." Gilpatric remembered that President Kennedy called the Joint Chiefs to the White House to meet with the National Security Council early in 1961; the subject of the meeting was what to do about Communist military advances in Laos and Gilpatric said that Kennedy got five different views from the five Joint Chiefs. Gilpatric also recalled that the Joint Chiefs split three ways in advice to Secretary McNamara during the Cuban missile crisis of 1962. According to Gilpatric, President Kennedy

IDEAS, CONCEPTS, DOCTRINE

nevertheless did not want to pursue any basic changes in the National Security Act, because he did not want to take on the two chairmen of the Armed Services Committees, Sen Richard Russell and Congressman Carl Vinson.[10]

As seen earlier, Secretary McNamara studied the 1958 defense legislation and opted for secretary of defense actions that were far short of the Symington committee recommendations. It seemed to McNamara that two major deficiencies needed action. He said:

> First, some of the combat ready forces had not been placed under the unified and specified command structure. Second, the Joint Chiefs of Staff had yet to be provided the organizational and management tools they needed to give the most effective day-to-day operational direction to the combat forces.[11]

McNamara therefore created the US Strike Command in 1961. Actions were already under way to form the Defense Communications Agency (DCA) and McNamara expanded its charter. The Defense Supply Agency (DSA) was formed to supervise the procurement of common items of supply for the several services. Service intelligence functions were consolidated under a new organization, the Defense Intelligence Agency (DIA). There were other actions such as assigning the Air Force responsibility for space research and development, a responsibility previously distributed among the three services. Another similar action was the assignment to the Air Force of the principal responsibility for managing missile ranges, a responsibility previously shared with the Navy.[12] The intelligence reorganization produced one voice speaking for defense in the US Intelligence Board, which produced national intelligence estimates. When there was dissatisfaction with the unitary intelligence estimates and intimation that DIA might be split up and returned to the services, Gen George S. Brown liked the DIA as "a reasonable organization." He said in February 1976:

> Personally, I think it would be a mistake to tear that house down and go back where we were years ago.... You know, you just look at the bomber count—we spent billions of dollars in air defense for this country when there wasn't any Soviet bomber fleet. We spent billions on missiles when there wasn't a missile gap. If there was a missile gap, it was because we had so many and they had very few, which was precisely the reverse of the picture that was put out.[13]

After the Bay of Pigs incident in 1961, Gen Maxwell Taylor recalled that President Kennedy was "very dissatisfied with the Joint Chiefs of Staff performance." Taylor said that Kennedy's primary complaint against the Joint Chiefs with regard to the Bay of Pigs "was that although they didn't think it would work, they never came to him and said so, because they weren't asked. The question wasn't put to them, so there was no response." After the Bay of Pigs, Taylor said of President Kennedy: "He felt that he would be more comfortable if he had a military man in the White House, someone beyond the military aide type, who could assist him in coping with the military questions in the future after the Bay of Pigs." In 1961–62 General Taylor served as military representative to the president, maintaining liaison to the president with the Pentagon and with the CIA. During this time Taylor recommended and Kennedy agreed that the Joint Chiefs should provide him with unfiltered advice but that it should not be purely military since all problems were affected by political, economic, and psychological factors as well as military ones. This idea was incorporated into a National Security Action Memorandum in 1961. The position of military representative to the president was not filled again when General Taylor was named chairman of the Joint Chiefs in 1962. Viewing his experience in retrospect, General Taylor concluded that the Joint Chiefs had never satisfactorily carried out their responsibility to serve as the principal military adviser to the president, the National Security Council, and the secretary of defense. Taylor said, "The fact is that the Chiefs have traditionally been loath to volunteer advice to higher authority, particularly if its substance would impinge seriously upon service interests. In my day, the slogan in the JCS was just answer the mail and nothing more."[14] He also recalled that President Eisenhower had understood staff work and was completely comfortable with the National Security Council. Taylor nevertheless concluded that Eisenhower gave the Pentagon less personal attention than did Presidents Kennedy or Johnson, both of whom elected to use the National Security Council as a vehicle for ratifying what had already been decided upon in the closer confines of the Oval Office. Both Presidents Nixon and Ford made more use of the National Security Council, but General Brown, who served under the two men, reported different reliance on military advice. Brown said President Nixon "had his mind on other matters, and the national security affairs were carried on pretty much according to existing policy and with the momentum they had gained. So the Joint Chiefs' relationship with President Nixon was rather *pro forma*. We didn't have much personal contact with the President." Brown said that President Ford used the National Security Council frequently and regularly in formal session: "The Joint Chiefs of Staff were represented at each and every one of those meetings, and either I or the acting chairman was expected to participate fully in the discussion. We had extensive personal contact both socially and in a business way with the President," Brown recalled.[15]

The Blue Ribbon Defense Panel

"I inherited a system designed for highly centralized decisionmaking," said Secretary of Defense Melvin R. Laird of his initiation to the Pentagon at the beginning of President Nixon's administration. Laird continued:

> Our centralization of decision making in so large an organization as the Department of Defense leads to a kind of paralysis. Many decisions are not made at all, or, if they are made, lack full coordination and commitment by those who must implement the decisions. The traffic from lower to higher echelons may be inhibited; relevant and essential inputs for the decision maker can be lost.[16]

IDEAS, CONCEPTS, DOCTRINE

According to Air Force Secretary Robert C. Seamans, Jr., the problem of overcentralization was endemic within the Air Force as well as within the OSD. And his swan song to the Senate Appropriations Committee in the spring of 1969, Gen John P. McConnell, retiring Air Force chief of staff, also had bewailed high centralization and the burden of providing more and more information to upper-level decisionmakers. McConnell said:

> In running flying units, I never had any trouble. When a squadron commander goofed, he was fired. In our procurement and development areas, I can't find anyone to fire. Too many people at too many levels have had too much to say about the program.[17]

During 1969 the Nixon administration sought to rejuvenate the National Security Council (NSC) and to make it a much more meaningful organization than it had become in the Kennedy-Johnson years, when many of the matters handled by President Eisenhower's NSC had been decided by the president and a single cabinet officer or group of government officials. In July 1969 President Nixon assembled a distinguished Blue Ribbon Defense Panel, headed by Gilbert W. Fitzhugh, chairman of the board of the Metropolitan Life Insurance Company. Nixon assigned the panel a very broad charter to study, report on, and make recommendations on the organization and management of the Department of Defense, including the Joint Chiefs of Staff, the defense agencies, and the military services. According to one congressional staff person, the Blue Ribbon Defense Panel was not incumbent, since "every incoming defense administration believes itself duty-bound to show that it has a new approach, one that will be vastly superior to the old ways, more conducive to economy, efficiency, and responsibility."[18] Adm Thomas Moorer, the Joint Chiefs of Staff chairman at the time, had a different explanation for the Blue Ribbon Defense Panel, saying: "This was a study motivated by disagreement between the Secretary of Defense and Henry Kissinger [the presidential national security adviser], the prime target being the Joint Chiefs of Staff who had nothing to do with the study in the first place."[19] Required to report within one year, the panel embraced its mission with enthusiasm engendered by a realization that its investigation was the first broad-scale study of defense organization since the commissions on the organization of the executive department chaired in the 1940s by former President Herbert Hoover. The panel had a large research staff which plumbed sources and conducted interviews both within and outside of government. At the outset of the work, President Nixon told the panel that what he was looking for was criticism. "I think it's important to remember that, because our report is critical, and it's not balanced for that reason," cautioned Fitzhugh.[20]

The Blue Ribbon Defense Panel completed its task within the year as specified, and after delivering copies of the report to President Nixon and Secretary Laird, Fitzhugh released the document at a news conference in the Pentagon on 27 July 1970. He spoke candidly of defects in the Department of Defense. Fitzhugh said:

The problems we found are not with people, it's with the organizational structure itself. Frankly, we think it's an impossible organization to administer. We are amazed it works at all, it's so big and cumbersome under the present organizational structure.... The basic difficulty we found was a diffusion of responsibility. There is nobody below the level of the Secretary and the Deputy Secretary that has the purview of the whole operations of the Department. The same people have an interest in everything, so that they are all bogged down with too much detail work, too many responsibilities, there are too many man killing jobs, and nobody really has the responsibility for anything.... Everybody is somewhat responsible for everything, and nobody is completely responsible for anything. So there's no way of assigning authority, responsibility and accountability. You can't hold anybody accountable. There is nobody you can point your finger to if anything goes wrong, and there is nobody you can pin a medal on if it goes right, because everything is everybody's business, and ... what is everybody's business is nobody's business.[21]

The Blue Ribbon Defense Panel Report — although perhaps influenced by the 12-month limit on its time of preparation — was the most exhaustive examination and commentary on the organization and operations of the Department of Defense. The report would continue to be cited and for this reason its nine-page executive summary carried thought for both immediate and future reflection.

BLUE RIBBON DEFENSE PANEL REPORT

EXECUTIVE SUMMARY

— The purpose of this summary is to provide a quick review of the six-chapter report resulting from the year-long study by the Blue Ribbon Defense Panel. The Panel's report offers recommendations in a number of areas including organization, management of materiel resources, management procedures, personnel management and conflicts of interest. This summary covers the major recommendations of the Panel in the area of the organization of the Defense Department and several of the more significant recommendations in the other areas.

As a result of its examination of the Defense Department, the Panel found that:

— Effective civilian control is impaired by a generally excessive centralization of decision-making authority at the level of the Secretary of Defense. The Secretary's ability to selectively delegate authority and decentralize management, while still retaining personal authority on major policy issues of the Department, is seriously inhibited by the present organizational structure.

— The President and the Secretary of Defense do not presently have the opportunity to consider all viable options as background for making major decisions, because differences of opinion are submerged or compromised at lower levels of the Department of Defense.

– There are too many layers of both military and civilian staffs, and staffs are too large in the Office of the Secretary of Defense (OSD), the Military Departments extending down through the field commanders, the Joint Chiefs of Staff and the Unified and Component Commands. The results are excessive paper work and coordination, delay, duplication and unnecessary expense.

– The present arrangement for staffing the military operations activities for the President and the Secretary of Defense through the Joint Chiefs of Staff and the Military Departments is awkward and unresponsive; it provides a forum for inter-Service conflicts to be injected into the decision-making process for military operations; and it inhibits the flow of information between the combatant commands and the President and the Secretary of Defense, often even in crisis situations.

– The Joint Chiefs of Staff could more effectively perform their important statutory role as principal military advisors to the President and the Secretary of Defense if they were relieved of the necessity of performing delegated duties in the field of military operations and Defense Agency supervision.

– The present combatant command structure does not facilitate the solution of many serious problems which materially affect the security of the nation. For example, recent advances in technology require much closer coordination in planning for and employing the forces of the Continental Air Defense Command and the Strategic Air Command than can reasonably be expected with two separate commands. Also, the present Unified Commands do not bring about unification of the Armed Forces, but rather are layered with Service component headquarters and large headquarters' staffs.

– There is substantial room for improvement and greater integration of management throughout the supply, maintenance and transportation systems of the Department. The most critical need for improved effectiveness is in the support of the Unified Commands.

– There is no organizational element within OSD with the capability or the assigned responsibility for objectively making net assessments of U.S. and foreign military capabilities.

– There is no adequate organizational element within OSD that is charged with the responsibility for long-range planning for the structuring and equipping of forces or for other similar purposes.

– No formal mechanism exists within OSD to assure adequate coordination among the various elements of the Department.

– The present functional assignments of Assistant Secretaries of the Military Departments contribute to duplication between the efforts of the Military Department Secretariats and the Service military staffs, and also between the Military Department Secretariats and OSD.

– The policies of the Department on development and acquisition of weapons and other hardware have contributed to serious cost overruns, schedule slippages and performance deficiencies. The difficulties do not appear amenable to a few simple cure-alls, but require many interrelated changes in organization and procedures.

— Operational test and evaluation has been too infrequent, poorly designed and executed, and generally inadequate.

— Procurement procedures do not sufficiently reflect the national need to maintain an adequate, but not excessive, industrial base.

— The promotion and rotation systems of the Military Services do not facilitate career development in the technical and professional activities, such as research and development, procurement, intelligence, communications and automatic data processing.

— The acquisition and retention of officers and enlisted men in the Armed Services are becoming increasingly difficult for a number of reasons, including (1) personnel policies with respect to compensation, promotion and retirement, and (2) the negative attitude of segments of the public.

— While policies on equal employment opportunity for military and civilian personne' and for contractors appear adequate, implementation responsibilities and functional assignments are fragmented and diffused and have impaired the achievement of effective results.

— The statutes and regulations regarding conflicts of interest are ambiguous, conflicting, and inequitable, and are not uniformly enforced.

To effect substantial improvement in these conditions, the Panel makes the following recommendations:

1. The functions of the Department of Defense should be divided into three major groupings:

(a) Military Operations, including operational command, intelligence, and communications (herein called Operations);

(b) Management of personnel and materiel resources (herein called Management of Resources); and

(c) Evaluation type functions, including financial controls, testing of weapons, analysis of costs and effectiveness of force structures, etc. (herein called Evaluation).

2. Each of these major groups should report to the Secretary of Defense through a separate Deputy Secretary. Appointees to these three positions should be drawn from civilian life, and should rank above all other officers of the Department of Defense except the Secretary. One of the three should be designated principal deputy. The General Counsel, the Assistant to the Secretary of Defense (Atomic Energy), the Assistant Secretary of Defense (Public Affairs), and the Assistant to the Secretary of Defense (Legislative Affairs) would continue to report directly to the Secretary of Defense. The staff of the Office of the Secretary of Defense should not exceed 2,000 people.

3. The Deputy Secretary of Defense for Management of Resources should be delegated responsibility for the following functions:

(a) The Military Departments, which should continue under the immediate supervision of their Secretaries;

(b) Research and Advanced Technology;

(c) Engineering Development;

(d) Installations and Procurement (a modification of the present Installations and Logistics);

(e) Manpower and Reserve Affairs;

(f) Health and Environmental Affairs;

(g) Defense Supply Agency; and

(h) Advanced Research Projects Agency.

There should be an Assistant Secretary of Defense for each of the functions (b) through (f) inclusive, who reports and provides staff assistance to the Secretary of Defense through the Deputy Secretary of Defense (Management of Resources). The position of Director, Defense Research and Engineering, should be abolished, and his functions reallocated between the Assistant Secretary of Defense for Research and Advanced Technology and the Assistant Secretary of Defense for Engineering Development.

Functions (g) and (h) should continue to be constituted as Defense Agencies, each under the immediate supervision of a Director.

The Advanced Research Projects Agency should be delegated the responsibility for all research and exploratory development budget categories. Funds for such research should be budgeted directly to this Agency, and the Agency should be authorized to assign or contract for work projects to laboratories of the Defense Department or in the private sector, as appropriate.

4. The Deputy Secretary of Defense for Operations should be delegated responsibility for the following functions:

(a) Military Operations;

(b) The Unified Commands;

(c) Operational Requirements;

(d) Intelligence;

(e) Telecommunications (and Automatic Data Processing);

(f) International Security Affairs;

(g) Defense Communications Agency; and

(h) Civil Defense Agency (if Civil Defense is to be retained in the Department of Defense).

Three new major Unified Commands should be created: (1) A Strategic Command, composed of the existing Strategic Air Command, the Joint Strategic Target Planning Staff, the Continental Air Defense Command, and Fleet Ballistic Missile Operations; (2) A Tactical (or General Purpose) Command, composed of all combatant general purpose forces of the United States assigned to organized combatant units; and (3) A Logistics Command, to exercise for all combatant forces supervision of support activities, including supply distribution, maintenance, traffic management and transportation. No Commander of a Unified Command should be permitted to serve concurrently as Chief of his Military Service.

The responsibilities now delegated to the Joint Chiefs of Staff by the Secretary of Defense to serve as military staff in the chain of operational command with respect to the Unified Commands, and all other responsibilities so delegated which are related to military operations and the Unified Commands, should be assigned to a single senior military officer, who should also supervise the separate staff which provides staff support on military operations and the channel of communications from the President and Secretary of Defense to Unified Commands. This officer should report to the Secretary of Defense through the Deputy Secretary of Defense (Operations). This senior military officer could be either the Chairman of the Joint Chiefs of Staff, as an individual, not ex-officio, the Commander of the Tactical Command, or some other senior military officer, as determined by the President and the Secretary of Defense.

There should be an Assistant Secretary of Defense for each of the functions (c) through (f), inclusive, who reports and provides staff assistance to the Secretary of Defense through the Deputy Secretary of Defense (Operations). The Defense Communications Agency and the Civil Defense Agency would each be under the immediate supervision of a Director.

All intelligence functions of the Department of Defense and all communications functions should report to the Secretary of Defense through the Deputy Secretary of Defense for Operations.

5. The following steps should also be taken:

(a) To provide the staff support on military operations, and the channel of communications from the President and the Secretary of Defense to the Unified Commands, an operations staff, separate from all other military staffs, should be created.

(b) The responsibilities now delegated to the Joint Chiefs of Staff by the Secretary of Defense to serve as military staff in the chain of operational command with respect to the Unified Commands, and all other responsibilities so delegated which are related to military operations and the Unified Commands, should be rescinded; and consideration should be given to changing the title of the Chief of Naval Operations to Chief of Staff of the Navy.

(c) All staff personnel positions in the Organization of the Joint Chiefs of Staff and in the headquarters military staffs of the Military Services which are in support of activities, such as military operations, which are recommended for transfer to other organizational elements, should be eliminated.

(d) The Organization of the Joint Chiefs of Staff should be limited to include only the Joint Chiefs of Staff and a reconstituted Joint Staff limited in size to not more than 250 officers augmented by professional civilian analysts as required.

(e) The Unified Commanders should be given unfragmented command authority for their Commands, and the Commanders of component commands should be redesignated Deputies to the commander of the appropriate Unified Command, in order to make it unmistakably clear that the combatant forces are in the chain of command which runs exclusively through the Unified Commander;

(f) In consolidating the existing area Unified Commands into the Tactical Command, major organizational and functional advantages will be obtained by:

(1) Merging the Atlantic Command and the Strike Command;

(2) Abolishing the Southern Command and reassigning its functions to the merged Atlantic and Strike Commands;

(3) Abolishing the Alaskan Command and reassigning its general purpose function to the Pacific Command and its strategic defense functions to the Strategic Command; and

(4) Restructuring the command channels of the sub-unified commands.

(g) The responsibilities related to civil disturbances currently delegated to the Army should be redelegated to the Tactical Command; and

(h) The Unified Commanders should be given express responsibility and capability for making recommendations to the Deputy Secretary of Defense for Operations, for operational capabilities objectives and for allocations of force structures needed for the effective accomplishment of the missions assigned to their Commands.

6. The Deputy Secretary of Defense for Evaluation should be delegated the responsibility for evaluation and control-type activities, including:

(a) Comptroller (including internal audit and inspection services);

(b) Program and Force Analysis (a modification of the present Systems Analysis Unit);

(c) Test and Evaluation;

(d) Defense Contract Audit Agency; and

(e) Defense Test Agency.

There should be an Assistant Secretary of Defense for each of the functions (a) through (c) inclusive, who reports and provides staff assistance to the Secretary of the Defense through the Deputy Secretary of Defense for Evaluation.

AF IN THE DEFENSE DEPARTMENT

The Defense Contract Audit Agency should be continued as a Defense Agency, under the immediate supervision of a Director.

A Defense Test Agency should be created to perform the functions of overview of all Defense test and evaluation, designing or reviewing of designs for test, monitoring and evaluation of the entire Defense test program, and conducting tests and evaluations as required, with particular emphasis on operational testing, and on systems and equipment which span Service lines. The Defense Test Agency should be under the supervision of a civilian Director, reporting to the Secretary of Defense through the Deputy Secretary of Defense for Evaluation.

7. The number of Assistant Secretaries in each of the Military Departments should be set at three, and except for the Assistant Secretaries (Financial Management), they should serve as senior members of a personal staff to the Secretaries of the Military Departments without the existing limitations of purview imposed by formal functional assignments. The Assistant Secretary (Financial Management) should become the Comptroller of the Military Department, with a military deputy, as in the current organization in the Department of the Navy.

The Secretaries and Service Military Staffs should be integrated to the extent necessary to eliminate duplication; the functions related to military operations and intelligence should be eliminated; line type functions, e.g., personnel operations, should be transferred to command organizations; and the remaining elements should be reduced by at least thirty percent. (A study of the present staffs indicates that the Secretariats and Service staffs combined should total no more than 2,000 people for each Department.)

8. Class II activities (Army), Field Extensions (Air Force), and Commands and Bureaus (Navy), all of which are line, rather than staff in character, which are now organizationally located under the direct supervision of staff elements in the headquarters military staffs of the Services, should be transferred to existing command-type organizations within the Services.

9. The Defense Atomic Support Agency should be disestablished. Its functions for nuclear weapons management should be transferred to the operations staff under the Deputy Secretary of Defense for Operations, and its weapons effects test design function should be transferred to the Defense Test Agency.

10. The administration functions presently assigned to the Assistant Secretary of Defense (Administration) should be assigned to a Director of Pentagon Services, reporting to the immediate office of the Secretary of Defense. He should be responsible for operating the facilities and providing administrative support for the Washington Headquarters.

11. A Net Assessment Group should be created for the purpose of conducting and reporting net assessments of United States and foreign military capabilities and potentials. This group should consist of individuals from appropriate units in the Department of Defense, consultants and contract personnel appointed from time to time by the Secretary of Defense, and should report directly to him.

12. A Long-Range Planning Group should be created for the purpose of providing staff support to the Secretary of Defense with responsibility for long-range planning which

integrates net assessments, technological projections, fiscal planning, etc. This group should consist of individuals from appropriate units in the Department of Defense, consultants and contract personnel appointed from time to time by the Secretary of Defense, and should report directly to him.

13. A Coordinating Group should be established in the immediate office of the Secretary of Defense. The responsibilities of this Group should be to assist the Secretary of Defense and the Deputy Secretaries of Defense in coordinating the activities of the entire Department in the scheduling and follow-up of the various inter-Departmental liaison activities; to staff for the Secretary the control function for improvement and reduction of management information/control systems needed within the Department and required from Defense contractors; and to assure that each organizational charter of the Office of the Secretary of Defense is of proper scope and coordinated and in accordance with the assigned responsibility of the organization. The responsibility for the Department's Directive/Guidance System, currently assigned to the Assistant Secretary of Defense (Administration), should be assigned to this group. The coordinating group should be headed by a civilian Director, who should also serve as executive assistant to the Secretary of Defense.

14. The Army Topographic Command, the Naval Oceanographic Office and the Aeronautical Chart and Information Center should be combined into a unified Defense Map Service reporting to the Secretary of Defense through the Deputy Secretary of Defense for Management of Resources.

15. A new development policy for weapons systems and other hardware should be formulated and promulgated to cause a reduction of technical risks through demonstrated hardware before full-scale development, and to provide the needed flexibility in acquisition strategies. The new policy should provide for:

(a) Exploratory and advanced development of selected sub-systems and components independent of the development of weapon systems;

(b) The use of government laboratories and contractors to develop selected sub-systems and components on a long-term level of effort basis;

(c) More use of competitive prototypes and less reliance on paper studies;

(d) Selected lengthening of production schedules, keeping the system in production over a greater period of time;

(e) A general rule against concurrent development and production efforts, with the production decision deferred until successful demonstration of developmental prototypes;

(f) Continued trade-off between new weapon systems and modifications to existing weapon systems currently in production;

(g) Stricter limitations of elements of systems to essentials to eliminate "gold-plating";

(h) Flexibility in selecting type of contract most appropriate for development and the assessment of the technical risks involved;

(i) Flexibility in the application of a requirement for formal contract definition, in recognition of its inapplicability to many developments;

(j) Assurance of such matters as maintainability, reliability, etc., by means other than detailed documentation by contractors as a part of design proposals;

(k) Appropriate planning early in the development cycle for subsequent test and evaluation, and effective transition to the test and evaluation phase; and

(l) A prohibition of total package procurement.

16. The effectiveness of Program or Project Management should be improved by:

(a) Establishing a career specialty code for Program Managers in each Military Service and developing selection and training criteria that will insure the availability of an adequate number of qualified officers. The criteria should emphasize achieving a reasonable balance between the needs for knowledge of operational requirements and experience in management;

(b) Increasing the use of trained civilian personnel as program managers;

(c) Providing authority commensurate with the assigned responsibility and more direct reporting lines for program managers, particularly those operating in matrix organizational arrangements; and

(d) Giving the program manager directive authority, subject to applicable laws and regulations, over the contracting officer, and clarifying the fact that the contract auditor acts in an advisory role.

17. Increased use should be made of parametric costing techniques for developments and procurements to improve the quality of original and subsequent estimates, and to help offset the difficulties of estimating the costs of unknowns.

18. A separate program category* should be established for test and evaluation, especially operational testing, and the responsibility for overview of all Defense test and evaluation efforts should be assigned to the Defense Test Agency.

19. Specialist careers should be established for officers in such staff, technical and professional fields as research, development, intelligence, communications, automatic data processing, and procurement.

20. In order to improve the process of acquisition and retention of military personnel, the Executive Branch should develop, and submit to the Congress for its consideration as necessary, a total military personnel program which coordinates and reconciles all the separate considerations, particularly including; (1) military compensation and

---

* Program categories are those categories of activities used for internal planning and management in the Department, e.g., strategic offensive forces, strategic defensive forces, research and development, intelligence, etc.

retirement, (2) personnel policies on promotion and rotation, and (3) acquisition programs, such as Reserve Officers Training Corps.

21. The duration of assignments for officers should be increased, and should be as responsive to the requirements of the job as to the career plan of the officer. Officers continued on an assignment for this reason should not be disadvantaged in opportunity for promotion.

22. Executive Orders and Department of Defense Directives with respect to matters of equal employment opportunity for Department of Defense military personnel, civilian employees and contractors, as set forth in the existing comprehensive programs for insuring equal opportunity, should be administered from a sufficiently high organizational level in the Department to assure effective implementation, and the procedures for assessing penalties for non-compliance should be reviewed and clarified.

23. The Secretary of Defense should recommend clarifying changes in conflict of interest statutes, should amend the regulations to clarify them, and should make certain administrative changes to insure uniform enforcement.[22]

The Blue Ribbon Defense Panel report was 237 pages and contained 113 specific recommendations. Fitzhugh remarked that 90 percent of the recommendations could be carried out without legislation, which meant that Secretary Laird could select ideas that he liked and use them. Many of the recommendations dealing with procurement already had been put into effect by Secretary Laird and Deputy Secretary Packard in the year that the report was in preparation. Three of the 14 members of the panel filed dissenting opinions, emphasizing disagreements about the proposed downgrading of the services, service secretaries, and service chiefs. These matters, together with the recommendation for three principal defense groups of military operations, resources, and evaluation, drew most rhetoric. Admiral Moorer, then chairman of the Joint Chiefs, later remarked that the Blue Ribbon Defense Panel report was "so bad that five of the members [actually only three, although two other members were compelled to leave the panel early] dissented.... Nothing of substance was ever accomplished by this study. But you will find it as a reference in every subsequent study," Moorer added. In mid-August 1970 it was reported that Admiral Moorer insisted on and got a no-holds-barred session for the Joint Chiefs with Laird and Packard. Moorer was said to have told Laird that the services, service secretaries, and service chiefs could not be downgraded; that strategic direction of the armed forces could not be workably separated from planning and from individual service responsibilities; that the unified command structure was satisfactory and did not require creation of super commands for tactics, strategy, and logistics; and that the Joint Chiefs of Staff machinery was highly efficient, had been perfected over the years, and should not be tampered with. Later on Moorer would caution that his service as JCS chairman at a time that the United States was heavily involved in a very unpopular war had convinced him that "organizations and procedures in the military command structure must be set up in such a way as to work particularly well in wartime rather than during an extended period of peace when the priorities of public interest in the military invariably get turned around."[23]

In a public commentary on the Blue Ribbon Defense Panel Report, Secretary Laird concurred in general with the panel's objectives, but preferred to implement new management concepts at a measured rather than precipitous pace. He remarked that he wanted "to avoid the tendencies toward increased staffing and overhead ... inherent in many of the specific Panel recommendations."[24] In a blunt talk in Los Angeles, Deputy Secretary Packard disavowed the recommendation for the three deputy secretaries of defense. He said: "The report greatly underrates the Joint Chiefs of Staff." He added: "We intend to give the Service Secretaries and their Services more responsibility so that they can do their jobs." Of the 113 recommendations of the Blue Ribbon Defense Panel, Packard reported acceptance of 48, conceptual implementation of 33 others, continued consideration of 21, and rejection of only 11. The 11 rejections out of hand had to do with the organization of the recommended major new unified strategic, tactical, and logistics unified commands and assignments of deputy secretariats.[25] In 1971 Secretary Laird implemented a number of changes in organization that were in part attributable to the Blue Ribbon Defense Panel. These included: establishment of the Office of Assistant Secretary of Defense (Intelligence) and of the Office of Assistant Secretary of Defense (Telecommunications), of the deputy director (Test and Evaluation) within the Office of the Director, Defense Research and Engineering; and establishment of the Central Security Service, Defense Investigative Service, Defense Security Assistance Agency, and Defense Mapping Agency.[26]

Although it was reported that Laird and Packard agreed at the meeting with Admiral Moorer and the Joint Chiefs in August 1970 that the Joint Chiefs of Staff ought to be left alone and not tampered with and that means ought to be found to decentralize authority to the service departments, these matters were kept under study during 1971. In the end, Laird announced that he did not share the Blue Ribbon Defense Panel's view that US military command structure was "unwieldy and unworkable in crisis and too fragmentary to provide the best potential for coordinate response to a general war situation." Experience in the first three years of the Nixon administration nevertheless demonstrated that improved management and control of forces was greatly needed. Deputy Secretary Packard and Admiral Moorer analyzed the problem and effected some solutions. In the command structure effected in 1958 the chain of command ran from the president to the secretary of defense to the commander in chief, unified and specified commands. In this same year, however, Secretary of Defense Neil McElroy directed that orders would be transmitted "through the Joint Chiefs of Staff." Thus the Joint Chiefs were an agent for transmitting orders; General Taylor pointed out that they had "a staff function" and no command authority over the CINCs. The

Blue Ribbon Defense Panel recommended that for clarity McElroy's direction should be rescinded.[27]

In 1972 Secretary Laird acknowledged that "limited advantages may perhaps be realized by separating the Joint Chiefs of Staff from the operational matters" but that "the total impact of this action must also be considered." The old procedure was kept in effect; however, in a revision of the Worldwide Military Command and Control System (WWMCCS), it was provided that critical, time-sensitive, instructions would go from the national command authorities to the chairman of the JCS who, acting for the JCS, would have authority to pass instructions directly to the operating forces. The role of the Joint Chiefs of Staff thus remained one of agency, not of command, and only the president or the secretary of defense could originate orders to the unified and specified commanders.[28]

Even before the Blue Ribbon Defense Panel met, the Department of Defense had begun to examine the US unified and specified command structure, particularly in view of President Nixon's new Nixon Doctrine and Strategy of Realistic Deterrence. On 1 January 1972, as will be seen, the US Readiness Command replaced the US Strike Command and the STRICOM's geographical areas of responsibility were reassigned. The Blue Ribbon Defense Panel recommended a very strong increase in the authority of unified commanders, namely:

> The Unified Commanders should be given unfragmented command authority for their commands, and the commanders of component commands should be redesignated Deputies to the commander of the appropriate Unified Command, in order to make it unmistakably clear that the combatant forces are in the chain of command which runs exclusively through the Unified Commander.[29]

Secretary Laird did not accept this recommendation, pointing out that unified commanders had maximum authority. Laird ruled:

> The current Unified Command Plan gives the commanders of Unified and Specified Commands maximum authority possible consistent with statutory requirements. This includes the authority to exercise operational command over all forces assigned to the command. The Unified Commanders have the authority to exercise those functions of command involving the control of assigned resources, composition of subordinate forces, assignment of tasks, designation of objectives, and full authoritative direction necessary to accomplish the mission of the command. In consonance with the National Security Act of 1947, as amended, each Military Department is responsible for the administration of its forces assigned by that department to the combatant commands. The Defense Department is operating under this system at the present time.[30]

Although congressional legislation provided the basic structure of national defense organization, every president had retained the authority to take military advice where he chose. "We can play with organizational charts all we want to," commented Sen John C. Culver, a key member of the Armed Services Committee, in 1978, "but what ultimately determines the process is what is congenial to the decision maker—that particular president's preference and most comfortable mode of operation."[31] In 1971–72 the handling of an appropriate response to increasing North Vietnamese aggression in Southeast Asia posed unusual complexities to the niceties of defense chart-books. In early May 1972 Admiral Moorer asked Chief of Naval Operations Adm Elmo Zumwalt to produce for President Nixon a concept for mining Haiphong and other North Vietnamese ports, this without the knowledge of Secretary Laird, who was strongly committed to Vietnamization and opposed to the commitment of additional US forces to the war.[32] When the increased US activity occurred, Secretary of the Navy John H. Chaffee said that he would have opposed the Hanoi and Haiphong minings, but he had had "no inkling" that such was planned. Secretary of the Air Force Seamans said that he first knew about the increase in air raids to take place against North Vietnam when he saw accounts of it on television. A little later, Seamans ruefully admitted that even though he had attempted to remain abreast of overall Air Force operations to perform his basic responsibility for managing resources and for acting as an adviser to the secretary of defense he never learned of diverted B-52 bombings into Cambodia until long after the fact. Embarrassed about being kept in the dark about Cambodian bombing, Secretary Seamans stated:

> I think a way should be found for the service secretaries to be more involved in operational activities. I think it is undesirable to be a service secretary and not know of something of this importance is going on.... I think the chain of command must be kept simple and straightforward, and I do not think the service secretary ought to be in the chain of command but I think that he should be involved in important operational matters in a timely way.[33]

After this, DOD regulations charged service chiefs to keep service secretaries informed on matters before the Joint Chiefs of Staff, but when he was queried about such matters Gen George Brown, JCS chairman, responded in 1976: "Today, the Service Secretaries are responsible for procurement, maintenance and training of forces. Once the forces are trained and equipped, they are turned over to the unified and specific commanders, who in turn operate under the Secretary of Defense."[34]

Personnel Cuts Affected Unified Commands and Organization

In the Defense Reorganization Act of 1958 Congress affirmed the validity and necessity of a unified command concept. With the advice and assistance of the Joint Chiefs of Staff, the president, through the secretary of defense, was authorized to establish unified or specified combatant commands for the performance of military missions and to determine the Army, Navy, and Air Force force structure to be assigned to the combatant commands for the performance of military missions. The importance of the structure was emphasized by the fact that the president personally approved and signed the Unified Command Plan, assigning missions and responsibilities to commanders in chief. The command plan was expected to

IDEAS, CONCEPTS, DOCTRINE

provide organizations that would permit an immediate application of defense forces in wartime, but the organization also had to reflect political accommodations to mold allied national forces into a cohesive unity. Effective on 1 January 1973 the Nixon-Laird administration revised the Unified Command Plan for the first time since 1963, and these worldwide command arrangements continued under scrutiny during the 1970s. In September 1977 President Jimmy Carter asked for an "unconstrained examination" of the national military command structure. The study, prepared by New York banker Richard C. Steadman, when released in July 1978, addressed the subject of the Unified Command Plan at some length but contained no "ultimate solutions" since it was thought possible "to draw up four or five alternative UCPs, each one about as good as the other." The report concluded, however, that "changes to the UCP are usually controversial, producing split opinions among the JCS."[35]

The National Command Plan organizational doctrines existing in the 1970s ran back to World War II. Each unified commander was expected to have a joint staff, comprised of officers from all military services which had forces assigned to the command. Although the unified commander exercised "operational command" over assigned forces, this was expected to be exercised through component commanders of military services having forces assigned. The component commander thus melded the "operational command" flowing from the national command authorities through the unified commander and the "service supervision" originating in military departments. This organizational doctrine was expensive in terms of general officers and headquarters personnel. Thus, in the NATO organization, the US European Command was located in Stuttgart, the US Army Command in Heidelberg, the US Air Force Command in Wiesbaden, and the US Navy Command in London. Europe also was divided into regions (North, Center, South, and Flanks), with land, naval, and air organizations for each region. In 1972 there were 37 headquarters in the Allied Command Europe, and the United States participated in 24 of them.[36] With the dissolution of USCINCMEAFSA effective on 1 January 1972, the area of responsibility of the US European Command was extended to include the Red Sea, the Persian Gulf, and the Middle East to the eastern border of Iran. This was intended to strengthen the planning capability for defense of the southern flank of NATO and for countering increased Soviet presence in the Mediterranean and Middle East areas. Also on 1 January 1972 the scope of responsibility of the Pacific Command was expanded to include the Indian Ocean to 62 degrees east longitude, those South American countries formerly holding membership in USCINCMEAFSA, the Aleutian Islands, and a portion of the Arctic Ocean. As has been seen, the US Pacific Command included component commands—ARPAC, NAVPAC, PACAF—and subunified commands—the Military Assistance Command, Vietnam (MACV), the Military Assistance Command, Thailand (MACTHAI), and US Forces Korea. Both Generals Westmoreland and Abrams were elected as COMUSMACV to serve as their own Army component commander. To overcome the deficiencies of the subunified command organizational structure,

COMUSMACV designated specified component commands as executive agents for common-user logistical support in specified corps areas in Vietnam and named the COMUSMACV for air as the executive agent for MACV air operations. In the 1 January 1972 delineation, the area of responsibility for the US Atlantic Command was expanded to include the international waters around Africa and South America. The Atlantic Command had no Army or significant Air Force forces assigned (one small Air Force unit was designated the Iceland Defense Force). The US Southern Command (SOUTHCOM) remained primarily responsible for defending the Panama Canal, offering military assistance activities in Latin America, and planning contingency operations that might be required in Latin America. The US Alaskan Command was assigned a geographical area of responsibility, but its principal mission was to participate in North American air defense.[37]

In 1973 Secretary James Schlesinger took note of the soaring costs of military manpower and ordered actions to review the superstructure of the Defense Department, field organizations, and major military command headquarters with a view to decreasing headquarters staffing. As a corollary activity, Schlesinger wanted to achieve a greater degree of force interdependence among the services without "going into the delicate area of roles and missions at this time." Schlesinger remarked, "At this stage, I would predict that the JCS and the military services will not willingly or readily volunteer for any traumatic experiences."[38] The assignment of review of the defense superstructure was given to William Brehm, assistant secretary of defense for manpower, who had close contact with Gen George Brown. Brehm said, "When I talked with General Brown, I found that he was very positive about the whole idea of conducting the review, particularly after he became chairman [of the Joint Chiefs of Staff]."[39] The Air Force's approach to reducing staffs was to streamline headquarters personnel in many cases to people absolutely needed for operations and matters of actual control of forces and to concentrate functions such as chaplain, legal, finance, comptroller, and civil engineering. Thus, the headquarters staffs of the Third Air Force in the United Kingdom, the Seventeenth Air Force in West Germany, and the Sixteenth Air Force in Spain were cut back by over 50 percent.[40]

At the urging of Secretary Schlesinger that the Army obtain more combat capability from the manpower resources, Gen Creighton Abrams developed planning to increase the Army's 13-1/3 active divisions to 16, chiefly by shifting manpower spaces from support to combat units. Abrams's plan involved closing seven Army headquarters around the world, including US Army, Alaska, and the US Army Southern Command. The question of closing the Army Pacific component command in Hawaii drew the most questions, and to these inquiries Abrams retorted: "The way things work, it has nothing to add and it is too far away to subtract."[41] Secretary Schlesinger would not agree to closing the Army Pacific Command unless General Brown was accepted as JCS chairman. "General Brown did support it," remembered Brehm, "and this was important in making the change come about."[42] ARPAC was disestablished effective 31 December 1974, at which

IDEAS, CONCEPTS, DOCTRINE

time a CINCPAC support group, headed by an Army major general began to provide some of the functions of an Army component commander such as liaison, advice, and assistance to PACOM, the Navy, and the Air Force component commanders. PACOM exercised operational command over Army units through subordinate unified commanders, the most important Army units being in Korea. In Korea, effective on 1 July 1974, Headquarters Eighth Army, the United Nations Command, and US Forces Korea were merged into US Forces Korea, which served as a PACOM subordinate unified command with a four-star Army officer in command.[43]

The Army's decision to eliminate Army component commands in the Unified Command Plan was said to have been applauded in the House Military Appropriations Subcommittee, and it was suggested that the Air Force and Navy might want to do the same. At that juncture, however, the Air Force already had made larger headquarters staff cuts than had the Army, though the Army's cuts were more dramatic. General Brown called for some caution in regard to reducing Air Force support for unified commands. "We can do lots of things in peacetime," he warned, "but we do not want to disrupt an organization that can support combat action."[44] In the Pacific, nonetheless, the Air Force followed a policy of reducing its presence as tensions diminished. In fiscal year 1974, Headquarters Fifth Air Force in Japan was reduced in size when Headquarters Pacific Air Forces (PACAF) took over a number of functions not directly related to operations and matters of actual control of US Air Force forces on Okinawa and in Korea. As it turned out, moreover, the commander, Fifth Air Force, commander, US Forces Japan, and as such had many functions other than purely Air Force business. In the command shuffles in Korea in 1974, there was some argumentation in the Air Force that Headquarters Fifth Air Force ought to move to Korea. But such a move would have severed the peacetime interface between Headquarters Fifth Air Force/US Forces Japan and the Japanese Self-Defense Forces. General Brown also said: "In my view . . . if it were in Korea and hostilities were to start, the first thing we would have to do would be to get the headquarters out of the way and get it back to Japan." Thus Headquarters Fifth Air Force remained in Japan in new facilities built for it at Yokota. In the command reorganization in Korea in 1964, the commander of US Air Forces Korea/314th Air Division reported to the commander of the Fifth Air Force, who was responsible to CINCPACAF as CINCPAC's Air Force component commander for the status of forces and training of air units in Korea. In time of war, the commander of the US Air Force Korea/314th Air Division would report immediately to the CINCUNC/COMUSKOREA, as the senior US officer in Korea, and would become the air component commander for him.[45]

In 1974 the Joint Chiefs of Staff worked on a revision of the Unified Command Plan that Secretary Schlesinger also undertook to find ways "to gain management effectiveness by reducing headquarters and support units, and at the same time improving command and control of combat units."[46] On 28 February 1975 Schlesinger announced disestablishment of the Continental Air Defense

Command (CONAD) and the Alaskan Command (ALCOM) as unified commands. CONAD was replaced by a specified air defense command. In a novel command arrangement, ALCOM was replaced by the Alaskan Air Command, whose commander gained a three-star billet and became the senior military officer in Alaska, the DOD coordinating authority there, and the commander of the Alaskan North American Air Defense region. As a part of this reorganization, Schlesinger announced that the concept of a joint task force would receive added emphasis in Alaska. In the event of a natural disaster, emergency, or hostilities, the Alaskan Air Force commander would command a reinforcing task force organization and would report directly through the Joint Chiefs of Staff to the national command authorities.[47] The Air Force did not plan to identify specific units to reinforce Alaska but instead to pull units for the purpose from available and combat-ready sources in various parts of the United States.[48]

When the Army had disestablished the US Army Pacific Command, General Brown had opposed a similar disestablishment of the Pacific Air Forces until work on revisions of the US Unified Command Plan jelled. There were some arguments, for example, that US Forces Korea ought to be made into a unified command for Northeast Asia or at the very best there should be an arrangement whereby the commander of US Forces Korea would remain under PACOM in peacetime but in times of crisis would report directly to Washington. In July 1974 Gen Louis L. Wilson, Jr., took command of PACAF and began to look to its future. In the drawdown of US forces in the Western Pacific, PACAF would retain the Fifth Air Force in Japan and the Thirteenth Air Force in the Philippines. In the Philippines the Thirteenth Air Force would have only one base—Clark Air Base on Luzon.

General Wilson was impressed with PACAF's remoteness from the Western Pacific—it was closer from Hawaii to the United States than to Korea or the Philippines. He wanted to relocate PACAF headquarters in the Western Pacific, but he could find no place for it. At this same juncture, Secretary of the Air Force John L. McLucas and Gen David Jones accepted "Tight Belt West" plans that PACAF should be disestablished and that the Tactical Air Command should assume the majority of Air Force management and support functions, conducted through senior Air Force commanders in the Pacific. General Jones stated:

> The Tactical Air Command has historically been the doctrinal "parent" of our tactical air forces, in the sense that among other responsibilities, TAC is the principal point of contact and coordination with the Army's Training and Doctrine Command, develops and tests combat tactics, trains all our tactical aircrews, and has operational control over the majority of the US based tactical air forces. We propose to move toward broadening TAC's direct role in tactical airpower world wide by extending its responsibilities to our tactical Air Force units in the Western Pacific.[49]

This "application of the single manager concept" promised to free approximately 2,000 headquarters and support personnel assigned to Headquarters PACAF. In December 1974 Secretary Schlesinger announced that he had approved the recommendation to disestablish Headquarters PACAF, but that this would not be done pending review of the entire Unified Command Plan. As it happened, Gen Robert Dixon, the TAC commander, was not in favor of the plan to have TAC take over the functions of PACAF, although he did not fight the project. General Wilson was also not in favor of the disestablishment. He noted that in the spring of 1975 somebody put the proposal to bed; he didn't know who. At any rate, it was apparently decided that TAC would write some basic policies and regulations, and the rank of CINCPACAF would be fixed at lieutenant general.[50]

Said Air Force Secretary Thomas C. Reed in February 1976:

> Because there is a finite amount of money, because the Soviet threats are very severe, and because the difficulties of penetrating to the Soviet targets are very difficult, we have had to make some very hard choices. The Air Force has faced up during the past 2 years to cutting out a great many things that are important. As the Department of Defense spokesmen said in their various appearances this year, we are past the point of cutting out fat, of cutting any support; we are now into substantive meat.[51]

In addition to other cuts, the Air Force in 1975 redesignated the Eighth Air Force on Guam to Barksdale AFB, Louisiana, where it replaced the Second Air Force, whose designation was retired. The Air Force kept the 3d Air Division on Guam. At about this same time the Air Force announced that the Air Force Communications Service (AFCS) at Richards-Gebaur AFB, Missouri, was to be moved to Scott AFB, Illinois, and merged with the Military Airlift Command (MAC). However, this merger did not take place. Instead, after it was moved to Scott AFB, AFCS continued as a separate command. MAC provided common, nontechnical support through a shared-staff arrangement. In 1976 Air Force Headquarters Command at Bolling AFB, Washington, D.C., was abolished. In 1977 the Air Force resisted a proposal to subdivide the Air Defense Command (ADCOM) among several other commands, including dual tasking of TAC's tactical fighters with an air defense/interception mission, but ADCOM's aerospace defense resources were transferred to other major commands within the Air Force in 1979.[52] The reductions in Army organizational structure affected by General Abrams also affected PACOM activities and command interrelations with the Air Force at the field army-tactical air force level. Some maintained that the Army component, US Army Pacific, should be reestablished; this headquarters was needed to provide more senior Army representation in military diplomatic activities in the large PACOM area where ground forces played important roles in many countries. General Abram's acceptance of a new Army doctrine that the Army corps would be the highest echelon for tactical maneuver and strategy decisions in effect eliminated the Army's group/field army; the Air Force found the "corps concept" to be short-sighted as it eliminated joint force interface at the component level of command.[53]

Secretary Brown and the Steadman Report

When President Jimmy Carter assumed office in 1977 he gave special attention to his selection of a secretary of defense. "The Pentagon needed some discipline," he reminisced, "and I wanted both a scientist with a thorough knowledge of the most advanced technology and a competent business manager, strong-willed enough to prevail in the internecine struggles among the different military services."[54] President Carter selected Harold Brown, who had served as director of Defense Research and Engineering and secretary of the Air Force during the Johnson-McNamara years. And so, Brown returned to high office in the Department of Defense after an eight-year absence and found that many old problems were still around. Brown remarked:

> If Government officials [would] stay in the executive branch long enough to have to live with the problems they have made, it would lead to more responsible behavior on their part. They would be more careful about making the same mistakes again. I hoped that I had avoided that by being away 8 years, but I find that in coming back I recognize not only the same general problems but also some of the same problems in the same programs....[55]

In regard to the needs to be faced in trying to organize the top military echelons, Brown conceived the problems revolved around planning and executing the operation of military forces in peace and war, how to get the best military advice into political-military decisions made generally by civilians, and how best to structure, equip, and train military forces. "Organization as such," Brown said, "cannot deal fully with any of these problems by itself, though poor organization makes each of them more difficult." Brown observed that in his judgment since the late 1950s no president or secretary of state had found defense organization satisfactory either in terms of planning and operations or of military advice. The question then was why had not Defense Department administrations—especially his own—put forward a plan for reorganization. He answered:

> Any such change requires a major expenditure or investment of political capital. It requires good relations with the Congress, and it requires strong Presidential backing.... Such changes are best proposed either by a departing or recently departed administration, which cannot be accused of self-aggrandizement. It requires also informed support by an incumbent administration.[56]

Early in his administration, Secretary Brown revealed his agreement with President Eisenhower's message that "separate ground, sea and air warfare is gone forever." In an address at the commissioning of the USS *Eisenhower* in 1977, Brown predicted that future operations would involve "coordinated efforts of land, air, and ... naval forces, in elements functionally configured ... led by officers who understand the functions and qualities that our armed services share, as well as the particular capabilities and traditions which enrich each of them."[57] Brown reiterated on another occasion:

> Almost all modern military operations are joint operations and have been so since World War II. Reconnaissance, target acquisition, and designation are now very largely done from the air, or even from space; the ranges of manned and unmanned attack vehicles, ballistic or aerodynamic, launched from land or sea, are much larger than they were before; the land and sea battles are now very strongly influenced, if not dominated, by control of the air; and air and sea forces need land bases.... For all these reasons, the operational commands charged with planning and executing combat operations

require a much closer integration of the different services than was necessary in the past, even in World War II.[58]

Secretary Brown recognized that improvement was needed but believed that an effort should first be made to achieve it without new legislative or massive reorganizations, the dominant theme being an emphasis on jointness. He believed there was no way a committee like the JCS could function in the chain of command, and so he used his chairman of the Joint Chiefs—Gen George Brown succeeded by Gen David Jones—as his agent to the unified and specified commands. "I practically never issued an order directly . . . almost always the . . . chairman sent it out. It was his responsibility to consult as much as he felt necessary with his colleagues."[59] One of Brown's early innovations was to require each CINC to send him every 90 days a personal letter describing the situation in the writer's command. In September 1977 President Carter signed a memorandum calling for an "unconstrained examination" of the national military command structure, and Secretary Brown was ready with a study director and a study plan. The "Report to the Secretary of Defense on the National Military Command Structure," prepared under direction of New York investment banker Richard C. Steadman, took the better part of six months before it was ready to be released in July 1978. The report did not recommend spectacular changes as the Blue Ribbon Defense Panel had done; for the most part it contained practical recommendations for making the system work better. The report noted:

> What emerged . . . was a consensus that, by and large, the system had been generally adequate to meet our national security needs in peacetime, crisis, and wartime. We did find, however, a general perception of some fundamental shortcomings which may make it incapable of dealing adequately with our future needs.[60]

The main thrust of the report looked toward strengthening the JCS chairman, particularly in providing national advice on program/budget and constrained force issues, and toward enhancing the role and effectiveness of the JCS joint staff. The report concluded that joint staff work could be improved, without structural change, by soliciting more guidance from senior officers prior to staffing; by having fewer requirements for service consensus, which resulted in watered-down compromises; by more analysis of alternatives; and finally by assigning more capable officers to the joint staff. At the end of the Steadman report an admonition was appended:

> In the event that these measures are not implemented, or if they should not prove effective . . . then solutions of a more fundamental nature directed at resolving the inherent tensions in the current organization, such as separating the joint advice and command functions from those of service administration, would become necessary. This might be accomplished by establishing a body of National Military Advisors entirely independent of Service responsibilities, although this would be drastic and controversial.[61]

As it happened both Secretary Brown and the Steadman report showed great concern about the status and prospects for US unified commands overseas. Secretary Brown wanted to give unified commanders greater control over his component commands that responded more to service headquarters in the Pentagon. This included initial planning for contingencies that ought to originate in the unified commands. The unified commanders needed to have an increased role in determining military requirements and budgets. Both Brown and Steadman were critical of the command chain in the Vietnam War. Brown said:

> In the Vietnam war . . . the Joint Chiefs as a group really had very little to say. That wasn't enough to win the war, but without it it would have been even worse. Certainly, the command chain in Vietnam, during the Vietnam war, was the most fouled up thing in recent history, in part because the Joint Chiefs refused to face up to the issue of how you organize command in the field for the most efficient operations.[62]

A major portion of the Steadman report was given over to a command by command evaluation of the US unified and specified commands. The report also focused on US experience in wartime/crisis handling since the defense reorganization of 1958. The report offered only general observations about DOD management of the Vietnam War:

> First, and most importantly, however imperfect our command arrangements may have been, few would make the case that the nature of the command system had any appreciably negative effect on the conduct of the war. . . . Second, in thinking about the future we should take little comfort in the fact that we were able to work with a jury-rigged command structure in Vietnam. . . . Third, Washington certainly was too deeply involved in the details of actually running the war, particularly the air war in the north. On the other hand, we believe that Washington failed to use the analytical tools available to evaluate with both overall policy and operational performance. Neither the reasonableness of stated objectives and the strategy for obtaining them, nor the cost-benefit analysis of various tactical options was subject to rigorous scrutiny. Moreover, Washington did not exercise independent judgment when evaluating requests from commanders in the field. There was a tendency to give the commander what he wanted. . . . If the US ever again is involved in a protracted war, its basic premises, its strategy, and its tactics should be subjected to rigorous analysis in Washington.[63]

In addition to the broad impression of the Vietnam War, the Steadman group studied 10 large and small crises: Middle East War (1967); sinking of the USS *Liberty* (1967); capture of the USS *Pueblo* (1968); Middle East War (1973); Cypress War (1974); Evacuation from Cambodia (1975); evacuation from Saigon (1975); seizure of the SS *Mayaguez* (1975); Beirut evacuations (1976); and the Korea tree-cutting incident (1976). The study concluded that crisis built around CINC's contingency plan "seemed to run more smoothly than those that were predominantly conducted *ad hoc*." There was, however, a notable tendency to bypass command channels, since communications advancements made it possible for a remote decisionmaker to talk directly with on-scene commanders. The report cautioned:

IDEAS, CONCEPTS, DOCTRINE

> In sum, military commanders must be aware that *any* use of military forces will be of interest to the command authorities and that employment of these forces may be closely directed from Washington. The civilian leadership, on the other hand, should be aware that by-passing the established chain of command does cause problems and may add some risks.[64]

Although unified and specified commanders prepared contingency plans, the Steadman report indicated that individual theater readiness or contingency plans were not collectively reconciled on a unified basis. The position of under secretary of defense for policy, created at Secretary Brown's behest in 1977, had been given staff responsibility for the interaction of foreign policy and defense policy, for planning, and for helping the secretary of defense evaluate the advice of the Joint Chiefs of Staff on military strategy and operations. Secretary Brown also had felt a need for a small operational staff—possibly best to be shared with the chairman of the JCS—to review the adequacy of military contingency plans.[65] The Steadman report recommended that the under secretary for policy should assure that national security policy and objectives were provided and reflected in JCS/Joint Staff plans for contingencies/crises, conventional wars, and tactical and strategic nuclear wars. Under a new planning guidance for contingency planning issued by Secretary Brown in 1979, the under secretary for policy was charged with reviewing JCS guidance for contingency planning as well as the plans themselves on the secretary of defense's behalf.[66]

In a reflection of his service in Washington both as chief of staff of the Air Force and the chairman of Joint Chiefs of Staff, Gen George Brown noted that Secretary Harold Brown "had me doing the things Steadman recommends" but that "the big difference is that I was not provided with any staff help; therefore I had to discuss these very important programmatic and weapons systems problems and draw on things I knew before I got the job, with no help from a staff."[67] In search of advisory and evaluation talent, General Brown as early as 1978 drew upon a study group of five retired flag officers—Gen William V. McBride, US Air Force; Gen Walter T. Kerwin, US Army; Adm Frederick H. Michaelis, US Navy; Gen Samuel Jaskilka, US Marine Corps; and Lt Gen Charles A. Corcoran, US Army—and one civilian, William K. Brehm. The group was known as the Special Study Group of the Chairman of the Joint Chiefs of Staff, and in 1978 it evaluated Nifty Nugget, which, as will be seen, was an influential mobilization and deployment exercise of US forces that resulted in substantial changes in the US Readiness Command. In 1980 the group evaluated follow-up check exercises called Proud Spirit. In these exercises the group's primary task was to determine the effectiveness of military operations planning and execution and of DOD crisis management under simulated major mobilization and deployment conditions. Following the evaluation of Proud Spirit for the Joint Chiefs of Staff, Gen David Jones, who had become JCS chairman, asked the group to analyze the overall JCS organization and procedures. He also asked the group to confer with the senior chiefs, the

CINCs, and other senior military officers to obtain their impressions and suggestions, and then to prepare a report for him.[68]

After a study involving a comparison of their own experiential views (three of the five military members had served lengthy tours as vice chiefs of their respective services) with the views of officers currently serving in highest positions of military leadership, the group members hammered out findings and recommendations in a long succession of meetings. Work that began in the spring of 1981 culminated in an unclassified report dated April 1982. The study group proposed several initiatives to increase "jointness" and "improve joint activities." Each initiative was judged important in its own right, but the steps had to be viewed collectively to appreciate their essential impact. The group also stressed that

> initiatives taken by the JCS to increase "jointness" and improve Joint activities will have maximum impact only if the civilian leaders—the President, the Secretary of Defense, and other Defense executives, both now and in the future—actively support the improved JCS organization, and solicit and use its products. Such support goes beyond pro forma meetings; it requires a basic change in approach on the part of the civilian leadership from the general pattern of the last 20 years or more. The Chairman must have a strong voice in defense councils, both formally and informally, representing the Joint community, including the CINC's. The advice of the Service chiefs, as a corporate group along with the Chairman, must be actively solicited on the wide variety of national issues to which they can contribute in unique ways.[69]

The recommendations of the group were: (1) Establish the position of vice chairman in the grade of general/admiral to act for the JCS chairman in the chairman's absence. (2) Refine the process of focusing the attention of the JCS on issues of major national significance and strengthen the chairman's authority to resolve other issues. (3) Require the Joint Staff to prepare the service chiefs for JCS meetings and to support the chiefs generally in the resolution of joint issues they address. (4) Change the practices and policies that result in overemphasis on the consensus-seeking "committee" approach to the development and approval of joint papers. (5) Improve the preparation and experience levels of service officers assigned to the Joint Staff and other Joint activities such as Unified Command headquarters. (6) Involve the CINCs and their staffs in Joint Staff activities. (7) Strengthen the Joint Staff through an organizational realignment that improves workload distribution. As part of the increased emphasis on preparation of officers for joint duty, the study group strongly endorsed a recommendation made by Gen Russell E. Dougherty, USAF, Retired, for the National Defense University's (NDU) Board of Visitors that a special NDU resident course be set up for all newly selected general and flag officers of the line to increase their sensitivity to and knowledge of Joint matters. The study group also recommended a special study of the unified command concept to determine how the role of the CINC could be increased in planning and operations, particularly in the relationships between the unified command headquarters and the component command headquarters and between the unified command headquarters and the Joint Chief of Staff/Joint Staff.[70]

Reorganization Proposals Foster Service Interdependency

In congressional hearings in early 1982, Gen David Jones skipped much of the usual chairman's thick posture statement because, he said:

> I think the most important issue facing us today in national security is the issue of the organization of the military. We do not have today an organization that can use ... essential resources as efficiently as it should.... We have made some progress, but the system is remarkably resistant to change. The system we have developed is a patchwork which grew out of our World War II experience and only has endured a few changes since the National Security Act of 1947.[71]

General Jones was completing four years as JCS chairman, and he said his perspective was quite different from when he had served as Air Force chief of staff. Jones stressed that the Joint Chiefs were a committee and that committees were "notoriously poor for running things," particularly when they were expected to act unanimously. Jones's specific recommendations were to make the JCS chairman—rather than the JCS—the principal adviser to the national command authorities, especially on issues where fundamental service interests clashed; to give the chairman more oversight of the readiness of the joint commands; to give the chairman a more direct hand in the selection, promotion, training, and assignment of people in joint positions; to provide for a deputy chairman; and to eliminate the service staffs' ability effectively to "veto" the content of joint advice. Although most of these specific recommendations dealt with the chairman, Jones emphasized that he was most interested in strengthening the joint system. "We have combat commanders in the field.... They don't have enough say in what is going on, whether it is in resource allocation or new programs. So it is the joint system that I would like to see strengthened," Jones emphasized. When asked for a personal example where his reforms would have resulted in a better product from the JCS, Jones replied: "During the Vietnam war there was a great fragmentation of air effort. We fought multiple air wars in Southeast Asia with only a loose coordination rather than an efficient central direction."[72]

In an article in *Armed Forces Journal International* published on 31 March 1982, Gen Edward C. Meyer, chief of staff, US Army, agreed with General Jones, but urged still more reform:

> My own personal judgment is that the changes urged by General Jones, while headed in the right direction, do not go far enough to correct what ails the JCS.... We must find a way to provide better balanced, sounder, and more timely advice from senior Service professionals in addition to strengthening the Chairman and the Joint Staff.[73]

Meyer subsequently stated that he wrote the article because "I consider the way in which we develop our forces and the way in which we provide the advice on those force developments to be a very elemental issue."[74] In the article and in subsequent congressional hearings, Meyer ticked off the basic changes he thought necessary:

> First, I believe we need to separate the service chiefs from the day-to-day operations of the Joint Staff. They would no longer be members of the JCS. . . . Second, in lieu of the current JCS, I would propose that we create a body of senior officers who would deal on a day-to-day basis with the kind of critical issues and the allocation of resource issues that are essential if we are to have a balanced military force. . . . Third, I believe we have to increase the role of the chairman so he is the provider of military advice concerning inter-service capabilities and requirements, and the provider of advice on operational matters. . . . Fourth, we need to increase the role of the unified commanders so that they are involved in contingency planning, as well as the determination of requirements. . . . Fifth, I believe there needs to be a decreased role for civilians below the level of the Secretary of Defense in providing military input on national security matters. . . . I believe the military must be charged with doing a better job so that military advice is better and therefore more acceptable to senior civilians. . . . Finally, there would be an improved opportunity for the service secretaries and service chiefs to work the very critical issues, today, of the right organization, the right equipment and the right tactics so that we have effective forces on the battlefield of the future.[75]

General Jones's rather unprecedented departure from custom in criticizing the existing JCS organization before the House Committee on Armed Services in February 1962 provoked extensive debate during the hearings of the committee's Investigations Subcommittee held in April–August 1982. The hearings more fully developed the views of Generals Jones and Meyer and brought testimony from the other service chiefs. Adm Thomas B. Hayward, chief of naval operations, reported that he was deeply offended by the slanderous criticisms of the Joint Chiefs. "While I am a naval officer first," Hayward said, "I am also well aware of my obligations and responsibilities as a member of the Joint Chiefs of Staff. I find scant difficulty in fulfilling my service obligations and those of the JCS objectively and simultaneously." "Reorganization," Hayward urged, "is simply not necessary. In fact, I have grave reservations that reorganization along the lines proposed would . . . be the first, dangerous step toward a general staff which the Congress clearly has not supported in the past, and which I do not support now."[76] Gen Lew Allen, chief of staff of the Air Force, agreed with the key feature of strengthening the role of the chairman of the JCS, but Allen opposed any change that would fail to ensure that the service chiefs remained an integral part of the joint process. Allen testified:

> I believe it is important that the Service Chiefs continue to perform the dual roles of head of a Service and a member of the JCS because they provide the essential linkage between joint strategic planning and the resultant force programming, equipping, and training performed by the Services. These two roles are not in conflict — on the contrary, these two responsibilities must be integrated to insure the Service can effectively and responsively satisfy joint requirements. It is incongruous to state that a chief has the time to concentrate on Service-related programming and budgeting issues — but not on the joint strategic planning issues which define and shape those same service programs. Effective joint planning cannot be done in a vacuum by a purely advisory group, free of the responsibility to implement or support those plans. Military advice is trusted most from those who are responsible and prepared to provide the capabilities to implement that advice.[77]

At the end of the three months' hearings, the House Armed Services Committee's Investigating Subcommittee drafted a bill which increased the authority of the JCS chairman somewhat, provided for a deputy chairman, and proposed to establish a senior strategy advisory board of 10 retired officers at the rank of general or admiral who should have served a term on active duty as a member of the Joint Chiefs of Staff. They would meet no less frequently than once a month and provide their advice and recommendations to the Joint Chiefs, the secretary of defense, and to the president on matters they would deem appropriate. In the Investigations Subcommittee, Rep Samuel S. Stratton of New York resolutely justified the senior strategy board:

> My idea would be to limit the board to a group of retired military experts. . . . I think what we need is to tap the experience of people like General Jones, Admiral Hayward... and someone like Admiral Moorer—people of that stature. . . . We have all kinds of acquisition people and research people and weapons development people, but nobody knows a damned thing about how to fight a war.[78]

The subcommittee of the House Armed Services Committee reported its bill which it designated as the JCS Reorganization Act of 1982. The bill passed in the House readily, but it died without action in the Senate at the end of the 97th Congress.[79]

In the summer of 1982 while the House hearings were under way on the proposed JCS Reorganization Act, Secretary Weinberger asked the newly appointed chairman of the Joint Chiefs, Army Gen John W. Vessey, Jr., to have the Joint Chiefs examine the proposals of General Jones and others relative to reorganization. "We agreed we would do that personally," Vessey later said, "and not engage staff officers." In the fall of 1982, the Joint Chiefs submitted their recommendations to Secretary Weinberger, some that would require changes in law and some that could be implemented without legal changes. In their discussions, the Joint Chiefs recognized three fundamental relationships that had to be cultivated: with the president and the secretary of defense, among the chiefs themselves, and with unified and specified commanders in the field. "In the past," Vessey noted, "the relationship of the chiefs to the President at times had been only through the Secretary of Defense," this despite the fact that by law the chiefs were the president's military advisers.[80] The chiefs persuaded President Reagan to meet with them regularly, around a table or over lunch, where they freely made known their defense philosophies. The president's "Star Wars" proposal, emphasizing strategic defense initiatives, was said to have arisen from a February 1963 meeting with the Joint Chiefs. The new Air Force chief of staff, Gen Charles Gabriel said: "This group of Chiefs is closer to the President than any I have seen."[81] General Vessey met with Secretary Weinberger as a daily practice, and once a week the chiefs all met with the secretary to discuss a previously agreed upon agenda. With Secretary Weinberger, General Vessey attended meetings of the National Security Council (NSC); Vessey additionally asked the individual chiefs to stand in, in quarterly rotation, for him in meetings with the secretary and the NSC that he was unable to attend, this in lieu of an authorized deputy chairman.

General Gabriel said of this practice: "It has been most revealing to me and a great education to be exposed to the N.S.C. and what goes on over there at those levels with the President."[82] To strengthen relations with the unified and specific commanders, Vessey asked each to come to Washington and tell the chiefs about their contingency plans. Vessey remarked: "We found some things that were not right, things of great strategic importance to the United States that had not been tended."[83]

The legal revision that the Joint Chiefs of Staff wanted was to modify the line of command running by law from the president, to the secretary of defense, to the unified commanders, with the Joint Chiefs serving only a staff function for passing command orders. Their recommendations that the chairman of the Joint Chiefs of Staff should be placed in the line of command and that the Joint Staff should be enlarged were proposed to Congress in April 1983. General Vessey was said to have gone somewhat further, endorsing an effort that would put the chairman in the National Security Council and perhaps change his title to something like "chief of defense staff."[84] Early in 1983 Rep Ike Skelton of Missouri worked in close collaboration with Gen Maxwell Taylor on a bill which was designed to reform the JCS. Numerous provisions of this bill were incorporated in a House Armed Services Committee bill that passed the House with broad bipartisan support in 17 October 1983. This bill, House Report (HR) 3718, Joint Chiefs of Staff Reorganization Act of 1983, established the chairman of the Joint Chiefs of Staff after the secretary of defense in the chain of combatant commands, made the chairman a member of the NSC, eliminated numerical restrictions on the size of the Joint Staff, and directed the secretary of defense to ensure the independence of the Joint Staff. It also gave each service chief and unified or specified commander an opportunity to comment on Joint Staff reports. The bill was referred to the Senate Committee on Armed Services, where, as had been the case a year earlier, there was no action on it.[85]

In a very penetrating analysis of the future of the Joint Chiefs of Staff appended to his testimony before the House Armed Services Investigating Subcommittee in 1962, John G. Kester, who had served a number of years in the Pentagon and then most lately as a special assistant to Secretary Brown in 1977 and 1978, pointed out that the Joint Chiefs of Staff had originated in World War II to model the chiefs of staff organization after Britain's high command. Kester reminded his readers: "The JCS are a product of history, not of logic. If we did not already have the Joint Chiefs of Staff, it is not clear that it would be necessary to invent them."[86] Early in 1964 proponents of reorganization of the US Joint Chiefs of Staff gained ammunition when, in Great Britain, Prime Minister Margaret Thatcher announced a sweeping reorganization of the British military hierarchy that would create much stronger central control of the military services. Gen David Jones expressed dislike for the British decision to centralize weapons procurement, arguing that this went too far in taking decisions away from the services that actually would use new weapon systems. But overall, in the joint command plan, Jones said: "In the joint arena, I think what they've done is the way we ought to go."[87] The controversy for and against reorganization of US defense was played out both in the public press and on the floor of Congress. Former Secretary of Defense James Schlesinger demonstrated that in the existing organization. He argued:

> The general rule is that no service ox may be gored.... The unavoidable outcome is a structure in which logrolling, back-scratching, marriage agreements and the like flourish. It is important not to rock the boat. This implies a built-in difficulty in formulating and executing military operations.... In all of our military institutions, the time-honored principle of "unity of command" is inculcated. Yet at the national level it is firmly resisted and flagrantly isolated. Unity of command is endorsed if, and only if, it applies at the service level. The inevitable consequence is both the duplication of effort and the ultimate ambiguity of command.[88]

Ex-Secretary of Defense Harold Brown and Gen David Jones were quoted as saying that the US command system had failed in crisis and war. Brown was quoted as saying, "Certainly, the command chain in Vietnam, during the Vietnam war, was the most fouled-up thing in recent history, in part because the Joint Chiefs refused to face up to the issue of how you organize command in the field for most efficient operations. We had problems in Korea in organization, and Vietnam was an organizational nightmare. All four services were in logistics in Vietnam, each service ran its own air war."[89]

In 1984 the US Navy and Marine Corps took the lead in opposing greater defense centralization. "It's a terrible, terrible move, terribly pernicious," said Navy Secretary John F. Lehman, who was said to have lobbied strenuously against the House bill. "It would very seriously diminish civilian control of the military." He said that to put the JCS chairman on the National Security Council as an equal to the secretary of defense would seriously threaten traditional military subservice to civilian authority.[90] "I recognize a Trojan horse when I see one," commented the former Marine Corps commandant, Gen Robert H. Barrow. "This is a dangerous proposition we are talking about here."[91] Retired Adm Thomas H. Moorer responded that the JCS should not be blamed for failures in Vietnam:

> It was not the Joint Chiefs of Staff who made the decision never to invade North Vietnam or overthrow Ho Chi Minh.... It was not the Joint Chiefs of Staff that put a 30-mile buffer zone along the Chinese border and thereby permitted the Chinese supplies to be assembled in large quantities, and then slide into Hanoi at night.[92]

Neither the Reagan administration nor the Republican-controlled Senate Armed Services Committee was reported to be enthusiastic about HR 3718, though the committee chairman, Sen John Tower, said he was interested in pursuing JCS reform as a part of a larger package for reorganizing all of DOD. Thus, unable to get consideration of its measure, the House Armed Services Committee attached an amendment to the fiscal year 1985 defense authorization bill to restructure the JCS by placing the chairman in the national military chain of command, allowing him to select the Joint Staff, making him a member of the National Security Council, and giving him unilateral authority to advise the president on military matters.[93]

Late in September 1984 a Senate-House conference committee hammered out a consensus from their respective revisions of the fiscal year 1985 defense authorization measure. The conferees agreed that the far-reaching aspects of JCS reorganization ought to await a more mature consideration of changes in other parts of the Defense Department. The conferees nevertheless adopted some of the provisions that the House wanted: These included empowering the JCS chairman to act as spokesman for the unified and specified commands, allowing him to set the agenda for the Joint Chiefs of Staff, and allowing him to select the officers to be assigned to the Joint Staff. The conferees also approved language highlighting the importance of the defense reorganization issue, especially for changes in the Joint Chiefs of Staff and the Office of the Secretary of Defense. In the 99th Congress that would take office in 1985, Sen Sam Nunn, the ranking Democrat on the Senate Armed Services Committee, expected that the reorganization and strengthening of the Joint Chiefs would be a matter drawing keen attention.[94] General Jones, for one, was not completely discouraged about the prospects for reorganization. "What we have been able to do over time is create a constituency in Congress. We have created a climate so when there is an administration that really wants reform, there is a constituency on the Hill to do it," he said.[95]

NOTES

1. Archie D. Barrett, *Reappraising Defense Organization* (Washington, D.C.: National Defense University Press, 1983), xxiii, xxv.

2. House, *Reorganization Proposals for the Joint Chiefs of Staff: Hearings before the Investigations Subcommittee of the Committee on Armed Services*, 97th Cong., 2d sess., 1982, 52–53.

3. Ibid., 442–44, 461–62.

4. Ibid.

5. Ibid.

6. Ibid.

7. Ibid.

8. Ibid., 442–78 passim.

9. Ibid., 630, 636–42.

10. Ibid., 479–83.

11. Ibid.

12. Senate, *Department of Defense Appropriations for Fiscal Year 1965: Hearings before the Subcommittee Department of Defense of the Committee on Appropriations and the Committee on Armed Services*, 88th Cong., 2d sess., 1964, pt. 1:297; House, *Department of Defense Appropriations for 1969: Hearings before a Subcommittee of the Committee on Appropriations*, 90th Cong., 2d sess., 1968, pt. 1:222–24.

13. House, *Department of Defense Appropriations for 1977: Hearings before a Subcommittee of the Committee on Appropriations*, 94th Cong., 2d sess., 1976, pt. 1:633 (hereafter cited as *1977 DOD Appropriations*).

14. House, *Reorganization Proposals for the JCS*, 801–17; John Charles Daly, moderator, *The Role of the Joint Chiefs of Staff in National Policy* (Washington, D.C.: American Enterprise Institute for Public Policy Research, 1978), 18, 24.

15. Daly, *The Role of the JCS in National Policy*, 24–26.

16. Senate, *Department of Defense Appropriations for Fiscal Year 1971: Hearings before a Subcommittee of the Committee on Appropriations*, 91st Cong., 2d sess., 1970, 13.

17. Senate, *Department of Defense Appropriations for Fiscal Year 1970: Hearings before a Subcommittee of the Committee on Appropriations*, 91st Cong., 1st sess., 1969, pt. 4:35–37; Claude Witze, "A Package Tied in Blue Ribbon," *Air Force Magazine*, September 1970, 27.

18. Witze, "A Package Tied in Blue Ribbon," 26; House, *Reorganization Proposals for the JCS*, 156.

19. House, *Reorganization Proposals for the JCS*, 156.

20. *Report to the President and the Secretary of Defense on the Department of Defense by the Blue Ribbon Defense Panel*, 1 July 1970, iv–vii; news briefing by Gilbert W. Fitzhugh at Pentagon, 27 July 1970.

21. *Report to the President*, 4.

22. Ibid., 1–9.

23. Witze, "A Package Tied in Blue Ribbon," 29; Col R. D. Heinel, Jr., "Laird Dumps Fitzhugh Findings after Secret Meeting with JCS," *Armed Forces Journal*, September 1970, 37; House, *Reorganization Proposals for the JCS*, 156.

24. Heinel, "Laird Dumps Fitzhugh Findings after Secret Meeting with JCS," 37.

25. Senate, *Department of Defense Appropriations for Fiscal Year 1972: Hearings before a Subcommittee of the Committee on Appropriations*, 92d Cong., 1st sess., 1971, pt. 1:140–54; House, *Department of Defense Appropriations for 1972: Hearings before a Subcommittee of the Committee on Appropriations*, 92d Cong., 1st sess., 1971, pt. 2:31–33.

26. Senate, *Department of Defense Appropriations for Fiscal Year 1973: Hearings before a Subcommittee of the Committee on Appropriations*, 92d Cong., 2d sess., 1972, pt. 1:348–63 (hereafter cited as *FY 1973 DOD Appropriations*).

27. Senate, *Fiscal Year 1973 Military Procurement Authorization: Hearings before the Committee on Armed Services*, 92d Cong., 2d sess., 1972, pt. 2:705–7 (hereafter cited as *FY 1973 Military Procurement*); Daly, *The Role of the JCS in National Policy*, 16; House, *Reorganization Proposals for the JCS*, 519; John G. Kester, "The Future of the Joint Chiefs of Staff," *American Enterprise Institute Policy and Defense Review*, 5; *Report to the President*, 35.

28. Senate, *FY 1973 DOD Appropriations*, pt. 1:356–57; Senate, *FY 1973 Military Procurement*, pt. 2:706.

29. *Report to the President*, 57; Senate, *FY 1973 Military Procurement*, pt. 2:706.

30. *Report to the President*, 57.

31. Daly, *The Role of the JCS in National Policy*, 17.

32. Elmo R. Zumwalt, *On Watch, A Memoir* (New York: Quadrangle Books of the New York Times Book Co., Inc., 1976), 384–89.

33. Senate, *Bombing in Cambodia: Hearings before the Committee on Armed Services*, 93d Cong., 1st sess., 1973, 90–91, 93.

34. Senate, *Strategic Arms Limitation Agreements: Hearings before the Committee on Foreign Relations*, 92d Cong., 2d sess., 1972, 115; Senate, *Bombing in Cambodia: Hearings before the Committee on Armed Services*, 93d Cong, 1st sess, 1973, 90–91, 93; House, *1977 DOD Appropriations*, pt. 1:601–2.

35. Senate, *FY 1973 DOD Appropriations*, pt. 1:354–55; *Report to the Secretary of Defense on the National Military Command Structure*, July 1978, sec. 2.

36. Senate, *FY 1973 Military Procurement*, pt. 2:711–14.

37. Senate, *FY 1973 DOD Appropriations*, pt. 1:354–55; *Report to the President*, 46–49.

38. House, *Department of Defense Appropriations for 1975: Hearings before a Subcommittee of the Committee on Appropriations*, 93d Cong., 2d sess., 1974, pt. 1:527 (hereafter cited as *1975 DOD Appropriations*).

39. Edgar F. Puryear, *George S. Brown, General, U.S. Air Force: Destined for Stars* (Novato, Calif.: Presidio Press, 1983), 239.

40. Ibid; House, *Department of Defense Appropriations for 1974: Hearings before a Subcommittee of the Committee on Appropriations*, 93d Cong., 1st sess., 1973, pt. 2:39.

41. *Report of Secretary of Defense James R. Schlesinger to the Congress on the FY 1976 and Transition Budgets, FY 1977 Authorization Request and FY 1976–1980 Defense Programs*, 5 February 1975, iii–39.
42. Puryear, *George S. Brown*, 239.
43. House, *1975 DOD Appropriations*, pt. 1:709.
44. Ibid., pt. 2:322.
45. Ibid., pt. 2:326–78.
46. "More Changes in the Unified Command Structure," *Air Force Policy Letter for Commanders: Supplement*, 15 March 1975.
47. *Report of Secretary of Defense Donald H. Rumsfeld, Annual Defense Department Report, FY 1977*, 27 January 1976, 236–37.
48. House, *Department of Defense Appropriations for 1976: Hearings before a Subcommittee of the Committee on Appropriations*, 94th Cong., 1st sess., 1975, pt. 2:168–69 (hereafter cited as *1976 DOD Appropriations*).
49. Senate, *Department of Defense Appropriations for Fiscal Year 1976: Hearings before a Subcommittee of the Committee on Appropriations*, 94th Cong., 1st sess., 1975, pt. 4:86.
50. Gen Louis L. Wilson, USAF Oral History Interview no. 1178, 7–8 November 1979, 201–7.
51. Senate, *Fiscal Year 1977 Military Procurement Authorization: Hearings before the Committee on Armed Services*, 94th Cong., 2d sess., 1976, pt. 2:963.
52. House, *1976 DOD Appropriations*, pt. 2:72–73, 171; Senate, *Department of Defense Appropriations for Fiscal Year 1977: Hearings before a Subcommittee of the Committee on Appropriations*, 94th Cong., 2d sess., 1976, pt. 1:855; House, *Department of Defense Appropriations for 1978: Hearings before a Subcommittee of the Committee on Appropriations*, 95th Cong., 1st sess., 1977, pt. 1:588–89 (hereafter cited as *1978 DOD Appropriations*); "New Approval to Aerospace Defense," *Air Force Policy Letter for Commanders: Supplement*, 15 April 1979, 2.
53. *National Military Command Structure Report*, July 1978; USAF Doctrine Information Publication 10, *Background Information on Air Force Perspective for Coherent Plans* (Command and Control of TACAIR), April 1981.
54. Jimmy Carter, *Keeping Faith* (New York: Bantam Books, 1982), 55.
55. House, *1978 DOD Appropriations*, pt. 2:47.
56. House, *Reorganization Proposals for the JCS*, 114–15.
57. Ibid., 109; Kester, "The Future of the Joint Chiefs of Staff," 13, citing remarks delivered at commissioning ceremonies of the USS *Dwight D. Eisenhower*, 18 October 1977.
58. Kester, "The Future of the Joint Chiefs of Staff."
59. House, *Reorganization Proposals for the JCS*, 122.
60. *National Military Command Structure Report*, July 1978, 1, 70, 76–77.
61. Ibid.
62. House, *Reorganization Proposals for the JCS*, 110, 124–25.
63. *National Military Command Structure Report*, July 1978, 24–26.
64. Ibid., 26–33.
65. Harold Brown, *Thinking About National Security* (Boulder, Colo.: Westview Press, 1983), 207.
66. *National Military Command Structure Report*, July 1978, 47; House, *Reorganization Proposals for the JCS*, 550.
67. Daly, *The Role of the JCS in National Policy*, 9.
68. House, *Reorganization Proposals for the JCS*, 702–9.
69. Ibid.
70. Ibid., 470–71, 707–62.
71. House, *Department of Defense Appropriations for 1983: Hearings before a Subcommittee of the Committee on Appropriations*, 97th Cong., 2d sess., 1982, pt. 1:14–15, 348–49.
72. Senate, *Department of Defense Appropriations for Fiscal Year 1983: Hearings before a Subcommittee of the Committee on Appropriations*, 97th Cong., 2d sess., 1982, pt. 1:31–32.
73. House, *Reorganization Proposals for the JCS*, 5–6.
74. Ibid.

75. Ibid.
76. Ibid., 97–101.
77. Ibid., 179.
78. Ibid., 971–1002.
79. Barrett, *Reappraising Defense Organization*, xvii.
80. House, *Department of Defense Appropriations for 1984: Hearings before a Subcommittee of the Committee on Appropriations*, 98th Cong., 1st sess., 1983, pt. 2:95.
81. Ibid.
82. Ibid.
83. Senate, *Department of Defense Authorization for Appropriations for Fiscal Year 1984: Hearings before the Committee on Armed Services*, 98th Cong., 1st sess., 1983, pt. 1:35–36; Richard Halloran, "Reshaping the Joint Chiefs by Way of Persuasion," *New York Times*, 29 June 1983, i–14.
84. Halloran, "Reshaping the Joint Chiefs by Way of Persuasion," i–14.
85. Extensions of remarks of Rep Ike Skelton of Missouri in the House, in *Congressional Record*, 28 September 1984, E 4083; "Bill Revamps JCS," *Defense Week*, 26 September 1983, 4.
86. John G. Kester, "The Future of the Joint Chiefs of Staff," *AEI Foreign Policy and Defense Review*, in House, *Reorganization Proposals for the JCS*, 516–37.
87. Gerald F. Seib, "Overhaul the Military Chain of Command," *Wall Street Journal*, 14 August 1984, 30.
88. James R. Schlesinger, "Reorganizing the Joint Chiefs," *Wall Street Journal*, 8 February 1984, 32.
89. Fred Hiatt, "The Wars Within," *Washington Post*, 23 July 1984, 1.
90. Ibid.
91. Ibid.
92. Ibid.
93. Martha Lynn Graver, "JCS Reorganization May Get Senate Ear at Last," *Air Force Times*, 18 June 1984, 28.
94. *Congressional Record*, 27 September 1984, S 1207 and S 1210; 28 September 1984, E 4083.
95. Seib, "Overhaul the Military Chain of Command," 30.

SS *Mayaguez*.

Neil H. McElroy,
secretary of defense.

Thomas C. Reed,
secretary of the Air Force.

John L. McLucas,
secretary of the Air Force.

Gen John W. Vessey, Jr.,
chairman of the
Joint Chiefs of Staff.

John F. Lehman, Jr.,
secretary of the Navy.

USS *Pueblo*.

CHAPTER 8

GLOBAL AIRMOBILITY FORCES

"Airlift is an exceedingly important function of the Air Force," Air Force Secretary Hans M. Mark remarked in 1980, "but it is one of those functions which is so all pervasive that people tend to forget about it." For his own part, Secretary Mark viewed an airlift enhancement program as second in importance only to the modernization of strategic nuclear deterrent forces.[1]

In its beginning in World War II, airlift was an adaptation of existing civil air transport aircraft to military usages in worldwide airway links. The Air Transport Command's Hump operations into China and the Military Air Transport Service's Berlin airlift, and its support for the Korean War—while notable operational undertakings—were makeshift operations and in no sense an application of ready forces according to an established plan. The MATS airlift of the 1940s and 1950s was conducted with aircraft similar to the commercial air transport industry and was designed primarily to provide logistical resupply, often of articles that had been neglected in forward deployment plans. Air transport customarily provided an emergency means of overcoming shorts in logistics. This point-to-point air transport operation was aptly described as "the eraser on the logistician's pencil."[2]

New Concepts and Requirements

In the 1950s in the Emergency War Plans premised on general nuclear war, the Strategic Air Command was accorded the first and overriding priority for MATS airlift to support its restrike capability. Airlift for Tactical Air Command's nuclear-capable elements came next. The remainder of airlift capability, if any, would be allocated to the Army. There were no formal provisions for limited war situations requiring massive ground force deployments, although it was assumed that in an emergency MATS would draw on its own resources and civil air transports for limited war airlift. The principal commitment of military funds to strategic bombers and ICBMs precluded the possibility of much increase of MATS capability through modernization of the airlift forces. After the Korean War, the Air Force used MATS to tighten its logistical accounts by rapid transportation of high-value parts and equipment, and MATS also had some success in persuading the Army and Navy to follow the same procedures. In 1958, however, the institution of the Airlift Service Industrial Fund required the military departments to pay for formerly gratis MATS airlift, and it became more difficult for MATS to "sell" its services. Already in a lesser priority to combat air forces,

MATS was jealously regarded by many civil air carriers who wanted government business. At an intratheater level, MATS was circumscribed by the long-standing existence of tactical troop-carrier aviation.[3] As has been seen, in the late 1950s congressional committees were very critical of the failure of the Air Force to prepare MATS adequately for a wartime mission not in competition with civil carriers. Later on, Air Force leaders would generously credit the House Special Subcommittee on National Military Airlift, and especially its chairman, Rep L. Mendel Rivers, with supplying the impetus beginning early in 1960 for the modernization of MATS. Congressman Rivers maintained this interest in airlift when he became chairman of the House Committee on Armed Services, insisting that the Military Air Transport Service be given the added prestige of a redesignation as the Military Air Transport Command. This was accomplished by congressional action in 1965 in the form of an amendment to the military procurement authorization bill, and on 1 January 1966 the name of MATS was changed to the Military Airlift Command (MAC).[4]

Although the Kennedy and Johnson administrations were committed to a military strategy of flexible response, it was by no way simple to determine how force—other than air power—could be easily projected to contingency conflict areas. As Alain Enthoven noted from a systems analysis viewpoint, "It was not easy . . . to get comprehensive and accepted estimates of how many forces we wanted to move, where we wanted to move them, and how fast." As this problem came under scrutiny, the most significant study was performed in 1963–64 under the leadership of the JCS Special Studies Group, and entitled "Rapid Deployments of Forces for Limited War," dated 10 July 1964. The study was predicated on the World War II-Korean War experience where in the first few months the enemy swept over a lot of territory that had to be retaken. If the free world had had an ability to reinforce rapidly, it could have checked the aggression and ended the wars more quickly. The study postulated countering enemy assaults in Europe, Korea, and Southeast Asia, comparing three strategies: (1) a "forward" strategy, emphasizing a capability to put fully equipped fighting men into action in a few days; (2) a "defensive" strategy, emphasizing only enough immediate capability to maintain a foothold; and (3) an "intermediate" strategy somewhere in between. The forward strategy required rapid deployment, the defensive strategy slow deployment, and the intermediate strategy a medium rate of deployment. In terms of the cost of a major conventional war, the study estimated that a forward strategy would save more than $10 billion. It reached a general conclusion that the optimum solution for rapid deployment would include prepositioning of equipment and with high-speed-ship sealift and airlift which included a projected C-5A transport plane that was still under study. These conclusions were confirmed in a joint Air Force/Army AIRTRANS 70's study, dated September 1964, and a Weapon Systems Evaluation Group Study, dated February 1965.[5] Secretary McNamara summed up the studies, saying: "All of our studies show that the length and cost of a war, as well as the size of the force ultimately required to terminate it favorably, are importantly influenced by how fast we can bring the full weight of our military power to bear on the situation." All things considered, McNamara favored a "strategy of a mobile central reserve supported by adequate lift capability and balanced prepositioning . . . as the preferred alternative for meeting the rapid response objectives." McNamara's plan for strategic mobility included emphasis of strategic airlift, the use of "forward floating depot" ships in which balanced stocks of equipment and supplies were maintained on stations overseas, and procurement of a new class of fast deployment logistics (FDL) ships that would be committed to a rapid deployment mission at all times.[6]

When Gen Howell M. Estes, Jr., assumed command of the Military Airlift Service in July 1964 he approached the challenge of developing what he conceived to be a kind of combat airlift without precedent, since it had never existed and did not then exist. The classic lesson of strategic mobility, he wrote, was that there was *"no classic lesson — except to be ready for anything, anywhere, at any time."* He advanced a thesis that modern combat airlift was fundamental to strategic mobility by which US armed forces could maintain a "kind of universal spatiotemporal readiness." He believed that the kind of strategic airlift that he envisioned was "as much conceptual as technological." Historically, the constraints on airlift had been combinations of at least nine factors: speed, range/payload trade-off, flexibility of employment, cubic capacity, load ability, self-sufficiency, terminal base requirements, full dependency, and direct operating costs. In airlift history, no single aircraft had made a significant improvement in alleviating the self-limiting constraints on strategic airlift, but at the outset of his command Estes conceived that the C-141 would begin a transition to the kind of strategic airlift he envisioned and that the giant C-5A would to a very great extent minimize the airlift limitations of the past. Estes predicted:

> It will for the first time permit the MAC force to respond without qualifications to total airlift requirements, including the maximum demand — the division-force move. And it will come much closer to putting airlift in a cost competitive position with surface transport.[7]

As Estes was ending his command of the Military Airlift Command in 1969, he took another look at the purpose of strategic airlift, drawing upon Sun Tzu's axiom, "There has never been a protracted war from which a country has benefited." The basic functions of a modern combat airlift force were to help prevent any type of war if possible and to help bring it to a swift conclusion if deterrence failed. Estes wrote:

> The role of modern combat airlift, then, is to airlift combat forces and all their battle equipment, in the size and mix required — with the greatest speed — to any point in the world, no matter how remote or primitive, where a threat arises or is likely to erupt.[8]

IDEAS, CONCEPTS, DOCTRINE

The strategic airlift force had to be so constituted and geared as to move sizable forces if necessary in opposite directions and keep them resupplied until surface lines of communication were operating at capacity. Estes maintained:

> Given the capability to satisfy this maximum demand, the airlift force can with lesser efforts operate jointly with sealift or prepositioned equipment or both, or in tandem with fast deployment logistic ships, once the initial rapid-reaction requirements have been fulfilled. But the basic requirement is invariant: to rush integral, combat-ready fighting forces anywhere, including the battle area itself, without a preliminary massing of logistics, within hours of the time a decision to commit has been taken; and to reinforce and sustain them for as long as airlift is the only practicable way to do it.[9]

As early as 1950, Gen William H. Tunner had proposed unsuccessfully that in the interest of economy and efficiency the Air Force ought to unify all air transport organizations, ending the historical distinction between tactical troop carrier and strategic air transport aviation. In 1964, the Tactical Air Command and the Military Air Transport Service were called upon to prepare new doctrinal manuals for troop carrier and airlift aviation, and a doctrine development committee in MATS proposed the time was right to end the distinction between tactical and strategic airlift. The committee proposed: "With the present and future capacity of MATS to perform all phases of the airlift mission, the concept of airlift need no longer be fragmented, but can now become an entity." In a letter to the Air Force on 23 September 1965 forwarding a proposed single airlift manual, General Estes agreed that multipurpose C-130, C-141, and soon the C-5A ended the distinction between the "two-manual" approach consideration of "assault" and "strategic" airlift. Estes wrote:

> Airlift is an instrument of national and military power in its own right, as well as an essential supporting element to strategic and tactical combat forces.... It is my opinion that the full functional capability of airlift must be addressed as an entity in order to exploit the flexibility of airlift forces. Such capability cannot in any way be considered divisible.[10]

On 7 January 1966, Maj Gen Arthur Agan, assistant deputy chief of staff for plans and operations, wrote Estes that Gen John P. McConnell, with advice from the Air Staff, wanted separate assault and strategic airlift manuals to be prepared by TAC and MATS working together to avoid duplication. Consequently, AFM 2-21, *Strategic Airlift*, published in September 1966, focused on intertheater airlift, but an introductory chapter did note that strategic airlift could augment tactical airlift forces. In fact, in limited wars, MAC's forces could introduce combat forces directly into battle areas and deliver supplies to deployed forces.

A new AFM 2-4, *Tactical Air Force Operations – Tactical Airlift*, was published in August 1966. It conceived that either strategic or assault airlift could augment the other, but that there normally would be an "interlock" or "interface" wherein strategic airlift would generally deliver goods and people to a rear base and tactical airlift would then deliver them, on a sustained basis, to the Army brigade level (battalion/company level if required), where the Army would redistribute with organic assets.[11] Later on, General McConnell would explain his distinction between strategic and tactical airlift. He conceived that strategic airlift provided the ton-mile capabilities allocated by the Joint Chiefs of Staff to move rapid deployments of men and materiel into an objective area. Tactical airlift had to satisfy a theater commander's needs that would depend upon many changing variables such as distance of forward movement, availability of surface transportation, tactical mobility requirements, and amounts of routine and emergency resupply and personnel movements.[12]

In view of the strategy of flexible response, the Air Force Aeronautical Systems Division looked to a transport aircraft to replace the old C-124 and C-133 cargo aircraft that had been long in service. The result was the C-141 Starlifter, selected for development in 1961. Based on planning in cooperation with the Army, the C-141A was configured to carry 98 percent of an airborne division for distances of up to 5,500 nautical miles at a speed of more than 440 knots. The first aircraft rolled out of the Lockheed factory in August 1963, and the first flight occurred on 17 December 1963. In its design phase, the C-141 was well conceived, but quite soon the problem of a heavy logistic support plane was back before the Aeronautical Systems Division, since the Army now wished to be able to get infantry divisions airlifted and a still larger "outsized" cargo transport was needed. The result was a capacious C-5A Galaxy design with advanced-technology engines providing the lowest specific fuel consumption of any Air Force power plant and therefore also providing a very economical airlift operating cost. As a result of studies which led to approval of the C-5A program and the letting of a novel total-package procurement contract to Lockheed in August 1965, it was determined to be more cost effective to reduce procurement of C-141s from a planned 20 to 14 squadrons and to procure a planned 6 C-5A squadrons with 96 unit equipment planes and a total buy of 120 of the giant but versatile transports.[13] The decisions to invest in large and expensive C-141s and C-5s called into question the likely vulnerability of such aircraft in combat environments. Secretary McNamara examined the danger, but he concluded that the large transports would be no more vulnerable than merchant ships that would move in by sea. The chief hazard to the planes would be in protecting them on the way to combat area airfields and assuring control over the place they landed. These were limitations, but there were similar limitations on sealift associated with submarine attack or other attacks at sea.[14]

It happened that the development of the Department of Defense plans for strategic mobility began to be affected in 1964 by increasing US military commitments in Southeast Asia. In fiscal year 1965, the airlift force of 517 MAC aircraft and 260 MAC-committed Air National Guard and Air Force Reserve aircraft was almost exclusively propeller-driven with the exception of 28 C-135 jet aircraft, these being aircraft that Secretary McNamara had diverted to MATS solely to provide an interim modernization of the airlift capacity pending delivery of more capable aircraft. In 1966, General Estes freely admitted that Southeast Asia was the only contingency operation he could handle.

> We don't really have the capability today . . . to meet the needs of one contingency operation to the extent we would like to . . . much less two. If we had another contingency, JCS would simply have to make priority determinations as to how the available airlift is going to be employed. . . . Further, we would certainly have to do such things as activate the Reserves, federalize the Guard, activate CRAF [Civil Reserve Air Fleet].[15]

As C-141s with their greater range, speed, and lift entered the MAC operational capability, the active airlift force of propeller-driven aircraft shrank. The C-141 would become the strategic air cargo workhorse airlifter of the Vietnam War; in the peak year of 1968 MAC mustered 224 C-141s and 170 propeller types into its active airlift force. The first three C-5s began operational service in 1970, and by that time the C-141 force was at full strength. The only other aircraft still in the active MAC airlift fleet were three dozen propeller-driven C-133s that were held on to handle outsized cargo.[16]

As a part of the plans and preparations for strategic mobility, a MAC wing/Army division affiliation program commenced in 1965, including exchanges of liaison officers and development of closer working relations between Air Force and Army units. MAC also entered on a very large body of studies, some in-house, but more in conjunction with OSD and the Army field forces. As an example of the studies, General Estes conceived that too much previous thought had been given to the use of major, sophisticated airfields. This had been the case in Big Lift, the highly touted "massive" reinforcement of NATO forces, with a full division deployed from Texas with little more than toothbrushes to marry with equipment already prepositioned in Germany. Estes conceived that airlift aircraft of the future were not going to enjoy sophisticated airfields like the Rhein-Main complex, but would fly troops and a major portion of their equipment to closer distribution points to the front lines. Thus it was important—and planning began—to learn how to unitize cargo carried by C-5s to permit full volume and weight utilization and still permit a cargo breakdown suitable to Army troops in forward areas. Another study was a tandem point examination of how to marry men and equipment delivered overseas by sea shipment with airlift to move them into the forward areas.[17]

The MAC strategic mobility planning fitted into the larger mobility studies of the OSD Systems Analysis Office, which by 1968 had developed a computer model that tied together some 3,000 separate mobility factors relating to the cost, capabilities, and limitations of each major component of US mobility forces. Assuming a certain fleet of ships and aircraft, certain readiness standards, and certain world deployment schedules, the best operational strategy could be computed. Under some circumstances, it was best to operate the FDL ships and C-5s in tandem; that is to have the FDL ships carry loads to ports and then have the C-5s fly the loads from ports to the combat zone. The analyses also suggested that a balanced mix of airlift, sealift, and equipment positioning to meet US deployment objectives consisted of 6 C-5A squadrons, 14 C-141 squadrons, and

30 FDL ships; prepositioned equipment in Europe and the Pacific; a civil reserve air fleet; and 460 commercial cargo ships. This was the posture that would support a two- and one-half war strategy and provide the capability of simultaneously reinforcing NATO forces and rapidly deploying general-purpose forces to counter a major conventional attack in Asia, as well as meeting a minor contingency in the Western Hemisphere.[18] Congress accepted the Air Force's requirement for C-141s and C-5As, although there was a reduction in support for the Galaxy as it became evident that the program was experiencing cost overruns Congress also initially accepted the FDL ship concept; the development and prospective procurement of 30 of these ships to be managed with the same "package-procurement" concept as was going to give trouble with the C-5A. Nevertheless, the FDL ship program was increasingly subjected to criticism from industrial, maritime, and congressional sources. Ship-building interests did not like the novel-design demands of the FDL ships which in effect were more akin to aircraft manufacture than ship building; the House Armed Services Committee was not convinced that FDL ships would not be used in competition with the private merchant marine; and there was also a growing disenchantment with American involvement in Southeast Asia and a feeling that the FDL ship would make it easier for a president to involve the United States in foreign military adventures. In 1968 during hearings on fiscal year 1969 military appropriations, the procurement of the FDL ships was disapproved in Congress on the basis of a lack of immediacy of need for the vessels in light of the stringent US fiscal situation. At this same time, the giant C-5A cargo airplane was becoming in some circles "a dirty word," mainly because of a large predicted cost overrun. The need for rapid deployment and systems to provide it came under a cloud since it appeared possible that the capabilities might result in, as Sen Richard Russell said, the United States assuming the function of policing the world.[19]

Strategic Airlift Support of Southeast Asia

In a generalized description of Military Airlift Command experience in support of US combat in Southeast Asia (SEA), a MAC briefer appearing before the House Armed Services Subcommittee on Military Airlift stated: "What was a transportation agency in the 1950's, is rapidly becoming a strategic combat airlift force for the 1970's."[20] Although strategic airlift requirements in support of Southeast Asia were built up relatively slowly, MAC began the SEA support period with 21 squadrons of C-124s, 3 of C-133s, 7 of C-130s, and 3 of C-135s. Of the new aircraft to be available, the C-141 began flying into SEA in August 1965, and by 1968 the last of 284 C-141s was produced. MAC received its first C-5 on 17 December 1969, and the first C-5 mission was flown in Vietnam in August 1971. The old C-124s took 95 hours to make the trip from Travis AFB, California, to Saigon and return, and at a mission utilization rate of 6.7 hours per day that came out to just over 13 days for one trip.[21] As the commander of MAC, General Estes said he wanted "every bit of airlift that I can get."²² Even in peacetime operations, MAC was programmed to increase its flying hours in a surge capability for national emergencies. In October 1965, the flying rate of MAC C-130s, C-135s, and C-141s was 5 hours a day per aircraft, with three crews per aircraft. The experience of the Air Force and MAC with the operation of large aircraft had always shown that the pacing item was not the ability of the airplane to meet high utilization demands, but it was the ability of the other parts of the airlift system to support the airplane itself. The principal pacing item was the aircrew and maintenance capability that generated the flying hours. Other constraints could occur in terms of load and offload capabilities, perhaps weather, and of course enemy action if it were encountered. To meet the airlift demands of Vietnam, beginning on 1 October 1965, MAC increased the flying rates of most of its aircraft from 5 to 6.5 hours per day by 1 April 1966 by going to a planned 48-hour workweek. On 1 July 1966, nearly a year after OSD established the surge requirement, MAC reached its objective of eight hours per day. This rate required four crews per aircraft, plus other manpower and resources; fortunately, the additional manpower was available because of the earlier than planned phaseout of certain Strategic Air Command B-47 and KC-97 units. As MAC viewed this experience of increasing its surge rate, certain facts became predictable. It was to be expected that economic constraints would preclude peacetime manning to support maximum attainable wartime utilization rates. Obviously, MAC would not be in so fortunate a position as to receive aircrews and maintenance personnel by transfer from the Strategic Air Command, nor would the Air Force be able to afford the time required to train the additional new personnel needed for an appropriate airlift surge rate.²³

At the onset of MAC's enlarged commitment to SEA support, the command was the gaining command for Air National Guard and Air Force Reserve units equipped with old propeller-driven transport planes, including such miscellany as C-97s, C-119s, C-121s, and C-124s. Although MAC drew upon the voluntary efforts of some of these units to take over cargo needs that permitted the transfer of the more productive MAC aircraft to the cargo needs of Vietnam, most of the Guard and Reserve transports, as Air Force Secretary Harold Brown said, were "just no good for strategic lift." As MAC was going to an all-jet force, the Reserve and Guard planes had peculiar support and en route base requirements that were becoming unavailable and economically infeasible. The Reserve and Guard squadrons, moreover, could not compete favorably with commercial airlift available for hire because their old aircraft were so expensive to operate. Initially, the Air Force intended to deactivate many of the Reserve and Guard squadrons and to convert a few of them to C-130 tactical air transport usages, but General Estes — faced with the prospect of possessing jet cargo aircraft whose flying-hour potential was considerably higher than the manpower MAC could expect to be authorized in peacetime — asked that Reserve units should be established to be associated directly with MAC C-5 and C-141 squadrons. The 1966 MAC planning for the Reserve associate program visualized that the associate groups would use

MAC aircraft and maintenance equipment and train with the MAC squadrons in peacetime. During emergencies, the Air Force Reserve personnel would augment MAC so that high utilization of the more productive jet equipment would be possible. General Estes submitted the associate unit plan to the Air Force in 1967 and after it was held up for a reevaluation of the whole Air Force Reserve program, the MAC associate program was approved by the Air Force and OSD. The first Air Force Reserve associate unit was activated at Norton AFB, California, on 25 March 1968 and in the next several years a Reserve associate unit complemented each of the 17 MAC active duty airlift squadrons. And eventually, 50 percent of MAC-authorized C-5 and C-141 crews would be air reservists, available in emergencies. The associate crews demonstrated their willingness to perform: the first C-5 to land in the Middle East in the 1973 crisis, for example, was manned by a Reserve aircrew.[24]

In addition to the Reserve associate program, other C-97 and C-124 groups provided voluntary fill-in flights to Vietnam. Twelve Reserve aerial port squadrons and six Reserve mobile en route support squadrons were assigned to MAC in 1966, and two additional Reserve en route squadrons were activated at Norton and Dover AFBs in 1968 to guard against multiple contingencies in addition to SEA. Personnel not needed in the associate program were used in forming the support units. During the Combat Fox airlift to Korea, incident to the seizure of the USS *Pueblo* by North Koreans in January 1968, 5 of the 19 Air Force Reserve C-124 groups were called to active duty primarily to backfill regular channel airlift requirements into Southeast Asia.[25]

The expansive requirements of the Southeast Asia conflict caused MAC to make heavy demands on CRAF, the contracted arrangement dating back to 1952 that provided civil augmentation of military air transport capability in time of emergency. Whereas the CRAF program in the decade after 1952 envisioned that it would be activated in its entirety in an emergency, the Air Force took steps in 1963 to convert CRAF to conditions of cold war, limited war, or contingency operations, whereby the civil airlift augmentation force would be capable of selective, discriminate, and flexible responses. In a change in policy, the Air Force took CRAF out of a wholly standby status and provided for portions of the capability to be used in daily augmentations of the military airlift force. Under this new concept, MAC negotiated peacetime contracts with CRAF carriers as agreeable between MAC and the carrier, while emergency stages I, II, and III required the carrier to commit airlift, by model and series, as appropriate to the emergency. The CRAF was composed of four segments: international long range, international short range, domestic, and Alaskan. Its major and most critical role was to augment the long-range military strategic airlift capability withdrawn from worldwide airlift operations when the military airlift was needed to support an emergency. It was the presidential, congressional, and defense policy that commercial airlift should be procured on a basis that would support a more viable, modern, civil air transport industry.[26]

At the time of the SEA force buildup, MAC airlift modernization was in its initial stages, and it would not be until August 1968 that the new C-141 force would become fully operational. As a result, MAC leaned heavily upon civilian augmentation, especially for the movement of passengers, a task best suited to civilian airliners. In view of the substantial growth of commercial air transportation between the Korean War and the SEA force buildup, conditions never warranted activating the compulsory contract features of CRAF; in the crisis period immediately following capture of the USS *Pueblo*, the carriers were asked to volunteer more expansion airlift to avoid declaring a Stage I CRAF emergency. They responded by providing nearly twice as much cargo airlift as in the preceding months. In the domestic CRAF, MAC contracted the LOGAIR and QUICKTRANS services to transport high-value cargo items between the Air Force Logistics Command and the Navy Supply Systems Command. CRAF aircraft also carried approximately 98 percent of defense mail. Although international CRAF flights transported cargo, the commercial carriers as a rule were reluctant to purchase aircraft suited to a full range of national defense cargo airlift needs, since such aircraft probably would be inefficient in commercial competition. Much military equipment could not be fitted through civil aircraft doors. In the beginning of the C-141 development, the Air Force had expected that this plane would be procured by commercial air carriers as a cargo carrier. The commercial carriers, however, considered that the tail-loading feature of the C-141 was a weight penalty for economical usage and did not try a version of the Starlifter. And, of course, there was no commercial usage economically feasible for a C-5 Galaxy. In Southeast Asia, the MAC operation was required to operate in a larger number of airfields than could the CRAF commercial aircraft. The Vietnam experience clearly demonstrated the divergent path taken by the military and civil aviation in the development of aircraft. Nevertheless, it was evident that civil airlift would continue to be needed to replace military airlift in routine-type functions throughout the world in times of emergency. But commercial airlift would not be routinely suited for the kind of unit deployments that MAC envisioned from the SEA experience.[27]

In the strategic airlift operations into Southeast Asia, MAC's review and modifications of aerial port/route structures yielded dramatic results. In the early stages of the conflict at the beginning of 1965, all MAC passengers and cargo bound for SEA went out of the aerial port at Travis AFB, California, bound for either Saigon or Bangkok. This created a tremendous loading problem at Travis and a redistribution problem in SEA. As SEA workload increased and the C-141s came on line, MAC operated regularly into 10 airfields and serviced an additional 16 airfields in SEA on an as-required basis, the objective being to deliver as close to the customer as possible. Whereas MAC aerial ports had formerly been at coast-out airfields in the United States—east coast for Europe and west coast for the Pacific—the longer-range MAC aircraft permitted a "multidirectional port concept." Routine channels over the northern Pacific were established between aerial ports of embarkation (APOEs) at Dover, Delaware; Charleston, South Carolina; and later McGuire AFB, New Jersey. In 1965, APOEs were also opened at Kelly, Norton, and McChord AFBs to support specific destinations in the western Pacific. The expansion of the multidirectional APOEs relieved airlift congestion and reinforced the source-to-user airlift concept. To minimize maintenance, refueling, and support requirements in SEA, MAC airlift inbound to SEA refueled at Clark Air Base in the Philippines, Yokota Air Base in Japan, or Kadena Air Base on Okinawa, completed their mission into SEA, and then recovered at Clark, Yokota, or Kadena. This pattern reduced MAC ground time and refueling needs at the forward airfields.[28]

During the heavy resupply into SEA, MAC operated approximately 73 flights (44 military and 29 commercial contract) per day into Southeast Asia with an average ground time of 1.8 hours. Tables 2 through 4 summarize MAC operations worldwide in 1961–74 with the principal activity of course being in the Pacific-Far East.[29]

In addition to the high-volume logistical airlift, MAC combat airlift also came into play in SEA and the Far East, flying integral battle units and their equipment into war areas in a de facto state of war. Between 23 December 1965 and 23 January 1966, a fleet of 88 C-141s, 126 C-133s, and 11 C-124s flew 231 missions in airlifting the 3d Infantry Brigade, 25th Division, from Hawaii directly to Pleiku Air Base, in the far interior of Vietnam. The operation was called Blue Light and, although initiated on only five days' notice, it went very smoothly. For one thing the MAC 1502d Air Transport Wing (renamed the 61st Military Airlift Wing) had been training with the 25th Division for some time. The missions were flown as scheduled flights over predetermined routes and although Pleiku Air Base facilities were rudimentary, the airfield was relatively secure. The Blue Light airlift gave first tests to the new C-141s, and these aircraft were fully used beginning on 17 November 1967 in Operation Eagle Thrust, wherein 391 airlift missions, in 8 noncontinuous increments, lifted 10,024 troops and 5,357 tons of equipment of the 101st Airborne Division, minus one brigade, from Fort Campbell, Kentucky, to Bien Hoa Air Base, Vietnam. Twenty-two C-133 missions flew outsized equipment and 369 C-141 missions lifted personnel and cargo. Using engine-running offloads at Bien Hoa during Eagle Thrust, the C-141 sorties were accomplished with an average offload time of 7.4 minutes, thus reducing ramp congestion and potential exposure to ground fire. C-133s were on the ground an average of about two hours. Eagle Thrust was leisurely flown in an elapsed time of 42 days; had such been required, General Estes remarked that even in this end-1967 time frame he could have massed his resources and completed the mission in two and a half days. Although Blue Light and Eagle Thrust hold implications for the future, Estes observed that they were not definitive laboratory experiments: "For one thing," he pointed out, "a good part of the massive logistical base had already been fairly well established; and, for another, the concept of the operation did not call for minimum closure times."[30]

TABLE 2
Military Airlift Command Passenger and Cargo Movement
(Ton-Miles)

Fiscal Year	Military	Commercial	Total	Percent Commercial
1961	1,069.7	281.7	1,351.4	20.8
1962	1,084.0	532.9	1,616.9	33.0
1963	1,168.8	595.0	1,763.8	33.7
1964	1,140.1	517.1	1,657.2	31.2
1965	1,449.3	722.3	2,171.6	33.3
1966	2,061.4	1,317.5	3,378.9	39.0
1967	3,163.9	2,275.4	5,439.3	41.8
1968	4,783.0	2,652.2	7,435.2	35.7
1969	4,369.7	2,792.0	7,161.7	39.0
1970	3,739.9	2,291.2	6,031.1	38.0
1971	3,228.4	1,548.5	4,776.9	32.4
1972	2,760.2	1,887.5	4,647.7	40.6
1973	2,488.1	1,021.3	3,510.0	29.1
1974	1,932.2	559.5	2,491.7	22.5

Source: Headquarters MAC.

TABLE 3
Consignment of Military Air Cargo: Fiscal Years 1960–75

Fiscal Year	MAC	Tons Consigned Commercial Airlines
1960	151,206	17,581
1961	133,291	26,409
1962	108,038	73,669
1963	115,282	69,077
1964	153,158	43,683
1965	187,325	66,067
1966	236,252	102,106
1967	397,297	201,905
1968	516,006	163,073
1969	577,719	147,603
1970	554,652	103,991
1971	469,614	57,143
1972	383,648	133,350
1973	366,468	84,674
1974	262,219	28,728
1975	254,572	18,752

Source: Headquarters MAC.

TABLE 4
MAC International Civil Airlift Procurement: Fiscal Years 1960–75
(In millions of dollars)

Fiscal Year	Revenues		
	Passengers	Cargo	Total
1960	47.9	41.9	89.8
1961	53.8	55.6	109.4
1962	77.2	104.8	182.0
1963	100.9	103.6	204.5
1964	98.7	88.1	186.8
1965	108.7	122.6	231.3
1966	188.3	166.2	354.5
1967	268.8	325.7	594.5
1968	332.6	244.9	577.5
1969	336.1	190.0	526.1
1970	320.6	120.5	441.1
1971	294.1	45.1	339.2
1972	222.0	146.3	368.3
1973	155.0	77.4	232.6
1974[1]	119.0	27.2	146.2
1975[2]	173.0	31.0	204.0

[1] Fixed buy for cargo was $30,000,000 but only $27,200,000 utilized for movement of cargo. Unused dollars were converted for movement of passengers during fiscal year 1974.

[2] Fixed buy for cargo was $20,500,000 which increased to $31,000,000 through expansion during fiscal year 1975.

Source: Headquarters MAC.

Later MAC airlifts in the Pacific-Southeast Asia were much more urgent. On 25 January 1968, MAC received an alert that a major force deployment reactive to the *Pueblo* incident would require movement of tactical air units from multiple onload points to diverse offloads in Korea. In Operation Combat Fox, beginning on 28 January, MAC supported the move of TAC fighters and C-130s and Air National Guard fighters from the United States, as well as moves of Pacific Command forces intratheater, into Korea. MAC C-124s, C-130s, C-133s, and C-141s flew more than 80 missions to Korea from the United States, SEA, and Japan. As seen already, President Lyndon Johnson directed a mobilization of five Air Force Reserve C-124 squadrons, which filled in regular channel airlift requirements, and commercial airlift was also called upon for assistance. Between 29 January and 17 February, MAC's deployed airlift control elements (ALCEs) at Osan, Kimpo, Kunsan, and Suwon, Korea, and at Misawa, Japan, and handled 1,036 aircraft, 13,683 tons of equipment, and 7,996 troops. Although Combat Fox was winding down, the Joint Chiefs of Staff alerted MAC on 12 February 1968 to begin deployment of additional forces to Vietnam within 48 hours to counter the

IDEAS, CONCEPTS, DOCTRINE

Tet offensive. The requirement of MAC Operations Order 9-68 was an airlift—code-named Bonny Jack—of an Army brigade from Fort Bragg, North Carolina, to Chu Lai and a reinforced Marine regiment from El Toro to Da Nang. As seen, MAC made a special appeal to commercial carriers, which responded with sufficient additional airlift to keep the backlog at MAC ports within acceptable limits while the combat airlift was in progress.[31]

In April 1972, when most US forces had been removed from Southeast Asia and it was necessary suddenly to redeploy air units from the United States to meet the North Vietnamese Easter offensive, the new capabilities of the Military Airlift Command were strikingly demonstrated. On 5 April Gen Creighton W. Abrams, Jr., urgently requested additional forces, and the Tactical Air Command started Constant Guard, a series of air deployments that numbered I through IV. As Constant Guard kicked off, a squadron of F-105Gs, two F-4 squadrons, and several EB-66s departed for Thailand, while 38 C-141s lifted 854 men and 400 tons of cargo in the move, and 4 TAC C-130s moved en route maintenance teams and their equipment. Constant Guard II was a similar move of two more F-4 squadrons to Thailand. Constant Guard III was the largest single move in the history of TAC, and four squadrons of F-4s moved to Thailand. In nine days, MAC C-5s, C-141s, and commercial carriers moved 3,195 personnel and 1,600 tons of cargo. In Constant Guard IV, two C-130 squadrons were moved to Taiwan, and MAC also took over the Pacific intratheater lifts so that the tactical C-130s could give full attention to in-country work. During this period, MAC also provided airlift support to SAC B-52 and tanker forces moving back to Guam and Thailand. Before the Easter offensive, giant C-5s had not operated in a combat environment, but on 3 May the US Military Assistance Command, Vietnam (MACV) asked for an emergency lift of six 49-ton M48 tanks from Yokota in Japan to the rocket-hazarded airfield at Da Nang in Vietnam. In expedited procedures, nearly all tie-down chains were removed during taxi, and as the C-5 cargo door opened and ramps were extended, the tank drivers started their engines. The tanks drove off under their own power, and the offloading sequence was timed at seven minutes. Ground times in the dangerous area were 30 minutes or less. Immediately after this lift, the C-5s moved 42 24-ton M41 tanks and eight 7.5-ton M548 tracked vehicles to Da Nang and Cam Ranh Bay. Altogether in 1972 the C-5s flew 303 missions into Southeast Asia.[32]

Early in 1975 when the Republic of Vietnam was collapsing under a North Vietnamese assault, this time not opposed by American air attack, MAC C-141s and C-5s rushed military assistance and lifted refugees from Vietnam. MAC flew Operation Babylift, the airlift of some two thousand orphans, most of them destined for homes in the United States. This humanitarian effort was unfortunately marred by the crash landing of a disabled C-5A shortly after takeoff from Tan Son Nhut Airfield on 4 April, killing 155 persons, mostly children.[33] The C-130 and C-141 transports evacuating South Vietnam in 1975 carried antiradiation devices to warn of surface-to-air missiles, but the employment of unarmed C-141s and especially C-5s in a combat situation raised some questions in Congress. In November 1975 Gen Paul K. Carlton, MAC commander, was asked how far forward the C-5 was going to operate. General Carlton answered:

> It depends on how much carrying the freight to that point is worth to the JCS. . . . We have already used the airplane both in Saigon and Danang . . . in very high risk zones. We have operated under the threat of the SAM . . . as well as air-to-air, under very unusual circumstances such as the second Tet offensive when we hauled tanks into Danang. We don't expose it unless the risk is worth it. We treat it very carefully and conservatively, but to answer your question, if the risk is worth taking to win the battle, we will take it. Just like we will with any airplane. . . . The JCS makes the decision on the use of the C-5 under almost all circumstances of risks.[34]

A New Maturity of Strategic Airlift: The C-5A Story

In the Department of Defense analyses of the impending revolution in worldwide force mobility so avidly sought after 1960, the gigantic but highly versatile C-5A Galaxy air transport was expected to provide a significant technological breakthrough. General Estes wrote in 1966:

> Although the C-5 . . . does not radically breach the state of the aeronautical art, it will to a very great extent minimize the airlift limitations of the past. It will for the first time permit the MAC force to respond without qualification to total airlift requirements, including the maximum demand — the division-force move. And it will come much closer to putting airlift in a cost competitive position with surface transport.[35]

For a time in 1969–70 and for a number of reasons the C-5A became "a dirty word, a lightning rod for pent-up resentments," and these resentments "put the need for rapid deployment and the systems that would provide it under a cloud."[36] Speaking to the problem of whether the Air Force had made a mistake in procuring the C-5A, Gen David C. Jones was going to say that the Department of Defense, the Air Force, and possibly the Congress had "collectively made an error" but it was not in trying the C-5 since it was a "fine airplane . . . a good aircraft." The errors in the C-5 program were found in the total program package in research and development and up through the procurement of aircraft to meet certain unattainable specifications, plus an Air Force "reluctance to come to Congress and say we have a problem and we ought to change our whole program."[37]

The Air Force's specific operational requirement (SOR) for a CX-HLS aircraft that became the C-5A originated with Military Air Transport Service visualizations of an aircraft large enough to move all Army equipment, thus ending the practice of "tailoring" combat units for air movement, often with a substantial loss of firepower. The major features designed into the C-5A enabled it to reach any part of the globe with minimum refueling stops or, if necessary, without stopping, with aerial refueling. Its high-flotation, 28-wheel landing gear would permit it to land on 4,000-foot unpaved fields. Its cargo deck was truck-bed height when the landing gear was made to kneel, and for vehicular loads the aircraft could drop each end of the cargo deck to provide ramps for easy exit or access. The aircraft had special avionics to permit it to follow terrain at low altitudes and to pinpoint targets for airdrop at night or in adverse weather. Although General Estes did not think the C-5 would strain the state of the art of aeronautics, this position was not shared by others later. In 1971 Deputy Secretary of Defense David Packard, who inherited the C-5 problem, declared that "the Air Force asked for more features on the C-5A than were really necessary. . . . There were a lot of things that I think everybody now realizes were not really necessary for this plane, and they added significantly to the cost."[38] On the other hand, the Air Force considered that the characteristics desired in the C-5A were justified by long airlift experience. Secretary Seamans said of the C-5: "It was based on all the operational experience derived from more than a decade of airlift usage in Berlin, Beirut, the Congo, Korea, and extensive development exercises in the field."[39]

In the development and procurement of new aircraft, the Air Force always had followed a procedure of completing a research and development phase amounting to about 20 percent of the total systems acquisition cost. The Air Force then negotiated the production requirements for aircraft, associated data, and equipment at a later date as best it could with the single contractor who had done the development work. This procedure virtually eliminated effective competition for 80 percent of the total acquisition costs involved. Moreover, the Air Force could not make a firm initial computation of the eventual total cost of a system. A new contractual concept to be used for the C-5A (and which would have been used for the fast deployment logistics ship) was put forward, namely a total-package procurement that envisioned that all development and production and as much support as was feasible would be procured under competition in one total package containing price and performance commitments. Three contractors—Boeing, Douglas, and Lockheed—competed for the aircraft and two—General Electric and Pratt and Whitney—for the engines. A total-system responsibility clause held the contractor responsible for the complete system performance, including the government-furnished engines, and the contractor was to be held responsible for taking any action, including correcting discrepancies, that might be required to obtain the guaranteed performance. Gen James Ferguson, commander of Air Force Systems Command, would say in 1970:

> The nature of this contract was one which placed major dependence on the contractor for management decisions after we told him what we wanted in the way of performance. The terms of the contractor were such that the Air Force had little control over the development. Putting it in oversimplified terms, we would meet him at the end of the runway and take a look at the first airplane. That is slightly overstated. That is the essence of it.[40]

In the aeronautical procurement environment of the early 1960s, there was a "buyer's market" since there was strong competition for the fewer aircraft systems that were being projected. In the bidding for the C-5A contract, General Electric successfully competed for the engines, and the Lockheed Company was the low bidder for the C-5A airframe; the contract award was announced in September 1965 with production to begin in fiscal year 1967. The Air Force liked the prospects of Lockheed building the C-5 because the company had a good record in building the C-130 and C-141 military transports. Even in September 1965 it appeared that Lockheed's management had underestimated costs and bid unrealistically low, but the management apparently conceived that the C-5 would be a scaled-up version of the C-141 and would present few production problems. This was not to be the case, and 1965 was right at the point where the US inflation trend was going to accelerate rapidly by virtue of the pressures for additional armaments for Southeast Asia. Lockheed had not included in its proposal a line item to cover its estimate of the impact of inflation, although it later appeared that the company had envisioned and provided for from $100 million to $150 million in inflation costs in the long eight-year program. In addition to increasing costs, the contractor also had to go back and make engineering changes to provide the airplane which he had contracted to deliver. These changes involved additional costs, and they also were going to affect the serviceability of the production plane. To meet aircraft weight requirements and payload specifications, Lockheed removed weight from the wing. This involved some degree of risk of weakening the wing, and it turned out that the result severely affected the lifetime of the C-5A.[41]

When Secretary of Defense Melvin Laird took office as a member of President Nixon's administration in 1969, he already had learned that the C-5A program was facing substantial cost-overruns, a matter which he also apparently thought had been attended to by Air Force officials in the previous administration.[42] Early in 1969 the Air Force figured the cost of the C-5A program, originally set at $3.1 billion not including spares in 1964, had climbed to a projected $4.348 billion, the gross unit flyaway cost increasing from $18 million to $26.9 million.[43] In the Joint Strategic Objective Plan 72-79, the Joint Chiefs of Staff stated a requirement for six squadrons of C-5s and 120 aircraft. The 120-aircraft fleet would include 96 unit equipment aircraft, enabling the basing of 32 unit equipment planes at Dover and Travis and 16 unit equipment aircraft each at Charleston and Kelly. The other planes would have been used for training and command and support. This program was already in doubt because of the cost-overrun projection when, on 13 July 1969, a C-5's wing cracked prematurely during the static load test. It was going to be impossible to incorporate a major redesign for improved wing-fatigue life since the earliest aircraft that could be caught in production would be the 75th. Therefore, MAC accepted the first production C-5 for operational use in December 1969 with the realization that the wing would restrict the aircraft to a maximum gross weight of 728,000 pounds instead of 769,000 pounds.[44]

During 1969, the maturation of National Security Study Memorandum 3 outlined a national strategy less demanding with regard to rapid deployment of US general-purpose forces, and Secretary Laird also took the increased cost and coupled wing problem of the C-5 in consideration. It was reported that Laird made

IDEAS, CONCEPTS, DOCTRINE

the decision to reduce procurement of C-5As to 81 aircraft in all, allowing for four squadrons of these planes. Laird said:

> We believe that these four squadrons of C-5As, together with 14 squadrons of C-141s in the active force and a Civil Reserve Air Fleet of about 450 four engine jet aircraft will be sufficient to meet our basic needs for intertheater airlift movement.[45]

With the reduction of the C-5 buy, the Air Force decided to operate the aircraft primarily from 3 major CONUS ports—32 at Travis, 22 at Dover, and 16 at Charleston—and 11 for training, command, and support. With the reduced force it was believed that initial deployments could be as rapid as ever, but the total amount of tonnage would be less.[46] The Military Airlift Command began operational use of the C-5A in June 1970, and in September 1970 it achieved initial operational capability with delivery of eight aircraft to Charleston AFB. In April 1972 when the planes were used during the Communist Easter offensive in Southeast Asia, 57 C-5As had been produced; 6 were in a flight-test program, 5 were used for training at Altus AFB, Oklahoma, 16 were assigned to Charleston, 18 to Travis, 10 to Dover, and 2 had been destroyed in ground accidents.[47]

As he looked back at the C-5A program, General Ferguson was quite sure that total-package procurement had been a mistake. If he were to do it again, he would have elected to contract for the development of the C-5, and then to look at the result and the cost of the program, and then to negotiate a contract for the production. In clearing up the contract with Lockheed, Deputy Secretary of Defense Packard was willing to let Lockheed settle for a $200-million fixed loss, which allowed the company to avoid bankruptcy and made the acquisition cost for the 81 aircraft about $4.5 billion. On 1 February 1971 Lockheed agreed to this settlement, including a new contract that allowed trade-offs in production as they seemed necessary.[48] The question of what to do about structural weaknesses of the C-5A went on before and after the contractual arrangements, and the problem seemed even more serious after 29 September 1971 when an outboard engine on a C-5A preparing for takeoff actually pulled free and tumbled back several hundred feet. In mid-1970 an ad hoc scientific advisory board committee chaired by Dr Raymond Lewis Bisplinghoff completed studies of the C-5A and concluded that with special care the plane could fill the strategic capabilities required of it. Whereas the service life of the plane had been expected to be 30,000 hours, the Air Force could expect to get 7,000 hours without extensive modifications. Additional structure tests revealed much the same conclusions as the Bisplinghoff committee. There were a number of ways to decrease wing fatigue such as through lighter loads, proper distribution of loads, and appropriate flight and fuel profiles. These inexpensive measures promised to give a C-5A over 20,000 hours of service life and did not preclude using the C-5 for higher loads and other mission profiles if these capabilities were needed. Such usage, however, would tax the plane's service life at a more rapid rate. Since the unmodified C-5As in 1972 were being projected to fly less than 1,000 hours a year, the Air Force delayed a decision to undertake an expensive retrofit of new and stronger wings.[49]

The Israeli Airlift of 1973

Early on the afternoon of Saturday, 6 October 1973, Arab armies of Syria and Egypt, massively equipped with Soviet-built tanks, artillery, and aircraft, attacked Israel from across the Golan Heights and the Suez Canal. The Israelis had known the Arabs were preparing to attack, but they did not preempt lest they appear the aggressor. Moreover, Israel was confident that a war could be ended in a matter of days, and it had stocked military consumables on such a basis. As already noted, however, the Israelis were badly surprised and compelled to expend materiel profligately to afford themselves time for mobilization. In Washington on the first day of the war, Gen George Brown, Air Force chief of staff, heard intelligence estimates that the Israelis were facing a high-rate-of-consumption war for which they were not prepared and that they would be out of major consumables in about seven days. Acting on his own initiative, Brown made a decision to prepare two F-4 fighter squadrons for immediate delivery of their aircraft to Israel and to begin moving ammunition to aerial ports of embarkation. When he had done this, he informed Secretary of Defense James R. Schlesinger of his actions.[50] The Israeli airlift—code-named Nickel Grass—commenced on 6 October, but according to the MAC commander, Gen Paul K. Carlton, Washington authorities, anxious about US oil supplies from the Persian Gulf, found it difficult to determine how supplies would be delivered from the United States to Israel. The result was several false starts. At first MAC was going to move all supplies to an east coast port, where the Israelis would take delivery. Then MAC was directed to plan to haul to the Azores, where Israeli El Al air carriers would pick up. Deputy Secretary of Defense William P. Clements, Jr., stated frankly that if there was any way to supply Israel without using MAC, he wanted to do it; he called a meeting of CRAF airline presidents and gave them a tough lecture. The presidents responded that they were willing to go if Clements would send MAC to lead the way, but that they would not fly alone, since by so doing they would lose every base right in countries not friendly to Israel. They wanted a declaration of national emergency and a promise of indemnity for all assets lost. Secretary Schlesinger was disappointed but not really surprised when the European allies did not accept the American view of the seriousness of the challenge to Israel; as a result, the United States did not ask for the use of European air bases for the airlift, but rather on 13 October elected to begin military flights through Portugal's Lajes Field in the Azores into Lod airfield in Israel. By this time the Soviets had begun an airlift resupplying Syria and Egypt.[51]

Both in the planning and operations, Nickel Grass was directed from a very high level through the Joint Chiefs of Staff but with no central top-level command post. General Carlton said:

IDEAS, CONCEPTS, DOCTRINE

> The concept of operating within an established command and control structure was isolated—the Air Force didn't set up a command post to handle our activity; yet, we were working for the Air Force. We found ourselves taking instructions primarily from JCS/J-4 Logistics. Command and control, or rather a lack of it, caused indecision.[52]

In view of the political complexity, MAC got no use from the European Command's command and control system that could have provided an interface with the US Navy in the Mediterranean. Instead, MAC worked directly with the US Sixth Fleet through the JCS to arrange codes, safe passage procedures, and diversion plans in case of hostile interceptions. In fact, the Navy tracked MAC transports from ship to ship from Gibraltar through the Mediterranean, keeping a ship on station every 300 miles and an aircraft carrier every 600 miles. Early on in the airlift, MAC needed to position airlift control elements and equipment, and movement of very small loads of a couple of thousand pounds incident to the airlift control element (ALCE) deployment and resupply was most feasibly done by C-130s belonging to USAFE and TAC. Midway in the operation, when Soviet threats caused the United States to go on a military alert, all C-130 assets were withdrawn from MAC control. Thereupon, General Carlton had to use C-141s to move very small loads for en route support, which, he said, "didn't make sense" and in the end proved to be "a powerful argument" for consolidating tactical airlift under MAC.[53]

To General Carlton a "vital lesson" of the Nickel Grass airlift was that "the C-5 wasn't a lemon."[54] Air Force Secretary McLucas agreed that the C-5 was a good system. McLucas remarked:

> I think a couple of years ago people were looking at this as an airplane that had experienced terrible technical difficulties and was costing more than it was supposed to. Now I think as a result of the Mideast experience we see it as an airplane that was very capable and did do the mission for which it was designed.[55]

When the national command authorities ordered an emergency resupply operation to Israel on 13 October, a MAC C-5 was en route within nine hours, loaded with 193,000 pounds of cargo. More MAC flights were staged from Dover AFB. The average nautical mile distance from the United States to Lod airfield via Lajes was 6,450 miles. All US equipment reaching Israel before the cease-fire arrived by air, and by the time the first resupply ship from the United States arrived in Israel on 2 November, nearly a week after the 24 October cease-fire, 566 MAC missions—421 C-141 and 145 C-5—had delivered 22,395 short tons of cargo for a total of 144.45 million ton-miles. On 29 of the C-5 missions, vitally needed M48 and M60 tanks were airlifted, a task that could only be accomplished by the C-5. The following table shows the US airlift/sealift in perspective:

TABLE 5
United States Airlift/Sealift
(85,108 Tons)

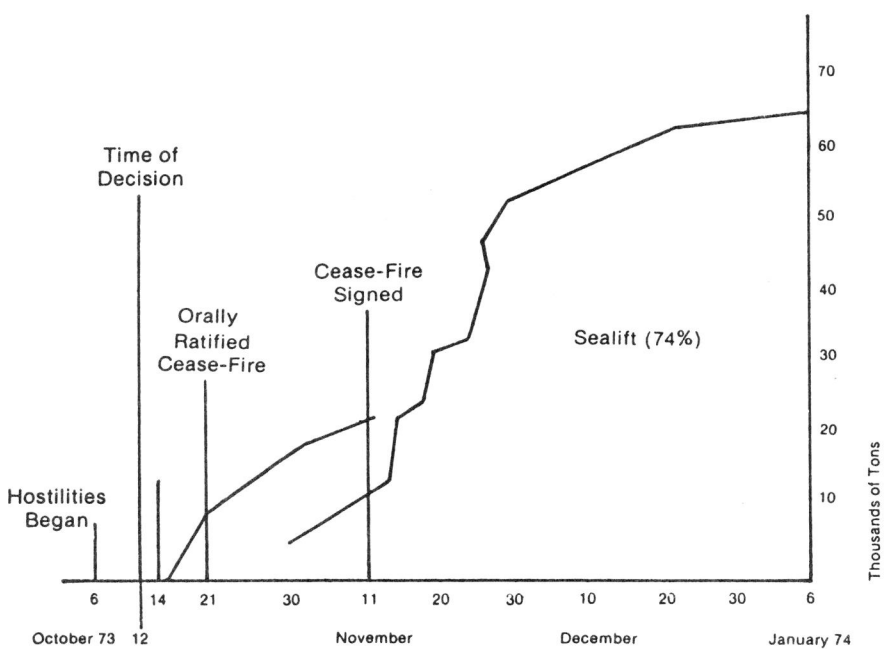

Source: House, *Hearings on the Posture of Military Airlift before the Research and Development Subcommittee on Armed Services*, 94th Cong., 1st sess., 1975, 31.

From 13 October to 14 November 1973, the C-5 utilization rate averaged 2.69 hours per day per aircraft, while the C-141 utilization rate was 5.14 hours. The C-5A averaged 74 tons of payload per mission, the C-141 27 tons. In addition to the MAC airlift, the Israelis made good use of their Boeing 707/747 airliners for handling cargo, comprised of mostly ammunition and bombs loaded and unloaded through passenger doors. There were 140 Israeli missions that lifted 5,500 tons for 34.30 million total ton-miles.[56]

Although it proved possible to mount Nickel Grass with only Lajes Field as an en route base, the limited facilities at Lajes and an about one-an-hour-refueling capacity at Lod forced a limitation of the MAC airlift flow eastbound to 36 C-141s and 6 C-5s, with a similar number returning westbound. The use of an alternative route in the North Atlantic for returning aircraft could have enhanced the efficiency of the operation. In his discussions of Nickel Grass, General Carlton revealed that his transports took more tons of fuel out of Israel than they took cargo

IDEAS, CONCEPTS, DOCTRINE

in. Fortunately, the Israelis had plenty of fuel; otherwise, it would have been bad news and the operation would have ground to a halt in a hurry. Carlton said:

> This is a lesson everyone has to keep in mind – that destinations should be kept within a radius of airlift aircraft, not simply within its range. Normally, you will want to make fast turnarounds there and not denude the people you're supporting of a critical resource.[57]

In talking about a strategic base for MAC, Carlton envisioned an airfield that could deliver a million gallons or more of fuel a day, equivalent to handling one strategic airplane every ten minutes. In the expedited delivery of fighter aircraft to Israel, KC-135 tankers proved the key to mobility. The tankers supported rapid delivery of F-4s and A-4s and in one case took eight Air Force F-4s nonstop from the United States to Israel. Within 15 hours after departing the United States, some of these F-4 aircraft had been accepted by Israel and were flying combat missions. Aerial refueling also would have been advantageous to MAC. C-5s were capable of air refueling, and MAC put five aerial-refueling-qualified crews at Dover, but aerial refueling was not used because of a fear of the results of aerial refueling maneuvers on the C-5's wing. Later it was evident that aerial refueling would have put less stress on the C-5 wing than the extra takeoffs and landings in the Azores. In the Israeli operation, General Carlton figured that with aerial refueling MAC could have delivered the same tonnage in 44 fewer C-5 missions, 57 fewer C-141 missions than MAC flew, and saved about 7 million gallons of fuel, including the fuel required to operate the tankers. There were, Carlton said, two apparent reasons aerial refueling had to be shared by MAC: "One of them is if you can't get there any other way.... The other is when you start to download cargo in order to get more range on the airplane to meet the range you have."[58] Without the requirement to land at Lajes, C-5s and C-141s could have replaced fuel reserves with added cargo loadings. Immediately after the Israeli operation, MAC began to train all its C-5 crews for aerial refueling operation. MAC also stated a requirement that its C-141 fleet be retrofitted for aerial refueling. The Air Force fleet of KC-135 tankers, moreover, had been designed principally to mate with SAC bombers and TAC fighters; the KC-135 was inadequate for refueling C-5s or C-141s, and there was now a requirement for a wide-bodied aircraft as an advanced tanker cargo aircraft.[59]

When sea shipments began to reach Israel, the MAC airlift was counted completed on 14 November 1973, though there were two more flights after this. Much later, a General Accounting Office study of the Yom Kippur War concluded that equipment on the ground determined the results of the war and that US airlift had no direct outcome on that conflict. The report noted that only a small amount of outsized equipment was delivered prior to the cease-fire. On the other hand, Air Force Chief of Staff Gen David Jones pointed out that the Israelis had asked for first priority to ammunition and spare parts. The outsized items that were airlifted were used to benefit Israeli morale. The outsized deliveries also demonstrated that the United States had the capability to deliver such equipment to Israel. Ample demonstration of the morale-building aspect of the airlift was provided by Prime Minister Golda Meir's dramatic outburst at the sight of the first tank arriving by C-5: "For generations to come, all will be told of the miracle of the immense planes from the United States."[60]

Airlift Consolidation and Specified Status for MAC

Said Secretary of Defense Schlesinger in February 1974:

> I believe that the mobility of our forces is extremely important. From the first day I walked into the Pentagon, I have been focusing on the subject, prior to any downturn in the economy, and prior to any war in the Middle East. This area has an enormous impact on our ability to help deter conventional conflict in Europe.[61]

As has been seen, one of the Air Force's Corona Harvest recommendations predicated upon experience in the SEA conflict was that steps should be taken to achieve a single airlift command as soon as possible. The principal airlift resources under consideration were the strategic airlift of MAC and the tactical airlift of TAC, but there was also a "support" category that included leased civil aviation services in the Navy's QUICKTRANS and the Air Force's LOGAIR systems, as well as congeries of C-118s, C-131s, T-29s, T-39s, C-97s, and so forth, assigned in ones and twos around the country for administrative support and proficiency flying. During the Middle East airlift of 1973, General Carlton found his task more difficult because he did not have clear title to the tactical C-130s, and the Arab oil embargo and cartel so greatly increased the cost of aviation fuel as to demand changes in support airlift. After much debate within the Department of Defense, Secretary Schlesinger issued a program decision memorandum on 29 July 1974, with amendment on 22 August 1974, that directed the consolidation of all airlift forces in the Department of Defense under a single manager by the end of fiscal year 1977, by which time the Military Airlift Command would become a specified command. The amendment made it clear that the directive included Department of Navy Fleet Tactical Support and Marine Combat Support Transport aircraft, the Air Force being directed to assume this airlift support starting in fiscal year 1977.[62]

On 29 August 1974 Gen David Jones informed every Air Force major activity of the decision to centralize defense airlift in the Military Airlift Command, specifically directing that all tactical C-130 aircraft and associated support in TAC, Alaskan Air Command, USAF South, USAFE, and PACAF would be transferred in place to MAC. A McLucas-Jones explanation of the meaning of the changes pointed out that they expected the consolidation to result in added tactical orientation for MAC, as well as additions of tactical planes to airmobility forces.

> As we have modernized our aircraft over the years, we have realized that the line between tactical and strategic airlift has blurred appreciably. For example, our C-130s have a strategic capability and can be used in this role (as, indeed, they have in the past).

> Similarly, our C-5s and our C-141s have a tactical capability. Therefore, we are transferring all tactical airlift aircraft to MAC—except, of course, for those in the Reserve forces, which will come under MAC's operational control if called up. The result will be one command responsible for both strategic and tactical airlift roles and for management of resources between them.[63]

In addition to this, the MAC charter was broadened by picking up responsibility for support aircraft. At this time, the Air Force ordered over 400 of the old support aircraft phased out. The more efficient T-39/C-135 support aircraft were retained but placed under MAC as the single manager. This streamlining promised to release over 6,000 manpower spaces and to reduce fuel consumption by roughly 150,000 gallons per day. The elimination of more than 400 support aircraft had a drawback since it posed a loss of continuation pilot proficiency; to offset this loss partially, the Air Force elected to increase T-39/C-135 utilization rates and to make proficiency training the primary mission of these aircraft. Initially, however, the planes were placed at operating locations throughout the United States, where they were available to provide a by-product airlift. Each command/separate operating agency was authorized to request MAC airlift on a priority basis through a central airlift scheduling facility where MAC consolidated the requests for their most efficient accommodation.[64]

In making the decision for the consolidation of airlift in the Military Airlift Command, Generals Jones and Carlton saw the need to "recognize and preserve the image and spirit" of the tactical airlift force. To this end, Carlton prepared a program designed both to retain the "tacticalness" of the C-130 units and to improve the tactical orientation of the C-5 and C-141 units.[65] One point of contention arose almost immediately in October 1974 when representatives of MAC and USAFE met to develop a plan for the "as is/where is" transfer of the resources of the two C-130 groups kept on temporary duty status in Europe. USAFE wanted to keep tasking authority directly to the individual flying units and crews, this to be exercised through an airlift control center (ALCC) collocated with USAFE headquarters at Ramstein Air Base. The aircraft were used to provide essential day-to-day tactical airlift for the European Command, such as airdrop training of US Army forces in Europe, deployment and redeployment of Air Force and Army tactical units for Central Europe to training/gunnery ranges in Southern Europe, and necessary carrier, mail, and priority support airlift within the European theater. MAC would not accept the level of detailed control USAFE wanted, but the debate generated a theater airlift manager concept, whereby a designated senior officer would exercise operational control of theater airlift for the Air Force component commander and also manage airlift for MAC.[66] Gen William G. Moore, Jr., who succeeded General Carlton as CINCMAC in 1977, was a tactical airlifter who had commanded the 834th Air Division in Vietnam. General Moore found some residual problems of force integration still lingering, particularly a "big MAC, little MAC" syndrome where many of the C-130 people felt they did not get the same level of support as the C-5/C-141 people. Because of distances involved, Moore also found it hard to get desired working relations with the theater air component commander. He needed a strong, on-the-scene command; accordingly, Moore reestablished the 322d and 834th Airlift Divisions at Ramstein and Hickam to ensure full airlift support in Europe and in the Pacific.[67]

"Becoming a specified command," said General Carlton, "followed very logically from airlift consolidation."[68] Said General Moore of MAC designation as a specified command,

> It was apparent that the commander of MAC had too many bases during contingency operations. For instance, during the Israeli Airlift, General Carlton found himself taking directions from too many sources. It became very apparent that MAC had to be the Air Force airlift spokesman in forums involving the JCS and unified commanders.[69]

General Carlton said that resistance to MAC's being designated a specified command directly responsible to the Joint Chiefs of Staff came from the theater commanders who wanted to own their own airlift fleets. As a matter of fact, the Air Force—while somewhat reluctantly agreeable to airlift consolidation—opposed designating MAC as a specified command. The influential Directorate of Doctrine, Concepts, and Objectives argued that such would begin a splintering of Air Force forces by mission, for example, a reconnaissance or a strike/attack or an interdiction specified command might be in order. Others argued that unified or specified commands should be combat oriented, whereas MAC's business was logistical. Some pointed out that the JCS, through the joint transportation boards, already could assure equitable application of airlift. On 13 March 1975 Air Force Secretary John L. McLucas accepted Air Staff recommendations and told Secretary Schlesinger that MAC should not be designated as a specified command but should remain an Air Force major command. The Joint Chiefs of Staff, less the chairman, concurred in the Air Force recommendation not to establish MAC as a specific command. But Gen George Brown, JCS chairman, wrote a separate memo to the secretary of defense recommending:

> Airlift resources are major assets for furtherance of our security policy, and the importance of airlift as a factor in planning for combat operations will be heightened by the consolidation of tactical and strategic systems. Under these circumstances, the MAC Commander should receive his strategic direction directly from the Joint Chiefs of Staff, who are charged with this responsibility under the law.[70]

As the discussion continued, MAC proposed that it would be a specified command reporting to the JCS and secretary of defense in all matters concerning war planning, contingency operations, and JCS exercises and a major command reporting to the Air Force secretary and chief of staff concerning peacetime operations and the budget. On 9 June 1976 Deputy Secretary of Defense Clements reaffirmed the decision to make MAC a specified command. The unified command plan (UCP) was appropriately changed, and on 16 December 1976 the president approved the UCP change, which finally went into effect on 1 February 1977.[71] According to General Moore, who as incumbent handled the change from

COMAC to CINCMAC, the transformation from major command to specified command was "a very smooth transition" since the procedures actually had been evolving for a number of years and the change had been clearly evolutionary rather than revolutionary.[72]

The Modern Airlift Era

Secretary of Defense Harold Brown stated in 1979:

> Given a desired schedule for the deployment of forces, the mobility forces required for initial deployment can be determined relatively easily. Likewise, given daily consumption ratios, the mobility forces required for sustaining support can be determined. It is much more difficult to make a judgement on how much capability to buy for the third function — movement in response to unpredictable shifts in the demands of combat — because this involves estimating how frequently exigent tactical situations will develop.[73]

Estimating Mobility Requirements Proves Difficult

In 1981 the congressionally mandated mobility study made by the OSD and JCS was prefaced with the twin observations:

> One of the major problems of any mobility analysis is that the results are very heavily influenced by assumptions. . . . Another problem of mobility analyses is that they tend to focus on the scenario. This is necessary to do the analysis but acts to obscure the military requirement for flexibility.[74]

Upon his arrival in office, Secretary of Defense Schlesinger's interest in airlift was directed toward its potential enhancement to US reinforcement of NATO. He wanted to be able to move a US division by air to Europe in 7 days instead of being confined to moving it in 19 days. He said, "I believe that we should expand our airlift so as to enhance our NATO reinforcement capability. That, in turn, should give us ample capacity for Pacific contingencies and the 'off design' cases."[75] During hearings on the posture of military airlift in November 1975, Brig Gen Jasper A. Welch, Air Force assistant chief of staff for studies and analysis, recalled that the thrust of mobility planning was still focused on Europe. Welch said:

> While our mobility forces give us the ability to project combat forces any place in the world, we naturally concentrate on priorities in Western Europe — where the ground forces of the United States and the Soviet Union are in the most approximate confrontation.[76]

With the strategic airlift force current in 1975, Welch computed that 14 days would be needed to move the 70,000 tons incident to one infantry division to Europe. With enhancements to airlift being requested and, Welch said, with an integrated sealift, airlift approach, we expect in the 30-day period to be able to deliver essentially all of the Active Army Forces and their closely associated and affiliated Reserve units, plus all of the Air Force equipment and units which we plan for deployment to NATO.[77]

Gen David Jones said:

Today we have a capability to move about 180,000 tons to Europe in a month with our airlift. That is about half of what we believe is necessary to get the fighting element over.... We are not trying to get a capability to deploy everything by air. The total requirement in a European conflict for initial movement and initial supplies is over 3 million tons. So what we try to do is to get a capability for about 370,000 tons by air, and the remainder by sea in that time period.[78]

Plans for the NATO airlift were coordinated with the European allies. In response to US queries, the allies stated in November 1973 that they had sufficient airlift to support their individual needs. In January 1975 US representatives held briefings and discussions with senior political and military representatives of NATO on strategic airlift. NATO officials agreed to press on with improving the reception capability of NATO airports and hoped to use NATO civil aircraft to speed US troops and equipment from the airports where they landed to the battle areas where they would be needed as fighting units.[79]

At a meeting of NATO heads of government in May 1978, President Carter reaffirmed that "the US is prepared to use all forces necessary for the defense of the NATO area." In fulfillment of this policy, Secretary of Defense Harold Brown announced a plan to speed reinforcements to Europe, this entailing a capability to triple US combat planes in the theater to 1,900 within a week and to increase US troop strength from 200,000 to 350,000 within two weeks. A key part of the plan would be to match up Army battalions with supplies and equipment in prepositioned overseas materiel configured to unit sets (POMCUS) storage in Europe. Brown said that the NATO-Warsaw Pact confrontation was "by far the most demanding contingency we consider[ed] in our planning" but that there were other areas in the world "such as the Middle East, the Persian Gulf, or Korea" warranting consideration in mobility planning. "Although we do not plan the capability for simultaneous all-out deployment to one of these locations and to Europe, our planning must account for the possibility that war in any one of them could lead to war in Europe." The two key areas in which mobility forces would have to be improved would include an ability to deploy additional US ground and air forces to Europe rapidly and an ability to deploy and support forces in limited contingencies without reliance on intermediate bases or overflight rights.[80] In October 1978 the United States conducted a first full-scale simulated computerized mobilization exercise in many years. Called Nifty Nugget, this 21-day marathon involved 24 military commands and 30 civilian agencies and examined the planned reinforcement of US combat units in Europe. The exercise was said to have demonstrated that after many years of talk, the United States was not prepared for a mobility reinforcement of NATO. There was no central mechanism for implementation and coordination of complex mobilization and deployments and of the activities of the Military Airlift Command, the Military Sealift Command, and the Military Traffic Management Command. The airlift part of the exercise suffered from a lack of coordination; moreover, plans called for many more aircraft than could be made available, particularly when contingency plans for more than one area had to be implemented simultaneously.[81]

Before 1979 the major concern of US defense mobility planning was a rapid reinforcement of NATO, but regional developments during 1979 broadened the spectrum of mobility requirements. The danger of the marked Soviet buildup of power against NATO continued to grow, but the collapse of a friendly government in Iran in January 1979 led to a chaotic revolution headed by the Ayatollah Khomeini and the seizure of US hostages in the American embassy in November 1979. In September 1979 it was revealed that a Soviet combat brigade was stationed in Cuba, and in December 1979 Soviet military forces initially invaded Afghanistan. In 1979 the United States also began to know "with considerable confidence" that in the 1970s the North Koreans had been engaging in a major military buildup that was not geared to defensive considerations. The full geopolitical importance of the Middle East was impressed upon the US government when President Carter in his State of the Union message in January 1980 stated: "Any attempt by any outside force to gain control over the Persian Gulf region will be regarded as an assault on the vital interests of the United States and such an assault will be repelled by any means necessary, including military force."[82] Robert W. Komer, under secretary of defense for policy, had been designated to head a DOD mobilization deployment steering group in the wake of Nifty Nugget. With the emerging power vacuum in the Persian Gulf, Komer pointed out that the United States was confronted with a three-front problem, instead of a two-front, or one-and-one-half front problem.

> In addition to our vital interest in Europe, our vital interest in Northeast Asia, we now have the problem of what to do to deter or defend Persian Gulf oil, particularly if the Soviets decided to take advantage of the enormous strategic gains they could achieve by meddling around in that particularly vulnerable area.[83]

Komer's studies suggested that "we ought to try to finesse one of the three fronts since we couldn't possibly handle three fronts simultaneously."[84]

In January 1979 Secretary Harold Brown's presentation of US mobility forces for the reinforcement of Europe banked heavily on programming to preposition military equipment in the NATO countries. A year later, Brown's solution for NATO reinforcement still hinged on prepositioning. He said:

> The Rapid Reinforcement Program will produce at M+14 a total of US ground firepower greater than is in the entire German Army and twice the number of air squadrons that are in the Luftwaffe. . . . The timely provision of this massive reinforcement depends in the first instance on our ability to preposition unit sets of equipment in Europe, fly troops over to them by passenger aircraft, and deploy our fighter squadrons to protected and well-stocked allied bases.[85]

Although prepositioning had advantages, it was not an entirely satisfactory solution to mobility shortfalls, even in Europe. Some items, such as helicopters and air defense systems with heavy use of electronics, were not suitable candidates for prepositioning. Moreover, no one knew how a crisis would develop. The United States might well want to shift forces to some place other than Europe's Central Front. No one knew where contingencies outside the NATO area might occur. Brown stated:

> It is possible that we would not get help from our NATO allies; there probably will be little or no prepositioned equipment and supplies; and, at least in some cases, we would be less willing to divert civil ships and aircraft from their normal business. Finally, operational problems will be greater. In particular, we may be operating over longer distances with few or no intermediate bases, and reception facilities may be limited. Improving our capabilities in such circumstances is an important objective of our program. In particular, we want to have the capability to deploy quickly (and support) at least a small force to distant locations without reliance on foreign bases or overflight rights.[86]

The emerging power vacuum in Southwest Asia demonstrated that US defense interests were no longer regional but had become global. Gen David Jones, the JCS chairman, expressed the Joint Chiefs' views:

> In the 1950s, 1960s and even in the 1970s, although with greater risk, we could afford to deal with issues on a regional basis. In the 1950s, in Korea we could literally decimate our military capabilities in much of the rest of the world and get by with it. In the 1960s, we could fight a war in Vietnam and rob Peter to pay Paul and get by with it. Now we need to address events on a global basis, and when we look at the greatest danger—several events occurring simultaneously—we have what the JCS have stated for a long time—a strategy/force mismatch, the inability to protect all our interests with the forces we have available. We also have a geographic asymmetry, in that we have vital interests close to the Soviet Union and far from us while they have no truly vital interests far from them and close to us. So they have a geographic advantage, particularly in Southwest Asia.[87]

According to Ambassador Komer, who said that he had "interfaced" with the Joint Chiefs and Joint Staff "very actively" to work out a Persian Gulf policy, the Joint Chiefs in 1980 were "terribly concerned that any major US-USSR regional clash anywhere in the world might quickly escalate to global war." Komer continued:

> And the JCS have been fascinated by what is called horizontal escalation—that if we are attacked someplace where we are vulnerable, let us say the Persian Gulf, instead of trying to contest the enemy where we are weakest and he is strongest, we should, in effect escalate by attacking him someplace else where we are stronger and he is weaker.[88]

Maxwell Taylor was often well informed on defense policy. In an interview in June 1950, he was emphatic that the Middle East was the wrong place to have a military confrontation with the Soviet Union since the United States no longer had the means to sustain military operations of any significant size on the periphery of the

Soviet Union. In the Middle East, however, it was important for the United States to sustain sufficient force to present the Soviets with a present risk of escalation.[89]

In part because of the identification of serious deficiencies in the ability of the United States to deploy combat forces to NATO that became apparent in Nifty Nugget and in part because of uncertainty over how to deal with other potential contingency areas, the Department of Defense military appropriations request for fiscal year 1981 asked for funds for a new airlift modernization program. In restructuring mobility objectives, the Air Force required funding for a new C-X airlift aircraft that would both project into a theater and meet intratheater airlift requirements. In the spring 1980 Department of Defense appropriations hearings, the House Armed Services Committee rejected development money for the C-X, questioning the pertinency of a new airlift plane that could carry only one XM-1 tank. The Senate had a better opinion of the C-X, but both the House and the Senate wanted the Department of Defense to give more attention to mobility planning. As enacted on 8 September 1980, the Department of Defense Authorization Act of 1981 required the secretary of defense to conduct an analysis of the mix of aircraft, sealift, and prepositioning required for the United States to respond to military contingencies in the Indian Ocean area and other areas of potential conflict during the 1980s. It also provided that no funds could be obligated or expended for a full-scale engineering development or procurement of the C-X or any other new transport aircraft until the secretary of defense certified in writing to Congress that US national security required the C-X; that the military cargo to be airlifted to the Indian Ocean was sufficiently well defined as to identify a deficiency of military airlift; that the military cargo was sufficiently well defined to provide justification and design for a new airlift aircraft; and that plans for a new airlift aircraft were sufficiently advanced as to make full-scale engineering development both economically and technically feasible.[90]

New Perspectives on Airlift Aircraft

In the first few years of the 1970s the volume capacity of Military Airlift Command's channel and special assignment airlift declined sharply with the reduction in support for Southeast Asia. In fiscal year 1975, it was only about 30 percent of the 7-1/2 billion ton-miles of fiscal year 1968, the peak year of Southeast Asian activity. These figures pointed to a major airlift problem: in wartime there was a much larger requirement for airlift than could be used in peacetime. In peacetime, moreover, the Department of Defense divided its limited passenger and cargo business between aircraft of the Military Airlift Command and the Civil Reserve Air Fleet. MAC's peacetime flying hours were necessary to maintain a crew proficiency suitable for a desired surge for emergencies, and MAC was customarily under congressional pressure to find a productive use for MAC's flying hours in peacetime, at the same time providing an incentive necessary for CRAF's commercial carriers to acquire significant numbers of wide-bodied jet cargo/

convertible aircraft for use in military augmentation. In the post-Vietnam years each of many mobility studies undertaken showed that there was an impending shortfall in both intertheater and intratheater airlift, particularly for "outsized" and "oversize" cargo. Outsized cargo was the air cargo that exceeded the loading capacity of C-130/C-141 aircraft and required use of C-5 aircraft. Typical outsized cargo items included the Army's M60 tank, 155-mm howitzer, and CH-53 helicopter. Oversize cargo required the loading capabilities of a C-130/C-141 aircraft and could not be carried in commercial aircraft without modification. Typical examples of oversize items were the UH-1B helicopter, standard Army 6-ton truck, and a 6,000-pound forklift. In 1975 the Air Force considered in regard to airlift capabilities:

> The greatest need is for capacity in long-range aircraft to move vehicles (particularly the smaller personnel carriers and trucks) which we call oversize cargo. Secondly, we could use a somewhat greater capacity for the outsize tanks, guns, and recovery and repair vehicles which only the C-5 can airlift today. We have ample passenger and bulk cargo capacity in the aircraft of the Civil Reserve Air Fleet.[91]

In hearings on the posture of military airlift in November 1975, the Air Force's airlift enhancement initiatives sought means less costly than procuring new transports for strategic airlift. The options included increased utilization rates for the C-5 and the C-141 aircraft; aerial refueling of the C-5 and the C-141 through new engines for KC-135s and obtaining a new fleet of advanced cargo/transport aircraft; stretching the cargo capacity of C-141s; using tactical C-130s to augment the strategic airlift force with eventual replacement of C-130s by more versatile advanced medium-short-takeoff-and-landing transport (AMST); and by motivating CRAF carriers to obtain and operate oversize-capable wide-bodied jets in their commercial inventories. In 1975 MAC intended to move military passenger traffic primarily by contract with CRAF airlines. Since the level of military cargo requirements was below that which could be handled by MAC in programed training, MAC expected to use its cargo capacity generated as a by-product of training before contracting with the airlines for substantial peacetime cargo service.[92]

In any prospective military airlift augmentation, General Carlton said in November 1975, CRAF was "a great national mobility asset. It has done yeoman service for us down through the years. It is the cheapest way to do the job, if the vehicle available will meet your requirements."[93] As the MAC commander, Carlton considered that he was responsible for any necessary mobilization of both the military and civilian airlift fleets. The military fleet had an adequate number of big C-5s and C-141s but an absolute minimum number of crews and supplies to make their flying hours go up to the 12 hours per day that would be desirable. The civil fleet had lots of crews and supplies and was operating aircraft from 8 to 10 hours every day, but the commercial passenger planes were unsuited to military cargo lift. In the early 1970s the Air Force had hoped that commercial cargo demands would result in the CRAF carriers buying wide-bodied cargo jets that would be available for government service. But the demand for commercial carriers capable of handling oversize cargo did not materialize. Beginning in 1974 the Air Force sought appropriations to compensate commercial carriers for modifying aircraft for freighter use; while the carriers were reported to be interested in this enhanced CRAF program, Congress rejected it in fiscal years 1975 and 1976.[94] When the enhanced civil cargo fleet did not materialize, the Air Force launched a new idea in fiscal year 1980 and submitted it to Congress in early 1979. This time, Gen Lew Allen proposed to subsidize the cost of cargo modifications when the aircraft were being constructed. Allen strongly urged that the enhanced CRAF would be "many, many times cheaper" than any other way of providing expanded strategic airlift, but in March 1981 he ruefully stated that the enhanced CRAF program had been, for reasons unknown to him, unable to work up much support. The airlines had been unwilling to buy any wide-bodied, cargo-capable aircraft. "It has been a source of enormous frustration that we have not, among us all, found the key to moving ahead with [the enhanced CRAF]," he said.[95] In May 1982, Allen remarked that the people who went to war in the future were going to go on commercial CRAF airliners but that there was still no arrangement whereby the airlines would convert their passenger airplanes quickly to cargo-capable airplanes, which meant strengthening floors, putting in larger doors, and doing other things that increased weight and operating costs in a commercial employment.[96]

A vital factor in airlift augmentation was to realize the full potential of existing resources. At the time that the C-141A production was on the line, it was evident already that the new plane had enough power to lift more cargo than the cubic content of its short fuselage could accommodate. The plane had been kept short to facilitate its operation from advanced shorter airfields. These facts were fully disclosed in congressional hearings in 1965, when it had been declared feasible to stretch the C-141s still in production by inserting plugs in their fuselages; at this time, the Air Force with Secretary McNamara's support would not accept the proposal since it asserted that C-141 production might be delayed for a year, the time required to make and test the changed version. The Air Force had hoped that commercial aviation would buy a civil cargo version of the C-141A, but airline companies would not accept a plane that would not be able to carry maximum cube ordinary cargo using the power that was available.[97] Based on its performance in operation, the C-141A "cubed out" before reaching its full weight carrying capability: the size or bulk of most cargo that could be airlifted in the C-141A exhausted the usable cargo volume before the aircraft reached its maximum allowable load. The lift in the Arab-Israeli conflict of 1973 clearly showed that the C-141A fleet was volume constrained. In fiscal year 1975 Congress authorized a technical feasibility prototype modification, adding 23 feet to the length of a C-141 fuselage, and also adding an aerial-refueling capability. The resultant C-141B had 13 pallet positions, 3 more than the C-141A. The modification program was completed in mid-1982, and of it Gen Robert E. Huyser, CINCMAC, said: "Other than CRAF the C-141 stretch program is the most cost effective airlift enhancement program in being today."[98]

Strictly speaking, the C-5A wing modification was not an enhancement to airlift, but it was essential to the preservation of the plane's strategic outsized-delivery capability. The life of a C-5A was projected to be 8,000 hours without wing modification, a severe reduction to a design goal of 30,000 hours. Even with reduced peacetime flying, the service life of the C-5A would run out in the mid-1980s. The unmodified wing was not hazardous in flight but certain restrictions were nevertheless practiced. The theoretical 200-foot terrain-following employment was abandoned, since at such altitude the rough air buffeted the vulnerable wing. The high-flotation landing gear was not used for any landings in plowed fields according to original design, since the rougher any landing, the worse the condition of a wing. The greatest strain was on what MAC called the "GAG cycle—the ground-air-ground cycle," so the rough field-landing capability was not used.[99] In December 1975, the Air Force began to design a modification to the C-5A wings that, in the end, involved a major rework of wing beams as well as surfaces. Replacement of the C-5A with a comparable field-landing capability, however, would have cost three times as much as the proposed modification. The modification program was finally set up whereby the wings would be modified as each C-5A went through scheduled inspection and repair as necessary (IRAN). The first production aircraft entered the Lockheed-Georgia facility in January 1982, and all 77 surviving C-5A aircraft were scheduled to have been modified by the end of fiscal year 1987.[100] Whereas it had originally been thought that the C-5A would be compatible with a small, austere forward airfield environment, this did not prove practicable even for a modified-wing aircraft. C-5 tests on unprepared surfaces at Harper Dry Lake and on matting at Dyess AFB were terminated because of runway and aircraft damage. Air Force Secretary Hans Mark wrote:

> The results of these tests plus the operational experience we have gained over the past 12 years have shown that the C-5 is not compatible with the small, austere airfield environment because of the aircraft size and operating characteristics. I know that originally we thought C-5s should be able to do that but we were wrong.[101]

The Air Force had bought KC-135 aerial-refueling aircraft to support Strategic Air Command's long-range bomber missions, and these planes had successfully extended the range of tactical aircraft in Southeast Asia. During the Israeli airlift in 1973, aerial refueling of C-141s and C-5s could have greatly benefited the hauling of cargo and also reduced congestion in the Azores and time-on-ground refueling at Lod airfield in Israel. It was obvious that aerial refueling of transport aircraft would speed a NATO deployment and preserve NATO fuel reserves, since the transports would not need to refuel at offload points. Whereas a reskinned and reengined KC-135 would continue to be effective in refueling bombers, experience showed that a wide-bodied transport/refueler would be needed to satisfy the fuel needs of C-5s and C-141s. In 1973 the Israelis flew a Boeing 747 with about 140,000 pounds of cargo nonstop from the United States to Israel, and Gen David Jones notes that that cargo capability could have translated into fuel to take fighters or transports directly into the Middle East. General Jones pointed out,"Operating from the US territory, either from the United States heading east or Guam heading west or southwest, we can refuel fighters, and we can take fighters en route to any, virtually any base in the world without support."[102] Air Force Secretary Thomas C. Reed added: "It is the concern about the unreliability of overseas bases that principally drives the Advanced Tanker Cargo Aircraft [ATCA]."[103] In an early estimate, the Air Force specified that about 65 of the ATCA would be appropriate for a European reinforcement scenario. By taking advantage of available commercial wide-bodied aircraft, the Air Force could have the new tanker/cargo plane with very little development effort. The mid-1975 lull in commercial aircraft purchases, moreover, provided a very competitive atmosphere for buying military transport aircraft off the shelf. In bidding for ATCA, McDonnell Douglas offered the Douglas DC-10 and Boeing offered the Boeing 747, both of which met the tanker/cargo criteria. In December 1977, the Air Force's source selection considered the DC-10 had more cost advantages and accepted it for purchase as a KC-10. As a notional number, the Air Force asked for 41 KC-10s, and Lt Gen Thomas P. Stafford recorded his surprise when the Ford administration upped the number to 92 aircraft. When President Carter took office the number first went to zero, but Secretary Harold Brown on reclama accepted a small program with 20 KC-10s. Before going further Brown wanted a better understanding about the feasibility of new engines for 615 KC-135s held by the Air Force. Although KC-10 planes could transport both fuel and cargo simultaneously, the refueling task was the major activity, and the planes were assigned to the Strategic Air Command as the single manager of a common user force. The refueling mission would be predominant. In 1982, the first eight KC-10s were in service at Barksdale AFB, and the Air Force program had settled on a 60-aircraft buy, each at a given price with discounts in the latter purchase years. In an interesting logistical support arrangement, the Air Force also bought into the billion-dollar pool of spare parts for the DC-10 existing worldwide and underwritten by the owners and operators of these planes.[104]

At the same time that Project Forecast recommended the CX-Heavy Logistics Support Aircraft that became the C-5, it also recommended a vertical short takeoff and landing (VSTOL) aircraft. By 1970, however, the Tactical Air Command could see no early availability for technology to admit a VSTOL plane. Moreover, the Army's inventory of thousands of helicopters had reduced the operational requirement for a frontline Air Force airlift vehicle. "We take a realistic view and admit," said an Air Force briefer in January 1970, "that the C-130 and its replacement should be operated more rearward to avoid heavy enemy fire, and that aircraft of lesser cost must handle the far-forward requirement."[105] At this time, the House Military Airlift Subcommittee accepted the TAC recommendations that while VSTOL was currently impractical there was nevertheless "an urgent requirement to develop a STOL aircraft with greater payload and operational capability than the existing C-130." The subcommittee added that this should have the "highest priority" in the Air Force budget for fiscal year 1972.[106] In response to Deputy Secretary of Defense Packard's case for increased use of prototyping to cut weapons development costs, the Air Force Systems Command did a prototyping study in 1971 for an advanced medium STOL transport (AMST), and in January 1972 requests for proposals were released calling for bidders to propose a technology demonstrator according to desired tactical airlift parameters. In January 1973 Boeing and McDonnell Douglas were given contracts to build and test two prototypes each. From the start of the AMST undertaking, the Air Force had trouble getting funds to keep the prototype development going—so much trouble in fact that the companies involved put significant amounts of their own money into the effort in the expectation that they would produce a plane that would have a substantial civil usage. Using a "sort of cut and paste" approach—a cockpit of a DC-10 and the landing gear of a C-141— McDonnell Douglas got its YC-15 on a first flight well ahead of schedule in August 1975, and Boeing's more sophisticated YC-14 flew a year later. The US Army was actively supportive of the AMST, and the Combined Arms Combat Developments Activity at Fort Leavenworth, Kansas, concluded in August 1977 that a tank-carrying AMST offered the Army the "most flexible and efficient tactical airlift system." MAC also was a strong supporter of the AMST, considering it responsive to all intratheater airlift needs as well as to the mobility and flexibility of forces engaged at or near the forward edge of the battle area.[107]

The flight-test program of the YC-14 and the YC-15 was completed in August 1977, and the Air Force wished to proceed to source selection of one or the other planes in anticipation of a contract award in April 1978. But the program continued to be in financial trouble: the AMST had started off with a projected average flyaway cost of $5 million per aircraft; with inflation the cost had grown to about $10 million; and by 1982 with continuing inflation it could be as high as a $20 million airplane. In December 1977, Secretary of Defense Harold Brown directed that the AMST be dropped from President Carter's fiscal year 1979 defense budget request. Brown estimated that the AMST program would cost $9 billion in procurement money. Brown explained:

> We decided that because we really had no confidence that we would spend the $9 billion of procurement money that would be needed to procure a fleet of those, that we would cancel the program. Now it may be that the contractors will still go ahead and develop something for a commercial use and we would then be willing to consider that. But our uncertainty about the justifiability of the procurement requirement caused us to conclude it was not fair to lead the contractors on further.[108]

A little later, Brown would add that the cancellation of the intratheater airlift AMST was based on an assumption that in a most likely European conflict a sophisticated transportation network would compete favorably with the "speed and responsiveness of tactical airlift." At the same time that he dropped the AMST, Brown directed the Air Force to work with the other services, particularly the

Army, on a study of the entire intratheater mobility problem. The study also would include all airlift and resupply-type operations and every conceivable way of doing the job, such as additional POMCUS, additional prepositioned supplies within the European theater, more use of strategic airlift, even CRAF, and moving tanks on tank carriers instead of by air. With zero money in the fiscal year 1979 budget, Gen David Jones saw very little prospect of resurrecting the AMST, but he added: "We have not foreclosed some day in the future having a widebody tactical airlift."[109] In 1979, with Gen Lew Allen as Air Force chief of staff, the Air Force still insisted that it was essential to produce a new wide-body tactical airlift aircraft to keep pace with Army requirements, but it felt unable to consider adding the beginning of such in its fiscal year 1980 budget requests because of other higher priority claims on prospective appropriations. The Military Airlift Command agreed with the Air Force's view. In January 1981 Gen Robert E. Huyser, CINCMAC, said:

> I have said before Congress that if we had all the money in the world and I was not physically constrained on how much I could spend on airlift . . . I would pick a larger AMST than was tested, and I would pick a modern updated C-5 type aircraft—two airplanes.[110]

The tactical airlift modernization study, ordered by Secretary Brown, showed that the AMST was the most cost-effective method of meeting intratheater airlift needs as stated by the using services, but it also admitted that the AMST had not been fully justified in terms of alternate intratheater transportation means. An odd thing nevertheless happened to the AMST before the project died. In 1978 Secretary Brown directed the Air Force to look at the AMST for an airmobile employment of MX intercontinental missiles. As already seen, this concept was discarded, but not before a good look was given to the McDonnell Douglas YC-15, particularly its propulsive lift technology. The potential was there to build a larger plane that would have a long-range deployment capability without compromising the excellent tactical performance demonstrated in the AMST prototypes.[111] As it happened, the growing chaos in the Persian Gulf and the Soviet invasion of Afghanistan late in 1979 focused Department of Defense and Air Force priorities back on intertheater airlift. Intratheater airlift, remarked Gen Lew Allen, was still important, but the first priority problem was intertheater airlift. In October 1979 the Air Force laid a purely intratheater AMST to rest with a decision to pursue a C-X, an aircraft larger than the C-141, smaller than the C-5A, and capable of both strategic and tactical missions. Since the C-X was in part derivative from AMST, there were those who said the Air Force abandoned the AMST to make room for the C-X. This was rebutted by Deputy Under Secretary of Defense for Research and Engineering Dale W. Church who in June 1980 pointed out that the AMST program "was on the rocks and about to go before the idea of a C-X was even created."[112]

GLOBAL AIRMOBILITY FORCES

Organizing for Strategic Mobility

When the US Strike Command (STRICOM) was established with headquarters at MacDill AFB, Florida, on 19 September 1961, it was intended to provide an integrated, mobile, highly combat-ready force to augment existing unified commands or to serve as a primary force in the Middle East or Africa. CINCSTRIKE also was designated as CINC Middle East, Africa, and South Asia (CINCMEAFSA). A small US Navy component—the Middle East Force—was deployed in the Persian Gulf-Indian Ocean area. There were two joint task forces: JTF-7, commanded by an Air Force major general, centered on the Middle East and South Asia and JTF-11, commanded by an Army major general centered in Africa. On 1 January 1972 Strike Command was reorganized as the US Readiness Command (REDCOM). The new REDCOM was a unified command with a primary mission of providing a general reserve of combat forces to reinforce other unified or specified commands. REDCOM lost geographical responsibilities outside the United States and the US Navy and Marine component units. Its command comprised the US Army Forces Command and the US Air Force Tactical Air Command and was responsible for exercising these forces for joint operations.[113]

Each year in the late 1960s, REDCOM conducted four Army-Air Force joint readiness exercises, and a concept of a rapid deployment of forces to Europe began to emerge when it appeared that POMCUS equipment in NATO could not be a total solution to expeditious reinforcement. This occurred because the Army could not store equipment for all units in Europe and suddenly found it had nothing to go anywhere else. According to Gen Volney F. Warner, CINCREDCOM, a concept of a rapid deployment Army force began shaping up around the 18th Airborne Corps (82d and 101st Airborne Divisions), which would not position materiel equipment in Europe. Nifty Nugget revealed that there was a great lack of coordination for emergency movements: MAC airlift was 20 percent underutilized; many of the deploying units were counting on the same airlift or sealift; in one scenario commanders wanted to make a major change in the flow of units overseas but the MAC computer system would not accommodate the change; in another scenario units arrived at a port and the ship for them was not there. Because of these identifications of defective organization, the Joint Chiefs of Staff following Nifty Nugget established the Joint Deployment Agency as their transportation management extension at MacDill AFB; assigned CINCRED the additional mission as director of the Joint Deployment Agency; and charged the agency with pulling together the lift of the Military Traffic Management Command, Military Airlift Command, and Military Sealift Command in conjunction with supported forces to ensure that overseas CINCs could receive reinforcements in desired sequences and in the time required.[114]

Although REDCOM was moving toward a conception of more rapid deployment, General Warner thought the command was just "bumping along" until the Middle East situation became a catalyst for vigor. As Soviet military sales of T62 and T72 tanks in the Middle East increased arms there by 400 percent, Warner saw a marked change in world affairs. He said, "The day that the 82d could charge off and cope with that problem on its own is probably over. The day that the Marines could do it on their own is over. The time for anointing a single service as the Rapid Deployment Force is over."[115] After the fall of the shah of Iran and the identification of a Soviet combat brigade in Cuba, Secretary Harold Brown directed in October 1979 the establishment of a joint task force. In March 1980 he established Headquarters, Rapid Deployment Joint Task Force (RDJTF), as a subordinate of the US Readiness Command to conduct planning and training for Southwest Asia. In August 1980 he directed RDJTF to focus exclusively on Southwest Asian contingencies.[116] Units from all services were earmarked for inclusion in the RDJTF, under the command of Marine Lt Gen Paul X. Kelley, thus conceptualizing a combination of the formerly divided RDFs, one a Marine force moved by the Navy and the second an Army force deployed by the Air Force.[117]

Since rapid response was the key to successful employment of a US rapid deployment force in most scenarios, Secretary Brown posited "that we must have more airlift, complemented by fast sealift, to meet the global challenges to our national interests."[118] In the winter of 1979–80, however, Brown did not agree that the additional airlift would need to be a new C-X: it could be an existing aircraft like the C-5 or a suitable modification of a plane like the Boeing 747. Since it would require a lot longer to take the AMST design and build a big airplane around it, he really leaned toward a C-5 or B-747 but he had promised the Air Force there would be at least paper competition between the two alternatives.[119] Ongoing airlift studies made it evident that there was a very real shortage of intertheater airlift for new Army weapons, which were projected to be larger than ever before. Although a C-X would be able to operate from short airfields, Secretary Brown doubted that it would be used for intratheater airlift very much, except perhaps after initial deployments had been made. Brown also pointed out that lengths of combat area airfields might not be as important as runway widths, which affect the ability of a transport to taxi and offload quickly.[120]

In planning for a C-X the Air Force rationalized that 85 percent of all transport aircraft were designed and built in the United States and that commercial industries were best qualified to design a military airlift plane. General Huyser, CINCMAC, considered this a wise decision, and he also wanted to take advantage of the new technology that was developed by Boeing and McDonnell Douglas in their AMST programs. Secretary Brown continued to insist that the Air Force must keep the option open to accept some modification of an existing aircraft. Even though the Air Force's specifications for the airlift plane it wanted numbered 2,400 pages, Brown said that if cost and schedule savings were enough a decision would follow that some of the requirements could go unmet. To both senators and congressmen, however, it appeared that the Air Force had not made an adequate case for a C-X, especially in the aftermath of the many problems that had occurred with the C-5. The Research and Development Subcommittee of the House Committee on Armed Services strongly favored strategic mobility but recommended the deletion of C-X funding since the C-X did nothing to address near-term lift deficiencies. In the Senate Armed Services Committee, there was objection that the 2,400 pages of specifications indicated that the Air Force did not know what it wanted, or else the Air Force was attempting to get a new airplane without looking at the option of using a modified plane.[121] As already noted, the Department of Defense Authorization Act of 1981, enacted on 8 September 1980, required the secretary of defense to submit a comprehensive report on US military mobility requirements to Congress and stipulated that no funds for a C-X would be forthcoming until the secretary of defense certified its necessity for national security.

The clarification and formalization of US strategic mobility requirements really started in mid-1980 during the congressional hearings and was anchored in the congressionally mandated mobility study (CMMS) of April 1981. In June 1980 Sen John Stennis, chairman of the Armed Services Committee, requested Secretary Brown's testimonial assurance on the need for the C-X and on mobility as it concerned the Persian Gulf. Stennis wrote Brown:

> The Committee needs to know whether or not a rigorous plan has been developed to allow our forces to be properly supported if they are called on to deploy to the Persian Gulf region. Do we yet know how best to spread the logistics load among airlift, sealift and prepositioning—given the special requirements in that part of the world?[122]

On 5 June 1980 Secretary Brown revealed to the Senate Armed Services Committee that the United States was developing an option to reduce deployment time into the Persian Gulf area by prepositioning combat materiel in a force afloat at an Indian Ocean anchorage, probably at Diego Garcia. In presenting the C-X, Brown addressed the overall strategic mobility picture.

> Analysis of scenarios for NATO, the Persian Gulf, and Korea show that prepositioning and sealift are very important, both for follow on force buildup and sustaining support. We cannot afford to preposition combat equipment everywhere and although shipping is the least expensive way to satisfy the heavy requirement in a protracted conflict, sealift is slow; it is measured in weeks rather than days. We can go into more detail . . . later on, but the key is getting there very quickly. This may be the determining factor and airlift has that advantage.
>
> Who is there first may be more important in deterring a conflict than who can get there with the most forces over a longer time. So, to meet time and transportation requirements, and to prevent the expensive loss of territory in the first few days of conflict, we must rely on airlift. Its key mission is to project and sustain combat forces until other means of transportation can follow on, but there are many threat situations

where airlift is the only means to provide a rapid response either as a result of geographical location of the threat area or the speed with which the threat develops.

Our organic airlift assets are the C-5A and the C-141. In time of war and national emergency, these assets would be augmented by the Civil Reserve Air Fleet. Our airlift must be adequate to meet requirements of a NATO-Warsaw Pact conflict in Europe simultaneously with a lesser non-NATO contingency.

Recent events have underscored our need for flexible, early, and rapid reinforcement. As we modernize Army and Marine Corps equipment to meet the continued Soviet building of conventional forces, even though we plan to miniaturize some of it to provide flexibility which comes with heavy equipment, our airlift requirements will exceed our capability, especially the capability to transport outsized cargo.

We need about [deleted] the organic airlift capability that we now have if we are to respond simultaneously in Europe and elsewhere.

Let me talk about the aircraft characteristics and this will be my final point. I believe the following are desirable for needed improvement of our airlift force:

Our studies have shown our current shortfall for intertheater airlift of outsized and nonoutsized cargo. For intratheater airlift the situation is not as obvious in terms of shortages in overall capacity, but our current fleet of intratheater airlift, the C-130, is aging and it can't carry outsized equipment. In fact, by 1986 these airlift shortages, particularly intertheater airlift, will be such that the major portion of Army firepower equipment cannot fit in anything except the C-5. The C-5 wing modification will keep the capability and it is very valuable in the present inventory, but it won't reduce our shortfalls.

Completing all our aircraft modification programs to enhance the present force will still leave our capability significantly short of mobility requirements.

There is no quick solution to the outsize lift requirement. Even a C-5 derivative would take several years.

We have two broad alternatives to remedy this shortfall by providing additional outsized cargo carrying capability: one is to buy an aircraft of new design; the other is to buy an existing or modified version of existing aircraft, with the C-5, and the Boeing 747, as examples.

A new design would have the advantage of better adaptability to operation in and out of small, austere fields. That would increase the number of air bases open to us and reduce crowding on larger ones. A fallout of this capability, which I don't put very heavy weight on, is that it would improve our intratheater capability. On the other hand, modifying an existing design would produce a somewhat earlier operational capability with correspondingly lower development costs and risk. It would also reduce dependence on en route bases for this particular portion of our air deployment requirements.

The balance between these two forces, in my judgment, depends on details of overall cost and capability which we won't have until we have firm evaluated contractor proposals after the first year of the program. So we have not made the choice between these alternatives, nor should we at this stage. Instead, we are asking for detailed proposals from industry for both alternatives and will make the choice after we receive and evaluate them, at which time we will have a much better handle on system cost and capabilities. In the interim, we will continue the operational evaluation of the C-5's ability to operate from small, austere air bases.

To summarize, we have a critical need for intertheater airlift of outsized cargo. We need to get started by requesting bids on alternative designs for C-X this year. What kind of aircraft in exact terms we will decide after a thorough review of the cost, schedule, and performance data generated by the contractors and firm proposals in response to our request for proposals.[123]

During House hearings, Gen Volney F. Warner, CINCREDCOM, supported the C-X as a Middle East necessity because it would operate into 70 percent of the available airfields whereas the C-141B could operate into only 43 percent of them. To meet the requirements of airlift users, Warner said that the C-X must be capable of deploying outsized loads directly into an area of operations, be air refuelable, be capable of performing intertheater airlift when required, and have night and weather capabilities to permit airdrop and air landings into austere areas under adverse conditions. The airdrop capability needed to be an integral part of the aircraft design.[124]

The congressionally mandated mobility study was forwarded to Congress by Secretary of Defense Weinberger on 30 April 1981. The study was done by OSD and the JCS with support from the Air Force and the other services. It analyzed four scenarios and concluded that the United States was short of all forms of mobility: airlift, sealift, and prepositioning. With specific regard to airlift, the congressionally mandated mobility study recommended that on a baseline of 1986 the United States should set as a minimum goal the possession of a combined intertheater airlift capacity of 66 million ton-miles per day over intertheater distances. The study recommended an increase of 25 million airlift ton-miles per day, of which at least 10 million should be of outsize airlift capacity.[125]

On November 1980 Deputy Secretary of Defense W. Graham Clayton approved a C-X mission element need statement with an added promise that the secretary of defense would have final say on the choice of a C-X or a derivative transport. Boeing, McDonnell Douglas, and Lockheed made proposals for the new airplane. At the same interval, the Air Force asked the same three companies to recommend an imaginative and innovative way to provide cheaper airlift. In the C-X competition Lockheed proposed that the Air Force should take advantage of the ongoing C-5 program and procure C-5N models (later designated the C-5B) that would have the new wing and other retrofitted changes that had been made in the C-5A. On 24 April 1981 Secretary of the Air Force Verne Orr advised Congress that the improved C-5 did not meet the requirements of the C-X. Orr nevertheless disclosed that he had "deep concern" about coming to Congress with another all-new weapon system and had not made up his mind about the C-X even though there was "a tremendous amount of enthusiasm" about the plane among his military associates.

When I look at the out-year costs of the MX and out-year cost of the [B-1] bomber, which I put at a higher priority than I do the C-X, when I consider there are some other airlift alternatives which may be weighed, I have deep concern about coming before Congress with another all-new weapon system. I haven't resolved that in my mind.[126]

Orr announced on 28 August that McDonnell Douglas was the C-X source selections choice, but the Air Force continued to study the C-5 and also a Boeing-747 option to the new airlifter that was called the C-17. The proposal that the Air Force buy passenger jets for conversion to cargo usages was economically permissive, but the B-747 freighter and its deck stood 16 feet above the ground and required special equipment to load, unload, and even fuel it. Such equipment was not likely to be found in small airfields. If civil airliners were to be used, the Air Force rationalized that they might as well be CRAF planes. In November 1981, the chiefs of staff of the Army and Air Force and the Marine Corps commandant informed Congress that they were in accord on the selection of the C-17, and on 7 December Secretary Weinberger certified to Congress that "the national security requirements of the United States for additional military airlift capability meant initiation of the C-X program." Meanwhile, sentiment in Congress was against a C-X research and development undertaking, and on 22 December 1981 Deputy Secretary of Defense Frank Carlucci told Secretary Orr that he had decided to postpone selection of an airlift aircraft pending a new Air Force systems analysis study of alternate proposals. This analysis endorsed the C-17, but for a short-term solution the Air Force indicated that it would accept a program procuring the 44 KC-10s which it had an option to purchase plus CRAF enhancements. In the long run, however, the Air Force wanted C-17s with a 1988 initial operational capability (IOC) since the aging C-130 and C-141 fleet would be needing replacements. Under the pressure of forming defense budget requirements for fiscal year 1983, Secretary Weinberger asked the Air Force to consider the C-5 and C-17 under the assumption that either aircraft could be funded at the fastest prudent pace, as justified by a more urgent national requirement for mobility. Until this time, the Air Force had considered that the advantage of earlier availability of a C-5B was more than offset by better military utility and the potential of the C-17 as the ultimate replacement of the C-130 and C-141 force. Under Weinberger's promise of faster funding for airlift, Secretary Orr noted that the C-5B would be operationally available about three years earlier than a C-17. Accordingly, in view of the CMMS conclusion that an airlift shortfall was serious already, Orr felt that the Air Force had to go with the most expeditious short-term fix, which was announced on 26 January 1982 by Lt Gen Kelly Burke, Air Force deputy chief of staff for research, development, and acquisition. The solution was to procure the remainder of the 44 KC-10s for which the Air Force had options and 50 new C-5Bs which Lockheed would produce on a firm fixed price proposal. This combination of aircraft would cost an estimated $11 billion and would provide the quickest near-term answer to the shortage of strategic airlift.[127] Secretary Orr said that his overriding consideration in the choice between the C-5 and C-17 is the conclusion—documented in the CMMS and numerous other studies over many years—that a significant shortfall exists now! Consequently, the objective is to increase airlift capability as quickly as possible. Hence, a good program soon was chosen over a somewhat better program later.[128]

To Secretary Weinberger the decision to procure the C-5s and KC-10s reflected the high priority that the Reagan administration was giving to projecting US military power worldwide rapidly. Air Force officials, nevertheless, remained staunchly supportive of the C-17. Gen James R. Allen, CINCMAC, wrote Weinberger on 5 April 1982 that the capabilities represented by the C-17 were needed both to alleviate remaining intertheater shortfalls and to satisfy initial intratheater requirements as a replacement for the aging C-130s and C-141s. The new C-5s would increase outsized capability by over 60 percent and the KC-10s added flexibility. Together they could deliver 1,870 tons of cargo a day to main operating bases in Southwest Asia, but this created an additional intratheater requirement of 1,235 tons a day for the already overworked C-130s that could not lift outsized cargo.[129] In testimony in June 1982, Deputy Secretary Carlucci said that the C-5/C-17 assessment was not an "either/or" proposition. The United States needed intertheater airlift immediately and the C-5 would provide that; the United States also needed an intratheater capability, but this requirement was not as urgent. Carlucci said that the C-17 would make an excellent replacement when the C-130s and C-141s began to phase out in the 1990s.[130]

On 29 September 1983 Secretary Orr and General Gabriel jointly released the US Air Force Airlift Master Plan. The plan was based on analytical and trade-off studies and provided force structure recommendations geared to the year 1998 and to the next century. The overall constraining factor in the master plan was the CMMS recommendation that the US airlift capability should be at least 66 million ton-miles per day. The master plan therefore outlined a requirement for 180 C-17s by 1998 to compensate for retirement of 180 older C-130s, retirement of the 54 oldest C-141s, and transfer of remaining C-141Bs to the air reservist forces. Active duty and Reserve forces would retain 114 C-5s. The CRAF program would retain a minimum of 11.3 million ton-miles per day, plus a minimum of 144.9 million passenger-miles per day. Over the longer term into the next century, the plan envisioned the replacement of the 180 C-141Bs in the reservist forces by 40 C-17s. To maintain the CRAF contribution at a constant level, the master plan stated that it "may be necessary for the military and civilian sector to jointly develop a new-technology advanced Civil/Military Aircraft (ACMA)."[131]

According to Secretary of Defense Weinberger, the Reagan administration inherited an obsolete defense policy that was "discredited by its failure to recognize and cope with the deterioration in the global military situation."[132]

> The 1-1/2 war or the short war . . . that you would have a short, sharp conventional exchange, followed by a rapid escalation to nuclear, are not likely or probable paths for us to follow. . . . It is necessary . . . for us to maintain our deterrent, not to try to be

IDEAS, CONCEPTS, DOCTRINE

> superior to them or anything of that kind, but to maintain a deterrent capability of resisting aggression in more than one part of the globe together with our allies.[133]

In the first year of the Reagan administration, services were instructed to equip and train a part of the total force for rapid response and flexible employment. The five-year objective for mobility forces was to develop the Rapid Deployment Joint Task Force to Southwest Asia within four to six weeks and continue preparations to deliver six more divisions in 10 days, to fall in on the POMCUS, and join the four US divisions there quickly. NATO reinforcements also included positioning 60 Air Force tactical air squadrons within 10 days. In the current capability of 1981, the strike force nominated for Southwest Asia would be an airlifted "show of force" that would serve, in General Warner's words, "to show we have the will to put them on the ground quickly so that if the Soviets bump up against them they will have the first US-Soviet confrontation we have had since 1917."[134] For viability the Southwest Asia force would depend upon airlifted supplies, then prepositioned supplies from Diego Garcia, and eventually ship delivery. In recognition of the need for a full-time major commander to develop detailed plans for a wide range of possible contingencies in Southwest Asia, the Rapid Deployment Joint Task Force (RDJTF) was chartered as a separate joint task force, reporting directly to the national command authorities through the Joint Chiefs of Staff. Its commander was given operational control over selected Army and Air Force units and assigned operational planning responsibility for Southwest Asia. On 1 January 1983 the RDJTF was upgraded to unified command status, and its commander was designated as the commander in chief, US Central Command (CINCCENT). The primary mission of the new command — with its headquarters remaining at MacDill AFB — was to deter Soviet aggression and protect US interests in Southwest Asia.[135]

The RDJTF/USCENTCOM was a four-service headquarters, with Army and Air Force components assigned and assurance that the Navy and Marines would operate in support when the task force deployed into an existing unified command's area. The Air Force designated specific units for inclusion, the composition and size of the force to be tailored to particular contingencies. The units identified were a SAC strategic projection force, four tactical fighter wings, and support forces including airlift, reconnaissance, and air rescue forces. The combat readiness of all these units was improved where necessary by drawing spare parts and munitions from other units. Of the capabilities of the RDJTF in mid-1962, Deputy Secretary Carlucci said: "Our assessment is that with adequate warning time and with the capability for air interdiction the RDJTF would represent an adequate deterrent to the Soviets in Southwest Asia."[136] SAC's Strategic Projection Force supported RDJTF in accordance with a Memorandum of Agreement affirming policies and principles and by the establishment of a SAC operating location at MacDill AFB. According to one scenario, the commander RDJTF/CINCCENT would receive an alerting message from the JCS for a deployment. He immediately would ask MAC for airlift and SAC for command

and control aircraft, these being expected to land at MacDill with their banks of radios that gave global communications.

In the Southwest Asia scenario, the SAC Strategic Projection Force of B-52H aircraft was planned to begin operations in advance of the tactical forces since they could be deployed within 24 hours and begin employment within 48 hours. Utilizing night, low-altitude tactics the B-52s would strike targets such as airfields and lines of communication. Upon deployment of tactical forces, the B-52s would be available in a support role. Under command relations, CINCSAC continued to command the Strategic Projection Force, but when it was deployed in support of the rapid deployment force (RDF) it came under the tactical command and control of the air component commander of the RDF, who had the authority and responsibility to develop plans and direct the targeting and tasking of the B-52s. Although the Strategic Projection Force supported the RDF, it also would stand alone in support of any theater commander since the force's B-52Hs (selected for long-range and low-altitude capabilities) were a fast, globally deployable capability that could respond quickly to national tasking. Until general-purpose forces could be deployed and employed in significant numbers, the SAC Strategic Projection Force could be the first response to contingencies at great distances from peacetime operating bases.[137] Gen W. L. Creech, as commander TAC, was also the air component commander of REDCOM. He met periodically with CINCREDCOM and the commanding general, Army Forces Command, for necessary activities. The Tactical Air Command had a full-time study group that, in Creech's words, "does nothing but worry about where we will bed down the RDF. We know all the potentialities, we know which bases can accommodate fighters, we know how much POL they have, we know the lengths of runways, even how much water is available, where we might bed down crews and maintenance people and the like."[138] TAC also conducted training deployments to Egypt and Saudi Arabia, as well as recurring Red Flag exercises specially designed for RDJTF designated units.[139]

The function of the Military Airlift Command in rapid deployment was primarily one of lifting the forces specified rapidly. In General Huyser's last appearance before the House Military Appropriations Subcommittee in June 1981, he discussed the strategic significance of airlift.

> I appreciate the opportunity... to discuss with you the airlift capability and what I think it does for the Rapid Deployment Force, which is to put the R in Rapid and make it a big R. I think that in the past this has not been given proper attention or proper priority. There were times in the last year when I felt that we finally were going to get around to understanding, that if we are going to have forces, that they are of little utility unless they can be properly projected and on a timely basis.... I would like to remind you of the things rapidity gives to forces. In my opinion, it offers the all important factor of having the potential to be a deterrent force, if you are there soon enough with enough. I guess it is the old statement of "he who is there fastest with the mostest is going to do the bestest." Secondly, I think it has the potential for containing conflict, if there are conflicts, to a manageable size. Thirdly, I think it reduces the number of forces required if you are timely enough. Fourthly, I think it gives you the opportunity to get into a

winning posture. So, I think these are four things that rapidity adds to the fighting forces.[140]

In an interview published in January 1982, Gen James Allen, who had become CINCMAC at Huyser's retirement, emphasized the same strategic significance of airlift.

> The nation's highest priority is to restore and maintain the strategic balance vis-à-vis the USSR. In my judgment, the second priority should be to improve our capability to project well equipped, highly trained, combat-ready land and air forces to overseas theaters. Within this priority, there needs to be a balance between deployable combat forces on the one hand and airlift deployment capability on the other. If we had 2000 C-17s and nothing to carry in them, the overall deterrent capability would be minimal. Conversely, the best equipped and trained CONUS-based forces aren't going to deter the Soviets if we don't have a manifest capability to deploy them when and where needed.[141]

Although the Air Force appeared to continue to regard the Military Airlift Command as a logistical support-service activity, actions taken in the 1970s for increased organizational savings provided MAC with diverse warfighting capabilities in addition to airlift. In 1976 the Air Force recognized that MAC and the Air Force Communications Service (AFCS) operated worldwide, frequently with small detachments at the same deployed locations. To save people and money, AFCS phased out many of its deployed detachments and shared sites and personnel with MAC. The savings accrued to the Air Force but MAC's worldwide stature was enhanced through integration of the airlift and communications missions.[142] In March 1983 the Air Force again sought savings by merging Special Operations Forces (SOF) that had been assigned to TAC with MAC's Aerospace Rescue and Recovery Services (ARRS). This move was expected to result in economies on both sides since the ARRS and SOF both employed C-130s, the one for rescue and the special forces for AC-130 gunships and MC-130 support aircraft. Both forces had helicopters in relatively small numbers. It also was anticipated that low-level tactics developed for MAC C-130s and C-141s would be useful in special operations. In January 1984 the 375th Aeronautical Airlift Wing joined ARRS and SOF under command of a new MAC air force—the Twenty-third Air Force. Unlike MAC's Twenty-first and Twenty-second Air Forces that commanded airlifters from McGuire and Travis AFBs, the Twenty-third had worldwide responsibilities for special operations, rescue and recovery, aeromedical airlift, weather reconnaissance, air sampling, drone recovery, space shuttle support, support for SAC missile sites, and the CONUS operational support forces.[143]

As it happened, the expansion of the Military Airlift Command mission to include special operations forces, although parsed for efficiency of administration and logistics, proved fortunate operationally in the US rescue operations in the Caribbean island of Grenada, where Cuban troops were building military installations and further threatening the Western Hemisphere. The activity in Grenada beginning on 25 October 1983 was conducted by a special

USCINCLANT joint task force which controlled the Marine forces on the northern part of the island and the Army forces to the south. MAC airlifted Army units to the island and then set up and controlled the airfield at Point Salines. It provided logistical resupply from a base of operations in Barbados. A new CINCMAC, Gen Thomas M. Ryan, Jr., described the overall performance of MAC units as "absolutely outstanding." He saw one of the significant aspects of the Grenada operation as involvement in almost every mission area for which MAC was responsible: Special Operations Forces' AC-130H gunships and MC-130E Combat Talons, weather, security police, audiovisual, aeromedical evacuation, and a combination of C-9, C-130, and C-140 airlift. Ryan said, "Everybody got a piece of the action and everybody performed very, very well." Ryan asserted that MAC's mission had shifted from one of essentially strategic logistical airlift to a mission based upon a national recognition of the tie-in between MAC and other US combat forces:

> It's become increasingly apparent to the leadership of this country that while we develop more capable conventional forces, we must concurrently develop the mobility resources to quickly deploy those forces into battle and, once deployed, resupply them. Since conventional forces have assumed a greater role in deterrence, as we attempt to raise the nuclear threshold, then the backbone of that deterrence must be the means of deploying them. So, I think the expression "MAC—The Backbone of Deterrence" accurately describes the current mission and goal of the command.[144]

NOTES

1. House, *Department of Defense Appropriations for 1981: Hearings before a Subcommittee of the Committee on Appropriations*, 96th Cong., 2d sess., 1980, pt. 2:292 (hereafter cited as *1981 DOD Appropriations*).

2. House, *Military Airlift: Hearings before the Subcommittee on Military Airlift of the Committee on Armed Services*, 91st Cong., 2d sess., 1970, 6349 (hereafter cited as *Military Airlift*).

3. Gen Howell M. Estes, Jr., "The Revolution in Airlift," *Air University Review*, March–April 1966, 5–6.

4. House, *Military Airlift: Report of Special Subcommittee on Military Airlift of the Committee on Armed Services*, 89th Cong., 2d sess., 1966, 7177–79 (hereafter cited as *Military Airlift: Report of Special Subcommittee*).

5. Alain C. Enthoven and K. Wayne Smith, *How Much Is Enough? Shaping the Defense Program, 1961–1969* (New York: Harper & Row, 1971), 234–36; Senate, *Fiscal Year 1970 Military Procurement Authorization: Hearings before the Committee on Armed Services*, 91st Cong., 1st sess., 1969, pt. 2:2027 (hereafter cited as *FY 1970 Military Procurement*).

6. House, *Department of Defense Appropriations for 1968: Hearings before a Subcommittee of the Committee on Appropriations*, 90th Cong., 1st sess., 1967, pt. 2:328 (hereafter cited as *1968 DOD Appropriations*).

7. Estes, "The Revolution in Airlift," 3–15; Estes, "Modern Combat Airlift," *Air University Review*, September–October 1969, 13–25.

8. Estes, "Modern Combat Airlift," 13–25.

9. Ibid., 18.

10. Ibid.

IDEAS, CONCEPTS, DOCTRINE

11. Maj Charles E. Miller, "Airlift Doctrine" (Maxwell AFB, Ala.: Center for Aerospace Doctrine, Research, and Education, 1984), draft manuscript, chap. 6, 1–7.
12. Senate, *Department of Defense Appropriations for Fiscal Year 1970: Hearings before a Subcommittee of the Committee on Appropriations*, 91st Cong., 1st sess., 1969, pt. 4:134 (hereafter cited as *FY 1970 DOD Appropriations*).
13. Maj Gen Harry E. Goldsworthy, "Aircraft Development: Its Role in Flexible Military Response," *Air University Review*, January–February 1969, 20–31; House, *Department of Defense Appropriations for 1965: Hearings before a Subcommittee of the Committee on Appropriations*, 88th Cong., 2d sess., 1964, pt. 3:8; Senate, *FY 1970 Military Procurement*, pt. 2:2093–94.
14. Senate, *Department of Defense Appropriations for Fiscal Year 1966: Hearings before the Subcommittee on Department of Defense of the Committee on Appropriations and the Committee on Armed Services*, 89th Cong., 1st sess., 1965, pt. 1:362–63 (hereafter cited as *FY 1966 DOD Appropriations*).
15. Senate, *Department of Defense Appropriations for Fiscal Year 1965: Hearings before the Subcommittee on Department of Defense of the Committee on Appropriations and the Committee on Armed Services*, 88th Cong., 2d sess., 1964, pt. 1:152.
16. Ibid.; House, *Department of Defense Appropriations for 1967: Hearings before a Subcommittee of the Committee on Appropriations*, 89th Cong., 2d sess., 1966, pt. 3:590–91; House, *Hearings on the Posture of Military Airlift before the Research and Development Subcommittee of the Committee on Armed Services*, 94th Cong., 1st sess., 1975, 457–58 (hereafter cited as *Hearings on the Posture of Military Airlift*).
17. House, *Hearings on the Posture of Military Airlift*; Estes, "Modern Combat Airlift," 22–23; House, *1968 DOD Appropriations*, pt. 5:709–10.
18. Enthoven and Smith, *How Much Is Enough?*, 234–35.
19. Ibid., 238–39; Comdr John L. Jones, "The Birth and Death of the Fast Deployment Logistics Ship (FDLS): A Case Study of Futility" (Carlisle Barracks, Pa.: Army War College, 28 February 1972).
20. House, *Military Airlift*, 6350.
21. Miller, "Airlift Doctrine," 42–43.
22. Ibid.
23. House, *1968 DOD Appropriations*, pt. 5:717; House, *Military Airlift*, 6249, 6260.
24. House, *1968 DOD Appropriations*, pt. 2:757–59, pt. 5:708–9, 716–21; House, *Military Airlift*, 6259–75; House, *Hearings on the Posture of Military Airlift*, 15, 576.
25. House, *Military Airlift*, 6273; Miller, "Airlift Doctrine," chap. 6, 53.
26. House, *Military Airlift: Report of Special Subcommittee*, 7182; House, *Military Airlift: Report by the Subcommittee on Military Airlift of the Committee on Armed Services*, 91st Cong., 2d sess., 1970, 9234–36 (hereafter cited as *Military Airlift: Report*).
27. House, *Military Airlift*, 6278–80; "The Requirement for Strategic Airlift," in Senate, *Fiscal Year 1973 Military Procurement Authorization: Hearings before the Committee on Armed Services*, 92d Cong., 2d sess., 1972, pt. 2:1154–57 (hereafter cited as *FY 1973 Military Procurement*); House, *Hearings on the Posture of Military Airlift*, 18–19.
28. Miller, "Airlift Doctrine," chap. 6, 44–46; House, *Military Airlift*, 6349–65.
29. House, *Hearings on the Posture of Military Airlift*, 103, 109.
30. Miller, "Airlift Doctrine," chap. 6, 49–52; Estes, "Modern Combat Aircraft," 24.
31. House, *Military Airlift*, 6339–40; Miller, "Airlift Doctrine," chap. 6, 53.
32. Miller, "Airlift Doctrine," chap. 6, 59–60.
33. Ray Bowers, *Tactical Airlift* (Washington, D.C.: Department of Air Force History, 1983), 640–41; Gen Paul K. Carlton, "The Military Airlift Command," *Strategic Review*, February 1975, 64–72.
34. House, *Hearings on the Posture of Military Airlift*, 88–89.
35. Estes, "The Revolution in Airlift," 9.
36. Enthoven and Smith, *How Much Is Enough?*, 238–39.

37. Senate, *Seminars, Service Chiefs on Defense Mission and Priorities, Task Force on Defense of the Committee on the Budget*, 94th Cong., 2d sess., 1976, 3:58–59 (hereafter cited as *Seminars, Service Chiefs on Defense Mission and Priorities*).

38. Senate, *FY 1970 Military Procurement*, pt. 2:2093–94; Senate, *FY 1970 DOD Appropriations*, pt. 6:28–29; House, *Department of Defense Appropriations for 1971: Hearings before a Subcommittee of the Committee on Appropriations*, 92d Cong., 1st sess., 1970, pt.2:41 (hereafter cited as *1971 DOD Appropriations*).

39. Senate, *FY 1970 DOD Appropriations*, 29.

40. Senate, *FY 1970 Military Procurement*, pt. 2:2093–94; House, *Department of Defense Appropriations for 1969: Hearings before a Subcommittee of the Committee on Appropriations*, 90th Cong., 2d sess., 1968, pt. 3:363–73; Senate, *Department of Defense Appropriations for Fiscal Year 1971: Hearings before the Subcommittee of the Committee on Appropriations*, 91st Cong., 2d sess., 1970, pt. 4:476 (hereafter cited as *FY 1971 DOD Appropriations*).

41. Senate, *FY 1971 DOD Appropriations*, 4:476; Senate, *FY 1970 Military Procurement*, pt. 2:2093–94; House, *1971 DOD Appropriations*, pt. 5:1018; Senate, *Seminars, Service Chiefs on Defense Mission and Priorities*, 3:58–60.

42. House, *Department of Defense Appropriations for 1970: Hearings before a Subcommittee of the Committee on Appropriations*, 91st Cong., 1st sess., 1969, pt. 7:438–39.

43. Ibid., pt. 2:805–7.

44. House, *1971 DOD Appropriations*, pt. 5:804–5; Senate, *Department of Defense Appropriations for Fiscal Year 1977: Hearings before a Subcommittee of the Committee on Appropriations*, 94th Cong., 2d sess., 1976, pt. 5:384–85 (hereafter cited as *FY 1977 DOD Appropriations*).

45. Senate, *FY 1971 DOD Appropriations*, pt. 1:44.

46. Ibid.; House, *1971 DOD Appropriations*, pt. 1:205–6, pt. 5:804–5.

47. House, *Department of Defense Appropriations for 1972: Hearings before a Subcommittee of the Committee on Appropriations*, 92d Cong., 1st sess., 1971, pt. 5:1012–13 (hereafter cited as *1972 DOD Appropriations*); House, *Department of Defense Appropriations for 1973: Hearings before a Subcommittee of the Committee on Appropriations*, 92d Cong., 2d sess., 1972, pt. 7:1139 (hereafter cited as *1973 DOD Appropriations*).

48. House, *1971 DOD Appropriations*, pt. 6:621; House, *1972 DOD Appropriations*, pt. 2:41, pt. 5:1012–13.

49. House, *1973 DOD Appropriations*, pt. 1:106–7, pt. 7:1179–80; Senate, *FY 1973 Military Procurement*, pt. 3:1481–97; House, *Department of Defense Appropriations for 1974: Hearings before a Subcommittee of the Committee on Appropriations*, 93d Cong., 1st sess., 1973, pt. 2:14–15; Senate, *Department of Defense Appropriations for Fiscal Year 1974: Hearings before a Subcommittee of the Committee on Appropriations*, 93d Cong., 1st sess., 1973, pt. 4:408–9.

50. Elmo R. Zumwalt, Jr., *On Watch, A Memoir* (New York: Quadrangle/New York Times Book Co., 1976), 432–33; Edgar F. Puryear, Jr., *George S. Brown, General, U.S. Air Force, Destined for Stars* (Novato, Calif.: Presidio Press, 1983), 222–23.

51. "Interview General Paul K. Carlton," *Airlift Operations Review*, July–September 1981, 1–7; Senate, *Department of Defense Appropriations for Fiscal Year 1975: Hearings before a Subcommittee of the Committee on Appropriations*, 93d Cong., 2d sess., 1974, pt. 5:124 (hereafter cited as *FY 1975 DOD Appropriations*).

52. Carlton interview, 2–3.

53. Ibid.

54. Ibid.

55. Ibid., 3; Senate, *FY 1975 DOD Appropriations*, pt. 4:11; House, *Hearings on the Posture of Military Airlift*, 460.

56. Senate, *FY 1975 DOD Appropriations*, pt.4: 30–31, 55–56; Senate, *FY 1975 DOD Appropriations*, pt. 1:173–74, pt. 4:84–85.

57. Carlton interview, 3–4.

58. Ibid.

IDEAS, CONCEPTS, DOCTRINE

59. Ibid.; House, *Hearings on the Posture of Military Airlift*, 77–79; Senate, *FY 1975 DOD Appropriations*, pt. 4:84–85.

60. Senate, *FY 1977 DOD Appropriations*, pt. 5:441; House, *Department of Defense Appropriations for 1977: Hearings before a Subcommittee of the Committee on Appropriations*, 94th Cong., 2d sess., 1976, pt. 1:127 (hereafter cited as *1977 DOD Appropriations*).

61. House, *Department of Defense Appropriations for 1975: Hearings before a Subcommittee of the Committee on Appropriations*, 93d Cong., 2d sess., 1974, pt. 1:340 (hereafter cited as *1975 DOD Appropriations*).

62. House, *Hearings on the Posture of Military Airlift*, 571–72; House, *Department of Defense Appropriations for 1976: Hearings before a Subcommittee of the Committee on Appropriations*, 94th Cong., 1st sess., 1975, pt. 2:31 (hereafter cited as *1976 DOD Appropriations*).

63. House, *Hearings on the Posture of Military Airlift*; House, *1976 DOD Appropriations*, pt. 7:823.

64. Ibid.

65. Miller, "Airlift Doctrine," chap. 6, 72–73 citing letter, Gen Paul Carlton, commander, Military Airlift Command, to Gen David C. Jones, chief of staff, US Air Force, 16 November 1964.

66. Miller, "Airlift Doctrine," chap. 6, 74–75; Senate, *Fiscal Year 1974 Authorization for Military Procurement: Hearings before the Committee on Armed Services*, 93d Cong., 1st sess., 1973, pt. 6:4388.

67. "Interview General William G. Moore, Jr.," *Airlift Operations Review*, April–June 1982, 4, 6.

68. Carlton interview, 5.

69. Moore interview, 6; Carlton interview, 5.

70. Miller, "Airlift Doctrine," chap. 6, 75–78.

71. Ibid.

72. Moore interview, 6.

73. Senate, *Department of Defense Appropriations for Fiscal Year 1980: Hearings before a Subcommittee of the Committee on Appropriations*, 96th Cong., 1st sess., 1979, pt. 1:152 (hereafter cited as *FY 1980 DOD Appropriations*).

74. Senate, *Department of Defense Appropriations for Fiscal Year 1983: Hearings before a Subcommittee of the Committee on Appropriations*, 97th Cong., 2d sess., 1982, pt. 3:10 (hereafter cited as *FY 1983 DOD Appropriations*).

75. House, *1975 DOD Appropriations*, pt. 1:160–61, 340.

76. House, *Hearings on the Posture of Military Airlift*, 230–32.

77. Ibid.

78. Senate, *Fiscal Year 1977 Military Procurement Authorization: Hearings before the Committee on Armed Services*, 94th Cong., 2d sess., 1976, pt. 2:960 (hereafter cited as *FY 1977 Military Procurement*).

79. Senate, *Fiscal Year 1975 Military Procurement Authorization: Hearings before the Committee on Armed Services*, 94th Cong., 1st sess., 1975, pt. 6:2723; House, *Hearings on the Posture of Military Airlift*, 177.

80. Senate, *FY 1980 DOD Appropriations*, pt. 1:38, 154.

81. James W. Canan, "Up from Nifty Nugget," *Air Force Magazine*, September 1983, 82–88.

82. House, *Department of Defense Appropriations for 1982: Hearings before a Subcommittee of the Committee on Appropriations*, 97th Cong., 1st sess., 1981, pt. 4:203 (hereafter cited as *1982 DOD Appropriations*).

83. House, *Reorganization Proposals for the Joint Chiefs of Staff: Hearings before the Investigations Subcommittee of the Committee on Armed Services*, 97th Cong., 2d sess., 1982, 560–61.

84. Ibid.

85. Senate, *FY 1980 DOD Appropriations*, pt. 1:155–56.

86. Ibid.; Senate, *Department of Defense Appropriations for Fiscal Year 1981: Hearings before a Subcommittee of the Committee on Appropriations*, 96th Cong., 2d sess., 1980, pt. 1:37.

87. Senate, *Department of Defense Appropriations for Fiscal Year 1982: Hearings before a Subcommittee of the Committee on Appropriations*, 97th Cong., 1st sess., 1981, pt. 1:42 (hereafter cited as *FY 1982 DOD Appropriations*).

88. House, *Reorganization Proposals for the JCS*, 561.

89. *U.S. News & World Report*, 23 June 1980, 52.

90. Public Law 96-34, *Department of Defense Authorization Act*, 1981, sec. 203; House, *Department of Defense Appropriations for 1981: Hearings before a Subcommittee of the Committee on Appropriations*, 96th Cong., 2d sess., 1980, pt. 3:934, 1009-11 (hereafter cited as *1981 DOD Appropriations*).

91. Senate, *Department of Defense Appropriations for Fiscal Year 1976: Hearings before a Subcommittee of the Committee on Appropriations*, 94th Cong., 1st sess., 1975, pt. 4:206; House, *Hearings on the Posture of Military Airlift*, 3-5.

92. House, *Hearings on the Posture of Military Airlift*, 2-7, 201-10.

93. Ibid.

94. Ibid., 500-3, 493, 495; House, *1977 DOD Appropriations*, pt. 1:126.

95. House, *Department of Defense Appropriations for 1980: Hearings before a Subcommittee of the Committee on Appropriations*, 96th Cong., 1st sess., 1979, pt. 2:413 (hereafter cited as *1980 DOD Appropriations*); House, *1982 DOD Appropriations*, pt. 2:261; Senate, *FY 1983 DOD Appropriations*, pt. 3:50-51, 60-63.

96. Senate, *FY 1983 DOD Appropriations*, pt. 3:50-51, 60-63.

97. Senate, *FY 1966 DOD Appropriations*, pt. 1:331-33, 1094-98.

98. House, *1982 DOD Appropriations*, pt. 4:290; Senate, *FY 1983 DOD Appropriations*, pt. 3:8.

99. House, *Hearings on the Posture of Military Airlift*, 37, 209.

100. Ibid.; Senate, *Department of Defense Appropriations for Fiscal Year 1978: Hearings before a Subcommittee of the Committee on Appropriations*, 95th Cong., 1st sess., 1977, pt. 1:936; Senate, *FY 1982 DOD Appropriations*, pt. 3:8.

101. Miller, "Airlift Doctrine," chap. 7, 53-54.

102. Senate, *FY 1975 Military Procurement*, pt. 6:2718-19.

103. Ibid.

104. Senate, *FY 1975 Military Procurement*, pt. 6:2718-19; House, *Hearings on the Posture of Military Airlift*, 204, 206, 607-8; Senate, *FY 1977 Military Procurement*, pt. 5:2918-20; House, *1980 DOD Appropriations*, pt. 3:707; House, *Department of Defense Appropriations for 1983: Hearings before a Subcommittee of the Committee on Appropriations*, 97th Cong., 2d sess., 1982, pt. 2:292 (hereafter cited as *1983 DOD Appropriations*); Senate, *Department of Defense Authorization for Appropriations for Fiscal Year 1983: Hearings before the Committee on Armed Services*, 97th Cong., 2d sess., 1982, pt. 4:2643; House, *1980 DOD Appropriations*, pt. 3:707-8.

105. House, *Military Airlift*, 6392-93.

106. Ibid.; House, *Military Airlift: Report of Special Subcommittee*, 9231.

107. House, *Hearings on the Posture of Military Airlift*, 277-80; Senate, *FY 1975 DOD Appropriations*, pt. 4:53-54, 24-25; Miller, "Airlift Doctrine," chap. 7, 28-35.

108. Maj Edward F. Whittel, ed., "Interview Robert E. Huyser, General," *Airlift Operations Review*, January 1981, 5.

109. Ibid.

110. Ibid.

111. Miller, "Airlift Doctrine," chap. 7, 36; House, *1980 DOD Appropriations*, pt. 3:700-1; House, *1981 DOD Appropriations*, pt. 2:357, 383.

112. Miller, "Airlift Doctrine," chap. 7, 36; House, *1981 DOD Appropriations*, pt. 9:353.

113. House, *1981 DOD Appropriations*, pt. 4:176, 209.

114. Ibid., 215.

115. Ibid., 194.

116. Senate, *FY 1983 DOD Appropriations*, pt. 3:281.

117. House, *1981 DOD Appropriations*, pt. 4:177.

118. *Department of Defense Annual Report Fiscal Year 1982* (Washington, D.C.: Government Printing Office, 1981), 198.

119. House, *1981 DOD Appropriations*, pt. 1:43, 526-27.

120. House, *1982 DOD Appropriations*, pt. 4:294-96.

121. Ibid.; Senate, *Department of Defense Authorization for Appropriations for Fiscal Year 1981: Hearings before the Committee on Armed Services*, 96th Cong., 2d sess., 1980, pt. 4:2626–27 (hereafter cited as *FY 1981 DOD Authorization*); House, *Department of Defense Authorization Act: Report No. 96–916, Committee on Armed Services*, 96th Cong., 2d sess., 1980, 90.

122. Senate, *FY 1981 DOD Authorization*, pt. 4:2612–14.

123. Ibid.

124. House, *1981 DOD Appropriations*, pt. 4:178.

125. Senate, *FY 1983 DOD Appropriations*, pt. 3:10–13; Edgar Ulsamer, "The Airlift Master Plan," *Air Force Magazine*, May 1984, 58–59.

126. Miller, "Airlift Doctrine," chap. 7, 18–23; "Air Force Position on the C–5/C–17 Issue," *Air Force Policy Letter for Commanders*, 15 February 1982.

127. Miller, "Airlift Doctrine," chap 7, 18–23; Ulsamer, "The Airlift Master Plan," 60–61.

128. Ulsamer, "The Airlift Master Plan," 60–61.

129. House, *1983 DOD Appropriations*, pt. 1:6–7, 192; Miller, "Airlift Doctrine," chap. 7, 24–25.

130. Senate, *FY 1983 DOD Appropriations*, pt. 3:310–11.

131. Miller, "Airlift Doctrine," chap. 7, 25–26; Ulsamer, "The Airlift Master Plan," 59.

132. House, *1983 DOD Appropriations*, pt. 1:6–7, 192.

133. Senate, *FY 1983 DOD Appropriations*, pt. 1:17.

134. Senate, *Department of Defense Authorization for Appropriations for Fiscal Year 1984: Hearings before the Committee on Armed Services*, 98th Cong., 1st sess., 1983, pt. 1:32–33, 303–8.

135. House, *1982 DOD Appropriations*, pt. 4:215–16.

136. Senate, *FY 1983 DOD Appropriations*, pt. 3:224–27, 280–87.

137. Senate, *Department of Defense Authorization for Appropriations for Fiscal Year 1982: Hearings before the Committee on Armed Services*, 97th Cong., 1st sess., 1981, pt. 7:3844–45; House, *1982 DOD Appropriations*, pt. 2:21, 156, pt. 4:377–78.

138. House, *1982 DOD Appropriations*, pt. 2:21, pt. 6:47.

139. Ibid.

140. Ibid.

141. Ibid., pt. 4:279; James Allen interview, January 1982, 3.

142. House, *1976 DOD Appropriations*, pt. 2:31.

143. "CINCMAC Discusses Airlift Issues," *Airlift*, Spring 1984, 5–6; "Military Airlift Command," *Air Force Magazine*, May 1984, 109.

144. "CINCMAC Discusses Airlift Issues," 5–6.

Gen Paul K. Carlton, commander of the Military Airlift Command.

Frank C. Carlucci, deputy secretary of defense.

Dale W. Church, deputy director of research and engineering for the Office of the Secretary of Defense.

William P. Clements, deputy secretary of defense.

Gen Robert E. Huyser, commander in chief of the Military Airlift Command.

John H. Chafee, secretary of the Navy.

CHAPTER 9

THE AIR FORCE IN SPACE

In the aftermath of the Soviet Sputnik, Air Force Chief of Staff Thomas D. White viewed the new realm of space as a continuum of the long-familiar atmosphere — the whole being describable as aerospace. To exert control over the land and the sea it had proven necessary to control the air. "We airmen who have fought to assure that the United States has the capability to control the air," White told the National Press Club in November 1957, "are determined that the United States must win the capability to control space."[1] As already seen, White subsequently amended his perception to note that the aim should be to exercise control *in* space rather than *of* space; this control was perhaps to be managed by a blockade of an adversary's entry into space. Air Force leaders also viewed desired space vehicles in terms of the old higher, faster, farther criteria applied to aircraft. The principal objective of the Dyna-Soar X-20 program undertaken in 1957 was to develop an experimental space glider and to demonstrate the feasibility and practical value of a pilot-controlled, maneuverable reentry and recovery from orbit at a time and place of a pilot's choosing. The Air Force's view was that man's discretion would be necessary for operations in space and that military superiority in space would be essential to an international enjoyment of space for peaceful purposes.

Discourse and Decisions on Manned Military Spacepower

President Eisenhower's willingness to keep space peaceful caused him to sponsor in 1958 the formation of the National Aeronautics and Space Administration (NASA). In his successful race for the presidency, John F. Kennedy voiced a belief that the United States was lagging behind the Soviets both in space and ballistic missiles. Early in his administration, Kennedy's National Aeronautics and Space Council, headed by Vice President Lyndon B. Johnson, recommended a NASA program to begin with suborbital and earth-orbital Mercury flights, followed by Gemini orbital flights to include rendezvous, docking, and extravehicular activity, and concluding with Apollo flights landing Americans on the moon. Kennedy approved the program, arguing that the lunar landing objective "would be a sufficiently difficult goal, and its achievement before the Russians would repair the US image and restore confidence in American technological superiority."[2] According to Deputy Secretary of Defense Roswell L. Gilpatric, the Kennedy administration was determined not to provoke an arms race in space. "An arms race in space will not contribute to our security," Gilpatric

IDEAS, CONCEPTS, DOCTRINE

stated in 1962. "I can think of no greater stimulus for a Soviet thermonuclear arms effort in space than a United States commitment to such a program. This we will not do."[3] Looking backward after twenty years' reflection, Gen Bernard A. Schriever recalled that the Kennedy administration's desire to attain an accommodation with the Soviet Union brought on the undebated effect of stifling military innovation. "Let's not have too much technology," Schriever said that the new administrators urged, "because it might force us into new systems programs. We were stifled and inhibited by policy, not technology and know-how."[4]

In the Defense Department, Secretary Robert S. McNamara established two fundamental criteria for the military space program. First, it had to mesh with NASA's program in all vital areas so that the Department of Defense and NASA programs, taken together, would constitute an integrated national program. Second, projects supported by the Defense Department had to hold a distinct promise of enhancing military power and effectiveness. McNamara was quite critical of what he described as the ongoing practice he found on taking office — of service initiation of "large projects with rather ill-defined purposes."[5] In 1963 both Secretary McNamara and Dr Harold Brown, then director of Defense Research and Engineering, were far from convinced that there was a defense requirement for man in space, and this skepticism translated into questioning about the X-20 Dyna-Soar. Early in 1963 McNamara got an agreement with NASA that the Gemini astronauts would perform some military space experiments, and, as has been seen, in December 1963 McNamara canceled further development of the Dyna-Soar. He simultaneously announced that the Air Force would commence development of a manned orbiting laboratory (MOL) that would allow the Defense Department to determine whether there would be a role for a military man in space.[6]

Also in 1963 the Air Force had sought approval for an Air Force space program, spelling out the two basic objectives of, first, augmenting by use of space systems the existing military capabilities of US terrestrial forces and, second, developing a military patrol capability for the protection of US interests in space. The Dyna-Soar had been a "key element" in the planned military patrol capability, and with its cancellation the principal Department of Defense undertakings in space were primarily support missions for terrestrial operations. Secretary McNamara also favored devoting a major part of the defense space budget to technological building studies and equipment developments that would comprise the building blocks of any future system that might be needed for operation in space. For the Air Force a Titan III missile booster put in development in 1961 for the purpose of launching Dyna-Soar was continued as a McNamara favored "building block" for a planned lift of the MOL and other possibly unforeseen usages.[7]

The feasibility of the building-block approach was tested in 1963–64 when President Kennedy was concerned that the Soviets were fielding an orbital bomb. He then directed development without delay of an active antisatellite capability. In just about a year the Air Force turned out Program 437, comprising a Thor missile booster and already-on-hand guidance. Practice firings placed simulated nuclear warheads within a lethal five-mile range of targeted space debris, and the satellite interceptor was counted as operational in 1964.[8] The Air Force seems also to have continued to look with some favor on the Bambi (ballistic missile boost intercept) concept of a satellite system capable of infrared homing on hostile missiles or satellites in their vulnerable boost phase; but Secretary McNamara dismissed the Bambi as "nothing more than a paper study of a very esoteric system."[9]

Both the Program 437 interceptor and the Bambi, in its original concept, would have used nuclear warheads in space. In 1970 Air Force Secretary Robert C. Seamans, Jr., was queried about the dangers of intercepting Soviet satellites with nuclear weapons. He made reference to the 1957 United States treaty pledging that the United States and other United Nations member nations would not orbit weapons of mass destruction.

> We have an international agreement not to use nuclear warheads [in a satellite interception employment], not even to test them except underground. This would open up Pandora's box again, and certainly give other countries latitude, say the Soviet Union, for further testing.[10]

Although the major focus of attention in the early 1960s was on manned space flights, the major Department of Defense applications in space were principally in support of terrestrial forces through the use of satellites for strategic intelligence surveillance, communications, navigation, weather, and other similar activities. Before 1961 the Defense Department freely acknowledged that it was developing photographic reconnaissance satellites that would replace the U-2 effort that was terminated in May 1960 with the Soviet shoot down of an American U-2. On 11 August 1960 Discoverer 13 successfully returned a photo-capsule, thus beginning the development of increasingly sophisticated surveillance of the Soviet Union. The Kennedy administration ordered complete secrecy on the subject, even though the Soviets initially complained and proposed a United Nations ban on reconnaissance from space. The Soviet Union started launching its own recon satellites in April 1962, and thereafter these surveillance flights came to be regarded by both sides as a stabilizing influence. In the antiballistic missile treaty of 1972 the USSR and the United States agreed not to interfere with "national technical means of verification" – a joint euphemism for the spy satellites.

President Carter made general reference to photoreconnaissance in a 1978 speech, and by 1980 US Air Force Secretary Hans Mark acknowledged that the space satellites had proven their worth as national technical means of treaty verification, arguing that strategic missile warning and surveillance "stand out as being of vital importance to national security."[11] In addition to surveillance, navigation and communications satellites provided vital support to terrestrial operations. The Navy's Transit family of navigation satellites reached full operational status in July 1964, allowing missile submarines to position themselves for accuracy within some 200 to 300 feet, close enough for the Polaris missiles to be effective against countervalue targets.[12] In another space application the Air Force began development of satellites for a defense communications system. This initial defense communications satellite program (IDCSP) got 19 satellites placed into near-synchronous equational orbit with communications to about 30 terminals deployed worldwide. The system provided sustained communications support to Southeast Asia and Seventh Fleet operations, and to the departments of defense and state during the Arab-Israeli conflict. In addition it furnished a previously unavailable capability—the transmission of high-quality photographs in a matter of hours rather than days.[13]

Although the capabilities of unmanned satellite applications were quickly offering potentially revolutionary support augmentations to military operations, a major US emphasis was still being applied to the possibility of manned space projections. "If you cancel the DYNASOAR, you cancel the Air Force," General White had warned. At his retirement as chief of staff, White made a short talk, stating:

> There was a time once when the people who controlled the known ground of the earth, controlled the world. Then the people who controlled the sea, controlled the world. Today people who control the air control the world, and I predict to you that tomorrow those who control space will control the world.[14]

In early 1965 an article in the *Journal of the Armed Forces* declared: "It is all but incredible that after 7 years of space research no manned military project has reached the hardware stage."[15] Gen John P. McConnell, who became Air Force chief of staff in 1965, was readily willing to admit that the United States had "made a mistake in not developing a weapons system which we could use in space," but he added:

> I think we are putting as much emphasis on space . . . as we can with the money that's available to us. I anticipate that we will continue to place appropriate emphasis on space. I am inclined to agree with General White that in the far distant future if we go to military usages of space, and this is way down the road in my opinion, that he probably will be right.[16]

In March 1965 Alexander Flax, assistant secretary of the Air Force for research and development, fended off a question about whether the building-block approach to space weapons development might not be too slow or too conservative by demonstrating that technological innovations of revolutionary portent came as reactions to a threat that would be countered or a clear application that would provide a great advantage. Flax added:

> Our problem in attempting to take the initiative in this space weapons area is in seeing a clear application that will obviously give us a great advantage, or a threat that must be countered. . . . Neither the people who look at the military side of this picture nor those who look at the technical side of the picture come up with a clear-cut application or threat of that nature, so that although we have numerous specialized military space programs, we have not seen any big new one that looks like we must embark on it right away. I think our proposed orbital laboratory program is intended to see what a man can do that we cannot do in the unmanned systems. This may not in fact turn up something we do not anticipate. But we do not at this time have a definite enough answer

to justify going ahead on more than just the elements of the building blocks of the system.[17]

The Air Force had started preliminary investigations of a space laboratory in 1958, well before Secretary McNamara's directive in December 1963 to design and use an experimental MOL to demonstrate to an on board pilot how could he add to the capabilities of military space systems. As defined by the Department of Defense in December 1963, MOL included a Titan III booster, a somewhat modified Gemini capsule, and a canister laboratory about 10 feet in diameter and 25 feet long in which two crew members would work at experiments for up to 30 days before reentering the Gemini capsule and recovering on earth. During 1964 the Air Force worked with 17 contractors studying experiments and subsystems to be incorporated in the MOL. In January 1965 the Department of Defense issued new and expanded instructions on the MOL, including a mandate for the Defense Department and NASA to compare configurations of the Apollo system with the Gemini/MOL configuration plan. The fiscal year 1966 defense budget included $150 million to fund initial MOL development efforts, and given early approval in 1965 to proceed with full-scale development the Air Force's estimate was that the first-manned orbiting laboratory could be launched in midfiscal year 1968.[18] In-depth DOD-NASA analysis recognized that major NASA systems such as Apollo could not effectively accomplish the desired MOL mission for the basic reason that the respective missions were too dissimilar. When this conclusion was made, President Johnson announced on 25 August 1965 that he had authorized the Department of Defense to proceed with the development of the MOL. Johnson then explained why the United States should explore outer space: "We dare not leave this area of our universe to become a monopoly in the hands of those who would destroy freedom. We must therefore obtain and maintain a leadership for the free world in outer space and we are trying to do that."[19]

As the MOL program gained approval, a manned space policy committee with equal representation from the Defense Department and NASA was formed in January 1966 to review areas of duplication between the MOL and Apollo programs. Despite this coordination, MOL was soon, and repeatedly, accused of being a duplication of NASA activities, especially when NASA outlined an Apollo follow-on to the lunar landings that would use the NASA Saturn booster and Apollo capsule for an orbital Apollo applications program, subsequently renamed Skylab.[20] In fiscal year 1966 the Air Force was unable to commit all of the $150 million appropriated for MOL, leading Secretary McNamara to conclude that the program was attempting to proceed faster than technology could support. For the MOL in fiscal year 1967 the Air Force initially requested $395 million, but it was evident soon that the schedule for development was going to slip nine months and only $230 million would be needed. Dr Harold Brown, now secretary of the Air Force, asked Secretary McNamara for the $230 million. "We were told," Brown said, "that if we asked for $395 million first and then could justify only $230 million we could not calculate very well."[21] McNamara thereupon allocated $150 million for fiscal year 1967 since he concluded that technology could not support more than this. When Brown reargued the matter he was told that he could reprogram Air Force funds if the MOL development warranted a larger expenditure. But Brown could see no way to use other scarce Air Force funds for MOL.[22] In fiscal year 1967 the Air Force completed design work, including the design of a necessary launch complex at Vandenberg AFB, and 12 MOL astronaut pilots were selected from among Air Force, Navy, and Marine Corps air officers. In fiscal year 1968 Secretary Brown was holding to an end-of-the-calendar-year-1969 date for first operations of the MOL, but he really doubted that this would be possible. In fiscal year 1969 the Air Force requested $600 million for major component development of the MOL and completion of the launch complex at Vandenberg AFB. With the MOL program in full-scale development, Brown predicted an initial launch of a two-man crew in mid-1971.[23]

After the mid-1960s competing US national requirements for support of the war in Indochina and for social concerns brought reduced support for national space endeavors. In his second term, President Johnson maintained interest in both the Apollo lunar landings and MOL, but several leading American scientists were beginning to argue that unmanned space technology could explore space far cheaper than a manned spacecraft. In the spring of 1968 an amendment to eliminate the MOL very nearly came up on the floor of the Senate. Although President Johnson reduced the NASA appropriations, he continued to support Apollo as a national goal. And the first lunar landing promised by President Kennedy came six months into the administration of President Richard M. Nixon, when Neil Armstrong and Edwin Aldrin, Jr., set foot on the moon on 20 July 1969.[24] The fiscal year 1970 defense budget prepared by the Johnson administration contained $576 million for the MOL. While a member of Congress, the new secretary of defense, Melvin R. Laird, not only had strongly supported the project but at one time had filed a mandatory report to the effect that the project was not being funded at a rapid enough rate. In February 1969 Laird conducted a thorough review of the MOL program, which could be reduced to two hardware qualification launches to qualify the Titan IIIM/Gemini B structural hardware and four 30-day manned flights. The elimination of one manned flight reduced the fiscal year 1970 requirement from $576 million to $525 million. The schedule called for the first unmanned launch in early 1971 and the first manned flight in early 1972.[25] In his 1968 election campaign, however, President Nixon had pledged to curtail NASA operations until the national economy could afford more funding, and in the spring of 1969 the House of Representatives had pressed for spending limits on government activities. Early in June Secretary Laird needed to cut back the defense budget, and he had a choice of reducing or terminating numerous small but important efforts or one of the larger, more costly programs. With the concurrence of President Nixon, Laird decided to cancel the Air Force's MOL program. The deputy secretary of defense, David Packard, announced the decision on 10 June 1969. Laird explained his reasoning:

> We were and still are confident that man's presence in orbit can enhance the effectiveness of equipment and speed its development for both manned and unmanned use in future systems. Man is unique in his talents, ability, and adaptiveness, as recent NASA flights have clearly demonstrated, but the cost of putting and sustaining him in space is very high.... The potential worth of the unique experiments planned for MOL plus the information expected on man's utility in space was not as valuable to Defense as the aggregate of other priority programs.... Since the MOL program was initiated, major advances have been made by both NASA and DOD in automated techniques for unmanned satellite systems.... These experiences as far as unmanned satellites are concerned have given us confidence that the most essential Department of Defense space missions can be accomplished with lower cost unmanned spacecraft.[26]

Secretary Laird stated that his decision to cancel the MOL did not reflect on the Air Force or the contractors of the program, which was, in his judgment, "practical and achievable." The Air Force then began to terminate the MOL within 24 hours after being so instructed; at this time, the launch facility at Vandenberg AFB was almost complete, and the Air Force elected to complete it for use in launching Titan III-type missiles for other purposes. Other technological items of interest to NASA were turned over for possible support of NASA's planned Apollo applications (Skylab) flights, which in 1973–74 would send three-man astronaut crews to work in a minispace station, the longest mission lasting 84 days. In terms of funding, $1.37 billion had been appropriated and obligated on the MOL program, and Secretary Laird estimated that the program would have cost an additional $1 billion or more in fiscal years 1971 through 1974.[27]

Although the decision to cancel the MOL was made at the highest levels, the Air Force apparently was not wholly dissatisfied with it. In the 1970 proposed program, the original amount allocated for military astronautics was about one-third of the total Air Force research, development, test and evaluation (RDT&E) program, and the manned orbiting laboratory accounted for one-half of the military astronautic request. Secretary of the Air Force Seamans made the point that the Air Force needed to press on with the F-15 fighter and C-5 airlift programs, as well as with improved air defenses. He said that "increasingly severe budgetary pressures ... and the rapid progress we have made with unmanned space vehicles, have finally resulted in the conclusion that the cost of a manned system is too great to be borne at this time."[28] A year later, Grant L. Hansen, assistant secretary of the Air Force for research and development, had much the same reasoning about the cancellation of the manned military space experiment. Hansen said:

> It is a fact of life ... that our aircraft fleet has gotten so behind the times that we have to have a great concentration of effort in that area to be able to get a modern fighter and bomber and airborne early warning system and combat air support aircraft. One of the things we are sacrificing in order to be able to afford to do those things ... is the further exploitation of capabilities in space for the things in the future.[29]

A New Air Force Policy of Space Applications

In the aftermath of the cancellation of the manned orbiting laboratory in mid-1969, Air Force policy shifted almost immediately from space in the abstract to the attainment of space applications. "Relative to priority in our efforts in space," stated Assistant Secretary Grant Hansen, "space is really not a program in the Air Force. It is a place where we do things and each project which utilizes space competes for funds on its own merit."[30] Gen James Ferguson, commander of the Air Force Systems Command and as such generally responsible for Air Force space projects, agreed with Hansen on the meaning of space.

> I think perhaps, the word has been distorted in the sense that space is [considered] separate from the rest of the environment in which we operate. What we are searching for are ways of performing our assigned missions more effectively. There are certain advantages in operating in space.[31]

In this "space applications" policy concept, the national space doctrine became generally expressed in the Pentagon in a single sentence: "Space is not a mission; it's a medium."[32]

In mid-1969 President Nixon charged a space task group headed by Vice President Spiro Agnew with conducting a study of post-Apollo activity. Secretary Laird was a member of the group and Secretary Seamans usually served as Laird's representative. In September 1969 the group made public three alternatives the nation could undertake, ranging downward in potential expense from a lunar base and manned flight to Mars to the least expensive option of an earth-orbiting space station and a reusable transport system to shuttle between the earth and the orbiting station. Until this time all recoveries from space had been directly down from orbit in a parachute mode. Secretary Seamans especially liked the space shuttle concept: "The shuttle will be able to come back from space much like an airplane, landing on a landing strip, and have considerably more maneuverability so there would be much more flexibility in bringing a package back from space at any time desired."[33] At this same time, the Air Force was also greatly interested in decreasing the costs of putting typical payloads into orbit, desirably by developing "a launch vehicle which we can recover and refurbish and use again and not throw it away every time."[34] In February 1970 the NASA Apollo applications program was trimmed down. On 7 March 1970 President Nixon's space policy emphasized applications in a carefully worded statement: "What we do in space from here on in must become a normal and regular part of our national life and must be planned in conjunction with all of the other undertakings which are also important to us."[35] In this milieu the Air Force got a go-ahead for development of an early warning satellite system, with two satellites over the Western Hemisphere and one over the Eastern Hemisphere, using infrared sensors to detect missile launches. Secretary Seamans nevertheless emphasized: "Our space activity is not an end in itself, but a means for accomplishing functions in support of existing forces and missions."[36] Because of national fiscal stringencies

President Nixon did not give a go-ahead for NASA's development of a space shuttle or space transportation system (STS) until January 1972 and then only because it would be of value to the Department of Defense and because it promised drastically to reduce launching and operational costs through reusable vehicles.[37]

"The high cost of space operations," Secretary Seamans observed in 1972, ". . . still prevents us from developing a space capability in all areas where we think satellites could enhance our national defense." For this reason the Department of Defense was very interested in NASA's space transportation system. Seamans expected the shuttle to be used to orbit the majority of DOD payloads, thus replacing expendable launch vehicles. Seamans added:

> The shuttle offers the potential of improving mission flexibility and capability by on-orbit checkout of payloads, recovery of malfunctioning satellites for repair and reuse, or resupply of payloads on orbit thus extending their lifetime. Payloads would be retrieved and refurbished for reuse and improved sensors could be installed during refurbishment for added capability.[38]

The Air Force was designated as DOD's executive agent for the space transportation system which was to be developed and tested by NASA. An agreement that was originally signed on 17 February 1970 and revised in August 1972 established a NASA/Air Force space transportation committee to report jointly to the NASA administrator and the secretary of the Air Force to maintain a continuing review of STS to ensure that it met DOD and NASA requirements.[39] Air Force responsibility for the STS as the DOD executive agent was placed in the Directorate of Space under the deputy chief of staff for research and development, through a shuttle program element monitor. The Air Force Systems Command was designated as the implementing command of the DOD shuttle program with a system program office established under the space and missile systems organization (SAMSO) in Los Angeles. A SAMSO deputy for launch vehicles managed the Air Force program activities.[40] In early projections, DOD planned to transition all of its spacecraft from launch on expendable boosters to launch on the NASA space shuttle during the period from FY 1980 through FY 1985; the change expected to result in a cost per launch of about half of that paid for launches with large expendable boosters.[41]

In an address in August 1975 Brig Gen Henry B. Stelling, Jr., Air Force director of space, predicted that for both the United States and the Soviet Union space systems were going to support virtually all military forces and could strongly influence the outcome of conflicts. He said there were four basic reasons for using military space systems:

> *Uniqueness*—some functions essentially can only be done from space, such as near real-time warning of a ballistic missile attack; *Economics*—some functions are more cheaply done from space, such as long-haul communications; *Functional Effectiveness*—some functions are more effectively done from space, like meteorology; and *Force Effectiveness Enhancement*—some space functions greatly enhance the effectiveness of terrestrial forces.[42]

The first three functions had been dormant, but Stelling predicted that in the late 1970s — "the Shuttle decade" — force effective enhancement would become increasingly important.[43] In an article published in late 1974, Gen Jacob E. Smart, who had served with NASA following his retirement from the Air Force, pointed to the "wide-range of tools" being provided by space-related technologies, but he questioned whether the United States was facing up to the challenges and opportunities of the space age. Smart wrote:

> Presently there are multiple agencies of the US government engaged in space related activities, each pursuing programs to fulfill its own missions. This of course is proper but points up the question: Does the sum of the individual agency's perceived roles adequately fulfill the total national need? There is no central policy coming from the top, guiding and coordinating these efforts.[44]

Smart said "we are witnessing the swift development of a new form of power which, like the air, land, and sea powers, will have applications that are political, military, economic and sociological."[45] In a further development of this same theme, Col Morgan W. Sanborn pointed out the view of space as a medium to be used for the enhancement of terrestrial forces that led back to the early days in which aviation was cut up without any common doctrine. There was no real organization or employment doctrine for space. In the Air Force, the Air Force Systems Command was responsible for the checkout and launch of DOD satellites, and it also operated certain space systems because it had the needed engineering talent to do so. The Aerospace Defense Command (ADC) operated space detection and tracking systems. The Strategic Air Command operated a meteorological satellite program. The Navy, along with the Air Force, was developing a Fleet Satellite Communications System, while the NAVSTAR (now global positioning system — GPS) program was being designed to support all three military services as well as civilian users. Sanborn wrote:

> The point is that space has become an amalgam of systems and users. . . . The need for a separate space command within the Air Force . . . seems obvious. This command could well develop into a space force when future requirements demand such a specialized and large-scale effort.[46]

According to Secretary Seamans in March 1970, the Air Force was "very much concerned about the presentation of our . . . satellite capability, because of its importance to our military posture."[47] On 19 October, 20 October, and 1 November 1968, the Soviets successively launched three cosmos satellites, the latter two making fly-by rendezvous with the first. Subsequently all three were observed to be accompanied by fragments. It was determined that "Soviet technical capabilities would permit them to develop any of several types of antisatellite systems during the next ten year period if they so desire."[48] The Soviets again flew satellite intercepts in 1970 and 1971. The US-USSR Antiballistic Missile Treaty of 1972 prohibited interference with reconnaissance satellite verification of treaty compliance and it prohibited the development, testing, or deployment of space-based ABM systems and their components.[49] In the Department of Defense satellite programs of the early 1970s it was evident that the greater part of program costs were not actually in space but in ground reception modes. Thus by increasing the size, power, and capabilities of satellites it was possible to achieve economy in the operation of forces. Thus, phase II of the defense satellite communications system consisted of only four high-power satellites in stationary equatorial orbits, each weighing almost 10 times as much as the smaller phase I satellites. The two phase II satellites launched in 1973 gave the DOD better long-distance capacity to the Pacific and Europe and the launching of the other two satellites completed the system in 1975.[50]

At first the Air Force viewed the Soviet antisatellite activity with concern but not with dismay. In 1972 Lt Gen Otto J. Glasser, deputy chief of staff for research and development, said it would be a "pretty tough problem" to knock out all satellites "simultaneously, or anything like simultaneously." "Of course you realize," he concluded, "that the minute any one of them is attacked that this raises everything else to a very high state of alert, so that all is not lost in one Wagnerian cataclysm."[51] Soviet space activities, nevertheless, continued to give concern, especially the rate of Soviet military space activity in comparison with that of the United States. The total number of Soviet launches surpassed that of the United States in 1971 and the rate of separation increased. In the first half of 1973 the USSR launched 42 satellites and the United States launched 9; in the first half of 1974 the USSR put 50 payloads into orbit compared to 15 for the United States. The Soviets stressed that their cosmos satellites were for scientific purposes, but there was no doubt that they also were for military data gathering, navigation, or position fixing. On 2 March 1977 the United States had 381 payloads in space; the remaining 3,842 objects in space consisted of 438 payloads of other nations (chiefly the USSR) and 3,404 pieces of debris. That the Soviets maintained a much higher rate of payload launches than the United States could indicate an inferiority of their satellite technology's longevity, on the other hand, it also showed a depth and high degree of launch capability to reconstitute satellite resources or replenish errant satellites.[52] In 1976 the USSR resumed testing of capabilities to inspect and destroy satellites, using three target satellites and four interceptors. In 1977 the same activity was repeated; single interceptors were flown in 1978 and 1980, while two were flown in 1981. In 1981 an intercept flight was made for the first time in large-scale Soviet maneuvers, which included missile launches and the launch of two other satellites for reconnaissance and navigation.[53] At the resumption of Soviet antisatellite activity in 1976, the Department of Defense intensified its studies of the effects of laser radiation and nuclear effects with a view to providing hardening to reduce damage to critical satellite components. In 1979, however, Lt Gen Thomas Stafford, Air Force deputy chief of staff for research, development, and acquisition, reported that the satellites were designed to perform their functions with stringent weight allowances that prohibited inclusion of burdensome defensive measures. These defensive measures would have negatively impacted a high level of survivability. To make the spacecraft ultimately hard and invulnerable would be a task that was beyond the scope of present expendable boost vehicles technology and even to the space shuttle when it became available.[54]

A presidential-level study of US military space policy began during the administration of Gerald Ford and was continued in the Carter administration. In the last year of the Ford administration, Congress passed the National Science and Technology Policy, Organization, and Priorities Act of 1976. This act established larger responsibilities in the Office of Science and Technology Policy (OSTP) within the Executive Office of the President, and this office began to play the dominant role in formulating space policy under President Carter. A series of joint studies involving the National Security Council, the Department of Defense, the Office of Science and Technology Policy, and NASA addressed the fragmentation of US space activities and sought a coherent national space policy. On 9 May 1977 Air Force Chief of Staff Gen David C. Jones signed out a letter to all major commands entitled "Air Force Space Policy." Referring to the growing US reliance on space operations, which was accompanied by a growing threat to the free use of space, the letter affirmed that activities in space relating to the development of weapon systems, military operations, and defense of the United States — conducted in accordance with national policy and international law — were among the prime Air Force responsibilities.

On 20 June 1978 President Carter issued a presidental directive 37 (PD-37) on national space policy. The directive established a policy review committee within the National Security Council (NSC) to provide a forum for considering space policy news and providing for a rapid referral of space issues to the president. Specifically, NASA was directed to pay virtually all the costs associated with the space shuttle; the Department of Defense was chartered to design survivability into space systems, develop an antisatellite (ASAT) capability, and to "bump" civilian payloads from scheduled shuttle flights if national security required. NASA rejected any claims to sovereignty over outer space and any limitations on the fundamental right to acquire data from space. It held that purposeful interference with space systems should be viewed as an infringement upon sovereign rights. It also stated that the United States would pursue activities in space for self-defense and would thereby strengthen national security, improve deterrence from attack, and help monitor arms control agreements. Concerning space systems survivability, PD-37 stated: "Identified deficiencies will be eliminated and an aggressive long-term program will be applied to provide more assured survivability through evolutionary changes."[55]

The heavy emphasis on military space in PD-37 caused consternation within the civilian space community. Consequently the NSC Policy Review Committee for Space recommended and on 11 October President Carter signed PD-42, "US Civil Space Policy." The thrust of this directive was summarized by its third tenet, which stated that the United States would not be committed to a high challenge such as Apollo. As resources from shuttle development phased down greater attention would be given to new space applications and explorations.[56]

Building a Space Command and Space Doctrine

Although General Jones had signed out the Air Force space policy declaring operations in space to be among the Air Force's primary responsibilities and President Carter had issued two directives on national space policy, Lt Col Charles H. MacGregor and Maj Lee H. Livingston, two Air Force officers who were completing three years of lecturing on space at Air University schools in the summer of 1978, declared that "our civilian leaders in the Department of Defense seem to understand the significance of military space systems better than the professional military." The two authors charged most Air Force officers with "professional parochialism" — an interest in airplanes and with attitudes that are "either indifference or a profound conviction that military space programs are merely flashy gadgetry." There was no single organization with primary space responsibilities: the Air Force Systems Command (AFSC), Air Defense Command, Strategic Air Command, and Defense Communications Agency all "had a piece of the pie." "Space systems," MacGregor and Livingston wrote, "have no high-ranking spokesman, no single manager to orchestrate our efforts, below the OSD." In January 1977 the Air Force director of space had conducted an Air Force space symposium to exchange ideas and concepts between the operating commands and the systems and development community, but MacGregor and Livingston charged that only the Air Defense Command was familiar enough with space systems to provide substantive requirements for future operational capabilities. The two men argued a need for a separate space command, plus an active participation of the operating commands in formulating requirements and shaping an evolving doctrine for space.[57] In a talk to an Air Force Association symposium in October 1978, Gen James E. Hill, commander of Air Defense Command, proposed that there should be a single point to deal with US space defense matters. "We are today at the point," he said, "where we must develop the doctrine and we must foster the visions which will give us security in the unbounded reaches of space."[58] Shortly before his retirement in 1979, General Hill wrote to the Air Force chief of staff that "unless we make an explicit organizational decision which assigns to a single organization the Air Force responsibilities in space operations once and for all, we will be faced with serious, negative, long-term impacts on resource management and planning."[59]

As it happened the formal mission statements for the Air Force in DOD Directive 5100.1 (June 1969) and in JCS Publication 2 (October 1974) had not mentioned space as a separate area of military operations. DOD Directive 5160.32 (September 1970) had been more specific in addressing space operations since it provided: "The Air Force will have the responsibility of development, production and deployment of space systems for warning and surveillance of enemy nuclear capabilities and all launch vehicles, including launch and orbital support operations."[60] An Air Force space mission organizational planning study completed in February 1979 concluded that there was consensus within the Air Force that it should actively seek designation as the executive agent within DOD for space and that it should improve its organizational structure to conduct space operations, this without any consensual agreement on timing or direction. When President Carter's PD-37 charged the Department of Defense with developing capabilities to monitor the situation in space, protect US and friendly space assets, and deny space as a sanctuary for potential enemies, a memorandum from the assistant secretary of defense for C^3I to the chairman of the Joint Chiefs of Staff and the chief of staff of the Air Force directed that the old NORAD space defense center would become ADCOM's space defense operations center (SPADOC). The NORAD space surveillance system operated a center in the Cheyenne Mountain Complex in Colorado Springs, Colorado, and maintained a catalog of all man-made objects in orbit. The OSD memo announced that SPADOC was viewed as a centralized management and operations center relative to space; Lt Gen Charles A. Gabriel, Air Force deputy chief of staff for operations, plans and readiness, demurred however and noted that when SPADOC achieved the capabilities visualized by OSD the Air Force would allow SPADOC to be the military focal point for DOD management of US space activity. For the time being, the Air Force was unwilling to impose authority on the individual space system owners and operators without their agreement.[61]

Air Force Manual 1-1, *Functions and Basic Doctrine of the United States Air Force*, printed on 14 February 1979, for the first time identified space operations as being of the nine basic operational missions of the Air Force. It provided: "The Air Force mission in space is to conduct three types of space operations: space support; force enhancement; and space defense." The space support operations included launch and recovery activities, on-orbit support, and satellite surveillance and control. The use of space systems was said to multiply the effectiveness of surface, sea, and aerospace forces by conducting global surveillance, serving as penetration aids, providing global communications capabilities, enabling operation of worldwide command and control systems, producing precise positioning and navigational data, and presenting detailed and timely meteorological information.[62] During 1979 the Air Force also heeded the recommendation of the space mission organizational planning study that the Air Force should acquire military capabilities in space. The chief organizational changes were in the Air Force Systems Command, where a need to isolate space systems from the acquisition of the MX missile demanded that the old space and missile systems organization (SAMSO) be divided. An Air Force space division was shredded out to be headed by an AFSC deputy commander for space operations. The space division's mission would be to develop new spacecraft and also to pioneer means by which payloads could be flown on the space shuttle. The Air Force also planned to construct a consolidated space operations center (CSOC) near SPADOC. The center would have a mid-1980s operational capability to serve as mission control for space shuttle flights related to national security. This center would control various satellites in orbit. Given these reorganizations, one camp of Air Force thinking urged that the space organization was sufficient; another camp said that more changes would need to be forthcoming, but it was too soon for major changes; and a third camp reasoned that a complete reorganization was long overdue. In the summer of 1980 the Air Force Scientific Advisory Board examined national space activities and Air Force organization for space operations. This report commended the Air Force for an outstanding job of evolving experimental space systems into reliable operational systems, but it concluded: "Given current capabilities and potentials of space systems, the AF organization for operational exploitation of space is inadequate. . . . There is insufficient emphasis on an integrated force structure in which space systems are included as essential elements."[63]

As secretary of the Air Force in January 1980, Hans Mark considered "enhancement of our ability to conduct operations in space" to be "exceedingly important" for the Air Force. Having considerable experience in space technology, Mark sometimes felt that no one listened to him because he advocated innovations in the space program. On a visit to the United States Air Force Academy in January 1980, Mark challenged the institution to apply its academic expertise to a study of a military space doctrine.[64] In his analysis of the Air Force organization for space, Lt Gen Richard C. Henry, commander of the AFSC's Space Division, explained the difficulty in separating acquisition from operations, the former being a normal AFSC responsibility and the latter operational function normally being the duty of a unified or specified command. Henry demonstrated that all spacecraft in orbit were highly technical in their construction and support. "There is," he wrote, "nothing routine about either launching or supporting spacecraft on-orbit and we still need to rely heavily on engineering talent for both functions."[65] The Air Force's talent of mostly young engineering officers was concentrated in AFSC, a group of men fresh from college who did not remain long on active military duty. Henry argued:

> The issue centers on our inability to define the line between acquisition and operations. It is very clear in a mission such as space defense. Yet, it is not so clear in the other mission areas where space systems are primarily in a supporting role to our operating forces: in communications, navigation, meteorology and the like. . . . We have a modicum of capability. We think we know what to do. We think we know how to do it. We don't yet, however, have the wherewithal—the direction—to get there. . . . What is important is that we move out in thinking our way through the basic strategy and doctrine for the military use of space. The alternative is to be captured by the technologists and the systems they develop. I sometimes think that we are in that situation today.[66]

Although the first applications in space may have been experiments tailored and supported by engineers, Lt Gen Jerome F. O'Malley—Air Force deputy chief of staff for plans, operations and readiness—could see a dawning of space operational activities. On 1 November 1980 he was addressing the Air Force Manned Space Flight Support Group assembled at the Johnson Space Center in Texas to work on the military applications of the space shuttle. O'Malley said:

> I believe the use of space by military forces is at a point paralleling the position of air power after WW I. . . . The potential for space to become a more hostile environment

is increasing. It is increasing for the very reason that air became an arena for hostilities: first, because space systems provide increasingly important support — some would say a decisive edge — to military forces; and second, the technology for space conflict is available.[67]

O'Malley argued that the Air Force must give organizational recognition to space:

> We must apply the same considerations to space systems as we do for other operations. We must design space assets, and structure their supporting organization in a manner responsive to the needs of operational forces — and integrate them into these forces — to allow field commanders to be confident that space capabilities will be there when they are needed.[68]

O'Malley was reminded of the maxim of Giulio Douhet: "Victory smiles upon those who anticipate the changes in the character of war, not upon those who wait to adapt themselves after the changes occur." "We would do well," O'Malley concluded, "to remember these words."[69]

In response to Secretary Mark's challenge at the United States Air Force Academy, the academy established a working group with expertise in astronautics, management, political science, and doctrinal development. An interdepartmental special topic course in space doctrine was organized and taught to cadets during the spring 1981 semester, and a USAFA Military Space Doctrine Symposium was convened and held on 1–3 April 1981. Solicited papers were published in *The Great Frontier: A Book of Readings for the Military Space Doctrine Symposium*, distributed a month prior to the symposium. The 246-person symposium was organized into three roundtable panels on US space operations doctrine, US space organization doctrine, and USSR/international space operations and organization doctrine. Each panel attempted to find consensus to questions posed to it. A pervading thought of the symposium directors was that it would be possible to learn from the past, decide where the Air Force must be in space by the year 2000, and articulate the doctrine that would assure a successful and logical progression toward the goal. In the end one panel member was outspokenly critical that "a gathering of 'space cadets' as was represented here is tantamount to 'preaching to the choir'." He recommended that future symposia include actual operational elements of the Air Force beyond the space community.[70] And since consensus was not reached on many pivotal organizational issues, participants recognized that the symposium served more as a stimulus than a response. The panel on space operations doctrine faltered when no commonly accepted definition of doctrine resulted from roundtable discussions, although, as will be seen, a weak consensus did emerge on specific characteristics that doctrine should possess. The chairman of the space organization doctrine panel provoked his group with an opening statement, contending that organization for space was *not* the problem; rather, what should we *do* in space was the precedent issue. There was a consensus that in the long run a dedicated space organization structure was inevitable, but there was also agreement that an optimum organizational structure would depend upon a clear conception of space itself, whether it would be a medium (place) or a mission.[71]

Early in 1981 an Air University air power symposium and the Air Force Academy Military Space Doctrine Symposium concluded that there was no space doctrine, that a space doctrine was needed, and that the Air Force needed to get its doctrinal house in order. Lt Col David E. Lupton pointed out after some reflection:

> These conclusions were not totally correct because there was a space doctrine, one that governed the employment of space forces even though it had not been officially published. The symposia attendees were correct in their criticism, however, because the doctrine, in effect, was a nondoctrine: that space should be a sanctuary, free from military forces. It is doubtful that many of the attendees at either space doctrine symposium would have accepted that the best way to employ space forces was not to have space forces.[72]

Lupton conceived that differences of opinion on possible space organization and what technologies to fund had resulted from differing fundamental beliefs that never had been broken out openly. He described four belief structures or schools of doctrinal thought relative to space. The first school had followed a "sanctuary" or "free skies" doctrine for space in which it was seen that space surveillance systems for mutual inspection of treaty compliance had a tremendous stabilizing influence on international relations and was too important to jeopardize by an intrusion of weapons into space. A second "survivability" school was similar to the sanctuary school but suggested that space applications—communications, meteorology, and surveillance—were effective in peacetime but could not serve wartime functions because of their inherent vulnerability. A third cluster of thinking was a "control" school, which suggested the value of space forces by using air power or sea power analogies and argued that the capability to deter war was enhanced by the ability to control space. A fourth school harked back to the old military axiom that domination of the high ground ensures domination of lower lying areas. The "high ground" school argued that global-coverage characteristics of space forces, combined with directed-energy or high-velocity-impact kinetic weapons, provided opportunities for radical new national strategies, including a space-based ballistic missile defense.[73]

At the opening address of the Air Force Academy Military Space Doctrine Symposium, Gen Bernard Schriever expressed confidence that the new administration of Ronald Reagan had a policy of realism toward the Soviet threat, that policy determinations that had stifled and inhibited developments in space would no longer stand in the way. "It seems to be a very propitious time to get going in space," Schriever said.[74] As viewed in short retrospect by Dr Robert S. Cooper, director of the Defense Advanced Research Projects Agency, the Reagan administration brought an intensified reaction to Soviet space activities that began to surge with the fielding of Soviet antisatellite and ocean surveillance capabilities. Cooper said:

> Up until a few years ago we had chosen not to build an antisatellite system . . . because nothing that the Soviets were doing in space was so threatening to our forces on the

> surface that we believed we needed to deny them the use of any specific spacecraft.... We were willing to fight all battles with the Soviet Union leaving their spacecraft in a sanctuary.[75]

In the late 1970s especially, Soviet writings viewed space as a military arena to be dominated to achieve victory in modern superpower warfare. The large Soviet space launch rate was estimated to be 85 percent military related, and there were a record 97 successful launches in 1981. The Soviets had considerable redundancy in their space vehicles, shorter lived satellites with more frequent replenishment, and a capability for rapid satellite replacement. "All of that space activity," Doctor Cooper said, "leads one to believe that the Soviets have some grand scheme or ulterior motive; they want to gain some kind of sovereignty in space."[76]

In May 1981 Lt Gen Kelly Burke, Air Force deputy chief of staff for research development and acquisition, welcomed the capability of the space shuttle as a high-volume multiuser transport, but he also summarized the risks inherent in the existing US space program. Burke said:

> With or without the shuttle the US military space program faces the following risks: —Loss of existing capability through failure to provide adequate redundancy or robustness of current systems. —Inability to quickly replace or backup key elements of existing systems lost either through natural disaster, normal wear out of on-orbit systems, or enemy action. —Loss of technological lead in key areas which, if fielded by the Soviets, would threaten our space infrastructure. —Inability to deter, defend, or retaliate effectively against actions hostile to our space infrastructure.[77]

Upon taking office in January 1981 President Reagan's team, as already seen, applied more interest to the prospects of discovering a space-based strategic defense against rapidly growing missile forces. Said James P. Wade, Jr., assistant to the secretary of defense for atomic energy and acting principal deputy under secretary of defense for research and engineering in March 1981:

> My observation is that with a new team coming aboard you will see an increased interest and emphasis on measures associated with active defense.... I believe personally the program has been underfunded over the past several years, in the sense of pushing technology and trying to understand what is the maximum potential in terms of where it could be applied and how and soon could it be applied to military problems.[78]

In an 18 September 1981 statement to Congress, President Reagan spoke of reordering the priorities of the space program, and his fiscal year 1982 NASA budget request was $600 million less than President Carter's. The space shuttle was exempt from cuts, and on 10 July 1981 former Secretary of the Air Force Mark was sworn in as deputy administrator for NASA. Soon afterwards, Maj Gen James A. Abrahamson, a fully trained astronaut in the old MOL program and a successful program manager for the F-16 fighter, was appointed associate administrator of NASA for the space shuttle program. The first space shuttle flight by the *Columbia* already had been accomplished successfully on 12 April 1981, and in reference to it President Reagan told Congress "the space shuttle did more than prove our technological abilities. It raised our expectations once more. It started us dreaming again."[79]

During 1981 and into 1982 centralization of management of space activities within the Department of Defense received much attention from senior management. A space operations committee was established within the Office of the Secretary of Defense, chaired by the secretary of the Air Force, and a department wide study looking toward production of a comprehensive DOD space policy was commenced under the chairmanship of the under secretary of defense for policy, Dr Richard D. DeLauer, who had been a program manager in the space program. Doctor DeLauer charged Dr Robert S. Cooper to act as the principal focus for review of space research and development across all mission areas.[80] In November 1981 Edward C. Aldrich, Jr., under secretary of the Air Force, spoke of "the direction we appear to be moving toward in establishing a policy for the DOD role in space." He said:

> The way in which we operate our space assets must be more coordinated and integrated in the future as we expand our space operations and commence routine launches of military satellites with the Shuttle. The right answer may be some form of a "space command" for the operation of our satellites and launch systems. The Air Force is moving in that direction.[81]

In November 1980 General O'Malley had spoken of the need to recognize that space was no longer a research and development environment only but should be considered an operational medium also. Late in 1981 the Air Staff formed a directorate of space operations within the Office of Air Force Deputy Chief of Staff for Plans and Operations. The Air Force also elevated commander in chief, North American Aerospace Defense Command (CINCNORAD) to a four-star level, commensurate with his responsibilities for space, missile, and aircraft defense of North America.

The Air Force Institute of Technology established a course in space operations.[82] In 1982, in preparation of the fiscal year 1983 budget's five-year defense projection, the Air Force stated its objectives in space: "Enhance space order of battle. Develop more survivable and enduring systems at all levels of conflict. Provide more evolutionary (rather than revolutionary) improvements. Exploit the STS to its fullest."[83] Brig Gen Bernard P. Randolph, director of space systems and deputy chief of staff for research, development, and acquisition, explained:

> The top two objectives address the fact that we in the Air Force consider space in terms of more military capability than we have used in the past; therefore, we wish to enhance our space order of battle, buy more, if you will, to assure that we have the necessary support, and assure that these systems we put on orbit as part of our space program will survive throughout the length of conflict.[84]

Early in 1982 the General Accounting Office (GAO) advised Congress to limit funds for the Air Force's planned consolidated space operations center (CSOC) until the Department of Defense came up with an overall plan for military exploitation of space. The report said that CSOC "could be used as a nucleus for a future space force" or a "future space command" and that it ought to be planned with that in mind.[85]

Whether "space" was a "mission" requiring the organization and functioning of "space forces," disparate and coequal with land, sea, and air forces, or whether "space" was a "place" was apparently actively debated in 1982. The outcome was that space was a place and not a mission and that "space systems compete with other types of systems in establishing the most effective means of accomplishing a given mission." To the Air Force, space continued as part of the operational medium where it could perform missions and specialized tasks.[86]

Space defense and an ASAT comprised a unitary Air Force mission, and the F-15-launched ASAT, working in cooperation with the Cheyenne Mountain SPADOC, was under development; but other ongoing space systems supported all military services. The backbone of military space communications in the late 1980s would be the military strategic and tactical relay satellite (MILSTAR), which would provide worldwide coverage for the strategic and tactical requirements of the Army, Navy, and Air Force. The NAVSTAR GPS navigation system would produce precise signals, allowing worldwide location to within 16 meters. The signals would be available to commercial users as well as the military services. A defense meteorological satellite program (DMSP) would provide instant weather information, even showing thunderstorms in progress.[87]

On 4 July 1982 President Reagan selected the occasion of the welcome home ceremonies for the final test-flight of the space shuttle to announce an awaited and revised national space policy. Major portions of the space policy paper were said to have borne security classifications, but a five-page fact sheet outlining the policy was issued by the White House. The basic goals of the national space policy were to strengthen national security, maintain US space leadership, exploit space for economic and scientific benefits, expand private investment and involvement in space, promote international activities in the national interest, and cooperate with other nations in maintaining the freedom of space. The policy emphasized the close coordination between NASA and the DOD, while keeping the civil and military space programs separate. Antisatellite capability was endorsed as a specific program for development with operational deployment as a goal. The policy also called for survivability and endurance of space systems for times of crisis and conflict and the development of attack warning, notification, verification, and contingency reaction capabilities to threats to US space systems. Early in his administration, President Reagan had abolished the Presidential Review Committee on space established within the National Security Council by President Carter; the new policy provided that space policy would be implemented by interagency mechanisms and a senior interagency group on space that would provide "orderly and rapid referral" to the president for decisions on space policy matters.[88]

On 21 June 1982 a few days before his retirement, Gen Lew Allen, Jr., announced the planned formation of a space command to be effective on 1 September 1982 with headquarters in Colorado Springs, Colorado. Air Force Space Command (SPACECMD) was formed as planned on 1 September 1982 with the mission of managing and operating assigned space assets, centralizing planning, consolidating requirements, providing operational advocacy, and ensuring a close interface between research and development activities and operational users of Air Force space programs. The commander of Space Command also was to serve as CINCNORAD and CINCADC. The commander of the Air Force Systems Command's Space Division was assigned the added duty SPACECMD's deputy commander. In a related reorganization, the Air Force established the Air Force Space Technology Center at Kirtland AFB, New Mexico, subordinate to the AFSC Space Division. Within this framework it was conceived that the Air Force Space Technology Center would work on basic technology; Space Division would be responsible for research, development, launch, and checkout; and the operational space commands then would assume in-orbit control, management, and protection responsibilities. SPACECMD immediately took over the space defense operations center already operating in the Cheyenne Mountain Complex; ground breaking occurred in May 1983 for the consolidated space operations center, which was to have the missions of controlling operational spacecraft and managing DOD space shuttle flights.[89]

In the autumn of 1982, Gen Charles A. Gabriel, Air Force chief of staff, explained the military significance of space. "Space is the ultimate high ground.... The magnitude and direction of the Soviet military space effort demands that we meet these challenges, employing the full range of aerospace assets in our nation's defense.... The nation's highest defense priority—deterrence—requires a credible warfighting capability across the spectrum of conflict."[90] Air Force Secretary Verne Orr developed the same theme:

> As in the 1920's when we were just learning about the possible uses of airpower, today we are still learning how space based capabilities can contribute to our national defense posture. And while some might view that space can be kept a weapons-free sanctuary free of military systems, history tells us that each time new technological opportunities present themselves, nations invariably employ them to avoid being placed in an inferior defense situation. Our nation will continue to pursue avenues to foster the peaceful use of space consistent with the President's national space policy. We and the Soviets are now ... highly dependent on space for many military support functions, e.g., warning, communications and command and control. This dependence will undoubtedly grow. As a minimum then we must ensure that our space systems can operate in a hostile wartime environment, survive and continue our defense requirements. As national use of and investment in space increases, protection of our resources will be essential. Because such protection introduces the possibility of space-to-space, space-to-earth, and earth-to-space operations, it is in our national interest to be prepared to accomplish them. Prudent preparations, such as ASAT, also give us a hedge against technological surprise, and ensure we are not placed in a permanent position of disadvantage by Soviet initiatives.[91]

IDEAS, CONCEPTS, DOCTRINE

In explaining why the Air Force had established Space Command, General Gabriel pointed out that it was

> mostly . . . a consolidation of what we had in being. A new way to organize with the operational beacon as opposed to just [a] technological driver. The operational will now be the driver. . . . What we have done is pull together the operational and technical—technological push was what we had before.[92]

Maj Gen Bruce K. Brown, vice CINCNORAD/assistant vice commander, Space Command, pointed out that several factors converged in 1982 to cause the Space Command's activation:

> These factors included the Soviet threat in space, our Nation's increasing dependence on space systems, an ever increasing national space resource commitment, and the need to take full advantage of the space shuttle to enhance man's presence in space. Lastly, on July 4, 1982, President Reagan announced that the most important goal of the United States space program was to strengthen national security. As a result, we now have a policy which underscores the need to move Air Force space programs out of the research and development community into the operational world.[93]

As early as 1977 drafting of a military space doctrine manual to be controlled as AFM 1-6 was begun in the Doctrine and Concepts Office of the Air Force Directorate of Plans (HQ USAF/XOX). The first drafts of this manual proposed that space forces be provided by an Air Force component commander to work within a joint force directed by a unified commander with authority from the national command authorities (NCA) through the Joint Chiefs of Staff.[94] The space manual had been projected for completion in 1981 so that it would be available to provide policy direction for the military space program but it was delayed, one reason being an argument over whether space was a medium or place or a mission. This argument was resolved, as explained by Maj Gen John H. Storrie, director of space, Air Force deputy chief of staff for plans and operations. Storrie explained:

> The bottom line is: space is a place; it is not a mission. We are going to continue to do those things in space that we do in the atmosphere and on the ground and on the seas. We are not going to go out and do those things in space just because the technology is there. . . . We are going to do them because we can do them better from space, or we can do them more cost-effective.[95]

Despite these decisions, the Air Force looked upon its Space Command as the initial step that could lay the foundation for the eventual integration of space systems into the unified/specified command structure. In early 1964 the joint statement of Secretary Orr and General Gabriel on the fiscal year 1985 Air Force posture strongly recommended a unified command for space, saying:

> We have developed the various space programs based on technological advances and mission requirements. However, no single military organization exercises operational authority over military space systems in peace, war, and the transition period from peace

to war. To make our space systems more effective and responsive, and to ensure a clear chain of command from the NCA to combatant forces, we proposed a unified command for space. This new command would exercise operational command over US military space systems which provide support to the combatant forces of the unified and specified commands. In the future, space-based systems may become available which will add a truly new dimension to conducting warfare. After an extensive review of command arrangements for space, the Air Force recommends a unified space command be formed soon.[96]

In support of the Air Force advocacy of a unified command for space, Gen Bernard Randolph, Air Force director of Space Systems and C^3, deputy chief of staff for research, development, and acquisition, argued that:

> First of all, it is the character of space systems to support a number of users. It is very difficult to say that a space system was an Air Force, Navy, or Army system because ... the way we work the space systems in the main is in fact jointly. ... I don't think the country can afford multiple organizations in space. Space is just too expensive. ... The Air Force strongly supports the idea of a unified command. We designed the kind of things that command would do to support all the fighting forces. ... There is no such thing as a unique Navy or Air Force system. Almost every space system applies to all the services.[97]

Although a US Navy spokesman agreed that the Air Force should take the lead in antisatellite programs for space defense, the Navy in 1983 organized a Naval Space Command of its own and appeared generally opposed to a unified space command. "I am having a hard time in my own mind defining what the mission of a unified command is in space," said Vice Adm Gordon R. Nagler, director of command and control, Office of Chief of Naval Operations. "For example, today the Air Force command in space is both acquisition and operations. I am not too sure if that is not in conflict a little bit."[98] Adm James D. Watkins, chief of naval operations, doubted the need for a unified command. Watkins was quoted as saying, "I would also worry unless there were significant improvements to be gained." Navy Secretary John F. Lehman, Jr., flatly disagreed with the need for a unified space command.[99] In March 1984 Admiral Watkins testified that he would not oppose a unified command at a right time. He said:

> I think that a unified command should be a command that has the potential to fight a war and if it is going to be a command established during a massive R&D program, then I don't really understand it. So I think there is confusion as to the need for a unified command at this particular time.[100]

In 1984, however, the Department of Defense accepted a unified US space command with Air Force, Navy, Army and Marine Corps participation as "the next evolutionary step." On 30 November 1984 a Department of Defense press release announced the activation of the new unified US Space Command (USSPACECOM). The announcement said that the new unified command would "better serve US interests and the needs of our allies worldwide by providing an organizational structure that will centralize operational responsibilities for more effective use of military space systems."[101] The Joint Chiefs of Staff established a joint planning staff for space (JPSS), a directorate on the Joint Staff, to develop transition plans.[102]

At the same time that the preparation of AFM 1-6, *Military Space Doctrine*, was perplexed by the question of whether space was a medium or a mission, there was a question as to whether the manual was to be a compendium of fundamental, unencumbered principles of space combat operations or a statement of restricted objectives in space. In a paper prepared for the Air Force Academy Military Space Doctrine Symposium in 1981, Lt Col Dino A. Lorenzini, who was assigned at the Naval War College, urged: "Military space doctrine should address . . . fundamental possibilities for space warfare now in the hope that we can plan more deliberately and prepare more decisively for the uncertain events that lie ahead."[103] In an article published in 1982 Lorenzini additionally proposed that two versions of space power doctrine might well be issued. An unencumbered version would be a "basic" space power doctrine relevant to the practice of warfare in space; a constrained version would be an "operational" doctrine taking into consideration national overall space policy decisions.[104] At the National Defense University, Col Casper J. Schichtle, while assigned as a senior research fellow, prepared a research report on space policy and organization which touched on space doctrine. His review of the January 1979 draft of the proposed AFM 1-6 brought his criticism that the Air Force was bound to a peaceful use of space whereas the Soviets were headed in another direction. He urged that the Air Force publish AFM 1-6:

> As a body of principles governing military activities in space for the foreseeable future, it should be a natural flowdown from stated national space policies. In addition, it should contain all but the most sensitive military space plans . . . and signify the defense establishment's desire to "come out of the closet."[105]

When AFM 1-6, *Military Space Doctrine*, was officially published on 15 October 1982 its first and longest chapter discussed, "National Space Policy, Executive Guidance, and Legal Constraints," and a lengthy bibliography basic to the chapter, was appended. The major thrust of the doctrine was that space systems would be consistent with national policy. As explained officially by Secretary Orr and General Gabriel the basic philosophy of the new space doctrine was to preserve free access to and transit through space for peaceful purposes for both military and civilian users. To do this, forces would need to be maintained that were capable and ready. Then, if conflict became unavoidable, the United States would be prepared to use the force necessary to secure resolution at the lowest level and on terms favorable to the United States. The basic military objectives in space as defined in the doctrine were:

> To maintain freedom of space; To increase effectiveness, readiness and survivability of military forces; To protect the nation's resources from threats in, through and from space; and To prevent space from being used as a sanctuary for aggressive systems by our enemies.[106]

In addition to AFM 1-6, the Air Force conceived that the Space Command would take a next step by creating more specific "operational space doctrine."[107] Secretary Orr defended AFM 1-6 as being a "strong emphasis" on doctrine and strategy for space. "The doctrine," he said, "provides a basis for determining strategy and will give focus and direction to the development of future space systems."[108] On the other hand, there was an apparent feeling in the ranks of young Air Force space enthusiasts — who were being called "space cadets" — that AFM 1-6 was so bound by national and international agreements as to provide incomplete forward-looking guidance for future conflict in space.[109]

President Reagan's Strategic Defense Initiative

Even before Ronald Reagan's election to the presidency he was known to favor a shift away from the effort to find US security in constant buildups of a strategic offensive military system. During a meeting with Reagan at the beginning of 1983, the Joint Chiefs of Staff raised the question of the lack of emphasis on ballistic missile defense (BMD), the lack of a clearly stated BMD goal, and no strong commitment of the nation's scientific talent to BMD. The Defense Department for several years had been passing up promising BMD proposals because of overall budget constraints, even though there had been "remarkable advances" in possibly pertinent technology. The chiefs were said to be "in total community" on examining a BMD initiative, and Reagan "showed considerable interest," ordering that the idea be developed further.[110] At the end of a speech devoted to promoting the fiscal year 1984 defense budget, Reagan on 23 March 1983 first sketched his Strategic Defense Initiative (SDI). He said that he was ordering "a comprehensive and intensive effort to define a long-term research and development program" aimed at defending the United States and its allies from ballistic missiles. The day following Reagan's speech, the White House announced that Secretary Weinberger would be responsible for an interagency study, with advice from outside the government, of what BMD technologies seemed most promising and how they would be used. The study was to be in the president's hand by the autumn of 1983, when the fiscal year 1985 defense budget would be under review. A White House spokesman explained that BMD would not be turned into a crash program but could be "a sketched-out crash program."[111]

The study request by President Reagan was accomplished under a senior interagency group-defense policy, chaired by Deputy Secretary of Defense Paul Thayer. A defensive technologies study team, headed by Dr James C. Fletcher of the University of Pittsburgh and including over 50 of the nation's top scientists and engineers, was formed both to assess the feasibility of achieving the BMD goal and to structure a research program for it. The principal finding of the Fletcher study was that, despite the uncertainties, new technologies held great promise for eliminating the threat of ballistic missiles to the United States and its allies. In the autumn of 1983, President Reagan's BMD projection, known properly as the Strategic Defense Initiative but popularly called "Star Wars," began to be

IDEAS, CONCEPTS, DOCTRINE

integrated into the fiscal year 1985 defense budget in notional steps visualized by the Fletcher panel. There was to be a research phase to the early 1990s when a future president and Congress could make a decision for full-scale engineering development looking in turn to sequential deployments of defensive systems. The Fletcher panel emphasized the importance of strong control management for the SDI, and accordingly, effective on 16 April 1984, Secretary Weinberger named Lt Gen James A. Abrahamson as director, Strategic Defense Initiative Organization (SDIO). The director of SDIO was chartered to report directly to the secretary of defense; he would prepare an integrated SDI objective memorandum that would be coordinated with service Program Objective Memorandums but would not be available for trade-offs to meet service or defense agency needs except upon decision of the deputy secretary of defense. General Abrahamson remarked:

> So our job is, with a small staff, somewhere around 80 people or so, to ensure that we have good central planning and good central direction, and then to encourage really effective ways to minimize the bureaucracy and make the most creative use of the talent that is there in each of the Services to proceed with the program. So what it means is that we will have authority for very direct and accelerated communications and direction down to each of the Service elements. We will have authority to use different contracting techniques... to try to streamline that operation so that we can operate in an aggressive way to move this technology ahead. So we have a central office, but [we are] relying on the talent that is already out in the Services.[112]

In the same months that the Strategic Defense Initiative was in projection, the Air Force was progressing with an Air Force space plan that reflected an intention to exploit the military potential of space, focus technological development, and redress deficiencies across all mission areas in space. In testimony in support of the Air Force portion of the fiscal year 1985 defense request in March 1984, Secretary Orr and General Gabriel spoke formally of the SDI, noting that the program would involve all three services' space programs and gather together money from them. The Air Force continued to voice support for a unified space command, stating:

> This new command would exercise operational command over US space systems which provide support to the combatant forces of other unified and specified commands. In the future, space-based systems may become available which will add a truly new dimension to conducting warfare.[113]

As of 1984, however, the Air Force endorsed "a Space System Operation Strategy that fully integrates space systems into the military force structure and provides sufficient survivability of our critical space systems to allow the US time to provide central support to our forces."[114] Secretary Orr and General Gabriel explained: "We emphasize space systems' survivability because effective military operations in the modern battlefield are increasingly dependent on satellite surveillance, warning, communications, meteorology information, and navigation."[115]

In revising AFM 1-1, *Basic Aerospace Doctrine of the United States Air Force*, as it was finally published on 16 March 1984, the Air Force summary of changes from the 1979 edition noted: "Space is a place, not a mission, and is described as part of the operational medium where the Air Force can perform all of its missions and specialized tasks." The 1984 manual read:

> Space is the outer reaches of the aerospace operational medium. In fulfilling U.S. national security objectives, the Air Force has the primary responsibility for maintaining the United States' freedom to act throughout the aerospace. Space, as a part of that medium, provides an unlimited potential and opportunity for military operations and a place where the Air Force can perform or support all of its missions and tasks.[116]

In the congressional budget hearings in March 1984, Secretary Orr and General Gabriel were in no hurry to extend military operations into space. The purpose of the F-15 ASAT program was defined as deterrence:

> The purpose of the F-15 ASAT program is to remove an asymmetry which exists between the US and Soviet military space capability. The current unilateral capability of the Soviets to threaten or negate US space systems with an ASAT could contribute to instability during a crisis. The primary mission of the F-15 ASAT is to assure our free access to and transit through space by deterring Soviet attacks against our space systems. If deterrence fails, our ASAT would provide us the capability to "respond in kind" to Soviet attacks on our space systems.[117]

The F-15 ASAT program was only one part of a comprehensive effort to reduce the vulnerability of US space systems. The Air Force rationalized:

> No satellite system can be made totally invulnerable to all threats any more than an airplane or ship can be made totally invulnerable. The objective is to ensure the satellite system can provide service to our combat forces through a predetermined level of conflict.[118]

In the Air Force's space systems architecture satellite survivability was a major consideration, and there were five major areas for increasing survivability: maneuver, hardening/shielding, possession of orbital spares, ability to replenish rapidly, and ability to fire back at attackers. The low-earth-orbit reconnaissance satellites were most vulnerable, and, as General Gabriel pointed out, both US and Soviet communications satellites in geosynchronous orbits at altitudes of 19,000 nautical miles above the earth along the equator were outside the range of the Soviet ASAT or the F-15 ASAT that the Air Force was projecting. In 1984 General Gabriel stated that the Air Force had no plans to select a capability to attack the high-altitude geosynchronous satellites that were so important to both the Soviets and the United States. Gabriel said:

> I would not . . . recommend that we build such a system. I would rather both sides not have a capability to go to geosynchronous with an ASAT. In fact I would like to be able to agree with the Soviets that we do not have any ASATs if we could verify it properly. Because we are an open society, we need our space capabilities more than they do.[119]

NOTES

1. Col Cass Schichtle, *The National Space Program: From the Fifties into the Eighties*, National Security Affairs Monograph 83-6 (Washington, D.C.: National Defense University Press, 1983), 62.
2. Ibid.
3. *A Compilation of Material Relating to U.S. Defense Policies in 1962*, 88th Cong., 1st sess., 77.
4. Keynote speech by Gen Bernard A. Schriever, USAF, Retired, 2 April 1981, in *The Great Frontier, Military Space Doctrine: The Final Report for the United States Air Force Academy Military Space Doctrine Symposium, 1–3 April 1981*, ed. Maj Paul Viotti, 26–27.
5. Senate, *Department of Defense Appropriations for Fiscal Year 1965: Hearings before the Subcommittee of the Committee on Appropriations and the Committee on Armed Services*, 88th Cong., 2d sess., 1964, pt. 1:170–74 (hereafter cited as *FY 1965 DOD Appropriations*).
6. House, *Department of Defense Appropriations for 1965: Hearings before a Subcommittee of the Committee on Appropriations*, 88th Cong., 2d sess., 1964, pt. 5:12–16, 70–76 (hereafter cited as *1965 DOD Appropriations*).
7. House, *Department of Defense Appropriations for 1966: Hearings before a Subcommittee of the Committee on Appropriations*, 89th Cong., 1st sess., 1965, pt. 3:170 (hereafter cited as *1966 DOD Appropriations*).
8. Ibid., pt. 2:373, pt. 5:150; Thomas Karas, *The New High Ground, Systems and Weapons of Space Age War* (New York: Simon and Schuster, 1983), 148–49.
9. House, *1966 DOD Appropriations*, pt. 5:150.
10. House, *Department of Defense Appropriations for 1971: Hearings before a Subcommittee of the Committee on Appropriations*, 91st Cong., 2d sess., 1972, pt. 1:623 (hereafter cited as *1971 DOD Appropriations*).
11. Karas, *The New High Ground*, 98–99; Marcia S. Smith, *Space Activities of the United States, Soviet Union, and Other Countries/Organizations, 1957–1982* (Washington, D.C.: Government Printing Office, 1983), CSR-20; Lt Col David E. Lupton, USAF, Retired, "Space Doctrines," *Strategic Review*, Fall 1983, 46.
12. House, *1966 DOD Appropriations*, pt. 5:8; Karas, *The New High Ground*, 130.
13. House, *1965 DOD Appropriations*, pt. 5:10–11; House, *Department of Defense Appropriations for 1969: Hearings before a Subcommittee of the Committee on Appropriations*, 90th Cong., 2d sess., 1968, pt. 2:129, 450 (hereafter cited as *1969 DOD Appropriations*).
14. Senate, *Status of U.S. Strategic Power: Hearings before the Preparedness Investigating Subcommittee of the Committee on Armed Services*, 90th Cong., 2d sess., 1968, pt. 2:257.
15. House, *1966 DOD Appropriations*, pt. 3:855.
16. Senate, *Status of U.S. Strategic Power*, pt. 2:257.
17. House, *1966 DOD Appropriations*, pt. 5:151.
18. Ibid., 197–201.
19. House, *Department of Defense Appropriations for 1967: Hearings before a Subcommittee of the Committee on Appropriations*, 89th Cong., 2d sess., 1966, pt. 1:478–79 (hereafter cited as *1967 DOD Appropriations*); House, *Department of Defense Appropriations for 1968: Hearings before a Subcommittee of the Committee on Appropriations*, 90th Cong., 1st sess., 1967, pt. 2:755–56 (hereafter cited as *1968 DOD Appropriations*).
20. Senate, *Department of Defense Appropriations for Fiscal Year 1969: Hearings before a Subcommittee of the Committee on Appropriations*, 90th Cong., 2d sess., 1968, pt. 4:2331–32 (hereafter cited as *FY 1969 DOD Appropriations*).
21. Ibid.
22. House, *1967 DOD Appropriations*, pt. 1:256–57.
23. House, *1968 DOD Appropriations*, pt. 2:749; Senate, *Department of Defense Appropriations for Fiscal Year 1968: Hearings before a Subcommittee of the Committee on Appropriations*, 90th Cong., 1st sess., 1967, pt. 2:623 (hereafter cited as *FY 1968 DOD Appropriations*); House, *1969 DOD Appropriations*, pt. 2:128–29; Senate, *FY 1969 DOD Appropriations*, 19.

24. Schichtle, *The National Space Program*, 66–70; Senate, *Status of U.S. Strategic Power*, pt. 2:256–57.

25. House, *Department of Defense Appropriations for 1970: Hearings before a Subcommittee of the Committee on Appropriations*, 91st Cong., 1st sess., 1969, pt. 4:359 (hereafter cited as *1970 DOD Appropriations*).

26. Ibid., 333; Senate, *Department of Defense Appropriations for Fiscal Year 1970: Hearings before a Subcommittee of the Committee on Appropriations*, 91st Cong., 1st sess., 1969, pt. 1:6–8 (hereafter cited as *FY 1970 DOD Appropriations*).

27. Senate, *FY 1970 DOD Appropriations*, pt. 1:7, pt. 4:673–79; Schichtle, *The National Space Program*, 74.

28. Senate, *FY 1970 DOD Appropriations*, pt. 4:25–26, 673–74.

29. House, *1971 DOD Appropriations*, pt. 6:615–16.

30. Ibid.

31. Ibid., 616.

32. Col Morgan W. Sanborn, "National Military Space Doctrine," *Air University Review*, January–February 1977, 75.

33. Senate, *Department of Defense Appropriations for Fiscal Year 1972: Hearings before a Subcommittee of the Committee on Appropriations*, 92d Cong., 1st sess., 1971, pt. 4:48 (hereafter cited as *FY 1972 DOD Appropriations*).

34. Senate, *FY 1972 DOD Appropriations*, pt. 4:48; Senate, *Department of Defense Appropriations for Fiscal Year 1973: Hearings before a Subcommittee of the Committee on Appropriations*, 92d Cong., 2d sess., 1972, pt. 4:94–95 (hereafter cited as *FY 1973 DOD Appropriations*).

35. Senate, *FY 1972 DOD Appropriations*, pt. 4:48; Senate, *FY 1973 DOD Appropriations*, pt. 4:94–95; Schichtle, *The National Space Program*, 71–76.

36. Senate, *FY 1972 DOD Appropriations*, pt. 4:48; Senate, *FY 1973 DOD Appropriations*, pt. 4:94–95; Schichtle, *The National Space Program*, 71–76.

37. Senate, *FY 1972 DOD Appropriations*, pt. 4:48; Senate, *FY 1973 DOD Appropriations*, pt. 4:94–95; Schichtle, *The National Space Program*, 71–76.

38. Senate, *FY 1973 DOD Appropriations*, pt. 4:77, 90.

39. *Air Force Policy Letter for Commanders*, 1 April 1973; Senate, *Fiscal Year 1974 Military Procurement Authorization, Research and Development, Construction Authorization for the Safeguard ABM and Active Duty and Selected Reserve Strengths: Hearings before the Committee on Armed Services*, 93d Cong., 1st sess., 1973, pt. 2:1027–28 (hereafter cited as *FY 1974 Military Procurement*); Senate, *Fiscal Year 1975 Military Procurement Authorization, Research and Development, and Active Duty, Selected Reserve and Civilian Personnel Strengths: Hearings before the Committee on Armed Services*, 93d Cong., 2d sess., 1974, pt. 6:2746–49 (hereafter cited as *FY 1975 Military Procurement*).

40. *Air Force Policy Letter for Commanders*, 1 October 1975.

41. Senate, *Department of Defense Appropriations for Fiscal Year 1978: Hearings before a Subcommittee of the Committee on Appropriations*, 95th Cong., 1st sess., 1977, pt. 5:182 (hereafter cited as *FY 1978 DOD Appropriations*).

42. *Air Force Policy Letter for Commanders*, 1 October 1975.

43. Ibid.

44. Gen Jacob E. Smart, "Strategic Implications of Space Activities," *Strategic Review*, Fall 1974, 19, 21.

45. Ibid.

46. Sanborn, "National Military Space Doctrine," 76, 77–78.

47. House, *1971 DOD Appropriations*, pt. 1:622–23.

48. Ibid.

49. Schichtle, *The National Space Program*, 11–12.

50. House, *1971 DOD Appropriations*, pt. 6:87; House, *Department of Defense Appropriations for 1976: Hearings before a Subcommittee of the Committee on Appropriations*, 94th Cong., 1st sess., 1975, pt. 2:13–14 (hereafter cited as *1976 DOD Appropriations*).

51. Senate, *Fiscal Year 1973 Military Procurement Authorization, Research and Development, Construction Authorization for the Safeguard ABM and Active Duty and Selected Reserve Strengths: Hearings before the Committee on Armed Services*, 92d Cong., 2d sess., 1972, pt. 3:1440 (hereafter cited as *FY 1973 Military Procurement*).

52. Smart, "Strategic Implications of Space Activities," 23; House, *Department of Defense Appropriations for 1978: Hearings before a Subcommittee of the Committee on Appropriations*, 95th Cong., 1st sess., 1977, pt. 2:370 (hereafter cited as *1978 DOD Appropriations*).

53. Smith, *Space Activities*, CSR-61 and 62.

54. Senate, *FY 1978 DOD Appropriations*, pt. 1:253, pt. 5:28–29, 189; House, *1978 DOD Appropriations*, pt. 2:370, pt. 3:533.

55. House, *Department of Defense Appropriations for 1980: Hearings before a Subcommittee of the Committee on Appropriations*, 96th Cong., 1st sess., 1979, pt. 3:307 (hereafter cited as *1980 DOD Appropriations*).

56. Schichtle, *The National Space Program*, 78–82; "The Air Force Space Policy," in *Air Force Policy Letter for Commanders*, 1 June 1977; "Air Force Is Developing and Protecting Assets in Space," *Air Force Policy Letter for Commanders*, 15 November 1978.

57. Lt Col Charles H. MacGregor and Maj Lee H. Livingston, "Air Force Objectives in Space," *Air University Review*, July–August 1978, 60–62.

58. "Air Space Defense and Operations Control Center," *Air Force Policy Letter for Commanders*, 1 December 1978.

59. Dr Charles W. Cook, deputy assistant secretary of the Air Force for space plans and policy, "Organization for the Space Force of the Future," 21 June 1981, in *The Great Frontier, Military Space Doctrine*, ed. Viotti, 2:472.

60. Maj Douglas H. May, "The Space Shuttle and Arms Limitation Verification," in *The Great Frontier, Military Space Doctrine*, ed. Viotti, 3:760.

61. Lt Col Robert S. Dickman, "A Doctrinal Look at SPADOC," December 1980, in *The Great Frontier, Military Space Doctrine*, ed. Viotti, 1:223–25.

62. AFM 1-1, *Functions and Basic Doctrine of the United States Air Force*, 14 February 1979, 2–6, 2–8, and 2–9.

63. Cook, "Organization for the Space Force of the Future," 2:472–76; House, *Department of Defense Appropriations for 1982: Hearings before a Subcommittee of the Committee on Appropriations*, 97th Cong, 1st sess., 1981, pt. 2:33 (hereafter cited as *1982 DOD Appropriations*).

64. Speech by Schriever, in *The Great Frontier, Military Space Doctrine*, ed. Viotti, 1, 24; House, *Department of Defense Appropriations for 1981: Hearings before a Subcommittee of the Committee on Appropriations*, 96th Cong., 2d sess., 1980, pt. 2:293.

65. Speech by Lt Gen Richard C. Henry in *The Great Frontier, Military Space Doctrine*, ed. Viotti, 61–70.

66. Ibid.

67. Ibid.; F. Clifton Berry, Jr., "Space Is a Place," *Air Force Magazine*, June 1982, 36–42.

68. Berry, "Space Is a Place," 36–42.

69. Karas, *The New High Ground*, 17–18; *The Great Frontier, Military Space Doctrine*, ed. Viotti, remarks of Lt Gen Jerome F. O'Malley to Manned Space Flight Support Group, Johnson Space Center, Texas, on 1 November 1980. Air Force Office of Information press release, November 1980; O'Malley, "The Air Force in the Space Era," *Air Force Policy Letter for Commanders: Supplement*, January 1981, 2–6.

70. Foreword by Lt Col Thomas J. Eller, professor and head, Department of Astronautics and Computer Science and chairman, Steering Committee, 1981 United States Air Force Academy (USAFA) Military Space Doctrine Symposium and Maj Charles D. Friedenstein, director, 1981 USAFA Military Space Doctrine Symposium in *The Great Frontier, Military Space Doctrine*, ed. Viotti, 1–3 April 1981, 1:iii–iv passim.

71. Ibid.

72. Lupton, "Space Doctrines," 40–41; this perceptive is extracted from *On Space Warfare: A Space Power Doctrine* (Maxwell AFB, Ala.: Air University Press, June 1988). See chapter 3 of this book.
73. Ibid.
74. Schriever speech, in *The Great Frontier, Military Space Doctrine*, ed. Viotti, 27.
75. House, *Department of Defense Appropriations for 1984: Hearings before a Subcommittee of the Committee on Appropriations*, 98th Cong., 1st sess., 1983, pt. 8:449 (hereafter cited as *1984 DOD Appropriations*).
76. Ibid., 433; Senate, *Department of Defense Appropriations for Fiscal Year 1983: Hearings before a Subcommittee of the Committee on Appropriations*, 97th Cong., 2d sess., 1982, pt. 1:389 (hereafter cited as *FY 1983 DOD Appropriations*); House, *Department of Defense Appropriations for 1983: Hearings before a Subcommittee of the Committee on Appropriations*, 97th Cong., 2d sess., 1982, pt. 4:459 (hereafter cited as *1983 DOD Appropriations*).
77. Senate, *Department of Defense Appropriations for Fiscal Year 1982: Hearings before a Subcommittee of the Committee on Appropriations*, 97th Cong., 1st sess., 1981, pt. 4:735 (hereafter cited as *FY 1982 DOD Appropriations*).
78. Senate, *Department of Defense Authorization for Appropriations for Fiscal Year 1982: Hearings before the Committee on Armed Services*, 97th Cong., 1st sess., 1981, pt. 7:4155 (hereafter cited as *FY 1982 DOD Authorization*).
79. Schichtle, *The National Space Program*, 82–84.
80. Senate, *Department of Defense Authorization for Appropriations for Fiscal Year 1983: Hearings before the Committee on Armed Services*, 97th Cong., 2d sess., 1982, pt. 7:4612–13 (hereafter cited as *FY 1983 DOD Authorization*).
81. Ibid.
82. O'Malley, "The Air Force in the Space Era," 6.
83. "Use of Space for National Security," *Air Force Policy Letter for Commanders*, 15 January 1982.
84. Senate, *FY 1983 DOD Authorization*, pt. 7:4854.
85. Karas, *The New High Ground*, 19.
86. Ibid., 19; Lupton, "Space Doctrines," 37, 45.
87. Senate, *FY 1983 DOD Authorization*, pt. 7:4853–64.
88. Schichtle, *The National Space Program*, 84; "Reagan Space Policy Endorses ASAT Development," *Airspace Daily*, 7 July 1982, 26–27.
89. Edgar Ulsamer, "Spacecom: Setting the Course for the Future," *Air Force Magazine*, August 1982, 48–55; Gen James V. Hartinger, "The New Space Command," *Signal*, March 1983, 23–26; "Space Command: Facts about the Formation," *TIG Brief*, 13 September 1982, 13–14; "Space Command," *Air Force Magazine*, May 1984, 112–13; AFR 23–51, *Space Command (SPACECMD)*, 25 July 1983.
90. AFM 1-6, *Military Space Doctrine*, 15 October 1982, Foreword.
91. House, *1984 DOD Appropriations*, pt. 2:129–30.
92. Ibid., 86–87.
93. Senate, *Department of Defense Authorization for Appropriations for Fiscal Year 1984: Hearings before the Committee on Armed Services*, 98th Cong., 1st sess., 1983, pt. 5:2666 (hereafter cited as *FY 1984 DOD Authorization*).
94. Maj Gen William R. Yost, "National Space Policy and Aerospace Doctrine," *Air Force Policy Letter for Commanders: Supplement*, January 1980, 14.
95. House, *1984 DOD Appropriations*, pt. 8:475.
96. House, *Department of Defense Appropriations for 1985: Hearings before a Subcommittee of the Committee on Appropriations*, 98th Cong., 2d sess., 1984, pt. 2:55 (hereafter cited as *1985 DOD Appropriations*).
97. House, *1984 DOD Appropriations*, pt. 8:466–68.
98. Ibid.
99. Ibid., 466, 477–78.
100. Ibid.
101. Ibid.

102. House, *1985 DOD Appropriations*, pt. 2:543, 683–84; *Air Force Policy Letter for Commanders*, 15 December 1984.

103. Lt Col Dino A. Lorenzini, "Military Space Doctrine Considerations," in *The Great Frontier, Military Space Doctrine*, ed. Viotti, 1:179.

104. Lorenzini, "Space Power Doctrine," *Air University Review*, July–August 1982, 18.

105. Col Cass Schichtle, *Policy and Organizations: The Next Step in the National Space Program* (Washington, D.C.: National Defense University Research Directorate, 1983), 48, 55–56.

106. AFM 1-6, *Military Space Doctrine*, 15 October 1982.

107. Ibid.; House, *1984 DOD Appropriations*, pt. 2:44, 130.

108. AFM 1-6, *Military Space Doctrine*, 15 October 1982.

109. House, *1984 DOD Appropriations*, pt. 2:44, 130; Maj Charles D. Friedenstein, "A Critical Analysis of the First Air Force Manual 1-6, *Military Space Doctrine*," report 83-0800 (Maxwell AFB, Ala.: Air Command and Staff College, 1983).

110. "Reagan Seeks Boost for 'Subcritical' BMD Program," *Aerospace Daily*, 25 March 1983, 145–46.

111. Ibid.

112. Pertinent papers and discussions of the Strategic Defense Initiative are included in House, *1985 DOD Appropriations*, pt. 5:665–829.

113. Ibid., pt. 2:24, 54–56, 162.

114. Ibid.

115. Ibid.

116. Draft AFM 1-1, *Basic Aerospace Doctrine of the United States Air Force*, October 1983, 4–10; AFM 1-1, 16 March 1984, para. 2-2.

117. House, *1985 DOD Appropriations*, pt. 2:190–96, pt. 5:434–41.

118. Ibid.

119. Ibid.

Maj Gen James A. Abrahamson, associate administrator of NASA for the space shuttle program.

Col Casper J. Schichtle, Jr., senior research fellow at the National Defense University.

Lt Gen Thomas P. Stafford, Air Force deputy chief of staff for research, development, and acquisition.

Maj Gen Henry B. Stelling, Jr., Air Force director of space.

Columbia.

James P. Wade, Jr., associate secretary of defense for atomic energy.

CHAPTER 10

THE NEVER-ENDING QUEST FOR AIR FORCE DOCTRINE

"Basic air doctrine," stated the first edition of AFM 1-2, *United States Air Force Basic Doctrine*, in 1 April 1953, "evolves from experience gained in war and from analysis of the continuing impact of new weapons on warfare. The dynamic and constant changes in new weapons makes periodic substantive review of the doctrine necessary." Immediately following these sentences, however, the manual promised: "The application of this doctrine to the roles and missions of the United States Air Force will promote the effective employment of air power in military operations."[1] Gen Hoyt Vandenberg signed the foreword of the manual. The April 1954 and April 1955 editions of AFM 1-2 signed for authentication by Gen Nathan Twining did not include the sentence specifying a need for "periodic substantive review" of the doctrine.[2] On the basis of the promise in the April 1953 edition that adherence to the prescribed doctrine would promote the effective employment of air power in military operations, Maj Rudolph P. Wacker, an Air Command and Staff College student in 1967, concluded that "there was apparently no doubt in any air staffer's mind that this early doctrine was infallible if applied. . . . The obvious implication was that we had applied all our past experiences and new weapons systems and had created an infallible doctrine."[3]

Recognition of a Need for Dynamic Doctrine

The basic text of the 1953 and 1954 editions of AFM 1-2 was virtually unchanged, and these manuals clearly reflected air experience in World War II. The main thrust of these manuals was that air power could be employed against the heartland of a nation and in peripheral areas of conflict; that weapons of mass destruction should be used in heartland attacks; that control of the air was essential in peripheral actions and desirable in heartland attacks; and that the final selection of targets must be based on military factors but that an enemy's emotional response to air attack must be considered for its psychological impact on his national will.[4]

The 1955 version of AFM 1-2 also stressed the lessons of World War II but reflected additional thinking from the Korean conflict and the cold war. The manual demonstrated the applicability of air power to deterrence but its main concentration was on how to apply force if deterrence failed. Air power's greatest opportunities lay in direct attacks against the enemy's heartland (his war-sustaining resources) but it could also conduct operations in his periphery (his air and surface efforts). This manual concluded with the admonition: "The paramount consideration for the security and well being of the United States is the timely provision of adequate air power."[5]

In the early 1950s Maj Gen Lloyd Hopwood's reformation of the Air Command and Staff School (ACSS) at Maxwell AFB gave good attention to Air Force doctrine in the curriculum for field grade officers to Air Force doctrine. Hopwood encouraged student thesis analysis of extant Air Force doctrine and also personally delivered a lecture on air doctrine, which Lt Gen George G. Loving, Jr., who had been a student in ACSS in 1955–56, would remember many years later as being "extraordinarily good" and a "real influence on me."[6] As has been seen, the Air Force in the aftermath of the Defense Reorganization Act of 1958 elected to relieve the Air University of the responsibility for preparation of Air Force basic doctrine and to retain the function in an air doctrine branch under the deputy director for policy, Directorate of Plans. At this juncture there was said to be a school of thought on the Air Staff that air doctrine written in the AFM 1-2 manuals was immutable, inflexible, and so fundamentally sound as to require neither further justification nor analysis, but the Air Staff did not object to the Air Command and Staff School studying air doctrine.[7]

Especially in 1958–59 Air Command and Staff School student analyses of air doctrine were quite critical. In his paper assaying the effects of intercontinental ballistic missiles, Maj William Y. Smith (whose subsequent career would culminate with four stars) demonstrated that the 1955 AFM 1-2 emphasized offensive action, basing its conclusion on five characteristics of aircraft that made them incomparable offensive weapons: range, speed, flexibility, mobility, and penetration ability. Smith showed that a ballistic missile lacked the manned aircraft's principal advantage: flexibility. On the other hand, missiles were powerful offensive weapons for reasons other than those which made the aircraft a unique offensive weapon. Since Soviet ICBMs would open the United States to attack, Smith urged that AFM 1-2 was deficient in the scant attention it gave to defense. He wrote:

> The point here is not that the present air defense system is completely inadequate. The point is that present teachings of the Air Force do not satisfactorily stress the urgent requirement for a sound defense. In neglecting this facet of doctrine, present USAF doctrine neglects a vital portion of the Air Force's war mission.[8]

Smith recommended that "studies be initiated immediately to develop a 'symmetrical' air doctrine that would refocus Air Force thinking to give defensive actions a priority equal to that given offensive ones."[9] A consolidation of other student theses on Air Force basic doctrine pointed to the main announced objective of air power as being control of the air, to be attained by offensive air strikes on enemy bases. This meant in operations in peripheral areas, air control would demand air strikes on Soviet bases.

> Our emphasis, springing from our doctrinal position, has been on the deterrent effect of nuclear striking power and an air force designed to attain control of the air. This emphasis, which dictates USAF operational requirements, is a natural result of our doctrine position. As a result, current theater commanders, faced with the prospect of limited wars of many categories, are not adequately equipped to plan for and conduct the wide range of actions necessary in this type of a conflict and must overcome by ingenuity the handicaps placed upon them by the inflexibility of our doctrinal position.[10]

Col Roy R. Walker offered still another recommendation in an Air War College thesis in April 1959, even though he recognized it was not likely to be adapted. Walker contended that AFM 1-2 be rescinded and not be replaced by any similar publication. Instead, the secretary of defense should require the Joint Chiefs of Staff to consider and recommend a national military doctrine for approval by the secretary of defense and the president. Following this, force doctrine — Army, Navy, and Air Force — should be written on a team principle within the parameters of the national military doctrine.[11]

As has been seen, the Air Staff refused to approve a suggested Air University revision of AFM 1-2 designed to reflect the impact of new weapons and defense reorganization, but a revised version of *United States Air Force Basic Doctrine* was issued under Gen Thomas D. White's authentication on 1 December 1959. This version contained very few changes from its three predecessors, the most notable exception acknowledging developments in missiles and space by replacing the words "air power" with "aerospace power." The new version described aerospace as the operational medium of the Air Force, "the total expanse beyond the earth's surface." To the list of predominant characteristics of aerospace forces — range, mobility, flexibility, speed, and penetration ability — was added "firepower delivery," manifested in accuracy, fast reaction, high rates of fire and launch, and the capability to employ maximum power weapons if necessary. Aerospace forces were to take advantage of every opportunity to exploit these characteristics. Thus it was said:

> Employment of Air Forces in the aerospace must be considered in terms of effects that are possible of achievement on the surface of the earth in both general and limited war, and effects to be achieved in space-oriented operations against hostile space vehicles, or in other operations not having a direct effect on earth areas and populations.[12]

The manual replaced the old words of necessity — gaining a "dominant position in the air" — with a new objective of getting "general supremacy in the aerospace." Its new concluding admonition was:

> The aerospace is a medium in which freedom to operate during war will be of vital military significance. That nation, or group of nations, which maintains predominance in the aerospace — not only in its military forces but also in its sciences and technologies — will have the means to prevail in conflict.[13]

IDEAS, CONCEPTS, DOCTRINE

The 1959 manual outlined a military scenario ranging from general through limited war, cold war, and peacetime explorations of aerospace to advance man's knowledge. Since national survival was paramount, preparation for general war must have precedence, although forces for general war were expected to have limited-war applications. The problem of identifying and preventing "wars of national liberation" soon to be met in Southeast Asia was not foreseen.[14] The 1959 manual was the first basic doctrine publication to touch on space. Writing in 1973 Lt Col Donald L. Cromer pointed out that the basic doctrine manual series failed

> to address where a space doctrine fits in let alone what it should be. . . . Leaving the subject as an implied part of doctrine runs the risk of misinterpretation, as well as requiring each individual or office to create his own doctrinal basis for space planning and employment. The fact that we do not have a codified space doctrine stands as mute testimony of this premise.[15]

Although the Air Force had mentioned keeping its doctrine "dynamic," the editions of AFM 1-2 issued in the 1950s were reminiscent of the state of past or present military art in that technology was driving doctrine rather than doctrine directing technology. Reminisced Eugene Zuckert, who became secretary of the Air Force in 1961:

> Frankly, I do not see quite the same degree of inventiveness in our concepts and doctrine that we have demonstrated in technology and in military adaptation to technological change. . . . We can't afford to let military science, which governs the use of weapons, fall behind the physical sciences that create those weapons. More than that, military science, which includes doctrine, ideally should stay well ahead of technology to give technology meaningful direction.[16]

Especially in 1961, as already noted, Zuckert maintained that some Air Force leaders "were still approaching top-level problems of national security in terms of the concepts, doctrine, and study methods of the early 1950s."[17] Zuckert evidently was enforcing a new rule that Air Force doctrine should be designed to support national policy and strategy, which was different from the view of a pure military aerospace doctrine based upon the absolute capabilities and limitations of aerospace forces in peace and war. In terms of President Kennedy's flexible response strategy, AFM 1-2 placed excessive emphasis upon massive retaliation and mass destruction and did not give adequate emphasis to the application of precisely measured power in limited or general war.

In the recognized Air Staff breakout of responsibilities for doctrine development, the task fell to the deputy chief of staff for plans and operations and was subdivided between the director of plans (HQ USAF/XPD) and the director of operations (HQ USAF/XOP). As it happened, Maj Gen Jerry D. Page, who had been responsible earlier on at Air University for preparing the April 1955 edition of AFM 1-2, was director of plans in 1963 and his office was the office of primary responsibility (OPR) for Air Force Regulation 1-1, *Responsibilities for Doctrine Development*, dated 20 March 1963. For the first time this regulation clarified the responsibilities for developing basic Air Force doctrine, operational doctrine, and unified doctrine. The regulation made Headquarters USAF/XPD responsible for preparing and disseminating basic doctrine and gave official guidance to the meaning of "basic aerospace doctrine" as follows:

> Basic aerospace doctrine sets forth the fundamental principles for employment of the US aerospace forces to support national objectives in peace and war. Directed toward the overall Air Force posture, it provides: (1) The fundamental reference authority for this employment, and thereby serves as the basis for all Air Force manuals dealing with the tactics and techniques in employment of aerospace forces. (2) Information for military instruction in various schools throughout the Air Force and in other military services. (3) Material for public and internal information programs. (4) Positions supporting budgetary and procurement programs, and negotiations with other services.[18]

The regulation provided that operational doctrine was "directed toward specific capabilities" and "developed in relation to specific categories such as tactical and strategic air operations." The responsibility for developing and submitting this doctrine was allocated to SAC, TAC, ADC, MATS, and the other operating commands, and the responsibility for monitoring the doctrine was assigned to Headquarters USAF/XOP. Unified doctrine was to be prepared for joint activities as directed by the Joint Chiefs of Staff. This directorate was responsible for determining the appropriate Air Force organization or command to develop doctrine required by JCS, and Headquarters USAF/XPD was responsible for monitoring the approval process through the Joint Chiefs. In a further allocation of responsibilities, TAC was made responsible for participating with the Army, Navy, and Marine Corps in the development of doctrine, procedures, tactics, techniques, training, publications, and equipment for joint operations that were the responsibilities of one of those services.[19]

Although AFR 1-1 was "official guidance," an ACSS student noted that the guidance was "sufficiently broad to permit vast interpretation in its formulation." "On the basis of this guidance, the basic doctrine could be presented in any number of ways: from a gigantic collection of tomes which happens to detail every foreseeable eventuality of employment, to a single page commander's concept of the 'don't shoot 'til you see the whites of their eyes' caliber."[20]

In 1963–64 Air Force Project Forecast made a comprehensive study of Air Force structure projectable into the 1965–75 time frame, and General Page headed the project's policy panel that sought to identify the goals of national policy that would influence development decisions within the Air Force. The findings of this panel became the grist for a new Air Force basic doctrine manual that would be written under Page's direction by Lt Col Richard C. Bowman, Lt Col George H. Sylvester, and Maj William E. Simons. Page explained to an interested interviewer that he felt strongly that "something new was needed." Although there was a precedent for doctrine to emerge from the scholarly efforts at the Air University professional schools, he considered that "there was a general lack of imagination and insight in the recent efforts from that quarter." As a consequence, Page said his group undertook the job unilaterally, got the blessings of General LeMay on it, and published AFM 1-1, *Aerospace Doctrine, United States Air Force Basic Doctrine*, on 14 August 1964.[21]

Even a cursory glance through the August 1964 edition of AFM 1-1 reveals its radical departure from the AFM 1-2 manuals of the 1950s. A discussion of the requirement to support national objectives with a strategy of flexible response drew emphasis throughout. This discussion posited a spectrum of conflict wherein national leaders would select the best use of strategic and tactical forces. "The guiding principle in all crises is to limit the use of force to that compatible with particular conflict issues." "Defeat of the enemy," the manual said, "is the attainment of our specific political objectives."[22] The August 1964 manual, unlike its predecessors, did not include a discussion of the principles of war. Whereas range, mobility, flexibility, speed, penetration ability, and (in 1959) firepower delivery had been described as predominant characteristics of aerospace forces, the 1964 manual described required aerospace force characteristics as survivability, command and control (control must be centralized at levels high enough to exploit these forces fully), penetration ability, selective target destruction, and recovery and recycling. Range, mobility, responsiveness, and tactical versatility were said to be "military advantages" if the aerospace medium were exploited properly. The manual also addressed employments of aerospace forces in general war (discussing counterforce, countervalue, active and passive defenses, and requirements for mixed manned and unmanned systems), in tactical nuclear operations, in conventional air operations, and in counterinsurgency. The three less intense forms of warfare required traditional missions of air superiority, interdiction, close air support, airlift, and reconnaissance. The advanced state of alert of the Strategic Air Command during the Cuban missile crisis of 1962 was cited as an illustration of the manner in which manned systems could provide cold war demonstrations in periods of international crises. This doctrinal statement also urged the Air Force to pursue vertical takeoff and landing capabilities when nuclear weapons were used; this injunction did not appear in subsequent versions of AFM 1-1.[23]

In explanation of the objective for the AFM 1-1 1964 basic doctrine manual, the Air Force inspector general explained:

> Objective of the project is to assure a cohesive and supportable delineation of aerospace power and principles for its employment by today's unilateral and unified forces.... A complete understanding of Air Force unilateral doctrine is required of all Air Force personnel responsible for developing doctrinal proposals with other services or unified commands. Since the views of other services are considered in the development of unified/joint doctrine, an understanding of basic issues which involve the Air Force is required.[24]

After the publication of AFM 1-1, the inspector general's brief called attention to the evolutionary change in Air Force concepts and doctrine: "Military concepts and doctrines undergo a constant process of evolutionary change to meet new times, new ideas, new kinds of weapons." It pointed to a need for a broadly capable aerospace force:

> In this thermonuclear age, the aerospace force must possess a broad range of combat and peacekeeping capabilities. It must be programmed and operated in close cooperation with the other services, each of which is a specialized increment of overall US military power.... In discussing the four main kinds of aerospace operations—general war, tactical nuclear, conventional, and counterinsurgency—emphasis is placed on our increased options for military response in support of national objectives.... For all confrontations and conflicts, the US aerospace force must have the superior, usable capabilities needed to convince an enemy that any escalating step on his part would place him at an increasingly critical disadvantage.[25]

The *Air Force Policy Letter for Commanders* called the new manual "timely reading." "The chapters on conventional air operations and counterinsurgency and the concluding chapter," the *Policy Letter* stated, "are worth reviewing."[26]

The Air Force Directorate of Doctrine, Concepts, and Objectives

In the same time span that the Air Force was enunciating AFM 1-1, the US Army was organizing its Training and Doctrine Command (TRADOC), effective on 1 July 1973, and this new combination of functional combat development centers collocated with Army educational institutions, plus a combat developments experimentation command, was going to be a fertile source of new Army doctrinal undertakings.[27] The shift to the strategy of flexible response was significantly increasing the role and size of general-purpose forces and generating new interservice roles and missions issues. Many of the initiatives of the other services appeared to infringe directly on Air Force roles and missions. Many observers concluded that the Air Force had been caught in a doctrinal and conceptual lag. It was against this background on 1 July 1966 in DCS/Plans and Operations that the deputy director of plans for advance planning was elevated in status and became the Directorate of Doctrine, Concepts, and Objectives (HQ USAF/XOD). The Directorate of Doctrine, Concepts, and Objectives was coequal with the Directorate of Plans and Directorate of Operations under deputy chief of staff for plans and operations. Headquarters USAF/XOD was given the mission: "To do hard thinking about the Air Force of the future... because of a continuing need for original, creative thought to help reason and guide the way to the future." This directorate included an aerospace doctrine division, concepts and objectives division, and an interservice liaison group.[28]

The initial director of doctrine, concepts and objectives was Brig Gen Richard A. Yudkin, who was promoted to major general on 1 July 1967. As remembered by Lt Gen George G. Loving, Jr., who, as a colonel in the Directorate of Doctrine, Concepts, and Objectives, was successively a staff officer, chief of the Doctrine Development Branch, and chief of the Aerospace Doctrine Division—the

IDEAS, CONCEPTS, DOCTRINE

directorate's work, like that of the Air Staff in general, was for a large part "always putting out fires." Loving said:

> Papers would come to be coordinated, and we would look at them from a doctrine viewpoint.... Fundamentally, we were defenders of the faith.... That was one aspect of the job, to try to defend our roles and missions in a rational way that would serve the Air Force well and serve the country well.[29]

Loving remembered that everyone in this directorate worked for General Yudkin on whatever needed doing. One of the first XOD studies was an analysis begun on 21 June 1966 to determine what areas of close air support were not being fulfilled by the Air Force to the satisfaction of the Army. Headquarters USAF/XOD completed the analysis on 14 August and briefed the Air Council on 25 August. As already noted, General McConnell signed off on the principal recommendation on 8 September 1966, namely that the Air Force take immediate and positive action to obtain a relatively inexpensive, rugged, highly specialized close-air-support aircraft (the A-X). Another major study of 1966 was the tactical rescue-intelligence system enhancement (TAC/RISE). The Credible Comet study was initiated in 1967 to develop a concept of operations and recommendations for tactical air electronic work. Project New Focus was organized on a temporary basis in mid-1965 and received a permanent charter in June 1967 to explore, refine, and reduce points of differences between the Army and the Air Force in close air support, tactical airlift, tactical reconnaissance, and tactical air control.[30]

In the view of General Loving, the Air Force's decision to build the A-X (A-10) close-air-support fighter and to be "more forthcoming" on other tactical air issues with the Army broke the Army's incursions into Air Force roles and missions. By 1969 the Air Force and the Army were "cooperating actively," much of the logjam on Army-Air Force doctrinal manuals having been broken in a flood of mutually agreeable publications.[31] Air Force operational doctrinal manuals were principally prepared and negotiated in the Air Force operating commands, and in view of the multiplicity of tasks it performed the Tactical Air Command prepared most of the AFM 2- manuals which, after approval by the Directorate of Doctrine, Concepts, and Objectives, were published by the Air Force. The Joint Chiefs of Staff also from time to time directed the services to develop joint doctrine (called "unified doctrine" in AFM 1-1, 14 August 1964) for interservice approval and final action by the Joint Chiefs of Staff. Thus, in 1965 the Joint Chiefs of Staff approved a concept for air-space control in a combat area and directed the Air Force to develop joint doctrine in coordination with the other services. In February 1967 the Joint Chiefs of Staff requested the Air Force to develop joint doctrine for close air support of ground forces, and the Air Force instructed TAC to develop a draft of this. After countless drafts and long negotiations, all service chiefs approved the agreement on "Doctrine and Procedures for Control of Air Space in the Combat Zone" by 17 December 1975, 10 years after the project was laid on. The Air Force illogically published *Doctrine and Procedures for Airspace Control in the Combat Zone* as AFM 1-3, on 1 December 1975, thus putting the manual in the "basic"

AFM 1- category along with AFM 1-1.³² By 1969 the proposed joint doctrine for close air support had been revised a fifth time; in 1972 deliberations on the joint CAS doctrine were still postponed. As has been seen, SACEUR requested that the NATO Military Agency for Standardization establish a working party to develop operational air doctrine for NATO. In some measure the preparation of NATO doctrine obviated some of the need for the stalled joint CAS manual. NATO doctrine was developed under the Military Agency for Standardization and was embodied in allied tactical publications (ATPs). The key Allied Tactical Publication (ATP) 33, *NATO Tactical Air Doctrine*, was ratified by the NATO nations and promulgated on 10 February 1975. Some 10 of NATO's subsequently published ATPs were of interest to the Air Force and were drafted in the beginning by working parties including Air Force representation. In the Pacific, an Air Standardization Coordinating Committee (ASCC) composed of members from the United States, Australia, New Zealand, Canada, and the United Kingdom, published combined doctrine as air standards (ASs). The Air Force was particularly concerned with AS 45-3, *Tactical Air Operations*, and AS 45-13, *Air Space Control in the Combat Zone*.³³

When high-priority jobs came into the Directorate of Doctrine, Concepts, and Objectives, people in the Aerospace Doctrine Division inevitably were pulled off doctrinal manuals, and revisions of AFM 1-1 moved forward very slowly. One of the earliest reviews of the August 1964 AFM 1-1 was conducted by an anonymous US Army officer, who remarked: "One of the problems is that doctrinal statements are habitually written to be specific, even dogmatic. The military writer's desire to assert the 'truth' often leads him to resolve imponderables with fortification."³⁴ To this reviewer the Air Force manual implied that there would be an easy escalation from conventional to nuclear weapons since it was written that "factors of geography and relative local force levels may require US forces to use nuclear weapons in order to assure the timely defeat of aggression and to use technology rather than human lives to end the conflict on favorable terms."³⁵ The reviewer considered that the experience of 20 years seemed to indicate that military professionals should know that any decision to go to nuclear weapons would be "a very grave one."³⁶ At the Air Command and Staff College, Lt Col Walter S. Van Cleve found the 1964 AFM 1-1 very hard to teach, and upon assignment as a staff officer in the Aerospace Doctrine Division Van Cleve provided a revised draft of the manual emphasizing easier readability. He also wrote a popularly published chapter on "Aerospace Doctrine in Modern Conflict" before his transfer and death in combat in Southeast Asia.³⁷

In the first half of 1967 a draft of AFM 1-1 representing experiences in Southeast Asia as well as old verities was circulated for comment to 21 selected senior officers, 35 air staff agencies, and key Rand personnel. A new draft was prepared in August 1967 incorporating the comments. Again in the spring of 1968 the draft was rewritten to improve format and language and "to improve the content." The lessons of the Middle East War of 1967, the Soviet invasion of Czechoslovakia in 1968, and progressive experience were inserted into the final preprint version of

AFM 1-1, circulated early in 1971. The revised manual was published on 28 September 1971 under the imprimatur of Gen John C. Meyer, Air Force vice chief of staff. This manual defined aerospace doctrine as "an authoritative statement of principles for the employment of United States Air Force resources."[38] The manual divided doctrine into basic doctrine (AFM 1-1), operational doctrine (AFM 2- and 3- series), functional doctrine, and joint (formerly unified) doctrine. Until this time no basic doctrine manual had envisioned "functional" doctrine that was designed to provide "guidance for the specialized activities of the Air Force such as research and development, personnel, training, professional education, communications-electronics, operations security, logistics, civil engineering, finance and budgeting, medical, intelligence, legal, chaplain, and administration."[39] Functional doctrine was published in subject series of manuals addressing specialized activities (for example, the 400- series for logistics).[40]

The September 1971 edition of AFM 1-1 extensively revised all chapters from previous editions, particularly those dealing with nuclear operations and special operations, this being the first version to devote an entire chapter to special operations and to elaborate on three elements: foreign internal defense, psychological operations, and unconventional warfare. Lessons from Vietnam and the Middle East War surfaced in an admonition:

> Though it is the keystone of the United States' deterrent posture, strategic sufficiency may not be a credible deterrent against hostile acts by small powers, whether such acts are initiated by those powers alone or while serving as proxies for larger powers. Deterrence of these threats comes from the maintenance of sufficient general purpose forces capable of rapid deployment and sustained operations combined with the national resolve to deploy and employ these forces. Thus, strategic and general purpose forces are complementary in providing an overall credible deterrent posture.[41]

The earlier categories of general and limited war were replaced by chapters on conventional, low-intensity nuclear, high-intensity nuclear, and special air force operations. This version iterated basic air power tasks as counterair, close air support, interdiction, reconnaissance, airlift, and strategic attack. For the first time, subelement activities were specified such as search and rescue, electronic warfare, air refueling, airborne command and control, and psychological operations, and supporting functions such as logistics, communications, intelligence, weather service, and installation security. For the first time, there was a specific section on "The Role of the Air Force in Space," which was to ensure that no other nations gain a military advantage through exploration of space. It asserted that aerospace systems operations into space were "a natural and evolutionary extension of US Air Force mission responsibilities and operational capabilities." The manual referred to the inherent characteristics of aerospace forces as being range, mobility, speed, versatility, and flexibility. There was no enumeration of the principles of war or principles of employment of air power, except that regardless of the level of conflict central allocation and local direction remained fundamental.[42]

In an analysis of the 1971 edition of AFM 1-1 an Air Command and Staff College study group reporting in May 1972 found the manual to be more attentive to recognition of Air Force roles and missions and descriptive of capabilities required to perform tasks—but not principles of employment—than previous basic doctrinal manuals had been.[43] This change in emphasis may have represented a recognition that the Department of the Air Force was no longer responsible for warfighting but rather for the preparation of Air Force forces for combat employments by unified or specified commanders. In one of his last briefings on doctrinal divergencies among the services, General Yudkin concluded his remarks with an admonition:

> It is evident from the course of events in recent years that historical precedents, parochial logic and official function papers will not be determinant in decisions on which service has what missions, procures what hardware, or achieves what force level. The race will normally go to the service that proposes the most in terms of imaginative concepts, substantial requirements, and forward looking solutions. This applies particularly in obtaining approval for initial or prototype hardware. Once that is achieved, the tangible nature of hardware can provide the basis for demonstration, persuasion and further approval toward a program. But the departure point for success—or if you prefer survival—is flexibility in our thinking, willingness to innovate and to change as we demonstrate the adaptability of our weapons systems and their unique responsiveness to changing news of national need. Starting from this departure point, we require highly developed capabilities to communicate and to focus our efforts in single-minded pursuit of identified objectives.[44]

In 1971 Col David M. Murane had been the principal Air Force representative in the NATO air doctrine working effort, and in 1972 he became chief of the Aerospace Doctrine Division in time to see the 1971 edition of AFM 1-1 go into effect. He was somewhat rueful that the manual had gone through as many as 27 drafts in the seven years required for its publication, and he provided a not entirely jocular list of the factors that influenced the writing and coordination process: command background of those who coordinate AFM 1-1, current ongoing air operations, different perspectives or semantics, orientation of original drafter, whims of those who coordinate existing and past AFM 1-1s, current interservice issues, perceived need to comment whether needed or not, the way action officers think their bosses think, and how important the players feel the manual is. Murane also suggested that one of the major benefits of the preparation of the basic doctrine manual was the coordination process which forced at least a portion of the senior Air Force officers to contemplate basic air doctrine.[45] During the drafting of the 1972 edition of the basic doctrine manual, Dr Alfred Goldberg of the Rand Corporation had lent assistance. He too explained: "The process [of coordinating and approving AFM 1-1] has come to dominate the product."[46]

New Program Directions for Air Concepts and Doctrine

Beginning in 1970 there were a number of perhaps unrelated changes in players and responsibility in the field of air concepts and doctrine. Following the retirement of General Yudkin, Maj Gen Leslie W. Bray, Jr., became director of doctrine, concepts, and objectives (HQ USAF/XOD) in February 1970. General Bray was interested in forward-looking air concepts, speaking to this subject on a number of occasions. In August 1970 the Concepts and Objectives Division (HQ USAF/XODC) was reorganized into a concepts development branch (XODCC) for long-range conceptual planning and an objectives assessment branch (XODCO). In 1971 it was apparent that XOD was a prestigious organization: Col Carl H. Peterson, who took over as chief, Aerospace Doctrine Division remarked: "We were virtually deluged with high-quality nominees for assignment to the Directorate."[47] In response to direction by the Air Force Advisory Group, Project Rand reoriented its efforts toward strategy and doctrine in 1971, devoting a much larger share of its resources in support of the deputy chief of staff for plans and operations (DCS/P&O).[48] After a year's assignment as a research associate with the Council on Foreign Relations, General Loving was assigned as commandant of Air Command and Staff College at the Air University in June 1970. He would remain there until reassignment in January 1973. As seen earlier in connection with the assignment of responsibilities for basic doctrine to Washington, Air University had organized a concepts division in the new Aerospace Studies Institute in 1959, but with the passing of time the ASI Concepts Division declined in prestige. In 1971 Lt Gen Alvan C. Gillem II, the AU commander, judged that the Concepts Division might as well be terminated if he could not get good officers to staff it for advanced thinking. Accordingly, on 30 June 1971 the Aerospace Studies Institute was inactivated with a not inconsiderable saving in manning authorizations.[49]

At the Air University, General Loving startled General Gillem with a question: "When are we going to put the war back in the Air War College?" Loving observed that the study of war had been disappearing from the curricula of Air University schools over the years since he had been a student there. In the Air Command and Staff College, Loving said: "I sought to introduce war subjects en masse. I offered seminars and electives . . . , hopefully, to educate people more broadly in the application of airpower and to stimulate discussion."[50] The Aerospace Doctrine Division asked ACSC to study basic doctrine as one of its priority projects, and ACSC Student Guidance for Research Studies, class of 1972, provided basic guidance for an ACSC basic study group of four students and two ex officio faculty advisers from the school's military strategy and doctrine branch. The initial research project was divided into three main parts: (1) to rewrite AFM 1-1, (2) to record background data and discussion, and (3) to write a draft magazine article for publication. The following year, 1973, an ACSC basic doctrine study group was similarly constituted but built on the previous year's work and turned out two products: (1) a rationale for the content and organization of AFM 1-1 and (2) specific recommended changes for certain sections of the manual that had been published in September 1971. Lt Cols Donald W. Smith and Haywood S. Hansell III were the ex officio faculty advisers on both years' work.[51]

The initial 1971–72 doctrine study group of Majs William R. Chambers, Don A. Clark, Geoffrey C. Davis, Jr., and Gerald W. Strut took as its starting point an investigation of the meaning and usage of basic air doctrine. It noted a statement made by Col Jerry D. Page in 1955 that basic doctrine was "the collection of essential fundamental truths of airpower." It also noted General White's dictum of 1955 that "the Air Force is a national instrument and evolves no doctrine, makes no plans and makes no preparations other than those clearly and unmistakably called for or anticipated by the national policy." The study group did not consider these two approaches to be mutually exclusive. It stated:

> Basic doctrine represents Air Force fundamental precepts which guide the employment of airpower within the framework of national policy.... Guidance from the President, Congress, and Secretary of Defense, combined with the Department of Defense budget process, has a major influence on Air Force doctrine. Therefore political constraints become significant in military strategy and as a result basic doctrine becomes responsive to external pressure. Basic doctrine achieves its value as a single, comprehensive listing of fundamental philosophical principles concerning employment of airpower.[52]

The ACSC 1971–72 study group undertook to prepare a new version of AFM 1-1 and to record its rationale for its thinking. The group's draft manual included three chapters: first, the environment in which air power would operate; second, the characteristics, capabilities, and employment principles of air power; and third, the employment of aerospace forces in modern conflict. Chapter 1 actually concerned the dynamics of modern conflict. It determined that deterrence was "the basic premise on which US Air Force doctrine is constructed." It adopted the continuum of conflict used by Secretary of Defense Laird—strategic nuclear war, theater nuclear warfare, theater conventional warfare, and subtheater or localized warfare—and added peaceful competition. This spectrum of conflict provided an added dimension to a continuum of warfare and found that the potential for limited objectives was implicit in multilevel conflict. The study group pointed out that chapter 4, "Aerospace Forces in High-Intensity Nuclear Operations," of the September 1971 AFM 1-1 was implicit in identifying winners and losers in conventional warfare, something that was outdated by the arrival of a US-Soviet mutual destructive capability. "The bargaining process," wrote Major Strut, "presents an alternative to nuclear confrontation and must be adopted as a cornerstone of our strategic strategy."[53]

In chapter 3 of the recommended AFM 1-1, Major Davis used a concept that aerospace forces had inherent characteristics that gave those forces unique capabilities which if properly employed could attain desired effects. Actually it was hard to separate "characteristics" from "capabilities." Nevertheless, the group agreed that speed, range, tactical versatility, and observation were characteristics of aerospace forces not possessed in the same degree by surface forces.

IDEAS, CONCEPTS, DOCTRINE

Capabilities of aerospace forces derived from these characteristics included flexibility, responsiveness, survivability, and surveillance. The group noted that the principles of war had not been included in Air Force basic doctrine since 1959. The principles had been violated considerably, particularly in Vietnam. The group urged that the principles of objective, offensive, concentration, surprise, security, and unity of effort were "Air Force basic beliefs and should be included in subsequent manuals. . . . Being guides for employment, these principles must be constantly interpreted in light of the changing capabilities of aerospace forces and the unique experiences of airmen." As a concomitant to the principles of war it was obvious that: "Aerospace forces are an entity, aerospace operations require centralized control and decentralized execution, and aerospace forces should be used in the offensive at the start of hostilities." Chapter 3 also demonstrated that aerospace forces produced desired military, political, and psychological effects, the interrelation of which was not always understood. Thus:

> A military victory can be a psychological defeat. The 1968 Tet offensive was a military victory by the United States but a political and psychological victory for the Viet Cong. The psychological effects of the Japanese bombing of Pearl Harbor united the American people against a common enemy. The psychological effects of all operations must be considered to ensure the proper employment of aerospace forces.[54]

Chapter 3 of ACSC draft AFM 1-1 was the principal responsibility of Major Chambers and essentially was an encapsulated combination of four chapters of aerospace oeprations in the 1971 basic doctrine manual. The draft chapter was organized to present (1) the dynamics of modern conflict, (2) the basic employment tasks, (3) the total force concept, (4) the mixed force concept, and (5) the five categories of conflict where air power might play a significant role. Chapter 3 also reflected a view that AFM 1-1s since 1959 had deviated from enunciation of basic doctrine by omitting principles of employment and emphasizing descriptions of operational tasks. To come to grips with the essence of air employment principles, Major Chambers rationalized:

> The Navy regards freedom of the seas as necessary in modern conflict. The Army considers mobility, firepower, and staying power to be prime factors. I believe that air superiority will be the decisive element in the majority of future conflicts. . . . The requirement for air superiority is most apparent when the enemy has the ability to conduct significant operations in the aerospace medium. If it is not possible to establish air superiority, we must, at least, have the capability to neutralize the enemy's effective use of aerospace. Otherwise, it may not be possible to conduct military operations of any type.[55]

In consideration of the early work of the Air University schools, the Aerospace Doctrine Division, now headed by Colonel Murane, in the last half of 1972, concluded that revisions of AFM 1-1 were needed to restate more clearly basic air doctrine in relation to changing national strategies and to take into account the impact of such things as arms control initiatives, new basic concepts, and technology. In 1971–72 the Directorate of Doctrine, Concepts, and Objectives was tasked to provide an Air Force definition of the Triad concept and an Air Force view of Secretary Laird's total force concept. The Southeast Asian War, the October 1973 War, and a growing focus on European defense spawned a proliferation of "deep strike," "deep interdiction," "air support of ground forces," and "general support of the battlefield" issues.[56] In an appearance at the Air Command and Staff College's block of instruction on air doctrine, Colonel Murane furnished a revision of AFM 1-1, which with a few exceptions followed the organization and language of the 1971–72 ACSC study group's draft manual. Added was a description of the strategic Triad which was the mixed offensive force of manned bombers, land-based missiles, and submarine-launched missiles. Also added was a description of the total force and the statement that: "US active duty, U.S. Reserve, and allied military forces and resources constitute an entity possessing capabilities that can be applied in unique and innovative ways to support deterrence and provide mutual security."[57]

In Washington in June 1974 a draft version of a new AFM 1-1 was at hand, and in September it was briefed to the Air Force Council where the vice chief of staff directed each member to read and comment on it. He also directed that a copy of the proposed revision be sent to Dr William W. Kaufmann, special assistant to the secretary of defense. The chief of staff approved the draft and changes on 4 November, and on 15 January 1975, AFM 1-1, *Aerospace Doctrine: United States Air Force Basic Doctrine*, was printed. In the foreword Gen David C. Jones stated:

> USAF Basic Doctrine is derived from knowledge gained through experience, study, analysis and test. It evolves from changing military environments, concepts, and technology; and through continuing analysis of military operations, national objectives and policy. This evolution must be a continuing process so that basic doctrine can remain a useful guide for the conduct of aerospace operations.[58]

The manual defined the kinds of doctrine as basic, operational, functional, joint, and combined. Doctrine for joint operations was established by the Joint Chiefs of Staff. Doctrine for combined operations was included for the first time in AFM 1-1 and constituted and established "the principles, organization, and procedures agreed upon between allied forces or agencies in combined operations." The philosophy of "sufficiency" was emphasized and the strategic Triad was identified as the highest national defense priority. There was new thought on the effectiveness of aerospace forces when evaluated in terms other than ability to destroy targets, as for example in deterrence, persuasion, and coercion. In this measure logistic support was directly influential on operational capability and so merited attention. Successful accomplishment of the Air Force mission was also predicated on the timely availability of trained and motivated people. In 1974 a Directorate of Doctrine, Concepts, and Objectives briefing on space for the Air Force Council left unresolved whether the Air Force should seek formal recognition of its space mission or whether the Air Force should diffuse space activities into operational commands. The 1975 AFM 1-1 noted that Air Force principles relating to space operations were consistent with the peaceful use of space. "There is, however, a need to insure that no other nation gains a strategic military advantage through the exploration of the space environment."[59]

In an exegesis of Air Force doctrinal development and the AFM 1-1 of 1975, Lt Gen John W. Pauly, deputy chief of staff for plans and operations, wrote:

> We assert that Air Force basic doctrine is alive and well. History shows that our doctrine has been responsive to changing times and philosophies while maintaining a consistent thread of fundamental principles. We can conclude that our doctrinal process is a discipline—a discipline for dealing with new concepts, technology, and roles and missions relationships with other services or allies. It serves to sharpen the debate by providing a framework of time-proven principles against which we can illuminate and test contending ideas now and in the future. However, in the final analysis, the most important function of doctrine is that it provides the fundamental guidance for the employment of aerospace forces in combat. In the experience of three major wars—World War II, Korea, Southeast Asia—we have seen a consistent thread of basic doctrine encompassed in the most fundamental of principles: that air power is an entity and is best employed under the centralized control of a single authority who is at a level that can best orchestrate the total air effort.[60]

After 1970, with Maj Gen Leslie W. Bray in charge, the Directorate of Doctrine, Concepts, and Objectives gave more attention to the development of Air Force concepts than to the recording of doctrine. In 1971 one way to develop ideas was conceived to be "think pieces" called concept development papers. One of these was on the development of long-range cruise missiles for the 1980s. In 1972 Col Kenneth L. Moll, chief of the Coordinated Action Plans Division, conceived of the preparation of an Air Force Future Concepts Project Workbook that would narrate where the Air Force should go and how to get there. This project proved to be "much tougher than originally conceived,"[61] but it provided basic thinking behind a "tactical counterforce" or second-echelon attack strategy. At General Bray's retirement on 30 September 1973 he was replaced as director of Doctrine, Concepts, and Objectives by Maj Gen William Y. Smith, who had prepared his Air Command and Staff School thesis in 1958–59 on the relationship of intercontinental missiles to conceptual air power. On 4 October General Smith told his division chiefs that he wanted to get approval for an ad hoc Air Staff study like Project Forecast to determine future long-term needs and priorities. As it happened the Air Staff was opposed to a large study, but in the latter part of 1974 an ad hoc Air Staff study group headed by Brig Gen John E. Ralph, who had replaced General Smith on 1 July 1974, laid on New Horizons II, 1985–2000. In the early months of 1975 seven study panels tackled such subjects as laser technology, future in space, and night/adverse weather technology. The results of New Horizons II were presented to the Air Force Council on 3 March and to the under secretary of the Air Force on 21 March. As has been noted, in September 1974 General Jones tasked an Air Staff ad hoc group to develop a reorganization plan for Air Force forces in the Pacific. These studies broadened into a concept propounded in the Directorate of Doctrine, Concepts, and Objectives and described as "Tight Belt East" and "Tight Belt West," in which the Tactical Air

Command would have been assigned all worldwide tactical air resources less operational control that would have been retained by CINCUSAFE and CINCPACAF. In 1974, it seemed that "Tight Belt West" would have disestablished PACAF and transferred management functions to TAC, but the proposition quietly fell through in 1975.[62]

On 24 November 1973 Gen George S. Brown as Air Force chief of staff signed a charter for an advanced concepts advisory group—which would be better known as the Air Force's six-man group—to explore new concepts, strategies, and programs for development and employment of US air forces in support of national policies. General Brown wanted in-house, free-flowing ideas, uninhibited by previous or current positions or parochialisms. In the months that he continued as chief of staff, General Brown frequently met with the group and exchanged ideas without attempting in the least to channel thinking. Members of the group, formally put on orders on 22 February 1974, were Cols John L. Piotrowski, Stuart W. Brown, Robert W. Kennedy, William H. L. Mullins, Robert H. Reed, and Leonard J. Siegert. After a review of several possible locations, the six-man group elected to settle in at the Air University to escape the "activity trap" of the Washington area. The group had free access to commands, activities, and staffs throughout the Air Force and after the first three months of visits throughout the Air Force it reported: "We are so preoccupied with day to day [concerns] that we have little focus on the future. Our strategic thought has stagnated. We may be letting contemporary doctrine, policies, international agreements and negotiations inhibit our vision of the future."[63] After visiting the commands, the group developed a master list of potential research subjects, many of which proved either too broad for the group or beyond the expertise of group members. During June–November 1974 individual members of the six-man group pursued subjects of their interest; in November 1974 a meeting between General Jones, now Air Force chief of staff, and Lt Gen Felix M. Rogers, Air University (AU) commander, put the group—reorganized into a four-man panel (4-M Panel A)—under General Rogers's operational control. The six-man group already had begun to use student researchers from the Air War College, and the employment of AU students on desired subjects, either individually or in panels with 4-M participants, was the practice. Under the new 4-M charter, 10 very significant concept feasibility studies were completed for the chief of staff. These studies focused on subjects such as Air Defense Command fighter force consolidation, alternatives to Air Defense Command functions and resources, disestablishment of the Air Force Headquarters Command, and realignment of the functions of the Air Force Directorate of Doctrine, Concepts, and Objectives. The original concept of the six-man group specified no particular length for its operation, and by January 1975 the Air Force decided to deactivate the group effective 1 June 1975. The most influential factor in this decision was the need to use a structured environment and to eliminate the free-thinking, unstructured aspect of the original idea.[64]

At its beginning the Directorate of Doctrine, Concepts, and Objectives (HQ USAF/XOD) had been established against a background of belief that the initiatives of the other services were infringing directly upon the Air Force's assigned roles and missions and that the Air Force was caught in a doctrinal and conceptual lag. One of XOD's principal functions was to be the formulation of long-range concepts, objectives, and strategy, but most of its work dealt with current and near-term issues relating to doctrine, roles, and missions. The doctrine development function of XOD, moreover, turned out to be rather narrow in scope, confined principally to Air Force basic doctrine and developing inputs to new joint or combined doctrine initiatives. In 1974 the Directorate of Doctrine was reported to be so busy putting out fires that there was little time to think at leisure: "Sometimes we feel we are so busy stamping ants," commented one officer in the division, "we let the elephants come thundering over us."[65] By 1974 the "review and comment" work of XOD was largely supportive of the Joint Chiefs of Staff process administered by the Directorate of Plans, and roles and missions issues were being handled routinely in the JCS process as a general rule. The importance of a Headquarters USAF/XOD "interface dialogue" with its component on the Army staff had been reduced when the Army decentralized its doctrinal and conceptual functions to the new Training and Doctrine Command (TRADOC), and the TAC-TRADOC connection became important in addressing and proposing resolutions to outstanding doctrinal and roles and missions issues. Perhaps more significantly, the centralization of decisionmaking in the Department of Defense and its attendant policy, planning, and programming process had tended to shift emphasis away from roles and missions arguments to broader-based decision factors such as costs, effectiveness, vulnerability, survivability, total force, force interdependence, mutual reinforcement, and strategic arms limitations talks. The four-man panel considered this background and proposed in its concept feasibility study on realigning the doctrine, concepts, and objectives functions and responsibilities, completed in January 1975, that the Directorate of Doctrine, Concepts, and Objectives be disestablished; that the directorate's day-to-day doctrinal, conceptual, and roles and missions be transferred to the Directorate of Plans (HQ USAF/XOX); and that a small doctrinal and conceptual studies center be established at Air University. In the shuffle it was proposed that the personnel of the Aerospace Doctrine Division be transferred intact to the Directorate of Plans.[66] The incumbent chief of the Aerospace Doctrine Division, Col Ray L. Thompson, was given the task of rebutting the four-man panel study, but the task of defending the status quo failed—though not to the extent recommended by the panel study. Aiming to get added conceptual thinking on the future of the Air Force, General Ralph put reorganization planning in motion before he was succeeded on 3 November 1976 by Maj Gen John S. Pustay. Two days later the Directorate of Doctrine, Concepts, and Objectives became the Directorate of Concepts (HQ USAF/XOC) under the Directorate of Plans (HQ USAF/XOX), deputy chief of staff, plans and operations. In this reorganization the doctrine development branch (HQ USAF/SOCDD) was placed under the Concept Implementation Division (HQ USAF/XOCD) of the Directorate of Concepts (HQ USAF/XOC).[67]

Another Air Staff reorganization effective on 30 June 1978 established the deputy chief of staff for operations, plans, and readiness, but left the doctrine junction under the Directorate of Plans, assistant deputy directorate for strategy, doctrine, and long-range planning. In this organization the Directorate of Plans remained the single point of contact for the development of all air doctrine, to include the Air Force's contribution to joint and combined doctrine. Headquarters USAF/XOX developed, coordinated, and published basic doctrine in the AFM 1-series. It maintained a doctrine coordinator to manage the development of operational doctrine by appropriate agencies within the Air Staff, the major commands, or the separate operating agencies. It also maintained a doctrine coordinator to manage the preparation, in conjunction with appropriate coordinating agencies, of joint and combined doctrine.[68] In continuing changes, the Doctrine and Concepts Division (XOXLD) was established on 8 January 1979, first under the Deputy Directorate for Long-Range Planning (XOXL) and then, effective on 15 October 1980, as the Doctrine and Concepts Division (XOXID) under the Deputy Directorate of Doctrine, Strategy, and Plans Integration. This latter organization functioned as the office of primary responsibility for Air Force positions on the formulation of basic, joint, and combined operational doctrine, US military strategy and national security policy, basic long-range objectives, war and mobilization planning, and policies and procedures for Air Force-wide mission area analysis.[69]

In January 1975 Col Ray L. Thompson, chief of the Aerospace Doctrine Division, conceived of an added undertaking to provide short, thought-provoking papers that would introduce and clarify long-term issues and stimulate discussion. This effort was known as the "Conceptual Issue Series," and it produced some publishable papers, one being Maj Dennis W. Stiles's "Air Power: A New Look from an Old Rooftop."[70] This beginning was expanded into a more formal "Concept Issue Papers" series and occasionally put out at security classifications no higher than secret to enable as wide a readership as possible. The Doctrine and Concepts Division prefaced this CIP series with the statement:

> Concepts are general ideas—dynamic in nature, open ended, and ever evolving. They are useful in understanding issues of today and tomorrow. They are the basic building blocks of doctrine, operational principles, and the planning process. They provide the glue to bind doctrine, technology, hardware, force structure, and force employment. Concepts found in the CIPs may be new or they may review and focus on old proven ideas of airpower employment. Ultimately, they will be used as a basis for changes in Air Force doctrine.[71]

On 25 August 1978, Lt Col Thomas A. Cardwell III of the Doctrine Section (HQ USAF/XOXFX), Assistant Deputy Directorate for Strategy, Doctrine, and Long Range Planning, issued the first of what would prove to be a substantial doctrine information publication (DIP) series. The DIP-1 was titled "So You Want to Know About JCS Pub 2." DIP-2, "How USAF Doctrine is Developed," soon followed on 5 October 1978. As will be seen shortly, DIP-2 was influential in defining the parameters of the new AFM 1-1 that would be published on 14 February 1979. The DIPs were printed and widely distributed; some were exhaustive documentation on the rationale of Air Force doctrine. DIP-10, "Background Information on Air Force Perspective for Coherent Plans (Command and Control of TACAIR)," dated 24 April 1981, was widely circulated to ensure that Air Force officers assigned to joint and combined staffs worldwide understood all warfighting and command provisions in JCS Pub 2, *Unified Action Armed Forces* (UNAAF). Current Air Force positions on unified and joint command were again broken out in DIP-12, "Command Relationships," published in June 1984.[72]

In the Aerospace Doctrine Division of the Directorate of Doctrine, Concepts, and Objectives, weekly discussions were held in July and August 1975 to determine why the Air Force needed an AFM 1-1 basic doctrine manual and whether the current 15 January 1975 version of AFM 1-1 satisfied Air Force needs. Whereas the 1975 edition had been designedly restricted to principles for employment of US air forces, it was concluded in the latter part of the same year that the manual was "too conceptual for the broad Air Force audience it should reach." It overlooked other fundamental Air Force responsibilities for organizing, equipping, and training Air Force forces. On 15 August 1975 an outline for a new expanded AFM 1-1 went to General Ralph, who approved it but wanted more coverage of the expanding Air Force role in space. Research on the new version was completed in February 1976, and a new draft was completed in May 1976. In September 1976 the draft was sent out to some 60 general officers. The draft sought to provide a document that was interesting, relevant, and useful to all Air Force organizational levels. Emphasis was given to simplified languages. A new approach was also followed, and graphics, illustrations, and quotes were used to break up the format.[73]

The ongoing version of AFM 1-1 during 1977 provoked questions about the Air Force's doctrine structure: the AFM 1- series for basic doctrine, AFM 2- for operational doctrine, and AFM 3- for mission employment tactics. If it were true that operational doctrine and mission employment tactics derived from basic doctrine, then it would have been expected that the subordinate manuals should change as basic doctrine changed. But after 1953 basic doctrine manuals had been revised on an average of every three and one half years whereas AFM 2- and AFM 3- manuals were seldom changed. "The absence of change in subordinate manuals," pointed out Lt Col Donald L. Hutchinson, special assistant to the ACSC commandant for doctrinal and conceptual matters, "suggests that there is no real thread running through our doctrinal manuals."[74] When officers attending the Air Command and Staff College were asked to review the in-work 20 May 1977 draft of AFM 1-1, they were unsure whether the changes incorporated in the draft were fundamental changes in Air Force beliefs or just a different author's approach. Many students observed that AFM 1-1 was trying to be all things to all readers.[75] Such reactions to the work of Washington doctrinal developers convinced them that the general problem with Air Force doctrine was that "there are simply no 'handles' on doctrine."[76] Early in 1977 the Directorate of Plans ordered an initiative to study the Air Force doctrine program with a view to establishing the appropriate identity of doctrine, locating problem areas, and recommending changes. The research phase involved Air University students and support from the US Air Force Academy, the work of Capt Robert C. Ehrhart of the USAFA History Department being notable. On 4 July 1977 Headquarters USAF/XOCDD published for review a study titled "Concept for Reasoned Change in Air Force Doctrine."[77]

Major Ehrhart would write on the basis of his work on the doctrine development initiative:

> A fundamental problem with Air Force doctrine is the absence of any real consensus as to what doctrine is and just what it is supposed to do. We want doctrine to reveal not only the capabilities of air forces but also to offer guidance on how best to use these capabilities. We demand that doctrine be both enduring and flexible, that it be valid over time yet responsive to change. We look to doctrine to provide guidance to Air Force personnel, while insisting that it remain open to interpretation. We want it to provide direction, yet not be too restrictive in its direction. We expect doctrine to guide research and development while at the same time it adjusts to technological innovations. And we insist that doctrine set out fundamental principles for the employment of air forces, while demanding it remain subordinate to national policy.... By trying to stretch a single term, "doctrine," to accommodate all things, we wind up with an amorphous concept that falls short in all areas. This criticism is not merely quibbling with semantics: The inability of Air Force people to understand the essence and purpose of doctrine is largely the result of trying to include too much under one umbrella word.[78]

Major Ehrhart proposed that the way to solve the complexity was to define doctrine more closely, namely:

> Air Force doctrine is the body of enduring principles, the general truths and accepted assumptions, which provide guidance and a sense of direction on the most effective way to develop, deploy, and employ air power. It should not encompass either political influences or specific instructions on the execution of these principles.[79]

In his participation in the doctrine development initiative, Lieutenant Colonel Hutchinson (then a major) agreed that a simplified definition of "doctrine" was in order. He would write:

> When the fancy wrappings are removed from the various official definitions of doctrine, two important and critical points remain. One is that doctrine is what we believe. There is active discussion concerning the process by which we arrive at this belief — whether it is derived from distilled experience or hypothesized in an analytical manner — and whether, based on the process, the belief is worthy to be titled doctrine.... The second point is that doctrine is what we teach. This includes both formal and informal instructions as well as the learning acquired through socializing. Therefore, doctrine, in a nutshell, is what we believe and teach.[80]

At ACSC in 1977–78, Major Hutchinson was research adviser to Maj Douglas S. Hawkins, who prepared a thesis, "Concept for Reasoned Change in Air Force Doctrine," that was a prescient analysis of the Air Force's need for an improved framework (taxonomy) for describing and categorizing doctrinal thought. Before assignment to ACSC, Hutchinson had been a planning and programming officer in the Concepts Directorate in Washington, and his analysis of the difficulty of the Air Force in recording its basic doctrine led him to suspect that the basic cause was the "inability to deal with the concept of varying levels of abstraction in our belief." He observed:

> Staff agencies, regardless of level of command, do not normally *develop* doctrine but merely *record* the lessons learned or the ideas developed by users and doers in a particular activity. . . . The recorder's job is to gather all pertinent information in a particular area and then, by a process of inductive reasoning, remove the essence at the appropriate level of abstraction to satisfy the needs of the organization. To me the most difficult task encountered by the recorder of doctrine is the establishment of the various levels of abstraction into which the beliefs of the organization will be classified. An equally difficult task is the grouping of beliefs that are on similar levels and then integrating these groups into the established hierarchy of doctrinal abstraction. It should be noted that this hierarchy of beliefs is a continuum and flows from the most abstract "truths" (basic doctrine) to very concrete notions (procedures). In the Air Force, we have failed to label beliefs at these lower levels as doctrine. We call them "tactics," "techniques," "standard operating procedures," "office policy," or some other well intended name. They all have one thing in common, however. They all reflect what we believe is the best way to accomplish a specific task and can, therefore, be considered doctrine.[81]

Hutchinson went on to attribute the difficulty in recording basic doctrine as being the usual attempt "to get agreement on beliefs at less than a general level, which has led to the inclusion of material to satisfy special interest. As a result, we have something we call 'basic doctrine' that is really a compilation of many subjects of which only one is doctrine."[82] "Basic doctrine properly recorded," Hutchinson said, "would be as useful to the Air Force as was the US Constitution's Bill of Rights is to the United States."[83]

The results of the doctrine development initiative were put on paper in "Concept for Reasoned Change in Air Force Doctrine." The study recommended a restructuring of Air Force doctrine by combining basic and functional doctrine, thus resulting in basic, operational, joint, and combined categories of Air Force doctrine.[84] These decisions were going to be incorporated in a new edition of Air Force Regulation 1-2. Meanwhile on 5 October 1978 Lt Col Thomas A. Cardwell III and Lt Col David R. McNabb published DIP-2, "How USAF Doctrine Is Developed," which incorporated and somewhat elaborated on the new AFR 1-2, *Assignment of Responsibilities for Development of Doctrine and Mission Employment Tactics*, which was published on 22 November 1978. The categories of doctrine were Air Force Basic Doctrine, which "states the fundamental principles for the employment of aerospace forces in support of US national objectives. . . . Additionally, AFM 1-1 provides guidance for the specialized activities of the Air Force"; and Air Force operational doctrine, which was "the expansion of the principles stated in the basic doctrine governing the organization, direction, and employment of aerospace forces in the accomplishment of the Air

Force missions." These categories of Air Force doctrine were accompanied by Joint Doctrine and Combined Doctrine. Air Force Mission Employment Tactics (the old AFM 3-series) were said to be logical extensions of Air Force doctrine. It was explained that:

> In short, USAF doctrine is what we believe concerning the use of aerospace forces. . . . Within the USAF, doctrine: (1) Defines and explains the roles, missions, and tasks of the Air Force; (2) Provides a guide from which weapons development decisions are made; (3) Provides guidance on the interrelationships of Service roles and missions; (4) Is the basis for mission area analysis and force planning; and (5) Provides a point of departure for every activity of the Air Force.[85]

AFR 1-2 assigned responsibilities for developing doctrine and mission employment tactics throughout the Air Force. DIP-2, on the other hand, gave an explanation of how doctrine was to be developed. And a follow-on, CIP 79-3, "Concept Development—What Is It? and Who Needs It?" issued in December 1979, further related concepts to doctrine. DIP-2 postulated that doctrine development was "a product of history—what has happened and what we believe—and today's environment—a systems approach to the present. It operates in a dynamic environment. Doctrine provides the bridge from our past through the present to the future."[86] A diagram provides a look at the historical approach to doctrine development:

Doctrine Development

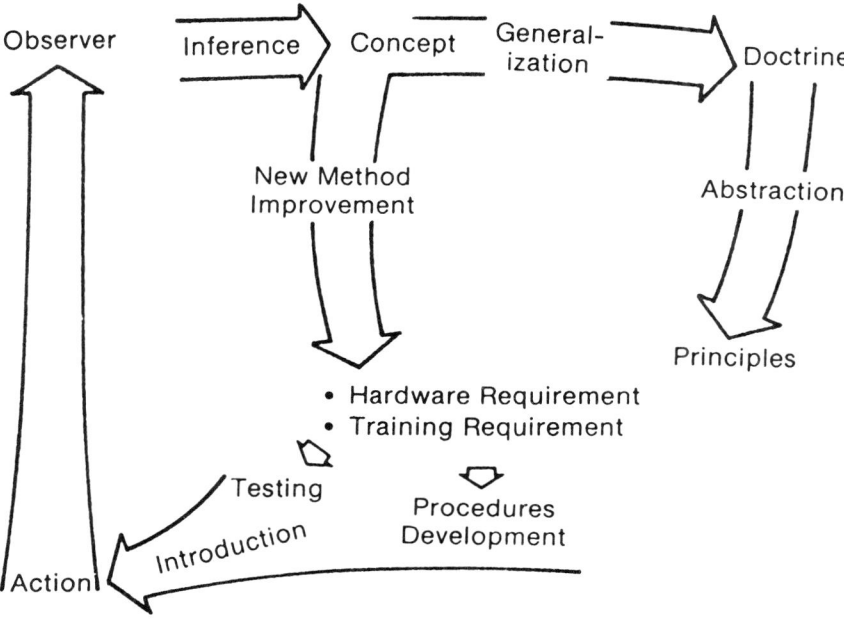

IDEAS, CONCEPTS, DOCTRINE

In terms of the diagram, development started when an observer saw an action that appeared to be about the same each time it occurred. For example in air-to-air combat, attacks from out of the sun or from six o'clock in a blind spot was a distinct advantage. This observation was inferred into a concept that to do this was wise, and a doctrine statement would have it that an attack should include a combination of deception, rapidity, and unexpectedness. CIP 79-3 used the same diagram to explain how "concept development is the forerunner of doctrine, and part and parcel of the doctrinal development process."[87] "Both conceptual and doctrinal development are logical aspects of the planning cycle. However, 'doctrine' builds on the past as well as on new concepts; and 'concepts' gropes for the future, with doctrine serving as a point of departure."[88] The CIP elaborated:

> The essential and important aspect of concept development in relationship to doctrine as well as long range planning is that it is *the* dynamic modifier of an otherwise more or less rigid set of rules and projections which serve as the basis for coherent and goal oriented action. Concept development is responsible for the continuous revision and update of doctrine. It insures that doctrine and planning never remain static and by so doing precludes it from becoming doctrinaire.[89]

But in addition to the historical genesis of doctrine, DIP-2 pointed out that doctrine also was shaped by environmental pressures external to the Air Force. The systems approach to doctrine development was compelled to examine events from the environment in a dynamic perspective. DIP-2 used this diagram to explain the influence of environment in doctrine: As the diagram indicates, national objectives and strategy provided the base, foundation, and anvil used to define doctrinal statements on issues, functions, missions, and the future.[90]

Environment for Doctrine Development

In the same months that the doctrinal development initiative was generating thinking, the doctrine development branch, Directorate of Concepts, was continuing the redrafting of the proposed AFM 1-1, which in the new frame of reference was to be titled *Functions and Basic Doctrine of the United States Air Force*. The composition of the manual would be quite different from its predecessors with large type, numerous headlines, catchphrases, line drawings, diagrams, portrait drawings, and numbers of quotations. It was designed for an expanded audience of career civilians, airmen, noncommissioned officers, military officers, and the general population. The manual was published on 14 February 1979, and in his signature letter Gen Lew Allen wrote: "Whether you are enlisted, an officer, or a civilian in the Air Force family, I believe this manual will help you to think sincerely about why we are in business — why we have an Air Force, and what it must be ready to do in the next 30 years and beyond."[91] Possibly because of language and format, there was an ongoing rumor that the 1979 edition of AFM 1-1 was written to "tell the Air Force Story" rather than as a doctrinal manual to prepare a military force and its commanders for war.[92] The manual focused upon the role of the Air Force in preparing air forces for combat, declaring: "The mission of the United States Air Force is to prepare our forces to fight to preserve the security and freedom of the people of the United States."[93] As a matter of fact, Headquarters USAF/XOCDD had originally conceived of battle doctrine as a chapter in the new AFM 1-1, perhaps fielding some of the ideas of Col John Boyd's *Patterns of Conflict*, or Col Jim Barton's *The Blitz Fighter*, but Air Staff consensus was not reached for inclusion of a chapter on battle doctrine.[94]

Viewed in retrospect, the 1979 revision of AFM 1-1 was described as "essentially a codification and expansion of the ideas that evolved over the years."[95] It stated that the national military objectives were to sustain deterrence, defend the United States, conduct warfare if called on to do so, and resolve conflict quickly and effectively. The levels of conflict were again redefined, this time as localized war, theater conventional war, theater nuclear war, and strategic nuclear war. The second chapter on Air Force functions and missions was the longest in the manual (30 pages), and the fourth chapter on organizing, training, equipping, and sustaining aerospace forces was second longest (14 pages). The chapter on functions and missions possibly ran to such extraordinary length because it was mostly a recall of particular legislative actions and functions papers. The nine basic operational missions were said to be strategic aerospace offense, space operations, strategic aerospace defense, airlift, close air support, air interdiction, counterair operations, surveillance and reconnaissance, and special operations. It was asserted that: "Aerospace forces are unique and can be decisive in combat."[96] However, air forces also had to "be effective in supporting the other services in their roles and missions."[97] And in a then-current matter under discussion, it was pointed out that the Air Force had a collateral role against enemy naval forces, this by neutralizing or destroying enemy naval forces, delivering mines, defending friendly naval forces, engaging in antisubmarine warfare, and conducting surveillance and reconnaissance. The characteristics of aerospace forces were given as speed, range, and maneuverability. The capabilities were flexibility, readiness, responsiveness, presence, destructiveness, survivability, and mobility. The principles for employing aerospace forces were centralized control; decentralized execution; coordinated effort of Army, Navy, Marine Corps, and allied forces with common doctrine and cooperation; and proper use of the principles of war, which were enumerated as objective, offensive, mass, economy of forces, surprise, unity of effort, maneuver, simplicity, timing and tempo, and defensive. The "timing and tempo" probably reflected Colonel Boyd's idea of dominating a battle by operating, as the manual read, "within the enemy's observation-orientation decision-action-feedback time cycle. . . . Maintaining a quicker tempo of action helps to disrupt the enemy's strategy and operations, by creating the confusion and disorder that can lead to the enemy's defeat."[98]

The 1979 edition of AFM 1-1 was hardly published before there was a growing dissatisfaction with it and a growing demand from inside the Air Force for a basic doctrinal manual that took a distinctive stand on how the Air Force was going to fight if the nation called upon it.[99] Wrote Dr Williamson Murray, an avid scholar on military affairs and one of the foremost American authorities on the German *Luftwaffe*:

> What strikes this reader is the emphasis throughout the manual on the role of the USAF in deterrence as opposed to its role as a combat force. . . . On the national level this undoubtedly reflects the basic assumption on which many of America's defense policies rest. Nevertheless, when a nation's military services become more concerned with deterrence than with their capability to *fight*, their real ability to deter comes into question.[100]

Professor Murray was also critical of the manual's drawings of aircraft, of contemporary people, and of simplified graphics which he wrote "hardly create a serious tone — the type of tone necessary for a manual discussing matters which in the final analysis involve life and death."[101]

In the aftermath of the publication of February 1979 — popularly referred to as the "picture-book" edition — one of the functions of the Doctrine and Concepts Division would continue to be the drafting of a less flamboyant version of the basic doctrine manual that would require several years to surface. According to Col David L. Hosley, who was deputy and later director of Headquarters USAF/XOXID in 1980–82, much of the division's work focused on NATO doctrine, the other projected volumes of the AFM 1- series, and efforts to get the AFM 2- manuals updated. As has been seen, the negotiation of NATO doctrine was already in progress and had resulted in Allied Tactical Publication (ATP) 33, *NATO Tactical Air Doctrine*, effective 1 October 1976, and also Allied Tactical Publication 40, *Doctrine and Procedures for Airspace Control in the Combat Zone*, effective in September 1977. ATP-33 was taken as the cornerstone of a series of publications on tactical air doctrine. Those of interest to the Air Force that were going to be printed included:

- ATP-8, *Amphibious Operations*
- ATP-27, *Offensive Air Support Operations*
- ATP-33, *NATO Tactical Air Doctrine*
- ATP-34, *Tactical Air Support of Maritime Operations*
- ATP-40, *Doctrine and Procedures for Airspace Control in the Combat Zone*
- ATP-41, *Airmobile Operations*
- ATP-42, *Counter Air Operations*
- ATP-44, *Electronic Warfare in Air Operations*

In NATO usage, doctrine was defined as "fundamental principles by which military forces guide their actions in support of objectives."[102] The spectrum of tactical doctrine included "basic doctrine" which set forth broad principles of warfare in a specific medium: land, sea, or air. The next level was "operational doctrine," which amplified basic doctrine in specific functional areas. The lowest level was "operational tactics," which dealt with the employment of forces in specific combat missions, such as how to attack a specific enemy formation. The NATO doctrines and procedures were theater specific and did not necessarily drive unilateral US doctrine and procedures worldwide. NATO terminology also was sufficiently different as to demand a *NATO Glossary of Terms and Definitions for Military Use*.[103]

As a result of the doctrine development initiative the Directorate of Plans (XOX) was committed in AFR 1-2, 22 November 1978, as the Air Force office of primary responsibility for not only AFM 1-1 but other basic airspace doctrinal manuals in the AFM 1- series. In this series, in addition to AFM 1-1, a joint manual, AFM 1-3, *Doctrine and Procedures for Airspace Control in the Combat Zone*, had been subjected to lengthy review but had been ultimately agreed upon by the service chiefs and published on 1 December 1975.[104] In the first half of 1977 the doctrine development branch of the Directorate of Concepts was tasked to begin work on an Air Force doctrine concerning the use of space and on another doctrine manual on theater nuclear operations. In the 1978 regulation, these were aligned as AFM 1-5, *Theater Nuclear Doctrine*, and AFM 1-6, *Military Space Doctrine*. The accounts of Air Force nuclear employment concepts, had been fragmented between various manuals, operational concepts and studies. A working group of officers from Air Force concepts, operations, and plans and the Defense Nuclear Agency pulled together a straw man draft that was reviewed and published as a secret classification manual AFM 1-5 on 20 April 1979. Later that year, AFM 1-7, *Chemical Warfare Doctrine*, was published on 26 September 1979 and AFM 1-9, *Doctrine for Electromagnetic Combat*, on 18 September 1979. The 1978 AFR 1-2 also projected AFM 1-2, which was to have been a command and control doctrine. This doctrine was not completed although the subject would be broken out at some length in the 1984 edition of AFM 1-1 and also in Headquarters USAF/XOXID's DIP-12, *Command Relationships*, dated June 1984. Another manual, AFM 1-10, *Combat Support Doctrine*, was projected on Theater Air Operations with the idea that it would describe the characteristics and warfighting principles of theater air operations in a high-threat combat environment. The draft version of the proposed AFM 1-10 met opposition within the Air Force, and the project was quietly dropped as too complex for completion.[105]

The task of working up an Air Force doctrine concerning the use of space as a military operating medium when assigned in 1977 involved the preparation of a first-of-a-kind doctrine intended to provide a broad overview of the utility of space for military use, a description of military missions in space, and an abbreviated statement of Air Force policy regarding its role and leadership in space. As an added complication the military usage of space was circumscribed closely by international agreements designed to keep space for peaceful purposes. After circulation of a preliminary draft, a review draft of AFM 1-6, *Military Space Doctrine*, was forwarded to the Air Staff and MAJCOMs for coordination in 1980.[106] At this juncture, the progress of the space doctrine foundered because of a doctrinal dispute as to whether space was a place or a mission, specifically whether space was a place where ongoing military missions were to be performed or whether it would be a distinct realm where space power would become coequal with land, sea, and air power. In a speech to the National Space Club in October 1979, Maj Gen William R. Yost, Air Force director of space systems in DCS/Research, Development and Acquisition, had reflected back to the early role of air doctrine in the early days of the airplane and had sensed an "analogy between today's challenge with the unknowns of space to the comparable challenges and unknowns associated with the airplane." To Yost the experience of "airpower's doctrinal founding fathers" pointed out "the requirement to keep doctrine and technology working toward a dynamic synthesis."[107] An Air University air power symposium conducted in 1981 offered similar conclusions: "There is no space doctrine.... We need space doctrine.... The Air Force needs to get its doctrinal house in order."[108] A few months later, in April 1981 a major military space doctrine symposium held at the US Air Force Academy advanced similar conclusions and moved them into a somewhat mystical view that space doctrine was a necessary prologue to Air Force space exploitation. One of the presenters at the academy was Lt Col Dino A. Lorenzini, an Air Force officer then assigned at the Naval War College. Lorenzini urged that doctrine was necessary:

> The development and articulation of doctrine serve as a focal point for discussion, challenge, and group consensus-building.... Once widespread acceptance is achieved, doctrine establishes a degree of permanence and organizational stability.[109]

He pointed out that space power doctrine would be different from air power doctrine, saying: "The application of space power doctrine is differentiated from that of air power doctrine by the atmospheric boundary above which aircraft cannot fly and below which spacecraft cannot operate."[110] Finally, he confronted the international limitations on military usages of space, proposing that an "unencumbered version" of space power doctrine would be referred to as *basic* space power doctrine, while a "constrained version that follows current administration policies and treaty obligations will be referred to as *operational space power doctrine*."[111] Lorenzini argued:

> Using basic space power doctrine as the starting point, we can decide exactly what we want to do militarily in space with an awareness of the benefits and risks involved.... Operational space power doctrine spells out the who, what, when, where, and how of military space activities. It should be consistent with the overall space policy decisions of our national leaders and compatible with our basic space power doctrine.[112]

As already noted, Lt Col David E. Lupton pointed out that there was a space doctrine as of 1981, even though it was an unpublished nondoctrine "that space should be a sanctuary, free from military forces . . . that the best way to employ space forces was not to have space forces."[113] On 15 October 1982 AFM 1-6, *Military Space Doctrine*, was published under Gen Charles A. Gabriel's authentication as Air Force chief of staff. "Space," Gabriel wrote, "is the ultimate high ground."[114] The manual accepted the proposition that space was not a mission but that "space is the outer reaches of the Air Forces's operational medium—the aerospace, which is the total expanse beyond the earth's surface. Space, then, is an operational environment that can be used for the conduct of Air Force missions."[115] Although the policy implications of the space manual have already been addressed, the manual offered an interesting revelation that, in the case of space, doctrine would need to catch up with technology. It stated:

> Our scientific, technological, and industrial communities have established a resource base from which this nation can logically proceed with expanded space operations. Within that framework, our doctrine and strategy must evolve to provide the vision, focus, and direction to guide the development of future space programs, systems, and operational practices.[116]

AFM 1-6 stated that the "attributes" of space systems included global coverage, economy, effectiveness, flexibility, efficiency, and redundancy. In AFM 1-1 of 1979, the "characteristics" of air power were said to be speed, range, and maneuverability, and a new 16 March 1984 edition of AFM 1-1 would list the air power characteristics as speed, range, and flexibility. Only flexibility (maneuverability) appeared on both the air power and space power lists, and the definitions of flexibility were different. Lupton pointed out that the environmental conditions of space operations were quite different from those of air operations. Perhaps the difference in characteristics meant that different operating environments (air and space) could not be logically treated under the umbrella term *aerospace*. He argued that the Air Force perhaps should consider air and space as distinct mediums with both shared and unique characteristics.[117]

In 1980 the Doctrine and Concepts Division reviewed the AFM 2- series (operational doctrine) manuals for accuracy and developed a long-range master plan to update them, this work to be prepared according to the 1978 AFR 1-2 by specified lead commands or agencies. Looking at the 1- series manuals as a whole, the average age of the 20 manuals in the series was almost eight years (94 months).

IDEAS, CONCEPTS, DOCTRINE

The oldest was AFM 2-31, *Aerospace Environmental Operations*, that had been published in December 1965 and the newest AFM 2-6, *Tactical Air Operations — Reconnaissance*. The 3- series (mission employment tactics) had been created in February 1966 but had never been very popular, and only six manuals in the series had been published, five of them applicable exclusively to tactical air forces. The 1978 AFR 1-2 provided that current publications would remain in effect until superseded by new documents, and none of the specific lead commands or agencies were quick to put through revisions. The Tactical Air Command had produced most of the 2- and 3- series doctrinal manuals, and the TAC-TRADOC interrelationship remained active. The TAC doctrine effort, however, went on record as preferring some more easily disseminated medium than the hard-to-get-coordinated doctrinal manuals. To Headquarters USAF/XOXID, however, the AFM 2- series operational manuals were important since they carried the burden of a presentation on how to fight. To rejuvenate aerospace doctrine, AFR 1-2, *Assignment of Responsibilities for Development of Doctrine*, was published on 25 July 1984. This regulation changed doctrinal categories to basic (AFM 1-), operational (AFM 2-), and tactical (AFM 3-), plus joint and combined. The Directorate of Plans was responsible for the overall policy, control, development, direction, and management of the entire scope of Air Force doctrine. The regulation specified a list of operational and tactical doctrines to be prepared and maintained, their currency to be guaranteed by an annual review and updating as required. Under this mandate the Tactical Air Command began the preparation in 1964 of an AFM 2-XC manual to replace three old manuals: AFM 2-1, *Tactical Air Operations — Counter Air, Close Air Support, and Air Interdiction*; AFM 2-7, *Tactical Air Operations — Tactical Air Control System* (TACS); and AFM 2-10, *Tactical Air Operations — Employment of Air Delivered Target Activated Munitions* (ADTAMS). This new level of doctrine was designed to provide basic guidance for the organization, mission structure, and command and control arrangements to be applied to the entire spectrum of tactical air operations.[118]

Facing the Future: Cooperative Armed Forces Doctrine

"Some doctrine," wrote F. Clifton Berry, Jr., editor in chief of *Air Force Magazine* in July 1983, "is dull as dishwater. A sort of 'motherhood and apple pie' topic studied as part of professional military education, then promptly forgotten in the press of the real world. Too many USAF people have treated doctrine that way. The process of neglect has had the effect of weakening the underlying rationale for building and operating USAF forces and equipment."[119] Berry saw hopeful signs in mid-1983 that the Air Force was not only rigorously engaged in self-examination of its basic doctrine but had taken the initiative to work more closely with its sister services in preparing the combat forces needed by the nation.[120]

On the basis of his experience in the US Air Force Directorate of Doctrine, Concepts, and Objectives, as well as in his doctrinal assignments in the Tactical Air Command, General Loving brought to the Air Command and Staff College in 1970–73 a conviction that "Air Force basic doctrine has evolved from experience."[121] In response to Loving's query about why the Air War College did not teach more about war, Lt Gen Alvan C. Gillem organized a broad study of the Air University curriculum in September 1972 which, among other issues, recommended that the Air War College ought not to try to develop a "blue suit think tank role" since this was a function of Headquarters USAF and such would require a very high priority for the best officers as students and faculty that only a personally extended priority of the chief of staff could provide. The study nevertheless recommended in March 1973 that the Air War College should attempt to support Air Force doctrinal and conceptual activities by emphasizing special student study groups on doctrine and concepts.[122] General Loving's interest ensured a surge of doctrinal studies in the Air Command and Staff College, and in 1972–73 in that school a separate lecture series on military history with a central focus on the role of air power was introduced for the first time.[123]

The prevalent mission of the Air War College would continue to be "to prepare senior officers for high command and staff duty." But on 5 July 1975, the Department of Defense's Committee on Excellence in Education, called the Clements Board after W. P. Clements, Jr., deputy secretary of defense, who headed it, ruled that the individual senior service colleges should specialize in service specialty warfare study—for example, air warfare in the Air War College. The Clements Board called upon each college to maintain or establish a program through which a few distinguished visiting professors would be available to impart their knowledge to faculty and students. The board demanded that the colleges place emphasis on research, saying "For the Senior Service Colleges to maintain excellence in their programs and meet their obligations to their Services, JCS and DoD, they must have active research programs focused on the particular mission of the college."[124] During the summer of 1974 Gen William W. Momyer already had recommended that the Air Force draw upon the personal experience of participants for a series of monographs on US Air Force activities in Southeast Asia, and this series was established in the Air War College.[125] The Air War College also had welcomed the opportunity to invite two civilian scholars to spend a year or more of residence with each of its four departments. In December 1978 the Air War College was being reduced to three departments, thus releasing spaces for two visiting scholars. In a briefing to the Employment of Air Power Planning Advisory Group, Col Thomas A. Fabyanic, chief of the AWC Military Studies Division, proposed to establish the Airpower Research Institute (ARI) at the Air University, using the two primary civilian research associates and other military research associates from the faculties of the AU school system. Both the Army and the Navy were funding research institutes, and Fabyanic urged that the Air Force should do no less.[126] The concept was approved and one of the first steps was to put the Southeast Asia Monograph Series under the incipient ARI. In 1979–80

ARI continued in an unofficial status, funded by resources of the Air University and its then parent Air Training Command. Finally, at the end of June 1980 the limited ARI was established with Colonel Fabyanic as director, two Air Force lieutenant colonels identified as the first military research associates, and two civilian research associates employed for the following academic year.[127]

Shortly after assuming command of Air University, Lt Gen Charles G. Cleveland began to explore new avenues through which the Air University could broaden and deepen its contribution to the Air Force mission. In September 1981 he established Project FLAME (Fresh Look At Mission – Education), and one of its recommended initiatives was to establish a center for aerospace strategic studies, incorporating ARI and other functions in it. In Washington, Lt Gen Jerome F. O'Malley, deputy chief of staff of operations, plans and readiness (HQ USAF/XO), reasoned that the responsibility for doctrinal development ought to remain in Washington since the Air Force needed a doctrine spokesman in the Pentagon to look after its interests. Similarly, Gen Bennie L. Davis, commander of SAC, was concerned that the operational commands not lose their role in developing doctrine. To reassure General Davis, Gen Thomas D. Ryan, Air Training Command commander, provided that ARI would be expanded to accommodate MAJCOM and special operating agency research associates sent to ARI to accomplish research topics desired by their commands while receiving credit for attending professional military education courses. In 1981–82 ARI was in operation while the negotiations for the larger organization – now being designated the Air University Center for Aerospace Doctrine, Research, and Education (AUCADRE) – were progressing. While manpower and personnel matters were still being worked out, Headquarters USAF provided for the designation and activation of AUCADRE, effective 3 January 1983. AFR 1-2, 25 July 1984, provided: "Air University, through the Air University Center for Aerospace Doctrine, Research, and Education (AUCADRE), provides advice, assistance, and research support for HQ USAF/XOX doctrinal development efforts, as required."[128]

The Headquarters USAF/XOX pamphlet DIP-2, "How USAF Doctrine Is Developed," acknowledged: "Doctrine development is a product of history – what has happened and what we believe – and today's environment. . . . Doctrine provides a bridge from our past through the present to the future."[129] On 5 February 1982, a few months before retiring as Air Force chief of staff, Gen Lew Allen, Jr., undertook "to create an environment where our people can learn from warfighting lessons of the past and use that knowledge to better prepare for the future."[130] "I believe," Allen wrote, "that a continuing study of military history, combat leadership, the principles of war, and particularly the application of airpower, is necessary for us to meet the challenges that lie ahead."[131] General Allen tasked General O'Malley to be the Air Staff's focal point for the project – Project Warrior – and in turn on 10 February 1982 O'Malley advised Air Force commanders that he had designated the Directorate of Plans, Doctrine and Concepts Division, as the focal point in his deputate. The goal was to create and maintain an environment for Air Force people to think and plan in warfighting terms. The objectives were to identify ways to improve the warfighting spirit and perspective of Air Force people, to encourage an improved understanding of the theory and practice of war, with particular emphasis on the contribution of air power, and to help toward better planning for the future. O'Malley enjoined all Air Force commanders to "continue the current trend of emphasizing the study and application of military history, warfighting skills, and combat leadership."[132]

One of the foci of Project Warrior was the study of war as a synergy of air, ground, and naval actions. Some of this same interrelationship of forces surfaced in a new view of doctrine published by Lt Col Dennis M. Drew, chief of the Warfare Studies Division at ACSC, in 1982. Here Colonel Drew rationalized that military history was the primary source of military doctrine and that observations of past success or failure could be generalized, tested over time, and abstracted into principles. Unlike most approaches, Drew advised his readers to seek a fundamental doctrine of war which would be the foundation for environmental doctrine (sea power, land power, and air power). The environmental doctrine would yield narrow organizational doctrines concerning the use of particular forces. In Drew's analysis AFM 1-1 was an example of organizational doctrine. As a teaching aid, Drew visualized a doctrine tree:

> The trunk of the tree is fundamental doctrine, the basis for all other doctrine types. The trunk, of course, has its roots in the ground, which represents history or experience, the primary source for doctrine. The tree branches represent environmental doctrine—each springing from the trunk, each individual yet all related. The leaves represent organizational doctrine—dependent on both the trunk and the branches, changing from season to season.[133]

Drew's conception that the development of doctrine should progress downward from a fundamental doctrine of war was somewhat different from a long-held partisan services view that joint and unified doctrine built upward by amalgamation of air, land, and naval doctrines, but it was not out of context with a new Air Force interest in a synergistic approach to war.

For more than a year, with the strongest direction from its top commanders, the Air Force examined its relations with the other services and its basic doctrine in 1962 and 1963. As has been seen, in the autumn of 1982 General Gabriel signed a Memorandum of Agreement (MOA) with the US Navy for closer cooperation in training and operations. In April 1983 Gabriel signed a memorandum of understanding (MOU) with the US Army designed to enhance joint employment of tactical forces. In May 1984 he signed a lengthy Memorandum of Agreement with the Army on joint force development to be pursued by both services. As a doctrinal undertaking these joint service agreements had significant benefits both in substance and in technique: they improved the effectiveness of joint operations, and they ironed out doctrinal differences between the Air Force and the Army. These were clear and concise doctrinal statements, related in time to existing doctrine, avoiding misunderstandings, and enabling commanders and staff to act on specific propositions. As doctrine the MOAs had at least one disadvantage in that they included both doctrine and procedures in single packages. In focusing upon battlefield operations—and particularly the extended battlefield—rather than doctrinal abstractions, the Army and Air Force were taking hard, critical looks at concepts and doctrines of most-likely theater war and reevaluating them in the light of fighting to win.[134]

As a part of the Air Force's self examination, AFM 1-1 was put under substantial review and revision during 1983 and was published on 16 March 1984 as AFM 1-1, *Basic Aerospace Doctrine of the United States Air Force*, with authentication by Gen Charles A. Gabriel. The writing of the manual was done by Maj Clayton R. Frishkorn, Jr., XOXID. In the new manual the drawings and flamboyant typography of the 1979 edition had been abandoned. The revision was significantly different in text from the 1979 predecessor in that it focused on warfighting rather than functions. A new chapter titled "Employing Aerospace Forces" discussed interacting fundamentals of warfighting (man, machine, and environment) to introduce the principles of war: objectives, offensive, surprise, security, mass and economy of force, maneuver, timing and tempo, unity of command, simplicity, logistics, and cohesion. In the words of the manual, "aerospace doctrine flows from these principles and provides mutually accepted and officially sanctioned guidelines to the application of these principles in warfare."[135] The new basic doctrine emphasized the role of aerospace forces as an essential element of the Armed Forces—a land, naval, and aerospace team employed in unified action. New attention was given to the Air Force's maritime support mission—recognition of the Air Force's ability to contribute to missions at sea. AFM 1-1 was aligned to AFM 1-6 on space doctrine and reflected the same emphasis, that many Air Force missions were potentially to be performed in space. The manual emphasized that a decision to commit US military forces in the conduct of war must consider the objectives desired, force capabilities, and the will of the people, the latter requirement rather clearly reflecting the US experience in Southeast Asia. Some old fundamental beliefs were reemphasized: air superiority was a first consideration in employing aerospace forces but it was a means to an end in that it permitted a freedom of action to air, land, and naval missions. Another old belief repeated was that air power could exploit speed, range, and flexibility better than land and sea forces and therefore could and should operate independently. Speed, range, and flexibility were most fully realized when air power was centrally controlled and decentrally executed. Possibly because clear control responsibilities would be vital to an Army-Air Force extended battlefield strategy, the manual emphasized unity of air power command in theater operations and a theater approach to warfighting. Although this theater approach had not changed significantly since 1947, it now was more vital than ever. The new edition of AFM 1-1 rather clearly reflected a new spirit of cooperation being found in the Pentagon in 1982–84. Nevertheless, in its concluding paragraph this ninth version of the Air Force's basic doctrine noted:

In sum, since 1943, several fundamental beliefs have remained embedded in Air Force doctrine. Airpower can exploit speed, range, and flexibility, better than land and sea forces, and therefore, it must be allowed to operate independently of these forces. These characteristics are most fully realized when airpower is controlled centrally but executed decentrally. The principal missions of airpower have evolved over the years and reflect what airpower does best. Although priorities in their application have shifted with changes in national policy, the beliefs about the proper employment of airpower have remained fundamentally constant in the face of profound changes in technology, strategy, and international relations.[136]

When earlier Air Force basic doctrine had sought to distill rather timeless attributes and principles of aerospace power for the guidance of the Air Force in being and the Air Force that would be, AFM 1-1 of 1984 emphasized:

> The Air Force continuously refines aerospace doctrine to make it relevant to present operations and viable for future contingencies. This process requires an open channel of communication between those headquarters' staffs charged with formulating doctrine and those echelons involved in the daily process of learning from experience. Feedback from these echelons is critical to evaluating and modifying existing doctrine and, when necessary, formulating new doctrine. AFM 1-1 is published, in part, to remind each and every individual in the Air Force of the obligation to keep aerospace doctrine useable.[137]

In other words, the Air Force recognized that it had always been and would continue to be in a search for its doctrine for the most effective employment of aerospace power both in peace and war.

NOTES

1. AFM 1-2, *Air Doctrine, United States Air Force Basic Doctrine*, 1 April 1953, i.
2. Ibid., 1 April 1954, ii; and 1 April 1955, ii.
3. Maj Rudolph F. Wacker, "Managing the Infinities of Basic Doctrine," research thesis (Maxwell AFB, Ala.: Air Command and Staff College [ACSC], June 1967), 49–50.
4. Ibid., 60–61.
5. AFM 1-2, 1 April 1955, passim.
6. Lt Gen George G. Loving, Jr., US Air Force Oral History Interview, 5–7 July 1983, 85–86.
7. Maj Gen Dale O. Smith, special assistant for arms control, Joint Chiefs of Staff, "Development of Air Force Doctrine," 15 April 1963.
8. Maj William Y. Smith, "The Effects of Intercontinental Ballistic Missiles on Air Doctrine," research thesis (Maxwell AFB, Ala.: ACSC, 17 April 1959), passim.
9. Ibid.
10. Lt Col R. H. Brundin, Lt Col F. R. Goldsberry, and Maj R. T. Adams, "United States Air Force Basic Doctrine," research thesis (Maxwell AFB, Ala.: Air Command and Staff School), 1959.
11. Col Roy R. Walker, "Is There Need for USAF Basic Doctrine?" research thesis (Maxwell AFB, Ala.: Air War College, April 1959), 53–54.
12. AFM 1-2, 1 December 1959, passim.
13. Ibid.
14. Wacker, "Managing the Infinities of Basic Doctrine," 70–71.

15. Lt Col Donald L. Cromer, "An Analysis of United States Air Force Space Doctrine," research thesis (Maxwell AFB, Ala.: ACSC, May 1973), 28.
16. "Secretary Zuckert's Air War College Graduation Address," *Air Force Policy Letter for Commanders: Supplement*, July 1965, 1–4.
17. Ibid.
18. AFR 1-1, *Responsibilities for Doctrine Development*, 20 March 1963.
19. Ibid.
20. Wacker, "Managing the Infinities of Basic Doctrine," 5.
21. Ibid., 72; AFM 1-1, *Aerospace Doctrine, United States Air Force Basic Doctrine*, 14 August 1964.
22. AFM 1-1, 14 August 1964, passim.
23. Ibid.; Annex A, "Evolution of Basic Doctrine," A-3 and A-4, in AFM 1-1, *Basic Aerospace Doctrine of the United States Air Force*, 16 March 1984.
24. "Updating Aerospace Doctrine," *TIG Brief*, 10 May 1963, 2.
25. "Aerospace Doctrine in the Thermonuclear Age," *TIG Brief*, 11 September 1964, 3.
26. "Understanding of Doctrine on Use of Air Forces (AFM 1-1)," *Air Force Policy Letter for Commanders*, 15 April 1965.
27. Gen William E. DePuy, "TRADOC (TRAining and DOCtrine Command): A New Command for an Old Mission," *Army Magazine*, October 1973, 31–34.
28. History, Directorate of Doctrine, Concepts, and Objectives, July–December 1966; History, Directorate of Concepts, July–December 1966, 3.
29. History, Directorate of Doctrine, Concepts, and Objectives, July–December 1966; January–June 1967; July–December 1967; Loving interview, 5–7 July 1983, 94–109.
30. Loving interview.
31. Ibid., 124.
32. History, Directorate of Doctrine, Concepts, and Objectives, January–June 1968, 55–57; January–June 1967, 26–27; July–December 1975, 30; Maj Douglas S. Hawkins, "Concept for Reasoned Change in the Air Force Doctrine Program," thesis (Maxwell AFB, Ala.: ACSC, 1978), 60, 71.
33. History, Directorate of Doctrine, Concepts, and Objectives, January–June 1971; January–June 1976, 62–63; House, *Department of Defense Appropriations for 1979: Hearings before a Subcommittee of the Committee on Appropriations*, 95th Cong., 2d sess., 1978, pt. 4:161–63 (hereafter cited as *1979 DOD Appropriations*); Directorate for Strategy, Doctrine, and Long-Range Planning, Doctrine Information Publication 3, *Combined Doctrine—What Is It?*, 1978.
34. Grant McClellan, "Doctrine: An Ever-Present Practical Necessity," *Army Magazine*, January 1965, 43.
35. Ibid.
36. Ibid.
37. Draft AFM 1-1, *United States Air Force Basic Doctrine*, 1 February 1966; Brig Gen Monro MacCloskey, *The United States Air Force* (New York: Frederick A. Praeger, 1967), 207–24.
38. Draft AFM 1-1, *United States Air Force Basic Doctrine*.
39. Ibid.
40. History, Directorate of Doctrine, Concepts, and Objectives, January–June 1967, 24; July–December 1967; January–June 1968, 53; January–June 1971; AFM 1-1, *Aerospace Doctrine, United States Air Force Basic Doctrine*, 28 September 1971, 1–1.
41. AFM 1-1, *Aerospace Doctrine, United States Air Force Basic Doctrine*, passim.
42. Ibid.
43. Maj William R. Chambers et al., "An Analysis and Study of United States Air Force Basic Doctrine," research study (Maxwell AFB, Ala.: ACSC, May 1972), 66.
44. Briefing on Doctrinal Divergencies in History, Directorate of Doctrine, Concepts, and Objectives, January–June 1968.
45. Lt Col Donald L. Cromer et al., "A Critical Analysis of USAF Basic Doctrine," research study (Maxwell AFB, Ala.: ACSC, May 1973), 20–21, quoting ACSC panel discussion on doctrine remarks, 15 February 1973.

46. Ibid.

47. History, Directorate of Doctrine, Concepts, and Objectives, January–June 1971; July–December 1971.

48. Ibid., 12.

49. History, Air University, Fiscal Year 1971, 1:19; conversation of the author with Lt Gen Alvan C. Gillem II, USAF, Retired.

50. Loving interview, 198.

51. History, Air Command and Staff College, 1 July 1972–30 June 1973, 19; Chambers et al., "An Analysis and Study of United States Air Force Basic Doctrine," iii–iv; Cromer et al., "A Critical Analysis of USAF Basic Doctrine," iii–iv.

52. Chambers et al., "An Analysis and Study of United States Air Force Basic Doctrine," 34–35.

53. Ibid., 36–48. Maj Gerald W. Street acknowledged his indebtedness to Ralph E. Strauch, *Winners and Losers: The Roots of Inadequacy in our Strategic Concepts*, Rand Corporation, July 1971, 1–32.

54. Chambers et al., "An Analysis and Study of United States Air Force Basic Doctrine," 54–59.

55. Ibid., 60–73.

56. History, Directorate of Doctrine, Concepts, and Objectives, July–December 1972, 21, 36; January–June 1974, 42–43.

57. Col Benjamin F. Ingram, chief, Military Employment Division, Directorate of Curriculum, ACSC, to students, class of 1973, letter, subject: Proposed AFM 1-1, 17 January 1973.

58. AFM 1-1, 15 January 1975; History, Directorate of Doctrine, Concepts, and Objectives, January–June 1975, 82; July–December 1974, 29.

59. AFM 1-1, 15 January 1975.

60. Lt Gen J. W. Pauly, "The Thread of Doctrine," *Air University Review*, May–June 1976, 3–10.

61. History, Directorate of Doctrine, Concepts, and Objectives, July–December 1972, 122; January–June 1973, 17; July–December 1973, 1; January–June 1974, 83; July–December 1974, 78; January–June 1975, 58–59, 70; July–December 1975, 46–48.

62. Ibid., January–June 1974, 83; July–December 1978, 78.

63. History, Directorate of Doctrine, Concepts, and Objectives, July–December 1973, 3; January–June 1974, 28–29; July–December 1974, 6–7; January–June 1975, 10; History, Air Force Six-Man Group, 1 April 1974–1 May 1975.

64. History, Air Force Six-Man Group.

65. I. B. Holley, Jr., "An Enduring Challenge: The Problem of Air Force Doctrine," US Air Force Academy, the Harmon Memorial Lectures in Military History no. 16, 1974, 11.

66. Four-Man Panel A, "Concept Feasibility Study on Realigning the Doctrine, Concepts and Objectives, Functions and Responsibilities"; History, Directorate of Doctrine, Concepts, and Objectives, January–June 1975, 10.

67. History, Directorate of Doctrine, Concepts, and Objectives, January–June 1975, 10; History, Directorate of Concepts, July–December 1976, 1–3; January–June 1978, vol. 1, pt. 1:1–3; Department of Air Force, Doctrine Information Publication 2 (DIP-2), "How USAF Doctrine Is Developed," 5 October 1978.

68. History, Directorate of Concepts, January–June 1978, vol. 1, pt. 1:1–3.

69. History, Directorate of Plans, January–June 1980, 1:84, 87, 110.

70. History, Directorate of Doctrine, Concepts, and Objectives, January–June 1975, 5; Maj Dennis W. Stiles, "Air Power: A New Look from an Old Rooftop," *Air University Review*, November–December 1975, 49–59.

71. Lt Col David L. Hosley, Doctrine and Concepts Division, Directorate of Plans, deputy chief of staff, Plans & Operations, to addressees, letter, subject: Concept Issue Paper, CIP 81-4, "Deterring Soviet Military Aggression in the 1980s."

72. History, Directorate of Plans, Deputy Chief of Staff/Operational Plans & Readiness, January–June 1980, 1:113; DIP-2, "How USAF Doctrine Is Developed," 5 October 1978; DIP-10, "Background Information on Air Force Perspective for Coherent Plans (Command and Control of TACAIR)," 24 April 1981; memorandum by Col Robert A. Norman, assistant director for joint and

National Security Council matters, Directorate of Plans, Deputy Chief of Staff/Operational Plans & Readiness, for agency chiefs and staff officers assigned to joint and combined staffs, 22 May 1981; DIP-12, "Command Relationships," June 1984.

73. History, Directorate of Doctrine, Concepts, and Objectives, July–December 1975, 24; January–June 1976, 55–56; History, Directorate of Concepts, July–December 1976, 62; and January–June 1977, 74.

74. Lt Col D. L. Hutchinson, "A New Look at an Old Problem," *Air University Review*, January–February 1979, 72.

75. Maj Douglas S. Hawkins, "Concept for Reasoned Change in the Air Force Doctrine Program," research report (Maxwell AFB, Ala.: ACSC, 1978), 17.

76. Ibid.

77. History, Directorate of Concepts, January–June 1977, 76–77; July–December 1977, 82–83.

78. Maj Robert C. Ehrhart, "Some Thoughts on Air Force Doctrine," *Air University Review*, March–April 1980, 30.

79. Ibid.

80. Hutchinson, "A New Look at an Old Problem," 69–73; Hawkins, "Concept for Reasoned Change in the Air Force Doctrine Program," passim.

81. Hawkins, "Concept for Reasoned Change in the Air Force Doctrine Program."

82. Ibid.

83. Ibid.

84. History, Directorate of Concepts, July–December 1977, 82–83.

85. DIP-2, "How USAF Doctrine Is Developed," passim; AFR 1-2, *Assignment of Responsibilities for Development of Doctrine and Mission Employment Tactics*, 22 November 1978.

86. DIP-2, "How USAF Doctrine Is Developed."

87. CIP 79-3, "Concept Development -- What Is It? And Who Needs It?" December 1979, 9–11.

88. Ibid.

89. Ibid.

90. Ibid., 6–10.

91. AFM 1-1, *Functions and Basic Doctrine of the United States Air Force*, 14 February 1979, i.

92. Dr Williamson Murray, "A Tale of Two Doctrines: The Luftwaffe's Conduct of the Air War and the USAF's Manual 1-1," *The Journal of Strategic Studies*, December 1983, 89.

93. Ibid.

94. History, Directorate of Concepts, January–June 1978, 51.

95. AFM 1-1, *Basic Aerospace Doctrine of the United States Air Force*, 10 March 1984, A-5.

96. Ibid.

97. Ibid.

98. Ibid., passim.

99. F. Clifton Berry, Jr., "USAF Doctrine Comes Alive," *Air Force Magazine*, July 1983, 35–36.

100. Murray, "A Tale of Two Doctrines," 89.

101. Ibid.

102. Col David L. Hosley interview, 9 January 1985.

103. Ibid.; House, *1979 DOD Appropriations*, pt. 4:137, 138, 161, 162; Tactical Air Conference, Langley AFB, Va., 11–15 April 1983; AFM 1-1, 16 March 1984, B-4.

104. History, Directorate of Doctrine, Concepts, and Objectives, July–December 1975, 30.

105. History, Directorate of Concepts, January–June 1977, 72–76; History, Directorate of Plans, January–June 1980, 1:110–11; July–December 1980, 1:87; January–June 1981, 1:84; Colonel Hosley interview, 9 January 1985.

106. History, Directorate of Concepts, January–June 1977, 72; July–December 1977, 81; History, Directorate of Plans, January–June 1980, 111; July–December 1980, 87.

107. Maj Gen William R. Yost, "National Space Policy and Aerospace Doctrine," *Air Force Policy Letter for Commanders: Supplement*, January 1980, 7–16.

108. Lt Col David E. Lupton, *On Space Warfare: A Space Power Doctrine* (Maxwell AFB, Ala.: Air University Press, June 1988), 43.

109. Maj Paul Viotti, ed., *The Great Frontier, Military Space Doctrine: The Final Report for the United States Air Force Academy, Military Space Doctrine Symposium, 1–3 April 1981*, 4 vols.; Lt Col Dino A. Lorenzini, "Space Power Doctrine," *Air University Review*, July–August 1982, 16–21.

110. Lorenzini, "Space Power Doctrine," 16–21.

111. Ibid.

112. Ibid.

113. Lupton, *On Space Warfare*, 43; see also Lupton, "Space Doctrines," *Strategic Review*, Fall 1983, 36–45.

114. AFM 1-6, *Military Space Doctrine*, 15 October 1982.

115. Ibid.

116. Ibid.

117. Lupton, "Space Doctrines," 37–38.

118. History, Directorate of Plans, January–June 1980, iii; Lt Col D. L. Hutchinson, "A New Look at an Old Problem," 72; Tactical Air Conference, Langley AFB, Va., 11–15 April 1983; AFR 1-2, *Assignment of Responsibilities for Development of Doctrine and Mission Employment Tactics*, 22 November 1978; AFR 1-2, *Assignment of Responsibilities for Development of Doctrine*, 25 July 1984.

119. Berry, "USAF Doctrine Comes Alive," 84.

120. Ibid.

121. Lt Gen Alvan C. Gillem II, commander, Air University, to commander, Air War College et al., letter, subject: The Lightner Board, 13 September 1972.

122. Air University, Review of Air War College and Air Command and Staff College, 22 March 1973, 24–25.

123. Ibid., 10.

124. Memorandum by W. P. Clements, Jr., chairman, Committee on Excellence in Education, to Department of the Army et al., subject: The Senior Service Colleges: Conclusions and Initiatives, 5 June 1975.

125. History, Directorate of Doctrine, Concepts, and Objectives, January–June 1975, 57.

126. History, Air War College, July 1978–June 1979, 39–40.

127. Ibid., July 1979–June 1980, 23–24.

128. History, Air War College, January–December 1981, 57–60; History, Air University Center for Aerospace Doctrine, Research, and Education, 1983, 1–9; AFR 1-2, 25 July 1984, 5.

129. DIP-2, "How USAF Doctrine Is Developed," 1978, 6.

130. Gen Lew Allen, Jr., chief of staff, US Air Force, to ALMAJCOM/SOA/CC, letter, subject: Project Warrior, 5 February 1982.

131. Ibid.

132. Lt Gen Jerome F. O'Malley, deputy chief of staff, Plans and Operations, to all major commands SOA/CC, letter, subject: Project Warrior, 10 February 1982.

133. Lt Col Dennis M. Drew, "Of Trees and Leaves: A New View of Doctrine," *Air University Review*, January–February 1982, 40–48.

134. Berry, "USAF Doctrine Comes Alive," 35; Col Thomas A. Cardwell III, "One Step Beyond—AirLand Battle, Doctrine not Dogma," *Military Review*, April 1984, 45–51.

135. AFM 1-1, 16 March 1984; "These Are the Air Force's Central Beliefs," *Air Force Policy Letter for Commanders*, 15 June 1984, 2; telephone conversation with Lt Col Clayton R. Frishkorn, Jr., 11 January 1985; Berry, "USAF Doctrine Comes Alive," 34–36.

136. AFM 1-1, 16 March 1984, vii.

137. Ibid.

Lt Gen George G. Loving, Jr.,
a student at the
Air Command and Staff School,
1955-56.

Col David R. McNabb,
publisher of DIP-2,
"How USAF Doctrine Is
Developed."

Col John L. Piotrowski,
member Six-Man Group.

Lt Gen Alvan C. Gillem II,
commander of Air University.

Col L. J. Siegert,
member Six-Man Group.

Gen Nathan F. Twining,
member Six-Man Group.

Maj Gen William Y. Smith,
director of doctrine, concepts,
and objectives.

INDEX

A-1: 208, 267, 301, 483
A-3D: 199
A-4: 485, 644
A-4D: 47, 288
A-4M: 520
A-6: 270, 276
A-6A: 520
A-7: 270, 276, 470, 473, 479, 482–83, 528–29, 556, 558, 563
A-7A (Ling-Temco-Vought): 121, 471–72, 482
A-7B: 482
A-7 Corsair II: 120
A-7D: 297, 472, 476, 482–83, 503, 526, 528–29
A-9: 528
A-10: 486, 498, 501, 503, 508–9, 529, 532, 543, 557, 559–63
A-11: 116, 431
A-37: 267, 275–76, 301
AAH: 530, 532
AC-1 Caribou: 181
AC-47: 307
AC-119: 310
AC-130: 130, 276, 294, 310, 668
AC-130A: 307
AC-130H: 669
AH-1G: 517, 519, 521, 527
AH-56: 472
AH-56A: 518–19, 521–27, 539
AV-8A Harrier: 520, 523–24, 526
ABCCC. *See* airborne battlefield command and control center
Abrahamson, James A.: 694
Abrams, Creighton W.: 262–65, 285, 530, 539, 602–3, 606, 636
Academic Instructor School: 318
ACSC. *See* Air Command and Staff College
Adams, Paul D.: 152–53, 190–91, 312–13
ADCOM: 690

ADC. *See* Air Defense Command
Addabbo, Joseph P.: 426, 489
Advanced aerial fire support system (AAFSS): 518, 522
Advanced ballistic reentry system (ABRES): 344
Advanced Civil/Military Aircraft (ACMA): 665
Advanced location strike system (ALSS): 483, 489, 545
Advanced manned precision strike system (AMPSS): 110
Advanced manned strategic aircraft (AMSA): 389, 392, 393–97, 399
design configuration of: 394
Advanced medium-range air-to-air missile (AMRAAM): 563, 565
Advanced medium STOL transport (AMST): 657–58, 660
Advanced Research Projects Agency: 317
Advanced tactical fighter (ATF): 563, 565–66
Advanced Tanker Cargo Aircraft (ATCA): 656
Advanced technology bomber (ATB): 373
Advanced technology stealth bomber: 377, 421–23, 425
Advisers
in Vietnam (US): 279
AEC. *See* Atomic Energy Commission
Aeronautics and Astronautics Coordinating Board
designed to: 141
responsibilities: 140
Aerospace
acceptance of term: 213
AFM 1–2, *United States Air Force Basic Doctrine* (1959), description of: 231

751

Aerospace Defense Command (ADCOM): 446, 448, 686, 697, 715, 727
  disestablishing of: 448
Aerospace forces
  AFM 1–1, *United States Air Force Basic Doctrine*, definition of, August 1964: 235
Aerospace Medical Division
  establishment of: 166
Aerospace Policy Division
  major functions of: 171
Aerospace Rescue and Recovery Services (ARRS): 668
Aerospace Studies Institute: 319
Aerothermodynamic structural systems environmental test (ASSET) project
  expansion of: 225
Afghanistan: 563, 650, 658
AFM 1–1, *Aerospace Doctrine, United States Air Force Basic Doctrine*: 716–23, 725–26, 730, 732, 734, 736–37, 739, 743–45
AFM 1–1, *Functions and Basic Doctrine of the United States Air Force*: 552, 690, 702
AFM 1–1, *United States Air Force Basic Doctrine*
  doctrinal change to concept of national security: 233
  14 August 1964 version of: 232
  publication of: 192
AFM 1–2, *United States Air Force Basic Doctrine*
  as of December 1959: 171, 231, 711–14, 716, 737
AFM 1–3, *Doctrine and Procedures for Aerospace Control in the Combat Zone*: 718, 737
AFM 1–5, *Theater Nuclear Doctrine*: 737
AFM 1–6, *Military Space Doctrine*: 698, 700–701, 737–39, 744
AFM 1–7, *Chemical Warfare Doctrine*: 737
AFM 1–9, *Doctrine for Electromagnetic Combat*: 737

AFM 1–10, *Combat Support Doctrine*: 737–38
AFM 2–Series: 739
AFM 2–1, *Tactical Air Operations—Counterair, Close Air Support, and Air Interdiction*: 551, 740
AFM 2–4, *Tactical Air Force Operations—Tactical Airlift*: 626
AFM 2–6, *Tactical Air Operations—Reconnaissance*: 740
AFM 2–10, *Tactical Air Operations—Employment of Air Delivered Target Activated Munitions*: 740
AFM 2–21, *Strategic Airlift*: 626
AFM 2–31, *Aerospace Environmental Operations*: 740
AFM 2–XC: 740
AFM 3–Series: 740
AFR 1–1, *Aerospace Doctrine: Responsibilities for Doctrine Development*
  description: 191
  issuance of: 191
AFR 1–1, *Responsibilities for Doctrine Development*: 714–15
AFR 1–2, *Assignment of Responsibilities for Development of Doctrine and Mission Employment Tactics*: 732–33, 739–40, 742
Agan, Arthur C.: 468, 471, 626
AGM (air-to-ground missile). *See* missiles, Hound Dog, and Skybolt
Agnew, Spiro: 684
AIM-7. *See* missile, Sparrow
AIM-9. *See* missile, Sidewinder
Air Assault 2 exercise: 188
Airborne battlefield command and control center (ABCCC): 283, 307
Airborne early warning (AEW): 505
Airborne warning and control system (AWACS): 296, 479, 503–6, 508, 538–39, 546
Air Command and Staff College (ACSC): 318
Air commands
  operations: 258
  training: 257

752

Aircraft nuclear propulsion (ANP) program
  cancellation of: 201
  description of: 200
  development expenditure on: 201
  JCS position on: 201
Aircraft research
  McNamara's views: 198
Air Defense Command (ADC/ADCOM): 289, 606, 689, 697
Air doctrine: 487, 500
  1963 commentary on: 172
  Smith's comments: 172
Air Doctrine Branch
  role of: 163
Air Force Advisory Group: 722
Air Force/Army Reconnaissance Force Study: 545
Air Force Communications Service (AFCS): 606, 668
Air Force Council: 725
Air Force doctrinal projects
  responsible agencies: 184
Air Force doctrine: 711–16, 720, 724–26, 728–41, 742–43, 745
"Air Force Doctrine on Air Superiority": 471
Air Force Future Concepts Project Worldbook: 726
Air Force Information Policy Letter for Commanders: 171–72, 717
Air Force Institute of Technology (AFIT): 695
Air Force Logistics Command (formerly Air Materiel Command): 632
  designation of: 166
  mission of: 167
Air Force Magazine: 551, 740
Air Force Reserve: 509, 556, 563–64, 627–28, 630–31, 635, 649, 665
Air Force Scientific Advisory Board: 481
Air Force/Space Digest
  on nuclear doctrine: 91
Air Force Special Air Warfare (SAWC)
  establishment of: 178
Air Force Systems Command (formerly Air Research and Development Command): 470, 481, 489, 561, 638, 657
  Council, establishment of: 171
  designation of: 166
Air Force Tactical Air Warfare Center: 555
Air Force 2000: 566
Air-ground doctrine
  development of: 178
  proposals for change: 174
Air interdiction: 469, 474, 476, 480–82, 487–88, 492, 494–95, 499, 520, 528–29, 532–33, 535, 538, 547–49, 551–52, 554–56, 565
  definition of: 298
AirLand Battle: 540, 543, 546–55, 566
"AirLand Battle 2000": 566
Air-land forces application (ALFA): 540–41, 554
Airlift: 623
  in Vietnam War: 311–16
Airlift control center (ALCC): 313
Airlift control element (ALCE): 313
Airlift Service Industrial Fund: 623
Air Materiel Command (AMC): 12–13
  reorganization of: 166
  responsibilities of (1950–51): 164
Airmobile concept
  testing of: 188
Airmobility concept
  evaluation of: 189
Air National Guard (ANG): 19, 21, 38, 45–47, 509, 556–57, 563–64, 627, 630, 635
Air power
  in Southeast Asia: 318
  in Vietnam War: 323
"Air Power: A New Look from an Old Rooftop": 729
Airpower in Three Wars: 321
Air Research and Development Command (ARDC)
  establishment of: 160
  functional organization of: 165
  responsibilities of (1950–51): 164
Airspace management: 541

Air Staff: 50, 318, 320–21, 468, 471, 473, 626, 647
  Board (formerly Systems Review Board)
    establishment of: 170
  reorganization, 1961
    alignment with AFSC and AFLC: 167
  reorganization, 1963: 170
Air Standardization Coordinating Committee (ASCC): 719
Air superiority: 468–71, 473–74, 476, 484–85, 487–88, 492–96, 501–3, 520, 528, 531–33, 539, 548, 551, 556, 559, 566
Air suppport operations center (ASOC): 300
Air supremacy: 474, 476, 532
Air-to-air combat: 486
Air Training Command (ATC): 742
Air Transport Command (ATC): 623
AIRTRANS 70: 624
Air University (AU): 317–22, 722, 727, 731, 738, 741–42
  Aerospace Studies Institute: 318
  doctrinal changes: 160
Air war
  in Vietnam, evaluations of: 316–23
Air War College: 318, 487, 546, 552
Alaskan Command: 605, 645
Aldrich, Edward C., Jr.: 695
Aldrin, Edwin, Jr.: 682
Allen, James R.: 665, 668
Allen, Lew, Jr.: 356, 359, 360–61, 366–68, 372–73, 387–88, 400–403, 420, 423, 447, 449, 451, 504, 509–10, 515, 538, 558, 561, 563–64, 566, 613, 654, 658, 697, 735, 742
Allied Air Forces Central Europe (AAFCE): 497–98, 500, 504
Allied Command Europe: 515, 602
Allied Forces Central Europe (AFCENT): 498
Allied Officer School: 318
Allied Tactical Publication (ATP) 8, *Amphibious Operations:* 737
Allied Tactical Publication (ATP) 27, *Offensive Air Support Operations:* 737
Allied Tactical Publication (ATP) 27(B), *Offensive Air Support:* 552
Allied Tactical Publication (ATP) 33, *NATO Tactical Air Doctrine:* 719, 736–37
Allied Tactical Publication (ATP) 34, *Tactical Air Support of Maritime Operations:* 737
Allied Tactical Publication (ATP) 40, *Doctrine and Procedures for Airspace Control in a Combat Zone:* 736–37
Allied Tactical Publication (ATP) 41, *Airmobile Operations:* 737
Allied Tactical Publication (ATP) 42, *Counter Air Operations:* 737
Allied Tactical Publication (ATP) 44, *Electronic Warfare in Air Operations:* 737
"All volunteer" military force: 478
ALQ-99: 297
Altus Air Force Base, Oklahoma: 640
AMPSS. *See* high altitude, advanced manned precision strike system
Analytic Services Inc.
  establishment of: 194
Anderson, George W., Jr.: 46, 55, 62, 136, 203
Anderson, Norman J.: 283
Anderson, Rudolph, Jr.: 80
Anderson, S. E.: 164–65
An Khe: 268
An Loc: 268, 274–75
Annam Mountain Range: 304
Anthis, Rollen H.: 281
Antiballistic missile (ABM) system
  signing of treaty: 438, 442
  Schlesinger's comments on development: 443
  studies of options: 439
  treaty: 344, 443
  treaty of 1972: 686
Antisatellite (ASAT)
  capability: 688, 696–97, 703
  program: 450–51

Antisubmarine warfare (ASW): 45
Apollo: 677, 681, 683–84, 688
Appropriations Act of 1962: 34
AQM-34: 544–45
Arab: 641
  armies: 641
  oil embargo: 645
Arab-Israeli conflict: 680
Arab-Israeli wars: 483
Armed Forces Journal International: 612
Armored personnel carrier (APC): 490–91
Arms control and limited nuclear test ban: 102
Armstrong, Neil: 682
Army. *See* US Army
Army Air Corps: 479
Army Air Forces. *See* Headquarters Army Air Forces
Army and Air Force Concepts, Strike Command Tests: 182
Army Forces, Atlantic: 78
Army of Vietnam (ARVN): 299, 300
Army War College
  objectives of: 173
Arnold, Henry H.: 340
AS 45–3, *Tactical Air Operations:* 719
AS 45–13, *Air Space Control in the Combat Zone:* 719
A Shau valley: 307
"Assured destruction": 338
ASW. *See* antisubmarine warfare
Atlantic Treaty Association Conference: 506
Atomic Energy Commission (AEC): 102
Attack helicopter controversy: 516–31
AWACS. *See* airborne warning and control system
Azores: 641, 644, 655

B-1: 344, 347, 354, 359, 366–67, 369, 377, 385, 389, 391, 396–98, 401–19, 421–26, 449, 479, 507, 564, 664
  Brookings Institution study of: 403
  cost-effectiveness alternatives: 401
  costs of (RDT&E and O&M): 397
  Dougherty's views on: 405
  fiscal year 1975 budget for: 398
  program: 402–3, 409, 417, 419
B-1A: 424
B-1B: 366, 373, 424–26
B-17: 34, 204
B-24: 204
B-26: 204
B-29: 34
B-36: 28, 34, 41
B-47: 28–29, 33–34, 37, 44, 58, 386, 535, 630
B-52: 8, 28–29, 33, 35, 37, 44, 51, 58, 62, 78, 97, 98, 109–10, 117, 260–61, 264–68, 270–71, 275, 282, 286–87, 294, 296–97, 301–3, 307, 309–10, 318–19, 334, 354, 359, 373, 377, 386–87, 390, 392, 394, 396, 401, 406–7, 410–12, 414–20, 422, 425, 481, 536–38, 601, 636, 667
B-52A: 392
B-52C: 392–93, 395, 396
B-52D: 395, 425–26, 536
B-52F: 392–93, 395–96
B-52G: 372, 392–93, 396, 410–11, 415–16, 418, 420, 425–26
B-52H: 51, 392–93, 396, 410–11, 415, 418, 420, 425–26, 538, 667
B-52I: 401, 414
B-52X: 417–18
B-57: 121
B-58: 28–29, 34, 44, 90, 98, 110, 334, 392–93, 395–96
B-66: 199
B-70: 22, 28–30, 33–35, 44, 51–52, 54–55, 90, 93, 100, 109–10, 165, 200, 334, 336, 340, 389–91, 395
  Brown's opposition to: 390
  controversy: 389–91
B-747: 660, 664
Backfire bomber: 438, 512–13, 538
Bai Phong: 267

755

Baker, Kemper N.: 317
Balance of terror: 88
Ball, George: 77
   and Cuban missile crisis: 82
Ballistic missile boost intercept (Bambi) concept
   use of: 218, 679
Ballistic missile defense (BMD): 701
Ballistic missile early warning system (BMEWS): 115
   station: 450
Bangkok: 632
Ban Karai Pass: 307
Ban Me Thuot: 274–75
Ban Raving Pass: 304
Barbados: 669
Barksdale Air Force Base, Louisiana: 656
Barrell Roll: 304
Barrow, Robert H.: 616
Barton, Jim: 735
Basic air cavalry concept
   1964 thoughts on: 235
   tests of: 177
Basic doctrine
   AFM 1–1, *United States Air Force Basic Doctrine*, definition of, August 1964: 235
Basic National Security Policy papers: 26
Bat Lake: 267
Battelle Memorial Institute: 319
Battlefield air interdiction (BAI): 551–55, 558
Bay of Pigs invasion: 36, 75, 586
Beach, Dwight D.: 190
Beck, Michael: 553
Beirut: 638
Bekáa Valley, Lebanon: 556
Belgium: 474, 496, 500, 503, 513–15
   air force: 468
Bell Aircraft Company: 527
Benelux: 475, 491
Berlin, Germany: 15, 35, 37–38, 638
   airlift: 15, 623
   crisis: 37–39, 42, 45, 468, 474
   West. *See* Germany

Berry, F. Clifton, Jr.: 740
Bien Hoa: 260, 314, 633
Big Lift: 122, 628
Binh Thuy Air Base: 276
Binh Trams: 305
Birchard, Glenn R.
   on C-141: 122
Biryuzov, S. S.: 220
Bison aircraft: 429, 536
Bisplinghoff, Raymond Lewis: 398, 640
   committee: 640
Bitburg Air Base, West Germany: 508
Blackhawk helicopter: 527
Blanchard, George: 550
Blitz Fighter, The: 735
Blue Gemini: 143
   vehicles: 219
Blue Light: 633
Blue Ribbon Defense Panel: 587–600
Bode, John R.: 528
Boeing: 28, 111, 473, 544, 638, 656–57, 660, 663
   707: 483
   747: 655–56, 660, 662, 664
Boerfink, West Germany: 498
Bombing
   Cambodia: 264, 272, 287, 601
   North Vietnam: 260, 264, 303, 306, 308, 323, 601
Bomb safety line: 552. *See also* fire support coordination line (FSCL)
Bonny Jack. *See* MAC, Operations Order 9–68
Boushey, H. A.: 212
Bowers, Ray L.: 311
Bowman, Richard C.: 232, 504, 715
Boyd, John: 735–36
Boylan, George S., Jr.: 475, 520, 556–57
Bradley, Mark E.: 164, 166, 173
Bray, Leslie W., Jr.: 546–48, 722, 726
Brehm, William: 603, 610
Brezhnev, Leonid I.: 335, 514
British Institute for Strategic Studies: 77
Brooke, Edward W.: 342–43, 345

Brooks, Overton: 213
Brown, Bruce K.: 698
Brown, George S.: 263, 347, 350, 353, 362, 390, 398, 416, 445, 482, 487, 489, 494, 496, 502, 529, 530, 532–33, 539–40, 542, 586–87, 601, 603–5, 608, 610, 641, 647, 727
Brown, Harold: 55, 62, 169, 197, 205, 207–8, 211, 218, 337–38, 340, 351–57, 360–63, 375, 390–95, 409–10, 416–19, 421–22, 432, 438–40, 447, 471, 480, 493, 507, 510, 513–14, 607–10, 615–16, 630, 648–51, 656–58, 660–61, 678, 681–82
  orbital weapons, views on: 226
  orbiting nuclear weapons: 107
  on pressing the state of the art (of aircraft design) too much: 101
  on visual light attack (VAL) aircraft: 120
Brown, Stuart W.: 727
Brussels: 506
Brzezinski, Zbigniew: 354, 362
Budget (US)
  1964: 91, 95
  1965, defense: 107
Buffalo. *See* CV-7
Bundy, McGeorge: 134
Burchinal, David A.: 48, 475, 491
Bureau of the Budget: 478
Burke, Arleigh: 6, 147
  on limited nuclear test ban treaty: 105
Burke, Kelly H.: 418, 424, 426–27, 515, 556, 561–62, 564–65, 664, 694
Burtenshaw, Edward C.: 317

C-5: 316, 683
C-5A: 123, 487, 624–26, 628–32, 636–40, 642–46, 653, 655, 658, 660, 662–65
C-5B: 663–64
C-5N: 663
C-7 Caribou: 314. *See also* Caribou
C-9: 669
C-17: 664–65, 668
C-46: 13
C-54: 258
C-97: 14, 38, 47, 630–31, 645
C-118: 38, 47, 645
C-119: 11–12, 630
C-121: 630
C-123: 11–12, 90, 313–14, 517
C-124: 11–12, 38, 47, 90, 123, 627, 629–31, 633, 635
C-130: 11–12, 20–21, 30, 122–23, 182, 187–89, 265, 274–76, 314–16, 483, 517, 626, 629–30, 633, 635–36, 639, 641–42, 645–46, 653, 656–57, 662, 664–65, 669
C-130A: 274, 307
C-130E: 90, 95
C-131: 645
C-133: 14, 20, 47, 123, 314, 627, 629, 633, 635
C-135: 20–21, 47, 123, 627, 629–30, 646
C-135B: 114
C-140: 669
C-141: 47, 90, 123, 182, 314, 316, 483, 487, 625–33, 635–37, 639–40, 642–44, 646, 653–55, 657–58, 662, 664–65, 668
C-141A: 122, 654
C-141B: 654, 663, 665
CH-47 Chinook: 189
CH-53: 653
CV-2 Caribou: 312–13, 518. *See also* Caribou
CV-7 Buffalo: 313, 518
C-X: 652, 656, 658, 660–61, 663–64
CX-HLS (cargo experimental heavy logistics support): 123, 637
Cambodia: 258, 260–61, 263, 271–72, 274–75, 287, 299, 304, 308, 315, 601
  bombing of: 264, 272, 287, 601
  diplomatic and military assistance to: 255
  US incursion into: 265
"Camel": 97

Camp New Amsterdam, Netherlands: 508
Cam Ranh Bay: 275, 314, 636
Canada: 501
 air force: 468
Canby, Stephen L.: 499, 500
Canedy, Charles R.: 545
Cannon, Howard W.: 520, 524–27, 529
Cape Canaveral range area
 management responsibilities as stated by McNamara and Webb: 143
Cardwell, Thomas A.: 729, 732
Carey, Gerald J., Jr.: 555
Cargo experimental heavy logistics support (CX-HLS) aircraft: 123
Caribou. *See also* CV-2 and C-7 transport planes: 177, 182
 Caribou I: 189
Carlton, Paul K.: 316, 637, 641–47, 653
Carlucci, Frank C.: 564, 664–66
Carpenter, John W.: 317
CASF. *See* composite air strike force
Carter, Jimmy: 352–54, 356, 358–60, 362–63, 369, 387, 391, 409–10, 417, 419, 421, 506–9, 538, 563, 602, 606–8, 649–50, 656–57, 679, 688–90, 696
 State of the Union message: 650
Castro, Fidel: 36, 75
 and Cuban missile crisis: 81
Casualties
 American, in Vietnam War: 264
Cease-fire
 in Vietnam War: 263, 271–73, 294, 316
Centalign B machines: 352
Central Highlands: 302
Centralization of authority
 secretary of defense: 156
Centralization of defense space activities: 141
Central Intelligence Agency (CIA): 263, 304
Chaff: 288, 295, 297, 298
Chaffee, John H.: 601

Chambers, William R.: 723–24
Chapman, Leonard, Jr.: 283–85
Charleston (Air Force Base, South Carolina): 639–40
Charyk, Joseph V.: 54, 202
CHECO (Contempory Historical Examination of Current Operations): 316–17, 322
Chemical warfare: 509
Cheyenne. *See* AH-56A
Cheyenne Mountain Complex: 696–97
China (People's Republic of): 52, 623
Chu Lai: 636
Church, Dale W.: 658
CIA. *See* Central Intelligence Agency
CINCMAC (commander in chief, Military Airlift Command): 646, 648, 654, 658, 660, 668
CINCMEAFSA: 659
CINCPAC (commander in chief, Pacific): 277–81, 285–87, 604
CINCPACAF (commander in chief, Pacific Air Forces): 285–86, 289, 299, 317, 604, 727
CINCPACFLT (commander in chief, Pacific Fleet): 285–86
CINCRED: 659
CINCREDCOM: 659, 663, 667
CINCSAC (commander in chief, Strategic Air Command): 286, 296, 585, 667
CINCSTRIKE: 659
CINCUNC/COMUSKOREA: 604
CINCUSAFE: 727
CIP 79-3, "Concept Development—What Is It? And Who Needs It?": 733–34
Circular error probable (CEP): 288
 accuracy: 340
Civil Aeronautics Board (CAB): 19
Civil Reserve Air Fleet (CRAF): 11, 14–15, 19, 21, 628–29, 631–32, 640–41, 652–55, 658, 662, 664–65
Clark Air Base, Philippines: 633
Clark, Don A.: 723
Clark, William P.: 370

Clarke, Albert P.: 322
Clay, Lucius D., Jr.: 286, 444–45
Clayton, W. Graham: 663
Clearwater: 122
Clements, William P., Jr.: 641, 647, 741
Cleveland, Charles G.: 742
Clifford, Clark M.: 145, 262, 395
Close air support: 469–70, 472–74, 476, 478, 482–89, 492, 494–95, 498–99, 501, 503, 508, 516–34, 541–42, 547, 552–59, 561
  aircraft (A-X): 718
  Army definition of: 518
  board, Air Force: 183
  board, Army: 183
  JCS definition of: 522
  joint doctrine for: 531–32
  in Vietnam War: 298–311
Close-support missions
  1950s controversy over: 174
Cobra helicopter. *See* AH-16
Cold war: 56
College Eye radar: 294
Collins, Harold E.: 484, 488–89, 529
Collins, J. Lawton: 173
Collocated operating base (COB): 508–10
Columbia: 694
Columbia University: 318
COMAC (commander, Military Airlift Command): 648
Combat air patrol (CAP): 289
Combat Fox airlift: 631, 635
Combat Lancer: 479
Combat operations center (COC): 313
Combined Arms Combat Developments Activity: 657
Command and General Staff College: 550
Command, control, communications, computing/information and intelligence (C^4I^2): 566
Commander in chief, Pacific. *See* CINCPAC
Commander in chief, Pacific Air Forces. *See* CINCPACAF

Commander in chief, Pacific Fleet. *See* CINCPACFLT
Commander in chief, Strategic Air Command. *See* CINCSAC
Commander, US Southeast Asia (COMUSSEASIA): 278
Commando Hunt: 262, 308–10
Committee on Government Operations: 17
Communists: 40–41
  forces: 56
  party: 23
  state: 57
  subversion in Laos: 36
  threat: 35
Communist China: 280, 303, 307, 310, 477, 491, 507
Communist insurgency
  in Vietnam: 299
Communist menace: 87
Communist Policy Towards Southeast Asia, 1954–1969: 319
Compass Cope: 544–45
Composite air strike force (CASF)
  deployments: 11
COMUSMACV. *See* US Military Assistance Command, Vietnam
COMUSSEASIA. *See* commander, US Southeast Asia
CONARC. *See* Headquarters Continental Army Command
Concept for Improved Joint Air-Ground Coordination: 300, 518
"Concept Issue Papers" (CIPs): 729, 733–34
"Concept of Operations for USAF Forces Collateral Functions Training, The": 536
Concurrency concept
  Brown, Harold, on: 169
  operational weapon systems: 168
  Wilson, Roscoe, description of: 169
Congo: 638
Congress (US): 6, 8, 17, 20–21, 23, 26–27, 34–37, 40–41, 43, 51, 53–55, 510, 512, 629, 637, 652, 654, 658, 661, 663–64

and Cambodia: 265
congressionally mandated mobility study (CMMS): 661, 664–65
and Vietnam War: 272–75
Consolidated space operations center (CSOC): 451, 690, 695–97
    objective of: 451
Constant Guard: 636
Constant Guard II: 636
Constant Guard III: 636
Constant Guard IV: 636
Contemporary Historical Examination of Current Operations. *See* CHECO
Continental Air Defense Command (CONAD): 604
Continental air and missile defenses: 113
Continental Army Forces: 78
Contingency planning for Southeast Asia: 278
Con Thien: 261
Controlled flexible response: 107
Control of space
    Boushey's comments: 212
    Pratt's comments: 212
    White's address: 212
CONUS (continental United States): 429, 433, 444–45, 447, 449, 640, 668
Coolidge committee: 2–3
Cooper, Robert S.: 693–95
Corcoran, Charles A.: 610
Corona Harvest: 315, 318–22, 645
    Steering Committee: 320–21
Cosmos satellites: 687
Coulee Crest: 300
Council on Foreign Relations: 722
Counterair: 469, 471, 488, 492, 494, 496
Counterforce strategy: 32, 59, 337
Counterinsurgency
    aircraft, 1963–64: 207
    course, AU: 178
    light armed reconnaissance aircraft (COIN/LARA), development of: 208

programs, establishment of: 178
    in Southeast Asia: 257
    in Vietnam: 259
Countervailing strategy: 352, 355, 362–63, 371–72
    Brown's idea of: 362
CRAF. *See* Civil Reserve Air Fleet
Credible Comet: 718
Creech, Wilbur L.: 508, 546, 554, 561, 562–66, 667
Creek Braille: 541
Crested CAP: 475
Cruise missile carriers (CMCs): 418
Cua Viet River: 273
Cuba: 650, 660
    Guantánamo Bay: 78
    Soviet missiles in: 75–76
    troops: 668
Cuban missile crisis: 75–87, 535, 716
    evaluations: 82
    politico-military effects: 86
Culver, John C.: 600
Currie, Malcolm R.: 335, 488, 490
Cushman, Robert E., Jr.: 283–84
Cutler, Robert: 133
Czechoslovakia: 475–77, 490–91

DHC-4 Twin Otter: 177
Dak To: 261–62, 268, 273
D'Amato, Alfonse M.: 562
Da Nang: 260, 273–75, 288, 290, 301, 316, 636–37
DASC. *See* direct air support center
Data base inventory (DABIN): 318
Davis, Bennie L.: 373, 388, 742
Davis, Geoffrey C., Jr.: 723
Davis, Lynn Etheridge: 353
Dayan, Moshe: 485
Dean, Fred M.: 183
DeBellevue, Charles B.: 296
Decker, George H.: 30, 45, 175
Defense Advanced Research Projects Agency: 693
Defense agencies
    establishment of: 156
    trend toward: 156

Defense Appropriations Act: 117
Defense Authorization Act, 1981: 426
Defense Communications Agency (DCA): 586, 689
  establishment of: 151
Defense Communications Planning Group (DCPG): 306–7
Defense of Europe, nuclear: 467–76
Defense Intelligence Agency (DIA): 304, 586
  establishment of: 151
Defense meteorological satellite program (DMSP): 696
Defense Reorganization Act of 1958: 155, 277, 584, 601
Defense research and development
  congressional changes in attitude toward: 211
Defense space program
  categories of projects: 222
Defense Supply Agency (DSA): 586
  establishment of: 156
Defense suppression: 487–89
Defense Systems Acquisition Review Council (DSARC): 517, 528–29, 540 DSARC-II: 358, 360
Defense unification
  changing Air Force views: 155
De Gaulle, Charles: 60, 474, 475
  and independent French nuclear deterrent: 91
DeLauer, Richard D.: 425, 695
Demilitarized zone (DMZ): 259–61, 266–69, 273, 277, 281, 294, 304–6, 308, 311, 323
Democratic party: 21
Denmark: 503
Department of Defense (DOD): 2, 6, 8–9, 11, 13, 15, 17, 19–26, 28, 30, 34–37, 40, 45, 47–48, 53–56, 60–61, 478, 490, 493, 500, 507, 514, 523, 526–27, 531–32, 537, 627, 637, 645, 650, 652, 657–58
  Appropriations Act for 1962: 34
  Authorization Act of 1981: 652, 661
  Close Air Support Report: 524

Committee on Excellence in Education (Clements Board): 741
  directives: 689
  North American Air Defense Master Plan: 449
  policymaking procedures: 135
  program package budget, establishment of: 149
  research and development, restricting of: 206
Department of State. *See* US State Department
DePuy, William E.: 531, 539–42, 548–49
Desert Strike: 300
Designated Systems Management Group
  establishment of: 168
Designated systems management procedures
  establishment of: 168
Deterrence
  Brown, Harold, comments on Soviet view of: 357
  national policy of: 349
  TACAIR resources in: 476–90
Deterrent or Defense: 1
Development concept paper (DCP): 517
DIA. *See* Defense Intelligence Agency
DIP-2, "How USAF Doctrine Is Developed": 732–34, 742
DIP-10, "Background Information on Air Force Perspective for Coherent Plans (Command and Control of TACAIR)": 730
DIP-12, "Command Relationships": 730, 737
Direct aerial fire support, Army definition of: 518
Direct air support center (DASC): 265, 300, 518–19
Directorate of air-land forces application (DALFA): 540
Directorate of Doctrine, Concepts, and Objectives: 647
Directorate of Space: 685

Disco. *See* EC-121T
Disosway Board
 report: 180
Disosway, Gabriel P.: 180, 473
Dixon, Robert J.: 488, 512, 530–31,
 539–42, 544, 558–59, 606
DMZ. *See* demilitarized zone
Dobrynin, Anatoly F.: 344
Doctrine
 Adam's definition of: 190
 NATO definition of: 500
 overseas area air defense
  agreement on (1962): 175
 Strike Command's definition of: 190
"Doctrine and Procedures for Airspace
 Control in a Combat Zone": 500
Dong Hoi: 267
Dotson, Robert S.: 551
Dougherty, Russell E.: 334, 404–9,
 537, 585, 611
Douglas: 638
Douhet, Giulio: 692
Dover Air Force Base, Delaware: 631,
 639–40, 642, 644
Doyle, John P.: 12
Draft presidential memorandum (DPM)
 on Tactical Air Forces: 476
Drew, Dennis M.: 743
"Dromedary": 97
 long-endurance aircraft: 55
Drysdale, Taylor: 161–62
 study groups: 161
Dual basing: 475
DuBridge, Lee A.: 212
Duc Phong: 274
Dulles, John Foster: 3
Duplication of tactical air: 531–32
Dutch air force: 498
Dyess Air Force Base, Texas: 655
Dyna-Soar: 142, 165, 219, 677–78, 680
 cancellation of: 225
 criticism of: 217
 examination of: 224
 termination of: 144

E-2: 504

E-2A: 431
E-3A: 445, 504–6, 508
E-3B: 447
EA-6B: 297
EB-66: 293, 636
EB-66C Brown Cradle: 290
EC-121: 289–90, 431, 506, 535
EC-121R: 307
EC-121T (Disco): 294
 radar control aircraft: 296
EF-111A: 489
Eade, George J.: 256
Eagle-Missileer project
 cancellation of: 200
 description of: 200
Easter offensive: 268–69, 274, 294,
 308–10, 323. *See also* Tet offensive
ECM. *See* electronic countermeasures
Economics Club of New York City: 9
Edwards AFB, California: 528, 561
Eglin AFB, Florida: 257, 555
Egypt: 483–84, 490, 641, 667
Egyptian Third Army: 485
Ehrhart, Robert C.: 731
18-nation disarmament conference: 103
Eighth Air Force: 606
8th Tactical Fighter Wing: 292
834th Air Division: 313–15
Eisenhower, Dwight D.: 1, 3, 6–7,
 9–10, 19, 21–22, 24–25, 27–30, 37,
 39, 155, 173, 196, 200, 279, 369,
 377, 438, 584, 587–88, 677
 and JCS: 86
 and voluntary suspension of nuclear
  tests: 102
Elbe River: 490
Electronic
 detection system: 307
 warfare: 488
Electronic countermeasures (ECM):
 274
Ellender, Allen J.: 211
Ellis, Richard H.: 321, 333, 359–61,
 366, 368, 372, 387, 389, 417–18,
 420–21, 423–24, 448, 538
El Toro: 636
Emergency War Plans: 623

Employment of Air Power Planning Advisory Group: 741
Enclave strategy
in Vietnam War: 260
England AFB, Louisiana: 559
Enhanced Tactical Fighter (ETF): 561
Enthoven, Alain C.: 288, 310, 470, 476, 547, 624
Essential equivalence, description of: 362
Estes, Howell M., Jr.: 625–26, 628–30, 633, 637–38
European Command: 646
Evans, William J.: 504
Everest, Frank F.: 152, 177

F-4: 119, 121, 147, 158, 200, 266, 268–70, 276, 291, 295, 297, 301, 305, 307, 310, 347, 444, 449, 468–70, 472–74, 479, 483, 502–3, 520, 529, 537, 556, 562, 563, 636, 641, 644
F-4 Pathfinder: 297
F-4A: 47
F-4B: 290
F-4C: 47, 90, 95, 116, 187, 288, 290–93, 430
F-4D: 294
F-4E: 295, 472, 485, 486, 489
F-4G: 542
F-4H: 46–47, 199
F-4H-1: 196
F-5: 175, 267, 276, 563
F-8U-3: 196
F-12: 431–33, 493
F-12A: 431
F-14: 276, 447, 502
F-15: 424, 447–49, 451–52, 479, 501–3, 508, 539, 556, 560–63, 565, 683, 696, 703
F-15E: 565–66
F-16: 447, 449, 502–3, 509, 515, 554, 556–58, 562–63, 566, 694
F-16E: 565
F-16XL: 565–66
F-18: 502, 561

F-84: 46, 511
F-86 Sabre: 199, 430, 435, 503
F-89: 430, 435
F-100: 121, 289, 291, 301, 430, 435, 469, 502, 556
F-100B (redesignated as the F-107A): 196
F-100F: 291, 305
F-101: 121, 432, 434–35, 445, 447
F-102: 121–22, 430, 434–35
F-104 Thud: 38, 174, 434–35, 468, 501
F-105 Thunderchief: 31, 46–47, 119, 121, 165, 196, 199–200, 268, 288–90, 292–93, 297, 469, 479, 556
F-105G: 291, 636
F-106: 164, 432–33, 444, 447, 449, 468
F-106X: 432–33
F-108: 116
F-110A: 47
F-111: 46, 270, 276, 334, 359, 392–93, 396, 424, 431, 468–69, 472, 476, 480, 482, 495, 503, 508, 515, 537, 554, 556, 558, 565–66
capabilities of: 479
problems with: 480–81
F-111 (TFX): 114, 119
F-111A: 121, 203–5, 469–70, 479, 481, 489
blind bombing system of: 480
F-111B: 203–5, 470, 473, 479
F-111D: 424, 480–81
F-111E: 481
F-111F: 481, 508
FB-111: 347, 359, 366–67, 387, 393–96, 401–2, 407, 411, 414, 418, 420, 422, 424
FB-111A: 393, 420–21
FB-111B: 367, 420–24
FB-111C: 367, 420–24
FB-111D: 420–21
FB-111G: 401
FB-111H: 419–20
FJ-Fury: 199
F-X: 470, 473–74
Fabyanic, Thomas A.: 741
FAC. *See* forward air controller

Fairchild Aviation: 561
Fairchild Hiller Corporation: 523, 528
Fairchild, Muir: 160
Falkland Islands: 556
Fan Song: 267
Farm Gate: 258
FEBA. *See* forward edge of the battle area
Federal Republic of Germany. *See* Germany, West
Feinstein, Jeffrey S.: 296
Felt, Harry D.: 277–78, 280
Ferguson, James: 61, 171, 207–9, 216, 218–20, 222–23, 227, 389, 467, 470, 481, 638, 640, 684
  and Air Force manned aircraft systems steering group: 97
  comment on man in space: 216
Fighter aces: 471, 498
Fighter aircraft, cost of: 492–93
Fighter Weapons School: 295
Fighting Falcon. *See* F-16
Finite deterrent (counterforce): 26
Finletter, Thomas K.: 145
Fire support coordination line (FSCL): 552–53
1st Air Division (South Vietnam): 275
1st Aviation Brigade: 312
1st Cavalry Division: 283
  Airmobile: 260, 311
1st Division (North Vietnamese army): 261
1st Division (South Vietnamese army): 265
1st Marine Air Wing: 283, 301
1st Marine Division: 283
"Fiscal Year 1984–88 Defense Guidance": 370
Fish, Howard: 508–9
Fishbed-J (MiG-21): 294. *See also* MiG-21
Fitter. *See* Su-17
Fitzhugh, Gilbert W.: 588, 598
Fixed-wing aircraft, controversy about: 516–31
Flaming Dart: 259

Flax, Alexander: 680
Fleet air defense system concept
  research and development of: 200
Fleet Marine Forces: 532
Fleet Satellite Communications System: 686
Fletcher, James C.: 701–2
Flexible and appropriate response strategy: 474
Flexible response: 10, 75
  strategy: 496, 506, 513
Flogger. *See* MiG-23
Flood, Daniel: 211
Focus 21: 566
Force de Frappé: 468
Force multiplier: 553
Ford, Gerald R.: 275–76, 349, 409, 587, 688
  administration: 656
Ford Motor Company: 22
Foreign Affairs: 123
"For New Victories of the World Communist Movement": 23
Fort Benning, Georgia: 260
Fort Bragg, North Carolina: 636
Fort Campbell, Kentucky: 314, 633
Fort Hunter Liggett, California: 543
Fort Leavenworth, Kansas: 550, 657
Fort Monroe, Virginia: 531, 540
Fort Riley, Kansas: 529
4400th Combat Crew Training Squadron: 257–58
Forward air controller (FAC): 265, 300–301, 304, 483, 486, 542–43, 553, 555
  FAC-X aircraft: 542
Forward edge of the battle area (FEBA): 498, 501, 528–30, 543, 545, 547, 549, 551, 561
Forward line of own troops (FLOT): 550, 553
Forward operating location (FOL): 508
Foster, John S., Jr.: 341, 346, 384, 394, 428, 439, 530
428th Tactical Fighter Squadron: 479
474th Tactical Fighter Wing: 481–82

Fourth Allied Tactical Air Force (4ATAF): 495–99, 504
France: 5, 474–75, 497
Freedom of the seas: 724
Freedom Train: 294
Freeman, Douglas Southall: 319
Frequent Wind: 276
Friedman, R. J.: 167
  on manned interceptors and unmanned missiles: 115
Frishkorn, Clayton R., Jr.: 744
FSS-7 radars: 450
Fulda Gap: 491
Future space systems
  importance of man in: 223
Future technological growth
  Holloway, Bruce, description of: 196

G.91 (reconnaissance aircraft): 174
Gabriel, Charles A.: 375, 377, 539, 551, 555, 565, 614–15, 665, 690, 697–98, 700, 702–3, 739, 743–44
Gagarin, Yuri: 215
Gaither committee: 2
GAO. *See* General Accounting Office
Gardner, Trevor: 214
Gates, Thomas S.: 3, 8, 19, 147, 151
GAU-8 cannon: 529, 559, 561
Gavin, James M.: 1–2, 176, 260
  and limited warfare: 91
Gayler, Noel: 286–87
GCI. *See* ground control intercept
Gemini program: 142, 677–78, 681–82
  planning board
    establishment of: 142
    responsibilities of: 142
General Accounting Office (GAO): 526, 644, 695
General Electric: 638
Germany
  East: 36, 39, 467, 474, 491, 495
    government: 39
  West: 36, 39, 467, 475, 491, 496, 498–99, 501, 505, 508, 512–15, 546, 549, 628
    air forces: 468
    Hanover: 558

Heidelberg: 498
West Berlin: 36
Wiesbaden: 497
General Dynamics: 111, 502, 565
Geneva Agreements: 273
  on Indochina: 255
  negotiations on nuclear test ban: 102
Geneva Conference: 257–58
Getting, I. A.: 222
  space race, view of: 222
Gia Lam
  airfield: 289
  International Airport: 297
Giap, Vo Nguyen: 261, 268
Gillem, Alvan C., II: 722, 741
Gilpatric, Roswell L.: 42, 60, 135, 139–40, 145, 148–49, 154–55, 161, 197, 220, 585, 677
  on orbiting nuclear weapons: 106
  on US defense needs: 123–24
Gilster, Herman L.: 298, 311
Ginsburgh, Robert N.: 255, 319, 535
Glasser, Otto J.: 335, 385–86, 389–90, 412, 481–82, 502, 521, 525, 529, 687
Gleason, Robert L.: 321–22
Glide bomb: 537
Global positioning system (GPS): 686
Golan Heights: 484–85, 641
Goldberg, Alfred: 721
Gold Fire I
  exercise, description of: 187
Goldwater, Barry: 404, 531
Goodpaster, Andrew J.: 500, 584–85
Graham, Daniel: 367, 381–83, 388
Great Britain (United Kingdom): 5–6
  and voluntary suspension of nuclear tests: 102
Great Frontier, The: A Book of Readings for the Military Space Doctrine Symposium: 692
Green Berets. *See* US Army, Special Forces
Greenland: 506
Greenland-Iceland-United Kingdom (GIUK) gap: 506, 508, 535
Grenada: 668

Ground control intercept (GCI): 289, 293–94, 298
Ground-launched cruise missile (GLCM): 511–15
Ground war
 in Vietnam: 260–63
Guam: 260, 268, 301, 477, 636, 656
Guantánamo Bay, Cuba: 78
Gulf of Tonkin: 288–90, 294

H-19: 517
H-21: 11, 517
Haig, Alexander: 512, 534
Haiphong: 266, 270, 289–90, 292, 295, 296, 303–4, 309, 311, 601
 harbor, mining of: 269
Hamilton, Fowler: 145
Hanoi: 266, 269–70, 286, 289–92, 295–97, 303, 309, 311, 481–82, 544, 601
Hansell, Haywood S.: 381, 723
Hansen, Grant L.: 492, 521, 683–84
Harkins, Paul D.: 280–81
Harpoon missile: 536
Harrier. *See* AV-8A
Harris, Hunter: 289, 317
Hartinger, James V.: 446, 452
Hawkins, Douglas S.: 731
Hawkins, W. M.: 193
Hayward, John T.: 538
Hayward, Thomas B.: 613
Headquarters Army Air Forces (AAF): 27
Headquarters Central Army Group (CENTAG): 496, 498
Headquarters Continental Army Command (CONARC): 18
Headquarters Eighth Army: 604
Headquarters Fifth Air Force: 278, 604
Headquarters Pacific Air Forces: 604. *See also* US Pacific Air Forces
Henry, Richard C.: 545, 691
Herter, Christian A.: 22
Herzfeld, Charles: 317, 439
Herzog, Chaim: 487, 489

Hickam (Air Force Base, Hawaii): 647
High altitude, advanced manned precision strike system (AMPSS): 97
Hill, H. S.: 533
Hill, J. M.: 184
Hill, James E.: 689
Hill, James J.: 530
Hilsman, Roger: 258
 on the Cuban missile crisis: 79
History of the War in Vietnam, October 1961–December 1963: 316
Hitch, Charles J.: 2, 26, 148, 150
 budget program packages: 148
 explanation: 150
Hittle, J. D.: 137
Hoa Lac airfield: 293
Hoang, Le Minh: 316
Ho Chi Minh: 255, 257, 304, 319
Ho Chi Minh trail: 257, 261, 263, 265, 272, 304–5, 308, 311
Hof/Cheb Gap: 491
Holland air force: 468
Holloway, Bruce K.: 152, 196, 317–18, 333, 343, 385, 510
 testimony on Minuteman: 343
Holloway, James L.: 536–37
Honolulu: 267
Hoopes, Townsend: 262
Hoover Commission on Governmental Organization: 13
Hoover, Herbert: 588
Hopwood, Lloyd P.: 161, 712
Horelick, Arnold L.
 on strategic weapons in Cuba: 76
Hosley, David L.: 736
House of Representatives: 652, 663
 Appropriations Committee: 7, 35, 49, 113, 523
 Appropriations Subcommittee: 10, 20, 31, 33, 51–52
 Armed Services Committee: 7, 20, 33–34, 49, 51, 53, 97, 100, 116, 613–16, 624, 629, 652
 Armed Services Subcommittee on Military Airlift: 629
 Defense Appropriations Subcommittee: 113

Military Airlift Subcommittee: 656, 667
Military Appropriations Subcommittee: 604
National Military Airlift Special Subcommittee: 20, 624
Research and Development Subcommittee: 661
Howze Board: 312, 517. *See also* US Army, Tactical Mobility Requirements Board
concept: 299
principal activities: 180
recommendations on airmobile Army units: 181
Howze, Hamilton H.: 176, 180
Hue: 268, 275, 302
Hughes helicopters: 528
Hungary: 477
Huntington, Samuel P.: 369
Hurricane Ella: 76
Hussein I: 486
Hutchinson, Donald L.: 730–32
Huyser, Robert E.: 654, 658, 660, 667–68

ICBM. *See* intercontinental ballistic missile
Iceland: 506, 539
Iceland Defense Force: 603
Igloo White: 307, 309
Ikle, Fred C.: 371–72
Ilyushin-28 bombers: 76
and Cuban missile crisis: 81
Imaging infrared (IIR): 560, 562
Indian Ocean: 537, 539
Indian River exercise
description of: 187
Inertial navigation system: 559
Infiltration Surveillance Center: 309
Initial defense communications satellite program (IDCSP): 680
Initial operational capability (IOC): 514
Institute of Defense Analysis: 305
improved manned interceptor (IMI): 114, 116

Integrated strike zone
in Vietnam War: 286
Intercontinental ballistic missile (ICBM): 4–6, 8–10, 24, 29, 32, 34, 41, 43–44, 52–53, 56, 60, 77, 623, 712
force, characteristics of: 358
Intermediate-range ballistic missile (IRBM): 5, 60, 77
and Cuban missile crisis: 81
Intermediate-range nuclear force (INF) missiles: 511
International Commission of Control and Supervision: 271
Intruder. *See* A-6
Iron Hand: 291
I-69 deployment plan: 441
Israel: 483, 486–87, 641, 643–45, 655
airlift: 647, 655
Israeli Air Force (IAF): 484–88, 555
Iran: 660
shah of: 660
Irvine, C. S.: 196
Italy: 513–15
air force: 468
Izvestiya: 76

Jackson, Henry M.: 3, 134, 337, 345, 442
Japan: 539, 635
Japanese Self-Defense Forces: 604
Jaskilka, Samuel: 610
Jason committee: 305–16
Jerusalem: 484
Johnson, Harold: 284, 300, 313–14, 518
Johnson, Lyndon B.: 2, 10, 259–60, 262–63, 279, 294, 308, 341, 393, 432, 440–41, 477–78, 587–88, 607, 624, 635, 677, 681–82
Johnson Space Center: 691
Johnson, U. Alexis: 77
Joint air weapon system (JAWS): 543
"Joint Attack of the Second Echelon (JASK)": 552

Joint Casualty Resolution Center: 287
Joint Chiefs of Staff (JCS): 6–9, 13–19, 21, 26, 30, 39, 42, 45, 51, 54–55, 59, 62, 86, 257–60, 263–64, 267, 279, 281, 284–86, 292, 297, 299, 306, 308, 316, 318, 467, 475–77, 485–86, 494, 505, 518, 521–23, 525, 531, 541, 547, 554–55, 557, 583, 585–88, 598, 600–605, 608, 610–17, 624, 628, 635, 637, 639, 641–42, 647–48, 651, 659, 663, 666, 690, 698, 700–701, 713, 715, 718, 728, 741
 Joint Strategic Capabilities Plan: 538
 on limited nuclear test ban treaty: 105
 and manned interceptor: 115
 and nuclear test ban treaty: 103
 Pub 2, *Unified Action Armed Forces:* 189, 521, 535, 689, 730
 Pub 8, *Doctrine for Air Defense from Overseas Land Areas:* 192
 Pub 9, *Doctrine for the United Defense of the US against Air Attack:* 192
 Reorganization Act of 1982: 614
 Reorganization Act of 1983: 615
 Special Studies Group: 610–11, 624, 627
Joint Command and Control Requirements Group, establishment of: 153
Joint Committee on Atomic Energy: 6
Joint Deployment Agency: 659
Joint doctrine: 531–32
 CINCSTRIKE: 178
 in Vietnam: 280
Joint Doctrine and Combined Doctrine: 733
Joint Military Transport Committee: 13
Joint OSD/Air Force Bomber Alternatives Study: 423
Joint Strategic Bomber Study: 401–3
 conclusions of: 402
 major observations of: 402
 McLucas's summary of: 413

Joint Strategic Objective Plan 72–79: 639
Joint strategic operations plan (JSOP): 557
Joint suppression of enemy air defenses (J–SEAD): 542, 555
Joint surveillance and target attack radar system (J–STARS): 555
Joint Task Force: 116, 278, 280, 306
Joint Test and Evaluation Task Force, organization of: 185
"Joint USN/USAF Efforts for Enhancement of the Joint Cooperation": 539
Jones, David C.: 52–53, 334–35, 349–50, 360, 390–91, 398, 403, 409, 414, 417, 443, 447, 493–97, 503, 512, 532, 536, 541, 560, 617, 637, 645–46, 649, 651, 655–56, 658, 687, 689, 725–27
Jordan: 486
Journal of the Armed Forces: 680
JTF-7: 659
JTF-11: 659
Jungle Jim. *See* 4400th Combat Crew Training Squadron

KB-50: 121
KC-10: 656, 664–65
KC-97: 630
KC-135: 14, 20, 30, 276, 425, 644, 653, 655–56
Kadena Air Base, Okinawa: 633
Kane, Francis X.: 196, 352, 378–81, 450–51
Katz, Amron H.: 319
Kaufmann, William W.: 337, 725
 on Secretary of Defense McNamara: 91
Kavanau, Lawrence L.: 222, 224
Keck, J. M.: 350
Keegan, George, Jr.: 302–4, 352, 353
Kelley, Paul X.: 660
Kelly Air Force Base, Texas: 633, 639

Kelly (Mervin J.) committee: 2
Kennedy, John F.: 1–2, 4, 10, 22–24, 26–27, 30, 35–37, 40, 43, 45, 47, 53, 55, 58, 60–61, 75–76, 133, 135–37, 140, 145, 147, 177, 179, 201, 214, 216, 258, 279, 280, 299, 333, 339, 390, 428, 468, 477, 478, 511, 517, 585–88, 624, 677–78, 682, 714
  administration: 26, 39, 60
  on basic national security policy: 137
  C-130E transports: 95
  and Cuban missile crisis: 75–76, 78–83
  and JCS: 86
  Korean War: 82
  on limited test ban treaty: 104
  on national objective in space: 137
  nuclear tests, on outlawing: 103
  nuclear weapons, on orbiting: 106
  obligational authority in Kennedy years: 91
  presidential campaign of 1960: 21
  rearmament program: 92
  space race: 214
  State of the Union message: 30, 36, 40
  on successful deterrent: 98
  on WWI: 82
  on WWII: 82
Kennedy-MacMillan communiqué: 83
Kennedy, Robert F.: 77
Kennedy, Robert W.: 727
Kent, Glenn A.: 385, 521
Kenyon, Richard D.: 546
Kep airfield: 293
Kerwin, Walter T.: 610
Kester, John G.: 615
Key West agreements: 526, 535
Key West, Florida: 539
Khe Sanh: 262, 265, 273, 283, 285, 301–2, 307, 314
Khmer Rouge: 271
Khomeini, Ayatollah: 650
Khrushchev, Nikita: 4, 23, 35–36, 39, 41–42, 76, 216, 257, 335–36
  and Cuban missile crisis: 79–81, 86

  and manned bombers: 113
Kidd, Isaac C.: 537
Kien An airfield: 293
Killian, James R.: 340
King Cobra helicopter: 527
Kinnard, Douglas: 303
Kissinger, Henry: 269, 344–45, 476–77, 588
Knowles, Thomas M., III: 483
Komer, Robert W.: 506, 509, 650, 651
Kompong Som (Sihanoukville): 265, 272, 308
Kontum: 261, 275
Korat (Royal Thai Air Force Base, Thailand): 278, 482–83
Korea: 469, 478, 495, 548, 631, 635, 638, 649, 651, 661
Korean War: 3, 11, 15, 288, 623–24, 632
Korth, Fred: 203
Kosygin, Aleksey: 441

L-101: 545
LaBerge, Walter B.: 413
Laird, Melvin: 263–64, 267, 269, 342–45, 375, 395–96, 398, 432–33, 438, 441, 477–78, 480, 493, 523, 526, 536, 556, 587–88, 598–602, 639–40, 682–84, 723, 725
Lajes Field: 641–44
LAMP. *See* low-altitude manned penetration aircraft
Lam Son 719: 265–66, 314, 316
Langley AFB, Virginia: 470, 531, 540
Lansdale, Edward G.: 317
Laos: 257–59, 261, 263–67, 272, 279, 281, 290–91, 294, 296, 299, 304–10, 315, 479–80, 482–83
  diplomatic and military assistance to: 255
Laser bombs: 310
Laser-guided bombs: 294–95, 309
Lavelle, John D.: 267
Lebanon: 16
Lehman, John F., Jr.: 538–39, 699

LeMay, Curtis E.: 5, 14, 45, 47, 50–52, 54, 56, 61–62, 155, 157–58, 161, 164–66, 170, 172, 175, 180–83, 186, 191, 202–4, 209, 211, 215–16, 218, 223–24, 226–28, 235, 259, 280–81, 312, 340, 390–92, 468, 470, 716
  on advanced manned precision strike system: 110
  and advanced manned strategic system: 109
  and B-70 program: 101
  on Berlin (1958): 85
  command of tactical aviation, views on: 181
  on counterforce: 98
  on Cuban missile crisis: 84
  and air power: 86
  on deficiencies in projected strategic forces: 95
  on deterrent force: 94–95
  on JCS: 86
  on Korean War: 85
  on Lebanon (1958): 85
LeMay-Decker agreement: 176
  on limited nuclear test ban treaty: 105
  on manned aircraft: 116
  on manned interceptor: 115
  on manned strategic weapon system: 96
  and missile program: 109
  and 1964 budget: 95
  and nuclear test ban treaty: 103
  on RS-70 and effective strategic deterrent force: 96
  and Soviet strategic capability: 114
  on Soviet threat: 93
  on strategic force deterrent: 97
  on strategic manned weapon system: 111–12
  on strategic power: 85
  on strategic superiority: 94
  on technology and flexibility: 94
  and TFX, visual light attack: 120
  on Thor missiles: 81

  views on US-Soviet space program: 228
Lemnitzer, Lyman R.: 18, 21, 26, 46, 136, 174, 176–77, 198, 211
Lessons learned
  in Vietnam War: 322
Leva, Marx: 145
Liddell Hart, Basil H.: 1
Limited Nuclear Test Ban Treaty
  of 1963: 103–4
  negotiations: 106
  opposition: 103, 105
  proposals: 102
Lindsay, Louis P.: 315
Lindsey Air Station, West Germany: 497
Linebacker I: 268, 294–96
Linebacker II: 270–71, 286, 295–98, 304, 483
Lippman, Walter: 75
Lisbon Conference: 467
Livingston, Lee H.: 689
Lockheed
  C-130E: 30. *See also* C-130
  Starfighter. *See* F-104
Lockheed Aircraft Corporation: 116, 473, 519, 523, 627, 638–40, 655, 663–64
Lockheed California Company: 545
Loc Ninh: 268
Lod airfield: 641–42, 655
Logistics airlift (LOGAIR): 13, 632, 645
Loiter capability: 472, 474, 482
London: 497, 506
Long Beach: 27
Long-range theater nuclear forces (LRTNF): 515
Loosbrock, John F.
  on nuclear doctrine: 91
LORAN (long-range aid to navigation): 297, 483
Lorenzini, Dino A.: 700, 738–39
Loving, George G., Jr.: 717–18, 722, 741

Low-altitude manned penetration (LAMP) aircraft: 97
Low-altitude navigation targeting infrared for night (LANTIRN): 561–63, 565
Low-altitude parachute extraction system, testing of: 188
Low, Andrew S.: 185
Luke AFB, Arizona: 482
Lukeman, Robert P.: 488, 528

MC-130: 668
MC-130E: 669
MAC. *See* Military Airlift Command
MacDill Air Force Base, Florida: 659, 666–67
MacGregor, Charles H.: 689
Machos, James A.: 551, 554
Maddox, William J.: 516, 520
Maginot Line: 33
Mahon, George H.: 398, 523
 on strategic manned systems: 113
Main operating base (MOB): 512
Man in space
 Brown's views: 223
 McNamara's views: 223
Man on the moon: 682
Manned bombers
 role in selective employment: 400
 value to NCA of: 399
Manned military space programs
 objectives of: 223
Manned orbital development system: 143
Manned orbiting laboratory (MOL): 678, 681–83
 initiation of: 225
 project: 144
Manned Space Flight Support Group: 691
Manned strategic bombers
 Dougherty, Russell, views on: 404–9
Marine Air-Ground Task Force (MAGTF): 534–35

Marine Amphibious Force (MAF): 282–83
Marine Combat Support Transport: 645
Marine Corps: 30–31, 36, 38, 43, 45, 62
Mark, Hans M.: 510, 623, 655, 679, 691–92, 694
Mark-17 (MK-17) MIRV: 341
Mark II avionics system: 480–81
Martin, Donald F.: 316
Massive retaliation: 339
Maxwell AFB, Alabama: 318, 487
Mayaguez: 287
McBride, William V.: 610
McCain, John S., Jr.: 286
McChord AFB, Washington: 633
McConnell AFB, Kansas: 529
McConnell, John P.: 189, 259, 270, 281–82, 284, 300, 303–4, 308, 313–14, 336, 341, 387, 391–96, 399, 429, 431–32, 439–40, 467–74, 476, 478, 518–19, 588, 626–27, 718
McConnell-Johnson agreement: 518–19
McCormack, John: 151
McCutcheon, Keith B.: 285
McDonald, David L.
 on attack aircraft carriers: 119
McDonnell Douglas: 563, 565, 656–58, 660, 663–64
 DC-10: 656–57
McElroy, Neil H.: 3, 5–6, 8, 193, 197, 599
McGuire Air Force Base, New Jersey: 633, 668
McKee, Seth J.: 429, 444
McKee, William F.: 170, 172, 184
McLaughlin, Burl W.: 314–15
McLucas, John L.: 346, 397–98, 412–13, 445, 490, 503, 529, 536, 605, 642, 645, 647
McMillan, Brockway: 142
McMullen, Thomas H.: 560
McNabb, David R.: 732
McNamara, Robert S.: 6, 22–24, 26–31, 33–47, 51–63, 134–36, 139–45, 148–

771

53, 156, 166, 170, 178–80, 182–83, 188–90, 196–207, 210–11, 217–19, 221–27, 259–60, 262, 278–79, 281, 288, 292, 302–3, 304–7, 310–12, 334–35, 337–41, 377–79, 381, 384, 387, 389–95, 410, 428–29, 431, 438–41, 468–71, 473, 475–77, 516–17, 586, 607, 624–25, 627, 654, 678, 681
  on advanced manned precision strike system: 110
  and aircraft carriers: 119
  and air defense: 113
  Air Force designated as military space program manager: 139
  Ann Arbor address: 58, 61
  and B-52: 117
  basic management philosophy: 135
  and Congress on strategy: 87
  control of space, response to: 221
  on cooperation between Defense Department and State Department: 87
  on cost-effectiveness of fighter aircraft: 95
  and Cuban missile crisis: 79–80, 82–84
  and damage limiting deterrent strategy: 98
  defense directive on research and development in space: 139
  defense research and development area, management change: 205
  on Department of Defense requirements, 1964: 90
  on Jupiter missiles: 81
  on Kennedy-Johnson defense strategy: 124
  Khrushchev, Nikita
    on intentions: 76
    position: 79
  on limited test ban treaty of 1963: 104
  and manned interceptor force: 114
  "McNamara's Ninety-Six Trombones": 26
  on missile reliability: 99
  military space program, beliefs on: 227
  on NATO: 88
  on 1964 budget: 91
  on a nuclear strike: 89
  on nuclear test ban treaty: 103
  on orbiting nuclear weapons: 106
  on overall objectives of United States: 89
  on overkill: 108
  on Soviet tactics: 88
  on Soviet Union and Communist China: 87
  on spreading freedom throughout the world: 89
  and strategic manned weapon system: 113
  strategy, Air Force questions: 91, 99
  on US military role: 89
McNaughton, John T.: 289, 305
  on orbiting nuclear weapons: 106
McNeil, W. J.: 3–4
Mediterranean Sea: 539
Medium altitude multimission RPV (MMRPV): 544
Medium-range ballistic missile (MRBM): 513
Meiningen Gap: 491
Meir, Golda: 645
Mekong River: 258, 305
Menu (B-52 strike): 264
Mercury flights: 677
Merritt, Jack N.: 256
Metropolitan Life Insurance Co.: 588
Meyer, Edward C.: 550–51, 553, 612–13
Meyer, John C.: 286, 296, 320–21, 347, 385, 720
Michaelis, Frederick H.: 610
Middle East: 468, 483–84, 489, 492, 529, 563
Middle East War of 1967: 719
Middle East Wars: 484–85, 488, 490, 548
M41 tank: 636

M48 tank: 636, 642
M60 tank: 653
M548 tracked vehicle: 636
MiG: 266–67, 273, 289–98, 471, 481
MiG-15: 75, 289, 294
MiG-17: 75, 289–92, 294
MiG-19: 75, 294–95
MiG-21: 291–95, 494, 556
MiG-21J: 484
MiG-23: 494, 504, 556, 563
MiG-25: 336, 493
Military Airlift Command (MAC): 275, 314–16, 606, 625, 628–37, 639–48, 650, 652–53, 655, 657–59, 666–69
  Operations Order 9–68: 636
Military Airlift Service: 625
Military Air Transport Command (MATC): 14, 47, 624
Military Air Transport Service (MATS): 11–17, 19–21, 47, 623–24, 626–27, 637, 715
Military assistance advisory group: 278–79, 281
Military Assistance Command
  Thailand (MACTHAI): 280–81, 602–3
  Vietnam: 602–3
Military Committee Document 14/2: 467, 474
Military Committee Document 14/3: 474, 499, 514
Military-industrial complex: 22
Military orbital development system (MODS)
  description of: 219
  development of: 219
Military potential of space
  Brown, Harold, views: 218
  McNamara, Robert, views: 218
  Zuckert, Eugene, views: 218
Military Sealift Command: 650, 659
Military space projects
  development of primary responsibility for: 197
Military space systems: 685
Military space weapon systems

Schrieber, Bernard A., description of basic capabilities: 219
Military strategic and tactical relay satellite (MILSTAR): 696
Military Traffic Management Command: 650, 659
Milton, Theodore R.: 258, 303
Minh, Tran Van: 274–75
Minimum essential facilities (MEF): 509–10
Mining
  of Haiphong harbor: 304
  of North Vietnamese ports: 268, 294
  of Vietnam: 272
Mirage aircraft: 485
Mirage IV A: 468
Missile gap: 2, 6, 10, 24, 77
Missiles
  A-3 Polaris: 210
  AGM-28 (Hound Dog): 410–11, 414
  AGM-86: 412
  AIM-7: 562–63
  AIM-7E2: 295
  AIM-9: 562
  AIM-9J: 295
  Air-launched cruise missile (ALCM): 412–16, 507, 513
    Jones's and Reed's description of: 414–16
  ALCM-A: 416
  ALCM-B: 416
  AT-3: 485
  Atlas: 6–8, 27, 44, 90, 100, 109, 165
  Atoll: 291, 293, 295
  A-X: 473, 479, 519–21, 523–30, 539, 556–57, 718
  Bomarc: 90, 115, 436
  Bullpup: 30
  C-3: 374
  C-4 (Trident I): 354, 359
  D-5 (Trident II): 374
  Discoverer: 214
  Galosh: 336–37
  Hawk: 78, 436, 485, 529
  Hercules: 436

773

Hound Dog: 41, 62
Jupiter: 5–6, 81
Lance: 549
Mace: 46, 60, 121, 209, 410, 511
Matador: 46, 60, 209, 410, 511
Maverick: 485, 489, 529, 559–62
Midas: 165, 214
"Midgetman": 376–77
Minuteman: 1, 7–8, 27–28, 33, 35, 43–44, 51, 62, 93, 100, 107–10, 165
  Rebasing Study: 357
Minuteman II: 90, 100, 109
Minuteman III: 339, 343–44, 350, 359, 363, 372
MX (Peacekeeper): 359–60, 364–66, 369, 374–78, 381, 388, 420, 564, 658, 664, 690
  basing: 367, 369, 375, 381
  costs: 379
  production: 377
Nike Ajax: 115, 436, 438
Nike Hercules: 38, 78, 90, 115, 438, 444, 446
Nike X: 90, 115, 439, 440
  ABM system: 341
Nike Zeus: 44, 90, 338, 438–39
Pershing: 209, 410
Pershing IA: 511–14
Pershing II: 511–15
Polaris: 1, 9, 27–28, 43, 62, 90, 109–10, 410, 679
Quail: 410–11, 414
Regulus: 410
Samos: 165, 214
Standard Arm: 291
  SA-1: 483
  SA-2: 75, 270, 273, 289–91, 315, 484, 487
  SA-3: 484, 487
  SA-5: 336
  SA-6: 484–85, 487, 490
  SA-7 Strela: 268, 273–74, 315, 483, 485, 487
SAM (surface-to-air missile): 637
Saturn: 681
Sidewinder: 290, 292, 295

Skybolt: 29–30, 35, 41, 44, 51, 60–62, 92, 165, 202
Snark: 29, 410
Sparrow: 290, 292, 294
Splendid Diad: 387
SS-3: 209
SS-4: 209
SS-5: 209
Strike: 32, 291
Thor: 5, 60, 81, 678
Titan: 6–8, 27, 32, 44, 90, 100, 109, 165
Titan II: 334
Titan III: 219, 681–83
  A: 217
  C: 217, 225, 227
  development of: 217
Tomahawk: 512, 514
Missile site radars (MSRs): 441
Mission element needs statement (MENS): 543, 561
Misty FAC: 305
MITRE Corporation
  beginnings of: 194
  establishment of: 195
MK-19 reentry vehicle: 345
MK-82 bombs: 425
Mobile medium-range ballistic missile (MMRBM): 60
  appropriations for: 210
  range of: 210
  story of: 209
Mobile midrange ballistic missile (MMRBM): 410
Mobile Minuteman concept
  development of: 202
Modernization of air defenses, Seamans, Robert, comments: 433
Mohawk aircraft: 177, 181, 189, 312–13, 517–18
Moll, Kenneth L.: 546, 726
Momyer, William W.: 204, 259, 261–63, 266, 276–77, 282–86, 290, 292, 298, 301, 303–4, 306–7, 310, 313–16, 320–21, 323, 469–70, 492, 516, 519, 523–24, 534, 554, 557, 741

Monkey Mountain: 290
Monroney, A. S.: 15
Moore, Joseph H.: 281, 289
Moore, William G., Jr.: 313, 646–47
Moorer, Robert A.: 560
Moorer, Thomas H.: 269–70, 272, 333, 341, 344, 346, 383, 438, 442, 469, 470, 472, 485, 525, 531, 547, 588, 598–99, 601, 616
Moorman, Thomas S.: 299, 316
Motel (radar control): 296
Mu Gia pass: 304, 306–8, 310
Mullins, William H. L.: 727
Multiple independently targetable reentry vehicle (MIRV): 512
Multi-purpose, long-endurance (MPLE) airplane: 97
Murane, David M.: 721, 724
Murmansk, USSR: 536
Murray, Williamson: 736
Mutually assured destruction strategy: 383
Myers, Gilbert L.: 187–88
Myrtle Beach AFB, South Carolina: 482, 508

N-156: 174
Nagler, Gordon R.: 699
Nakhon Phanom Royal Thai Air Force Base: 287, 296, 307, 309
Napoleon [Bonaparte]: 1
Nassau conference: 83
National Aeronautics and Space Act
  amendment of: 140
National Aeronautics and Space Administration (NASA): 677–78, 681–86, 688, 694
  Apollo project: 143
  defense interface: 137
  NASA-DOD interface
    arrangements and agreements: 142
    McNamara policy directive: 141
  Tactical Aircraft Research and Technology Conference: 560
National Aeronautics and Space Council

  revitalized: 140
National command authorities (NCA): 399, 698–99
National Command Plan: 602
National defense organization, some change in Air Force attitudes: 155
National Defense University: 611, 700
National Intelligence Board (NIB): 9
National Military Command Center
  establishment of: 154
National Range Division
  establishment of: 144
National Science and Technology Policy, Organization, and Priorities Act of 1976: 688
National Security Act of 1947: 277, 516, 533
National Security Council (NSC): 6, 318, 477, 491, 585, 587–88, 614–16, 688, 696
  changes: 133
  Johnson subcommittee comments on process: 134
  Operations Coordinating Board
    abolishment of: 134
    composed of: 133
    established by: 133
  purpose of: 133
National Security Decision Memorandum (NSDM) 242: 346
National Security Study Memorandum 3: 639
National space policy: 688
National space requirements, Kennedy administration: 133
NATO (North Atlantic Treaty Organization): 1, 5, 10, 42–43, 60–61, 76, 84, 91, 122, 467–69, 474–76, 480–81, 483–84, 491–501, 503–4, 506–16, 533, 535–36, 538, 541, 543, 545, 547, 548, 550–52, 558, 562–63, 566, 602, 628–29, 649–52, 655, 659, 661, 666, 719, 736, 737
  airborne early warning and control (AEW&C): 506
  Council of Ministers: 474, 497, 499

Military Agency for Standardization: 500
ministerial meeting, December 1962: 81, 83
missiles in Turkey and Cuban missile crisis: 80
nuclear weapons, Council of Ministers: 118
Parliamentarians Conference, Paris, November 1962: 82
Triad: 510, 515
NATO Air Defense Ground Environment (NADGE): 497, 503–5
"NATO Tactical Air Doctrine": 500
Naval Space Command: 699
Naval War College: 700, 738
NAVSTAR: 686, 696
Navy. *See* US Navy
Nellis AFB, Nevada: 295, 479, 481, 563
Netherlands: 498, 501, 503, 513–15
Neutralist forces: 257
New Frontier: 123
  strategy, AFM 1–2 description of: 231–32
New Horizons II, 1985–2000: 726
Nha Trang: 276
Nichols, David L.: 511
Nickel Grass: 641–43
Nifty Nugget: 649–50, 652, 659
Nimrod: 504, 506
9th Marine Expeditionary Brigade: 260
Nitze, Paul H.: 26, 134, 284–85, 333, 511–12, 514
Nixon, Richard M.: 21, 263–66, 268–72, 294, 342–43, 345–46, 348, 395, 441, 477, 478, 491, 587–88, 599–602, 639, 682, 684–85
  Doctrine: 264, 477, 491
Nol, Lon: 264
Norstad, Lauris: 60, 174, 209, 211, 427–28, 444–45, 446, 450
North American Air Defense Command (NORAD): 78, 690, 695, 698
  agreement: 446
  organization of: 427

  studies of change of: 445
North American Aviation Company: 100–101, 111, 473
North Atlantic Treaty Organization. *See* NATO
North German Plain: 475, 480
North Korea: 286, 507
North Koreans: 631, 650
North Vietnam: 259, 261, 263, 266, 269–70, 272–73, 275–76, 281, 285, 288, 290–91, 293–96, 299, 303, 306–8, 469, 473, 478–79, 481–83, 492, 548, 636
  air attacks against: 259–60
  air interdiction: 269
  bombing of: 262–63, 269, 270, 480
North Vietnamese: 636
North Vietnamese army (NVA): 262, 306, 308
Northeast Asia: 650
Northern Army Group (NORTHAG): 496, 498
Northrop Corporation: 502, 523, 528
Norton Air Force Base, California: 631–33
Norway: 501, 503
NSC. *See* National Security Council
Nuclear. *See also* Limited Nuclear Test Ban Treaty
  B-61 bomb: 515
  bombs in Southeast Asia: 257
  detonation detection and reporting system (NUCDETS): 115
  H-bomb: 105
  Schlesinger, James, views on strategy: 345
  test ban: 102–7
    test ban negotiations transferred from Geneva to Moscow: 103
  weapons, tactical: 468
Nunn, Sam: 499–500, 617

O-1: 305
O-2: 543
OV-10: 543

O'Donnell, Andrew W.: 534
Office of Assistant Secretary of Defense for Civil Defense
  establishment of: 150
Office of Organizational and Management Planning Studies
  establishment of: 148
Office of Science and Technology Policy (OSTP): 688
Office of the Secretary of Defense (OSD): 469, 472, 476, 507, 523–24, 536, 628, 630–31, 647–48, 652, 661, 664–65
  Systems Analysis Office: 470, 628
Okinawa: 278, 314, 539
O'Malley, Jerome F.: 691–92, 695, 742–43
101st Airborne Division: 314
173d Airborne Brigade: 260
On Strategy: 256
Operation
  Arc Light: 260, 301, 307, 318–19
  Babylift: 636
  Blue Light: 314
  Bolo: 292
  Combat Fox: 635. *See also* Combat Fox airlift
  Eagle Pull: 276
  Eagle Thrust: 314, 633
  FRELOC: 475
  Neutralize: 261
  Niagara: 262
  Proud Deep: 267
  Reforger: 475
Operational doctrine
  definition of: 184
Orbital bomb: 678
Orbiting nuclear weapons: 106
Organic Army aviation
  employment of: 176
Organizational deficiencies: 583, 589–600, 602, 608–9, 614
Organization of American States (OAS): 78–79
Organization of Consultation: 78
Orr, Verne: 367–68, 451, 539, 663–65, 697, 698, 700–703

Over-the-horizon backscatter (OTH-B) radars: 430, 449
Over-the-horizon radars: 115

P-47: 204
P-51: 204
Packard, David: 256, 342, 493, 501, 521–26, 536, 598–99, 638, 640, 657, 682
Pacific Air Forces (PACAF). *See* US Pacific Air Forces
Pacific Command (PACOM). *See* US Pacific Command
Pacific Fleet (PACFLT). *See* US Pacific Fleet
Page, Jerry D.: 56, 172, 192, 232, 714–15, 723
Palmdale, California: 545
Paris: 260
  air show: 503
  negotiations during Vietnam War: 263, 269, 271
Paris Agreement: 271–72, 274, 287, 316
Paris: Or the Future of War: 1
Parrish, Noel F.: 173
Partridge, Earle E.: 153
  recommendations: 153
  report on national military command and control systems: 153
Paschall, Lee M.: 450, 505
Pathet Lao: 257
Patrick, Mason M.: 1
Patterns of Conflict: 735
Pauly, John W.: 726
Pave Strike: 489
PD-37: 688, 690
PD-42: 688
PD-59: 363
Pearl Harbor: 9
Peled, Benjamin: 484, 486
Pell, Claiborne: 371
Pentagon Papers: 318, 320
Perimeter acquisition radar (PAR): 441
Perle, Richard N.: 426, 443

Perry, William J.: 335, 355, 419–20, 422, 559
Persian Gulf: 563, 650–51, 658–59, 661
Peterson, Carl H.: 722
Phantom. *See* F-4
Phelan, Roger E.: 319
Philippines: 276, 278, 314, 633
Phillips, Samuel C.: 143–44
Phnom Penh: 271, 276
Phuc Yen: 293
  airfield: 289
Phuoc Long: 274–75
Piotrowski, John L.: 727
Piraz: 289
Plain of Jars: 304
Pleiku: 260, 275, 314, 633
Point Salines: 669
Pokrovsky, G. I.: 214
Poland: 477, 495
Polaris submarine: 6, 22–23, 27, 35, 44, 61–62, 78, 81, 90
Political restrictions in Vietnam War: 289
POMCUS (Prepositioned Overseas Materiel Configured to Unit Sets): 508, 649, 658–59, 666
Poseidon MIRV: 337, 339, 374
Powell, Herbert B.: 152
Power, Thomas S.: 7–9, 26, 161
  on arms race: 93
  and Minuteman program: 109
  opposition to limited nuclear test ban treaty: 105
Pratt and Whitney: 638
Precision emitter locator strike system (PELSS): 544
Precision-guided munitions: 269–70, 297
Precision location strike system (PLSS): 545–46, 555
Presidential review memoranda–10: 353
President's Scientific Advisory Committee
  on limited nuclear test ban treaty: 106
Pritchard, Gilbert L.: 178

Program 437: 678
Project CHECO: 316. *See also* CHECO
Project FLAME: 742
Project Forecast: 192, 410, 469, 656, 715
  description of: 228
  establishment of: 158
  findings of: 229–30
  initiation of: 228
  policy panel, discussion of: 232
Project High Frontier: 381–83
Project Loyal Look: 318
Project New Focus: 718
Project Rand: 722
Project STRAT-X: 357
Project Warrior: 742–43
Proud Spirit: 610
Pustay, John S.: 728
Putt, Donald L.: 193–94, 212

Quang Lang: 267
Quang Tri: 265, 268, 275, 284, 302, 311
Quarles, Donald A.: 16, 21, 340
Quesada, Elwood R.: 277, 302–3
Quick-reaction alert (QRA): 511–12, 515
Quick-strike reconnaissance (QSR): 544
QUICKTRANS: 13, 632, 645
Qui Ninh: 273

RB-66: 121, 187
RF-4C: 47, 90, 95, 544
RF-101: 187
RF-105: 47, 165
RF-111: 121
Radar control: 296
Radar homing and warning (RHAW): 290–91
RAF (Royal Air Force): 5, 60, 468, 505, 520, 552
RAF Bentwaters, England: 508
RAF Lakenheath, England: 508

RAF Mildenhall, England: 497
RAF Upper Heyford, England, 481
RAF Woodbridge, England: 508
Ralph, John E.: 726, 728, 730
Ramstein Air Base, West Germany: 497–98, 540, 646, 647
Rand Corporation: 2, 319, 721
  initiation of: 194
  responsibilities of: 194
Randolph, Bernard P.: 695, 699
Rapid deployment force (RDF): 667
"Rapid Deployment of Forces for Limited War": 624, 660
Rapid Deployment Joint Task Force (RDJTF): 660, 666
  CINCCENT: 666
  USCENTCOM: 666
Rasmussen, Robert D.: 552
Ready Reserve: 37
Reagan, Ronald W.: 364, 367–69, 372, 374–75, 381, 383, 388, 423, 425, 451, 538, 564, 616, 693–94, 696, 701
  administration: 665–66
  Commission on Strategic Forces: 375
  nuclear strategy: 371
  plans for US strategic forces: 368
  rearmament program: 374
  strategic modernization program: 425
Reconnaissance/surveillance: 543
Red China
  and war in Southeast Asia: 257
REDCOM. *See* US Readiness Command
Red Crown radar: 294–96
Red Flag: 563
Red-line management review concept
  effectiveness of: 169
  Schriever's comments: 169
Reed, Gordon C.: 19
Reed, Robert H.: 727
Reed, Thomas C.: 375, 403, 414, 606, 656
Remotely piloted vehicle (RPV): 489, 540, 544–45, 556
Republican party: 10, 21–22

Republic of Vietnam. *See* South Vietnam
Research Studies Institute: 163
Resor, Stanley R.: 521
Reston, James: 4
Reykjavik, Iceland: 506
Richardson, Elliot L.: 272, 345, 443
Richardson, Robert C.: 379–80, 383
Ritchie, Richard S. "Steve": 296
Ritland, O. J.: 142
Rivers, L. Mendel: 20–21, 624
Rivet Haste: 295
Robertson, Reuben B., Jr.: 195
Rogers, Bernard W.: 509–10, 515
Rogers, Felix M.: 321, 727
"Role of Military Air Transport Service in Peace and War, The": 19
Rolling Thunder: 259–60, 269, 285–86, 289, 292, 305–6, 310
  coordinating committee: 286
Root, Elihu: 155
Roser, Hans F.: 487
Rosson, William B.: 185
Rostow, Walt W.: 258
  on accidental nuclear war: 92
Royal Air Force. *See* RAF
Royal Australian Air Force: 487
Royal Navy: 505
Royal Netherlands Air Force: 508
Royal United Services Institute (RUSI): 487
Rubel, John H.: 141, 207, 220–21
RS-70: 51–56, 58, 92, 96, 97, 100–101, 202, 389, 390–91
Rules of engagement
  in Laos: 304
Rumsfeld, Donald H.: 349–50, 408, 446
Rusk, Dean: 22, 26, 36, 77, 133–36, 173, 258, 260, 279
  and Cuban missile crisis: 79, 82, 86
  on limited nuclear test ban treaty: 102, 104
  on US security: 98
Russ, Robert: 563
Russell, Lord Bertrand
  and Cuban missile crisis: 79

Russell, Richard B.: 32, 53, 147, 226, 399, 586, 629
  Senate Armed Services Committee: 101, 211
Ryan, John D.: 303–4, 334–35, 342–44, 398, 411, 438, 479–80, 502, 521, 536, 556
Ryan, Thomas M., Jr.: 669

SR-71: 117, 431
Su-17 Fitter: 494, 504
Saber Armor-Alpha: 528
Saber Armor-Charlie: 528
Saber Penetrator IV Study: 412
SAC. *See* Strategic Air Command
Safeguard plan: 342
SAGE. *See* semiautomatic ground environment
"Sagebrush" maneuver: 11
Sagger. *See* AT-3
Saigon: 261–65, 267–68, 274–75, 278–81, 287, 289–300, 316–17, 629, 632, 637
  surrender of: 276
Saint: 165
SALT I agreement: 344, 348
SALT II treaty: 360
Sams, Kenneth: 317
Sanborn, Morgan W.: 686
Sandy search and rescue mission: 483
Satellite inspection and negation (SAINT): 450
Saudi Arabia: 563
Savannakhet: 258
Schelling, Thomas C.
  on deterrent strategy: 93
Schichtle, Casper J.: 700
Schlesinger, James R.: 315, 345–51, 385, 401, 412, 443–45, 447, 491, 493, 499, 502–3, 505, 557–58, 603, 605, 616, 641, 645, 647–48
Schriever, Bernard A.: 7, 24, 141–42, 144, 158, 160, 164–66, 168–69, 171, 185, 195, 204, 213–14, 219, 228, 230, 678, 693

Science and technology
  Air Force military analysts' views: 193
  McElroy's views: 193
  Putt's views: 193
Scowcroft, Brent: 375–76
Sea lines of communication (SLOC): 538
Seamans, Robert C., Jr.: 335–36, 342, 395–98, 429, 433, 478–79, 480–81, 501–2, 521, 523, 527, 556, 588, 601, 638, 679, 683–86
Search-and-destroy strategy in Vietnam War: 260
Search and rescue (SAR): 483, 518
2d Advanced Echelon (ADVON): 280
2d Air Division (Vietnamese air force): 280–82, 285–86, 300
Second Air Force: 606
Second Allied Tactical Air Force (2ATAF): 496–97, 499, 504, 508
Second echelon attack: 546–55
Second-strike deterrent strategy: 343
Secretary of Defense
  Office of: 51
  Office of Assistant (Supply and Logistics): 15
Seeking, locating, annihilating, and monitoring (SLAM): 261
Selective employment of air and ground alert (SEAGA): 387
Selectivity and flexibility in targeting: 342, 346
  Meyer, John, comments on: 347
Sembach Air Base, West Germany: 497
Semiautomatic backup intercept control system: 90
Semiautomatic ground environment (SAGE): 37, 44, 90, 115, 497
Senate. *See* US Senate
Sentinel ABM system: 342, 440–41
  systems management: 441
Seventeenth Air Force: 497, 603
Seventh Air Force: 260, 265, 267, 282–83, 286–87, 289, 291–92, 295–97, 301–2, 305, 307, 313

Seventh Army: 38
Seventh Fleet: 680
SHAPE (Supreme Headquarters Allied Powers Europe): 467, 511, 585
Sharp, Dudley C.: 15, 19
Sharp, Ulysses S. Grant: 262, 279, 281, 283–86, 303–4
Short-range air missile (SRAM): 296
Short-range attack missile (SRAM)
  development of: 229
Shoup, David M.: 62, 182
Siegert, Leonard J.: 727
Signal intelligence (SIGINT): 544
Sihanouk, Norodom: 264
Sihanoukville: 263
Sikorsky: 527
Simons, William E.: 232, 715
Sinai desert: 484, 487, 559
Singapore: 274
Single integrated operational plan (SIOP): 296, 536, 538
  SIOP I: 339
  SIOP II, options of: 339
Single manager
  concept in Vietnam: 285
  plan in Vietnam: 284
  system: 301
Sixteenth Air Force: 497, 603
6th Air Division (South Vietnam): 275
Skylab: 681, 683
Slay, Alton D.: 419, 447, 490, 503, 544–45, 562
Smart bombs. *See* precison-guided munitions
Smart, Jacob E.: 280, 686
Smith, Dale O.: 172–73, 182, 192
  on arms control rationale: 93
Smith, Donald W.: 723
Smith, Frederic H., Jr.: 48–49, 156, 170
Smith, Joseph: 14
Smith, William Y.: 712, 726
Sokolovsky, V. D.: 220
  and aviation: 113
Sorenson, Theodore: 77
South Korea: 468, 508

South Ruislip, Great Britain: 497
South Vietnam: 257–69, 271–76, 278–87, 289, 299–304, 307–10, 315–16, 469, 478, 517, 547, 636
  diplomatic and military assistance to: 255
  evacuation of: 275–76
  US advisory assistance to: 257–59
South Vietnamese Air Force: 267–68, 273–75
South Vietnamese Joint General Staff: 273
Southeast Asia: 468–69, 471, 478–79, 482–84, 489, 507, 527, 529, 539–40, 542, 544–45, 547–48, 556, 564, 628–33, 635–36, 639–40, 645, 652, 655
  insurgency in: 255–323
  military operations in: 277–323
  military organization in: 277–323
  objectives in: 255–77
  strategy in: 255–77
  war in: 255–323
Southeast Asia Coordinating Committee (SEACOORD): 279
Southeast Asia Monograph Series: 741
Southeast Asia Treaty Organization (SEATO): 255, 257
Southwest Asia: 563, 565, 651, 660, 665–67
Soviet Union: 8–10, 23–24, 32, 35–37, 39–43, 49, 52, 59–61, 303, 307, 468, 474, 476–77, 483–84, 488, 491, 493, 500, 511–12, 514, 641–42, 648, 650–52, 658, 660, 662, 665–66, 668
  armed forces: 23, 58–59
  Bear aircraft: 429, 535
  Beauty swept-wing jet: 41
  Blinder jet: 41
  Bounder jet: 41
  Cuba
    Cuban missile crisis: 87
    missiles in: 75–76
  ICBM sites: 88
  invasion of Czechoslovakia: 719
  military strategy, discussion of: 220
  missile program: 336

missiles
- SS-9: 335–36, 342
- SS-17: 348
- SS-18: 348, 351–52, 355
- SS-19: 348, 351–52
- SS-20: 512–14

missile threat, early military analysis of: 333
Navy: 538
and nuclear technology: 103
Red Army: 23, 62
and sophisticated nuclear technology: 102
and voluntary suspension of nuclear tests: 102
and war in Southeast Asia: 257
Space defense operations center (SPADOC): 690, 697
Space and missile systems organization (SAMSO): 685, 690
Space-based ABM system: 687
Space doctrine: 689, 692–93, 696, 698, 700–703
Space operations committee: 695
Space shuttle: 684–86, 691, 694
Space transportation system (STS): 685
Spasm war: 26
Special Air Warfare (SAW): 518
Special forces: 260
Special operational requirement (SOR): 20, 470
Special Operations Forces (SOF): 668
Special Warfare Center: 178
Sprague committee: 2
Sputnik: 10, 677
Stafford, Thomas P.: 562, 656, 687
Starbird, Alfred: 306
Starry, Donn A.: 549, 550
Steadman, Richard C.: 602, 608–10
Stealth program: 422
Steel Tiger: 304–5
Stelling, Henry B., Jr.: 685–86
Stennis, John C.: 414, 524, 661
Stetson, John C.: 447–48
Stever, Guyford H.: 163
Stiles, Dennis W.: 729

Storrie, John H.: 698
Strategic Air Command (SAC): 7–10, 14, 22, 26, 28–29, 37–38, 78, 260, 270, 282, 286, 296–98, 321, 468, 471, 537, 585, 623, 630, 636, 644, 655–56, 666–68, 686, 689, 715, 742
- Advanced Echelon (SACADVON): 286
- and Cuban missile crisis: 80, 83

Strategic Army Command (STRAC): 38
Strategic Army Corps: 17
Strategic bomber program: 100
Strategic debates, 1963: 87
Strategic defensive forces, interceptor forces: 434–35, 436
- active: 434
- Air National Guard: 435
- control and surveillance: 437
- surface-to-air missiles: 436

Strategic Defense Initiative (SDI) "Star Wars": 701–2
Strategic nuclear forces, basic objectives of: 349
Strategic Projection Force: 666–67
Strategic retaliatory program: 90
Strategic space force
- LeMay's views on: 227

Strategic superiority: 91
Strategic Triad concept: 384
"Strategy of Realistic Deterrence": 477
Stratton, Samuel S.: 614
Strike Command. *See* US Strike Command
Strike Eagle. *See* F-15
Strut, Gerald W.: 723
Stuka: 492, 529
Submarine-launched cruise missile (SLCM): 411–12, 512–13, 538
Subsonic cruise armed decoy (SCAD): 411–12
Suez Canal: 641
- West Bank: 487

Summa Corporation: 528
Summers, Harry G.: 256
Sun Tzu: 625

Supplement to the Information Policy Letter for Commanders: 171
Supreme Allied Commander, Europe (SACEUR): 496, 500, 512, 514–15, 534, 719
Supreme Headquarters Allied Powers Europe. *See* SHAPE
Supreme Soviet: 79, 80
Sweeney, Walter C., Jr.: 185, 191, 470
Swift Strike III: 300
Sylvester, George H.: 232, 715
Symington, Stuart: 9, 133, 145, 147, 211, 442, 470, 471, 526, 527, 585
  committee
    defense management: 145
    objectives in modernizing Department of Defense: 145
    recommendations: 146
  report, Navy reaction to: 147
Syria: 483–84, 490, 641
Syrian Air Force: 556
Systems Review Board (formerly Weapons Board)
  establishment of: 168

T-28: 207–8
T-29: 645
T-37: 207–8
T-38: 174
T-39: 645–46
TR-1: 545–46, 555
Tactical air
  US Marine Corps: 531–39
  US Navy: 531–39
Tactical Air Command (TAC): 11, 18, 47, 78, 263, 287–88, 315, 320–21, 473, 479, 483, 488–89, 492, 502, 506, 508, 512, 514, 523, 530–31, 537, 539–46, 552–53, 555–66, 605–6, 626, 635–36, 642, 645, 656, 659, 667, 715, 727
  and NATO: 84
Tactical Fighter Tactics and Weapons System Panel: 470
Tactical Air Control Center (TACC): 290, 300, 313, 519

Tactical air control party (TACP): 300
Tactical Air Control System (TACS): 505
Tactical airlift
  in Vietnam War: 314–15
Tactical airlift liaison officer (TALO): 313
Tactical air reconnaissance (TAR): 552
Tactical Air Reconnaissance Center
  organization of: 185
  responsibilities of: 185
Tactical air support element (TASE): 300
Tactical air warfare
  Army and Air Force concept papers: 186
  LeMay, Curtis, comments: 186
  Myer, Gilbert, description of: 187
Tactical counterforce: 546–47
Tactical expendable drone system (TEDS): 544
Tactical fighter wings: 469
Tactical rescue-intelligence system enhancement (TAC/RISE): 718
Taiwan: 16, 314, 636
Takhli Air Base, Thailand: 479–82
Tally Ho: 304–5
Talon Vise: 276
Tanks
  M41: 636
  M48: 636, 642
  M60: 653
  T62: 484, 660
  T72: 660
Tan Son Nhut: 314, 316
  Air Base: 287, 313, 636
  airfield: 276
Target identification system electro-optical (TISEO): 295
Task Force 77: 285–86, 288
"Tasks of Combat Air Support": 521
Tate, Grayson D.: 381
Tate, Robert F.: 161–62
Taylor, Maxwell D.: 1–2, 6, 9–10, 16–17, 36, 40, 59, 134, 136, 151, 157, 258, 279, 586–87, 599, 651

appointed as military representative to Kennedy: 136
and Soviet nuclear technology: 103
Tchelpone: 258, 265, 304, 308, 310
Teaball (radar control): 296, 298
Technipols: 136
Tehran, Iran: 563
Teledyne Ryan Company: 544
Teller, Edward
    on nuclear war: 105
    opposition to limited nuclear test ban treaty: 105
Terrain contour matching (TERCOM) navigation system: 412
Terrain following radar: 479–80
Tet offensive: 262, 267, 269, 283, 301, 307–8, 636–37, 640, 724
TFX (tactical fighter): 113, 116. *See also* F-111
    contracting of: 203
    design of: 199
Thailand: 258, 265, 268, 276, 278–82, 287–91, 296, 301, 309, 636
Thanh Hoa: 269
Thatcher, Margaret: 615
Thayer, Paul: 701
Thien, Nguyen Van: 269, 271, 273–75
Think Tank
    Excom: 77
    War Council: 77
3d Air Division: 606
Third Air Force: 497, 603
Thirteenth Air Force: 258, 278, 280, 282–83, 285, 287, 605
32d Tactical Fighter Squadron: 508
36th Tactical Fighter Wing: 508
Thompson, Ray L.: 728–29
Thompson, Robert: 271
304th Division (North Vietnamese army): 262
314th Air Division: 604
315th Air Division: 314
325C Division (North Vietnamese army): 262
354th Tactical Fighter Wing: 482–83
Three Pairs exercise: 300

Thua Thien: 268, 283–84
Thud. *See* F-105
Thunderchief. *See* F-105
Tibbets, Paul W.: 154
Tiger Hound: 304–5
Tight Belt East: 726
Tight Belt West: 605, 726–27
Titov, G. S.: 216
Tonkin, Gulf of. *See* Gulf of Tonkin
Tornado aircraft: 515
Torrejón Air Base, Spain: 497
Total force: 725
    concept: 478, 527–28, 556, 564
Tower, John: 616
Townes, Charles: 367
Training and Doctrine Command (TRADOC): 717, 728
Transport aircraft
    in Vietnam War: 311–16
Travis Air Force Base, California: 629, 632, 639–40, 668
Triad: 375, 377, 385–87, 400, 427, 725
    NATO: 510, 515
    term: 385
    review of concept: 388
    Weinberger's summary of significance: 388
Trident submarine: 344
Trilateral force: 385
Triservice fighter: 200
Truce talks
    during Vietnam War: 260
Tube-launched, optically directed, wire-controlled (TOW) missile: 527
Tunner, William H.: 12, 14, 16, 20, 626
Tupolev Backfire (bomber): 429
Turkey: 5–6, 76
    air force: 468
24th Division: 475
25th Infantry Division: 314
Twining, Nathan F.: 9, 14–16, 711
    on limited nuclear test ban treaty: 105
    on nuclear technology: 102
    study group on nuclear test ban: 102

U-2: 75–76, 511, 679
  Anderson, Rudolph, Jr.: 80
  photography: 333
U-2R: 545
UE aircraft: 557
UH-1B: 653
UM-1 Iroquois: 189
Udorn Royal Thai Air Force Base: 287
Ulsamer, Edgar: 551
Uncertain Trumpet, The: 9
Unified Command Plan (UCP): 601–2, 604–6, 647
United Kingdom: 474–75, 513–14
United Nations: 679
  and Cuban missile crisis: 80
United Nations Command: 604
United Nations General Assembly
  and orbiting nuclear weapons: 107
United States: 6, 9, 11–13, 19, 22–23, 25, 31–32, 36, 38–45, 49, 54, 56–58, 60–61, 625, 628–29, 632, 635–36, 639, 641–42, 644–46, 648–52, 655–56, 659–61, 663–66, 668–69
  concerns about Soviet missiles: 336
  nuclear forces, four purposes for: 371
United States Army Air Forces. *See* US Army Air Forces
University of Pittsburgh: 701
Upham, John S., Jr.: 183
US ambassadors
  and military activities in Southeast Asia: 279
USAF. *See* US Air Force
"USAF Concept for Limited War, The": 56
USAFE. *See* US Air Forces in Europe
USAF Terms of Reference: 317
US Air Force: 8–14, 17–19, 21, 28–29, 31–35, 37–39, 42, 45, 47–49, 51–56, 58, 60–62, 471, 473, 623–24, 626, 628–32, 637–42, 644–48, 652–58, 660–61, 663–66, 668
  Aeronautical Systems Division: 627
  Airlift Master Plan: 665
  Chief of Staff: 478
  continental air defense study group: 114

  Headquarters Command: 602, 727
  and joint operations: 277
  Korea: 604
  manned aircraft systems steering group: 97
  organizational adjustments to defense reorganization: 160
  policy: 717
  Project Blue Lance: 380–81
  reorganization: 728–29
  research and development organization
    report of: 163
  Reserve: 12, 19, 21, 38–39, 46–47
  Scientific Advisory Board: 691
  South Command: 645
  Space Command (SPACECOM): 452, 697–98, 701
    mission of: 452
  Space Study Committee
    assembly of: 214
    report of: 214
  Space Plan, description of: 216
  space program
    Ferguson's defense of: 220
    basic objectives of (1963): 219
  Space Technology Center: 697
  Systems Command: 685–86, 689–91, 697
  XOD: 715, 717–18, 722, 727–28
US Air Force Academy: 317, 692, 731, 738
  Military Space Doctrine Symposium: 692–93, 700
US Air Forces in Europe (USAFE): 473, 493–94, 496–98, 505, 537, 540–41, 543, 642, 645–46, 727
US Alaskan Command: 603
US Army: 10–11, 18–19, 21, 30–31, 37–39, 42–43, 45, 55, 183, 512, 518, 623, 626–28, 636–37, 646, 649, 653, 656–60, 662, 664, 666–67, 669
  airmobility concept: 182
  Alaska: 603
  aviation: 312–13
  Combat Developments Command
    activation of: 179

divisions: 38
doctrine, principal center for: 173
11th Air Assault Division: 311
5-year strength, 1964 budget: 90
Materiel Command
    operational date and responsibilities: 179
Pacific Command: 603, 605
Provisional Corps, Vietnam: 284
Southern Command: 603
Special Forces: 257
staff: 566
Strategic Studies Group
    Army's doctrinal role: 178
Support Command: 282
Support Group: 282
Tactical Mobility Requirements Board: 311. *See also* Howze Board
Vietnam: 282
weapons: 22
US Army Command: 602
US Army, Europe (USAREUR): 496, 540–41, 543
US Army Field Manual 100-5, *Operations*: 549–50
US Army Forces Command: 659
US Army Pacific (ARPAC): 278
US Army Training and Doctrine Command (TRADOC): 531, 539–46, 548–50, 558
US Army XXIV Corps: 284
US Atlantic Command: 603
US Central Command (CINCCENT): 666
USCINCLANT: 669
USCINCMEAFSA: 602
US European Command (USEUCOM): 475, 491, 496, 511, 515, 602
US Forces Japan: 604
US Forces Korea: 602, 604–5
US Forces Vietnam: 279
US Fourth Infantry Division: 302
US Intelligence Board: 586
US Marine Corps: 531–39, 636, 659–60, 662, 664, 666, 669

US Military Assistance Activity: 321
US Military Assistance Command, Vietnam (COMUSMACV): 260–62, 280–87, 300–301, 313, 319, 602–3, 636
US National Guard: 468, 478
US Naval Forces, Vietnam: 282
US Navy: 10, 12–14, 30, 37, 42–43, 45–47, 531–39, 623, 642, 659–60, 666
    Component Command: 282
    Fleet Tactical Support: 645, 659
    Supply Systems Command: 632
    Task Force 77: 282
US Navy Command: 602
US Navy, Europe (USNAVEUR): 496
US Office of Management and Budget: 551
US Pacific Air Forces (PACAF): 12, 278, 280, 285–86, 289, 299, 308, 314, 316–17, 321, 473, 537, 605–6, 645, 727, 729. *See also* Headquarters Pacific Air Forces
US Pacific Command (PACOM): 277–81, 285–87, 479, 602, 604–6
    forces: 635
US Pacific Fleet (PACFLT): 278, 285–86
US Readiness Command (REDCOM): 552, 610, 659, 667
US Reserve: 468, 478
USS *Eisenhower*: 607
US Senate: 21, 32, 54, 59, 652
    Appropriations Committee: 19
    Appropriations Subcommittee: 21, 52–54
    Armed Services Committee: 32, 49, 53–54, 100–101, 116, 494, 499, 524, 528–29, 588, 615–16, 661
    Preparedness Investigating Subcommittee of: 474
    Close Air Support Special Subcommittee: 522, 525, 531
    Commerce Committee: 15
    Committee on Foreign Relations: 104–5

Foreign Relations Committee: 105
Preparedness Investigating Subcommittee: 105
US Seventh Fleet: 260, 295
US Southeast Command: 280, 603
US Space Command (USSPACECOM): 699
USS *Pueblo*: 631–32, 635
US State Department: 23, 258, 263
US Strategic Bombing Survey: 317
US Strike Command (USSTRICOM): 152, 178–79, 182–83, 185–88, 190–91, 260, 278, 300, 311–13, 586, 600, 659
  establishment of: 152
  functional responsibilities: 152
  joint doctrinal recommendations: 191
  principal tasks: 152
US Support Activities Group: 287
U-Tapao: 297
U-Tapao Royal Thai Air Force Base: 276
US XXIV Corps: 265

Vance, Cyrus: 181, 312, 377, 379
Van Cleve, Walter S.: 719
Vandenberg-Collins agreement, operational control of the air: 175
Vandenberg, Hoyt: 711
Van Duyn, John E.: 321–22
Vertical short takeoff and landing (VSTOL): 526, 656
Vertical takeoff and landing (VTOL): 230, 520–21, 526
Vessey, John W., Jr.: 375, 614–15
VFAX aircraft: 473
Victor bomber: 468
Vientiane: 304–5
Vietcong: 261–62, 303, 306, 308
Vietnam: 469, 477, 479, 495, 499, 530, 540, 548, 646, 651, 653
Vietnamese air force (VNAF): 268, 273, 276, 299–301, 316, 322
Vietnamization: 263–66, 268, 287, 316
Vietnam War: 266–77, 520, 628–29, 630–32, 635

  air power in: 256, 266–71
  casualties, American: 264
  cease-fire: 263, 271–73, 294, 316
  electronic sensors: 306
  evaluations of: 478
  forward air controllers: 274
  helicopter: 265–66, 311–16
  hugging tactics: 266
  neglect of strategy in: 256
  popular support of: 256
  restrictions on: 276
    military: 478
  rules of engagement: 266–67, 276
  spoiling operations: 262
  spring invasion: 266–71
US military limitations in: 256
Vinh; 267
Vinson, Carl: 20, 34, 53, 147, 197, 586
  and House Armed Services Committee: 100
Visual light-attack (VAL) aircraft: 120, 157, 210, 470–71
Vogt, John W., Jr.: 286–87, 296, 482–83, 498, 500–501
Von Neumann, John: 214
VO-67 Squadron: 307
Vulcan bomber: 60, 468
Vung Tau: 260

Wacker, Rudolph P.: 711
Wade, Horace M.: 321
Wade, James P., Jr.: 355, 426–27, 451, 694
Walker, Roy R.: 713
Walleye glide bomb: 485
Walsh, John B.: 350
Warfare, research on the science of: 161
Warner, Volney F.: 659–60, 663, 666
War Powers Resolution: 272
War reserve materiel: 510
Warsaw Pact: 468, 474–75, 477, 480, 484, 533, 540–44, 546–49, 551, 558, 566, 649

Soviet threat, US response to: 490, 516
Wass de Czega, Huba: 550–51
Watergate: 272
Watkins, James D.: 538–39, 699
Weapon Systems Evaluation Group Study: 624
Weapon Systems Study Group
   Bradley plan: 164
   Schriever's objections to: 165
Webb, James E.: 140–43
Weinberger, Caspar W.: 276, 352, 364, 367, 369, 370–71, 373–76, 378, 388, 424–26, 538, 554, 556, 614, 663, 664–65, 701–2
   on defense policy: 364
   on hard-target kill capability: 373
Welch, James A., Jr.: 558
Welch, Jasper A.: 648
Welsh, Edward C.: 140, 145
Westmoreland, William C.: 260–62, 279, 281–84, 289, 300–302, 519, 527, 602
Weyand, Frederick C.: 275, 541
Weyland, Otto P.: 11
Wheeler, Earle G.: 55, 62, 175, 181, 189, 259–60, 263–64, 281–85, 303–4, 306, 339, 341, 396, 468, 477
   on Army strength: 118
   and tactical aircraft: 120
   on US Army in Cuban missile crisis: 83
White Sands, New Mexico: 559
White, Thomas D.: 6–8, 10–11, 16, 18–19, 21, 28–29, 31–35, 146, 151, 155–56, 163–67, 175, 193, 201, 212–13, 215, 221, 677, 680, 713, 723
   defense unification, comments on: 146
Wickam, John A., Jr.: 555
Wiesner, Jerome B.: 133, 209
   Ad Hoc Committee on Space: 137
      recommendations: 138
   on accidental nuclear war: 92
Wild Weasel: 286, 291, 297, 489, 542

Williams, Robert R.: 312, 517, 521, 548
Wilson, Charles E.: 175, 196, 340, 516
   roles and missions directive: 176
Wilson, Louis L.: 605–6
Wilson, Roscoe C.: 169, 201, 213–14
Wood, Robert J.: 177
World War II: 27, 82, 624
Worldwide Military Command and Control System (WWMCCS): 600
Wright-Patterson AFB, Ohio: 502

X-15: 116, 230
X-20: 224
XB-70: 28–29, 54, 389
XB-70A: 101
XM-1: 652

YB-70: 28
YC-14: 657
YC-15: 657–58
YF-12A: 116, 431
YF-16: 502
YF-17: 502
Yokota Air Base, Japan: 633
Yom Kippur War: 479, 483, 485–88, 490, 529, 542, 555, 559, 644
York, Herbert F.: 26, 35, 195, 199, 209, 214, 384
   on objectives of defense efforts in space: 214
Yost, William R.: 738
Young, Milton R.: 490
YQM-94A: 544
YQM-98A: 544
Yudkin, Richard A.: 255, 717–18, 720, 722

Zuckert, Eugene M.: 31, 51–54, 155, 158–59, 166–68, 170, 196, 203–4, 209, 211, 215, 218–19, 226, 228–32, 235, 312, 430, 714

on advanced manned precision strike system: 111
air doctrine guidelines, description of: 231
on arms control: 107
on deterrence: 108
on manned interceptor: 116

national defense organization address: 159
and 1964 budget: 95
ZSU-23-4 antiaircraft guns: 484, 490
Zumwalt, Elmo R., Jr.: 344, 384, 536, 601